917.91 B261A
BARNES
  ARIZONA PLACE NAMES                    EV.

                              11.50

917.91 B261A
BARNES
  ARIZONA PLACE NAMES                    EV

                              11.50

# ARIZONA PLACE NAMES

WILL C. BARNES'

# ARIZONA
# PLACE
# NAMES

*Revised and enlarged by*
BYRD H. GRANGER

*Illustrated by*
ANNE MERRIMAN PECK

THE UNIVERSITY OF ARIZONA PRESS
TUCSON

*Sixth printing 1977*

THE  UNIVERSITY  OF  ARIZONA  PRESS

I. S. B. N. 0-8165-0009-6
L. C. No. 59-63657

# PREFACE

When the present volume was first considered, it was believed that the new book would be a revision of the original *Arizona Place Names* produced in 1935 by one of the state's most eminent pioneers, Will C. Barnes. However, it became increasingly apparent that Will Barnes had done a job unique in tone and content. There were, nevertheless, sound reasons for placing a "revised" work before the public. Among them was the fact that Barnes himself was aware of certain areas which needed additional work, and had he lived no doubt he would himself have undertaken the task. This was made apparent by an examination of Barnes' personally annotated copy of his book, which Mrs. Will C. Barnes very kindly made available. It proved an invaluable aid in preparation of the present volume.

A second factor calling for a "revised" volume was the passage of almost a quarter of a century during which Arizona enjoyed a tremendous surge in population and a consequent increase in place names. Thus there was much new material needing attention. Also, scholarship in the United States had made accessible resources not readily available when Barnes was writing his book. Another factor was the realization that as each month dropped from the calendar, it took with it pioneers who alone knew stories about many place names. To garner their wealth of knowledge, the present had to be seized. The purpose of interviewing old timers, of reading new materials on place names, and of analyzing hundreds of maps is, of course, to amass that information in a single place — a book. This volume is the compounded result.

It goes without saying that the present editor owes a heavy debt to Will C. Barnes for his years of work and interest in place names. Time and again Barnes' name will be found under entries in this volume, indicating that his work was the source of information. In certain instances materials similar to his will be found, but the list of references will go back to the original sources, for some may be interested in checking, for instance, what Spanish missionaries had to say about place names. It is believed that the method of annotation used will make such a course possible.

A book such as this is the product of many minds working together. The editor wishes it were possible personally and fully to acknowledge the vast amount of help given by many people in every part of Arizona. At the end of this volume will be found a section of "Biographical Sketches" which in part does acknowledge assistance. It does not include those who, not having place name information themselves, took time and trouble to hunt up pioneers and documents which erased many question marks concerning place names.

The editor is particularly grateful to Mrs. Alice B. Good and the staff of the State Department of Library and Archives in Phoenix. Thanks are due also to Mrs. Norman Garrett of Prescott for her help when the editor was at the Sharlot Hall Historical Museum of Arizona. The library of the Arizona Pioneers' Historical Society in Tucson was a primary source, and to its staff and most particularly to Mrs. Edith O. Kitt, its "secretary emeritus," the editor extends heartfelt thanks. Mrs. Kitt spent hours making notes and locating source materials. The staff of the Library of the University of Arizona has at all times been extremely helpful,

# PREFACE

particularly its Reference Department under Donald Powell. To Dr. Louis Shellbach, until late 1957 Naturalist at the Grand Canyon, special thanks are given for his opening the files at the Naturalist's Headquarters, wherein were found otherwise unobtainable items. The staff of the Museum of Northern Arizona at Flagstaff has contributed materially to the contents of this book, and grateful acknowledgment is made to Dr. Harold S. Colton, its now retired director, and to Miss Katharine Bartlett of its library, for their able assistance.

Individuals by the score have contributed to the present book, some by interviewing old timers in remote corners of their own counties. Among such people Mrs. Clara G. Woody of Globe stands out. Mrs. Woody knows the history of Gila County and is well acquainted with its pioneers, many of whom she personally interviewed. The same may be said of Miss Elizabeth Shannon, Miss Harriet Sweeting and Mr. James Monroe Patton of Clifton. In Coconino County Mr. and Mrs. William Corey contributed their efforts through their close association with the Northern Branch of the Arizona Pioneers' Historical Society. Mrs. Corey was the editor's right hand in locating pioneers who had the knowledge being sought. Robert Lennon of Patagonia was extremely helpful all along the line. Having lived in and mapped both Yuma and Santa Cruz Counties, Mr. Lennon was able to save the editor weeks which otherwise might have had to be devoted to basic research. What worth the Tombstone section of this volume may have can be attributed in no small part to the work of Mrs. Edna G. Landin, President of the Tombstone Restoration Commission, whose tireless and enthusiastic help the editor now gratefully acknowledges. Albert H. Schroeder, author of many articles on the Southwest and at that time an archaeologist on the staff of the Southwestern National Monuments, time and again came forward with specific help and suggestions.

The present volume contains information on post offices, including their dates of establishment, names of the first postmasters, changes in name of the office, and the date of discontinuance if known. Also included is information on Wells Fargo Stations. The accumulation of such information takes years, but that time was telescoped for the present work by the generous contributions of Mr. and Mrs. John Theobald of Phoenix, both of whom have spent literally years searching old newspapers, microfilms of official post office records, and other sources covering the territorial period 1863-1912. Information for the period 1912-1930 on post offices was taken from a microfilm of official documents which the Theobalds kindly permitted the editor to use.

Maps by the hundreds have been searched with magnifying glass and dividers. Through the kind assistance of Senator Carl Hayden, copies of old maps were made at the National Archives in Washington and shipped to the editor. Thanks are due to Senator Hayden for his assistance on many questions. The correspondence with his office has been voluminous and endlessly productive.

Carl H. Mapes, Chief Map Editor of Rand McNally and Company, provided the editor with copies of old Rand McNally maps and also of the *Business Atlas* information to accompany the maps. It was these maps which contained places not shown elsewhere, and thanks are due to Mr. Mapes for his courtesy and cooperation. Phil Townsend Hanna provided a copy of the excellent "Indian Country" map produced by the Automobile Club of Southern California, which proved extremely helpful. As for elevations contained in this volume, many were taken from aerial maps supplied through the courtesy of Senator Barry

# PREFACE

Goldwater. The editor gratefully acknowledges help given by those who have made it possible to cover locations for entries in this book. Where no map locations could be given, information concerning locations is sometimes given by range and township, sometimes by descriptions taken from source materials.

The decision to include pronunciations in the present volume automatically imposed certain problems. The editor was extremely fortunate in enlisting the aid of Dr. C. F. Voegelin, head of the Department of Anthropology of Indiana University and a noted linguist, in working out a phonemic system which will be found under the "Pronunciation Guide." During his sojourn in Flagstaff, Dr. Voegelin also tape recorded Hopi place name pronunciations. Indian place names brought in a specialized field. Expert help was procured in several areas, notably from Alden Jones, assistant superintendent of the Papago Indian Agency and author of a book on Papago place names. Robert W. Young, who is assistant superintendent of the Navajo Agency and who writes the annual report on Navajo affairs, spent many hours with the editor going over Navajo place names. Valuable information and lines of communication exist in other Indian areas: with the Mojave Indian Council, with the Hualapais, with the Pimas, and others, but lack of time has precluded thoroughgoing research which the editor hopes to accomplish on Indian place names in the future. Spanish pronunciations and those of English names with an "Arizona twist" are given phonemically under the entries concerned. Dr. M. D. Clubb of the University of Kansas, an expert on the Grand Canyon, provided pronunciations for names in that area.

Material in the main body of many entries has come not only from books and interviews and old newspapers, but also from personally annotated copies of the first edition of *Arizona Place Names*. As mentioned, Will C. Barnes' own copy contributed materially. Also used was the personal copy of the late Dr. Sidney Pattison, provided by Mrs. H. Harwood Pattison of Santa Fe, New Mexico. A third was that of Mr. Roscoe Willson of Phoenix, well known for his weekly columns on Arizona history.

The editor wishes to express to Dean Francis Roy of the Liberal Arts College of the University of Arizona thanks for making available the great amount of help to produce the manuscript. Thanks are also due to Dr. Desmond Powell as chairman of the Place Names Committee which helped solve problems. To the many students who, while working their way through the university helped with the Place Names project, the editor says "thank you," particularly to Miss Janet Veith for her accurate analysis of maps, to Mrs. C. J. Barker, a graduate student in Speech, for her help on pronunciations, and to Mrs. Richard Sutton, and Mrs. John Dotis for their endless patience and accuracy in compiling the index and in other matters.

The present volume does not pretend to be complete. In the place names card files are hundreds of additional names on which much work remains to be done. There are many pioneers still to be interviewed. It is the editor's sincere hope that the current book on place names will arouse the interest of those who have information so that they may step forward to communicate what they know. Place names are like quick-silver: they refuse to be still. For that reason the editor realizes that ultimately there must be another and still another revision of place names. Meanwhile, may the present book serve its purpose and may it prove a stimulus to centralization of information on the place names of Arizona.

# HOW TO USE THIS BOOK

Entries are largely self-explanatory. However, the following notations may prove helpful.

**Use of the Index**

To locate a place name, look it up alphabetically in the Index. i.e., for Adair:

ADAIR      NAVAJO      look up the entry under the section on Navajo County. Entries are given alphabetically by county.

For Adair Wash:

Adair Wash      See: ADAIR, NAVAJO      Navajo

This indicates that the name has a common origin with that of Adair. Therefore look up the entry listed in capital letters.

**Elevations:**

Maximum elevations have generally been used for mountains. Average elevations have been used for mesas and plateaus.

**Pronunciations:**

The "Pronunciation Guide" will prove simple to use after a brief familiarization with the symbols used for the English letters.

**Locations:**

Maps are included for each section in the book. On these the approximate location of a place may be checked. For accurate locations, see what map is given as having contained the name in question. Where a place has not been mapped by others on maps examined by the editor, the township and range or other helpful information will be given in the entry.

**Maps:**

Numbers have been used to indicate map sources. Thus "E-20" will be found listed under the section on "Bibliography: Maps" at the back of the book, where E-20 will be found to be the Smith map of 1879.

**Ref.:**

Books have been listed by number. The name of the source can be found by checking its number in the section on "Bibliography: Books."

Names of individuals interviewed are given. Information concerning them will be found under "Biographical Sketches."

**Variant Names:**

These are names which are used less frequently than the main entry, or which are corruptions of the main entry names.

**Associated names:**

This lists names which have origins in common with that of the main entry.

# PRONUNCIATION GUIDE

The following phonemic system was worked out for *Arizona Place Names* by Dr. C. F. Voegelin, head of the Department of Anthropology of Indiana University, and a noted linguist. It is based on the International Phonetic Alphabet.

| ENGLISH LETTER | PHONEMIC SOUND | ENGLISH WORD | PHONEMIC WRITING OF THE ENGLISH WORD |
|:---:|:---:|:---|:---|
| a | /ey/ | Apex | /éypeks/ |
| b | /b/ | Benson | /bénsən/ |
| c,s | /s/ | Cibola | /síbowlə/ |
| d | /d/ | Davis | /déyvis/ |
| e | /iy/ | Easter | /íyster/ |
| ui | /iy/ | Mesquite | /meskíyt/ |
| i | /iy/ | Pima | /pimə/ |
| f | /f/ | Finney | /fíniy/ |
| ph | /f/ | Phoenix | /fíyniks/ |
| g | /ǰ/ | Geronimo | /ǰeránimow/ |
| j | /ǰ/ | Jerome | /ǰerówm/ |
| h | /h/ | Holbrook | /hówlbruk/ |
| g | /h/ | Gila | /híylə/ |
| ay | /ay/ | Kayenta | /kayéntə/ or /kayentéy/ |
| ai | /ay/ | Kaibab | /kaybæb/ |
| i | /ay/ | Pine | /payn/ |
| k | /k/ | Kingman | /kíŋmən/ |
| c | /k/ | Cline | /klayn/ |
| q | /k/ | Queen | /kwiyn/ |
| l | /l/ | Lowell | /lowl/ or /lówəl/ |
| m | /m/ | Montezuma | /mòntəzúmə/ |
| n | /n/ | Needles | /níydlz/ |
| ng | /ŋ/ | King | /kiŋ/ |
| oa | /ow/ | Oak Creek | /owk kriyk/ |
| o | /ow/ | Otis | /ówtis/ |
| o (pure sound) | /o/ | Pedro | /péydro/ |
| p | /p/ | Parker | /párker/ |
| r | /r/ | Ray | /rey/ |
| er | /er/ | Water | /wáter/ |
| ir | /er/ | Fir | /fer/ |

# PRONUNCIATION GUIDE

| ENGLISH LETTER | PHONEMIC SOUND | ENGLISH WORD | PHONEMIC WRITING OF THE ENGLISH WORD |
|---|---|---|---|
| ur | /er/ | Fur | /fer/ |
| t | /t/ | Taylor | /téyler/ |
| y | /y/ | Yuma | /yúwmə/ |
| ll | /y/ | Mogollon | /məgiyówn/ |
| v | /v/ | Verde | /vérdiy/ |
| w | /w/ | Walker | /wɔ́ker/ |
| z | /z/ | Zuñi | /zúwni/ |
| ch | /č/ | Childs | /čayldz/ |
| th | /ɵ/ | Thatcher | /ɵǽčer/ |
| th | /ð/ | The Captains | /ðə kǽptənz/ |
| sh | /š/ | Show Low | /šowlow/ |
| ch | /š/ | Chevelon Creek | /ševlṇ kriyk/ |
| si | /ž/ | Artesia | /artíyžə/ |
| a | /æ/ | Babbitts | /bǽbəts/ |
| i | /i/ | Clip | /klip/ |
| wh | /hw/ | When | /hwen/ |
| e | /e/ | Helvetia | /helviyšə/ |
| u | /u/ | Bullard Peak | /bulerd piyk/ |
| oo | /u/ | Holbrook | /hówlbruk/ |
| u | /uw/ | Bruce | /bruws/ |
| o | /a/ | Robbins | /rábənz/ |
| a | /a/ | Ajo | /áho/ |
| au | /ɔ/ | Audrey | /ɔ́driy/ |
| a | /ɔ/ | Walker | /wɔ́ker/ |
| ou | /aw/ | House | /haws/ |
| oy | /oy/ | Moyer | /móyer/ |
| u (accented) | /ʌ/ | Upper | /ʌper/ |
| o | /ʌ/ | Other | /ʌðer/ |
| a | /ə/ | Above | /əbʌv/ |
|  |  | Apache | /əpǽci/ |
| h | /hy/ | Huge | /hyuwj/ |

x

# PRONUNCIATION GUIDE

In addition to the basic phonemic guide, listed below are sounds which were encountered in rendering Indian and Spanish place names. Navajo, for instance, is a highly inflected language. The guide was worked out by Mrs. C. J. Barker, a graduate student at the University of Arizona.

| PHONEMIC SYMBOL | ENGLISH WORD | PHONEMIC WRITING OF THE ENGLISH WORD | PURPOSE OF THE SYMBOL |
|---|---|---|---|
| ‿ (above the word) | Man | /mæn/ | Nasalized at times. |
| : (after a letter) | This city | /ðis:iˆ/ | To show lengthening as though the consonant sound is made twice its expected length. In isolated cases the sound is held longer, while being made so softly that only a little is heard. (See Navajo.) |
| · (after a letter | | | For a vowel to show half-lengthening beyond usual length. |
| | | /a:y/ | For a diphthong, when half of it is held longer than the other. |
| · (under a letter) | Button | /bʌtṇ/ | When the sound is made as a syllable by itself. |
| | Little | /lítḷ/ | |
| ° (under a letter) | | /z̦/ | A de-voicing symbol. /z/ has an "s"-like quality, but is not quite an "s." |
| | | /b̦/ | Has a "p"-like quality, but is not quite a "p" as in the word *exponent* in which a little of the sound is heard but not in regular duration. |
| ˆ (above and to the right of a letter) | | | Raises the sound so that it is made higher in the mouth, but not high enough to become another phonemic sound. |
| ˇ (above and to right of a letter) | Ligurta | /liyˇgertə/ | Lowers the sound so that it is made lower in the mouth. |

XI

# PRONUNCIATION GUIDE

| PHONEMIC SYMBOL | ENGLISH WORD | PHONEMIC WRITING OF THE ENGLISH WORD | PURPOSE OF THE SYMBOL |
|---|---|---|---|
| > (above and to right of a letter) | | | Fronts the sound so that it is made farther toward the front of the mouth, as "s" is made closer to the front than is "t." |
| ' | Accent | /ǽksent/ | Primary accent. |
| ` | Montezuma | /mòntəzúmə/ | Secondary accent. |
| ? | Ouch | /ʔawč/ | Glottal stop. The way most people say *ouch!* |
| /gh/ | | /rogʰar/ | As an exponent. The Spanish g *(rogar)* made far back in the throat. |
| /æl/ | Corral | /koræl/ | |
| /ær/ | Care | /kær/ | |
| g | | | Vocalized g |
| i | | | Nasalized i |

Throughout this volume where Navajo place names occur, variant spellings will be noticed. Navajo until recently was not a written language, and the many ways in which place names are rendered represent attempts by non-Navajos to spell what the ear — often faulty — has heard. Preference in such cases has been given to the spellings used at the Navajo Agency headquarters.

# ARIZONA'S PLACE NAMES

Arizona is the sixth largest state in the nation, encompassing 113,810 square miles in which the elevation varies from 137 feet above sea level to the lofty San Francisco Peaks, rising 12,610 feet. The state contains violent contrasts, from burning desert floor to evergreen-clad mountains with running streams. Arizona's topography has, of course, had a primary effect on her place names. Roughly the state divides into three areas. The first is the Arizona (also called the Coconino, Plateau, some 45,000 square miles in the northern and eastern part of the state, where the general elevation is 6500 feet. The area has several volcanic summits over 10,000 feet high. Vast gorges and profound canyons slice the plateau. The most spectacular, of course, is the Grand Canyon. Toward the south the plateau slopes to its rim, the great Mogollon escarpment, which drops abruptly hundreds of feet into the Basin area of the State.

The Basin Range encloses about 68,000 square miles in southern Arizona, spreading across to the state's eastern boundary. The Basin is considered to have two divisions: (1) the Mountain District between the Arizona Plateau and (2) the Plains, a region of 27,000 square miles. Range upon range of mountains cut across the Mountain District, while the Plains contain both mountains and desert. The vast plateaus, the great canyons, the rich valleys and mineral-laden mountains, the dry desert stretches have all governed the course of men and the origin of place names. The presence or absence of water, however, has always been the controlling influence. For this reason the rivers of Arizona loom large in her history.

Chief among the rivers is the great Colorado. Whereas other streams in the state have either dried up from natural causes or have been dammed so that their lower stretches are dry, the Colorado remains a running stream, although a controlled one now in contrast to its earlier violence in flood. Because the Colorado has always been the most important stream in the region, something of its history bears discussion.

The first white man known to have seen the mouth of the Colorado River was Capt. Fernando Alarcon in May 1540, whose assigned task it was to take supplies to the Coronado expedition which was making its way overland. Perhaps for this reason Alarcon dubbed the stream El Río de Buena Guía (The River of Good Guidance). It proved not to be such a good guide, however, for the two parties did not meet. His name for the river did not survive, nor did any of several given to the stream by other explorers and by the Indians on its banks. The name finally settled upon is a translation of Fr. Francisco Garcés' Río Colorado, now called the Colorado River. Whatever name it has borne, the Colorado River has always been important to Arizona as an avenue of transportation and a means of irrigation. Along its banks and in its Grand Canyon are hundreds of place names. The same is true of two other principal streams, the Gila River and the Little Colorado, both now dry along much of their length.

Not boating water, however, but drinking water has been of primary importance. Early explorers, particularly those in the 1840's and 1850's, reported that fish were abundant in many small running streams and that grass, which grew belly high to a horse, promised a land rich for raising cattle and for farming. Explorers, emigrants to the West Coast, miners, soldiers, cowmen — all looked first for water. In consequence, the smallest well in the dry desert was of great importance and place names for the guidance of the thirsty traveler became attached to water holes. Sometimes in the rainy season there was too much water and

XIII

gentle streams went on rampages which wiped out settlements, Indian and white. Gradually the streams dried up. Gone are the silvery fish, the running rivers, the high-waving grass. The causes are obscure, although unquestionably over-grazing added to the havoc wrought by continual drought.

That the rivers have run and dried before in prehistoric times may be adduced from the number of Indian ruins which mutely reveal that hundreds of years ago another great drought must have dessicated the land, forcing out the Indian farmers. Although place names have not, of course, come down from the deserted ruins to the present day, the Indian influence both prehistoric and contemporary is strong. From about 1100 A.D. to 1400 A.D. thousands of Indians roamed what is now Arizona, leaving a criss-crossing of paths from pueblo to pueblo and camping site to camping site. Indian trade, according to archaeological indications, was brisk. When white men came, they followed Indian paths. The deserted Indian irrigation ditches — literally by the mile — were put back to work. And though the great number of Indians thought to have been in the area at one time were gone, thousands of Indians of various tribes still remained. Contacts with Indians, peaceful and otherwise, have left their imprint on Arizona place names.

The lure of quick-and-easy wealth has from the first attracted white men to Arizona. It was this which drew the expedition of Francisco Vasquez de Coronado in 1540 after Fr. Marcos de Niza returned to Mexico City in 1539 with rumors of the fabled Seven Cities of Cibola. Spaniards believed in the possibility that the towns existed, for in their own background was the legend of the bishop who fled from the Arabs, taking with him vast treasures and establishing seven cities in the unexplored world. Why should not the fabled Seven Cities be those far to the north of Mexico City? Excited by the possibility, Coronado set off for the wilds with hundreds of soldiers, hundreds of Indians, hundreds of horses, cattle and sheep. The journey was neither quick nor easy and failure lay at its terminus, but from the reports of the expedition came the first recording of place names in today's Arizona.

The disappointed Spaniards did not again enter the region for many years. Then in 1595 Juan de Oñate set out to colonize Pueblo Land. When he crossed the Río Grande in 1598, Oñate took formal possession of New Mexico in the name of Philip II, King of Spain. Other explorations followed, their delineation not being within the scope of this volume, since they had little or no influence on Arizona place names. As for the Spanish maps, their makers exhibited an almost joyful haphazardness in tracing the features of the *terra incognita*.

Spanish missionaries became active in the early 17th century in the Hopi villages and New Mexican pueblos. Toward the end of the century they entered southern Arizona from Sonora. Of prime importance among the latter group was Fr. Eusebio Kino, a Jesuit. As a young man, on what threatened to be his deathbed, Kino vowed to devote his life to God's service in the event he lived. His intention was to missionize in China, but he was sidetracked into Mexico, going from there to the frontier of Christendom, Pimería Alta or "Upper Pima Land," in the mid-1690's. The tireless Kino explored from east to west and north to south, going down the Gila River, recrossing the desert, visiting tribes on the present-day San Pedro River, spreading the Word of God. The records kept by Kino and his lieutenant, Juan Mateo Manje, survive as do some, at least, of his maps, and they are replete with place names, many of which are still in use. Kino died in 1711.

Meanwhile, to the north in the Hopi villages other Spanish missionaries had been at work. The Indian's dislike of the domineering Spaniards grew to seething hatred. Revolt flared in 1680 and for a time no living Spaniard was seen in the region. The Spaniards returned to the New Mexican pueblos, which proved tractable, but never again did they successfully enter Hopi land. Perhaps fearing reprisals for their slaughter of the Spaniards, the Hopis deserted their valley villages for the impregnable high mesas where they live today.

In southern Arizona the missionaries who succeeded Kino did not have his magic touch with the Indians. The priests had trouble controlling the cruel rapacity of the Spanish military units. Revolt was slower to develop but come it did, in 1751. Two years later it was over with Spanish dominion again in force.

During the days of Spanish rule, the name applied to what is now southern Arizona was Sonora, whereas what is now northern Arizona was then a part of New Mexico (as southern Arizona came to be when the United States made the Gadsden Purchase in 1853). Sonora was a rich mining region. Because of its size it became necessary to apply a place name to clarify what part of Sonora was being referred to in reports. Thus the term "District of Arizonac" was given to that part of Sonora now occupied in part by Pima County, Arizona. The name was that of a station of the Saric Mission, called Arizonac, near which were valuable silver mines. Ores found in the Baboquivari Mountains and near Arivaca, for instance, were taken to Arizonac and shipped from there to Mexico City. The word *arizonac* is derived from Papago Indian words, *ali* ("small") and *shonak* ("place of the spring"), or "place of the small spring." Arizona historian James H. McClintock said that Padre Ortega in 1754 referred to the Real de Arizona as "the town in whose district were silver mines" in 1751. McClintock said that the Spaniards dropped the letter *c* and adapted the Indian name to Spanish phonetics. He set the location of Arizonac as west of Old Sasabe about eight miles and south of the international boundary about a mile at a place called Banera. Here, according to an Arizona pioneer named Isaac D. Smith, the Indians used a small stream which they called Aleh-zon ("young spring"). Smith told McClintock that the Spaniards destroyed the village of Arizonac c. 1790.

In 1821 Mexico broke free from Spain. Until 1825 her State of Sonora stretched to the Gila River. The portion which is now Arizona was separated for a brief period and then again joined to Sonora. There it remained until the Gadsden Purchase of 1853 when upper Sonora became part of the United States, being known as Doña Ana County, Territory of New Mexico. By the purchase the United States moved her boundary line far south of the Gila River, but missed by several miles the original plan to secure a seaport on the Gulf of California. She acquired a region which was already dotted with place names of Spanish and Indian derivation.

The Gadsden Purchase brought new riches and new troubles to the United States. Part of the trouble stemmed from the Gold Rush in California. Americans by the thousands swarmed to the West Coast, some by way of Cape Horn, some across the Isthmus of Panama or across central Mexico, and others by struggling across the unexplored vastness of lands beyond the Mississippi and in the great Southwest. The clamor for safer and better routes led to a series of explorations by military engineers and topographers. Armed with transit and chain these men searched for possible routes for sturdy wagons, for suitable terrain to hold rails of shining steel, for information about water, without which men in the desert dropped and died. First came Lt. Col. Philip St. George Cooke with his peaceful Mormon Battalion in 1846-47. Many of these men noted the high waving grass and rich hills, and many returned to settle in Arizona. In 1847 came Lt. Col. William H. Emory, searching for the new international boundary line. Inevitably as white men made inroads on Indian territory troubles developed. To the north and east in 1849 came Lt. James Hervey Simpson to carry out American promises made in 1848 under the Treaty of Guadelupe Hidalgo, to subdue the unruly Navajo. In 1851 young Lt. Lorenzo Sitgreaves made his lonely way through heat, hail, and freezing cold across the vast Arizona Plateau, nearly succumbing to starvation and thirst along his route to the Colorado River. Next was Lt. Amiel W. Whipple sighting for the Pacific Railroad Survey along the 35th parallel in 1853-54.

To the south the Boundary Survey Commission was at work, and Lt. John G. Parke inched eastward through hostile Apache land, establishing a route later followed closely by the Southern Pacific Railroad. While naked Indians squatted on the banks of the Colorado River and watched, Lt. Joseph Christmas Ives and his party in 1857 steamed up the Colorado River in the *U.S.S. Explorer.* When the vessel smashed on rocks, Ives and his men swung overland. They dropped down a trail for a visit with the Havasupai Indians in a side gorge of the Grand Canyon. The trail was so steep and dizzy that many of the men had to crawl cautiously from their mules and lie flat to overcome vertigo. In the wake of the military men came the prospectors, the miners, the settlers. Steamers began to ply the Colorado, bringing in supplies for the mines, riding downstream with their holds loaded with ores for San Francisco and Liverpool. All of these activities left their mark on Arizona place names.

As gold was playing out in California, it was being found in placers near Yuma and in veins to the north in the Cerbat Mountains. Prospectors flocked in with sturdy burros and pick and shovel. Where they made rich finds, they sold out to miners, and, overnight, ramshackle tent cities took shape. Inevitably, the Indians objected and United States soldiers established forts to protect the rights of white men. In most areas the military succeeded in subduing the native Indians, but not so in south-eastern Arizona where strike-and-run Apaches put an end to many mining ventures and attempts at settlement. The renegade Mexicans were, if anything, more deadly than the Apaches, but from the pioneers' viewpoint, for a more practical reason. Mexicans attacked to rob, whereas the Indians attacked to protect land they could not hope to hold.

A favorite place for Mexican attack was the string of stage stations from border to border. There were no banks, and station keepers of necessity kept in their stations what funds they had. The stations were the ganglia in the system of communication in Arizona. They were ports of call not only for stage coaches, but for freighters and emigrant parties. For twenty-two years, various stage lines served Arizona, disappearing when the railroad men pounded the last spike into place. Greatest of the stage lines was the Butterfield Overland Mail, which at one time employed two thousand men along its route from St. Louis to San Diego. Operations began in September, 1858, and within a year there were stations on an average of one every twenty miles along the entire route. In Arizona, where the line roughly followed the path laid down by the Mormon Battalion, stations often were no more than nine miles apart. The men who built the stations and ran the line sometimes gave their posts names reminiscent of home towns in faraway New York. With the coming of the Civil War, the Butterfield line through Arizona was dropped. Many of the stations fell into decay, while others continued to be used. Their place names dot the early maps.

In 1863 Abraham Harlow Peeples organized a prospecting party under the guidance of the scout Pauline Weaver. Setting out from Yuma the group made its way overland until it arrived at what is now known as Antelope Peak. Here early one morning Mexicans in search of straying pack animals found nuggets of gold. Before breakfast Peeples picked up over $7,000 in nuggets. The immediate result was a surge of the mining population toward Antelope Hill and to the gulches near what is now Prescott. More rich finds were made and the hills literally swarmed with mining men. Names were placed on the land, hundreds of them, as mining camps took shape, and the hills and valleys resounded to the thud and clang of miner's pick and shovel.

In other parts of the recently acquired Gadsden Purchase miners were also at work. Rich copper ores at Ajo were being shipped for smelting. Men seeking to file claims in remote places complained because they had to go too far to take care of paper work under the government of New Mexico. They grumbled too because the governing agencies were remote from the centers of trouble between white men and red. For such practical reasons men began agitating to have their land set apart from the Territory of New Mexico. In 1858 New Mexico first expressed her willingness to free Arizona. In Washington, D.C., Charles Debrille Poston, a leading spirit in the development of mines in southern Arizona, was working hard to create an Arizona Territory. He was to earn the nickname "Father of Arizona." Poston took advantage of the absence of southerners from Congress to see that a bill for the creation of Arizona Territory should be submitted. Following an oyster supper at which Poston treated his guests royally to win their support, the bill passed, and on February 23, 1863, the Territory of Arizona became a political fact. President Lincoln appointed John A. Gurley territorial governor, but Gurley died before getting west of the Mississippi. His successor was John N. Goodwin.

The gubernatorial party soon started its westward trek. On November 26, 1863, it left Santa Fe; in mid-December it left Albuquerque. There was need for haste. The governor had to be sworn in on Arizona ground before the first of the coming year. On December 27 the party crossed the 109th meridian into Arizona, but since there was doubt that they were actually in Arizona, the men hastened to a spot known to be in the new territory. There at Navajo Springs on December 29 John N. Goodwin took the oath of office and the government of the new territory was officially formed in the open wilds. From Navajo Springs the party went to a small army post near what is now Prescott. Mining activities in the hills of that area led to the decision that the territorial capital should be established there, and in very short order the name Prescott was added to the Arizona map.

A major problem facing the new government was to provide protection for her citizens against those Indians who had not yet been subdued. This was a job for military men, and the story is a long and bloody one. To the west of Prescott were the far from subdued Hualapai Indians. Between them and Prescott were troublesome Yavapai Indians. In the southern part of the territory Apaches of various tribes were flaying settlers alive or roasting them to death. Only the Pimas, the Papagos and the Maricopas were friendly to white men. The need for protection existed almost everywhere in the new territory, and there were too few military men to get the job done. Easterners, their own troubles with native Indians having reached into the past, made sympathetic noises about the plight of the poor Indian. Arizonans worked their mines or plowed their fields with guns at the ready and stated flatly that the only good Indian was a dead one. Caught between the extremes of opinions were the generals in the field, who had terms as commanders in Arizona as brief as those of many French cabinet leaders. Some military men were able and some were not, but the best of the lot was General George Crook, the only one to be called back for a second assignment in the nation's Indian trouble-spot. The military men, the Indian massacres and battles, the victims on both sides, left their heritage in Arizona place names.

One by one the Indian tribes gave in to the overpowering force of the white men who came increasingly to Arizona. As predicted, cattlemen raised enormous herds. They sold their beef to agents for Indian reservations, to residents in the growing villages, to the great slowly snaking mass of railroad construction crews laying tracks across desert and plateau. The brands used by the cattlemen and their own names — like those of the railroaders — remain in many places.

As the railroad tracks were spiked into position, the post office known as Terminus rolled slowly forward from west to east across Arizona. On January 27, 1879, Frank B. Wightman took up his duties as postmaster on the railroad car which was to accompany the construction crews from Yuma to New Mexico. Also on board was a Wells Fargo Station. Mile by slow mile Terminus moved across the southern part of the territory until finally the last letter had been distributed to the last worker and the post office ceased to exist on April 11, 1881. The two-year trip of the post office on wheels probably holds the record for the slowest ever made by a railroad car.

Along the new rails in southern Arizona and along the line of the Atlantic and Pacific railroad to the north, the steam engines rolled, pausing periodically to take on water for their boilers. In many places wells had to be dug through the dry crust of the earth to find water. Necessarily, section houses were built where wells existed. Around the section houses communities often grew, for where there was water, men settled. Added to this source of place names was the fact that the government had subsidized the railroads to insure that the transcontinental lines would be laid. In consequence, the railroads were given every other section of land along their rights of way. These sections were named, often for reasons which seem lost.

Arizona was beginning to settle down into the pattern of contemporary civilization. In 1886 her citizens saw the last of Apache bloodshed. Rich mining discoveries such as those at Globe and in Tombstone attracted not only miners, but settlers. At approximately the same time members of the Church of Jesus Christ of Latter-day Saints began establishing colonies along the Little Colorado River, moving from there deeper into Arizona when the river colonies failed. Mormons settled at Mesa, near Phoenix, and along the San Pedro in southeastern Arizona. As the population increased Arizona's citizens began thinking of her in terms of a state. Arizona became the nation's forty-eighth state on February 14, 1912.

The Arizona kaleidoscope continues to change. Places vanish, but their names and stories remain. Diesel power replaced steam on the railroads and the towns around the wells crumbled. Floods washed away some villages; controlled irrigation now creates others. Old mines cave in and gnarled mesquite grows in the openings. Uranium is discovered and the Navajo frowns at the intruders' uprooting old Indian names. Swift modern transportation erases the importance of old watering places, but creates new names where fishermen alight on flight strips for a day's angling on the Colorado or a week's sojourn in the high, cool mountains. Arizona's place names are a folk history of her people and her cultures, and, as such, their origins are often as attractive and ephemeral as a rainbow following a desert shower.

# CONTENTS

# APACHE

*White House ruins in Canyon de Chelly — Apache wickiup and cattle — McNary lumbering.*

## APACHE:
Pro.:   /əpǽči/

On February 24, 1879, Apache County was created out of Yavapai County, one of the four original Arizona counties. The area assigned to Apache County was not to remain undisturbed, for in 1881 that part of it between the Black and Gila Rivers was cut off to form part of what is now Graham County. Apache also lost a great stretch of land when Navajo County was formed. Apache County's present area is 7,151,360 acres. The county seat is St. Johns *(q.v.)*.

Apache County was named for the Apache Indians of.Arizona and New Mexico. The first reference found to the name *Apache* is in an account of the 1581 Espejo Expedition, in which they are called *Apichi*. The word *Apache* is derived from the Yuman *apa* ("man"), *ahwa* ("war; fight; battle"), and *tche,* which pluralizes the combination. As a nation the Apache Indians did not exist, the term being applied comprehensively to many tribes. According to Cortez, who wrote about this matter in 1799, the Spaniards included as Apaches the Tonto Apaches, the Chiricahuas, Gilenos, Mimbrenos, Taracones, Mescaleros, Llaneros, Lipanes and the Navajos.

Almost from their initial contact with white men, the Apaches dealt death and destruction to the invading race. Their usual method of attack was to ambush individuals or small groups, their primary intent being to steal and, if necessary to kill in order to steal. This early haphazard approach soon changed to vengeful and purposeful killing after the Apaches themselves had been repeatedly attacked and slaughtered by early Spanish-Americans and later by Americans. However, the warlike Apaches also included among their enemies the peaceful Pimas and Maricopas, who lived along the Gila and Salt Rivers.

One by one the Apache tribes were either decimated until they were no longer able to withstand the incursions of settlers, or they were subdued in large groups and herded onto reservations set aside for their use, such as the Fort Apache Reservation *(q.v.* Navajo) and the Navajo Reservation *(q.v.* Apache).

Apache County is a cattle-raising and lumbering area in that portion which has not been assigned to Indian reservations. Many sheep are raised on the Navajo Reservation, a large portion of which is in Apache County. Other agricultural activities are conducted in the county.

## ADAMANA

El.: c. 5600'  Loc.: Apache 2, B-10
Pro.: /ǽdəmǽnə/
This place name is a contraction of the name of Adam Hanna, who with Jim Cart grazed cattle in the area. Hanna's ranch on the Rio Puerco was at Adamana. Hanna later sold out, moving to Farmington, New Mexico, where he died. The station named *Adamana* was erected by the A.T. & S.F. R.R. c. 1890 for use by early tourists who wished to visit the nearby Petrified Forest.

P.O. est. January 21, 1896. Adam Hanna, p.m. Discont. 1910. Wells Fargo Station, 1904.

Ref.: Grigsby; Barnes; *Arizona Times*, February 18, 1947 (State Library Files). Maps: C-14; GI-19.

## AGATE BRIDGE

El.: 5575'  Loc.: Apache 2, BC-11.2
A partly buried petrified rock, one hundred and eleven feet long, Agate Bridge is the largest piece of petrified wood in the Petrified Forest National Monument. A concrete support prevents it from breaking.

Ref.: 4, p. 312. Maps: GI-8; GI-9.

## AGUA SAL CREEK

El.: c. 5000'  Loc.: Apache 1, EH-6-8
Pro.: /ǽgwəsǽl/  Spanish: "salt water"
The unpalatable water of the stream suggested the name.

Ref.: Barnes; 71, p. 91. Maps: C-12; GA-25.

## ALCOVE CANYON

El.: c. 6000'  Loc.: Apache 1, GE-5-3
Herbert Gregory selected this name because of the many alcoves in the canyon walls.

Ref.: 71, pp. 31, 190. Maps: D-4.

## ALLENTOWN

El.: 6000'  Loc.: Apache 2, HI-6.6
Allan Johnson, who had been with the A.T. & S.F. R.R. during its construction period, settled near here and ran cattle. A shipping station was established c. 1900 and a little community developed. The place was deserted for many years. It has now completely disappeared as a result of Navajos' carting away the buildings for their own use.

P.O. est. October 11, 1924. Joseph A. Grubbs, p.m. Discont. June 2, 1930.

Ref.: Grigsby; P.O. Records; David H. Clark, letter, May 11, 1956. Maps: C-11; GA-1.

## ALPINE

El.: c. 8000'  Loc.: Apache 3, H-9
Descriptive. The town of Alpine is located in a piny area. Alpine developed from a log house (known as Fort Bush) owned by Anderson Bush, who in 1876 came into what is today called Bush Valley, in which Alpine is located. Bush sold out c. 1879 to William Maxwell and Fred Hamblin, Mormons, who in turn sold to Mormon settlers from Luna, New Mexico. Fred's brother, the famous Mormon explorer Jacob Hamblin, is buried at Alpine. In 1880 the settlers built a log-house fort about a mile southeast of the present Alpine.

Bush Valley is said to be the highest place in the United States where farming is successful.

P.O. est. January 7, 1885. William G. Black, p.m.

Ref.: Noble; 167, p. 128; 112, pp. 186, 187; 4, p. 429; Evans Coleman File, APHS; "Record of Heber Ward, Luna, N. M.," Ms. Map: C-6.

## AMBERON FLAT

El.: c. 8300'  Loc.: Apache 3, E-7.
At junction of East and West Forks.
Pro.: /ǽmberan/
The first settler in the area of the present town of Greer was Amberon Englevson, who in 1877 began grazing his horses in the valley. Englevson, a freighter, built a corral for his horses on Amberon Flat, a name which came into existence following the Norwegian's death in 1880 when his horses stampeded in the corral and killed him.

Ref.: Butler; Wentz. Maps: None.
a.n. Amberon Point  Apache

## ANTELOPE HOUSE

El.: c. 6000'  Loc.: Apache 1, F-10.75
About seven miles from the entrance to Canyon de Chelly is a large eleventh-century ruin named because of pictographs of red and white antelope painted on the canyon wall above it. The painting, however, is modern, having been done by a Navajo in the mid-nineteenth century.

Ref.: 4, p. 420; 167, p. 23. Map: GA-26.
a.n. Antelope Point  El.: 6189'. Map: GA-2.  Apache

## APACHE LAKE

Loc.: Near north fork of White Mountain River
Pro.: /əpǽči/
Mentioned by Gilbert of Wheeler's expedition (1873) as a pond characterized by its holding water just a short time.

Ref.: 175, III, 538; 85, p. 477. Maps: None.

## APACHE NATIONAL FOREST

Loc.: Southeastern part of Apache County and northern part of Greenlee County.
Pro.: /əpǽči/
An area of high timbered country, clear streams, deep ravines, and pleasant mountain meadows, Apache National Forest was established on August 17, 1898, as the Black Mesa Forest Reserve, named for Black Mesa. On July 1, 1908, the forest was given its present name. The Arizona portion of this forest covers 677,823 acres, with additional acreage in New Mexico.

Ref.: 120, pp. 34, 36. Map: GA-1.

## BALDY, MOUNT

El.: 11,590'  Loc.: Apache 3, C-7
Descriptive. The current name replaces the older historic name, Mount Thomas.

When Capt. George M. Wheeler passed here in 1873, he noted that the view from the summit was "the most magnificent and effective of any among the large number that have come under my observation. Outstretched before us lay the tributaries of seven principal streams . . . four main mountain peaks . . . valley lands far surpassing any I have before seen. The view of the landscape to the east is of the most marvelous beauty of form and color. Mountain, forest, valley, and stream are blended in one harmonious whole . . . Few world-wide travelers in a lifetime even could be treated to a more perfect landscape, a true virgin solitude, undefiled by the presence of man."

Wheeler established camp here on what he referred to as "Thomas Peak." The mountain was named for Gen. Lorenzo Thomas (d. March 2, 1875) who served in the war against Mexico. He was made a major general in 1865.

Ref.:   175, I, 63, 64. Maps: GA-25; E-20; C-5.

## BALUKAI MESA

El.: 7630'                         Loc.: Apache 1, AC-12-15
Pro.: /ḫa:lók:ʔa:y/               Navajo: *Baa lo'k'aa'i,*
                                  "a place with reeds on it"
Descriptive. This is a summer Navajo range.

v.n. Salahkai Mesa
Ref.:   167, p. 129; 73, p. 18; 71, p. 49. Maps: C-6 through C-14.
a.n. Balukai Wash                                    Apache

## BANNON

El.: 7000'                         Loc.: Apache 3, BC-4.1
James Bannon was an early settler and cattleman.

P.O. est. March 19, 1920. Elizabeth S. Marble, p.m. Discont. December 31, 1942.
Ref.:   Hayden; P.O. Records. Maps: A-7; C-12.

## BAT CANYON

El.: c. 6000'                      Loc.: Apache 1, F-11
                 Navajo: *jaá abaní há atiin,* "bat trail"
The canyon takes its name from Bat Rock on the Bat Trail at the point where the canyon begins to flatten out. This rock is said to be infested with bats. The American name is a translation of the older Navajo place name.

Ref.:   167, p. 22. Map: GA-2.

## BATTLEGROUND

El.: c. 8000'                      Loc.: Apache 3, G-9.25.
                 On Black River near Sprucedale Lodge.
Some years after his arrest for cow stealing, followed by his escape from jail, young Bill Smith came back into home territory to see his brothers, Al, George and Floyd. They made the mistake of showing up at Crosby's store, sixteen miles south of Eagar. After the Smiths left, Crosby organized a posse to track Bill down. The Smiths were found in a sunken marshy meadow where a fierce gun battle ensued. Bill and two of the posse were killed. The place is now called the Battleground.

Ref.:   Thompson. Map: None.

## BATTLESHIP, THE

El.: 5530'                         Loc.: Apache 2, AB-11.25
Descriptive. This is a butte with several petrified logs jutting from its sides like big guns.

Ref.:   Branch. Maps: C-11; GI-8; GI-9.

## BEAUCHAMP PEAK

         Loc.: White Mtn. Ind. Reser. "a high round
         mountain, the end of a range, s.w. of Black River."
On July 25, 1864, J. W. Beauchamp left the main camp of the King S. Woolsey expedition to take bearings from the top of a nearby mountain. Woolsey reported that Beauchamp "was waylaid by six Indians, shot through the chest with a rifle, lanced, stripped, and left for dead. He lived some fifteen or twenty minutes, however, after we reached him, but died before we could get him to camp. We buried him at the foot of the mountain, which we named Beauchamp Peak . . . "

Ref.:   *Arizona Miner,* September 21, 1864, 1:2. Map: None.

## BEAUTY, CAMP

El.: c. 6000'                      Loc.: Apache 1, EI-10
                                   In Canyon de Chelly
Capt. George M. Wheeler's report of 1873 has a photograph of Camp Beauty, where the canyon walls are estimated to be one thousand feet high. A trail led from it to Fort Defiance, thirty-five miles away.

Ref.:   175, I, 75. Maps: None.

## BECKER LAKE

El.: c. 8000'                      Loc.: Apache 3, F-5.75
The Becker brothers — Julius and Gustav — created this lake by damming up a natural spring hole in 1882 for irrigation purposes. Several outlaws are buried at the bottom of this lake.

Ref.:   Becker (Gustav's son); Willson; Wiltbank. Map: GA-25.

## BEKIHATSO LAKE

El.: c. 6000'                      Loc.: Apache 1, DC-12
Pro.: /béy:ki?hatzów/             Navajo: *Be'e k'id hatsoh,*
                                  "big pond"
Bekihatso Lake is a sink-hole in Chinle Wash Valley. Although it has been known to hold water throughout the summer months, it is normally the largest dry lake in the region. The Navajo water monster is said to have appeared here. Old Navajos are reported to have been afraid to approach this place because sometimes the water made a groaning sound.

Ref.:   71, p. 36; 167, p. 8. Map: C-12.

## BENNY CREEK

El.: c. 8000'  Loc.: Apache 3, EF-7.3. Just north of Greer.
Benny and Rosey Creeks, lying side by side, memorialize a romance which didn't materialize. Prior to 1900 Rosey Thompson was set to marry Benny Howell, or so he thought, but while he was away getting the license, she ran off with Fred Hoffman and married him.

Ref.:   Wentz. Map: None.

## BIBO

El.: c. 5800'                      Loc.: Apache 2, C-10
Sol Bibo had a trading post here from 1880 to 1890.

Ref.:   Barnes. Map: C-12.

## BIG CAVE

El.: c. 6000'  Loc.: Apache 1, EI-10. 2 miles up Canyon de Chelly, from Cross Canyon trail.

This is one of the largest caves in Canyon de Chelly.

Ref.: 167, p. 25. Map: GA-2.

## BIG LAKE

El.: c. 10,000'  Loc.: Apache 3, F-9

In 1923 this area was merely a slough, but was even then called Big Lake. A dam built in 1934 created a true lake. The dam level was raised ten feet in 1954 so that it is now approximately fifty feet high. When the lake was still a shallow slough, wild game used to stand in it, finding refuge from the stinging bites of summer insects. Today the deeper waters are a haven for lake trout.

Ref.: Becker; Wentz; Wiltbank. Map: GA-25.

## BILLINGS

El.: c. 6000'  Loc.: Apache 2, C-9.75

This station on the A.T. & S.F. R.R. was named for an engineer with the first railroad construction party, according to one story. However, the Billings Cattle Company was established here c. 1883 by A. E. Henning, and it seems more likely that the name derived from that fact.

Ref.: Barnes. Maps: C-5; C-7.

## BITSIHUITOS BUTTE

El.: c. 8000'  Loc.: Apache 1, A-7

Pro.: /bətzíʰhwitᵈẓʔa>ˊs/  Navajo: *Bitsu'h hwits'os,* "tapered formation at its base" (i.e. at base of Yale Point)

Descriptive.

Ref.: 71, pp. 138, 190. Map: C-14.

## BLACK CREEK

El.: c. 6000'  Loc.: Apache 2, HI-7-1

Pro.: /bey:ᵏhatči^dǽ:uwʰliyˊniyˇ/  Navajo: *Be'ek'id halchu déé',* "flows from Red Lake"

At one time this important fifty-mile drainage flowed from its source in Black Lake at the west end of the Chusca Range, and from this lake it probably took its name. Later its waters were diverted into the present Red Lake reservoir.

Ref.: 71, pp. 33, 87, 88, 89; 167, p. 9; 73, p. 24.

Maps: D-1; D-4; D-7; C-4; C-11; C-12; C-6; C-10 (Bonito Valley and Defiance Creek).

a.n. **Black Creek Canyon**
Loc.: Between Oak Springs and Houck  Apache
Ref.: 73, pp. 104, 24.
  **Black Creek Valley**
  Loc.: Lies between Black Lake and Houck, Fort Defiance and St. Michaels  Apache
  In this valley are the oldest permanent white settlements within the Navajo Reservation. In 1850 Capt. James Hervey Simpson mentioned the valley as having attractive features.
  Ref.: Richard Van Valkenburgh & Frank Walker, *Masterkey,* 19: 89-94, May 1945. 71, pp. 26, 32, 33.
  **Black Lake**  Maps: D-4; C-12  Apache
  When Capt. Simpson in 1849 first saw this lake, the waters looked almost black. Its Spanish name was "Laguna Negra" (Black Lake). It was also known as El Salitre Negro (Spanish: "black saltpeter") and as Cieneguilla Chiquita.
  Ref.: R. Van Valkenburgh and Frank Walker, *Masterkey,* 19: 89-94, May, 1945.

## BLACK FOREST

El.: c. 5600"  Loc.: Apache 2, BC-9

Pieces of black petrified wood by the thousands give this area its name.

Ref.: Branch. Maps: GI-8; GI-9.

## BLACK MESA

El.: c. 6500'  Loc.: Apache 1, EA-10-15; Apache 2, EA-1
  Navajo: *Dziti'jiin,* "mountain extends black"

The name "Black Mesa" is the translation of the Navajo name, meaning "black streak mountain." The mesa is a land-locked island sharply defined by cliffs, with Salahkai Mesa forming its southeastern end.

v.n. **Zilh-le-jini** ("Black Mountains")  Map: D-1  Navajo
Ref.: 71, pp. 40, 190. Map: None:

## BLACK PINNACLE BUTTE

El.: c. 8500'  Loc.: Apache 1, HI-9.3

Pro.: /čéyžinih/  Navajo: *chézhiní,* "black rock"

The American name is a translation of the Navajo and is descriptive. Navajos use the name, sometimes spelled *tse-zhini,* for the black rock of many places. They also call this particular place *shashdits' inih* ("where the bear lived"). Black Pinnacle Butte is a volcanic ridge which towers above the pine forest.

v.n. **Sajini Butte**
  **Sezhini Butte**
  **Mal-pais Butte**

Ref.: 71, pp. 34, 190, 195; 167, p. 11. Map: D-4.

## BLACK RIVER

El.: c. 8000'  Loc.: Apache 3, FA-9-13

In 1826 James Ohio Pattie explored some eighty miles above the mouth of the fork of the Black River. Pattie called the middle or upper Salt River the "Black River." Today's Black River heads high on Mount Baldy, tumbling through canyons from twelve hundred to fifteen hundred feet deep. The canyon sides are lined with rugged black volcanic precipices. The Black River is over one hundred feet wide in places and runs for more than one hundred and fifty miles. It is in country so wild that the river is crossed by only two roads.

Lt. William Emory on October 26, 1846, called this stream the "Prieto" (Spanish: "black" or "dark").

King S. Woolsey in his report of September 21, 1864, gave the "Negrita" as one of the points of travel for his expedition. An editorial in the *Arizona Miner* notes that the name has been translated by the editor to "Black River," since Col. Woolsey felt the Negrita and Black were the same. The editor also noted the river was sometimes called the "Prieta."

Ref.: Schroeder; *Arizona Miner,* September 21, 1864, 1:4; Wentz; 87, p. 284; 22, p. 440.

Maps:. C-8; C-13; C-2 (South Fork Salt River).

a.n. **Black River Mountains**  Apache
There was an army skirmish with Indians here on October 18, 1886.

Ref.:   Schroeder.
**East Fork of Black River**
   Loc.: Heads in wet season at Crescent Lake        Apache
**v.n. North Fork**   (so called by Forest Service)
Ref.:   Wentz.
**West Fork of Black River**
   Loc.: Joins East Fork in Sec. 11 T. 4.5 N., R. 28 E., Apache
This is the highest stream in the White Mountains, rising
two hundred feet below the top of Mount Baldy. It used to
be called Buffalo Creek, hence today's name for Buffalo
Crossing.
Ref.:   Wentz.

## BLACK ROCK

El.: c. 6000'                          Loc.: Apache 2, I-1
Descriptive. This is a translation of the Navajo name (see
Black Pinnacle Butte for similar translation of the name).
The volcanic dyke known as Black Rock, which rises over
one hundred fifty feet, forms a jagged ridge.
Ref.:   167, p. 12. Map: D-4.
**a.n. Black Rock**   El.: 6664'. Maps: GA-25; GA-18   Apache
**v.n. Black Rock Point**

## BLUE FOREST

El.: c. 5500'                          Loc.: Apache 2, B-10.25
John Muir, the naturalist, named this forest because of its
bentonite (blue) clay. Petrified wood is many colors, but
never blue. Blue Forest is a lowland area with petrified logs,
chips, and pieces scattered on the blue sand.
Ref.:   Branch; 4, p. 312. Maps: C-11; GI-8; GI-9.

## BLUE RANGE

El.: c. 7000'                          Loc.: Apache 3, DF-7.9
This range lies next to the White Mountains, between it
and the Escudilla Mountains. Across these ranges and adjacent ones lies an area of timber unbroken for a stretch of
about four hundred miles. This may be the same as the
Sierra Azul of the Spaniards.
Ref.:   Becker. Maps: None.

## BOG CREEK

El.: c. 8000'                          Loc.: Apache 3, BC-7-8
Lying athwart the old road which connected the Springerville area with Fort Apache, this creek came by its name
because of its boggy nature in the wet season. Here more
than one freighter cursed stridently as he struggled with
teams and wagons hub-deep in gummy mud. The round
trip from Springerville to Fort Apache took six days in
good weather, and from ten to twelve otherwise. The Becker
brothers of Springerville, who accepted barter from local
farmers for store goods, had the farmers deliver their barter
of oats and hay at Fort Apache, thus saving the merchants
the possibility of being stuck in Bog Creek.
Ref.:   13, pp. 4-5, 7; Wentz. Maps: GA-25; B-9.
**a.n. Little Bog Creek**        Map: B-9                Apache

## BONEYARD, THE

El.: c. 9000'
                          Loc.: Apache 3, FG-8.
                          Sec. 27, T 6 N, R 29 E.
In the fall of 1887, the Chriswell family arrived from
Arkansas and camped south of St. Johns. Because of an
abundance of grass, water, and timber in the little valley
now called the Boneyard, the family moved there where
just before Christmas they built a two-room log cabin.
Then came the snows, and they were heavy. With only a
few cattle and no salt, the family subsisted through the
severe winter by eating beef. They threw the bones out
through a hole cut in the side of the house and closed it
with a clapboard shutter. When spring came and the snows
at last melted, the bones began their many years' bleaching
on the hills north of the house. Since the spring of 1878,
the place has been called "The Boneyard."
Ref.:   Evans Coleman File, APHS. "How the Boneyard Up
        West of Alpine Got Its Name," Box 2.   Map: None.

## BONITO CANYON

El.: c. 8000'                          Loc.: Apache 2, CI-1
Pro.: /bániytə/          Spanish: "pretty canyon"
Bonito Canyon was so called before Capt. James H. Simp-
son's visit in 1849, when he referred to the "beautiful strati-
fied walls of Cañoncito Bonito" where his party camped on
September 11. The walls are nearly four hundred feet high.
This canyon was the site of a battle between mounted
riflemen and Indians on October 17, 1858. Soldiers called
this place "Hell's Gate" during the campaign against the
Navajos. Through it runs Bonito Creek.
Ref.:   71, pp. 33 (Note 2), 190; 73, p. 42; 148, p. 84; Burcard;
        85, p. 404.  Map: E-1.

## BONITA CREEK

El.: c. 10,000' to 8000'              Loc.: Apache 3, F-7-9
Pro.: /bániytə/                      Spanish: "pretty"
Descriptive. The Little Bonita joins the Big Bonita about
twenty-five miles from the source of the latter.
Ref.:   Wiltbank; Wentz. Map: GA-25.

## BONITO CREEK

El.: c. 7000'                          Loc.: Apache 1, I-15
Pro.: /bániytə/                      Spanish: "pretty"
Descriptive. The presence of this five-mile stream was the
reason for establishing Fort Defiance and its gardens where
they were located.
Ref.:   71, p. 89. Map: E-1.

## BUELL PARK

El.: c. 8000'                          Loc.: Apache 1, HI-13
Pro.: /byuwəl/          Navajo: *nírhaldzis*,
                        "hollow place in the ground"
Maj. Buell had a camp here in the 1860's during the Navajo
campaign. It is a rock-walled basin of about ten square
miles, its only entrance being a canyon two hundred feet
high and seventy feet wide. The Navajos regard this as a
sacred place, and here they begin their Wind Ceremony.
**v.n. Bule Park, Yule Park, Jewell Park.**
Ref.:   73, p. 37; 71, pp. 33, 112, 190; 167, p. 14. Maps: D-4;
        C-12.
**a.n. Buell Park Springs**                              Apache
Ref.:   71, p. 151.

## BUTLER CANYON

El.: 8000'  Loc.: Apache 3, D-7.25. Near Greer. Jacob Noah Butler (b. Iowa, April 26, 1852; d. May 7, 1919) moved from Utah, where he helped build Mormon temples at St. George and Salt Lake City, to Arizona in 1888 and located with his nineteen children in Butler Canyon.

Ref.: Mollie Butler, Letter, May 28, 1956. Map: None.

## CANBY, FORT

El.: c. 6000'  Loc.: Apache 2, I-1
A military map of indeterminate date (1860-?) shows a route followed by Canby. According to Sabin (II, 950) this post was dismantled in 1864. Despite the map, Fort Canby was probably in New Mexico.

Ref.: Farmer. Map: E-22.

## CARNERO LAKE

El.: c. 8000'  Loc.: Apache 3, E-7
Pro.: /karnéro/  Spanish: "sheep"
The lake is on Carnero Creek, the name of which may have come from the fact that Navajos brought sheep to water here. Below the fork this creek is called Green Spot Draw because Henry Barrett had a patch of green alfalfa growing here.

Ref.: Davis. Maps: C-13; GA-25.

## CARRIZO

El.: 5222'  Loc.: Apache 1, HI-2
Pro.: /kəriyɣo/  Spanish: "reed"
The name probably comes from the fact that a small band of Apaches known as the "Carriso or Arrow-reed People" lives in the nearby Carrizo Mountains. An Indian mission school and a village are at Carrizo.

P.O. est. September 19, 1914. Nellie Van Alen Bell, p.m. Discont. January 31, 1920.

**v.n. Sierra de Chegui** (Dominguez-Escalante Map, 1776)
**Sierra de Carriso** (McComb Map, 1860)
Ref.: 88, I, 208; 130. Map: D-4.

**a.n. Carrizo Wash**  Loc:. T. 14 N., R. 27 E.  Apache
**Carrizo Creek**  Apache
In 1881 a large Apache rancheria was on this creek and here there was held a conclave of many tribes under the fanatic, Noch-ay-del-Klinne.
There is another Carrizo Creek to which Lt. Amiel W. Whipple applied the term, as did also Lt. Edward Fitzgerald Beale, who camped on it on September 2, 1857. This creek is now called the Dead River, near Pinta.
Ref.: 26, III, 55; 39, p. 94; 177, pp. 152, 153 (Note 6).

**Carrizo Mountain**
El.: 8743'. Maps: GA-14; GA-12; GA-18  Apache
The Navajo name is Dzil naozill ("whirling mountain"; i.e. mountain surrounded by mountains).
Ref.: 71, p. 96; 167, p. 7; 73, pp. 24, 43.

| | | |
|---|---|---|
| **Carrizo** | El.: c. 5500'. Map: C-5 | Navajo |
| **Carrizo Butte** | Map: GA-16 | Navajo |
| **Carrizo Ridge** | Map: B-7 | Navajo |
| **Carrizo Wash** | Map: GA-16 | Apache |

This is currently considered to consist of two branches — Big Carrizo Wash and Little Carrizo Wash.

## CARSON MESA

El.: c. 6000'  Loc.: Apache 1, C-9-10
In the fall of 1863 Col. Christopher (Kit) Carson took on the task of subduing the Navajos, which he accomplished by the spring of the following year (cf. Canyon de Chelly, Apache). The mesa was named for him.

Ref.: 71, p. 190. Map: D-4.

## CERRO GORDO

El.: c. 7000'  Loc.: Apache 3, DC-6
Pro.: /cero górdo/  Spanish: cerro, "hill"; gordo, "fat"
Descriptive.

Ref.: Wiltbank. Map: GA-25.

## CERRO MONTOSO

El.: c. 8000'  Loc.: Apache 3, C-6
Pro.: /cero montówso/  Spanish: cerro, "hill"; montuoso, "hilly" or "mountainous"
Descriptive. Mexicans in the area say the name means "brushy mountain."

Ref.: Wiltbank. Map: C-12.

## CHALCEDONY PARK

El.: c. 6000'  Loc.: Apache 2, B-12
Petrified National Forest, q.v.
This is the third park in the Petrified Forest National Monument. The name is descriptive, chalcedony being a variety of translucent quartz, frequently greyish in hue, which is found in Chalcedony Park.

Ref.: 92, p. 114. Maps: D-7; C-11 (Third Forest).

## CHAMBERS

El.: 6000'  Loc.: Apache 2, DE-7.25
Charles Chambers ran a trading post here for years before the railroad came in 1881. He remained at least until 1888. Later the name was changed to Halloysite, after a bentonite clay which was mined four miles northeast. The mine was active in 1955. Halloysite is a clay-like kaolin used in the manufacture of fine china. On June 1, 1930, the name again became Chambers.

P.O. est. June 22, 1907. Frank T. Hathorn, p.m. Rescinded November 27, 1907. Est. December 5, 1907. Joseph Root, p.m. Changed to Halloysite, December 9, 1926. Spencer Balcomb, p.m. Name changed to Chambers, May 10, 1930. Wells Fargo Station, 1908.

Ref.: Grigsby; Richards; 167, p. 36; 71, p. 34; MNA. Maps.: C-10; F-3; GA-1.

**a.n. Chambers Wash**
Loc.: Drains Padres Mesa on Defiance Plateau  Apache
Ref.: 71, p. 34.

## CHELLY, CANYON DE

El.: c. 6000'  Loc.: Apache 1, EI-9-12
Pro.: /dəšéy/  Navajo name for area: tséyi', "among the cliffs"
The name for the canyon is a corruption (not connected in any way with the French language) of the Navajo name. Navajos who live in the canyon today are still called ceyi' ni ("Canyon de Chelly people"). Spanish-speaking invaders slurred the Navajo designation to its present form.

One of Arizona's most magnificent canyons. Canyon de Chelly was carved over the ages by Oak Springs. The canyon first came into the white man's ken in modern times in 1805 when Navajos fought Spanish forces which had been led into the canyon by Lt. Antonio Narbona, later to become governor of New Mexico. The branches of the canyon had long served as a home for Indians, as is demonstrated by many prehistoric ruins lining its red sandstone walls.

The first American officer to visit the canyon was Capt. James Hervey Simpson, who made camp in the canyon in August 1849. In conversation with Señor Donaciano Vigil, secretary of the province, Simpson learned the Indian origin and pronunciation of the canyon name. The first written description of the canyon was that of Capt. Alexander William Doniphan, who spelled the name Canon de El Challe. There was apparently at one time an encampment for United States troops in the canyon (called a "fort" by Heitman), but the camp does not appear on maps examined. In 1863-64 Col. Kit Carson dispatched Capt. Albert Pfeiffer with a detachment of soldiers into the canyon to subdue the unruly Navajos. Pfeiffer's troops went through Canyon del Muerto (q.v.) and guarded its entrance to Canyon de Chelly while Capt. A. B. Carey came up through the main gorge. The pincer action and the Sherman-like campaign of devastation resulted in the surrender of the Navajos and their removal to Bosque Redondo, New Mexico.

On February 14, 1931, Canyon de Chelly National Monument was set aside. It contains 83,840 acres.

v.n. **Canyon Chennele**
Ref.:    167, p. 108; 7, p. 285; 88, p. 242; 73, p. 42; 5, p. 4; 166, p. 109; 148, p. 24; 71, pp. 18, 35 (Note 2); 4, pp. 414-415; 85, p. 485.  Maps: E-1; GA-2.

a.n. **Rio de Chelly**
Loc.: In Canyon de Chelly. Flows out of canyon and n. to San Juan River                                      Apache
This is the old name for the wash which today is known as Chinle Wash.

## CHINDE MESA
El.: c. 6000'                           Loc.: Apache 2, B-8
Pro.: /číndíy/                           Navajo: "haunted"
Navajos avoid hogans where a death has occurred, believing them to be haunted. According to a local story, a geologist was with a field-mapping crew and accidentally fell into some water. He went into a deserted hogan, stripped and was drying himself when some Navajos rode up. Suddenly the geologist appeared in the darkened doorway. The Indians took one startled look at his ghostly white figure hovering within and rode off in a rush, shouting "Chinde! Chinde!" The mapping crews then applied the name to the mesa.

Ref.:    Branch. "U.S.G.B. Decisions, July 1, 1936-June 30, 1937," p. 8. Map: GA-15.

## CHINLE
El.: 5058'                              Loc.: Apache 1, D-10
Pro.: /čʔin:liˆ/ or /činliy:/
                                        Navajo: ch'ínlíh,
                                "at the mouth of the canyon" or
                                "it flows from the canyon"

Descriptive. Located at the mouth of Canyon de Chelly, Chinle has long been a trading center. Traces of Spanish war and trade began to be left here in the early nineteenth century. In 1864 a peace conference between Navajos and Col. Kit Carson was held on the knoll near the present Canyon de Chelly Monument Headquarters. The conference marked the official end of Navajo warfare with whites.

In 1882 the first trading post at Chinle was begun in a tent. A small trading camp was built under new proprietors in 1885. Missionaries arrived in 1904 and a small government school was opened in 1910.

P.O. est. as Chin Lee January 15, 1903. Charles L. Day, p.m. Name changed to Chinle, April 1, 1941.

Ref.:    Burcard; 71, p. 35; 167, p. 39; P.O. Records.
Map: GA-2.

a.n. **Chinle Creek**              Map: D-4                Apache
This is the contemporary name for old Rio de Chelly.
**Chinle, Fort**            Map: GA-2               Apache
**Chinle Valley**           Map: GA-24              Apache

## CHUSCA MOUNTAINS
El.: 8808'                              Loc.: Apache 1, H 5
Pro.: /tšóšga:y/   Navajo:  Chosga'i', "white spruce" or "fir"
A report of Capt. Alexander William Doniphan's expedition in 1846-47 makes the first written reference to the Chuska (sic) Mountains. Lt. James Hervey Simpson (1850) also mentions them, separating them on his 1851 map into a northern portion (Sierra de Tunecha), and a southern (Sierra de Chusca). In 1892 the U. S. Geological Survey mapping party added a third division at the northern end, terming it Lukachukai (q.v.). The U. S. Geographic Board has since approved the name Chusca for the entire range.

v.n. **Choiskai**
**Tunitcha**
**Carrizo**                 (71, p. 93)
**Tchensca**                (Doniphan)
Maps: C-6 (Lu-ka-chu-kai); E-11 (Tunechan); E-23; E-20; GA-17.

a.n. **Chuska Valley**                                   Apache
Ref.:    71, p. 24.
**Doniphan Pass**                                        Apache

## CIENEGA AMARILLA
El.: c. 6000'      Loc.: Apache 2, I-2.2, Near St. Michaels.
Pro.: /siyénəgə æmariy'yə/     Spanish: "yellow meadow"
Water from two short canyons dampens this area so thoroughly that native grass is luxuriant when there is rain. It dries to a golden shade in the meadows. There are also a multitude of yellow flowers here following rains.

Ref.:    71, p. 133.. Maps: None.

## COLTER
El.: c. 8000'                          Loc.: Apache 3, FG-7-8
James G. H. Colter came to Arizona from Eau Claire, Wisconsin, in 1872, settling about four miles from the present Springerville.

P.O. est. September 5, 1913. Duge Colter, p.m. Discont. September 15, 1922.

Ref.:    84, p. 10; 112, p. 185. Map F-2.

a.n. **Colter Creek**  Loc.: Sec. 29, T. 7 N., R. 30 E.     Apache
**Colter Reservoir**        Map: C-13              Apache

## COMB RIDGE

El.: c. 6000'                    Loc.: Apache 1, AC-1-4
The abruptly serrated red peaks of this ridge make it look somewhat like a comb.

Ref.:    71, pp. 37, 48; 65, p. 15. Maps: A-7; GA-24; GA-22; GA-21.

## COMMERCE

El.: c. 6300'                    Loc.: Roughly in the upper end
                                 of Round Valley
William B. Gardner planned to have a post office called Commerce, but he was unable to raise the money for his bond and the office never opened.

P.O. est. March 19, 1887. William B. Gardner, p.m. Discont. April 18, 1887.

Ref.:    Wiltbank; 84, p. 10. Map: None.

## CONCHO

El.: 5000'                       Loc.: Apache 3, C-2
Pro.: /kánčo/                    Spanish: "shell"
In the late 1860's, a Mexican community sprang up in the shell-like basin west of the present St. Johns. Here in 1879 came Mormons, including William J. Flake who with Bateman H. Wilhelm had purchased land from J. F. Chaves of New Mexico. A Mormon ward was organized approximately a mile west of Concho in 1880 and was named Erastus, for Erastus Snow, who later became one of the twelve apostles of the Church of Jesus Christ of Latter-day Saints. The settlement had been made under Snow's supervision. The Mexican village retained the name of Concho. In 1890 the Mormon settlement adopted the name Concho.

P.O. est. as Erastus, May 26, 1881. Sixtus E. Johnson, p.m. Name changed to Concho, March 21, 1890. Leandro Ortega, p.m.

Ref.:    Wiltbank; Stemmer; 112, p. 183; 4, p. 428; 55, p. 576; *Weekly Arizona Miner,* July 23, 1879, 3:5; P.O. Records. Maps: C-6 (Erastus); C-7 (Concho).

a.n. Concho Creek    Loc.: In valley of Concho        Apache
v.n. Sepulveda Creek        Map: B-9
Pro.: /sæpáliver/
    Vernon Creek
            Loc.: An upper branch of Concho Creek
    Both Vernon and Sepulveda Creeks enter the Sinks, where they disappear, to emerge at a big spring at Concho.
Ref.:    Wiltbank; "U.S.G.B. Decisions July 1, 1939-June 30, 1940," p. 38.

## CORNFIELDS

El.: c. 5000'                    Loc.: Apache 2, D-4
Navajos raise much corn here.

P.O. est. August 4, 1922. William M. Black, p.m. Discont. March 15, 1934.

Ref.:    Barnes; P.O. Records. Map: F-2.

## COVE

El.: c. 6800'                    Loc.: Apache 1, GH-4
This ancient Navajo rendezvous has many well-concealed red sandstone canyons and coves. Capt. John G. Walker passed through the area in 1859 after making the first successful American military crossing of the Lukachukai Mountains (*q.v.*) He was followed in the same year by Maj. James Hervey Simpson.

Ref.:    167, p. 45. Maps: GA-7; GA-10; GA-17; GA-20.
a.n. Cove Mesa       Maps: GA-7; GA-10; GA-20        Apache
    Cove Wash        Maps: GA-17; GA-20               Apache

## COYOTE CREEK

El.: c. 8000'                    Loc.: Apache 3, HI 6-4
Pro.: /kayówti˘/ or /káyot/
A stockman, St. George Creaghe, caught coyotes here and hence named the creek. Miles of Indian ruins line both sides of Coyote Creek, indicating the former plentifulness of water in this now dry stream bed.

Ref.:    Barnes; Wiltbank; Wentz. Maps: C-10; GA-1.
a.n.
        The use of the word *coyote* occurs frequently in place names, but in most instances the reason for using the word has been lost. A few such place names are listed below:
        Coyote Hill    Loc.: E. of Kingman 5 miles        Mohave
Ref.:    4, p. 336.
        Coyote Holes
        Loc.: E. of Camp Mohave on road to Prescott        Mohave
        This is an old name dating back at least to 1869.
Ref.:    169, p. 87.
        Coyote Spring         Map: B-5                    Mohave
        Coyote Mountains    Loc.: T. 16, 17 S., R. 8 E.   Pima
        Coyote Peak
            Loc.: N. of Little Horn Mts. c. 25 miles w. of Maricopa
        County line                                       Yuma
        Coyote Peak    Loc.: S.E. of Wellton 12 miles     Yuma
        Coyote Wells    Loc.: E. of Vicksburg 16 miles    Yuma

## CRAIG

El.: c. 6000'                    Loc.: Apache 2, EF-3.25
A Dr. Craig, sheepman and county physician, had his summer camp here.

P.O. est. January 24, 1911. Ellis W. Wiltbank, p.m. Discont. September 30, 1912.

Ref.:    Barnes; P.O. Records. Maps: C-11; C-12.

## CRESCENT LAKE

El.: c. 10,000'                  Loc.: Apache 3, DE-9
Descriptive. When the Civilian Conservation Corps crew built dams at Big Lake and at this point in the mid-1930's, Ed Becker of Springerville named the latter Crescent Lake because of its shape.

Ref.:    Becker. Map: GA-25.

## CROSS CANYON

El.: c. 6000'                    Loc.: Apache 2, FG-2
A Navajo trail crossed this canyon.

Ref.:    Barnes; 71, p. 151 (table). Maps: A-7; C-12.

## DEAD RIVER

El.: c. 6000'                    Loc.: Apache 2, BC-7-10
Dead River is a place name which has shifted position somewhat on maps. On GLO 1883 it is shown next to Carrizo Creek, but by GLO 1933 its location had changed to its current position next to Lithodendron Wash, in the position formerly occupied by Carrizo Creek.

Locally a story is told that "Old Man" Lynn and his two little girls lived in a wagon, roaming up and down this ten-mile river from its junction with the Puerco River. Neither the father nor his children were very intelligent, and the man kept the girls in seclusion. One day one of the children wandered into Adamana saying that something seemed to be wrong with her father, because he would not get up. Something was discovered to be definitely wrong. The old man had been dead for several days.

**v.n. Dead Wash**

Ref.:   Grigsby; G.E.P. Smith. Maps: GA-15; C-5; C-13.

## DEFIANCE, FORT

El.: 6862'                              Loc.: Apache 1, I-15

In what was later to become part of Arizona, Navajo troubles broke out when the Indians stole cattle and sheep from settlers in the Rio Grande Valley. When New Mexico became a territory of the United States, Americans promised to control the Navajos, and in 1849 Col. John Washington, military governor of New Mexico, led an expedition into the Canyon de Chelly region. On his return journey he rested in the lovely meadow of Cañoncito Bonito (See Bonito Canyon), the situation of which made it an ideal spot for a military fort.

Col. Edwin V. Sumner became military governor of New Mexico in April 1851. One of his first acts was the breaking up of the dissolute post at Santa Fe. He marched in August to the Navajo country, where Fort Defiance was constructed under his direction. It became a full fledged post on September 18, 1851. Fort Defiance was the first permanent military post in the present Arizona. Having been sent to defy the Navajos, the soldiers dubbed their log and adobe barracks and buildings Fort Defiance. Sumner left Maj. Electus Backus in charge of the new outpost, which rapidly became the center of efforts to subdue the Navajos. In 1860 two thousand Indians attacked the fort, but were driven off by one hundred fifty soldiers.

Early military maps show Fort Defiance in New Mexico, even after the creation of the territory of Arizona, but by 1869 Fort Defiance is shown clearly in its correct location. During the Civil War, troops were withdrawn on April 25, 1861, and sent to Fort Fauntleroy, New Mexico. In the summer of 1863, Col. Christopher (Kit) Carson was assigned to conquer the Navajos. He established Fort Canby as a base camp, but its location is not yet entirely clear. However, it was probably a few miles east of Fort Defiance. Carson's campaign ended with the complete subjugation of the Navajos as a result of the American scorched-earth tactics. Fort Canby was then abandoned.

Fort Defiance has the distinction of being the first post office in what is now Arizona, preceding that at Fort Buchanan (q.v., Santa Cruz) by a few months. When the final treaty was arranged with the Navajos in 1868 at Fort Sumner, New Mexico, old Fort Defiance became the new Navajo Indian Agency, with Maj. Theodore Dodd as agent. In 1870 missionaries established a school in an abandoned adobe house. The Fort Defiance boarding school was completed in 1883, thus becoming the first to be established on the Navajo Reservation.

P.O. est. April 9, 1856. John E. Weber, p.m.

Ref.:   167, pp. 57-58; 111, p. 149; 177, p. 128, Note 8; 183, p. 103, Note 8; 166, p. 140; 75, p. 131; 52, I, 308-09; 71, p. 33; 105, p. 58. Maps: E-1 to present; A-1 (Fort Canby).

**a.n. Defiance Plateau**
Loc.: W. of Black Creek Valley, E. of Chinle Valley and Pueblo Colorado Valley                         Apache
Herbert Gregory applied this name in 1907.
Ref.:  . 71, p. 191; 150, p. 34, Note 1.

## DENNEHOTSO

El.: c. 6000'                    Loc.: Apache 1, BC-3-6
Pro.: /dénaha<'tzo/          Navajo:   "green line ends up" or
                                          "upper end of the meadow"
Descriptive. Approximately five hundred Navajos make a summer encampment here.

**v.n. Dinnehotso**
Ref.:   167, p. 51. Map: GA-23.

## DIAMOND FIELDS

                        Loc.: Apache 1, E-3. Supposedly south
                        of Hopi villages, near Little Colorado.
Great excitement arose with the report in 1872 that diamond and ruby fields — open, exposed, and ready for plundering — had been found in Arizona by men named Arnold and Slack. A company was capitalized at ten million dollars and title to three thousand acres of land obtained. All was ready for a gigantic swindle when Clarence King, a geologist, visited the fields and reported them liberally salted with rough diamonds from places thousands of miles distant. While the fraud was labelled the "Arizona diamond swindle," the fact is that the so-called rich fields had been salted in northwestern Colorado. Despite this, some maps carried the notation "Diamond Fields" in the extreme central northeastern section of Arizona.

Ref.:   7, pp. 591-92. Maps: C-4; E-21; E-18.

## DINNE MESA

El.: c. 6000'                              Loc.: Apache 1, F-2
Pro.: /dinéy/     Navajo:     "Navajo; the Navajo people"
Herbert Gregory applied this name in 1907, replacing an earlier name, Gothic Mesa. Apparently "Gothic" referred to the way the land had eroded. The Navajo name for this area is descriptive. It is /tow? adindahazkáʰ/ meaning "no water mesa."

Ref.:   71, pp. 90 (Note 2), 31, 191, 192. Map: A-7.
**a.n. Gothic Wash**         Map: Macomb, 1865              Apache

## EAGAR

El.: c. 7000'                              Loc.: Apache 6, F-6
Pro.: /íyger/
John Thomas Eagar (b. December 20, 1851; d. March 12, 1942) with his brothers Joel and William and the Robertsons took up homesteads in Round Valley (q.v.) early in its recorded history. The date on their deed is 1878. John had moved to Fort Milligan and from there to the site of the town of Eagar where he lived for twenty-five years. The town was established in 1888 on ground given by the Eagar

brothers for that purpose. At first the community was called Union, but the name soon changed to Eagarville, which was retained until December 1892, when the "ville" was dropped in renaming the school district.

A notable battle of outlaws took place on the hill back of what is now the Eagar cemetery. Nine men of the Snider gang were killed.

P.O. est. February 4, 1898. Emma Udall, p.m.

Ref.:   Wiltbank; Unidentified clipping, State Library Files, George H. Crosby, Jr., "Something About Names"; 84, pp. 7, 21; 112, p. 185; P.O. Records.   Map: GA-25.

## EAGLE ROCK

El.: c. 5500′                    Loc.: Apache 2, B-11
In the loop of the road that traverses the First Forest of the Petrified Forest National Monument is a thirty-foot pedestal on which there was formerly an eagle's nest. The nest has long since fallen.

**v.n. Eagle Nest Rock**
Ref.:   Branch; 4, p. 312. Map: GA-15.

## ECKS MOUNTAIN

El.: c. 6000′                    Loc.: Apache 3, B-4.25.
                                 Sec. 14, T. 10 N, R. 24 E.
Ecks Nicholls had a ranch near here.
Ref.:   Barnes. Map: None.

## EMIGRANT SPRINGS

El.: c. 5800′                    Loc.: Apache 2, FG-5.5
Westbound emigrants found good water which induced them to camp here.
Ref.:   Barnes. Maps: C-9; C-12.

## ESCUDILLA MOUNTAIN

El.: 10,877′                     Loc.: Apache 3, GH-8
Pro.:   /eskuwdíyə/             Spanish: "a porringer"
Local Spanish-speaking residents say this means "dark blue pot." The mountain is described in Wheeler's reports as a rounded summit with a high rim and a craterlike bowl, although having no volcanic crater structure. It is about ten miles across this bowl. The mountain has a noticeable blue tinge in certain lights.

**v.n. Sierra Escudillo**
Ref.:   Noble; Wiltbank; 175, I, 67; 175, III, 529. Map: C-3.

## FIGUEREDO CREEK

El.: c. 6000′                    Loc.: Apache 2, I-2
Pro.:   /fiygeréydo/
Only a small part of this creek lies in Arizona, the remainder draining the Chusca Valley in New Mexico. The creek was named for Roque de Figueredo, a missionary to the Zuñi Indians in 1629.
Ref.:   71, pp. 91, 191. Map: D-1.

## FIRST FOREST

El.: c. 5756′                    Loc.: Apache 2, B-11
Lying about six miles south of Adamana, the First Forest was the initial area of the Petrified Forest which early visitors saw. This was before the days of automobiles, when tourists rode in horse-drawn coaches. The names of the various forests have no relation to geological time.

Ref.:   Branch; Grigsby; 92, p. 114. Maps: GA-15; GA-25.
**a.n. Second Forest**      Map: GA-15      Apache and Navajo
     **Third Forest**        Map: GA-15              Navajo
     **Fourth Forest**                      Apache and Navajo
     (Rainbow Forest) Loc.: N.W. of Third Forest 2 miles

## FLAT ROCK

El.: c. 5700′                    Loc.: Apache 1, FG-10
                         Navajo: /tsént^s eyl/ "broad rock"
Descriptive. Navajos once took refuge here from their enemies. Possibly it is the "fort" of early documents, but it has not been used since 1864, the end of Kit Carson's campaign against the Navajos.
Ref.:   167, p. 24. Map: GA-2.

## FLAT TOP MOUNTAIN

El.: c. 9000′                    Loc.: Apache 3, G-7
Descriptive.

**v.n. Table Top Mountain**
Ref.:   Barnes. Maps: C-12; GA-25.

## FLATTOPS, THE (sic)

El.: c. 5600′                    Loc.: Apache 2, BC-12
Descriptive. An expedition from the Museum of Northern Arizona (Flagstaff) found pit houses near these two mesas in 1953.
Ref.:   Branch. Map: GA-15.

## FLUTED ROCK

El.: c. 8500′                    Loc.: Apache 1, GH-13
Pro.:   /dzi˙^stdatsá?ani/        Navajo: zildassáani,
                                 "mountain sitting upon itself"
Fluted Rock is a high mesa faced with fluted columns. During the campaign against the Navajos (1863-1864), Fluted Rock was the site of a heliograph station. The American name is a translation of the Navajo.

**v.n. Zilh-Tusayan**
     **Black Rock**
     **Zildassaani**
Ref.:   71, pp. 34, 91; 167, p. 56. Maps: C-6 through C-14 (except C-12)

## FOUR CORNERS

El.: c. 4500′                    Loc.: Apache 1, I-1
Utah, Colorado, New Mexico, and Arizona come together at this point. The Four Corners Monument lies beyond the cottonwood circle (see below).

Ref.:   72, p. 60; 73, p. 129. Map: GA-11.
**a.n. Tees Nos Pos**      Map: GA-11                  Apache
Pro.:   /t?iysnʌzbão/      Navajo: "cottonwood in a circle"
**v.n. Teec Nos Pos**      Ref:. 183, p. 18
     **Teecnospos**        Map: GA-11
     **Tisnasbas**         Ref.: 71, p. 302
     **Carrizo**           Map: GA-25. Ref.: 73, p. 296
**a.n. Tisnasbas Creek** Ref.: 71, p. 92
     **Teec Nos Pos Wash**   Map: GA-11                Apache

## GANADO

El.: 6400'                              Loc.: Apache 2, DE-2
Pro.: /gənádo/                         Spanish: "cattle"
The first trading post at Ganado Lake was built in 1871 by
Charles Crary. "Old Man" William B. Leonard soon opened
another. At that time it was apparently called Pueblo Colo-
rado, but when the post was sold in 1876 to Juan Lorenzo
Hubbell (b. Pajarito, N.M., November 27, 1853; d. No-
vember 12, 1930), the new owner changed the name to
Ganado, after Ganado Mucho, a Navajo.

Ganado Mucho was the last peace chief of the Navajos and
was the twelfth to sign the peace treaty of 1868 (See Fort
Defiance). He remained chief of the western Navajos until
he died in 1892. He had flocks of sheep and herds of cattle
for miles along the nearby stream, the Pueblo Colorado.

A Presbyterian mission at Ganado in 1901 built a school
and a hospital. The Sage Memorial Hospital is a descendant
of the earlier mission hospital.

P.O. est. February 15, 1883. Charles Hubbell, p.m.
**v.n. Wukopakabi**
          (Hopi: "great reed or arrow house")
          Locally called Pueblo Ganado and Pueblo Colorado, this
          ruined pueblo was inhabited by the Reed people of the Hopi
          who migrated from here to Awatobi (q.v. Navajo).
Ref.:  4, p. 409; 88, I, 976; 166, p. 139; 167, pp. 64, 65; P.O.
Records. Map: C-7.

## GIGANTES, LOS

West butte: 6460'; East butte, 6490'  Loc.: Apache 1, FG-6
                                        Spanish:  "the giants",
                          Navajo:  ce'ezde'lzah, "stone juts out"
Descriptive.
**v.n. Los Gigantes Buttes**
Ref.:  71, p. 152; 73, p. 187. Maps: E-18; C-10.

## GOBBLERS PEAK

El.: c. 9000'                          Loc.: Apache 1, H-9.25
There are two Gobblers Peaks. There used to be many wild
turkeys at both, but there are now no more here than elsewhere in the region.
Ref.:  Wentz; Noble. Map: C-14.
**a.n. Gobbler Peak**       Map: C-14                   Apache

## GREASEWOOD

El.: c. 6000'                          Loc.: Apache 2, C-5
Pro.: /dəwúžiˈbiyˈ:to/     Navajo: díwózhii biiˈtó,
          "water in the greasewood" i.e. Greasewood Spring
Descriptive. This is a Navajo settlement beside Greasewood
Spring. There are several "Greasewood Springs" on the
Navajo Reservation.
Ref.:  73, p. 142; 167, p. 69; 71, p. 192. Map: D-1.
**a.n. Greasewood Flat**   El.: c. 5000'. Map: GA-24   Apache

## GREEN'S PEAK

El.: 10,210'                           Loc.: Apache 3, DE-6
Col. John Green was commandant at Fort Apache (cf. Fort
Apache Indian Reservation, Navajo).
Ref.:  Wiltbank; 175, I, 300. Maps: E-21; C-14.
**a.n. Mount Green**        Map: C-3                    Apache

## GREER

El.: c. 8000'                          Loc.: Apache 3, DE-7
The Willard Lee family (See Lee's Ferry, Coconino) arrived in the present Greer area in 1879, giving the locality
the name of Lee Valley. Gradually a community developed
and with it the need for postal service. The residents wanted
the name "Lee Valley," but the Post Office Department requested a shorter name. Americus Vespucius Greer (b.
Alabama, 1832; d. Provo, Utah, April, 1896) had laid out
the town of Amity (see Round Valley) and then moved to
Lee Valley. Residents selected "Greer" in his honor. The
locality is now a fishing and resort center.
P.O. est. March 12, 1898. Hannah M. Wiltbank, p.m.
Ref.:  112, p. 186; 84, p. 18; *St. Johns Herald,* April 9, 1898,
          4:1. Map: C-9.

## HALL CREEK

El.: c. 8000'                          Loc.: Apache 3, DE-7-6.5
John Hall settled on this stream just north of Greer.
Ref.:  Wentz. Map: GA-25.

## HARDSCRABBLE WASH

El.: c. 6000'                          Loc.: Apache 2, EH-12-14.25
In this wash is a seep-type spring which belonged to the
Wabash Cattle Company. Cows watering at the spring had
to scrabble hard to get out of the wash.
Ref.:  Grigsby. Maps: A-9; C-12.

## HARRIS CAVE

El.: c. 6000'                          Loc.: Apache 3, C-5.5
In 1883 Will M. Harris (b. 1866) found this cave. Will
was wrestling with his brother and they tumbled into a
creek. They then walked a short distance and Will suggested
they dry their clothes on a rock. As they were spreading their
clothing to dry, Will noticed an opening in the flat ground,
partially concealed by large rocks. The boys dropped into
the opening and discovered two caves, one about eighteen
hundred feet long and the other over a thousand feet long.
Around the remains of ancient Indian fires within the cave
they found over two hundred pots, a jar filled with turquoise, and another filled with shell earrings. Will Harris
filed a claim to the land at the cave.
**v.n. Pottery Cave**
Ref.:  Will M. Harris. Maps: B-9; C-12; A-7.
**a.n. Harris Lake**   Loc.: Sec. 30, T. 9 N., R. 26 E.      Apache

## HASBIDITO CREEK

El.: c. 5600'                          Loc.: Apache 1, E-5
Pro.: /hašbidí:tò/               Navajo: "dove spring"
**v.n. Hospitito**
Ref.:  71, p. 191. Maps: C-12; GA-7; GA-8; GA-10.
**a.n. Hasbidito Spring**   Map: GA-10                 Apache

## HAYSTACKS, THE
El.: c. 5400'          Loc.: #1 – Apache 2, B-11.
          #2 – Apache 2, I-2. S. of Window Rock 1 mile.
Descriptive. The Haystacks are a group of small, rounded hillocks.
Ref.:   167, p. 174; 4, p. 409. Maps: #1 – GA-15.

**a.n.** Haystack Cienega     Map: B-9          Apache
     Haystack Mountain     Map: B-9          Apache
**v.n.** Senecky          Map: B-9

## HELENA CANYON
El.: c. 5800'          Loc.: Apache 2, HI-7-6
The origin of this name, as well as that of its earlier name of Quirino, has not been determined.
The name first appears on Smith 1879 as Quirino, but on GLO 1883, 1887, and 1892 it has changed to Helena Canyon. There is a possibility that Quirino is a corruption of Cariño (See Pine Springs), but even so the Spanish meaning of "tenderness" does not shed any discernible light on the origin of the name. On the 1880 Rand McNally map there is a small railroad station named Querino between Allantown and Sanders, which would seem to indicate that the construction crew picked up the name from the canyon in 1879 and applied it to what was probably a work station on the line.

**v.n.** Querino Canyon
Ref.:   Maps listed in entry. Maps: C-5; C-6; C-7; E-21; A-2; E-20.

## HOPE WINDOW
El.: c. 6000'   Loc.: Apache 1, CD-9-10. T. 6 N., R. 11 W.
Herbert Gregory named a hole in a large rock for a Columbia University student volunteer assistant, Edna Earl Hope.
Ref.:   71, p. 192. Map: None.

## HORSESHOE CIENEGA
El.: c. 8000'          Loc.: Apache 3, BC-7-8
Pro.: /se'nəkə/
This is a horseshoe bend in Bog Creek.
Ref.:   Wiltbank. Maps: B-9; GA-25.

## HOUCK
El.: 6000'          Loc.: Apache 2, GH-6.25
Pro.: /hawk/
In 1874 Houck was a mail carrier from Prescott to Fort Wingate, New Mexico. In 1877, he set up a trading post called Houck's Tank. It was the scene of the murder of William Walker and William Smith by Indians in 1880. Houck moved away in 1885. Currently Houck consists of a store, post office and service station.
P.O. est. as Houck's Tank, December 16, 1884. James W. Bennett, p.m. Changed to Houck, November 23, 1895. Wells Fargo Station, 1907.
Ref.:   Barnes; Grigsby; 73, p. 159; 167, p. 76; 55, pp. 609, 552; 4, p. 310; P.O. Records. Maps: A-7; C-6 (Houck's Tank); C-9.

## HUNT
El.: c. 6100'          Loc.: Apache 3, C-1
After leaving service at Fort Apache on June 20, 1872, Col. James Clark Hunt (b. July 21, 1836; d. March 29, 1890) settled downstream from St. Johns about seventeen miles. An agricultural settlement developed, with Thomas L. Greer having a ranch a mile to the east, from which the area took the name Greer Valley.
P.O. est. July 12, 1902; John H. Greer, p.m. Discont. September 13, 1927.
Ref.:   Wiltbank; 112, p. 184. Map: C-9.

## HUNTER'S POINT
El.: c. 6800'          Loc.: Apache 2, I-2.2
John G. Hunter was Navajo agent at Leupp in 1927.
Ref.:   167, p. 77. Map: C-12.

## HURRICANE CREEK
El.: c. 8000'          Loc.: Apache 3, CD-9-10
          Rises on Mount Baldy and flows s.
A high wind sometime in the early 1880's is said to have blown down trees on both sides of this creek, hence its name.
Ref.:   Barnes. Map: GA-25.

## JACOB'S WELL
El.: c. 6000'          Loc.: Apache 2, F-8
          Navajo:   'aah hoyoolls'il, "tank of water"
          'axoyolcil, "hollow pool"
"Well" is a misnomer for the small lakes used by early travelers and stockmen in Arizona. Lt. Amiel W. Whipple in 1853 noted a "spring" which was a "conical pit, about three hundred feet wide at top, and one hundred and twenty-five feet deep" containing a pool of water about thirty yards wide, called by the Navajos "Wah-nuk-ai-tin-ai-e." A few years later on September 1, 1857, came Lt. Edward Fitzgerald Beale with his camels to this water-hole, which he called by its present name of Jacob's Well. The many Indian trails down to it, which Whipple noted, were gone and only one remained down the steep sides to the water. By 1938 eroding winds had deposited silt in the hole so that its depth was a mere five feet.
Ref.:   167, p. 79; 73, p. 172; 87, pp. 381-382; 177, p. 150; 12, p. 39; 103, p. 18; 178, p. 72; Burcard. Maps: E-11; C-1.

## JIM CAMP WASH
El.: c. 5400-5500'          Loc.: Apache 2, B-12
The stone foundation for the cowboy camp which gave the wash its name was still in existence in 1955. Three cowboys named Jim used to camp here (Jim Donoghue, Jim Walker, and Jim Bowen).
Ref.:   Grigsby. Maps: GI-8; GI-9.

## KINLICHEE
El.: c. 7500'          Loc.: Apache 2, G-2
Pro.: /kin:ãẓíni?/          Navajo: Kin dah lichi'i,
          "red house in the distance" "place of the red spot house"
A pueblo ruin nearby gave the name of Kinlichee. The ruins have largely disappeared in recent years. In 1863-64, Camp

Florilla was located beside the large spring in the neighborhood. The camp was used as a remount outpost.

v.n. Kin Lichee
Ref.:   Farmer; 73, p. 175; 167, p. 84; Burcard. Map D-1.

## KIN TIEL
El.: c. 5800'                              Loc.: Apache 2, F-5
Pro.: /kinhʸeyl/        Navajo:   kin, "pueblo" tyel, "broad"
Covering thirty acres, Kin Tiel is one of the largest pueblo ruins in Arizona. Beams taken from the ceilings indicate that its rooms were built between 1264 A.D. and 1285 A.D.

v.n. Kin Teel
Ref.:   88, I, 698. Map: D-1.

## KLAGETOH
El.: c. 6000'                              Loc.: Apache EF-4.5
Pro.: /sˢey:it'o?/              Navajo:   teeghi'to'
                                       "water in the ground"
The day school and settlement lie just west of Klagetoh Wash. There is a twelfth century Indian ruin here.

P.O. est. July 24, 1934. William H. Rush, p.m. Discont. April 15, 1944.
Ref.:   167, p. 84; P.O. Records. Maps: D-1; F-6.

## KNOB MOUNTAIN
El.: c. 8000'                              Loc.: Apache 3, C-6
Descriptive.
Ref.:   Barnes. Map: C-12.

## LANG CREEK
El.: c. 8000'        Loc.: Apache 3, DE-7. Near Greer.
Tommy Lang settled here in 1879. This creek is now dry.
Ref.:   Wentz. Map: None.

## LITHODENDRON CREEK
El.: 5800'                              Loc.: Apache 2, BE-7-6
Lt. Amiel W. Whipple named this in 1853. Herbert Gregory notes that the name may be attributed to a petrified forest which Whipple found here.

v.n. Carrizo Creek
     Lithodendron Wash
Ref.:   177, p. 153; 71, pp. 193, 34 (Note 2).
Maps: E-11; C-1; C-5 and C-10 (show Lithodendron as Carrizo, while Carrizo becomes Dead River); C-11 (Lithodendron shown correctly); C-12 (Both Carrizo and Dead River have disappeared); C-13 (Lithodendron shown correctly. Carrizo and Dead River combined into Dead River).

## LUKACHUKAI MOUNTAINS
El.: 9460'                          Loc.: Apache 1, FH-5-7
Pro.: /lók?aǰuwˇga:y/        Navajo:   Loka cogai,
                                   "place of slender reeds" or
                    "white patch of reeds extends out of the pass"
Descriptive. The patch of reeds is in a cove at the western base of Lukachukai Pass. Nearby is Lukachukai settlement, with a trading post which was established in 1892 by George N. Barker, and a mission school which was established in 1906. The school became a government school in 1933.

Navajos use water from Lukachukai Creek for irrigation. The creek is the dividing line between the Chusca and Lukachukai Mountains.

P.O. est. July 27, 1916. Ralph S. Hicks, p.m.
Ref.:   73, p. 187; 167, p. 88; 71, p. 90; P.O. Records. Maps: A-7; GA-20.

## LUPTON
El.: 6165'                              Loc.: Apache 2, I-6
Pro.: /lʌptən/          Navajo:   tséjijoolí, "round rock"
G. W. Lupton was trainmaster at Winslow in 1905. Lupton is a small settlement at the mouth of Helena Canyon (q.v.). Near here Col. John Washington followed the old Zuñi-Mexico trading trail in 1864 in his Navajo campaign (q.v., Fort Defiance).

P.O. est. May 25, 1917. Joseph D. Gorman, p.m.
Ref.:   167, p. 89; 4, p. 310; P.O. Records. Maps: C-9; C-11.
a.n. Lupton Wash        Loc.: At Lupton                    Apache

## LYMAN DAM
El.: c. 6500'                              Loc.: Apache 3, E-4
A controversy with Mexico over use of Little Colorado River water ended with the Mormons being allocated the use of three-fifths of such water. A large dam referred to locally as Salado Reservoir was built south of St. Johns in 1886. After seventeen years of service, it was washed out in the big flood of 1903. The second dam, called Lyman Dam for Francis M. Lyman (a Mormon bishop), lasted a dozen years, disappearing under pressure of the flood of 1915. State aid helped build a dam which has endured. It is sometimes referred to incorrectly as "Slough Reservoir." There is now a town of Lyman below the dam.

v.n. Lyman's Project
     Lyman's Reservoir
Ref.:   Wiltbank; 4, p. 76, 428-29. Map: GA-1.

## MAL PAI
                                       Loc.: Not known.
Pro.: /mǽlpay/            Spanish:   "bad land"
"Malpais" usually refers to the rocky or volcanic nature of the surroundings.

P.O. est. June 7, 1890. John W. Phipps, p.m. Discont. August 4, 1890.
Ref.:   P.O. Records. Maps: None.

## MANSFIELD, CAMP
El.: c. 7000'                              Loc.: Apache 2, I-2.
                                       S. of Ft. Defiance 7 miles.
Camp Mansfield may have been named for Maj. Gen. Joseph King Fenno Mansfield (d. September 18, 1862) who was cited for gallantry and meritorious conduct in the defense of Fort Brown, Texas, and who became a major general on July 18, 1862. He died at the battle of Antietam just before this camp was established.

Ref.:   85, p. 522. Maps: None.

## MANY FARMS

El.: c. 5800'  Loc.: Apache 1, D-8
Pro.: /daʔákeyhaláni/  Navajo: *Da'ak'chalani,*
"many farms"
The American name is a translation of the Navajo and is descriptive. Nearly seven hundred acres are cultivated by Navajos here. The Indians began putting the last five hundred acres under irrigation in 1937.
Ref.: 167, p. 92; 73, p. 189; Burcard. Map: D-1.

## MATTHEWS PEAK

El.: 9403'  Loc.: Apache 1, H-8
Herbert Gregory named this for Washington Matthews, an ethnologist, author of *Navaho Legends.*
Ref.: 71, p. 193. Maps: D-4; C-12.

## MAVERICK MOUNTAIN

El.: c. 6000'  Loc.: Apache 3, C-11
Pro.: /mǽverik/
This mountain is rough country and wild cattle (mavericks) take refuge here, resulting in cattlemen's naming the mountain Maverick.
Ref.: Barnes; Wiltbank. Maps: D-3; GA-1.
**a.n. Maverick Lake**  Apache
This is a small mud lake near the mining camp known as Maverick.
P.O. est. August 16, 1948. Mrs. Grace I. Chambers, p.m.
Ref.: Davis; P.O. Records.

## MAX

Loc.: "Somewhere in southern Apache County" (Barnes).
P.O. est. February 24, 1881. Redden A. Allred, p.m. Discont. May 13, 1881.
Ref.: Barnes; P.O. Records. Map: None.

## McKAY'S PEAK

El.: 9171'  Loc.: Apache 3, A-7
Alex McKay was a supervisor of Sitgreaves National Forest, later becoming a prominent cattleman.
Ref.: Barnes. Maps: C-12; C-14.

## McNARY

El.: 7200'  Loc.: Apache 3, A-4.5
A company sawmill town, McNary is the name which replaced the earlier name of Cooley when the McNary Lumber Company (James G. McNary) bought the property in 1924. The name *Cooley* was applied by the lumber company to the post office in 1919, in honor of Corydon E. Cooley. The location prior to that time had been known as Cluff Cienega for Mormon Bishop Benjamin Cluff, who from 1879 to 1880 cut wild hay here for delivery to Fort Apache.
Corydon E. Cooley (d. March 18, 1917) was a scout for Gen. George Crook. He married an Apache woman and established a ranch and haven for travellers at Showlow (*q.v.* Navajo). His place was noted for the excellence and variety of its food, the beauty of its flowers, and its solid

comfort. Capt. George M. Wheeler mentions stopping here in 1871 near Cooley's Park.
P.O. est. January 7, 1919. James C. Webster, p.m. Changed to McNary, January 11, 1924.
**v.n. Clough Cienega**
**Cooley's Ranch**
Ref.: Wiltbank; 112, p. 169; 22, pp. 178, 179; 92, p. 142; 158, p. 123; 152, I, 62; P.O. Records.
Maps: E-18; E-20 (Cooly); C-12 (Colley); C-13 (McNary).
**a.n. Cluff Peak**  Loc.: Sec. 35, T. 6 S., R. 21 E.  Graham

## MEADOWS, THE

El.: c. 6200'  Loc.: Apache 2, EF-14.5
N.W. of St. Johns 7 miles.
The first to build a dwelling at The Meadows was Frank Walker, an express carrier on the route between Fort Wingate, New Mexico, and Fort Apache. Walker constructed a shack here in 1870 at the point where the route crossed the Little Colorado River.
In late 1879 missionaries to the Indians—Ira Hatch, Thomas Brookbank, E. C. Richardson, and J. B. Wakefield — built a house around which a small settlement quickly developed. It was soon abandoned, but the area was used for raising grain at a later date.
Ref.: 55, p. 576; 112, p. 184; 167, p. 128. Map: None.

## MERIDIAN BUTTE

El.: c. 5500'  Loc.: Apache 1, A-1.5
Herbert Gregory gave the butte this name because it lies near the 110th meridian.
Ref.: 71, p. 193. Maps: C-12; GA-22.

## MEXICAN WATER

El.: c. 5000'  Loc.: Apache 1, DE-1
Pro.: /na:ka‹ʼi:tó/  Navajo: *Naakaii tó hadayiiznili,*
"Mexicans dug shallow wells"
The American name is a translation of the Navajo. In 1907 the trading post at Mexican Water was known as *Nokaita* Despite the translation of the Navajo name, one source says that the trading post was named because the lower middle section of Walker Creek used to be called Mexican Water. It may be, of course, that the wells were dug in this area and have since disappeared. This seems likely since the trading post is located where the 1879 Mormon Road crossed the creek. The present crossing is about three miles west of the trading post, and came into being when a steel bridge was completed on July 1, 1939. The abrupt drop off at the older point made it impossible to cross easily there as erosion made the drop increasingly deeper.
**v.n. Noki**
Ref.: 71, pp. 31, 91, 194; 167, p. 99. Map: C-12.
**a.n. Nokaito Canyon**  Loc.: Same as trading post  Apache

## MILKY WASH

El.: c. 6000'  Loc.: Apache 2, EB-11-13
The limestone and bentonite clay formation of the floor and walls of the wash give a milky color to run-off water during the wet season.

Ref.: Branch. Maps: C-13; GI-8; GI-9.

**a.n. Milky Wash Ruin**

Loc.: On Milky Wash E. of Petrified Forest 9 miles, Apache
This prehistoric pueblo ruin has largely disappeared by gradually falling over the crumbling bluffs into the wash. The houses were small. Stone fire altars were a feature of this ruin.

Ref.: 88, I, 863; Branch.

## MINERAL CREEK

El.: c. 7500'            Loc.: Apache 3, BC-5
Pro.: /mínerǽl/
Alkali in abundance gave the creek the name. Mineral Creek flows north near Harris Cave (q.v.) and disappears in The Sinks (See Concho).

Ref.: Wiltbank. Map: C-6.

## MONUMENT CANYON

El.: c. 6000'            Loc.: Apache 1, FG-11-12
Two huge rock columns where Monument Canyon joins Canyon de Chelly give this canyon its name. Navajo legend says that Spider Rock (about nine hundred feet high) is the home of a great spider which is the bogeyman of naughty Navajo children. When boys and girls misbehave their parents inform the woman on Speaking Rock (over eight hundred feet high) across the canyon. She tells the spider, which then descends, takes the children to the top of his forty-foot square home and devours them. It is said the bleaching bones are what give the white color to the top of Spider Rock. Other spires of red sandstone are found in Monument Canyon.

Ref.: 4, p. 418; 5, Charles D. Wyatt, "Canyon de Chelly"; "Canyon de Chelly National Monument," U. S. Dept. of Interior, n.d., pp. 2-3. Map: GA-2.

## MORMON BEND

Loc.: Top of mountain where road from old Ft. Apache to Round Valley drops down.
A tree with a chair-like bend in its trunk was used to mark the place at the top of the mountain where the road from Round Valley to Fort Apache began its drop down into the valley.

Ref.: Becker. Maps: None.

## MUERTO, CANYON DEL

El.: c. 6000'            Loc.: Apache 1, EH-9-10
Pro.: /delmwérto/       Spanish: "of the dead"
Canyon del Muerto fell upon its most evil day when Lt. Antonio Narbona led Spanish soldiers into Canyon de Chelly in 1805 to subdue the Navajos. The wily Indians concealed themselves high in the walls of the canyon and watched silently as the detachment threaded its way below. Among the Indians was one old woman who had been a Spanish slave. The temptation to scream insults at the Spaniards was more then she could resist, and her high nasal deprecations revealed the Indians' hiding place to the troops. Unable to shoot directly at the Indians, the soldiers ricocheted bullets from the roof of the hiding place, and immediate slaughter was the result. On January 25, Narbona reported that his men had killed ninety bucks, twenty-five

women and children, and had in addition captured thirty women, thirty horses, and thirty sheep.

The bones of the slain are still in the cave. James Stevenson, an archaeologist, in 1886 found bones and gave the name to the canyon. Navajos call it by a descriptive name, either *sehili* ("it flows into the canyon") or *'ane'etseghi* ("back of in-between the rocks"), because its stream is a tributary to Chinle Wash in Canyon de Chelly.

**v.n. Massacre Cave**

Cañon Trigo (Spanish: "calamity; misfortune").

Ref.: Display, Canyon de Chelly Monument Headquarters; Richard Van Valkenburgh and Frank Walker, *Masterkey*, 132; 89-94, May 1945; 4, p. 421; 166, p. 116; 7, p. 285, note; 5, p. 7; 71, p. 35. Map: GA-2.

## MUMMY HOUSE

El.: c. 6200'            Loc.: Apache 1, G-9
The largest and most spectacular prehistoric ruins in the Canyon del Muerto, Mummy House lies in two large caves joined by a thin ledge three hundred feet above the bottom of the canyon. In 1893 the ruin was found to have ninety rooms and three kivas, with low buildings and a tower on the connecting ledge. Charcoal dating has established that this ruin holds the record of the longest occupany of any place yet known in North America; it apparently began as a dwelling at least as early as 348 A.D. and was still in use as late as 1284 A.D. In its early days it was used by the Basketmakers, distinguished by their use of a dart thrower (instead of the later bow and arrow) and their manufacture of excellent woven sandals and baskets, as well as by their use of circular houses during the Indians' later existence. Pueblo Indians later built their homes over the centuries-old pit houses.

**v.n. Mummy Cave**

Ref.: 4, pp. 420-421; 167, p. 25; "Canyon de Chelly National Monument," U. S. Dept. of the Interior, n.d., p. 3. Map: GA-2.

## NAVAJO INDIAN RESERVATION

Loc: Apache 1 & 2 (all). Navajo 1 (all); Navajo 2 (top half). Coconino 1 (N.E. portion); Coconino 5 (N. part)
Pro.: /nǽvəho/
The largest Indian Reservation in the United States is that assigned to the Navajos, which occupies much of northern Arizona and parts of New Mexico and Utah as well. The land is cut by numerous canyons and much of its 25,000 square miles is barren desert.

The reservation was established by Executive Order and Treaty of June 1, 1868, thus ending almost two decades of troubles with the Navajos. (cf. Fort Defiance and Canyon de Chelly). Amendments have been added to the acreage from time to time, the last occurring on January 28, 1908, when 82,500 acres were appended. The additions were made because the Navajos — who had always occupied the territory and had no concept of artificial boundaries — roamed the areas concerned anyway. There are 10,185,802 acres of this reservation in Arizona, and 4,324,594 acres in Utah and New Mexico.

At the time the reservation was established, about seven thousand exiled Navajos returned to their native land from Fort Sumner, N. M. By 1954, their population had increased to approximately 81,000, a fact which has resulted in many bare-subsistence problems for the Navajos.

Ref.:  111, p. 27; 29, p. 18; 88, I, 374; 16, p. 104; "Annual Report of the Arizona Commission of Indian Affairs, 1954, 1955, 1956," pp. 7-8. Maps: D-1; D-6; D-7.

## NAVAJO SPRINGS
El.: 5700'                               Loc.: Apache 2, E-9
Pro.: /nǽvəho/

When Lt. Amiel W. Whipple went through this region in 1853, he found that the Navajos made use of the "fine pool of water which breaks out at the surface of a valley." This was Navajo Springs. Here on September 1, 1857, Lt. Edward Fitzgerald Beale in search of a wagon road for emigrants reported finding traces of Whipple's trail. In the years which followed, emigrants to the opening frontiers of the West found a resting place at Navajo Springs. In 1863 Maj. G. B. Willis laid out the route as an official trail with Navajo Springs still an important stopping place. In his tracks followed the governor's party for the newly created Arizona Territory.

In late summer 1863, the first gubernatorial party with a military escort left for the West. On December 27, the group finally crossed the line of New Mexico and in a snowstorm entered Arizona. There was some uncertainty as to whether the men were actually in Arizona. Therefore to avoid possible legal troubles, the party went to Navajo Springs, which was known to be in Arizona. Here on December 29, Richard C. McCormick, Secretary of the new Arizona Territory, raised the United States flag and administered the oath of office to Gov. John N. Goodwin and other officials. Goodwin had been appointed governor upon the death of John Gurley, first appointee to the office.

Ref.:  177, p. 151; 12, p. 39; 167, p. 106; 105, p. 150; 52, III, 69-70; 87, p. 42. Maps: A-7; E-11.

**a.n. Navajo**   Loc.: T. 20 N, R 26 E. on AT SF RR. El.: 5700' First called Navajo Springs, this trading post lies about three miles from the springs. Lewis and Hugh Lynch owned a trading post here for many years.

P.O. est. as Navajo July 3, 1883. J. A. Smith, p.m. Wells Fargo Station, 1885.

Ref.:  P.O. Records; Barnes.

## NAZLINI
El.: c. 7000'                            Loc.: Apache 1, E-13
Pro.: /kínsˢəgá<ˆ:y/          Navajo: *Názlíni,*
                              "flows in crescent shape"

The trading post at Nazlini lies on Nazlini Creek, which follows a roughly curved streambed up Nazlini Canyon, along the deep gorge of which are found many Indian ruins and old Navajo camp sites. Erosion has long since forced Navajos out of the canyon.

**v.n. Nashlini**
Ref.:  167, p. 107; 71, pp. 90, 194. Map: D-1.

## NELSON RESERVOIR
El.: c. 6000'                        Loc.: Apache 3, G-7.8
                                          T. 6 N., R. 30 E.

Nelson Reservoir is on Nutrioso Creek. In 1918 it was owned by Edmund Nelson, who first used the waters of the creek in 1891. The capacity of this small reservoir is five hundred acre feet.

Ref.:  C. H. W. Smith, Engineer, Surface Water Division, State of Arizona. Letter, April 26, 1956. Map: None.

## NERO
El.: c. 7000'                            Loc.: Apache 3, D-5

A place without name in 1955, the former Mormon settlement of Nero still has a few families residing along the banks of the Little Colorado River. The locality is sometimes referred to today as Richville. Richville in turn appears to be a corruption of the earlier name of Richey, which took its name in 1892 from the fact that Joseph B. Richey settled here. Since the post office was established under the name Richville in the same year, apparently the name Richey was extremely short-lived.

Prior to having the name Richey, the locality was called Walnut Grove, a descriptive name. Still earlier, it bore the name Nero, given to it by a small and temporary colony of Mormons in 1883 for a reason not yet uncovered.

P.O. est. as Nero February 15, 1883. James W. Wilkins, p.m. Discont. May 5, 1883. Re-est. as Richville, June 23, 1892. William H. Sherwood, p.m. Discont. May 24, 1907.

Ref.:  Wiltbank; Becker; Wentz; MNA. Maps: C-5 (Nero); C-9 (Richville).

**a.n. Richville Valley**
    Loc.: Part of valley of Little Colorado between St. Johns and Springerville above Lyman Dam          Apache

## NEWSPAPER ROCK
El.: c. 5500'                       Loc.: Apache 2, BC-10.25

It is merely a supposition that Indians used picture writing to convey the news, but this assumption is the origin of the white man's name for some petroglyphs in the Petrified Forest. Since the pictures are located near an ancient pueblo of about one hundred twenty-five rooms, and are even closer to a cave which may have served as a room in which women gave birth, it is entirely possible that the picture writing is a form of doodling by idle and restless fathers-to-be. The cave is called the Origin-of-Life Cave.

Ref.:  Branch; 4, p. 312. Map: GI-9.

## NOBLE MOUNTAIN
El.: c. 8000'                          Loc.: Apache 3, G-8.5

Edward A. Noble, a farmer and cattleman, homesteaded near the base of this mountain in 1881. He is buried at Alpine (d. November 1909). The Forest Service gave his name to the mountain.

Ref.:  Noble (son). Maps: GA-1; GA-25; C-13.

## NUTRIOSO

El.: c. 8000'                    Loc.: Apache 3, G-8
Pro.: /núwtri owso/
At the south end of Dry Valley is Nutrioso. The settlement
was named because the first settlers killed a beaver (Spanish: *nutria*) and a bear (Spanish: *oso*). James G. H. Colter
(cf. Colter) located in Dry Valley in 1875.
Nutrioso became a haven for Mormons seeking safety from
marauding Indians, and as other nearby settlements were
laid waste, Nutrioso grew in importance. In 1880 settlers
built a fort. By 1883 the settlement rated a post office.
P.O. est. April 12, 1883. John W. Clark, p.m.

**v.n. Neute Rosa**  (corruption: Hinton map, 1883)

Ref.:   Wentz; Butler; 112, pp. 185, 186; P.O. Records. Map:
        C-6.

**a.n. Nutrioso Creek**      Loc.: At Nutrioso            Apache

## ODART MOUNTAIN

El.: c. 6000'                    Loc.: Apache 3, C-10.5
This mountain was the summer range for a New Mexico
cattle outfit which used the O-dart brand (o ➡).

Ref.:   Barnes; Davis. Map: D-3.

## ORD, MOUNT

El.: 10,860'                     Loc.: Apache 3, CD-8
The third highest peak in Arizona is named for Maj. Gen.
Edward Otho Cresap Ord (cf. Apache, Fort, Navajo). He
was in charge of the Department of California and was
noted for his uncompromising attitude as an exterminator
of Apaches.

Ref.:   52, VIII, 22. Maps: C-5; C-6; GA-25.

**a.n. Ord, Mount**      Maps: B-7, C-6      Gila and Maricopa

## ORTEGA LAKE

El.: c. 7000'                    Loc.: Apache 3, A-2.3
Pro.: /orteyɡə/
Leandro Ortega owned the ranch purchased by the Mormons at Concho (*q.v.*). The lake was a noted lambing area in
the 1880's.

Ref.:   Wiltbank; Barnes. Maps: C-13; GA-25.

**a.n. Ortega Draw**      Map: B-9               Apache
**v.n. Ortega Wash**

## PADDY CREEK

El.: c. 5800'                    Loc.: Apache 1, C-10.8-12
Paddy Creaghe was killed by Apaches in the early 1880's.

Ref.:   Barnes. Map: D-3; GA-25.
        Loc.: #2 Between Eagar and Alpine            Apache
        Paddy O'Dell was an early settler in this area.

Ref.:   Wiltbank. Map: None.

## PADRES MESA

El.: c. 6000'                    Loc.: Apache 2, CD-6
Pro.: /pádreyz/
Herbert Gregory named this area for "the Spanish padres."
They were the first white men to settle among the Indians,
several giving their lives in defense of the Christian faith.
(cf. Hopi Villages, Navajo).

Ref.:   71, p. 194. Map: C-12.

## PAINTED DESERT

El.: c. 5500'                    Loc.: Apache 2, A-8.25
                Navajo:  *Halchíítah,* "amidst the colors"
A vast treeless area of brilliantly colored sand and stone, the
Painted Desert was called El Desierto Pintado by Spaniards
who passed through in 1540.
In 1936 the most brilliant portion of the Painted Desert was
made a part of the Petrified Forest National Monument.
There are, however, no well-defined boundaries to the area
known as the Painted Desert.

Ref.:   29, p. 4; 167, p. 111; 4, p. 311; 151, p. 581. Maps: A-7;
        C-1; GI-9.

## PARK

                                 Loc.: Not known
The origin of this name has not yet been ascertained.
P.O. est. February 5, 1885. James F. Wallace, p.m. Discont.
June 19, 1886.

Ref.:   P.O. Records. Map: None.

## PASTORA PEAK

El.: 9420'                       Loc.: Apache 1, HI-3
Pro.: /pæstórə/
Lying in the northeastern part of the Navajo Reservation
where there was once good grazing, this mountain was
named by W. H. Holmes in 1875, because of its pasturage.

**v.n. Pastura Peak**

Ref.:   Barnes; 71, p. 158. Map: GA-14; C-6.

## PAT KNOLLS

El.: c. 9000'                    Loc.: Apache 3, F-8
                                 Sec. 30, T. 7 N., R. 29 E.
Pat Trainor ran cattle on these smooth hills in the 1880's.
Trainor was tried thirteen times for rustling, but was never
convicted.

Ref.:   Becker. Maps: None.

## PEARCE MOUNTAIN

El.: c. 8000'                    Loc.: Apache 3, B-6
The Pearce family lived here, keeping sheep. James Pearce
was the first Mormon settler on Silver Creek. He was the
son of the man who established Pierce [*sic*] Ferry ( *q.v.*
Mohave). His brother Joe also was at Pearce Mountain.

Ref.:   Barnes. Map: B-9.

**a.n. Pierce (sic) Wash**      Map: B-9      Navajo
**Pearce Spring**              Map: B-9      Apache

## PETRIFIED FOREST

                                 Loc.: Apache 2
Vandalism led to the establishment of the 93,000 acre tract
of the Petrified Forest National Monument on December
8, 1906. Prior to that time, the petrified giants of the forest
were being removed by the trainload to make fireplaces,
table tops, and other articles, but when a Denver firm came
to Adamana (*q.v.*) and began crushing the ancient irreplaceable logs to make wheels for abrasive purposes, public senti-
ment was roused. Thousands of visitors had seen the forest
since Lt. Lorenzo Sitgreaves in 1851 reported the presence
of petrified wood in the northern part of the future Arizona.
Lt. Amiel W. Whipple in 1853 wrote of encountering the

forest in the Painted Desert region on a vast, nearly treeless plateau.

On the plateau, according to geologists, about one hundred and fifty million years ago a great basin of water covered the earth, and the fallen trees gradually became water-logged and covered by layers of sand and gravel. Mineral-laden waters replaced the original wood, forming great columns of agate and carnelian. Gradually as the surface of the earth shoved upward, erosion did its work, exposing the petrified logs. In the deep washes, logs have been found three hundred feet below the surrounding land.

Ref.: 4, pp. 311, 312; 92, p. 113; 5, p. 1; 167. p. 112. Maps: GI-8; GI-9.

## PHELPS BOTANICAL AREA

El.: 9500'     Loc.: Apache 3, DE-7.25. One-half NW¼ Sec. 10 and NE¼ Sec. 9, T. 6 N., R. 27 E.
A reserve for botanical students was set up on Phelps' homestead when Apache National Forest (q.v.) was created in 1898.

Ref.: Phillips. Map: None.

## PINE SPRINGS

El.: c. 6000'     Loc.: Apache 2, G-5
Navajo: t'iis'íí'ahi, "standing cottonwood"
A band of Navajos noted for its particularly fine weaving lives at Pine Springs in Carino Canyon (see Helena Canyon). The trading post, church, and school are located at a spring in the midst of juniper and piñon which give the community its American name.

v.n. Agua Vibora (1860)
Carino Canyon

Ref.: 73, p. 221; 167, p. 113. Map: GA-25.

## PINEYON

El.: c. 7000'     Loc.: Apache 3, C-6
Pro.: /pinyówn/     Spanish: piñon: a variety of conifer, bearing edible nuts
The name Pineyon results from anglicizing the Spanish name. The settlement is surrounded by piñon timberland.

P.O. est. June 26, 1918. Mary A. Calaway, p.m. Discont. August 15, 1929.

Ref.: Wiltbank; P.O. Records. Map: F-3.

## PINTO

El.: c. 6000'     Loc.: Apache 2, D-9
Pro.: /pínto/     Spanish: "painted" (with reference to a horse)
Its location in the heart of the Painted Desert country probably gave Pinto its name though it may have been named for a horse, considering the name derivation. It appears as "Pinto" on maps from 1880 to 1923, but by GLO 1933 it had been changed to "Pinta."

P.O. est. February 27, 1902. Celia F. Henning, p.m. Discont. May 23, 1922.

Ref.: None. Maps: C-9 (Pinto); C-13 (Pinta).

## PLENTY

El.: c. 6000'     Loc.: Apache 3, G-5
There is a story that when it came time to name the post office, the names of village girls were voted on. That of Floy Greer won and the community was originally named Floy. Confusion in the mails between Eloy (q.v. Pinal Co.) and Floy caused the name of the latter to be changed to Plenty. Never a large community, Plenty now has only one or two houses remaining.

P. O. est. as Floy, November 28, 1919, Rosa Despain, p.m. Changed to Plenty, May 1, 1933. Discont. July 15, 1937.

Ref.: P.O. Records; Noble; Wiltbank; 63, p. 9. Maps: C-12 (Floy); F-6.

## POKER MOUNTAIN

El.: c. 8000'     Loc.: Apache 3, B-12.5
Cowpokes in winter camp devoted more time to poker than they did to cows. In the mid-1880's several cattle outfits wintered in the gap lying between two mountains, and the names Poker Mountain and Poker Gap were as natural to the cowboys as drawing breath. They called the stream Freezeout Creek.

Ref.: Barnes. Map: C-12.

a.n. West Poker Mountain
Loc.: S. of Poker Mountain 6 miles     Apache

## POLE KNOLL

El.: c. 7000'     Loc.: Apache 3, C-7.5
Before this knoll burned over, it was covered with aspen used for poles by settlers.

Ref.: Wentz. Map: GA-25.

## POOL KNOLL

El.: c. 7000'     Loc.: Apache 3, B-11.5
Customarily, cattlemen join forces during roundup time, driving cows into a corral or area where they are then separated into their respective herds. On Pool Knoll such a corral existed for the use of several large cattle outfits which pooled their forces in the early 1880's for spring roundups.

Ref.: Wiltbank. Map: GA-25.

## POTTER MESA

El.: c. 6000'     Loc.: Apache 2, CD-12. On Milky Wash E. of Petrified Forest National Monument
Potter Mesa was named after Potter's Well, developed and used by Albert F. Potter as a horse camp. The location was originally made by William Garland in 1885.

Ref.: Paul F. Roberts, Letter, March 25, 1957. Map: None.

## PUEBLO COLORADO

El.: c. 6500'     Loc.: Apache 2, E-1
Pro.: /pwéblo calarǽdo/     Spanish: "red village" "red house"
A red sandstone pueblo ruin called by the Navajos kin dah lichi'i ("red house in the distance") was mentioned as the Pueblo Colorado by Gen. James H. Carleton in a letter of 1863. For a time it was a trading post, earning notoriety by having an official total of two votes, but turning in over eighty votes in the election of 1879.

Ref.:   55, p. 645; 167, p. 64. Maps: C-7 (Ruins); C-8.

**a.n. Pueblo Colorado Valley**                Apache and Navajo
Lt. Joseph C. Ives and Dr. John S. Newberry in 1858 were
the first to use this name. It includes the valley of Leroux
Wash and the Pueblo Colorado Wash. Over a thousand
miles of the Defiance Plateau is drained by the Pueblo
Colorado Wash.
Ref.:   Bartlett; 71, pp. 89, 194.

**Pueblo Colorado River**  Maps: C-9, C-5 (Creek)    Apache

## PUERCO RIVER

El.: c. 6800'-5600'     Loc.: Rises in N. M. Enters Ariz. at
Lupton. Joins Little Colorado east of Holbrook.
Pro.:  /pérko/ or /pwǽrko/       Spanish: "dirty"
At flood stage the Puerco takes on a dirty color and carries
much trash. Lt. James William Abert, who was with Beale's
expedition, in 1848 noted that the Puerco for almost two-
thirds of its one hundred and forty mile length was deep
with sand and had perpendicular banks often thirty feet
high. This showed what torrents flowed through its channels
at certain seasons.

**v.n. Rio Puerco of the West**  (Map: C-1)
Ref.:  1, p. 59. Map: E-11.

**a.n. Puerco River Indian Ruin**
(partially excavated). Map: GI-8                Apache

## QUARTZITE CANYON

El.: c. 6000'                Loc.: Apache 1, I-15
Branch of Bonito Canyon at Fort Defiance
Quartzite Canyon is a geologically descriptive name which
replaced the inappropriate name "Blue Canyon."
Ref.:  71, pp. 89, 194. Map: None.

## REDONDO MESA

El.: c. 6000'                Loc.: Apache 2, A-2.5
Pro.:  /reydóndo/       Spanish: "round flat land"
Descriptive.
Ref.:  Wiltbank. Maps: GA-25; C-12.

## RED LAKE

El.: c. 6000'                Loc.: Apache 1, I-3
Navajo: Be'ek'id halchíí', "red lake"
The American name for this semi-artificial lake is a transla-
tion of the Navajo.
Ref.:  167, p. 121. Maps: E-22; E-23; C-4; C-5; C-10; C-11;
C-12; D-1; D-7.

## RED ROCK

El.: 6371'                Loc.: Apache 1, H-4.5
Pro.:  /tsesˢičíˆ:dáhˀaᶎkáni/       Navajo: Tse ichii'
dah 'azkani, "red rock mesa"
Red Rock is a sandstone peak three hundred eighty-six feet
high. Near it is the community of Red Rock where a trading post was established in 1906. Numerous springs were
found by Lt. W. C. Brown in this region during his water
survey of 1892.
Ref.:  Burcard; 73, p. 242; 167, p. 122. Map: GA-19.

**a.n. Red Rock Valley**  Maps: GA-19; GA-18; GA-17   Apache
**Red Rock Wash**        Map: GA-19                    Apache
**Red Wash**             Maps: GA-19; GA-17            Apache

## RESERVATION CREEK

El.: c. 5000'                Loc.: Apache 3, AB-12-13
Its location on the Indian Reservation gives this stream its
name.

**v.n. Rio Nutrioso (1864)**
Ref.:  Barnes. Maps: D-3; E-12.

## RICE

El.: c. 6400'                Loc.: Apache 2, B-9.6
The origin of this name has not yet been ascertained.
The current name for this little town is Old Stage Coach
Tavern, after the former stage station just north of nearby
Lithodendron Wash, where horses were changed. The stage
line was a Star Route road.
Ref.:  Grigsby. Map: GI-9.

## ROCK POINT

El.: 4000'                Loc.: Apache 1, CD-4
Pro.:  /tséntsa:de:zˀáhí/       Navajo: Tsé ntsaa deez'áhí,
"big rock extends"
Descriptive. A trading post and a day school mark Rock
Point, where Chinle Creek begins to pass between high
sandstone walls.
P.O. est. June 10, 1926. Raymond C. Dunn, p.m. Discont. June
4, 1930.
Ref.:  167, p. 124; P.O. Records. Maps: F-3; GA-25.

**a.n. Rocky Point**    Loc.: On Highway 66          Apache
There is a trading store here.
Ref.:  73, p. 249.

## ROOF BUTTE

El.: 9835'                Loc.: Apache 1, I-4
Pro.:  /ˀadá:ˀ dikˀá/       Navajo: 'adáá' dik'á,
"roof shaped mountain on the run"
or dziłdah neeztínii,
"mountain lying up at elevation"
Descriptive. This is the highest point in the Lukachukai
Mountains.
Ref.:  167, p. 127; Young; 71, p. 117. Map: C-6.

## ROUND ROCK

El.: 6020'                Loc.: Apache 1, D-5
Pro.:  /tsénikàˆni/   Navajo: Tsé nikání, "desk-like rock"
Descriptive. Round Rock is actually a mesa with two sections. The Round Rock trading post is at the base of one of
the mesas. The American name is a rough translation of
the Navajo.

**v.n. Round Peak**
**Round Rock Butte**
Ref.:  167, p. 127; 71, pp. 29, 34. Maps: C-12; GA-25.

## ROUND VALLEY

El.: c. 6500'                Loc.: Apache 3, B-2.5
Spanish: valle redondo, "round valley"
Descriptive. In 1869 Dionicio, Elalio, and Juan Baca, and
Gabriel Silva came to this valley with Tony Long, William
R. (Tony) Milligan, Marion Clark, and Johnny McCul-
lough with supplies from Pueblo, Colorado, for what is
now Fort Apache. To weather the severity of the winter,
the men built the first house in the valley. Milligan and

Long built additional houses (Fort Milligan) in the spring of the year, while the Mexicans by 1872 had established their own colony, known as Valle Redondo, at the north end of the valley.

To this valley in 1875 rode Julius Becker, followed by his brother Gustav in 1876, to become farmers. In August 1876, Julius established a store which is now the third oldest in Arizona. The Beckers found Round Valley occupied by Mexicans and by outlaws who used it as a haven. The first Mormons (Americus V. Greer and Harris Phelps, from Texas) came to the valley in 1879, followed in the same year by William J. Flake, who had John Burk and Adam Greenwood as herd boys for his cattle. First known as Alma Ward, in 1882 the valley area was divided into two wards. Part was named Omer Ward, which was then laid out as a community, Omer, with Amity Ward, site of Fort Amity, a Mormon town (Sec. 7, T. 8 N., R. 28 E.), in the upper end of the valley. Omer is one of the *Books of Mormon*. By 1885 disputes had arisen concerning the townsite of Omer and parts of Amity Ward. One result was the formation of Union Ward from Amity and Omer Wards. The town of Eagar (q.v.) developed and Omer became Springerville (q.v.).

Ref.: Wiltbank; George H. Crosby, Jr., "Something About Names." Unidentified clipping (State Library Files); "Becker's 75th Anniversary Number," *Apache County Independence News,* XXXIX (August 31, 1951), 2:1:1; 13, pp. 3, 4, 6, 7, 8; 112, p. 185. Map: E-20 (Milligan's and Springerville).

## RUDD CREEK

El.: c. 8000'　　　　　　　　Loc.: Apache 3, FG-8-7

Dr. William Mann Rudd (b. Tennessee, September 27, 1827; d. February 1915) came to Arizona from Arkansas in 1876. En route, the Rudd family met a man named Springer (see Springerville) who advised them that the Springerville area was the place for settlers. Only two families of the original emigrant party stuck out the long journey to Springerville from Arkansas. The other family was that of Anderson Bush (see Alpine).

Soon after his arrival, Rudd bought a ranch on Rudd Creek, which either he or his wife named. Dr. Rudd was a man of multiple talents. He first worked as a tanner. Following the Civil War he studied medicine and practiced in Arkansas for ten years. When Apache County was created, a district attorney was needed, so Dr. Rudd studied law and was admitted to the bar. He served both as county attorney and as county judge. He was also a cattleman.

Ref.: Noble; Velma Rudd Hoffman (granddaughter), Letter, July 10, 1957. Map: GA-25.

a.n. **Rudd Knoll**　Loc.: Sec. 25, T. 7 N., R. 28 E.　　Apache

## ST. JOHNS

El.: 5725'　　　　　　　　　　　Apache 3, EF-1.6

At the site of the future St. Johns the crossing of the Little Colorado River was called El Vadito (Spanish: "the little crossing") by Spaniards who first explored that section of the country. From 1864 on Solomon Barth, a trader to the Indians, packed salt from the Zuñi salt lake to miners at Prescott and came to know the St. Johns region well. In a poker game in 1873 he won enough cattle and land from the Mexicans to permit him to forsake an itinerant trader's life and to settle down with his brothers Nathan and Morris to help him. He changed the name from El Vadito to San Juan (Spanish: St. John). One story says that the name came from that of the first woman resident, Señora Maria San Juan Baca de Padilla. Another asserts that the name comes from the annual feast of San Juan on June 24, which Spanish-Americans still celebrate in St. Johns as they do in other communities. In 1866 William R. Milligan (see Round Valley) came to the area, followed in 1870 by Frank Walker, who settled near the present St. Johns (see The Meadows, Apache q.v.). Soon a settlement began to grow at the crossing on the Little Colorado. By 1872 Spanish-Americans had established an agricultural community where St. Johns is today. In 1874 Juan Sedilla erected a stone cabin here.

Sol Barth sold out his interests in 1875 to Ammon M. Tenney, a Mormon agent who located on the G Bar or Sedro Ranch some thirty-five miles north of St. Johns. Following on Tenney's heels came Wilford Woodruff, president of the Church of Jesus Christ of Latter-day Saints, who on March 29, 1880, located a Mormon settlement approximately one mile north of St. Johns, but on September 19, 1880, Erastus Snow advised moving the settlement to high ground adjacent to the Mexican settlement. The name Salem was selected for the new location and steps were taken to establish a post office, which, however, never opened because of hostility to the Mormon settlement.

St. Johns was made the county seat in 1879, but in 1880 was superseded by Springerville. However, in 1882 St. Johns again became the county seat, retaining that honor to the present.

P.O. est. as Saint John's, April 5, 1880. Sixtus E. Johnson, p.m. Name changed to St. Johns, April 18, 1893.

Ref.: Shreve; Evans Coleman File, Box #2, APHS; *Arizona Weekly Enterprise* June 7, 1890; (State Library Files) 167, p. 128; 112, pp. 165, 177, 178. Maps: E-20 (St. John); C-3.

## ST. MICHAELS

El.: c. 7000'　　　　　　　　Loc.: Apache 2, I-2.5
　　　　　　　　　Navajo: *Tso hotso,* "yellow meadow"
　Early Spanish name:　Cienega Amarilla ("yellow meadow")

Flowers at the end of summer here are yellow, hence the name. The grass also turns yellow in the summer heat.

The first written mention of this area was made by Lt. James Hervey Simpson in 1850; he called it "Sieneguilla de Maria." Here on a hillside sometime during the early 1850's, Mexicans planned to ambush some Navajos by hiding a cannon and firing it into the Indians. A Navajo named Syphilis (sic), who was with the Mexican party, betrayed their plan to his own people. He rejoined his tribesmen, later becoming a chief using the name Delgadito. It was he who signed the final treaty for the Navajos.

The present Franciscan Mission at St. Michaels was begun in 1896, using funds supplied by Rev. Mother Katharine

Drexel, founder of the Sisters of the Blessed Sacrament. On October 11, 1897, Rev. Juvenal Schnorbus, assisted by Rev. Anselm Weber, arrived to take over the work. They changed the name from the Navajo *Tsohotso* to St. Michaels. The mission encompasses four hundred forty acres. Here a Navajo ethnologic dictionary was prepared and published in 1910 by Fr. Berard Haile.

P.O. est. July 29, 1902. John Walker, p.m.

Ref.:   71, pp. 33, 33 (Note 2); 73, p. 283; 167, p. 129; 88, II, 412. Map: C-9.

## SANDERS

El.: 5800'                          Loc.: Apache 2, GH-7.25
C. W. Sanders, office engineer of the A.T. & S.F. R.R., may have given his name to this station, but locally it is believed that the name is a corruption of Saunders, for Art Saunders, who had a trading post near this small station on the railroad. Since there was already a station called Sanders on the line, the name on the railroad was changed to Cheto. However, Sanders is still a small community just off the railroad on the main highway.

P.O. est. as Sanders, December 15, 1915. Orville L. Hathorn, p.m.

Ref.:   Richards; 167, p. 131. Maps: C-6 (Saunders); C-10 (Sanders).

## SAWMILL

El.: c. 8300'                        Loc.: Apache 1, H-14
Pro.: /niʔiˆːjihi/                   Navajo: *Ni'iijihí*, "sawmill"
The Navajos operate their own sawmill here, using timber cut from Navajo reservation land. During 1954, 13,954,000 board feet of ponderosa pine were logged on the Fort Defiance Plateau. A trading post has been at Sawmill since 1907.

P.O. est. as Niegehe, September 6, 1941. Genus Alex Baird, p.m. Rescinded December 30, 1941. Re-est. as Sawmill, November 3, 1952. Mrs. Myrtle B. Lee, acting p.m.

v.n. Nehiegee

Ref.:   167, p. 139; 16, p. 34; 71, p. 36; P.O. Records. Maps: A-7; D-1; GA-25.

## SEGETOA SPRING

El.: c. 2100'                        Loc.: Apache 1, F-14
Pro.: /tsiˆʰyiˆʔtohi/                Navajo: *Tsiyi't óhí*,
                                     "spring in the forest"
Descriptive.

v.n. Tsegitoe
      Segatoa Spring

Ref.:   71, pp. 151, 194. Maps: C-12, A-7.

## SETSILTSO SPRING

El.: c. 6100'                        Loc.: Apache 1, C-3
Pro.: /čéčʔiltsoʰ/                   Navajo: *Chech'il tsoh*, "big oak"
Descriptive.

v.n. Tsetsiltso
      Tsatsiltoo
      Salltso
      Saletso
      Sueltso C-11 (Springs)

Ref.:   71, p. 195, 152. Maps: A-7, C-12.

## SHEEP CROSSING

El.: c. 9000'      Loc.: Apache 3, D-7.6. Upper crossing on
                            West Fork of Little Colorado.
Descriptive. The herding of sheep requires that they be shifted from low, hot areas to summer coolness for grazing in the mountains. To drive the sheep along an old, established trail from Phoenix to their destination in the White Mountains takes three months. There was a time when tremendous sheep herds migrating to summer or winter quarters cropped forage so close that cattle were hard put to find food. It was this which caused trouble between sheepmen and cattlemen. Currently, at least one sheep company uses Sheep Crossing.

Ref.:   Becker. Map: None

a.n. Sheep Springs            Map: C-14                Apache
      This is the highest point between Eagar and the White Mountains. Company herds of sheep formerly used this spring.

## SHEEP DIP CREEK

El.: c. 6000'                        Loc.: Apache 1, CD-8, F-9.3
The creek takes its name from a sheep dipping vat which the government built for use by Navajo sheep herders. The water of the creek is drinkable.

Ref.:   Barnes; 71, p. 91. Maps: A-7; C-12.

## SIMPSON CREEK

El.: c. 8000'      Loc.: Apache 1, H-8-11. T. 4 N., R. 6 E.
Herbert Gregory named this stream to honor Capt. James Hervey Simpson (d. March 2, 1883), who kept a journal and made a map of the route followed by the first white men to cross the Lukachukai and Chusca Mountains in 1849-50. Simpson Creek, an intermittent stream, rises in Washington Pass and empties into Black Lake.

Ref.:   71, pp. 71, 91, 28 (Note 3). Map: None.

## SITGREAVES NATIONAL FOREST

                   Loc.: Southern boundaries of Apache,
                            Navajo and Coconino Counties.
Created on July 1, 1908, Sitgreaves National Forest was formed from parts of Black Mesa Forest Reserve and Tonto National Forest. The Black Mesa Forest Reserve in turn had been established on August 17, 1898, and the Tonto National Forest on October 3, 1905. Sitgreaves National Forest was named in honor of Lorenzo Sitgreaves (d. May 14, 1888), who as a lieutenant made the first topographical military trip across northern Arizona in 1851. Gross acreage is 883,919.

Ref.:   120, p. 36. Map: B-9.

## SNOWSTAKE CREEK

El.: c. 8500'                        Loc.: Apache 3, C-7
Stakes used to be located in this area to measure snowfall. This stream is now known as Becker Creek which, with Snake Creek, makes the White River. Ord Creek (cf. Mt. Ord) heads between Ord and Mount Thomas and comes in below this stream.

Ref.:   Wentz. Map: A-7.

## SONSELA BUTTE

El.: 8733'              Loc.: Apache 1, I-10.5
Pro.: /só?silà/       Navajo: *So' s ilá*, "stars set"
Descriptive.

**v.n. Sonsola**
  **Sonsala**
  **Sonsila**

Ref.: Burcard; 71, pp. 34, 195; 73, p. 272. Maps: C-6; GA-25.

## SPONSELLER LAKE

El.: c. 6500'          Loc.: Apache 3, A-7
Joseph Sponseller grazed sheep here in 1883.
Ref.: Barnes. Map: GA-25.

**a.n. Sponseller Mountain**     Map: B-9     Navajo and Apache

## SPRINGERVILLE

El.: 6856'            Loc.: Apache 3, F-5.9
Merchants were not slow to see the need for a store in the recently settled Mormon wards of Omer and Amity in Round Valley (*q.v.*). Mexicans were potential customers, as were also the outlaws who made a profitable business of stealing horses in southern Arizona, rebranding them in Round Valley, and selling them to northern Arizona ranchers. The outlaws reversed their procedure when in the north. To Round Valley in the fall of 1875 came Harry Springer, with merchandise from Albuquerque, to establish his store two miles west of the site of Omer across the Little Colorado River. The place was known as Springer's Store. Springer made the sad mistake of trusting outlaws with feed and seed and as a result soon went broke. In the area less than a year, he departed from a joshing group which, when it came time to select a name for the post office, chose "Springerville." For two years (1880-1882) Springerville was the county seat. The town moved in 1885 when the Mormons moved from Omer to Eagar, the name of Omer then changing to Springerville.
In this same area on August 20, 1876, Julius Becker set up his first store. The Becker brothers, Gustav and Julius, brought their goods into Round Valley by way of Belen and American Valley, New Mexico, taking sixty days for the round trip. The Beckers continued using ox trains until about 1890, when they changed to horses and mules. After 1895 the freight haul was shortened by the completion of a branch railroad spur to Magdalena, New Mexico. Trucks were first used in 1918.
Julius W. Becker (Gustav's son) was active in seeking to establish the transcontinental highway through Springerville. In 1910 A. L. Westgard drove through Springerville in the first automobile (a Pathfinder) to make the transcontinental journey. For many years Springerville lay on the only transcontinental automobile route.
The statue of the Madonna of the Trail in the center of Springerville was dedicated by the National Old Trails Association and the D.A.R. on September 29, 1928, to commemorate a pioneer trail across the United States. There are in the nation a total of twelve such statues commemorating National Old Trails. Cast by sculptor August Lienback, the statues are of algonitestone, a composite poured mass of great density and durability.

P.O. est. October 29, 1879. Charles A. Franklin (alias A. F. Banta), p.m.
Ref.: Becker; Wiltbank; 175, I, 70-71; 13, pp. 3, 9; "Becker's Seventy-fifth Anniversary Number," *Apache County Independence News*, XXXIX (August 31, 1951), 2:1:3; 2:5:3; 112, pp. 165, 184-185; 108, p. 399; 105, p. 340; George H. Crosby, Jr. "Something About Names,"; unidentified clipping (State Library Files). Maps: C-5; GA-1; GA-25; E-20.

## STEAMBOAT CANYON

El.: c. 6000'          Loc.: Apache 1, A-15
About a mile from the settlement of Steamboat Canyon is an eroded sandstone formation which resembles an old-fashioned river steamboat. On the walls of the canyon is an inscription which reads "A[20] Abril 20, Ano de 1666. P[o] de Montoya." At the spring located in the canyon may be seen many petroglyphs and English notations.
Ref.: 71, p. 195; 167, p. 151; Burcard. Maps: D-1; C-12.

**a.n. Steamboat Wash** Loc.: Same as above     Apache

## STONE AXE RUIN

El.: c. 5000'     Loc.: Apache 2, B-10. Near Puerco and
                  Little Colorado River divide.
Numerous stone axes were found when this prehistoric ruin was excavated in 1901. Unfortunately, the ruin has since been grossly vandalized, part of it being used to construct a dam.
Ref.: 88, II, 638; Branch. Map: None.

## S U KNOLLS

El.: c. 10,000'     Loc.: Apache 3, E-8.5. T. 6 N., R. 28 E.
                    One on each side of Crescent Lake.
Stevens, Upshur and Burr had a summer camp for the S U Cattle company here in the 1880's. Their brand was S U.
Ref.: Barnes; Becker. Map: None.

## SUNRISE SPRINGS

El.: c. 6000'          Loc.: Apache 2, C-3
The origin of this name has not yet been learned. A white settlement existed here as early as 1907.
Ref.: 71, p. 37; 71, p. 152. Maps: A-7; F-2.

## SURPRISE VALLEY

El.: c. 5000'          Loc.: Apache 2, BE-14. 6-11.3
The origin of this name has not yet been learned. A small Mormon settlement once existed in this valley.
Ref.: Barnes. Maps: A-7; C-9.

**a.n. Surprise Creek**
  Loc.: Enters Little Colorado River, T. 15 N., R. 25 E., Apache.

## SWEETWATER

El.: c. 6000'          Loc.: Apache 1, G-2
Pro.: /tóssika<'n/     Navajo: *Tółikan*, "sweet water"
The name is a translation of the Navajo. There is a trading post here.
Ref.: Burcard; 73, p. 289. Map: D-1.

**a.n. Sweetwater Wash** Maps: GA-6; GA-4; GA-3     Apache

## TANNER SPRINGS

El.: 5685′                          Loc.: Apache 2, C-6
Tanner Springs in 1884 was the scene of bloody skirmishing between white cowboys and Navajos, both of whom wished to use its waters. Known to early explorers as La Xara Springs (1851), Ojo La Xara (1859) and as Jara Spring (1876), it assumed its current name when Seth B. Tanner had a trading post here.

v.n. La Xara Spring
    Jara Springs          (Map: C-3)
    Java Springs          (Map: C-5)
Ref.:   73, p. 295; 167, p. 154. Maps: E-11; C-1; C-6 (Tanner Springs).

## TEEPEES, THE

El.: c. 5600′                       Loc.: Apache 2, B-10
Located in the Blue Forest of the Petrified Forest National Monument, these eroded sandstone formations resemble Indian teepees.
Ref.:   4, p. 312; Branch. Map: GI-8.

## THOUSAND CAVE MOUNTAIN

El.: c. 6000′                       Loc.: Apache 3, G-1.6
Since there are numerous caves in this mountain, the name is descriptive. Many Indian relics have been found in several of the caves.
Ref.:   Barnes; Wiltbank; Shreve. Map: C-10.

## TODOKOZH SPRING

El.: c. 6000′                       Loc.: Apache 2, F-3
Pro.: /tódik?ow:z/   Navajo: To dikóózh, "bitter water"
Descriptive. Navajos use this name for many springs on their reservation.
Ref.:   71, pp. 152, 158, 196. Map: A-7.

## TSEHILI

El.: c. 6200′                       Loc.: Apache 1, G-6
Pro.: /tse:hyili/              Navajo: Tsééhyílí,
                  "flows into the rocks" (i.e., into a box canyon)
Descriptive. A variant descriptive name for the stream by this name is Spruce Brook. A trading post was established at Tsehili settlement in 1885 but was abandoned in 1890 when heavy snows forced Navajos to move their flocks of sheep down lower into Chinle Valley.

v.n. Sehili
    Tsaile
    Tse-a-lee
    Salee
    Tsalee Creek
    Brook Creek
Ref.:   Burcard; 71, pp. 90, 150, 195; 167, p. 161. Maps: A-7; C-12.
a.n. Tsehili Butte   Loc.: S. of Tsehili Creek      Apache
    This igneous pinnacle is climbed by Navajo medicine men seeking medicines or offering prayers.
v.n. Tsalee Butte
    Tsalee Pinnacle
Ref.:   167, p. 161.

## TULE

El.: c. 6500′                       Loc.: Apache 3, F-5
Pro.: /túwli/                       Spanish: "reed"
Many reeds grew in this area. El Tule was a small Mexican settlement.
P.O. est. September 7, 1898. Severo Chavez, p.m. Discont. August 20, 1903.
Ref.:   P.O. Records; Wiltbank. Maps: E-20 (Tule Springs); C-9.

## TUNITCHA MOUNTAINS

El.: c. 6200′                       Loc.: Apache 1, F-6
Pro.: /tóntsa:/        Navajo: Tóntsaa, "big water"
In 1849 Lt. James Hervey Simpson designated these mountains as the Sierra de Tunecha (cf. Chusca Mountains). Simpson's Journal states he picked up the name from a work called "Doniphan's Expedition," adding that Simpson found no granite as described in the work mentioned.
Two battles with Navajos took place in these mountains, the first on November 14, 1859, and the second on October 3, 1860.

v.n. Tunicha
Ref.:   71, pp. 27, 196; 85, pp. 404-405; 148, pp. 47, 62. Maps: E-1 (Tune-Chah, 1851); C-3.
a.n. Tunecha Valley      (Simpson, 1849)           Apache

## TURKEY CREEK

El.: c. 8400′                       Loc.: Apache 3, AC-13-11
Wild turkeys formerly abounded in this locality.
Ref.:   Barnes. Maps: A-7; GA-25; D-3.

## TUYE SPRING

El.: c. 6000′                       Loc.: Apache 1, A-14.7
Pro.: /toye:?/        Navajo: Tóyéé, "scant water"
The Navajos commonly use the name tuye for springs at the heads of box canyons. Fr. Haile says they employ the name for watering places which attract lightning.

v.n. Togay
    Togai
    Tuyey
Ref.:   Barnes. 71, pp. 113, 149, 154, 196. Map: C-12.

## TWENTY-FOUR DRAW

El.: c. 9100′                       Loc.: Apache 3, D-8
Prior to 1900, the big 24 Land and Cattle Company maintained a corral here. Owned by Smith, Tee, and Carson (Englishmen), the "24" outfit was the biggest in that part of Apache County. In 1881 the 24 Ranch fifteen miles north of Springerville had fifteen thousand cattle. It used the following brand: 24 . The notorious Clantons had the H Bar V Ranch just across the line in New Mexico, using the "74" brand: 74 . The ease with which the Clantons could and did alter the 24 brand to their own led to trouble between the two outfits. This did not stop the Clantons, who did a profitable business driving cattle and horses south in winter, where they made a name for themselves in the Tombstone area. Once when the Clantons returned to Springerville (q.v.), Commodore Owens had warrants for a dozen of their group. In three years, most of the warrants were served, some on dead men.
Ref.:   Wiltbank; Becker. Map: GA-25.

## TWIN BUTTES

El.: c. 6000'                    Loc.: Apache 2, E-13
Descriptive.

Ref.: Barnes; Wiltbank. Maps: A-7; C-7.

## VENTANA MESA

El.: c. 6000'                    Loc.: Apache 1, B-11
Pro.: /ventánə/                  Spanish: "window"
There are several natural windows in this mesa.

Ref.: 71, p. 196. Map: C-10.

## VENTO SPRING

El.: c. 6500'                    Loc.: Apache 1, H-5
Pro.: /vénto/
Barnes says that the name means "an opening or vent."

Ref.: Barnes; 71, p. 149. Maps: A-7; C-12.

## VERNON

El.: c. 6500'                    Loc.: Apache 3, B-4
B. H. Wilhelm settled here, naming it in 1894 for W. T. Vernon. The location became important as a sawmill town, but as activity diminished, the place lost its residents. At one time a Mormon ward, Vernon was disorganized by the Church of Jesus Christ of Latter-day Saints in 1954 when Vernon's sawmill activity finally moved to the vicinity of Lakeside.

P.O. est. October 25, 1910. Fannie Northrup, p.m.

Ref.: Noble; APHS files. Map: C-11.

## VIEW POINT

El.: 9430'                       Loc.: Apache 1, G-6
Descriptive. From this highest point in the Lukachukai Mountains, one can see deep into neighboring states and back into Arizona.

Ref.: 71, p. 29. Map: C-12.

## WAHL KNOLL

El.: 8000'                       Loc.: Apache 3, EF-7.75
John C. Wahl ran cattle on this knoll west of Springerville in the early 1880's. He lived in Springerville.

Ref.: Barnes. Map: GA-25.

## WALKER CREEK

El.: c. 6200'                    Loc.: Apache 1, D-1
Herbert Gregory named this stream for Capt. John George Walker (d. July 20, 1893) of Macomb's expedition in 1859; Walker was apparently the first to cross this stream.
Gregory notes that the Navajos call the upper portion of Walker Creek *Chinlini* ("place where water comes out of a canyon"), and the canyon it traverses is, of course, Chinlini Canyon. Its lower middle section is Mexican Water *(q.v.)*.

v.n. Gothic Wash  (name discarded by Gregory)
   To chinlini (Canyon)

Ref.: 71, pp. 191, 90 (Note 2). Maps: A-7; C-10 (Gothic Wash); C-12 (Walker Creek).

a.n. Walker Butte    El.: 6033'. Map: GA-6         Apache
   Walker's Church                                 Apache
   Walker Creek Valley                             Apache

Ref.: 71, p. 90.

## WASHINGTON PASS

El.: c. 8150'                    Loc.: Apache 6, I-13
Lt. Col. John Macrae Washington (d. December 24, 1853) was in charge of the second military expedition into the northern part of the newly annexed territory which was later to become Arizona. The pass was first reconnoitered by Maj. Henry Lane Kendrick (d. May 24, 1891) on August 30, 1849. Kendrick reported it was difficult and dangerous. Lt. James Hervey Simpson (d. March 2, 1883) called it Pass Washington in honor of his commanding officer. An earlier expedition in 1846 had been led through this pass by Col. Alexander W. Doniphan.

Ref.: 166, pp. 136-37; 148, pp. 60, 61, 62; 71, p. 28 (Note 2); 111, p. 25. Maps: E-1; E-18.

## WATER CANYON

El.: c. 7000'                    Loc.: Apache 3, G-6
The Eagar brothers (cf. Eagar) used water from this canyon for irrigation. The canyon parallels waterless Dry Canyon.

Ref.: Wiltbank. Map: GA-25.

## WHEATFIELDS CREEK

El.: c. 7500'                    Loc.: Apache 1, IH-10
In 1909 the government set up an irrigation project here where Navajos raise wheat, hence the name.

v.n. Cieneguilla de Juanito   (Simpson, 1849)

Ref.: 71, p. 35 (Note 3); Barnes; Richard Van Valkenburgh, *Masterkey*, 19: 89-94, May 1945. Maps: D-4; GA-2; C-13; C-14.

a.n. Wheatfields Canyon   Loc.: Same as for creek        Apache

## WHISKEY CREEK

El.: c. 6150'                    Loc.: Apache 1, F-10
                Navajo: *Tó di. di hi déé' nłiinnii*,
                "flows from Whiskey Creek, dark water"
The Navajo name for this creek in translation means "dark water," and in fact from certain angles this stream does appear to have the color of whiskey, although when scooped up it is perfectly clear and sparkling. The apparent color is attributable to the growth of a brownish under-water plant.

Ref.: Young; Burcard; 71, p. 90; 73, p. 318. Maps: A-7; C-12; C-13; C-14; GA-2.

## WHITE HOUSE RUINS

El.: c. 6700'                    Loc.: Apache 1, F-11
Pro.: /kiniˆ:ˀnaʔigaˊy/          Navajo: *kinii'na'igai*,
                "horizontal white streak in the middle of the house"
Visitors to Canyon de Chelly National Monument today stand near the place where Lt. James Hervey Simpson on September 8, 1849, looked on the quietly sleeping ruins of Casa Blanca, known today as White House Ruins. Capt. George M. Wheeler called it White House in 1873, because of "a long wall in the upper part of the ruin . . . plastered with white clay."
The tiny rooms when in use were reached only by ladders. Study of the annual growth rings in beams taken from this ruin reveal its earliest construction date as 1066 A.D.

Ref.: Burcard; 175, I, 75; 4, p. 419; 5, pp. 8-9; 73, p. 319; 148, p. 75. Map: GA-2.

## WHITE MOUNTAINS

Loc.: Apache 3, AH-6-13

Spanish name: *Sierra Blanca,* "white mountains"

The Spanish name for these mountains was probably used because snow caps the summits for seven months of the year. The highest peaks are Mount Baldy and Mount Ord (*q.v.*). The White Mountains form part of the largest unbroken virgin pine forest in the United States. The pines stretch from the Mogollon Mountains in New Mexico to the San Francisco Peaks near Flagstaff, Arizona.

Ref.   Becker; 87, p. 309; 92, p. 134. Maps: E-1; E-18; C-1.

**a.n. White Mountain Reservoir**   Map: C-12                    Apache
Appropriation date, 1894.
Ref.:   84, p. 29.

## WIDE RUIN

El.: c. 6000'                          Loc.: Apache 2, E-5

Pro.:   /kinᵗʰʸey:l/          Navajo: *Kin nteel,* "wide house"
(probably referring to ancient ruins)

Apparently the anglicized name resulted from the fact that this ruin was indeed "wide," for it consisted of the remains of a prehistoric "palace" at least four hundred feet square, built across Wide Ruin Wash. There is now a store and settlement at Wide Ruin.

P.O. est. March 20, 1934. Mrs. Dora W. Balcomb, p.m. Discont. March 31, 1938.

**v.n. Kintgel**

Ref.:   Burcard; 71, p. 35 (Note 1); 73, p. 319; 4 F, p. 224 (Note 72). Map: D-1.

**an. Wide Ruin Wash**
Loc.: Heads 10 miles n.e. of ruin in T. 24 N., R. 28 E., Apache
    **Wide Ruin Valley**   Loc.: Same as wash               Apache

## WINDOW ROCK

El.: c. 4000'                          Loc.: Apache 2, I-2

Descriptive. In 1933 the newly appointed Commissioner of Indian Affairs, John Collier, turned his attention to helping the Navajos. His first step was the consolidation of the five separate areas and agencies of the Navajo reservation under a single general superintendent, with new headquarters at Window Rock. By 1936 the huge window in the sandstone cliffs to the north of the new buildings looked down upon the completed headquarters. It was first planned to call the location Ni'alnii'gi ("earth's center"), but the Navajos were averse to profaning a ceremonial name. This led to the substitution of the name Window Rock.

P.O. est. as Navajo Agency, January 30, 1936. William H. Daley, p.m. Name changed to Window Rock, August 1, 1936.
Ref.:   167, p. 174; 177, pp. 243-244. Map: D-1.

## WISHBONE MOUNTAIN

El.: c. 9000'                          Loc.: Apache 3, B-6
Descriptive.
Ref.:   Barnes. Map: GA-25.

## WOLF MOUNTAIN

El.: c. 6000'                          Loc.: Apache 3, C-5

The early name was Tamar Mountain, taken from the fact that the Tamar Sheep Company had a summer camp nearby. The name was lost with the passage of time. The newer name was applied by the Forest Service.

Ref.:   Barnes. Map: C-13 (Wolf Mountain); Tamar Mountain: None.

## WOOLSEY LAKE

El.: c. 7000'                          Loc.: Apache 3, A-8

Theodore S. Woolsey, Jr., was the first supervisor for the Black Mesa Forest Reserve (cf. Sitgreaves National Forest).

Ref.:   Barnes. Map: C-12.

## YALE POINT

El.: 8050'                             Loc.: Apache 1, BC-7

Herbert Gregory named this place for Yale University.

Ref.:   71, p. 197. Maps: D-1; C-12.

## ZUNI RIVER

Loc.: Apache 2, DI-14-9.5

Pro.:   /zúwnyiˆ/

Zuñi Indians live on this river in New Mexico. The first white men to see it were the Spaniards who explored in 1540. According to Casteñada, they called the stream the Colorado ("red"). Some authorities think the Zuñi corresponds with the Rio Vermejo or Jaramillo, but Bandelier does not agree with this. (cf. Little Colorado River, Navajo).

**v.n. Rio de Pescado**   (Simpson, 1849, Spanish: "fish river")

Ref.:   182, p. 482 (Note 1); 148, p. 89. Maps: E-1; E-11; C-1.

**a.n. Zuni Lake**                                               Apache

Loc.: 30 miles above Milligan settlement on N.M. line.

Noted for its salt deposit from a spring at the base of a large eighty foot volcanic cone at the southern part of the lake. It was this salt which Sol Barth (cf. St. Johns) used to haul to Prescott in the 1870's.

Ref.:   89, pp. 236-237.

## ZUNI WELL

El.: 5392'                             Loc.: Apache 2, B-9

Pro.:   /zúwnyiˆ/

The Zuñi Oil Company, prospecting for oil, in 1917 or 1918 drilled a well here. At three hundred feet, the drill hit petrified wood, which is so dense that no drill then available could go through it. The well was shifted and a shaft sunk. Not oil, but salt water, was struck. The abundance of salt water caused the cementing of the well to a depth of one thousand feet so that water could be drawn from it for sanitary facilities of the Petrified Forest National Monument.

Ref.:   Branch. Map: GI-9.

# COCHISE

*Indians lurking above wagon train in Apache Pass — cattle raising.*

## COCHISE COUNTY:

Pro.: /kowčíys/

Cochise County was named upon its creation on February 1, 1881, for the famed Chiricahua Apache leader. The county was carved from Pima County, one of the four original counties in the territory of Arizona. Tombstone *(q.v.)* was its county seat until 1929, but today Bisbee is the county seat. The area of this county is 4,003,840 acres. Although it is only ninth in size among the Arizona counties, it is still the equivalent of Connecticut and Rhode Island combined. The county is a leader in mining and in livestock raising and other agricultural pursuits.

The history of Cochise County is one of the most interesting in the state, inasmuch as its remoteness from law and order at one time made it a haven for outlaws. This, added to the fact that Tombstone was the mining mecca of wealth seekers from 1879 for the next several years (and also the most cultured city in the entire West or Southwest), adds to the glamour of the Cochise County story.

## ADAMS PEAK

El.: 5840'  Loc.: Cochise 1, C-3-4.6

The Adams family arrived in this locality from Texas and established the Adams Ranch at the base of this peak. David Adams was the first of the family to arrive (cf. Texas Canyon).

Ref.: Bennett. Map: GB-10.

## AJAX HILL

El.: 5327'  Loc.: Cochise 1, C-6-8.6

According to an undated clipping from the *Bisbee Review,* this hill was named after an old prospector who had a number of claims in the 1880's covering most of the hill. This led to other miners' calling the place Ajax's Hill.

Ref.: State Library Files. Maps: GB-1; GB-20.

## ANTELOPE SPRING

El.: 4800'  Loc.: Cochise 1, E-5—8.6

As late as 1896, there were still antelope here. The spring was a watering place used by both Indians and cattlemen. A heliograph station near Gleeson created a camp here for soldiers in pursuit of Geronimo in 1886.

Ref.: Barnes; Bennett; Macia. Map: GB-16.

## APACHE

El.: 4330'  Loc.: Cochise 2, F-8.8
Pro.: /əpæčiˆ/

Little remains of the small community called Apache. Here may be seen the monument dedicated April 29, 1934, to commemorate the surrender of Geronimo in 1886. The surrender, however, took place several miles to the southeast (cf. Skeleton Canyon).

P.O. est. May 22, 1908. John W. Richhert, p.m. Discont. August 15, 1943.

Ref.: Barnes; P.O. Records. Maps: GB-5; F-3.

## APACHE PASS

El.: 5115'  Loc.: Cochise 2, B-3
Pro.: /əpæčiˆ/

In 1849 the Fremont Association party passed through what they called the Puerto del Dado. This was the same name used in 1854 by Lt. John G. Parke when he made his survey for a railroad route from the Mississippi to the Pacific.

Apache Pass earned a reputation for being one of the most dangerous locations for encounters with Indians in the whole of Arizona. The Butterfield Overland Stage established a station here in 1857. Substantial adobe buildings were erected, but nothing remains of these today except mounds. The pass itself is a deep gorge about four miles long. Apaches took advantage of the heights above in order to watch the passage of emigrant wagon trains. It was said that the road for miles on either side of the pass was littered with the bones of horses, mules, and oxen, and wreckage of wagons lay for fourteen miles on either side of the pass, so thickly that one was never out of sight of them. There were also many graves along the trail. At one time

Apache Pass was known as Ewell's Pass (cf. Ewell's Station). Fort Bowie (q.v.) was located in this pass.

Ref.: 48, pp. vii; 184, Note 20; 34, pp. 18-19; 32, II, 132; 99, p. 41; *Arizona Miner,* October 22, 1870, 2:2; 111, pp. 169-170; 2, p. 149. Map: GB-6.

a.n. Apache Peak  El.: 7684'. Map: GB-1  Cochise

Apache Spring  Map: GB-8  Cochise

## ARIZMO

Loc.: Not Known

People from Missouri homesteaded here and coined the word.

P.O. est. September 19, 1903. Louis A. Gregory, p.m. Discont. August 17, 1906.

Ref.: Barnes. Map: None.

## BABOCOMARI

El.: 4600'-3800'  Loc.: Cochise 1, B-7—9
Pro.: /bábəkəmári/ or  Papago: "caliche hanging over in
/bárbəkomə/  little cell-like formations"

The meaning of the name is as given by Joe, a Papago Indian, to Dr. Frank Lockwood.

The Babacomari (sic) Land Grant was called the San Ignacio del Babacomari (sic). The grant was made on December 25, 1832, by the government of Mexico to Ignacio Eulalia Elias. The United States courts confirmed the grant at 34,707 acres. Here was erected an hacienda which rapidly became the center of an important cattle raising ranch. Depredations by Apaches forced its abandonment, and by 1851 when it was visited by members of the Boundary Commission, it had already begun to fall into ruins. In 1855 the old ranch was still being used as a fort by people in the San Pedro Valley. By 1856 only the walls were still standing. Visitors to the old hacienda noted that it was situated on the bank of a running stream known as the Babocomari River or as Babocomari Creek. It was not unusual to catch fish in this stream.

v.n. Babaconora

Ref.: Barnes; 67, p. 42; 101, p. 51; 52, V, 195; 23, p. 322; 55, p. 428; APHS Names file. Maps: GB-1; E-18 (Creek); E-12.

## BAKERVILLE

El.: 5000'  Loc.: Cochise 1, E-7—11.4

A Dutch baker named Jake Perung settled here in the 1880's and built a rooming house and hotel.

Ref.: C. E. Mills, Manager, Copper Queen Branch, Phelps Dodge Corporation, Bisbee, Letter, April 14, 1956. Map: None.

## BALLARD, MOUNT

El.: 7200'  Loc.: Cochise 1, E-11.3

W. H. Martin and John Ballard bought the option to the Copper Queen claims on April 5, 1880. These men were promoters who never saw Bisbee (q.v.), but sent Ben and Lewis Williams to act for them while they supplied machinery and furnaces.

Ref.: Burgess. Map: GB-2.

## BENSON

El.: 3585'                          Loc.: Cochise 1, BC-5.3

When the S.P.R.R. came through southern Arizona in 1880, the town of Benson was founded. The new town, at a somewhat different location from that of the earlier stage station (see Ohnersorgen Stage Station), was the rail shipping point for the booming new town of Tombstone to the south.

Benson was named for Judge William B. Benson of California, a friend of Charles Crocker, president of the railroad. Judge Benson spent many years in the mining regions of the West.

P.O. est. July 26, 1880. John Russ, p.m. Wells Fargo Station, 1885.

Ref.:   112, pp. 235-236; *Arizona Miner,* April 16, 1880 (APHS Files); *The Oasis,* April 4, 1896, 1:1. Map: GB-1.

**a.n. Benson Pass**
El.: 4300'. Loc.: Pass to west of Benson              Cochise

Ref.:   122, p. 200.

## BISBEE

El.: 5300'                          Loc.: Cochise 1, ED-11.3

In 1877 while in pursuit of Apache Indians three army scouts camped in Mule Pass. One was John Dunn, who at that time found samples of rich ore. Since his duties would not permit him to work on his claims, Dunn grubstaked a man named George Warren, sending him into Mule Gulch. Warren seems to have been a first-class alcoholic as well as a pick-and-shovel man. To these two men belonged the Copper Queen Mine, so named because of the fame of the Silver King Mine in Pinal County, which it was hoped the Copper Queen would rival.

In 1880 a small eastern mining firm known as Phelps Dodge and Company sent Dr. James Douglas (cf. Douglas) to purchase copper prospects in Arizona. He bought property close to the Copper Queen. The richest ore lay where the Copper Queen and Phelps Dodge properties joined. Rather than pursue litigation over the ores, the two companies merged as the Copper Queen Consolidated Mining Company.

Among the men who promoted the Copper Queen were Ben and Lewis Williams. A shareholder in the company was Judge DeWitt Bisbee, who was also the father-in-law of one of the brothers. The Williams brothers and Judge Bisbee became interested in the property when Edward Reilly, who had an option on the Copper Queen, went to San Francisco where he enlisted the aid of John Ballard and William Martin to supply funds to purchase the mine. Bisbee, Williams and Company undertook to develop the Copper Queen. Judge Bisbee never visited the town which bore his name.

In 1929 Bisbee became the county seat for Cochise County.

P.O. est. September 7, 1880. Horace C. Stillman, p.m. Incorporated January 9, 1902.

Ref.:   3, p. 9; 4, p. 174; *Arizona Republic,* August 8, 1954, "Arizona Days and Ways," p. 23. Map: GB-2.

**a.n. Bisbee Junction**      Map: C-12                    Cochise
The first name for Bisbee Junction was Osborne, so named for William Church Osborne of the Phelps Dodge Corporation. The place was sometimes also referred to as New Osborne. Wells Fargo Station, 1907.

Ref.:   APHS Names File; Barnes. Map: GB-2 (Osborn).

## BLACK DIAMOND

El.: 5000'                          Loc.: Cochise 1, EF-6.8

The nature of the black silver ore at the Black Diamond Mine gave the name to the post office.

P.O. est. February 12, 1902. William H. Schofield, p.m. Discont. August 7, 1908.

Ref.:   Larriau; P.O. Records. Map: C-11.

**a.n. Black Diamond Peak**   El.: 6000'. Map: GB-16      Cochise

## BOOT HILL

El.: 4400'                          Loc.: Cochise 1, CD-8.
                                    Northwestern part of Tombstone.

The term "boot hill" was frequently applied to grave yards in the West where those who died with their boots on were buried. In the early days this particular grave yard had the appropriate name Tombstone Cemetery. Here victims of the Wyatt Earp and McLowery-Clanton Feud are buried. All but one of the original wooden grave markers have deteriorated or disappeared. It is a curious fact that the names of the dead were painted on headboards and that as weathering occurred, the painted portions became embossed, being raised as the weathering board wore away.

Ref.:   35, p. 54; 4, pp. 250-251. Map: None.

## BOQUILLAS

El.: 3994'                          Loc.: Cochise 1, B-7.3
Pro.:   /bokíyəs/                   Spanish: "little mouths"

This small railroad location was so named because it was adjacent to the San Juan de Boquillas y Nogales land grant. The fact that there are three or four little streams which come together on the Babocomari Creek led to the descriptive name for the several small arroyo mouths which debouched into the larger stream. Formerly all had living water. In 1853 Ignacio Elias Gonzales and Nepomuceno Felix purchased this grant. The United States Land Court recognized 17,355, but rejected 29,721 acres of the total claim.

Ref.:   Bennett; Barnes. Map: GB-1.

## BOSTON MILL

El.: c. 4000'                       Loc.: Cochise 1, C-10

In 1882 Boston Mill was one of the voting places in Cochise County. At that time it had a population of eighty-six. It is possible that the name derived from the fact that several Bostonians may have erected the mill.

**v.n. Emery City**

Ref.:   Larriau; Macia; *Tombstone Epitaph,* July 15, 1882, 3:5. Map: None.

## BOWIE

El.: 3762'                Loc.: Cochise 2, BC-1.1
Pro.: /búwiy/ or /bówiy/
The town of Bowie is located fourteen miles west of Fort Bowie. The first name for this location was Tres Cebollas (Spanish: "three onions"). Capt. James H. Tevis (b. Wheeling, West Virginia, July 11, 1835; d. August 29, 1905) homesteaded here. He had served with Confederate forces in 1860 as a captain with the Arizona Scouts, and was mustered out as a second lieutenant at Hempstead, Texas, 1865. In 1879 he moved to Austin, Texas, and began laying plans for his return to Arizona. He arrived in Fort Bowie January 1, 1880, where he opened a sutler's store. He donated ground for the mill and offices of the Cochise Mining and Milling Company, the mines for which were located sixteen miles to the south. One member of the firm, Capt. John Hancock, suggested that a post office be established so that mail would not have to be brought fourteen miles each day from Fort Bowie. At first the post office was in a tent but later was moved to Tevis's store when it was completed. Hancock named the new post office Teviston in honor of Capt. Tevis.
Late in 1881, Superintendent Bean of the railroad company talked to Tevis about naming the railroad station Bean City. Tevis replied that the residents had beans three times a day every day and were sick of the word. Insulted, Bean walked out saying he would call the place Bowie Station. The result was that the place was known as Teviston and also as Bowie Station until 1910. Apparently Bean was angered enough so he applied his own name, despite Tevis, to the location when a post office was secured.

P.O. est. as Bean, September 28, 1881. Henry A. Smith, p.m. Changed to Teviston, December 27, 1881. William L. Martin, p.m. Changed to Bowie, June 11, 1908. Homer Henrich, p.m. (Appointed January 4, 1908). Wells Fargo Station, 1885.

Ref.:   Riggs; 130; pp. 1, 2, 4, 7, 8, 233-34. Maps: GB-4; C-6; C-11 (Bowie); C-10.

   (Teviston P.O. and Bowie Station, in same place).

## BOWIE, FORT

El.: c. 6000'                Loc.: Cochise 2, BC-3.2
Pro.: /búwiy/ or /bówiy/
The Butterfield Overland Stage encountered so much difficulty with Apache Indians at Apache Pass (q.v.) that early in 1858 President Butterfield of the stage line asked the federal government to establish an army post in the pass. One year after the Butterfield Overland Stage suspended operations in southern Arizona, on July 28, 1862, Fort Bowie was established a half mile east of the Apache Pass mail station. Capt. L. E. Mitchell of the California Column selected the site. The place was named for Gen. George W. Bowie of the Fifth California Cavalry. The location was probably selected because of the proximity of a spring from which the old stage station had obtained its water, and there was also a strip of tableland where a fort could easily be constructed.
The post was garrisoned initially by the Fifth Infantry of California Volunteers with some members of Company A, First Cavalry, California Volunteers. The post was estab-

lished under Brig. Gen. James H. Carleton when the California Column passed on its way to Santa Fe. At that time Bowie was a colonel of the regiment.
Fort Bowie rapidly became important as an army post in the warfare against Apache Indians. It was in Apache Pass that Lt. G. W. Bascom in 1861 had his disastrous meeting with Cochise, from which Cochise escaped to spend many years wreaking vengeance on white men. The graveyard at the post filled rapidly with the bodies of men tortured and slain by Indians. Not until the end of the Civil War were enough troops available for a concentrated and organized campaign against the Apaches. In 1872, however, a truce was made with Cochise. When he died in 1874, his Chiricahua Apaches were sent to the San Carlos Reservation where their unhappiness led them to break out of the reservation. During Gen. Nelson A. Miles' campaign against the Indians, Fort Bowie served as headquarters and also as station number one in his heliograph system.
When the leaders of the San Carlos rebel Indians were shipped out of Arizona, Fort Bowie began its gradual decline. It was abandoned as a military establishment on October 17, 1894. In June 1911, the United States Government sold the twenty-four hundred acres of the Fort Bowie Military Reservation at public auction.

P.O. est. as Apache Pass, December 11, 1866. George Hand, p.m. Name changed to Fort Bowie, June 22, 1880. Sidney R. Delong, p.m. Discont. November 30, 1894.

Ref.:   75; p. 125; 32, II, 138-139; 161, p. 94; 111, pp. 154, 155; 52, II, 121; 7, p. 515. Maps: E-10; E-12; C-1; C-4 (Camp Bowie Military Reservation); C-6 (Camp Bowie and Apache Pass); C-7 (Apache Pass); GB-6.

a.n. Bowie Mountain   El.: 6943'. Map: GB-6                Cochise
Ref.:   Barnes.

## BRANNOCK

El.: c. 5000'                Loc.: Cochise 2, C-5
The several Riggs brothers owned extensive cattle and mining interests in this area. The post office for the headquarters of the Riggs Ranch was so named after the first name of one of the brothers.

P.O. est. August 16, 1887. Brannick Riggs (sic) p.m. Discont. April 1, 1891.

Ref.:   Riggs; Barnes. Maps: C-7; C-8.

## BREWERY GULCH

El.: 5900'                Loc.: Cochise 1, E-11
Brewery Gulch is the second most important canyon in Bisbee, joining the main Mule Pass Gulch at a right angle. Its name reflects the fact that at one time drinking sprees were held in this gulch.

Ref.:   4, p. 173; Map: GB-2.

## BROOKLINE

El.: 4100'                Loc.: Cochise 1, B-8.6
The now-vanished community known as Brookline was located at a point where the S.P.R.R. crossed a brook.

Ref.:   Barnes; Macia. Maps: GB-1; C-10 through C-14.

## BROPHY WELL

El.: c. 4000'                          Loc.: Cochise 1, F-8
The Brophy brothers established a ranch here, calling it
Soldier Hole Ranch.
The name for Soldier Hole Ranch came from the fact that
United States troops used to stop here where water was
found close to the surface. Because there was abundant
water, Soldier Hole was also used by teamsters hauling
lumber and timber from sawmills in the Chiricahua Mountains to Tombstone and Bisbee. The ranch house served
meals and dispensed whiskey over a bar.
Jim Brophy c. 1881 was running cattle at Soldier Hole.
His brother, Frank C. Brophy, joined him in Tombstone
and the two men went out to the ranch and began digging
what is now known generally as Brophy Well. They took
turns, one working at the bottom of the well while the
other remained, rifle in hand, at the top using field glasses
to keep a sharp lookout for Apaches. The man up top
also operated the windlass. Before long Frank Brophy
decided the cowman's life was not for him. He went to
Bisbee, just then emerging into prominence as a mining
camp. Jim Brophy remained as a cattleman at Brophy Well.
In 1892 a petition was sent to the Post Office Department
asking for a postal station at Soldier Hole. The receipt of
the petition in Washington caused a small furor, the Assistant Postmaster General being somewhat staggered by the
name. An explanation was sought and was found when it
was explained that the waterholes had for years been used
by soldiers in pursuit of Apaches. Mr. Wannamaker, who
was also consulted, thereupon seized a Spanish dictionary.
He thumbed through the pages and came to the word
*descanso,* meaning "a haven of rest." This name was thereupon substituted. Descanso was a tiny mining town where
Mexican turquoise was found.
P.O. est. as Descanso, May 23, 1892. William O. Abbott, p.m.
Discont. May 2, 1894.
Ref.:   140, p. 131; Frank C. Brophy, Letter, May 25, 1956.
        Riggs; *Weekly Arizona Enterprise,* 1892 (APHS Files).
        Maps: C-6 through C-12.

## BUENA

El.: 4400'                            Loc.: Cochise 1, B-10
Pro.: /bwéynə/                        Spanish: "good"
The origin of this name has not been ascertained.
P.O. est. as Bueno, October 26, 1910. John H. Downer, p.m.
Discont. October 31, 1919.
Ref.:   Barnes. Maps: GB-1; C-12.

## BUENA VISTA PEAK

El.: 8826'                            Loc.: Cochise 2, DE-5.8
Pro.: /bwéynə vistə/ or              Spanish: *buena,* "good"
      /bwéynə viystə/                        *vista,* "view"
Descriptive name applied by geological survey mapping
party.
Ref.:   Barnes. Maps: GB-5; C-12.

## BULL RUN

El.: c. 4000'                         Loc.: Cochise 1, BC-5.2
In 1847 when the Mormon Battalion under Col. Philip St.
George Cooke came to a small tributary creek of the San

Pedro River, they stopped to offer prayers of thanks for
water. Wild bulls used the river as a watering place. Pro-
voked by the intruders, the bulls attacked fiercely. There
ensued the only battle experienced by the Mormon Battalion — Arizona's "Battle of Bull Run."
Ref.:   Macia; 52, I, 140. Map: E-1.

## BRUNCKOW MINE

El.: c. 5000'                         Loc.: Cochise 1, D-9
Frederick Brunckow, an exile from Germany, was a well-
educated engineer and scientist. By 1858 he had arrived in
Arizona and had begun to develop a mine at this location.
Before long Brunckow was murdered by Mexicans who
then threw his body down the mine shaft.
Brunckow's cabin was on a little mound which gave it a
vantage point for viewing the surrounding country. For
this reason the place after his death became a rendezvous
for badmen and soon earned the reputation of being "the
bloodiest cabin in Arizona's history." One peaceful visitor,
however, was Ed Schieffelin, who camped here when he
was first prospecting in the Tombstone region (q.v.). The
Brunckow cabin gradually fell to pieces as portions of it
were carried away for use in other cabins. Part of it still
remains.
Reports that Brunckow's mine was rich led to claim jumping on several occasions, but the mine has never paid off.
v.n. Broncho (corruption)
Ref.:   Macia; H. C. Stillman, Letter to George H. Kelly, De-
        cember 8, 1924 (State Library Files); 167, p. 282; 170,
        p. 99. Maps: E-20 (Broncho); C-4; C-5 (Bronkow).

## CALUMET

El.: 3958'                            Loc.: Cochise 2, AB-12.3
Calumet is a small railroad siding for loading ore cars.
Martin Costello of Tombstone, who owned the Calumet
claims, set their value at a half million dollars. Leasing the
Costello claims, a development company was started by
the Calumet and Hecla Mining Company of Calumet,
Michigan, in March 1889. From this developed the Calumet
and Arizona Mining Company, which operated a smelter
northwest of the Copper Queen. In late 1931 and early
1932, this company was merged with Phelps Dodge.
Ref.:   *Douglas Dispatch,* "Fiftieth Anniversary Edition," Sec.
        4, 4:1, 2; 61, p. 62. Maps: GB-9; C-12 through C-14.

## CARR CANYON

El.: 6000'                            Loc.: Cochise 1, A-11
This place was named for James Carr, who was a horse
rancher in 1886.
Ref.:   *Arizona Star,* June 6, 1886, n.p. Maps GB-13; C-11.
a.n. Carr Peak         El.: 9214'. Map: GB-13         Cochise

## CASCABEL

El.: c. 3000'                         Loc.: Cochise 1, A-2.5
Pro.: /kǽskəbèl/                     Spanish: "rattlesnake"
Alex Herron had a ranch and a store. When he applied for
a post office he wanted to call it Pool after Joseph Pool, a
neighbor who was giving up a post office on his own ranch.
Pool was turned down by the post office authorities. On

his way to Benson, Herron met a Mexican with a large rattlesnake which the man had killed. He asked the Mexican the name for the snake and the reply was "Cascabel." Thereupon Herron decided to call his post office by that name.

P.O. est. June 13, 1916. Alexander Herron, p.m. Discont. July 15, 1936.

Ref.:   APHS Files. Maps: GB-18; C-13; C-12; C-14.

## CASTLE DOME

El.: 5805'                              Loc.: Cochise 2, BC-10.1
Descriptive.

Ref.:   Burrall. Map: GB-5.

## CASTLE ROCK

El.: c. 3000'                           Loc.: Cochise 1, E-11
Descriptive.

Ref.:   92, p. 414. Map: GB-3.

## CATHEDRAL ROCK

El.: 6985'                              Loc.: Cochise 2, EF-6.8
Descriptive.

Ref.:   1, p. 81, illustration. Map: GB-5.

## CAVE CANYON

El.: 5350'                              Loc.: Cochise 1, A-12—12.7
There are many caves along this canyon.

Ref.:   Bennett. Map: GB-13.

## CAVE CREEK

El.: 4396'                              Loc.: Cochise 2, F—9-6
The first settler was a man named Reed who arrived in this area c. 1878. He sold the place to the Hand brothers after his wife's death. The Hand brothers, John, Frank, and Alfred, were Englishmen who arrived c. 1888.

This colorful canyon of stone bluffs with smoothly eroded faces in pink, red, green, buff, and gold is pock-marked with caves of every size from that of a fist to caverns. However, the name actually comes from the existence of a very large underground cavern called Crystal Cave.

Ref.:   Riggs. Maps: B-2; GB-5.

## CHAMISO

El.: c. 4000'                           Loc.: Cochise 1, A-5
Pro.:   /kəmíyso/          Spanish: "half-burned wood"
A pile of mesquite cord wood caught fire and burned at this location c. 1890.

Ref.:   Barnes. Maps: C-13; C-14.

## CHARLESTON

El.: 4300'                              Loc.: Cochise 1, BC-9
In 1880 Charleston (cf. Galeyville) was a mill town with reduction works for the Tombstone Milling and Mining Company. A wild river camp, smaller and tougher than Tombstone, Charleston was a center not only for rustlers, but for soldiers on a tear from Fort Huachuca.

Charleston owed its beginning to the fact that there was no water at Tombstone to work the reduction facilities, so the new town was established on the banks of the San Pedro River. Curiously, it was an abundance of water in the wrong place – in the mine shafts at Tombstone – which put an end to Charleston.

P.O. est. April 17, 1879. Charles D. Handy, p.m. Discont. October 24, 1888. Wells Fargo Station, 1885.

Ref.:   P.O. Records; 76, p. 32; 170, p. 98; 35, p. 235. Maps: GB-1; C-7; C-8; C-11; C-13; C-14.

**a.n. Millville**
       Loc.: Across river from Charleston. Map: C-4, Cochise

P.O. est. May 26, 1879. John B. Allen, p.m. Discont. May 3, 1880.

Ref.:   Macia; P.O Records.

## CHINA PEAK

El.: 7125'                              Loc.: Cochise 1, DE—6.3
The China Mine near this peak was financed and worked by Chinese from California, hence the name.

Ref.:   Barnes. Map: GB-13.

## CHIRICAHUA MOUNTAINS

El.: 9795'                              Loc.: Cochise 2, DE—7.3—5
Pro.:   /číyrəkaw/ or          Apache: *tsil* "mountain";
        /číyrikáwə/                    *kawa*, "great"
The Chiricahua Mountains were so named because they were the home of the Chiricahua Apaches. This most war-like band of the Apaches ranged far into Mexico on raids. Their favorite ambush spot for American wagon trains was in Apache Pass *(q.v.)*.

Gen. O. O. Howard, who came to Arizona in April 1872, visited Cochise, the Chiricahua Chief, in these mountains to receive the submission of the tribe. In October the Chiricahua Indian Reservation was set aside for these Indians with Thomas Jefferson Jeffords as agent. The first headquarters for this agency was at Sulphur Springs *(q.v.)*. Unfortunately, white men named Rogers and Spence had a ranch and a store where they sold whiskey to the Indians. As a result, there were serious disorders and the Chiricahuas forsook the hard-earned peace to wage a severe war on white men between 1876 and 1882. In the latter year the remaining Chiricahuas were removed to Florida from Arizona, and on October 30, 1876, the Chiricahua Reservation again became a part of the public domain.

**v.n. Chiricahues** (Cortez, 1799)
      **Chiricagui**
      **Chiricahui, Sierra**

Ref.:   9, I, 370 (1851); 178, III, 119; 88, I, 282; 35, p. 459, Note 14; 55, p. 532; 7, p. 554; 9, I, 369-70. Maps: GB-5, GB-6; E-22; E-12 (Chi-ri-ca-hui); E-1; C-1 through 14.

**a.n. Chiricahua**       El.: 4671'. Map: C-13       Cochise
      This is a cattle shipping point on the railroad northeast of Douglas. There was formerly a settlement at this point.

P.O. est. September 14, 1907. Henrietta Powell, p.m. Discont. January 31, 1921.

**Chiricahua National Monument**   Map: GB-5       Cochise
Late in 1886 ex-sergeant Neil Erickson, who had a homestead here, went in pursuit of Col. Hughes Stafford's horse which had been stolen by an Apache named Massai. Erickson related he followed the hoof-prints and foot-prints until night came on and in returning to his home, found the huge fantastic formations of rocks almost overpowering. Erick-

son did not do much exploration, leaving that for his son-in-law, Ed Riggs, who with his wife Lillian spent many hours exploring the hundreds of acres of giant rhyolite pillars, balanced rocks, and other strange formations. Through the efforts of Riggs, this area was set aside by Presidential Proclamation in April 1924 as the Chiricahua National Monument.

According to geologists, at one time the relatively level land experienced a violent upheaval with molten lava bursting through the earth to spread over the plains. Sometimes hundreds of years elapsed before another eruption occurred, but apparently there were many such earthquakes and lava outbreaks. Slowly the earth lifted and tilted to form mountains. Erosion then did its slow work to create the fantastic forms to be seen today. In the Monument descriptive names abound, such as The Chinaman's Head, The Bishop, The Ugly Duckling, The Boxing Glove. Riggs himself named Duck-on-a-Rock, Balanced Rock, Thor's Hammer and the Totem Pole. Friends and guests of the Riggs named others.

Ref:. Riggs; 5, Dodge, "Refreshing Interlude," pp. 7, 8; 4, p. 375. Maps: C-13; C-14; C-9 (Chiricahua Forest Reservation).

**a.n. Massai Point**           Map: GB-6                    Cochise
Pro.: /mǽsiy/
Massai was the last surviving member of the Chiricahua tribe, which was transported out of Arizona in 1876. Massai returned to the area intending to kill Col. Hughes Stafford, but Stafford's keen eyes noted the Indian's tracks in the road. Stafford went back to find out where the Indian had come from, not where he had gone to, and this saved Stafford's life. When Neil Erickson was following this Indian through the canyon in pursuit of Stafford's stolen horse, he found the place where Massai and his wife had camped to cook ribs from one of Louis Cruz's cows. This place was close to Massai Point. This occurred c. 1892, and it is the last report of Chiricahua Apaches being in the area. The horse was recovered several months later. This is the place which the Apaches themselves referred to as Yahdesut ("Point of Rocks"). Later Riggs asked that the place be named for the Indian.

Ref.: Riggs; *Douglas Dispatch,* "Fiftieth Anniversary Edition (1952)," Sec. 6, 7:8.

**v.n. Massai's Canyon**                                    Cochise
    **Masies Canyon**
    **Chiricahua Peak**   El.: 9795' Map: GB-5              Cochise
At one time this peak was called Round Mountain. The name was changed by government action in 1904.

Ref.: Barnes.
    **Chiricahua Wild Area**
    El.: 1700' to 9795'. Loc.: To Summit, Chiricahua Mountains.                                                 Cochise
This is no place for a tenderfoot. There are no roads and it is truly wild frontier.

Ref.: 122, p. 14.

# CHOLLA
El.: 3700'                           Loc.: Cochise 2, B-1
Pro.: /čoyə/                         Spanish: "skull"
Cholla is thicker than usual here.

Ref.: None. Maps: GB-11; C-13; C-14.

# COCHISE
El.: 4225'                           Loc.: Cochise 1, E-3
Pro.: /kowčíys/
Cochise (d. June 8, 1874) was a famous Chiricahua Apache chief. Raiding Mexican territory was considered fair game by this chief, but he gave no trouble to Americans until, in 1861, under a flag of truce with other chiefs he visited Lt.

George Bascom in Apache Pass *(q.v.)* to deny any part in the abduction of a white child. Bascom, a young and inexperienced lieutenant, lost his temper and made captives of the visiting chiefs because they refused to confess. In an attempt to escape, one was killed and four were caught, but Cochise disappeared with three bullets in his body. He immediately began a ceaseless campaign of vengeance for the lives of his companions, who had been hanged at once by the troops. Cochise was caught in 1871, but when he was ordered transferred to New Mexico, he escaped with two hundred of his band and did not again capitulate until the establishment of the Chiricahua Reservation in 1872. The railroad station known as Cochise was established in 1887. It came abruptly into the news on September 9, 1889, when a S.P.R.R. train was held up here in a robbery notable because it was planned by Bert Albord, constable of Willcox, and by William Downing, a cattleman. The robbery itself was executed by Matt Burts and Billy Stiles (another law officer) of Pierce. Three-fingered Jack gave information leading to the solution of this crime, but he does not seem to have participated in it.

P.O. est. August 28, 1886. Silas H. Gould, p.m. Wells Fargo Station, 1903.

Ref.: 4, p. 439; 88, I, 317. Maps: C-6; C-14; GB-7.

**a.n. Cochise Head**   El.: 8109'. Map: GB-6              Cochise
    This formation in the Chiricahua National Monument strongly resembles an Indian profile, in which a large pine tree serves as an eyelash. The profile itself is more than a mile long.

**v.n. San Simon Head**

Ref.: 32, II, 232; 1, p. 86.

    **Cochise Memorial Park**
    El.: 7512'. Loc.: In Stronghold Canyon, Dragoon Mountains.                                               Cochise
    It is a tradition that when Cochise died he was buried in this area. On the night of his death his followers ran their horses up and down Stronghold Canyon to erase all traces of his grave.

Ref.: 4, p. 440.

    **Cochise Peak**   El.: 6500'. Map: GB-16              Cochise
    This is the same as Cochise Memorial Park. It was so named because Cochise and his men used this area as a hiding place. The stronghold was near the center of the Chiricahua Indian Reservation.
    It was in this canyon that Capt. Gerald Russell, Troop K, Third Cavalry, was watering his horses when attacked by Cochise and his band. His guide, Bob Whitney, was killed by the first shot.

Ref.: Barnes. 22, p. 174.

# COLLEGE PEAK
El.: 6385'                          Loc.: Cochise 2, C-11.5
Locally this peak was called The Nipple, a descriptive name; it was so called at least as late as 1880 by the cavalry unit camped at White Springs. On GLO 1883, the mountain appears by name for the first time and is called College Peak. It may be that as women moved into the area they objected to the earlier name, but no documentation has been located to authenticate this. There are two peaks, one known as North College Peak and the other known as South College Peak.

Ref.: Riggs; Macia. Maps: GB-17; B-2; C-5 through C-14.

## CONTENTION

El.: 3792'  Loc.: Cochise 1, B-7.5

Hank Williams, a prospector, was among the thousands of miners who flocked to Tombstone when the word got around that Ed Schieffelin had struck it rich. Williams was camped close to Schieffelin. One of Williams' mules got loose and while following it, Williams noted that the dragging halter chains were scraping metallic ore. He immediately staked a claim. It was hotly contested by Dick Gird, Schieffelin's partner. Gird and Schieffelin bought out Williams and as a result of the argument named their mine the Contention.

There was no water with which to work the rich ores and for this reason Contention City was established at the nearest available water, on the San Pedro River. When the mines flooded at Tombstone, Contention soon became a ghost town.

P.O. est. April 5, 1880. John McDermott, p.m. Discont. November 26, 1888. Wells Fargo Station, 1885.

Ref.:  55, p. 545; 27, pp. 20-21; 105, pp. 208-209; Larriau. Maps: GB-1; C-5; C-7; C-8.

## COPPER CENTER

El.: c. 4000'  Loc.: Cochise 1, CD-11.6.
On the San Pedro near Hereford.

There was a smelter at this location at one time (date not known).

P.O. est. October 14, 1901. Rengwald Blix, p.m. Discont.?

Ref.:  Larriau; P.O. Records; Barnes. Map: None.

## CORONADO NATIONAL MEMORIAL

El.: 6827'  Loc.: Cochise 1, AB-12.5
Pro.: /cáronado/ or /coronado/

This international park was named for Francisco Vasquez de Coronado, the first to introduce cattle, sheep, and horses to Indians in the Southwest. On the four hundredth anniversary of Coronado's 1540 expedition, plans were made to set up a monument at or near the International Boundary where Coronado probably crossed into what is now Arizona. On July 9, 1952, the Coronado National Monument (2,745 acres) was created by presidential signature. Of eleven national memorials, it is the only one in Arizona.

Ref.:  *Bisbee Daily Review,* "Ft. Huachuca Get-Acquainted Edition," July 31, 1951; Grace M. Sparkes, Letter, March 7, 1956; 120, p. 33. Map: A-13.

a.n. Cochise Peak
El.: 6800'. Loc.: International Memorial area  Cochise

## CORTA

El.: 5166'  Loc.: Cochise 1, EF-12
Pro.: /córtə/  Spanish: "felled wood"

This was a station for loading firewood which used to be cut nearby.

Ref.:  Barnes. Maps: C-10; C-11; C-12; F-2.

## COURTLAND

El.: 4604'  Loc.: Cochise 1, F-7.5

Courtland Young was one of the owners of the Great Western Mining Company, established in 1909 by his brother, W. J. Young.

P.O. est. March 13, 1909. Harry Locke, p.m. Discont. September 30, 1942. Wells Fargo Station, 1910.

Ref.:  Barnes. Maps: GB-16; C-11 through C-14.

## CROTON SPRINGS

El.: 4137'  Loc.: Cochise 1, E-3

These springs were so named as early as 1849 because the water tasted like croton oil. In 1881 Thomas and Lizzie Kirkland Steele had a home at this point, which also served as a stage station. According to Fish, the Steeles were here in 1874.

Ref.:  Lizzie Steele File, APHS; 48, pp. 188-189; 55, p. 586. Maps: GB-7; C-7; C-8; C-3; E-6; E-12; E-11.

## CURVO

El.: 3836'  Loc.: Cochise 1, BC-5.4
Spanish: "crooked"

The railroad makes a sharp turn here, hence the name.

Ref.:  Barnes. Map: GB-1.

## DAHL

Loc.: Not known.

There is a possibility that this post office was established at the Dial Ranch, owned by Robert Dial, in the South Pass of the Dragoon Mountains.

P.O. est. as Dahl, September 9, 1905. John A. White, p.m. Discont. ?

Ref.:  Larriau; Macia; P.O. Records. Map: None.

## DIXIE CANYON

El.: 5939'  Loc.: Cochise 1, E-11

At one time a Negro called Nigger Dick lived at springs in this canyon, where he farmed and had cattle. Gradually the canyon come to be known as Dick's Canyon, and finally as Dixie Canyon.

Ref.:  Barnes. Map: GB-2.

## DON LUIS

El.: 5000'  Loc.: Cochise 1, E-11.7
Pro.: /dan luwíys/

Lewis Williams with his brother Ben promoted the development of the mines in the Bisbee area (cf. Bisbee). Mexicans called him Don Luis.

P.O. est. January 27, 1903. John J. Mercers, p.m. (deceased). Mary I. Hull appointed p.m., October 7, 1903. Discont. August 31, 1933. Wells Fargo Station, 1904.

Ref.:  Barnes; APHS Names File. Maps: GB-2; C-12; C-13; C-14.

## DOS CABEZAS PEAK

El.: c. 8000'  Loc.: Cochise 2, D-2.4
Pro.: /dos cabéysos/  Spanish: "two heads"

The descriptive name for two bald summits known as Dos Cabezas was in existence in the late 1840's.

Ref.:  124, p. 23; 89, p. 33. Maps: GB-8; C-2; C-3; C-8.

a.n. Dos Cabezas  El.: 3900'. Map: GB-8
The early name for this location was Ewell's Springs (cf. Ewell's Station), one half mile east of the present town. The springs served as a watering spot for the Boundary Survey

party in August 1851. In 1857 a stage station was created here for the Birch Route. The Butterfield route passed to the southwest. The first school in Cochise County was built at Ewell's Springs.

P.O. est. January 1, 1949. Wells Fargo Station, 1885.

Ref.: John J. Howard, Letter to Mrs. E. Macia, June 10, 1928. 32, II, 139. Map: GB-8.

### Dos Cabezas Mountains
Maps: GB-6; GB-8; GB-11; GB-23                    Cochise

## DOUBLE ADOBE
El.: 4354'                    Loc.: Cochise 1, FG-11.4
                              E. of Bisbee 6½ miles
Pro.: /ədówbí/

This now nearly-abandoned little community was named because of a two room adobe building with eighteen-inch walls having several gun openings. The Double 'Dobe Ranch was in existence when Tombstone was flourishing as a mining camp in the 1880's. The ruins of the building are still in existence.

Ref.: *Douglas Dispatch,* "Fiftieth Anniversary Edition," Sec. 5, 8:1; 24, p. 39. Map: None.

## DOUBTFUL CANYON
El.: 5200'                    Loc.: Cochise 2, FG-5

The pass through this canyon was called Doubtful Pass because the Indians were so thick it was always doubtful whether emigrants or soldiers would make their way safely through it. There was a Butterfield stage station (twenty-one miles east of Apache Pass), here, called the Doubtful Pass Station. The map shows one Doubtful Canyon running east and west and another running north and south.

Ref.: Schroeder; 99, p. 31. Map: GB-19.

## DOUGLAS
El.: 3980'                    Loc.: Cochise 2, B-12.5

In 1878 the place where the town of Douglas now exists was known as Black Water, so called because of a dirty water hole. Nevertheless, water was so scarce that Black Water was much used.

Parke Whitney, Charles A. Overlocke and J. A. Brock in 1901 located a town which they named for Dr. James Stewart Douglas (b. Quebec, June 19, 1868; d. January 2, 1929). Others joined with the small group and in February 1902 the Douglas Improvement Company was incorporated to operate and maintain public utilities.

Douglas moved to Bisbee (*q.v.*) in 1889 where he became assayer for the Copper Queen Mining Company. He married the daughter of Lewis Williams on November 11, 1891. In 1900 he became the superintendent of a mine in Sonora for Phelps Dodge.

P.O. est. March 5, 1901. Charles A. Overlocke, p.m. Wells Fargo Station, 1904. Incorporated May 15, 1905.

Ref.: H. A. Merrill File, APHS; *Douglas Dispatch,* "Fiftieth Anniversary Edition," Sec. 4, 4:1-3; Sec. 3, 1:5; *Arizona Republic,* "Arizona Days and Ways," August 8, 1954, p. 26. Maps: GB-9; C-9 through C-14.

## DRAGOON MOUNTAINS
El.: 7000'                    Loc.: Cochise 1, D-5.4
Pro.: /drægúwn/

The Dragoon Mountains were so named because it was here that the 3rd U. S. Cavalry, known as Dragoons, was stationed. Their name came from the fact that they used heavy carbines rather than the usual sabre and revolver associated with cavalry troops.

Ref.: None. Maps: GB-7; GB-10;; GB-16; GB-1; E-18.

### a.n. Dragoon Pass    El.: 4613'. Map: GB-10    Cochise
The Butterfield Overland Stage had a station here in 1858. The stage station, called Dragoon Springs, is two miles southeast of the present Dragoon post office. The springs, first located by scouts of the U. S. Dragoons in 1856, had dried up by 1879 when William Fourr took over the stage station property. The old stage station walls are still in existence, as are also the graves of several people murdered by Indians.

It was at this place that in September 1858 the Butterfield agent, Silas St. John, was in charge of a crew constructing buildings for the station at Dragoon Springs. The men were attacked at night by three Mexican laborers, and three Americans were killed. St. John fought off the assailants, despite the fact that he had a deep axe wound in his hip and his left arm had been severed by an axe blow. The Mexicans left. For three days St. John defended himself and his dead or dying associates from coyotes and buzzards. At noon on the fourth day troops arrived and a surgeon was sent for from Fort Buchanan (Santa Cruz County).

The surgeon, Dr. B. J. Irwin, rode one hundred sixteen miles and succeeded in saving St. John's life.

Ref.: Nuttall; Macia; 111, p. 272; 32, II, 140-142; 52, II, 5.

### Dragoon    Map: GB-10    Cochise
This is the small town on the S.P.R.R. two miles from the old Dragoon Springs Station. In 1882 Dragoon Summit, or Summit as it was called, served as a voting place with a registered population of twelve.

P.O. est. June 20, 1881. Cassius M. Hooker, p.m. Wells Fargo Station, 1885.

Ref.: Larriau; *Tombstone Epitaph,* July 15, 1882, 3:5.

### Dragoon Peak    El.: 6533'. Maps: GB-7; GB-16    Cochise
### Dragoon Wash    Maps: GB-1; GB-16    Cochise
### Little Dragoon Mountains    Map: E-20    Cochise
### v.n. Limestone Mountain    Map: GB-5    Cochise

## DREW'S STATION
El.: c. 3700'                    Loc.: Cochise 2, E-2
                              Probably near Drew Tank.

In 1881 this was a stage station owned by Harrison Drew about fifteen miles north of Tombstone on the road to Benson. It was at this place that Doc Holliday killed Bud Philpot.

Ref.: Larriau. Map: GB-6 (Drew Tank).

## DUNN SPRINGS
El.: c. 4100'                    Loc.: Cochise 1, FG-3.6

Jack Dunn was an army scout in the 1870's. During his scouting days he took time out to prospect for mining claims (cf. Bisbee). He later had a cabin at this spring.

Ref.: Barnes. Maps: GB-6; B-2; C-4; C-5; C-8; C-12; C-13; C-14.

### a.n. Dunn Springs Mountain    El.: 6503'. Map: GB-6    Cochise

## EAST PEAK

El.: 6648'                    Loc.: Cochise 1, A-6.5
Descriptive.
Ref.: Barnes. Maps: C-12; C-14; GB-1.

## ECHO PEAK

El.: c. 6000'                 Loc.: Cochise 2, CD-4.5
At one place on the trail in Echo Canyon in Chiricahua National Monument there is a notable echoing quality. This place was named by J. J. P. Armstrong or perhaps by Ed Riggs in 1924.
Ref.: Riggs. Map: GB-6.

## ELFRIDA

El.: c. 4000'                 Loc.: Cochise 2, A-8.6
Pro.: /élf:raydə/
G. I. Van Meter named this community Elfrida after his mother. The origin of his mother's name was Danish transplanted to England; it is not Spanish. Van Meter donated the right of way across his land to the railroad, and the company named this station at his request.
P.O. est. July 24, 1915. Marie H. Leitch, p.m.
Ref.: G. I. Van Meter, Letter to John Curry, January 10, 1937. Maps: GB-16; C-12.

## EMIGRANT CANYON

El.: c. 5000'                 Loc.: Cochise 2, CD-3.5
This was the place where emigrants left the main transcontinental trail to pitch temporary camp in order to recuperate.
Ref.: Riggs. Map: GB-6.

**a.n. Emigrant Hills**   El.: 4396' and 4443'. Map: GB-6   Cochise
There are two hills at this location.

**Emigrant Pass**   El.: 6200'. Map: GB-6   Cochise
This pass lies between two peaks in the Chiricahua Mountains. One is 6226' and the other is 6279'.

## ERICKSON

El.: 7900'                    Loc.: Cochise 2, DE-7.8
Neil Erickson (b. April 22, 1859; d. October 1937) served as a sergeant with the U. S. Army before homesteading in this area. He later served as the first ranger in the Chiricahuas for a quarter of a century.
Erickson, a native of Sweden, lived with a single purpose in his early life. While working for the railroad, his father (an emigrant to the United States) had been killed by Indians in Minnesota. The young boy took an oath to avenge his father's death. Years later he landed in Boston, staying only until he had learned English. He then enlisted "to fight Indians," not caring where, but only that it should be as soon as possible. He carried out his vow, serving with the cavalry during the Geronimo campaign from 1881 through 1886.
Ref.: Lillian Erickson Riggs (Daughter). Map: GB-5.

## EWELL'S STATION

El.: c. 4500'                 Loc.: Cochise 2, O-3.1
Pro.: /íywelz/
Capt. Richard S. Ewell of the First Dragoons established this station early in 1859. It was a change station on a relay route between Apache Pass and Dragoon Springs. As there was no water at this station, it was hauled in from nearby Dos Cabezas Springs.
Little remains today to mark this spot.
Ref.: 32, II, 139-140; 161, p. 182. Map: E-20.

## FAIRBANK

El.: 3800'                    Loc.: Cochise 1, BC-8.1
N. K. Fairbank organized the Grand Central Mining Company in Tombstone, where he resided. He was one of the stockholders in the railroad line from Benson to Mexico, and this place on the railroad — where there was a branch line to Tombstone — was named for him.
P.O. est. May 16, 1883. John Dessart, p.m. Wells Fargo Station, 1885.
Ref.: Barnes; Macia; Larriau; APHS Names File. Maps: GB-1; C-6 through C-14.

## FENNER

El.: c. 4000'                 Loc.: Cochise 1, B-5
Dr. Hiram W. Fenner of Bisbee was for many years Chief Surgeon of the Tucson Division of the S.P.R.R.
Ref.: Barnes. Map: GB-1.

## FIFE CANYON

El.: c. 6000'                 Loc.: Cochise 2, C-5
Fife Canyon was named for a polygamous Mormon who lived here with two wives and intended to bring in a third. One day a Mexican employee asked one Mrs. Fife for food. He shot her in cold blood as she was setting food on the porch for him. Hours later the murderer was caught skulking in the grass near Fort Bowie and was taken to the Riggs Home Ranch, thence to Fife's place where he was identified and forthwith lynched.
Ref.: Riggs. Map: GB-5.

**a.n. Fife Peak**   El.: 6810'. Map: GB-5   Cochise
**Fife Springs**   Map: GB-5   Cochise
**Fife Creek (Five Mile Creek)**   Map: GB-5   Cochise
Fife Creek, Five Mile Creek, and Witch Creek are identical. It is five miles along this creek from the Riggs Home Ranch to the Fife Ranch.
**Five Mile Canyon**   Cochise

## FITTSBURG

El.: c. 4000'                 Loc.: Cochise 1, F-6
When the town of Pearce began to grow c. 1905, George Fitts of Tombstone planned an addition to the west of Pearce to be called Fittsburg. It was short-lived.
Ref.: Barnes. Map: None.

## FLICKNER CANYON

El.: c. 6000'                 Loc.: Cochise 2, D-4.7
This road was named by Ed and Lillian Riggs for Frank Flickner c. 1930. On the basis of a personal survey and report, Flickner was largely responsible for locating the present road in the Chiricahua National Monument.
Ref.: Riggs. Map: None.

## FLY'S PEAK

El.: 9759'                    Loc.: Cochise 2, DE-7
John Fly was a photographer in Tombstone when that town
was first getting started in the late 1870's. He accompanied
Gen. George Crook on several campaigns. Fly's pictures of
the early days in Arizona, particularly of Indians, are
famous.

Ref.:   Barnes. Maps: GB-5; C-12.

## FORREST

El.: c. 4000'                 Loc.: Cochise 2, AB-12.3
Henry Forrest raised both cattle and sheep. His place was
a regular stopping point for freighters hauling timber
from Turkey Creek to the Copper Queen Mine. Forrest
maintained a large water trough for their use. Forrest and
his wife are buried on his ranch site.

P.O. est. May 8, 1914. Josie C. Clyman, p.m. Discont. November
15, 1917.

Ref.:   Burgess. Maps: F-2; C-9.

## FOURR CANYON

El.: c. 5000'                 Loc.: Cochise 1, D-5
Pro.: /fer/
William Fourr (b. Missouri, July 11, 1842; d. 1935) came
to Arizona in 1863 as a prospector. He bought the Kenyon
and Burke Stage Station, establishing a ranch at Oatman
Flat (q.v.). He left Oatman Flat to move to Dragoon Pass
in June 1879, living there until his death.

Ref.:   Nuttall; William Fourr File, APHS; Arizona Sentinel,
        June 28, 1879, n.p. Map: GB-1.

## FRENCH JOE CANYON

El.: c. 6000'                 Loc.: Cochise 1, A-7
What French Joe's last name was seems to have slipped
into oblivion. French Joe lived with his partner on a ranch
in this canyon. The Indians killed his partner and French
Joe never went back to the ranch, but moved at once to
a place on the Babocomari Creek.

Ref.:   Bennett. Maps: GB-1.

a.n. French Joe Peak   El.: 7684'. Map: GB-1        Cochise

## GALEYVILLE

El.: 5700'                    Loc.: Cochise 2, E-5
In November 1881 John H. Galey, a Pennsylvania oil man,
opened the Texas Mine and built a smelter at Galeyville.
Galeyville was laid out in 1880 and soon had four hundred
residents, most of whom were gone by 1882. The place
was extremely isolated, being high in the Chiricahua Mountains, twenty miles from the nearest railroad, close to the
Mexican boundary, and about as far from the arm of the
law as was possible to get. Mining activities zoomed and
died like a skyrocket, but the fireworks introduced by lawless men went on for several years. Cattle rustlers used
nearby gulches to harbor stolen cattle while brands were
altered. Galeyville was at least eighty miles away from
another tough spot known as Charleston (q.v.) and the resi-

dents of the two places did not often mingle, but when
they did, law-abiding citizens were safer elsewhere.

In 1888 the San Simon Cattle Company forced out or
bought out squatters in the area. What remained of old
Galeyville, which had been devastated once by fire, was
carried away piece by piece to build new structures in
nearby Paradise (q.v.).

P.O. est. January 6, 1881. Frank McCandless, p.m. Discont. May
31, 1882.

Ref.:   Macia; Larriau; 76, p. 32; 27, pp. 88-89; 105, p. 282.
        "Bad Men March Through Arizona's History," Arizona
        Daily Star, March 27. 1932. APHS; Gazette, April 1,
        1881, 2:2. Map: C-5.

## GARCES

El.: c. 4000'                 Loc.: Cochise 1, B-11.2
Pro.: /gárseys/ or /garséys/
The first name for this now-vanished mining camp was
Reef, so named for the Reef Mine. The name came from a
very conspicuous reef of rock which was a well-known
landmark. Somewhat later the name was changed to Palmerlee because the land was owned by Joseph S. Palmerlee.
Why the name was changed to Garcés has not yet been
ascertained. Barnes says it was so named for Garcés National Forest. The forest was in turn named for Fr.
Francisco Garcés (1738-1781) who came to the Southwest
in 1768. He was a noted mission builder who lost his life
in an Indian revolt in 1781.

P.O. est. as Reef, January 7, 1901. Mark Walker, p.m. Name
changed to Palmerlee, December 7, 1904. Joseph S. Palmerlee,
p.m. Name changed to Garcés, April 12, 1911. Richard M. Johnson, p.m. Discont. May 24, 1926.

Ref.:   Macia; Barnes; APHS Names File; P.O. Records. Maps:
        GB-13 (Reef); C-9 (Reef); C-10 (Palmerlee); C-11
        (Reef).

## GARFIELD PEAK

El.: c. 6500'      Loc.: In Chiricahua National Monument
Garfield (d. c. 1882) was a member of the Tenth Cavalry
during the Civil War. When the Tenth Cavalry men, his
former comrades, were at the Riggs Ranch in 1886, they
built a monument to Garfield and carved their own names
on the stones. When the monument began to weather badly,
the Riggs family moved its stones into their own home,
using them to face the fireplace.

Ref.:   Riggs. Map: None.

## GATEWOOD

El.: c. 6000'                 Loc.: Cochise 2, DE-2.5
This place in the San Simon Valley was named for Lt.
Charles B. Gatewood, Sixth U. S. Cavalry. In 1886 Gate-
wood was successful in convincing the Apache chief
Geronimo that he should confer with Gen. Nelson A. Miles
and surrender. Gatewood spoke the Apache language and
knew the Indians well. Because of his prominent nose, the
Apaches called him Bay-chin-day-sin ("long nose").

P.O. est. June 7, 1890. Joseph M. Hooker, p.m. Discont. February 5, 1894.

Ref.:   Barnes. Maps: C-7; C-8.

## GLEESON

El.: 5000′  Loc.: Cochise 1, F-8
John Gleeson (b. Ireland, November, 1861) and his wife
were an Irish couple who came to Arizona from Iowa and
Colorado. They worked in the mines at Pearce — he as a
miner and she as a boarding house keeper in the early
1890's. Gleeson grub-staked a crippled friend and the man
re-located the old mines at Turquoise. He sold out by 1914.
Long before white men appeared in this area Indians were
mining turquoise on Turquoise Mountain. Tiffany and
Company of New York continues to work the mine when
the demand warrants. The remnants of the older community of Turquoise came back to life in 1900 for a brief
building boom, and there are still restricted mining operations here.

P.O. est. as Turquoise, October 22, 1890. James W. Lowery,
p.m. Discont. September 17, 1894. Re-established as Gleeson,
October 15, 1900. Frank A. O'Brien, p.m. Discont. March 31,
1939. Wells Fargo Station, 1910.

Ref.: Macia; 88, II, 840; 4, p. 441; *Tombstone Prospector,*
March 14, 1901, 4:2. Maps: GB-16; C-7 (Turquoise);
C-9 (Gleeson).

## GLENN, MOUNT

El.: 7512′  Loc.: Cochise 1, DE-5.4
Calvin Glenn (d. c. 1918) was manager for the Chiricahua
Cattle Company c. 1888. This highest peak in the Dragoon
Mountains was named for him. Glenn remained with the
company until c. 1905.

Ref.: Barnes; APHS Names File. Maps: GB-16; C-12.

## GOODWIN CANYON

El.: c. 4500′  Loc.: Cochise 2, CB-2.5
The first name for this canyon was Cochise Canyon and
it was so known when the stage lines ran through Apache
Pass. The canyon is behind the old Apache Pass stage
station. It was called Cochise because it was here that the
Apache chief camped with seven hundred of his tribe
while another chief, known as Old Jack, camped five
hundred men in front of the station at what is known as
Goodwin Springs. By 1889 the places were known as
Goodwin Spring and Goodwin Canyon. It is reported
that Gov. John N. Goodwin stopped here.

Ref.: Barnes; 161, p. 95. Maps: GB-6; B-2.

**a.n. Goodwin**  Loc.: Unknown  Cochise
P.O. est. March 5, 1875. Thomas McWilliams, p.m. Discont.
October 18, 1880.

## HALFMOON VALLEY

El.: c. 6000′  Loc.: Cochise 2, CD-8-10
William Lutley of Tombstone lived in this valley in the early
1880's and named it descriptively for its crescent shape.

Ref.: Barnes. Map: GB-5.

## HAMBURG

El.: c. 7000′  Loc.: Cochise 1, A-11.4
Henry Hamburg was a German from St. Louis who had
a mining camp here for several years.

P.O. est. October 5, 1906. Louise deVere Hamburg, p.m.
Discont. ?
Ref.: Barnes; APHS Names File. Maps: GB-13; C-12.

## HANDS PASS

El.: c. 7000′  Loc.: Cochise 2, DE-5
Frank H. Hands (1862-1936) was one of three brothers
interested in mining who came to this area from England
in 1888. Two of the brothers developed the Hilltop Mine
(cf. Hilltop). Frank settled in the valley and is buried at the
bottom of the pass beside the road. Hands and his brother
John were instrumental in getting the road put through from
Pinery Canyon (*q.v.*) to Portal (*q.v.*) and the pass was
named for them.

Ref.: Riggs. Maps: GB-5; C-11.

## HARRIS MOUNTAIN

El.: c. 5000′  Loc.: Cochise 2, EF-5
The name of this mountain commemorates the death of a
pioneer emigrant and his family who were murdered by
Apaches in 1873. Harris, on his way west, was looking for
a short cut. Despite warnings, he left the emigrant party
at San Simon Cienega, where Apaches with whom he had
been talking told him of a short cut through the Chiricahuas.
That was the last heard of Harris. The whole family simply
disappeared.

Many years later one of his daughters was rescued by
army men and was brought back from Mexico. She told
the story of what happened. Following her directions, the
army men found the bones of the family in Hunt Canyon,
where the Indians had killed Harris, his wife, and two
children, carrying off his fifteen year old daughter. One
soldier took time to carve a crude head board, "Here lie
the Harris family killed by Apaches 1873." The headboard
was made of hardwood, probably from a whiskey cask.
Such boards were often used for grave markers.

Ref.: Macia. Maps: GB-5; C-12.

## HELEN'S DOME

El.: 6377′  Loc.: Cochise 2, BC-3.1
In the 1850's Helen's Dome was known as Cow Peak
because there was a live oak tree at the top of this mountain which, when viewed from Apache Pass stage station
looked like a cow.

Old timers still sometimes refer to this conical mountain
as Helen's Doom, and it was so known at least as early as
1875. According to the post trader at Fort Bowie, Sidney
DeLong, it was named for Mrs. Helen Hackett, wife of
Capt. Hackett, stationed at the post. Accompanied by some
friends she climbed the peak and it was named for her.

Ref.: Riggs; Barnes; 161, pp. 94, 95. Maps: GB-6; E-20; C-12.

## HEREFORD

El.: c. 4000′  Loc.: Cochise 1, CD-11.1
Pro.: /hérferd/
William Herrin put up a smelter around which a small com-
munity developed. Herrin named the place for his friend,
Benjamin J. Hereford, an attorney of Tucson in the 1870's

and later. After the smelter shut down and later was destroyed by fire, this place was deserted until c. 1892 when Col. William Greene started a cattle ranch here.

P.O. est. April 4, 1904. Ben Snead, p.m. Wells Fargo Station, 1904.

Ref.:   Barnes; APHS Names File. Maps: GB-13; C-10.

## HILLTOP

El.: c. 7000'                              Loc.: Cochise 2, CD-5
The Hilltop Mine was established by Frank and John Hands (cf. Hands Pass). They later sold it to a man in St. Louis who developed it into an active mine. Its location near the top of the hill resulted in the descriptive name. The town of Hilltop was started first on the west side of the mountain. Then a tunnel was put through to the east side where an even larger town was established.
This mine has been inactive for several years. During part of the period of inactivity, Hilltop was a summer colony. Today it is a ghost town.

P.O. est. January 26, 1920. Raleigh O. Fife, p.m. Discont. June 30, 1945.

Ref.:   Riggs; P.O. Records. Maps: GB-5; C-13.

## HOLT

El.: c. 4000'                              Loc.: Cochise 2, C-1.3
Col. J. M. Holt of Montana shipped cattle from here 1887 to c. 1892.

Ref.:   Barnes. Maps: GB-4; C-12.

## HOOKER'S HOT SPRINGS

El.: 4008'                                Loc.: Cochise 1, B-1
The springs known as Hooker's Hot Springs were discovered by a Dr. King in April 1881, and were named for Henry C. Hooker, who had the nearby Sierra Bonita Ranch (q.v., Graham). Dr. King was killed by Apaches in 1884.

Ref.:   Barnes; Henry C. Hooker File, APHS. Maps: GB-24; C-10 (Hot Springs); C-12.

a.n.  **Hot Springs Creek**        Map: C-12                      Cochise
       **Hot Spring Canyon**       Map: GJ-17                    Cochise

## HORSEFALL CANYON

El.: c. 4000'                           Loc.: Cochise 2, CD-5-5.3
In the early 1900's a forest ranger, on his way to fight a fire, was mounted on the lead horse of the pack train. He stumbled off the trail and was killed, hence the name.

Ref.:   Riggs. Map: B-2.

## HORSESHOE CANYON

El.: c. 6000'                            Loc.: Cochise 2, EF-7.2
The big arc shape of this canyon results in the descriptive name. The Apaches used this canyon as one of their several strongholds. The impenetrable nature of the country in southeastern Arizona's mountains made it next to impossible for the cavalry to catch up with Indians, and the Apaches were on the move for seven years. When they finally surrendered, they did so of their own accord and not because they had been captured.

It is a misnomer to call one particular area of the southeastern Arizona mountains "Cochise Stronghold." The fact is that the entire area served as a stronghold for Cochise and the Chiricahua Apaches.

Ref.:   Riggs; Burrall. Map: GB-5.

## HUACHUCA, FORT

El.: c. 4800'                             Loc.: Cochise 1, A-10
Pro.:  /wačúkə/
The name Huachuca was apparently first used for a Pima Indian village on what came to be the Babocomari Land Grant.
Camp Huachuca succeeded Camp Wallen (q.v.) as a military post of principal importance in Arizona. Camp Huachuca was established on March 3, 1877, at the mouth of what was known then descriptively as Central Canyon, in the Huachuca Mountains. Increasing difficulties with Apaches added to the importance of the camp and in 1882 it was made a permanent post. Following the surrender of Geronimo in 1886, the post was relatively inactive until the Madero revolt in Mexico in 1911. Camp Huachuca then became headquarters for troops along the border. It reached its maximum importance during World War II when 22,000 soldiers and 8,000 civilians swarmed on the military reservation. In 1949 Fort Huachuca was transferred to the state of Arizona for use by the National Guard. For a brief period it was abandoned as a military establishment. The growing importance of military electronic devices caused the reactivation of the post as a federal project in the early 1950's.

P.O. est. as Camp Huachuca, November 24, 1879. Fred L. Austin, p.m. Name changed to Fort Huachuca, February 5, 1891. Wells Fargo Station, 1885.

Ref.:   75, p. 137; 4, p. 392; 1, p. 76; 38, pp. 345-346, Note 9; 20, p. 248, Note 2. Maps: GB-1; GB-14; E-20 (Camp Huachuca); C-5.

a.n.  **Huachuca Canyon**     Maps: GB-1; GB-14                  Cochise
       **Huachuca Mountain**
       El.: 7604'. Maps: GB-1; GB-13; GB-14                      Cochise
v.n.  **Wachupe Mountains** (1859)
Ref.:   64, p. 27.
       **Huachuca Peak**   El.: 8406'. Maps: GB-13               Cochise

## HUNT CANYON (No. 1)

El.: c. 5500'                           Loc.: Cochise 2, CB-10-9.5
The Hunt Canyon which is located in the Chiricahua National Monument was named for Gov. George Wylie Paul Hunt following his first and only trip into the Wonderland of Rocks. William Riggs advised the governor against the selection of a certain horse which was known for its weak knees. However, the governor, who was completely dressed in white riding clothes despite the fact that it was a rainy day, insisted on riding the horse. In this canyon the horse's knees buckled, and the governor tumbled off, with sad results to the white riding habit. The governor went no farther into the Wonderland of Rocks, but left his name and his dignity in the canyon.

Ref.:   Riggs. Maps: C-13; GB-5.

# HUNT CANYON (No. 2)

El.: c. 6000'  Loc.: Cochise 2, CD-8-9

Zwing Hunt (b. Texas) showed up in Tombstone in the early 1880's as a law-abiding freighter. Before long the profits to be had by rustling cattle proved too great a temptation and Hunt changed professions. In the fall of 1881, he was indicted for rustling and at once disappeared into Mexico, not to reappear until March 1882, on a night when a Mr. Peel was murdered at the Tombstone Mill. Hunt was reported as being present. The next word of Hunt came from Chandler's Ranch where there had been a shooting ruckus with one dead and several wounded. Again Hunt was involved. He was captured and brought to the county hospital for treatment of a wound in his lungs. From here he was quietly taken one night in a wagon and was not seen again. A report came in that he had been killed by Apaches. His brother, Hugh Hunt, led a party of scouts to the place where Zwing was buried. The body was found, not mutilated in the usual Apache fashion, buried in a grave by a juniper tree, on the trunk of which was carved Zwing Hunt's name and the date of his death. From that time, the canyon was known as Hunt Canyon.

Hunt was supposed to have been one of the men who took part in the massacre in Skeleton Canyon (q.v.). He was said to have buried his treasure from that massacre in the canyon where he himself is buried. Many treasure seekers have dug hundreds of holes searching for Hunt's treasure.

Ref.: 119a, pp. 218-219; 108a, pp. 154-155, 156, 157, 159, 160; 27, p. 120. Map: GB-26.

# JHUS CANYON

El.: c. 7000'  Loc.: Cochise 2, DE-5
Pro.: /juws/

Jhus was one of the Indian leaders who was responsible for leading Chiricahua Apaches off the San Carlos Indian Reservation in the early 1880's on prolonged and destructive raids throughout southeastern Arizona.

Ref.: Burrall. Map: GB-5.

# JOHNSON

El.: c. 5000'  Loc.: Cochise 1, D-3.8

Copper ores were discovered in the vicinity of the future Johnson before the railroad came through in 1881. In 1883 the Peabody Company took over the mine and began rejuvenating it under a general manager named Johnson. The resultant community was named for him. It was at that time that the old hotel at Russellville (q.v.) was moved to the new town. In 1944 zinc began to exceed copper production at Johnson, the mines having been taken over by the Coronado Copper and Zinc Company in 1942. That company still owns the mine and the community.

P.O. est. April 5, 1900. William De H. Washington, p.m. Discont. November 29, 1929.

Ref.: *Daily Republican,* March 9, 1883, 2:3; *Douglas Dispatch,* "Fiftieth Anniversary Edition," Sec. 4, 4:3. Maps: GB-10; C-9.

**a.n. Johnson Peak**  El.: 6644'. Map: GB-10  Cochise

# JONES PEAK

El.: 8415'  Loc.: Cochise 2, E-6

In 1923 a seventeen-year-old boy named Lawrence Jones of Coolidge lost his life here en route to join a forest fire crew.

Ref.: 151, p. 401. Map: GB-5.

# KANSAS SETTLEMENT

El.: c. 4000'  Loc.: Cochise 1, F-4

In 1910 a group of homesteaders from Kansas settled in this area. There is a store here, but no community.

Ref.: Riggs. Map: None.

# KARRO

El.: 3593'  Loc.: Cochise 2, DE-1.6

This place is said to have been named for a grading contractor named Carr.

Ref.: Barnes. Map: GB-4.

# KELTON

El.: c. 4000'  Loc.: Cochise 2, A-7.8

Capt. C. B. Kelton once served as sheriff for Cochise County. Kelton took up a homestead where the S.P.R.R. right of way to Mexico was to run, and the railroad location bearing his name is on his former property. The place was constructed in 1909. In 1878 Kelton was living in Tucson.

P.O. est. February 10, 1915. Bailey A. Taylor, p.m. Discont. January 31, 1928.

Ref.: Robert Alpheus Lewis File, APHS; APHS Names File; Barnes; *Bisbee Review,* n.d., n.p. (State Library Clipping File). Maps: GB-16; C-12.

# KENTUCK

El.: c. 4000'  Loc.: Cochise 1, DE-3.5

"Kentuck" was the nickname of Marcus Flenoy Herring (b. Kentucky, September 23, 1823; d. May 22, 1910), who was serving with the military in 1862, stationed at Fort Bowie until January 1863. Following his discharge c. 1878, Herring prospected in the Mule Mountains and was associated with George H. Eddleman in locating some mining claims. In 1884 he was registered as a voter at Bisbee.

Ref.: Marcus Flenoy Herring File, APHS. Map: E-20.

# LAND

El.: 3656'  Loc.: Cochise 1, B-6.7

William C. Land (b. Texas c. 1838) first crossed the Southwest when he drove cattle to California in the 1850's. In 1880 he came to Arizona where with a man named Hayse he purchased the Babocomari Land Grant. Land ran about forty thousand head of cattle, but the drought of 1890-1892 put him out of business.

P.O. est. July 15, 1911. Lou C. Woolery, p.m. Discont November 20, 1913.

Ref.: Edward W. Land File, APHS. Maps: GB-1; C-11.

## LARAMITA

El.: c. 4000'                    Loc.: Cochise 1, F-11.4
Pro.: /larəmíytə/
Laramita was the first point of entry from Mexico c. 1894 before Douglas and Naco came into existence. When Naco was built, the point of entry moved to that place. The foundation and marker can still be seen at Laramita.
Ref.: Burgess. Map: None.

## LAUB                                      Loc.: Not known.

The origin of this name has not been ascertained.
P.O. est. November 15, 1900. Earl S. Peet, p.m. Discont. February 16, 1901.
Ref.:   P.O. Records. Map: None.

## LAVENDER PIT

El.: 5000'                       Loc.: Cochise 1, E-11.3
The mine pit with the poetic name was named for Harrison Horton Lavender (b. South Dakota, October 31, 1890; d. March 21, 1952). Starting as a miner for the Calumet and Arizona Mining Company, Lavender in 1931 (when the company merged with the Phelps Dodge Corporation) was named mine superintendent of the Copper Queen at Bisbee. He was appointed general manager in 1937.
Lavender Pit is so extensive that entire residential areas and businesses in Bisbee had to be relocated, as did also the main highway, when it was planned to mine this pit. It is the one which can be seen from the highway.
Ref.:   98a, p. 59; *Arizona Republic,* "Arizona Days and Ways," August 8, 1954, p. 2. Map: None.

## LECHUGUILLA PEAK

El.: 5009'                       Loc.: Cochise 1, A-2.3
Pro.: /lèčuwgiyə/           Spanish: "century plant" or "lettuce" (the century plant looks like a fringed head of lettuce)
Many century plants grow in this locality.
Ref.:   Barnes. Map GB-12.

## LESLIE CANYON

El.: c. 5000'                    Loc.: Cochise 2, BC-9.5
Franklin Nashville Leslie (b. Galveston, Texas) was known in southeastern Arizona as Frank Leslie, although his father's name was Kennedy. He used his mother's name following trouble with his father. For a time Leslie served as an army scout under Gen. George Crook and Gen. Nelson A. Miles. Because he was a dandy and a lady's man, Leslie was known as Buckskin Frank. In 1882 he was a bartender in Tombstone.
Leslie is known to have killed at least three people, the last in 1889 being Mollie Williams, his supposed wife, at Leslie's ranch following a drinking spree in which they were joined by James Neal. He shot her twice while she was talking to Neal. He then shot Neal, making the curious comment, "Now don't get excited; they are just blanks." They were potent blanks, so much so that Leslie believed he had killed Neal. The latter, however, struggled to Tombstone from Leslie's place and reported the murder of Mollie Williams and the attempt on his own life. So cer-

tain was Leslie that he had killed Neal that when the deputy sheriff came to get him, Leslie said that Neal had killed Mollie Williams and that Leslie shot Neal in self-defense. Leslie was sent to prison in Yuma, but the story does not end there. A romance via mail developed between Leslie and a Mrs. Belle Stowell, a wealthy woman in San Francisco who had just divorced her husband. She was instrumental in having Leslie released from prison and they were married on December 1, 1897.
Ref.:   119a, p. 95; Bennett; Frank Leslie File, APHS; *Arizona Daily Star,* May 4, 1897, 1:4. Map: GB-5.
a.n. Leslie Creek              Map: GB-16                    Cochise

## LEWIS SPRINGS

El.: c. 4000'                    Loc.: Cochise 1, C-9.9
The first name for these springs was Fritz Springs, after Fritz Hoffman who located them on June 6, 1878.
Robert Alpheus Lewis (b. 1858, Kentucky; d. February 15, 1900) was the fifteenth miner to arrive in the Tombstone area. Lewis came to Arizona from San Francisco in November 1878, to the vicinity of Bisbee, to look into claims made by a man named A. C. Smith that he knew where rich silver was to be found. Despite the fact that Lewis soon learned Smith had never been to Arizona, Lewis liked both the country and Smith; he remained in Arizona, keeping Smith with him.
In April 1878, Lewis went to Fort Huachuca for tobacco and there he heard about rich ores in the hills where Tombstone was soon to develop. He settled at Lewis Springs, naming it for his father, and remained there until 1884. Lewis died as a result of a bob-sledding accident in Oregon.
P.O. est. January 11, 1905. Virginia P. Clark, p.m. Discont. September 30, 1933. Wells Fargo Station, 1904.
Ref.:   APHS Names File; Robert A. Lewis File, APHS. Maps: GB-1; C-12.

## LEWISTON                                  Loc.: Unknown

P.O. est. July 25, 1881. William L. Martin, p.m. Discont. November 11, 1881.

## LIGHT

El.: c. 4500'                    Loc.: Cochise 2, B-5.9
The now-vanished community of Light was settled between 1902 and 1910 by homesteaders from Kansas, California, and Texas. John W. Light, a native New Yorker and a Civil War veteran, was one of these dry farmers. He had the post office in his store.
P.O. est. March 22, 1910. George W. Waters, p.m. Discont. September 30, 1927.
Ref.:   Riggs; APHS Names File. Maps: GB-16; C-11.

## LOWELL

El.: 5250'                       Loc.: Cochise 1, EF-11.3
In 1901 the Lowell Mine was just getting started. It was owned by a New England merchant, and it might well be that the community which developed derived its name from Lowell, Massachusetts.
P.O. est. August 1, 1904. Edward F. Kelsey, p.m. Discont. June 17, 1907. Wells Fargo Station, 1909.
Ref.:   Burgess. Maps: (Lowell Mine) C-12; GB-2.

## LUCKY CUSS MINE

El.: c. 4000'  Loc.: Cochise 1, CD-8.2.
Near Tombstone.
The Schieffelin brothers, Al and Ed, were disappointed with their first search for ores in the future Tombstone area. One morning Ed showed some ore to Al, saying it looked good, but Al could not be bothered inasmuch as he was on his way to hunt deer. Later Al came back with a fat buck and found Ed erecting a mining monument while shouting he had struck it rich. At this Al said, "You're a lucky cuss." From this came the name of the mine.
Ref.: 27, pp. 19-20. Map: None.

## MacDONALD

El.: c. 4000'  Loc.: Cochise 1, B-6.
S. of St. David.
In 1882 Henry J. Horne, Jonathan Hoopes, and others established a settlement which was actually a southern extension of St. David. They named it for Alexander F. MacDonald, then president of the Maricopa Stake of the Church of Jesus Christ of Latter-day Saints.
Ref.: 112, p. 236. Map: None.

## MANZORA

El.: c. 4000'  Loc.: Cochise 1, DE-4
Pro.: /mansórə/ or /mǽnsorə/
This was the shipping point for ore from the Golden Rule Mine. The origin of the name has not been ascertained.
P.O. est. December 23, 1916. Harry O. Miller, p.m. Discont. March 30, 1918.
Ref.: Bennett; P.O. Records. Maps: GB-7; B-2.

## MASCOT

El.: c. 6000'  Loc.: Cochise 2, AB-2
The Mascot Copper Company was established in 1915 to run the Mascot Mine, discovered by Charles Roberts. The canyon leading from the mine was called Mascot Canyon. This mine, which changed hands many times and existed under various names, was a speculators' paradise, stock being sold first under one name and then under another.
P. O. est. December 11, 1916. Lilly A. C. Hauser, p.m. Discont. October 15, 1918.
Ref.: APHS Names File. Map: C-12.

## McALISTER

El.: c. 4000'  Loc.: Cochise 1, DE-.07
The McAlister family settled as farmers in this area.
P.O. est. March 3, 1911. Mary F. McAlister, p.m. Discont. November 30, 1920.
Ref.: APHS Names File; *Bisbee Review*, n.d., n.p. (State Library Clipping File). Maps: A-1; C-11.

## McNEAL

El.: c. 4000'  Loc.: Cochise 2, A-9.5
McNeal was established on the Truit Ranch. Truit was a pioneer cattleman. One of the first settlers was Judge Miles McNeal, from Missouri, who homesteaded here c. 1908.
P.O. est. as Truit, March 25, 1909. James H. Latimer, p.m. Name changed to McNeal, October 1, 1909. Josephine A. Lane, p.m.
Ref.: *Bisbee Review*, n.d., n.p. (State Library Clipping File); *Douglas Dispatch*, "Fiftieth Anniversary Issue," 1952, Sec. 8, 3:4. Maps: GB-16; C-10 (Truitt); C-11 (Truitt & McNeal); C-12 (McNeal).

## MESCAL

El.: 4058'  Loc.: Cochise 1, O-5
Pro.: /meskæl/  Spanish: "century plant"
Descriptive.
P.O. est. April 25, 1913. Frank D. Black, p.m. Discont. August 26, 1931.
Ref.: Barnes. Maps: GB-1; C-10.

| a.n. Mescal Canyon | Map: GB-8 | Cochise |
| Mescal Creek | Map: GB-2 | Cochise |
| Mescal Spring | Map: GB-2 | Cochise |

There were two companies of colored troops stationed at this point in 1885 to furnish escort to travelers.
Ref.: *Daily Tombstone*, December 14, 1885, 3:3. APHS Names File.

## MIDDLEMARCH

El.: c. 4000'  Loc.: Cochise 1, DE-7
Middlemarch is in the middle pass of the Dragoon Mountains. It was the half-way point on the route used by the military from the Sulphur Springs Valley to Tombstone. In the 1880's, the Middlemarch Mine was established and run by the Middlemarch Copper Co.
P.O. est. May 10, 1898. Charles M. Lawrence, p.m. Discont. December 31, 1919.
Ref.: Larriau; Macia; APHS Names File. Map: C-9.

| a.n. Middlemarch Canyon | Map: GB-16 | Cochise |

## MIDWAY

El.: c. 4000'  Loc.: Cochise 1, F-7
Established in 1909, this location on the Arizona-Eastern Railroad lay midway between Pearce and Kelton. It was abandoned in 1926.
Ref.: Barnes. Map: C-12.

## MILLER PEAK

El.: 9445'  Loc.: Cochise 1, B-11.9
John J. Miller, (d. c. 1916) a rancher in this area, raised and sold produce to the people in Bisbee.
Ref.: Burgess. Map: GB-13.

| a.n. Miller Canyon | Map: GB-13 | Cochise |

## MILLION DOLLAR STOPE

El.: 4539'  Loc.: Cochise 1, CD-8.2.
In Tombstone.
The name for the Million Dollar Stope came from the fact that nearly one million dollars in ore was mined in the tunnels of the Grand Central Mine.
The great gaping hole which now exists developed in 1908 when the shaft caved in. At that precise moment a horse pulling an ice wagon was crossing the shaft and of course fell in. The wagon was completely ruined but, aside from astonishment, the horse was untouched. It was led out through an underground passage to an old mouth of the mine, a quarter of a mile away.
Ref.: 27, p. 381. Map: None.

## MIRAMONTE

El.: 4000'                          Loc.: Cochise 1, O-5.2
Pro.: /mirəmántey/
People from St. David settled at Miramonte in 1913. The
reason for the name is not known.
P.O. est. May 14, 1918. Rebecca Lolgreen, p.m. Discont. July
31, 1919.
Ref.: Barnes. 112, p. 236. Maps: GB-1; C-12.

## MONTE VISTA PEAK

El.: 9373'                          Loc.: Cochise 2, D-7.1
Pro.: /mántevístə/ or                          Spanish:
        /mántevíystə/                  "mountain view"
Descriptive.
Ref.: Barnes. Maps: B-2; C-12.

## MOORES SPUR

El.: 4600'                          Loc.: Cochise 2, EF-9.2
The reason for the name of this railroad siding has not been
ascertained.
P.O. est. as Moors Spur (sic), October 25, 1913. James R. Phil-
lips, p.m. Discont. February 28, 1914.
Ref.: P.O. Records. Map: GB-5.

## MUD SPRINGS

El.: 4660'                          Loc.: Cochise 2, BC-10.6
Descriptive. There is a series of springs lying at the entrance
to Mud Springs Canyon. It was at this point that Gen.
George Crook spoke of visiting with Lt. George M. Wheeler
at the latter's camp. The area lies low in the valley and
becomes muddy when cattle come in during the rainy
season.
Ref.: Macia; Burgess; 38, p. 261. Maps: GB-24; GB-5.

a.n. **Mud Springs Canyon**    Map: GB-24              Cochise
      **Mud Springs Draw**      Map: GB-16              Cochise

## MULE MOUNTAINS

El.: 7000'                          Loc.: Cochise 1, DF-10.8-11.5
While it is not known what the precise origin of the name
for these mountains is, there are several conjectures worth
considering. It may be that army horses and mules went
AWOL here, with the result that these mountains had more
than their share of mules. It has also been suggested that
Indians who stole stock in Mexico drove the animals
through the pass, which came to be known as La Puerta
de las Mulas ("Mule Pass"). On the other hand, at least
one source has noted in two peaks to the west a resemblance
to a pair of mule's ears.
The name first appears on GLO 1879 as Mule Pass Mountain. There is also a Mule Pass shown. In the same year the
Smith map shows "Puerta de las Mulas," but calls the
mountains Sierra de San Jose.

Ref.: 119a, p. 14; 4, p. 380; Barnes' Notes. Maps: GB-1; GB-
      2; GB-16; E-20 E-18 (Mule Pass Mountain); C-4 (Mule
      Pass and Pureto (sic) de los Muelas); C-5 (Mule Moun-
      tains).

a.n. **Mule Gulch**            Map: GB-2               Cochise
      Bisbee lines both sides of Mule Gulch. An early name still
      frequently used for this gulch is Mule Pass Gulch.

## NACO

El.: 4590'                          Loc.: Cochise 1, E-12.7
Pro.: /nákow/
This community on the international border was so named
because the railroad line on which it was built was con-
structed principally to reach mines at Nacosari, Mexico.
Naco was built in the early 1890's, at which time the port
of entry was transferred to it from Laramita (q.v.).
Indians call the fruit of the barrel cactus naco; they collect
the spring crop, cook the fruit until it is tender, and then
dry it in the sun and use it for seasoning.
P.O. est. January 1, 1899. Joseph E. Curry, p.m. Wells Fargo
Station, 1904.
Ref.: Barnes; P.O. Records; 72, pp. 36-37; *Weekly Arizona
      Enterprise,* February 18, 1892, 4:7. Maps: GB-2; C-9.

a.n. **Naco Hills**            Map: GB-2               Cochise
      **Naco Peak**            Map: B-2                Cochise

## NUGENT'S PASS

El.: c. 4000'                       Loc.: Cochise 1, B-3
Nugent's Pass was named probably in the 1850's for John
Nugent, a member of Col. Hays' party.
Ref.: 48, p. vii. Maps: E-18; C-6.

## OAK GROVE

El.: 4447'                          Loc.: Cochise 1, F-1
Oak Grove had its name as early as 1869 when an encounter with Indians is reported to have taken place here.
This was the place where in 1872 Henry C. Hooker camped
with cattle "left over" after he had filled government contracts (cf. Sierra Bonita Ranch, Graham). From here
Hooker located the spring where he established a stage
station.
Ref.: 85, p. 433; 105, p. 231; 87, p. 237. Maps: E-20, E-18.

a.n. **Oak Grove Canyon**     Map: GB-24              Cochise

## OCHOA

El.: 4333'                          Loc.: Cochise 1, C-5.2
Pro.: /očóə/
Until 1859 Estaban Ochoa (b. Mexico 1829) was a partner
with Pedro Aguirre (cf. Aguirre, Pima). By 1870 Ochoa
was freighting from Tucson to Camp Ord (cf. Fort Apache,
Navajo). Active in politics, Ochoa served as mayor of
Tucson in 1875. Later, in 1879 he was in partnership with
P. R.Tully. The firm of Tully & Ochoa had many enterprises, but the chief were ranching and freighting.
To provide room for his tremendous sheep flocks, Ochoa
established a ranch with a settlement called Ochoaville on
the Elias Land Grant two miles from Camp Huachuca. The
community had six dwellings, a store, and a population of
about seventy-five.
Ochoaville is not the same place as Ochoa Siding, which
was four miles from Tully (q.v.), both places being named
to commemorate the prominence of the two men. Ironically,
the coming of the railroad nearly put the men out of business.
P.O. est. as Ochoaville, November 11, 1879. Estaban Ochoa,
p.m. Discont. September 4, 1885.

Ref.: Lenon; *Arizona Daily Star,* September 11, 1879, 3:1; Estaban Ochoa File, APHS; P.O. Records. Maps: GB-1; C-5 (Ochoaville).

**a.n. Ochoa**          Map: A-3          Santa Cruz

This station on the branch railroad to Nogales was short-lived.

## OHNESORGEN STAGE STATION

El.: 4300′          Loc.: Cochise 1, AB-5.1
                    N. of Benson c. 1 mile.

An early name for this location was San Pedro River Station on the east bank of the San Pedro River. In 1852 the river ordinarily flowed in a shallow bed nearly level with the surrounding plains. However, it was subject to flooding conditions and in 1859 a strong bridge was built across it at the old fording place. This bridge was used by the First California Volunteers on June 23, 1862, on their march to New Mexico. This was the date on which they noted that the old station had been burned.

William Ohnesorgen (b. Germany 1849) came as a child in 1853 to America with his family to live in Texas. In 1867 he went with his uncle to Mesilla, New Mexico, and in February 1868, went on to Arizona where he clerked in Tucson for Charles Lesinsky. In 1871 his brother bought out the old Duncan, Renshaw, and Fowler Stage Station on the San Pedro about a mile north of where the present town of Benson is located. This station became an overland stage stop. The station house consisted of a hollow square with thick adobe walls containing portholes for guns in case of attack. Eight soldiers were stationed here.

In 1878-79 Ohnesorgen built a toll bridge across the San Pedro. This place began to pay for itself in 1880 when mining supplies had to be hauled to Fairbank, Contention, and Charleston. Meanwhile Ohnesorgen had started a stage line from Tucson to Tombstone; he sold it in 1880. The old stage station washed away in high flood waters in 1883.

Ref.: William Ohnesorgen File APHS; 32, II, 149. Map: None.

## ONION SADDLE

El.: 7600′          Loc.: Cochise 2, DE-6.4

At one time there used to be a creek that headed close to where the road through Pinery Canyon tops the mountain. This was Onion Creek. Originally the saddle was called Onion Creek Saddle — descriptive of the wild onions which grew along the creek.

Ref.: Riggs. Map: None.

## ORANGE BUTTE

El.: 5257′          Loc.: Cochise 2, E-1
Descriptive.

Ref.: Barnes. Maps: E-20; C-4; C-12.

## OUTLAW MOUNTAIN

El.: 5070′          Loc.: Cochise 1, F-8.4

Outlaw Mountain earned its name by serving as a hide-out for many outlaws, including the Clanton gang.

Ref.: Barnes; APHS Files. Maps: GB-16; B-2; C-12.

**a.n. Outlaw Spring**     Maps: GB-6; GB-16          Cochise

## OVERTON

El.: c. 6600′          Loc.: Cochise 2, D-4

Capt. Gilbert E. Overton, Sixth U. S. Cavalry, is said to have camped here in 1886.

P.O. est. November 26, 1917. Jean C. Wilder, p.m. Discont. May 31, 1918.

Ref.: Barnes; P.O. Records. Map: None.

**a.n. Overton Canyon**     Map: GB-6          Cochise

## PACKSADDLE MOUNTAIN

El.: 6310′          Loc.: Cochise 2, C-9.7
Descriptive.

Ref.: Barnes. Map: GB-5.

## PALOMINAS

El.: 4300′          Loc.: Cochise 1, C-12.1
Pro.: /palomíynəs/

At one time this was a small community serving as a supply town for nearby mines. It has since disappeared.

Ref.: Larriau; Map: GB-13.

## PARADISE

El.: 5398′          Loc.: Cochise 2, E-6

One of the Reed Daughters (cf. Cave Creek) married George A. Walker. The young couple moved to an isolated location which, because of their happiness, they named Paradise. In 1901 the Chiricahua Development Company located a vein of ore here and spent nearly half a million developing it. The isolation of Paradise was replaced by a mining town which was a Paradise for roisterers. It is now a ghost town.

P.O. est. October 23, 1901. George A. Walker, p.m. Discont. September 30, 1943.

Ref.: Riggs; *Arizona Daily Star,* "Bad Men March Through Arizona's History," March 27, 1932, n.p. (APHS). Maps: GB-5; C-9.

## PAT HILLS

El.: c. 5000′          Loc.: Cochise 2, AB-5

In 1878 a man named Pat Burns or Bierne located at a small spring called the Pat Burns Cienega where he ran cattle for several years before moving to Colorado.

Ref.: Barnes. Maps: GB-8; C-12.

## PAUL SPUR

El.: 4189′          Loc.: Cochise 2, O-11.9

A cement plant and small community are located at this place on the railroad where there is also a section house. It was so named for Alfred Paul, Sr. (b. Germany, 1878), who came to Arizona in 1885. Paul helped lay out the site of Douglas. The fact that the Calumet and Arizona Mining Company was using the flotation process to extract copper led to Paul's putting in a lime kiln at this place after 1914 because lime was needed to neutralize acid in the ore. Currently this place is producing cement.

P.O. est. July 24, 1930. Bert Whitehead, p.m. Discont. May 2, 1958.

Ref.: *Douglas Dispatch,* "Fiftieth Anniversary Edition," 1952, Sec. 9, 2:5; 112, III. Map: C-13.

## PEARCE

El.: 4255'                              Loc.: Cochise 1, EF-6

John Pearce, a rancher, struck gold in this vicinity in 1894 and the Commonwealth Mine was begun. The railroad station opened in 1903.

For several years Pearce and his wife lived in Tombstone where he was a miner and she managed a boardinghouse. They saved their money and began a ranch in the Sulphur Springs Valley. It was while riding the range that Pearce stopped to rest at the top of a small hill and here he discovered rich ore. Pearce sold out for $250,000. The peak of production at the mine was reached in 1896. However, the mine was worked until 1904 when shaft cave-ins caused a shutdown. With the erection of a cyanide plant in 1905, the mine went back into operation. It is now inactive.

P.O. est. March 6, 1896. Thomas Chattam, p.m. Wells Fargo Station, 1885.

Ref.: Barnes; 4, pp. 440-441. Maps: GB-16; C-9.

a.n. Pearce Hill        Map: GB-16              Cochise
     Six Mile Hill      Map: GB-16              Cochise
     In 1894 James Pearce, while rounding up cattle, rode to this hill where he picked up an ore specimen containing free gold. This led to the discovery of the Pearce Mine about a mile away.
Ref.: Barnes.

## PERILLA MOUNTAINS

El.: 5927'                              Loc.: Cochise 2, C-11.7
Pro.: /períyə/                          Spanish: "saddle horn"
Descriptive.

v.n. Peri Mountains (Smith 1879)
Ref.: Lenon. Maps: B-2; E-20; C-5.

## PICK-EM-UP

El.: c. 4000'                           Loc.: Cochise 1, BC-8.
                                        Near Fairbank.

A small settlement grew up around what was known as the Brady House, also called the First Chance Saloon since it was the first chance for a drink on the road from Charleston to Tombstone.

The name Pick-em-up was applied to the settlement as a result of an occurrence in which Johnny O'Rourke, a tinhorn gambler known as Johnny-Behind-the-Deuce, was the central figure. He earned his nickname by consistently backing his favorite card. In a fit of petulant temper in Charleston, Johnny-Behind-the-Deuce shot Henry Schneider, a mining engineer, and was promptly arrested. Just at that moment the mining mill whistle began to blow. Miners poured into the streets where blood still ran. They wanted to lynch the murderer, but the constable aimed to get Johnny-Behind-the-Deuce safely behind bars in Tombstone. The constable and his prisoner set out hell-bent-for-leather with a team of horses. The miners were not to be put off. They mounted every available horse, climbed into buggies and wagons, and took after the constable and Johnny-Behind-the-Deuce.

Two miles out of Tombstone at Jack McCann's Saloon a racing mare was standing. McCann was preparing her for a race at the Watervale Track nearby. The constable shouted urgently to McCann that the miners wanted to lynch Johnny-Behind-the-Deuce and yelled to the saloon-keeper to "Pick 'em up!" Off went the tinhorn gambler and the saloon keeper on the mare with the mob in close pursuit. Johnny-Behind-the-Deuce arrived in Tombstone where the sheriff faced the would-be lynchers with a shotgun. They dispersed and Johnny-Behind-the-Deuce was safe for the time being.

Ref.: Larriau; 27, pp. 62-63; *Tombstone Epitaph*, August 9, 1890, 3:3. Map: None.

## PICKET CANYON

El.: 5200'                              Loc.: Cochise 2, CD-4.7
When the Riggs family began improving their ranch, they cut cypress trees in this canyon, to be used for pickets around their yard.

Ref.: Riggs. Map: GB-6.
a.n. Picket Park        Map: GB-6              Cochise
     A natural park exists at the south end of this area.

## PINERY CANYON

El.: c. 4800'                           Loc.: Cochise 2, CD-4.7
It was in this canyon that the military in the early days cut lumber for use at Fort Bowie. For this reason it was known as the pinery, hence the name. At one time the agency for the Chiricahua Apaches was located in this canyon.

Ref.: Riggs; 52, VIII, 15. Maps: GB-6; E-20; C-5.
a.n. Pinery Creek       Map: GB-8              Cochise
     Pinery Peak        Map: GB-5              Cochise

## PIRTLEVILLE

El.: 3955'                              Loc.: Cochise 2, AB-12
The post office at Pirtle was named for Elmo R. Pirtle (b. Tennessee, May 5, 1868; d. August 1920), who owned the property and established the settlement. He came to Douglas as a real estate dealer in 1901.

P.O. est. as Pirtle, February 8, 1908. Cassius C. Hockett, p.m. Changed to Pirtleville, March 30, 1910. Jefferson J. Langford, p.m.

Ref.: Barnes; 112, III; APHS Names File; P.O. Records. Maps: C-11; GB-8.

## PITTSBURGH

El.: c. 5000'                           Loc.: Cochise 2, F-5.
                                        N.e. of Paradise 6 miles.
In 1905 the Cochise Consolidated Copper Company, which had home offices in Pittsburg, Pennsylvania, in a petition for a post office named a new townsite Pittsburgh. The land had been under development by the company since 1903.

P.O. est. June 18, 1906. Harry Alexander, p.m. Rescinded, October 9, 1906.

Ref.: *Arizona Silver Belt*, October 26, 1905, 4:2. Map: None.

## POINT-OF-MOUNTAIN

El.: c. 4000'                           Loc.: Cochise 1, F-1
In 1874 Thomas Steele (b. Missouri, September 8, 1844; d. August 28, 1916) was running a stage station at this location. Steele came to Phoenix in 1870. In 1873 he built a

stage station between Tres Alamos and Fort Grant. It was at this point that the stage road to Globe took off from the main east-west route. In 1876 the place was operated by Tom Williams, and by 1880 it was called the Point-of-Mountain Stage Station under the ownership of William Whalen (b. Canada 1843; d. 1908) who came to Arizona in 1889. He abandoned it when the railroad came through.

Ref.: Barnes; William Whalen File, APHS; Lizzie Steele ms., APHS; Thomas Steele File, APHS; *Arizona Citizen*, October 10, 1874, 4:2. Map: E-20.

a.n. Steele Hills       Map: GB-10       Cochise

## POMERENE

El.: 3540'       Loc.: Cochise 1, AB-4.9
This settlement is said to have been named for Senator Pomerene of Ohio.

P.O. est. October 27, 1915. Henry M. Kimmel, p.m.
Ref.: Barnes. Maps: GB-12; C-12.

## POOL

El.: c. 4000'       Loc.: Cochise 1, A-1.5
Dr. Josiah Pool (b. November 10, 1830) came to Arizona in 1882, serving as a rancher, camp cook, cowpuncher and bookkeeper. He established a ranch south of Tucson on the Santa Cruz. In 1883 he located another ranch thirty miles north of Benson on the San Pedro River. In 1894 he was at Mammoth, later at Winkleman, and still later at Phoenix.

P.O. est. February 12, 1902. John J. Pool, p.m. Discont. July 15, 1913.
Ref.: Frank M. Pool File, APHS. Maps: GB-25; C-9.

a.n. Pool Wash       Map: GJ-17       Cochise

## PORTAL

El.: 4773'       Loc.: Cochise 2, F-6
Pro.: /pórtəl/
The name Portal is descriptive of the fact that the little community lies at the entrance to Cave Creek Canyon. The word is English, not Spanish. The place was founded by Otto Duffener and his brother c. 1900. The two men were prospectors who lived at Paradise for a number of years, thereafter moving to their home between Paradise and Portal.

In 1955 the Southwestern Research Station was established at Portal. It is operated by the American Museum of Natural History to provide research facilities in all branches of science which can be investigated through the "utilization of the faunal, floral, and geological features of the area."

P.O. est. June 14, 1905. Edward F. Epley, p.m.
Ref.: Riggs; "The Southwestern Research Station of the American Museum of Natural History," New York, 1955. Maps: C-10; C-12.

a.n. Portal Peak       Map: B-2       Cochise

## POTTER MOUNTAIN

El.: 6525'       Loc.: Cochise 1, E-10.4
Tuck Potter (d. c. 1950) was a highly respected pioneer who did much to help build the Bisbee area. This mountain was named for him.

Ref.: Burgess. Map: GB-16.

## PRICE, CAMP

El.: c. 4000'       Loc.: Cochise 2, D-12.3
Camp Price lay just over the divide from Camp Rucker (See Rucker Canyon) at the head of Tex Canyon. Here in 1881 there was a military outpost which was also known as Camp Supply. When Gen. George Crook was in Arizona on his second tour of duty, there was a military telegraph station here.

The camp may have been named for Lt. Col. William Redwood Price (d. December 30, 1881), Sixth Cavalry. He had been very active in the campaign against the Hualpai Indians, receiving his colonelcy on December 10, 1868, for service during an engagement with Indians near Walker Springs.

Ref.: 85, I, 807; APHS Names File; 22, pp. 444-445. Map: E-20 (Old Camp Supply); C-5.

## PROSPECT

El.: c. 4000'       Loc.: Cochise 1, A-1.25
Prospect was a mining camp. Its name was descriptive of the prospect holes dug by hopeful miners. Prospect was still in existence in 1903.

It was probably in this vicinity that Fr. Kino c. 1697 visited a rancheria of the Sobaipuri, which he called Rosario and also referred to as Jiaspi.

Ref.: Barnes; Burrall; 88, I, 631. Map: C-6.

## QUIBURI

El.: 3792'       Loc.: Cochise 1, BC-7.5
The name *Quíburi* is derived in part from the plural of *Ki*, which in the Nevome dialect means "houses."

In 1692 Fr. Eusebio Kino undertook his first formal expeditions into this part of what is now Arizona. One section of his party proceeded along one route under Lt. Cristobal Martín Bernal and the other under Kino and Lt. Juan Matheo Manje. The two parties met at Quíburi. This Indian town was that of Chief Coro, so called by the Spaniards because his strong voice had as much force as that of a chorus. Coro more than once kept Apaches from invading Pimeria (cf. Pima County, Pima).

In 1760-64 Quíburi was a *visita* of Suamca (in Mexico).

variants (corruptions):

    Kiburi (Kino Map 1702)
    San Pablo de Quiburi (Garces Diary)
    San Ignacio Guipori (c. 1702)

Ref.: 7, p. 355; 20, p. 269; 19a, p. 70; 88, II, 339. Map: None.

## RAILROAD PASS

El.: 4291'       Loc.: Cochise 1, A-1
In 1856 Lt. John G. Parke, seeking a feasible railroad route across the Southwest, noted that the lowest point between the Valle de Sauz (San Simon Valley) and the Valle de las Playas (Sulphur Springs Valley) was located at what he suggested be called The Railroad Pass.

Ref.: 124, p. 20. Maps: GB-11; C-3; E-20.

## RAMSEY CANYON

El.: 5000'                    Loc.: Cochise 1, AB-12-11
Frank Ramsey, after whom this canyon is named, worked with his father for a cattle company at least as early as 1900.
Ref.:   Larriau; Choat File, APHS. Maps: GB-13; C-8.
**a.n. Ramsey Peak**        Map: B-3                        Cochise

## RAVENS PEAK

El.: c. 8000'                    Loc.: Cochise 2, E-5.5.
                    At head of main fork, Cave Creek.
This peak was named by Harry D. Burrall in 1906 because ravens nested here in the summertime.
Ref.:   Burrall. Map: None.

## REILLY PEAK

El.: 7631'                    Loc.: Cochise 1, D-1
James Reilly (b. Ireland, October, 1830; d. 1906) came to New York City in 1848 and to Arizona as a soldier in 1857. He was honorably discharged in Texas in 1859, where he remained as a freighter until stolen out of business by the Indians. In 1861 he came as a freighter to Fort Buchanan, freighting from there to Magdalena, Sonora, until Indians again stole him out of business in 1862. Reilly then lived in Mexico until he killed a Mexican and was exiled to La Paz in Baja California, where he remained until 1866. From that point he went to Yuma as freighter and prospector, later having a hotel and store there until 1874. An energetic man, Reilly studied for and was admitted to the practice of law. "63" Reilly, as he was known, was a man of many talents. In 1878 he was publishing *The Expositor* in Phoenix. By 1880 he was in Tombstone where he was appointed a Justice of the Peace. It must have been in this period that he established his ranch near Reilly Peak.
Ref.:   James Reilly File, APHS. Map: FB-24.
**a.n. Reiley Canyon (sic)**    Map: GB-24                        Cochise
**Reilly Creek**        Map: GB-24    Cochise and Graham
**Reilly Hill**        El.: 5485'. Map: GB-24            Graham

## RHYOLITE CANYON

El.: 6000'                    Loc.: Cochise 2, D-4.9
This is a descriptive name for the rock formation in the canyon. It was so named by Mr. and Mrs. Ed Riggs.
Ref.:   Riggs. Map: GB-6.

## RIGGS CANYON

El.: 5000'                    Loc.: Cochise 2, CD-4.8
Ed Riggs, who was the first to explore the area of the Chiricahua National Monument, named this canyon for his father.
Ref.:   55, p. 586. Map: None.
**a.n. Ed Riggs Mountain** ,
        El.: 6153'. Loc.: Chiricahua Nat'l. Mmnt.            Cochise
        Ed Riggs (b. 1885; d. June 1950) was born at the Riggs' Home Ranch, the oldest son of the oldest of several Riggs brothers, first settlers in this area. The mountain was named for him soon after his death. He was the discoverer of a great many of the scenic features in the Chiricahua Na-

tional Monument. With his wife Lillian he built the first trail into the area and was instrumental in having the Wonderland of Rocks established as the Chiricahua National Monument (cf. Chiricahua Mountains, **a.n.**).
Ref.:   Riggs.
**Riggs Seep**        Map: GB-24                        Cochise

## ROBERTS CIENEGA

El.: c. 4000'                    Loc.: Cochise 2, B-5.
                About 6 miles from mouth of West Turkey
                    Creek in Sulphur Springs Valley.
Pro.:   /raberts siyénəgə/
This location was named for Lt. Col. Joseph Roberts, an aide to Gen. George Crook from 1870-1873. There was a temporary military camp in this cienega during the days of the campaign against Vitorio in the early 1880's.
Ref.:   Barnes; Barnes' Notes. Map: None.

## ROCKFELLOW DOME

El.: 6542'                    Loc.: Cochise 1, DE-5.6
John A. Rockfellow (b. New York, January 30, 1858) when twenty years old arrived by rail at Yuma. His first months in Arizona were at the mines in Signal (*q.v.,* Mohave) moving from there to Tombstone. Later he became a stockman from 1883 to 1890. After his marriage he was a school teacher for three years while employing someone to look after his ranch.
Ref.:   140, p. 199. Map: GB-16.

## RUCKER CANYON

El.: c. 6000'                    Loc.: Cochise 2, C-8
    Pro.:   /rˇker/
The violence of flash floods during the rainy season in Arizona is notorious, for flash floods have taken many lives. One such incident occurred on July 11, 1878, in White River Canyon when Lt. John A. Rucker noticed a fellow officer, Lt. Austin Henely, caught in a raging flash flood. According to newspaper reports, Rucker plunged in on horseback to save Henely, but both men drowned. After the flood subsided, the bodies were recovered and taken to Fort Bowie for military burial.
According to the story told by the Apache Indian scout John Rope, who was with Rucker's party when the officers were drowned, Rucker and Henely met two citizens at a saloon "on the left fork" where all four remained until the hard rain abated. The two citizens then mounted their mules and swam across the flooded river. The officers followed on horseback but made the mortal error of riding side by side. The swift current knocked one horse against the other and the officers fell off. The men safely ashore threw ropes to the officers, but in vain. The scout reports that during the search for the bodies, the Indians worked in water up to their armpits. The bodies were recovered during the ensuing night.
In honor of Rucker, the name of Camp Supply where he had been stationed was changed to Camp Rucker on April 29, 1879. This camp was not the same as the Camp Supply located on the other side of the same mountains (see Camp Price). During the early 1880's Camp Rucker was one of

the most important military stations in the campaign against the Apaches.

Gradually a community grew up around the camp. One of its pioneer families was named Powers, and when the post office was established it was called Powers. The name was changed to Rucker four years later. For a number of years the post office was out of existence, but was re-established as Rucker Canyon in 1918.

P.O. est. as Powers, December 1, 1887. Jane M. Powers, p.m. Changed to Rucker, June 20, 1891. Joseph H. Cogswell, p.m. Discont. September 28, 1906. Re-established as Rucker Canyon, October 15, 1918. Robert S. Grier, p.m. Discont. August 15, 1929.

Ref.: *Arizona Sentinel,* July 27, 1878, 1:4; *Salt River Herald,* January 1, 1879, 2:2; "Experiences of an Indian Scout: Excerpts from the Life of John Rope, an 'Old Timer' of the White Mountain Apaches," (as told to Grenville Goodwin); *Arizona Historical Review,* VII (January 1936), 44-46; P.O. Records; 75, p. 151. Maps: C-5 (Camp Rucker); C-7 (Powers); GB-5.

## RUSSELLVILLE

El.: 4707'          Loc.: Cochise 1, D-4.2
                    Sec. 2, T. 16 S., R. 22 E.

While it may not be the origin of the name for Russellville, it is worth noting that Capt. George Briggs Russell in April 1871, battled with Cochise and one hundred and fifty well-armed Apaches near what later became Benson. Capt. Russell in command of about eighteen men emerged with one killed and one wounded, whereas Cochise lost fifteen men during the retreat of the Indians from the open plains to the mountains where they entrenched themselves. At this point the Indians were better able to fight and Capt. Russell had to send for re-enforcements.

The place known as Russell or Russellville was a mining community which in 1883 was described as being an "old town." When the town of Johnson (*q.v.*) was established in the same year, Russellville began its gradual disappearance from the map. It was at Russellville that John A. Rockfellow (cf. Rockfellow Dome) taught for three winter terms, beginning in 1886.

Ref.: Lenon; Macia; 52, VIII, 208; Russellville File, APHS; Johnson File, APHS; 140, p. 130. Map: None.

## RUSTLER PARK

El.: 8784'          Loc.: Cochise 2, DE-6.4

During the late 1870's and the early 1880's rustlers made a good thing of the level area with good grass and fine springs on top of the mountains in what is now the Chiricahua National Monument. Here they held stolen cattle while changing brands and waiting for the hair to grow, before attempting to sell the beasts. Today Rustler Park is a popular recreation area.

Ref.: Riggs; 33, p. 13. Map: GB-5.

**a.n. Rustler Canyon**     Map: GB-5          Cochise

Actually there is no Rustler Canyon as such, but the name has come to be applied to this canyon adjacent to Rustler Park.

Ref.: Riggs.

## SACRAMENTO PIT

El.: 5250'          Loc.: Cochise 1, F-11.3

Where there is now a tremendous hole, there was once a place called Sacramento Hill with an elevation of 5656 feet. The man-made pit was created when copper ores were removed from the Sacramento Pit. The stripping of the ores began in 1918 and was completed within ten years. Meanwhile, more than thirty-four million tons of earth had been removed. It is not yet known why the name Sacramento was applied to this location.

Ref.: 98a, pp. 58, 59. Map: GB-2.

## SAGE PARK

El.: 7500'          Loc.: Cochise 2, DE-7.5

This peak was named for Harley H. Sage, a forest ranger who died on November 13, 1918, while serving his country. A copper shield on this mountain commemorates his death.

Ref.: Barnes; 151, p. 56. Map: GB-5.

## ST. DAVID

El.: 3850'          Loc.: Cochise 1, B-5.9

The origin of this name has not yet been ascertained.

Philemon Merrill (b. New York, November 12, 1820) was adjutant general of the Mormon Battalion.

When his and four other Mormon families separated from the colony at Jonesville (cf. Lehi, Maricopa) in August 1877, they moved southward, first working for Tom Gardner (See Gardner Canyon, Santa Cruz), moving from there on November 29, 1877, to found the town of St. David. During the first year at St. David the colonists built a small rock fort measuring sixty feet and forming a hollow square. The fort was three miles south of the present town. The old town was a half mile south of the present town, but the site was moved because malaria was too prevalent at the first location. The first town MacDonald (cf. MacDonald) was named for Alexander F. MacDonald, a Mormon apostle, who was killed by the same mob which killed Joseph Smith in Missouri.

P.O. est. July 24, 1882. Joseph McRae, p.m.

Ref.: Philemon Merrill File, APHS; 112, p. 235; 55, pp. 584-586. Maps: GB-1; C-5; C-7.

## SAMPLE

El.: 3585'          Loc.: Cochise 1, AB-5.5

The post office known as Sample was named for Comer W. Sample. A man of unsavory reputation, a known rustler, he was hanged for his part in the so called Bisbee Massacre of December 8, 1883.

P.O. est. July 26, 1886. Pablo Rebeil p.m. Discont. October 31, 1887.

Ref.: Barnes; P.O. Records. Map: None.

## SANDY BOB CANYON

El.: 5700'          Loc.: Cochise 1, E-10

Sandy Bob had a ranch near this location. In 1881 he owned a stage line to Tombstone.

Ref.: 103, p. 159. Map: GB-16.

## SAN BERNARDINO LAND GRANT

El.: c. 3800'                    Loc.: Cochise 2, DE-12.5
Pro.: /sǽn bèrnadíyno/
The San Bernardino Land Grant lay partially in the United States and partially in Mexico. It was awarded in 1822 to Ignacio Perez by the newly created Mexican government. At that time the grant consisted of 73,240 acres. In 1853 as a result of the Gadsden Purchase part of this land grant was annexed to the United States, and the United States courts later confirmed 2,336 acres of the grant.

The ranch headquarters were at the San Bernardino Hacienda. For many years prior to the building of the hacienda, the location was important to those who lived in or passed through the region, because of the existence of San Bernardino Spring. Here at least as early as 1697 Spanish and the citizen soldiers of Sonora began their habit of stopping en route between the garrisons of Janos and Fronteras. By 1846 when Lt. Col. Philip St. George Cooke and his Mormon Battalion passed here, San Bernardino Hacienda was in ruins. Some thirty years later the land was being used by John Slaughter and his family. He is said to have purchased the land in 1884.

John Horton Slaughter (b. Louisiana October 2, 1841; d. February 15, 1922) grew up in Texas. After serving as a soldier with the Confederacy, he became an Indian fighter and a Texas Ranger. He first visited Arizona in 1877. Two years later he moved his herds to southern Arizona, settling with his bride first to the south of the old Hereford Stage Station in the San Pedro Valley. Later he took up the San Bernardino Ranch.

P.O. est. September 15, 1906. Elizabeth McAlister, p.m. Discont. June 15, 1918.

Ref.: 134, pp. 295-96, 302, 306; 55, p. 428; 27, p. 350; *Arizona Star*, May 2, 1878, 3:1; 50, p. 555; 20, p. 245; 22, p. 472; 55, p. 670. Maps: GB-17; C-9; C-12; E-20 (San Bernardino Spring and Flat).

**a.n. Avansada, Mesa de la**                    Cochise
    Loc.: This is the mesa near the old Spanish presidio at San Bernardino. Descriptive. The name means "Mesa of the Advanced Guard."
    Ref.: 134, p. 351.

**Bernadina**        Maps: GB-5; GB-17        Cochise
    This former post office and small community have disappeared, only a large cattle loading corral and chute remaining. This place may have been named for the San Bernardino Land Grant.
P.O. est. as Bernadina, September 16, 1915. N. V. Clanch, Jr., p.m. Discont. December 15, 1917.
Ref.: Barnes; APHS Files; P.O. Records.

**San Bernardino Valley**    Maps: GB-5; GB-17        Cochise

## SAN PEDRO

El.: 4100'                    Loc.: Cochise 1, C-10.6
Pro.: /san peʸdro/ or /sǽn pédrow/
The town of San Pedro came into existence in 1879 when it was staked out along the right-of-way of the S.P.R.R. This would appear not to be the same as the earlier San Pedro Crossing or, as it was sometimes called, the San Pedro Settlement. The earlier San Pedro was in existence at least as early as 1870 when it was reported in the census to have a population of eighty. This may have been a slight exaggeration, inasmuch as a newspaper article in early 1872 reports that there were then sixty men living at the place, or four times more than were there the year before. This community was still in existence in 1875. GLO 1876 shows a San Pedro Settlement a few miles west of the San Pedro River and approximately southeast the same distance from Cienega on the old stage road. In 1879 a place called San Pedro is shown on the east bank of the river, a few miles southeast of the older San Pedro. It is noted on earlier maps as San Pedro Springs. It lies to the south of two crossings called Upper Crossing and Middle Crossing.

Neither San Pedro discussed above is close to the outlet of Bronco Creek, several miles to the south on the San Pedro River. On the Smith Map (1879) the old Presidio of San Pedro is located at the mouth of Bronco Creek on the San Pedro River. This clearly places it in a location different from that of either of the San Pedro settlements above. This presidio was first garrisoned by Mexican soldiers in 1840. The ruins of the hacienda were noted by Gray in 1856; he had named San Pedro Springs in 1851. Smith (1879) also shows a Lower Crossing on the San Pedro at Hooker's Springs on the main overland route.

In 1857 Capt. Richard Ewell was searching for Mrs. Joseph Pennington Page, and Capt. John Tevis (who was with Ewell's party) wrote of passing by old Fort Babocomari, which he spoke of as being used as a ranch. It had a wall about fifteen feet high encircling adobe buildings within an acre of ground. This is supposed to have been the old Indian village of Santa Cruz de Gaybaniptea, so called by Fr. Francisco Garcés. This place was supposed to have been a league and a half from Quíburi.

P.O. est. March 22, 1872. Jacob Schaublin, p.m. Discont. June 8, 1880.

Ref.: 87, p. 43; 101, pp. 50, 51; 161, p. 71 (Note 3), 76; 105, p. 40; 35, 465, Note 118; *Arizona Sentinel*, June 14, 1879, 2:3; *Arizona Citizen*, February 17, 1872, 3:3; April 24, 1875, 1:4; *Arizona Star*, November 7, 1879, n.p. (APHS Names File). Maps: GB-13; C-3.

**a.n. Fitz Ranch**        Maps: E-20; C-7        Cochise
    This ranch, also known as Fitz Jefferson's Ranch, was on the site of the old San Pedro Presidio.
Ref.: Barnes. Map: None.

## SAN PEDRO RIVER

El.: c. 4500'-2000'    Loc.: Traverses Cochise County from its southern boundary to its northern boundary; then traverses Pinal County to Gila River.
Pro.: /san peʸdro/ or /sǽn pédrow/
At one time the San Pedro River was the second largest tributary to the Gila River from the south. Geographically this is of course still true, but the San Pedro is no longer a continually running stream.

Coues thinks the San Pedro River is the same as that called the Rio Nexpa by the 1540 Coronado expedition. However, its first clearly recorded name is Rio de San Joseph de Terrenate or de Quíburi, names applied by Fr. Kino in September 1692. Kino does not use the name San Pedro.

In 1763 the name in use was Sobahipuris *(sic)*, derived from the name of the Indians residing on its banks.

Why or when or how the name San Pedro came into use has not yet been definitely ascertained. That it has a fairly late origin is indicated by the fact that Col. Graham in 1850 referred to it as the Rio Puerco (Spanish: "dirty river"), although in 1846 Lt. Col. Philip St. George Cooke called it the Jose Pedro River. The name was apparently then in transition. Coues believes that the ultimate name derived from the Casas de San Pedro just over the Sonora border in Mexico in 1853. The Boundary Survey map (1853) shows this location; it also shows mountains in the area called Sierra de San Jose. On the undated Fifth Military District map (E-12) a river in the same vicinity is called Rio Terrenate, with part of it within the United States bearing the title of Rio San Pedro. The Smith map (1879) further confuses the situation by showing what is apparently a small Mexican village, El Terrente, as well as the old San Pedro Presidio on the river in Arizona.

Ref.:   19, I, 123; 19, II, 248; 21, p. 447; 72, pp. 13-14; 35, p. 482, Note 29; APHS Names File.

**a.n. San Pedro Valley**                                          Cochise

The portion of the valley lying to the north of Benson is often referred to as the Lower San Pedro Valley, and it was in this region that the first settlements were made on the San Pedro River in late 1865 when Mark Aldrich, John H. Archibald, F. Barthod, Jarvis Jackson, and others from Tucson put in crops of wheat and barley. These early families endured many depredations at the hands of Indians. By 1875 there were no residents left in the area. Nevertheless, when the land was thrown open for homesteading in 1878 several communities developed.

Ref.:   51, p. 423; 119, p. 23. Maps: GB-18; E-7; B-3; C-1.

## SAN RAFAEL DEL VALLE LAND GRANT

El.: 4100'                                    Loc.: Cochise 1, BCD-9.6-11.3
Pro.: /sæn rafáyəl del váye/           Spanish: "Saint Rafael
/san rafáyel del váye/                          of the Valley"

The United States courts confirmed at 17,474 acres that portion of this Mexican land grant lying within the Gadsden Purchase. The title of the grant had been vested in the Camou brothers of Sonora. The entire tract prior to its division consisted of 20,034 acres.

Ref.:   Barnes; 55, p. 428. Maps: B-2; C-5.

## SAN SIMON VALLEY

El.: c. 4200'                                    Loc.: Cochise 2, FG-8-9
Pro.: /sæn si^mówn/ or             Spanish: "Saint Simon"
/san si^mówn/

It is impossible to discuss the origin of the name for the San Simon Valley without taking into consideration the way early white travelers viewed the living stream which at one time traversed this valley. This is best done by considering changes in name on various maps.

The living stream which formed that portion of the San Simon River roughly north of the future S.P.R.R. was known to Spanish speaking people in the 1840's as the Rio San Domingo. It was also known as the Rio de Sauz, no doubt because willows grew along its banks and in the upper swamps connected with the valley. (Spanish: *sauz,* "willows"). When Robert Eccleston and his party encountered

the stream in 1849, they found no name for it on any map in their possession and therefore applied the name Welcome Creek to it, but this name did not stick. The stream has no name on the map prepared by Lt. John G. Parke in the early 1850's. In that same year the Boundary Survey party under Commissioner Bartlett crossed the southern part of what is now Cochise County. Along the upper portion of the river there was no living stream, but the ground was distinctly marshy and had willow groves, thus making the term *cienega* applicable. The Cienega de Sauz (Spanish: "willow swamp") first appears on the Leach Map for 1857, on which also appears the term "Rio San Domingo or Rio de Sauz." The latter two names are used on the Boundary Survey map of 1853. Maj. William H. Emory refers to this stream as the Suanca and by the other names mentioned above.

Obviously the waters of this once living stream began to dry up, for in 1879 Smith uses the term San Simon Cienega for that part near the Mexican border and marks the rest of the river course "Underground Passage of Rio de Sauz." The name San Simon Valley also appears for the first time on this map. Curiously enough, on GLO 1879, it shows as the San Simeon Valley and the Sauz River.

Obviously in the years since Eccleston's trip in 1849 the living stream had died. In the years between, however, the fact that permanent water was to be found along its course made the San Simon River of great importance to early American travelers. For this reason a station for the Butterfield Overland Stage line was established early in 1859 at a place called San Simon (T. 133, R. 31, E, Sec. 38). It was a small station for changing teams. John Cremony noted that the San Simon Creek sank into the ground about a mile south of the stage station. Still later the railroad came through and the community of San Simon began to grow. Whether the post offices listed were both on the railroad is not known, but if so, apparently there must have been a period of years when the post office was out of existence.

P.O. est. as San Simon, March 16, 1881. Francis B. Austin, p.m. Re-established May 20, 1930. Mrs. Anna M. Hall, p.m. Wells Fargo Station, 1885.

Ref.:   48, pp. vi, 180; 51, p. 93; 101, p. 42; 32, II, 130; 111, p. 115; 9, I, pp. 366, 371; 37, p. 171. Maps: GB-19; GB-4; GB-5; GB-8; GB-11; GB-22; E-7 (Rio de San Domingo); E-18 (San Simon Valley); C-3 (Sauz River); C-4 (San Simon); E-20.

**a.n. La Puerta**                                             Cochise

In 1851 Gray referred to La Puerta as being the pass into the Valle de Sauz.

Ref.:   68, p. 45.

**San Simon Head**

El.: 5715'. Maps: C-13; GB-6; GB-13               Cochise

A prominent land mark.

**San Simon Peak**   Loc.: T. 11 S., R. 31 E.         Cochise

## SARAH DEMING CANYON

El.: 6000'                                    Loc.: Cochise 2, CD-4.7

When Ed Riggs in 1923 took the first party into what is now the Chiricahua National Monument to show them the famous Balanced Rock, which only he had seen before that time, the only out-of-state woman in the party was Sarah Deming. A place name came into being when she slipped and tore a big hole in the seat of her pants. Aunt Martha Riggs, a pioneer woman who — like all pioneer women — did not consider herself dressed unless she was wearing an apron, grabbed her apron and hastily handed it to Miss Deming, who quite as hastily tied it on backwards.

Ref.:   Riggs. Map: None.

**a.n. Sarah Deming Trail**                                    Cochise
    Loc.: In Sarah Deming Canyon

## SAWMILL

El.: 4065'                    Loc.: Cochise 2, B-12.2
Sawmill is a part-time post office established c. 1952 to provide service for lumbermen working at this camp.

Ref.:   Prather. Map: B-3.

## SEMBRICH

El.: c. 4000'                    Loc.: Cochise 1, A-11.2
This place was named for a settler who lived in the Huachuca Mountains c. 1879.

P.O. est. December 31, 1915. John W. Noel, p.m. Discont. November 15, 1916.

Ref.:   Barnes. Maps: C-12; F-2.

## SENTINEL PEAK

El.: 9490'                    Loc.: Cochise 2, DE-7.9
Because of its shape, this peak is sometimes referred to as Square Peak. Both names are descriptive.

Ref.:   Barnes. Maps: GB-5; C-13.

## SERVOSS

El.: c. 4000'                    Loc.: Cochise 1, EF-4.5
Walter Servoss (b. Rochester, N. Y.; d. 1908) was a boyhood friend of John Rockfellow (cf. Rockfellow Dome). The two men came to Arizona in 1883. Servoss went to South America where he engaged in mining for several years and later came back to become a partner with Rockfellow on the NY Ranch.

P.O. est. December 30, 1911. Robert A. Hutchinson, p.m. Discont. April 15, 1920.

Ref.:   140, pp. 42, 199; P.O. Records. Map: C-10.

## SIERRA VISTA

El.: 4600'                    Loc.: Cochise 1, A-10
Pro.:  /siyéra vísta/          Spanish: "mountain view"
       /siyéra víysta/
The canyon at the mouth of which this community is located was first known as Garden Canyon because it contained the produce gardens for Fort Huachuca. It was also sometimes referred to as Hayes and Tanner Canyon by old-timers because two men by those names had a sawmill in the canyon.

When it became necessary to provide post office facilities for civilians near Fort Huachuca, the name Garden Canyon was selected. This was later changed to Fry, after Oliver Fry, who had come to the area toward the end of the

nineteenth century with a group of homesteaders. In 1955 the name of the town was changed to Sierra Vista by petition of its citizens.

P.O. est. as Garden Canyon, March 4, 1919. William Carmichael, p.m. Name changed to Fry, April 1, 1937. Incorporated as Sierra Vista, August 9, 1955.

Ref.:   Bennett; Macia. Maps: GB-14; C-12 (Garden Canyon); F-2 (Fry).

## SKELETON CANYON

El.: 4985'                    Loc.: Cochise 2, FG-10
The isolated and very rugged nature of mountains and canyons in the extreme southeastern corner of Arizona on the Mexican boundary made the area a perfect passage for smugglers. Thieves' honor meant nothing to the gang of American bandits which in 1881 ambushed a Mexican smuggler pack train here. The Americans were led by Curly Bill and Old Man Clanton, both of whom figured more than once in badman encounters in southern Arizona. The men made a rich haul at the cost of the brutal murder of a number of Mexican vaqueros, estimated at six to nineteen. The bodies of the dead were left where they fell. Coyotes and buzzards did their work and the bare bones remained to give the name to the canyon. The place where Curly Bill's men murdered the Mexicans is known as Devil's Kitchen. The five white men involved were said to have captured $75,000 in Mexican silver, with which they proceeded to whoop it up in Charleston and Galeyville (q.v.). The *Tombstone Epitaph,* writing of the event on August 5, 1881, put the death list at four and the treasure at $4,000. It also reported that there were twenty rifles fired by the Americans, indicating a band of that number, and that there were sixteen Mexicans involved.

Mexicans who escaped from this slaughter vowed vengeance. Twenty miles northeast of Skeleton Canyon they found it in Guadalupe Canyon which traverses a small part of Arizona. Here in retaliation Old Man Clanton was ambushed and murdered with four other members of his party.

Ref.:   55, p. 622; 119A, p. 119; 180a, p. 142; 27, pp. 283, 352. Map: GB-5.

## SNOWSHED PEAK

El.: 5000'                    Loc.: Cochise 2, DE-7
Actually the Snowshed, as it is known locally, is merely a ridge of the main Chiricahua Mountains. The formation is such that when there is a lot of snowfall, it collects along the ridge which literally becomes a snowshed when the whole snow mass breaks off in one small avalanche.

Ref.:   Riggs. Map: GB-5.

## SOUTHERLAND PEAK

El.: 8500'                    Loc.: Cochise 1, A-10.5
                             Sec. 22, T. 23S., R. 20E
Jim Southerland, a native of Idaho, was a cattleman who had a ranch in Hayfield Canyon. He was known as the homeliest man in Arizona. He died when he fell into a well he was digging.

Ref.:   Barnes. Map: None.

## SQUARE MOUNTAIN

El.: 5692'    Loc.: Cochise 1, DE-1.6
Descriptive.

Ref.: None. Map: GB-23.

**a.n. Square Top Hills**    Maps: GB-16; C-12    Cochise

## STARK

El.: 4380'    Loc.: Cochise 1, D-12.2
A now-vanished station on the old El Paso and South-western Railroad was named for William Stark, who with his wife had a store and post office at this place. The Starks homesteaded here in the late 1870's.

P.O. est. May 23, 1914. Solomon F. Pyle, p.m. Discont. February 15, 1921.

Ref.: Burgess. Maps: GB-13; C-10.

## STOCKTON HILL

El.: 5589'    Loc.: Cochise 1, DE-8.2
Eugene Edmonds was nicknamed "Stockton" Edmonds because he was a survivor of the Stockton Indian massacre in California. With his family he settled at the Stockton ranch, which soon became a favorite stopping place for freighters and outlaws on the road from Tombstone to the Chiricahua Mountains.

Ref.: 27, p. 115; Macia. Map: GB-16 (Stockton Ranch).

## SULPHUR SPRINGS VALLEY

El.: c. 4000'    Loc.: Cochise 1, EF-1-2
Although current maps examined show the name as Sulphur Spring, documentary evidence points to the fact that there was more than one spring. Despite the name, the water was apparently palatable. It was noted, however, that wherever it stagnated a trace of hydrogen sulphide developed from the decay of vegetables and the chemical action on gypsum in the water.

The early name for the valley was Valle de las Playas and it so shows on the military map for 1859. In 1868 two Americans named Rogers and Spence homesteaded at Sulphur Springs. This led to some difficulty when the Chiricahua Reservation was established by Gen. O. O. Howard in October 1872. The two white men were able to substantiate their squatters' claim and were given a quarter section where Rogers kept a trading post until his death. It was here, on April 6, 1876, that the Apaches were sold as much vile whiskey as they wanted. A fight developed among the Indians themselves and the trading post keepers were killed. The Indians fled to Mexico. This was the beginning of six years of Apache depredations (cf. Chiricahua Mountains).

The stage station at Sulphur Springs was on the road from Tucson to Camp Goodwin.

By 1875 the name Sulphur Springs Valley had come to be applied to the entire valley, the largest in Cochise County, which extends from the Mexican boundary northward into Graham County. It averages more than twenty miles in width.

Ref.: 28, p. 177; 175, III, 592; *Tucson Citizen,* October 19, 1872, 2:1; 55, VIII, 14; 87, p. 532; 92, p. xxxi; 83, p. 401. Maps: GB-23; E-17; E-18; E-20.

**a.n. Sulphur Hills**    El.: 5156'. Maps: C-12; GB-16    Cochise
**Sulphur Peak**    El.: 7401'. Map: B-2    Cochise

## SUNGLOW

El.: c. 6000'    Loc.: Cochise 2, C-6.8
This place was named in 1920 by Jeff P. Thomason, Sr., reportedly because when the sun strikes this area in the early morning, it envelopes it in a golden glow.

Johnny Ringgold, commonly called Ringo, is buried about one and one-half miles from the old Sunglow post office. His body lies within a few hundred feet of where he was shot. Ringo, a notorious badman, was found sitting propped in the fork of a tree with a bullet in his head. Curiously, his feet were bare. No sound of shots had been heard. His body was found a few hours after his death and his horse was only a mile or two below. The circumstances surrounding his death are still shrouded in mystery. The coroner's jury brought in a verdict of suicide, more than somewhat dubious considering that Ringo's revolver was fully loaded when found.

Today nothing remains at Sunglow except a dwelling or two.

P.O. est. December 2, 1922. Jeff Thomason, p.m. Discont. December 30, 1933.

Ref.: 102, p. 83; Riggs. Map: C-13.

## SUNNYSIDE

El.: 6500'    Loc.: Cochise 1, A-11.6
In the 1880's, a Scotsman named Sam Donnelly was one of the better patrons of the tough waterfront bars in San Francisco. His regeneration began when he overheard men plotting skullduggery and suggesting that Scotty accomplish the deed at the cost to them of a drink of whiskey. Scotty saw through his alcoholic haze clearly enough to give the men a tongue lashing, after which he wandered out to stumble into a Salvation Army meeting. He became a Salvation Army officer and street preacher whose path finally took him to Tombstone. There he ran into a man named Sinclair, the locator of the Copper Glance (sometimes incorrectly referred to as Glance) Mine in the Huachuca Mountains. Plans developed for a religious colony, to be christened Sunnyside, at the mining prospects. The mining locations paid off and the community prospered. All went well until the late 1890's when Brother Sam died. He was irreplaceable. Added to that, the mines played out, debts accumulated, and the honest people of Sunnyside gave the creditors the mines.

P.O. est. July 16, 1914. Lucy Langford, p.m. Discont. March 15, 1934.

Ref.: 140, pp. 150-152; P.O. Records. Maps: GB-13; C-12.

**a.n. Sunnyside Canyon**    Map: B-3    Cochise

## SWISSHELM MOUNTAINS

El.: c. 7000'    Loc.: Cochise 2, B-8.9
The first name for the Swisshelm Mountains on early maps was the Pedregosa Mountains. John Swisshelm (d. c. 1908)

was a miner who, with Henry Hudson and J. W. Fleming, prospected in these mountains c. 1878.

   **v.n. Pedregosa Mountains**     Spanish: "rocky" or "stony"
     Descriptive. At the extreme south end of these mountains, Geronimo surrendered in Skeleton Canyon in 1866.
   Ref.: Barnes; *Arizona Star,* February 22, 1920, 5:2. Maps: GB-9; GB-16; GB-5; C-6; C-7; E-12 (Swisshelm District).
   **a.n. Swisshelm Peak**   El.: 7183'. Map: C-12     Cochise
     This is probably the same peak which was named by the three prospectors Fleming Peak for J. W. Fleming.
   Ref.: Barnes.
   **Swisshelm**                 Cochise
P.O. est. December 12, 1904. Wilson R. Holland, p.m. Discont. April 9, 1908.

## TAYLOR BUTTE

El.: 4633'             Loc.: Cochise 2, AB-10.1
A man named Taylor owned a stone quarry at the butte which bears his name. Actually, there are two buttes here which are known descriptively as Twin Buttes.
Ref.: Barnes. Maps: GB-16; C-12.

## TEXAS CANYON

El.: c. 5000'          Loc.: Cochise 1, BCD-5.2-4.2
The Adams family from Texas was on its way to the West Coast but got no farther than the canyon now known as Texas Canyon, where Indians stole David Adams' team and left him completely up against it. With his brothers, Will and Wilbur, Dave settled down on what is known as Adams' Flat to make a go of it. He and his family succeeded.

Texas Canyon, through which the main highway across southern Arizona runs, has scenery to whet the most jaded tourist's appetite. The road climbs up and through a mass of jumbled rocks piled upon each other in incredible shapes. Depending upon the time of day, their color varies from pink to deepest amethyst.
Ref.: Nuttall; Bennett. Map: GB-10.

   **a.n. Tex Canyon**     Map: GB-5     Cochise
     The canyon at the southern end of the Chiricahua Mountains was named for Scott (Tex) Whaley, one of two white men who accompanied Lt. Charles B. Gatewood into Geronimo's camp in 1886 (cf. Gatewood). Tex homesteaded in this canyon.
   Ref.: APHS File.

## THREE SISTERS BUTTES

El.: 4650'             Loc.: Cochise 1, FG-5.1
These three buttes, descriptively named, have been so called since at least the 1870's. They resemble each other.
Ref.: 87, p. 231. Maps: C-12; GB-7; GB-16.

## TINTOWN

El.: c. 6000'           Loc.: Cochise 1, EF-11.4
Mexican workers in the Bisbee mines c. 1904 erected houses made of flattened tin cans, oil containers, and scraps of discarded lumber to form a community where they could be as gay as they wished without disturbing others. Tintown's houses were close together, with two or three families living in each shanty. The place has nearly disappeared.
Ref.: 4, pp. 378-379. Map: GB-25.

## TOMBSTONE

El.: 4539'          Loc.: Cochise 1, CD-8.2
There is a difference between the prospector and mining man. A prospector is marked by his love of the search for precious metals, whereas the miner is he who takes over what the prospector locates. Ed Schieffelin (d. May 12, 1897) was primarily prospector. He was at Signal (*q.v.* Mohave) when he had a chance to go through Indian-infested southeastern Arizona with some military men. Not himself a soldier, Schieffelin packed his few belongings and set off. In the fall of 1877, he was at Camp Huachuca, at that time in the heart of Apache land, and a bloody land it was. The bare, richly colored hills to the northeast looked good to Schieffelin, and his prospector's dreams made him disregard the warning that if he went alone to find mineral wealth, he would find his tombstone. Schieffelin was careful. Cautious and alone, he camped at night without fires. He made no move without searching the landscape for Apaches. At night Schieffelin crawled silently to the seep where he got water, then crept back again among the boulders to sleep.

In winter of 1877, Ed Schieffelin hit his first strike and named it Tombstone. Needing help, he hurried north to Signal to have the ore assayed by Richard Gird and to enlist the aid of his brother Al Schieffelin. Gird reported that the find was a rich one and he, Al, and Ed left for the latter's location. Once in southern Arizona, they settled their new belongings at a place which in 1879 was called Gird Camp. Soon the boom was on. Miners streamed in from Signal where the word spread that Schieffelin had struck it rich. A community began to grow up near what was called Tank Hill, about three miles from the present Tombstone.

The lack of water was a major problem. There was a running stream at Tank Hill, and one after another concrete foundations for tent houses appeared. On the hill there was a big tank for storing water. Near the base of the hill was a community known as Watervale; from it water was pumped to the tank. At its best Watervale was a temporary community (Loc.: T 22 S, R 19 E; three miles north of Tombstone). It lacked room for building permanent structures, and hordes of newcomers sought a level place for a town. Tombstone was the result.

The indefatigable John B. Allen, who seems to have established stores in mining communities throughout southern Arizona, was referred to in 1879 as the "founder of Tombstone City" where he was once again in the van of those creating a community. By the end of 1879 Tombstone had about one hundred permanent residents, plus at least one thousand others camped on nearby hills. A year and a half later Tombstone was emerging as one of the largest cities in the West. The badmen whooped it up at Tombstone but their noise was nothing compared to the ruckus they created at nearby Charleston (*q.v.*) or far across the valley at Galeyville (*q.v.*). While it is true that badmen flocked to Tombstone's saloons and gambling houses and that the Earp-Clanton feud is a famous one, it is often overlooked that Tombstone was probably the most cultivated city in the

West and Southwest. Tombstone was at that time larger than San Francisco and whatever cultural opportunities there were in the West could be found at Tombstone. With a population of 15,000 the community erected an opera house where the best of the world's musicians and actors could be heard.

Ironically, it was water which drowned Tombstone's hopes and plans. As the mining shafts plunged ever deeper into the rich earth, moisture began to appear. When the shafts reached five hundred feet, it became necessary to begin pumping. This was of little avail. To add to difficulties, the surface pumps at the Grand Central and Contention Mines burned in 1886 and in 1887, and the mining shafts filled rapidly with water. As the mines flooded, the town began to shrivel. By 1890 Tombstone was nearly dead. In 1901 another effort was made to pump out the mines. This had barely achieved partial success when in 1909 the everlasting water penetrated the boilers, extinguishing the fires, and again the mine shaft flooded. The prohibitive cost precludes abstracting the rich ores known to be hundreds of feet deep in Tombstone's earth. Tombstone, however, did not die. For years it led an anemic existence, barely tottering along. As the past has receded, the town has become of increasing interest to the present, and today Tombstone is a flourishing tourist attraction known as the "Town Too Tough to Die."

As for Ed Schieffelin, his life came full circle when his body was buried near where years before he had crept at night to obtain water. He once said that the two most glorious nights he had ever known were those during which he had slept on the hill where he is now buried, and he left a written request in his records that he be buried at that spot. Ever the prospector, he had long since wandered to other fields and in one of them in the Northwest he died, his body being brought back for burial to the place he loved.

In 1881 Tombstone became the county seat for Cochise County. It continued to be so until 1929 when the county seat was moved to Bisbee.

P.O. est. December 2, 1878. Richard Gird, p.m. Wells Fargo Station, 1885. Incorporated January 3, 1881.

Ref.: Nuttall; Macia; 76, p. 35; 4, p. 245; *Bisbee Review*, n.d. (State Library Clipping File); *Weekly Arizona Star*, March 13, 1879, 3:2; September 17, 1879, n.p. Maps: GB-1; C-5.

| | | |
|---|---|---|
| **a.n. Tombstone Gulch** | Maps: GB-1; GB-20 | Cochise |
| **Tombstone Hills** | Maps: GB-1; GB-20 | Cochise |

The earlier name for this group of hills seems to have been Burros, an indication of their smaller size as distinguished from the nearby and much larger Mule Mountains.

Ref.: 119A, pp. 14-15.

| | | |
|---|---|---|
| **Tombstone Canyon** | Map: GB-2 | Cochise |
| **Richmond** | Loc: ¼ mile e. of Tombstone | Cochise |

This is reported to have been the planned location of Tombstone. It was so named by Virginians who came to Arizona after the Civil War. However, Tombstone developed on the more level land where the community lies today.

Ref.: Larriau; 170, p. 91.

## TRES ALAMOS

El.: c. 2500'  Loc.: Cochise 1, B.3
Pro.: /tréys ǽləmos/  Spanish: "three cottonwoods"
Before there was a stage station at this location it was known as Rio de Tres Alamos. The name Tres Alamos does not appear on maps examined until GLO 1879. Nevertheless, it was being called by this name at least ten years earlier, when it was noted that there was a settlement here where seven men had been murdered within the year, thus causing its abandonment. It never again was important as a community of any sort although a stage station was operated here c. 1877 by Thomas Dunbar. On Smith 1879 this accounts for the name Dunbars. Dunbar hired a man named Montgomery to run the post office, hence the name is sometimes found as Montgomery's. The name Tres Alamos continues to be found from GLO 1879 until GLO 1903, from which it has disappeared.

P.O. est. December 2, 1874. John Montgomery, p.m. Discont. September 15, 1886.

Ref.: 111, p. 204; 55, p. 285. Maps: A-3; E-20; C-4.

| | | |
|---|---|---|
| **a.n. Tres Alamos Wash** | Maps: GB-10; GB-12 | Cochise |

## TUFA

El.: c. 4500'  Loc.: Cochise 2, C-10.8
Pro.: /túwfə/
This small place on the railroad may refer to a form of chemical sedimentary stone known as *tufa*.

P.O. est. January 29, 1903. Katie Hines, p.m. Order rescinded August 1, 1903.

Ref.: P.O. Records. Map: GB-17.

## TULLY

El.: c. 4000'  Loc.: Cochise 1, C-5.1
P. R. Tully was a partner in Tully, Ochoa and Company of Tucson (cf. Ochoa). It is probable that as the railroad was being constructed, Tully and Ochoa established a supply point for the construction crew. This place was referred to as Tullyville, or by its post office name of Tully.

P.O. est. June 21, 1880. John O'Dougherty, p.m. Discont. November 8, 1880.

Ref.: Barnes; P.O. Records. Map: GB-1.

| | | |
|---|---|---|
| **a.n. Tully Peak** | Loc.: T. 14S., R. 16 E. | Cochise |

Tully Peak first appears on the 1893 Roskruge Map.

## TURKEY CREEK

El.: c. 5000'  Loc.: Cochise 1, BC-1-6
From 1880 to 1884 a man named Morse had a sawmill on Turkey Creek where he prepared lumber for use in the Copper Queen Mine at Bisbee. The timbers measured one foot in diameter, and Turkey Creek was the only place where timbers of such size could be found. Morse is said to have named Turkey Creek for the wild turkeys found along it.

Ref.: Riggs; Burgess. Maps: GB-16; GB-5; E-20.

| | | |
|---|---|---|
| **a.n. Morse Canyon** | Map: B-2 | Cochise |
| | Morse had his sawmill here. | |
| **Turkey Creek Canyon** | Map: GB-14 | Cochise |
| **v.n. Turkey Canyon** (corruption) | | |
| **a.n. Turkey Creek Ridge** (corruption) | | |

## TURNER

El.: c. 4000'                                   Loc.: Cochise 1, A-9.1

The post office called Turner was established following a series of incidents in connection with affairs at Fort Huachuca itself. Briefly, the new post office came into existence when the commanding officer at the fort discovered that the postmistress at the fort post office (wife of a Civil War veteran) was bootlegging whiskey to the soldiers. The civilian family was ordered to leave the military reservation at once. However, the Civil War veteran declared the might of the Post Office Department was greater than that of the United States Army and that the commanding colonel would have a hard time forcing the fort post office and its postmistress to vacate the premises.

Infuriated, the colonel retorted that transport wagons would be sent and the family had better be ready to leave peacefully or it would do so as a result of force. The wagons came, only to find postmistress and family adamant, whereupon the United States Army moved the United States post office bodily outside the north gate of Fort Huachuca to what was called Huachuca Siding on the railroad.

The matter came to the attention of postal authorities, who applied the name Turner to the new post office in honor of Tom Turner, well known cattleman and third sheriff of Santa Cruz County (1901-1904). The office was moved to another location a short distance farther from the fort, with a new postmaster.

Nothing daunted, the ex-postmistress and her belligerent husband set up a saloon near the north entrance to Fort Huachuca.

P.O. est. as Turner, March 30, 1898. Horace H. Temple, p.m. Discont. December 31, 1919.

Ref.:   Lenon; Larriau. Map: C-9.

## TURTLE MOUNTAIN

El.: 8152'                                      Loc.: Cochise 2, D-7.1

Harry D. Burrall built the trail to this peak c. 1906. He named the peak because of its resemblance to the head and body of a turtle.

Ref.:   Burrall. Map: GB-5.

## UNCLE SAM HILL

El.: 4813'                                      Loc.: Cochise 1, C-8.5

This hill was named for the Uncle Sam Mine.

Ref.:   Barnes. Map: GB-20.

| a.n. Uncle Sam Gulch | Map: GB-2 | Cochise |
| Uncle Sam Mine | Map: GB-2 | Cochise |

## VANAR

El.: c. 4000'                                   Loc.: Cochise 2, F-2.2

This location on the S.P.R.R. near the New Mexico line appears on Rand McNally 1898 for the first time as Vanarman. GLO 1909 shows it shortened to Vanar and it so appears thereafter. The origin of the name has not been ascertained.

P.O. est. June 5, 1914. Alfred D. Wallace, p.m. Dicont. October 14, 1916.

Ref.:   P.O. Records. Map: GB-22.

| a.n. Vanar Wash | Map: GB-22 | Cochise |

## VOTA

El.: c. 6000'                                   Loc.: Cochise 1, A-11.5

The origin of this name has not been ascertained.

P.O. est. April 21, 1881, Ira J. Richards, p.m. Discont. February 26, 1883.

Ref.:   P.O. Records. Map: C-5.

## WALLEN, CAMP

El.: c. 4000'                                   Loc.: Cochise 1, A-9.25

Pro.:  /wálən/

When Camp Wallen was first established, it was referred to by its garrison as New Post. This name was officially changed on May 9, 1886, to Fort Wallen after Col. H. D. Wallen, who commanded the Northern Arizona Military District (1866-1867). It seemed to be a smart move to occupy old ranch buildings for this camp, but it proved a poor one in that the land was part of the privately-owned Babocomari Land Grant. This made abandonment of the post essential. This was done on October 31, 1869.

It is interesting to note that many years before, there was an Indian village here known as Huachuca, ruled by an Indian called Taravilla ("the prattler"). This same name was used by United States troops when Camp Huachuca (q.v.) was established on March 3, 1877.

The next known occupants of old Fort or Camp Wallen were the Messrs. McGarey with their 7,000 sheep.

Ref.:   APHS Names File; *Arizona Enterprises,* January 18, 1890, 1:4; *Arizona Citizen,* August 15, 1874, 1:4; 75, p. 159; 20, p. 360; 87, pp. 234-235. Maps: E-18; C-2; C-4; E-20.

## WARREN

El.: 5250'                                      Loc.: Cochise 1, ED-11.3

George Warren (b. 1845) was grubstaked by John Dunn to work on the claim in Mule Gulch (cf. Bisbee). The town of Warren is next to Bisbee.

P.O. est. July 10, 1907. Harry B. Hansom, p.m. Wells Fargo Station, 1908.

Ref.:   P.O. Records; APHS Files. Map: GB-2.

## WEBB

El.: c. 4000'                                   Loc.: Cochise 2, AB-8

This location was first called Tyler, so named by Robert M. Tyler c. 1909. However, the post office requested a shorter name and Mr. Tyler suggested the name Webb after J. D. Webb, his wife's father.

P.O. est. November 19, 1909. Robert M. Tyler, p.m. Discont. August 5, 1938.

Ref.:   Barnes; APHS Names File; P.O. Records. Maps: C-11; C-12.

## WHETSTONE MOUNTAINS

El.: c. 6000'                                   Loc.: Cochise 1, A-8-6.5

On the Smith map (1879) these mountains appear for the first time, labelled Mustang Mountains. On GLO 1883 the range is called the Whetstone Mountains, and its southern extremity is called Mustang Mountains. Lt. John G. Bourke said that in the 1870's these mountains were known by both names — Mustang and Whetstone. The latter name was due to the fact that in the mountains there was a ledge of novaculite (a fine-grained, hard rock used for whetstones). He also noted that Mexicans called the range the Mestinez (Spanish: "mustang") because in 1870 the hills sheltered a herd of about sixty wild ponies. These ponies may have been descendants of the stock brought into the region by Fr. Kino. In 1697 Kino and Manje made a trip up the San Pedro Valley. They were somewhat suspicious of the Sobaipuri Indians because some of the Indians rode horses, which it was rumored they must have stolen. However, Manje said in 1687 that several stock ranches near the future Pima County border had been abandoned because of Indian raids. The unclaimed stock went wild and soon became "mesteña" or mustangs, and the Sobaipuri Indians captured and used the horses.

Ref.: 22, p. 102; 20, p. 358. Maps: GB-2; C-5; E-20.

## WHITEWATER

El.: c. 4000'    Loc.: Cochise 2, A-10.8

This stream, sometimes called White River, was so named because the presence of alkali in the water left a white sediment along the bank. The creek runs down the mouth of Rucker Canyon to the Sulphur Springs Valley and thence across the international boundary into Mexico. Currently it is called Whitewater Draw. That part of Whitewater Draw close to the present Douglas used to be a favorite rodeo ground. Because of its ample supply of water it was selected as the site for the Douglas smelter.

P.O. est. April 2, 1907. Alsworth A. Crawford, p.m. Discont. August 16, 1918. This was the post office for the Whitewater ranch.

Ref.: *Bisbee Review*, n.d., n.p. (State Library Clipping File); APHS Names File; 98A, p. 61; 151, p. 816. Maps: GB-16; C-10.

## WILGUS

El.: c. 5000'    Loc.: Cochise 2, C-6.5

The first name for this now-vanished community was Aztec, but the reason for the name is not known. When the post office was re-established several years later, it was named Wilgus. B. F. Smith was an early homesteader at this location. The first postmaster was William Wilgus Smith, brother of B. F. Smith. Will Smith was killed by Indians and his body found under snow; his small dog was keeping vigil nearby. Although the post office has been discontinued at this place, there are still a few people living here.

P.O. est. as Aztec July 21, 1887. William W. Smith, p.m. Name changed to Wilgus, February 21, 1888. Discont. January 31, 1911.

Ref.: Riggs; Miles Rutherford Choat File, APHS; P.O. Records. Maps: GB-5; C-7.

## WILLCOX

El.: 4163'    Loc.: Cochise 1, F-2

The first name for the present community of Willcox was Maley *(sic)*, after James H. Mahley (b. 1850), who in 1882 was a resident of Dos Cabezas. Maley was so called because the railroad right-of-way went through Mahley's ranch. The legend concerning the change in name is that when the first train came through, Gen. Orlando B. Willcox (1823-1907), then commander of the Department of Arizona (1877-1882), was on board and received an ovation. Since its beginning as a railroad point, Willcox has been important as a cattle shipping center.

P.O. est. September 13, 1880. John F. Row, p.m. Name changed to Wilcox, October 19, 1880. Name changed to Willcox, November 23, 1889. Wells Fargo Station, 1885.

Ref.: APHS Files; P.O. Records; 4, p. 437. Maps: GB-7; GB-23; C-5.

**a.n. Willcox Playa**    Map: GB-7    Cochise

In 1854 Lt. John G. Parke named this enormous shallow dry lake bed the Playa de los Pimas, stating that it lay immediately to the west of Dos Cabezos *(sic)*. When he passed the lake bed on February 28, 1854, and again on July 30, 1855, the lake bed was hard, smooth, and level. Another officer found several inches of water here on his return to California in October.

The Mexican name for such dry lakes without plant life is *playa*. This is the place which Hinton referred to as Soda Lake. It has also been called Lake Cochise. On many early maps it is called simply Playas. In 1879 Smith rather laconically called it Dry Lake and GLO 1883 is no more imaginative with its "Alkali Flats." As can clearly be seen, all names are descriptive. The mirages observed at this dry lake are astonishing. At times the playa appears to be a vast expanse of deep water. During World War II this led to an embarrassing incident for two navy flyers who were ferrying a flying boat across the country; where there seemed to be water, there was none. Their unauthorized landing was a rough one.

Ref.: 124, p. 24; 87, p. 242; 12, p. 46; 92, p. 9.

**Maley Canyon**    Map: GB-8    Cochise

## WINCHESTER MOUNTAINS

El.: c. 5000'    Loc.: Cochise 1, DC-2-1

The name for the Winchester Mountains first appears on GLO 1921. This throws in doubt the origin of the name. It is possible that these mountains may have been named for Josiah Winchester, a miner and prospector in southern Arizona. On the other hand, there is also the possibility that they were named for 1st Lt. Hiram F. Winchester, Sixth Cavalry, who died on May 29, 1881. Documentary evidence for either one has not yet been uncovered. There is a third possibility that the mountains were named for Henry D. Winchester, after whom the Winchester District was named in 1882. This seems the most likely of the three, since a community named Winchester served as a voting place for the population of fifty-one in 1882.

Ref.: Barnes; 85, I, 1049; *Tombstone Epitaph*, April 3, 1882, 1:7; July 15, 1882, 3:5. Maps: GB-10; GB-23; GB-24.

# COCONINO

*San Francisco Peaks — beginning of Flagstaff — sheep raising — lumbering and sawmill.*

## COCONINO COUNTY:

/kowkowníynow/ or /kowkǝnıynow/

Coconino County is Arizona's largest county and is the second largest county in the United States. Its 11,886,720 acres lie in central-northern Arizona on both sides of the Grand Canyon with Kanab Creek and a portion of the Colorado River as its western boundary.

Coconino County was carved from Yavapai County, one of the four original counties in Arizona. In 1887 William H. Ashurst of Flagstaff introduced a measure in the 14th Legislative Assembly to create a "Frisco County," but the measure was defeated. In the following year Frank Rogers (See Rogers Lake) took up the fight, and introduced the bill again in 1889. It passed through the House and the Council, but was vetoed by the governor. The House then passed over the veto, but the Senate failed to follow through. By 1891 the time was right for the creation of Coconino County and on February 19, 1891, it came into being. The name *Coconino* was suggested by Dan M. Riordan (See Riordan). The name is that of the Coconino Indians, of whom today's Havasupai are descendants. Lt. Lorenzo Sitgreaves interpreted the name as Cojnino, a not very great departure from the name Cosninas, as noted by Fr. Francisco Garcés in 1776. Actually, the word is the Hopi designation for Havasupai and Yavapai Indians.

Coconino encloses country of great contrast, including the magnificence of the Grand Canyon, the beautiful wooded San Francisco Peaks, and the escarpment of the Painted Desert. North of the Grand Canyon lies the area of Arizona referred to as the Arizona Strip, a large part of which also lies in Mohave County. This area is relatively virgin territory since it is not easily accessible. Coconino is largely an agricultural, lumbering, and livestock area. The county seat is at Flagstaff.

# AGASSIZ PEAK

El.: 12,340'                          Loc.: Coconino 5, A-4
Pro.: /ǽgəsiy/
Jean Louis Rodolphe Agassiz (1807-1873) made the fossil
reports for the Pacific Railroad surveying expedition of
1855-1860. Agassiz, a Swiss, was a famed zoologist at
Harvard. The peak was named by Gen. W. J. Palmer in
his "Report on Surveys of 1867-1868." The peak had previously been called San Francisco Mountain (q.v.)

Ref.:   16, p. 319; 177, p. 175 (Note 16); 143, p. 1. Maps: C-
12; GC-3; GC-9; E-20.

a.n. **Agassiz**          Map: C-10                     Coconino
There used to be a railroad station three miles west of Flagstaff. Its name was changed to Milton (cf. Flagstaff).

# ALDER CANYON

El.: c. 5000'                         Loc.: Coconino 5, G-15
This canyon heads at Alder Lake, so named because of
alder trees around it.

Ref.:   Barnes. Map: GC-9.

a.n. **Alder Lake**       Maps: B-8; GC-9               Coconino
Following the Battle of Big Dry Wash (q.v. Navajo), the
troops camped here to recuperate.

Ref.:   Barnes.

# ALLAN LAKE

El.: c. 8000'                         Loc.: Coconino 5, B-10
"Broncho Jim" Allan was a pioneer horseman here.

Ref.:   Barnes. Maps: B-8; GC-9.

# ANDERSON CANYON

El.: c. 5000'                         Loc.: Coconino 5, G-7
Jim Anderson, a partner of William H. Ashurst, came with
the influx of Californians bringing livestock into the Flagstaff area.

Ref.:   Barnes; Anderson. Maps: B-8; GC-2.

a.n. **Anderson Mesa** Loc.: Sw. of Flagstaff 20 miles   Coconino
**Anderson Spring**       Map: B-8                      Coconino
**Anderson Point**                                     Coconino
Also called Truman Point by the Forest Service, after a
local settler.

Ref.:   11, pp. 23-24.

# ANGELL

El.: c. 5000'                         Loc.: Coconino 5, D-5.5
Pro.: /éynǰəl/
Trains used to take on water at this place, which is now a
section house. It was named for the first assistant superintendent of the A. & P.R.R.

Ref.:   Barnes. Maps: B-8; C-12.

# ANITA

El.: c. 6000'                         Loc.: Coconino 1, DE-13.8
The Anita Mines (T. 22 N., R. 2 E.) six miles west of this
small station were named by their owner, Ferd Nellis, after
a member of his family. The mines were first opened about
1898. The branch railroad to the Grand Canyon reached
Anita and ceased construction until 1899 (completed to
Rim September 1901). In the meantime, stages from Bass

Camp (q.v. Grand Canyon) met tourists here.

P.O. est. August 17, 1914. Grace E. Lockbridge, p.m. Discont.
August 31, 1918.

·Ref.:   Barnes; 168, p. 41; 93, p. 15; P.O. Records. Maps: C-
10; GC-9; D-1.

# ANTELOPE LAKE

El.: c. 7000'                         Loc.: Coconino 4, F-5.5
Among its measures to assure a water supply, the town of
Williams counts the effort in 1934 to create a lake by damming a site some seven miles to the southeast. The dam,
named Kennedy Dam in honor of James Kennedy (a
prominent citizen of Williams) was found by 1936 to have
a volcanic "sieve bottom," and efforts to make a satisfactory
lake were abandoned.

Ref.:   61, p. 147. Map: B-6.

# A ONE (A 1) MOUNTAIN

El.: 8300'                            Loc.: Coconino 4, IJ-5
The Arizona Cattle Company used the A 1 brand at this
location in the early 1890's. Capt. Ben Bullwinkle, a former
insurance fire patrol chief from Chicago, was company
manager. An inexperienced and wild horseman, Bullwinkle
customarily rode from the ranch headquarters into Flagstaff at full speed. In 1896 he rode a horse to its death on
the road to town. Bullwinkle was killed in the animal's
death plunge.

v.n. **A One Crater**

Ref.:   Barnes; Slipher. Maps: GC-3; GC-2.

a.n. **A 1 Ranch Spring**
Loc.:. Above Tanner Crossing on Little Colorado River, 5
miles.                                                Coconino

Ref.:   71, p. 158.

# APACHE MAID MOUNTAIN

El.: 7315'                            Loc.: Coconino 5, A-11
Pro.: /əpǽči/
The name of this mountain is one which naturally gives rise
to legends. One story says that c. 1873 troops from Camp
Verde fought Indians here, killing an Apache woman and
taking her baby to the fort with them. This agrees well with
the story of Saxton Seth Acker, called "Boss" Acker, who
moved to this place in 1884. His story was that a young
Apache girl came along with the troops from Camp Verde,
c. 1874, so it was decided to name the mountain for her. A
third version says that emigrants to the region set a scout
ahead to send up a "smoke" when he had found a route,
and when the fire was started, it attracted a lost and starving
young Apache girl who was adopted by one of the travelers.
In 1908 the Forest Service proposed changing the name to
Bronco Mountain, but was not successful.

Ref.:   Barnes; Bunch. Maps: C-9; GM-21.

a.n. **Bronco Mountain**       Maps: C-8; C-12          Coconino

# APEX

El.: c. 6000'                         Loc.: Coconino 1, E-13
This place was named because it is the highest on the Grand
Canyon branch of the railroad.

Ref.:   Barnes. Map: C-10.

## AREY

El.: c. 7000'                    Loc.: Coconino 4, H-5
This little station was named for R. J. Arey, engineer with
the Albuquerque and Arizona division of the S.F.R.R., with
headquarters at Williams in early 1905.
Ref.:   James R. Fuchs, Letter, April 30, 1956. Map: GC-3.

## ASHURST RUN

El.: c. 7000'                    Loc.: Coconino 5, C-8
Ashurst Run was the name given the ranch of William
Henry Ashurst, a pioneer cattleman in the 1870's. The
Ashurst family was a typical example of pioneer courage
and endurance. Ashurst was caught in a snowstorm while
away from the ranch, and during his absence his little
daughter choked to death, probably from diphtheria. Mrs.
Ashurst prepared the child for burial and made a coffin. Her
husband arrived, after a bitter struggle through the snow,
in time to help dig the small grave.
In 1900 Ashurst died of exhaustion when unable to extricate
himself from under a dislodged boulder while prospecting
in the Grand Canyon.
Ref.:   Henry Fountain Ashurst, Letter, December 12, 1955.
        Maps: B-8; GC-2.

a.n. Ashurst Lake        Map: B-8              Coconino
     Ashurst Spring      Map: B-8              Coconino

## AUBREY SPRING

El.: c. 6000'                    Loc.: Coconino 3, B-7.25
This spring was named for Francois X. Aubrey (cf Aubrey
Landing, Mohave).
Ref.:   Barnes. Map: C-12.

## BABBITT BILL TANK

El.: c. 6000'                    Loc.: Coconino 5, B-7.5
Babbitt Bill Tank was named for William Babbitt, who came
to Arizona in 1886 with his brother David. Three other
brothers — Charles J., George, and Edward J. — later joined
them. The Babbitt brothers were noted northern Arizona
cattlemen and merchants who owned and used the spring at
Babbitt Bill Tank.
v.n. Rabbit Bill Tank (corruption)
Ref.:   Kelly; 27, III. Maps: GM-1; GC-3.

a.n. Babbitt Spring      Map: GC-3             Coconino
     This location at the south end of Elden Mountain was first
     known as Elden Spring until one of the Babbitt brothers be-
     gan raising foxes and changed the name of the spring.
     "Elden Spring" then moved as a place name to the former
     Schulz Spring location.
     Ref.:   Sykes.
     Babbitts             Map: C-7             Coconino

## BADGER CREEK

El.: c. 3000'                    Loc.: Coconino 1, A-3-5
Jacob Hamblin, noted Mormon missionary, killed a badger
on this creek. The animal was carried to another nearby
creek and was put in a kettle to boil. By the next morning
the alkali in the water had combined with the animal fat
to form soap, from which the second creek took its name
of Soap Creek.

v.n. Clear Creek
     Spring Creek
Ref.:   Barnes; 4, p. 158. Map: GC-9.
a.n. Badger Canyon        Map: B-5             Coconino

## BAKER'S BUTTE

El.: 8077'                       Loc.: Coconino 5, C-14
In 1882 Lt. John G. Bourke, aide to Gen. George Crook,
told Will C. Barnes that this butte was named for an army
surgeon named Baecker. Locally, it is believed that the butte
was named for a man who owned and worked a mine here.
He was said to have had several Indian sons.
Ref.:   Barnes. Maps: GC-2; GC-9.
v.n. Baecker Butte              (E-20)

## BARBERSHOP CANYON

El.: c. 7000'                    Loc.: Coconino 5, E-13.5
A local stockman had a sheep shearing plant at a spring on
the east slope of the ridge bearing his name, Dick Hart
Ridge. One of his crew served as a barber for the men,
which resulted in the name of the canyon and of Barbershop
Spring.
Ref.:   Barnes. Maps: GC-2; GD-12.

## BAR M CANYON

El.: c. 6000'                    Loc.: Coconino 5, A-9
The Bar M cattle brand was used by Matt Burch, who ran
stock here.
Ref.:   Barnes. Map: B-8.
a.n. Bar M Spring        Map: B-8              Coconino

## BARNEY FLAT

El.: c. 5000'                    Loc.: Coconino 4, EF-6.3
George Barney started the Bar Heart cattle outfit here c.
1905.
Ref.:   Benham. Maps: B-6; GM-21.

## BARNEY PASTURE

El.: c. 5000'                    Loc.: Coconino 4, I-8
James Barney operated a horse ranch here. David and Peter
Strahan and John Loy helped Barney construct a fence
nearly four miles long between Sycamore and Oak Creek
Canyon to confine the horses to this large area. David
Strahan ran cattle in the same pasture.
Ref.:   Earl C. Slipher, Letter, February 29, 1956. Maps: B-6;
        GM-21.
a.n. Barney Ridge        Map: B-5              Coconino
     Barney Spring       Map: GM-21            Coconino

## BELLEMONT

El.: 7132'                       Loc.: Coconino 4, I-5
At first called Volunteer (cf. Volunteer Mountain), the
name of this small lumbering community on the A.T. & S.F.
R.R. was changed to Bellemont in September 1882. From
early territorial days, the site was the location of a stage
and relay station on the northern Arizona route. The ruins
of two inns still remained as late as 1930. The current name
is said to have been coined to honor Miss Belle Smith,

daughter of F. W. Smith, general superintendent in charge of railroad construction in the early 1880's.

P.O. est. March 2, 1887. Frank W. Payne, p.m. Discont. August 1, 1957. Wells Fargo Station, 1887.

Ref.: APHS Files; James R. Fuchs, quoting *Prescott Weekly Courier*, September 9, 1882, 2:3; Barnes; P.O. Records. Maps: GC-2; GC-3; C-6.

**a.n. Bellemont Prairie**     Map: GC-9     Coconino
Ref.: 139, p. 17.

## BIG SPRINGS

El.: 7850'     Loc.: Coconino 1, D-5
In 1882 Maj. Clarence Dutton wrote of a spring in Stewart's Canyon, stating that the Big Springs yielded "several times as much water as all the other" dozen springs known to exist on the Kaibab Plateau.

Ref.: 47, p. 130. Maps: GC-3; B-6; GC-9.

## BILL WILLIAMS MOUNTAIN

El.: 9256'     Loc.: Coconino 4, E-5.5
A double-peaked lava-cone formation, Bill Williams Mountain appears on the map made for the Sitgreaves' survey by Richard H. Kern in 1851. In Arizona during the year 1837, Antoine Leroux, a famous guide, met the rugged "mountain man" after whom the mountain is named. At that time Williams was in Arizona alone on the river which now bears his name. He had traveled through the Mogollon and Little Colorado River region, living off the land and trapping beaver. Leroux reports that Williams headed north across the Colorado River, thus completing his only known visit to what is now Arizona.

William Sherley Williams (b. North Carolina, January 3, 1787; d. March 14, 1849) served as an itinerant preacher for nine years, followed by twelve on the frontier and an additional seven as a plainsman and mountain man, according to Zebulon Pike, who knew him. Pike described Williams as a hunter and trapper who was tall, gaunt, red-headed, and said he was fairly well educated. While transporting baggage for the Fremont expedition, Williams was killed by Ute Indians in 1849. Two years later Kern used information given by Antoine Leroux in placing the name of Bill Williams on a mountain and a river in Arizona.

**v.n. Santa Maria**     (Disturnall Map, 1847)
**Jock-Ha-We-Ha**     (Mojave: "covered with cedar")
**Hue-ga-woo-la**     (Havasupai: "bear mountain")
**Ives Mountain**

Ref.: 135, p. 63; 92, pp. 379-380; 4, p. 321; 53, pp. 107, 18, 77, 144, 52, III, 292.
Maps: GC-2; E-22; GH-11; C-1.

**a.n. Bill Williams Fork**     Mohave
**Bill Williams River**     Map: GN-16     Mohave and Yuma
The Bill Williams River, or Bill Williams Fork, is formed by the junction of the Big Sandy (*q.v.,* Mohave) and the Santa Maria River (*q.v.,* Mohave). Bill Williams River forms the boundary line between Yuma and Mohave counties. In 1604 the river was called by Juan Mateo de Oñate, Rio de San Andres because Oñate first saw the stream on St. Andrew's day (November 30). In 1744 Jacobo Sedelmayr called the river the Rio Azul. On October 23, 1851, Lt. Lorenzo Sitgreaves noted that trappers called it Bill William's *(sic)* Fork.

**Williams Canyon**     Loc.: On Santa Maria River     Mohave
Where the Santa Maria River narrows to an eight-mile gorge, there is a canyon. It is sometimes called Banded Canyon because of the laminated gneisses and schists in its walls.

**Williams Fork**     (cf. Aubrey Landing, Mohave)     Mohave
Five votes were cast at this election precinct on November 8, 1870.
Ref.: William Todd, Letter (APHS).

**Williams Mountains**     Map: C-12     Mohave
Ref.: 7, p. 348; 150, p. 13; 100, pp. 54, 29.

## BISHOP SPRINGS

El.: c. 6000'     Loc.: Coconino 4, B-1. Near Bishop Lake
                 (Map: C-13)
Samuel A. Bishop (d. 1877) left Los Angeles in February 1859, to make his way east, where he met the exploring party under Lt. Edward Fitzgerald Beale. Bishop encountered the party at the San Francisco Mountains and took over part of the chore of handling the camels used by Beale. Beale went with Bishop and a small retinue to the Colorado River to obtain cached supplies, but found them gone and had to hurry to Los Angeles to obtain supplies for the entire expedition.

Years later Bishop died on the Upper Colorado from heat, exposure, and debility. He is buried at Kenyon Station.

Ref.: Samuel A. Bishop File, APHS; "Arrival of Lieut. Beale," *Weekly Alta California,* May 21, 1859. Map: None.

## BITTER SPRINGS

El.: c. 6000'     Loc.: Coconino 2, A-5
Despite the descriptive name, the water here is not as bad as one might conclude.

Ref.: Colton. Maps: GC-2; C-10.

## BLACK BILL PARK

El.: c. 6000'     Loc.: Coconino 5, B-4.5
William West (d. c. 1926), a bar keeper of Flagstaff, was known locally as "Black Bill." When the railroad surveyed to run rails north from the main line to the Grand Canyon, Black Bill speculated by homesteading a quarter section where the railroad had to go. The railroad, however, did not go through his land.

**v.n. Black Bill Flat**
Ref.: Colton. Map: B-8.

## BLACK FALLS

El.: c. 4500'     Loc.: Coconino 5, D-1
Lava fields at one time spread out west of the Little Colorado River with the result that tongues of malpais extend from the San Francisco Mountain group to several falls on the Little Colorado. At Black Falls the river runs over several fingers of black lava.

Ref.: 71, pp. 42, 43. Map: B-9.

**a.n. Black Knob**     Loc.: Near Long. 111°30'     Coconino
**v.n. 1. Pogue Butte**     (in Painted Desert)
       **2. Lava Butte**
       **3. Black Peak**
Ref.: 151, p. 149; 71, pp. 43, 190.

**Black Hills**     Loc.: East of San Franciso Mt.          Coconino
This is a thickly clustered group of small cones.
Ref.:   139, p. 16.

**Black Point**
Loc.: Upstream from Cameron 20 miles          Coconino
According to Navajo legend, the Western Clans stopped
here on their migration to Navajo Mountain.
Ref.:   71, p. 43; 167, p. 11.

## BLAZED RIDGE

El.: c. 7200'          Loc.: Coconino 5, CD-14.2-3
Trees on this ridge were blazed to mark the site of one of
the last Indian fights to take place in the vicinity of Pine.
Ref.:   Hart. Map: GD-11.

## BLUE CANYON

El.: c. 4000'          Loc.: Coconino 2, H-10.5
Blue Canyon, a trading post on Moenkopie Wash, takes its
name from a beautifully colored canyon (cf. Blue Can-
yon, Navajo). The post office was known as Algert, after
Charles H. Algert.
P.O. est. as Algert, March 27, 1900. Cirrilla E. Needham, p.m.
Discont. December 15, 1904.
Ref.:   Barnes; 4, p. 421; P.O. Records. Maps: GC-2; C-9
        (Algert).

## BLUE RIDGE

El.: c. 6000'          Loc.: Coconino 5, D-12
The angulation of this ridge from northwest to southeast
has placed it in a position so that the afternoon haze produces an unusual blue cast.
Ref.:   Keeley. Maps: GC-2; B-9; C-12.

**a.n. Blue Ridgels**          Map: B-9          Coconino
**Blue Mountain**     Loc.: T. 26 N., R. 9 W.          Coconino

## BLUE SPRING

El.: c. 5000'          Loc.: Coconino 2, C-10.5
Blue Spring is indigo colored. Its stream is reported to be
three feet deep and probably produces more water than any
other spring in Navajo country.
Ref.:   167, p. 173. Maps: GC-2; C-13.

## BLY

                       Loc.: Coconino 1, F-15
Fletcher D. Bly was a sheepman whose ranch extended from
Williams to the Grand Canyon.
Ref.:   Mrs. Nathan S. Bly, Notes (APHS). Map: GC-2.

## BODOWAY MESA

El.: c. 6000'          Loc.: Coconino 2, B-8.5
Pro.:  /bə?ádiwey/
*Ba adowe* was a Piute Indian chief who came with his band
into the Arizona Strip country c. 1850. His name was
applied to the area in which the group lived. The rendering
of the name is the Navajo pronunciation anglicized.

**v.n. Bodaway Mesa**

**Broadway Mesa (corruption)**
Ref.:   71, p. 42; 167, p. 14. Maps: GC-2; C-12.

## BONITA LAVA FLOW

El.: c. 6000'          Loc.: Coconino 5, B-3.5
Pro.:  /bʌníytə/
An indescribable jumble of lava rock, the Bonita Lava Flow
gives many viewers the feeling that they are sojourners on
the cold, dead surface of the moon. Long ago the volcanic
flow escaped from a vent melted through an older flow and
spread over a basin, leaving it piled with rough lava.
Ref.:   5, p. 7. Map: GC-2.

**a.n. Yaponcha Crater**
Loc.: At the central point of the flow          Coconino
Hopi legend says a crevice in the Bonita Lava Flow is the
home of their Wind God, Yaponcha.
Ref.:   5, p. 7.

## BOOT LAKE

El.: c. 8000'          Loc.: Coconino 5, C-8
This lake is descriptively named because it is shaped like a
long hip boot. It used to be called Borne Lake, but the reason for the former name is not known.
Ref.:   Barnes. Maps: C-13; C-10 (Lake Borne); C-6 (Lake
        Born).

## BOTTOMLESS PITS

El.: c. 5000'          Loc.: Coconino 5, A-5.5
In the early 1880's when the A. & P.R.R. tracks were laid
here without a culvert to allow drainage under the tracks,
trash gradually accumulated. Eventually it formed a dam
which backed up to create a lake south of the roadbed. One
night c. 1888 Stanley Sykes camped at this small lake in
order to avoid danger to his horse from loco weed farther
along the route. During the night he heard a weird sucking
noise and in the morning noted that the lake had dropped
about two feet. It continued to drop rapidly. The bottom of
the limestone basin had dissolved under the accumulated
water, permitting it to drop through. Sykes gave the name to
the locality.
Ref.:   Sykes; 139, p. 16. Maps: B-8; GC-2.

## BRECKENRIDGE SPRING

El.: 8000'          Loc.: Coconino 4, FG-3.5
On September 13, 1857, Lt. Edward Fitzgerald Beale passed
north of Mount Sitgreaves and while en route to Mount
Kendrick passed two springs, issuing from the north side of
Sitgreaves. He named the first Breckenridge and the second
Porter, after members of his party. Breckenridge, Jr., was
in charge of Beale's camels at the beginning of the expedi-
tion.
Ref.:   12, pp. 51-52. Map: None.

**a.n. Porter Spring**          Map: B-9          Coconino

## BURNED PUEBLO

El.: c. 5000'          Loc.: Coconino 5, E-3.5
Pro.:  /pwéblo/
This prehistoric ruin contains adobe melted by intense heat
from the burning of stored corn. Visitors have often taken
the adobe to be lava. The name refers to a fire which
obviously occurred here in the remote past.
Ref.:   29, p. 41. Map: D-1.

## CALL OF THE CANYON

El.: c. 4000'                    Loc.: Coconino 4, I-7
The ruins of Zane Grey's log cabin are still to be found at
the place where Grey wrote *The Call of the Canyon*. The
place was the "Lola Mae" Lodge (not on the property of
the Call of the Canyon Resort) where Grey was a guest
while doing his writing. It is just across the creek from Call
of the Canyon.

Ref.: Schnebly; Mrs. Florence Smythe, Call of the Canyon
Resort, Letter, June 11, 1957. Map: D-1.

## CAMERON

El.: 4200'                       Loc.: Coconino 2, C-14
In 1911 when the bridge across the Little Colorado River
was built, Scott Preston, a Navajo, had a store where
Cameron is today. In the same year Hubert Richardson be-
gan a settlement and named it for U. S. Senator Ralph
Cameron, last territorial delegate for Arizona to the U. S.
Congress (cf. Bright Angel Creek, Grand Canyon).

P.O. est. July 7, 1917. Elizabeth Halderman, p.m.
Ref.: 4, p. 285; 167, p. 16; P.O. Records. Map: C-12.

## CANYON LODGE

El.: c. 6000'                    Loc.: Coconino 5, E-6.5
Descriptive.

P.O. est. November 20, 1924. Earl M. Cundiff, p.m. Discont.
May 14, 1926.
Ref.: P.O. Records. Map: F-3.

## CARR LAKE

El.: c. 7000'                    Loc.: Coconino 5, F-15
Originally called Lake No. 2, this was renamed by cowboys
c. 1886 for E. R. Carr, general manager of the Waters Cattle Company.

Ref.: Barnes. Maps: B-9; B-7; GC-2.

## CASNER MOUNTAIN

El.: 6843'                       Loc.: Coconino 4, H-7.5
Pro.: /kǽzner/
G. R. Casner grazed sheep here in early days.

v.n. Cashner Cabin
Ref.: Lester. Map: GC-2.
a.n. Casner Park           Map: GM-21           Coconino
    Casner Cabin           Map: GC-3            Coconino

## CASTLE BUTTE

El.: c. 6000'                    Loc.: Coconino 2, E-10
Descriptive.

Ref.: Barnes. Maps: GC-2; C-12.

## CATARACT CANYON

El.: c. 1500'                    Loc.: Coconino 1, A-10
There is a series of beautiful waterfalls on the creek in this
canyon (cf. Havasu Canyon, Grand Canyon).

v.n. Rio de San Antonio
    (Garcés, 1774) McClintock thinks this is the same as Cata-
    ract Cascade Canyon.
    Cascade Creek    (Ives, 1858). Map: E-4

Havasu Canyon
Ref.: Barnes. Maps: B-5; GC-2.
a.n. Cataract Creek          Map: B-4            Coconino
    Fr. Francisco Garcés on June 19, 1775, called this the Rio
    Jabesúa.
Ref.: 113, p. 11.
    Cataract Plains                               Coconino
    Loc.: Extend from Red Butte to Valle n. to Fraziers' Well
    and Cataract Canyon.
Ref.: Morse.

## CEDAR RIDGE

El.: c. 6000'                    Loc.: Coconino 2, B-8
This small trading post is situated on top of a high ridge
covered with juniper and piñon. There used to be a Cedar
Ranch about twenty-one miles north of Flagstaff where the
two stage routes to Grand Canyon joined.

Ref.: 167, p. 28; 4, p. 285; *Arizona Enterprise*, October 6,
1892, 1:5-6, Map of G.C. region. Maps: GB-2; C-12.

## CHALENDER

El.: c. 7000'                    Loc.: Coconino 4, G-5
Pro.: /čǽlənder/
George F. Chalender was Superintendent of Motive Power
for the A. & P.R.R.

P.O. est. May 2, 1883. Harry L. Harris, p.m. Discont. August
27, 1897.

v.n. Challendar
Ref.: Barnes; P.O. Records. Maps: GC-2; B-4; C-6.
a.n. Chalender Lake          Map: B-8            Coconino

## CHARLIE DAY SPRING

El.: 5000'                       Loc.: Coconino 2, DE-10.9.
                                 Outskirts of Tuba City.
The spring takes its name from the nearby hogan of Charlie
Day, a blind Navajo, who once served as an army scout. In
the summer of 1928, Charlie Day Spring was developed and
walled with concrete. Fossils of bison, camels and elephants
were found in the spring while the work was progressing.

Ref.: 164, pp. 1-2. Map: None.

## CHAVES PASS (sic)

El.: c. 6000'                    Loc.: Coconino 5, D-11
Pro.: /šávez/
Col. J. Francisco Chavez was a member of New Mexico
Cavalry Volunteers, 1861-1864. In 1863 he commanded
the military escort for the first gubernatorial party to arrive
in Arizona Territory. Later Col. Chaves (sic) was ordered to
locate a shorter route to Prescott via Antelope Springs
(Flagstaff). The Chaves Road ran from Camp Verde to the
Little Colorado River near the present Winslow, going
through the pass which bears his name. A way station was
in the pass.

v.n. Chavez Pass
    Chevez Pass
    Jarvis Pass (corruption)
    Snow Lake
    Scene of a cavalry fight with Indians, November 25, 1875.
Ref.: 85, p. 441; 87, p. xxxvi. Maps: GB-2; B-8; C-4.

a.n. **Chaves Crossing**        Map: B-8              Coconino
   **Chaves Pass Ruin**                                Coconino
   The Hopi call this Chubwichalobi (q.v.).
   **Chave (sic) Spring**     Map: B-7              Coconino
Ref.:   167, p. 37.

## CHUBWICHALOBI

El.: c. 6000′                   Loc.: Coconino 5, GH-10-11.
                                      20 m. s.w. Winslow.
                                Hopi: "antelope notch place"
On the hill above Chavez Pass lie ruined pueblos which the
Hopi say were built by their ancestors.
**v.n. Chavez Pass Ruin**
Ref.:   88, I, 293. Map: None.

## CIENEGA CANYON

El.: c. 8000′                   Loc.: Coconino 5, C-14
Pro.:  /sénəkiy/               Spanish:   "marshy place"
Descriptive.
Ref.:   Hart. Map: B-9.

## CINCH HOOK BUTTE

El.: 7427′                      Loc.: Coconino 5, B-14
As early as 1890, settlers called the butte by this name because of its cinch hook shape, which shows up clearly on
topographical maps.
Ref.:   Barnes. Maps: B-8; GC-2; GD-11.

## CITADEL, THE

El.: c. 5000′                   Loc.: Coconino 5, B-1
A pueblo ruin which apparently at one time was a fortification of fifty or more rooms, the Citadel occupies the top of
a small mesa visible for miles. The name is descriptive of its
former function and commanding position. It is in Wupatki
National Monument.
Ref.:   29, p. 28; 5, David L. Jones, "Red Ruins in the Black
        Cinder," Illustration, p. 4. Map: D-1.

## CLARK VALLEY

El.: c. 7000′                   Loc.: Coconino 5, B-7
John Clark (b. Maine, March 13, 1839) at one time was a
settler here. Clark migrated to California in 1859 where he
raised sheep. When the railroad spoiled the free range there,
Clark moved his five thousand sheep to Arizona. Two
thousand perished during the three month's trip. Clark remained near the present-day Williams for a year (until
1877) when he settled in Clark Valley. He stayed here
until 1883. During wet years, this section of the valley is
covered by Lake Mary.
**v.n. Clark's Valley**
Ref.:   APHS Place Names File; 112, III. Map: GC-2.

## CLARKVILLE

                                Loc.: Not known
The name is that of the post master.
P.O. est. December 15, 1898. Marion Clark, p.m. Discont.?
Ref.:   P.O. Records. Map: None.

## CLAY PARK

El.: c. 6367′                   Loc.: Coconino 5, A-9
Ben Clay located at this spot in the early 1880's. At that
time it was called Jack's Ranch (cf. Jack's Canyon, Yava-

pai). Many people now call this place Powell Park, for
William Dempsey Powell, who came to Arizona in 1875.
Ref.:   Barnes; Schnebly; Frier. Maps: GM-21.

## CLIFFS

El.: c. 5000′                   Loc.: Coconino 5, A-5
Nearby cliff dwellings give this location its name.
P.O. est. August 9, 1907. James M. Rose, p.m. Discont. Jan-
uary 31, 1916.
Ref.:   Barnes; P.O. Records. Maps: C-21; GC-3.

## CLINTS WELL

El.: c. 5000′                   Loc.: Coconino 5, C-13
Named for Clint Wingfield, who was killed by the bandit
Black Jack Ketcham (See Black Jack Canyon, Greenlee).
Ref.:   Hart. Maps: B-9; GB-2.

## CLOSTERMEYER LAKE

El.: c. 5000′                   Loc.: Coconino 4, I-1.5
William Clostermeyer was a pioneer who settled here.
Ref.:   APHS Place Names File. Maps: GC-2; C-12; B-9 (Klo-
        stermeyer).

## COAL MINE CANYON

El.: c. 6000′                   Loc.: Coconino 2, EF-13-11
Coal is mined just below the rim at the head of a west fork
of this canyon. Odd and variegated formations dot the canyon, the sands of which are used by Navajo medicine men
in sand paintings.
**v.n. Coal Canyon**
Ref.:   4, p. 413; 29, p. 47; 128, p. 42; 167, p. 42. Map: D-4.

## COCKS COMB

El.: c. 7000′                   Loc.: Coconino 1, G-8
Descriptive.
Ref.:   Barnes. Map: B-5.

## COCONINO NATIONAL FOREST
## (and KAIBAB NATIONAL FOREST)

                 Loc.: Central portion of Coconino County.
Pro.:  /kowkəníynow/        /kaybæb/
Coconino National Forest was formed on July 2, 1908,
from parts of Black Mesa (established August 17, 1898),
Tonto, and Grand Canyon Forest Reserves (established
February 20, 1893), and all of the San Francisco Mountains Forest Reserve (established August 17, 1898). The
word "reserve" in the original names held an implication of
resources withdrawn from use by the people, and this resulted in misunderstanding of the purpose of the forestry
program. The term was dropped and "national forest" substituted. Present acreage is 1,915,850.
Tusayan National Forest (1,141,259 acres) was established
on June 28, 1910, from the western part of Coconino
National Forest. Meanwhile, Kaibab National Forest was
taking shape, being formed from part of Grand Canyon
National Forest (north of the Colorado River) on May 22,
1908. On July 2, 1908, Kaibab was formally created. Dixie
National Forest (Mohave) was added to it on March 18,
1924. Tusayan National Forest went out of existence as an
entity when it was consolidated with Kaibab National Forest

on August 4, 1934. Today Kaibab National Forest has a gross area of 1,999,470 acres, of which 194,070 are privately owned.

Headquarters for both Coconino and Kaibab National Forests are at Williams.

Ref.: Bade; Keeney; 120, pp. 30, 34, 35. Maps: B-9; GC-3; GD-12.

## COFFEE CREEK

El.: c. 6000'  Loc.: Coconino 4, I-7
Slurring of the original name of Coffer Creek has resulted in the present local name Coffee Creek. Coffer is supposed to have lived in the area many years ago.

Ref: Barnes; MNA. Map: B-1.

## COLCORD SPRING

El.: c. 6000'  Loc.: Coconino 4, G-7.5
Pro.: /kálkerd/
Col. W. R. Colcord settled near Potato Butte c. 1886, moving up the Mogollon Rim about a year later, where the spring took on his name.

Ref.: Woody (information from *Hoofs and Horns,* July 1886). Map: B-6.

## COLEMAN LAKE

El.: 5526'  Loc.: Coconino 4, F-6
T. A. ("Dad") Coleman is probably the same Coleman who in 1875 left Visalia, California, driving thousands of sheep to this location in Arizona. When he arrived, he still had four thousand sheep despite very heavy losses along the route.

On May 12, 1876, he settled at the place which bears his name, building a dam to impound runoff water.

v.n. Collins Ranch  Map: C-4
  McCullum Ranch
    Correct spelling should be McCollum, after Nehemiah McCollum, who settled near Coleman's place in 1878 or 1879. (cf. McCollum Ranch).

Ref.: Fuchs, Letter, April 30, 1956; Benham; Mark Smith; 61, p. 50, (Note 83); p. 53. Map: B-5.

## CORE RIDGE

El.: c. 10,500'  Loc.: Coconino 5, A-4
The prominent ridge between Fremont Saddle (10,800') and Mount Humphrey (12,794') is a true core of rocks which fill the vents through which, long ago, lava and ashes burst to create the higher peak.

Ref.: 29, p. 61. Map: None.

## CORN CREEK

El.: c. 3500'  Loc.: Coconino 5, G-5
Both Hopi and Navajo Indians have long used this area for raising corn.

Ref.: 71, p. 39. Map: GC-2.

## CORVA

El.: c. 6000'  Loc.: Coconino 4, CD-4.8
Pro.: /kórvə/  Spanish: "ham"; "ham shaped"
Section station on railroad. A butte nearby is so shaped that the name *Corva* is descriptive.

Ref.: Barnes. Map: B-4.

## COSNINO CAVES

El.: c. 5000'  Loc.: Coconino 5, B-5.5
Pro.: /kazníyno/
"Cosnino" is the name applied by the Hopi to the Havasupai Indians (cf. Havasu Canyon, Grand Canyon).

Lt. Amiel W. Whipple in 1853 was the first white man known to have visited the caves and the nearby natural water tanks. He called the caves Cosnino Caves after Indians then living in the vicinity.

On September 10, 1857, Lt. Edward Fitzgerald Beale noted the "Cosnurio Caves" in his journal, describing them as being large and divided into apartments by walls. They were then still being used by Indians. Beale also calls them the "Cosmino Caves," and discusses on February 10, 1858, visiting the water tank about a quarter of a mile distant (sec. 35, T. 22 N., R. 9 E), the Turkey Tanks, an important water hole on the route to points along the Little Colorado River. Later (c. 1873) Capt. George M. Wheeler called the caves the Coconino Caves.

Ref.: 12, pp. 48-49; 177, p. 168; 178, p. 181; 29, p. 41; 88, I, 538; 175, III, 629; 167, p. 100. Maps: GC-9; E-11.
a.n. Cosnino  Loc.: Near Cosnino Caves  Coconino
    This is a section house on the railroad.
  Coconino  Loc.: On r.r. to Grand Canyon  Coconino

## CRATER

El.: c. 5800'  Loc.: Coconino 5, FG-6.8
The location of this point close to Meteor Crater is suggestive of the possibility that the post office may have existed in connection with operations at the crater, but this has not been definitely established as yet.

P.O. est. December 23, 1920. Dorothy E. Hogue, p.m. Discont. July 15, 1921.

Ref.: P.O. Records. Map: F-3.

## CUMMINGS MESA

El.: c. 6000'  Loc.: West of Forbidding (Bridge) Canyon, partially in Utah.
Cummings Mesa was named for Byron Cummings (d. May 21, 1954), a well-known archeologist who accompanied John Wetherill and a man named Berheimer on a trip to Rainbow Natural Bridge (Utah). Cummings is said to have been the first white man to see the huge arch.

Ref.: 65, p. 237; 76, p. 7. Map: None.

## DANE CABIN

El.: c. 7000'  Loc.: Coconino 5, F-15
Frank Dane was a sheepman here c. 1920 or a little earlier.

Ref.: Hart. Maps: B-7; GO-12.
a.n. Dane Canyon  Maps: B-9; GD-12  Coconino
  Dane Ridge  Maps: B-9; GD-12  Coconino
  Dane Spring  Maps: B-9; B-6  Coconino

## DAVENPORT HILL

El.: c. 7500'  Loc.: Coconino 4, F-5.5
James Davenport (d. November 30, 1947) lived in Williams after terminating his ranch activities south of the town, c. 1891. Davenport Lake is a wet weather lake which Jim Davenport at one time attempted to drain by cutting a ditch, but he was unsuccessful.

Ref.:   Fuchs, Letter, quoting the *Williams News,* December 4,
1947; Kennedy; Benham. Maps: B-6; GC-2.

**a.n. Davenport Peak**   Loc.: Sec. 36, T. 8N., R. 7 E.          Yavapai
A "Jake" Davenport is reported to have lived here in the
1870's.

**Davenport Ranch**                                    Maricopa
**Davenport Wash**
           Maps: GG-3; GM-19      Maricopa and Yavapai

## DAZE
El.: c. 6500'                        Loc.: Coconino 5, D-10-5
Pro.: /dá<zi˄/
William Daze (d. c. 1938) was an old-time railroad engineer who was promoted to road foreman, then to master
mechanic. At his own request he returned to being a road
foreman, a position he held until his death. Little remains
today to show that Daze ran sheep here in the 1880's.

Ref.:   Slamon; Kelly. Map: B-8.

**a.n. Daze Lake**       Map: B-8                    Coconino

## DEADMAN FLAT
El.: c. 6000'                        Loc.: Coconino 5, A-2
Any location with the name "Deadman" is a temptation to
the tellers of tall tales. Stories about Deadman Flat are no
exception, ranging from an account of an attack by Indians
on men who were driving horses between California and
Colorado (a fracas which resulted in the death of one Indian), all the way to a legend about a foreigner — scarcely
able to speak English—who wandered into Flagstaff seeking
help for his sick companion whom he had left alone on the
trail. His partner was found murdered when a rescue party
finally reached him.
A straightforward account is that of W. H. Switzer of Flagstaff, who as a boy of fourteen knew a trapper who asked
young Switzer to accompany him on a trip. The boy refused. The trapper with his pack horse set out for the flats
where he set his traps. However, his horse got loose. When
the trapper's body was found propped up against that of
his dead horse, the story was easy to reconstruct by following the telltale tracks. Apparently the trapper tried for hours
to catch the animal, with the horse keeping just out of reach.
Finally the man shot the horse. Then he sat down with his
back against the horse and shot himself.

Ref.:   29, p. 28; 4, p. 285; Barnes; Switzer; Anderson. Maps:
C-12 (Deadman's Wash); GB-2.

**a.n. Deadman Wash**    Maps: GC-3; C-12           Coconino
**Deadman Tank**    Map: GC-3                Coconino
**Deadman Wells**   Map: GC-3                Coconino

## DEER LAKE
El.: c. 5000'                        Loc.: Coconino 5, G-15
This lake was a favorite watering place for deer. F. Pius
ran horses at Deer Lake and used it for camping in early
days. Travelers on the Verde road used it as a stopping
place.

Ref.:   Barnes. Maps: B-7; B-9; GC-2.

## DENNISON
El.: 5002'                           Loc.: Coconino 5, G-6.8
An early settler named Dennison is said to have lived close

to this point on the railroad. Barnes, however, says it may
have been named for a man called Denny who was an assistant roadmaster for the railroad for a number of years.

Ref.:   106, p. 31; Barnes. Map: GC-9.

## DEVIL DOG HILLS
El.: c. 5000'                        Loc.: Coconino 4, D-6
Locally, it is said that the name may come from the fact
that these hills are extremely rough.

Ref.:   Benham. Map: GC-2.

**a.n. Devil Dog Tank**       Map: B-6              Coconino

## DIABLO, CANYON
El.: 5429'                           Loc.: Coconino 5, E-6
Pro.:  /kænyən dáyblo/ or         Spanish: "Devil's Canyon"
       /kæn yən di˄ablo/
Lt. Edward Fitzgerald Beale on September 8, 1857, wrote
that Cañon Diablo was so referred to by his guide and that
its gorge was an obstacle that could not be crossed, thus
causing his party to deviate about forty miles to the west
from its intended path.
F. W. Voltz (cf. Woolf Crossing) opened a trading post
here in the 1890's.
The first known meteorites in northern Arizona were found
in 1886 by sheepherders near Canyon Diablo, about two
miles west of Meteor Crater *(q.v.).*
P.O. est. November 15, 1886. Charles H. Algert, p.m. Discont.
February 28, 1918. Wells Fargo Station 1885.

**v.n. Canon Diable**

Ref.:   12, p. 46; 59, p. 19. Maps: C-6 (Trading Post of Canyon
Diablo); C-5; GC-2; B-8; E-11 (Cañon Diablo).

## DINOSAUR CANYON
El.: c. 3000'                        Loc.: Coconino 2, C-13
Three-toed dinosaur tracks were discovered here in 1928 by
Hubert Richardson. An American Museum of Natural His-
tory Expedition checked this in 1929. The tracks are esti-
mated to be three million years old.

Ref.:   167, p. 51; 4, p. 413. Map: D-1.

## DONEY PARK
El.: c. 7000'                        Loc.: Coconino 5, B-4
Pro.:  /dówni˄/
Originally called Deadman Flat, this area may have a story
connected with it which has since become confused with
one told about the present Deadman Flat *(q.v.).* Ben Doney
(d. 1932) settled on the flat, giving it the name Doney Park.
A northern Civil War veteran, Doney came west to prospect. The four little craters northwest of Wupatki where he
did most of his prospecting are known as Doney Craters.
Doney had heard a legend about a Spanish mine at a red
hill near a blue mountain. He spent his life digging the bottoms out of Indian pit houses, thinking them to be openings
to old mine shafts.
P.O. est. May 16, 1922. Frank J. Smith, p.m. Discont. May 31,
1924.

Ref.:   29, p. 27; 139, p. 35; 167, p. 51; Bartlett; P.O. Records;
MNA. Maps: B-8; GC-2.

**a.n. Doney Mountain**                              Coconino
**v.n. Doneys Cone**

## DOVE SPRING

El.: c. 7000'                    Loc.: Coconino 5, C-9
Great flocks of wild doves give this place its name.
Ref.:   Barnes. Map: B-8.

## DOYLE SADDLE

El.: c. 9000'                    Loc.: Coconino 5, A-4
This is the saddle connecting Agassiz and Fremont Peaks.
Allen Doyle (b. Detroit 1850; d. 1920) was a cattleman
and a guide. He came to Prescott, Arizona, as a miner.
From there in 1881 he drove cattle to Flagstaff.
Ref.:   Slipher; Barnes; 112, III; Map: GC-2.

**a.n.** Doyle Peak        Map: B-4                    Coconino

## DRY BEAVER CREEK

El.: c. 7000'                    Loc.: Coconino 5, A-10
The name arose to differentiate this stream bed, which was
often dry, from that which it joined, which, never being
dry, was called Wet Beaver Creek (Yavapai).
Ref.:   Barnes. Maps: GN-21 (Wet Beaver); C-9; GC-2.

## DRY LAKE

El.: 7020'                       Loc.: Coconino 5, G-16
The shallow lake on top of Dry Lake Mountain fills with
water in the rainy season, but normally the lake is dry.
Locally the mountain is sometimes called Little Mount
Elden, which is a misnomer since its location is not correct
for such a name. The five small volcanic cones which com-
prise the Dry Lake Hills lie between San Francisco and
Elden Mountain.
Ref.:   Colton; 139, p. 70. Maps: B-9; GC-3.

**a.n.** Dry Lake Hills       Map: GC-3                   Coconino
     Dry Lake Wash       Map: B-8                    Coconino

## DUTTON HILL

El.: 7666'                       Loc.: Coconino 4, H-7
Maj. Clarence E. Dutton was a geologist who explored the
Grand Canyon in 1880. This may be the same hill which is
now called Sliker Hill after Gene A. Sliker (d. c. 1954), a
resident of Flagstaff.
Ref.:   Barnes; Conrad. Map: GC-3.

## EAGLE NEST MOUNTAIN

El.: c. 6000'                    Loc.: Coconino 4, B-3
Named by a cattleman who found an eagle's nest in the
cliffs of this prominent butte.
Ref.:   Barnes. Maps: GC-2; B-4.

## EBERT MOUNTAIN

El.: c. 7000'                    Loc.: Coconino 4, H-1
J. Franklin Ebert (b. 1851; d. September 21, 1907) came
to Arizona in 1870, raising stock and spending the remainder of his life in the Flagstaff and Williams areas.
Ref.:   Fuchs, Letter, quoting *Williams News*, September 21,
        1907; May 9, 1908. Maps: GC-2; B-8.

**a.n.** Ebert Spring         Map: B-4                    Coconino

## ECHO CLIFFS

El.: 5360'                       Loc.: Coconino 2, AC-4-6
These cliffs lie near Echo Peak on the east side of the Colorado River opposite the mouth of the Paria near Lee's
Ferry. Frederick Dellenbaugh relates how for amusement
he shot his Remington revolver into the river. The resulting
violent report was followed by silence and the echoing and
re-echoing of the sound began "with a rattle like that of
musketry." Powell's party then named the place Echo
Peaks.
Another name for the long line of strikingly colored cliffs
is better known today — Vermillion Cliffs — which is the
name given to them by Maj. John Wesley Powell.
Ref.:   41, pp. 150-151; 132, pp. 112-113; 42, pp. 292-293.
        Maps: C-12; C-3.

## ELDEN MOUNTAIN

El.: 9280'                       Loc.: Coconino 5, A-5
The mountain was named because of Elden Spring at its
base. The spring in turn was named after a sheepman who
established headquarters here in the early 1880's when he
had a contract to cut ties for the new railroad. Two of his
children died during the relatively brief time Elden was
located here, and their bodies are buried near the spring.
Elden had moved on by 1883. The volcanic summit of
Mount Elden, as it is often called, is north of the spring.
According to one source, Elden Spring is the same as San
Francisco Spring on the trail laid out by Maj. G. B. Willis
in 1862 (cf. Babbitt Bill Tank, *a.n.* Babbitt Spring).
Ref.:   151, p. 285; Switzer; Anderson; 167, p. 142. Maps: GC-
        3; B-8; B-6; C-10.

**a.n.** Elden Pueblo
     Loc., E. of Flagstaff 6 miles on Hwy. 66.      Coconino
     Only the ruins of the walls remain standing.
     Little Elden Spring   Map: B-8                Coconino
     Bear Spring           Map: B-6                Coconino
     Barnes says Lt. Edward Fitzgerald Beale gave this name to
     what is now Elden Spring, four miles northeast of Flagstaff.
Ref.:   77, p. 1; 4, p. 317.

## ELEPHANT LEGS

El.: c. 5000'                    Loc.: Coconino 2, G-8
It takes no more than a glance at these huge eroded formations to note their resemblance to the massive legs and big-
toed feet of elephants.
Ref.:   None. Maps: GC-9; D-1; C-13.

## ESPEJO SPRING

El.: c. 5000'                    Loc.: Coconino 2, D-12.5
Pro.:  /espéyho/        Spanish: "mirror; windowpane"
Herbert Gregory gave this name to the spring to honor
Antonio de Espejo, who explored in this country in 1582
(cf. Jerome, Yavapai).
Ref.:   71, p. 191; 151, p. 293. Maps: GC-2; D-4.

## FAIN MOUNTAIN

El.: c. 7000'                    Loc.: Coconino 5, A-10
William Fain ran the 16 brand here, using Fain Spring at
the foot of the mountain. Sixteen Springs takes its name
from the brand.
Ref.:   Barnes. Maps: GC-2; B-9 (Sixteen Springs).

## FAIR VIEW

El.: c. 6000'          Loc.: Coconino 4, C-5
Descriptive.

Ref.: Barnes. Map: C-12.

## FERN MOUNTAIN

El.: c. 9000'          Loc.: Coconino 4, I-4
Otto Platten named this mountain because of the bracken which grows heavily on its slopes.

Ref.: Colton. Map: B-4.

## FIVEMILE LAKE

El.: c. 5000'          Loc.: Coconino 5, G-14.5
This lake lies five miles from the Mogollon Rim. This name was not in use until after 1895.

**v. n. Five Mile Lake**

Ref.: Barnes. Maps: B-9; GD-11.

**a.n. Five Mile Pass**          Map: B-8          Coconino

## FLAGSTAFF

El.: 6894'          Loc.: Coconino 5, A-5.5
Many legends surround the name of this northern Arizona city. The first settler was Edward Whipple, who operated a saloon near Flagstaff Spring in 1871. In 1876 the second white man to settle in the area arrived. He was F. F. Mc-Millen, who settled north of the present Flagstaff. On earlier military maps, the only springs noted in this area are Leroux Spring and San Francisco Spring, but on G.L.O. 1879 appears the name Antelope Spring, which was probably that used by McMillen.

A few months after McMillen arrived, a group of scouts camped near the spring. They were the advance party for a contingent of settlers who had signed up in Boston as prospective settlers in the West. The scouting group found an open valley in which was a lone pine. The tree was too great a temptation to be passed by, so the youths lopped off its branches, placed a leather hoop at the top and ran an American flag up the pole. A clipping (no date or name of paper given) in the State Library files said in a story written by Al Doyle of Flagstaff that the flag was raised late in May 1876. Others claim it was raised to celebrate the centenary of the signing of the Declaration of Independence. In any event, the emigrants did not remain in the area, but pushed westward. A third version is that a military detachment en route may have been responsible for stripping a tree and thus creating a flagstaff. Earl O. Slipher of Flagstaff has an old photograph which shows such a topped tree with a plank nailed to it and with signs of having had a flag attached to the tree. This is authenticated by the reminiscences of Lee Newman, a pioneer, who told of seeing such a tree west and north of Old Town Spring, near the point of the present Mars Hill. Newman was acquainted with all the original settlers in the area, who numbered fewer than twenty in 1880. A fourth account, written five years after Flagstaff was established, states definitely that the flagstaff was still one mile east of town and that it had been erected by Lt. E. F. Beale's men in 1859. Five years later (1892) the pole was gone.

The name of the spring at the old location underwent several changes, starting with Antelope, then Flagstaff, and then — with the creation of the new town on the railroad — becoming Old Town Spring. In 1882 there were ten buildings at Old Town, but in 1883 business moved to the new railroad depot and by 1884 Old Town was almost deserted. When the post office was established at the new location, the name Flagstaff was a natural choice.

In 1891 Flagstaff became the seat of the newly-created Coconino County.

P.O. est. February 21, 1881. Thomas McMellon, p.m. Wells Fargo Station, 1885. Incorporated as a town, June 4, 1894; as a city, 1928.

**v.n. Beachville**

This name was given by the railroad to honor C. W. Beach of Prescott, but the name did not take hold.

Ref.: 4, p. 189; 167, p. 55; 127, p. 159; 55, p. 578; 162, p. 6; *Arizona Journal Miner*, April 10, 1899, 4:2; *Arizona Gazette*, May 6, 1881, 3:1 (Beachville).

George H. Tinker, *A Land of Sunshine: Flagstaff and Its Surroundings* (1887).

Maps: C-6; GC-3.

**a.n. Milltown**          Loc:. Now part of Flagstaff          Coconino

The sawmill settlement east of Flagstaff was named Milton by Michael J. Riordan to honor the poet Milton. Riordan wanted to call the connecting road to Flagstaff "Mike's Pike," but Flagstaff residents called it Milltown Road, and Milton came to be known as Milltown.

**Agassiz**          Coconino

Loc.: R.r. station at Milton. See above. Map GC-3.

Ref.: Slipher.

## FLOYD, MOUNT

El.: 7446'          Loc.: Coconino 4, A-3
On October 4, 1857, Lt. Edward Fitzgerald Beale wrote that he had named this place Floyd's Peak. John B. Floyd at that time was Secretary of War and later transmitted Beale's report to the Speaker of the House (May 10, 1858). Floyd was also responsible for the organization of the Ives Expedition to determine the navigability of the Colorado River. However, in view of Beale's habit of naming places for members of the expedition, this was probably named for Dr. Floyd, the expedition physician.

Ref.: 12, p. 66; 52, pp. 11, 17. Maps: C-12; C-2.

## FOREST LAGOONS

El.: c. 7500'          Loc.: Coconino 3, B-5
The lagoons were evidently flood-water lakes in the pine forest on a trail made by Lt. Joseph Christmas Ives, who gave them the name; they lay at his Camp 74.

Ref.: Barnes; 121, p. 110. Map: E-20.

## FORT VALLEY

El.: 7400'          Loc.: Coconino 4, I-7-4.7
Leroux Spring (q.v.) in 1877 became the location of John W. Young, a son of Brigham Young, who with members of his party built a cabin. When the A. & P.R.R. tracks were being laid in 1881, Young contracted to make ties, as did also over fifty other Mormon workers who pitched their tents on what they called LeRoux Prairie. Reports of

Apache Indians on the warpath led the group to erect a log house sixty feet long, forming one side of a stockade one hundred feet square made of railroad ties. Young named the structure Fort Moroni, after the Angel Moroni of the *Book of Mormon*. (Said to have been a mortal who died c. 421 A.D. Moroni kept a legend of his people on gold plates which he buried near Palmyra, New York, which Joseph Smith discovered and translated into the *Book of Mormon*.)

When the transitory threat of Indian attack had passed, Young used the fort as headquarters for his Moroni Cattle Company and to house his six wives. A photograph of the place shows a line of six rooms, each with a separate door. In 1883 Young sold the Moroni Cattle Company to the Arizona Cattle Company (A-1 Cattle Company) and the name of the place was changed to Fort Rickerson in honor of Charles L. Rickerson, treasurer of the cattle company.

When the first forest experiment station in the United States was set up here in 1908, Prof. J. G. Lemmon suggested the name be changed to De la Vergne Park, but the name did not take hold. The old fort was torn down in 1920. Today the area is known simply as Fort Valley.

v.n. Fort Maroni

Ref.: Slipher; 112, pp. 153, 154; 92, p. 377; 29, p. 49. Maps: C-6 (Fort Moroni); C-12 (Exp. Station); GC-3 (Fort Valley).

## FREDONIA

El.: c. 3500'        Loc.: Coconino 1, B-1
Pro.: /fríydoniə/

In 1885 a number of Mormon families left Utah seeking freedom from efforts to suppress polygamy. McClintock says Hardscrabble was the first name for Fredonia where they settled.

Erastus Snow is said to have suggested the name "Fredonia" as representative of the families who were seeking freedom from federal laws. The name is viewed locally as having an additional implication in that the Spanish word for wife is "doña" and that men living three miles north across the line in Utah sent their extra wives to this place to escape law enforcement.

P.O. est. April 6, 1892. William S. Lewis, p.m. Incorporated, March 5, 1956.

Ref.: P.O. Records; Barnes. Maps: B-5; D-1; GC-2.

## FREMONT PEAK

El.: 11,940'        Loc.: Coconino 5, A-4

John Charles Fremont (b. Savannah, Georgia, January 21, 1813; d. July 13, 1890) earned fame as the "Pathfinder" of trails in the great West. In 1842 Fremont began his explorations for an overland route to the Pacific. He was appointed first commissioner of the U. S. Boundary Commission to survey the boundary between the United States and Mexico, but gave up that position in 1846 to serve as governor of California. In 1878 Fremont was appointed governor of Arizona, serving until 1882. Fremont never saw the peak which was named in his honor.

v.n. Mt. Fremont

Ref.: 4, p. 319; 159, p. 255; 29, p. 61. Map: GC-9.

## FULTON

El.: c. 7000'        Loc.: Coconino 5, B-9.5

The Riordan brothers (Michael J. and Timothy A.) were Flagstaff lumber men who built the Arizona Central Railroad on which Fulton was a station. It was named for Harry Fulton, who ran sheep here in the 1890's.

Ref.: Barnes; Slipher. Maps: GC-2; C-7.

a.n. Fulton Spring        Map: GC-3        Coconino

## GARLAND PRAIRIE

El.: c. 5000'        Loc.: Coconino 4, H-6

The earliest name attached to this open park in the pines was apparently Snider Prairie. The name Snider in turn probably came from Snider's Water Hole, where Companies C and F of the First California Volunteers cached their stores in order to speed up the march during the bitter winter of 1863. Fred G. Hughes was detailed with ten men to remain with the stores until relief arrived. The detachment named the spot Snider's Water Hole.

William Garland with his partner Ross bought out the L. O. Ranch and ran cattle in this region c. 1888 to 1895. L. O. Spring takes its name from the old ranch.

P.O. est. as Snyder's Hole, February 24, 1881. S. M. Gray, p.m. Discont. May 16, 1881.

Ref.: 61, p. 60 (Note 7); 52, pp. 111, 42; P.O. Records. Maps: GC-2; GC-3.

a.n. Garland Spring        Map: GC-3        Coconino
     Little L. O. Canyon   Loc.: S. of Maine        Coconino
     Little L. O. Spring Canyon    Map: GC-3        Coconino
     Garland        Loc.: T. 20 N, R. 5 W.        Yavapai
     On P. & ACRR, all of which has vanished.

## GASH MOUNTAIN

El.: c. 7000'        Loc.: Coconino 5, B-9.5

John Gash, a cattleman, settled in the flat at the base of this mountain in the 1870's. When the Van Deren family located at the same place later, they named both the flat and the mountain for the first settler.

Ref.: Barnes; Slipher. Map: GC-9.

## GENERALS SPRINGS

El.: c. 7000'        Loc.: Coconino 5, D-14

Gen. George Crook discovered these springs. He had a narrow escape from the Apaches near this point c. 1871.

Ref.: Barnes; 22, p. 145. Maps: GC-9; GD-12; GD-11.

a.n. Generals Springs Canyon        Map: GD-12        Coconino

## GENTRY CANYON

El.: c. 7500'        Loc.: Coconino 5, BC-12-14

A settler named Gentry (b. Redding, Calif.) grazed sheep, using Gentry Spring as his headquarters. Gentry came to Arizona in the 1880's.

Ref.: McKinney; Barnes; Davis. Map: GB-12.

a.n. Gentry Cabin        Map: GB-12        Coconino
     Gentry Creek        Map: B-7        Gila
     Gentry Mountain     Map: B-7        Gila

### GERONIMO, MOUNT

El.: 7634'                    Loc.: Coconino 5, C-8.5
Pro.: /jeránimo/ or /heránimo/
Named for the Apache outlaw (cf. Geronimo, Graham).
Ref.: Barnes. Map: GC-2.

### GLEN CANYON

El.: c. 3000'                    Loc.: Coconino 2, B-1.2
Glen Canyon is deep and narrow, forming the site of the
Glen Canyon Dam on which construction began in 1957.
The town of Page (q.v.) was constructed to provide homes
for workers and their families.
Ref.: None. Map: GD-2.

### GOVERNMENT PRAIRIE

El.: c. 7000'                    Loc.: Coconino 4, H-3
Locally it is believed that the name is derived from the fact
that the military stationed at Prescott pastured their horses
on this prairie during the summer months. Others think the
name comes from an old government trail which passed
close to the mountain.
Ref.: Bartlett. Maps: C-14; GC-2; GC-3.

a.n. Government Hill          El.: 8490'. Map: GC-3    Coconino
     Government Knolls    El.: 7593'. Maps: C-12; GC-3   Coconino
     Government Mountain     El.: 8347'. Map: GC-3    Coconino
     Government Cave
     El.: c. 7000'. Loc.: W. of San Francisco Peaks at n. end of
     Fort Valley.                                      Coconino
     Government Cave is a lava tunnel nearly a mile long and at
     places about fifty feet wide and nearly forty feet high.
     Lumbermen named the cave after nearby Government
     Prairie. The cave for years served as a source of ice for
     ranches in the neighborhood.
Ref.: 66, p. 1; 4, p. 320.

### GRAND FALLS

El.: c. 3500'                    Loc.: Coconino 5, E-3
Lt. Lorenzo Sitgreaves discovered Grand Falls in 1851,
naming the falls for a magnificent drop of one hundred and
eighty-five feet (higher than Niagara). Normally dry, the
Grand Falls reveal the reason for their name when they
become what has been termed a "chocolate Niagara" with
a yellow mist rising from the gorge at its bottom.
During the period of volcanic activity, Rodin's Cone (lying
between the San Francisco Peaks and the falls) emitted a
fiery molten stream which plunged over the canyon rim into
the channel of the Little Colorado River, forcing it into a
new course around the end of the lava. Today one can
discern where the lava rolled downstream almost twenty
miles.
v.n. Cascades          (McComb map, 1860)
Ref.: 30, p. 1; 29, p. 41. Maps: GC-2; D-1; E-20; C-4.

### GRAPEVINE SPRING

El.: c. 7000'                    Loc.: Coconino 5, C-9
Wild grapevines are not uncommon in Arizona. Their presence at the spring and downstream along Grapevine Canyon
results in the name.
Old-timers used to pick grapes for winter jelly in this beautiful and rugged canyon, so rough that the only place where

cattle can be crossed is at what is known as the old Mormon
Crossing, which is locally believed to have been used by
wagons coming from the east en route to Mormon Lake.
The stream joins Canyon Diablo.
Ref.: Tom Pollock, Letter, December 13, 1955. Maps: GC-9;
      B-8; C-13.

### GREENHAW

El.: c. 6000'                    Loc.: Coconino 5, A-5.3
This was the post office for a lumber mill which used to
exist two or three miles east of Flagstaff. It was named for
a prominent resident of Flagstaff.
P.O. est. July 13, 1903. James C. Brodie, p.m. Discont. January
4, 1904.
Ref.: P.O. Records. Map: None.

### HAMBLIN CREEK

El.: c. 5000'                    Loc.: Coconino 2, B-10
Jacob Hamblin (b. Ohio, April 2, 1819; d. August 31,
1886), a Mormon missionary, had charge of early colonization by Mormons along the Little Colorado River. He
served as guide to Maj. John Wesley Powell over the Lee's
Ferry route along the base of the Echo Cliffs in the early
1870's. The creek is on this route.
Ref.: 71, p. 42 (Note 2). Map: GC-2.

### HAPPY JACK

El.: c. 7000'                    Loc.: Coconino 5, C-7.5
Near the present summer logger's camp of Happy Jack
there was water used by bees, from which came the name
Yellow Jacket. This name was used for a Forest Service
Camp. In 1947 the name was changed to Happy Jack by
the new forest supervisor, who had come from Happy Jack,
Montana. When a lumber camp with a post office was estab-
lished across the road from the Forest Service workcamp,
the summer settlement took its name from that of the
forestry camp.
P.O. est. April 1, 1950. Mrs. Grace M. Edmunds, p.m.
Ref.: Platt Kline, Flagstaff. Map: B-8.

a.n. Yellow Jacket Spring     Map: B-8                Coconino

### HART CANYON

El.: c. 5000'                    Loc.: Coconino 5, F-13.5
D. F. Hart ran cattle on the range in upper Oak Creek in
1887.
Ref.: Barnes; Less Hart (no relation). Maps: GC-2; B-7; B-9.
a.n. Hart Mountain                                    Coconino

### HART PRAIRIE

El.: c. 8000'                    Loc.: Coconino 4, I-8
Frank Hart (d. c. 1888) was a sheepman who located in an
open space on the San Francisco Peaks where he found
springs on both sides of the prairie. His partner, John
Clark, was the first to come to the area from California on
horseback to look over the land, but Clark returned to the
West Coast. Hart brought in sheep and settled.
v.n. Harte Prairie
Ref.: Barnes; 127, p. 159; 29, p. 63 (Map); Anderson. Map:
      E-20 (Harts).

## HAY LAKE

El.: c. 5000'                    Loc.: Coconino 5, D-10
Stage teams on the Santa Fe-Prescott route in the early days fed on wild hay cut at this point.
Ref.:   Barnes. Maps: C-12; GC-2.

## HEARST MOUNTAIN

El.: c. 7500'                    Loc.: Coconino 4, E-4
Hearst Mountain was named by the Hearst-Perrin cattle outfit in 1887. This same outfit also had holdings in Santa Cruz County. The Hearst was William Randolph Hearst.
Ref.:   Barnes; APHS. Maps: GC-2; B-4; C-13.

## HIBBARD

El.: c 5000'                     Loc.: Coconino 5, D-5.5
I. L. Hibbard was superintendent of the S.F.R.R., later becoming its general manager.
Ref.:   Barnes. Map: GC-2.

## HOBBLE MOUNTAIN

El.: c. 7000'                    Loc.: Coconino 4, G-2
Finding stolen calves hobbled here many years ago caused a man named Kinsey to name the mountain.
Ref.:   Barnes. Maps: GC-2; B-8.

## HOGBACK MOUNTAIN

El.: c. 6500'                    Loc.: Coconino 5, C-5.5
"Hogback" describes the high narrow ridge forming the mountain near Winona. By late 1955 railroad crews had gouged out the middle section for bed cinders, with every indication that the hill may ultimately disappear.
**v.n. Cinder Hill**
Ref.:   Sproat. Map: None

## HOLDEN LAKE

El.: c. 5000'                    Loc.: Coconino 4, E-4.5
An early Arizona Territorial Ranger, T. F. (Fred) Holden ran the TFH brand of cattle here.
Ref.:   Benham; Kennedy. Maps: GC-2; B-4.

## HORSESHOE LAKE

El.: c. 7500'                    Loc.: Coconino 5, E-15
One source says the shape gives this wet weather lake its name. Another states that the lake is named after the One Horseshoe Ranch which existed c. 1890 on Beaver Creek.
Ref.:   Barnes; Hart. Maps: B-9; C-13; GB-12.
**a.n. Horseshoe Hill**                              Coconino

## HOUSE ROCK

El.: c. 5000'                    Loc.: Coconino 1, F-2.5
On the Mormon Road (a trail from the Mormon settlements in Utah to the Hopi country) travelers found shelter where two large rocks had fallen together. In 1870-1880 Jacob Hamblin and his party used this trail about once a year and on one trip some unknown person used charcoal to inscribe on the top of the rocks the words "Rock House Hotel." Other travelers soon inverted the name to its present form. They also applied the name to a nearby spring.

Ref.:   42, pp. 304, 305; 41, p. 160. Maps: GC-4; B-5.

| **a.n.** House Rock Canyon | Map: GC-4 | Coconino |
| House Rock Wash | Map: GC-4 | Coconino |
| House Rock Valley | Map: GC-4 | Coconino |

Contemporary travelers are sometimes startled by the sight of buffalo in this valley. They are descendants of a herd once owned by "Buffalo" Jones and James T. Owens, who in 1928 sold them to the State of Arizona. During the day the buffalo stay in the shade. They are not easily seen except at morning or in the evening. An annual buffalo hunt is held to keep the herd from becoming too numerous.
Ref.:   29, p. 34; 61, p. 130 (Note 92); 4, pp. 293-294.

## HOWARD HILL

El.: c. 5000'                    Loc.: Coconino 1, D-14.5
Charles E. Howard (b. June 6, 1856; d. March 14, 1922) arrived in Flagstaff in 1881. In 1893 he established the Howard Sheep Company, later moving its headquarters to Ashfork.
Ref.:   Fuchs, Letter, April 30, 1956, quoting *Williams News*, March 24, 1922; Benham. Maps: B-4; GC-2.

| **a.n.** Howard Lake | Maps: B-4; D-1 | Coconino |
| Howard Mesa | Map: B-4 | Coconino |
| Howard Mountain | Map: B-8 | Coconino |
| Howard Seep | Map: B-9 | Coconino |
| Howard Spring | Map: B-8 | Coconino |
| Howard Tank | Map: GC-3 | Coconino |

## HULL MOUNTAIN

El.: c. 7500'                    Loc.: Not definitely known
Philip Hull and his sons were ranching in this area at least by the early 1880's.
Ref.:   *Arizona Enterprise*, October 6, 1892, 1:5, 6; 61, p. 51. Map: None.

| **a.n.** Hull Spring | Map: C-6 | Coconino |
| Hull Wash | | Coconino |

Ref.:   139, p. 15

## HUMPHREYS PEAK

El.: 12,670'                     Loc.: Coconino 5, A-4
An extinct volcano, Humphreys Peak is the highest in Arizona. It is one of three peaks forming a rough U shaped valley known as the Inner Basin or Interior Valley. G. K. Gilbert in 1873 named the peak for his superior officer, Brig. Gen. Andrew Atkinson Humphreys, who had been with the Ives Expedition as a captain in 1851.
The valley was once noted for its continually flowing springs, but a disastrous fire c. 1876 destroyed its splendid stand of Engelmann spruce, with the probable result that the springs are now intermittent.
**v.n. San Francisco Peak**   (early maps)
Ref.:   4, pp. 9, 319; 175, I, 32; 143, pp. 1-2. Maps: GC-3; GC-2; D-1.

## HUTCH MOUNTAIN

El.: 8650'                       Loc.: Coconino 5, C-10
A man named Hutchinson, who was generally referred to as "Hutch," was a sheepman here.
Ref.:   Barnes. Maps: B-8; GC-9.

## INDIAN GARDENS

El.: c. 5000'                          Loc.: Coconino 4, I-8
At one time there were Indian wickiups in this area. An ancient trail is said to have crossed the divide here west to Sycamore Canyon.

Ref.: 29, p. 53. Maps: D-1; GM-21.

## INSCRIPTION HOUSE

El.: c. 5000'                          Loc.: Coconino 2, G-3
Just prior to 1910, the ruins of an Indian pueblo were discovered here. What made the ruin exceptionally interesting was a half-obliterated, non-decipherable inscription, obviously placed on it by Spaniards. John Wetherill in 1909 was able to discern the letters *CHOS* and the date *1661 A d n.*

Ref.: 65, p. 162; 5, Brewer, "Navajo National Monument," p. 6. Maps: C-12; D-1; GC-2.

## JACOB LAKE

El.: 7921'                          Loc.: Coconino 1, E-4
In the 1860's and 70's, Jacob Hamblin (b. Ohio, April 2, 1819; d. August 31, 1886), a Mormon missionary, explored this area in search of possible sites for settlement by Mormons. Hamblin began missionary work in Arizona in 1858, when he visited the Hopi. He also scouted through the Little Colorado River country searching for settlement sites. During the 1870's, Hamblin established an emigrant road from Utah to the Little Colorado country, the trail being called the Mormon Road. Hamblin is buried at Alpine, Apache County.

Jacob Lake is shallow, but nearly always contains some water. It is used by stockmen. Nearby is a small settlement and camp ground of the same name.

P.O. est. January 10, 1933. Harold Bowman, p.m. Discont. June 30, 1955.

Ref.: P.O. Records; 4, pp. 488, 105. Maps: GC-4; GC-2; C-12.

a.n. Jacob Canyon        Map: GC-4              Coconino
Jacob's Pools      Loc.: Approx. T. 38 N, R. 5 E.      Coconino
On route used by Hamblin annually to get to Hopi area. Hamblin was first white man to camp at this place. There are two pools, each about eight feet long.

Ref.: 41, pp. 158, 159, 160.

## JAYCOX MOUNTAIN

El.: c. 7000'                          Loc.: Coconino 5, D-10
Henry H. Jaycox (b. New York c. 1834; d. January 20, 1884) was a scout and guide who served as a member of King S. Woolsey's second and third expeditions in 1864 (cf. Bloody Tanks, Gila). Jaycox camped at Jaycox Tank, from which the mountain was named. In 1870 he was farming on the Verde River.

Ref.: Barnes; 52, III; Willson; Henry H. Jaycox File (APHS). Maps: B-8; C-4 (Jaycox Tank); C-13 (Jaycox Mountain).

## J D DAM

El.: c. 5000'                          Loc.: Coconino 4, G-7
One of the oldest dams in the vicinity of Williams, J D Dam was constructed by J. D. Douglas, who had headquarters nearby.

Ref.: Benham. Maps: GC-2; B-8.
a.n. J D Dam Wash        Map: B-6              Coconino

## JOHNSON CREEK

El.: c. 3000'                          Loc.: Coconino 1, C-1.5
For a few weeks, W. D. Johnson was the photographer for the second expedition led by Maj. John Wesley Powell into the Grand Canyon in 1871-1872. There is a question whether he is the same Johnson who settled on the creek in 1871 with his four brothers some ten miles from Kanab, from whom it is possible that the creek and Johnson Canyon took their names.

Ref.: Barnes. Maps: GC-2; C-10 (in Utah); C-13.

a.n. Johnson Canyon   Loc.: Near Williams        Coconino
Capt. George Johnson (d. prior to June 1885) maintained a sheep ranch in this canyon in the late 1870's and early 1880's. Johnson also had another ranch about nine miles west of Williams.

Ref.: Kennedy; 61, p. 44 (Note).

## KABITO PLATEAU

El.: c. 6000'                          Loc.: Coconino 2, BD-4
Pro.: /kʔaˁˇybiyˇːtó/ or          Navajo: "willow spring"
     /kabíyto/
Kabito Spring lies twenty-two miles north of Wildcat Peak. The name given to the entire plateau is that of the spring.

v.n. Kaibito Plateau
     Kaibito Spring

Ref.: 151, p. 407; 71, pp. 41, 157; 73, p. 174. Maps: GC-2; C-12.

## KANA-A CREEK

El.: c. 8000'                          Loc.: Coconino 5, A-4
                          Heads at Sec. 24, T. 23 N., R. 8 E.
Kana-a Creek runs through the valley of the same name, which contains a lava flow named for the Hopi Kachinas of the Kana-a.

Ref.: Colton; Barnes. Map: None.

## KENDRICK PEAK

El.: 10,418'                          Loc.: Coconino 4, H-2.5
Four separate lava flows created Kendrick Peak, which originally was about 4800' high. Erosion lowered the cone nearly one thousand feet, developing three canyons in its sides. Lt. Amiel W. Whipple named the peak in honor of Maj. Henry Lane Kendrick (d. May 24, 1891), Second U. S. Cavalry, who was in charge of the escort for the Sitgreaves Expedition in 1851. Later Kendrick was commandant at Fort Defiance, Apache County.

v. n. Mount Kendrick

Ref.: 139, p. 58; 177, p. 175 (Note 16); 85, I, 592; 159, p. 239. Maps: GC-2; GC-3; C-7.

a.n. Kendrick Park        Map: GC-3              Coconino
     Kendrick Spring      Map: GC-3              Coconino

## KERLINS WELL

El.: c. 5000'                    Loc.: Coconino 4, A-4
George Beale, a brother of Lt. Edward Fitzgerald Beale,
accompanied the military party and reported that on July
13, 1859, this watering place was discovered and named
for F. C. Kerlin, Lt. Beale's clerk. In June 1881, Coues
found the name "kerlin" inscribed on the rocks at the
spring.

v.n. Cullen's Wells
Ref.: Barnes; 35, p. 342. Maps: GC-2; C-7.

## KINDER SPRING

El.: c. 5000'                    Loc.: Coconino 5, D-13
Runyon C. Kinder ran sheep in the late 1880's in this
region.
Ref.: Barnes. Maps: B-9; GC-2.

a.n. Kinder Crossing        Map: B-9                  Coconino

## KINNIKINICK LAKE

El.: c. 7500'                    Loc.: Coconino 5, D-9
Pro.: /kínəkinik/
Less Hart, an old-time stockman, put a ditch into an old
dry lake bed in 1902 for his Hart Cattle Company. According to Mr. Hart, the name originated from Kinnikinick
Spring where a shrub by that name was growing. The shrub
is shiny-leafed Arctostaphylos (Bearberry), called "kinni-
kinic" by the Indians.
Ref.: 151, p. 429. Map: B-8.

a.n. Kinnikinick Canyon     Map: B-8                  Coconino

## LAKE NO. 1

El.: c. 7000'                    Loc.: Coconino 5, G-16
When United States troops built the Crook Road in 1873,
they found so many lakes along the route that they began
identifying them consecutively toward the east by numbers
rather than by name. Most numbers have since given way
to names of settlers. The road from Fort Verde to Fort
Apache along the Mogollon Rim was known as the Verde
Road and as Crook's Road or Crook's Trail. It ended at
Corydon E. Cooley's Ranch (cf. McNary, Apache).
Ref.: Barnes. Map: B-9.

a.n. Lake No. 4         Maps: B-9; GD-12             Coconino

## LANDERS

P.O. est. November 24, 1896. Dayton T. Crofut, p.m. Discont.
January 16, 1897.
Ref.: P.O. Records. Map: None.

## LAVA BEDS

El.: 8000'                    Loc.: Coconino 5, A-3.7
Lava at one time covered a large portion of the region
around Flagstaff. The use of the name "lava" in place
names is descriptive.
Ref.: Schnebly. Maps: C-10 (Lava); C-11.

a. n. Lava Caves
    Loc.: Between Kendrick Peak and Flagstaff      Coconino
    Very high ceilinged and extensive caverns, where ice used
    to be obtained by residents of Flagstaff.

### Lava Spring

Loc.: 10 miles from New Year's Spring             Coconino
Lt. Amiel W. Whipple described this spring as being at the
head of a lava canyon. The spring had a basin nearly thirty
feet across.
Ref.: 42, p. 224; 177, p. 184.

## LEE'S FERRY

El.: 3170'                    Loc.: Coconino 2, A-2
Jacob Hamblin, a Mormon missionary, arrived in 1860 at
the mouth of the Paria River, seeking to find a safe crossing place on the Colorado. He was unsuccessful in his first
attempt, but did cross the Paria safely on a raft in 1864.

In less than a year a Mormon settlement had been established at the mouth of the Paria. Later, a ferry was established about three miles above the present bridge across
the Little Colorado River. In 1872 John Doyle Lee,
a central figure in the Mountain Meadow Massacre in Utah,
built a log cabin at the mouth of the Paria and secured
rights to run the ferry. He called his small ranch Lonely
Dell. (The massacre at Mountain Meadows was an attack
in 1857 by white men disguised as Indians, upon an emigrant train. One hundred and fifteen were killed.) Although
Lee was at the ferry location only two years, the name Lee's
Ferry became attached to the place. Lee was captured by
United States marshals in 1874. He was shot standing in his
coffin, protesting his innocence, in 1877. One of his widows
ran the ferry until the Mormon church bought it in 1877,
after which it was operated by Warren M. Johnson.

In 1909 the ferry was again sold, this time to a cattle company. Coconino County took over the ferry in 1916 and ran
it until the opening of the bridge in 1929. All that remains
of the original settlement today is the old cemetery.

P.O. est. April 4, 1879. Warren M. Johnson, p.m. Discont.
March 2, 1923.
Ref.: 151, p. 454; 112, pp. 90, 91; 41, p. 211; 4, pp. 284-285;
    P.O. Records; 29, p. 34. Maps: B-5; E-20; GC-2.

a.n. Lee's Ferry Road                                 Coconino
    Established by Hamblin from the ferry to the Little Colo-
    rado River colonies.
Lee Canyon  Loc.: Sec. 31, T. 32 N., R. 3 W.          Coconino
    John Lee lived here several years before moving to Lee's
    Ferry.
Lee Mountain    El.: 6607'. Map: GM-21                Coconino
Lee Park            Map: GM-21                         Coconino
Lee Spring          Map: GM-21                         Coconino
    John Lee and his brother are reported to have lived at
    Camp Verde in the 1870's.
Ref.: 112, p. 82.

### Lee's Lookout

El.: 3170'. Loc.: Opposite Lee Ranch on left bank of Paria
River                                                 Coconino
At the top of this mound is a circular wall of rock which
commands an excellent view in all directions. Whether Lee
used it is not known.
Ref.: 98, pp. 181-82.

## LEFEVRE CANYON

El.: c. 7000'                    Loc.: Coconino 1, E-3.5

The Lefevre family grazed sheep here.

Ref.: Barnes. Map: GC-4.

**a.n. Lefevre Ridge**                              Coconino

## LEONARD CANYON

El.: c. 5000'                    Loc.: Coconino 5, F-13-B-9

W. B. Leonard was a sheepman who, in the mid-1870's, had a trading post at Ganado (q.v. Apache). His last home for several years was near Navajo Springs.

Ref.: Barnes; Schnebly. Maps: GC-2; GC-12; B-9.

| **a.n.** Leonard Crossing | Map: B-9 | Coconino |
|---|---|---|
| Leonard Point | Map: B-8 | Coconino |
| Middle Leonard Canyon | Map: B-9 | Coconino |
| West Leonard Canyon | Map: B-8 | Coconino |

## LEROUX SPRING

El.: c. 7000'                    Loc.: Coconino 4, I-4.5

Pro.: /lərúw/

Lt. Amiel W. Whipple in 1853 mentioned stopping at Leroux Spring, which he named in honor of his guide, Antoine Leroux. The spring was much used as a camping place by travelers and military detachments, including Lt. Edward Fitzgerald Beale in 1857. It was also used by the King S. Woolsey expedition, as reported by Henry Clifton, who noted that Gen. T. J. Palmer had renamed the spring Christmas Springs. Ammon M. Tenney said that Leroux Spring was known to Mormons along the Little Colorado River as San Francisco Spring.

Antoine Leroux (b. St. Louis, Mo., c. 1801; d. June 30, 1861) emigrated to New Mexico in the early 1830's, where he married Juana Catarina Vigil of Taos. Leroux was a trapper during the 1830's, exploring between New Mexico and California. In 1846 he served as guide for the Mormon Battalion. After completing a stint with the U. S. Boundary Commission 1849-51, he was with Lt. Lorenzo Sitgreaves' expedition. Leroux was also a guide for Lt. Amiel W. Whipple (see above), and in 1857 for Lt. Beale.

**v.n.** Lereax Spring    (Udell, 1858, pp. 31, 57)

  Little Leroux Spring    (Map: B-8)

Ref.: 151, p. 455; 159, p. 237; 177, pp. 166, 156; 128, p. 2; 112, pp. 152, 154; 71, p. 34; *Arizona Journal Miner,* November 20, 1869, n.p. (State Library Files). Maps: GC-3; GC-2; C-1; E-18; B-8.

**a.n.** Leroux Prairie    (cf. Fort Valley, Coconino, *a.n.*)

  Leroux Wash    Loc.: T. 21 N., R. 23 E.         Navajo

  Whipple named this wash "Leroux's Fork."

  Leroux Crossing    Loc.: Probably on Leroux Wash    Navajo

  The *Citizen* for August 9, 1873 (1:5), mentions "new settlements" here.

## LEUPP

El.: c. 3000'                    Loc.: Coconino 5, F-4.5

Pro.: /luwp/

Francis E. Leupp (b. New York City, January 2, 1849; d. November 19, 1918) served as Commissioner of Indian Affairs, 1904-1909. His interest in Indian affairs dated from his early manhood.

In 1908 a sub-agency for the Navajos was established at this location. It has since been consolidated with the single Navajo headquarters at Window Rock (Apache).

P.O. est. September 14, 1905. John G. Walker, p.m.

Ref.: A. McF. Greenwood, Asst. Commissioner, Bureau of Indian Affairs, Letter, April 10, 1956; C. E. Lamson, Chief, Branch of Personnel, U. S. Dept. Int., Letter, April 26, 1956; P.O. Records. Maps: C-11; GC-2.

**a.n. Leupp Corners**

  Loc.: Turn-off from main highway to Leupp    Coconino

## LIMESTONE CANYON

El.: c. 7000'                    Loc.: Coconino 5, E-14

The word "limestone" is descriptive of this and other locations carrying the name.

Ref.: Hart. Maps: GD-12; GM-9.

| **a.n.** Limestone Pasture | Maps: B-7; BC-9 | Coconino |
|---|---|---|
| Limestone Spring | Map: B-8 | Coconino |

  The pasture and the spring are all one.

  **Limestone Tanks**

  Loc.: N. Cedar Ridge Trading Post 6 miles    Coconino

  Jacob Hamblin used this as a watering place on the Mormon Trail to the Little Colorado River settlements. (cf House Rock, Coconino).

Ref.: 167, p. 87.

## LOCKETT LAKE

El.: c. 7000'                    Loc.: Coconino 1, H-12.5

A pioneer sheepman, Henry ("Hank") Lockett, used this for watering his flocks.

Ref.: Barnes. Map: B-4.

**a.n. Lockett Tank**

  Loc.: South of Coconino Point, well concealed under a bench.                                        Coconino

  Water pouring over a bluff knocked out a huge basin. Still standing are the walls of an old rock house used by horse thieves as a hangout.

Ref.: Mercer.

## LOCKWOOD SPRING

El.: c. 7000'                    Loc.: Coconino 4, I-7

Opinions differ concerning the origin of this name. One source says the name probably derives from that of Lt. D. W. Lockwood, a member of the Wheeler surveying party in 1871. Another notes that it was named for a stockman murdered some years ago.

Ref.: 61, p. 159 (Note 5). APHS. Map: GC-2.

**a.n. Lockwood Park**        Map: B-8              Coconino

## LOCUST CANYON

El.: c. 7000'                    Loc.: Coconino 1, D-7.5

Descriptive.

Ref.: Barnes. Maps: GC-2; B-5; C-10.

**a.n. Locust**                                      Coconino

  Barnes says this is a r.r. station.

  **Locust Spring**        Map: B-5              Coconino

## LONG TOM CANYON

El.: c. 8000'  Loc.: Coconino 5, H-16-15
A hunter and sheepherder named Woolf (cf. Woolf Crossing) camped here c. 1882 and named the canyon. In 1885 in this canyon Will C. Barnes constructed a cabin which was later used by forest rangers.

Ref.:  Barnes. Map: GC-2.

## LONG VALLEY

El.: c. 7000'  Loc.: Coconino 5, C-12.5
Descriptive.

Ref.:  Hart. Maps: C-12; B-9; GC-2.

**a.n.** Long Lake  Map: B-8  Coconino

## LOWELL OBSERVATORY

El.: c. 7500'  Loc.: Coconino 5, A-5.5
Dr. Percival Lowell (1855-1916) came home from Japan in 1893, determined to take up the work of Schiaparelli, the Italian astronomer, whose failing eyesight was putting an end to his studies of Mars. Since the planet was to be closer to Earth in 1894 than it would again be until 1956, Lowell was determined to place a well-equipped observatory in operation before the event.

After taking observations at Tucson, Phoenix, Tombstone, and Flagstaff to determine which would be the best site, Lowell selected the northern Arizona city. Appropriately, Lowell called the hill on which the new observatory was constructed Mars Hill. For the next twenty-two years, Lowell devoted himself to activities at the Lowell Observatory which he endowed. Dr. Lowell c. 1915 calculated the course of an unknown planet which in 1930 was discovered where Lowell said it would be at that time. The planet is Pluto.

Mars Hill is a part of Observatory Mesa, which stretches from Fort Valley to the site of the observatory. Although Mars Hill may at first have been called Observatory Hill, the latter name has long since vanished.

Ref.:  153, p. 170; 69, pp. 360, 358, 359; 4, p. 319; 139, p. 69; Slipher. Map: GC-3.

## MAHAN MOUNTAIN

El.: c. 7000'  Loc.: Coconino 5, C-10
Pro.:  /meyhən/
A. J. T. Mahan patented his claim to land on the east slope of the mountain in 1889.

Ref.:  Barnes. Maps: B-8; GC-2.

## MARSHALL LAKE

El.: 7133'  Loc.: Coconino 5, A-6.5
John Marshall in 1892 homesteaded here; later he patented the land.

Ref.:  Frier. Maps: GC-2; GC-3; C-12.

## MARY, LAKE

El.: 6850'  Loc.: Coconino 5, A-6.5
Lake Mary is an artificial lake created in 1903 to supply water for a sawmill. The spillway was built lower than the mill so that water had to be pumped up to the mill. Timothy A. Riordan, president of the lumber company, named the lake for his eldest daughter, Mary. Some years afterwards when the mill was abandoned, the owners of the lake gave it to Coconino County to be a recreational area.

**v.n.** Mary Lake
  Mary's Lake
Ref.:  Sykes; 29, p. 55; 4, p. 451. Maps: GC-2; GC-3.
**a.n.** Lake Mary Spring  Map: B-8  Coconino
  Lake Mary Valley  Map: GC-3  Coconino
  Also formerly sometimes referred to as Little Valley.
  Upper Lake Mary  Map: B-8  Coconino

## McCLINTOCK RIDGE

El.: c. 7000'  Loc.: Coconino 5, E-14.5
W. W. McClintock, a cattleman, homesteaded on the ridge in 1904.

Ref.:  Barnes. Maps: GD-12; B-9.

**a.n.** McClintock Canyon  Map: B-7  Coconino
  McClintock Draw  Map: GD-12  Coconino

## McCOLLUM RANCH

El.: c. 6000'  Loc.: Coconino 4, EF-6.5
  Seven miles s. of Williams.
A cattleman, Nehemiah McCollum, settled at this ranch in either 1878 or 1879, selling out to the Perrin Land and Cattle Company in 1886.

P.O. est. February 24, 1881. Robert McCollum, p.m. Discont. May 16, 1881.

Ref.:  61, p. 53; P.O. Records. Map: None.

## McLELLAN

El.: c. 5000'  Loc.: Coconino 4, E-5
C. T. McLellan was on the survey gang for the railroad. There used to be a section house, water station, and telegraph office at this now-abandoned point on the railroad. When double tracking for the railroad was completed in 1912, McLellan began to lose importance.

Ref.:  Kelly. Maps: GM-1; GC-2; B-4.

**a.n.** McClellan Tank  El.: c. 5000'. Maps: B-6; GC-2  Coconino
  While it is possible that this name is a corruption of "Mc-Lellan," the tanks may also have been named either for William C. McClellan, a member of the Mormon Battalion who settled at Sunset in 1876, or for John McClellan, an early stockman. The tank is on the old Mormon Road (q.v.). Maps which carry the name as "McClellan" show it in a location identical to that of McLellan.

Ref.:  Barnes; APHS Files.
  McLellan Dam  El.: c. 5000'  Coconino
  McLellan Reservoir  El.: c. 5000'. Map GM-1  Coconino

## MEDICINE VALLEY

El.: 8000'  Loc.: Coconino 5, A-4
  (Sec. 5-8, T. 23 N., R. 8 E.)
In 1929 the Museum of Northern Arizona excavated a cave in this valley. While doing so, the party found a medicine man's kit and named the location Medicine Cave, from which the valley takes its name.

Ref.:  Colton; Bartlett. Map: None.

## MERRIAM CRATER

El.: c. 5000'                          Loc.: Coconino 5, D-4
This crater is named in honor of Dr. Clinton Hart Merriam
(1855-1942), a naturalist and author of a biological survey
in the San Francisco Peaks and Little Colorado desert areas.
Ref.:   157, p. 514. Maps: B-8; GC-2.

## MERRILL CRATER

El.: c. 5000'                          Loc.: Coconino 5, D-5
Dr. George P. Merrill (1854-1929) was the first scientist
to prepare a report on Meteor Mountain. He served as
curator of geology for the United States National Museum
and wrote many papers on meteorites.
Ref.:   151, p. 514. Maps: B-8; GC-3.
a.n. Merrill Mountain   (in which crater is situated)      Coconino

## MESA BUTTE

El.: c. 5000'                          Loc.: Coconino 4, I-1
Descriptive.
Ref.:   Barnes. Maps: GC-2; C-13; E-20.

## METEOR CRATER

El.: 6900'                             Loc.: Coconino 5, F-7
Meteor Crater is well known to tourists on the transcontinental highway across northern Arizona. It is the second
largest of the world's eleven accepted craters and clusters
of craters. (Chubb Crater in northern Quebec is assumed
to be the largest, although proof of its meteoritic origin has
not yet been uncovered.)
Meteor Crater was known by white men merely as a landmark as early as 1871, but it was not an object of particular
interest until 1886. In that year, sheepherders came upon
the first recognized meteorites near Canyon Diablo. Five
years later in 1891 a party from the U. S. Geological Survey
ruled out the possibility of volcanic origin for the crater
because no volcanic materials were found near it by geologists. However, its meteorite origin was not surmised until
1903 when Daniel Moreau Barringer (1860-1929), a mining engineer, felt so certain that the crater had been formed
by a meteorite that he filed mining claims for the site.
Samples of drillings were 75% mineral. Repeated attempts
to drill, however, met with failure, attributable to the
extreme hardness of the metals in the crater and the quality
of drill bits then available. The stock market crash in 1929
put an end to mining attempts. However, scientific interest
in the crater has maintained a high level.
In 1951 a survey by Princeton University with a Worden
Gravimeter finally revealed the immensity of the meteorite
mass. The size of the meteor buried six hundred feet under
the surface of the crater is at least 1,700,000 tons. A study
by Carnegie Institute of Technology indicates that on first
impact the mass probably weighed between 2,600,000 and
7,800,000 tons, most of it exploding and scattering when it
hit the earth, to form the rim of the present crater. The
resulting rim was over one hundred feet above the previous
ground level. At the time when the meteor plunged to strike
the earth at an angle (roughly fifty thousand years ago),
the surrounding plain was approximately flat. Even after

thousands of years of silt accumulating in the crater bowl,
the crater is still nearly six hundred feet deep and almost a
mile across from rim to rim. Prehistoric pit houses exist
inside the crater rim.
P.O. est. April 27, 1906. Samuel J. Holsinger, p.m. Discont.
April 15, 1912. Wells Fargo Station, 1907.
v.n. Barringer Crater
    Great Arizona Crater
    Crater Mound
    Coon Mountain
    Meteor Mountain
Ref.:   59, pp. 14, 23, 25, 18-19; P.O. Records. Maps: GC-2;
        C-11.

## MILLER CANYON

El.: c. 7000'                         Loc.: Coconino 5, D-14
Miller Canyon was formerly called McCarty Canyon for
an old trapper who was found dead in the canyon c. 1902.
The name was changed when P. C. Miller built a cabin in
the canyon and raised cattle.
v.n. Millers Canyon
Ref.:   Barnes; Hart. Maps: GD-11; GC-9.

| a.n. McCarty Draw | Map: B-9 | Coconino |
|---|---|---|
| East Miller Canyon | Map: B-9 | Coconino |
| Miller Ridge | Map: GD-11 | Coconino |
| Miller Spring | Map: B-9 | Coconino |
| Miller Wash | Map: B-4 | Coconino |
| Miller Cabin Seep | Map: B-4 | Coconino |

## MILOS BUTTE

El.: 7525'                            Loc.: Coconino 5, A-9
Pro.:  /máylows/
An old-timer named Milos was in this area, but had his
headquarters at Flagstaff.
Ref.:   Corey. Maps: B-8; GC-2; GM-21.

## MOE AVE

El.: c. 5000'                         Loc.: Coconino 2, C-11
Pro.:  /mównaviˆ/
Fr. Francisco Garcés in 1776 was the first white man to
visit this location. He found Havasupai Indians living here.
In 1871 Jacob Hamblin (cf. Jacob Lake) founded a Mormon colony in the little oasis at Moe Ave Springs. By 1900
only three families remained and in 1903 the land was sold
to the Bureau of Indian Affairs. There is now no settlement
and the springs have disappeared. (cf. Moenkopi.)
v.n. Moa Ave
    Moenave
    Moen Abi
    Moehavi
Ref.:   71, p. 144, 193; 167, p. 100; 112, p. 158. Maps: D-1
        (Moenave); GC-2; C-5, 8.

## MOENKOPI

El.: 4550'                            Loc.: Coconino 2, D-11
Pro.:  /mównkapiˆ/       Hopi: "place of running water"
The Navajo name for this small settlement means "Little
Oraibi," deriving from the fact that in the 1870's TIvi
(called "Toobi" and also "Tuba"), a chief of Old Oraibi,
founded a Hopi village at this place, naming it for the
springs. The Hopi village was erected where an earlier

village had existed — probably that which Juan de Oñate in 1604 called Ranchera de los Gandules. Fr. Garcés refers to it as Concabe, an attempt to render the sound of the name in Spanish.

It was through TIvi's friendship that the Mormons were able to establish a colony at Moe Ave (q.v.) in 1879. John W. Young, a son of Brigham Young, in that year built a woolen mill, with the understanding that the Indians would be his labor supply. The project was soon abandoned. In 1903 when the Church of Jesus Christ of Latter-day Saints sold its holdings in the area to the Indian Department, the Mormon settlement vanished.

v.n. Moencopie
   Moenkapi
   Moyencopi

Ref.: 151, p. 526; 167, p. 100; 63, p. 30; 112, p. 161; 88, I, 919. Maps: C-5 (Moen Copie Settlement); C-7 (Moencopie); D-1; GC-2.

a.n. Moenkopi Plateau                 Coconino
Triangular area bounded by Dinnebito and Moenkopi washes and cliffs facing the Little Colorado River.

Ref.: 71, p. 39.

   Moencopi Wash                 Cononino
Name changed to this form by Mormons, from its original Spanish name of Cosonias Wash (Cominguez-Escalante map, 1776). *Cosninas* was the Hopi name for the Havasupai Indians who then lived in this area.

Ref.: 167, p. 164.

## MOGOLLON RIM

El.: c. 7000'          Loc.: Coconino 5, BH-14-16
Pro.: /mʌgiyówn/
Rising abruptly above the valley floor is the majestic rim of the Mogollon Plateau, which is also shown on some maps as Mogollon Mesa. The name comes from that of Juan Ignacio Flores Mogollon, governor of New Mexico, 1712-1715. The precipitous two-hundred-mile escarpment of the Mogollon Rim (commonly referred to as "The Rim" and in one part as the "Tonto Rim") is the result of a geologic faulting from southeast to northwest across Arizona. Gradually the top leveled to form the Mogollon Plateau on which waters run northward, while below the Rim the drainage is southerly.

v.n. Black Mesa

Ref.: G.E.P. Smith, letters to Board on Geographic Names, January, 14 and 22, 1942; APHS Files; Schnebly; 88, p. 919. Maps: C-5; GC-2; GD-12; GM-19; E-20.

a.n. Mogollon Buttes               Coconino
Ref.: 92, p. 366.

## MONUMENT MOUNTAIN

El.: c. 6000'          Loc.: Coconino 5, G-1.8
There is a stone government marker at the top of this mountain.

Ref.: Barnes. Map: C-12.

## MOONEY MOUNTAIN

El.: c. 8000'         Loc.: Coconino 4, FG-5.5
A pioneer stockman is said to have camped at the base of this mountain. However, it has been suggested that the

name has some connection with the prospector whose name is associated with Mooney Falls in Havasupai Canyon (q.v. Grand Canyon).

Ref.: Barnes. Map: C-12.

a.n. Mooney Trail        Map: GC-3        Coconino

## MOQUI SPRING

El.: c. 6000'          Loc.: Coconino 5, E-12
Pro.: /mówkiˆ/
An abundance of water at this spring made it a favorite camping place. It was named by E. R. Carr, manager of Waters Cattle Company, c. 1884.

The name "Moqui" may represent an early attempt to put the pronunciation of "Hopi" in Spanish. On the other hand, there is a Navajo word *mogi* ("dead"), which was used by the Navajos as a term of contempt for the peaceful Hopis, and perhaps the Spaniards picked up the appellation rather than *Hopitu,* the name the Hopi apply to themselves, meaning "the peaceful ones."

Ref.: Barnes. Maps: B-9; C-12.

a.n. Moqui                     Coconino
Loc.: On old A.T. & S.F. R.R. 7 miles w. of Winslow.
This section house is now gone.

## MORITZ LAKE

El.: c. 7000'          Loc.: Coconino 4, H-3
Pro.: /morts/
Joe Moritz, a stockman, made an artificial lake at this place c. 1910.

Ref.: Benham; McKinney; Terry; 151, p. 532. Maps: C-10; C-12; D-1; GC-2; GC-3.

a.n. Moritz Hill        Map: B-4        Coconino

## MORMON CROSSING

El.: c. 6000'          Loc.: Coconino 5, FG-13-14
      (approximate: at upper end of Chevelon Canyon)
In 1879 Mormon settlers from Sunset and Brigham City (q.v. Navajo) moved into this area, grading a road into the canyon from the forks. This was called "Mormon Crossing." However, Chevelon Creek failed to provide sufficient water for a permanent settlement, and the "Valley of Agalon," as the Mormons termed their settlement, failed to endure.

Ref.: Barnes. Map: None.

## MORMON MOUNTAIN

El.: 8440'          Loc.: Coconino 5, A-8
Mormon Mountain, the smallest of the volcanic mountains in the Flagstaff area, rises about fifteen hundred feet above Mormon Lake. Both locations are named because of their proximity to Mormon enterprises on the west side of the lake where in 1878 Mormons established a dairy as a joint undertaking by Sunset, Brigham City, and St. Joseph (q.v. Navajo). Mormon Dairy was situated in what was then called Pleasant Valley. Today Mormon Dairy Spring carries on the name. A second enterprise was a sawmill established at Pine Spring at a place called Millville in 1876. The sawmill was sold in 1882 and moved to Pinedale.

Mormon Lake was used as a grazing area for the dairy's

one hundred and fifteen cows. By 1900 the drainage channels for the grazing field had become clogged so that water collected, thus forming a shallow lake four miles long by three wide. During drought cycles, the lake disappears. This may account for the fact that on the military map (Carleton's) of 1864 a lake is shown here with the name Carleton Lake, named for Gen. James Henry Carleton (d. January 7, 1873), who was then in command of troops in the Territory of New Mexico. This lake is not on subsequent military maps.

Mormon Mountain at one time was called Mount Longfellow because near its foot was a Central Arizona R.R. station named Longfellow by Michael J. and Timothy A. Riordan of Flagstaff to honor the New England poet.

Other names are derived from the activities of members of the Church of Jesus Christ of Latter-day Saints, such as Mormon Ridge, which forms the drainage divide between Navajo and Moencopie Creeks on the Kaibito Plateau where the Mormons were the first white settlers. This may be the same as the ridge-backed mountain known among Mormons as Lee's Backbone, since it lies on the route from Lee's Ferry to Moencopie.

P.O. est. as Pine Springs, March 20, 1879. Hugh Marshall, p.m. Discont. July 27, 1882. Re-est. as Mormon Lake, May 18, 1925. Chauncey D. Lewis, p.m.

Ref.:   139, p. 15; 71, pp. 41, 193; 171, pp. 18-19; APHS Files; 4, p. 451; 29, p. 55; Barnes; P.O. Records. Maps: C-7; C-12 (Longfellow); GC-2; GM-21.

**a.n. Mormon Canyon**          Map: B-8                    Coconino
**Mormon Road**
(cf. Jacob Lake, Coconino)                    Coconino and Navajo

## MUNDS PARK

El.: 6812′                         Loc.: Coconino 5, A-10

The name "park" to urban dwellers implies a place for recreation, but in the West it is usually a natural clearing with a park-like aspect. Munds Park is named for James T. Munds (b. Roseburg, Oregon) who came to Arizona with his parents in 1875. In 1883 he homesteaded at this place.

Ref.:   127, p. 129. Maps: GC-2; GM-21.

**a.n. Munds Canyon**       Maps: C-14; GM-21              Coconino
**Munds Mountain**   El.: 6812′. Map: GM-21                Coconino
**Munds Spring**        Maps: B-8; C-13                    Coconino
**Munds Trail**                          Coconino and Yavapai
Jim Munds built a trail so that he could get his cattle from the Mogollon Rim down into Oak Creek. It still carries his name.

**Munds Draw**          Map: GM-5                    Yavapai
This is named for John L. Munds, a stockman who served two terms as sheriff of Yavapai County.

Ref.:   Barnes.

**Munds**       Loc.: N. of Kingman 8 miles        Mohave
Also named for John L. Munds, a station on the Chloride branch of the A.T. & S.F. R.R.

Ref.:.  Barnes.

## NAIL CANYON

El.: c. 6000′                       Loc.: Coconino 1, D-4

Alvin and Casper, two sons of an early settler named Nagel, anglicized their name to *Nail*.

Ref.:   Barnes. Map: GC-2.

## NAVAJO BRIDGE

El.: c. 3000′                       Loc.: Coconino 2, A-3
Pro.:  /nǽvǝho/

After being shown under a variety of names on maps, this bridge over the Colorado River has finally settled down to its present name. The bridge is eight hundred and thirty-four feet long and lies four hundred and sixty-seven feet above the river bed. It was opened for use on January 12, 1929.

Ref.:   Barnes. Maps: B-5; D-1; C-13 (Grand Canyon Bridge).

## NAVAJO MOUNTAIN

El.: 10,416′ (peak in Utah)        Loc.: Coconino 2, GH-1
Pro.:  /nǽvǝho/

Although only the base of this commanding peak lies in Arizona, its history is so closely allied with that of Arizona that its inclusion as a place name in this volume is warranted. Long prior to the coming of white men in the West, it is probable that the Navajos referred to it by the name they still use — *na'cis'á·n,* meaning "enemy hiding-spot."

The highest point on the Navajo Reservation, the mass of Navajo Mountain rises solitarily above the plain. Its base is a series of bare rock pinnacles and promontories, seemingly impassable. When Maj. John Wesley Powell came through Glen Canyon in 1872 on his second exploration of the Grand Canyon, his party found carved on a rock the names of Seneca Howland, his brother O. G. Howland, and William Dunn, the three men who left the first party and were killed by Indians in 1869. Powell climbed out of the canyon, saw the massive mountain nearby and named it Mount Seneca Howland, not knowing that it was already being called Navajo Mountain. Earlier, the same peak had been called Sierra Panoche (Spanish: *pinocha,* "pine leaf") (Macomb map, 1859).

During the campaign to subdue the Navajos, a heliograph station on Navajo Mountain was used to flash messages across the reservation.

Ref.:   Burcard; 73, p. 205; 6, p. 7; 41, p. 141; 71, p. 45; 47, (Note 1); 167, p. 105. Map: C-10 (In Utah).

**a.n.**

Several Arizona place names incorporate the word "Navajo."
**Navajo Creek**                                Coconino
Named by Powell's party.

**Navajo National Monument**    Map: C-12        Coconino
Established March 2, 1909. (cf. Betatakin, Navajo; Kiet Seel, Navajo; Inscription House, Navajo).

**Navajo Spring**        Map: B-8                Coconino
The old Mormon Trail had a camping place here which is now used by Navajos.

Ref.:   41, p. 149; 71, p. 158; 167, p. 106.

## NEVIN

El.: c. 7000′                      Loc.: Coconino 4, H-5

A. G. Nevin was a general manager of the S.F.R.R.

Ref.:   Barnes. Map: GC-2.

## NEWBERRY MESA

El.: c. 5000' Loc.: Coconino 5, EH-1-5
The first geologist to study and record his observations of the Grand Canyon was Dr. John Strong Newberry (b. 1822; d. 1892), who served both as surgeon and geologist for the Ives Expedition in 1857-58 during its exploration of the Colorado River and northern Arizona. Newberry described the mesa which bears his name.

**v.n. Newberry Terrace**
 **Wotan's Throne** Map: GC-7 Coconino
Ref.: 71, pp. 38; 38, (Note 2); Photo. caption, Naturalist's Hq., Grand Canyon; 151, p. 825; 93, p. 37. Maps: D-4; C-12.

**a.n. Newberry Butte** Map: GC-7 Grand Canyon
 **Newberry Point** El.: c. 5000'. Map: GC-6 Grand Canyon

## NEW YEAR'S SPRING

El.: c. 8000' Loc.: Coconino 4, GH-4.75
Lt. Amiel W. Whipple mentions visiting this spring on January 1, 1854, describing it as a pool nearly twelve feet across. The date of his stopping here determined its name.
Ref.: Fuchs, Letter, April 30, 1956; 177, p. 177; 178, Part II, 47. Map: E-20.

## NINE MILE VALLEY

El.: c. 3500' Loc.: Coconino 1, AD-1.4-3
This valley extends south from Fredonia, the distance indicated in its name. This valley first shows on GLO 1876.
Ref.: Barnes. Maps: E-20; C-5.

## NORTH CANYON

El.: c. 5000' Loc.: Coconino 1, G-7
Two canyons head near each other, with their creek courses running thereafter nearly parallel. From this arises their respective names of North and South Canyon.
Ref.: Barnes. Maps: B-5; GC-2.

**a.n. North Creek** Coconino
 **South Canyon Spring** Map: B-5 Coconino

## O'LEARY PEAK

El.: 8925' Loc.: Coconino 5, A-3
Dan O'Leary served as a guide for Gen. George Crook, being present when the Hualapai Indians made an attempt to kill Crook at Date Creek. O'Leary was serving as interpreter (cf. O'Leary Pass, Mohave, and Camp Date Creek, Yavapai).
Ref.: 151, p. 571. Maps: GC-2, GC-3.

## O'NEAL SPRING

El.: c. 6000' Loc.: Coconino 5, A-6
 Sec. 20, T. 21 N., R. 7 E.
In March 1888, Jim O'Neal established a homestead at this spring where he raised sheep. Michael J. and Timothy A. Riordan bought the place and ran a pipeline to Flagstaff to supply water for their lumber mill. The city of Flagstaff used it to tide over an exceedingly dry spell.
Ref.: Willson; Slipher. Map: None.

## ORDERVILLE CANYON

El.: c. 7000' Loc.: Coconino 1, F-3.5
When the Mormons were first settling in the Little Colorado Valley in 1878 and thereafter, there was a popular movement among the members of the various groups to form "The United Order," a cooperative in which all property belonged to the community rather than to individuals. From this, one community took the name of Orderville. The settlement has vanished, but the name remains attached to the canyon. The United Order did not endure very long.
Ref.: Richards. Maps: GC2; GC-4.

## PADILLA MESA

El.: c. 6000' Loc.: Coconino 2, GH-14-15
Pro.: /padíyə/
Fr. Juan de Padilla was with Don Pedro de Tobar in 1540 when the men were sent by Coronado to investigate the country west of the Seven Cities of Cibola (cf. Hopi Villages, Navajo). Padilla was later killed by Hopi Indians.
Ref.: 71, pp. 39 (Note 1); 194. Map: GC-2.

## PADRE, CANYON

El.: c. 6000' Loc.: Coconino 5, C-7.5
Pro.: /pádrey/ or /pædrey/
At one time Canyon Padre was known as Hennessey Canyon after John Hennessey, who lived in it. Locally, the opinion is expressed that its present name comes from the fact that there was already a Canyon Diablo (q.v.) and that a canyon bearing such a name should have a Canyon Padre to balance it. Others think the name refers to the early Spanish expeditions to the region. Canyon Padre joins Canyon Diablo seven miles before the latter enters the Little Colorado River.

**v.n. Pudre Canyon (sic)** (Map: C-7)
Ref.: Colton; Sykes; Hart; Slipher. Maps: GC-2; C-7.

## PAGE

El.: c. 3000' Loc.: Coconino 2, B-1
Page is a community erected to provide homes and community life for construction workers of the Glen Canyon Dam, begun in 1957. The town was named for John Chatfield Page (b. Nebraska, October 12, 1887; d. March 23, 1955), who served as Commissioner of Reclamation, 1937-1943. Commissioner Page devoted many years to development of the upper Colorado River.
Ref.: Ref. Dept., U. of A. Library. Map: None.

## PARIA RIVER

El.: c. 4000' Loc.: Coconino 2, A-2
Pro.: /payríyə/ Piute: "elk water"
Before the coming of white men, the Paria Valley was noted for its herds of elk. However, by the mid-1850's few elk remained on the Paria Plateau.
In 1872 Capt. George M. Wheeler noted a crude wagon road from Utah along the course of the Paria River to its mouth (cf. Lee's Ferry). It was, of course, the Mormon Road (cf. Jacob Lake).

**v.n. Pahreah River**
Ref.: 151, p. 589; 70, p. 37; 175, I, 54-55. Maps: C-4; GC-2.

## PARKS

El.: c. 7000'                    Loc.: Coconino 4, H-5

The history of Parks is typical of the evolution of place names. Originally the small settlement was not where Parks is today, but was on the railroad where a section house existed under the name of Rhoades. Since there is still a Rhoades Tank south of Williams about ten miles, where water pours off a twenty-foot cliff into the natural tank, it is probable that both were named for a man who lived in the area. John T. Dennis, a former resident of the state of Maine, located a sawmill at Rhoades. A boxcar was used as a depot at this place, and mail was taken care of at the sawmill. With the establishment of the highway, the small settlement was relocated two miles east of the older railroad point, with the store at the original place gradually coming to be known as Old Maine. At the newer location, the name Maine gave way to Parks when a man by that name constructed a store.

The school district is still known as Maine.

P.O. est. as Rhodes, April 26, 1898. William L. Bliss, p.m. Name changed to Rhoades, date unknown, but prior to October 1907. Name changed to Maine, October 3, 1907. John T. Dennis, p.m. Discont. June 11, 1910. P.O. re-est. as Parks, December 14, 1914. James W. Evans, p.m. Discont. May 31, 1957.

Ref.:  Benham; Best; Sykes; P.O. Records; APHS Files. Maps: C-9 (Rhoades); C-10, C-11 (Maine); C-12 (Parks); F-2 (Parks); GC-2.

## PARRISSAWAMPITTS SPRING

El.: c. 7000'                    Loc.: Coconino 1, E-7
                                Piute: "boiling water"

Descriptive of the way the spring bubbles out of the ground.

v.n. Parishawampitts Canyon

Ref.:  Barnes. Maps: B-5; GC-2.

a.n Parrissawampitts Canyon      Map: B-5            Coconino

## PARTRIDGE CREEK

El.: c. 5000'                    Loc:. Coconino 4, B-4

On April 21, 1857, Lt. Joseph Christmas Ives pitched camp in what he called Partridge Ravine. However, he says that to the south lay Mount Floyd, which may indicate it is not the same as the Partridge Creek which was named by Lt. Amiel W. Whipple (1854) on his map. Mollhausen, a member of the Ives expedition, noted in his diary that many partridges existed along the creek. Whipple also noted the great number of the birds seen along the creek.

Ref.:  169, p. 31; 177, pp. 181 (Note 25); 185 (Note 2); 178, p. 88. Map: GC-2.

a.n. Partridge Wash                                Coconino

## PINE SPRINGS

El.: c. 6000'                    Loc.: Coconino 4, E-5

Descriptive. Fr. Francisco Garcés on June 19, 1775, called this Pozo de la Rosa. (Spanish: "rose well").

Ref.:  35, p. 335, (Note 19). Maps: B-6; GM-1.

a.n.

The word "pine" occurs descriptively in many place names. A few are listed below.

| Pine Hollow | | Map: B-5 | Coconino |
|---|---|---|---|
| Pine Creek | | (cf. Natural Bridge, Gila) | Gila |
| Pine Creek | | Loc.: s.e. corner Baca Float #5 | Yavapai |
| Pine Creek | | Loc.: Sec. 3, T. 16 N., R. 6 W. | Yavapai |
| Pine Creek | | Loc.: Sec. 15, T. 3 N., R. 11 E. | Maricopa |
| Pine Mountain | El.: 5761'. Loc.: T. 5 N., R. 9, 10 E. | | Yavapai |
| Pine Butte | | Loc.: Sec. 4, T. 7 N., R. 9 E. | Gila |
| Pine Springs | | | |

Maps: C-11; B-8; E-20; C-4. (cf. Mormon Mountain, Coconino)                                Coconino

## PITMAN VALLEY

El.: c. 7500'                    Loc.: Coconino 4, H-5

Elias E. Pitman (b. Tennessee, 1826; d. 1888) went to California via the Horn in 1858. He moved from California to Arizona in 1862, establishing a cattle ranch in the valley which bears his name, at what is now Chalender. Pitman sold out to William Garland (cf. Garland Prairie) in 1885 and moved to California where he died.

Ref.:  Fuchs, Letter, April 30, 1955; Mrs. Guy Pitman Taylor (daughter), Letter, April 4, 1956; 61, pp. 53-54. Map: E-20.

## PITT

El.: c. 5000'                    Loc.: Coconino 4, F-4

William Pitt, a sheepman, maintained a livestock loading platform on the railroad at this point.

Ref.:  Barnes. Maps: C-13; GC-2.

a.n. Pitt Spring

Loc.: On Williams side of Whitehorse Lake       Coconino

## PIVOT ROCK CANYON

El.: 6901'                    Loc.: Coconino 5, BC-13.6

The canyon is named because in it is Pivot Rock, which is descriptively named.

Ref.:  Barnes; Schnebly. Map: GD-11.

a.n. Pivotrock (sic) Spring    Map: GD-11           Coconino

## PLATTEN SPRINGS

El.: c. 8000'                    Loc.: Coconino 4, G-3.5

Fred Platten (b. 1849; d. March 2, 1939) served as a forest ranger in the vicinity of Williams for many years. He won a Congressional Medal of Honor while a sergeant with Troop H, Sixth Cavalry, for gallantry in action against Sioux Indians on April 23, 1875.

Ref.:  Mrs. Mary Ford Platten (widow). Map: None.

## PRESTON MESA

El.: c. 6000'                    Loc.: Coconino 2, E-8

Named for Sam Preston, a Navajo trader.

Ref.:  Barnes; 71, p. 157. Maps: D-1; GC-2.

## PROMONTORY BUTTE

El.: 8078'                    Loc.: Coconino 5, F-15

Descriptive. This point on the Mogollon Rim overlooks the Tonto Basin.

Ref.:  Barnes. Maps: C-4; E-20; GC-2; GD-12.

## PROSPECT CANYON

El.: c. 5000'  Loc.: Coconino 3, D-3.2-1.5

When John Conners and Franklin French of Holbrook were prospecting, they named this canyon in order to be able to identify it.

Ref.: Barnes. Maps: A-7; GC-6.

## PUMP HOUSE WASH

El.: c. 5000'  Loc.: Coconino 4, I-8

The lumber mill at Flagstaff needed water for the A. & P. R.R. It was pumped through the wash to the railroad from the former spring where the concrete bridge now crosses Oak Creek.

Ref.: Sykes. Map: None.

## QUAYLE

El.: c. 6000'  Loc.: Coconino 5, E-11

The Quayle family lived at this point for several years. P.O. est. October 19, 1914. Selma H. Quayle, p.m. Discont. October 31, 1916.

Ref.: Barnes; P.O. Records. Map: F-2.

## RAINBOW PLATEAU

El.: c. 6000'  Loc.: Coconino 2, FG-1, 2

Descriptive. Lying partially in Utah, the Rainbow Plateau is the least known and most inaccessible portion of the Navajo Reservation. Red rock canyons varying from two hundred to two thousand feet in depth slice the rugged terrain, with the entire area abounding in domes, buttes, and mesas in endless variety, so close to each other that passage between them is often impossible.

Ref.: 71, p. 44; 151, p. 631. Map: C-12.

a.n. Rainbow Plateau  Map: B-5  Coconino

## RAIN TANK

El.: c. 6000'  Loc.: Coconino 1, EF-13

A tank which catches rainwater in flood, Rain Tank is used for watering stock. It lies at the foot of Rain Tank Wash.

Ref.: Terry. Maps: B-4; C-5; E-20.

## RATTLESNAKE TANKS

El.: c. 4000'  Loc.: Coconino 5, A-8.5
Sec. 17, 8. 16 N., R. 7 E.

As is to be expected, the name "Rattlesnake Tank" is derived from the fact that people camped near here killed several rattlers. In 1875 the watering place was known as "Updyke's Tanks," according to Martha Summerhayes. Mrs. Summerhayes was perhaps slightly in error on the spelling, for in the store books kept by C. C. Bean at Camp Verde, there is a single entry for supplies sold to one George Opdyke. Opdyke died in Prescott in 1891.

v.n. Opdyke Tanks

Ref.: Barnes; C. C. Bean, "Journal of Accounts at Camp Verde," (ms.); Gardner; John H. Marion File APHS; 158, p. 139. Map: None.

## RED BUTTE

El.: 7600'  Loc.: Coconino 1, I-2.25

Called by the Havasupai Indians *hue-ga-da-wi-za,* or "Mountain of the Clenched Fist," this place was described by Lt. Edward Fitzgerald Beale on September 15, 1857, as "the most prominent landmark in view . . . of curious form, rising out of the plain and entirely isolated . . . the sides . . . quite red about half way up, and the shape of the whole somewhat resembles a bishop's mitre." Beale adds that he named the butte for Lt. C. E. Thorburn, U.S.N., who made the itinerary report for Beale's expedition. While searching for firewood, Thorburn picked up a rattlesnake, but the reptile was so torpid with cold that Thorburn quickly dropped it without harm to himself. Beale then shot the snake.

On his expedition up the Colorado, Lt. Joseph Christmas Ives spoke of Red Butte as having been described by Lt. Amiel W. Whipple in 1854.

Ref.: 12, pp. 54, 57; 92, p. 385; 93, pp. 13-14; 169, p. 25. Maps: B-4; B-5; C-3; E-23; E-11.

a.n. Red Hill  Map: GC-3. El.: 7750'  Coconino
　　Red Mountain  Map: B-8  Coconino
　　Red Mountain  Map: GL-3. El.: 6350'  Santa Cruz

Composed of reddish rhyolite, Red Mountain is a castle-shaped mass clearly seen from the road northeast of Patagonia. The Mexicans call it Sleeping Mountain, descriptive of its aspect from nearby Crittenden.

Ref.: Lenon; 133a, p. 240.

a.n. Red Rock Canyon  Map: GL-3  Santa Cruz

## RED HORSE WASH

El.: c. 6000'  Loc.: Coconino 1, BG-13-14

Ordinarily a dry wash, Red Horse Wash became a raging torrent on July 29, 1915, washing out the railroad bridge on the line to Grand Canyon. The night train from the Canyon was wrecked, the single casualty being Fred Terry, fireman on the train. The wash was named because of its proximity to Red Horse Tank, now disappeared.

v.n. Pozo de Santa Isabel  (Garcés: camped here July 1776)

Ref.: Barnes, quoting Coues; Hart; Terry (no relation). Map: B-4.

## RED LAKE

El.: c. 6000'  Loc.: Coconino 4, DE-3.2

This small lake contains water nearly all year. It is markedly red following a rain. During a brief period while the railroad to the Grand Canyon was being constructed, there was a post office at the small settlement called Red Lake.

P.O. est. June 16, 1888. Adah F. Stone, p.m. Discont. September 3, 1888.

Ref.: Benham; P.O. Records. Map: C-9.

## RED ROCK COUNTRY

El.: c. 4000'  Loc.: Coconino 4, I-8-9

The name "Red Rock Country" is descriptive of the outcroppings in the lower part of Oak Creek Canyon. Many parts of the area are wild and exceedingly rugged which, coupled with the red coloring, has led cowboys to call the region Hell's Hollow.

Ref.: 92, p. 57; 139, p. 22. Maps: None.

## RIMMY JIMS

El.: c. 6000'                    Loc.: Coconino 5, DE-11
                                Near Meteor Crater
Although Rimmy Jims is a small store and trading post on the highway, it is worthy of mention because of the origin of its name. The store was begun many years ago by an old cowman famous in northern Arizona for his dry wit. When he first came into the country, local cowboys noticed that his saddle rigging was attached far back rather than having the cinch belt fastened to the center of the saddle skirt or both front and back (double rigged). The analogy of this to rim-firing led to his being called Rimmy Jim and the name stuck. When he retired, he built his little store, which of course was called Rimmy Jim's. The owner was famous with motorists along the transcontinental highway, for Rimmy Jim could be counted on, not only for very casual car servicing, but for regaling his guests with the tallest of tales in endless variety.

Ref.: Present owner. Map: None.

## RIO DE FLAG

El.: 6000'-7500'                Loc.: Coconino 4, I-4.2;
                                Coconino 5, A-2-5.5.
Locally, the name Rio de Flag vies with the appellation "River de Flag" in popularity. The origin of the local name in the opinion of many is sly humor, since the stream usually runs only following heavy rains or when the snows are melting. However, since every city of importance is located on a river, residents place Flagstaff on one, thus implying the presence of additional commerce.

Apparently the stream used to run, for Lt. Lorenzo Sitgreaves' map (1851) names the stream Rio de San Francisco and shows it originating in the San Francisco Mountains and joining the Gila, an error due no doubt to the fact that its course was guessed at rather than explored. Lt. Amiel W. Whipple (1854) added to the guesswork by estimating that the stream probably formed the main branch of the Rio Verde, and on the 1859 Military Map it is called "Rio Verde or San Francisco." To avoid confusion which might arise from the fact that there was another San Francisco River in central-eastern Arizona, Whipple suggested that Sitgreaves' name for the stream be retained. He also indicated that Antoine Leroux was the one who told Sitgreaves the local name which Sitgreaves used on his map.

Ref.: Bartlett; 177, p. 167. Maps: GC-3; C-2 (Verde River); E-11 (Rio Verde or San Fernando); E-1 (San Francisco or Verde River).

a.n. San Francisco Wash                    Coconino
     Wash de Flag (Barnes)
     Flag Wash          Map: B-8          Coconino

## RIORDAN

El.: c. 8000'                    Loc.: Coconino 4, I-5.5
Pro.: /ríyrdṇ/
The Riordan brothers were successful lumbermen in the Flagstaff area. Timothy A. (b. Chicago, January 1, 1858) arrived in Flagstaff in 1884 where he joined his brother, Dan M. Riordan (b. Chicago). They were joined by

Michael James Riordan (d. October 7, 1930). The site of a former lumber camp, the settlement of Riordan was named for Dan M. Riordan after the brothers left the area. They sold their lumber interests in 1897. Dan Riordan was the Indian agent at Fort Defiance (q.v. Apache) 1880-1884.
P.O. est. June 18, 1917. Howard V. Haeberlin, p.m. (declined). Veronica McGonigle, p.m. February 25, 1918. Discont. September 25, 1925.
Ref.: Anderson; Timothy A. Riordan File, APHS; 112, III; P.O. Records. Maps: GC-2; GC-3; C-12.

## ROBBER'S ROOST

El.: c. 6000'                    Loc.: Coconino 3, AC-8-7.1.
                                Roughly in T. 27 N., R. 8 W.
Asa ("Ace") Harris tracked a train robber, Jim Parker, to this place where Parker was hiding out. Parker had robbed the train at Peach Springs. The two men had a gun battle, but Parker escaped.
Ref.: Harris; 169, p. 236. Map: GC-2 (Canyon).

## ROBINSON MOUNTAIN

El.: c. 8000'                    Loc.: Coconino 5, AB-3.3
Henry H. Robinson (1873-1925) wrote the *San Franciscan Volcanic Field* after surveying the area for the United States Government.

v.n. Robinson Crater
Ref.: 151, p. 645. Map: B-8.

## ROCK TOP MOUNTAIN

El.: 7359'                    Loc.: Coconino 5, AB-9.3
A big, broken malpais cap with boulders the size of dining tables gives Rock Top its descriptive name.
Ref.: Bill Corey. Maps: GM-21; C-7.
a.n. Rock Top Spring          Map: B-8                    Coconino

## RODEN SPRING

El.: c. 6000'                    Loc.: Coconino 5, D-3.1
Pro.: /rówdṇ/
In 1884 William D. Roden, Sr., with his family drove about two hundred cattle from Texas to Arizona, stopping for the winter at the Grand Falls on the Little Colorado River. In the springtime, three Hopis with burros passed Roden's camp, but — despite the fact that water was rare — did not stop to take water with them. Curious, Roden followed them toward the San Francisco Peaks. On the route he found a sign made with stones, near which was an iron bush. Crawling under the bush, Roden found moist ground, scraped out a hole and watched water come at once to the surface. The next day he returned to the seep with men and tools, dug the hole deeper and found enough water to warrant his moving to the place which bears his name. The Hopis were frequent and welcome visitors during Roden's many years' residence at Roden Spring.
Ref.: Switzer. Maps: B-9; C-13.

## ROGERS LAKE

El.: 7244'                    Loc.: Coconino 4, I-6.5
Charles Thomas Rogers (b. Maine 1829) came to Arizona in 1864. He had a cattle range near the present Rogers Lake

from May 1878 until he moved, either in late 1878 or early 1879, to the site of what was to become Williams. Rogers and his son Frank ran cattle in the vicinity of Williams during the 1880's and 1890's, using the 111 brand. Rogers dammed runoff waters to form the lake. Today it is bisected by the main highway, and the lake bed is dry.

Ref.: Benham; Sykes; 61, p. 54; Charles Thomas Rogers File APHS. Map: GC-3.

## ROSEBUD FLAT

El.: c. 8000'      Loc.: Coconino 4, G-4.3
Stanley Sykes (d. 1956) was sawmill foreman here and named the flat because of its blanket of wild roses.

Ref.: Sykes. Map: C-11 (springs).

## ROSE WELLS

El.: c. 6000'      Loc.: Coconino 3, E-6.5
Bill Rose owned these twin wells in the early days. They were dug by "Banjo Joe," an immense, tall fellow with black whiskers, who was always smiling and laughing and was noted for playing the banjo whenever he could find a moment. The wells were as unlike as possible in quality, one having sweet, potable water while the other had gypsum water. Rose Wells Ranch for many years had the only water in the area.

Ref.: Morse. Maps: A-13; GC-9.

## ROSS SPRING

El.: c. 6000'      Loc.: Coconino 4, H-7.3
From c. 1888 to 1895, Tom Ross was a partner with William Garland (cf. Garland Prairie) in the cattle business.

Ref.: Barnes. Maps: B-6; GC-3.

## ROUNDY CREEK

El.: c. 4000'      Loc.: Coconino 2, BA-9.4
Lorenzo W. Roundy was a Mormon bishop who was actively seeking to help establish colonies along the Little Colorado River. On May 28, 1876, he drowned during an attempted crossing of the Colorado River at Lee's Ferry.

Ref.: Barnes; 71, p. 42 (Note 1). Maps: GC-2; GC-9; D-4.

## RYAN

El.: c. 8000'      Loc.: Coconino 1, D-4
Aquilla Nebeker and his partner, a man named Ryan, worked mines in this locale c. 1900, calling their camp Coconino. When Nebeker sold out to Ryan, the latter changed the name.

P.O. est. February 6, 1902. Cass Lewis, p.m. Discont. October 23, 1903.
Ref.: Barnes; P.O. Records. Maps: B-9; C-9.

## ST. JOE SPRING

El.: 8000'      Loc.: Coconino 5, H-15.1
Mormon Bishop Joseph Hill Richards' sons, Will and Parley, lived at this point c. 1883, selling out c. 1888 to sheepmen. The two young men named it for the settlement of St. Joseph (q.v., Navajo).

Ref.: Barnes; 171, pp. 41-42. Map: B-9.
**a.n. St. Joe Canyon**      Map: B-9      Coconino

## SALMON LAKE

El.: c. 6000'      Loc.: Coconino 5, AB-14.
                          Sec. 18, T. 13 N., R. 8 E.
"Old Man" Williams, butcher at Camp Verde in 1880, was noted as a spinner of tall tales. He told a group leaving Camp Verde for a turkey hunt that they would not need to carry much grub because Williams had recently hidden a case of canned salmon in a tree near a small lake. Turkeys were scarce; the non-existent salmon could not be found, and the group nearly starved. Thereafter the lake was always referred to as Salmon Lake.

Ref.: Barnes. Map: None.

## SAN FRANCISCO MOUNTAIN

El.: c. 12,000'      Loc.: Coconino 5, A-3.6
San Francisco Mountain is of particular interest because its glacial deposits are one of the southermost indications of ice action in the United States. See San Francisco Peaks.

Ref.: 139, p. 32; 151, p. 666. Maps: GC-3; E-11; C-1.

## SAN FRANCISCO PEAKS

El.: 6000' to 12,000'      Loc.: Coconino 5, A-3.6
Sometimes referred to as the San Francisco Mountains, the group of peaks on the rim of what is also referred to *in toto* San Francisco Mountain, includes Agassiz, Fremont, and Humphreys. Their group name is an ancient one, dating back to c. 1629 when the Franciscans at Oraibe named the peaks to honor the founder of their order, St. Francis of Assisi. Farfán and Quesada called them Sierra Sinagua in 1598. In 1776, Garcés called them Sierra Napoc. Coues thinks this is an error for "Napao," or Navajo. There is a possibility that the Spanish name for the group ("Sierra Cienega") dates back to the name used in 1598, since phonetically the two are closely allied. Another name found on old Spanish maps is Sierra de los Cosninos, after Indians living in the area (cf. Cosnino Caves).

The San Francisco Peaks are the center of extinct volcanic activity which included an area of about three thousand square miles. The three principal mountains are important in the folklore of both the Navajo and the Hopi Indians. The Hopi regard the peaks as the home of their spirits. It has been suggested that the name San Francisco was applied by the missionaries at Oraibe to combat the importance of the peaks to the Hopi Indians. Although this naming method was often used by Franciscan missionaries, there is no documentary evidence which supports the naming of the San Francisco Peaks in this manner.

The desirability of the area at the base of the San Francisco Peaks for settlement has long been recognized. More than one effort was made to start colonies before Flagstaff flourished. In 1872 a group arrived from Colorado Territory, but its history beyond the mention of its arrival is not known. The so-called Boston Party in 1877 headed west for the same approximate location. Each man in the group paid $140 to the Arizona Colonization Company of Boston for transportation west, and each took with him his own provisions for ninety days, his own tools, and his own clothing. However, the group did not remain long in the area (cf. Flagstaff).

Ref.: *Citizen*, June 29, 1872, 1:4; 4, p. 319; 31, p. 352; 35, pp. 352, 353 (Note 32); 87, p. 50; 143, p. 1; 167, p. 134; 177, p. 166. Maps: E-11; C-1; C-5.

*a.n. San Francisco Wash        Map: B-8                    Coconino*

## SCHNEBLY HILL

El.: 6349'                    Loc.: Coconino 4, I-8.8
Theodore Carlton Schnebly (b. Hagerstown, Maryland, December 29, 1868; d. March 13, 1954) came to Arizona from Gorin, Missouri, on October 12, 1901. Among the first settlers in Oak Creek Canyon, he bought his place from Frank Owenby, who was the first settler in the area. In 1902 Schnebly put in the road which goes over the hill bearing his name. The road goes up over the Mogollon Rim from Oak Creek Canyon.

Ref.:   Schnebly (son). Maps: B-1; GM-21.

## SCHULTZ PASS

El.: 8000'                    Loc.: Coconino 5, A-4
Between the San Francisco Peaks and the Dry Lake Hills and Mount Elden lies Schultz Pass, named for Charley H. Schultz, a sheepman. Schultz Peak (also known as Schulz Mountain) c. 1922 was the site of a temporary observatory set up by the Lowell Observatory.

Ref.:   Anderson; Slipher; Sykes. Map: GC-3.

*a.n. Schultz Spring*

Loc.: E. end of road through Schulz Pass        Coconino
When the Babbitt brothers began raising foxes at the site of the first Elden Spring, the name was changed from Elden to Babbitt Spring. Thereafter the name "Elden Spring" was applied to the location of Schultz Spring. (cf. Babbitt Bill Tank, *a.n.* Babbitt Spring).

## SEDONA

El.: 4500'                    Loc.: Coconino 4, I-9.3
Pro.: /siydównə/
Sedona is a thriving community in Oak Creek Canyon. It was named by Ellsworth Schnebly for his sister-in-law, Sedona M. Schnebly (b. February 24, 1877; d. November 13, 1950). Mr. and Mrs. Theodore Carlton Schnebly arrived from Gorin, Missouri, in October 1901. They arrived in Arizona with their household goods on a freight car via the narrow gauge railroad to Jerome.

P.O. est. June 26, 1902. Theodore C. Schnebly, p.m.
Ref.:   Schnebly (son); P.O. Records. Maps: B-5; C-9; GM-21.

## SHEEP HILL

El.: c. 7115'                Loc.: Coconino 5, A-4.7
In all probability white men noticed Navajo sheep lying on this hill and applied a translation of the Navajo name (*dibé shijéé'í*: "where sheep lie down"). There is another possibility that mountain sheep may have used the hill, since Henry Clifton in 1869 noted such sheep at a place which he termed Sheep Tanks north of the Little Colorado River.

Ref.:   *Arizona Miner*, November 20, 1869, 2:1; 167, p. 142. Map: GC-3.

## SITGREAVES, MOUNT

El.: c. 8000'                Loc.: Coconino 4, G-4
Capt. Lorenzo Sitgreaves headed an expedition which crossed northern Arizona in 1851 in search of a feasible wagon road for emigrants who sought to reach California and its fabled wealth.

*v.n. Sitgreaves Peak*
Ref.: 177, p. 175 (Note 16). Maps: B-2; B-9; C-1; GC-3.

*a.n. Sitgreaves National Forest            Coconino and Yavapai*
In July 1908, parts of Black Mesa and Tonto National Forests were combined to form Sitgreaves National Forest.
Ref.: 120, p. 36.

## SLATE MOUNTAIN

El.: 8209'                    Loc.: Coconino 4, H-2
Rising nearly one thousand feet above the surrounding area is about a square mile of eroded slate formations which give this place its name.
Ref.: 139, p. 85. Map: GC-3.

*a.n. Slate Lakes        Map: B-9                    Coconino*

## SMOOT LAKE

El.: c. 6000'                Loc.: Coconino 4, F-2.3
William H. Smoot (d. 1902), a cattleman, who had lived in Prescott since 1877, arrived in the Williams vicinity c. 1881 and remained there until his death.
Ref.:   61, p. 53 and Footnote. Maps: B-4; C-13.

## SNAKE GULCH

El.: c. 5000'                Loc.: Coconino 1, BC-3.5-A-5
This narrow, long, twisting canyon literally snakes its way through the countryside.
Ref.:   Barnes. Map: B-5.

## SOLDIER LAKE

El.: c. 6000'                Loc.: Coconino 5, D-10
On the regular route from Fort Whipple to New Mexico, this lake was probably used by the military as a stopping place. Capt. Charles King and his men rested here after a battle with Apaches in October 1874.
Ref.:   Barnes. Maps: B-8; C-13.

## SQUARE BUTTE

El.: c. 6000'                Loc.: Coconino 2, FG-4
Descriptive.
Ref.:   Barnes. Map: C-12.

## STONEMAN LAKE

El.: 6722'                    Loc.: Coconino 5, A-10
In the early days of the Arizona Territory, this body of water in the crater of an old volcano was known as Chavez Lake (See: Chavez Pass, Navajo) a name which was later changed by John F. Marion to Stoneman's Lake.

Gen. George Stoneman (1822-1894) first saw Arizona when he was a lieutenant with Lt. Col. Philip St. George Cooke and the Mormon Battalion in southern Arizona in 1846. When a military department was formed in 1869 for southern California and Arizona with headquarters at Fort

Whipple, Gen. Stoneman was assigned to the command, taking his post in mid 1870. Following criticism of his rigid policies of punishment for Indians and also of his establishing new posts and improving old ones, he was replaced by Gen. George Crook in June 1871. It was largely through Stoneman's efforts that truces were made with the Mohaves, Wallapais (Hualapais), Yavapais and the so-called Apache-Yumas. Stoneman served as governor of California 1883-1887.

P.O. est. April 22, 1924. Phillip J. Morin, pm. Discont. December 2, 1939.

Ref.: 52, VIII, 97, 104; 4, pp. 451-452; 7, p. 558; 127, p. 7; 159, pp. 152, 242; P.O. Records. Maps: GM-21; C-9.

## SUMMIT MOUNTAIN

El.: c. 8500′                              Loc.: Coconino 4, E-6.3
Descriptive. The top of this mountain is nearly flat, with two points (one lying east and the other west) giving a marvelous view of the surrounding country. A main Forest Service lookout has been here since c. 1915.

Ref.: Benham. Map: B-6.

| a.n. Summit Spring | Map: B-6 | Coconino |
| Summit Valley | Map: B-5 | Coconino |

## SUNSET CRATER

El.: 8000′                              Loc.: Coconino 5, AB-3.5
Maj. John Wesley Powell named the crater in 1892 because of the cinder colors which grade downward from the summit through shades of yellow, orange, red, and deep red into the black volcanic ash on the lower part of the cone. Sunset Crater National Monument was established on May 26, 1930. The crater rises about one thousand feet above the area at its base. A foot trail winding up the side of the cone leads the visitor to a view of the four-hundred-foot deep crater, which was formed c. 1066 A.D. by volcanic eruption.

Interesting to visitors are the Bonita Lava Flow (q.v.) and the Ice Caves. Ice caves were formed when the hot mass on the surface cooled, leaving a crust, while the molten lava underneath flowed away. A poor conductor of heat, lava retains cold air which settles into the cave, and ice is a year-round phenomenon. In the 1880's, ice from this and similar lava caves was used in homes and saloons in Flagstaff. The Sunset Crater Ice Caves have an extremely rough interior and have never been fully explored.

Ref.:4, p. 286; 5, p. 7; 167, p. 153. Maps: GC-3; C-13; C-9; C-7 (Sunset Peak).

## SUNSET PASS

El.: c. 6000′                              Loc.: Coconino 5, GH-8-9
The old Hopi trail to southern parts of the present Arizona crossed the Little Colorado River near Sunset Crossing and then proceeded to Sunset Pass or Gap. The pass lies between two lava-topped mesas known as Table Mountain (descriptive) and Sunset Mountain. From that point, the trail went to Chavez Pass (q.v. Navajo). Sunset Pass was the scene of Capt. Charles King's battle with Apaches (October, 1874), in which King received such severe wounds that he

was retired from service, later writing an account of his experiences published under the title The Sunset Pass.

Ref.: 11, p. 24; Barnes. Maps: E-18; E-20; C-4.

## SUNSHINE

El.: c. 6000′                              Loc.: Coconino 5, FG-6.8
When operations began at Meteor Crater (q.v.) it was necessary to have a shipping station on the railroad. At first this was called Sunset, but in 1902, the name had to be changed because of another station under that name already on the line. S. J. Holsinger named it Sunshine.

Ref.: Barnes. Map: C-10.

## SUPAI

El.: c. 6000′                              Loc.: Coconino 4, E-5
Pro.: /súwpay/
This place is a section house for the S.F.R.R. It is named for the Havasupai Indians (cf. Havasu Canyon, Grand Canyon).

Here westbound trains stop to make a brake test before dropping over the western end of the long Mogollon Rim (q.v.) to lower elevations to the west.

P.O. est. September 5, 1896. Rufus C. Bauer, p.m.

Ref.: Terry; P.O. Records. Maps: C-8; D-1.

## SWITZER MESA

El.: c. 6000′                              Loc.: Coconino 5, A-5
Pro.: /swáytzer/
William Asa Switzer arrived in Flagstaff in 1884.

Ref.: Sykes (née Switzer). Map: GC-3.

## TABLE MOUNTAIN

El.: 7708′                              Loc.: Coconino 5, AB-3.7; T. 23 N., R. 8 E.
"Table" as a name occurs descriptively in several place names. The Table Mountain in Coconino County along with Sunset Mountain forms Sunset Pass (q.v.) through which the old trail went from the Hopi Villages to the Verde Valley.

Ref.: 41, p. 198; 11, p. 24. Map: None.

| a.n. Table Mountain | Loc.: T. 2 S., R. 28 E. | | Greenlee |
| Table Mountain | Map: C-12 | | Mohave |
| Table Top Mountain | Map: C-12 | | Pinal |
| Table, The | Map: C-12 | | Gila |

Sam Hill, a prospector, had a cabin near this mountain, which he named.

| Table Mountain | Map: GK-30 | | Pinal |
| Table Mountain | Map: GK-15. El.: 6158′ | | Pinal |
| Little Table Mountain | Map: GK-15 | | Pinal |
| Little Table Mountain | Map: GE-5. El.: 6254′ | | Pinal |
| Tabletop Mountains | Map: GK-1 | | Pinal |

v.n. Table Mountain

Table Rock Mountain

| Little Table Top Mountain | Map: GG-17. El.: 2900′ | Pinal |
| Table Top Mountain | Map: GG-17. El.: 4200′ | Pinal |

Table Top Valley

Loc.: Boundaries: West-Vekol Valley; South-Vekol Mountains; East-Santa Rosa Valley (ridge); North-Table Top Mountains.                              Pinal

Ref.: 128, p. 19.

| Tabletop | Map: GK-1. El.: 4373′ | Pinal |
| Tablelands, The | Map: GK-6. El.: 3725′ | Pinal |

## TANNER CROSSING

El.: c. 4000'                     Loc.: Coconino 2, C-14
Seth B. Tanner of Tuba City was a Mormon who helped establish the Tanner-French trail into the Grand Canyon. The crossing on the Little Colorado River near Cameron was a rocky ford which permitted pioneers to avoid the treacherous quicksands of the river bottom.

**v.n. Tanners Crossing**
Ref.:   93, p. 36; 151, p. 743. Map: C-12.

## TENNEYS GULCH

El.: c. 6000'                     Loc.: Coconino 1, AD-5
Ammon M. Tenney, a Mormon missionary in 1879, was instrumental in purchasing land at St. Johns (*q.v.* Apache) for Mormon colonization. Earlier (1870) he had explored the country with Maj. John Wesley Powell and the Mormon guide and explorer, Jacob Hamblin.

Ref.:   Barnes; APHS Names File. Maps: C-5; E-20.

**a.n. Tenneys Spring**        Map: C-7                     Coconino

## THOUSAND WELLS

El.: c. 6000'                     Loc.: Coconino 2, FG-10
Maj. John Wesley Powell said "Thousand Wells" comes from the fact that the area contains a number of water pockets.

Ref.:   132, p. 189. Maps: A-3; C-3; C-20 (Tousand Wells).

## THREE MILE LAKE

El.: c. 6000'                     Loc.: Coconino 4, E-4.2
A wet weather lake, Three Mile Lake is three miles from Williams, hence its name.

Ref.:   Benham; Barnes. Maps: B-4; C-13; C-14.

## TOLANI LAKES

El.: c. 4000'                     Loc.: Coconino 5, H-2.3
Pro.:   /tósʼsani/ Navajo:    *to,* "water"; *lani,* "many bodies"
Several fresh water lakes occur in seven basins at the divide which separates Jadito, First Mesa and Oraibe washes (See Tonolea).

Ref.:   151, p. 760; 71, pp. 39, 117. Maps: C-2; D-4; GC-2.

## TOLFREE

El.: c. 7000'                     Loc.: Coconino 1, I-12.5
Lyman H. Tolfree, first postmaster for this place, gave it his name. He had a hotel at Grand Canyon on the Hance Trail.

P.O. est. August 13, 1894. Discont. February 2, 1896.
Ref.:   Barnes; APHS Names File; P.O. Records. Map: C-8.

## TONOLEA

El.: 6457'                        Loc.: Coconino 2, G-7.5
Pro.:   /tóniˇhēlíˆ/
A typical Indian trading post, Tonolea is perched on a small hill overlooking an ephemeral sink which has been dammed so that it is now a storage lake. The old name for Tonolea was Red Lake, a name so common in the Navajo country that the present name was selected as more distinctive.

P.O. est. as Tonolea, January 21, 1926. James P. O'Farrell, p.m.
Ref.:   4, p. 422; 71, p. 117; P.O. Records. Maps: C-10 (Red Lake); C-13; D-4.

## TOMS CREEK

El.: c. 7000'                     Loc.: Coconino 5, B-13
Tom Maitell was the first settler on this stream. Locally, he was known as "Greasy Tom."

Ref.:   Barnes. Map: B-7.

## TOWER BUTTE

El.: 6000'                        Loc.: Coconino 2, D-0-1
Flat-topped mesas from which this takes its name form the old surface into which nearby canyons have been carved by erosion.

Ref.:   71, p. 44. Maps: GC-9; C-10; C-12.

## TUBA

El.: 4450'                        Loc.: Coconino 2, D-11
Pro.:   /túwbə/
Because of the presence of over thirty springs in this area, Indians were cultivating land near the present Tuba City when Fr. Francisco Garcés visited the place in 1776. This included Havasupai and Hopi from Oraibe. Hopi Indians were still there when Jacob Hamblin, the Mormon explorer and missionary, passed through during the 1850's and 1860's. The name of the chief was TIvi, whose name was pronounced both as Tocobi and Tuba by his Mormon friends. In November 1870, Hamblin took him on a visit to Utah. In 1873 Horton D. Haight with his Mormon emigrant party remained for some time at the site of the present Tuba City, but passed on to settle on the Little Colorado River. In 1875 James S. Brown arrived with Mormon settlers, but it was not until 1878 that Erastus Snow laid out the present site of the town near Musha Spring, two miles north of the Mormon settlement at Moencopie (*q.v.*). Unwittingly, the colonists were establishing themselves on Indian land. In 1903 the U. S. government purchased improvements made by the Mormons, who then moved out.

P.O. est. as Tuba City July 31, 1884. Thomas W. Brookbank, p.m. Name changed to Tuba, April 4, 1894.
Ref.:   71, p. 143; 167, pp. 163, 100; 112, pp. 80, 158; 164, p 1; P.O. Records. Maps: G-6; C-8; GC-2; GC-8.

**a.n. Tuba Butte**        Loc.: N.e. of Tuba 10 miles        Coconino
**Tuba Springs**           Loc.: At Tuba                       Coconino

## TUCKERS PASS

El.: c. 6500'                     Loc.: Coconino 5, E-10.7
Lt. Edward Fitzgerald Beale mentions traveling through this pass and joining his train at Floyd's Peak (*q.v.*) about twelve miles away.

Ref.:   Barnes. Maps: None.

## TUNNEL, THE

El.: c. 8000'                     Loc.: Coconino 5, CD-14
In 1885 the Arizona Mineral Belt Railroad attemped to put in a line joining Globe and Flagstaff. This necessitated some

means of getting the line up over the Mogollon Rim. So great was the belief in its future success that young men who worked on the project took their pay in grub stake and stock while they used their mules digging a tunnel to be used by the railroad. However, in 1887 Alec Pendleton, surveyor for the road, found what he considered a better way to reach the Rim, and the tunnel was abandoned. The ambitious young men held the stock until 1888 or 1889 when the road was sold by the Yavapai County sheriff to the Riordan Lumber Company of Flagstaff. By that time more than forty miles of the road had been completed. As late as 1920 there were piles of ax-hewn ties still lying along the proposed right of way south of Mormon Lake. In the intervening years the history of the seventy-five foot tunnel has become obscured.

Ref.: Croxen; Woody. Map: None.

## TURKEY CREEK

El.: 7000′      Loc.: Coconino 5, FE-14-15

An abundance of wild turkeys in Arizona led many people to apply the name "Turkey" descriptively to various places. One creek was named by Lt. Amiel W. Whipple; it is probably the present Pine Creek (Coconino), which is not the same as the one for which a location is given here.

Ref.: 177, pp. 190-191 (Note 8); 40, p. 6; 4, p. 317. Maps: B-9; GD-12.

| a.n. Turkey Butte | El.: 7304′. Map: B-6 | Coconino |
|---|---|---|
| Turkey Creek | | Yavapai |
| Turkey Creek | | Cochise |
| Turkey Creek | Loc.: T. 5. N., R. 25 E. | Navajo and Apache |
| Turkey Mountain | Map: B-8 | Coconino |
| Turkey Mountain | Loc.: W. of Morenci 8 miles | Graham |
| Turkey Mountain | | |
| | El.: 6736′. Loc.: Sec. 1, T. 1 S., R. 29 E. | Greenlee |
| Turkey Hills | Map: GC-3 | Coconino |

Named by Stanley Sykes, who used to hunt turkeys here.

Turkey Hill Ruin    Loc.: E. of Flagstaff 9 miles    Coconino

The mound covers what is thought to be one of the largest and most recently abandoned pueblos in the region.

## TUSAYAN

El.: c. 6000′      Loc.: Coconino 1, F-13.2

Pro.: /túwsayan/

The name "Tusayan" was that given by Spanish explorers in the sixteenth century to the Hopi Villages (q.v.).

P.O. est. April 24, 1934. Jay Vincent Galindo, p.m. Discont. February 27, 1937.

Ref.: P.O. Records. Map: F-6.

## TUTHILL, FORT

El.: 6907′      Loc.: Coconino 5, A-6

Camp Tuthill, created in 1928 when the Arizona legislature provided funds for the project at this area, was named for Brig. Gen. Alexander MacKenzie Tuthill, commander of the Arizona National Guard which formerly used the camp as headquarters. On April 11, 1955, Gov. Ernest McFarland signed papers which created from it the present Coconino County Park and Recreational Area. Virgin timber in the area towers two hundred feet.

Ref.: Barnes; Mrs. Corey; Sykes. Map: B-8.

## TWENTY-NINE MILE BUTTE

El.: c. 6500′      Loc.: Coconino 5, B-14

When military routes were being established, it was customary to name locations by their distances from army posts. Twenty-nine Mile Butte is that distance on the Crook road from Camp Verde.

Ref.: Barnes; Goddard. Maps: C-13; C-14.

| a.n. Twenty-nine Mile Lake | | |
|---|---|---|
| Loc.: Sec. 36, T. 13 N., R. 9 E. | | Coconino |
| Twenty-seven Mile Lake | | |
| Loc.: Sec. 23, T. 13 N., R. 9 E. | | Coconino |

## TWIN SPRINGS

El.: c. 8900′      Loc.: Coconino 4, EF-5.8

Originally the main spring was known as Andrews Spring after Tom Andrews who took up a claim here in 1903. Andrews moved to Williams c. 1905. The springs lie about twenty yards apart, the one to the east drying each summer.

Ref.: Smith; Benham. Map: B-6.

## VAIL LAKE

El.: 7161′      Loc.: Coconino 5, B-6.7

At one time sheepmen used this area for lambing, from whence came the name Lambing Lake. However, Jim Vail later established a cow camp beside the lake and the name gradually changed to Vail Lake.

v.n. Lambs Lake

Ref.: Barnes. Maps: GC-3; B-5; C-12 (Lambing Lake).

## VALLE

El.: 6000′      Loc.: Coconino 4, F-1

Pro.: /váyey/ or     Spanish: "valley"
/væli^/             prado, "meadow"

The Spanish name for this small open valley was changed in the mid-1920's to Prado when the name was used for the small railroad station at this point. Because there was already another "Prado" on the Prescott-Phoenix ("Peavine") Railroad, the name soon was changed back to Valle. Apparently it had been called Prado at an earlier date also.

Ref.: Benham; Terry. Maps: B-4; C-10.

## VINEYARD CANYON

El.: 5000′      Loc.: Coconino 5, DE-14-15

John Allen Vineyard was an early settler in this vicinity.

Ref.: Agnes Ollsen (daughter of Vineyard). Map: B-7.

a.n. Vineyard Mountain     Map: B-7     Gila

## VOLUNTEER MOUNTAIN

El.: 8057′      Loc.: Coconino 4, H-5.5

The origin of the name "Volunteer" is still obscure. Hinton noted Volunteer Spring as a station on the road from the Colorado River (mouth of the Paria) to Prescott, indicating that the name has been attached to the area for many years.

Ref.: 87, p. xxxvii. Maps: C-11; GC-3.

a.n. Volunteer Canyon     Map: GC-3     Coconino

## WALKER LAKE

El.: 7910'                    Loc.: Coconino 4, HG-4.4
Walker Lake was so called as early as 1878 when settlers in
the Flagstaff area were very few. The origin of the name is
obscured, but it is reported that a man named Walker for
many years farmed at the base of the mountain bearing
the name.
Ref.:   Daniel O'Leary File, APHS; Slipher; *Arizona Enterprise,*
        September 18, 1878. Map: GC-3.

## WALNUT CANYON NATIONAL MONUMENT

El.: 6500'                    Loc.: Coconino 5, AB-5.5-6
On February 6, 1858, Lt. Edward Fitzgerald Beale wrote
of arriving at Walnut Creek where his party breakfasted
and spent the day. Beale visited the ancient Indian ruins,
learning that what he had thought to be mere piles of
stones were actually ruins of houses.

A creek runs through Walnut Canyon. The gorge, about
four hundred feet deep, has eroded in a series of ledges on
which prehistoric Indians constructed one-room dwellings
utilizing the overhanging ledges for ceilings. These curious
houses were first fully investigated by a white man in 1883
by James Stevenson. Walnut Canyon soon became a happy
souvenir hunting ground for residents from Flagstaff and
its vicinity. The extreme vandalism led to measures to protect the ruins, with the result that Walnut Canyon National
Monument was created on November 30, 1915.

Walnut Creek changes name to San Francisco Wash *(q.v.)*
at its juncture with the S.F.R.R. It is probable that this is
the same creek which Capt. Amiel W. Whipple called
Pueblo Creek because of the numerous Indian ruins along
its banks.
Ref.:   Sykes; MNA; 5, "Monument to Vandalism," pp. 2, 5, 6;
        12, p. 82; 177, p. 191, (Note 8). Maps: C-12; GC-3; C-2
        (Walnut Creek)
a.n. **Walnut Canyon Wash**                              Coconino

## WARD TERRACE

El.: 5000'                    Loc.: Coconino 2, C-12.5
Lester F. Ward's work "in the Painted Desert region marked
the beginning of detailed stratigraphic studies for the
Navajo Reservation," reports Herbert Gregory, who applied
the name to the area.
v.n. **Ward Mesa**
Ref.:   71, p. 40 (Note 1); 29, p. 36. Map: D-4.

## WELCH

El.: c. 6000'                 Loc.: Coconino 4, C-5
Welch was a former section house on the S.F.R.R. It was
named for the Welch family, all of whom have since left.
Ref.:   Slamon. Maps: C-13; GM-1.

## WEST CLEAR CREEK

El.: c. 6000'                 Loc.: Coconino 5, B-13-14
Descriptive. Formerly referred to as Clear Creek, the name
is now West Clear Creek to eliminate confusion with the
Clear Creek which flows into the Little Colorado River.
Ref.:   Barnes. Map: CM-21.

## WET BEAVER CREEK

El.: c. 7000'                 Loc.: Coconino 5, B-10-A-11
Two neighboring creeks bore the name "Wet Beaver." How-
ever, one usually was dry while the other was wet most of
the time. Hence, the names Dry Beaver Creek and Wet
Beaver Creek.
Ref.:   Barnes. Maps: C-9; GC-2; C-5 (Beaver Creek).

## WHITE HILL

El.: c. 6000'                 Loc.: Coconino 4, FG-1.2
This hill is limestone.
Ref.:   Barnes. Map: B-4.

## WHITE HORSE HILLS

El.: c. 9000'                 Loc.: Coconino 5, A-3
Cowboys of the A-1 Cattle outfit named the hills c. 1885
because of the presence of a cream-colored mare which
ranged in the hills for more than twenty years.
v.n. **Marble Hills (Robinson)**
Ref.:   Barnes. Map: GC-3.
a.n. **White Horse Spring**        Map: B-9               Coconino
    In 1888 Mrs. George (née Mary Baker) Hochderffer, wife
    of a pioneer rancher, discovered this spring, which for sev-
    eral years was known as Mary's Spring. Its location in the
    White Horse Hills caused a gradual shift in the name.

## WHITE HORSE LAKE

El.: c. 6000'                 Loc.: Coconino 4, GH-6
In September, 1934, plans were completed for the creation
of a community lake to be formed by a dam on a tributary
to Sycamore Canyon. The dam was finished in early 1935.
Run-off from heavy snows nearly ruined the dam, which
was saved by quick and concerted action by residents of
Williams. In 1951 the dam was raised to double its capacity. It is a popular recreation area.
Ref.:   61, p. 147. Map: B-6.

## WHITE MESA

El.: c. 6500'                 Loc.: Coconino 2, EF-5
James White claimed to have gone through the Grand Can-
yon on a raft in 1857, prior to Maj. John Wesley Powell's
expedition. According to his story, his two companions
(Capt. C. Baker and Henry Strole) lost their lives, but
White managed to emerge from the canyon. His story is
considered not true (cf. Whites Butte, Grand Canyon).
Ref.:   71, p. 41. Maps: C-1; GC-2; E-20.

## WHITE SAGE WASH

El.: c. 4000'                 Loc.: Coconino 1, DC-1-1.5
The wash runs through a white sage flat.
Ref.:   Barnes. Map: B-5.

## WHITING                                    Loc.: Not known.

This place was probably named for the family of the first
postmaster.
P.O. est. July 12, 1944. Mrs. Mabel Whiting Shumway, p.m.
Rescinded, October 21, 1944.
Ref.:   N. R. Abrams, Asst. P.M. Gen., P.O. Dept., Letter,
        March 28, 1956. Map: None.

## WHITMORE POOLS

El.: c. 6000'                    Loc.: Coconino 2, EF-7
Dr. James M. Whitmore (d. January 8, 1866) settled in 1863 at Pipe Springs (*q.v.* Mohave). A stockman, he had several water holes in the region. He was killed by Indians.

Ref.:   71, p. 157. Maps: C-3; C-7; GC-2.

a.n. Wittmore Springs      Map: C-7                    Coconino

## WILDCAT CANYON

El.: c. 6000'                    Loc.: Coconino 5, H-13.5-16
Robert (Bob) Casbeer, a sheepman, named this canyon because in it a wildcat raided his sheep, killing several in a single night.

Ref.:   Barnes. Map: B-9.

## WILDCAT PEAK

El.: 6648'                    Loc.: Coconino 2, FG-7.5
                    Navajo: *náshdoits'o'i*, "mountain lion"
The American name for this huge igneous needle is a translation of the Navajo.

Ref.:   71, pp. 41, 197. Map: GC-9.

## WILLAHA

El.: c. 6000'                    Loc.: Coconino 1, DE-15
                    Supai: "watering place"
Despite the name of this location, the tanks ordinarily were dry, which made it necessary to haul water from Williams via the railroad to Grand Canyon for use by stockmen at this place. In 1956 a test mining operation for low grade copper and uranium was being conducted here.

Ref.:   Terry; Barnes. Maps: C-10; C-12.

## WILLIAMS

El.: 6792'                    Loc.: Coconino 4, EF-5
The location of Williams at the base of Bill Williams Mountain (*q.v.*) accounts for its name. First white men in the area were Sam Ball and John Vinton, who arrived in 1876. However, their interests were bought by Charles Thomas Rogers (b. Maine, 1827) who arrived in 1877.

With the coming of the railroad, Williams began its long history of prosperity and poverty followed by more prosperity, gradually becoming an important lumbering and railroad town, which is known today as the "Gateway to the Grand Canyon."

P.O. est. June 14, 1881. Charles T. Rogers, p.m. Wells Fargo Station, 1885.

Ref.:   P.O. Records; 55, p. 578. Maps: C-5; C-12; GC-2; GC-9.

## WILLOW CREEK

El.: c. 8000'                    Loc.: Coconino 5, EF-14-12.5
In 1885 many willows were growing at the head of this canyon.

Ref.:   Barnes. Map: B-7.

a.n. Willow Spring           Map: B-9                    Coconino
     Willow Springs Canyon   Map: B-7                    Coconino
     Willow Valley           Map: B-8                    Coconino

Once used by Hopi for farming, this area formed part of the Mormon Trail established by Jacob Hamblin and others in the 1860's and 1870's. The wash runs into Hamblin (after Jacob Hamblin) Canyon where many pioneer travelers who watered stock at these springs have carved their names. A mile south are some of the finest petroglyphs in the Southwest.

v.n. Oakley Springs      (Gilbert, 1879; on Mallory map)

Ref.:   MNA; 71, p. 145; 167, p. 173.

## WILSON MOUNTAIN

El.: 7116'                    Loc.: Coconino 4, I-8.5
This mountain was named for a man killed in nearby Wilson Canyon.

Ref.:   Barnes. Map: GM-21.

a.n. Wilson Canyon
     Loc.: T. 18 N., R. 6 E., s.w. corner          Coconino

## WILSON PUEBLO

El.: c. 6000'                    Loc.: Coconino 5, E-6.5
                    At Two Guns, ¼ mile north of U.S. 66.
The Museum of Northern Arizona was in charge of excavating this Indian ruin, built c. 1050 A.D. It was named for Ida G. Wilson, librarian at the state college in Flagstaff, who was responsible for interesting the museum staff in the excavation.

Ref.:   Bartlett; 167, p. 26. Map: None.

## WING MOUNTAIN

El.: c. 9000'                    Loc.: Coconino 4, H-4.5
In 1884 this mountain was referred to as Mount Wainwright, after Ellis Wainwright, who had an interest in the A 1 Cattle Company. The name was apparently changed later to honor another owner in the company, "Old Man" Wing, who also owned the Wing Cattle Company.

v.n. Mount Wing

Ref.:   Barnes; Sykes; Conrad; Dietzman. Maps: B-3; C-7; C-12; GC-3.

## WINONA

El.: c. 6000'                    Loc.: Coconino 5, C-5.6
Pro.: /wáynównə/
The first name for this station on the railroad was Walnut, a descriptive name. It was changed to Winona in 1886, but the origin of the name is not known at present. In 1910 the only family living here was named Sproat. What was probably one of the first tourist camps in the United States was started here c. 1920 by Billy Adams on the old Santa Fe trail. When the highway was moved, the small settlement died.

Children in this area attended school in the summer because heavy winter snows precluded their following the usual schedule.

P.O. est. June 19, 1924. Mrs. Myrtle Adams, p.m. Discont. August 15, 1943.

Ref.:   Sproat; Mr. and Mrs. Adams; P.O. Records. Maps: GC-2; C-12.

## WOODS CANYON

El.: c. 9000″                    Loc.: Coconino 5, FG-15
J. X. (Jack) Woods (d. California 1925) of Winslow
grazed sheep in the 1880's in this region. He was a railroad engineer, retiring c. 1900.

Ref.:   Barnes. Maps: B-7; B-9.

## WOOLFS CROSSING

El.: c. 4000′                    Loc.: Coconino 5, E-3.5
A trading post and mission used to exist here, known as
Tolchico or also as Tolchaco. Woolfs Crossing was one of
the places where the Little Colorado River could be forded.
The name "Tolchico" in Navajo means "Red Water Wash."
The name Woolf came from the fact that a trapper, Herman
Voltz or Woolf (b. c. 1810; d. January 1899), settled here
after a life as a "mountain man." After 1865 he maintained
a one-room post, trading goods with the Indians for the
beaver pelts they brought to him.

P.O. est. as Tolchaco, March 31, 1903. Charles Robinson, p.m.
Discont. August 31, 1922.

Ref.:   MNA; 167, pp. 159, 176; 71, p. 39; 29, p. 41; P.O.
        Records. Maps: D-4; C-10 (Tolchaco); GC-2 (Woolfs
        Crossing); C-6 (The Crossing); C-12 (Wolf Crossing).

## WUPATKI NATIONAL MONUMENT

El.: c. 6000′                    Loc.: Coconino 4, AD-1-2
Pro.:   /wopátki^/              "red ruins in black cinder"
The first expedition into the part of the Southwest newly
annexed from Mexico was made by Lt. Lorenzo D. Sitgreaves in 1851. His group camped at Wupatki.
On December 9, 1924, the area was set aside as a national
monument containing many Indian ruins, the principal ones
of which are Wupatki (a red sandstone ruin of 125 rooms);
Teuwalanki (Hopi, "citadel"), which is atop a small mesa;
and Nalakihu (Hopi, "house alone"), at the foot of the hill.

Ref.:   5, p. 7; 4, pp. 38, 285-86. Maps: B-9; C-13.

## YEAGER CANYON

El.: c. 9000′                    Loc.: Coconino 5, DE-13-15
As this canyon was named before Louis D. Yeager came
into the area, the origin of the name remains doubtful.

Ref.:   Stemmer. Map: CD-12.

a.n. Yeager Lake            Map: B-8                    Coconino

# GILA

*Roosevelt Dam — mining — the big chunk of silver ore that gave Globe its name.*

## GILA COUNTY:

Pro.: /híylə/

Gila County was formed from parts of Maricopa and Pinal counties on February 8, 1881, and was extended eastward to the San Carlos River by petition in 1889. It contains 3,040,000 acres. The county was named for the Gila River, which forms part of its southern boundary. The county seat was established at what was originally called Globe City, now Globe *(q.v.)*, an important copper mining center.

The elevation of Gila County varies from 2,123 feet at Roosevelt Dam to 7,153 feet at Mount Ord. Over half of the county is occupied by the San Carlos Indian Reservation (cf. San Carlos River), which in turn extends into Graham County for half its own area. The principal industries of Gila County have always been and continue to be mining and the raising of livestock.

## ALISO CREEK

El.: c. 2500'  Loc.: Gila 2, CA-8.2
Pro.: /alíyso/  Spanish: "alder tree"
Descriptive. This name was in use at least as early as 1864. On the San Carlos Indian Reservation map Aliso Creek shows as a small tributary to Gilson Creek, but on the Gila County map and one forest map (B-7) it shows as a larger creek but not labelled. The name Gilson appears only on one map.

Ref.: *Arizona Miner*, May 11, 1864, 3:3. Maps: C-12; C-14; B-7; E-18; C-4.

## AMSTER
Loc.: Northeast of Globe a short distance.
N. L. Amster was president of the Shannon Copper Company.

Ref.: 102, p. 10. Map: None.

## ANCHA, SIERRA

El.: c. 5000'  Loc.: Gila 1, CH-4-8
Pro.: /siyérənčə/  Spanish: "broad mountain"
The name of these mountains is derived from the fact that their base is not cut by canyons. This gives the range a broad quality before it separates into peaks which include McFadden, Baker, Aztec, Center, and McFadden Horse Mountain. The Mohaves called the mountains *Ewee-Tha-Quaw-Ai*, meaning "Wide Ranges of Rocks." These mountains concealed camps for many bands of Apaches. The fact that the mountains harbored many Indians is reflected in the great number of skirmishes recorded in official army records, the first occurring in 1864 and the last in 1875.

Ref.: 85, p. 692; Woody; 52, III, 304; 85, pp. 441, 447; *Weekly Arizona Miner*, August 13, 1864 (State Library Files). Maps: GD-2; GD-9; GD-17; C-2; E-20.

a.n. **Sierra Ancha Experimental Forest**
Maps: GD-6, GD-14  Gila
**Sierra Ancha Forest Reserve**  Maps: GD-6, GD-14  Gila
In 1900 it was recommended that this reserve be established.
Ref.: 55, p. 729.

**Sierra Ancha Mines**  Map: B-7  Gila
The white spots visible on the sides of the Sierra Ancha are not snow but evidences of the asbestos mine located in the mountains. The gradual accumulation of dust on the ore dump is slowly changing color so that it no longer looks as white as snow.
Ref.: 4, p. 365; Woody.

## ANGORA

El.: c. 6000'  Loc.: Gila 1, C-1
John F. Holder, first and only postmaster at this place, had angora goats.

P.O. est. June 25, 1900. John F. Holder, p.m. Discont. February 5, 1908.

Ref.: Barnes. Map: C-10.

## APACHE PEAKS

El.: c. 4500'  Loc.: Gila 1, H-9
Pro.: /əpǽči/
At one time Apaches roamed through what were known as the Apache Mountains, where at least two skirmishes with troops occurred in 1870 and 1871. The name no longer applies to the mountains, but only to the four peaks which are grouped closely together.

Ref.: 85, pp. 435, 436; Barnes. Maps: C-12; B-7.
a.n.
Many place names use the word "Apache." A few are given below.

| | | |
|---|---|---|
| **Apache Canyon** | Map: GB-23 | Graham |
| **Apache Spring** | Map: GB-23 | Graham |
| **Apache Peak** | Map: GK-30 | Pinal |

## APACHE TRAIL

El. c. 4000'  Loc.: Gila 1, EH-8.5-12
Pro. /əpǽči/  Maricopa 2, EI-5-6
The Apache Trail was late-born. When the trail finally developed, it followed Tonto Trail, referred to at times as the Yavapai Trail because members of the latter tribe lived along the north Tonto Creek which the trail followed.

The first part of the later automobile highway was built in connection with the construction of Roosevelt Dam in 1905, when the Reclamation Service cleared a road from Mesa to connect with the settlement of Roosevelt at the dam. The road was carved along the sides of mountains, through canyons, and over plateaus by Apaches under the direction of Louis C. Hill, supervising engineer. The Apache Trail Stage Company was incorporated on October 8, 1914. It was this stage line which hauled passengers who disembarked at Globe from the railroad, to Phoenix where they again boarded the train. The company did its best to make the trip as entertaining as possible. In many instances this included putting up numerous road signs bearing place names with fabulously interesting and entirely inaccurate stories. Stage passengers were enthralled by the tall tales of the Wild West, told by the drivers. The charter for the stage company expired on October 8, 1939.

The Apache Trail is one of the most beautiful in Arizona.

Ref.: Woody; 112, p. 218; State Library Archives. Map: A-13.

## ARMER

El.: c. 4000'  Loc.: Gila 1, F-8
Pioneer cattlemen, the Armer family conducted the post office at Armer.

P.O. est. March 12, 1884. Lucinda Armer, p.m. Discont. May 13, 1895.

Ref.: Barnes; P.O. Records. Map: C-6.

a.n. **Armer Gulch**  Map: B-7  Gila
**Armer Mountain**  Map: B-7  Gila
**Armer Wash**  Loc.: Same as Armer Gulch  Gila
**Armer and Tanner Winter Camp**  Map: B-7  Gila

## ARRASTRA GULCH

El.: c. 4000'  Loc.: Gila 1, C-2
Pro.: /arǽstrə/ or  Spanish: "drag-stone mill"
/ərǽstrə/
Early miners in Arizona ground their ores by means of what was known as an *arrastra*. An *arrastra* was constructed by making a circular pit into which the ore was dumped. It was then ground by means of a large rock, usually fairly flat, to which was attached a stout limb from a mesquite or

other tree. A pole, set at right angles to this central pole which was upright in the grinding stone, was hitched to a mule which spent its day going around in a circle while the ores were slowly ground down to dust. Occasionally water was poured over the ore to ease the work.

The wide-spread use of *arrastras* led to the use of the word in many place names. Two examples are given below.

Ref.:   Woody; Croxen. Map: GD-9.

**a.n. Arrastra Lake**

      Loc.: On Colorado River few miles n. of Yuma     Yuma

     **Arrastra Wash**     Map: GN-18     Yuma

## ASH CREEK

El.: c. 4000′     Loc.: Gila 2, AB-3

King S. Woolsey led an expedition against the Indians in 1864. The members of the expedition named this creek because of the ash trees found on its banks.

Ref.:   *Arizona Miner,* May 11, 1864, 3:3. Maps: GD-1; GD-11; GD-6; E-20.

The word "ash" is used descriptively in several Arizona place names, several examples of which are given below.

**a.n. Ash Creek Flat**   Loc.: Not ascertained     Gila

     A band of Chiricahua Indians under Chief Loco was defeated in a skirmish here with cavalry under Capt. Overton on May 7, 1880.

Ref.:   55, p. 617; 85, p. 446.

**v.n. Ash Creek Valley**     Gila

**a.n. (continued)**

| | | |
|---|---|---|
| **Ash Spring** | Map: B-7 | Gila |
| **Ash Spring Wash** | Map: GD-14 | Gila |
| **Ash Creek** | Maps: GE-3; GE-6 | Graham |
| **Ash Flat** | Map: C-14 | Graham |
| **Ash Creek Canyon** | Map: GB-24 | Cochise |
| **Ash Creek Spring** | Map: B-7 | Gila |
| **Ash Creek Black Hills** | Map: GE-6 | Graham |
| **Ash Creek** | Map: GD-15 | Maricopa |
| **Ash Creek** | Maps: GK-3; GK-6; GK-26; GK-31; GK-5 | Pinal |
| **Ash Canyon** | Map: GL-3 | Santa Cruz |
| **Ash Creek Station** | | Yavapai |
| **Ash Creek** | Maps: GJ-8; GJ-14 | Pima |
| **Ash Wash** | Map: GJ-8 | Pima |

## AZTEC PEAK

El.: 7694′     Loc.: Gila 1, G-7

Aztec Peak, in the Sierra Ancha, is a narrow rock chimney which makes the mountain top a point easily defended. Signs that the place was used as a point of defense by Indians are still evident.

Before archaeologists had investigated the pre-historic Indians of Arizona, it was commonly believed that the Aztecs had inhabited the region. This belief was supported by the work of the eminent historian Prescott, and for this reason settlers who came to Arizona in the 1860's and 1870's sometimes applied the name Aztec to places.

Ref.:   McKinney. Maps: C-13; GD-3; GD-6.

## BAKER MOUNTAIN

El.: 7579′     Loc.: Gila 1, G-6.9

According to one story Ned Baker, the pack master for a military Indian scouting party, was killed in an ambush in 1868 near the top of the "jump-off" constructed down this mountain.

A second story is to the effect that John H. Baker, a cattleman, c. 1885, had a cabin on the side of this mountain and ranged his cattle in the Sierra Ancha.

When the King S. Woolsey expedition passed through this area in 1864, it named a peak in this region Lookout Mountain. It may well have been Baker Mountain, which is still sometimes called Lookout Peak. It is said that a military heliograph station existed on the mountain at one time.

Ref.:   McKinney; 151, p. 115; 52, V, 273-274; 115, p. 109; APHS Files; Woody. Maps: GD-6; C-12.

## BARNES PEAK

El.: 5028′     Loc.: Gila 1, G-10.9

F. L. Ransome, author of a work on geological formations in this area (1903) named Barnes Peak because it was composed of Barnes conglomerate. Barnes was a prospector whose mine was located near the initial discovery of the type of conglomerate which bears his name.

Ref.:   135, p. 30; Barnes (No relation). Maps: C-9; GD-4; GD-5.

| | | |
|---|---|---|
| **a.n. Barnes Spring** | Map: GD-5 | Gila |
| **Barnes Tunnel** | Map: GD-5 | Gila |
| This was the location of the mine. | | |
| **Barnes Wash** | Maps: GD-5; GD-14 | Gila |

## BARNHARDT CANYON

El.: c. 4000′     Loc.: Gila 1, CB-3-4

The old Barnhardt Ranch, which gave this canyon its name, has now vanished.

Ref.:   Pieper. Map: GD-9.

## BELLEVUE

El.: c. 5000′     Loc.: Gila 1, H-12.5

The fine view from this location was the reason for its name. The place was named by the Whelan brothers.

P.O. est. July 30, 1906. Edward P. Whelan, p.m. Discont. April 7, 1927.

Ref.:   Barnes; Woody. Maps: C-12; GD-10.

## BIG JOHNEY GULCH

El.: c. 4000′     Loc.: Gila 1, H-11

Pro.:   /jániy/

The first of the many rich claims to be located in the Globe District was recorded in Big Johney Gulch in 1870 by Cal Jackson and members of his party. The first location was called the Pinal Discovery, which later became a part of the Old Dominion Mining Property.

The gulch was apparently named for a miner known as Big Johney. His name has been corrupted to other spellings which are listed below. In this same gulch were also located the Ramboz (See Ramboz) and Rescue Mines as well as the first Miami Mine (See Miami).

**v.n. Big Johnny Canyon**

     **Big Jonnie Canyon**

Ref.:   Barnes; Woody. Map: GD-8.

**a.n. Big Johnny Mine**     Map: GD-8     Gila

## BISHOP KNOLL

El.: 4848'                     Loc.: Gila 1, D-3

When Gisela (q.v.) was a Mormon settlement this knoll was named for the bishop who was in charge.

Ref.:   Barnes. Map: GD-9.

## BLACK WARRIOR

El.: c. 4000'                  Loc.: Gila 1, G-11.6

Silas Tidwell located and named this mine. A post office was established for the convenience of the miners. The Black Warrior was purchased by the Inspiration Mining Company (See Inspiration) and the old community is now under a tailings dump.

P.O. est. August 26, 1899. David A. Abrams, p.m. Discont.?
Ref.:   Woody. Maps: C-9; GD-4.

## BLOODY TANKS

El.: c. 4000'                  Loc.: Gila 1, G-12

Bloody Tanks is located at the head of what is known as Bloody Tanks Wash, which prior to the Battle of Bloody Tanks was known as the West Branch of Pinal Creek. Just above the Tanks on January 24, 1864, King S. Woolsey and his expedition of men from Prescott, including fifteen Maricopa Indians, pitched camp. On a nearby hill some Apaches also pitched camp. Woolsey was convinced that these Indians were hostile. They were persuaded to enter Woolsey's camp and a parley was held. The Woolsey party suddenly opened fire and massacred the visiting Indians. Their blood mingled with the water of the stream and gave the place its name of Bloody Tanks.

This incident has also been referred to as Piñole Treaty because of the legend that the Indians were not shot, but were murdered by giving them poisoned piñole (flour). While it is apparently true that the Indians were given piñole, there is no evidence to demonstrate that it was poisoned. On the contrary, it is reported that the members of the Woolsey expedition trailed the fleeing survivors and picked up tobacco and piñole which the men had handed to the Indians before the massacre. There is little likelihood that the members of the expedition would have sought to retrieve poisoned piñole.

Ref.:   Woody; 25, p. 121; 4, p. 348. Maps: GD-4; GD-5; GD-7.
a.n.  Bloody Tanks Wash                                          Gila
   (See Miami, a.n.). Maps: GD-4; GD-5; GD-7; GD-10.

## BLUE HOUSE MOUNTAIN

El.: 6417'                     Loc.: Gila 2, B-1

The origin of this name has not been determined.

Ref.:   None. Map: GD-1.

## BLUE RIVER

El.: c. 4000'                  Loc.: Gila 2, CE-7-6

The upper portion of this river contains water which has a blue appearance.

Ref.:   Woody. Maps: C-11 (Blue Creek); GD-3.

## BOARD TREE SADDLE

El.: 6007'                     Loc.: Gila 1, G-5.5

In the saddle of the Sierra Ancha Mountains the trees were large enough to permit the making of boards, hence the name.

Ref.:   Voris (Bob). Map: GD-6.

## BUCKHORN CREEK

El.: c. 2500'                  Loc.: Gila 1, DC-8.9

Prior to 1870, a hunter is said to have found the heads of two bucks with their horns in a death-lock, from whence came the name of the creek. The area through which the creek flowed was known as the Buckhorn Basin. It was here that a mythical "massacre" of miners was said to have taken place. This story was one of the rumors in Arizona towards the close of Gen. George Crook's assignment in Arizona (cf. Crook National Forest). Crook ordered every such rumor investigated. The so-called Buckhorn Basin massacre was investigated by Maj. William C. Rafferty of the 6th Cavalry. He found no basis for the story.

Ref.:   Barnes; 22, pp. 454-455. Map: GD-15.

## BURCH MESA

El. c. 6000'                   Loc.: Gila 1, C-1.8

William Burch settled first in Big Green Valley (See Little Green Valley) and later moved to this place.

v.n.  Birch Mesa
Ref.:   Barnes. Maps: B-7; GD-16.

## BURCH PUMPING STATION

El.: 2500'                     Loc.: Gila 1, H-11.5.
                    Two miles from Globe on Apache Trail.

Kenyon Burch was a mining engineer and an official of the Miami Copper Company. The pumping station for mines at Globe was named for him.

Ref.:   Woody. Map: None.

## BUZZARD ROOST CANYON

El.: c. 6000'                  Loc.: Gila 1, E-4

Cowpunchers in this area used to camp here. They referred to each other and to themselves as "buzzards." The location was also noted as a place "where men on the dodge flopped in order to hide."

Ref.:   Packard; McInterff. Maps: B-7; GD-2.
a.n.  Buzzard Roost Mesa       Map: GD-2                          Gila

## CANYON CREEK

El.: c. 4000'                  Loc.: Gila 2, A-3.4

The name of the creek is descriptive. In his survey of 1871, Capt. George M. Wheeler noted particularly that the Indian ruins in Canyon Creek had not yet been explored. This is still true.

Canyon Creek was the scene of several battles between Indians and soldiers, the first being recorded on April 25, 1873, and the last on November 3, 1881.

Ref.:   Davis; 175, I, 43; 85, pp. 438, 447. Maps: B-9; C-1; E-20; GD-1; GM-19.

## CAPITAN, EL

El.: c. 4000'                    Loc.: Gila 1, G-13.9
Pro.: /el kæpitæn/        Spanish: "the captain"
El Capitan was a mine which had a post office. The mine may have been named for the commanding peak known as El Capitan Mountain.

P.O. est. December 5, 1919. Frankie Wood, p.m. Discont. September 15, 1924.

Ref.: Barnes; P.O. Records. Maps: A-7; GD-13.

a.n. Capitan Canyon, El     Map: GD-13          Gila
     Capitan Mountain, El   El.: 6564'. Map: GD-13   Gila
v.n. Capitan Peak            Map: C-11
a.n. Capitano Creek          Map: C-7             Gila
     Capitan Pass    Loc.: Just off Highway 77 at peak   Gila
     Capitan Pass Spring    Map: GD-10            Gila

## CARR PEAK

El.: 7604'                       Loc.: Gila 1, G-7
Carr Peak took its name from the Carr Ranch.

Ref.: Woody. Maps: GD-6; A-7.

a.n. Carr Mountain    El.: 7619'. Map: GD-6      Gila
     Carr Mountain is west of Carr Peak and is also on the old Carr Ranch.

## CASSADORE MESA

El.: c. 4000'                    Loc.: Gila 2, A-7.5
Pro.: /kæsədor/
Cassadore was a sub-chieftain of the San Carlos Apaches. He lived in this area during the height of the Apache troubles in 1873. Troops were sent to capture Cassadore with orders to "take no prisoners." Cassadore and his band fled, only to be overtaken in the hills by the troops. The Indians of their own free will came to the army camp and surrendered with the explanation that white people had been killed, not by Cassadore's band, but by some "bad Indians." When the Indians told Capt. J. M. Hamilton that their food was gone, their moccasins so worn out that their feet were leaving blood on the rocks, and that they preferred to die by bullets rather than by hunger, the army man fed them and sent word to headquarters of their plight. The order to kill them was rescinded and the surrender of Cassadore's band was accepted on February 18, 1874. The Indians were taken back to their homes by the troops and left there.

The use of the name "Cazadero" does not seem warranted, inasmuch as there are today among the Apaches descendants bearing the Cassadore family name.

Ref.: Jennings; Woody; 4, pp. 446-447; Barnes. Map: B-7.

a.n. Cassadore Creek    Loc.: Twelve miles n. San Carlos   Gila
     Cassadore Springs   Loc.: Same as Creek               Gila
     Cassadore Mountain  Loc.: T. 19 E., R. 2 N            Gila
     Cazador     Map: GB-17                          Cochise
     A siding on the railroad.

## CATALPA

El.: c. 2500'                    Loc.: Gila 1, G-8.8
A man named Peter Robertson in 1877 brought the first sheep into the Little Salt River Valley (now under Roose-velt Lake). His location shows on the Smith Map of 1879 as "The Grove of Robinson." The name "Catalpa" was given to the post office because of the many catalpa trees in the Little Salt River Valley.

P.O. est. December 4, 1885. Peter C. Robertson, p.m. Discont. October 17, 1888.

Ref.: Woody; Barnes. Maps: B-7; C-6; E-20 (Grove of Robinson).

## CATHOLIC PEAK

El.: c. 6000'                    Loc.: Gila 1, A-4
The resemblance of this peak to a huge cross led to the application of the name.

Ref.: Barnes. Maps: B-7; C-12.

## CENTER MOUNTAIN

El.: 6789'                       Loc.: Gila 1, G-6.4
The position of this mountain in the Sierra Ancha midway between McFadden Horse Mountain and Baker Mountain led to naming it Center Mountain.

Ref.: Barnes. Maps: B-7; GD-6.

## CHERRY CREEK

El.: c. 4000'                    Loc.: Gila 1, GH-9-4
Wild cherry trees account for the name of this creek. The canyon through which the creek runs boxes for about ten miles above its confluence with the Salt River and in this stretch there are extensive cliff ruins.

Ref.: Barnes; Woody. Maps: C-4; E-18; E-20; GD-6; GD-11; GD-14.

a.n. Cherry Flat Recreational Area    Map: GD-10        Gila
     This recreational area in the Pinal Mountains was opened for citizens of Miami.
     Cherry Springs    Maps: GD-5; GD-2               Gila

## CHILITO

El.: 4000'                       Loc.: Gila 1, H-15.5
Pro.: /čiylíyto/          Spanish: "little peppers"
The London-Arizona Mining Company had its headquarters at this place. According to one source, the Mexicans called the first postmaster "Chilito" because of his fiery temper, and from this came the name of the post office.

P.O. est. June 11, 1913. George B. Chittenden, p.m. Discont. July 15, 1918.

Ref.: George Ketenbach (Patterson Notes). Map: C-12.

## CHIRICAHUA BUTTES

El.: c. 7000'                    Loc.: Gila 2, EF-5.9
Pro.: /čiyriykáwə/        Apache: tsil, "mountain";
                                   kawa, "great"
Apaches of the Chiricahua band are said to have lived in this area.

Ref.: Barnes. Map: D-9.

## CHRISTMAS

El.: 2990'                       Loc.: Gila 2, A-11.6
The rich copper mines at this location were first discovered in the early 1880's by three prospectors, one of whom was Dr. James Douglas. However, the original locators were

unable to maintain their claim because the land lay within the San Carlos Indian Reservation.

Several years later, George B. Chittenden (See Chilito) became interested in the property. He succeeded in having Congress pass a bill which changed the lines of the reservation, thus opening the property to re-location. Chittenden arranged that he would receive news of the passage of the bill via telegraph to Casa Grande and then by messengers riding on horseback in relay. The news came to his hands on Christmas Day, 1902, his birthday. Wasting no time, he rode immediately to locate the property, naming it Christmas.

For several years the mine was inactive, but by 1956 it had re-opened and developmental work was in progress.
P.O. est. June 17, 1905. William W. Swingle, p.m. Discont. March 30, 1935.
Ref.: Woody; Barnes; State Library Files, Unidentified clipping; 4, p. 346. Maps: A-7; C-10; GK-6.

## CHRISTOPHER CREEK
El.: c. 6000'                          Loc.: Gila 1, F-1.3
Isadore Christopher located his CI ranch on the creek which bears his name.

In July 1882, Christopher killed a bear, skinned it, and hung the skin in one of his cabins. The next day, while Christopher was away, the Apaches came along and burned his two log houses. The next visitors were troops which arrived while the cabins were still burning. The story spread that the soldiers solemnly buried the remains of the bear, thinking the Apaches had skinned "poor old Christopher."
Ref.: Barnes; Woody; Croxen. Maps: B-7; C-13; GD-12.
a.n. Christopher Mountain   Map: GD-12                  Gila

## CHROMO BUTTE
El.: c. 4000'                          Loc.: Gila 2, A-7
The use of the word *chromo* is descriptive.
Ref.: Woody. Maps: B-7; C-12.

## CHRYSOTILE
El.: 4600'                             Loc.: Gila 2, B-4
Pro.: /krisotayl/
Chrysotile, or asbestos as it is more commonly called, is mined at this location, hence the name. Chrysotile is unique in that it is the only asbestos in the United States which is white, a fact attributed to its being iron-free.

The asbestos mines at Chrysotile were found by Tom West in October 1911. They were finally sold to the Johns-Manville Company, which at first refused to purchase the property because the company's customers were used to the brown asbestos from Canadian mines and would not buy white asbestos.

Some confusion has arisen concerning the spelling of the name Chrysotile, which is occasionally misspelled "Chrysolite." Chrysolite, however, is a magnesium iron silicate, not an asbestos. One variety of chrysolite is an olive green stone used as a semi-precious gem called peridot. Peridot stones are found near Peridot (*q.v.*).

P.O. est. June 27, 1916. Nels A. Nelson, p.m. Discont. July 15, 1933.
Ref.: Woody; P.O. Records. Maps: A-7; C-12.

## CITY CREEK
El.: c. 4000'                          Loc.: Gila 1, C-2
In the late 1870's, Mormons had a colony called Mazatzal City on the Verde River at its juncture with this creek. When the Mormons moved to Pine (*q.v.*) c. 1882, the creek retained the name City Creek.
Ref.: Croxen; Barnes. Maps: B-7; GD-9.

## CLAYPOOL
El.: c. 4000'                          Loc.: Gila 1, H-11.5
The settlement at Claypool was developed by Senator W. D. Claypool (d. 1956) and his brother-in-law, George Wilson.
P.O. est. July 21, 1917. Frank E. Hall, p.m.
Ref.: Barnes. Maps: A-7; C-12.

## CLINE
El.: 2192'                             Loc.: Gila 1, D-7
Christian Cline settled here c. 1876 and ran cattle. The name Cline is a common one in the area today; his sons, grandsons, and great grandsons have populated the area, but the original settlement has disappeared.
P.O. est. January 11, 1886. Thomas J. Cline, p.m. Discont. August 15, 1912.
Ref.: Woody. Maps: C-8; GD-15.
a.n. Cline Creek        Map: GD-15                      Gila
    Cline Mesa        Map: GD-2                       Gila

## COLCORD MOUNTAIN
El.: 7690'                             Loc.: Gila 1, H-2
Pro.: /kálkerd/
William C. Colcord with his brother Harvey and their mother arrived in 1886 and established a ranch under the Mogollon Rim (*q.v.* Coconino). Later they moved to Colcord Canyon. The name was applied to the mountain by the Forestry Service.
Ref.: Mrs. William C. Colcord. Map: B-7.

## CONLEY POINTS
El.: c. 4000'                          Loc.: Gila 1, C-1.2
In the early 1880's, the Conley family settled near these small peaks. An Indian woman once filed a homestead claim on the same flat, which led to the name "Indian Delia's Place," long since changed to Conley Points.
Ref.: Barnes. Map: B-7.

## COOLIDGE DAM
El.: c. 2500'                          Loc.: Gila 2, B-10.5
One of several important and interesting dams in Arizona, Coolidge is unique in that it was the first and largest egg-shaped, multiple-dome dam ever built. The top of the dam lies 259 feet above bedrock.

One of the delays encountered in constructing the dam was opposition by Apache Indians, who objected strenuously to the disinterment of bodies lying in the Apache graveyard over which waters of the dam would collect. A concrete slab was laid over the principal burying ground, which is now covered by the waters of San Carlos Lake.

When the dam was dedicated on March 4, 1930, it was formally named for President Calvin Coolidge. Among the guests was the humorist Will Rogers. The water which had already collected was just sufficient to cause a luxuriant growth of grass in the valley. Rogers said to Coolidge, "If this was my lake, I'd mow it."

P.O. est. May 7, 1928. Welford C. Rupkey, p.m. Discont. January 31, 1956.

Ref.:   4, p. 345. Maps: B-7; C-13.

## COON CREEK

El.: c. 4000'                    Loc.: Gila 1, GH-8-9
In 1864 King S. Woolsey named this Sycamore Creek. The name *Racoon* was used by Lt. John G. Bourke, who reported that settlers had a brush with Apaches near a prehistoric ruin on its banks. Settlers themselves said that racoons used to live along the lower portion of the stream.

Ref.:   Woody; Shroeder; 111, p. 222; 20, p. 186. Maps: C-12 (Racoon Creek); GD-16; GD-14; GD-6; A-7; C-4; E-18.

a.n. Coon Creek Butte      Map: GD-6                    Gila

## COPPER HILL

El.: c. 4000'                    Loc.: Gila 1, H-11.4
The mining camp for the Iron Cap, Arizona Commercial, and Superior and Boston mines was at a place known as Copper Camp or Copper Hill. It was also referred to as Copper Gulch, although actually the gulch was the site of the road which led to the camp and the place in which many early strikes were made. Copper Hill was on the south side of the hill, whereas another community known as Copper City was on the north side of Black Peak in Big Johney Gulch. Copper City was the older of the two settlements, having been mentioned in newspapers at least as early as 1884. All traces of both settlements are now gone. The names, of course, were descriptive of the type of ore found.

P.O. est. June 18, 1908. Ruth Hayden, p.m. Discont. February 15, 1933.

Ref.:   Woody; Barnes. Maps: A-7; C-10.

## CROOK NATIONAL FOREST

El.: c. 4000'      Loc.: Gila 1, FH-9-16; Gila 2, AG-3-12
Crook National Forest was set aside as a reserve in 1908. It was named for Gen. George Crook (b. Dayton, Ohio., September 23, 1829; d. March 21, 1890), who led a successful campaign against Apache Indians while he was in command of the military department of Arizona in 1872-1873. Crook was again in Arizona from 1882 to 1886. The forest covered the Santa Teresa, Pinaleno, and Galiuro Mountains, and the Mount Graham area. In 1953 this forest was abolished, becoming parts of Coronado, Tonto and Gila National Forests on July 1 of that year.

According to Lt. John G. Bourke, Gen. Crook did many things in addition to improving the lot of the Indians. Notable was the fact that he re-organized and relocated the defi-

cient and unhealthy army posts, among them Camp Grant. He did what he could to improve the quarters of the military and he saw to it that good water was available at every camp. Furthermore, he established first class roads over which wagons and ambulances could journey safely between the various posts. Under his direction the military telegraph line, which originated at San Diego and came through Fort Yuma, California, was brought on to Maricopa Wells where it branched, with one line going to Fort Whipple and the other to Tucson and thence to San Carlos and the crossing of the Gila, fifteen miles from San Carlos.

Ref.:   22, p. 252; 4, p. 346; 92, p. 130. Maps: A-7; C-10.

## CROWLEY

Loc.: In Apache Mountains near Globe.
Con Crowley was a cattleman and miner. He ran cattle near Crowley, which was named for him.

P.O. est. April 30, 1907. Charles N. Thorsen, p.m. Discont. February 14, 1911.

Ref.:   Barnes; Woody. Maps: None.

a.n. Con Canyon                                        Gila

## CUTTER

El.: c. 3500'                    Loc.: Gila 2, A-8.2
E. Al Cutter was a member of the board of directors of the company which constructed the Gila Valley, Globe, and Northern Railroad in the 1890's. Later he served as vice-president. Currently, Cutter is a section station at the foot of a grade where at one time extra engines were hitched on to help haul freight loads of heavy grain over the divide between the Salt and Gila River watersheds.

Ref.:   Woody. Maps: C-10; A-7.

## DAGGER PEAK

El.: 3260'                    Loc.: Gila 1, H-8.4
The name derived from the fact that the Spanish or "dagger" yucca grows abundantly in this region.

Ref.:   Alfred Devore. Map: GD-14.

a.n. Dagger Basin       Map: GD-14                    Gila
     Dagger Canyon      Map: GD-14                    Gila
     Dagger Spring      Map: B-7                      Gila

## DEAD BOY POINT

El.: c. 4000'      Loc.: Gila 1, D-3. Sec. 4, T. 8 N., R. 11 E.
During the days of unpleasantness between cattlemen and sheepmen, two young boys named Wiley Berry and Juan Rafael were in John Berry's sheep camp at this point. Here on December 22, 1903, Zack Booth, a disreputable cowboy, killed the boys, hence the name. Booth was hanged at Globe.

Ref.:   Barnes. Map: None.

## DEL SHAY BASIN

El.: c. 5000'                    Loc.: Gila 1, E-5
Pro.: /del šey/                    Apache: "red ant"
Del Shay Basin derived its name from the fact that it was at one time the stamping grounds for one of the most notorious of Apache chiefs, a man whose name has been spelled Delche, Del-che, and Del Shay. The Indian and his

band roamed the country from 1870 until his death in mid-1874.

One story concerning the application of the name to the basin area is that Charles Douchet was stationed at Fort Reno and that Del Shay, chief of the so-called Tonto Apaches, was brought wounded into camp. Douchet made friends with the Indian, who later showed the white man where a gold mine lay in the basin. Still later, Douchet and Al Sieber located the Del Shay Gold Mine, from which the basin is said to have taken its name.

Apparently Del Shay was not fairly dealt with by the white man. The Report of the Commissioner of Indian Affairs for 1871 states that at one time while Del Shay was at Camp McDowell, he was shot in the back; at another time an attempt was made by the post doctor to poison the Indian. Deeds such as these apparently did not increase Del Shay's love for the paleface and he fought back with extreme fierceness. On April 22, 1873, following capture by Captain Randall in the Sierra Ancha, Del Shay and his band were herded onto the reservation. He escaped and continued his depredations.

According to Barnes, Dr. Warren S. Day, who was post surgeon at Camp Verde, bribed Del Shay's brother by tossing Mexican dollars onto a blanket until the sum became so great that the Indian could no longer resist. Thus bribed, he and the scouts went out after their chief and returned with his head on July 29, 1874.

Ref.:   Mrs. Laura Cliff Griffen; Woody; Barnes; APHS Files, Letter from Charles M. Clark, May 25, 1935; 111, pp. 226, 227. Map: B-7.

**a.n. Del Shay Creek**          Map: GD-9                          Gila

## DEVORE WASH

El.: c. 4000'                          Loc.: Gila 1, GH-10
Pro.: /dəvór/
When John Kennedy drove stock into this area in 1875, his nephew, David Devore (b. Kentucky, 1856), helped handle the stock. Devore was a rancher and miner who settled in Prescott in 1873. In 1880 he moved to Globe, where in 1892 he disposed of his mining interests.

Devore Wash forms part of the old trail through the Tonto Basin.

Ref.:   Woody; 112, III. Maps: GD-5; GD-14.

## DIAMOND POINT

El.: 6381'                          Loc.: Gila 1, E-1.4
Crystals found in the rock and on the ground are called locally "Arizona Diamonds."

Ref.:   Barnes. Maps: B-7; GD-12.

## DOAK

El.: c. 6000'                          Loc.: Gila 1, H-13.1
The origin of this name has not been ascertained.

P.O. est. February 19, 1919. Margaret L. Tanner, pm. Discont. March 3, 1921.

Ref.:   P.O. Records. Maps: A-7; C-12.

## DRIPPING SPRING

El.: c. 3000'                          Loc.: Gila 1, H-15
At one time Dripping Spring was a cattle ranch which had a stage station for the Florence to Globe line. The ranch took its name from the springs issuing from the cliff some four miles east of the ranch headquarters.

P.O. est. November 13, 1886. Mrs. Mary R. Strockey, p.m. Discont. February 6, 1890.

Ref.:   Barnes. Map: C-6.

## DRIPPING SPRING RANGE

El.: c. 5000'                          Loc.: Gila 1, H-14-16
F. L. Ransome notes that the name Dripping Spring Mountain in 1903 was applied to a vaguely defined area including the ridges south of the old settlement of Pioneer. The county line runs along the top of these hills.

Ref.:   135, pp. 32, 18; Woody. Map: A-7 (Dripping Spring Mountain).

## DRIPPING SPRING WASH

El.: c. 2500'          Loc.: Gila 1, H-15-16; Gila 2, A-11.5
Lt. William H. Emory called this Disappointment Creek. On November 5, 1846, Lt. Emory wrote that his border surveying party had been struggling through the mountain stronghold of the Apaches at a great cost to the expedition's mule power. At this creek Emory had looked forward to the Apaches' bringing him fresh mules. Emory said, "The failure of the Apaches was a serious disappointment and entirely justifies the name given to the creek where they agreed to meet us. Besides being the only means of transportation, they are in extremity, to serve us as food, and the poor suffering creatures before us gave no very agreeable impression of the soup which they were to furnish . . ."

The Dripping Springs which gave the creek its name lie more than a mile away.

Ref.:   50, p. 76; Woody. Maps: A-7; C-12.

## DUDE CREEK

El.: c. 4000'                          Loc.: Gila 1, D-1
Frank McClintock, a rancher on this creek, gave it its name, but his reason for so doing is not known.

Ref.:   Barnes. Maps: B-9; GD-11; GD-12.

## DUTCH WOMAN BUTTE

El.: 5000'                          Loc.: Gila 1, EF-7.3
There are at least two possibilities concerning the origin of the name Dutch Woman Butte. The first is that the name is descriptive. A map of 1890 shows this as Dutch Man's Butte. The butte does bear a resemblance to a dutch wooden shoe. The *Phoenix Herald* (July 21, 1888) said the butte looked like a Dutch woman sitting down.

The second story is that the Apaches captured a Dutch woman and soldiers rescued her in a fight on this butte. One soldier was reportedly killed and buried at the location, and the military report listed the place as Dutch Woman Butte. Official records examined do not bear this out, though it may possibly be true.

Ref.:   Barnes; Woody. Maps: B-7; C-10; GD-15.

## EAST VERDE RIVER

El.: c. 4000'                              Loc.: Gila 1, AC-3-1
Pro.: /vérdiy^/                           Spanish: "green"
On August 28, 1864, King S. Woolsey reported to the Governor of Arizona on Woolsey's third exploratory trip. He stated that his party had named a stream the "East Fork of the Verde."

In the late 1870's, Mormons settled about ten miles west of the present Payson, calling their location the East Verde Settlement. They abandoned it c. 1882, moving to Pine (*q.v.*). The original settlement now belongs to the Doll Baby and N. B. ranches. (Sec. 17, T. 10 N., R. 9 E.)

Ref.:  Croxen; Woody. Maps: GD-9; GD-11; GM-19; C-1; E-20.

## EDWARDS PEAK

El.: 5770'                                Loc.: Gila 1, C-7
Charles Edwards settled on a ranch near what was in the early days called Reno Mountain (cf. Camp Reno). Edwards was fatally shot near Cline's Ranch, but the murderer was never found.

Ref.:  Barnes. Maps: C-13; GD-15.

**a.n. Edwards Park**     Loc.: T. 6 N., R. 9 E.        Gila
This park covers about four hundred acres of fairly open ground in the Mazatzals, one of the roughest ranges in Arizona.

Ref.:  Barnes.

**Edwards Spring**        Map: B-7                      Gila

## ELLISON

El.: c. 4000'                             Loc.: Gila 1, H-7.9
Jesse W. Ellison (b. Texas, September 22, 1841) came to Arizona in 1885. He arrived at Bowie Station (*q.v.* Cochise) by rail with his eighteen hundred cattle. There he found so little water that his cattle stampeded. Many went pell mell into arroyos and were killed. Others were rounded up by people in the area, and with the remnants of his herd Ellison headed toward Gila County, going first to Big Green Valley. He registered his brand as a Q.

In 1885 bad luck hounded him. His house burned, and he left the ranch to start another in Star Valley. Ellison started the Q Ranch on what had been the Newton Ranch, the new name coming from Ellison's brand. Here he lived with his family until 1915 when he sold to Pecos McFadden. As his children grew up and went into the cattle business, their brands were their initials plus a smaller Q. Ellison died January 21, 1934.

P.O. est. July 27, 1894. Jesse H. Ellison, pm. Discont. March 16, 1907.

**v.n. Q Ranch**                         (B-7)
Ref.:  McKinney; Woody; 112, III. Maps: B-7; C-9; GD-6.
**a.n. Ellison Creek**    Maps: GD-11; GD-12            Gila

## FIVE POINT MOUNTAIN

El.: c. 4000'                             Loc.: Gila 1, F-13
Descriptive.

Ref.:  Woody; Barnes. Map: B-7.

## FLAT TOP MOUNTAIN

El.: c. 5000'                             Loc.: Gila 2, G-11
Descriptive.

Ref.:  Barnes. Map: GD-5.

## FOSSIL CREEK

El.: c. 4000'                             Loc.: Gila 1, A-1
The second King S. Woolsey expedition in March and April 1864 followed this stream. The name is descriptive of fossil remains found in the creek bed. Lummis reports that Fossil Creek is so heavily charged with minerals that objects which drop into it — such as twigs — are rapidly coated with layers of travertine and that it was this which led to the naming of the stream.

Ref.:  Woody; Barnes; 107, p. 143. Maps: A-7; C-1; E-17 (Fossill).

**a.n. Fossil Springs**   Map: GM-19                    Gila

## GERALD WASH

El.: c. 3500'                             Loc.: Gila 1, G-10.8
James F. Gerald (b. Massachusetts, 1837) came to Arizona in 1877 from western Canada, where he had been a miner. For a while he was a hotel man in Globe, but purchased land and established a cattle ranch, working it until his retirement in 1911. The wash runs across the old Gerald ranch.

Ref.:  Woody; 112, III. Map: GD-5.

**a.n. Gerald Hills**     Map: GD-5                      Gila

## GIBSON PEAK

El.: c. 5000'                             Loc.: Gila 1, D-2.3
Three Gibson brothers — Arthur, Wash and Joe — had a ranch in the area. The brothers were Mormons.

Ref.:  Barnes; Pieper. Map: GD-9.

**a.n. Gibson Creek**     Map: GD-9                      Gila
**Gibson Wash**           Maps: CD-13; GK-6             Gila

## GILA PUEBLO

El.: c. 4000'                             Loc.: Gila 1, H-12.1
Pro.: /híylə pwéblo/
The first name for this location was Healy Terrace because Charles Healy explored here for Indian ruins. The Gila Pueblo is the site of a big prehistoric Indian village which was sold to the Medallion Society c. 1930. The Society developed headquarters here for the study of Indian ruins in the region. In 1956, the former Healy Terrace was the headquarters for the Southwestern Monuments Park Service.

Ref.:  Woody; 4, p. 39. Maps: B-7; C-13.

## GILA RIVER

Loc.: The Gila traverses the southern third of Arizona.

Pro.: /híylə/
The most important tributary to the Colorado River at one time was the Gila River; it rises in New Mexico and forms part of the boundary of Gila County, to which it gave its name. The Gila River was never dry, and is now so in its lower stretches largely because of dams along its principal

tributaries. It was the first stream of any size encountered by white men, certainly having been crossed by Fr. Marcos de Niza in his trip in 1539. The first man to see its mouth was Capt. Fernando Alarcon in 1540, who sailed up the Colorado and dubbed the future Gila "Miraflores." In 1604 Juan de Oñate called it the Rio del Nombre de Jesus.

Meanwhile, events were shaping up in New Mexico, the area which Oñate governed. In 1630 a province of New Mexico was named Xila, or Gila, a Spanish word encountered on maps of Spain itself and used in the language as an idiomatic expression: *de Gila,* a "steady going to or from a place." Fr. Kino in 1694 was calling the river the Rio de los Apostoles ("Apostles' River"), but in 1697 he became the first to record the name Gila for the river. Other names applied to this stream seem to have been Rio Jaquesila, so called by Fr. Francisco Garcés in 1775, and El Rio de los Balsas ("River of the Rafts") near its juncture with the Colorado, where the Indians used rafts to cross. It was, however, to have many different ways of rendering its name of Gila, including Hila, Hyla, Chila, Hela, Helah, and Helay.

Ref.: 7, pp. 163 (Note 41), 348, 349, 355; 125, p. 85, 125 (Note 51); 76, p. 12; 20, p. 422; 35, pp. 541, 544, 136 (Note 48); 141, pp. 65, 66; 42, pp. 80, 82; 21, p. 275; 19, I, 127, 171, 194-195; Mary B. Aguirre File, APHS. Maps: All in area crossed by river.

## GILLILAND GAP

El.: c. 5000'  Loc.: Gila 1, E-1.2
John Gilliland (b. Texas, 1859; d. January 3, 1937) was foreman for the Stinson outfit. He came to Arizona in 1879. During the Pleasant Valley unpleasantness, he rode to the Tewksbury ranch one day where young boys were repairing a twenty-two rifle. It went off and hit Gilliland in the back of the neck. (See Pleasant Valley.)

Ref.: McKinney. Map: GD-12.

## GILSON'S WELL

El.: c. 4000'  Loc.: Gila 2, A-8
Sam T. Gilson was an employee of the Indian Agency. He had the Indians dig a well and then took possession of it, following which he established a stage station and sold water to travelers. He made a good living out of this for many years. The Indians finally succeeded in having the well assigned for their use. The place is now a stockyard and a loading station for San Carlos Reservation cattle.

Ref.: Woody. Maps: D-9; C-13; GD-16.

## GISELA

El.: c. 2500'  Loc.: Gila 1, D-3.3
Pro.: /gaysílə/ or /gaysílyə/
The first settlers at the place which came to be known as Gisela were David Gowan and two others who arrived in 1880 (See Natural Bridge). At that time the location was referred to as Upper Tonto. The men dug an irrigation ditch and began ranching. In 1881 the three men sold their holdings to Mormons who also remained but a short time. The local school teacher, Mrs. Frederick Stanton, selected the name for the post office, using that of a heroine of a book called *Countess Gisela.*

P.O. est. April 9, 1894. Fred Stanton, p.m. Discont. August 31, 1911.
Ref.: Barnes; 55, p. 595. Maps: A-7; C-8.
a.n. Gisela Mountain  Map: GD-2  Gila
Grass Valley  Gila
Loc.: Valley in which Gisela was located

## GLOBE

El.: 3524'  Loc.: Gila 1, H-11.9
Although there are several fascinating legends concerning the possible origin of the name Globe for the mining community which is the county seat of Gila County, the fact seems to be that the name came from the Globe Mine. The Maricopa Book of Mines shows that the Globe Ledge was recorded on September 19, 1873. The mine was located in that year by Ben Reagan, Robert and David Anderson, Isaac Copeland, William Sampson, William Long, T. Irwin, and others. The first settlement in the newly opened mining area was at the Ramboz Mine (cf. Ramboz Peak). Here the Globe Mining District was organized in November 1875 in the Globe Hills. Ramboz settlement was moved prior to 1878 to Globe, probably because there was ample water at the latter place and because it was also better situated as a general distributing point.

As for the origin of the name for Globe, one story relates that D. B. (Gip) Chilson and Henry Wagner were prospecting in the Apache Peaks for a large silver mine they had heard of as being the source for the silver bullets reputedly used by Apache Indians. They found such a place and called it Globe because of its immense size. One of its locators said after its discovery that it was as big as the globe.

A second version states that a small settlement was barely begun where Globe is today when cavalry men, riding through near what became the Old Dominion Mine, *(q.v.)* found a large and perfectly round boulder, hence the name. Still another legend says that at the site of the new community a globe-shaped boulder of nearly pure silver was found. However, this story seems to have originated from the finding of what is referred to as "Munson's chunk," which was actually found after the community was a going concern. The first story, that the community took its name from the Globe Ledge and Globe Mine, seems the most tenable.

When the community was initiated it was referred to as Globe City, a name which continued until the publication of the *Arizona Silver Belt* on May 2, 1878 (the first edition), in which the editor suggested that the word "city" be dropped.

The townsite had been laid out earlier by Alec Pendleton. In October 1880, Globe was incorporated as a village, but this fact seems to have been forgotten after 1884. The result was that the town of Globe was again incorporated in 1905. Its citizens found city government too expensive and disbanded the incorporation within a year. It was reincorporated as a city in 1907.

P.O. est. December 22, 1876. Edwin M. Pearce, p.m. Wells Fargo Station, 1885.

Ref.: *Maricopa Book of Mines*; Woody; *Arizona Record,* July 21, 1929, 1:1; 7, p. 626, (Note 11), 135, p. 116; 25, p. 263. Maps: E-20; C-4 (Globe City); GD-4.

**a.n. Globe Hills**          Map: GD-4                        Gila

## GORDON

El.: c. 6000′                              Loc.: Gila 1, G-1.4
A man named Gordon lived here c. 1885.

P.O. est. September 10, 1913. Katie L. Payne, p.m. Discont. November 15, 1915.

Ref.: P.O. Records; Barnes. Map: GD-2.

**a.n. Gordon Canyon**          Map: GD-2                      Gila

## GRAPEVINE SPRING

El.: c. 2500′                              Loc.: Gila 1, E-8.9
On his third exploratory expedition, King S. Woolsey in June 1864 applied the name descriptively to this spring because of the many wild grapevines. The men of the expedition located it in their attempt to find water because that of the Salt River was too brackish for drinking purposes.

Grapevine Spring is actually on the south side of the Salt River, a little east of the confluence of Tonto Creek with Salt River.

Ref.: Woody. Maps: B-7; C-1.

**a.n. Grapevine Canyon**      Map: GD-14                      Gila
    **Grapevine Spring**      Map: GD-5                       Gila

## GRAVEYARD CANYON

El.: c. 6000′                              Loc.: Gila 1, G-4
During the war in Pleasant Valley (*q.v.*), John Tewksbury and young Jacobs were ambushed and murdered in this canyon. They were killed in sight of their house, but the enemy refused to permit anyone to bury their bodies. The result was that range hogs tore the bodies badly. When it was finally possible to bury them, they were placed in an Arbuckle coffee case and buried in a single grave.

Ref.: McKinney. Map: B-7.

## GREENBACK VALLEY

El.: c. 4000′                              Loc.: Gila 1, E-6
The first settler in what came to be known as Greenback Valley was David Harer. Harer was a man who literally followed a dream. Harer had dreamed of finding a beautiful valley in which there was a spring and a running stream. He reported his dream to an army officer who later during scouting expeditions came across such a valley. When the officer told Harer about the discovery, Harer laid plans to visit his dream valley, despite warnings that the area harbored unfriendly Apache Indians.

One good look at the little valley was enough for Harer. In 1875 he moved in, built a cabin, and made friends with the Indians. Two years later he brought in his family. Harer employed Indians to help him clear his land, giving one Indian a five dollar bill. The Apache either did not know

how to use the money or had no desire for it and consequently stuck the bill into the blaze of a tree. Later Harer found the money and decided that a fitting name for his valley was Greenback.

Ref.: Packard (interviewed by Woody). Maps: C-10; GD-15.

**a.n. Greenback Creek**          Map: GD-15                   Gila
    **Greenback Peak**   El.: 5555′. Map: GD-15           Gila

## GRIFFIN FLAT

El.: c. 2000′                              Loc.: Gila 1, F-8.7-8.2
C. C. (Cliff) Griffin came to Arizona from Virginia in the 1880's. He owned the 76 Ranch and also the 44 Ranch.

Ref.: Woody. Map: GD-14.

## GUN CREEK

El.: c. 4000′                              Loc.: Gila 1, CE-5.2-4.8
An early settler is said to have found an old gun somewhere along the creek.

Ref.: Barnes. Maps: GD-2; GD-9; GD-15.

## HAIGLER CREEK

El.: c. 6000′                              Loc.: Gila 1, EF-3
Pro.: /héygler/
Joseph Haigler acquired a ranch on this creek c. 1880 from Bob Sixby. Haigler was killed by Indians on his ranch. Haigler Creek is notable for the number of springs which gush above its surface at intervals along it.

Ref.: State Library Files; McKinney. Maps: C-13; GD-2.

## HARDSCRABBLE MESA

El.: c. 6000′                              Loc.: Gila 1, A-1
The name for this area is descriptive since the terrain is black volcanic rock which makes for difficult travel. The name dates back at least to September 23, 1873, when army records include a report of a skirmish with Indians on Hardscrabble Creek. The trail from Tonto Basin to Camp Verde crossed this mesa.

Ref.: McKinney; Barnes; Woody; 85, p. 439. Map: GM-19.

**a.n. Hardscrabble Canyon**   Maps: B-7; GM-19                Gila

## HAYDEN

El.: 2051′                                Loc.: Gila 1, H-16.5
Pro.: /héydən/
Hayden, Stone and Company operated mines near this community. The ores were brought to this point where a mill and smelter had been built to process the ores. The community was named for Charles Hayden of the mining company.

P.O. est. December 3, 1910. Harry C. Adams, p.m. Incorporated 1956.

Ref.: Barnes; Woody. Maps: C-11; GK-32.

**a.n. Hayden Junction**                                     Pinal
    Loc., On Gila River where road from Hayden joins S.P.R.R.
P.O. est. November 8, 1913. Joseph B. Boughton, p.m. Wells Fargo Station, 1910.

Ref.: P.O. Records.

## HAYES MOUNTAIN

El.: c. 4000' Loc.: Gila 2, A-10
W. C. Hayes ran cattle on the San Carlos Indian Reservation from the early 1890's until reservation cattle leases were cancelled and the land turned to use by Indian cattle.
Ref.: Woody. Map: D-9.

## HELL'S GATE

El.: c. 4000' Loc.: Gila 1, B-2.7
Hell's Gate is the beginning of an extremely rough and dangerous trail called the Hell Gate Trail running from Green Valley to the junction of Tonto and Haigler Creeks.
Ref.: McKinney. Map: B-7.
**a.n. Hell's Gate Ridge** Gila
El.: c. 6000' Maps: GD-2; C-13 (Hell's Gate Crossing)

## HELL'S HOLE

El.: c. 4000' Loc.: Gila 1, A-1.1
Herbert Wertman (See Workman Creek) had a ranch in this area. Part of Workman Creek runs through a canyon which is locally referred to as Hell's Hole.
The name Hell's Hole is also applied to an extremely rough area (Sec. 4, T. 11 N., R. 7 E.) at the forks of Hardscrabble Canyon.
Ref.: Barnes. Maps: GD-9; GM-19.

## HENDERSHOT PLACE

El.: c. 6000' Loc.: Gila 1, D-7.1
It was in this place that in July 1882 a band of Apaches under Nan-tia-tish attacked the Meadows family, killing the elder Meadows and wounding his two sons. The Indian band also attacked McMillan (See McMillanville), the Middleton ranch, and other places at this time.
Ref.: Barnes; Woody. Map: B-7.

## HESS CREEK

El.: c. 4000' Loc.: Gila 2, A-4-5
Hess settled and ran cattle along this creek.
Ref.: Barnes. Maps: B-7; C-13.
**a.n. Hess Flat** Loc.: Same as creek Gila

## HILLCAMP

El.: c. 6000' Loc.: Gila 1, CD-5
The short-lived Hillcamp P. O. was created on the site of the old sawmill camp on the San Carlos Indian Reservation. The place was also referred to as Hill Top. The name Hillcamp came from that of the first and only postmistress.
P.O. est. May 9, 1927. Mrs. Zoma Lee Hill, p.m. Discont. October 4, 1927.
Ref.: Woody; Barnes; P.O. Records. Map: F-3.

## HOLDER

El.: c. 4000' Loc.: Gila 1, C-1.5
The first and only postmaster after whom the place was named, ran goats in this area until about 1905. He then moved out because of the decision that sheep and goats could no longer be run in the Tonto Forest Reserve.
P.O. est. September 5, 1896. John T. Holder, p.m. Discont. August 6, 1897.
Ref.: Barnes. Map: B-7.

## HORSE MOUNTAIN

El.: c. 5000' Loc.: Gila 1, F-2
Bill McFadden and his son Pecos raised horses. They ran them on the mountain which is now called Horse Mountain.
Ref.: McKinney; McInturff. Maps: GD-2; GD-12.
**a.n. Horse Camp** Map: GD-6 Gila
Horse Camp was the summer pasture for McFadden's horses on top of Horse Mtn.
Ref.: McKinney.

| Horse Camp Canyon | Map: B-7 | Gila |
| Horse Camp Creek | Map: GD-6 | Gila |
| Horse Camp Seep | Map: B-6 | Gila |
| Horse Canyon | Maps: GD-1; GD-6 | Gila |
| Horse Tank Canyon | Map: B-7 | Gila |

Natural pot-holes were used by horses which got water here.
Ref.: McKinney

## HORSESHOE BEND

El.: c. 3000' Loc.: Gila 1, H-9
There is a bend in the river at this point.
Ref.: Barnes; Woody. Maps: C-12; GD-14.

## HORTON CREEK

El. c. 6000' Loc.: Gila 1, F-1
Willis B. Horton (b. Mississippi 1850) was living on this creek in the early 1880's. He also lived in Tucson, where in 1879 he testified in connection with assessment for the Total Wreck Mining Company (q.v. Pima).
Ref.: APHS Files. Map: GD-12
**a.n. Horton Spring** Loc.: At head of Horton Creek Gila

## HOSFELT PEAK

El.: 5770' Loc.: Gila 1, D-6
Charles Hosfelt had the Hosfelt Ranch in Tonto Basin near the head of Roosevelt Lake.
Ref.: Barnes. Map: B-7.

## HOUDON MOUNTAIN

El.: c. 6000' Loc.: Gila 1, E-3.4
Pro.: /huwdán/
Lewis Houdon was a Swiss prospector who mined along the creek in this area with Bob Sixby. He was killed by Apaches in July 1882, during the attack by Nan-tia-tish (cf. Haigler Creek, Gila.)
Ref.: Barnes; Woody. Maps: C-13; GD-2.

## HOUSTON MESA

El.: c. 5000' Loc.: Gila 1, C-1.5
Pro.: /hyúwstən/
The Houston family settled in this area and grazed cattle here in the early 1880's. One of the family, Sam, was accidentally killed when riding alone. His rein fell off the horn, hitting the pistol in the scabbard. The pistol discharged, shooting him in the leg. He bled to death before he could reach help.
Ref.: Woody. Maps: C-13: GD-11.
**a.n. Houston Creek** Maps: GD-2; GD-9; GD-11 Gila
**Houston Pocket** Map: GD-2 Gila
The Houstons used this for their winter horse range.
Ref.: Barnes.

## ICEHOUSE CANYON

El.: c. 5000'                    Loc.: Gila 1, H-12-13

August Pieper (d. 1931) arrived in Globe in 1883 from Silver City, New Mexico. He dug tanks in what came to be known as Icehouse Canyon. When these were filled with water and froze, Pieper cut and stored the ice. He hauled it into Globe by ox team and sold it for 25c a pound, mainly to saloons.

Ref.:   Ernest Pieper (son). Map: GD-4.

## INDIAN GARDENS

El.: c. 6000'                    Loc.: Gila 1, F-1

Indian Gardens is so named because it was one of many small farming spots used by the Apaches for raising pumpkins, beans, corn, and other produce. Similar plots existed at Wheatfields and Rice and near the Inspiration Mine.

Ref.:   Barnes; Woody. Map: B-9.

## INSPIRATION

El.: c. 4000'                    Loc.: Gila 1, G-11.7

Inspiration is the post office for the Inspiration Mine. The mine was owned by Isaac Copeland and William Scanlon. The story is that the owners of the mine were at one time pressed for money and had an "inspiration" to borrow from a bank. The success of the ensuing operation led to the naming of the mine. Another story says that Copeland was a spiritualist who had a dream or a vision of the mine. The various parts of the company-owned community include Moonshine Hill and the remains of the former Mexican village, Los Adobes, which was evacuated when the undermined ground began to cave in.

P.O. est. May 11, 1917. John H. Kelley, p.m.

Ref.:   Barnes; 4, p. 347; APHS Files. Maps: C-12; GD-5; GD-7.

## INSPIRATION POINT

El.: c. 4000'                    Loc.: Gila 1, E-8.6

Formerly the S.P.R.R. maintained a hotel at this spot. Only a few cement blocks and part of a floor mark the site today. The name for the place is descriptive of the impression created by the view from this location.

Ref.:   Barnes; Woody. Map: B-7.

## JACK'S MOUNTAIN

El.: 5681'                       Loc.: Gila 1, G-7

A mule with a liking for this mountain was the reason for its name. The mule, named Jack, belonged to Bill Lewis. The animal frequently ran away and was always found on top of Jack's Mountain.

Ref.:   Barnes. Map: GD-6.

**a.n. Jack's Spring**          Map: B-7                    Gila

## JACKSON BUTTE

El.: 6539'                       Loc.: Gila 2, A-5

William Jackson, a stockman, ranched at this butte.

Ref.:   Barnes. Map: B-7.

## JERKED BEEF BUTTE

El.: 5950'                       Loc.: Gila 1, FG-3.5

Estevan Ochoa was a leading citizen of Tucson in the 1870's and 1880's. At one time the Apaches took him temporarily out of the trading business by rustling all his draught oxen. The Apaches drove the animals before them until both animals and Indians had crossed the Salt River. The marauders then stopped and on the slope of a high mesa killed and jerked the beef, hence the name.

Ref.:   76, p. 77. Maps: C-4; E-18.

## JIM SAM BUTTE

El.: c. 6000'                    Loc.: Gila 1, F-4.5

Jim Sam Haught (d. 1945) was an early settler in Arizona. He moved from Payson to the butte which bears his name c. 1918.

Ref.:   McKinney. Map: GD-2.

## J K MOUNTAINS

El.: c. 4482'                    Loc.: Gila 1, F-11.2

The name of the mountain came from the brand on cattle which ran here. This may have been the brand of John Kennedy, who arrived in the area in 1875.

Ref.:   Craig; Woody. Maps: GK-14; GK-29.

**a.n. J K Spring**          Map: B-7                        Gila

## JUMP-OFF CANYON

El.: c. 3000'                    Loc.: Gila 2, A-4.5

This is a spot on the road into the adjacent valley where the trail drops down off the Mogollon Rim. The drop is so sudden and steep that it is known as a jump-off. It is still necessary to tie a wagon to a tree to slow the vehicle's descent. It is also necessary at this point to lower freight by means of a rope hand over hand. The jump-off opens from the old military road between Fort Apache and Fort Whipple.

Ref.:   Woody. Map: GD-14.

## KELLY BUTTE

El.: c. 6000'                    Loc.: Gila 2, F-3

Sergeant Kelly was stationed at Fort Apache in the 1890's, apparently having been there for many years previously. There is no record of his having been killed by Apaches (a suggested origin for the name). The butte is said to bear a resemblance to Kelly's notable Roman nose.

Ref.:   Davis; Patterson, Notes. Maps: D-3; E-20 (Kelly's Peak, 1879); C-4; E-18.

## KINISHBA

El.: c. 6000'                    Loc.: Gila 2, G-3.2
                                 Four miles west of Fort Apache.

Pro.:  /kiníšbà/

Formerly this extensive ruin was known as the Fort Apache ruin. It was partially restored from 1935 through 1942 under the direction of Dr. Byron Cummings of the University of Arizona. Since that time the elements have done their work and the buildings currently show marked signs of returning to a ruined condition.

Kinishba stands on flat ground at the edge of a deep wash. The buildings are two and three stories high with open courts and passage ways. The structures were probably built between 1232 A.D. and 1328 A.D. and have been occupied by at least three main cultural groups.

Ref.: 4, p. 444. Map: None.

## KIRBY

El.: c. 2500'                    Loc.: Gila 1, F-9.1
The Kirby family arrived with Mormon settlers who came into this valley between 1878 and 1884. At a later date Mrs. Kirby served as postmistress.

P.O. est. September 21, 1914. Amelia Kerby (sic) p.m.
Ref.: Woody. Map: C-12.

## KOHL'S RANCH

El.: c. 6000'                    Loc.: Gila 1, F-1.1
The post office at this location took its name from the owners of the ranch.

P.O. est. April 28, 1939. Mrs. Laura B. Kohl, p.m.
Ref.: P.O. Records. Maps: F-7; GD-12.

## LAUFFER MOUNTAIN

El.: c. 5000'                    Loc.: Gila 1, F-5.9
Jake Lauffer was a cattleman and prospector who ran a ranch in this vicinity in the 1880's. He was wounded by outlaws at this mountain on August 3, 1888.

Ref.: Barnes. Maps: C-10; GD-15.

## LEWIS, CAMP

El.: c. 4000'                    Loc.: Gila 1, BC-2
This camp was probably named for Col. Charles W. Lewis (b. Virginia, 1825; d. San Diego, California, 1871). Lewis was in command of troops at Calabasas (q.v. Santa Cruz) in 1865. In the same year he was appointed colonel in the 7th Regiment of California Volunteers. Lewis, who had lived in San Diego since 1846, returned there probably in March 1869.

Ref.: 27, p. 157; Charles W. Lewis File, APHS. Map: C-1.

## LITTLE GIANT

El.: c. 3500'                    Loc.: Gila 2, A-11
George H. Stevens was nicknamed "the Little Giant." He was an active politician in the 1880's. Stevens had an Indian wife. Their several sons and their descendants are today highly respected leaders among the San Carlos Indians (cf. Stevens Ranch, Greenlee).

P.O. est. April 1, 1879. Samuel A. Lowe, p.m. Discont. April 28, 1882.
Ref.: Barnes; Woody. Map: C-4.

## LITTLE GREEN VALLEY

El.: c. 5000'                    Loc.: Gila 1, F-2
There are two valleys north of Payson, both of them being noted in the early days for their luxuriant meadows surrounded by timbered hills. The larger was called Big Green

Valley and the smaller naturally followed with its current name. The first settlers were William Burch and John Hood in 1876.

Ref.: Barnes. Maps: E-20; GD-12.

## LITTLE TROUGH CREEK

El.: c. 4000'                    Loc.: Gila 2, CD-4.5-3
The name derives from the Indian service having placed a watering trough in the canyon through which this creek runs.

Ref.: Barnes. Maps: C-13; D-3.

## LIVEOAK

El.: c. 4000'                    Loc.: Gila 1, G-11
Descriptive. It is possible that this post office was established in connection with the mining operations in the vicinity.

P.O. est. November 3, 1905. Rey A. Hascal, p.m. Rescinded February 10, 1906.
Ref.: P.O. Records; Barnes. Map: A-14.

a.n. Liveoak Shaft          Map: GD-5          Gila
    Liveoak Gulch          Maps: GD-4; GD-5          Gila

## LIVINGSTON

El.: c. 4000'                    Loc.: Gila 1, G-9
Charles Livingston arrived in Arizona in the late 1870's. He ran the Flying V Ranch at the community which later bore his name. When Gila County annexed its upper portion from Yavapai County, a conflict arose with the Flying V brand of that county, owned by Jerry Vosburg. Livingston relinquished his use of the brand.

Later in 1888, Livingston homesteaded at the mouth of Pinto Creek. A small community soon sprang up. When it became necessary to have a post office, the name Curnutt was considered along with the name Livingston, since Curnutt was also an early settler in the region.

The community of Livingston was noted for the many and exciting horse races which occurred there. When Roosevelt Dam was completed and waters began to collect in the lake, Livingston was abandoned. It is now completely covered by a dense growth of willow and mesquite trees.

P.O. est. as Livingstone September 19, 1896. James H. Curnutt, p.m. Discont. June 20, 1907.
Ref.: Cooper; Barnes; Woody. Map: C-9.

## LOUSY GULCH

El.: c. 5000'                    Loc.: Gila 1, C-2.6
Ben Cole with his sons Emer and Link worked a mine at this location one winter in the 1880's. All became lousy, hence the name.

Ref.: Barnes. Maps: GD-9; GD-16.

## MARSH CREEK

El.: c. 5000'                    Loc.: Gila 1, EF-3
This creek was dammed by beaver and every flat along it became a marsh until the beavers were destroyed.

Ref.: McKinney. Map: GD-2.

## MARYSVILLE

El.: c. 4000'                          Loc.: Gila 1, C-2.
                              About four miles w. of Payson.
This short-lived mining camp came into being in March
1880. It was named for its first woman settler, Mrs. Mary
Pyeatt. The town lasted about three years.

Ref.: Croxen. Map: None.

**a.n. Marysville Hill**        Map: GD-9                    Gila

## MAZATZAL MOUNTAINS

El.: c. 6000'                        Loc.: Gila 1, BD-7-9
Pro.: /mǽzitsˢæl/
The Mazatzal Mountains form the dividing line between
Gila and Maricopa County, west of Roosevelt Lake. The
name was applied to the mountains at least as early as May
18, 1867, when army records list a skirmish with Indians in
these mountains.

**v.n. Mazatzal Range**

Ref.: Barnes; 85, p. 428. Maps: C-2; E-20; GD-9; GD-15.

**a.n. Mazatzal City**        Map: E-20                    Gila
      A small mining camp which had a brief existence here in
      the late 1870's, but never amounted to much. McClintock
      wrote of visiting a placed called Mazatzal City in September
      1889. However, this was apparently East Verde Settlement
      (*See* East Verde River).

Ref.: Croxen; 112, p. 174.

**Mazatzal Peak**        Map: GD-9                    Gila

## McDONALD FORT

El.: c. 4800'                          Loc.: Gila 1, C-2
Mort McDonald, a merchant who had a string of saddle
horses, arrived in eastern Arizona in the late 1870's. The
small butte which bears his name was used by residents of
Payson and Marysville as a point of security during an
Indian scare in 1882. Hence the name "Fort."

Ref.: Barnes; Gillette; Woody. Map: GD-9.

**a.n. McDonald Mountain**    Map: GD-2                    Gila

      **McDonald Pocket**        Map: GD-2                    Gila
      McDonald wintered his horses here in a basin enclosed by
      the mountain.

Ref.: Barnes.

## McFADDEN HORSE MOUNTAIN

El.: 7523'                          Loc.: Gila 1, GH-6.4
Bill McFadden and his red-headed wife, Nancy, settled on
McFadden Creek south of McFadden Peak. The McFad-
dens raised horses and used the top of McFadden Horse
Mountain as a pasture. Their brand was a circle. McFadden
died January 7, 1929; Nancy McFadden died in 1930.

Ref.: McKinney; Woody. Map: GD-6.

**a.n. McFadden Peak**    Maps: GD-6; C-11                    Gila
      Nancy McFadden drove the first wagon and team over the
      Sierra Ancha into Pleasant Valley.

      **McFadden Spring**        Map: B-7                    Gila

## McMILLANVILLE

El.: c. 4000'                          Loc.: Gila 2, A-5.4
In the spring of 1876, Charles McMillan. and Theodore
(Dore) H. Harris located a silver mine which they named

the Stonewall Jackson. Legend says that McMillan had
made a night of it in the roaring saloons of the new community of Globe. The next day he and Harris set out to
prospect, but McMillan took time out to sleep it off while
his partner waited. Harris poked around and in the poking
found some soft sticky ore. He woke McMillan, who was
not too hung-over to realize that the find was a rich one.
The two men staked out their claim on March 6, 1876, but
soon sold out to a California company.

A boom-town developed at McMillan's camp as other locations were staked. Within a short time, three hundred people
were living at the place. In 1879 a five-stamp mill was
erected. By 1880, the population had increased to fifteen
hundred. The prosperous miners are reported to have
decorated a Christmas tree that year with "cigars, tobacco,
dynamite fuses, grub, and bottles of whiskey."

In July 1882, Nan-tia-tish and his band of Apaches included
McMillanville in their series of attacks. However, the
villagers were expecting the attack and all women were
placed in the Stonewall Jackson Mine tunnel for safety. The
pioneers were so well prepared that the Indian attack was
not successful and the Apaches soon left, heading for a
second attack on the Middleton and other ranches (See
Hendershot Place). This was the band which was finally
overtaken at Big Dry Wash (*q.v.*, Navajo).

By 1885 the silver in the mines was exhausted and Mc-
Millanville faded rapidly into a ghost town, having but a
single inhabitant in 1890. Currently there is a sign on the
highway marked "McMillan," which is actually the site of
the old mine. The village lay a half mile east and south of
the highway. Little remains today to mark the site.

P.O. est. December 12, 1877. Charles T. Martin, p.m. Name
changed to McMillan October 11, 1878. Discont. October 12,
1882.

Ref.: Woody; 87, p. 464; 135, p. 115; 170, p. 89; 4, p. 468.
Maps: C-12 (McMillenville); E-20.

## MEADOW VALLEY CREEK

El.: c. 5000'                          Loc.: Gila 1, FE-5-3
Descriptive. Barnes says a military outpost existed here in
1866 for Ft. McDowell. Such a post is not listed in any of
the books examined, but a skirmish with Indians occurred
here on February 28, 1867.

Ref.: 85, p. 427; Barnes. Map: E-20.

## MESCAL MOUNTAINS

El.: 4390'                          Loc.: Gila 1, H-14
Pro.: /meskǽl/
Lt. William H. Emory in 1846 referred to this range as the
Sierra Carlos Range. In the Wheeler report of 1873, Gilbert
called it the Gila Range.

Ref.: 175, III, 513; Barnes. Maps: GD-13; GK-6.

**a.n. Mescal Warm Spring**    Map: GK-6                    Gila
      Ref.: Woody.

## MESQUITE SPRING

El.: c. 4000'        Loc.: Gila 1, D-8
Pro.: /meskíyt/
Archie McIntosh established a ranch here after the Apache Indian troubles had quieted down somewhat. This was the spot visited by Gen. George Crook's men in the early 1870's. McIntosh was a scout for Crook.

Ref.: 22, p. 43; Barnes. Map: E-20 (Black Mesquite Spring and McIntosh).

## METHODIST CREEK

El.: c. 3000'        Loc.: Gila 1, E-7-8
Will Vineyard found a wild bee colony in a tree on this creek c. 1890. As he reported it, when he robbed the honey comb the bees went after him in a way that "would make a Methodist preacher swear."

Ref.: Barnes. Map: B-7.

**a.n. Methodist Mountain**        Map: B-7        Gila

## MIAMI

El.: 3438'        Loc.: Gila 1, H-11.8
Pro.: /mayǽmə/
Black Jack Newman located the Mima Mine, naming it for his fiancée, Mima Tune, whom he later married. This mine was east of the Old Dominion Globe Mine in Big Johney Gulch (q.v.). Almost simultaneously, James F. Gerald, who represented a group of men from Miami, Ohio, constructed a custom mill on what was then called the West Branch of Pinal Creek, but later Miami Wash. The mill was on a hill which is cut by the railroad where it crosses the Apache Trail, near the present Burch Pumping Station (q.v.). The flat in front of the mill was called Miami Flat for the Miami Copper Company, which owned the mill and mine.. Gradually, the names Mima and Miami became so blended that the original intention to call the new community Mima was overlooked.

Beginning in 1907, the town of Miami came into existence practically overnight, and its growth was insured by the Inspiration Mine Company (See Inspiration), which began constructing a huge reduction plant in 1909. Miami is sometimes referred to as the "Concentrator City."

P.O. est. September 25, 1908. Albert E. Hull, p.m.

Ref.: Woody, quoting Mrs. Jerry Copeland, friend of the Newmans; 4, p. 204. Maps: C-10; GD-5.

**a.n. Miami Flat**        El.: 3349'. Map: GD-4        Gila

**Miami Wash**        Loc.: Crosses Miami Flat        Gila
In early days this wash was known as Bloody Tank Wash (See Bloody Tank, a.n.). Now that the banks of this wash have been concreted, it is often referred to as the Miami Canal.

Ref.: 4, p. 202.

## MILK RANCH POINT

El.: c. 7500'        Loc.: Gila 1, BC-1
A Mormon family established a small dairy here at a spring and sold dairy products to construction camps along the railroad.

Ref.: Barnes. Map: B-7.

## MISTAKE PEAK

El.: c. 5200'        Loc.: Gila 1, E-5.8
This peak has such a vastly different appearance when viewed from the Tonto Basin (appearing as part of the main range) and when viewed from the other side, (looking like a separate peak), that people call it Mistake Peak.

Ref.: Barnes. Map: B-7.

## MOODY POINT

El.: c. 5500'        Loc.: Gila 1, GH-5.7
Ed Moody (b. California, 1878) was living in Globe in 1908.

Ref.: Barnes; Gila County Great Register. Map: GD-6.

## MOORE CREEK

El.: c. 7000'        Loc.: Gila 1, BC-1
Rance Moore had cattle at the Moore ranch in 1886.

Ref.: Barnes; Woody. Map: GD-12.

## MULE HOOF BEND

El.: c. 3900'        Loc.: Gila 2, B-3
This bend on the Salt River is shaped like a mule hoof.

Ref.: None. Map: GD-1.

## MYRTLE

El.: c. 7000'        Loc.: Gila 1, C-1
Mr. and Mrs. E. F. Pyle named this ranch for their daughter Myrtle, who died at their ranch and is buried near Bonito Creek.

P.O. est. December 23, 1899. Elfonso Landry, p.m. **Discont.** August 15, 1911.

Ref.: Pieper; P.O. Records. Map: C-9.

| a.n. Myrtle Lake | Map: GD-12 | Coconino |
|---|---|---|
| Myrtle Point | Map: GD-12 | Coconino |
| Myrtle Trail | Map: GD-12 | Gila and Coconino |

## NAEGLIN CREEK

El.: c. 6000'        Loc.: Gila 1, GH-2
Pro.: /néylən/ or /níylən/
Lewis and Henry Naeglin located in what is known as Naeglin Canyon c. 1886. The two men helped bury many killed during the Pleasant Valley feud. Lewis was present when Al Rose was shot. He reported the killing (cf. Rose Creek, Gila).

Ref.: Barnes; Woody; McInturff. Map: GD-16.

**a.n. Naeglin Rim**        Map: B-7        Gila

## NATANES PLATEAU

El.: c. 6000'        Loc.: Gila 2, EG-6-7
Pro.: /nətǽneys/ or /nətǽnəs/        Apache: "Chief"
This plateau was so referred to by Gilbert in the Wheeler report of 1873.

Ref.: 107, III, 27. Map: E-20.

**a.n. Natanes Peak**        Maps: E-20; C-3        Gila

## NATURAL BRIDGE

El.: 4533'        Loc.: Gila 1, B-1
Natural Bridge is one of the wonders, not only of Arizona, but of the world. It was found in 1880, according to Barnes,

by L. W. Snow, William Nelson, and Irvin L. House. Here in 1881, Snow and a Scot named David Gowan (d. December 1929) homesteaded. Gowan built his little house and planted an orchard on the twenty-five acres which form the top of Natural Bridge. From this place one would not realize that he was standing on top of a tremendous natural bridge. At one spot on the top of the bridge there is a water hole worn through, down which one can peer deep into the gorge below. The journey to the bottom of the enormous gorge is arduous but rewarding. It is, however, not to be taken except with a guide, for Gowan himself reported that he was lost for three days within a hundred yards of his own house. From the bottom of the wild gorge with its huge boulders, one can look up at the towering limestone arch with a span of over five hundred feet, roughly five times that of the famous Virginia Bridge. The breadth of the bridge is twelve times greater than that of the Virginia Bridge. This enormous span is supported by a column more than one hundred feet in circumference, which rises from the floor of the gorge to the roof. Beneath the arch is the Great Basin, described as a "solid rock bowl, some seventy-five feet in diameter and ninety in depth; and so transparent that a white stone rolled down the strange natural trough over one hundred feet long in the side of the basin, can be seen in all its bubbling course to the bottom of that chilly pool." The pool receives its water from a white falls about thirty feet high.

Gowan became sole owner of this natural wonder. A description of it was published extensively in Scotland. Some of Gowan's relatives read the account, wrote to him, and later migrated to Arizona, where they succeeded Gowan as owners of the Natural Bridge.

Ref.: 12, pp. 142-153; Barnes. Maps: C-7; GD-11.

## NATURAL CORRAL CREEK

El.: c. 4000'                                    Loc.: Gila 2, BC-7-8
A natural corral here is used by Apache cattlemen.
Ref.: Barnes. Maps: B-2; C-13.

## NUGGET

El.: c. 4500'                                    Loc.: Gila 2, A-6.5
The Nugget Mine lay about two miles southwest of Richmond Basin. It was not unusual for people to pick up silver nuggets or even good-sized silver boulders near the mine. Within the past ten years, for instance, a nearly pure silver nugget weighing sixty-four ounces was found in this area. As the Nugget Mine developed, it became necessary to have a post office for the miners.

P.O. est. January 7, 1881. George Santan, p.m. Discont. March 10, 1884.
Ref.: Woody; 135, p. 115. Map: C-5.
a.n. Nugget Wash          Map: GD-14                                    Gila

## OLD DOMINION MINE

El.: c. 3500'                                    Loc.: Gila 1, H-11.2
The Old Dominion Mine, reportedly named by Mrs. Alec Pendleton for her native state of Virginia, had ores which were worked in a smelter close by. The vein of the mine

was apparently inadequate, for the smelter was moved to Globe and the Old Dominion Company in May 1884 purchased the Globe Mine (cf. Globe, Gila.) After 1884, the former Globe Mine became generally known as the Old Dominion, whereas the original mine carrying the name was to all intents and purposes abandoned.

Ref.: Woody; 150, pp. 116, 117, 134. Maps: GD-4; GD-8.
a.n. Old Dominion Smelter    Map: GD-8                                    Gila
          This was the approximate location of the original Old Dominion Mine.

## ORD, MOUNT

El.: 7155'                                    Loc.: Gila 1, BC-6
Gen. Edward O'Connel Ord commanded troops in Arizona in 1869, at which time Camp Reno was located at the foot of the mountain bearing the general's name. A heliograph station was located on this mountain in 1886.

Ref.: Barnes; Woody. Maps: C-5; GD-15.
a.n. Ord Mine          Loc.: Near Mount Ord                                    Gila
          Cinnabar is currently mined here.

## OXBOW HILL

El.: c. 5000'                                    Loc.: Gila 1, D-2.8
In June 1871, Charles B. Genung was on an expedition with troops in this area. As they straggled along, they came upon several ox yokes on the mountain, apparently removed from oxen which had been run off by Apaches from settlers during raids. Genung's party named the place Ox Yoke Mountain. The Indians were noted for stealing horses and cattle which they would drive off to particular locations where they would proceed to kill the animals, roast them, and gorge themselves.

It was here that Genung encountered a typical instance of the wily actions of Apaches. The Mexican guide warned the party that the Indians might set fire to the brush. The men immediately rushed their horses down the trail, but not quickly enough. Despite the fact that the trail lay along the north side of the mountain and that the brush and grass did not burn readily, the onrushing fire cut off nearly all the soldiers. They had to abandon the trail and make their way as best they could.

The Oxbow Mine came into existence sometime after this incident, and a post office was established for the mining camp.

P.O. est. as Oxbow, March 17, 1895. Elizabeth H. St. John, p.m. Discont. June 23, 1908.
Ref.: Dugas; 52, VIII, 174-175. Maps: B-7; C-8; GD-9.

## PAYSON

El.: 5000'                                    Loc.: Gila 1, C-5
Payson was founded as Union Park in 1882. People in the area called it Green Valley until the post office was established. Then the postmaster, Frank C. Hise, named it for Senator Louis Edward Payson, who as congressional chairman of Post Office and Post Roads was responsible for Hise's having the appointment.

P.O. est. March 3, 1884. Frank C. Hise, p.m.
Ref.: P.O. Records; Barnes; 4, p. 453. Map: GD-9.
a.n. Green Valley Creek                                    Gila
          Green Valley Hills                                    Gila

## PERIDOT

El.: c. 4000'                          Loc.: Gila 2, C-8.7
Pro.: /peýridat/ or /peýrədat/
Peridot is the location of the Lutheran Mission on the San
Carlos Indian Reservation. It is so named because of the
semi-precious olive green gems known as peridot found in
this vicinity.
P.O. est. May 27, 1943. Leonard A. Malone, p.m.
Ref.: Jennings; Mrs. Harvey C. Osborne, Letter, April 19,
      1956. Maps: C-14; F-10; GD-16.
**a.n. Peridot Hill**     Loc.: At site of Peridot          Gila

## PETERS MOUNTAINS

El.: c. 3000'                          Loc.: Gila 1, D-8
Dave Peters at one time ran the 3-(Three Bar) Brand in
this area.
Ref.: Barnes. Map: B-7.

## PICACHO COLORADO

El.: 4777'                             Loc.: Gila 2, A-3.5
Pro.: /pikáčo/                         Spanish: "red peak"
Descriptive.
Ref.: Barnes. Map: B-7.

## PINAL CREEK

El.: c. 4500'                          Loc.: Gila 1, H-12-14
Pro.: /pinǽl/
The three branches which form this stream come together
at the upper end of the Wheatfields, one from the west and
two from the east end of the Pinal Mountains, from which
the creek takes its name. It winds its way through the town
of Globe. However, the creek, which formerly held water,
now is a dry bed, its waters having leaked into the shafts of
the Old Dominion Mine (q.v.).
The stream was named on June 13, 1864, by the King S.
Woolsey expedition. The night before, men in the party
traveled to a camp which they pitched toward midnight
beside a stream. The next morning they realized that they
were in a "beautiful valley covered with corn and wheat
fields."
Ref.: Woody; 151, p. 604; Arizona Miner, September 7, 1864,
      3:4; 4, p. 194. Maps: GD-4; GD-8; GD-14; C-4; E-18;
      E-20.

## PINAL MOUNTAINS

El.: c. 7800'                          Loc.: Gila, GH-13
Pro.: /pinǽl/
Numerous skirmishes with Indians occurred in the Pinal
Mountains. Army records report the first battle on April 1,
1868. The last occurred on March 15, 1874. The name
Pinal Mountains was known at least as early as 1864, when
the Woolsey expedition named the creek Pinal Creek (q.v.).
These mountains were inhabited by the so-called Pinal
Coyoteros, a tribe of Apaches, who were also referred to
as the Pinalenos.
Ref.: 85, pp. 430-440. Maps: GD-10; GD-4; E-18; C-2.
**a.n. Pinal Peak**     El.: 7850'. Map: GD-4              Gila
      Pinal Peak was named by the King S. Woolsey expedition
      of 1864.

Ref.: Barnes.
**Pinal**            Map: C-10                          Gila
      A railroad point on the Gila Valley railroad.
Ref.: Barnes.
**Pinal Peak**  El.: 6488'. Maps: C-12; GF-2          Greenlee

## PINE

El.: 5448'                             Loc.: Gila 1, B-1
The settlement of Pine began in 1879 when Riel Allen led
a group of Mormons to this spot. Many of them were
settlers who had been in the East Verde Settlement (q.v.).
The community is located in pine timber country, hence
the name.
P.O. est. April 8, 1884. Mary D. Fuller, p.m.
Ref.: 112, p. 174. Maps: C-6; GD-11.
**a.n. Pine Valley**                                   Gila

## PINTO CREEK

El.: c. 4500'                          Loc.: Gila 1, FG-9-11
Pro.: /pínto/           Mexican-Spanish: "painted"
In June 1869, this stream was referred to as the Rio Pinto
in an account of an Indian skirmish which occurred on its
banks. The variegated coloring of the high banks and of the
hills along its course gave it this name.
Ref.: 85, p. 433. Maps: C-4; E-18; GD-4; GD-5; GK-14.

## PIONEER

El.: c. 4000'                          Loc.: Gila 1, FG-14
The Pioneer Mine was located by George Scott and John
Brannaman in 1876 on the west side of Pinal Mountain
above Silver Creek. From the mine the Pioneer Mining
District took its name. The mine was soon bought by an
eastern company, the Howard Mining Company, and developed into a very active mine. The post office at the mining camp was called Pioneer. During the 1940's there were
still a few people living at this place.
Like most mining camps, Pioneer had its rough and ready
times. The climax of one of these came on Christmas night,
1882, when a twenty-two year old man named Hartnett
was challenged by a smaller and older man — Tom Kerr —
to try pinning down the latter's shoulders. Hartnett did so,
not only once, but twice, which made Kerr so furious he
shot the younger man four times and beat his head to a
pulp. Kerr, an ex-constable of Pinal County, then claimed
self defense. The flagrant lie did not keep him from an
immediate lynching.
P.O. est. April 24, 1882. Thomas A. Lonergan, p.m. Discont.
September 4, 1885.
Ref.: Woody; 135, p. 116. Map: C-5.
**a.n. Pioneer Creek**     Map: GD-13                   Gila
      **Pioneer Mine**       Map: B-7                      Gila

## PIONEER MOUNTAIN

El.: 5982'                             Loc.: Gila 1, H-13
The Pioneer Mining District in which the Silver King Mine
was located came into existence in 1875. While part of it
was in Pinal County, the greater portion lay in Gila County.
Pioneer Mountain, located out of the district near Globe

several miles to the east, was probably named for the district. The district is not to be confused with the community of Pioneer, located several miles to the southeast and not within the district itself.

Ref.: Woody. Maps: GD-13; E-20
**a.n. Pioneer Basin         Map: GD-4                    Gila**

## PIONEER STAGE STATION

El.: c. 4600'                         Loc.: Gila 1, H-14
The Pioneer Stage Station served as a point at which travellers to and from the old Pioneer Mine could take the stage to either Globe or Phoenix.

Ref.: Woody. Map: GD-13.

## PLEASANT VALLEY

El.: c. 6000'                         Loc.: Gila 1, F-4
The beautiful little valley with its descriptive name was known as Pleasant Valley at least as early as 1874, when two encounters with Indians are listed in army records.

For a number of years Pleasant Valley was perhaps the most uncomfortable spot for settlers in the United States. This was because of a fierce and bitter feud between the Grahams and the Tewksburys. Literally dozens of people were killed during the Pleasant Valley War, far bloodier than the noted feuds of Hardin County, Kentucky.

The first settler in the valley was Al Rose, a Dane, who put up a small stockade here in 1877. Very few others had settled before John Tewksbury arrived in Globe in 1879. He returned shortly thereafter to California for his sons and livestock, after which he settled in Pleasant Valley. The Grahams came from Texas about three years later. In 1877 the Tewksburys helped protect a band of sheep being driven over the Mogollon Rim. Cattlemen reacted violently to the incursion of sheep. The battle was soon joined by all hands. The feud came to its end in 1892 when the last of the Grahams was killed in Tempe. Meanwhile, guns had sounded not only in Pleasant Valley but as far north as Holbrook. During the feud Pleasant Valley was almost deserted. Settlers drifted back slowly.

Ref.: 55, p. 595; 4, p. 456; Woody; 85, p. 439. Maps: C-9; E-20; B-7.

## POINTED BUTTE

El.: c. 4000'                         Loc.: Gila 2, CD-3
Descriptive.

Ref.: Barnes. Map: C-12.

## POLLES MESA

El.: c. 4250'                         Loc.: Gila 1, AB-1.8
Pro.: /pówliˆz/
Polle Chilson raised cattle on this mesa.

Ref.: Gillett; Barnes; Pieper. Map: GM-19.

## PORPHYRY MOUNTAIN

El.: c. 5400'                         Loc.: Gila 1, G-1̂1.2
Descriptive. There is also a mine by this name.

Ref.: Woody. Maps: GD-4; GD-5.

## POTATO BUTTE

El.: 6180'                            Loc.: Gila 1, F-4.6
This butte looks like a potato standing on end.

Ref.: Barnes. Maps: C-12; GD-2.

## PRINGLE WASH

El.: c. 3000'                         Loc.: Gila 1, H-8
This wash crosses the Pringle Ranch, which is on Pinal Creek. It was owned by the three Pringle brothers who came into the area in the early 1880's. Robert Pringle (b. Scotland, 1848) emigrated to America in 1868 and to Arizona in 1882. In 1914 he rented his ranch near Globe to the Gardners.

Ref.: Woody; 112, III. Maps: GD-1; GD-6; GD-14.

## PUEBLO CANYON

El.: c. 4000'                         Loc.: Gila 1, H-7
Pro.: /pwéblo/
Pueblo Canyon derives its name from a group of cliff dwellings which as yet have been only partially explored. The Pueblo Mine takes its name from this canyon. It is an asbestos mine.

Ref.: 111, p. 14. Map: GD-6.
**a.n. Pueblo Mine Spring    Map: B-7                     Gila**

## QUAIL SPRING CANYON

El.: c. 3600'                         Loc.: Gila 1, H-7.5
Quail in great numbers frequent this canyon and Quail Spring, which is in it.

Ref.: Ralph De Vore (interviewed by Woody). Map: GD-6.
**a.n. Quail Spring          Map: B-7                     Gila**
Ref.: Hicks.
    **Quail Springs Wash   Map: GD-14                   Gila**
Ref.: McInturff.

## QUARTSITE PEAK

El.: c. 4800'                         Loc.: Gila 2, A-6.9
"Quartsite" ore is found in the mine here.

Ref.: Barnes. Map: B-7.

## R-14 RANCH

El.: c. 4000'                         Loc.: Gila 2, EF-2.2
The Apaches who became scouts with the soldiers were given numbers. R-14 was a well-known scout whose family name was Altaha. The Indians frequently used soldiers' names for surnames. These they attached to their army numbers. R-14 was a very prosperous rancher and cattleman.

Ref.: Davis. Map: D-3.

## RAGGED TOP

El.: c. 6000'                         Loc.: Gila 2, D-2
Descriptive.

Ref.: Barnes. Map: GD-16.

## RAMBOZ PEAK

El.: c. 5300'                    Loc.: Gila 1, H-11
Pro.: /rǽmbowz/
Henry Ramboz' mining claim was one of the first to be filed in the Globe area. Ramboz (d. c. 1930) lived with his partner, J. D. Wilson, at Ramboz Camp and Spring. He came to Arizona c. 1875. Wilson remained but a short time, but Ramboz stayed on. A small store was erected at the camp by John Clum and George H. Stevens. It was at this point that the Globe Mining District was formed in November 1875.

Ref.:   Woody; 55, p. 594. Map: GD-4.

## RAMER RANCH

El.: c. 6000'                    Loc.: Gila 1, H-1
Pro.: /réymer/
H. J. Ramer (b. 1850) bought his ranch c. 1887 from Andy Cooper, a participant in the Pleasant Valley war, who was later killed in Holbrook. The original name for the place was the Cooper Ranch.

Ref.:   Barnes; Woody. Maps: C-7 (Rayners); A-7.

## RANCH CREEK

El.: c. 4000'              Loc.: Gila 2, A-10.5-8.4
The location of the Hayes Ranch on the west bank of Aliso Creek into which this small stream flows gave it its name.

Ref.:   Barnes. Map: B-7.

## REDMAN MESA

El.: c. 6000'                   Loc.: Gila 1, F-5.5
Joseph Redman had a big ranch on the Sierra Ancha, a ranch south of Globe and some land in the Roggenstroh Mountains. He operated a meat market in Globe.

Ref.:   Webb. Map: B-7.

a.n. Redman Mountain   Map: GD-14 ("Redmond")         Gila

## RENO, CAMP

El.: c. 4000'                   Loc.: Gila 1, C-6.1
A sub-station of Fort McDowell (q.v. Maricopa), Camp Reno was named for Brig. Gen. Marcus Albert Reno, who had served as a colonel with the 12th Pennsylvania Cavalry. Camp Reno was established in July 1868 in what was then called Green Valley. By September 22, five companies were stationed at the camp in an effort to hold the Apaches in check in the Tonto Valley.

The post was poorly located. It was fully exposed to raiding Indians because the camp was on an open mesa. On either side were two deep canyons containing water and brush which afforded excellent concealment for raiding Indians. The post was abandoned c. 1870.

Ten years later a post office by the name of Reno was opened, indicating that a small settlement was there after the withdrawal of troops.

P.O. est. October 20, 1880. Isaac R. Prather, p.m. Discont. July 24, 1894.

Ref.:   52, V, 262, 307, 253; 111, p. 153; 85, p. 431; 52, VIII, 70, 71; *Phoenix Republican,* September 30, 1891, 1:6. Maps: B-7; C-2; E-18; E-20.

a.n. Reno Canyon
Loc.: On road between Camp McDowell and Reno in Four Peaks (*q.v.,* Maricopa) area.                    Gila
Reno Creek          Map: GD-15          Gila
Camp Reno was located on this creek.
Reno, Mount         Map: C-12          Gila

v.n. Parker Butte      Loc.: T. 7 N., R. 11 E.          Gila
A Texan named Parker settled on a ranch near this butte in the 1880's.

Ref.:   Barnes.

a.n. (continued)

Parker Creek         Map: GD-6          Gila

Reno Pass      El.: 4724'. Maps: C-12; GD-15          Gila
The military road through this pass was named for Camp Reno. It was built c. 1868. The road was so rough and its grade so steep that it required at least two teams to take a loaded wagon through the pass and exceptional brake power to take it down grade.

Ref.:   111, 153; Woody.

## REPPY

El.: c. 4000'                   Loc.: Gila 2, B-8.1
This point on the railroad was named for Charles D. Reppy (1846-1946). Reppy was a noted newspaper man, his first job in Arizona being that of editor of the *Arizona Bullion* in Harshaw during the paper's six month's existence. He was associated with the *Tombstone Epitaph* from late 1880 until July 1882. In 1885 he bought the *Florence Tribune,* with which he was associated through 1909. He served as chief clerk of the House for the 18th State Legislature.

Ref.:   Estelle Lutrell, *Newspapers and Periodicals of Arizona, 1859-1911;* Tucson, Arizona: University of Arizona, 1949. Map: GD-16.

## REYNOLDS CREEK

El.: c. 6000'                   Loc.: Gila 1, FH-6.5
Glenn Reynolds built the first house on the creek which bears his name. For many years he was a prominent Gila County cattleman. In 1888 he was elected sheriff of Gila County. On November 2, 1889, he was escorting Apache prisoners to the railroad en route to prison. He was killed by the Apache Kid on that trip.

Ref.:   Barnes; McKinney; Woody. Map: GD-6.

## RICHMOND BASIN

El.: c. 5600'                   Loc.: Gila 1, H-10.2
In 1876 Mack Morris was the locator of the Richmond Mine in what came to be known as Richmond Basin. This area first came to attention when nuggets of native silver were found in the depression of the ground (basin) where Morris located his mine. The women obtained pin money by picking up such nuggets. The Richmond Mine produced high-grade silver ore until 1882, the ore being treated in a mill at Wheatfield.

Morris was later killed in Tucson when his horses ran away with him.

Ref.:   Mrs. Dudley Craig; 76, p. 64; 135, p. 115. Map: GD-14.

## RIGG, CAMP

El.: c. 4000'                    Loc.: Gila 2, C-8.3

Lt. Col. Edwin A. Rigg received his rank on March 24, 1865. He had come to Arizona in May 1864 from New Mexico to fight the Apaches. In the report of the Woolsey expedition, King S. Woolsey says that his party was preparing for a raid on Signal Mountain when an order was received to abandon the proposed raid. Woolsey heard of this while he was at Camp Rigg and started back at once to Fort Goodwin to try to get Col. Rigg to rescind the order. Camp Rigg is not listed among the official posts of the military in Arizona. This may indicate that it was a temporary camp.

Ref.: *Arizona Miner*, September 21, 1864, 1:3; *Tucson Citizen*, July 3, 1875, 4:3; 55, p. 405; Jennings. Map: C-1.

## ROBERTS MESA

El.: 6669'                    Loc.: Gila 1, E-1

In the 1880's, Jim Roberts ran the Pendleton brothers' ranch at this location. He did not stay in the area long enough to prove up land in his own name. The land was later patented by Elam Bales.

In 1928 when Roberts was seventy-two years old, he served as deputy sheriff in Clarkdale. During this term in office, Roberts shot and killed a bank robber who was escaping in an automobile.

Ref.: McKinney; Woody; Barnes. Map: GD-12.

**a.n. Roberts Draw**                                    Gila

## ROCK HOUSE SPRING

El.: c. 5000'                    Loc.: Gila 1, D-5.3

The presence of a rock house at this point gives the spring its name. There is also another rock house in the vicinity.

Ref.: McKinney. Map: B-7.

| **a.n. Rock House** | Map: GD-6 | Gila |
| **Rock House Creek** | Map: GD-1 | Gila |
| **Rock House Canyon** | | Gila |
| **v.n. Tank House Canyon** | Map: B-7 | |
| **Rock Horse Canyon (Corruption)** | | |

## ROCKINSTRAW MOUNTAIN

El.: 5385'                    Loc.: Gila 1, F-1.4

Pro.: /rógənstr)/

George Rudolph Roggenstroh (b. Germany 1856) was naturalized an American citizen in Globe on September 18, 1882. He established a ranch and in 1891 assigned a mining deed to his land at what is now known as Rockinstraw Mountain. While he was alone at his ranch one time, he was shot accidentally through his hand. A neighbor, John McComb, arrived shortly after the accident and took Roggenstroh to town where his hand was amputated.

Rockinstraw Mountain is located at the south end of the Apache Mountains. The Apache Mountains were so called at least as early as 1870 when an army skirmish is recorded as having occurred there. The mountains are also sometimes referred to as the Sierra Apache.

Ref.: Woody; Gila County Great Register (1886); 85, p. 435. Maps: C-13; GD-14.

## ROOSEVELT DAM, THEODORE

El.: 2146'                    Loc.: Gila 1, E-8.7

Years before Roosevelt Dam was thought of, its future location was used as a ford across the Salt River at the mouth of Tonto Creek. From at least 1882 on, this point was called The Crossing by ranchers and farmers. Inevitably a settlement developed at this location. Today it is under the waters impounded by Roosevelt Dam.

The first name for the future dam was Tonto Dam. The first stone in the masonry dam was laid on September 20, 1906, and nearly five years later on February 5, 1911, the structure was completed. Theodore Roosevelt dedicated the dam on March 18, 1911, pressing a button which began the collection of water in the reservoir for the future irrigation of land in the Salt River Valley. Nearly four years later on April 15, 1915, water overflowed the dam for the first time. The spillways were raised c. 1936.

Roosevelt Dam is 284 feet high, and its base is 184 feet thick. Roosevelt Lake is twenty-three miles long. The rising of the waters in the lake and the construction of the dam itself made it necessary to re-locate the settlement at The Crossing. The town of Roosevelt was consequently moved. The name of the dam was changed by Congress to Theodore Roosevelt Dam in August 1959.

P.O. est. January 22, 1904. William A. Thompson, p.m.

Ref.: Woody; State Library Files; 4, pp. 147, 366; 39, pp. 159-160. Maps: C-10 (dam); C-12; GD-15.

**a.n. Salt River Bird Reservation**                                    Gila

Roosevelt Lake was at one time a national bird preserve.

## ROSE CREEK

El.: 5800'                    Loc.: Gila 1, G-6.9

Al Rose, a member of the Graham faction during the Pleasant Valley war, was rounding up his cattle preparatory to leaving the valley when he was killed in October 1887. Rose Creek is said once to have been called Connor Creek after Sam Connor, the first person to locate in this vicinity.

Ref.: Barnes; Woody. Map: GD-6.

**a.n. Connor Canyon**        Map: GD-6                Gila

## RUSSET HILLS

El.: c. 5000'                    Loc.: Gila 2, DE-2.5

These hills are brown.

Ref.: Barnes. Map: E-20.

## RYE CREEK

El.: c. 3000'                    Loc.: Gila 2, CD-3-4

Wild rye grew noticeably along this creek as late as 1879.

**v.n. Wild Rye Creek**        (Map: C-6)

Ref.: Barnes. Maps: C-6; GD-9.

**a.n. Rye**        Loc.: T. 9 N., R. 10 E.                Gila

The settlement at Rye was a crossing point on the creek. During the Pleasant Valley war the town of Rye was a neutral refuge for feuders on both sides. Gilliland, wounded by one faction, rode thirty miles to this point to have a bullet cut out of his neck with a razor. He recovered (cf. Gilliland).

P.O. est. October 14, 1884. Mary E. Boardman, p.m. Discont. October 9, 1907.

Ref.: 16, p. 453; Woody. Maps: C-6; C-8.

## ST. JOHNS CREEK

El.: c. 4000'  Loc.: Gila 1, BC-2.6

William O. St. Johns patented a ranch at this location. It served as a general stopping place on the road from Globe to Payson.

Ref.: Barnes. Map: GD-9.

## SALOME CREEK

El.: c. 4000'  Loc.: Gila 1, EF-5.5-8.2

Pro.: /sǽliˆmey/ or /séləméy/

The first American settlers changed the Spanish pronunciation of the creek name to "Sally May." The legend grew that a pioneer had married two different women, and having settled on this creek, named it after his wives. Another version is that he had two daughters so named. Probate records fail to substantiate the stories.

**v.n.** Sallymay
    Salumay                                              Gila

Ref.: Place Names Committee, Arizona Pioneers Historical Society, 3rd annual report, December 29, 1937; 22, p. 451. Maps: C-10; C-13; (Sallymay); GD-15.

**a.n.** Sally May Canyon  Map: GM-19  Gila

## SALT CREEK

El.: c. 3500'  Loc.: Gila 2, D-9

There is a large salt spring on this creek.

Ref.: Barnes. Maps: A-7; B-9; C-12.

**a.n.** Salt Mountain
    Loc.: T. 2 S., R. 20 E. W. side of Salt Creek  Gila

## SALT RIVER

El.: c. 4000'-1100'  Loc.: Gila 1, HG-9; Gila 2, EA-2.8-4.5
    Maricopa 2, KA-6.

The largest tributary of the Gila River, the Salt River rises approximately twenty miles west of Fort Apache and flows for over two hundred miles southwesterly to its junction with the Gila about twelve miles southwest of Phoenix. The Salt River winds through deep gorges in a mountainous terrain.

Each explorer seems to have given the Salt a different name. Fr. Kino in 1698 sighted the stream from a mountaintop and called it the Salado ("Salt"). He also referred to this branch of the Gila as one of the rivers which he named for the evangelists. He named it Matthew. In 1736 or 1737, Padre Ignacio Xavier Keller viewed the Verde and Salado Rivers and apparently named their union point and the stream below there, the Asuncíon ("Assumption").

Fr. Jacobo Sedelmayr in 1744 arrived at its banks and dubbed it the Rio de la Asuncíon. That section of it which is formed by the joining of the Verde River with the Salt River was termed by the writer of the *Rudo Ensayo* (1766) as the Rio Compuesto ("Put Together River"). On November 3, 1775, Fr. Francisco Garcés called it the Rio de la Asumpción, a variant of the name applied by Fr. Sedelmayr.

By 1852 the river was being referred to as the Salado or Salinas. The upper portion of the river was called the Black River, as is true today. Capt. George M. Wheeler in 1873 refers to it by two names: the Prieto ("Black") and the Salt River.

The name for the river derives from the fact that its waters, particularly when the stream is low, have a brackish taste. This is due to several large salt springs along its upper regions where the water may be described as a weak brine. Much of the saltiness comes from the Salt River Draw (T. 5 N, R. 17 E). King S. Woolsey is reported to have attempted to establish a salt mine at this location and the military map for 1879 shows a salt works located at the extensive Salt Banks.

The Salt River Canyon through which the river winds was the scene of many engagements with Apaches, the first occurring according to army records on August 28, 1866.

Ref.: Woody; 141, p. 64; 35, p. 142, (Note 56); p. 110, (Note 15); 7, pp. 357, 362; 145, pp. 5, 20, 46; 9, p. 240; 125, p. 130, (Note 63); 87, p. 75; 161, p. 147; 89, p. 235; 85, p. 426; State Library Files. Maps: GK-14; C-1; E-1; E-11 (Rio Salinas).

**a.n.** Salt River Mountains  Map: GD-14  Gila

Salt River Mountains  Map: GG-14  Maricopa

The Indian name for these mountains is *Mohatuk*, meaning "greasy mountain." The rocks look greasy when they are wet. Barnes relates an interesting Pima legend concerning how the mountain became greasy. When the great flood was over, Elder Brother emerged as the ruler and Coyote as his subordinate. Coyote was sent to liberate the animals which were shut up in a dark cave. Rabbit had died, and the other animals wanted a way to dispose of the body so that Coyote would not get him. They decided to burn Rabbit as a ruse to get Coyote away. Coyote was sent to the Sun to get fire. When he looked back he saw smoke and returned at once to find the people burning Rabbit's body. They formed a circle to shut Coyote out. Coyote ran around trying to find an opening and suddenly found a way in by leaping over two short men. He immediately bit out Rabbit's heart and ran away northward across the Gila. There he stopped and ate the heart, and as he did so, grease fell out among the stones of the mountain and the marks last to this day.

**v.n.** Salt River Range  (Map GG-12)

Ref.: Barnes, quoting Frank Russell of Smithsonian Institution, 1902.

**a.n.** Salt River Peak  El.: 4857'. Map: GD-14  Gila

## SAN CARLOS RIVER

El.: 2635'  Loc.: Gila 2, GC-10-7

Pro.: /sæn kárlos/

On the military map of 1851 there is a Rio San Carlos. This stream was named by Fr. Francisco Garcés on November 4, 1775. As was customary, the stream was named because it was San Carlos' day. Coincidentally Carlos III was then King of Spain. It was he who in May 1782 authorized the formation of Franciscan missions in the Southwest. Fr. Garcés also referred to the Gila river as being joined by the Rio de Carlos. Maj. William H. Emory in the late 1840's renamed it the San Francisco River and it appears on subsequent military and GLO maps under that name. On GLO 1869 it appears as Williams Creek. By 1874 the Public Surveys map was showing it as the Rio San Carlos. By that year, of course, the San Carlos Indian Reservation was in existence. The military map of 1875 shows it as the San Carlos River.

Prior to the establishment of the San Carlos Indian Reservation, the military had a sub-post of Fort Grant called San Carlos. Maj. William B. Royall selected the place for the new camp on the east bank of the San Carlos River approximately three miles above its junction with the Gila River. On June 22, 1872, Lt. Jacob Almy was given orders to establish the San Carlos post at once.

The San Carlos Indian Reservation was established by Executive Order on November 9, 1871, and was enlarged thereafter several times. It also suffered a reduction in territory when the Globe Mining District was formed. Rich minerals were on the Indian Reservation, and the land was removed by Executive Order. The reservation was established to be a catch-all for the various bands of Apaches as well as other Indians. Included were the Mojaves and the Yumas. Apache bands included the Arivaipa, Chiricahua, Coyotero, Mimbreno, Mogollon, Pinaleno, San Carlos, Tonto, and Tsiiltaden. The total acreage was 1,834,240. Gen. George Crook protested against herding so many different tribes onto a single reservation, and the Indians themselves resented it, since their various tribes were not united in any way, but rather in many instances were openly suspicious and hostile toward each other. In March 1875 Crook left Arizona.

Matters at the reservation went from pretty bad to awful. Not only were the Indians discontented, but a struggle developed between the army officers and the Indian agent as to who should have control over Indian affairs and actions. Added to this was the unhappy fact that private citizens in many instances could not refrain from meddling. Typical was the so-called gang of "Tombstone Toughs." According to Lt. John G. Bourke, "They represented all the rum-poisoned bummers of the San Pedro Valley," and took it upon themselves to plan an invasion of the reservation and the murder of the Apaches. Their ill-conceived plans came to an abrupt halt after the gang fired at one old Indian and then ran away. Their action left the settlers in the area to bear the evil results of swift Apache vengeance.

The struggle between the military and the Indian agent was well handled by John P. Clum (b. 1851, d. 1932). A very young man when he took on the assignment as Indian agent at the reservation, Clum was full of energy and courage. He served from 1874 to 1877. One of the first acts was the purchase of forty-two hundred sheep, two hundred cows, two hundred goats and two hundred burros, which, he reported, gave the Apaches work enough to do so that they had no time left to think about marauding. This meant that no troops were needed and on October 9, 1875, Gen. August V. Kautz removed the troops from San Carlos and abandoned Fort San Carlos. This was only a temporary move, however, since the fort was soon reoccupied.

P.O. est. at San Carlos October 22, 1875. George H. Stevens, p.m.

Ref.:  *Weekly Arizona Miner,* June 29, 1872, 2:1; 157, p. 79; 88, II, 374; 105, pp. 183, 187; 22, p. 456; 35, p. 139; 141, p. 63; 28, p. 164; Estelle Lutrell, *Newspapers and Peri-*

*odicals of Arizona,* 1859-1911. Tucson, Arizona: University of Arizona, 1949, p. 79. Maps: E-1; E-11; C-2 (Rio San Carlos); E-20; E-18.

**a.n. Talklai**          Maps: C-9; C-10; C-11          Gila

This post office was named for Talklai (d. March 4, 1930), half-brother of the San Carlos Chief, Distalin. Talklai was one of the members of the Indian police unit developed by John P. Clum. On December 22, 1875, Distalin, apparently crazed, attacked Clum and other agency officials, but was killed by two members of the Indian police, one of whom was Talklai. From its location on the GLO 1903 map, it would seem that Talklai may have been established as a post office in Tiffany's store.

P.O. est. December 19, 1900. James W. Balmer, p.m.

Ref.:  Barnes.

**Rice**          Map: C-10          Gila

Three months prior to the establishment of a post office at Talklai, one was established at Rice, a station on the railroad. According to Barnes, Lt. Sedgwick Rice was Indian agent for several years at San Carlos, and when the Indian School was built it was named for this man. The railroad station adopted the name of the school. It is also reported that a Lt. Rice was in charge of the Agency in 1894-1895 when the railroad finally obtained a right-of-way by vote of the Indians.

Prior to 1909 both Rice Station and Talklai are shown as being on the west bank of the San Carlos.

P.O. est. September 7, 1900 as Rice. James H. Stevens, p.m. Name of Talklai changed to Rice, February 16, 1909. (This coincides with the information on GLO 1909).

When Coolidge Dam was built, it was anticipated that the waters would collect and cover the older location of San Carlos. For this reason the headquarters of the agency were moved to the location of Rice, and the name of Rice was changed to San Carlos on September 1, 1930. The old San Carlos post office was discontinued on May 28, 1929, just prior to the move. Wells Fargo Station (at old San Carlos), 1903.

Ref.:  Woody.

**San Carlos Lake**          Gila

The waters impounded by Coolidge Dam were named San Carlos Lake after the old military post and town which it was anticipated would be covered by water, but as yet this has not proved to be the case.

## SAW MILL CREEK

El.: c. 4000'          Loc.: Gila 2, C-3-4

This stream rises at the location of a former government saw mill.

Ref.:  Barnes. Maps: C-12; C-13.

## SCHELL GULCH

El.: c. 2500'          Loc.: Gila 1, F-7.2-8.5

Robert H. Schell (b. Canada 1845) was naturalized in Nevada in 1866. He was listed as a resident of Gila County in 1886 and probably lived on the gulch which bears his name.

Ref.:  Gila County Great Register (1886). Map: B-7.

## SCHULTZ RANCH

El.: 3906'          Loc.: Gila 1, H-13

Charles Schultze bought out the first homesteader at this location. He lived in Globe prior to the time that he and his brothers and their parents moved to the ranch. It is still owned by the same family. The name "Schultz" is a corruption.

P.O. est. as Schultze July 12, 1894. Lizzie Schneider, p.m. Discont. April 21, 1902.

Ref.: Woody; Barnes. Maps: GD-4; GD-10.

## SEVENMILE CANYON

El.: c. 5000'                          Loc.: Gila 1, EF-5.5
This canyon lay seven miles from Young on the old wagon road to Globe.

Ref.: McKinney. Map: GD-2.

**a.n. Seven Mile Mountain**     Map: B-7                    Gila

## SEVEN MILE CREEK

El.: c. 4000'                          Loc.: Gila 2, BC-8
The name describes the length of the creek.

Ref.: Barnes. Maps: B-7; C-13.

**a.n. Seven Mile Crossing**                                Gila
Apparently this was the crossing on Seven Mile Creek where it joins the San Carlos River.

Ref.: 4, p. 447.

## SIDDLE RANCH

El.: c. 6000'                          Loc.: Gila 1, D-1
Pro.: /sayélə/
Henry Siddle was the first settler on the East Verde. During the 1880's he crouched on a hill above his ranch while he watched Apaches burn his cabin.

Ref.: Barnes. Map: None.

## SIEBER CREEK

El.: c. 5000'                          Loc.: Gila 1, C-3
Pro.: /síyber/
Al Sieber (b. Germany, February 29, 1844; d. February 19, 1907) was brought up in Pennsylvania and served in the Civil War. He came to Arizona in 1868. Sieber earned a fine reputation as a guide and scout for the military and was well-thought of by the Apaches. A fearless man, Sieber did not hesitate to enter an Indian encampment to reprimand Apaches crazy-drunk on tizwin. He was twice wounded in Indian skirmishes and became permanently crippled as a result.

During the construction of Roosevelt Dam, Sieber was accidentally killed by a rolling boulder in 1907. A monument beside the road stands close to the spot where this accident occurred. The monument had to be moved from the accident location because high waters sometimes covered it.

Ref.: Barnes; Woody. Map: E-20.

## SILVER BUTTE

El.: c. 6000'                          Loc.: Gila 2, F-2
The young juniper on this butte at night look as though tipped with silver.

Ref.: Davis. Map: D-3.

## SILVER CREEK

El.: c. 4000'                          Loc.: Gila 1, H-13-14
A silver camp on this creek gave it its name.

Ref.: Woody. Map: GD-13.

## SINGLE STANDARD GULCH

El.: c. 4600'                          Loc.: Gila 1, C-2.6
The gulch takes its name from the mine.

Ref.: Barnes. Maps: GD-9; B-7 (Single Standard Mine).

## SLATE CREEK

El.: 3500'                             Loc.: Gila 1, BD-5.5
Slate rock is found here.

Ref.: Cooper. Map: GD-15.

## SLEEPING BEAUTY PEAK

El.: 4890'                             Loc.: Gila 1, H-11
From the southeast this mountain looks very much like a reclining woman with long hair streaming backwards from her forehead.

Ref.: Woody. Maps: GD-4; GD-5.

**a.n. Sleeping Beauty Spring**  Map: GD-5                  Gila

## SNOWSTORM MOUNTAIN

El.: 5162'                             Loc.: Gila 1, C-2
The mountain took its name from the nearby Snowstorm Mine. According to legend, the location was made during a very bad snowstorm.

Ref.: Barnes. Map: GD-9.

## SOLDIER CAMP WASH

El.: c. 4000'                          Loc.: Gila 1, HG-7.5
In the early 1870's, soldiers in pursuit of Apaches used Soldier Hill as a camping spot.

Ref.: McKinney; Barnes. Map: GD-6.

**a.n. Soldier Camp Creek**     Map: GD-2                   Gila
**Soldier Creek**               Map: GD-1                   Gila
**Soldier Camp Mountain**       Map: GD-2                   Gila

## SOMBRERO PEAK

El.: 6436'                             Loc.: Gila 1, H-6.8
Pro.: /sombréro/                       Spanish: "hat"
A descriptive name.

**v.n. Sombrero Butte**
                (Ref. 146, p. 706) (Map: C-9)
Ref.: Barnes. Maps: C-9; GD-6.

## STANTON

El.: c. 3000'                          Loc.: Gila 1, H-8.8.
                        In Richmond Basin (q.v.)
In 1880 Stanton was a stage station at the Mack Morris Mill. It was a small settlement with ranches strung out along the nearby creek where much farming was being done. All that remains is a high rock wall and one house. Its school has been bought out by the Inspiration Copper Company for water rights.

P.O. est. May 14, 1880. Thomas L. Johnson, p.m. Discont. November 1, 1882.

Ref.: Woody; Barnes. Map: None.

## STAR VALLEY

El.: 4554'                         Loc.: Gila 1, C-3.4
When Andrew M. Houston and his brother Samuel arrived
in 1878, they found a man named Star living in the valley
and named it for him.
Ref.: Barnes; APHS Files. Map: GD-2.

## STEWARD POCKET

El.: 4875'                         Loc.: Gila 1, D-2.1
Ben Steward was the first settler in this pocket. It joins
Houston Pocket on the west.
Ref.: Barnes; Gillette. Map: GD-9.

## STORM CANYON

El.: 3072'                         Loc.: Gila 1, HG-9
In November 1898 Jack Knighton, Bob Sloan and J. B.
Henderson camped here while out rounding up cattle.
Snowed in, they nearly starved. Because they lost their
horses, they had to walk to McMillan through snow six to
seven feet deep and drifts which they estimated to be fifty
feet deep.
Ref.: Barnes; Woody. Map: GD-14.

## STRAWBERRY VALLEY

El.: 6047'                         Loc.: Gila 1, B-1
Wild strawberries gave the name to this location. In 1864
Henry Clifton, who was a member of King S. Woolsey's
second expedition, reported that the party called the valley
Wah-poo-ata because it was the home of a Tonto chieftain
by that name. He was referred to by Prescott citizens as
Big Rump. Later when Mormon settlers came into the
region from Utah, the name Strawberry was applied to the
valley.
P.O. est. December 13, 1886. Lafayette P. Nash, p.m. Discont.
December 31, 1904.
Ref.: Barnes; Woody; 26, p. 596; 29, p. 58. Maps: GD-11;
GM-19; C-6.

a.n. Strawberry Canyon        Map: GD-11            Gila
     Strawberry Creek                                Gila
     Strawberry Mountain  El.: 6794'. Map: GD-11     Gila

## TAM O'SHANTER PEAK

El.: c. 8000'                     Loc.: Gila 1, HG-16
The crest of this peak looks like a tam o'shanter.
Ref.: Barnes. Maps: C-13; GD-13.

## TIDWELL'S MILL

El.: c. 4000'                     Loc.: Gila 2, A-6.6
The ores from the mines near McMillanville were handled
at a relatively unsuccessful mill built by Silas Tidwell in
the late 1870's.
Ref.: Barnes. Maps: B-7; E-20.

## TIMBER CAMP MOUNTAIN

El.: c. 4000'                     Loc.: Gila 2, AB-5.8
In the late 1870's, a sawmill on this mountain cut timber
for use in the mines.
Ref.: Barnes; 3 A, p. 135. Maps: B-7; C-11.

## TONTO

El.: 2488'                        Loc.: Gila 1, C-5.5
Pro.: /tánto/                     Spanish: "fool"
At the foot of the trail called The Jump-off, a post office
was located for the Cross-Seven Cattle Company. The
ranch was also often referred to as Howell's Ranch.
P.O. est. February 25, 1884. James B. Watkins, p.m. Discont.
June 6, 1902.
Ref.: Barnes. Maps: C-7; GD-15.

## TONTO BASIN

El.: c. 2500'                     Loc.: Gila 1, CD-6.3
Pro.: /tánto/                     Spanish: "fool"
The Tonto Basin, which is hemmed in by surrounding
mountains, contains some of the roughest country in the
United States. It was used as a stronghold by the Indians,
who knew it so well that they had no trouble ambushing
pursuers. Nevertheless, the military was gradually able to
subdue the Apaches, and the last of the Tonto Basin Indians
surrendered in April 1873.

The name *Tonto* derives from the fact that the basin was
inhabited by the so-called Tonto Apaches, dubbed erroneously because of their supposed foolishness. In the nineteenth century the name Tonto Apache was applied by
writers to nearly all the Indians in the territory between the
White Mountains and the Colorado River. This included
the members of at least two linguistic families. Therefore,
the term "Tonto Apache" cannot be considered applicable
to a particular tribe.

The first exploration of the basin by men seeking places to
settle was made in July 1876 by William C. Allen, John
Bushman, Pleasant Bradford and Peter Hansen. These men
reported unfavorably. Nevertheless, in March 1878, John
H. Willis herded cattle into the upper part of the basin.
Attempts by the Mormons to settle in the basin met with
defeat because of the irregular water supply and the rough-
ness of the terrain, which made land holdings small. On
August 14, 1890, the Mormons were authorized to abandon
all their Tonto Basin settlements. The basin remains largely
uninhabited to this day.

Ref.: 38, p. 179; 88, II, 783; 89, p. 236; 112, pp. 173, 174.
Maps: GD-2; GD-9; GD-11; GD-12; E-20; C-5; E-18.

a.n. Tonto Creek   Maps: GD-2; GD-9; GD-12, GD-15      Gila
     This stream was named by King S. Woolsey on June 8,
     1864. From 1867 through 1878 many skirmishes with In-
     dians were fought along its banks.
Ref.: Barnes; 85, pp. 430, 434.

     Tonto Mountain                                    Gila
     Tonto Mountain                                    Yavapai
     Tonto National Forest              Gila and Maricopa
     This forest was created on October 3, 1905. In 1955 it had
     approximately 2,812,060 acres. Its purpose is to protect the
     watershed of Theodore Roosevelt Reservoir.
Ref.: Barnes; Woody.

     Tonto National Monument   El.: 2300'. Map: C-12      Gila
     The 1120 acres of the Tonto National Monument were set
     aside in December 1907 to preserve an abandoned pre-
     historic Indian village. There are two major ruins. The
     Upper Ruin lies two hundred and fifty feet above the lower
     and is nearly twice its size. However, visitors customarily
     see only the Lower Ruin nestled in a cave about forty feet

deep by eighty-five long. The ruin was occupied by the Salado people c. 1200 A.D. These people apparently arrived in the Roosevelt and Tonto Basins a hundred years or so earlier, then living in small pueblos near the river.

Ref.: Peavy, *Arizona's National Monuments*, pp. 3, 4, 5, 6.

**Tonto Natural Bridge** El.: 4660' Gila
The span at Natural Bridge (*q.v.*) is known by this name.

**Tonto Spring** Map: GD-12 Gila

**Packard's** El.: 2300'. Map: F-7 (Tonto Basin) Gila
A small settlement at Tonto Basin is sometimes referred to as Packard's, after an early rancher, Amanda Packard, who settled at Packard Spring and who later had a store on Tonto Creek where he advertised he had "grub-hay-grain" for sale. It is also referred to as Pumpkin Center and Punkin Center.

P.O. est. as Tontobasin, and Punkin Center May 8, 1929. Lillian L. Colcord, p.m. Name changed to Tonto Basin, May 2, 1930.

**a.n. Packard Wash** Map: B-7 Gila

Ref.: Woody; APHS Names File; 4, p. 454.

## TORNADO PEAK
El.: 4483' Loc.: Gila 1, HG-15.7
The peak takes its name from the Tornado Mining Company, which made a gold strike nearby in March 1927. The company apparently got its name because in its early existence a tornado swept through the area.

Ref.: Barnes. Map: GD-13.

## TRIPLETS
El.: 5376' Loc.: Gila 2, D-8.5
Descriptive.

**v.n. Three Peaks** (Map: C-2)
**Triplets Peaks** (Map: C-12)
**Mount Triplet** (Maps: C-13; C-14)

Ref.: Uplegger. Maps: C-1; E-20.

## WEBBER CREEK
El.: c. 5000' Loc.: Gila 1, CD-1-1.6
A man named Webber was the chief packer for an army outfit which mapped the Tonto Basin in 1879.

Ref.: Barnes. Maps: GD-11; E-20.

## WEBSTER MOUNTAIN
El.: 5776' Loc.: Gila 1, G-11
John R. Webster (b. Wisconsin, 1842) was listed in the Gila County Great Register of 1886 as living in Globe. The mountain is probably named for him.

Maps: GD-4; GD-5

**a.n. Webster Gulch** Maps: GD-4; GD-5; GD-7 Gila
**Webster Spring** Map: GD-5 Gila

## WET-BOTTOM CREEK
El.: c. 4000' Loc.: Gila 1, A-2.5-3
The bottom of this creek is now only occasionally moist.
Ref.: Gillette. Maps: B-7; GM-21.

**a.n. Wet-Bottom Mesa** Map: GM-19 Gila

## WHEATFIELDS
El.: c. 6000' Loc.: Gila 1, G-10
In August 1864, the King S. Woolsey expedition found an extensive Indian wheat field ready for harvesting. Woolsey reported that his men gathered as much wheat as they wished, threshing it and making it into piñole, thereafter letting their horses eat what was left. The Woolsey party named the place Wheat Field.

Hinton noted that there was much agricultural activity in this region, where irrigation was used. He also noted the presence of malaria, common in early Arizona. The various farms were later bought up by the Inspiration Consolidated Copper Company both for the water rights and for the protection of the company in case its tailings dams should ever break.

P.O. est. October 20, 1880. E. F. Kellner, p.m. Discont. March 17, 1881.
Ref.: Woody; 105, p. 141; 87, p. 264.
Maps: E-20; A-15; C-1 (Wheat Camp).

## WHITE RIVER
El.: c. 4000' Loc.: Gila 2, GE-3.
Navajo 3, IG-8-11.
The name probably originated from the fact that the stream came from the White Mountains.

**v.n. White Mountain Creek**
**White Mountain River**

Ref.: Barnes. Maps: C-2; E-18; E-20.

## WILLIAMS CAMP
Loc.: Not known.
The origin of this name has not yet been ascertained.
P.O. est. September 20, 1927. Mrs. Alice Mistler, p.m. Discont. June 1, 1928.
Ref.: P.O. Records. Map: None.

## WINDY HILL
El.: 2457' Loc.: Gila 1, F-8.5
This is a descriptive name. The winds are usually blowing around this high point which projects into Roosevelt Lake.
Ref.: Cooper; Woody. Map: GD-15.

## WINDSOR SPRING
El.: 6500' Loc.: Gila 1, B-4.1
Walter Windsor (d. March 14, 1947) arrived in this area in the late 1880's and established a ranch and mining claim.
Ref.: Goode. Maps: B-7; GD-9.

**a.n. Windsor Camp** Map: GD-9 Gila

## WINKELMAN
El.: 1947' Loc.: Gila 2, A-12
The history of Winkelman has to be traced back through that of two other small communities which formerly existed in its vicinity.

The first of these was Dudleyville, near the mouth of the San Pedro River. It was in this region that a large number of farmers settled following the survey of 1877 and 1878. Among these people was Dudley Harrington, who established his ranch in 1879. The trip to Florence for supplies and mail became increasingly onerous to the settlers and remained so even when mail was brought to Riverside within twenty miles of the settlers. This situation was remedied in 1881 when a post office was established for the agricultural settlement. The name for the post office was taken from the first name of Dudley Harrington, whose son was the first postmaster.

By 1890 the dangers of overgrazing by cattle on the hills which surrounded the valley became evident. With no grass roots to absorb and hold the rains which fell to the earth, floods washed down from the hills across the valley and into the San Pedro River, which broadened with every flood. Several times the store at Dudleyville was moved to prevent its being washed away by the river.

The coming of the railroad in 1903 resulted in the establishment of an entirely separate post office. The railroad line ran near the ranch owned by Peter Winkelman, a stockman. The third community was that known as Feldman, which was located on the Pusch Ranch of which Henry Feldman was manager. Although the post office records say that the name of Dudleyville was changed to Feldman, it is obvious that Feldman was another location.

P.O. est. as Dudleyville May 9, 1881. William D. Harrington, p.m.

P.O. est. as Winkelman March 8, 1905. Ernest A. Spann, p.m. Wells Fargo Station, 1906.

P.O. est. as Feldman November 22, 1911. Hugh H. Ballinger, p.m. Discont. May 15, 1928.

Ref.:   Barnes; APHS Files; 119, pp. 32, 44. Maps: C-11; GK-31; GK-32; GK-33. All three communities (Feldman, Dudleyville, and Winkelman) show on all maps, except that Feldman is not on GK-30.

**a.n. Ojio**                                                    Pinal
   This was a Sobaipuri rancheria which Fr. Kino visited in 1697. Next to Quiburi, it was at that time the largest settlement on the San Pedro River, containing about three hun-

dred and eighty people living in seventy houses. This place was called by the Spaniards La Victoria because the padre's party had made its way safely through a region where, it had been thought, the natives were cannibals with a fondness for white meat.
Ref.:   88, II, 112; 20, pp. 336, 367.

## WORKMAN CREEK

El.: c. 5400'                                  Loc.: Gila 1, EG-6-7
The name "Workman" is a corruption of the name of Herbert Wertman, who lived about four miles below Workman Creek near the falls in the 1880's. He was a packer for the army pack trains at Fort Apache in 1880. According to Barnes, Wertman was tall and thin, being over six feet tall and weighing about one hundred and forty pounds. He occasionally wore his long yellow hair tied with a blue ribbon. He claimed that he was born at Bald Knob, Michigan.
Ref.:   Barnes. Map: GD-6

**a.n. Workman Creek Falls**   Map: GD-6                        Gila
   These falls are about one hundred and eighty feet high.
Ref.:   Barnes.

## YOUNG

El.: 5070'                                       Loc.: Gila 1, G-3.5
With the coming of peace after the Pleasant Valley war, settlers returned to the valley and gradually the need arose for a post office. At first it was planned to call this place Pleasant Valley, but there was already a post office by that name southeast of Flagstaff. Therefore, the post office was named Young for the first postmistress, the daughter of Silas Young. It was she who homesteaded on the Graham place after he took his cattle out of the valley between 1887 and 1892. Silas Young in turn had another place in the valley.

P.O. est. June 25, 1890. Olla Young, p.m.
Ref.:   McKinney. Maps: B-7; C-7.

# GRAHAM

*Safford valley and Gila River — Solomon's pioneer store — cattle raising.*

## GRAHAM COUNTY:

On March 10, 1881, Graham County was created from parts of Apache and Pima counties. The supposition is that Graham County was so named from the prominent mountain peak of the same name. Isadore E. Solomon started the county seat in his sawmill, but the seat of county government was not destined to remain at his little community. The first county seat was at Safford (q.v.), but in 1883 it was moved to Solomonville. In 1915 when Greenlee County was permitted to pull away from Graham County, it is said that the move was allowed provided that Safford was voted to be the county seat. This, in fact, occurred. Graham County is largely an agricultural area, consisting of 2,950,400 acres.

## ALGODON

El.: c. 3500'  Loc.: Graham 2, C-11
Pro.: /ǽlgədówn/  Spanish: "cotton"
Algodon is a small settlement located on land originally
included in the Goodspeed Ranch. The ranch was bought
in 1900 by John A. Lee and William Franklin Lee. Soon
thereafter other Mormon families joined the Lees and a
small community began to grow. When or why its name
became Algodon is not known at present. Locally the
name Algodon has fallen into disuse and the area can no
longer be considered a community.

The name frequently applied to the vicinity is Lebanon or
Lebanon Hot Springs. However, according to one source,
Algodon was a separate community lying approximately a
mile from Lebanon. Today even the name Lebanon is fall-
ing into disuse, being replaced gradually by the name
Cactus Flat, which is descriptive.

The first artesian well water in the vicinity was not found,
as has sometimes been said, at Artesia (q.v.), but at Lebanon. The well was located in September 1897 by F. E.
Merrill and N. D. Beebe.

P.O. est. at Lebanon, July 18, 1907. George A. Tanner, p.m.
(deceased). Rescinded November 20, 1907. P.O. est. at Algodon, June 30, 1915. Effie Lee, p.m. Discont. December 30,
1921.

Ref.: 180, pp. 48-56; Jennings. Maps: C-12; GE-2.

## ARAVAIPA

El.: 4563'  Loc.: Graham 1, A-11.9
Pro.: /ærəváypə/
The first name for this post office was Dunlap, so named
for the first postmaster, on whose ranch the post office was
located. Burt Dunlap ran cattle, using this ranch as headquarters from 1882 to 1896. It was purchased by the Dowdle
family c. 1916 and is still in their hands. The name was
changed to Aravaipa because there was another Dunlap post
office.

P.O. est. as Dunlap, March 22, 1883. Burt Dunlap, p.m. Name
changed to Aravaipa, April 18, 1892. Discont. September 15,
1893.

Ref.: Jennings; Barnes. Maps: GE-5; C-6 (Dunlap); C-7.

## ARKILL

El.: c. 4000'  Loc.: Graham 2, CD-14.
Fourteen miles n. of Bowie on old r.r.
Seth T. Arkills was a pioneer locomotive engineer who
worked on the Arizona Eastern Railroad between Globe
and Bowie. The building of the road began in February
1894 and was completed in February 1899. Arkills ran
the work train during the construction period and later
brought the first train into Globe. Service was so irregular
that oldtimers called the line the tri-weekly or "try-weakly,"
and said that they would "go down one day and try to get
back the next."

Ref.: Mrs. Seth T. Arkills, APHS Files; Woody. Map: None.

## ARTESIA

El.: c. 3500'  Loc.: Graham 2, C-11.8
Pro.: /artíyžə/
Despite the fact that the name Artesia implies the sinking
of the first deep well in this location of Graham County,
such a well was actually first sunk at Lebanon (q.v.). However, Artesia is in the same area and the name probably
derives from the fact of the well.

P.O. est. September 29, 1904. William Randolph, p.m. Rescinded February 8, 1905. Re-est. January 31, 1912. Discont.
May 14, 1926.

Ref.: Jennings; P.O. Records. Maps: GE-2; C-12.

## ASHURST

El.: 2739'  Loc.: Graham 2, A-8.5
Redlands, the first name for this location, was derived from
the color of the soil. However, when a farm community
developed at this spot, the residents decided to name it for
Henry Fountain Ashurst, U. S. Senator from Arizona.

P.O. est. January 8, 1919. Gilbert S. Richardson, p.m. Discont.
August 31, 1955.

Ref.: 4, p. 343; Jennings. Maps: GE-2; C-12.

## BASSETT PEAK

El.: c. 6000'  Loc.: Graham 2, B-11
Bob Bassett ran cattle in this vicinity.

Ref.: Barnes. Maps: GE-2; C-11.

## BIG CREEK

El.: c. 7000'  Loc.: Graham 2, BC-13.12
Descriptive.
Ref.: None. Map: CE-3.

## BISCUIT PEAK

El.: 6539'  Loc.: Graham 1, A-8.5
Descriptive.
Ref.: Jennings. Map: GE-1.

## BLUEJAY PEAK

El.: 8889'  Loc.: Graham 1, D-9.3
This peak is noted for numerous bluejays.
Ref.: Jennings. Map: GE-6.

## BONITA

El.: 4531'  Loc.: Graham 2, A-13.1
Pro.: /boníˆtə/  Spanish: "pretty"
When Fort Grant was in its heyday Bonita was a town just
outside the military reservation where the soldiers poured
in every payday and made the place really roar. There were
then about one thousand people living at Bonita — Mexicans
and families of Negro soldiers stationed at the post, cowpunchers and merchants. The residents were said to own
"hog ranches," meaning that they kept places which had
hogsheads of whiskey. Bonita was not frequented by officers
and their wives, who made Hooker's Bonita Ranch their
place of call.

Payday for the soldiers occurred three times a year. Approximately one thousand soldiers descended on the town.

Added to this were the girls who flocked in from Willcox. The eight or ten saloons did a rush business, as did the girls.

Today Bonita is a quiet and sleepy spot.

P.O. est. February 25, 1884. Edward Hooker, p.m. Discont. September 30, 1955.

Ref.: Jennings; "Bonita, The One-Time Rip Roaring Camp" *Arizona Daily Star* n.d., n.p. in APHS Files. Maps: GE-6; C-6.

## BONITA CREEK

El.: c. 3500'                    Loc.: Graham 2, EB-9-5
Pro.: /boníyt/
When this creek is running, it helps supply water for Safford. The Indians who broke out from the San Carlos Indian Reservation in April 1882 were pursued by troops who overtook them on Ash Creek Flat, but the Indians defeated the soldiers and continued their march to the Bonito (Greenlee County).

v.n. Gila Bonita        (Maps: C-12; E-20)
   Rio Bonito         (C-1; E-11)

Ref.: Jennings. Maps: GE-2; C-1; E-11 (Rio Bonito or Shaleys Fork); E-20.

## BRYCE

El.: 3500'                    Loc.: Graham 2, B-9.1
In January 1883, Ebenezer Bryce and his sons began constructing a ditch on land where they had established squatters' rights. The same family still has the land.

P.O. est. August 5, 1891. Nephi Packer, p.m. Discont. February 28, 1922.

Ref.: 112, p. 249; 180, p. 60; Jennings. Maps: GE-2; C-8.

a.n. Bryce Peak
   Loc.: Sec. 3, T. 5 S., R. 25 E.                    Graham

## BUFORD HILL

El.: c. 6000'                    Loc.: Graham 1, A-7.1
Clay Buford served as an Indian Agent at San Carlos. He retired to live on his ranch in Aravaipa Canyon. The ranch was called Spring Gardens (See Beauford Mountain, Maricopa.)

Ref.: Barnes. Map: GE-2.

a.n. Buford Canyon        Map: GE-5        Graham

## BYLAS

El.: c. 3500'                    Loc.: Graham 1, C-3.8
Pro.: /báyləs/        Apache: "one who does all the talking"
Bylas is a strange mixture of typical Indian wickiups and small houses which comprise a trading point for Indians on the San Carlos Indian Reservation. It was named for an Indian chief.

P.O. est. September 13, 1917. Theodore E. Reed, p.m.

Ref.: Jennings; 102, p. 19. Maps: GE-2; C-10 (Bilas); C-12.

## CALVA

El.: c. 3500'                    Loc.: Graham 1, BC-3.2
Pro.: /kælvə/
This station on the Arizona Eastern Railroad was established in the 1890's under the name of Dewey, probably

for Admiral Dewey who was in the news at that time. When this station was washed out by a big flood, it was rebuilt and renamed. The second name was Calva. It was named for a local sub-chief who lived at this point and had a farm on the river.

It was anticipated that waters impounded by Coolidge dam would cover Calva. Therefore it was abandoned as a settlement. However, as yet the waters have never reached Calva. It is today only a shipping pen for cattle.

P.O. est. October 13, 1938. Charles Brown Hall, p.m. Discont. June 30, 1941.

Ref.: Jennings; Barnes. Maps: GE-2; C-10; C-14.

## CEDAR SPRINGS

El.: c. 5500'                    Loc.: Graham 1, AB-10.7
Cedar Springs and the area surrounding it figure prominently in two events in the 1880's. The first involved an attack nearby in the fall of 1881 by Apaches on a wagoners' spring. The Apaches under Nachez and Juh had left the San Carlos Reservation about two hundred strong on September 30. During their raids, they attacked a wagon train, killing Bartoles Samaniego and six of his teamsters. The name henceforth given to the place was The Battleground. While on their way elsewhere from this massacre, the Apaches met and killed a telegraph repair crew of five men. The second event occurred in 1889 when Maj. Joseph W. Wham, the paymaster, was waylaid not far from the springs by bandits rolling rocks onto the road, thus compelling the paymaster's party to stop at the barrier. This happened on May 11, 1889, with the robbers escaping with about $22,000. They were later caught and jailed.

Military parties frequently stopped at Cedar Springs to rest. The post office was at the springs; it was the headquarters ranch of Norton and Stewart Cattle Company.

P.O. est. September 20, 1887. Bernard E. Norton, p.m. Discont. April 8, 1892.

Ref.: 55, pp. 691-692; P.O. Records; 85, pp. 447, 448. Map: GE-1.

## CENTRAL

El.: 2900'                    Loc.: Graham 2, BC-10
In the fall of 1882, six families from Forestdale (*q.v.*, Navajo) settled on land adjacent to that irrigated by the Central Canal. They extended the canal about a mile west to their community. The families included those of Joseph Cluff, George Clemens, John Young, John Whitbeck, and A. Lambson. In February 1883, this community with several others was organized into the St. Joseph's Stake of the Church of Jesus Christ of Latter-day Saints.

P.O. est. January 11, 1886. William Asay, p.m.

Ref.: 55, p. 592; Barnes; 7, p. 533. Map: C-6.

## CLARK PEAK

El.: 9006'                    Loc.: Graham 2, A-11.8
This place was named for the Clark Mining District.

Ref.: Barnes. Map: GE-3.

## COBRE GRANDE MOUNTAINS

El.: 7150′        Loc.: Graham 1, B-5.7
Pro.: /kówbreygrándiy/ or      Spanish: "big copper"
      /kówbrey grándey/
The reason for this name has not yet been ascertained.

Ref.: None. Map: GE-5.

## COLUMBINE

El.: c. 9000′       Loc.: Graham 2, A-11.8
The presence of columbine flowers on the meadows gave
the name to this forest ranger station.

Ref.: Jennings. Map: GE-3.

## CORK

El.: c. 2500′       Loc.: Graham 2, AB-9
The contractor who built this branch of the Arizona Eastern
Railroad was named William Garland. Having been born
in Cork, Ireland, this son of the old sod took pleasure in
giving Irish names to Arizona places. Cork was one. Another was Limerick, which is in the vicinity of Emery (q.v.),
but where there was apparently never a railroad station.
According to Barnes he named another, Dublin.
The only one of the three which seems to have had any
pretense to being a settlement was Cork.
P.O. est. November 22, 1916. Mary Stapley, p.m. Discont. November 30, 1918.

Ref.: Jennings; Barnes. Maps: C-12; F-2.

## CRYSTAL PEAK

El.: c. 6000′       Loc.: Graham 1, B-4.9
Silicon dioxide crystals in the rocks gave the name to this
mountain.

Ref.: Barnes. Map: C-12.

## DEADMAN'S CANYON

El.: c. 3500′       Loc.: Graham 2, AC-11-12
Lt. John G. Bourke described the death of one of the army
packers, Presilino Monje, who caught cold when crossing
the Mazatzal Mountains. The cold developed into pneumonia. The party attempted to get the packer back to camp
by carrying him in a chair made of mescal stalks attached
to his saddle, because he was too weak to sit up. On March
23, 1873, a little after midnight Monje took a turn for the
worse. He died before dawn and was buried in a pretty
spot in this canyon which the military party named Deadman's Canyon.

v.n. Graveyard Canyon     (GE-2)
Ref.: 22, pp. 211, 212. Map: GE-3.

a.n. Deadman's Peak      El.: 6338′. Map: GE-3    Graham
     Deadman Ridge       Map: GE-3           Graham

## EDEN

El.: c. 2500′       Loc.: Graham 2, A-8.7
Early in 1881, Mormons who had been unable to establish
a permanent settlement in Apache County, arrived at what
is today Eden. They had come from Brigham City (q.v.,
Navajo). The group included William R. Hawkins, Lehi
Curtis, Moses Curtis, and Moses M. Curtis. Of the group
only Lehi Curtis had no family.

As was customary, the group built a large stockade of
cottonwood poles. By the fall of 1882, eight families were
living at Curtis. This was one of the places which was
organized into the St. Joseph's Stake (See Central) in
May 1883. At that time Curtis was renamed Eden, the
present townsite of which was located on May 10, 1883.
It has been suggested that the name Eden was selected
because of the agricultural possibilities.
P.O. est. May 23, 1892. William T. Oliver, p.m.

Ref.: 180, pp. 15, 34; 55, p. 591; 102, p. 34; 112, p. 248. Maps:
     GE-2; C-8.

## EMERY

El.: c. 2500′       Loc.: Graham 1, CD-3.5
The little community of Emery was established by the
Holyoke family at least as early as 1888. The name dropped
out of use, probably because the community is so close to
Fort Thomas that it could well be taken for a part of it.

Ref.: Mrs. Virgie Holyoke. Map: None.

## ENTERPRISE

El.: c. 4000′       Loc.: Graham 2, E-10
Enterprise is a Mormon settlement near San Jose about
eight miles east of Safford. The origin of the name has
not yet been ascertained.

Ref.: Barnes; Jennings. Map: None.

## EPLEY'S RUINS

El.: c. 2500′       Loc.: Graham 2, D-10.3
These large prehistoric ruins of the pueblo type on the Gila
River were so named after the owner of the ranch on which
they were located. They are on the outskirts of Solomonville.

Ref.: 88, I, 430. Map: None.

## ESCALA

El.: c. 3500′       Loc.: Graham 2, CD-14.6
Pro.: /eskálə/           Spanish: "ladder"
This point on the railroad was located at the summit of a
hill which the track climbed zig-zag fashion like a ladder.

Ref.: Barnes. Map: C-10.

## EUREKA SPRINGS

El.: c. 4000′       Loc.: Graham 1, BC-9.2
Pro.: /yúwrikə/
Hinton notes Eureka Springs as a stopping point on the
route from Tucson to Camp Goodwin. It was the head-
quarters for the Leitch cattle ranch, known as the Eureka
Cattle Company.

Ref.: Barnes; Jennings; 87, p. xxxi. Maps: A-7; C-5; C-12.

a.n. Eureka Mountain      Map: C-12        Graham

## FOUR MILE PEAK

El.: c. 5000′       Loc.: Graham 1, A-8.4
This mountain lies four miles southeast of Biscuit Peak,
from whence the name is probably derived.

Ref.: Barnes. Map: GE-1.

a.n. Fourmile Creek      Maps: GE-1; GE-5      Graham

## FREEZEOUT CREEK

El.: c. 6000'     Loc.: Graham 2, DC-2
During roundups, supplies for cowboys were packed on mules, a single pack train frequently containing over one hundred mules. One day while cowboys of the Double Circle Ranch were herding cattle on the San Carlos Indian Reservation, the mules stampeded, scattering packs in all directions. The cowboys waited in vain that night for supper and bedding. About dark the weather became bad, with rain and snow and increasing cold. During the night three cowboys quit and rode out of camp. The others stuck it out, but thereafter whenever the men made camp at the same creek, they referred to it as "Freezeout."
Ref.:   C. A. Smith, Jr. (interviewed by Woody). Map: D-9.

**a.n. Freezeout Mountain**     Map: D-9     Graham

## FRYE

El.: c. 4000'     Loc.: Graham 2, AC-13
Albert A. Frye owned a lumber yard six miles from Safford. He obtained lumber from a mill in the canyon which bears his name. A dam in the canyon helps provide water for Thatcher and Safford.
Ref.:   Jennings. Map: GE-3.

**a.n. Frye Creek**     Map: GE-3     Graham
The creek has its course in Frye Canyon.

## GALIURO MOUNTAINS

El.: c. 5000'     Loc. Graham 1, AD-8-11
Cochise 1, CE-1-4; Pinal 2, H-8-12
Pro.:  /gəléro/
In 1854 Lt. John Parke reported that this mountain chain was called the Calitro and that he had obtained this information from the oldest inhabitants of Tucson. He added that he thought it might be a corruption of *Calizo* ("lime"), as there was an abundance of lime in the mountains so named. By the time Capt. George M. Wheeler came into the area the name had become corrupted slightly and was spelled by him Caliuro. On maps the name can be traced through its various corruptions as follows: from Salitre ("nitrate") to Calitre to Calitro (Parke); then to Caliuro and its contemporary spelling, Galiuro. There is evidence that the range was already being called Galiuro in 1871, since there is a record of an Indian skirmish in the Sierra Galiuro Mountains on February 13, 1871.
Ref.:   121, p. 23; 175, III, 591; 2, p. 141; 169, p. 173, (Note 32); 16, p. 436. Maps: GE-5; C-2; E-20; GJ-17.

## GERONIMO

El.: 3700'     Loc.: Graham 1, D-4.3
Pro.:  /jeránimo/ or /heránimo/
This community on the railroad was named for Geronimo, the Apache who led a band of Chiricahuas off the San Carlos Reservation in a series of devastating raids in the early 1880's. In the summer of 1885, Geronimo and Nachez left the White Mountain Reservation with a band of one hundred and twenty Apaches. After many months of marauding, Geronimo was cornered in January 1886 in Mexico. Capt. Crawford, in charge of the military expedi-

tion, was killed and his second in command bumbled in setting up a meeting between Gen. George Crook (then in Arizona for his second tour of duty) and the Indian chief. This caused Crook's replacement on April 11, 1886, by Gen. Nelson A. Miles.

Miles went into immediate action, setting up heliograph signal points so that he could be kept constantly aware of the movements of the Indians. In August Lt. Charles Gatewood was successful in arranging a truce with Geronimo, who submitted to capture and was sent with other Apaches to Florida.

Geronimo's Apache name was Gokliya. He was dubbed Geronimo by Mexican *Rurales* (soldiers). The Apaches, ever quick, noticed that the Mexicans referred to the Indian leader fearfully as "Geronimo" and this led to the Indians' screaming the word during an attack on Mexicans. This was at the battle of Kiskaya. Thus "Geronimo" became a kind of battle cry. After this battle it is said that the Apaches themselves dropped the Apache name for their chief and thereafter called him Geronimo.

The community of Geronimo is close to the ruins of original Camp Thomas *(q.v.)*. The place is today a center of agricultural activities.
P.O. est. April 30, 1896. George Rayfield, p.m. Discont. May 31, 1956.
Ref.:   157, pp. 130, 133-134; 28, p. 29. Maps: GE-2; C-9.

## GILLESPIE

El.: c. 4000'     Loc.: Graham 2, C-13
Gillespie is the site of the old Gillespie ranch on the east side of Stockton Pass *(q.v.)*. The old house and corrals are still in existence. As the place lay halfway between Safford and Fort Grant it was used as a way station by people on that route. Horses were watered here at ten cents per head.

Contrary to some stories, there is no evidence that Curly Bill of Tombstone had any connection with this ranch. He confined his activities as a bandit to Cochise County.
Ref.:   Jennings. Map: None.

**a.n. Gillespie Wash**     Map: GE-7     Graham

## GLENBAR

El.: c. 2500'     Loc.: Graham 2, AB-9.2
The first name of this location was Matthewsville. It was derived from the fact that early in 1880 Joseph and David Matthews left Round Valley (cf. Eagar, Apache) and made their way to this spot where they bought land from Mrs. Patterson. In the following year Solomon T. and Charles Matthews joined their brothers. David was the first to build a log cabin.

Despite the fact that in 1883 a flour mill was erected near this spot, the place had a very slow growth. The Matthews Ward of the Church of Jesus Christ of Latter-day Saints was created in 1888. As time passed the residents of Matthews scattered and the post office closed. Nevertheless, a few years later, the remaining residents apparently petitioned to re-open the post office. Because of the post office rule that the same name could not be used again, it was re-opened under the descriptive name of Fairview. Apparently this name had been in use for some time, since a Wells Fargo Station was established under the name Fairview in 1887. The fact that there was another post office by the name of Fairview led to choosing the final name of Glenbar. The name Glenbar was selected because a number of residents were Scots and preferred that name. It was sometimes called Hogtown by others.

P.O. est. as Matthews February 9, 1897. Hulda Blair, p.m. Discont. May 1, 1906. P.O. re-est. as Fairview, January 13, 1909. Ephraim Larson, p.m. P.O. changed to Glenbar, November 8, 1917. Discont. May 31, 1956.

Ref.: Barnes; Jennings; 55, p. 247; 112, p. 247; 180, pp. 13, 48. Maps: C-8 (Matthewsville); C-9 (Matthews); C-10 (Fairview); C-12 (Glenbar).

## GOODWIN, CAMP

El.: c. 2500'          Loc.: Graham 1, D-4.3
On June 21, 1864, a military post was established to provide protection for Americans at the end of the Gila Valley. King S. Woolsey said it was on a stream called the Tulerosa. The camp was named after Arizona's first territorial governor, John N. Goodwin. The site selected was at a spring in Goudy Canyon. From the beginning, Camp or Fort Goodwin was ill-fated. Unscrupulous contractors put up a few poorly built adobe houses at a cost estimated at $150,000. One of these contractors was Henry C. Hooker, who later established the Sierra Bonita Ranch (q.v.). Camp Goodwin was extremely unhealthy. Malaria-carrying mosquitoes swarmed and the soldiers sickened. This necessitated the abandonment of the post. The commanding officer, Maj. John Greene, in 1870 established Fort Apache (q.v. Navajo) as a temporary camp until something could be done about a new location for a post in the valley. Old Camp Goodwin was vacated permanently on March 14, 1871. A new post was established.

The post office at the new post in the valley was called Camp Goodwin (cf. Thomas, Fort, Graham). In 1881 the original Camp Goodwin was serving as a sub-agency of the San Carlos Apache Reservation with about three hundred and seventy-five Apaches under Juh, Geronimo, Nana and Loco. Geronimo and Juh caused an uprising in which the chief of police of the agency was killed and an attempt was made upon the sub-agent's life.

Ref.: *Arizona Miner*, September 21, 1864, 1:1; Jennings; 55, p. 405; 75, p. 135; 111, p. 185; 39, p. 31. Maps: C-1; E-22.

a.n. Goodwin Wash     Map: C-12 (Goodwin Canyon)    Graham
    Goudy Creek                                     Graham
    Loc.: East side of Merrill Creek in Graham Mountains.
Pro.: /gódiy/
Grant Goudy lived here for several years.
Ref.: Barnes; Jennings.
    Goudy Canyon          Map: GE-3             Graham
    This is the canyon through which Goudy Creek runs.
    Grant Goudy Trail     Map: GE-3             Graham

## GRAHAM

El.: c. 2500'          Loc.: Graham 2, BC-9.9
The now-vanished community of Graham was begun in November 1880 by Jorgen Jorgenson, George W. Skinner, Andrew Anderson, and James Wilson. These men are reported to have bought four quarter sections of land said to have been occupied by horse thieves and speculators who had a small house. It was known as the Rustler's Ranch and in 1879 was owned by the notorious Powers brothers and a man named Snyder (see Kielberg Peak). It was four miles east of the present-day Pima.

In January 1881 the settlers arrived and the little community began to take shape. It was one of those included in the organization of the Saint Joseph Stake of the Mormons in February 1883. The townsite was surveyed in 1884 and a meeting house constructed of mesquite poles with a dirt roof and walls of heavy unbleached muslin.

P.O. est. March 17, 1882. Thomas Weirs, p.m. Discont. September 24, 1885.

Ref.: 112, pp. 246, 247; 100, p. 14; 55, p. 592; 7, p. 533; 180, p. 9, (Note 13). Map: None.

## GRAHAM, MOUNT

El.: 10,713'          Loc.: Graham 2, AB-12
Despite the fact that Mount Graham bears one of the oldest place names in Arizona, the origin of the name remains shrouded in doubt. Lt. William H. Emory referred to it by its present name on October 28, 1846, thus lending strong support to the possibility of its having been named for William A. Graham, Secretary of the Interior and later (1848-1851) Secretary of War ad interim. Another possibility is that it was named for Major Lawrence Pike Graham, 2nd Dragoons, who in 1848 journeyed from Santa Cruz to San Diego. Still a third — but least likely because of the dates involved — is the name of Col. James Duncan Graham, a member of the Boundary Survey party in 1851. Col. Graham is less likely a prospect from another point of view: the dissension which existed between him and Commissioner Bartlett over survey matters.

Lt. John G. Bourke noted that in the early 1870's the Mexicans called the mountains Sierra Bonita.

Ref.: 67, pp. 6, 20, 44, 72, 76; 7, pp. 626-27, (Note 12); 50, p. 67; 20, p. 207. Maps: E-1; E-26.

## GRAND REEF MOUNTAIN

El.: c. 4000'          Loc.: Graham 1, A-6
The Granite Reef Mine is on this mountain. The name came from the fact that the ground at the mine is solid granite. The mine was abandoned c. 1918. It had produced silver and lead. The name "Grand Reef" is a corruption.

Ref.: Barnes; Jennings. Map: C-12.

## GRAND VIEW PEAK

El.: c. 6000'          Loc.: Graham 2, A-11.2
Descriptive.
Ref.: Barnes. Map: C-13.

## GRANT, FORT

El.: c. 5000'                    Loc.: Graham 2, A-10.8

The unhealthy location of Old Camp Grant (q.v., Pinal County) and the tarring of its reputation because of the massacre there, were among factors which led the military to seek a new location. Therefore in October 1872, Col. William B. Royall and a detachment of thirty men scouted in the vicinity of Mount Graham for a new location for the two hundred and seventy-five men stationed at Old Camp Grant. A place for the new post was found on a plain about fifteen miles wide and many miles long, on a mesa with an abundance of wood, grass, and good water. The date of the official shifting from Old Camp Grant to new Camp Grant is indefinite. Officially three dates are listed. They are December 19, 1872, January 1873, and March 31, 1873. Among troops shifted to the new spot were those from Camp Crittenden (q.v., Santa Cruz).

Life at the new location was much healthier than that at the old. The town of Bonita (q.v.) offered rough and tough recreation for the soldiers. The ranch of Col. Henry C. Hooker offered more genteel recreation for the officers and their ladies.

On April 5, 1879, Camp Grant became Fort Grant, but it was already waning in importance as Fort Huachuca (q.v., Cochise) began to emerge as the key post in southern Arizona. The last commander at Fort Grant was Capt. John M. Jenkins, with one trooper of the Fifth Cavalry. Fort Grant was abandoned on October 4, 1905, and the post office closed two days later. All that remained was one lone caretaker. In May 1908, Col. William F. Stewart and his cook joined the caretaker. Stewart, an army veteran of forty years, had refused to retire and so was sent to his new post duties at Fort Grant.

In 1912 the state of Arizona took steps necessary to take over Fort Grant and to move the Industrial School to that place.

P.O. est. August 19, 1869. George Cox, p.m. (Old Camp Grant, Pinal County). Name changed to Fort Grant, June 23, 1879. Discont. October 6, 1905.
Ref.: 87, p. 311; 157, pp. 101, 123, 152, 155-156; 111, p. 151. Maps: C-1; C-2; E-22; GE-3.

| a.n. Grant Creek | Map: GE-3 | Graham |
| Grant Hill | El.: 9250'. Map: GE-3 | Graham |

## GREASEWOOD MOUNTAIN

El.: 7092'                    Loc.: Graham 2, BC-14.2

There is a dense stand of creosote bush, locally called greasewood, on this mountain.

Ref.: Barnes. Map: GB-23.

## GRIPE

El.: 3211'                    Loc.: Graham 2, DE-10.6

The men stationed at this Arizona State Agricultural Inspection Point gave the name to their small building as being significant of what they did a large part of the time.

Ref.: 4, p. 341. Map: None.

## HAECKEL

El.: c. 4000'                    Loc.: Graham 2, DE-11.5

The Irishman who owned the railroad from Bowie to Globe was named Haeckel. This place was named for him.

Ref.: Jennings. Maps: GE-7; C-10.

## HELIOGRAPH PEAK

El.: 10,028'                    Loc.: Graham 2, B-12.8
Pro.: /híyləgræf/

When Gen. Nelson A. Miles established his heliograph system to keep check on the movements of the Indians (cf. Geronimo), Station No. 3 of his system was established on the top of this peak. The soldiers used a mirror and sunlight in order to flash signals.

Ref.: Jennings; Barnes. Map: GE-3.

## HUBBARD

EL.: c. 2500'                    Loc.: Graham 2, BC-10

Elisha F. Hubbard, Sr., was the Mormon first ward bishop of this community. A settlement developed from the older Graham and Bryce Wards, which puts Hubbard at a rather late date, probably in the late 1890's. The current name for this locality is Kimball. It is so called for a dam built by the Mormons below Graham. The dam burned.

P.O. est. as Hubbard, June 13, 1902. John Hancock, p.m. Discont. March 31, 1912.
Ref.: 112, p. 249; Jennings. Maps: C-9; F-2.

## INDIAN HOT SPRINGS

El.: c. 2500'                    Loc.: Graham 2, A-8.2

The name for this location is derived from the fact that the Indians used the waters medicinally. There are four large springs and several smaller ones. It was here that an attempt was made by the Alexander brothers to start a health resort in 1899. They purchased what was known as the Holladay Hot Springs and constructed a hotel and other buildings. They also changed the name to Indian Hot Springs. Today the springs are owned by a doctor and two others (names not known).

The names of the four springs are Beauty Springs, Iron Springs, Mud Springs, and Magnesium Springs, which has a temperature of 81°; the others have temperatures from 116° to 119°.

Ref.: Jennings; *Arizona Bulletin*, May 26, 1899, 3:3; 4, p. 343. Map: C-12 (Hot Spring).

## JACKSON MOUNTAINS

El.: c. 5000'                    Loc.: Graham 1, C-6

Bill Jackson ranched cattle near the base of this mountain c. 1900. He had been wagon boss and ranch foreman for the Arizona Land and Cattle Company at Holbrook from 1890 to 1895.

Ref.: Barnes. Map: C-12.
a.n. Jackson Butte            (cf. Gila County)

## KIELBERG PEAK

El.: 6680'                          Loc.: Graham 1, A-11.2
Pro.: /kíylberg/
From 1875 to 1920 a Danish prospector named Kielberg lived in the vicinity of the peak bearing his name. Kielberg Peak was the site of the murder of the sheriff by the Powers brothers, who were themselves slain at their cabin in Rattlesnake Canyon on February 11, 1918.

Ref.:    Jennings; G.E.P. Smith, "List of Place Names Submitted for Decision," June 21, 1931, Place Names Committee, APHS. Maps: GE-1; C-12.

| a.n. Kielberg Canyon | Map: GE-1 | Graham |
| Kielberg Creek | Loc.: T. 10 S., R. 18 E. | Graham |

## KLONDIKE

El.: 3647'                          Loc.: Graham 1, A-7.4
A number of men returning from Alaska settled at this point and named it to commemorate their experiences in the Klondike.

P.O. est. July 22, 1907. John F. Greenwood, p.m. Discont. August 31, 1955.

Ref.:    Barnes. Maps: GE-5; C-10.

| a.n. Klondike Wash | Map: GE-5 | Graham |

## LADYBUG PEAK

El.: 8773'                          Loc.: Graham 2, B-12.6
There are so many ladybugs in the Lady Bug Saddle on this mountain that the local farmers go to this place to scoop buckets of ladybugs to use in their gardens.

Ref.:    Jennings; Barnes. Maps: GE-2; GE-3.

## LAYTON

El.: c. 2500'                       Loc.: Graham 2, C-10.2
The first settler at Layton was Hyrum H. Tippets, who came to this location on January 13, 1883, from Brigham City, Utah. Other settlers in 1884 were John Walker, Adam Welker, Benjamin Peel, and Charles Warner. The new residents in the valley named their community for Christopher Layton (b. England, March 8, 1821; d. August 7, 1898). The community of Layton is now consolidated with Safford. Formerly it was considered as a separate unit to the south of the railroad tracks.

Ref.:    112, pp. 249-250; 55, p. 592; 7, p. 533; Jennings. Map: None.

## LOMPOC

El.: c. 4000'                       Loc.: Graham 2, A-14.5
The now-vanished community at Lompoc was settled by people from Lompoc, California.

P.O. est. June 27, 1913. Sheldon S. Hardenbrook, p.m. Discont. June 15, 1915.

Ref.:    Barnes. Maps: C-12; F-2.

## LONE STAR

El.: c. 2500'                       Loc.: Graham 2, CD-10.7
The Lone Star Mine uses this siding on the railroad to ship its ores. The mine lies nine miles north of the siding.

Ref.:    Jennings. Map: None.

a.n. Lone Star Mountain   El.: c. 4000'. Maps: GE-2; C-12 Graham
The Lone Star Mine near this mountain was inactive for several years. However, it was reorganized in 1950 and is now in operation. The mine lies one and a half miles east of the mountain.

Ref.:    Jennings.

## MARIJILDA CANYON

El.: c. 5000'                       Loc.: Graham 2, BD-12-11
Pro.: /mǽrəhɑ́ldə/
This canyon is named for Marijilda Grijalva, a scout for Gen. George Crook. Grijalva had a ranch in the Gila Valley for many years.

Ref.:    Barnes. Map: GE-3.

| a.n. Marijilda Creek | Map: GE-7 | Graham |

## MARTINSVILLE

El.: c. 4000'                       Loc.: Graham 2, A-13.75
William Garfield Martin used the brand WGM on the horses which he ran in this area. After he established his ranch, a number of other discharged Negro soldiers and their families settled nearby. Many of their descendants still live in the vicinity.

Ref.:    Jennings. Map: E-22 (Martin).

## MAXEY

El.: c. 2500'                       Loc.: Graham 2, A-8
Maxey came into being because of the relocation of Camp Goodwin at Fort Thomas, of which Maxey was the civilian adjunct. Maxey was named by J. B. Collins, who served under Maj. Gen. Samuel B. Maxey in the Confederate army. With Globe and Solomonville, Maxey earned a reputation as a spot where government supplies could be bought from the Indian traders. In 1880 Maxey was thoroughly disreputable. It consisted for the most part of saloons and houses of prostitution.

P.O. est. as Camp Thomas, March 2, 1877. Frank Staples, p.m. Name changed to Fort Thomas, February 28, 1883. Name changed to Maxey, June 21, 1886. William Hibberd, p.m. Name changed to Fort Thomas, February 8, 1887.

Ref.:    Barnes; Jennings; 22, p. 441; P.O. Records. Map: C-6.

## MERRILL PEAK

El.: 9285'                          Loc.: Graham 2, A-11.8
According to one source, this peak was named for the P. C. Merrill family (cf. St. David, Cochise). Another source says that it was named for forest ranger Gerald Merrill, who erected the first lookout tower on its top.

Ref.:    U. S. G. B. Decision No. 5003, pp. 1-2; Barnes. Map: GE-3.

| a.n. Merrill Creek | Loc.: On Merrill Peak | Graham |

## MINGVILLE

El.: c. 4000'                       Loc.: Graham 2, A-6.75.
                                    Sec. 28, T. 6. S., R. 19E.
Mingville was named for Dan H. Ming, a cattleman. The post office was on his ranch. Ming (b. 1841; d. November 1925) was called "Big Dan." He was six feet four inches tall. During a severe drought in 1885 the cattlemen held a

meeting. One suggested that, like the Hopi Indians, the gathering should pray for rain. Dan was called upon. First he made the men remove their hats. Then he proceeded, "Oh Lord, I'm about to round you up for a good plain talking. Now, Lord, I ain't like these fellows who come bothering you every day. This is the first time I ever tackled you for anything, and if you will only grant this, I promise never to bother you again. We want rain, Good Lord, and we want it bad; we ask you to send us some. But if you can't or don't want to send us some, then for Christ's sake don't make it rain up around Hooker's or Leitch's ranges, but treat us all alike. Amen."

P.O. est. January 26, 1881. Thomas I. Hunter, p.m. Discont. December 16, 1881.

Ref.: Daniel H. Ming File, APHS. Map: None.

## MORRISTOWN

El.: c. 4000'          Loc.: Graham 1, CD-7-8

T. D. Morris laid out a mining town, but it never developed. The location was on the stage road in the Clark Mining District.

Ref.: *Weekly Arizona Enterprise,* May 23, 1891, 2:8. Map: None.

## NACHES

El.: c. 2500'          Loc.: Graham 1, A-3.2
Pro.: /næčez/

Naches was the son of Cochise and therefore chief of the Chiricahua Apaches after Cochise's death. Cheis (called Cochise by white men) was the son of Naches.

Ref.: Barnes; 88, I, 317. Map: C-10.

## PELONCILLO MOUNTAINS

El.: c. 6000'          Loc.: Graham 2, FH-9-14;
                       Greenlee AC-10-15; Cochise 2, EF-1-2
Pro.: /pelənsíyo/          Spanish: "sugar loaf"

The Peloncillo Range shows on the boundary survey map for the Gadsden Purchase of 1854. On the Parke Map of 1851 it is referred to as the Black Mountains. On August 10, 1851, at the northern end of the Black Mountains, the surveying party had pointed out to them a mountain which their guide referred to as El Peloncillo, to which a party was dispatched for further investigation. Gradually the name of the single peak was extended to apply to the entire range.

Ref.: 9, I, 363, 364, 367. Maps: A-7; C-11.

## PIMA

El.: 2848'          Loc.: Graham 2, B-9.2
Pro.: /píymə/

The first name of the present community of Pima was Smithville. In February 1879, a group of Mormons, including W. R. Teeples, John William Tanner, Lem Pierce, and Hyrum Weech, searched for a place in the Gila Valley to settle where it would be feasible to construct a canal. They located such a place at the site of Smithville, so called in honor of Pres. Jesse N. Smith, a Mormon leader. Here on March 16, 1879, a settlement was begun by Joseph K. Rogers and his party. Apparently more settlers arrived on April 8, 1879, when the village was laid out in sixteen blocks of four lots each. The usual troubles encountered in the valley — malaria and lawless men — beset the settlers. Nevertheless, they stuck it out. The name of the community was changed to Pima when the post office was established.

P.O. est. August 23, 1880. William R. Teeples, p.m. Wells Fargo Station, 1903.

Ref.: 112, p. 245; 55, p. 590; 7, p. 593; 180, p. 11. Maps: GE-2; C-5.

## PINALENO MOUNTAINS

El.: c. 8000'          Loc.: Graham 1, CD-8-11;
                       Graham 2, AB-10.2-14
Pro.: /pínəléyno/          Apache: *pinal,* "deer"

This is the range of mountains which has Mount Graham as its highest point. Lt. William H. Emory in 1846 talked to Indians who said that they belonged to the tribe of the "piñon lanos." He applied the name to the mountains where they lived. The Whipple report refers to these same mountains as the Pinal Leno. In 1856 Gray interpreted the name as meaning "the Pine Plain Mountains." It is now known that the word *pinal* means "deer," so that the interpretation should be "deer mountains" or "deer people."

Ref.: G.E.P. Smith; U. S. G. B. Decision No. 5003, p. 2; 50, pp. 71, 73; 177, p. 196; 101, p. 46. Maps: GB-11; GB-23; GE-6; C-4; E-1 (Pinon Leno); E-11; E-20.

## PINNACLE RIDGE

El.: 7275'          Loc.: Graham 1, B-6.9
Descriptive.

Ref.: Barnes. Map: GE-5.

## POINT OF PINES

El.: c. 5000'          Loc.: Graham 2, C-4.2

In 1945 Dr. Emil Haury, head of the Department of Anthropology at the University of Arizona, and E. B. Sayles, curator of the Arizona State Museum, spent the summer evaluating the possibilities of a field school for the archeology department at Circle Prairie where Point of Pines now exists. By the end of the summer they had catalogued two hundred ruins covering a great period of time. With the approval of the San Carlos Apache Tribal Council, a summer program of the University of Arizona Department of Anthropology was begun. In the ensuing years students working with staff members established that people were in that region as early as 2000 B.C. They have also uncovered the fact that the Point of Pines Ruin had at least eight hundred rooms on the ground floor alone. The date for this ruin has not yet been established, although it is known that it was begun some time after 1000 A.D. and had become fairly large by 1250 A.D.

Ref.: Emil Haury, "Operation: Pick 'n Shovel," *Arizona Alumnus,* XXXIV (January, February 1957), pp. 10-11. Map: GE-7.

## POST CREEK

El.: c. 7000'          Loc.: Graham 2, A-12

This creek was so named because it helped furnish water for the post at Fort Grant.

Ref.: Barnes. Map: GE-3.

## PUEBLO VIEJO

El.: c. 2500'                     Loc.: Graham 2, D-10.8
Pro.: /pwebloviyého/             Spanish: "old town"

In 1873 prehistoric Indian ruins were reported to cover a tract one-half mile by two miles wide at this place. Hodge has conjectured that the ruin, which he referred to as Buena Vista (Spanish: "pleasant view"), on a high bluff on the Gila River a few miles northeast of San Jose was the reason for the name Pueblo Viejo being applied to the Gila River valley in this area. Some writers have said that possibly the ruin was the one referred to as Chichilticalli (Nahuatl: *chichiltic*, "red"; *calli*, "house") in the reports of the Coronado Expedition in 1540.

v.n. **Upper Gila Valley**

Ref.: 88, I, 168-169; Lizzie Steele File, APHS; 89, pp. 45, 186; *Arizona Citizen,* March 8, 1873, 2:2. Maps: A-2; C-1; E-11; E-18; E-20.

## SAFFORD

El.: 2914'                        Loc.: Graham 2, CD-10.2

In 1874 a group of farmers who were tired of having their ranches washed out by the river at Gila Bend made their way up the Gila River to found the first American colony in the Gila Valley of eastern Arizona. They settled at the site of Safford, naming it for Gov. Anson Pacely Killen Safford, who was currently a visitor in the valley. C. M. Ritter located the townsite on January 28, 1874. Joshua E. Bailey arrived in the same month and established the first store in the new settlement. A post office was set up in his store.

Safford served as the county seat until 1883, after which the function was moved to Solomonville *(q.v.).* It was returned to Safford in 1915.

P.O. est. March 5, 1875. Joshua E. Bailey, p.m. Wells Fargo Station, 1903.

Ref.: Joshua E. Bailey File, APHS; 55, p. 588; 112, pp. 242, 574. Maps: C-4; E-20.

## SANCHEZ

El.: c. 2500'                     Loc.: Graham 2, E-10
Pro.: /sánčez/ or /sænčez/

Lorenzo Sanchez settled at this location in February 1889. He had twelve children and c. 1891 succeeded in having a school established, all the pupils of which were his own children. When the post office was established, it was natural to name it Sanchez since practically everyone in the town bore that name.

P.O. est. August 19, 1901. Hignio Costales, p.m. Discont. November 19, 1903.

Ref.: Barnes; Jennings. Map: C-9.

## SAN JOSE

El.: c. 4000'                     Loc.: Graham 2, DE-10.3
Pro.: /sanhowzéy/ or /sæn howzéy/

The first settlers in the Graham County portion of the Gila Valley were Mexicans who moved there in 1873. The place was first called Munsonville because William Munson started a store which he sold in 1874 to I. E. Solomon. A community developed around an old adobe ruin, the village consisting of about twenty-five adobe huts in 1879.

Near San Jose was the place where Mormons used prehistoric irrigation canals in the system they called the Montezuma Canal after the long-vanished Indians. The canals supplied water to Lehi eleven miles away. Over one hundred and twenty-three miles of old Indian canals were thus employed. In July 1873 the San Jose settlement (probably in existence during the construction period of the Mormon canals) was called in a newspaper dispatch Montezuma.

P.O. est. as San Jose, December 12, 1877. Jules Griego, p.m. Discont. August 1, 1878. Re-est. March 30, 1904. Abelino Mejia, Jr., p.m. Discont. November 21, 1904.

Ref.: Lilly Kirkland File, APHS; 89, p. 587; 180, p. 9; 112. pp. 213, 214; 55, p. 587; *Tucson Citizen,* July 5, 1873, 2:3. Maps: C-4; C-12; E-20.

a.n. **Munson Cienega**   Loc.: 9 miles from Solomonville   Graham
This is probably where Munson established his ranch after selling his store to I. E. Solomon.

## SANTA TERESA MOUNTAINS

El.: c. 4000'                     Loc.: Graham 1, AC-6-7.5
Pro.: /sánta teréysa/

These mountains had this name at least as early as 1870. The origin of the name is not known.

Ref.: None. Maps: GE-5; C-4; E-20.

## SAW BUCK MOUNTAIN

El.: c. 5000'                     Loc.: Graham 1, CD-3

The name is descriptive of the resemblance of this mountain to a pack saddle of the saw buck type.

Ref.: Barnes. Maps: GE-2; C-13.

## SIERRA BONITA RANCH

El.: c. 4400'                     Loc.: Graham 2, A-14
Pro.: /siyéraboníyta/            Spanish: "beautiful mountains"
                                          or "pretty mountains"

The Sierra Bonita was a ranch noted for its fine appointments and open hospitality. It was established by Henry C. Hooker (b. New Hampshire, January 10, 1828; d. December 5, 1907). Hooker came to Arizona in 1866. He made a small mint of money as a government contractor (cf. Camp Goodwin). Following the completion of his contracts, he was in California for a while but returned to become a contractor again. In 1872 while encamped at a place called Oak Grove with a herd of cattle which were "left over after he had filled his government contracts," Hooker and his men were disturbed when the herd stampeded. The cowboys followed the cattle to a spring. The location appealed to Hooker and he homesteaded there, calling it Sierra Bonita. In the days before fencing when the land belonged to the government, a man could range his cattle over endless miles. Actually, Hooker controlled a range nearly thirty miles square.

The Sierra Bonita Ranch was the place of call for officers and wives from Camp Grant about eight miles distant. Hooker was very much interested in blooded stock, both cattle and horses, and was famous for some of the race horses he brought to Arizona.

Ref.: Henry C. Hooker File, APHS; 55, p. 585; 105, p. 231. Maps: GE-6; E-20.

## SLAUGHTER MOUNTAIN

El.: c. 5000'                    Loc.: Graham 2, C-7
Pete Slaughter was a cattleman in this area. He grazed cattle on the San Carlos Indian Reservation c. 1885.

Ref.: Barnes. Maps: GE-2; C-12.

## SOLOMONVILLE

El.: 3000'                    Loc.: Graham 2, D-10.6
In 1876 Isadore E. Solomon, who was suffering from tuberculosis, came to Arizona with his brother and Mrs. Solomon. The family bought several thousand acres in the Pueblo Viejo Valley and the small adobe house and store built in 1873 by Munson. The Solomons built mesquite charcoal pits in order to produce fuel to be used at the Clifton mines. Isadore also added to the Munson building and opened a store. When a post office was to be established for the growing community, the mail carrier, William Kirkland, suggested the name Solomonville and this was adopted. At a later date the name was corrupted to Solomonsville. The manner in which this came about was probably as follows: Postmasters made up their own hand-cancellation stamps which they used when sending out the mail. One such postmaster carved an "s" into Solomonville and was stubborn about correcting the name to its proper form. Solomonville in 1883 served for a brief time as county seat for Graham County.

P.O. est. Solomonville, April 10, 1878. Isadore E. Solomon, p.m. Wells Fargo Station, 1903. Changed to Solomon, April 7, 1950.

Ref.: Theobald; G. E. P. Smith; 112, pp. 242-244; 39, p. 50; 126, p. 15. Maps: C-4; E-20.

**a.n. Solomon**          Map: GE-2              Graham
   This was the railroad station for the town.
   Ref.: Barnes.

## STANLEY BUTTE

El.: c. 5000'                    Loc.: Graham 1, A-5.5
A Lt. Stanley was stationed at Fort Grant in the 1880's. This butte was named for him.

Ref.: Barnes. Map: C-10.

**a.n. Stanley**          Map: C-10              Graham
P.O. est. November 5, 1906. John Blake, p.m. Discont. September 13, 1926.

## STOCKTON PASS

El.: c. 5000'                    Loc.: Graham 2, A-12
The name Stockton Gap was in use at least as early as 1885 when it was so referred to in an account concerning an attack by Geronimo's band of marauding Apaches on the Williamson Ranch near the gap. The pass was named Stockton after a cattleman.

**v.n. Eagle Pass**
   This name is associated with Eagle Rock Peak. (Sec. 12, T. 9 S., R. 24 E.)

Ref.: 157, pp. 128-129; Barnes. Maps: C-4; E-20.

**a.n. Stockton Pass Wash**    Map: GM-3          Graham
   **Stockton Creek**          Map: C-12          Graham

## SUNSET

El.: 4811'                    Loc.: Graham 1, B-11
This location may have taken its name from its proximity to Sunset Peak.

P.O. est.? Discont. January 1, 1932.
Ref.: P.O. Records. Maps: GB-6; C-13; C-14.

**a.n. Sunset Canyon**          Map: GE-1                Graham
   **Sunset Peak**     El.: 7094'. Map: GE-1      Graham

## SWIFT TRAIL

Loc.: Graham 1, AC-11
When Theodore Swift (b. Iowa, December 20, 1871; d. 1955) was Forest Service Supervisor, he was successful in having this road established to the top of Mount Graham, thereby opening a new and beautiful recreation area.

Ref.: 112, III; Jennings. Map: GE-3.

## TANQUE

El.: c. 4000'                    Loc.: Graham 2, E-12.9
Pro.: /ténkiy/                    Spanish: "tank"
The railroad company put in a water tank at this place.

Ref.: Barnes. Maps: GE-2; C-10.

## TAYLOR PASS

El.: 7181'                    Loc.: Graham 1, D-8.5
John Taylor was a Mormon bishop in this area.

Ref.: Barnes. Map: GE-6.

## THATCHER

El.: 2929'                    Loc.: Graham 2, C-10.1
In July 1881, John M. Moody bought the Conley Ranch where in 1882 he was joined by four other Mormon families. Layton selected the first townsite on May 13, 1883, but in 1885 chose a new townsite one half mile to the south on higher land that he purchased October 9, 1885. The name had already been selected as a result of a Christmas visit by the Mormon Apostle Moses Thatcher together with Apostle Erasmus Snow in 1882.

P.O. est. March 10, 1888. Mrs. Elizabeth Layton, p.m. Wells Fargo Station, 1903.
Ref.: 112, p. 249; 180, pp. 15, 42. Map: C-7.

## THOMAS, FORT

El.: 2705'                    Loc.: Graham 2, A-8
When the troops were moved from Camp Goodwin (q.v.) to what was later known as Fort Apache (q.v., Navajo) because of the unhealthy conditions at old Camp Goodwin, there was a lapse of some time until a new camp was established in the Gila River Valley to replace old Camp Goodwin. However, a healthy spot was found and Fort Thomas was established there on August 12, 1876, three-fourths of a mile south of the Gila River and six miles east of the old location. As the name Camp Thomas had been replaced by the name Camp Apache in 1871, there was nothing to hinder applying the name Camp Thomas to the new post in Graham and this was done. The name was changed to Fort Thomas on May 18, 1877.

The fact that old Camp Goodwin had been planned as a permanent post resulted in expensive fraud, and this led to great caution in establishing Fort Thomas as a decent post. Goodwin was a total loss and consequently funds were not forthcoming for the new post. In 1879 Fort Thomas consisted of two adobe barracks, one two-room adobe shack for the commanding officer and his family, a guard house, and an adjutant's office. These were constructed by the soldiers themselves at no expense to the government. Only the post trader had decent quarters. In 1884 funds were finally made available and a handsome post came into existence. The surrender of Geronimo in 1886 was the beginning of the end for Fort Thomas. It was abandoned on November 22, 1892.

Meanwhile, a community had grown up around the post (cf. Maxey). In 1887 the name of Maxey was changed to Fort Thomas. It was here in the summer of 1895 that the railroad line met an impasse in its construction plans to cross the Gila Valley. The Apache Indians steadfastly refused to permit the line to cross the reservation. Work was held up for over a year.

Today Fort Thomas is a good-sized community.

Apparently there was a post office within the post itself as well as in the town of Maxey. The post office at Camp Thomas still bore the name Goodwin, probably to facilitate delivery of mail since the name Camp Goodwin was better known than that of Camp Thomas.

P.O. est. as Camp Goodwin, March 5, 1875. Thomas Mc-Williams, p.m. Discont. October 18, 1880. P.O. in community of Maxey est. as Camp Thomas, March 2, 1877. Frank Staples, p.m. Name changed to Fort Thomas, February 28, 1883. (See Maxey for further information.) Wells Fargo Station, 1903.

Ref.: P.O. Records; 75, p. 157; 39, pp. 29, 31; 111, p. 156; 180, p. 52. Maps: C-3 (Camp Goodwin); C-4; E-20.

## TURNBULL, MOUNT

El.: 7700'          Loc.: Graham 1, B-4.4

On October 30, 1846, Lt. William H. Emory remarked on the fact that at three o'clock in the afternoon his party passed around the base of this mountain.

Lt. Charles Nesbit Turnbull, (b. Washington, D. C., August 14, 1832), an army enginner, was a member of the Gadsden Purchase Boundary Survey party in 1854. As he was only fourteen at the time of the naming of Mount Turnbull in 1849, it seems more likely that the mountain was named for his father, William Turnbull (1800-1857), who designed the famous Washington Aqueduct Bridge which was built (1832-1843) to carry water to the city. It was a notable feat. However, there is no documentary evidence to demonstrate that Mount Turnbull was named for either member of the Turnbull family mentioned.

Ref.: 50, p. 69; State Library Files; Copy of information received from F. Wadel, APHS. Maps: C-1; D-9; E-1; E-11.

## WEBB PEAK

El.: 10,029'          Loc.: Graham 2, A-11.7

Wilfred T. Webb was a well-known cattleman, farmer, and politician of the Gila Valley.

Ref.: Barnes. Map: GE-3.

## WEBBER PEAK

El.: c. 5000'          Loc.: Graham 2, D-9.
                        Sec. 36, T. 5 S., R. 26 E.

John Webber was an early settler of the Gila Valley.

Ref.: 151, p. 806. Map: None.

## WEST PEAK

El.: 8685'          Loc.: Graham 1, D-8.5

The name is descriptive of the location of this peak at the west end of the Pinaleno Mountains.

Ref.: Jennings. Map: GE-6.

## WHITLOCK VALLEY

El.: c. 3500'          Loc.: Graham 2, F-13

Captain Whitlock (first name not known) prior to 1880 is said to have commanded U. S. troops in a fight with Apaches at Whitlock Cienega, now called Whitlock Valley. This shows as Whitelock on GLO 1869.

Ref.: Barnes. Maps: C-4; E-20.

**a.n. Whitlock Hills**
Loc.: East end upper San Simon Valley          Graham

**Whitlock Peak**
Loc.: Peloncillo Mountains on line between Graham and Greenlee counties.          Graham

**Whitlock Sink**          (see below)          Graham

**Parks Lake**          Loc.: T. 10 S., R. 30 E.          Graham
Jim B. Parks, a cattleman, was well known. This is an earlier name for Whitlock Sink (see above).

Ref.: Barnes; Jennings.

## WILD HORSE CANYON

El.: c. 3000'          Loc.: Graham 1, AB-1-3

A band of wild horses used to roam in this canyon. They were rounded up and exterminated about 1910 in the campaign to prevent dourine among Indian ponies.

Ref.: Barnes. Maps: C-13; D-9.

ARIZONA PLACE NAMES

# THE GRAND CANYON

*Grand Canyon — Discoverers and Explorers — Indian, Spaniard, Friar, Mormon Pioneer, Mountain Man.*

## THE GRAND CANYON:

One of the most spectacular of nature's wonders lies entirely in Arizona. It is the Grand Canyon, the most beautiful part of which—one hundred and five miles long — is in the Grand Canyon National Park. The Grand Canyon is an area of violent contrasts, varying in depth from three thousand to six thousand feet and in width from four to fifteen miles, with the North Rim being higher than the South Rim. Any attempt to describe the innumerable sculptured chasms, buttes, and terraced walls must inevitably fail, for there is no way to put into words the tremendous variety of colors and shapes.

The many formations have been carved during eons of time. The fact that the entire region in which the Grand Canyon lies was long, long ago raised high above the surrounding country reveals that the Colorado River has cut into it, exposing a record of geological time which is scientifically second to none now known to man. The Grand Canyon was formed as the Colorado River cut its narrow channel vertically downward. While this was going on, the exposed rock walls were subjected to erosive forces. According to Francois E. Matthes, the erosion occurred principally from the bottom up, each cliff being undercut by the removal of soft shale and the resulting overhang then spalling. Fractures extending vertically have caused slipping, and along the fault lines side canyons and amphitheaters have developed. The so-called temples, lacking such faults, have formed from blocks of strata.

The first white man to see the Canyon was Garcia Lopez de Cardenas, a member of the Coronado Expedition in 1540. He was sent to locate the large river which Pedro de Tobar had reported that Indians said lay far to the west of the Hopi villages. It was many years before the Grand Canyon was deemed worthy of investigation, but once exploration began, many expeditions followed. Lt. Amiel W. Whipple in 1854 followed the lower Colorado River up to the mouth of what he called Big Canyon. In 1857 Lt. Joseph Christmas Ives, after locating what he considered the headquarters of navigation of the Colorado River, went overland and reached the edge of the main gorge. Dr. John S. Newberry, geologist and surgeon for the Ives expedition, was the first to give a detailed description of the great canyon and to point out the significance of its geological formations.

Maj. John Wesley Powell, a one-armed Civil War veteran, was the first to lead an expedition through the entire length of the Grand Canyon, using boats, in 1869. In 1871-72 Powell made a second and more thorough exploration of the Big Canyon, as it was then known, and changed the name soon thereafter in his report to Grand Canyon. Powell was the first of many scientists who have investigated the vast chasm, and his expedition members applied many place names still in use. Others were applied by Maj. Clarence E. Dutton, Charles E. Walcott (both c. 1880), and Francois E. Matthes with Richard Evans (1902). The place names of the Grand Canyon reflect not only Indian life in that region, but also events and names of pioneers in Arizona history.

## ABYSS, THE

El. c. 6000'                    Loc.: East BC-9.75
Descriptive.
Ref.: None. Map: GC-7.

## AGATE CANYON

El.: 3250'                      Loc.: West L-10.9
Several places in the Grand Canyon region are named for semi-precious stones. This one was named by Richard T. Evans of the U.S.G.S. in 1903.
Ref.: Kolb. Map. GC-8.

## AKABA, MOUNT

El.: 4500'                      Loc.: West E-3.5
An Indian family by this name lived in the vicinity of this butte.
Ref.: 151, p. 184. Map: GC-8.

## ALARCON TERRACE

El.: 4750'                      Loc.: West FG-5
Pro.: /ǽlersán/
This canyon was named for Capt. Juan Hernando de Alarcon, who left Acapulco, Mexico on May 9, 1540, and went northward until he reached the headwaters of the Gulf of California, thus being the first white man to explore beyond the mouth of the Colorado River. He carried supplies for the Coronado Expedition then en route overland to the Seven Cities of Cibola, but the two groups failed to join.
Ref.: *Nature Notes*, III, No. 10 (June 30, 1929), p. 2; 182, p. 403. Map: GC-8.

## ALLIGATOR, THE

El.: c. 5700'                   Loc.: East C-9
This low-lying ridgeback is descriptively called The Alligator.
Ref.: Kolb. Maps: GC-7; GC-1.

## ALSAP BUTTE

El.: c. 7000'                   Loc.: East HI-4
John T. Alsap (b. Kentucky, 1832; d. 1886) settled near Phoenix in 1869, where he was a lawyer, becoming both county and district attorney. He was later a probate judge. Alsap is often called the "Father of Maricopa County."
Ref.: Barnes. Map: GC-7.

## APACHE POINT

El.: 5850'                      Loc.: West G-6.5
Pro.: /əpǽči/
Named for the Apache Indians of Arizona (cf. Fort Apache, Navajo).
Ref.: Barnes. Map: GC-8.
**a.n. Apache Terrace**   Map: GC-8   Grand Canyon, Coconino

## ARROWHEAD TERRACE

El.: c. 5000'                   Loc.: West J-3
Descriptive of the shape of this terrace.
Ref.: Barnes. Map: None

## ASBESTOS CANYON

El.: c. 4000'                   Loc.: East HI 9-11
William Bass discovered an asbestos vein here.
Ref.: Kolb. Map: GC-7.

## AWATOVI CREEK

El.: 4250'                      Loc.: East JL-5.5-4.5
Pro.: /awátʔowbíˆ/   Hopi: "high place of the Bow people"
This place was so called for the ancient and vanished pueblo known as Awatovi (*q.v.* Coconino).
**v.n. Awatuvi Creek**
Ref.: Shellbach. Map: GC-7.
**a.n. Awatubi Crest**   Map: GC-7   Grand Canyon, Coconino

## AYER POINT

El.: c. 5000'   Loc.: East H-10, to right of Hance Canyon
Mrs. Edward E. Ayer, wife of a prominent Flagstaff lumberman, was the first white woman to visit the Grand Canyon (1883) and the first white woman to go down into the canyon at this point via the Hance Trail (*see* Hance Creek, a.n.). Accompanying Mrs. Ayer on her trip to the Grand Canyon was her daughter and a young Miss Sturgis. Mrs. Ayer translated the *Memorial of Fray Alonzo de Benavida, 1630* (published 1916).
Ref.: Slipher; 168, p. 19; 20, p. 418, (Note 1). Map: None.

## BANTA POINT

El.: 5250'                      Loc.: East JK-5
Will C. Barnes named this point for Albert Franklin Banta (b. Indiana 1846). Banta came to Arizona in 1863 under the name Charles A. Franklin with Gov. John N. Goodwin's party (*see* Navajo Springs, Apache). In the ensuing years he acted as a scout for Gen. George Crook (1865-1871) and as a guide for the Wheeler expedition of 1871-73. He later lived in Apache County where he served as district attorney and as a probate judge. He was a member of the Tenth Arizona Legislature and was influential in creating Apache County.
Banta, a teller of extremely tall tales, was the Kilroy of territorial Arizona.
Ref.: Barnes; APHS File; 52, VIII, 31. Map: GC-7.

## BARBENCETA BUTTE

El.: 4463'                      Loc.: East IJ-2.25
Pro.: /bárbnsíytə/
On November 2, 1870, the noted Mormon explorer and missionary, Jacob Hamblin, met with Barbenceta, principal chief of the Navajos. In 1871 Hamblin introduced this Indian to Maj. John Wesley Powell to enlist the aid of the Indians for the Grand Canyon exploration. Powell later named the butte for the Indian.
Ref.: Shellbach. Map: GC-7.

## BASALT CLIFFS

El.: c. 4000'                   Loc.: East JK-8-9
There is a dark basaltic formation below the top of the plateau.
Ref.: Kolb. Map: GC-7.
**a.n. Basalt Creek**   Map: GC-7   Grand Canyon, Coconino

## BASS CAMP

El.: 6652'                                    Loc.: West J-8

William Wallace Bass (b. Shelbyville, Indiana, October 2, 1841; d. March 7, 1933) settled near Williams (Coconino County) in 1883. Bass did not take up residence at Grand Canyon until about 1889.

The early history of the Grand Canyon centers largely around William Bass. In 1884 Bass went on a hunting trip which led him to the top of the Havasupai trail to Mount Huethawali. The same Indian after whom Burro Camp is named, Captain Burro, showed William Bass where the hidden springs lay. Bass was surprised, because the spring was very close to a spot which he thought he had searched thoroughly, hence the name Mystic Spring.

Bass looked for a definite trail into the canyon because he had located an Indian fortress about fifteen feet square on the very edge of the canyon and so believed a trail must exist. He found it and extended the trail down into the canyon and built Bass Camp where he set up tent houses for guest accommodations. He named the trail the Mystic Spring Trail, and completed it prior to 1900. On December 2, 1937, the U. S. Board on Geographic Names designated it Bass Trail.

When the railroad put in a branch line for shipping ores from the mines in the Grand Canyon, tourists began to arrive in greater numbers. By 1902 Bass was well equipped to take care of them. He also was working copper and asbestos mines near his camp. Bass met his guests with his own stage at a stop on the railroad known as Bass Station, about five miles southwest of the present Grand Canyon Village. On December 11, 1925, Bass sold his camp to the Santa Fe Land and Improvement Company.

Ref.: "McKinney Expedition Papers," *W. W. Bass Materials,* Wickenburg (Shellbach File); 4, pp. 485-486; 93, pp. 77, 78, 181; 168, pp. 45, 46; 61, p. 77; Writings of Mrs. Bass, *W. W. Bass Materials,* Wickenburg (Grand Canyon Files). Map: GC-1.

a.n. **Bass Cable Ferry Crossing**          Grand Canyon, Coconino
In 1908 Bass built a ferry across the Colorado River in the Grand Canyon. The ferry was a cage swinging on a wire cable and was used to carry horses, cattle, sheep, and human passengers.

v.n. **Bed Rock Camp**
Ref.: Shellbach; 72, p. 148.

a.n. **Bass Canyon**       Map: GC-8   Grand Canyon, Coconino
**Bass Rapids**      Map: GC-8   Grand Canyon, Coconino
**Bass Tomb**       El.: 6710'. Map: GC-8
                                        Grand Canyon, Coconino
When Bass died in 1933, he left orders for his body to be cremated. This was done and his ashes were scattered from an airplane over Holy Grail Temple, also known as Bass Tomb. Apparently this place was called Bass Tomb prior to Mr. Bass's death in 1933, because George Wharton James in 1910 noted that the then-current name was Holygrail Temple, "formerly Bass Tomb."
Ref.: 93, p. 80; *W. W. Bass Materials,* Wickenburg (Shellbach File).

**Heuthawali, Mount**
El.: 6280'. Map: GC-8          Grand Canyon, Coconino
Pro.: /wiýčaliy/

## BEALE POINT

El.: 6695'                                    Loc.: West G-4.5

Beale Point was named for Lt. Edward Fitzgerald Beale, who in 1857-58 was in charge of the survey party for a wagon road along the 35th Parallel. Beale used camels for pack animals.
Ref.: 12. Map: GC-8.

## BEDIVERE POINT

El.: 7750'                                    Loc.: East A-4

Grand Canyon nomenclature based on characters in the Arthurian legends was introduced by Richard T. Evans in 1902. Evans found that the magnificent scenery of the canyon inspired thoughts of the Holy Grail legends.

Ref.: Francois E. Matthes File, Envelope No. 6, Letter to chairman, Geographic Board, May 6, 1925, Grand Canyon Files. Map: GC-7.

a.n. **Elaine Castle**      Map: GC-8   Grand Canyon, Coconino
**Galahad Point**     Map: GC-7   Grand Canyon, Coconino
**Gawain Abyss**     Map: GC-8   Grand Canyon, Coconino
**Gunther Castle**    Map: GC-7   Grand Canyon, Coconino

**Guinevere Castle**
El.: 7255'. Map: GC-8                Grand Canyon, Coconino

**King Arthur Castle**
El.: 7315'. Map: GC-8                Grand Canyon, Coconino

**Lancelot Point**    Map: GC-8   Grand Canyon, Coconino
**Merlin Abyss**                  Grand Canyon, Coconino
**Modred Abyss**     Map: GC-8   Grand Canyon, Coconino

## BED ROCK CANYON

El.: c. 4000'                                  Loc.: West JG-3.5

This is a rock-walled, shallow and waterless canyon.

Ref.: "Bulletin No. 82, *B.A.E.,* Washington, D. C. 1926, p. 133 (Shellbach File). Map: GC-8.

a.n. **Bed Rock Rapids**    Map: GC-8   Grand Canyon, Coconino

## BOUCHER CREEK

El.: c. 4000'                                  Loc.: West L-10

Pro.: /búwčer/ or /buwšéy/

Louis D. Boucher (b. Sherbrook, Canada) arrived at the Grand Canyon in 1891 and established a tourist camp. He built the Boucher Trail on which, at Dripping Springs (which he also named) he had two tents and a corral. His was the last trail to be constructed (c. 1902-5).

v.n. **Long Creek**
Ref.: Shellbach File; 93, pp. 46, 47, 48. Map: GC-8.

a.n. **Boucher Rapids**    Map: GC-7   Grand Canyon, Coconino
**Boucher Trail**      Map: GC-7   Grand Canyon, Coconino

## BOULDER CREEK

El. c. 3500'                                   Loc.: East EF-11-10

This creek bed is filled with boulders.

Ref.: Kolb. Maps: GC-7; GC-1.

## BOUNDARY RIDGE

El.: 7000'                                     Loc.: East GJ-2

Richard T. Evans proposed this name because the ridge follows the northern boundary of Grand Canyon National Park.

Ref.: Ed McKee, Park Naturalist, Letter to Francois Matthes, USGS; Matthes File, Grand Canyon. Map: GC-7.

## BOURKE POINT

El.: 6537′                    Loc.: East I-3.25

In the early 1870's Lt. John G. Bourke served as aide to Gen. George Crook. Bourke later wrote several books about Arizona. The name for this location was suggested by Will C. Barnes to honor Bourke.

Ref.: Barnes. Map: GC-7.

## BOYSAG POINT

El.: 5589′                    Loc.: West A-2.75
                              Piute: *boysag*, "bridge"

This point is in Grand Canyon National Park on the North Rim. Because it can be reached only by a small artificial bridge, the Indian word for bridge was used.

Ref.: 151, p. 161. Maps: GC-8; GC-6.

## BRADLEY POINT

El.: c. 5000′                 Loc.: East F-8

G. Y. Bradley was a member of Maj. John Wesley Powell's first expedition through the Grand Canyon in 1869.

Ref.: Barnes. Maps: GC-1; GC-7.

## BRADY PEAK

El.: 8009′                    Loc.: East H-4

Peter R. Brady (b. Washington, D.C., 1825) was a graduate of the Naval Academy in 1844. He resigned his commission in 1846, thereafter serving with the Texas Rangers in the Mexican War. He first came to Arizona in 1854, and was later instrumental in establishing a company to work the mines at Ajo (*q.v.* Pima). He served as a territorial senator.

Ref.: Barnes. Map: GC-7.

## BRAHMA TEMPLE

El.: 7554′                    Loc.: East FG-7.5

The fantastic shapes of many of the buttes in the Grand Canyon led to their fanciful names. Brahma Temple is an example. It was named after "the first of the Hindu Triad, the Supreme Creator, to correspond with the Shiva Temple . . . Shiva, the destroyer; Brahma the creator."

Ref.: 93, p. 30; 151, p. 162. Map: GC-7.

## BREEZY POINT

El.: 3500′                    Loc.: East B-9

This point was named by Emery C. and Ellsworth Kolb because the breeze is so strong here that it blows gravel.

Ref.: Kolb. Maps: GC-1; GC-7.

## BRIGHT ANGEL CREEK

El.: c. 4500′                 Loc.: East GD-4-8.5

On August 16, 1869, Maj. John Wesley Powell during his first exploration of the Grand Canyon reported that his party had just endured four days of rain which resulted in great floods pouring over the canyon walls, bringing in quantities of mud and making the Colorado River "exceedingly turbid." The party found a clear little creek or river which, in contrast to the Dirty Devil River in Utah, named for the bad angels, they called the Bright Angel River.

Ref.: 132, p. 86. Maps: GC-1; GC-7.

**a.n. Bright Angel Canyon**    Map: GC-7 Grand Canyon, Coconino

**Bright Angel Amphitheatre**    Grand Canyon, Coconino
Maj. Clarence E. Dutton in 1882 described this amphitheatre as being the "longest and deepest of any, and . . . the narrowest."

Ref.: 47, p. 173.

**Bright Angel Plateau**    Grand Canyon, Coconino
Part of the Tonto platform running from Indian Gardens to Plateau Point.

Ref.: 93, p. 33.

**Bright Angel Point**
El.: 8153′. Maps: GC-7; GC-1    Grand Canyon, Coconino

**Bright Angel Spring**
Maps: GC-1; GC-7    Grand Canyon, Coconino

**Bright Angel Trail**    Map: GC-1 Grand Canyon, Coconino
The Bright Angel Trail was originally called Cameron Trail. It was constructed in 1891 by P. D. Berry, Robert Ferguson, C. H. McClure, and Niles J. Cameron in order to have access to their mines in the canyon. Berry filed this location as a toll road. In 1890 Ralph H. Cameron and Berry had acquired all mines in the vicinity; they sold out in 1902 to the Canyon Copper Company.

Ralph Cameron (b. Southport Maine, October 21, 1863) owned a hotel on the canyon rim until 1910, when he was elected delegate to the United States Congress. The railroad, which was attempting to force Cameron to release his holdings at the Canyon, moved its station one thousand feet to the east in order to attract tourists away from Cameron's Trail.

Conflict over the Bright Angel Trail was carried on from 1901 through 1928. It spread four ways, involving the citizens of Coconino County, the railroad, the county government, and the federal government. The trail was sold by Coconino County on May 22, 1928, to the United States Government. Cameron Trail was changed officially by the U. S. Board on Geographic Names on December 2, 1937, to Bright Angel Trail.

Ref.: 168, pp. 29, 30, 44, 45, 50, 59, 60.

**a.n. Bright Angel Wash**    Grand Canyon, Coconino
**Devil's Corkscrew**    Grand Canyon, Coconino
This portion of the Bright Angel Trail winds and twists downward for twelve hundred feet.

Ref.: 93, p. 63.

## BUDDHA TEMPLE

El.: 7218′                    Loc.: East D-7

Buddha was the founder of Buddhism.

Maps: GC-1; GC-7.

**a.n. Buddha Cloister**
Loc.: Below Buddha Temple    Grand Canyon, Coconino
This name was in use at least by 1900.

Ref.: 93, p. 30.

## BURRO CANYON

El.: c. 3500′                 Loc.: West J-5-6

Thousands of wild burros used to flock to this canyon for water.

Ref.: Kolb. Map: GC-8.

**a.n. Burro, Mount**
El.: 5692′. Map: GC-8    Grand Canyon, Coconino
This is said to have been the name of an Indian family.

Ref.: 151, p. 177.

## CAPE FINAL

El.: 7919'                               Loc.: East I-7.5
In 1880 Maj. Clarence E. Dutton named this view point.
It was at the end of a five-mile ride which brought him out
to a view at the head of the Grand Canyon. As Dutton
describes it, "Point Final is doubtless the most interesting
spot on the Kaibab. In pure grandeur, it is about the same
as Point Sublime [but] the two differ much in the characteristics of the scenery."
Ref.: 47, pp. 176, 181. Map: GC-7.

## CAPE ROYAL

El.: 7876'                               Loc.: East H-8
This point was named by Maj. Clarence E. Dutton in 1882.
In his words it is a "congregation of wonderful structures,
countless and vast, profound lateral chasms."
Ref.: 47, p. 176; Map: GC-7.

## CAPE SOLITUDE

El.: 6157'                               Loc.: East LM-6
Descriptive. So called at least as early as 1900.
Ref.: 93, p. 71. Map: GC-7.

## CARBON BUTTE

El.: c. 4000'                            Loc.: East K-6.5
Carbon Butte was named by Charles E. Walcott because
of its position between the fork of Carbon Creek and the
Colorado River.
Ref.: Francois Matthes, Letter to Geographic Board on
        Names, November 27, 1926. Map: GC-7.
a.n. Carbon Creek     Map: GC-7    Grand Canyon, Coconino
     Carbon Canyon    Map: GC-7    Grand Canyon, Coconino
Named by the Birdseye expedition in 1923.

## CARDENAS BUTTE

El.: 6264'                               Loc.: East JK-10
Pro.: /kardeynəs/
Garcia Lopez de Cardenas, the second son of a Spanish
nobleman, came to South America in 1535. He later went
to Mexico City, where a distant relative by marriage, Mendoza, was Viceroy. In 1540 Cardenas was a member of
the Coronado Expedition to the Seven Cities of Cibola.
He was commissioned by Coronado to check on an Indian
story that a great canyon lay to the west of the Hopi villages. While investigating this report, Cardenas became the
first white man known to have seen the great gorge of
the Grand Canyon.·
Ref.: 18, p. 55. Map: GC-7.
a.n. Cardenas Creek    Map: GC-7    Grand Canyon, Coconino

## CEDAR MOUNTAIN

El.: 7057'                               Loc.: East M-10.5
Descriptive.
Ref.: Barnes. Map: GC-7.
a.n. Cedar Spring
     Maps: GC-1; GC-7              Grand Canyon, Coconino

## CHEMEHUEVI POINT

El.: 6626'                               Loc.: West I-7.5
Pro.: /čémɔèyvĭ/
Named for Chemehuevi Indians, a branch of the Piute
tribe (see Chemehuevi Valley).
Ref.: 151, p. 212; 93, p. 82. Map. GC-8.

## CHEOPS PYRAMID

El.: 5350'                               Loc.: East D-8
Cheops was the Egyptian pharaoh who built the Great
Pyramid, using relays of one hundred thousand men every
three months. The Great Pyramid is the oldest of the seven
wonders of the ancient world and the only one which still
survives. George Wharton James says that Cheops Pyramid
at the Grand Canyon has "a peculiar shape as of some
quaint and Oriental device of symbolic significance."
Ref.: 93, pp. 30-31. Map: GC-7.

## CHEYAVA FALLS

El.: c. 7000'                            Loc.: East H-7.25
Pro.: /čeyávə/               Hopi: "intermittent"
This falls in Clear Creek Canyon was first visited by the
Kolb brothers (Emery C. and Elisworth) in 1903. The falls
was pointed out to them by William Beeson in May 1903,
Beeson saying he saw a "big sheet of ice." The Kolbs
examined it through their telescope and found that it was
actually a large falls; they then made the trip. Ellsworth
Kolb named it because the falls existed only intermittently.
Ref.: "Cheyava Falls" Grand Canyon Natural History Notes,
        Bulletin 2, November 1935, pp. 10, 15. Map: GC-7.

## CHIAVRIA POINT

El.: 6100'                               Loc.: East IJ-6.5
Juan Chiavria was a Maricopa chief present at the battle
of Bloody Tanks (q.v. Gila).
Ref.: Barnes. Map: GC-7.

## CHIKAPANGI MESA

El.: 4250'                               Loc.: West BC-2.3
Pro.: /čĭkəpənágiy/
An Indian family named Chikapangi lived on this Mesa,
which was named for them.
Ref.: 151, p. 216; 92, p. 237. Map: GC-8.
a.n. Chikapanagi Point  Map: GC-8   Grand Canyon, Coconino

## CHUAR BUTTE

El.: 6250'                               Loc. East K-6
Pro.: /čúar/
This is the shortening of the name of a young chief of the
Kaibab tribe called Chuaroompek. This man was intro-
duced by the Mormon missionary and guide, Jacob Ham-
blin, to Maj. John Wesley Powell.

Over Chuar Butte in 1956 two transcontinental airliners
collided at 21,000 feet altitude. Parts of the wreckage fell
onto Chuar Butte. This incident triggered an investigation
for the improvement of air safety.
Ref.: 151, p. 220. Map: GC-7.
a.n. Chuar Creek                   Grand Canyon, Coconino

## CLEMENT POWELL BUTTE

El.: c. 5500′      Loc.: East E-7

Clement Powell was the assistant photographer of the second exploration of the Grand Canyon, 1871-1872.

Ref.: Barnes. Maps: GC-1; GC-7.

## COCHISE BUTTE

El.: c. 5000′      Loc.: East J-5.5

Pro.: /kočiys/

Cochise was chief of the Chiricahua Apaches in the 1870's. (*See* Cochise, Cochise).

Ref.: None. Map: GC-7.

## COCOPAH POINT

El.: c. 6000′      Loc.: East A-9

Pro.: /kówkopa/

This place was named for the former Indian tribe of Cocopahs, whose home was along the Colorado River below Yuma.

Ref.: None. Map: GC-7.

## COLORADO RIVER

Loc.: Enters Arizona from Utah in north-central Arizona. Traverses south, then west and northwest, then south, forming western boundary of Arizona.

Pro.: /kaloрádow/ or /kowloræedo/ or /kaleрédow/

Spanish: "red"

The first white man known to have seen the delta of the Great Colorado River was Francisco de Ulloa in 1539. In 1540 Capt. Fernando Alarcon was told to take supplies via the river to meet the Coronado expedition, then going overland. He called the river El Rio de Buena Guía ("The River of Good Guidance") but failed to make connections with Coronado, whose route was far to the east of the Colorado River. *Buena Guía* was the motto on Viceroy Mendoza's coat of arms.

In 1541 Capt. Melchoir Diaz traveled overland through northern Sonora to the same river. There he noted Indians along the shores, keeping themselves warm by holding burning brands in their hands close to their abdomens. He therefore called the stream Rio del Tison ("Firebrand River"). With the failure of the Coronado expedition, the two names vanished as Spaniards lost interest in what was later to become Arizona. It was years before another white man saw the stream.

When a white man next saw the Colorado, he was far from its mouth. In 1604 Juan de Oñate called the river, which he saw from near the present mouth of the Bill Williams River, the Rio Grande de Buena Esperanza ("The Great River of Good Hope"). Again many years passed. Then Fr. Eusebio Kino, who also noticed the Indians and their firebrands near the mouth of the river, gave it another name: Rio de los Martires ("River of the Martyrs"). In 1699 his lieutenant, Juan Mateo Manje, learned from the natives something of how enormous the river must be, and he then referred to it as the "true Rio del Norte of the ancients . . . the fertile Colorado River." It was to be many years, however, before the name Colorado took firm hold. Meanwhile every newcomer gave it another name.

Fr. Hernando Escalante called it the Rio del Cosnina after the Coconino Indians, forerunners of the contemporary Havasupais.

Fr. Jacobo Sedelmayr c. 1746 seems to have been the first to note that the Indians themselves had their own names for the river. The Pimas called it the Buqui Aquimuri ("Red River"), and the Cocomaricopas called it the Gritetho, the equivalent of the Spanish term Rio Grande ("Great or Grand River"). Fr. Francisco Garcés in 1774 said that the Yumas called the stream the Javill or HahWeal ("Red") because the entire region through which it flowed was a reddish color. Much later, George Wharton James c. 1910 noted that the Havasupai Indians called the river the Hackatai. The Piute name was Pa-ha-weap ("water deep down in the earth"), for in their territory the river cut through the Grand Canyon. The Navajos are reported to have called the Colorado Pocket-to.

White men added still more names when Americans first began to travel along its banks. James Ohio Pattie in the 1830's called it the Red River. Others called parts of it (to the north) the Grand River. Maj. John Wesley Powell's men in 1869 referred to it as the Colorado River of the West. The name finally settled upon was a translation of Garcés' Rio Colorado, the Colorado River.

Ref.: 76, p. 12; 7, pp. 35, 39, 155, 182, pp. 404, 574; 42, pp. 28-29, 82; pp. 272-273; 177, I, 205; 125; 125, p. 119; 20, p. 415; 145, p. 28; 35, pp. 144 (Note 58), 431, 431 (Note 19); 19, II, 244; 151, p. 230. Maps: All of the region traversed by the river.

## COLTER BUTTE

El.: 7258′      Loc.: East J-4.5

James G. H. Colter (b. Nova Scotia 1844) was an Arizona pioneer who settled on the Little Colorado River in 1872. (See Colter, Apache).

Ref.: Barnes. Map: GC-7.

## COMANCHE POINT

El.: 7079′      Loc.: East L-9

Pro.: /kəmǽnčiy/ or /komǽnčiy/

George Wharton James called this place Bissel Point for an early official of the A.T.&S.F.R.R. James also refers to it as Comanche Point. The Kolb brothers, who traveled through the Grand Canyon in 1911, also referred to this place as Bissel Point. Later, the U.S.G.B. officially changed it to Comanche after a tribe of Plains Indians.

Ref.: 93, p. 70; 151, p. 231. Map: GC-7.

**a.n. Comanche Creek**      Map: GC-7      Grand Canyon, Coconino

## CONFUCIUS TEMPLE

El.: 7128′      Loc.: East AB-6.5

Confucius (c. 551-478 B.C.) was the most famous sage of China.

This formation at the Grand Canyon embodies another instance of the fancied resemblance of great buttes to temples associated with the prophets and originators of the world's religions.

Ref.: 93, p. 46. Map: GC-7.

## CONQUISTADOR AISLE

El.: c. 3000'                          Loc.: West FG-5.75
The bed of the Colorado River travels through a dark chasm which has been named to honor explorers of the South Rim region. These explorers include Lt. Joseph C. Ives, Capt. George M. Wheeler, Lt. Edward F. Beale, Dr. A. H. Thompson, and Dr. John Newberry.
Ref.: 93, p. 83. Map: GC-8.

## COPE BUTTE

El.: 4540'                                Loc.: East B-9
Edward Drinker Cope (1840-1897) was a noted American paleontologist. In the 1870's he investigated the cretaceous and tertiary strata of the West.
Ref.: None. Map: GC-7.

## CORONADO BUTTE

El.: 7120'                              Loc.: East H-11.5
Pro.: /karonádo/ or /koronádo/
Francisco Vasquez de Coronado came to Arizona with the Viceroy, Mendoza, in 1535, becoming a legal citizen of the City of Mexico in 1537. On April 18, 1539, the King of Spain signed the appointment of Coronado as governor of New Galicia. It was here that Coronado entertained Fr. Marcos de Niza when the priest was on his way northward in the spring of 1539. In the middle of summer, Marcos came back and Coronado joined him, going to Mexico City. There Coronado took part in preparations for a great expedition to the fabled Seven Cities of Cibola. On February 23, 1540, Coronado's army set out. There were three hundred thirty-six Spanish military men, the wives and children of some of the soldiers, and hundreds of Indians in the expedition. The army had five hundred and fifty-nine horses. Not only were there Spaniards in the expedition, but there were also five Portuguese, two Italians, one Frenchman, one Scot, and one German. The Spaniards, wearing brightly burnished armor, proceeded along their route with all the pomp, panoply, and trappings of courtly warfare. Their hardships were many, but finally on July 7, 1540, the expedition entered the Zuñi villages. The houses were stone and mud, for such the fabled Seven Cities turned out to be. Coronado returned to Mexico City "very sad and very weary, completely worn out and shamefaced." The expedition had been a complete failure as far as its avowed search for wealth was concerned. Coronado died September 22, 1554.
Ref.: 182, pp. 379, 380, 381, 382, 389, 402; 18, pp. 68, 69. Map: GC-7.

## CREMATION CREEK

El.: c. 4000'                          Loc.: East E-10-8.5
This creek lies at the bottom of Cremation Point (the second above Yavapai Point). Here Indians claim they used to cremate bodies and throw the ashes over the cliff.
Ref.: Kolb. Map: GC-7.

## CRYSTAL CREEK

                                      Loc.: East CA-2-7.5
This creek has extremely clear water. The first pilots to fly an airplane in the Grand Canyon dropped down below the Rim here when looking for the honeymooning Hyde couple in 1927. The couple attempted to go through the canyon in a boat, always a perilous feat. They perished.
Ref.: Kolb. Maps: GC-1; GC-7.
a.n. Crystal Rapid          Map: GC-1      Grand Canyon, Coconino

## DANA BUTTE

El.: 5025'                                Loc.: East C-8.75
This butte was named for the American geologist, James Dwight Dana (1813-1895). Dana wrote more than two hundred scientific books and papers.
Ref.: 93, p. 39. Map: GC-7.

## DARWIN PLATEAU

El.: 5500'                                Loc.: West I-7
This plateau was named for Charles Darwin, the evolutionist.
Ref.: 93, p. 81. Map: GC-8.

## DE MOTTE PARK

El.: c. 8000'                          Loc.: Coconino 1, F-7.8
Although De Motte Park is not actually at the Grand Canyon, it is seen by every automobile visitor to the North Rim. This open glade on the Kaibab Plateau was named by Maj. John Wesley Powell in August 1872, for a personal friend of Powell's, Dr. Harvey C. De Motte, professor of mathematics at Wesleyan University. Dr. De Motte traveled with the Grand Canyon exploration group for a short while. At one time this valley was referred to as V T Park. Here Van Slack and Thompson grazed cattle using the V T brand c. 1886. The brand belonged to the Valley Tannery of Orderville, Utah, where the two cattlemen lived. The range was abandoned in 1919 and the name De Motte Park re-established.
Ref.: *Utah Historical Quarterly*, VII, 1939, p. 91, (Shellbach flie); Notes of Uncle Jim Owen, Interview with Ernie Appling, July, 1951; History File; Grand Canyon Files; 181, p. 261; 42, pp. 318, 319. Map: B-5.

## DESERT VIEW POINT

El.: 7450'                                Loc.: East K-10
Descriptive.
Ref.: 151, p. 262. Map: GC-7.

## DEUBENDORFF RAPIDS

El.: c. 2500'                          Loc.: West GH-3
Deubendorff, a boatman for the 1909 Galloway-Stone Expedition, capsized in this rapid. The expedition used four boats, running from Green River, Wyoming, to Needles, California. Its trip was the fastest on record, taking two months and one week.
Ref.: Kolb. Map: GC-8.

## DE VACA TERRACE

El.: 4750'                                Loc.: West H-6
Pro.: /dəváka/
Cabeza de Vaca was a Spanish explorer who was lost c. 1528-1536 among the Indians on the Gulf of Mexico coast.
Ref.: *Nature* Notes III, No. 10, June 30, 1929 (Shellbach File). Map: GC-8.

## DICK PILLAR

El.: 6400'                    Loc.: West K-7,
                 at extreme end of Grand Scenic Divide
This rocky pillar was named for Robert Dick, a Scots baker-geologist who gave much assistance to Hugh Miller during the latter's studies of Old Red Sandstone at the Canyon.
Ref.:  93, p. 82. Map: None.

## DOX CASTLE

El.: 4000'                    Loc.: West K-6
Miss Virginia Dox was an early visitor to this location.
Ref.:  Barnes. Map: GC-8.

## DUNN BUTTE

El.: c. 5000'                 Loc.: East G-9
William H. Dunn was a member of Maj. John Wesley Powell's first Colorado River Expedition in 1869. He was killed with the Howland brothers by Indians. (cf. Howlands Butte).
Ref.:  A. H. Thompson, "Diary," *Utah Historical Quarterly*, p. 54 (Shellbach File). Map: GC-7.

## DUPPA BUTTE

El.: 6708'                    Loc.: East IJ-4.25
Bryan P. D. Duppa (b. France 1834, but a subject of England) served in the English army as a colonel. Following a duel with a fellow officer, he resigned and in 1863 emigrated as a remittance man to Arizona. In Arizona he was known as Darrel Duppa (*See* Gillette and Phoenix, Maricopa).
Ref.:  Barnes. Map: GC-7.

## DUTTON POINT

El.: 7555'                    Loc.: West J-5
This point was named for Maj. Clarence E. Dutton, a famous geologist and author of the *Tertiary History of the Grand Canyon District* (1882). Dutton was responsible for many place names in the Grand Canyon. Dutton Point was named by George Wharton James.
Ref.:  93, p. 40; 47. Map: GC-8.
**a.n. Dutton Canyon**     Map: GC-8     Grand Canyon, Coconino
Ref.:  151, p. 277.

## EHRENBERG POINT

El.: 6000'                    Loc.: East H-3.5
Herman Ehrenberg was a German engineer who emigrated to Arizona where he was a noted and highly respected mining engineer. (*See* Ehrenberg, Yuma).
Ref.:  None. Map: GC-7.

## ELVES CHASM

El.: 3200'                    Loc.: West G-7
This chasm contains fantastic forms of travertine. A trip into this beautiful little canyon is like a visit to fairyland.
Ref.:  Kolb. Map: GC-8

## ESCALANTE CREEK

El.: c. 3500'                 Loc.: East JI-10
Pro.:  /eskəlántey/
Maj. John Wesley Powell wrote that during the exploration of the Grand Canyon in 1869 his party came across a stream of which they believed themselves to be the discoverers. They named it to honor Fr. Hernando de Escalante, calling it Escalante River and the country which it drains, Escalante Basin. Dellenbaugh places this river a half day's journey from the San Juan River, which probably puts it in Utah, but there is nevertheless an Escalante Creek in the Grand Canyon named for the same explorer. Fr. Escalante explored the Hopi Village area either in 1774 or 1775 when he spent eight days at the Hopi villages and attempted to reach the Rio Grande de Cosninas (Colorado River). Hernando de Escalante Fontañeda left Santa Fe, New Mexico, in 1776 and traveled northwest through Utah, from whence he went southward, crossing the Grand Canyon probably at what is now Lee's Ferry or at the mouth of Kanab Wash. After crossing the Colorado, Fr. Escalante went to the Hopi and Zuñi villages, thence to Santa Fe. Herbert Gregory says that according to tradition, Escalante crossed the Colorado River at the Crossing of the Fathers (El Vado de Los Padres), at the upper end of Glen Canyon, Utah. Gregory notes that if this is true, Escalante was a very daring adventurer.
Ref.:  132, p. 138; 41, p. 210; 7, p. 216; 71, p. 17. Map: GC-7.
**a.n. Escalante Butte**     Map: GC-7     Grand Canyon, Coconino

## ESPEJO BUTTE

El.: c. 5750'                 Loc.: East LM-8
Pro.:  /espéyho/
Antonio de Espejo was a Spanish explorer who emigrated to America in search of riches. On November 10, 1582, with Fr. Bernardino Beltran, he led an expedition of many peons, one hundred fifty horses, and supplies to visit the tribes in northern Mexico. Ultimately, he arrived at the Zuñi villages where he heard about a great lake sixty day's journey away. He traveled on and is believed to have visited in the area of the present-day Jerome, (*q.v.*, Yavapai) before returning to Mexico City.
Ref.:  *Enciclopedia Universal Illustrada;* 11, pp. 22, 23. Map: GC-7.
**a.n. Espejo Creek**     Map: GC-7     Grand Canyon, Coconino

## EXCALIBUR

El.: 3500'                    Loc.: West L-5.5
This sharp, thin ridge about four hundred feet high bears a fancied resemblance to King Arthur's sword, Excalibur.
Ref.:  21, p. 295. Map: GC-8.

## FAN ISLAND

El.: 5100'                    Loc.: East J-5
                     N.W. of Shinumo Creek 1.5 miles
This is an isolated flat topped, fan-shaped butte.
Ref.:  Barnes. Map: None.

## FARVIEW POINT

El.: 8300'          Loc.: East G-2. Near Point Imperial
There is a broad view of the Painted Desert from this point.

**v.n. Fairview Point (corruption)**     Ref.: Shellbach
Ref.:    4, p. 491. Map: None.

## FISHTAIL CANYON

El.: c. 3000'                    Loc.: West EF-1-2
The upper end of this canyon branches like a fishtail.
Ref.:    Kolb. Map: GC-8.

**a.n. Fishtail Point**     Map: GC-8     Grand Canyon, Coconino

**Fishtail Rapids**     Map: GC-8     Grand Canyon, Coconino

## FOURMILE SPRING

El.: 5600'                    Loc.: East B-9.5
This large spring is four miles from Diamond Creek.
Ref.:    Kolb. Maps: GC-1; GC-7.

## GALLOWAY CANYON

El.: 3750'                    Loc.: West JG-3
Nathan Galloway was a Mormon trapper who made a trip
with William Richmond through the Grand Canyon in
two boats which they had constructed. They started near
the present Arizona state line on January 12, 1897, and
emerged from the canyon on February 3, reaching Needles
on February 10, 1897. Later Galloway made another trip
with the Julius F. Stone expedition.

Ref.:    "Hand Written List of 'Explorations of Colorado River',"
Matthes File, Envelope #2, Grand Canyon Files; 98, pp.
238-239. Map. GC-8.

## GARCES TERRACE

El.: c. 5000'                    Loc.: West G-4.5
Pro.: /garséys/
Fr. Francisco Garcés in 1775 made an exploratory and
missionizing trip among the Havasupai and other Indians
south of the Grand Canyon. While he was serving as
priest at the mission near the present-day Yuma, he was
killed by Indians on July 17, 1781.
Ref.:    None. Map: GC-8.

## GARDEN CREEK

El.: c. 4000'                    Loc.: East D-9.5-8.5
At the lower end of this creek Indians ran irrigation ditches
for their gardens, hence the name.
Ref.:    Kolb. Maps: GC-1; GC-7.

## GATAGAMA POINT

El.: 6102'                    Loc.: West DE-2
Pro.: /gǽtəgámə/
This is the name of an Indian family.
Ref.:    151, p. 319. Map: GC-8.

## GEIKIE PEAK

El.: 4750'                    Loc.: West L-9.1
Named for the Scots geologist, Sir Archibald Geikie (1835-
1924). He was director-general of the Geological Survey

for the United Kingdom. Deeply interested in volcanic geology, Geikie spent time studying geology at the Grand
Canyon where he found evidence to support his theories
concerning erosion.
Ref.:    151, p. 320. Map: None.

## GRAND CANYON (VILLAGE)

El.: 6866'                    Loc.: East D-10
This is the main tourist accommodation point and park
administration area for the Grand Canyon.

P.O. est. as Grandcanyon, March 14, 1902. Martin Buggeln,
p.m. Wells Fargo Station, 1904.

Ref.:    P.O. Records. Map: GC-7.

## GRAND SCENIC DIVIDE

El.: 5650'                    Loc.: West J-7-7.5
Here the granite of the Inner Gorge disappears from the
Grand Canyon, thereby at once effecting a vast change
in the scenery. To the east lie the magnificent buttes of the
canyon, while to the west the view is so different as to
seem scarcely the same canyon, hence the name.
Ref.:    93, pp. 81-82. Map: None.

## GRAND VIEW TRAIL

El.: 5000'                    Loc.: East G-10.5-12
Descriptive. The Grand View Trail was begun in June 1892
by Pete Berry (See Bright Angel Creek, a.n.), who built the
trail for access to his copper mine. He completed it in
February 1893. Berry and his partner sold out to the Canyon Copper Company in 1901.

The first hotel, the Grand View, was built at the Grand
Canyon in 1904. Meanwhile in 1902, the Grand Canyon
National Park had been created and the government undertook to force out private individuals in the area. This was
accomplished in connection with the Grand View Hotel in
1908. The old frame hotel has since been destroyed by
the Park Service.

P.O. est. as Grandview, November 27, 1903. Harry H. Smith,
p.m. Discont. November 30, 1908.

Ref.:    Theobald; P.O. Records; 93, p. 67. Map: GC-7.

**a.n. Grand View Caves**          Grand Canyon, Coconino
These caves were discovered in 1897 by Joseph Gildner,
who was camp cook for the Canyon Copper Company. The
first cave is over three hundred feet long and varies in height
from ten to eighty-five feet; the second cave is the same
length but higher.
Ref.:    93, p. 68.

**Horse Shoe Mesa Cave**          Grand Canyon, Coconino
By decision of the U. S. Geographic Board on Names December 2, 1937, the caves on the Grand View Trail were
designated Horse Shoe Mesa Caves. They are on the west
side of Horse Shoe Mesa.
Ref.:    Shellbach.

**Grandview Point**
El.: 7406'. Map: GC-7          Grand Canyon, Coconino
Ref.:    93, p. 66.

## GRANITE GORGE

El.: c. 3000'  Loc.: East KA-10-7; West LG-9-1
Large masses of pink and white granite give this forty-mile gorge its name.

Ref.: 4, p. 492; 151, p. 334. Map: GC-7; GC-8.

**a.n. Middle Granite Gorge**
Loc.: 10 miles below Granite Gorge. Four miles long.
Grand Canyon, Coconino

**Lower Granite Gorge**
Loc.: 100 miles below Granite Gorge. Fifty miles long, the upper six miles being in Coconino County.
Grand Canyon, Mohave and Coconino

Ref.: 151, p. 477.

**Granite Narrows** Map: GC-8 Grand Canyon, Coconino
**Granite Rapids**
Maps: GC-1; GC-7 Grand Canyon, Coconino

**v.n. Monument Rapids**
A barrier of boulders was tumbled down here from Monument Creek, a side tributary.

Ref.: 4, p. 484; 98, p. 225.

## GREAT THUMB POINT

El.: 6755'  Loc.: West FG-2
Descriptive.

Ref.: None. Map: GC-8.

**a.n. Great Thumb Mesa** Map: GC-8 Grand Canyon, Coconino
Ref.: Barnes.

## GREENLAND SPRING

El.: c. 3000'  Loc.: East FG-4
Descriptive.

This spring lies on what is known as the Greenland or Walhalla Plateau (See *a.n.*).

Ref.: Shellbach File. Maps: GC-1; GC-7.

**a.n. Greenland Lake** Coconino

**Greenland Point** Coconino

**Walhalla Plateau** Map: GC-1 Coconino
This is the name which has been designated as the correct one for what is sometimes called the Greenland Plateau. "Walhalla" was suggested by Francois Matthes in 1902. He did not at that time know that the Mormon cattlemen referred to the plateau as Greenland.

Ref.: 146. p. 799; Francois Matthes, Letter (copy,), Chairman of Geographic Board, May 6, 1925; Envelope No. 6, Grand Canyon Files.

## HAKATAI CANYON

El.: c. 3700'  Loc.: West IJ-5-6
Pro.: /hákətay/
This is the Havasupai name for the Colorado River.

Ref.: 93, p. 230. Map: GC-8.

**a.n. Hakatai Rapids** Map: GC-8 Grand Canyon, Coconino

## HALL BUTTE

El.: c. 4500'  Loc.: East G-9
Andrew Hall was a member of Maj. John Wesley Powell's expedition through the Grand Canyon in 1869.

Ref.: Barnes. Map: GC-7.

## HANCE CREEK

El.: c. 3500'  Loc.: East HI-12-10.5
Hance Creek was named for John Hance, a pioneer resident on the South Rim. No reference to the history of the Grand Canyon would be complete without mentioning "Captain" John Hance (b. Tennessee 1839; d. January 6, 1919), who was one of Arizona's most colorful characters. Hance served as a Confederate during the Civil War until he was taken prisoner, whereupon he switched sides and fought with the boys in blue. After the war Hance moved to Arizona from Missouri. For many years he hauled fodder for stock at the army post at Camp Verde.

In 1884 Hance took up a homestead on the South Rim of the Grand Canyon. He was quick to see the appeal the canyon would have for tourists, although at the time he himself was more interested in locating mines in the canyon. With an eye toward both the tourist trade and the hauling of ores, Hance widened an old Indian trail, which became the first tourist trail down to the river bed from the South Rim. The first tourist to use the Hance Trail was Edward E. Ayer (*see* Ayer Peak, Coconino) in 1885. In the same year Hance constructed the first tourist accommodations, a log cabin at Glendale Springs.

Hance's ready wit and endless supply of stories made him popular with tourists. According to Hance, for instance, he dug the Grand Canyon and put the dirt into making the San Francisco Peaks.

Ref.: Hart; 168, pp. 19, 20, 21; 153, p. 162; Caption on Hance picture, Naturalists Headquarters, Grand Canyon. Map: GC-7.

**a.n. Hance Rapids** Grand Canyon, Coconino

**v.n. Red Canyon Rapids**

**a.n. Hance Trail** Map: GC-7 Grand Canyon, Coconino
**Tourist** Map: C-10 Grand Canyon, Coconino
The first post office at the Grand Canyon had the appropriate name of Tourist. Its postmaster was Capt. John Hance, who had the office at his ranch.

P.O. est. May 10, 1897. John Hance, p.m. Discont. April 12, 1899.

Ref.: Theobald; P.O. Records.

## HANCOCK BUTTE

El.: 7629'  Loc.: East GH-4
Capt. William Augustus Hancock (b. Massachusetts, May 17, 1831; d. March 24, 1902) arrived at Fort Yuma in 1864 as a private with the California Volunteers. He was promoted to a second lieutenancy in 1865. After serving as post trader at Camp Reno, 1869-1870, Hancock moved to the Salt River Valley in August 1870, where he surveyed Phoenix townsite and erected its first house. He served as the first sheriff of Maricopa County.

Ref.: APHS Files. Map: GC-7.

## HANSBROUGH POINT

El.: 5000'  Loc.: East L-2.6
In Marble Canyon below Vasey's Paradise (*q.v.*) Hansbrough Point lies squarely in the middle of a rapid. The Point towers over seven hundred feet. Cut on the huge shaft is the name of Peter Hansbrough, a member of

the Robert Brewster Stanton expedition in 1890 (*see* Stanton Point). Hansbrough, while attempting to push his boat off an overhanging shelf on which it had lodged, was drowned when his boat overturned. His body was found the next day and was buried near the shaft on which his name is carved.

Ref.:   42, pp. 361, 335-356; Shellbach File. Map: None.

## HATTAN TEMPLE

El.: c. 5500′                                 Loc.: East EF-7

Andrew Hattan served as a cook and hunter for Maj. John Wesley Powell's second expedition through the Grand Canyon in 1872.

**v.n. Hattan Butte**

Ref.:   Barnes. Maps: GC-1; GC-7.

## HAVASU CANYON

El.: c. 3500′                                 Loc.: Coconino 1, AB-10-11
Pro.: /hǽvəsuw/                      Havasu: *haha*, "water"; *vasu*, "blue";
                                                          ("blue water")

The end of Havasu Canyon which is closest to the bed of the Colorado River bears the name, but that part lying closer to the plateau south of the Grand Canyon has for years been called Cataract Canyon (*q.v.*, Coconino).

Fr. Francisco Garcés in 1776 is the first white man known to have journeyed down from the canyon rim to visit the Havasupai Indians. Garcés' name for the creek was Rio Jabesua de San Antonio and also Rio Cabezua. The creek is the largest stream from the south feeding into the Colorado River.

The Havasupai Indians apparently resided at one time in the Little Colorado Valley east of the San Francisco Peaks, where the Hopi Indians referred to them as Cosninos. Although Garcés reported the tribe in Havasu Canyon in 1776, some members were still in the Little Colorado Valley as late as 1850. When Maj. John Wesley Powell visited the valley in c. 1870, a Havasupai chief showed him ruins once inhabited by the Havasupai. The peaceful Havasupaia were driven by other Indians to seek security in the depths of the canyon.

Powell referred to Havasu Creek as Coanini Creek (variation of Cosnino). Dr. A. H. Thompson of Powell's party said he believed Coanini Creek and the one called Cataract Creek by Lt. Joseph C. Ives were the same.

**v.n. Lee's Canyon**

John D. Lee (*See* Lee's Ferry, Coconino) hid in the canyon to avoid capture for his part in the Mountain Meadows Massacre.

Ref.:   42, p. 382; Schroeder; A. H. Thompson, "Diary," Entry for July 21, 1872, *Utah Historical Quarterly* (Shellbach File); 88, I, 537; 112, pp. 69-70; 24, p. 57; 132, p. 197; 139, p. 12. Map: GC-8.

**a.n.**

There are five falls in Havasu Canyon.

**Fifty Foot Falls**                            Grand Canyon, Coconino
Loc.: First in the series. It was created in 1932 by a flash flood.

Ref.:   24, p. 659.

**Navajo Falls**
Loc.: Second in the series. Map: GC-8
                                                    Grand Canyon, Coconino

**Bridal Veil Falls**   Loc.: Third falls. Grand Canyon, Coconino
The lacy streamers of these falls are one hundred seventy feet high and five hundred broad.

**v.n. Havasu Falls**

**a.n. Mooney Falls**
Loc.: Fourth in the series              Grand Canyon, Coconino
James Mooney was a prospector who in 1880 attempted to descend the two hundred twenty foot falls by sitting in a loop of rope while Indians lowered him over the cliff. The rope caught in a crack and Mooney swung helpless for two days while everything possible was done to save him. On the third day he fell to his death. Four years later his remains were still at the foot of the cliff. They were later recovered and buried at the top of the falls which are named for the ex-sailor.

Ref.:   Barnes; 4, p. 488.

**Beaver Falls**          Map: GC-8          Grand Canyon, Coconino
Many beaver used to be at this fifth falls in the series.

**a.n. Beaver Canyon**       Map: GC-8       Grand Canyon, Coconino

**Havasu Rapids**       Map: GC-6       Grand Canyon, Coconino

**Supai**
El.: 3201′. Map: GC-6              Grand Canyon, Coconino
This is the official name for the Havasupai village which is the center of tribal activities. This village is subject to severe floods. In 1911 a rim-to-rim forty-foot wall of water swept away all buildings while the Indians clung to the cliff sides and watched the raging torrent.

Ref.:   24, p. 671; 22, p. 655.

**Havasupai Reservation**              Grand Canyon, Coconino
A "Suppai" reservation was created on June 8, 1880, but the area underwent later changes, with the present 518 acres finally being set aside on March 31, 1882, for the "Yavai Suppai" Indians. An estimated two hundred thirty-five Havasupai are on the reservation. The tribe also has allotted for its use 2540 acres in Cataract Canyon.

Ref.:   88, II, 374; "Annual Report of the Arizona Commission of Indian Affairs, 1954, 1955, 1956," p. 16.

**Havasu Hilltop**      El.: 5415′      Grand Canyon, Coconino
From this point the fourteen-mile narrow Topocoba Trail twists and drops from the rim into Havasu Canyon. In the first mile and a half it descends over one thousand feet, during which the traveler encounters at least twenty-nine switchbacks. The trail was built in the last several years to replace an old wagon road once used by canyon miners.

Ref.:   24, pp. 655, 656; 93, p. 55.

**Topocoba Spring**      El.: 4975′      Grand Canyon, Coconino
This spring is at the base of the first abrupt drop via the Topocoba Trail.

**v.n. Tope Kobe Spring**

**a.n. Topocobya Canyon**                 Grand Canyon, Coconino
This is the side canyon of Havasu Canyon through which the Topocoba Trail descends and in which Topocoba Spring is located.

Ref.:   93, p. 174.

**Havasupai Point**              Grand Canyon, Coconino
The former name for this place was Hotel Point or Bass Hotel Point.

Ref.:   W. W. Bass Materials, Wickenburg, Arizona (Shellbach File).

## HAWKINS BUTTE

El.: c. 5250′                                 Loc.: East FG-9

W. R. Hawkins served as hunter and cook for Maj. John Wesley Powell's first Grand Canyon expedition in 1869.

Ref.:   Barnes. Maps: GC-1; GC-7.

## HAYDEN MOUNTAIN

El.: 8350′ Loc.: East H-3

Charles Trumbull Hayden (b. Conn. 1825) came to Arizona in 1857 on the first Butterfield Overland stage. In 1870 he established Hayden's Ferry, now called Tempe (q.v., Maricopa).

Ref.: Barnes. Map: GC-7.

## HERMIT BASIN

El.: 3500′ Loc.: East B-9

Louis Boucher was a French-Canadian who settled at Dripping Spring (see Boucher Creek). He established Hermit Camp to provide sleeping and eating accommodations for tourists who came down the trail to the Colorado River bed. His was the first provision for travelers near the river.

Ref.: Emery C. Kolb, Letter, February 27, 1947, State Library Files; 93, p. 76. Maps: GC-1; GC-7.

a.n. Hermit Creek   Maps: GC-1; GC-7 Grand Canyon, Coconino
   Hermit Rapids   Maps: GC-1; GC-7 Grand Canyon, Coconino
   Hermit Rim   Map: GC-7   Grand Canyon, Coconino
   Hermit Trail   Maps: GC-1; GC-7 Grand Canyon, Coconino
   This trail was constructed by the S.F.R.R. and the Fred Harvey System in 1912. It was named by Mary Jane Colter, architect of the El Tovar Hotel.

Ref.: Kolb; 93, pp. 73, 74, 75.

## HILLERS BUTTE

El.: c. 5500′ Loc.: East DE-7.4

John K. Hillers was a photographer on the second Grand Canyon expedition under Maj. John Wesley Powell in 1871-1872.

Ref.: Barnes; Kolb. Maps: GC-1; GC-7.

## HINDU AMPHITHEATER

El.: c. 4500′ Loc.: East AC-6

In 1882 Maj. Clarence E. Dutton wrote that this amphitheater was marked by its "profusion and richness [which] suggests an oriental character."

Ref.: 47, p. 169. Maps: GC-1; GC-7.

## HOPI POINT

El.: 7071′ Loc.: East C-9.5

Pro.: /hówpiˆ/ Hopi: Hopitu, "peaceful ones"

This point was named for the Hopi Indians, who live on the Hopi Reservation (see Hopi Villages, Navajo).

v.n. Rowe's Point   (cf. Rowe's Well)

Ref.: None. Maps: GC-1; GC-7.

a.n. Hopi Wall   Map: GC-7   Grand Canyon, Coconino

## HOTOUTA CANYON

El.: c. 3150′ Loc.: West JL-6.7

Pro.: /howtᵃwtθ/

Tom Hotouta was the son of the last great Havasupai chief, "Navaho," according to George Wharton James.

v.n. Hotauta Canyon (corruption)

Ref.: 93, p. 78. Map: GC-8.

a.n. Hotouta Amphitheater   Grand Canyon, Coconino

## HOWLANDS BUTTE, THE

El.: 5584′ Loc.: East FG-8.5

Seneca and W. R. Howland (brothers) were members of Maj. John Wesley Powell's first Grand Canyon expedition in 1869. When the party encountered a severe rapid after several harrowing experiences, the Howland brothers and William H. Dunn refused to proceed through the canyon, believing that their lives were in extreme danger. They obtained permission from Powell to leave the expedition, whereupon they clambered up the canyon walls to the rim. Here they were killed by Indians on Shivwits Plateau.

Ref.: A. H. Thompson, "Diary," Utah Historical Quarterly, p. 54, footnote (Shellbach File). Maps: GC-1; GC-7.

## HUALAPAI CANYON

El.: c. 3700′ Loc.: West AB-8-7

Pro.: /wálpay/

The Hualapai Indians, for whom this canyon was named, today live on a reservation set aside for them (see Hualapai Indian Reservation, Mohave). In early Arizona territorial days, the Hualapai Indians were even more fierce than the dreaded Apaches.

Ref.: None. Map: GC-8.

## HUBBELL BUTTE

El.: 6450′ Loc.: East IJ-6

Juan Lorenzo Hubbell (b. Pajarito, N.M., November 1853; d. November 11, 1930) settled on the Navajo Indian Reservation in 1871 as a pioneer trader. During his lifetime he served as Coconino County sheriff and also as a member of the 17th Territorial Government and the first State Senate. His descendants are prominent traders in the Navajo country, with headquarters at Ganado. This butte was named at the suggestion of Will C. Barnes.

Ref.: Barnes. Map: GC-7.

## HUTTON BUTTE

El.: 5500′ Loc.: East I-4.25

Oscar Hutton (b. Virginia, c. 1830; d. Tucson, 1873) was an Arizona pioneer reputed to have killed more Indians than any other man in Arizona. Hutton came to Arizona in 1863. A year later he was at the Mowry Mine (q.v., Santa Cruz). Hutton served with the Arizona Volunteer Infantry at Calabasas as a second lieutenant, the only officer in the company. From that time on, Hutton's life was devoted to service as a military man, Indian fighter, interpreter, guide, and packer. In December 1864, Hutton and his men moved to Camp Date Creek. On August 13, 1866, they battled at Grapevine Springs with Indians, killing twenty-three. Discharged on November 3, 1866, Hutton then returned to southern Arizona where he served as a packer and interpreter. In 1871 he was a guide at Camp Grant where in court he came to the defense of the Indians against an accusation that those at Camp Grant were involved in Indian raids on settlers and emigrants. Hutton Butte and Hutton Peak in Gila County are named for him.

Ref.: Oscar Hutton File, APHS. Map: GC-7.

## HUXLEY TERRACE

El.: 5500'                          Loc.: West J-7

Huxley is the center plateau of three named after evolutionary scientists. The others are Darwin and Wallace. Thomas Henry Huxley (1825-1895) was an English biologist and philosopher on whom the publication in 1859 of Charles Darwin's *The Origin of the Species* had a tremendous effect. Huxley's lectures and essays in support of Darwin's theory won him the nickname of "Darwin's bulldog."

Ref.:   93, p. 82. Map: GC-8.

## IMPERIAL POINT

El.: 8801'                          Loc.: East GH-2.5

This is the highest point along either rim of the Grand Canyon. It may, therefore, have been called "imperial."

Ref.:   None. Map: GC-7.

## INDIAN GARDEN

El.: 3876'                          Loc.: East D-9

George Wharton James wrote that Indian Garden lay in the center of what was called Angel Plateau, and that the garden had been cultivated by a Havasupai family years before white men saw the spot. It is today a happy resting point for those who make the descent into the canyon along the Bright Angel Trail.

Ref.:   93, p. 33. Maps: GC-1; GC-7.

## ISIS TEMPLE

El.: 7028'                          Loc.: East C-8

George Wharton James said that this temple-like formation was named for the goddess of the Egyptians, and that in front of it are two notable great cloisters.

Ref.:   93, p. 31. Map: GC-1.

## IVES POINT

El.: 6600'                          Loc.: West H-5

Lt. Joseph Christmas Ives was the first military man to explore the Colorado River to its headwaters for navigation. He then made a surveying trip from west to east across Arizona (1851).

Ref.:   None. Map: GC-8.

## JEFFORDS POINT

El.: c. 5500'                       Loc.: East IJ-5

Thomas Jefferson Jeffords (b. Chautauqua County, New York, 1832; d. February 19, 1914) came to Arizona in 1862. The redheaded and red-bearded Jeffords served as an Indian trader and government scout. He was a close personal friend of the famous Chiricahua chief, Cochise. Jeffords took the message from Gen. O. O. Howard to Cochise in 1870 offering to make a peace with the Indians and to create a reservation. When the Chiricahua Reservation came into being, Jeffords served as its first Indian Agent.

Ref.:   Barnes; APHS Files. Map: GC-7.

## JOHNSON POINT

El.: 5100'                          Loc.: East E-7.6

Fred Johnson was a Grand Canyon National Park Ranger who drowned accidentally in 1929 near here while in performance of official duties.

Ref.:   Barnes. Maps: GC-1; GC-7.

## JONES POINT

El.: 5300'                          Loc.: East EF-7.75

S. V. Jones was a member of Maj. John Wesley Powell's second Grand Canyon expedition (1871-1872).

Ref.:   Barnes. Map: GC-7.

## KAIBAB PLATEAU

El.: 8200'              Loc.: East AH-2-6; West JL-1-2.5
Pro.:  /káybæb/         Piute:  *kaiuw*, "mountain";
                                *a-vwi*, "lying down"

In his progress report dated April 30, 1874, Maj. John Wesley Powell noted that the great plateau forming the North Rim of the Grand Canyon was called by the Indians *kai-vav-wi* ("a mountain lying down"). This was rendered phonetically in English as Kaibab Plateau. Early white settlers referred to it as Buckskin Mountain or as Kaibab Mountain. The Piutes refer to the great forests lying on this plateau as the Kaibabits.

Ref.:   133a, p. 26; Shellbach File. Maps: GC-1; GC-7; GC-8.
a.n. **Kaibab National Forest**   Maps: GC-1; GC-7; GC-8  Coconino
        This national forest was created by presidential signature in 1908.
      **Kaibab Trail**   Maps: GC-1; GC-7  Grand Canyon, Coconino
        This is the trail down from the North Rim of the canyon.
      **Kaibab**                  Grand Canyon, Coconino
        This was the first name of the post office later known as North Rim.
P.O. est. June 16, 1926 as Kaibab. Woodruff Rust, p.m. Rescinded October 12, 1926. P.O. re-est. November 16, 1927. Harry E. Brown, p.m. Name changed to Kaibab Forest, January 28, 1928. Name changed to North Rim, June 1, 1947. Discont. August 31, 1955.

## KANAB CANYON

El.: c. 8000'                       Loc.: East A-3.5
Pro.:  /kənáb/ or       Piute:  *Kanab*, "willows"
       /kənǽb/

It was at the mouth of this canyon that the Powell Grand Canyon expedition met Joe Hamblin, George Adair, and Nathan Adams — packers for the expedition — who had traveled down the canyon and waited with badly needed rations for the explorers.

Ref.:   41, p. 241; APHS Names File. Map: GC-7.
a.n. **Kanab Creek**
        Maps: GC-2, B-5, C-3. Grand Canyon, Coconino and Utah
        Many willow trees along this creek give it its name.
      **Kanab Desert**            Grand Canyon, Coconino
        This is a term used by Maj. Clarence E. Dutton in 1882 to describe the area in the center of which Kanab Canyon is located.
Ref.:   47, p. 124.
      **Kanab Rapids**   Map: GC-8   Grand Canyon, Coconino
      **Kanav Spring**            Grand Canyon, Coconino
        A. H. Thompson on August 10, 1872, located this place as ten miles southeast of Rock Springs and seven miles north of the Colorado River.
Ref.:   Shellbach File.

## KANGAROO HEADLAND

El.: 6055' Loc.: West D-3-4

The outline form of this headland resembles a kangaroo.

Ref.: Barnes. Map: GC-8.

## KIBBEY BUTTE

El.: 7500' Loc.: East GH-5

Joseph H. Kibbey (b. Indiana) came to Arizona in 1887. A distinguished jurist, Kibbey specialized in laws pertaining to irrigation. On August 5, 1889, he was appointed to the Arizona Supreme Court, but resigned in order to accept an appointment as governor in May 1905. He served until 1909. Kibbey was a prime mover in the formation of the Salt River Valley Water Users Association. The butte was named by Will C. Barnes.

Ref.: Barnes; APHS Files. Map: GC-7.

## KOLB NATURAL BRIDGE

El.: 5420' Loc.: East J-3

Joe Hamblin served as a packer for Maj. John Wesley Powell in 1871-1872. In 1920 Jack Roak talked to John Brown, who was with Joe Hamblin when the two men saw this natural bridge in 1871. The bridge was forgotten for many years until Sen. Barry Goldwater, while flying over the Grand Canyon in December 1953 noticed the great span about twenty-five hundred feet below Point Imperial on the North Rim. It was several months before Goldwater visited the place (October 1954), but he did so in a helicopter to establish definite location.

The natural bridge has a span of two hundred feet at its base, and it is at least two hundred feet to the underside of its arch. The bridge was named for Emery C. Kolb (b. Wilkinsburg, Pa., 1881). Ellsworth Kolb, his brother, was the first to arrive at the Grand Canyon, where Emory joined him in 1902 to work in an asbestos mine. However, the mine was closed and Emory bought a camera outfit. With it in 1903 he moved permanently to the Grand Canyon, where he is known to thousands for his pictures and for his daily lecture. The Kolb brothers made the trip through the Grand Canyon twice and have made hundreds of explorations within the canyon walls.

Ref.: Letter (copy), Jesse L. Nusbaum, Sr., to Otis T. Marsten, September 6, 1955, Grand Canyon Files; *Chicago Tribune*, November 30, 1954, n.p.; Kolb; 59, pp. 30-31. Map: GC-7 (Nankoweap Butte).

a.n. Kolb Point Grand Canyon, Coconino

## KWAGUNT VALLEY

El.: c. 5000' Loc.: East KM-2-6
Pro.: /kwágənt/

Maj. Clarence E. Dutton referred to this place in 1880 by the name Quagunt Valley. It was so called by Maj. John Wesley Powell in 1869 after an Indian named Quagunt (or Kwagunt) who was very friendly to the exploring party. The Piute Indian said that he owned the valley, which his father, who occupied it before him, had given to him.

Ref.: A. H. Thompson, *Diary*, October 22, 1872 entry, *Utah Historical Quarterly*, p. 102, (Shellbach File); 47, p. 180. Map: None.

a.n. Kwagunt Butte
El.: 5000'. Map: GC-7 Grand Canyon, Coconino
Kwagunt Canyon Map: GC-7 Grand Canyon, Coconino
Kwagunt Creek Map: GC-7 Grand Canyon, Coconino
Kwagunt Hollow Map: B-4 Grand Canyon, Coconino
Kwagunt Rapids Map: GC-7 Grand Canyon, Coconino

## LAVA FALLS

El.: 4000' Loc.: East K-8

This was so called by members of the Powell Grand Canyon expedition on August 25, 1871. According to Dellenbaugh, the canyon apeared to have been once filled with lava to a depth of fifteen hundred feet. They named the descent Lava Falls. Maj. Clarence E. Dutton in 1882 wrote that lava had burst forth at both sides of the canyon, damming up the river to a height of about eight hundred feet but that the river broke through again, creating the canyon and the Lava Falls Rapids. The lava flow extends down the river about sixty miles. This is probably the place which Thompson in his "Diary" for March 31, 1872, refers to as Lava Ridge.

Ref.: A. H. Thompson, "Diary" March 31, 1872, *Utah Historical Quarterly*, p. 73 (Shellbach); 41, p. 192; 42, p. 224; 47, plate XIX. Map: GC-6.

a.n. Lava Canyon Map: GC-7 Grand Canyon, Coconino
Lava Creek Map: GC-7 Grand Canyon, Coconino
Lava Butte Map: GC-7 Grand Canyon, Coconino

## LE CONTE PLATEAU

El.: c. 3500' Loc.: West K-8

Dr. Arnold Guyot before 1916 named this plateau to honor Prof. Joseph Le Conte, a famous geologist who took observations with a stationary barometer during Guyot's explorations in this locality.

Ref.: 151, p. 453. Map: GC-8.

## LIPAN POINT

El.: 7400' Loc.: East JK-11
Pro.: /líypan/ or /lípən/

This is another instance of a point being named to commemorate an Indian tribe. The first mention of the Lipan Indians occurred in 1699 when they were named as allies of the Comanches. During the 18th century the tribe occupied the area drained by the San Saba and Colorado Rivers in Texas. Their name has been rendered in phonetic spelling as Lee Pawnee, Seepan, Sinapan, and Gipanes, in addition to numerous others. Francois E. Matthes in 1902 changed the name of this point from Lincoln to Lipan.

Ref.: 35, p. 460, (Note 14), No. 8; Shellbach File. Map: GC-7.

## LOOKOUT POINT

El.: c. 4500' Loc.: East B-9.25
Descriptive.

Ref.: None. Maps: GC-7; GC-1.

## LYELL BUTTE

El.: c. 6800'                        Loc.: East EF-10
Sir Charles Lyell (1798-1875) was a British geologist whose
noted work, *The Principles of Geology* (published 1830
and 1832) was a direct forerunner of the theory of evolution advanced by Charles Darwin.
Ref.: None. Map: GC-1.

## MAIDEN'S BREAST, THE

El.: 5400'                          Loc.: East CD-9.5
George Wharton James noted that the Havasupais gave
the name meaning "maiden's breast" to a formation at the
end of Maricopa Point. The name came from the fact
that the formation was crowned with "a small nipple in
red sandstone." Regarding its size, James adds that it was
"quite a height for any earthly maiden."
Ref.: 93, p. 32. Map: None.

## MALLERY GROTTO

El.: c. 5000'                        Loc.: East B-10
Just under the rim at the extreme west of the El Tovar
Amphitheater is a cave about one hundred fifty feet long.
It contains Indian pictographs. The grotto is named for
Garrick Mallery, the "great authority on the pictographs
of the North American Indians."
Ref.: 93, pp. 23, 24. Map: None.

## MANU TEMPLE

El.: 7192'                          Loc.: East DE-6.5
This formation was named for the great law giver of the
Hindus.
Ref.: 93, p. 30. Maps: GC-1; GC-7.

## MANZANITA POINT

El.: c. 5000'                        Loc.: East FG-6
Pro.: /mǽnzəníytə/ or              Spanish: "little apple"
  /mánzəníytə/
Col. John White in the 1920's lived at the Grand Canyon.
Late one season he visited the North Rim and while ascend-
ing Bright Angel Creek, he noticed a large manzanita
bush. There he wrote on a piece of wood "Manzanita
Point." When Stephen Jones later showed White on a map
where Manzanita Point was supposedly located, White said
that his point was farther down Bright Angel Creek. When
Jones next crossed the canyon and ascended Bright Angel
Creek, he watched for manzanita bushes and located a large
circular cluster about a mile down from where Manzanita
Point shows on the map. The manzanita point named
by White is approximately opposite the mouth of The
Transept.
Ref.: Stephen P. Jones, Letter, February 7, 1930, Grand Can-
      yon Place Names File. Maps: GC-1; GC-7.
**a.n. Manzanita Creek**     Map: GC-1     Grand Canyon, Coconino

## MARBLE GORGE

El.: c. 3500'                        Loc.: East JL-2-6
Maj. John Wesley Powell on August 9, 1869, wrote that
his exploring party passed between cliffs of marble in which
were a great number of caves, eroded on a grand scale.

He named the gorge Marble Canyon, noting that the walls
towered hundreds of feet in the air, rising at least to thirty-
five hundred feet at the canyon's lower end. The distance
through this canyon measured nearly sixty-one miles, during which the party ran through a rapid per mile. The men
made four portages with their boats, using ropes, through
extremely swift currents and whirlpools.
Ref.: A. H. Thompson, "Diary," August 22, 1872, *Utah His-
      torical Quarterly*, p. 94 (Shellbach File); 132, pp. 76-77,
      79; 151, p. 501. Map: GC-7.
**a.n. Marble Canyon**                Grand Canyon, Coconino
      This post office formerly existed at the trading post on the
      north side of Navajo Bridge across the Colorado River.
      P.O. est. October 12, 1927. Mrs. Florence L. Lowery, p.m.
      **Marble Flats**      Map: GC-7      Grand Canyon, Coconino

## MARCOS TERRACE

El.: 5000'                          Loc.: West H-7
Pro.: /márkos/
Fr. Marcos de Niza (b. Nice) was the first white man to
enter what is now Arizona. In the spring of 1539, he left
Mexico City on a missionizing trip to the north. He got
almost within sight of the Zuñi Villages and believed them
to be the fabled Seven Cities of Cibola, but Marcos did
not visit the Zuñi Villages. He was prevented from doing
so by the fact that his advance agent, the Negro Estevan,
had been killed by the Indians and Marcos feared to continue his journey alone. He carried back to Mexico rumors
of wealth which the Negro through various Indians had sent
to him. He returned to Mexico in mid-summer 1539, where
he met Coronado as he passed through New Galicia. The
friar's story sounded like the answer to the Spaniard's
prayer for untold and easily obtained wealth, and Coronado
was soon in charge of an expedition to go to the seven cities.
Ref.: 182, pp. 381, 382, 346, 361. Map: GC-8.

## MARICOPA POINT

El.: 7050'                          Loc.: East CD-9.5
Pro.: /mǽrikowpə/
This point was named to honor the Maricopa Indians, a
peaceful tribe living in south central Arizona.
Ref.: None. Map: GC-7.

## MARION POINT

El.: 6000'                          Loc.: East H-1.3
Will C. Barnes named this point for John H. Marion (b.
Louisiana 1835; d. July 27, 1891), who published the
*Arizona Miner* at Prescott for many years. (See Marion,
Yavapai.)
Ref.: Barnes; APHS Files. Map: GC-7.

## MARSH BUTTE

El.: 4730'                          Loc.: East A-8
George Wharton James named this place for the American
paleontologist, Othniel Charles Marsh (1831-1899). Marsh
investigated fossils of the western United States. Among
his numerous discoveries were the fossilized early ancestors
of horses in America. For many years Marsh was in charge
of the division of vertebrate paleontology of the U.S.G.S.
Ref.: 93, p. 40. Maps: GC-1; GC-7.

## MASONIC TEMPLE

El.: 6200'                                        Loc.: West J-5
This is one the masons didn't build.
Ref.: 151, p. 506. Map: GC-8.

## MATKATAMIBA CANYON

El.: 3750'                                        Loc.: West CB-5.5-3
Pro.: /mætkǽtəmiybə/
Matkatamiba is the name of an Indian family.
Ref.: 151, p. 507. Map: GC-8.

**a.n. Matkatamiba Mesa**   Map: GC-8   Grand Canyon, Coconino
   **Matkatamiba Rapids**
   El.: 2985'. Map: GC-8                 Grand Canyon, Coconino

## MATTHES POINT

El.: 7864'                                        Loc.: East H-7.75
                  Second point west of Cape Royal, North Rim.
Pro.: /mǽθis/
In 1902 Francois E. Matthes was in charge of the making
of the topographic map of the Grand Canyon and was
responsible for those eminences named for mythological
deities as well as for those named for southwestern Indian tribes.
Ref.: Harold C. Bryant, Letter, April 9, 1956, Grand Canyon
     Names File. Map: None.

## MESCALERO POINT

El.: 6635'                                        Loc.: West L-10
Pro.: /méskəléro/
The Mescalero Apaches were a tribe living in southwestern
New Mexico.
Ref.: 151, p. 515. Map: GC-8.

## MILLET POINT

El.: c. 6000'          Loc. West GH-1. Sec. 18, T. 35 N.,
                       R. 1 W., Grand Canyon National Park
Barnes associates the name of Francis David Millett (1846-
1912), an American artist who drowned when the *Titanic*
sank, with this place. Aside from Barnes' suggestion, the
editor has been unable to unearth further evidence linking
to the Grand Canyon the name of this artist, whose water
colors and oils are part of many public collections.
Ref.: Barnes. Map: None.

## MIMBRENO POINT

El.: c. 6000'                                     Loc.: West L-10
Pro.: /mimbréynyo/          Spanish: "willow twigs"
The Mimbreño Apaches lived in southwestern New Mexico.
Ref.: 151, p. 521. Map: GC-8.

## MOHAVE POINT

El.: 7000'                                        Loc.: East C-9.5
Pro.: /mowháviy/          Mohave: "three mountains"
The Mohave Indians lived along the Colorado River. Their
name came from the fact that the tribe lived near The
Needles (*q.v.*, Mohave).
Ref.: None. Maps: GC-1; GC-7.

## MONUMENT CREEK

El.: c. 3000'                                     Loc.: East BC-9.5-8.5
A single shaft about a hundred feet high is visible from the
rim at this point.
Ref.: Kolb. Maps: GC-1; GC-7.

**a.n. Monument Rapids**          Grand Canyon, Coconino
   These rapids are also called Granite Falls.

## MORAN POINT

El.: 7157'                                        Loc.: East I-11.5
Thomas Moran was an artist who first visited the North
Rim in 1873 with Maj. John Wesley Powell. His paintings
of the Grand Canyon are masterpieces. One hangs in the
nation's capitol in Washington. This painting was largely
responsible for making the American public aware of the
wonders of the Grand Canyon.
Ref.: 98, p. 219; 93, p. 57. Map: GC-7.

## MUAV CANYON

El.: c. 5000'                                     Loc.: West JK-3-6
Pro.: /múwæb/             Piute: "divide," "pass"
This canyon was probably so named because of the presence of the Muav Saddle (El.: 7050', Map: GC 8), a pass
in the canyon rim at the top of the north wall. Powell spoke
of it by this name in 1869.
Ref.: Barnes' Notes; 47, p. 265; 151, p. 534. Map: GC-8.

## NAJI POINT

El.: 6250'                                        Loc.: East H-6
Pro.: /náčiy/ or /náji/
Natchi, the son of the Chiracahua chief Cochise, in 1876,
succeeded his father as chief of the Chiracahua tribe. Ten
years later he was sent with other Chiracahua Apaches
in exile to Florida.
**v.n. Natchi Point**
Ref.: Barnes; 151, p. 542. Map: GC-7.

**a.n. Natchi Canyon**
   Loc.: S.W. of Naji Point ½ mile.   Grand Canyon, Coconino

## NANKOWEAP BUTTE

El.: 6321'                                        Loc.: East K-2-3
Pro.: /nǽnkowiyp/         Piute: "place where Indians
                                     had [a] fight"
According to information on file at the Grand Canyon,
a Piute Indian named Johnny said that a fight between
Indians took place at Big Saddle at the head of Nancoweap
(*sic*). It was so called when Maj. John Wesley Powell went
through in 1871-1872.
Ref.: Shellbach; 42, p. 326. Map: GC-7.

**a.n. Nankoweap Canyon**  Map: GC-7   Grand Canyon, Coconino
   **Nankoweap Creek**     Map: GC-7   Grand Canyon, Coconino
   **Nankoweap Mesa**      Map: GC-7   Grand Canyon, Coconino
   **Nankoweap Rapids**    Map: GC-7   Grand Canyon, Coconino
   **Nankoweap Valley**                Grand Canyon, Coconino
   This was the valley called by A. H. Thompson on October
   19, 1872, the Nankoweep Valley.
Ref.: A. H. Thompson "Diary," October 19, 1872, *Utah His-
     torical Quarterly*, p. 102 (Shellbach File).

   **Little Nankoweap Creek**  Map: GC-7 Grand Canyon, Coconino

## NEAL SPRING

El.: 8175'                              Loc.: East F-4
This spring at the head of Bright Angel Canyon was named for a cowpuncher.
Ref.: Kolb. Map: GC-7.

## NOVINGER BUTTE

El.: 6000'                              Loc.: East GH-4.25
Simon Novinger (b. Pennsylvania, 1832; d. January 24, 1904) arrived in Arizona from California in 1871. He was a pioneer in the Salt River Valley.
Ref.: Barnes. Map: GC-7.

## OBI POINT

El.: 8000'                              Loc.: East G-7
Pro.: /óbiy/          Piute: "pine nut tree"; "piñon"
Descriptive.
Ref.: Barnes; 93, p. 62. Map: GC-7.
**a.n. Obi Canyon**                    Grand Canyon, Coconino

## OCHOA POINT

El.: c. 4300'                          Loc.: East JK-8.25
Pro.: /očowə/
Estevan Ochoa (b. New Mexico) was a prominent Arizona pioneer merchant and freighter. *(see Ochoaville, Cochise)*.
Ref.: Barnes; APHS Files. Map: GC-7.

## 140 MILE CANYON

El.: 2250'                             Loc.: West EI-2-1
The Powell Grand Canyon expeditions named several canyons according to their distance from the party's entrance to the Grand Canyon.
Ref.: 133. Map: GC-8.
**a.n. 150 Mile Canyon**   Map: GC-8   Grand Canyon, Mohave
    **135 Mile Rapids**    Map: GC-8   Grand Canyon, Coconino
    **237 Mile Rapids**    Map: GH-1   Grand Canyon, Mohave

## O'NEILL BUTTE

El.: 5700'                             Loc.: East D-9
William O. (Bucky) O'Neill came to Prescott in 1879, where he became a court reporter and established the western livestock magazine *Hoofs and Horns*. O'Neill was mayor of Prescott at the time he organized a company of Rough Riders for service in the Spanish-American War, in which he lost his life.
O'Neill's connection with the Grand Canyon was as a promoter of copper mines and the railroad to the Grand Canyon.
Ref.: Barnes; Shellbach File; 93, p. 36. Maps: GC-1; GC-7.

## O'NEIL SPRING

El.: 4000'                             Loc.: East GH-11
This spring was named for Jim O'Neil, a scout for Gen. George Crook. In 1880 O'Neil was living in Prescott.
Ref.: APHS Files; 127, p. 159. Map: GC-7.

## OSIRIS TEMPLE

El.: 6637'                             Loc.: East BC-7-8
According to one legend, Osiris was a wise and beneficent king who reclaimed Egyptians from savagery, teaching them handicrafts. His brother Seth invited him to a banquet and had him enter a cunningly contrived coffin, immediately nailing down the lid. Isis, Osiris' wife, found and took his body after a long search. Seth again got the body and cut it into fourteen pieces. Isis finally reclaimed the remains. Horus, Isis' son, avenged his father's murder and deposed his uncle.
Ref.: 151, p. 576; 93, p. 32. Map: GC-7.
**a.n. Horus Temple**
    El.: 6150'. Map: GC-7          Grand Canyon, Coconino

## PAGUEK WASH POINT

El.: 5655'                             Loc.: West BC-2
                                       Piute (?): "fishtail"
Descriptive.
Ref.: Barnes; 151, p. 581. Map: GC-8.

## PALISADES OF THE DESERT

El.: c. 5000'                          Loc.: East LM-6-8
Descriptive. These bold cliffs are at the western border of the Painted Desert. The name was proposed by Francois E. Matthes in 1902.
Ref.: 151, p. 583; 109, p. 2. Map: GC-7.
**a.n. Palisades Creek**   Map: GC-7   Grand Canyon, Coconino

## PANAMETA TERRACE

El.: c. 4000'                          Loc.: West CD-3-4
This place was named for an Indian family.
**v.n. Panameta Point**
Ref.: 151, p. 585. Map: GC-8.

## PANYA POINT

El.: c. 4200'                          Loc.: West B-7.5
Pro.: /pañyə/
This is the name of an Indian family.
Ref.: 151, p. 587. Map: GC-8.

## PAPAGO POINT

El.: c. 7000'                          Loc.: East J-11
Pro.: /pǽpəgo/
This point was named for the Papago tribe of southern and southwestern Arizona and northern Sonora *(cf.* Papago Indian Reservation, Pima).
Ref.: 151, p. 587. Map: GC-7.
**a.n. Papago Creek**   Map: GC-7   Grand Canyon, Coconino

## PATTIE BUTTE

El.: 5000'                             Loc.: East EF-9.25
James Ohio Pattie was a fur trapper with his father. The two men entered Arizona and trapped along the Gila River in 1825. Pattie was the first American citizen to see the Grand Canyon.
Ref.: 125. Map: GC-7.

## PAYA POINT

El.: 5500'          Loc.: West CD-3.9
Pro.: /payə/
This point was named for Lemuel Paya, a Supai Indian.
Ref.: 151, p. 593. Map: GC-8.

## PHANTOM RANCH

El.: 2500'          Loc.: East D-8.25
The Phantom Ranch is the only one in the Grand Canyon.
Here those who descend the trails from the rims find
guest accommodations.
Here in 1903 David Rust established a camp for travelers
and hunting parties, calling it Rust's Camp. In 1907 Rust
put in a cable sixty feet above the stream across the Colorado. Rust's tramway furnished a safe way to cross the
turbulent river. In 1913 this place was referred to as Roosevelt's Camp because Theodore Roosevelt stayed here. In
1921 the present resort was constructed at the old Rust
Camp by the Fred Harvey Company. Phantom Ranch
was named by Mary Jane Colter, the architect for the Fred
Harvey establishments at the Grand Canyon.
Ref.: Emery C. Kolb, "Cheyava Falls," *Natural History Notes,*
Bulletin No. 2 p. 11; Kolb; 98, pp. 174, 215; 168, p. 75.
Map: GC-1.

**a.n. Phantom Creek**   Map: GC-1   Grand Canyon, Coconino
   **Kaibab Trail**                   Grand Canyon, Coconino
When the Park Service failed in its attempt to buy the
Bright Angel Trail from Coconino County (See Bright
Angel Creek), it built a new one called the Kaibab or Yaki
Trail three miles east. This trail led to the Colorado River
exactly opposite the mouth of Bright Angel Creek. Three-
quarters of a mile up the creek the Fred Harvey Company
constructed Phantom Ranch.
Ref.: 168, p. 75.

## PIMA POINT

El.: c. 5750'          Loc.: East B-9.5
Pro.: /píymə/
The Pima Indians are a peaceful, agricultural tribe living
in south central Arizona. *(see Pima Indian Reservation,
Pima).*
Ref.: 151, p. 604. Map: GC-7.

## PIPE CREEK

El.: c. 3000'          Loc.: East DE-10-8.25
In 1894 Niles and Ralph Cameron, Peter H. Berry, and
James McClure were exploring for mining locations. Ralph
Cameron found a meerschaum pipe lying on the ground.
As a joke he scratched a date one hundred years earlier
on it and placed it where the other men in his party would
discover it. They did and from this incident Pipe Creek
was named.
Ref.: Emery C. Kolb, *Grand Canyon Nature Notes,* VIII,
No. 3 (June 1933). Map: GC-7.

## PIUTE POINT

El.: 6632'          Loc.: West K-10
Pro.: /páyuwt/
The Piute Indians are the tribe native to the area north
of the Grand Canyon.
Ref.: Barnes; 146, p. 607. Map: GC-8.

## POSTON BUTTE

El.: c. 5500'          Loc.: East J-6.25
Pro.: /pówstən/
Charles DeBrille Poston has been called the "Father of
Arizona" *(see* Poston Butte, Pinal).
Ref.: None. Map: GC-7.

## POWELL PLATEAU

El.: 7680'          Loc.: West GJ-3.5
Maj. John Wesley Powell (d. September 23, 1902) is in-
separably associated with the Grand Canyon, for it was
he who in 1869 led the first successful expedition through
its towering walls and dangerous rapids, and named it the
Grand Canyon. In 1871-72, Powell again explored the
canyon, making scientific records.
Later Powell became first director of the U.S.G.S. and
of the Bureau of American Ethnology. A monument at
Powell Point commemorates his achievements in the Grand
Canyon.
Maj. Clarence E. Dutton named the plateau.
Ref.: 132; 133; 47, p. 164; 93, p. 79. Map: GC-8.
**a.n. Powell Spring**   Map: GC-8   Grand Canyon, Coconino

## PUTESOI CANYON

El.: c. 5000'          Loc.: West EB-6-7.5
This is the name of an Indian family.
Ref.: 151, p. 625. Map: GC-8.

## RA, TOWER OF

El.: 6079'          Loc.: East B-7
Ra was the ancient Egyptian god of the sun, a principal
deity. The pharaohs claimed to be Ra's incarnation.
Ref.: None. Maps: GC-1; GC-7.

## RETREAT, POINT

El.: c. 3000'          Loc.: East JM-2-6
This point in Marble Canyon was named by Frank Stanton
because it was the one via which the Stanton party left
the river following the upset which drowned two members
of the Brown party in 1889.
Ref.: Shellbach File. Map: None.

## RIBBON FALLS

El.: 3750'          Loc.: East E-7-6.75
Slightly more than one-third of the way up the trail from
the canyon bed to the North Rim is Ribbon Falls. Actually
it is a single fall which drops down in a cut over an overhang. It deposits travertine. At the bottom of the falls the
ground slopes down so that the water makes a moss-green
track with the water spraying over it. It makes a very
beautiful spot against the red wall of the canyon.
Ref.: Kolb. Map: GC-7.

## ROARING SPRINGS

El.: c. 5500'          Loc.: East F-5.75
These springs at the head of Bright Angel Creek gush
with such force from the canyon wall that the result is a

true roaring sound. The water then plunges four hundred feet down a fern-covered slope.

Ref.: Kolb; 4, p. 494. Maps: GC-1; GC-7.

**a.n. Roaring Springs Canyon**
Maps: GC-1; GC-7                          Grand Canyon, Coconino

## ROWES WELL
El.: 6681'                                Loc.: East B-10.75
Pro.: /ráws/
In June 1890 Sanford Rowe (b. Oklahoma, date not known; d. October 1929), a pioneer stockman and guide, had a talk with Capt. John Hance about where Rowe might find water near the Grand Canyon. Hance told him there was water in the wash near the present Rowe Well. As an experienced guide, Rowe was quick to notice many deer tracks and the fact that the dirt stood up between the hoof marks, thereby indicating moisture. He began digging, hitting solid rock when down only eighteen feet. In order to establish his claim Rowe placed a mining monument of rocks at his well since he had already used up his homestead right. He later developed Rowe's Well into an auto camp. Rowe maintained his interest until a short time before his death.

Ref.: Grand Canyon History File; 93, p. 13; 61, p. 74, (Note 80). Maps: GC-1; GC-7.

**a.n. Rowe Knob**
El.: 7071'. T. 31 S., R. 2 E.            Grand Canyon, Coconino

## SADDLE MOUNTAIN
El.: 8420'                                Loc.: East HI-2.5
Descriptive.

Ref.: Barnes. Map: GC-7.

**a.n. Saddle Canyon**  Map: GC-8     Grand Canyon, Coconino
This canyon originates at Saddle Mountain.
Ref.: Shellbach File.

## SANTA MARIA SPRING
El.: 6250'                                Loc.: East B-10
Pro.: /sǽtəməríyə/ or /santəmaríyə/
This spring about twenty-one hundred feet down the Hermit Trail was named by Mary Jane Colter, the architect for the El Tovar Hotel.

Ref.: Kolb. Maps: GC-1; GC-7.

## SAPPHIRE CANYON
El.: c. 3500'                             Loc.: West KL-10-9
Maj. John Wesley Powell named this canyon for its coloring.

Ref.: Barnes. Map: GC-8.

## SET, TOWER OF
El.: 5997'                                Loc.: East BC-8
Set was the Egyptian god of war. This location was named by the artist, Thomas Moran, c. 1879.

**v.n. Set, Temple of**
Ref.: 93, p. 53. Maps: GC-1; GC-7.

## SHANUB POINT
El.: 5500'                                Loc.: West B-2
                                          Piute (?): "dog"
The reason for this name has not yet been ascertained.

Ref.: 151, p. 685. Map: GC-8.

## SHINUMO ALTAR
El.: c. 6000'                             Loc.: Coconino 1, I-7.25
Pro.: /šínəmo/        Piute: "old people; cliff dwellers"
Frederick Dellenbaugh named Shinumo Altar. He said that the formation, which towers six hundred feet above the surrounding terrain, looked very much like "a great altar." He also said that the Piute Indians called the former occupants of the country the Shinumo and Dellenbaugh therefore applied the name Shinumo Altar, purely on a descriptive, not on an archaeological, basis. Dr. A. H. Thompson spelled this name Sheno-mo.

**v.n. Mesa Butte**
  **Shenomo Altar**
Ref.: 71, p. 43; 42, p. 310; Shellbach. Maps: A-7; C-6; D-4.

**a.n. Shinumo Amphitheater**
Map: GC-8                                 Grand Canyon, Coconino
Ref.: 47, p. 167.

**Shinumo Canyon**                        Grand Canyon, Coconino
Dellenbaugh notes that the party named this canyon because it found "indications of the former presence of that tribe." The older name for Shinumo Canyon is Snake Gulch. It was so referred to by A. H. Thompson on March 4, 1872. However, the name had been changed by 1886 on the U.S.G.S. map.
Ref.: Shellbach File; 41, p. 184.

**Shinumo Creek**    Map: GC-8            Grand Canyon, Coconino
**Shinumo Gardens**                       Grand Canyon, Coconino
William Bass owned this garden where he raised cantaloupe, onions, corn, beans, squash, and radishes, as well as peaches. It was reported to be a prehistoric garden. In the wall behind it are several cliff dwellings.
Ref.: 93, p. 87.

**Shinumo Rapids**    Map: GC-8           Grand Canyon, Coconino
**Shinumo Trail**
Loc.: From Bass Cable Ferry to Powell Plateau.
                                          Grand Canyon, Coconino
Ref.: 93, p. 57.

## SHIVA TEMPLE
El.: 7650'                                Loc.: East BC-6-7
Shiva Temple is a wooded butte which eons ago was part of the North Rim, from which it is now sliced off. Shiva Temple was named by Maj. Clarence E. Dutton in 1880. Dutton described it as "the grandest of all the buttes, and the most majestic in aspect, though not the most ornate . . . All around it are side gorges sunk to a depth nearly as profound as that of the main channel. It stands in the midst of a great throng of cluster-like buttes . . . In such a stupendous scene of wreck, it seemed as if the fabled 'Destroyer' might find an abode not wholly uncongenial." The member of the Hindu triad known as the Destroyer is Shiva.

Ref.: 4, p. 484; 93, p. 31; 47, p. 150. Maps: GC-1; GC-7.

## SIEBER POINT

El.: c. 6000'                                    Loc.: East H-1-2

This point is named for the Indian scout, Al Sieber. The name was suggested by Will C. Barnes (cf. Sieber Creek, Gila).

Ref.:  Barnes. Map: GC-7.

## SINKING SHIP

El.: 7344'                                       Loc. East H-12

The tilting of the strata in this formation gives it the appearance of a sinking ship.

Ref.:  Barnes. Map: GC-7.

## SINYALA CANYON

El.: 3750'                                       Loc.: West BA-5-3.5

Pro.: /sinyálə/

George Wharton James had as a guide a Havasupai named Sinyela (sic).

Ref.:  93, p. 154. Map: GC-8.

a.n. Sinyala Mesa          Map: GC-8          Grand Canyon, Coconino

Sinyala Mountain
El.: 5455'. Map: GC-8                         Grand Canyon, Coconino

v.n. Sinyala Butte

a.n. Sinyala Rapids        Map: GC-8          Grand Canyon, Coconino

## SIXTY-MILE CREEK

El:. 4250'                                       Loc.: East IK-6-5

This creek is about sixty miles below Lee's Ferry. Apparently this name was suggested by Francois E. Matthes, Richard F. Evans and J. R. Evans.

Ref.:  151, p. 697; Letter to Chairman U. S. Geographical Board, November 27, 1926, from Matthes and Evans (Grand Canyon File; Matthes File). Map: GC-7.

a.n. Sixty Mile Canyon                        Grand Canyon, Coconino

## SOCKDOLAGER RAPIDS

El.: 3250'                                       Loc.: East HI-10

The rigors undergone by the Powell expedition into the Grand Canyon are almost unimaginable. Their encounter with Sockdolager Rapids is an instance of the violence of the Colorado. It began with their hearing a sullen and increasingly thunderous roar in the waters ahead. Suddenly the river seemed to drop out of sight. Stopping their tiny boats, the men stepped out to stare at the fearful rapids. As Dellenbaugh describes it, "The narrow river dropped suddenly and smoothly away and then beaten to foam, plunged, and boomed for a third of a mile . . . The boats rolled and pitched like a ship in a tornado, as we flew along . . . I . . . could look up under the canopies of foam pouring over gigantic black boulders, first on one side and then on the other . . . the boats . . . leaping at times almost one half their length out of the water, to bury themselves quite as far on the next lunge." It is no wonder the men selected *Sockdolager* to describe these rapids; it is slang used to indicate a "heavy or knock-down blow" or a "finisher."

Ref.:  *Oxford English Dictionary;* 41, pp. 226, 227; 42, p. 330, Map: GC-7.

## SPENCER TERRACE

El.: 5450'                                       Loc.: West I-7

This most westerly of the plateaus associated with **Darwin Plateau** is named for a close friend of the evolutionist, Herbert Spencer (1820-1903), an English philosopher of the great scientific movement of the second half of the 19th century. His work is marked by a belief in progress as the law of the universe, based on a mechanical conception of matter and motion which lends materialistic coloring to his concepts.

Ref.:  93, p. 82; 151, p. 713. Map: B-4.

## SPOONHEAD, MOUNT

El.: 5775'                                       Loc.: West D-7

In 1902 a Havasupai Indian named Spoonhead was engaged in digging a trail under orders from the Indian agent.

Ref.:  Kolb; 151, p. 714. Map: GC-8.

## STANTON POINT

El.: 6315'                                       Loc.: West F-3.5

This point was named by Robert Brewster Stanton (1846-1922). Stanton was in charge of an exploration by boat into the Canyon for the Denver, Colorado Canyon, and Pacific R. R. Company in 1890 to investigate the feasibility of a railroad to run through the canyon.

Ref.:  151, p. 718. Map: GC-8.

a.n. Stanton Rapids                           Grand Canyon, Coconino
One of Stanton's boats was wrecked at the point called by him No. 241.

Ref.:  93, p. 86.

## STURDEVANT POINT

El.: c. 5000'                                    Loc.: East D-7.75

Glen E. Sturdevant was a park naturalist who drowned in the Colorado River just below this point in 1929.

Ref.:  Barnes. Maps: GC-1; GC-7.

## SUBLIME, POINT

El.: 7464'                                       Loc.: East A-5.6; West L-6

Maj. Clarence E. Dutton spent many hours on this point, writing descriptions of Grand Canyon scenery. He is said to have called it "the most sublime of the earthly spectacles." He named the promontory in 1880.

Ref.:  93, p. 85; 47, p. 143. Maps: GC-1; GC-7; GC-8.

## SULLIVAN POINT

El.: 8324'                                       Loc.: East GH-3.5

J. W. (Jerry) Sullivan (b. Canada 1844) arrived in Arizona at Prescott on December 2, 1868. He was a noted stock raiser, banker and politician in northern Arizona. This peak was named by Will C. Barnes.

Ref.:  Barnes. Map: GC-7.

## SUMMER BUTTE

El.: 5100'                                       Loc.: East EF-8

John C. Summer was a member of Maj. John Wesley Powell's 1869 expedition into the Grand Canyon.

v.n. Sumner Point (corruption)

Ref.:  Barnes; APHS. Map: GC-7.

## SWILLING BUTTE

El.: 7258'                                    Loc.: East HI-4.5
Jack W. Swilling (b. Georgia 1831; d. August 12, 1878)
came to Arizona in 1859 (*see* Gillette, Maricopa).

Ref.: APHS Files. Map: GC-7.

## TAPEATS CREEK

El.: c. 3500'                                  Loc.: West HI-12
Dr. A. H. Thompson of the Powell Grand Canyon Expedition wrote in his diary on September 6, 1872, that Ta Pits
was the name of this creek. Dellenbaugh refers to it under
the name which is used today, stating that it was so called
because a Piute Indian claimed ownership.

**v.n. Thunder River**          Map: B-4
   Locally Tapeats Creek is called Thunder River because it
   thunders through a rocky gorge at the point where it is fed
   by Thunder Spring.
Ref.: Shellbach File.

Ref.: A. H. Thompson "Diary," September 6, 1872, *Utah
   Historical Quarterly*, p. 98 (Shellbach File); 41, p. 240.
   Map: GC-8.

**a.n. Tapeats Rapids**     Map: GC-8     Grand Canyon, Coconino

**Thunder Spring**     Map: GC-8     Grand Canyon, Coconino

**Tapeats Terrace**     Map: GC-8     Grand Canyon, Coconino

**Tapeats Trail**                       Grand Canyon, Coconino
   Maj. Clarence E. Dutton wrote that this trail on the north
   side of Tapeats Amphitheater was constructed in 1876 following a rumor of placer gold to be found in the Colorado
   River bed. Although the trail had already begun to go to
   pieces, it was used by Dutton's party in 1880.
Ref.: 47, pp. 159, 160.

## THOR'S HAMMER

El.: 7400'                                      Loc.: East G-12
                             On South Rim near Grand View
George Wharton James said that he named this formation
because of its resemblance to a hammer huge enough to
be used by the god Thor.

Ref.: 93, p. 56. Map: None.

**a.n. Thor Temple**     Map: GC-7     Grand Canyon, Coconino
Ref.: 151, p. 753.

## THOMPSON CANYON

El.: 8250'                                       Loc.: East E-5
Two cattlemen named Van Slack and Thompson ran cattle
in this vicinity, using the VT brand (*see* DeMotte Park).
Ref.: Barnes. Maps: GC-1; GC-7.

**a.n. Thompson's Spring**              Grand Canyon, Coconino
   Maj. Clarence E. Dutton wrote that in 1880 a basin was
   dug here and made watertight to preserve the small flow
   from Thompson's Spring.
Ref.: 47, p. 171

## THOMPSON POINT

El.: 6750'                                     Loc.: West H-4.5
This point was named for Dr. A. H. Thompson of Maj.
John Wesley Powell's second Grand Canyon expedition
(1871-1872).

Ref.: 93, p. 83. Map: GC-8.

## TILTED MESA

El.: 5500'                                        Loc.: East IJ-2
This formation is notably tilted. George Wharton James
called it the "Tilts." Francois E. Matthes suggested the
name Tilted Mesa for the sloping table land west of
Marble Gorge.

Ref.: 93, p. 71; 109, p. 2. Map: GC-7.

## TITHUMIJI POINT

El.: 5811'                                        Loc.: West C-7
This point was named for an Indian family.

Ref.: 151, p. 759. Map: GC-8.

## TOLTEC POINT

El.: 6470'                                        Loc.: West H-8
Pro.: /tóltek/ or /táltek/
One early archaeological theory concerning Indians in Arizona said that Toltec Indians from Mexico lived as far
north as the Gila River.

Ref.: 151, p. 761. Map: GC-8.

## TONTO TRAIL

El.: c. 3500'          Loc.: East AH-7.5–10.5; West IL-7-9
Pro.: /tánto/                               Spanish: "fool"
This trail is on the South Rim near Granite Gorge. It was
named for the so-called Tonto Apaches, a term which included members of several tribes. (*See* Tonto Basin, Gila).

Ref.: 151, p. 762. Maps: GC-7; GC-8.

## TOPAZ CANYON

El.: c. 3500'                                    Loc.: West A-10
This is another canyon bearing the name of a semi-precious
stone.

Ref.: 151, p. 763. Map: GC-8.

## TOVAR TERRACE

El.: 5000'                                       Loc.: West G-5-6
Pro.: /towvár/
Pedro de Tobar (or Tovar) was the son of the lord high
steward of Queen Doña Juana and Lope de Samaniego, who
was keeper of the arsenal of Mexico City. Pedro de Tobar
accompanied Coronado on his expedition in 1540. Tobar
learned of the existence of the Grand Canyon in his con-
versations with Hopi Indians. When he reported this to
Coronado, Cardenas was sent to investigate. (*See* Cardenas
Butte).

**v.n. Tobar Terrace**

Ref.: *Grand Canyon Nature Notes*, III, No. 10 (June 30,
   1929) (Shellbach File); 182, p. 477. Map: GC-8.

**a.n. Tovar Point, El**     El.: 7050'     Grand Canyon, Coconino
   This point is the end of the amphitheater in which El Tovar
   Hotel is located. From here there is a fine view of the hotel,
   hence the name of the point.
   Currently this is called Grandeur Point.
Ref.: 93, pp. 25, 38.

**Tovar Amphitheater, El**              Grand Canyon, Coconino
   This is the area below El Tovar Hotel. Down through it the
   Bright Angel Trail winds to Indian Gardens.
Ref.: 93, p. 25.

**Tovar Hill, El**                          Grand Canyon, Coconino
   This hill leads up to the head of the Bright Angel Trail.
Ref.: Shellbach File.

## TOWAGO POINT

El.: c. 4000'     Loc.: West CD-7. S.E. of Supai 4 miles.
This is the name of an Indian family.
Ref.: 151, p. 764. Map: None.

## TRANSEPT, THE

El.: 4750'     Loc.: East EF-5-6
Maj. Clarence E. Dutton in 1882 wrote that the portions of the Grand Canyon close to Vulcan's Throne had "arms of a transept, the main chasm being regarded as the nave. Vulcan's Throne is . . . almost exactly at the intersection." He added that The Transept was among the second or third "order of magnitude among the lateral excavations along the Grand Canyon," but that even so, it was much larger than Yosemite.
Ref.: 47, pp. 92, 172. Maps: GC-1; GC-7.

## TRAVERTINE CANYON

El.: 3000'     Loc.: East A-9
Waters heavily charged with calcium carbonate leave a deposit of smooth soft green stone called travertine. Seepage has deposited travertine all over this canyon wall, hence the name.
Ref.: Kolb. Map: GC-1.
a.n. Travertine Creek    Map: GC-7    Grand Canyon, Coconino

## TRITLE PEAK

El.: 6750'     Loc.: East I-5
Pro.: /tréytl/
Frederick A. Tritle was appointed territorial governor of Arizona in 1885 and served until 1889. Considering the fact that previous governors retired and did not remain in Arizona, Tritle is unique in that he was the first to retire and stay in Arizona. (*See* Mount Tritle, Yavapai). He remained for health reasons.
Ref.: None. Map: GC-7.

## TURQUOISE CANYON

El.: 3500'     Loc.: West JL-10.9
This is another canyon named for a semi-precious stone.
Ref.: None. Map: GC-8.

## TUSAYAN RUIN

El.: 6800'     Loc.: East DE-9.75
Pro.: /tuwsáyan/
This is the small ruin which lies back of the Wayside Museum on the South Rim of the Grand Canyon. It was built by pueblo dwellers probably c. 1200 A.D. It remained relatively undisturbed after its abandonment c. 1400 until excavated in 1930, when the Tusayan Ruin was named by Harold S. Gladwin.

The name Tusayan was that used by the Spaniards for the Hopi Mesas and villages.
Ref.: 4, p. 482; Shellbach File. Map: None.
a.n. Tusayan Hill
    Loc.: West of Coconino Wash near Maricopa Point.
                        Grand Canyon, Coconino
Ref.: 93, p. 74 (Shellbach File).

## TAHUTA POINT

El.: 6485'     Loc.: West FG-2
Pro.: /tahúta/
Tahuta was the name of an Indian woman.
Ref.: 151, p. 738. Map: GC-8.
a.n. Tahuta Terrace    Map: GC-8    Grand Canyon, Coconino

## TANNER CANYON

El.: c. 4000'     Loc.: East KL-10.5-8.5
In 1889 Seth B. Tanner, a man named French, and others built a trail from the South Rim down into the canyon to the Colorado River where it joined the Nankoweap Trail up to the North Rim, built in 1882 under Maj. John Wesley Powell. The trail followed Tanner Canyon.
Ref.: 93, p. 55; 4, p. 483. Map: GC-7.

## UKWALLA POINT

El.: 5840'     Loc.: West B-5
Pro.: /úkwalə/ or /ʃkwalə/
This is the name of an Indian family.
Ref.: 151, p. 780. Map: GC-8.

## UNCLE JIM POINT

El.: 8250'     Loc.: East F-5
Uncle Jim Owens was a pioneer who settled near here.
Ref.: 151, p. 782. Maps: GC-1; GC-7.

## UPSET RAPIDS

El.: 3250'     Loc.: West B-2.25
In 1923 the Birdseye Expedition mapping the Grand Canyon had its first boat upset of the trip in this hither-to unnamed location.
Ref.: Shellbach File; 151, p. 784. Map: GC-8.

## VASEY'S PARADISE

El.: c. 5000'     Loc.: East JL-2.6
George W. Vasey (1822-1893) served as a botanist with the United States Department of Agriculture 1872-1893. The description written of Vasey's Paradise (in Marble Canyon) on August 9, 1869, by Maj. John Wesley Powell covers the subject nicely:

"The river turns sharply to the east and seems enclosed by a wall, set with a million brilliant gems . . . On coming nearer we find fountains bursting from the rock, high over head, and the spray and the sunshine forms the gems which bedeck the wall. The rocks below the fountain are covered with mosses and ferns, and many beautiful flowering plants. We name it Vasey's Paradise, in honor of the botanist who traveled with us last year."

The opinion of Dr. A. H. Thompson is expressed as follows, "The Major thinks that the place is called 'Vasey's Paradise' but if it is, it is a Hell of a Paradise."

Ref.: 132, p. 76; A. H. Thompson "Diary," Entry for Aug. 20, 1872, *Utah Historical Quarterly*, Footnote p. 93 (Shellbach Files). Map: None.

### VENUS TEMPLE

El.: 6286'                           Loc.: East IJ-8
Venus was the Roman goddess of gardens and springtime
and was believed to be the mother of the Roman people.
At a later date she became the Greek goddess of love.
Ref.:   151, p. 788. Map: GC-7.

### VESTA TEMPLE

El.: 5200'                           Loc.: West L-10
Vesta was the Roman goddess of the burning hearth, wor-
shipped in every Roman household.
Ref.:   151, p. 79. Map: GC-8.

### VISHNU TEMPLE

El.: 7535'                           Loc.: East IJ-9
In Hindu mythology, Vishnu is a god of primary importance, being ranked as one of the supreme trinity with
Brahma and Shiva. He is considered a preserver of men
against evil and misfortune. The butte was named in 1880
by Maj. Clarence E. Dutton, who said that it resembled
an oriental pagoda. Dellenbaugh adds that Vishnu Temple
is "without doubt the most stupendous mass of nature's
carving in the known world."
Ref.:   47, p. 148; 93, p. 37. Map: GC-7.
**a.n. Vishnu Creek    Map: GC-7         Grand Canyon, Coconino**

### VISTA ENCANTADORA

El.: 8500'                           Loc.: East G-4.25
Pro.:  /viəstá enkántadorə/      Spanish: "enchanting view"
In 1941 the original name of Vista Encantada was changed
by Dr. Harold C. Bryant, then supervisor of the Grand
Canyon National Park, to Vista Encantadora, a more suit-
able name. Dr. Bryant felt that *encantada* ("enchanted")
was better rendered as *encantadora* ("enchanting.")
Ref.:   Harold C. Bryant, Letter, April 9, 1956. Map: GC-7.

### WALTENBURG CANYON

El.: 3000'                           Loc.: West IH-5.6
John Waltenburg worked with William Bass as a helper
and occasionally as a partner for about eighteen years.
He came originally from Wisconsin. He spent a month c.
1917 with Levi Noble of the U.S.G.S. making the Shinumo
geological survey. He got along so well with Noble that
after the survey was completed, Waltenburg went to work
for the geologist in Southern California, where until his
death he was in charge of Noble's farm.
**v.n. Walthenburg Canyon (corruption)**
Ref.:   Shellbach File, H. C. Bryant Memo, March 3, 1950;
        William W. Bass Materials, Wickenburg, Arizona; Grand
        Canyon History Files. Map: GC-8.
**a.n. Waltenburg Rapids                 Grand Canyon, Coconino**
**v.n. Walthenburg Rapids (corruption)**

### WATAHOMIGI POINT

El.: 5640'                           Loc.: West A-5.75
                On South Rim 1½ miles s. of Havasu Falls.
Pro.:  /watowhowmiygiy/
This point was named for an Indian family.
Ref.:   151, p. 804. Map: None.

### WESCOGAME POINT

El.: 5250'                           Loc.: West A-7
Pro.:  /weskowgámiy/
This point was named for an Indian family, members of
which still live nearby.
Ref.:   151, p. 808. Map: GC-8.

### WHEELER POINT

El.: 6500'                           Loc.: West H-6
In 1871 Capt. George M. Wheeler made his surveying
trip across northern Arizona, during which he explored
portions of the Grand Canyon.
Ref.:   175. Map: GC-8.

### WHITE'S BUTTE

El.: 4750'                           Loc.: East B-8.75
This butte was named for a prospector at the Grand Canyon.
Ref.:   Kolb. Map: GC-7.
**a.n. White Creek        Map: GC-8      Grand Canyon, Coconino**
        White built the upper portion of the trans-canyon Bass Trail.
Ref.:   *Grand Canyon Nature Notes*, VIII, No. 6, (Sept. 8,
        1933), 193.

### WIDFORSS POINT

El.: 7650'                           Loc.: East E-6
The name of this point was established by the U. S. Geographic Board on Names in December 1937. It had been
known as McKinnon Point (*sic*) since June 7, 1928, when
a note was found in a tin can on this point. The note read
as follows: "Point MacKinnon, November 26, 1892, present Colonel H. MacKinnon, Gren.Gds. London; Colonel
W. S. Cody (Buffalo Bill) . . ." and others. Colonel Mac-
Kinnon had visited this point after killing his first buck on
the Kaibab. The name was changed to honor Gunnar
Mauritz Widforss (b. Sweden, October 21, 1879; d. at the
Canyon Rim, November 30, 1934). Widforss' magnificent
paintings of the Grand Canyon have never been equalled.
Ref.:   Shellbach File; Kolb. Maps: GC-1; GC-7.
**a.n. Widforss Trail**
        Loc: From Bright Angel Point to Widforss Point.
                                Grand Canyon, Coconino

### WODO, MOUNT

El.: 5125'                           Loc.: West B-7
Pro.:  /wodo/
This was named for an Indian family.
Ref.:   151, p. 823. Map: GC-8.

### WOOLSEY POINT

El.: 7225'                           Loc.: East H-3
King S. Woolsey was a noted Arizona pioneer (*See Agua
Caliente, Maricopa*).
Ref.:   None. Map: GC-7.

## YAKI POINT

El.: 6800'                          Loc.: East E-10
Pro.: /yáki^/ or /yǽki^/
This point was named just prior to 1910 when the Yaqui Indians of Mexico were struggling with the Mexican government against being transported from their home to the tropical climate of that country. Many Yaquis fled for refuge to the United States (*See* Guadeloupe, Maricopa).
Ref.: 93, p. 36; 151, p. 827. Maps: GC-1. GC-7.

## YAVAPAI POINT

El.: 6600'                          Loc.: East D-9.25
Pro.: /yǽvəpay/
This point was named for the Yavapai Indians of Arizona.
**v.n. O'Neil Point**
Ref.: None. Map: GC-7.

## YUMA POINT

El.: 6250'                          Loc.: East A-9.25
Pro.: /yúwmə/
The Yuma Indians are a tribe inhabiting the lower reaches of the Colorado River where Yuma is today (*See* Yuma, Yuma).
Ref.: None. Map: GC-7.

## YUMTHESKA POINT

El.: 4290'                          Loc.: West A-5
This point was named for an Indian family.
Ref.: 151, p. 832. Map: GC-8.
**a.n. Yumtheska Mesa**
Maps: GC-6; GC-8                     Grand Canyon, Coconino

## YUNOSI POINT

El.: 5600'                          Loc.: West A-6.5
Yunosi was the wife of Hotouta. After her husband's death, she had visions of his spirit. Curiously, during such moments she spoke in the crude English taught to her by her husband, calling out to him as "Big Chief Tom." Speaking in this English, she would turn to others and inquire of them in a shriek, "You no see? You no see?" Thus her name, Yunosi.
**v.n. Yonosi Point**
Ref.: 94, pp. 250, 255-256. Maps: GC-6; GC-8.

## ZOROASTER TEMPLE

El.: 7136'                          Loc.: East F-8
Zoroaster was the founder of what was for generations the national religion of the Perso-Iranian people. He is believed to have been alive c. 700 B.C. Zoroaster, founder of the wisdom of the Magi, rejected the myriad gods of his age in favor ot concentration on the spirit of good.
Dellenbaugh describes the vast angular mass of Zoroaster Temple as keeping guard to the right of Bright Angel Creek.
Ref.: 93, p. 30. Maps: GC-1; GC-7.
**a.n. Zoroaster Canyon**
Maps: GC-1; GC-7                     Grand Canyon, Coconino

## ZUNI POINT

El.: 7284'                          Loc.: East IJ-11
Pro.: /zúwnyi^/
This point was named for a tribe of Indians which lives in New Mexico near the Arizona border northeast of Springerville.
Ref.: 151, p. 834. Map: GC-7.

ARIZONA PLACE NAMES

# GREENLEE

*Copper smelter and mill at Clifton — mountain men in forest.*

## GREENLEE COUNTY:

Mason Greenlee (b. Virginia, 1835; d. April 10, 1903) was one of the first settlers in the county which today bears his name. Greenlee made the first location in the Greenlee Mining District north of Clifton. He had come first to the Clifton area in 1874, but was forced to leave by Indians. He returned in 1879 and never again left the area.

Greenlee County was created from the eastern part of Graham County by act of the 25th Territorial Legislature on March 10, 1909, but not until 1911 was the new county finally organized as an active unit. The delay was caused by political difficulties between the mother county and the new county. The youngest county in Arizona, Greenlee is principally a mining and stock raising area containing 1,199,360 acres. The county seat is at Clifton *(q.v.)*.

## ALDER CREEK

El.: c. 5000'  Loc.: Greenlee BC-5

Alder Creek was named by Fred Fritz, Sr. (d. 1916), because of the many alder trees which he found when he homesteaded in 1890. Fritz used alder logs to build his cabin. The logs were fully one foot square after they were hewn. Today no trees remain of the same size and length. Mr. Fritz is buried at the creek, in response to his own request.

Ref.: Mrs. Fred Fritz. Maps: GF-2; GF-3.

a.n. Alder Peak  Maps: GF-2; C-14  Greenlee

## ALMA MESA

El.: c. 6000'  Loc.: Greenlee D-4.6
Spanish: *alma,* "soul"

Alma Mesa is close to the New Mexico line and not far from the community of Alma, New Mexico, on the San Francisco River. The New Mexico community was named by Morris E. Coates after a town of the same name in Colorado, from which he came.

Ref.: Barnes. Maps: GF-2; C-13.

## APACHE GULCH

El.: c. 5000'  Loc.: Greenlee AB-8.5-9.2
Pro.: /əpǽči/

At a place called Apache Grove on Apache Creek which runs through this gulch, there are Indian ruins as well as additional ruins on the mountain.

Ref.: Scott; Reilly. Maps: GF-1; GF-2.

## ASH PEAK

El.: c. 4000'  Loc.: Greenlee B-11.3

The ash trees which once grew in abundance at this location are now entirely gone. A particularly beautiful grove of ash trees was located at Ash Spring, a place which was noted because it formed a natural ambush pocket and also served as an Apache waterhole. It was here that Horatio Merrill and his fourteen-year-old daughter were killed by Indians on December 3, 1895.

Ref.: Cosper; Empie; 28a, p. 70; Barnes. Maps: GF-3; A-3; C-8.

## BALDY MOUNTAIN

El.: 6415'  Loc.: Greenlee D-7.6
Descriptive.

Ref.: None. Maps: C-12; GM-2.

## BAT CANYON

El.: c. 4000'  Loc.: Greenlee B-9

Descriptive. Bat Cave on Eagle Creek southwest of Morenci is used as a source of bat guano fertilizer.

Ref.: Simmons. Maps: GF-2; GF-3.

## BEAR CREEK

El.: c. 5000'  Loc.: Greenlee B-5.6

John H. Toles Cosper (cf. Cosper) killed over four hundred bear in this vicinity. According to his nephew, he would kill one bear in the morning and another in the afternoon almost daily.

Ref.: Cosper (nephew). Map: GF-3.

a.n. Bear Canyon  Map: GF-3  Greenlee
    Bear Canyon  Map: GF-2  Greenlee

Bear Mountain  Loc.: N.w. corner T. 2 N., R. 30 E.  Greenlee

Not only are bear plentiful in this area, but from certain directions the mountain resembles a bear lying down.

## BENTON

El.: c. 5000'  Loc.: Greenlee C-5.2
At junction of Blue and Little Blue River.

Benton (first name not known) had a cattle ranch at this spot. He was killed in the first Apache raid on the Blue River in 1889 or 1890. The little settlement of Benton was a lumber center where Ira Harper had a sawmill three and one-half miles above the junction of the Little Blue and the Blue River. The community had a blacksmith shop, store, post office, school, and a few simple houses for lumber haulers. Ranchers customarily moved into Benton during the winter in order to send their children to school. The floods from 1904 through 1906 washed away most of the settlement. In 1906 the Balke family moved away and the post office was closed. Benton is now included in the Rail HU Ranch on the east side of the Blue River.

P.O. est. October 10, 1903. Max A. Balke, p.m. Discont. October 10, 1907.

Ref.: Mrs. Fred Fritz, Jr.; Mrs. Fred Fritz, Sr.; Sweeting; Mr. and Mrs. Eddie Fritz. Map: None.

## BIG LUE CANYON

El.: c. 6000'  Loc.: Greenlee D-8-7
Pro.: /biglúw/

Eugene Johnson owned the ranch holdings which he sold to Abe and Dick Boyles (c. 1906). Johnson was in the area at least by 1884. His brand was LUE and the name for the ranch, the Big Lue Ranch, derived from this. The Boyles in turn sold the ranch in 1911 to Bud Stacey.

"Stuttering Charlie" Johnson settled in Johnson Canyon on the lower Blue River in 1886. He had been a Texas Ranger, and then a cattleman at Silver City, New Mexico. His first brand on the Blue was 333, but later he used the LUE brand.

Ref.: Fred Fritz, Sr., Notes; Mrs. Fred Stacey; Mrs. Fred Fritz. Map: GF-2.

a.n. Big Lue Mountain  Map: GF-2  Greenlee

## BINGHAM PEAK

El.: 7070'  Loc.: Greenlee B-4.2

Lt. Theodore Alfred Bingham in the early 1880's started through this area with troops from Fort Apache. Bingham was appointed a second lieutenant of Engineers on June 13, 1879, becoming a first lieutenant two years later.

Ref.: Barnes. Map: GF-3.

## BLACK JACK CANYON

El.: c. 5000'  Loc.: Greenlee DC-8-7

Black Jack Ketcham was a notorious bandit who in 1899 murdered two store keepers named Rogers and Wingfield at Camp Verde. Ketcham maintained a hideout at Black Jack Spring. He continued his depredations, committing many robberies, including one of a train in New Mexico. He was caught, tried and convicted and was hanged at Clayton, New Mexico, on April 26, 1901.

Ref.:   Patterson; Mrs. Fred Fritz, Sr.; 51, p. 694. Map: GF-2.

## BLUE

El.: c. 6000'                    Loc.: Greenlee D-2.2
The first name of this location was Whittum.

Whittum was the site of the third ranch established by Fred Fritz, Sr. Here he lived with Nat Whittum, an older man who had been an Indian scout. In 1891 Fritz went to Clifton for supplies and upon his return found Nat kneeling by the bed in the cabin, dead. He had apparently been reaching for his gun and died in that position. From the house Fritz followed the trail of blood which led to the spring and horse corral. This indicated that the killer had watched Nat leave the cabin, go out to the horses, and then had shot him unarmed early in the morning. It was thought that Nat was killed by the Apache Kid, a renegade Indian.

While C. D. Martin was acting as postmaster at Whittum, he circulated a petition to have the name changed to Blue because everyone knew where the Blue River was, but Whittum was a name not known other than locally.

The spot at which Whittum is buried is now called Old Base Line, because it is the forest service boundary line.

P.O. est. as Whittum, July 21, 1894. Isaac F. Castro, p.m. Name changed to Blue, November 3, 1898. Max A. Balke, p.m. (cf. Benton.)

Ref.:   Cosper; Mrs. Fred Fritz, Sr.; *Arizona Bulletin,* April 28, 1899, 2:1. Maps: C-8 (Whittum); C-9.

## BLUE RIVER

El.: c. 6000'                    Loc.: Greenlee DC-1-2
The Spanish name for this stream was Rio Azul "Blue River." In 1870 Sylvester Mowry wrote deploring the changes in place names, citing the Americanization of Rio Azul into Blue River. Both names probably derive from the fact that the stream heads in the Sierra Azul or Blue Mountains.

Ref.:   Barnes; *Arizona Citizen,* December 10, 1870, 1:5; Becker. Maps: GF-2; C-4; C-9; E-12.

**a.n. Blue Creek**          Map: GF-2                    Greenlee

   **Blue Range**   Loc.: W. side of Blue River          Greenlee
   This short range has Rose Peak at its southern end.

## BOYLES

El.: c. 4000'                    Loc.: Greenlee C-1-6.9
Dick and Abe Boyles located a ranch at the juncture of the Blue with the San Francisco River. Cowboys and travelers did not find a free welcome at the ranch, such as was customary elsewhere. Mrs. Boyles was reputed to charge even for a cup of coffee, but the cowboys evened things up by roping a Boyle maverick and putting a neighbor's brand on it for revenge whenever they were so charged. After Benton was flooded in 1904-1906 (cf. Benton) Mr. and Mrs. Dick Boyles started a post office, store, and saloon at Boyles on the old Carpenter Ranch.

P.O. est. as Carpenter, March 30, 1904. Roda H. Carpenter, p.m. Changed to Boyles, November 14, 1904. Laura L. Boyles, p.m. Discont. October 31, 1905.

Ref.:   Mrs. Fred Fritz, Sr.; Fred Fritz Notes; P.O. Records. Maps: GF-2; C-10.

## BULLARD PEAK

El.: 7862'                    Loc.: Greenlee D-5.8
The first prospectors and miners to arrive in the vicinity of the present-day Clifton included Jim Bullard, a cousin of the Shannon brothers. Bullard, a retired cavalry lieutenant and Indian scout, accompanied Metcalf, Stevens, and others on a prospecting party from Silver City. Since he was a man who preferred solitude, Bullard built himself a small cabin and began prospecting around what was then called Galinas Peak. He was asleep in his cabin when Apaches slipped up and shot him. It is not known whether he is buried at the base of the peak or is interred in the Shannon plot at Silver City.

Ref.:   Shannon; Mrs. Fred Fritz, Sr. Maps: GF-2; C-12.
**a.n. Bullard Canyon**          Map: GF-2                    Greenlee

## BURNT STUMP MESA

El.: c. 6000'                    Loc.: Greenlee D-7.7
A burnt stump, apparently struck by lightning, gave the name to this mesa.

Ref.:   Scott. Map: GF-2.

## BUZZARDS ROOST CANYON

El.: c. 5000'                    Loc.: Greenlee D C-8.9
Since the early days of American settlement, this location has been noted as a buzzard's roost.

Ref.:   Scott. Map: GF-2.
**a.n. Buzzard Roost Wash**                    Greenlee

## CAMPBELL'S BLUE

El.: c. 7000'                    Loc.: Greenlee CD-2
William Campbell was a cattleman and sheriff of Apache County in 1888. He ranged cattle along this stream.

Ref.:   Barnes; Noble. Maps: C-13; C-14.

## CHASE CREEK

El.: c. 5000'                    Loc.: Greenlee A-5.6
Chase Creek is reported to have been named after Capt. Chase (first name not known), who was not the same person as the prospector, George Chase. Capt. Chase left Silver City, New Mexico, in pursuit of Apaches in 1870. He hired the two Metcalf brothers, Bob and Jim, for scouts. The party camped in the vicinity of Clifton, perhaps on what is now known as Chase Creek.

Later Chase Creek was the site of a small Mexican furnace called the Stone House, which Henry Lezinsky *(sic)* caused to be built in the late 1870's. As the town of Clifton grew, buildings were constructed along this narrow twisting canyon. Chase Creek earned an unsavory reputation in the 1880's and 1890's when Clifton was often called the second wildest camp in the West.

Ref.:   Farnsworth; Patton; 126, pp. 7-8, 102; 75, p. 36; 126, pp. 13-14. Maps: GF-1; GF-2; GF-3.

## CHIMNEY ROCK CANYON
El.: c. 5000'                    Loc.: Greenlee D-7
Descriptive.
Ref.:  Simmons. Map: GF-2.

## CLIFTON
El.: 3464'                       Loc.: Greenlee B-8.7
Lt. John G. Bourke related that when he was with the army c. 1869 on a scouting expedition, he was in a group which was among the first to note the rich copper deposits in the vicinity of what later became Clifton. The men took pieces of nearly pure copper ore back to Tucson. However, it was not until c. 1872 that a group of prospectors and miners from Silver City, New Mexico, explored the area and established copper mines. Among these was Charles M. Shannon, Charles Lezinsky, and Lezinsky's brother.

There is little reason to doubt that the location of the new community in the midst of towering cliffs led to its descriptive name, probably a shortening of "Cliff Town." The situation of the town was such that it was subject to dangerous floods which time and again took lives and destroyed property. The greatest flood occurred on December 4, 1906, when it rained continuously for thirty hours. This gave the people forewarning of what might happen and most of them took refuge on higher ground. Nevertheless, eighteen people were killed by this flood.

No serious flood has occurred since 1916.

P.O. est. March 1875. Charles Lezinsky, p.m. Wells Fargo Station, 1885. Town incorporated March 11, 1909.
Ref.:  22, pp. 98-99; 126, pp. 21, 115-116, 117, 119, 124. Maps: GF-1; GF-2; GF-3; C-4; C-5; E-20.
**a.n. Clifton Hot Springs**                  Greenlee
At one time a bath house and swimming pool existed in the center of Clifton so that people could bathe in Clifton Hot Springs. The building is now gone. The springs are in back of the present post office.
Ref.:  4, p. 43; Reilly.

## COALSON CANYON
El.: c. 5000'                    Loc.: Greenlee D-6-7
Coalson Canyon takes its name from the nearby Coalson Ranch which was patented by Nick Coalson c. 1930. Coalson raised stock and caught wild horses.
Ref.:  Reilly; Simmons; Fritz. Map: GF-2.

## COPPER KING MOUNTAIN
El.: 6826'                       Loc.: Greenlee B-8.1
Here the New England Copper Company had a mine named the Copper King.
Ref.:  Simmons. Maps: GF-1; GF-2.

## COPPER MOUNTAIN
El.: 5410'                       Loc.: Greenlee A-8.4
Copper Mountain was apparently one of the first places to be named by Americans in the Clifton area. It was so called at least as early as August 1872, when miners and prospectors in the newly-opened area organized the Copper Mountain Mining District. The organization of the district made it possible for miners to record their claims at Clifton thereafter, thus obviating additional trips to Prescott.

Copper Mountain is the site of Morenci. The copper has long since been mined out.
Ref.:  126, p. 15; Simmons. Map: GF-1.

## COPPERPLATE GULCH
El.: c. 5000'                    Loc.: Greenlee AB-8
Ambrose Burke had the Copper Plate claims in this gulch.
Ref.:  Simmons. Maps: GF-1; GF-2.

## CORONADO MOUNTAIN
El.: 7400'                       Loc.: Greenlee A-2.8
Pro.: /kárənado/ or /kórənado/
Dan J. Grant, a miner, named Coronado Mountain for Francisco de Coronado, who is thought by many to have passed through the vicinity of Clifton on his way to the legendary Seven Cities of Cibola. Adjacent to Coronado Mountain is the Coronado Mine. In order to transport ore from the mines on the mountain to its base and also to take supplies to the small community of Coronado on the mountain, the Coronado Railroad was built from the base of the mountain to the community. The track lay along what was called the Coronado Incline, an extremely steep grade thirty-three hundred feet long. The miners used to ride the ore cars to work. On August 15, 1913, sixteen men climbed on top of an ore car to come down the incline. A drawbar broke and the car hurtled down at great speed. Seven men jumped, escaping with minor injuries. The others clung to the speeding car and were dashed to death when it smashed against the mountain on the opposite side at the foot of the incline.

Ref.:  Scott; Simmons; Farnsworth; Reilly; 126, p. 109; 75, p. 80. Maps: GF-1; GF-2; C-9.
**a.n. Coronado**          Map: GF-2          Greenlee
This was the community owned by the Arizona Copper Company at the top of the Coronado Incline.
P.O. est. August 21, 1912. Samuel F. Lanford, p.m. Discont. November 30, 1919.

| | | |
|---|---|---|
| Coronado | Map: C-12 | Greenlee |
| Coronado Creek | Map: GF-2 | Greenlee |
| Coronado Gulch | Map: GF-1 | Greenlee |
| Coronado Ridge | El.: 6500'. Maps: GF-1; GF-2 | Greenlee |

## COSPER
El.: c. 6000'                    Loc.: Greenlee C-3.4
John H. Toles Cosper was a beloved cattleman of Greenlee County. He came to the vicinity of the Blue River from Luna, New Mexico, in 1885, and built up a large herd of cattle. His ranch was famous for dances which lasted not only through one night, but several days and nights. He kept a fiddler on his payroll so that there would never be a lack of music when anyone felt the urge to start a dance.
P.O. est. August 26, 1914. Lu Ella Cosper, p.m. No additional data. Probably never in operation.
Ref.:  Fred Fritz Notes. Map: GF-3.

## DARK CANYON

El.: c. 6000'                               Loc.: Greenlee C-7.3
                                           N. of Granville 1 mile
Descriptive.

Ref.: Patterson; Scott. Map: None.

## DIX CREEK

El.: c. 6000'                               Loc.: Greenlee C-7.8
The Dix Ranch at the mouth of the Blue River belonged
to Dick Boyles. "Dix" is a corruption.

Ref.: Mrs. Fred Fritz, Sr. Map: GF-2.

a.n. Dix Mesa              Map: GF-2                    Greenlee

## DORSEY GULCH

El.: c. 6000'                               Loc.: Greenlee B-8
Hank Dorsey was a prospector who arrived in the vicinity
of Clifton prior to August 1872, and established claims
in the gulch which bears his name.

Ref.: Fitzgerald; Sweeting. Maps: GF-1; GF-2.

## DOUBLE CIRCLE RANCH

El.: c. 5000'                               Loc.: Greenlee A-5.5
George H. Stevens located a sheep ranch at this place c.
1880. Stevens, a former sergeant of the Fifth Cavalry,
married a high-caste Apache woman named Mollie and
established his ranch on Eagle Creek in 1879, or perhaps
earlier. The place was known as Little Steve's Ranch and
also as the Eagle Ranch. Stevens sold to Joe H. Hampson,
who owned the ranch from 1884 to 1908. Hampson in
turn sold half interest to Tom Wilson and to a Major Drum
of Kansas City. These two men in 1909 organized the
Double Circle Ranch, naming it for their brand. They
purchased the remainder of Hampson's interest in 1912.

The Double Circle Ranch is of interest, not only because
it is one of the oldest in the state, but also because it was
a completely self-sustaining unit and was thus typical of
early ranches. Everything had to be packed in. The fur-
nishings included a piano which was lugged over rough
mountainous country by Mexicans a few steps at a time.

P.O. est. January 5, 1921. Anna E. Hoffman, p.m. Rescinded
February 2, 1921.

Ref.: 4, p. 432; 39, pp. 46, 47. Map: GF-2.

## DUNCAN

El.: 3643'                                  Loc.: Greenlee D-12.6
In 1883, when the Arizona and New Mexico Railroad was
built to connect Clifton with the main railroad line, two
of the men who sold out their interest to the Arizona
Copper Company were brothers, Duncan Smith and Sheriff
Guthrie Smith. There is a possibility that this railroad
point was named for one of these men. On the other hand,
there is also a story that two brothers named Duncan
settled in this locality and were killed by Apaches c. 1885.
Duncan was not the same place as Purdy (q.v.). When the
railroad was established, the post office at Purdy was closed
and its affairs transferred to Duncan.

P.O. est. October 11, 1883. Charles A. Boake, p.m. Wells Fargo
Station, 1885.

Ref.: 28a, p. 78; Cosper. Maps: GF-3; C-7.

## EAGLE CREEK

El.: c. 6000'                             Loc.: Greenlee A-3.5-9.8
In the early 1880's, when this area was the scene of many
scouting expeditions by soldiers, several eagles' roosts
were found in the rhyolite bluffs bordering the creek.
The Double Circle or Eagle Ranch (q.v.) was located on
Eagle Creek.

v.n. Prieto Creek              (C-4)

Ref.: Farnsworth; 58, pp. 65, 69, 70. Maps: GF-1; GF-2; C-4;
      C-10; E-20.

## ELEVATOR MOUNTAIN

              Loc.: East side of Eagle Creek on w. boundary
                                       San Carlos Reservation
Descriptive. The mountain slopes gradually up from the
valley floor on one side and then drops abruptly from its
top on the other side like an elevator.

Ref.: Simmons. Map: None.

## ENEBRO MOUNTAIN

El.: c. 7000'                               Loc.: Greenlee A-7.6
Pro.: /enéybro/           Spanish: "juniper tree"
Juniper grows somewhat densely on this mountain. A local
Mexican name for juniper and cedar is tasquite. However,
the Spanish word for juniper is the one which has been
attached to this mountain for many years.

Ref.: Simmons. Maps: GF-1; GF-2.

## ESPERO

El.: c. 7500'                               Loc.: Greenlee B-1
Pro.: /espéyro/     Spanish: "hope, waiting or expectation"
E. H. Patterson established a dude ranch at this location
and gave the place its name. Whether he felt it was descriptive is not known. Currently the place still operates as a
guest ranch under the name of Sprucedale.

P.O. est. January 11, 1919. Sophia J. Taylor, p.m. Discont.
February 28, 1934.

Ref.: Wiltbank; Reilly; 102, p. 35. Map: C-12.

## EVANS POINT

El.: 3541'                                  Loc.: Greenlee B-8.1
The name for this point of land came from the fact that
it was owned by one of the partners in the Evans-Van
Hecke Mining Company in 1899. As was customary, the
mining company issued script rather than United States
currency to its employees. Some of this script is still in
existence and bears the inscription "Evans Point, Arizona."

P.O. est. April 4, 1899. Mongo R. W. Parks, p.m. David M.
Evans, p.m. (apptd. April 22, 1899. Neither commissioned.)
Discont. April 13, 1900.

Ref.: Sweeting; P.O. Records. Maps: GF-1; GF-2.

## FOUR BAR FOUR MESA

El.: c. 6000'                               Loc.: Greenlee A-5.9
The cattle which graze on this mesa have the 4 brand.
John Joseph Filleman (b. Texas, May 2, 1861; d. July
10, 1942) in 1912 acquired the ranch from the Battendorf
brothers, who had established it. Filleman had originated
the 4 brand in Texas. He came to Arizona in 1886.

Ref.: Barnes; Fred Fritz Notes; Mrs. Harris Martin, Letter,
      May 11, 1956. Map: GF-2.

## FRANKLIN

El.: 3676'                    Loc.: Greenlee D-13.1
In 1895 a group of Mormons from Utah emigrated to
this location. They named the town for Franklin D. Richards, an apostle of the Mormon Church. This name was
given in 1898 when the community was visited by officials of the Mormon Church.

P.O. est. May 17, 1905. Nephi Packer, p.m. Discont. March
14, 1958.

Ref.:   180, p. 48; 112, p. 250. Map: F-6.

## FRISCO CANYON

El.: c. 5000'                 Loc.: Greenlee DA-7-10
This canyon forms the channel of the San Francisco River,
hence its name.

Ref.:   Barnes. Map: None.

## FRITZ CANYON

El.: c. 4000'                 Loc.: Greenlee B-6.1
In the spring of 1887 Fred Fritz, Sr. (d. 1916) brought
in sixty head of cattle to a spot one mile below the canyon
which bears his name. Fritz had visited the area in 1885
with a prospector named Irie Townsend. At that time
Fritz was trapping for beaver.

Ref.:   Mrs. Fred Fritz, Sr. Map: GF-2.

## GARFIELD

El.: 4813'                    Loc.: Greenlee A-7.9
The little community of Garfield consisted of a store and
five or six houses, now all vanished. The reason for its
name is not known at present.

Ref.:   Scott; Reilly. Maps: GF-2; C-13.

a.n. Garfield Gulch        Map: GF-1          Greenlee

## GOAT RANCH

El.: c. 6000'                 Loc.: Greenlee AB-6.8
The Zorrilla family of Clifton had a goat ranch at this
point at one time.

Ref.:   Reilly; Patterson. Maps: GF-2; GF-3.

## GOBBLER POINT

El.: c. 7000'                 Loc.: Greenlee A-2.2
The killing of a very large gobbler at this location led to
the name. Wild turkeys are still plentiful here.

Ref.:   Barnes. Map: GF-3.

## GOLD GULCH

El.: c. 5000'                 Loc.: Greenlee A-8.5
Gold used to be panned in this gulch.

It was in this gulch that in 1882 a party of miners from
Silver City was ambushed by Apaches. Several of the men
were slain, including Capt. Slauson, J. R. Risque, a man
named Truscott (Trescott?), and one other, unnamed. A
Capt. Frink hid under a bush and although the Apaches
came within a few feet of him, he escaped their notice.

Ref.:   Scott; Patterson; 28a, p. 72; 111, p. 236. Maps: GF-2;
        GF-3.

a.n. Placer Gulch          Map: GF-1          Greenlee
Ref.:   Scott.

## GRANT CREEK

El.: c. 6000'                 Loc.: Greenlee BC-2.3-3.2
William Grant was a wiry Scotsman who had arrived in
Clifton by 1881. There is a possibility that this well-known
prospector and miner was the same person who settled
and ranched on the creek which today bears the name
Grant Creek.

Ref.:   28a, p. 68; Reilly. Map: C-14.

## GRANVILLE

El.: c. 6000'                 Loc.: Greenlee B-7.2
Granville is said to have been the name of a pioneer
prospector in the area.

A small community sprang up at the location where timbers were cut for use in the mines at Metcalf. There were
also mines at Granville. The teams which hauled ore
through the community used to be shod at the blacksmith
shop in Granville. There is nothing left of Granville today,
but a recreation area has been created at this location on
the Coronado Trail.

Ref.:   Reilly; Farnsworth; Barnes; Scott. Maps: GF-1; GF-2;
        C-14.

## GRASSY MOUNTAIN

El.: 6334'                    Loc.: Greenlee D-7.6
The name is descriptive of the former condition of this
mountain which at one time had abundant grass, as did
many mountains in the vicinity. However, all such grass
has disappeared.

Ref.:   Simmons. Map: GF-2.

## GREY'S PEAK

El.: 7077'                    Loc.: Greenlee A-6.8
A prospector by the name of Grey is said to have lived
near the foot of this peak. Mexicans refer to Grey's Peak
as Pistola Peak, because the mountain looks something
like a pistol.

Ref.:   Barnes; Simmons. Maps: GF-1; C-3; C-12 (Gray); E-20.

## GUTHRIE

El.: c. 4000'                 Loc.: Greenlee B-9.8
In 1883 when the Arizona Copper Company built the railroad to the mines at Clifton, it brought the interest of two
brothers named J. Duncan Smith and Guthrie Smith. The
small railroad location is said to have been named for
Sheriff Guthrie Smith (cf. Duncan). According to another
story, it is possible that the location was named for a
settler called Guthrie, who first lived north of the present
Duncan on the river and later established the community
on the railroad.

P.O. est. February 6, 1901. Ellen J. Brown, p.m. Discont.
August 15, 1922. Wells Fargo Station, 1904.

Ref.:   28a, p. 74; Cosper. Map: C-10.

a.n. Guthrie Peak
        Loc.: In Peloncillo Mts. w. of York near county line.
                                              Greenlee

## HANNEGAN MEADOW

El.: 9092'                                    Loc.: Greenlee B-1.8
Robert Hannegan *(sic),* a cattleman, is described as having
been a "big fat old fellow." His cattle holdings were in
New Mexico, but in the mid-1880's he camped for a
single summer on these beautiful meadows with his cattle.
Ref.:   Cosper; Patton. Map: GF-3.

**a.n. Hannegan Creek**   Loc.: Sec. 3, T. 3 N., R. 29 E.    Greenlee

## HARDEN CIENEGA

El.: c. 5000'                                 Loc.: Greenlee D-7
Pro.:   /hardn siyénəgə/
The origin of this name has not yet been learned.
The name for this creek dates back to at least 1885 when
the Jerry Stockton family located on it after emigrating
from Trinidad, Colorado.
Ref.:   Mrs. Fred Fritz, Sr. Map: GF-2.

## HARDY

El.: c. 4000'         Loc.: Greenlee B-12.2. At Ash Peak
Joe Hardy was a miner in the area of Duncan. He operated
the Ash Creek Mining property as late as 1938.
P.O. est. January 10, 1938. Mrs. LaVada McEuen, p.m. Re-
scinded February 15, 1938.
Ref.:   Empie. Map: None.

## HELL HOLES

El.: c. 6000'                                 Loc.: Greenlee D-9.3
The extremely rough character of the country led to this
name. If cattle once got in, it was plain hell to get them out.
Ref.:   Scott; Patterson; Barnes. Map: GF-2.

**a.n. Hells Hole Peak**       Map: C-13              Greenlee

## HONEYMOON CABIN

El.: c. 6000'                                 Loc.: Greenlee A-3.6
A young forest ranger, Johnny Wheatly, took his bride
to this forest ranger's cabin, hence the name.
Ref.:   Barnes; Shannon. Map: GF-2.

## HORSE CANYON

El.: c. 6000'                                 Loc.: Greenlee DC-5.5
Fred Fritz, Sr. used this small and rough canyon to corral
and pasture his stock one winter.
Ref.:   Mrs. Fred Fritz, Sr. Map: GF-2.

## JUAN MILLER CREEK

El.: c. 6000'                                 Loc.: Greenlee B-6
Pro.:   /wanmiler/
The name of the camp site and creek on the Colorado
Trail is a corruption of the name of an old German, Von
Muellar, who lived in this area for many years.
Ref.:   Mrs. Fred Fritz, Sr. Map: GF-2.

## KING CANYON

El.: c. 6000'                                 Loc.: Greenlee BC-8
The King Mine at Metcalf was the origin of the name for
this canyon. The mine was owned by the Arizona Copper
Company.

Ref.:   Simmons. Map: GF-2.

**a.n. King Creek**         Map: GF-2                Greenlee
 **King Gulch**         Maps: GF-1; GF-2           Greenlee

## LIGHTNING MESA

El.: c. 5000'                                 Loc.: Greenlee CD-7.7
The fact that lightning strikes noticeably more often in
this area than elsewhere led to the naming of the mesa.
Ref.:   Scott. Map: GF-2.

## LONGFELLOW INCLINE

El.: c. 5000'                                 Loc.: Greenlee AB-8.6
The Longfellow Mine was one of the earliest prospects
uncovered in the Clifton area. According to the Wheeler
Report in 1873, the Longfellow Mine was unlike anything
found thus far in copper formations. The report noted
that the copper-bearing outcrops indicated a vast amount
of ore under the surface, but despite the attempts of miners
to find the vein, all that they managed to uncover was the
fact that the mountain was practically pure copper. The
ultimate result was the creation of an open-pit mine.
The Longfellow Incline was used for hauling groceries to
the mercantile company store in Morenci. Part of the
incline is still in existence.
Ref.:   28a, p. 54; 87, pp. 82-83; Scott. Maps: GF-1; E-20
        (Longfellow Copper Mines).

## LYDA CREEK

El.: c. 6000'                                 Loc.: Greenlee D-9
                              Runs into Blackjack Canyon
This creek was named for an old cheesemaker who used
to bring his products into Clifton via the Black Jack Canyon
sawmill road.

**v.n. Lida Creek**
Ref.:   Mrs. Fred Fritz, Sr. Map: None.
**a.n. Lyda Springs**    Loc.: At site of Lyda Ranch    Greenlee

## MALEY CORRAL

                        Loc.: North of and between Honeymoon
                              Ranger Station and Black River
Pro.:   /méyley/
The Maley brothers had a ranch at this location in 1884.
Ref.:   Scott. Map: None.

**a.n. Maley Gap**                                  Greenlee

## MALPAIS MOUNTAIN

El.: c. 6000'                                 Loc.: Greenlee C-7.5
Pro.:   /mæl pa:is/                           Spanish: "bad place"
Descriptive.
Ref.:   Reilly; Patterson. Maps: GF-1; GF-2.

## MAPLE CANYON

El.: c. 5000'                                 Loc.: Greenlee DC-5
A large grove of mountain maple still grows in this canyon.
In the early days settlers used to tap the trees for maple
sap which they then boiled to maple sugar. Plugs can still
be seen in some of the tree trunks.
Ref.:   Mrs. Fred Fritz, Sr. Map: GF-2.

**a.n. Maple Peak**        El.: 8302'. Map: GF-2          Greenlee
 Red mountain maple abound here.
Ref.:   Shannon.

## MARKEEN MOUNTAIN

El.: c. 6000'     Loc.: Greenlee B-8.1
The Markeen Copper Comany had a camp on this mountain.

Ref.:   Sweeting. Maps: GF-1; GF-2.

## MAVERICK HILL

El.: 7457'     Loc.: Greenlee D-9
Maverick Basin is a very brushy and rough location where wild cattle take refuge. Maverick Hill is located in the basin.

Ref.:   Barnes. Map: GF-2.

## METCALF

El.: 4431'     Loc.: Greenlee AB-8.2
Bob Metcalf and his brother Jim served as scouts under Capt. Chase who was in pursuit of Apaches in 1870 (cf. Chase Creek). The party camped near what was to become Clifton. Bob Metcalf scouted alone and located rich deposits of copper and later staked the Metcalf claims.

In 1889 the Shannon Copper Company was organized and bought claims near those held by Metcalf. The company began producing copper in 1901 and a community named Metcalf soon existed. By 1910 nearly five thousand people lived there. Ores were shipped for smelting to Clifton. After 1915 ores in the Metcalf area began to play out. The Arizona Copper Company purchased the holdings in 1918 and Metcalf gradually died away. Today all that remains of interest to the casual visitor is the old cement bank vault.

P.O. est. August 25, 1899. Sophie E. Shirley, p.m. Discont. May 15, 1936.

Ref.:   Scott: Patterson; Reilly; Shannon; Farnsworth; Simmons; 126, pp. 13-14, 77-78, 79. Maps: GF-2; C-9.

## MITCHELL PEAK

El.: 7947'     Loc.: Greenlee A-6.9
A man named Mitchell was killed in Metcalf c. 1899. Mitchell, superintendent of the Metcalf Mine, was the Justice of the Peace. A Mexican came into a store for money and Mitchell, who had been looking for the man, said the Mexican owed a fine he must pay. An argument ensued. The Mexican left the store, got a pistol and shot Mitchell as he emerged from the store.

Ref.:   Simmons; Farnsworth. Maps: GF-1; C-12.

## MODOC MOUNTAIN

El.: 5226'     Loc.: Greenlee A-8.5
This mountain is largely composed of modoc limestone.

Ref.:   Simmons. Map: GF-1.

## MORENCI

El.: 4838'     Loc.: Greenlee A-8.6
Pro.:  /morénsîˆ/
The town of Morenci is located on the site of a mining camp owned and operated by a man named Joy. By 1881 William Church was interested in financing mining here. He visited the Phelps Dodge offices in New York City, seeking a loan of fifty thousand dollars and offering as security his copper mine and smelter at Morenci. The mining company asked Dr. James Douglas to investigate the property. His report was so favorable that the Detroit Mining Company was formed with William Church as president and general manager. It is reported that Church named the location after his hometown in Michigan. In 1887 Church sold his half of the company to Phelps Dodge.

Open pit operations were begun at Morenci in 1937. By the end of 1955 five hundred seventy million tons had been moved, leaving the uppermost level at five thousand feet and the lowest at forty-four hundred.

P.O. est. March 3, 1884. George W. Davison, p.m. Wells Fargo Station, 1904.

Ref.:   Barnes; 126, pp. 74-75. Maps: GF-1; GF-2; GF-3; C-6.

**a.n. Morenci Gulch**     Map: GF-1     Greenlee
    **Morenci Hot Springs**
    Loc.: Sec. 26, 27, T. 5 S., R. 29 E.     Greenlee

## MUD SPRINGS CANYON

El.: c. 5000'     Loc.: Greenlee D-5-6
Descriptive.

Ref.:   Scott. Map: GF-2.

## MULLIGAN PEAK

El.: 5615'     Loc.: Greenlee B-8.4
A prospector named Morris Mulligan is said to have worked in this area.

Ref.:   Patton; 102, p. 61. Maps: GF-1; GF-2; C-9.

## N O BAR MESA

El.: c. 6000'     Loc.: Greenlee A-6.1
Although the N O Bar Ranch is said to have been homesteaded originally by Ed Laney, the N O - brand was originated by Cap Smith and his brother Bill, who sold out to the Battendorf brothers.

Ref.:   Fred Fritz Notes; Patterson. Map: GF-2.

## OREJANO CANYON

El. c. 5000'     Loc.: Greenlee AB-6.7-7.3
Pro.:  /oreyháno/     Spanish:  "maverick"
The term for unbranded cattle is "maverick," or in Spanish, orejano. Orejano Canyon was used as a branding place for mavericks.

Ref.:   Simmons. Map: GF-2.

## OROVILLE

El.: c. 4000'     Loc.: Greenlee A-8.2
Pro.:  /órovil/
George Wells established a ranch across the river from the location of the Oroville post office. In addition to Well's ranch there were many farms operated by Chinese who supplied Clifton residents with fruits and vegetables. The Well's ranch was farmed in 1886 by Charlie Wing. The name Oro is said to have come from the discovery of gold in the area. The main street of Clifton in the old records was referred to as Oro Street.

Several Chinese at Oroville were murdered by Mexicans. The Mexicans knew that the Chinese hoarded money in order to pay their passage back to China and in January 1904, some Mexicans set off a dynamite blast to force the Chinese out of their homes so that the homes could be looted. Three or four Chinese were killed as they dashed toward safety.

P.O. est. as Oro, October 19, 1880. Joseph T. Yankie, p.m. Discont. June 12, 1882.

Ref.:   Barnes; Patterson; Patton. Maps: C-5 (Oro); C-6.

## PARSONS PEAK

El.: c. 6000′                    Loc.: Greenlee BC-11.8
Alexander Graves in 1871 established a small dairy ranch in Parson Canyon. Both the peak and the canyon were named because Graves was a minister.

Ref.:   Barnes. Map: C-10.

## PAT CREEK

El.: c. 4000′                    Loc.: Greenlee BC-6.7
Pat Slaughter was an early settler on this creek.

Ref.:   Shannon. Map: GF-2.

a.n. Pat Mesa           Map: GF-2              Greenlee
     Pat Mountain       Map: GF-2              Greenlee

## PIGEON CREEK

El.: c. 5000′                    Loc.: Greenlee BC-6.9-6.3
Early settlers in the 1880's found flocks of wild pigeons living on this little stream.

Ref.:   Fred Fritz Notes; Scott. Maps: GF-2; C-13.

## PIPESTEM CREEK

El.: 6000′                       Loc.: Greenlee B-6-5
This creek is shaped like the stem of a meerschaum pipe.

Ref.:   Simmons. Map: GF-2.

a.n. Pipestem Mountain
     Loc.: At foot of Pipestem Canyon, through which stream
     runs.                                       Greenlee

## PURDY

El.: c. 4000′                    Loc.: Greenlee D-12.6
A rancher named Purdy located across the river from the current Duncan. When the increasing number of residents in the area petitioned for a post office, it was established on Purdy's ranch. However, when the railroad came through in 1883, the location of the post office was shifted across the river to the newly established Duncan. Purdy sold his holdings shortly after 1887 to Warden Courtney.

P.O. est. April 2, 1883. George B. Atchelder, p.m. Moved to Duncan, October 11, 1883.

Ref.:   Cosper. Map: A-4.

## RATTLESNAKE BASIN

El.: c. 7000′                    Loc.: Greenlee B-2.8
John H. Toles Cosper, a cattleman, said that while he and a companion were camped at this spot years ago they killed between sixty and seventy rattlesnakes in a single week.

Ref.:   Barnes. Map: GF-3.

a.n. Rattlesnake Camp      Map: GF-2           Greenlee
     cf. Stray Horse Creek.
     Rattlesnake Canyon    Map: GF-2           Greenlee

## RED MOUNTAIN

El.: c. 6000′                    Loc.: Greenlee A-4.1
All of this mountain is red.

Ref.:   Simmons. Map: GF-2.

a.n. Red Hill              Maps: C-12; GF-2              Greenlee

## ROCKY GULCH

El.: c. 4000′                    Loc.: Greenlee C-6.4
Descriptive.

Ref.:   Sweeting. Maps: GF-1; GF-2.

## ROSE PEAK

El.: 9525′                       Loc.: Greenlee A-4.3
An abundance of wild roses has led to the naming of this peak.

v.n. Red Peak

Ref.:   Scott. Maps: GF-2; C-4; E-20.

## ROUSENSOCK CREEK

El.: c. 6000′                    Loc.: Greenlee AB-4.2
Pro.: /ráwzənsak/
A German prospector named Rousensauc (sic) and his partner (named Rose) staked out claims around the peak that bears the German's name.

Ref.:   Mrs. Fred Fritz, Sr.; Simmons; Barnes. Map: GF-2.

a.n. Rousensock Canyon                                  Greenlee

## SALT SPRING

El.: c. 4000′                    Loc.: Greenlee B-9
Descriptive.

Ref.:   Patton. Maps: GF-1; GF-2.

## SAN FRANCISCO RIVER

El.: c. 5000′-2500′              Loc.: Greenlee DB-5.5-8.5
James Ohio Pattie on January 1, 1825, named this stream the St. Francisco. Locally, it is referred to as the Frisco River.

Few place names in Arizona have shown the shifts in location and name which are associated with this stream. On Smith (1879) it is the San Francisco River, but on GLO 1876, it has an East Branch. On Smith and GLO 1879 Los Platos River is the same as the later Blue Creek of GLO 1921. The stream shows as the Francisco River on the General Surveys Map of 1874.

Ref.:   125, p. 90. Maps: C-3; E-20; C-1 (Los Platos River); C-2 (Francisco River).

## SANTA ROSA GULCH

El.: c. 4000′                    Loc.: Greenlee A-8
The Santa Rosa Mine at the head of this gulch resulted in the name for what is also called Santa Rosa Wash. The mine is located on Santa Rosa Mountain at the head of the gulch. The gulch is now filled with mine waste.

Ref.:   Simmons; Patton. Map: GF-1.

## SARDINE CREEK

El.: c. 5000'                    Loc.: Greenlee AB-7
The steep and narrow character of this canyon resulted in its descriptive name.
Ref.:   Scott. Maps: GF-1; GF-2.

**a.n. Sardine Saddle**                                        Greenlee

## SAWED OFF MOUNTAIN

El.: c. 8000'                    Loc.: Greenlee B-2.6
                                 Sec. 30, T. 3 N,. R. 30 E.
The fact that this mountain has a point which looks as though its tip had been sawed off led John H. Toles Cosper to give it its descriptive name in 1883.
Ref.:   Barnes; Simmons. Map: None.

## SHANNON MOUNTAIN

El.: c. 5000'                    Loc.: Greenlee AB-8
Charles and Baylor Shannon were among the earliest mining men to arrive in the Clifton area. They were nephews of Robert and Jim Metcalf. Baylor became a cattleman, but Charlie was a prospector at heart and located claims both on Chase Creek and at the place which later became Metcalf. He built the Shannon Smelter for the Shannon Copper Company on the hill which bears his name.
Ref.:   Reilly; Scott; Shannon; 126, pp. 77-76, 7. Maps: GF-1; C-10; C-11.

## SHEEP WASH

El.: c. 5000'                    Loc.: Greenlee A-5.2-6.7
Before cattle were brought into this area, there used to be sheep along this wash.
Ref.:   Simmons. Maps: GF-2; C-13.

## SHELDON

El.: c. 4000'                    Loc.: Greenlee C-11.7
A former railroad station at Sheldon is now gone and all that remains of the community is the cemetery and a few farmers' holdings. The place is said to have been named for Gov. Lionel Sheldon, who was governor of New Mexico in 1883-84. There is, however, a possibility that it may have been named for an engineer on the railroad.
P.O. est. August 27, 1908. John F. Holder, p.m. Discont. November 29, 1919.
Ref.:   102, p. 79; Barnes; Simmons. Maps: GF-3; C-10; C-12.

## SQUARE BUTTE

El.: c. 4000'                    Loc.: Greenlee AB-8.9
Descriptive.

**v.n. Square Mountain**
Ref.:   Scott. Maps: GF-1; GF-2.

## SQUAW CREEK

El.: c. 6000'                    Loc.: Greenlee BC-4
Many place names incorporate the word "squaw," for reasons which more often than not have been lost. This is the case with Squaw Creek as well as with the majority of names listed below.

Maps: GF-2; C-13.

| a.n. Squaw Butte | Map: B-7 | Yavapai |
|---|---|---|
| Squaw Butte | Map: B-7 | Gila |
| Squaw Canyon | | Gila |

The King S. Woolsey expedition battled Indians here.
Ref.:   *Arizona Miner*, April 20, 1864, 2:2.

| Squaw Creek | Maps: GE-1; GE-5 | Graham |
|---|---|---|
| Squaw Creek | Map: GM-21 | Yavapai |
| Squaw Creek, Middle Fork | Map: GM-21 | Yavapai |
| Squaw Creek, North Fork | Map: GM-21 | Yavapai |
| Squaw Creek, South Fork | Map: GM-21 | Yavapai |
| Squaw Creek | Map: C-12 | Greenlee |
| Squaw Creek Mesa | Map: GM-3 | Yavapai |
| Squaw Flat | Map: GG-7 | Maricopa |

This is an old Indian camping ground on the Salt River.

| Squaw Mesa | El.: 6103'. Map: GD-6 | Gila |
|---|---|---|
| Squaw Mountain | Loc.: Sec. 36, T. 9 N., R. 3 E. | Yavapai |
| Squaw Mountain | Maps: B-6; C-12 | Cochise |
| Squaw Peak | Loc.: T. 28 N., R. 19 E. | Mohave |
| Squaw Peak | Map: C-12 | Gila |
| Squaw Peak | El.: 4786'. Map: GD-14 | Maricopa |

Barnes says named by Dr. O. A. Turney c. 1910.

| Squaw Peak | El.: 6533'. Map: GM-21 | Yavapai |
|---|---|---|
| Squaw Peak | Map: GM-6 | Yavapai |
| Squaw Peak | Map: C-12 | Yavapai |

Barnes says Dudley Brooks named this peak before 1882 while a military telegraph operator at Camp Verde. Brooks on his discharge took up a ranch near here.

| Squaw Peak | Map: C-12 | Yuma |
|---|---|---|
| Squaw Tank | Loc.: Approx. sec. 15, R. 17 W., T. 1 S. | Yuma |
| Squaw Tit | El.: 4371'. Map: GM-21 | Yavapai |
| Descriptive. | | |
| Squaw Tit Peak | Loc.: T. 9 S., R. 2 W. | Maricopa |
| Descriptive. | | |
| Squaw Tits | El.: 2478'. Map: GC-7 | Maricopa |
| Descriptive. | | |

## STRAY HORSE CREEK

El.: c. 7000'                    Loc.: Greenlee A-2.1
At one time this place was known as Rattlesnake Creek. However, it was a camping area and the Forest Service changed the name because campers showed a definite reluctance to stop at a place bearing the name Rattlesnake. A story developed that a stray horse wandered around this vicinity for many years and that was the origin of the substitute name.
Ref.:   Reilly; Barnes.

| a.n. Stray Horse Divide | Map: GF-2 | Greenlee |
|---|---|---|
| Rattlesnake Camp | Map: GF-2 | Greenlee |
| Rattlesnake Gap | Map: GF-2 | Greenlee |

## SUN FLOWER MESA

El.: c. 4000'                    Loc.: Greenlee C-7
Descriptive.
Ref.:   Scott. Map: GF-2.

## SUNSET PEAK

El.: 6983'                       Loc.: Greenlee BC-7.8
The last thing the sun hits in the canyon is this peak. It was used in 1886 as a signal station during Gen. Nelson A. Miles' campaign against the Apaches.
Ref.:   Barnes. Maps: GF-2; C-12.

## THOMAS CREEK

El.: c. 6000'                    Loc.: Greenlee B-9.4
Charlie Thomas was a cattleman who kept his steers on
Thomas Creek during the winter.
Ref.:   Mrs. Fred Fritz, Sr.; Reilly. Map: GF-2.

## THUMB BUTTE

El.: c. 4000'          Loc.: Greenlee B-11 T. 7 S., R. 29 E.
Descriptive. "Thumb" is used descriptively in many place
names. A few are listed below.
Ref.:   Barnes. Map: None.

**a.n. Thumb Butte**
    Loc.: S. side of Union Pass road, half way up west slope of
    summit.                                    Mohave
    **Thumb Butte**    Loc.: Sec. 28, T. 23 S., R. 12 E.    Santa Cruz
    **Thumb Butte**                                    Yavapai
    Probably the best known Thumb Butte in Arizona is that
    which looms like a gigantic hand doubled into a fist, thumb
    slightly bent, behind the city of Prescott.
    **Thumb Butte**       Loc.: T. 5 S., R. 17 W.          Yuma

## WARD CANYON

El.: c. 4000'                      Loc.: Greenlee B-9
In the early 1900's, Johnnie Ward ran a slaughter house
in this canyon, hence its name.
The old railroad from Clifton to Lordsburg passed through
what later became Ward's Canyon. In April 1880, a stage
party en route to Lordsburg met Mexicans just outside of
Clifton, who warned them that Apaches were active along
the route. The stage party went with a posse and in the
canyon found a party of Mexicans with one dead and
scalped as a result of an Apache attack.
Ref.:   28a, p. 57; Patterson. Maps: GF-1; GF-2.

## WEBSTER SPRING

El.: c. 6000'                    Loc.: Greenlee A-1.7
It has been suggested that this spring was named for Frank
and Reece Webster of Central (Graham County), who
hauled logs for the Arizona Copper Company mine workings. These men had a corral on the upper part of Eagle
Creek. On the other hand, a number of informants say
that Judd Webster, first supervisor of Greenlee County,
located at this spring.
Ref.:   Mrs. Jay Kleinman, Letter, May 16, 1956; Cosper; Reil-
        ly; Scott. Maps: GF-1; GF-2.

## WILD BUNCH CANYON

El.: c. 4000'                    Loc.: Greenlee CB-7.7
This is a rough canyon where wild cattle hid out.
Ref.:   Mrs. Fred Fritz, Sr. Map: GF-2.

## WILLOW SPRINGS CANYON

El.: c. 4000'                    Loc.: Greenlee D-15
Descriptive.
Ref.:   Simmons. Map: GB-19.

## WOOLAROC

El.: c. 6000'                    Loc.: Greenlee A-5
Pro.:   /wúwlərak/
Woolaroc is the post office which was located on the Double
Circle Ranch (q.v.).
Among the names suggested for the new post office to
be established here was that of Woolaroc. It was submitted
by W. Ellis Wiltbank, who was prompted to do so because
that was the name of the airplane which won the Dole
Honolulu-to-San Francisco Flight at that time. The name
of the plane in turn was taken from that of Frank Phillips'
estate in northern Oklahoma which had Woods, Lakes
and Rocks, hence the name.
P.O. est. May 24, 1924. Willard L. Mabra, p.m. Discont. June
14, 1930.
Ref.:   Barnes; Shannon. Map: C-13.

## YORK

El.: c. 4000'                    Loc.: Greenlee C-11
York was a location on the railroad from Clifton to Duncan. It was named for the nearby George R. York Ranch
on the bend between Duncan and Clifton. York had this
ranch in the early 1880's. It was attacked by the same
band of Apaches which in 1882 killed seven Mexicans at
Guthrie. York gave them a hot reception, and they abandoned the attack on his place. Soon after, York was trailing
some of his horses and was ambushed and killed by Indians
in Doubtful Canyon.
P.O. est. as Yorks January 16, 1882. Lou M. Butler, p.m. Discont. July 9, 1883. Re-est. as York May 9, 1911. Lotte Rubey,
p.m. Discont. February 28, 1920.
Ref.:   55, p. 617; 28a, p. 75. Maps: A-3; C-5.

# MARICOPA COUNTY

*The river made the life of Salt River Valley — Hohokam farmers and their irrigation — Jack Swilling's ditch — glimpse of modern fertility and the capitol.*

## MARICOPA COUNTY:
Pro.: /mærikópə/

The first county in Arizona to be carved from the original four (Pima, Yuma, Mohave, and Yavapai) was Maricopa County on February 12, 1871. The new county was named for an important Yuman tribe known to have been living with and below the Pima Indians at least as early as 1775, according to Fr. Francisco Garcés. Maricopa was the name applied to them by the Pimas (Maricopas called themselves *Pipatsje,* "people"). Apparently the Maricopas moved gradually from the Gulf of California to the location noted by Fr. Garcés. Col. Kit Carson found them at the mouth of the Gila in 1826.

A reservation for the Maricopa Indians was established on February 28, 1859, on the Gila River, the area being enlarged by various executive orders thereafter. No treaty was ever made with the Maricopa or Pima Indians, they having always been friendly toward the white men.

The county seat of Maricopa is Phoenix, the state's largest city, also the site of the Arizona State Capitol. Maricopa County is a rich agricultural district, irrigated in large part by the waters of the Salt River impounded in Roosevelt Lake, Apache Lake, and Canyon Lake. A number of mountain ranges cross the county. The area of the county is 5,904,640 acres.

## ADAM'S MESA

El.: 2515'  Loc.: Maricopa 2, F-4.9
Jeff Adams, a cattleman, had a ranch near this location.
Ref.: Barnes. Map: GG-11.

## AGUA CALIENTE

El.: c. 600'  Loc.: Maricopa 1, A-16.4
Pro.: /agwəkaliˆente/  Spanish. "hot water"
In 1744 Fr. Jacobo Sedelmayr while exploring the Big Bend
region of the Gila River visited an Indian rancheria which
he called Santa Maria del Agua Caliente, noting that it
would be a fine site for a mission. Several years later, on
November 14, 1775, Fr. Francisco Garcés again used the
name Agua Caliente (see a.n.)
The first American to settle at Agua Caliente was King
S. Woolsey (b. Alabama, 1832; d. June 29, 1879). Woolsey came to Arizona from California in 1860, serving for
a time as a mule driver and hay contractor for the military
post at Fort Yuma. Probably in the spring of 1865 he arrived at Agua Caliente in partnership with George Martin.
In 1863 Woolsey had been with the Walker party prospecting along Lynx Creek (q.v. Yavapai). It was after this
that he took up ranching in the Salt River Valley and later
moved to Agua Caliente. The partnership with Martin at
Agua Caliente did not last long. Martin sold out to Woolsey c. 1868 and Woolsey took charge of a stage station
nearby (See Burkes).
Woolsey was active in territorial politics and won a reputation as an Indian fighter (See Bloody Tanks, Gila).
When Woolsey took up his claim at Agua Caliente he
noted a fact recorded also by Sedelmayr many years
earlier — that Indians made use of the warm water springs
for medicinal purposes, using the mud to soothe their
pains. By 1873 Agua Caliente had developed into a prominent health resort. Woolsey sold out part of his holdings to
David Neahr. On Woolsey's death the land went to Neahr
with the water rights reserved by Woolsey's heirs.
P.O. est. March 12, 1867. Patrick McKannon, p.m. Discont.
June 24, 1867. Re-est. March 17, 1888.

v.n. Ojo Caliente
Ref.: Arizona Graphic, March 24, 1900, p. 1; Arizona Star,
March 21, 1920, 1:2; Citizen, May 31, 1873, 1:5; 7, pp.
365-366, 367; 35, p. 118; 145, p. 40; 105, pp. 138-139,
142; 25, p. 81. Maps: A-11; GG-15.

a.n. Agua Caliente Mountains
El.: 1250'. Map: GN-2  Maricopa and Yuma

San Bernardino  Maricopa
This now-vanished Maricopa rancheria was at Agua Caliente. It was visted and named by Fr. Francisco Garcés in
1775.

v.n. San Bernardino del Agua Caliente
Ref.: 88, II, 426.

## AGUA FRIA

El.: c. 1000'  Loc.: Maricopa 2, A-4
Pro.: /agwə fríyə/  Spanish: "cold water"
The stage station at this location was owned and operated
in 1879 by Martin Heald Calderwood, who was building
a residence for his family and for use by travelers. By
August 15, 1884, Calderwood had sold his station.

Ref.: Arizona Miner, August 29, 1879; Prescott Courier,
August 15, 1884 (APHS). Map: E-20.

a.n. Agua Fria River
Maps: All since 1880.  Maricopa and Yavapai

## AGUILA

El.: c. 1000'  Loc.: Maricopa 1, AB-0.5
Pro.: /agiˆlə/  Spanish: "eagle"
This small settlement on the railroad is named for the
nearby eminence, Pico del Aguila (Spanish: "eagle's beak.")
Up until at least mid-1909, there was apparently little at
Aguila other than a small railroad station. In that year,
however, F. H. Kline, a mining promoter, laid plans for
the development of a town at Aguila. Kline and his asso-
ciates planned to erect a community complete from bar-
bershop to hotel. The plans came to very little, but the
results were more than had previously existed here.
P.O. est. March 30, 1910. Frank Sperger, p.m.
Ref.: Arizona Gazette, June 11, 1909, 13:6; Willson. Maps:
C-10; GG-19.

## ALDER CREEK

El.: c. 3500'  Loc.: Maricopa 2, HI-4.5-5.5
Descriptive.
Ref.: Barnes. Maps: GD-15; GG-3.

## ALHAMBRA

El.: c. 1000'  Loc.: Maricopa 2, AB-6.5
Josiah Harbert, a native of Alhambra, California, owned
the land on which the town of Alhambra was built. He
named both this place and the one in California.
P.O. est. January 13, 1893. Arthur E. Hinton, p.m. Discont.
November 15, 1918. Wells Fargo Station, 1903.
Ref.: Barnes; P. O. Records. Map: GG-14.

## ALICIA

El.: c. 1000'  Loc.: Maricopa 2, A-9.8
This location on the Arizona Eastern Railroad was named
for Alice Masten, daughter of N. K. Masten, first president of the Maricopa and Phoenix Railroad.
Ref.: Barnes. Map: GG-9.

## ALLAH

El.: c. 1100'  Loc.: Maricopa 1, F-1
This railroad station was established on Brill's ranch. The
name of the ranch was changed to Garden of Allah, that
being considered descriptive of its resemblance to the desert
portrayed in the novel of the same name.
P.O. est. May 4, 1918. William C. Hyatt, p.m.
Ref.: Barnes; 102, p. 10; APHS Names File; G. E. P. Smith;
P.O. Records. Map: GG-19.

## ALMA

El.: c. 850'  Loc.: Maricopa 2, C-7.6
Sec. 21, T. 1 N., R. 5 E
The first name of Alma was Stringtown, because the houses
were strung out along a country road bordered for miles
by cottonwoods. There is a possibility that the name Alma
is a corruption of the Spanish word alamo ("cottonwood").
Today Alma is a part of Mesa (q.v.).
Ref.: 112, p. 218. Map: None.

## ALPHA

El.: c. 600'  Loc.: Maricopa 1, A-11.6
The origin of this name has not yet been ascertained. (cf. Burkes Station).

P.O. est. May 1, 1894. Tennie Cameron, p.m. Discont. March 8, 1898.

Ref.: P.O. Records. Maps: A-16; C-8.

## APACHE CAVE

El.: 4619'  Loc.: Maricopa 2, HI-5.4
Pro.: /əpǽči/
On December 27, 1872, troops under Maj. William Brown overtook and vanquished Yavapai Indians hiding in a cave. Lt. John G. Bourke, who was with Brown's party, said that the band of Indians was under the command of Nani-chaddi and that an Apache scout called Nantaje led the troops to the cave. When Brown arrived on the spot, the battle was already in progress between the Indians and an advance party under an officer named Ross. The wails of Indian women and the crying of Indian children and babies hit by bullets richocheting from the cavern roof led Brown to order a cease-fire so that the Indians might have a chance to surrender. Instead of yielding, the Indians began their weird, half-exultant death chant and about twenty Indian warriors leaped over the rampart of the cave toward the troops. Seven Indians were killed at once and the rest retreated.

Meanwhile, a third contingent of soldiers under officers named Burns and Thomas heard the battle and came to the top of the precipice and looked down. Burns harnessed two of his men with the suspenders of other soldiers, helping the two soldiers to lean down over the precipice and to fire directly at the Indians. The other soldiers at the top of the cliff rolled huge boulders on the Indians. The mingled thunder of crashing boulders, the screams of the dying Indians, and the volleys of gunfire made a frightful din. Again Maj. Brown signalled for a halt in the offensive. All was still. When the troops entered the cave they found about thirty survivors, none of whom had any thought of further fighting. The bodies of the dead were left in the cave, hence the names sometimes applied, Skeleton or Skull Cave.

Ref.: 22, pp. 190, 191, 196, 197, 199. Map: B-7 (Cave).

a.n. Skull Mesa  Map: GG-3  Maricopa
The fact that Apaches of various tribes were active throughout this part of Arizona has led to the use of the name Apache in several instances, some of which are listed below.

Apache Creek  Map: GG-3  Maricopa
Apache Gap  Map: GD-15  Maricopa
Probably so named because it is on the Apache Trail.

Ref.: 151, p. 99.

Apache Lake (cf. Horse Mesa, a.n.). Map: B-7  Maricopa
Apache Peak  Map: B-7  Maricopa
Apache Spring  Map: B-7  Maricopa
Apache Trail (q.v., Gila)  Maricopa and Gila

## APIARY WELL

El.: c. 250'  Loc.: Maricopa 1, BC-10.4
Although wild bees were noticeably thick at many wells in this area, there is no indication that any one well was particularly designated Apiary Well locally.

Ref.: Parkman. Map: A-7.

## ARLINGTON

El.: 800'  Loc.: Maricopa 1, EF-7.6
The Arlington Valley includes the area from Gillespie Dam to the present community of Arlington. The valley and community were named by Mrs. Moses Clanton, a native of Missouri and wife of the man who helped build the Buckeye Canal in 1900. Mrs. Clanton said she had no reason for suggesting the name except that she liked the sound of it.

P.O. est. November 23, 1899. Moses E. Clanton, p.m.

Ref.: Parkman; P.O. Records. Maps: GG-19; GG-18 (Arlington Valley).

a.n. Arlington Mesa
Loc.: N.e. end of Arlington Valley on Gila River.
Ref.: 141, p. 69.  Maricopa

## ASHDALE

El.: c. 4000'  Loc.: Maricopa 2, C-1.4
Ash trees on Cave Creek gave the name to this location.
Ref.: Barnes. Map: GG-19.

## ASHER HILLS

El.: 2050'  Loc.: Maricopa 2, DE-3.9
These hills were probably named for nearby Asher's Ranch.
Ref.: None. Map: GG-11.

## AVONDALE

El.: c. 1000'  Loc.: Maricopa 1, IJ-6-4
The story of Avondale is so closely allied with that of a place called Coldwater that the two must be treated simultaneously.

Billy Moore had a freight station on the west bank of the Agua Fria River (Spanish: "cold water") where he had a well with clear, cold water. For both these reasons he called his place Coldwater, although many old-timers referred to it simply as Billy Moore's. Billy's place was near a ranch known as Avondale.

When the railroad established a station in the area, it was a mile west of Coldwater. The new station on the Avondale Ranch, however, was called Litchfield, and around it a community took shape. Moore's lost its importance as a freighting station so that the name Coldwater was gradually abandoned. It is not known why the post office was not named Litchfield when it was re-established after a lapse of six years, but the name Avondale was used instead of Coldwater because of the post office rule that once-used post office names could not be re-instated.

P.O. est. as Coldwater July 2, 1896. Mary V. Jones, p.m. Discont. October 3, 1896 (never in operation). Re-est. December 29, 1897. John M. Van Horn, p.m. Discont. July 11, 1905.

P.O. re-est. as Avondale, March 23, 1911. Henry E. Weaver, p.m.

Ref.: Barnes; Parkman; 141, p. 13; P.O. Records. Map: GG-2.

## BARNES BUTTE

El.: 1475'                    Loc.: Maricopa 2, BC-7
This butte was named in 1937 for Will C. Barnes (b. 1859; d. 1936), noted Arizona pioneer and historian. A plaque was erected in his honor by members of the Forest Service in 1937.

While in army service with the Signal Corps in Arizona, Barnes earned a Congressional Medal of Honor. After he was discharged, he spent a busy life as a stockman, legislator, forester, and author.

Ref.:   State Library Files. Map: GG-12.

## BARTLETT DAM

El.: c. 3000'                  Loc.: Maricopa 2, EF-2.3
Bartlett Dam, which was completed in 1939, is the highest multiple-arch, impounding dam in the world. The arches are seven feet thick at the bottom and more than two feet thick at the top.

Ref.:   4, pp. 55, 147. Map: B-7.

## BEARDSLEY

El.: c. 850'                   Loc.: Maricopa 1, I-3.5
Will H. Beardsley began an irrigation project at this location in 1888.

Ref.:   Barnes; 141, p. 202. Map: A-7.

## BEAUFORD MOUNTAIN

El.: 5239'                     Loc.: Maricopa 2, D-1.2
Clay Beauford (b. 1848; d. 1929) was serving as a Confederate soldier in 1863 at the age of fifteen. He came to Arizona in 1870, still as a soldier, but this time with the Fifth U. S. Cavalry. He served as chief of scouts and captain for the San Carlos Indian Police from 1874 to 1880. In January 1879, he re-adopted his legal name of Welford Chapman Bridwell.

**v.n. Humboldt Mountain**

Ref.:   Barnes. Maps: C-6; E-10 (Mt. Buford); GG-3.

## BELL BUTTE

El.: 1372'                     Loc.: Maricopa 2, B-7.6
Descriptive.

Ref.:   Barnes. Map: GG-12.

## BIG HORN MOUNTAINS

El.: c. 2500'                  Loc.: Maricopa 1, AB-2.5-5
In 1854 Antisell referred to the Big Horn or Goat Mountains, where mountain sheep abounded.

Ref.:   2, p. 131; 9, p. 197. Maps: C-2; C-12; E-18; E-20.

**a.n. Big Horn**     El.: c. 1800'. Map: GG-7     Maricopa
Little remains today to mark the location of a former small settlement which took its name from the nearby Big Horn Mountains. The community was on the old Buzzard Ranch.

P.O. est. September 24, 1930. Wesley W. Matteson, p.m. Discont. June 29, 1935.

Ref.:   P.O. Records; Johnson.

## BLUE PLATEAU

El.: 2921'                    Loc.: Maricopa 2, H-13.5
Descriptive of appearance of this plateau.

Ref.:   4, p. 224. Map: GG-8.

## BLUE POINT

El.: c. 1500'                 Loc.: Maricopa 2, E-6
This steep bank at the end of the Tonto Sheep Trail has a blue clay face, hence the name.

Ref.:   Barnes. Map: B-7.

## BOSQUE

El.: c. 1000'                 Loc.: Maricopa 1, GH-5.7
                              Spanish: "forest grove"
In 1895 a shipping point was established here by the Phoenix Wood and Coal Company. The company was cutting ironwood and mesquite, thick in this area, hence the name. The work was on government land, and the company was sued by the United States Government and made to pay twenty-five cents an acre for "cutting timber on public lands."

Ref.:   Barnes. Map: GG-8.

## BUCKEYE

El.: 960'                     Loc.: Maricopa 1, G-7.1
Thomas Newton Clanton, G. L. Spain, and M. M. Jackson were responsible for the name Buckeye for this post office. Jackson built the Buckeye Canal, naming it for his home state, Ohio. In the midst of the agricultural land to be irrigated by the canal, Clanton gave a quarter section for a townsite. Jackson was a native of Sydney, Ohio, and the new town was known as Sydney. By 1889 the townsite had been laid out. When the post office was established two years later, it was set up in Clanton's house with his daughter as postmistress. Curiously enough, although the town by 1895 was being referred to as Buckeye, deeds were made out under the name of Sydney until the town was incorporated c. 1931. It was then necessary to obtain a special order from the State Supreme Court officially to change the name from Sydney to Buckeye.

P.O. est. March 10, 1888. Mrs. Cora J. Clanton, p.m.

Ref.:   Parkman; *Arizona Star*, May 17, 1889, 4:2. Maps: C-7; GG-19.

**a.n. Buckeye Hills**   El.: 1750'. Maps: GG-18; GG-4   Maricopa
**Buckeye Valley**       Loc.: W. of Buckeye              Maricopa
Ref.:   141, p. 67.

## BURGER WELL

El.: c. 400'                  Loc.: Maricopa 1, C-7
John Burger dug the old Burger Well on the stage road to Agua Caliente. The well has long since caved in. Formerly there was a small station named Burger on the Phoenix branch of the S.P. R.R. east of Signal Butte. Only a signboard marks this spot today.

Ref.:   Barnes; Mercer; 141, p. 204. Map: A-7.

## BURKES STATION

El.: c. 500'         Loc.: Maricopa 1, A-11.3
Burkes Station was established on the Butterfield Overland Stage Route in September 1858. It was named for Patrick Burke, its first keeper.

Apparently the station fell into disuse, for in 1864 J. Ross Browne called it a "former overland mail station," which in Browne's day was occupied by two soldiers who took care of government hay stored there. Later the stage station was again in use, for in July 1874 G. R. Whistler had purchased it from Billy Fourr (cf. Oatman Flat) and was acting as station keeper. Whistler employed Ventura Nuñez as a stableman. The Mexican murdered Whistler. Nuñez then fled, but was caught by King S. Woolsey ninety miles away and brought back to Burkes Station where Nuñez was immediately hanged. His body was left dangling as a warning to other potential malefactors. When the remains finally dropped to the ground, Mexican traders buried them. The coming of the railroad was the end of Burkes Station, which reverted to being a part of a ranch. In 1900 the name for Burkes Ranch had changed to Alpha, but the reason for the change has not yet been learned.

Ref.: 111, pp. 273-74; 32, II, 181; 25, p. 99; 35, p. 119, (Note 26); Maps: C-1; C-4; E-18; E-20; E-21 (Berk's Station); E-24 (Bark's Station).

## BURNT WELLS

El.: c. 400'         Loc.: Maricopa 1, BC-5.2
A brush fire is said to have occurred over a quarter of a century ago at this location.

Ref.: Barnes. Map: A-7.

## BUTTERFLY MOUNTAIN

El.: c. 4000'         Loc.: Maricopa 1, JI-8.4
This word may have come from *mariposa* (Spanish: "butterfly").

Ref.: Barnes. Map: GG-10.

## CALDERWOOD

El.: c. 1500'   Loc.: Maricopa 1, J-4.3. T. 5 N., R. 1 E.
In 1865-66 M. H. Calderwood (d. May 15, 1913) served with the California Volunteers in what later became Santa Cruz County. Calderwood subsequently established a stage station where the Agua Fria River intercepted the road from Phoenix to Wickenburg, a site often used for stage stations. Calderwood served in the state legislature in 1877 and again in 1895.

P.O. est. January 26, 1892. Amer D. McGinnis, p.m. Discont. February 26, 1894.
Ref.: 111, p. 278; Barnes; P.O. Records. Map: E-20 (Agua Fria Station).

**a.n. Calderwood Peak**     Loc.: T. 5 N., R. 1 E.     Maricopa

## CAMELBACK MOUNTAIN

El.: 2700'         Loc.: Maricopa 2, B-6.2
Descriptive.
Ref.: None. Map: GG-1.

## CAMP CREEK

El.: c. 2500'         Loc.: Maricopa 2, DF-1.5-3.4
Camp Creek is a camping spot used during summer months.
Ref.: Barnes. Maps: GD-15; GG-3.

## CARL PLEASANT DAM

El.: c. 2000'   Loc.: Maricopa 1, J-1.5; Maricopa 2, A-1
Carl Pleasant Dam was named for its engineer and contractor-builder. The dam, completed in 1927, is two hundred fifty feet high and was constructed on the multiple arch plan.

As a result of the completion of the dam, waters collected in what is sometimes called Lake Pleasant, but more commonly Pleasant Lake. The lake is eight miles long.

A post office was in existence during the construction period.
P.O. est. as Lake Pleasant September 30, 1926. James G. Tripp, p.m. Discont. February 27, 1928.
Ref.: 4, p. 356. Maps: A-13; C-13; GG-19.

## CASHION

El.: 991'         Loc.: Maricopa 1, J-6.3
Pro.: /kǽšiyən/
Jim Cashion, a native of Canada, was a railroad construction superintendent. In 1900 Cashion owned an entire section (640 acres) of land where the town of Cashion is located today. The railroad passed through the Cashion Ranch, which accounts for the name of the depot on the railroad at this place. The town came into existence c. 1910.
P.O. est. November 27, 1911. Fred L. Bush, p.m.
Ref.: Parkman; P.O. Records. Map: GG-2.

## CASTLE DOME

El.: 5316'         Loc.: Maricopa 2, J-6.2
Descriptive.
Ref.: Barnes. Map: GD-15.

## CAVE CREEK

El.: c. 2500'         Loc.: Maricopa 2, BC-2.8
The name Cave Creek dates back at least to October 1870 when John H. Marion of Prescott wrote of having traveled along this route with Col. George Stoneman's party. The name probably derived from the presence of a few rather large caves used by Indians. At least three skirmishes between soldiers and Indians occurred along this creek.

The community of Cave Creek came into existence prior to 1890.
P.O. est. April 28, 1890. William B. Gillingham, p.m. Discont. November 20, 1895. Re-est. as Cavecreek, January 9, 1896.
Ref.: APHS Files; 85, pp. 439, 440, 441. Map: GG-3.

## CEMENT WELL

El.: c. 1500'         Loc.: Maricopa 1, F-5.5
In the arid desert country of southwestern Arizona, the presence of a water hole has often meant the difference between life and death. This accounts for the importance placed on naming all such water holes to aid travelers in locating them. Cement Wells was used by the Flower Pot Cattle Company. The well was so named because its sides were cemented.

Ref.: 141, p. 205. Map: C-12.

## CHANDLER

El.: 1210'                  Loc.: Maricopa 2, DE-8.8
Alexander John Chandler (b. near Coaiticock, Canada, July 15, 1859; d. May 8, 1950) came to Arizona in August 1887. He was appointed the first veterinary surgeon for the Territory of Arizona. Meanwhile, severe drought had set in and Arizona cattle were perishing rapidly. After only thirty days as state veterinarian in Prescott, Chandler resigned, intending to go to California. On his wagon trip down the Black Canyon Road, Chandler became convinced he was doing the right thing. However, the night he arrived in Phoenix it began to rain and Chandler changed his mind. He reconsidered his resignation as veterinary surgeon and took up the job again, keeping it until 1892.

Chandler became one of the largest landholders in the Salt River Valley, having nearly eighteen thousand acres which formed the Chandler Ranch in the early 1890's. While Roosevelt Dam was being constructed, Chandler was becoming an expert in irrigation. He surveyed his acreage into agricultural plots of from ten to one hundred sixty acres, and in 1911 advertised his land for sale. The response was immediate. A year later the town of Chandler was established to provide a community for the newcomers.

P.O. est. April 11, 1912. Ernest E. Morrison, p.m. Incorporated February 16, 1920.

Ref.:   156, pp. 18, 19, 20, 17, 42, 48, 192. Map: GG-12.

**a.n. Chandler Heights**                      Maricopa
In the late 1920's Dr. Chandler, C. A. Baldwin and others created a corporation for the growth of citrus thirteen miles southeast of Chandler. A community developed at this place.

P.O. est. August 12, 1938. Mrs. Teresa M. Binner, p.m.

**Chandler Junction**        Map: GG-12            Maricopa

## CHOLLA MOUNTAIN

El.: c. 2500'                   Loc.: Maricopa 1, J-1
Pro.: /čóyə/                    Spanish: "skull"
Cholla cactus grows abundantly on this mountain. Members of the cholla group include the so-called teddy-bear, stag horn and "jumping" cholla.

Ref.:   Barnes. Maps: C-10; C-12.

## COLEDON

El.: c. 500'                  Loc.: Maricopa 1, FG-11.8
This point on the S.P.R.R. appears on GLO 1909 as Cole. In 1921 it shows as Coledon. After 1921 it disappears from subsequent GLO maps.

The original name was that of a railroad engineer. It was shortened to facilitate telegraphing.

Ref.:   Barnes. Map: GG-19.

## CONTINENTAL MOUNTAIN

El.: 4535'                  Loc.: Maricopa 2, C-2.2
The Continental Mine gave its name to this mountain.

Ref.:   Barnes. Map: GG-3.

## CORGIAT WASH

El.: c. 1200'               Loc.: Maricopa 1, JG-7.9-7.2
Pro.:  /koẃrjɔt/
A one-armed French farmer named Corgiat farmed along this wash in 1915. A few years later he moved away.

**v.n. Corgett Wash (corruption)**
Ref.:   Parkman. Map: GG-2.

## COURT HOUSE BUTTE

El.: c. 500'                  Loc.: Maricopa 1, A-6
Descriptive.

**v.n. Cathedral Rock**
Ref.:   141, p. 206. Map: A-7.
**a.n. Court House Well**  Loc.: Sec. 16, T. 2 N., R. 10 W.   Maricopa

## CRABB WELL

El.: c. 2500'                 Loc.: Maricopa 1, CD-1.5
D. D. Crabb dug this well about ten miles southeast of Aguila (q.v.).

Ref.:   Barnes. Map: None.

## CRAMM MOUNTAIN

El.: c. 3000'                 Loc.: Maricopa 2, C-1
In 1882 a prospector and miner named Cramm lived at the foot of this mountain.

Ref.:   Barnes. Map: GG-3.

## DEADMAN GAP

El.: c. 1500'                 Loc.: Maricopa 1, DE-14.8
The body of a man who died of thirst was found in this pass c. 1913. Locally it is believed that he died while in pursuit of his horses which had gotten away. His grave can still be seen in the gap.

Ref.:   Kirk Bryan Notes; Stout. Map: C-12.

## DELOSSA

El.: c. 600'                  Loc.: Maricopa 1, B-12.7
Pro.:  /dəlósə/
A siding existed here until 1920. The name came from that of the De la Ossa family, well-known in Lochiel, Santa Cruz County and in Santa Cruz, Sonora.

Ref.:   Lenon. Map: None.
        Listed in Rand McNally 1898 *Business Atlas.*

## DESERT STATION

El.: c. 1500'                 Loc.: Maricopa 2, C-8
Desert Station was established on the Butterfield Overland Stage route in late 1858. The name was descriptive, for Desert Station was located in the middle of the stretch known as the Forty-mile Desert. Water had to be brought to it from twenty miles on either side.

Ref.:   32, II, 172; "Letter of Mr. Wallace, June 15, 1860," *Daily Alta Californian,* July 1, 1860. Maps: A-4; E-18; E-20; E-21.

## DESERT WELL

El.: c. 1600'                          Loc.: Maricopa 2, EF-8.8
This well was dug in 1885 and was considered an important one on the route from Mesa to Florence.
Ref.: 101, p. 40. Maps: C-10; GG-6.

## DIAMOND MOUNTAIN

El.: c. 4500'                          Loc.: Maricopa 2, FG-2.4
The Diamond Cattle Company, which used a diamond brand on the left hip of cattle, ran a large herd here at one time.
Ref.: Barnes. Map: GG-3.

## DIVIDE

El.: c. 2500'                          Loc.: Maricopa 1, D-1
Divide lies on the line between Maricopa and Yavapai Counties, hence the name. Barnes says it is the crest of the watershed between the Colorado River on the west and the Gila to the east and south.
Ref.: 102, p. 32; Barnes. Map: C-10.

## DIXIE

El.: c. 500'                           Loc.: Maricopa 1, DE-7.2
This location on the railroad took its name from the Dixie Mine in the Gila Bend Mountains.
Ref.: 141, p. 33. Maps: C-13; GG-19.

## DOS PALMAS WELL

El.: c. 500'                           Loc.: Maricopa 1, G-3
Pro.: /dospálməs/              Spanish: "two palms"
Two large yucca palms near the well gave it its name. In the early 1930's, practically everything associated with this watering spot washed away. It had at that time already been abandoned for several years.
Ref.: Barnes. Map: A-7.

## DOUBLE BUTTE

El.: c. 1500'                          Loc.: Maricopa 2, BC-8
Descriptive. This butte is about four miles south of Tempe.
**v.n. Gregg Buttes**
    This name came from that of Dr. A. J. Gregg.
Ref.: Barnes. Map: None.

## EAGLE EYE MOUNTAIN

El.: c. 2000'                          Loc.: Maricopa 1, B-1.2
Stage coach drivers named the hole in the mountain which gave this mountain its name.
Ref.: 4, p. 359. Maps: C-10 (Eagle Peak); C-12.

## EASTER

El.: c. 1100'                          Loc.: Maricopa 2, BC-8.9
The town of Easter came into being in 1915, a mile north of Hansen. In that year there were sixty-five people over thirteen years old living at the place, and a petition for a post office was presented. The town served as a community for the Easter Mine, which was discovered on an Easter Sunday.

P.O. est. June 3, 1915. Della S. Miller, p.m. Discont. August 13, 1917.
Ref.: *Tucson Citizen,* July 15, 1915, 6:4; Barnes; Parker (Prescott). Maps: C-12; F-2.

## ECHO CANYON

El.: c. 1100'                          Loc.: Maricopa 2, B-6
In certain parts of this canyon on the north side of Camelback Mountain, there is a notable echoing quality. The Echo Canyon Bowl, a natural amphitheater, is located in the canyon.
Ref.: Theobald. Map: None.

## EDITH

Loc.: Near Phoenix, but not definitely ascertained.
When a post office was established at the Judson Mine, the postmaster named it for his wife.
P.O. est. July 6, 1888. Judson S. Todd, p.m. Discont. December 28, 1888.
Ref.: Barnes; P.O. Records. Map: None.

## ENGLE WELL

El.: 2500'                             Loc.: Maricopa 1, CD-1
                    N.E. ¼, S.E. ¼, Sec. 1, T. 7 N., R. 8 W.
This well was owned by Zagel Engle, but was still incompleted in 1918, although work was under way on it at that time.
Ref.: 141, p. 207. Map: None.

## ENNIS

El.: c. 1400'                          Loc.: Maricopa 2, IJ-4
A Mr. Ennis once owned land here.
Ref.: Barnes. Map: GG-19.

## EUCLID

Loc.: Not known.
The origin of this name is not yet known.
P.O. est. December 18, 1895. Charles W. Prange, p.m. Discont. June 18, 1896.
Ref.: P.O. Records. Map: None.

## FALFA

El.: c. 1300'                          Loc.: Maricopa 2, CD-8.3
Pro.: /fǽlfə/
Alfalfa is raised in this region in large quantities. Falfa, a contraction of alfalfa, is a hay-loading station.
Ref.: Barnes. Map: GG-12.

## FISH CREEK

El.: c. 3000'                          Loc.: Maricopa 2, HJ-5.6-7
This stream was reported by Jack Fraser (see *a.n.*) as being filled with fish c. 1881.
Ref.: Barnes. Maps: GD-15; GK-10; GK-29; GK-16.
**a.n. Fish Creek Canyon** Loc.: Forms bed of Fish Creek   Maricopa
    The fact that this forms almost a perfect box canyon has led some to use the name Box Canyon.
    **Fish Creek Mountain**      Map: GD-15                    Maricopa
    **Fraser's Station**     Maps: A-7; GK-10; GK-16       Maricopa
    This station was established by Jack Fraser c. 1881.
Ref.: Barnes.

## FOREPAUGH

El.: c. 1150'  Loc.: Maricopa 1, BC-0.4
Pro.: /fórp)/
Forepaugh is said to have taken its name from that of an old-time miner, referred to as a "desert rat," who lived on the mountain nearby. Nothing remains at this place except a deserted service station of ancient vintage.
P.O. est. April 25, 1910. Charles B. Genung, p.m. Discont. July 15, 1916.
Ref.: Barnes; P.O. Records. Map: A-7.
a.n. Forepaugh Peak  Loc.: T. 6 N., R. 17 W.  Yuma
Ref.: Barnes.

## FOUR PEAKS

El.: 7645'  Loc.: Maricopa 2, HI-4.4
Descriptive. Four Peaks in the Mazatzal Mountains was the scene of an army skirmish with Indians in 1867 and another in 1874.
Ref.: 89, p. 234; 85, pp. 428, 440. Map: GD-15.

## FOURTH OF JULY WASH

El.: c. 800'  Loc.: Maricopa 1, BC-8.3-10.3
In the 1890's, a group of people went on a camping trip and had a memorable party on the Fourth of July. A member of the party promptly suggested the present name for this hitherto unnamed wash.
Ref.: Parkman. Map: GG-5.
a.n. Fourth of July Butte  Map: C-12  Maricopa

## FRAESFIELD MOUNTAIN

El.: 3054'  Loc.: Maricopa 2, CD-3.8
The origin of this name has not been ascertained.
Maps: GG-3; GG-1.

## FRANKENBURG

El.: c. 1200'  Loc.: Maricopa 2, C-7.5
A cattleman and farmer named Frankenburg had large land holdings here at the turn of the century.
Ref.: Barnes. Map: GG-12.

## FROG TANKS

El.: c. 1500'  Loc.: Maricopa 1, J-1.5
The first Americans in this area found a natural tank used by large frogs. On maps examined, this appears to be the same location as Pratt (q.v.)
Ref.: Barnes. Maps: E-18; E-20.

## GALLETA WELL

El.: c. 1000'  Loc.: Maricopa 1, CD-7.4. T. 1 S., R. 7 W.
Pro.: /gayeyéta/  Spanish: type of grass found on ranges
Galleta Well was a watering place for the Flower Pot Cattle Company herds.
Ref.: Barnes. Map: None.

## GAVILAN PEAK

Loc.: In upper New River Canyon region, but not definitely known.
Apache: "hawk"; Spanish: gavilan "sparrow hawk"
In the 1870's, Tonto Apaches had a stronghold on this peak. In the early 1880's, Charles Mullen, Sr., established a homestead below this mountain on the only open permanent water on New River. The Indians, anxious about the water, raided and ran him out. The U. S. Cavalry immediately raided the Indians in retaliation, and a pitched battle progressed up the river to Gavilan Peak, where the Indians were cornered in a blind canyon. Apparently the peak was named at that time.
Ref.: Letter from Frank T. Alkire to G. E. P. Smith, December 21, 1937. Map: None.

## GIBSON

Loc.: On lower New River, north of Phoenix, but not definitely known.
Jack Gibson ran cattle and raised horses in the early 1890's in this area.
P.O. est. August 18, 1900. William D. Piles, p.m. Discont. December 15, 1900.
Ref.: Barnes; P.O. Records. Map: None.

## GILA BEND

El.: 777'  Loc.: Maricopa 1, F-12
Pro.: /híylə/
The fact that the Gila River makes a sweeping 90° bend to the west at this point has been noted by many travelers, some of whom called it the Big Bend.
Here in 1774 Fr. Francisco Garcés found an Indian rancheria which he called Santos Apostales San Simon y Judas. Many years later a colony of white men began a settlement at or near the old rancheria, where they began raising grain in 1865 for use by freighters. This colony at the Big Bend soon came to be known as Gila Bend. It was located at the turning point of the river where there was a stage station. The town location later shifted. This was due to the fact that the railroad in 1880 laid track away from the river bank. Gradually the original settlement shifted from the deserted stage station to the new railroad depot. Meanwhile, the river itself was changing course to the east, thus in part eliminating the old Big Bend. However, by 1945 the Gila River began to show signs of reverting to its old course.
Gila Bend is today a prosperous agricultural town.
P.O. est. May 1, 1871. Albert Decker, p.m. Wells Fargo Station, 1885.
Ref.: 111, p. 274; Logan; P.O. Records. Map: GG-8.
a.n. Gila Bend (Papago Indian) Reservation
Maps: GG-4; GG-8  Maricopa
This reservation was established on December 12, 1882. At one time it had 22,391 acres, but it now consists of 10,297 acres. The acreage was decreased on June 17, 1909.
Ref.: 88, II, 374; "Annual Reports (1954, 1955, 1956) of the Arizona Commission of Indian Affairs," p. 13.
a.n. Gila Bend Mountains
El.: 3170'. Maps: GG-4; GG-5; GG-18
Maricopa and Yuma

## GILA RANCH

El.: c. 775'  Loc.: Maricopa 1, F-12.6
Pro.: /híylə/
Gila Ranch was built in the summer of 1858 to serve as a time-table station on the Butterfield Overland Stage

route. The place was destroyed by Indians in February 1860 but was later rebuilt.

The ranch was established on the site of a Maricopa Indian village which was noted by Lt. N. Michler in 1854 under the name Tezotal. The desert ironwood tree is listed as *Olneya tesota* in Dr. John Torrey's botanical report for the U. S. Boundary Survey Commission in 1854. The Spanish translation of the Papago name Uupatoitak is Tesota, meaning "cat-claw field." Eight Papago families were living at Uhupat Oidak (*q.v.*) in 1910, although all traces of the old Gila Ranch had vanished.

Ref.:   Schroeder; Kirk Bryan Notes; Phillips; 32, II, 173; 51, p. 117; 50, p. 602; 124, p. 39. Maps: E-2; E-11; E-12; E-17 (Tezotal); E-20 (Gila Station); E-21 (Gila Bend Station).

## GILA RIVER INDIAN RESERVATION

El.: c. 1200'                     Loc.: Maricopa 2, A-9
Pro.: /híylə/
On February 28, 1859, a reservation was established for the bands of Pima and Maricopa Indians living near the Gila River, with additional land being added from time to time until a slight reduction in area was made on July 19, 1915. Total acreage is currently 372,000, with the reservation being bisected by the Gila River. Approximately five thousand Indians live on the reservation.

Ref.:   135, II, 372; "Annual Report of the Arizona Commission of Indian Affairs (1954-1956)," pp. 4-5. Map: GG-12.

## GILBERT

El.: 1273'                     Loc.: Maricopa 2, D-8.3
Robert Gilbert donated the land on which the railroad station and community carrying his name is located.

P.O. est. August 22, 1912. Davis H. Butler, p.m.

Ref.:   Barnes; P.O. Records. Map: GG-12.

## GILLESPIE DAM

El.: c. 600'                     Loc.: Maricopa 1, CD-8.7
The Peoria Dam, of wood and rock, (cf. Peoria) was washed away here by a flood in 1900. The many attempts to dam the Gila below the mouth of the Hassayampa River added another dam in 1906, when the owners of the Enterprise Ranch built one of earth and brush at the site of the old Peoria Dam, in order to divert water into the Enterprise Canal, constructed in 1886.

Frank A. Gillespie of Oklahoma constructed a concrete dam at this location in 1921. The Gillespie holdings in 1956 amounted to eighty-two thousand acres near Gila Bend. In that year a new community with the old name of Arizona City was proposed by H. C. McMullen, who had an option to buy the land for eight million dollars.

P.O. est. August 24, 1925. Edward F. Holland, p.m. Discont. November 30, 1927.

Ref.:   4, p. 463; 141, p. 70; *Arizona Star,* January 26, 1956, 3:3. Maps: C-12 (Peoria Dam Site); F-4; GG-18; GG-19.

## GILLETTE

El.: c. 2000'                     Loc.: Maricopa 1, JK-0.7
The mill site for the Tip Top Mine was located at a town named by D. B. Gillett (or Gillette), Jr. The town is associated with the history of an Arizona pioneer, Jack Swilling, who was living three miles away from Gillette when it was founded. The Swilling Mine was located near Gillette and its owner moved to the new community.

Jack Swilling is said to have been a lieutenant in the Texas Rangers under Capt. Sherod Hunter in 1862, during which year he traveled into Arizona as far as Maricopa Wells. In 1863 Swilling joined the second Joseph Walker prospecting party at Mesilla, New Mexico. He accompanied the group into Arizona and settled in the Salt River Valley where in 1865 he organized the Swilling Canal Company. His was the first irrigation canal utilizing waters of the Salt River. In 1871 Swilling organized the company which built the Tempe Canal. Shortly thereafter, he moved to Black Canyon where he farmed until his change of residence to Gillette. In 1878 while he was living at Gillette, Swilling went to Snively Holes, disinterred the body of Col. Jacob Snively, a prospector, and removed it for reburial at Gillette.

Swilling was a heavy drinker. When he was in his cups, he was prone to confess to deeds which he had not committed. The first recorded instance of this took place at Piños Altos, New Mexico, when he "confessed" to shooting a close friend. A second instance of the same kind occurred when Swilling "confessed" to committing a stage robbery and murder while bringing Snively's remains to Gillette. Unfortunately, Swilling's story was believed and he was committed to the penitentiary at Yuma where he died. His innocence was proved shortly thereafter.

P.O. est. as Gillette, October 15, 1878. John J. Hill, p.m. Discont. August 11, 1887.

Ref.:   *Arizona Sentinel,* February 9, 1878, 1:3; 111, p. 107; 105, p. 144; 52, II, 273; 161, p. 202-204. Maps: C-4; C-5; E-20; GM-3.

## GLENDALE

El.: 1100'                     Loc.: Maricopa 2, A-6
Glendale was established in 1892 by the New England Land Company. The residents were members of the Church of the Brethren of Illinois, who sent B. A. Hatzel as their advance agent. He selected the location and named the town, but his reason for selecting "Glendale" has not been ascertained.

P.O. est. June 27, 1892. Samuel B. Stoner, p.m. Wells Fargo Station, 1903.

Ref.:   Barnes; P.O. Records. Maps: C-8; GG-19.

## GOLDEN

El.: c. 1100'                     Loc.: Maricopa 1, A-1
In the 1880's there was a mining camp named Golden in the Harquahala Mountains, twenty miles south of the railroad.

Ref.:   Barnes. Maps: A-7; C-10.

## GOLDFIELD MOUNTAINS

El.: c. 2500'                    Loc.: Maricopa 2, F-6.5
The Goldfield Mountains take their name from the community of Goldfield and the Goldfield Mine.

**v.n. Oronai Mountain**

**Harosoma Ridge**                    Maricopa and Pinal
Ref.:   151, p. 328. Maps: GG-6; GG-11.

**a.n. Goldfield**          Loc.: Unknown
P.O. est. October 7, 1893. James L. Patterson, p.m. Discont. April 6, 1894.

## GOODYEAR

El.: 1152'                    Loc.: Maricopa 1, IJ-6.3
In 1916 the Goodyear Tire and Rubber Company purchased and leased land in the Salt River Valley to produce Egyptian cotton. The company purchased one tract twenty-seven miles ·southeast of Phoenix and about four miles south of Chandler. The Chandler Branch of the Arizona-Eastern R.R. entered it in the center of Sec. 29 at a station called Casaba. (See *a.n.*). The main town, a mile and a half to the north, was for a short time called Egypt, probably because the company planned to produce Egyptian cotton. The name Goodyear was soon given both to the town and to the ranch.

In 1944 the Goodyear Tire and Rubber Company sold its property. The name Goodyear, however, was transferred from the discontinued post office to the new town of Goodyear.
P.O. est. January 8, 1919. G. Lindley Gollands, p.m. Discont. February 15, 1941. Re-est. in new location as Goodyear, November 22, 1944.
Ref.:   K. B. McMicken, vice-president, Goodyear Farms, Letter, March 28, 1956; 92, p. 436-437; P.O. Records. Map: GG-2.

**a.n. Casaba**          Map: GG-9          Maricopa
The Spanish word for "melon" is *casaba*. Melons were raised here.

## GRANITE REEF DAM

El.: c. 1700'                    Loc.: Maricopa 2, E-7.3
Descriptive.
Granite Reef Dam is a diversion dam on the Salt River below the junction of the Verde and the Salt fifteen miles northeast of Mesa. The dam was completed in 1908. It is one thousand feet long and constitutes the point from which water is diverted into canals on the north and south side to irrigate 340,000 acres of land in the Salt River Valley.
Ref.:   Gertrude Hill, Museum of New Mexico, Letter, August 6, 1955; 156, p. 26. Map: GG-11.

## GUADALUPE

El.: c. 1200'                    Loc.: Maricopa 2, B-8
Pro.: /wadəlúwpe/
Yaqui Indians fled from Mexico to avoid subjugation by Porfirio Diaz, who planned to exile them from their home in northwestern Mexico to the tropical region of Yucatan. Many sought refuge in Arizona where they established villages. The Indian village of Guadalupe is one. It was named for the Virgin of Guadalupe, the patroness saint of Mexico.
Ref.:   4, p. 352; Barnes. Map: GG-12.

## HANSEN

El.: c. 1200'                    Loc.: Maricopa 2, C-8.9
This location on the railroad was named for a farmer in the vicinity.
Ref.:   Barnes. Map: GG-12.

**a.n. Hansen Junction**          Map: GG-12          Maricopa

## HAPPY CAMP

El.: c. 900'                    Loc.: Maricopa 1, H-11.3
An early traveler in territorial Arizona noted the anomaly implied in the name Happy Camp, since it was located in a dreary and barren tract of land. It served as a stage station to which water was hauled from the Gila River and sold to travelers.
Ref.:   31, p. 311. Map: E-20.

## HARDIN

Loc.: On Black Canyon stage route where it crossed Arizona Canal, but not more definitely located as yet.
The reason for this name has not yet been ascertained.
P.O. est. May 9, 1898. Frank Moody, p.m. Discont. October 27, 1898.
Ref.:   P.O. Records. Map: None.

## HASSAYAMPA RIVER

El.: c. 1000'-300'                    Loc.: Maricopa 1, E-G-F-0-7.8
Pro.: /hæsiyǽmpə/          Mohave: *ah*, "water"; *si-am*,
                                        "big rocks"; *pa*, "place of"
In mining folklore the Hassayampa River came to be associated with anyone who was known to be a liar, and prospectors, who understandably were evasive when asked direct questions about their finds, explained their lies by saying that anyone who drank the waters of the Hassayampa was unable to tell the truth. This fact also accounted for the bragging which men did about their finds, particularly since the Vulture Mine (*q.v.*) was such a rich one that the men who worked in the region were prone to tell tall tales about it.

**v.n. Hesiampa (1864)**

Ref.:   Charles S. Genung File, Sharlot Hall Museum; 92, pp. 362, 363; 4, p. 162; 52, IV, 44; *Arizona Miner*, March 9, 1864, 2:3. Maps: A-7; E-20 (Hassayampa Creek); E-21 (Rio Hassayampa).

**a.n. Hassayampa**          Loc.: T. 1 S., R. 5 W.          Maricopa
The small community of Hassayampa developed around a garage owned by Osie Bales and an associate where the main road to Yuma forked at the lower end of the present town of Buckeye. The little community was so named because at this point the Hassayampa River drains into the lower Gila region.

Ref.:   Parkman.

**Hassayampa Plain**                    Maricopa
Ref.:   141, pp. 14, 17.

**Hassayampa Sink**   Loc.: At Wickenburg          Maricopa
This was the local name for the area in early 1864.

## HAT MOUNTAIN

El.: 3482'                    Loc.: Maricopa 1, FG-15.8
The round flat-topped mesa descriptively called Hat Mountain dominates the surrounding plain.

**v.n. Tea Kettle Mountain**
Ref.: 34, p. 212; Kirk Bryan Notes. Maps: C-12; GG-19.

## HERDER MOUNTAIN

El.: c. 3000'                  Loc.: Maricopa 2, F-3.3
Herder Mountain is located on a sheep trail used by sheep migrating between the Tonto Basin and the White Mountain country. The sheep are wintered in the lower and warmer levels. The mountain is used by herders to locate other flocks along the trail in order to prevent one over-running another.
Ref.: Barnes; APHS. Map: GG-11.

## HIEROGLYPHIC HILL

El.: c. 900'                   Loc.: Maricopa 1, B-10.8
                  On Gila River 24 miles n.w. of Gila Bend.
Hieroglyphic Hill was mentioned in several accounts by early travelers in Arizona. Indian pictographs are found in many places in Arizona. This has led to the use of the word "hieroglyphic" in some place names.
Ref.: Barnes. Map: None.

**a.n. Hieroglyphic Canyon**      Map: GM-19      Yavapai and Gila
**Hieroglyphic Tanks**      Map: GM-19      Yavapai and Gila
**Hieroglyphic Canyon**
Loc.: Phoenix Mountain Park                     Maricopa
**Hieroglyphic Mountains**
Loc.: West of Castle Hot Spring      Maricopa and Yavapai

## HIGLEY

El.: c. 1200'                  Loc.: Maricopa DE-8.7
S. W. Higley was concerned with construction work for the Phoenix and Eastern Railroad, on which the community of Higley is located.
P.O. est. January 11, 1910. Lawrence H. Sarey, p.m.
Ref.: Barnes; P.O. Records. Map: GG-6.

## HOOVER

El.: c. 1000'                  Loc.: Maricopa 1, HI-5
The origin of this name has not yet been ascertained.
P.O. est. February 1, 1915. Norman H. Morrison, p.m. Discont. July 31, 1915.
Ref.: P.O. Records. Map: A-7.

## HORSE MESA

El.: c. 4000'                  Loc.: Maricopa 2, HI-6
During the twice-yearly sheep trek sheep were sometimes herded near here. The herders grazed saddle and pack horses on the mesas, hence the name.

**v.n. Vaquero Mesa**
    This name appears only on the 1927 Tonto National Forest Map. It is not known why the Forest Service should have changed into Spanish a location name which had for half a century been known as Horse Mesa. Vaquero ("cowboy") is not in general use.
Ref.: Barnes. Map: GD-15.

**a.n. Horse Creek**          Map: GD-15                    Maricopa
**Horse Mesa Dam**   Loc.: Sec. 21, T. 3 N., R. 10 E.   Maricopa
This subsidiary to Roosevelt Dam was completed in 1927. The backing up of waters behind it created Apache Lake, (cf. Apache Cave) which is seventeen miles long. A post office existed during the construction period for this dam.
P.O. est. as Horse Mesa, December 20, 1926. Daniel J. Jones, p.m. Rescinded September 2, 1927.
Ref.: 4, p. 367; P.O. Records.

## HUDSON

El.: c. 2000'                  Loc.: Maricopa 2, A-1
The origin of this name has not yet been ascertained.
P.O. est. April 23, 1891. Henry C. Hodges, p.m. Discont. July 3, 1893.
Ref.: P.O. Records. Map: C-7.

## HUMMING BIRD SPRING

Loc.: In Big Horn Mts. 17 miles from Palo Verde Mine, but not more definitely known.
This spring was named for the nearby Humming Bird Mines, owned by E. R. Cartwright.
Ref.: 141, p. 210. Map: None.

## HUTTMAN WELL

El.: c. 500'                   Loc.: Maricopa 1, AB-13.
                               Sec. 18, T. 7 N., R. 9 W.
Hugo Huttman owned some wells here.
Ref.: Barnes. Map: None.

## INITIAL POINT

El.: c. 1000'                  Loc.: Maricopa 1, J-7.1
The United States surveyor with the boundary survey group prior to the Gadsden Purchase was A. B. Gray. He established (c. 1853) a triangulation station at Initial Point for a survey along the Gila River. When the territory of Arizona was organized, Levi Bashford was appointed the first surveyor general, and on July 2, 1864, Congress made Arizona part of the Surveying District of New Mexico, providing for surveying operations within Arizona. Surveys within the new territory were begun at Initial Point. A stone monument eight feet in diameter at the base, four feet at the top, and eight feet high was placed on the summit of a hill about one hundred and fifty feet high above the surrounding terrain, on the south side of the Gila opposite the mouth of the Salt River.
Nearly all public surveys within Arizona have been started at this point.
Ref.: Lenon; 52, IV, 303-304. Map: GG-2.

## JACK-IN-THE-PULPIT

El.: 2638'                     Loc.: Maricopa 1, H-14
Jack-in-the-Pulpit is a descriptive name for one of three irregular ridges created by the erosion of lava beds. It is a pinnacle of volcanic rock with its base resting in lava.
Ref.: 34, p. 225. Map: GG-8.

## JEAGER TANKS

El.: c. 500'  Loc.: Maricopa 1, A-16
Pro.: /yéyger/
Louis John Frederick Jaeger (sic), a native of California, used Jaeger Tanks (sic) as a watering stop for the teams he employed in hauling ore from the Gunsight Mine to the main road to Yuma.

Apparently the location of the tanks close to the Eagle Mountains, coupled with lack of information on the part of newcomers concerning Jaeger, gradually resulted in a corruption of the place name to Eagle Tank.

**v.n. Yaeger Tank**

Ref.: Jordan; 112, III. Map: C-12 (Eagle Tanks).

## JOKAKE

El.: c. 1400'  Loc.: Maricopa 2, BC-5.9
Pro.: /jokákiy/  Hopi: "mud house"
This winter resort was built of sun-dried adobes made on the site. A Hopi Indian construction laborer suggested the name.

P.O. est. May 11, 1936. Robert Evans, p.m. Discont. August 31, 1954.

Ref.: Barnes; P.O. Records. Map: F-8.

## KENDALL

El.: c. 1200'  Loc.: Maricopa 2, BG-7.2
This location on the Phoenix and Eastern Railroad was named for Frank Kendall, treasurer of the Phoenix and Maricopa Railroad, which came into existence in the early 1880's.

Ref.: Barnes. Map: GG-12.

## KENTUCK MOUNTAIN

El.: 5005'  Loc.: Maricopa 2, D-1.7
Jim Kentuck was a cattleman in this vicinity.

Ref.: Barnes. Map: GG-3.

**a.n. Kentuck Spring**  Map: B-7  Maricopa

## KENYON STATION

El.: c. 700'  Loc.: Maricopa 1, CD-12
Prior to the establishment of the Butterfield Overland Stage route in 1857, a young man was traveling along the route under the charge of his guardian. The two camped at this spot. To the horror of members of an immigrant train already on the scene, the young man in a fit of temper shot his guardian. He was immediately executed for his crime. From that moment the place was known as Murderer's Grave.

Three years later, after the establishment of the Butterfield Overland route, the name of the station was changed to Kinyon Station, so named for Marcus L. Kinyon, who in 1858 was in charge of this division of the Butterfield route. By a curious coincidence many years later (1872), a man named Charles H. Kenyon (b. New York, 1840; d. February 16, 1885) was superintendent of Moore and Carr's stage between Yuma and Tucson. The change in name to Kenyon probably occurred then.

It was at this station on August 18, 1873, that two Mexicans killed Ed Lumley by stabbing and torturing in an attempt to make him reveal where his money was hidden. The problem of such attacks was one which all stage station keepers had to face. Because there were no banks, there was nothing to do but to hide money which came in to stage stations from travelers and by other means. It was also a well known fact that money was secreted at stage stations. This led not only to robbery and murder, but also to legends of buried treasure.

**v.n. Rancherias de San Diego**
Named by Fr. Francisco Garcés, November 12, 1774. Coues believes that this place was "very likely Kenyons."

Ref.: 32, II, 174; Charles H. Kenyon File, APHS; 111, p. 274; 112, III. Maps: E-20; E-21; E-24 (Kinyon).

## KYRENE

El.: c. 1500'  Loc.: Maricopa 2, CD-9
Pro.: /kayríyn/
It is believed locally that the name Kyrene was selected merely to match the classical name of Tempe nearby. The name is that of Cyrene in Carthagenia.

Kyrene is a small community with a store and a school. Since it was not a station on the railroad, it was served by Peterson's switch, a siding and a section house named for Nils Peterson, who had a cotton gin at this location. Cattle and hay were also shipped from Peterson's.

Ref.: Theobald; Barnes. Maps: C-6 (Indian Village) C-7.

## LA BARGE CANYON

El.: c. 3000'  Loc.: Maricopa 2, HG-7-6.5
John LeBarge (sic) (b. Canada, 1856) was naturalized in 1876 at Springfield, Massachusetts. By 1890 he was living in Pinal County where he was a prospector. It is reported that he was a companion of Waltz of the Lost Dutchman Mine (q.v., Pinal).

Ref.: APHS Files; Barnes; 151, p. 442. Map: GK-10.

**a.n. La Barge Creek**  Map: GD-15  Maricopa

## LAMBLY STATION

El.: c. 2500'  Loc.: Maricopa 1, FG-1.6
A man by this name kept a stage station at this point in 1872.

Ref.: Weekly Arizona Miner, December 7, 1872, 2:5; Theobald. Map: E-20.

## LAVA

El.: c. 600'  Loc.: Maricopa 1, C-12.7
Black volcanic bombs lie thickly on the ground here. The name is descriptive.

Ref.: Barnes. Map: GG-19.

**a.n. Lava Spring**  Loc.: T. 1 S., R. 6 W.  Maricopa

## LAVEEN

El.: c. 1500'  Loc.: Maricopa 2, A-8.4
This small settlement was named for its first postmaster.

P.O. est. September 30, 1913. Roger G. LaVeen, p.m.

Ref.: P.O. Records. Maps: C-12; F-2.

## LEHI

El.: c. 800'                    Loc.: Maricopa 2, CD-7
Pro.: /líyhay/
Settlements in the Salt River Valley were begun by Mormons in March 1877 when nine families came to this location from St. George, Utah. The seventy-one persons in the party were under the presidency of Daniel W. Jones. By July the settlers had extremely limited funds and went heavily into debt while building an irrigation ditch. The result was that the majority of the group became dissatisfied. Most of them left under the leadership of Philomen C. Merrill (cf. St. David, Cochise). Some remained at what they called Camp Utah.

The Mormons of Camp Utah laid out a village known as Utahville, the land for which was located by four different persons, each of whom agreed to furnish an equal amount of land for the village lots. Utahville came to nothing because one of the locaters refused to cooperate and went so far as to close up the streets on his land. This led to Jones' laying out a small community on his own land, and in 1880 the name Jonesville was voted for his place. It was in the same year that the area was referred to by the *Phoenix Herald* as Bottom City because of its location near the Salt River.

When the post office refused to accept the name Jonesville for the community, the name Lehi — Lehi was a prophet in the *Book of Mormon* — was supplied by Brigham Young, Jr.

P.O. est. May 26, 1884. James L. Patterson, p.m. Discont. March 5, 1904.

Ref.:   174, p. 204, 207; Daniel W. Jones, "Letter," *Phoenix Herald,* July 27, 1880, 1:1,2; P.O. Records. Map: GG-12.

## LEWIS AND PRANTY CREEK

El.: c. 2500'                    Loc.: Maricopa 2, I-6.3
Lewis and Pranty were the first men to settle on this creek which bears their name. Pranty began prospecting and mining in the Tonto Basin c. 1900. Twenty-five years later he disappeared, leaving his belongings and cabin undisturbed.

Ref.:   Barnes; 151, p. 547. Map: GD-15.

## LIBERTY

El.: 879'                    Loc.: Maricopa 1, H-7
The post office which was ultimately to be known as Liberty was first called the Toothaker Place. This was due to the fact that the post office was established apparently in the home of its first postmistress, Harriet Toothaker. The official name, however, was Altamount, but for what specific reason has not yet been ascertained. The reason for establishing the post office is probably that a cotton gin was built at the Toothaker Place and neighboring farmers naturally made it a point of call. However, the farmers and other settlers did not live close to Altamount and the post office was later moved somewhat to its new location where it was re-established under the name Liberty.

P.O. est. as Altamount, July 16, 1895. Harriet Toothaker, p.m. Discont. May 28, 1898. Re-est. as Liberty, February 15, 1901. James Phillips, p.m. Discont. June 30, 1942.

Ref.:   Parkman; P.O. Records. Maps: GG-2; C-9.

## LISCUM

El.: c. 4000'                    Loc.: Maricopa 2, C-1.5
Liscum was the post office for the Phoenix Mine. It was named by the mine manager, Sam Hunnington, for Col. Emerson H. Liscum, an army officer who served in Arizona from 1880 to 1884.

P.O. est. March 29, 1901. Sam H. Purcell, p.m. Discont. December 30, 1902.

Ref.:   Barnes; P.O. Records. Map: A-7.

## LITCHFIELD PARK

El.: 1044'                    Loc.: Maricopa 1, IJ-5.7
In 1916 the Goodyear Tire and Rubber Company purchased and leased two tracts of land to grow Egyptian cotton (cf. Goodyear). One tract was west of the Agua Fria River and was for a short time referred to as the Agua Fria Ranch. The name Litchfield was given to it in honor of Paul W. Litchfield, vice-president of the company. The main office of the Southwest Cotton Company was moved to Litchfield Park in September 1927.

P.O. est. as Litchton, January 7, 1919. William W. Burke, p.m. Changed to Litchfield Park, June 18, 1926.

Ref.:   K. B. McMicken, Vice-President, Goodyear Farms, Letter, March 28, 1956. Map: GG-2.

## LOUDERMILK WASH

El.: c. 1300'-550'                    Loc.: Maricopa 1, AB-8-10.7
A well reportedly dug by men working on the state highway was owned by a settler named Loudermilk, after whom the wash was named.

Ref.:   Parkman; Barnes; 141, p. 222. Map: GG-5.

## MARINETTE

El.: 1080'                    Loc.: Maricopa 1, J-5.2
Marinette was so named by homesteaders for their hometown of Marinette, Wisconsin.

P.O. est. April 25, 1912. Edward J. Halsley, p.m.

Ref.:   Barnes; P.O. Records. Maps: C-13; F-2.

## MARYSVILLE

El.: c. 1500'                    Loc.: Maricopa 2, EF-6.2
In 1868 William Rowe established a place known as Rowe's Station. Here in 1865 Charles Whitlow had settled with his family in order to be near the newly established Camp McDowell (cf. Fort McDowell). Whitlow kept a general store and supplied the post animals with forage. In 1874 Whitlow moved to Florence. Rowe was still a resident of Marysville in 1875.

Meanwhile a little community had grown up at the former Rowe's Station. To honor his daughter, Mary Elizabeth Whitlow (b. Kentucky, 1853), Whitlow named the place Marysville. In 1877 Mormons from Utah crossed the Salt River at this point (cf. Lehi). Their use of the name Maysville is a corruption of the true name of the place.

P.O. est. April 25, 1873. Charles Whitlow, p.m. Discont. January 4, 1874.

Ref.:   Mary E. Bailey File, APHS; *Arizona Miner,* January 22, 1875, 2:3; 87, pp. 280-281. Maps: C-3; E-18; E-20.

## MATTHIE

El.: c. 2500'                    Loc.: Maricopa 1, E-1
A superintendent of the S.F. R.R. was killed in an automobile accident at this point, which was then given his
name.

Ref.: Barnes. Map: C-13.

## MAVERICK BUTTE

El.: 4576'                    Loc.: Maricopa 2, D-1.3
Pro.: /mǽvariyk/
A cattle rancher named J. M. Cartwright and his associates
found mavericks in this area many years ago. They branded
the animals and named the mountain because of this.

Ref.: Barnes. Map: GG-3.

## McDOWELL, FORT

El.: c. 1500'                    Loc.: Maricopa 2, E-5
On Setember 7, 1865, five companies of California Volun-
teers officially established what was then called Camp Mc-
Dowell. The camp was named for Maj. Gen. Irvin Mc-
Dowell, who had been decorated for his services at the
battle of Buena Vista, Mexico, and had been appointed
major general on March 18, 1865, for his services at Cedar
Mountain, Virginia.

Camp McDowell was one of the most important military
posts in the Southwest. Because of its position adjacent
to several Apache trails, it was possible for troops from
McDowell to make fast military expeditions whenever
there was trouble with Indians. Despite its importance, four
years after Camp McDowell was established, the post was
still a very rough camp as far as facilities were concerned.
It never did develop into a well organized and equipped
post. On April 12, 1867, the name was changed to Fort
McDowell. By 1874 its importance had diminished con-
siderably. Nevertheless, Fort McDowell continued to exist
until its abandonment on April 10, 1891.

P.O. est. as McDowell, August 9, 1869. James A. Moore, p.m.
Discont. November 15, 1917. Re-est. as Fort McDowell, July
10, 1923. Discont. June 30, 1928.
Ref.: Stanton D. Kirkham File, APHS; 75, p. 144; 111, p.
153; 87, p. 313; 38, p. 176; P.O. Records. Maps: C-1;
E-20; GG-19.

### a.n. McDowell Canyon                    Maricopa
This was the canyon through which soldiers passed going
to and from Camp McDowell. Because Indians liked to
harass soldiers in this canyon, the soldiers did not like to
pass through it.
Ref.: 158, p. 224.

### McDowell, Fort, Indian Reservation

Loc.: At old Fort McDowell.                    Maricopa
A reservation of 24,971 acres for the Yavapai, Mohave, and
Apache Indians was created by Executive Order on Sep-
tember 15, 1913.
Ref.: 88, II, 374.

| McDowell Mountains | Map: GG-1 | Maricopa |
| McDowell Mountain | El.: 2828'. Map: GG-11 | Maricopa |
| McDowell Pass | Map: GG-11 | Maricopa |
| McDowell Peak | El.: 4002'. Map: GG-1 | Maricopa |

## McQUEEN

El.: 1225'                    Loc.: Maricopa 2, CD-8
A. C. McQueen was a livestock agent for the A.T. & S.F.
R.R. in the 1890's.

Ref.: Barnes. Map: GG-12.

## MEAD

                    Loc.: Not known.
The origin of this name has not yet been ascertained.

P.O. est. January 21, 1904. Charles Dickens, p.m. Order
rescinded some time after April 5, 1904.

Ref.: P.O. Records. Map: None.

## MERIDIAN

El.: 975'                    Loc.: Maricopa 1, JG-7.3
The fact that this settlement existed near the crossing of
the Gila and Salt River Meridian and the Gila and Salt
River Base Line resulted in its name.

P.O. est. August 13, 1894. Edward K. Buker, p.m. Discont.
July 11, 1895.

Ref.: Barnes; P.O. Records. Map: None.

## MESA

El.: 1273'                    Loc.: Maricopa 2, C-6-7.6
Pro.: /meysə/                    Spanish: "table"
The present-day city of Mesa was founded by Mormons
from Bear Lake County, Idaho, and from Salt Lake County,
Utah. A combined party arrived in Arizona via the Lee's
Ferry route to Camp Verde and then to the Salt River
Valley. Here on the broad tableland (from whence the
place derives its name) T. C. Sirrine in May 1878 located
a section of land, deeding it for a Mormon community to
Trustees C. R. Robson, G. W. Sirrine, and F. M. Pomeroy.
Mail for the community came in via Hayden's Ferry until
the new community petitioned for its own post office. The
name Mesa was turned down by the Post Office Department because of the prior existence of a community called
Mesaville in Pinal County. Therefore, the colonists named
their community Hayden to honor Charles Trumbull Hayden (cf. Tempe). Despite the fact that by that time
Hayden's Ferry had changed its name to Tempe, there
ensued so much confusion in the mails between the two
post offices of Hayden and the old Hayden's Ferry that
in 1886 the name of the former (now Mesa) was changed
to Zenos, after a prophet in the Book of Mormon. In 1888
the Pinal County community of Mesaville went out of existence as a post office, whereupon the name Zenos was
quickly changed to Mesa.

### v.n. Mesa City
P.O. est. as Hayden, June 27, 1881. Fanny V. McDonald, p.m.
Name changed to Zenos, May 15, 1886. Name changed to Mesa,
June 19, 1889. Wells Fargo Station, 1903. Mesa incorporated
July 15, 1883.

Ref.: 112, pp. 211, 216-17; 7, p. 532; P.O. Records. Maps:
C-5 (Hayden); C-6 (Zenos); C-7 (Mesa); GG-12; E-20
(Mesa City).

## MIDMONT

El.: c. 1500'                    Loc.: Maricopa 2, AB-6.8
This post office was about midway between Phoenix and
Camelback Mountain, which probably accounts for the
name.
P.O. est. January 7, 1919. Louise Osborne, p.m. Discont. May
15, 1920.
Ref.: Barnes; P.O. Records. Map: None.

## MIDWAY

El.: c. 800'                    Loc.: Maricopa 1, DG-15.6
This place was halfway between the two terminals of Tuc-
son and Gila Bend.
Ref.: Barnes. Map: C-12; GG-18.

## MIRAGE, EL

El.: c. 2000'                    Loc.: Maricopa 1, I-4.3
Pro.: /el miraĵ/
The origin of this name has not yet been ascertained. This
is not a Spanish, but a coined name.
P.O. est. October 1, 1947. Clayton F. Glaser, p.m.
Ref.: P.O. Records. Map: F-11.

## MOBILE

El.: 1230'                    Loc.: Maricopa 1, I-11
In 1925 a group of forty Negroes from Mobile, Alabama,
homesteaded here, naming the community for their native
city.
P.O. est. August 5, 1925. Mrs. Elsie B. Luny, p.m.
Ref.: 4, p. 387; P.O. Records. Map: GG-13.

## MOIVAVI

El.: c. 1000'                    Loc.: Maricopa 1, GH-15.6
Pro.: /moy vwáhya/              Papago: moi, "many";
                                vaxia, "well, water hole"
This is a small winter rancheria which has a well thirty-
two feet deep.
v.n. Mayvaxi
     Mueykava (Wheeler)
Ref.: Kirk Bryan Notes; 34, p. 397. Maps: D-8; D-11 (Moi-
     vaxia).

## MONTEZUMA'S HEAD

El.: 4337'                    Loc.: Maricopa 1, A-9.5
The name Montezuma's Head dates back at least as early
as 1872 when it was described as being the stone face
at the southeastern end of Maricopa Mountain. The resemblance of the formation to a head is notable.
v.n. Face Mountain
Ref.: Arizona Miner, January 20, 1872, 2:5; 34, 221. Map:
     GG-5.
a.n. Montezuma    Map: GG-5. (A railroad siding.)  Maricopa
     Montezuma Sleeping    Map: GG-10             Maricopa
     This is a descriptive name for a formation in the Estrella
     Mountains.
Ref.: Barnes.

## MONTGOMERY

El.: c. 900'                    Loc.: Maricopa 2, A-5
John Britt Montgomery (b. Illinois, January 4, 1839; d.
December 24, 1916) migrated to California in 1853, going

from there to Idaho in 1862. In December 1864, he arrived at Wickenburg where he soon became noted as the
only man who knew how to whipsaw lumber. Later he
established the Montgomery Addition, now a part of Phoenix. Still later, he became a cattleman near the mouth of
the Hassayampa River, using a flower pot as his brand.
The post office was established prior to his death by his
descendants.
P.O. est. November 20, 1913. Arminda J. Montgomery, p.m.
Discont. January 31, 1920.
Ref.: John Britt Montgomery File, APHS; P.O. Records.
     Map: A-7.

## MOORE GULCH

El.: c. 3000'                    Loc.: Maricopa 2, A-0.6-0.9
In 1877 William Moor (sic) had Moore Camp five miles
east of Gillette (q.v.).
Ref.: Barnes. Map: GM-3.

## MORMON FLAT

El.: 1547'                    Loc.: Maricopa 2, G-6.4
In the 1880's, Mormons from the Salt River Valley sometimes brought stock to graze on this flat at the junction
of the Salt River and LaBarge Creek. When the Apache
Trail stage drivers (cf. Apache Trail, Gila) drove train
passengers past this spot, the passengers heard harrowing
and completely mythical stories about massacres of Mormons by Apaches.
Ref.: Barnes; G. E. P. Smith; 151, p. 532. Map: GD-15.
a.n. Mormon Flat Dam    El.: 1671'. Map: GG-19    Maricopa
     Completed in 1925, this dam is two hundred twenty-nine
     feet high and six hundred twenty feet long. The waters im-
     pounded by it form Canyon Lake, ten miles long.
Ref.: 16, p. 368.

## MORRISTOWN

El.: 1719'                    Loc.: Maricopa 1, G-1.5
The first name for the present-day community of Morristown was Vulture Siding, but in 1897 after the importance
of the Vulture Mine (q.v.) had faded, the name of this
place was changed to Hot Springs Junction because at this
station passengers disembarked from the train to take a
stage to Castle Hot Springs. The name was later changed
to Morristown to honor the first inhabitant at the place,
George Morris, the discoverer of the Mack Morris Mine
in Gila County.
P.O. est. December 30, 1897. Lee H. Landis, p.m. Wells Fargo
Station, 1903. (Hot Springs Junction).
Ref.: Barnes; Arizona Journal Mining, November 4, 1897,
     4:2; 16, p. 356; P.O. Records. Maps: C-9; C-12 (Hot
     Springs Junction).

## MUERTOS, LOS

El.: c. 1500'   Loc.: Maricopa 2, BC-8. S. of Tempe 7 miles
Pro.: /los mwắrtos/              Spanish: "the dead"
Frank Hamilton Cushing in 1887 excavated Indian ruins
to which he gave the name Los Muertos.
Ref.: 111, p. 11. Map: None.

## MULLEN WELLS

El.: c. 500'                    Loc.: Maricopa 1, B-7
John Mullen owned these wells.
Ref.:  Barnes. Map: C-12.

## NEPHI

El.: c. 1250'                   Loc.: Maricopa 2, C-7.6
Pro.: /niýfay/
In August 1887 the majority of Mormons then living in
Tempe moved to Nephi. At that time the settlement was
called Johnsonville because the land was owned by Ben-
jamin F. Johnson. The name was changed to Nephi after
Nephi Johnson, one of those who testified against John
D. Lee (cf. Lee's Ferry, Coconino).

Another possibility concerning the name is that Nephi is
the name of the Mormon prophet who recorded the *Book
of Mormon* on plates of gold (cf. Cumora, Apache). The
fact that Nephi was close to Lehi also may have some
significance, inasmuch as according to Mormons Lehi was
the father of Nephi.

P.O. est. February 19, 1889. Frank C. Johnson, p.m. Discont.
August 11, 1892.
Ref.:  112, p. 220; Barnes; APHS Names File. Map: C-7.

## NEW RIVER

El.: c. 2000'                   Loc.: Maricopa 2, A-1.6
The reason for the name New River has not yet been
ascertained.

New River was a stage station owned by Darrel Duppa,
who arrived in Arizona in the early 1860's. Lt. John G.
Bourke called it Duppa Station. The station earned the
reputation of being infested with Mexican robbers and
border outlaws so that it was practically impossible to get
an agent to remain there. Possibly for this reason the station was abandoned in 1875.

There is now a service station and bar at this place. Part
of the old station joins the home of the present owners.

P.O. est. as Newriver, May 9, 1898. Ephraim Tomkinson, p.m.
(deceased). P.O. never in operation.
Ref.:  25, p. 308; *Arizona Sentinel*, September 25, 1875, 3:2;
       22, p. 172. Map: C-13.

**a.n.** **New River Mesa**        Map: GG-3              Maricopa
    **New River**     Map: GM-19      Yavapai and Maricopa
    **New River Mountains**
        Maps: GM-3; GM-19
                        Yavapai and Maricopa
    **New River Peak**       Map: B-6               Yavapai

## NIGGER WELL

El.: c. 2500'        Loc.: About 12 miles from Wickenburg
                          north of White Tank Mountain.
A Portuguese who was part Negro was running a bakery
at Wickenburg c. 1866. He saved his money and decided
it would be a paying proposition to dig a well between
the Salt and Hassayampa Rivers, where there was no water
to be found on the surface. He began digging the well and
got down about thirty feet when the work ceased. Passersby
noticed that the well was caved around the top and that
the camp had been robbed. The Portuguese was never

seen again, nor was the well cleaned out to ascertain
whether he was buried in the hole. The place from that
time forth was called Nigger Well.

Another story is that a freighter whose wagon broke
down temporarily stored twenty-six hundred pounds of
dynamite under canvas beside the road. A man named
"Frenchy" DeBaud noticed coyotes smelling around the
canvas. He stopped his team to take a pot shot at the
coyotes. He hit the dynamite instead, but the effect was the
same if not more so since it not only wiped out the varmints
but included the creation of what the Frenchman referred
to as "one damn beeg hole."

Nigger Well earned an evil reputation. In addition to
murders which occurred there, a Chinese was held up by
three Mexicans, and in 1881 Indians killed Gus Swain
at this spot.

Ref.:    52, II, 69; Barnes; *Arizona Star*, September 20, 1889,
         1:2; September 26, 1889, 4:2; *Arizona Weekly Enter-
         prise*, April 21, 1888, 3:2. Map: None.

## OATMAN FLAT

El.: 560'                       Loc.: Maricopa 1, B-11.3
In March 1851, Royse Oatman, his wife, and seven children
were making their way across Arizona en route to California. The Oatman family was with a party of fifty immi-
grants, some of whom dropped off at Tucson. The others
reached the Pima Villages where they stopped to rest.
Oatman was coming to the end of his resources and felt
that he had to push on at once to California. The family
got as far as what is now Oatman Flat without untoward
incident and pitched camp for the night. A party of Indians showed up. They were friendly at first, but their visit
ended in slaughter. Lorenzo Oatman, twelve years old, was
thrown over the edge of the flat and left for dead. The
other members of the family were murdered, with the
exception of two daughters, Mary Ann and Olive, whom
the Indians took with them and later sold as slaves to
Mohaves.

Lorenzo slowly and painfully made his way to safety, knowing that his sisters were alive. He refused to give up the
search for them. Olive was finally rescued in 1856, but
her sister had died in captivity.

The bodies of the Oatman family, found at the spot of the
massacre, are buried in a common grave near where they
fell.

Ref.:    7, pp. 484-86; 25, p. 87. Map: GG-5.

**a.n.** **Artutoc**
    This vanished Maricopa rancheria on the north side of the
    Gila was visited by Fr. Jacobo Sedelmayr in 1744, and by
    Fr. Francisco Garcés in 1775.
Ref.:    88, I, 86; 35, p. 118, (Note 25).

    **Rinconada**                                       Maricopa
    Spanish: "corner."
    The Gila River makes a bend here, on the north edge of
    Oatman Flat.
Ref.:    88, I, 87.

    **Oatmans**      Loc.: T. 5, 6 S., R. 8, 9 W.        Maricopa
Oatmans was a station established at Painted Rocks (*q.v.*)
several miles to the east of Oatman Flat. It was here that

the road from Yuma branched to go to Phoenix or to Tucson. This place is not to be confused with the stage station constructed by William Fourr in 1869 at Oatman Flat.

Ref.:   APHS File.

**Oatman Mountain**   El.: 1649'. Map: GG-5          Maricopa
**Oatman**                                                    Mohave
Refer to main entry under this name, Mohave County.

## OCAPOS

El.: c. 1200'                     Loc.: Maricopa 1, H-11.5
Reversing the first two letters of *So*uthern *Pa*cific *Co*. resulted in this name. The location on the railroad was established about 1890.

Ref.:   Barnes. Map: C-12.

## OTERO CREEK

El.: c. 4000'-2500'               Loc.: Maricopa 2, HE-3-4
Pro.:   /otéro/
Jesus Otero had a cattle ranch here from 1884 through 1890.

Ref.:   Barnes. Maps: GD-15; GG-11 (Otero Ranch).

**a.n. Otero Canyon**       Map: GG-3                 Maricopa
**Otero Spring**       Map: B-7                 Maricopa

## OVERTON

El.: c. 2500'                     Loc.: Maricopa 2, AB-2.
          About 30 miles n. of Phoenix near Cave Creek.
The origin of this name has not yet been ascertained.

P.O. est. October 6, 1880. Josiah Woods, p.m. Discont. October 3, 1881.

Ref.:   P.O. Records. Map: None.

## OZBORN

Loc.: Not known.
The origin of this name has not yet been ascertained.

P.O. est. January 20, 1900. Frederick E. Aarnden, p.m. Rescinded October 5, 1900.

Ref.:   P.O. Records. Map: None.

## PAINTED CLIFFS

El.: c. 2500'                     Loc.: Maricopa 2, HG-5.4
These cliffs have rock strata in shades of green.

Ref.:   151, p. 581; 4, p. 367. Map: GD-15.

## PAINTED ROCKS

El.: 1195'                        Loc.: Maricopa 1, C-10.8-11.6
The Painted Rock Mountains are so named because they contain possibly one acre of rocks about fifty feet high which are covered with petroglyphs of snakes, turtles, birds, men, and other figures. These figures may have been painted by modern Indians, which — if so — makes them singular. It has been suggested that these pictures were inscribed as a kind of treaty boundary to make clear a separation point between the lands of the Yumas and those of the Maricopas.

These are the mountains which Fr. Kino in 1699 referred to as the Sierra Pinta (Spanish: "painted mountains"). Fr. Jacobo Sedelmayr visited this same place on October 26,

1754. He wrote that his group climbed "Sierra Sibupuc" to eliminate the bend in the Gila River which occurs here. In 1849 this solitary little hill was noted by the Fremont Association.

**v.n. Picture Rocks**          (Emory, 1854)
   **Sierra Escritas Piedras Pintadas**   (Spanish: "painted rocks")
Ref.:   145; 20, p. 420; 111, p. 17; 48, p. 218; 35, p. 117, (Note 24). Maps: GG-5; GG-15.

**a.n. Painted Rock**                                        Maricopa
   This was the name of a former location on the railroad between Gila Bend and Sentinel.

Ref.:   145, p. 65.

## PALO VERDE

El.: c. 650'                      Loc.: Maricopa 1, EF-7.2
Pro.:   /palo vérdi/ or          Spanish:  *"palo*, "stick";
        /pǽlo vérdi/                       *verde*, "green"
Milis Benson, a Dane, suggested the name for this location because of the palo verde trees in the wash to the east of the post office.

P.O. est. January 4, 1910. William Walton, p.m.

Ref.:   Parkman; 141, p. 216. Map: GG-19.

**a.n. Palo Verde Hills**   Loc.: T. 1 S., R. 6, 7 W.        Maricopa

## PAPAGO (STATE) PARK

El.: 1450'                        Loc.: Maricopa 2, BC-7.3
Pro.:   /pǽpəgo/
On April 13, 1892, Charles Debrille Poston filed a homestead claim for what he called Hole-in-the-Rock. The large hole in the red rock hill gradually became the site of a recreation and picnic area which spread over two thousand fifty acres of land set aside in 1914 as the Papago Saguaro National Monument. The Act of Congress creating this monument was recalled on August 7, 1930, and the place then become Papago State Park or, as it is popularly called, Papago Park.

Ref.:   Theobald; 131; 151, p. 369; 34, p. 385. Map: GG-12.

## PARADISE VALLEY

El.: c. 1350'                     Loc.: Maricopa 2, BC-5
In 1899 Frank Conkey was manager for the Rio Verde Canal Company. The promoters of this project saw this valley first when it was covered with spring flowers and palo verde in bloom. They therefore named it Paradise Valley.

Ref.:   Barnes. Map: GG-1.

## PEORIA

El.: 1400'                        Loc.: Maricopa 1, JK-4.5
One of the first settlers in this area was Chauncey Clark, who came from Peoria, Illinois, c. 1896. There were already some people in the area who had put in a dam, but the dam was washed out and the early residents left (cf. Gillespie Dam). The land was then taken over by men named Murphy and Christy, who sold it to Clark, Mr. and Mrs. Albert J. Straw, Mr. and Mrs. James McMillan and their children, W. T. Hanna, and Mr. and Mrs. Jack Copes and their daughter. The townsite for this location was

planned by D. S. Brown and J. B. Greenhut of Peoria, Illinois.

P.O. est. August 4, 1888. James McMillan, p.m. Wells Fargo Station, 1903.

Ref.: Robert J. Straw ms., APHS; 102, p. 68; P.O. Records. Maps: C-7; F-2.

## PEROXIDE WELL

El.: c. 350'  Loc.: Maricopa 1, DE-6.4

In 1910 a well was dug to be used by stock belonging to the Flower Pot Cattle Company. The taste of the water led the cowboys to call the well Peroxide Well.

Ref.: Barnes; 141, p. 219. Map: A-7.

## PERRYVILLE

El.: c. 1000'  Loc.: Maricopa 1, H-5.3

By curious coincidence, the town of Perryville was started by a man named Perry L. Carmean in the early 1920's, but the community now has as prominent residents members of the Perry family who moved there in 1929. Carmean had, meanwhile, left the area.

In 1875 William H. Perry (b. Massachusetts 1846; d. 1929) with his partner George Helm brought sheep from California to the vicinity of Williams in northern Arizona. Perry sold his sheep in 1880 and then brought in cattle from Utah to the Agua Fria River east of Cordes. In 1929, his family moved to Perryville.

Ref.: Perry (son). Map: GG-2.

## PHOENIX

El.: 1080'  Loc.: Maricopa 2, A-7.2
Pro.: /fíyniks/

In 1865, J. Y. T. Smith, a contractor, established Smith's Station about four miles from the center of the present Phoenix on the road to Camp McDowell. Smith Station was a hay-supply point for the camp. In September 1867, Jack Swilling (cf. Gillette) visited Smith and quickly noticed that the Salt River was potentially a great source of irrigation waters. Swilling then organized the Swilling Irrigation Canal Company, the members of which included Henry Wickenburg and "Lord" Darrell Duppa, a well-educated and venturesome Englishman.

Although the new company began operations near the present Tempe, it soon moved its headquarters to Smith's place. The need for a specific address to speed the delivery of supplies led the group to discuss name possibilities. Swilling, a southerner, suggested Stonewall. Someone else suggested Salina because the company planned to use water from the Salt River, but this was vetoed because of the implication that the region might be a salt marsh. Duppa noted the presence of ancient canals and villages of a vanished civilization. He therefore suggested the name Phoenix because a new city could be expected to rise upon the ashes of the old, just as the legendary Phoenix, when consumed by fire, rose from its own ashes. The name Phoenix was agreed upon.

Within a short time, irrigation in the Salt River Valley attracted settlers. The future Phoenix began to rise. On October 15, 1870, its citizens held a meeting and selected an official townsite. On December 23, 1870, town lots were sold.

Three miles to the east, William B. Helling built a flour mill in early 1871. At first the small community, of which the mill was the nucleus, was called Helling's Mill or Mill City. Its juxtaposition to Phoenix, however, soon led to the name East Phoenix. It was ultimately engulfed by Phoenix. In 1889 the seat of Arizona's government was moved from Prescott to Phoenix, where it still remains. In 1891 there was imminent danger that Phoenix would be consumed, not by fire, but by water, when the flooding Salt River swept through the entire southern end of the city, in some places covering office desks. The danger from the Salt River floods is now past, since the erection of Bartlett Dam (q.v.) has eliminated water in the river at Phoenix.

P.O. est. at East Phoenix, August 19, 1871. Edward K. Baker, p.m. Discont. July 11, 1876.

P.O. est. at Phoenix, June 15, 1869. John W. Swilling, p.m. Wells Fargo Station, 1879. Incorporated January 3, 1881.

v.n. Salt River
    Phenix

Ref.: 55, pp. 443, 598; 7, p. 623; 4, pp. 217, 219, 221; 87, pp. 259, 260; *Weekly Arizona Miner*, August 27, 1870, 1:3-4; January 7, 1871, 1:2; January 14, 1871, 3:4; February 3, 1872, 2:4. *Tucson Citizen*, April 20, 1872, 4:2-3; October 29, 1870, 4:3; January 7, 1871, 4:3. Map: GG-14.

a.n. Phoenix Mountain  El.: 2000'. Map: GG-1  Maricopa
Camelback is the southern point of a group of hills called Phoenix Mountain.

    **Phoenix South Mountain Park**
    Loc.: S. of Phoenix c. 5 miles  Maricopa

## PIEDRA

El.: c. 700'  Loc.: Maricopa 1, CD-12.4
Pro.: /piˆédrə/  Spanish: "stone"

The ground around Piedra is covered with volcanic rocks.

Ref.: Barnes. Map: GG-16.

## PINACLE MOUNTAIN

El.: 3170'  Loc.: Maricopa 2, C-4
Descriptive.

Ref.: Barnes. Map: GG-1.

## PINYON MOUNTAIN

El.: 5256'  Loc.: Maricopa 2, JG-5.5
Pro.: /pínyown/

Pinyon is a type of pine tree which grows thickly on this mountain.

Ref.: 151, p. 606; Barnes. Map: GD-15.

## POPPER WELL

El.: c. 1500'  Loc.: Maricopa 1, BC-7.
    Six miles w. of Palo Verde Mine.

Richard Popper owned this well jointly with the Harquahala Livestock Company.

Ref.: 141, p. 220. Map: None.

## POWERS BUTTE

El.: c. 800'                          Loc.: Maricopa 1, DG-8
Col. J. C. Powers, a native of Mississippi, was in this area
in the 1880's before any colonization had begun in the
vicinity of Buckeye. Noted for his assiduous canal building,
Powers constructed one canal at the west end of Powers
Butte.

Ref.:   Parkman. Map: A-7.

## PRATT

El.: c. 1500'                         Loc.: Maricopa 1, J-1.5
William B. Pratt owned a mine for which Pratt was the
mail and supply station. The community was on the site
of Frog Tanks (q.v.)

P.O. est. May 5, 1890. Eugene E. St. Claire, p.m. Discont.
August 25, 1896.

Ref.:   Barnes. Map: C-7.

## QUIEN SABE CREEK

El.: c. 4000'                         Loc.: Maricopa 2, C-1
Pro.: /kiˆen sábe/                    Spanish: "who knows?"
This creek was named for a mine in the area.

Ref.:   Barnes. Map: GG-3.

a.n. Quien Sabe Springs        Map: B-7               Maricopa
     Quien Sabe Peak    Loc.: Sec. 14, T. 7 W., R. 5 E.    Maricopa

## RAINBOW VALLEY

El.: c. 1000'                         Loc.: Maricopa 1, JG-8.2
The origin of this name has not yet been ascertained.

P.O. est. June 24, 1931. Jerome L. Brown, p.m. Discont. October
9, 1933.

Ref.:   P.O. Records. Maps: GG-2; GG-4.

## REAVIS

El.: c. 5500'                         Loc.: Maricopa 2, I-6.8
Pro.: /révəs/
E. M. Reavis (b. 1827; d. 1896) established his ranch c.
1875 where he lived like a hermit, always carrying a long
rifle, and letting his hair and beard grow. Reavis was last
seen alive on April 20, 1896. His badly decomposed and
partially devoured body was found on May 5, 1896, by
James Delabaugh. There was no indication of foul play.
In 1935 the old Reavis Ranch was known as Pineair.

Ref.:   Woody (undated, unidentified clipping). Map: GK-16.

a.n. Reavis Creek    Maps: GK-10; GK-16    Maricopa and Pinal
v.n. Reevis Creek

## RITTENHOUSE

El.: c. 1500'                         Loc.: Maricopa 2, E-9.3
In 1919 C. H. Rittenhouse formed the Queen Creek Farms
Company. A railroad station was established at this location.
Ref.:   156, p. 122. Map: GG-19.

## ROBERTS BUTTE

El.: c. 800'                          Loc.: Maricopa 1, E-7.7
Roberts Butte illustrates a shift which sometimes occurs
in place names. The original name was Robbins Butte, and

it so appears on GLO maps until 1921. However, on January 1, 1886, G. A. Roberts homesteaded at the foot of
the butte and locally his name has become attached to it.
Ref.:   Parkman; 151, p. 644. Maps: C-8; C-12; GG-19.

## ROUND TOP BUTTE

El.: 1800'                            Loc.: Maricopa 1, H-13.8
This is a rounded butte at the northeast end of Blue
Plateau (q.v.).

Ref.:   34, p. 225. Map: GG-8 (Round Butte).

## SAINT CLAIRE SPRING

El.: c. 1800'                         Loc.: Maricopa 2, DE-1.9
William St. Clair (sic) was a miner and cattleman who
lived with his family at this spring.

Ref.:   Barnes. Maps: B-7; GG-3.

a.n. Saint Claire Mountain    El.: 3219'. Map: GG-3    Maricopa
     Saint Claire Peak       El.: 4220'. Map: GG-3    Maricopa

## SALT RIVER (P. O.)

El.: c. 1500'                         Loc.: Maricopa 2, C-6.75
The adjacency of this small community to the Salt River
led to the name.

P.O. est. as Saltriver, August 21, 1912. Effie C. Coe, p.m. Discont. October 15, 1916.

Ref.:   P.O. Records. Map: F-2 (town).

## SALT RIVER INDIAN RESERVATION

El.: c. 1500'                         Loc.: Maricopa 2, E-6.5
On June 14, 1879, the Salt River Indian Reservation (near
Scottsdale) was set aside for use by Maricopa and Pima
Indians. Although the agency headquarters are at Sacaton
(q.v., Pinal), the tribal offices are on the Salt River Reservation. The extent of the reservation has been increased and
modified from time to time. Currently it consists of 47,007
acres on which approximately fourteen hundred Indians live.

Ref.:   88, II, 374; "Annual Report of the Arizona Commission
        of Indian Affairs (1954, 1955, 1956)," p. 6. Map: GG-
        11.

## SALT RIVER VALLEY

El.: c. 1500' Loc.: Maricopa 1, IJ-5-7; Maricopa 2, AE-5-9
This is the rich agricultural valley of the Salt River. Roughly oval, the valley is about forty miles from east to west
by twenty from north to south. The city of Phoenix is
located in the Valley.

Ref.:   4, p. 217. Map: None.

## SAND TANK MOUNTAINS

El.: c. 2800'                         Loc.: Maricopa 1, HG-13-14
When Kirk Bryan was exploring this region c. 1920, he
learned that tanks in these mountains were called locally
Sand Tanks. Bryan then extended the name to the mountains.

Ref.:   Kirk Bryan Notes. Map: GG-8.

a.n. Sand Tank Wash        Maps: GG-7; GG-8                Maricopa

## SAN PABLO

El.: c. 1150′     Loc.: Maricopa 2, BC-7.4
Pro.: /san páblo/ or     Spanish: "St. Paul"
   /sæn pǽblo/
In 1873 residents of Tempe (q.v.) laid out a town next to Hayden's Ferry for the Mexican population. The proceeds from the sale of town lots was to be devoted to constructing a Catholic church. William Kirkland (cf. Kirkland Valley, Yavapai) donated seventy acres of land for the Mexican village.

Ref.: *Tucson Citizen*, May 31, 1873, 1:5, 4:3; Barnes, quoting *Arizona Sentinel*, May 3, 1873. Map. None.

## SANTO DOMINGO TANK

El.: c. 2500′     Loc.: Maricopa 1, F-1.2
    N. of Hot Springs Junction c. 7 miles.
Pro.: /sánto domíngo/
The reason for the name of this tank is not known.

Ref.: 141, p. 221. Map: None.

**a.n. San Domingo Wash**
    Loc.: S. of Wickenburg c. 6 miles     Maricopa
    George Monroe, once owner of Castle Hot Springs, had a cabin on this wash.

**v.n. San Domingo Gulch**
Ref.: *The Prospect*, May 5, 1905, 5:1-2.

## SAUCEDA MOUNTAINS

El.: c. 2500′   Loc.: Pima 1, G-1; Maricopa 1, CF-14.5-17
Pro.: /saséydə/     Spanish: "little willows"
The mountains apparently are named because of the presence of willow trees. Willows occur at a winter Papago rancheria in Sauceda Wash. The name of the village, which is in the Pima County portion of the mountains, is Tshiulikami or Chiulikan (Pro.: /čⁱúˡəkəm/), meaning "where the willow grows." The town is also known as Saucida.

Chiulikan is the same as or is immediately adjacent to Vokivaxia (Papago: "red well") which is also known as Pozo Colorado (Spanish: "red well"). The line of demarcation, if any, between Chiulikan and Pozo Colorado is not clear.

**v.n. Salceda Mountains**
Ref.: Lenon; Kirk Bryan Notes; 151, p. 674; 32, p. 404; 128, p. 8. Maps: A-7; GG-16.

**a.n. Sauceda Wash**   Maps: GG-8; GG-16   Maricopa and Pima
**Papago Mountains**
    Loc.: West end of Sauceda Mountains   Maricopa
Ref.: Kirk Bryan Notes.

## SAWIK MOUNTAIN

El.: 2135′     Loc.: Maricopa 2, DE-6.2
The origin of this name has not yet been ascertained.

**v.n. Sheldon Mountain**
Ref.: 151, p. 674. Map: GG-1.

## SCOTTSDALE

El.: 1261′     Loc.: Maricopa 2, BC-6.7
Scottsdale is named for Maj. Winfield Scott, an army chaplain (b. Michigan, February 26, 1837; d. October 16, 1910). In 1881 Scott first saw the area which was later to carry his name. He homesteaded, taking out a patent in 1891. Meanwhile, Scott was serving at Fort Huachuca while his brother George was in charge of the ranch. Following Scott's retirement from army life, he promoted the vicinity of his ranch as a health and agricultural center. The name Scottsdale became official in 1896 when a school district was established to serve families of the relatively few settlers in the area. Scott did not live to see his dreams of a health center at Scottsdale fulfilled. He moved to San Diego in 1909, returning to Phoenix for an operation in 1910.

Scottsdale was relatively slow to develop until the years following the end of World War II. Since that time it has expanded rapidly until today it is a thriving community noted as an arts and crafts center.

P.O. est. February 20, 1897. James L. Davis, p.m. Incorporated June 25, 1951.

Ref.: Byrd Howell Granger, *The True and Authentic History of Scottsdale*, Scottsdale, Arizona: n.p., 1956. Maps: C-9; GG-12.

## SENTINEL

El.: 858′     Loc.: Maricopa 1, AB-13.7
The small community of Sentinel was named because of its adjacency to Sentinel Peak. The hill stands above the surrounding plain like a sentinel.

P.O. est. June 20, 1880. William H. Burke, p.m. (cf. Burkes Station). Wells Fargo Station, 1888.

Ref.: Barnes. Map: GG-15.

**a.n. Sentinel Hill**   El.: 1715′. Map: GG-6   Maricopa
**Sentinel Wash**   Map: GN-2   Maricopa
**Sentinel Butte**   El.: 3343′. Loc.: T. 15 S., R. 17 T.   Pima

## SIL MURK

El.: c. 600′     Loc.: Maricopa 1, F-11.5
Pro.: /siýəl muk/     Papago: *sil* (corruption of Spanish *silla*), "saddle"; *mok*, "burned"
In the late 1890's, fourteen Papago families emigrated from Sauceda to this place where they established a village. The reason for the name is not known.

**v.n. Siilimok**
Ref.: Kirk Bryan Notes; 128, p. 39. Map: GG-8.

## SKUNK CREEK

El.: c. 1800′   Loc.: Maricopa 1, IJ-5-9; Maricopa 2, A-2
The origin of this name has not yet been ascertained.

Ref.: None. Map: GG-19.

## SMITH'S MILL

El.: c. 2500′     Loc.: Maricopa 1, FG-2.5
W. C. Smith built a mill at this location for reducing ores from the Vulture Mine (q.v.).

P.O. est. June 27, 1874. Peter Taylor, p.m. Discont May 1, 1877.

Ref.: Barnes; *Tucson Citizen*, July 18, 1874, 4:3; 87, p. xxi. Maps: C-4; E-20.

## STANWIX

El.: 554′     Loc.: Maricopa 1, A-13
In 1858 the name of this Butterfield stage station was "The Dutchman's." However, two years later a traveler noted it as Stanwix's station, the residence of Mr. Wash.

Jacobs, road agent for the overland stage. Stanwix is said to have been the name of a pioneer in the region, but whether he was a Dutchman is not known. Still later, this same place was being called Grinnell Station, but for what reason has not yet been learned.

Confederate troops under Capt. Sherod Hunter occupied Stanwix in April 1862. The southerners withdrew when it was learned that the California Column was nearing the station. Several years later, in 1877, Stanwix housed the operator for the military telegraph line.

**v.n. Stanvix Hall**

Ref.: Lenon; Barnes; 31, p. 186; *Weekly Arizona Miner*, December 3, 1875, 4:1; "Letters from Notes of the Trip Overland," *Daily Alta Californian*, June 24, 1860. Maps: C-2 (Grinnell Station); C-4; C-5 (Shown for first time in Maricopa rather than in Yuma County. Not on subsequent maps examined.); E-18; E-20 (Stanwix).

## STEWART MOUNTAIN

El.: 2990'              Loc.: Maricopa 2, FG-5.3
From 1880 to c. 1900 Jack Stewart ran cattle from his ranch near this mountain. When a dam was constructed as part of the Salt River Valley Reclamation Project, the dam was named Stewart Mountain Dam. The dam, completed in 1930, is two hundred twelve feet high. The waters which back up behind the dam form Saguaro Lake, approximately ten miles long. It is also called Stewart Mountain Lake.

Ref.: Barnes; 4, p. 350. Map: GG-11.

## SUGARLOAF MOUNTAIN

El.: 2880'              Loc.: Maricopa 2, FG-4.2
Descriptive. The fact that some eminences look like mounds of unrefined sugar has resulted in similar descriptive names elsewhere.

Ref.: Barnes. Maps: C-9; GG-19.

| a.n. Sugar Loaf Mountain | El.: 1800' | Mohave |
|---|---|---|

Loc.: One-half mile s. of Hoover Dam.

| Sugarloaf Mountain | El.: 7307'. Map: GB-6 | Cochise |
|---|---|---|
| Sugar Loaf Hill | El.: 5140'. Map: GB-16 | Cochise |
| Sugarloaf Hill | El.: 8281' | Coconino |

Loc.: On e. slope of San Francisco Mountain.

| Sugarloaf Peak | El.: 9281'. Map: GC-3 | Coconino |
|---|---|---|
| Sugarloaf Mountain | | |
| El.: 3190'. Maps: GG-3; GG-11 | | Maricopa |
| Sugarloaf Peak | El.: 675' | Yuma |

In the Laguna Mountains, this peak (also called Squaw Peak) is 1¾ miles s. of Laguna Dam and is a prominent landmark.

## SUNDAD

El.: c. 800'              Loc.: Maricopa 1, A-9.1
The now-vanished small community of Sundad was once proposed as a desert sanatorium. The origin of the name has not yet been ascertained.

Ref.: Theobald. Map: GG-5.

## SUNFLOWER VALLEY

El.: c. 3300'              Loc.: Maricopa 2, G-2.3
Sunflower Valley was so named because of the masses of sunflowers growing there. It was in this valley that Capt. George B. Sanford camped on November 15, 1866.

The Sunflower Creek referred to in newspaper dispatches in 1875 may well have been in this valley. The newspaper writer stated that he found white families camped there, but that all the men were over on "Tonto Creek looking for eligible places to locate ranches." The correspondent also noted that the women were badly frightened because a horse returned to camp shot full of arrows and a man had come in to advise the women to leave immediately despite the fact that their menfolk were elsewhere. The writer of the dispatch said that the horse was not attacked by Indians, however, but by a member of the "Indian ring," which wanted to prevent settlement in the area.

In later years the Sunflower Ranch was established in the valley. There was also a store and post office at Sunflower.

P.O. est. April 28, 1943. Walter B. Davis, p.m. Discont. April 30, 1949.

Ref.: Barnes; 52, V, 197; *Weekly Arizona Miner*, October 1, 1875, 2:2; 85, p. 439; 87, p. 281. Maps: E-20; GD-11 (Sunflower Ranch).

## SURPRISE WELL

El.: c. 1500'              Loc.: Maricopa 1, CD-8
The fact that most wells in this area had to be sunk from one hundred to three hundred feet for water led to the naming of this well when good water was found at forty feet.

Ref.: Barnes. Map: C-12.

## TALIESIN

El.: c. 1800'              Loc.: About 24 miles n.e. Phoenix
Pro.: /tælī´ésən/              Welsh: "shining-brow"
Taliesin, or Taliesin West as it is often called, is the winter quarters of Frank Lloyd Wright's Taliesin Fellows, a group of architectural apprentices. The buildings were constructed in 1939 of native materials. Taliesin is a world-famous embodiment of some of Wright's architectural principles. Taliesin was a poet of King Arthur's Round Table; he sang of the glories of Fine Arts. The Wright family has customarily used Welsh names for their places.

Ref.: 4, p. 146; Frank Lloyd Wright, Letter, July 3, 1957. Map: None.

## TARTON

El.: c. 700'              Loc.: Maricopa 1, BC-12.7
The origin of this name has not been ascertained.

Map: GG-15.

## TELEGRAPH PASS

El.: 1980'              Loc.: Maricopa 2, A-8.7
The military telegraph line from Maricopa Wells to Phoenix ran through this pass in the Salt River Mountains.

Ref.: Barnes. Map: GG-14.

## TEMPE

El.: 1159'  Loc.: Maricopa 2, BC-7.5
Pro.: /tempíy/
In 1871 Charles Trumbull Hayden (b. Connecticut, April 4, 1825; d. February 5, 1900) left Tucson, where he had lived since his arrival in 1857 on the first Butterfield Overland mail coach. He moved to the site of the future Tempe. Here he established a flour mill, around which grew a small community. He also established a ferry across the river, hence the name Hayden's Ferry.

Because of its proximity to a nearby butte the location was sometimes referred to as Butte City. In time, however, the butte became known as Hayden's Butte. Both the community and the butte had their names changed again. In 1875 a newly-arrived group of Mormons was advised to go to Tempe or Hayden's Mill, thus indicating that both names were in use at that time. On July 23, 1882, the Mormons purchased Hayden's eighty acres of land between the ferry and the Mexican town of San Pablo. The name Tempe was suggested by Darrel Duppa (cf. Phoenix) and was applied not only to Hayden's Ferry, but also to the small village of San Pablo (q.v.). Duppa is said to have suggested the name because of the similarity of the countryside to the Vale of Tempe in Greece.

P.O. est. as Hayden's Ferry, April 25, 1872. John J. Hill, p.m. Changed to Tempe, May 5, 1879. Incorporated November 26, 1894. Wells Fargo Station, 1888.

Ref.: *Arizona Miner*, November 9, 1872, 1:2; *Phoenix Herald*, November 27, 1894, 1:7; 105, p. 143; 55, ms, p. 465, (Note 6), p. 466; 112, pp. 198, 219. Maps: C-4; E-18; E-20 (Haydens); GG-12.

**a.n. Tempe Butte** El.: 1496'. Map: GG-12  Maricopa
According to a Pima Indian calendar stick, in the 1850's this butte was the scene of a battle between Apaches and Maricopas, in which the Apaches were defeated.

Ref.: 111, p. 32.

## THEBA

El.: c. 500'  Loc.: Maricopa 1, D-12.1
The origin of this name has not been ascertained.
Ref.: None. Map: GG-16.

## THOMPSON PEAK

El.: 3980'  Loc.: Maricopa 2, CD-4.9
The origin of this name, which dates back at least to c. 1910, has not yet been ascertained.
Ref.: None. Maps: C-10; C-12; GG-1.

## TOLLESON

El.: 1100'  Loc.: Maricopa 1, JK-6.3
W. G. Tolleson named this place in 1912.
P.O. est. July 14, 1913. Leon H. Tolleson, p.m. Incorporated 1929.
Ref.: Clipping File, State Library Archives. Map: GG-2.

## TONOPAH

El.: c. 1500'  Loc.: Maricopa 1, D-5
The origin of this name has not been ascertained.
P.O. est. June 15, 1934. John H. Beauchamp, p.m.
Ref.: P.O. Records. Map: GG-19.

## TORRANCE WELL

El.: c. 2500'  Loc.: Maricopa 1, D-1
Clay Torrance owned the Torrance Well.
Ref.: 141, p. 224. Map: C-4 (Blank Tank).

## TORTILLA FLAT

El.: 1600'  Loc.: Maricopa 2, H-6.3
Pro.: /tortíyə/  Spanish: "pancake; omelet"
The giant rocks in this area look like a platter of tortillas.
P.O. est. February 15, 1928. Mathis Johnson, p.m.
Ref.: 4, p. 368. Maps: B-7; GD-15.

**a.n. Tortilla Creek**  Maps: GK-10; GD-15 Maricopa and Pinal
**Tortilla Mountain**  Map: GK-10  Maricopa

## TOTOPITK

El.: c. 1800'  Loc.: Maricopa 1, JK-16.1
Pro.: /topt/  Papago: "crooked; lopsided"
Totopitk is a summer rancheria where about eight families live each year near what was sometimes referred to as Totobit Tanks (potholes and plunge pools worn in the black lava and conglomerate).

**v.n. (corruption) Toapit**
**(corruption) Tauabit**

Ref.: Kirk Bryan Notes; 26, p. 378; 128, p. 16; 34, p. 96. Maps: A-7 (Toapit: shows in Pima County, an error); C-12; C-13 (Shows in Pinal County, an error); D-8; GG-17.

## TWO-BAR RANCH

El.: c. 4000'  Loc.: Maricopa 2, JK-5.9
Earl Bacon, a freighter in Pleasant Valley (q.v., Gila) in the 1880's, established this ranch and used the Two-Bar brand.
Ref.: Cooper. Map: B-7.

**a.n. Two-Bar Mountain**  Gila
**v.n. Cathedral Peak**
**Cathedral Rock**
**a.n. Two-Bar Canyon**  Map: B-7  Maricopa
**Two-Bar Ridge**  El.: c. 3000'. Maps: B-7; C-12  Maricopa

## UHUPAT OIDAK

El.: c. 500'  Loc.: Maricopa 1, F-11.3
Pro.: /úwpə? óyda?/  Papago: "cat's claw field"
This is a very old temporary summer village used by the Papagos. Here Gila Ranch (q.v.) was located a century ago.
Ref.: 128, p. 39. Map: D-11 (Uupatoitak) (Tesota).

## UNION

El.: c. 1000'  Loc.: Maricopa 1, J-6.7
The origin of this name has not yet been learned. All that remains to mark what was once Union is the location of the Union School.
P.O. est. June 20, 1887. E. J. Elzy, p.m. Discont. October 30, 1888.
Ref.: P.O. Records. Map: GG-2.

## UPASOITAC

El.: c. 500'  Loc.: In Great Bend of Gila River
Fr. Francisco Garcés visited this Maricopa rancheria in 1775 and gave it the name of San Simon y San Judas. The

meaning of the Maricopa name for the community is not known. This is not the same location as that called San Simon y San Judas by Fr. Kino in 1700, the latter being located in Sonora, Mexico.

**v.n. Oparsoitac**
Ref.: 88, II, 871; 35, p. 113. Map: None.

## USERY MOUNTAIN

El.: 2970'                    Loc.: Maricopa 2, E-6.3
This mountain was named for King Usery, a rancher here c. 1879.

Ref.: Barnes. Maps: GG-11; GG-6.

## VALLEY HEIGHTS

El.: c. 1500'                    Loc.: Maricopa 2, A-5.5
Descriptive.

P.O. est. May 13, 1914. Thomas J. Crowl, p.m. Discont. December 9, 1919.

Ref.: P.O. Records; Barnes. Maps: C-12; F-2.

## VILLA BUENA

El.: c. 500'                    Loc.: Maricopa 2, A-9
Pro.: /víyə bwéynə/          Spanish: "good town"
This location was named descriptively by Dr. O. A. Turney. It is a prehistoric ruin.

Ref.: Barnes. Map: C-10 (Indian Village).

## VULTURE

El.: c. 2500'                    Loc.: Maricopa 1, E-2.9
In 1879 James Seymour, a New Yorker, bought the supposedly worked-out Vulture Mine *(q.v.)*. He built a mill at Seymour and laid out a townsite, making his venture pay well. Maps indicate that Seymour and Vulture were at least seven miles apart.

P.O. est. as Seymour, June 20, 1879. Isaac H. Levy, p.m. Name changed to Vulture, October 4, 1880. Discont. April 24, 1897.

Ref.: Barnes; P.O. Records; 87, p. 260. Maps: C-5; C-15.

## VULTURE MINE

El.: c. 2500'                    Loc.: Maricopa 1, E-1.9
In 1863 Henry Wickenburg (cf. Wickenburg) discovered the Vulture Mine, one of the richest in Arizona's territorial history. There are various stories concerning how Wickenburg stumbled across the mine. One is that he shot a vulture and on picking it up noticed nuggets lying on the ground. The second says that his burro ran away and in anger Wickenburg threw rocks at it until he noticed that one of the rocks contained gold. Another reports that Henry Wickenburg noticed a number of buzzards hovering over this peak at the time that he made his discovery.

During the Civil War there was a great demand for gold and the Vulture Mine helped supply the need. By the end of the war there were forty mills in operation at the mine, and another four were built on the Hassayampa in the ensuing year. Others were added later. Wickenburg sold the mine at an early date and so did not share in the vast wealth taken from it.

Ref.: 4, pp. 57, 358; 87, p. 144. Maps: A-7; C12; E-20.

**a.n. Vulture Range**                                    Maricopa
This was at one time the name for the range in which the Vulture Mine was located.
Ref.: 141, p. 13.

## WADDELL

Loc.: Exact loc. unknown. On Ashfork and Phoenix R.R.
P.O. est. February 19, 1937. Mrs. Lola M. Taylor, p.m.

## WATERMAN WASH

El.: c. 600'                    Loc.: Maricopa 1, JH-15-7.2
In the 1880's, a Col. Waterman (first name not known) explored most of the country in the Buckeye and Arlington region looking for canal locations. It is reported that he is buried in the wash which carries his name.

Ref.: Parkman. Maps: GG-13; GG-2.

## WEBB MOUNTAIN

El.: 1879'                    Loc.: Maricopa 1, D-9.1
This mountain was named for Sam Webb who had a ranch at the head of Arlington Valley. (See *a.n.*)

Ref.: Barnes. Map: GG-18.

**a.n. Webb Valley**                                    Maricopa
This small valley forms a divide between waters flowing northeast to the Gila near Arlington and those flowing southwest to the Gila west of Gila Bend.
Ref.: 141, pp. 71-72.

**Webb Well**          Maps: C-13; GG-18          Maricopa
The Webb Well was dug in 1917 to supply water for the Arizona Gold Hill Mining Company. It is from this well that the mountain and valley take their name.
Ref.: 141, p. 226.

## WHITE PICACHO

                              Loc.: E. of Vulture about 20 miles.
Col. Jacob Snively was prospecting near this point when he was murdered by Apache Indians (cf. Gillette).
Ref.: 111, p. 189. Map: None.

## WHITE TANK

El.: c. 1800'                    Loc.: Maricopa 1, J-14.1
The White Tank used to be in the White Tank Mountains and was the source of the name for the mountains. The big tank was located at the northeast corner of the mountains where water pouring down fifteen hundred feet had dug out a hole as big as a house which used to have water in it the year round. Some time between 1898 and 1902 a cloudburst on top of the mountain apparently rolled huge rocks over the bluff, together with tons of dirt, and the hole filled quickly. That was the end of the tank. The rock in and around the former tank was a whitish color, hence the name.

Ref.: Parkman; 141, p. 227. Maps: C-4; E-20; GG-7.

## WICKENBURG

El.: 3000'                    Loc.: Maricopa 1, F-1
Heinrich Heintzel, or Henry Wickenburg (b. Austria 1820; d. 1905), fled from his native country because in all innocence he had sold coal from his father's property in-

stead of turning it over to the state, and as a result was being pursued by the police.

Wickenburg arrived in Arizona in 1862. Two years later he discovered the Vulture Mine *(q.v.)*, but in the same year sold his interest in the mine in order to devote himself to ranching. He established his ranch near the site of the future town of Wickenburg. The name was first used while James A. Moore was a guest at the ranch. Moore, in writing to Gov. John N. Goodwin, dated his letters "Wickenburg Ranch," and that name was used thereafter for the locality.

Wickenburg was not a successful rancher. His place was in what in 1864 was called the Hassayampa Sink, a land of sand and rocks and too little water, where only four men lived at the time. As the Vulture Mine developed, so did Wickenburg village as a supply point for the mine, and by 1870 there were four hundred seventy-four people in Wickenburg. The area was plagued by Indians. The most noted Indian event was the so-called Loring or Wickenburg massacre in which young Henry Loring, a member of the 1871 Wheeler surveying expedition, and a stageload of his companions were brutally slain.

While the town of Wickenburg prospered, the man himself did not. Discouraged and tired, Wickenburg shot himself in 1905, fifty-one years to the day after the first ore from the Vulture Mine had been crushed.

P.O. est. June 19, 1865, B. F. Howell, p.m. Town surveyed and platted April 10, 1897. Wells Fargo Station, 1903.

Ref.: APHS Names File; *Weekly Arizona Miner,* December 26, 1868, 2:2; November 18, 1871, 3:1; *Oasis,* April 10, 1897, 2:1; 170, p. 67; 4, p. 357; 52, IV, 44; 87, p. 44; 22, pp. 166-67. Maps: C-1; E-17; E-23; E-24.

**a.n. Wickenburg Mountains**
Maps: GG-18; C-14                     Maricopa and Yavapai

## WILLIAMSPORT
Loc.: Not known
The origin of this name has not been learned.

P.O. est. October 16, 1866. William Thompson, p.m. Discont. June 13, 1867.

Ref.: P.O. Records. Map: None.

## WINTERS WELL
El.: c. 800′                     Loc.: Maricopa 1, D-6.1
This was the well for the E. H. Winters Ranch. Winters owned this ranch from 1895 to 1925.

Ref.: 141, p. 227; Barnes. Map: A-7.

**a.n. Wintersburg**                     Maricopa
This is the community that developed next to Winters Well.
P.O. est. January 22, 1931. Mace L. Kentch, p.m. Discont. July 17, 1941.

## WITTMAN
El.: c. 1800′                     Loc.: Maricopa 1, H-2.8
The first name of this location was Nadaburg (Spanish: *nada,* "nothing"). The name Nadaburg was given to the location on the railroad because there was nothing there; however, a community gradually developed and the name was changed to Wittman to honor the man who financed the rebuilding of the Walnut Grove Dam.

P.O. est. as Nadaburg, December 2, 1920. John P. Berry, p.m. Changed to Whittman, February 1, 1929. Changed to Wittman, March 1, 1935. Order rescinded March 4, 1935.

Ref.: Barnes; P.O. Records. Map: GG-19.

## WOOLSEY BUTTE PEAK
El.: 3170′                     Loc.: Maricopa 1, C-9.1
This peak was named for King S. Woolsey. (cf. Agua Caliente).

Ref.: 4, p. 463. Map: GG-18.

**a.n. Woolsey Tank**
Loc.: Near Woolsey Peak (GG-18)                     Maricopa
There was an old camp ground and a natural rock tank at this location. Near this tank was the location of the prospect hole owned by the Flower Pot Cattle Company and called the Perhaps Mine. The mine hole was ten feet deep. It contained drinking water in 1918.

Ref.: 141, p. 229.

**Woolsey Wash**     Maps: GG-5; GG-18                     Maricopa

## YELLOW MEDICINE BUTTE
El.: 2308′                     Loc.: Maricopa 1, BC-8.5-10.5
The origin of this name has not yet been ascertained, but it may come from nearby Yellow Medicine Tank.

Ref.: Barnes; 141, p. 229. Map: GG-5.

**a.n. Yellow Medicine Wash**
Loc.: Same as for butte                     Maricopa

## YOUNGTOWN
El.: 1400′                     Loc.: About 16 miles northwest of Phoenix. Maricopa 1, J-5
In 1955 a real estate development for approximately one thousand retired people was begun at this location with the euphemistic name of Youngtown.

Ref.: *Arizona Republic,* "Days and Ways," January 25, 1959.

# ARIZONA PLACE NAMES

# MOHAVE COUNTY

*Hoover Dam — mining — early railroading.*

## MOHAVE COUNTY:

Pro.: /mowhávíˆ/

On November 8, 1864, Mohave County was one of four created in the new Territory of Arizona. Its name was taken from that of the Mohave Indians, a tribe related to the Yuma Indians; the Mohaves lived along the Colorado River in the southwestern part of the county. The name Mohave means "three mountains," (from *hamol,* "three," and *avi,* "mountains") and has reference to the center of tribal activities in the vicinity of The Needles *(q.v.).*

As originally created, Mohave County consisted of the entire northwestern region of Arizona. The county seat was first at Callville but when that portion of Arizona was given to Nevada in 1865, the county seat was removed to Mohave City in 1866 and then by 1872 to Hardyville *(q.v.).* It was changed from there to the mining center of Cerbat in 1871 and thereafter to Mineral Park in 1873. In 1887 with the completion of the railroad through Kingman, the county seat was moved to Kingman where it has remained.

Mohave County encompasses 8,486,400 acres, making it the second largest county in Arizona and the third largest in the nation. Mining and ranching are the principal industries. A large portion of the county is contained in the Hualapai Reservation.

## AHAPOOK CREEK

Loc.: Mohave 6, FG-2-4; Yavapai 2, A-3-5
Hualapai: *A' Ha'a*, "water"; *Pook*, "head"
Descriptive. This stream rises near Cygnus Peak and flows south into Spencer Creek.

Ref.: Dobyns. Map: C-7 (Ah-ah-pook).

## ALEXANDER, CAMP

El.: c. 500'     Loc.: Mohave 3, A-11. Above Hardyville
1.5 miles on Colorado River
The origin of this name has not yet been learned. Camp Alexander was in existence at least as early as January 9, 1868, when Capt. S. B. M. Young of the Eighth U.S. Cavalry mentioned in his report that he had intended camping here with his detachment on a scouting expedition. Capt. George M. Wheeler in September 1871 said the camp was the highest point at which the Colorado River was then crossed by ferry.

Ref.: 169, p. 52; 175, I, 157. Map: None.

## AMBOY

El.: c. 500'     Loc.: Mohave 5, E-8. Mouth of Bill
Williams River
The origin of this name has not been learned.
Charles Debrille Poston in 1865 suggested that a military post be established at this point.

Ref.: Barnes. Map: None.

## AMBUSH WATER POCKET

El.: c. 6000'     Loc.: Mohave 1, F-11.3 (approximate).
When William H. Dunn and Seneca and W. H. Howland (brothers) withdrew from the Powell Grand Canyon exploration party in 1869, the three men clambered up out of the canyon to the Shivwits Plateau. They then went north to a large water pocket where they came upon a camp of Ute Indians. They were well received and fed, but during the night other Indians arrived with tales about outrages by miners against Indians. The band immediately jumped to the conclusion that the three men could never have emerged from the canyon as they claimed and were the guilty miners. In the morning as the three white men came up from the water pocket after filling their canteens, the Indians ambushed them. Because of this, Frederick S. Dellenbaugh gave the name Ambush Water Pocket to the location.

Locally, the place had been referred to as Pen Pockets because cattlemen corralled wild horses here.

Ref.: 42, pp. 228-230; Barnes. Map: None.

## AMERICAN FLAG

El.: c. 4000'     Loc.: Mohave 6, AB-1.5
During boom mining days, a new mining camp took the name of the first big mine—the American Flag—located by a group of Cornishmen. All traces of the mines have disappeared.

Ref.: Babcock; Harris. Map: E-20.

## ANDRUS SPRING

El.: c. 6000'     Loc.: Mohave 1, F-8
Capt. James Andrus developed this seep for watering his stock c. 1866. Andrus led the pursuit of Indians who murdered Dr. James M. Whitmore (cf. Whitmore Pools, Coconino).

Ref.: Barnes. Map: GH-6.

a.n. Andrus Draw                                    Mohave
Although not topographically a canyon, this is sometimes called Andrus Canyon.

Upper Andrus Spring     Map:C-12          Mohave
Lower Andrus Spring     Map:C-12          Mohave

## ANNADALE

El.: c. 2500' Loc.: Mohave 4, CD-7.5. Just e. of Hackberry.
Currently three families live at a small settlement begun c. 1945 by Mrs. Anna McCaw, whose first name was used in naming the locality. Mrs. McCaw sold her interests c. 1951.

Ref.: Clarence Schaefer, Valentine. Map: None.

## ANTARES

El.: 3608'     Loc.: Mohave 4, B-7
Pro.: /ænteýrĭys/
Antares is the name of the brightest star in the constellation of Scorpio, but no evidence has been uncovered to associate the name of this place with that of the star.
Any former settlement at this place has disappeared, there remaining currently only a section house on the railroad.

Ref.: Barnes; Harris. Map: GH-6.

## AQUARIUS MOUNTAINS

El.: c. 5000'     Loc.: Mohave 6, F-5.5
Capt. Amiel W. Whipple named this range in 1854 because his party found numerous streams flowing from the mountains. Although Whipple in one place calls the mountains "the Aquarius range" and in others "Aquarius Mountain" or "Mount Aquarius," these are not the same as the Aquarius Range in T. 16 N., R. 11 W.

Ref.: 177, pp. 201, 202; 71, p. 46; 169, p. 7 (Note 8); Dobyns. Maps: C-2; E-12; E-20; GH-8.

a.n. Aquarius Cliffs                                 Mohave
Loc.: From Aquarius Mts. on Bill Williams River to Colorado River.
This almost continuous cliff rim takes its name from the mountains.

Cottonwood Cliffs                                    Mohave
Loc.: Ts. 21, 22, 23 N., Rs. 11, 12 W.
These are the cliffs called by Whipple the White Cliffs, because of dense groves of cottonwoods and also because of the fantastically shaped white cliffs in the area. (cf. White Cliffs Creek).

White Cliff Valley
Loc.: Along course of White Cliff Creek.          Mohave
Ref.: 177, p. 202.

## ARK BASIN

El.: 3800' Loc.: Mohave 3, CD-9. S. W. Mineral Park in
low foothills at western base of the range
and the border of Sacramento Valley.
Prior to 1906, a series of mines in this area was owned by the Ark and San Antonio Mining Company.

Ref.: 62, p. 87. Map: None.

## ARMISTEAD CREEK

Loc.: "Somewhere west of Truxton Springs" Lt. Edward Fitzgerald Beale on July 4, 1859, reported that the creek was named for Maj. Lewis Addison Armistead (d. July 3, 1863, in Battle of Gettysburg, as a brigadier general in the Confederate Army), who had been breveted major in 1847 for gallant action in the war with Mexico.

Ref.: 85, I; Barnes. Map: None.

## ARTILLERY MOUNTAINS

El.: c. 2500'          Loc.: Mohave 6, DE-7-8

A small group of mountains near the head of the Bill Williams River is a southern extension of the Aquarius Cliffs. Lt. Amiel W. Whipple in 1854 noted a volcanic cone which he called Artillery Peak (T. 12 N., R. 13 W.), probably because of its resemblance to a cannon.

The name of this group of mountains has shifted from time to time. GLO 1912 shows both Artillery Mountains and Rawhide Mountains as two different ranges, whereas on GLO 1909 only Artillery Peak and Artillery Mountains are shown. By GLO 1921 the two groups (Rawhide and Artillery Mountains) are shown separately, as is also Artillery Peak, on the northeast side of the Rawhide Mountains.

Ref.: 100, pp. 13, 22; 177, p. 217. Maps: C-10; E-11; E-20.

## AUBREY LANDING

El.: c. 500'          Loc.: Mohave 6, A-9

From the Mexican border to the entrance of the Grand Canyon there used to be boat landings along the Colorado River in the days when the river ran with enough water to float shallow-draft steamers. Aubrey Landing was an important shipping point. The settlement was begun at the mouth of the Bill Williams River near many mining operations as the result of a town meeting on August 4, 1864, when the name Aubry (sic) was selected to honor the "Skimmer of the Plains." The "Skimmer" was Francois Xavier Aubrey, who earned his title by galloping eight hundred miles on horseback in five days and thirteen hours from Independence, Missouri, to Santa Fe.

Aubrey (b. Maskinonge, Canada, December 4, 1824; d. August 20, 1854) was a noted freighter. In 1852 he drove thousands of sheep across Arizona to California, returning via the Mohave River. In 1853 he located gold in a gulch near the Colorado River. A year later he was the first to explore a wagon route along the 35th Parallel, taking a wagon from San Jose, California, to Santa Fe. At the end of this journey he was killed by Maj. R. H. Weightman in a barroom brawl in Santa Fe.

Aubrey City, as the landing was sometimes called, was abandoned after 1865 when the market for copper broke. By 1878 all that remained was a post office, saloon and hotel—all under one roof—and a unique ship's cabin converted into a residence where William J. Hardy, agent for a steamboat company, held open house. All traces of Aubrey Landing are now gone.

P.O. est. October 2, 1866. Henry J. Lightner, p.m. Discont. November 3, 1886.

v.n. Abray Landing

Ref.: *Arizona Miner,* September 7, 1864, 4:1; 105, p. 198; 111, p. 119; 52, I, 353; 169, p. 10, (Note 15); 29, p. 20; *Arizona Sentinel,* June 15, 1878, 4:2; 100, p. 44; P.O. Records. Maps: C-1; E-4.

a.n. Aubrey Canyon                              Mohave
Near s. end Chemehuevis Valley.
Aubrey Hills                                    Mohave
Loc.: S. of Hualapai Mts. between Big Sandy and Sacramento Valleys.
Aubrey Cliffs                                   Mohave
The Colorado (Arizona) Plateau has cliffs which limit it on the south — the Aubrey Cliffs. They are so named because Aubrey sandstone is "their most conspicuous stratigraphic member." From the description given by Gilbert of Wheeler's expedition, this is probably what Beale called the Aulick Range on October 6, 1857.

Ref.: 12, p. 66; 175, III, 47.
Aubrey Spring       Loc:. T. 28 N., R. 8 W.     Coconino
Aubrey Valley       Map: C-12                    Coconino
Aubrey                                          Yavapai
Loc.: 11 miles w. Seligman. Maps: C-1; E-20.
This name was changed at the request of the railroad because another Aubrey was already on the line. This name is sometimes given as Audley.

Ref.: Barnes.

## BANGS MOUNTAIN

El.: 7500'          Loc.: Mohave 1, B-2.1

Clarence King, an eminent geologist, named this for James E. Bangs, clerk with his party.

v.n. Mount Bangs          Maps: C-9; C-12

Ref.: 41, p. 194; Barnes. Maps: C-9; C-12.

## BATTLESHIP MOUNTAIN

El.: c. 3000'          Loc.: Mohave 3, B-11.8

Descriptive.

v.n. Battle Mountain

Ref.: 62, p. 180; Barnes. Maps: C-12; GH-8.

## BEALE SPRINGS, CAMP

El.: c. 4000'          Loc.: Mohave 3, EF-10.5

Two springs quite close together were visited by Lt. Edward Fitzgerald Beale, U.S.N., on October 8, 1857, but he left them unnamed. By 1867, however, the springs were being referred to in reports of skirmishes with the Hualapai Indians as Beale Station, and later in the same year, as Beale's Springs. Lt. Col. William Redwood Price, making his report on January 20, 1868, stated that the Hualapai Indians were "not subdued, nor desirous of Peace," and cited their attacking the mail station at Beal's (sic) Spring on December 10, shooting all the stock belonging to the mail company. Troubles such as these led to the establishment on March 25, 1871, of a small "tent fort" at Beale Springs, commanded by Capt. Thomas Byrne, Twelfth Infantry, a red-headed Irishman who handled the Indians with consummate skill. He had a small contingent of men, but a "'deludherin' tongue" with which he beguiled the Indians in the cause of peace.

Despite "Old Tommy" Byrne's skill in keeping the peace, Dr. J. A. Tonner, the Indian agent on the Colorado River Reservation, made trouble. In his annual report for 1873,

Tonner complained that the Hualapais refused to come down from the high elevations to the reservation on the river's edge, that they were settled on the direct line of travel west, in the midst of increasing mining operations, and that the only way to avoid serious future trouble was to remove the Hualapais from Camp Beale Springs to the river. By July 1873, orders had been issued for the abandonment of the camp. It was finally abandoned on April 6, 1874. (see Cherum Peak.)

P.O. est. March 17, 1873. Benjamin S. Spear, p.m. Discont. March 30, 1876.

Ref.: 85, p. 479; 169, pp. 5 (Note 5), 50; 22, p. 161; Farmer; 169, p. 96; *Tucson Citizen*, July 19, 1873, 2:1; 75, pp. 124, 161; P.O. Records. Maps: C-1 (Real Spring); C-2; C-7; E-20.

## BERGEMEYER COVE

El.: c. 400'     Loc.: Near Katherine Boat Landing; only deep cove on Arizona side, 1 mile s. of power line.
Frederick R. Bergemeyer (b. Mason City, Iowa, 1913; d. August 23, 1953) was the first ranger in charge of the National Park Service activities in the Katherine Wash district near Bullhead City. He was serving as assistant chief ranger of Zion and Bryce Canyon National Parks when he was fatally injured in a motor accident while en-route to a forest fire in Zion National Park.

Ref.: Burns; Paul R. Franke, Supt., Zion and Bryce Canyon Nat'l Park, Letter, March 23, 1956. Map: None.

a.n. Bergemeyer Wash     Mohave
Loc.: Drains into Bergemeyer Cove.

## BIG BEND

El.: c. 500'     Loc.: Mohave 3, A-11
Descriptive name for bend on Colorado River.

Ref.: Burns; 100, p. 43. Map: GH-4.

## BIG SANDY RIVER

El.: c. 1500'     Loc.: Mohave 6, D-1-8
Descriptive.
Lt. Amiel W. Whipple reported in 1854 that Capt. Joseph R. Walker was supposed to have named this stream. Whipple himself called the stream the Williams River and descended it to the point where it joined the Santa Maria to form the true Bill Williams River. The initial portion Whipple traveled along is now known as the Little Sandy, and the lower section is the Big Sandy. The names derive from the fact that the stream runs through a sandy valley (Big Sandy Valley) extending from Hackberry south to the Bill Williams River. The Big Sandy Wash which forms the stream bed runs along the foot of the Aquarius Cliffs to the site of Signal (q.v.) and then passes through Signal Canyon.

There were many mining prospects in the vicinity of the Big Sandy, which may account for the fact that a short-lived post office was established, possibly to serve the miners.

P.O. est. June 7, 1890. Thomas H. Hunt. p.m. Discont. November 21, 1890.

Ref.: 177, pp. 211, 211 (Note 19); 100, pp. 50, 52; P.O. Records. Maps: C-1 (Bill Williams Fork); C-2; E-22; GH-8.

## BLACK MOUNTAINS

El.: c. 3000'     Loc.: Mohave 3, A-1-11
Mohave 5, BCD 1-3.5
Lying like a black barrier along the westernmost edge of Mohave County is the range of mountains which is known by various names, the most accepted of which is the Black Mountains. The name is descriptive of the dark and forbidding hills which stretch all the way from the northern edge of the state southward to Union Pass. From the pass to the end of the range at Sacramento Wash, the name Black Mesa has often been applied, since in this region the range is more markedly an ancient volcanic plateau sliced into individual hills by erosive forces. The name Ute Mountains at one time was applied to the entire length of the range, but this name has fallen into disuse.

Fr. Francisco Garcés is apparently the first white man to record having seen these mountains, which in 1775 he called the Sierra de Santiago. Later, Lt. Amiel W. Whipple (1854) wrote of finding himself in a wide valley bounded on the west by the Blue Ridge Mountains. Meanwhile, Lt. Joseph C. Ives had struggled up the turbulent Colorado River in the *S. S. Explorer* and had passed through a rock gorge nearly twenty miles long with walls of black-appearing rhyolite, which caused Ives to give it the name Black Canyon. Lt. Mallory extended the name to include the portion of the Black Mountains in that vicinity, calling it the Black Canyon Range. Coues says that in his time (1865) the range was called the Sacramento Range because it bordered the Sacramento Valley. He adds that the mountains gradually came to be called the Black Mountains because Ives had so named the canyon of the Colorado through the volcanic range.

v.n. Colorado Range
(Wheeler Report)
Ref.: 100, pp. 25, 27; 62, p. 23; 151, p. 147; 169, p. 5; 177, p. 203; 42, p. 167; Barnes. Maps: GH-9; GH-4; GH-14.

a.n. Blue Ridge Wash     Mohave

## BLACK ROCK SPRING

El.: c. 5000'     Loc.: Mohave 4, B-5.5
There is a black rock near this spring.

Ref.: Barnes. Maps: GH-6; GH-8.

## BONELLI'S CROSSING

El.: c. 1100'     Loc.: Mohave 3, A-1
On September 29, 1871, Capt. George M. Wheeler noted that two settlers had just arrived at the mouth of the Virgin River on the Colorado River, where they were establishing a ferry for use by those wishing to travel to or from Utah via northwestern Arizona. One of these two settlers was probably Jim Thompson who sold the ferry c. 1875.

The purchaser was Daniel Bonelli, a Swiss who had arrived in Utah with Brigham Young and a party of Mormons. Bonelli was a stonemason, and after he had purchased the ferry from Thompson, Bonelli built a stone house. Waters of Lake Mead now cover the stone building and the Bonelli farm, but a duplicate of his house exists in Kingman.

Ref.: Harris; Housholder; 175, I, 160; 127, p. 138. Maps: GH-6 (Bonelli Landing); GH-8.

## BORIANNA MINE

El.: c. 6000'     Loc.: Near Yucca Flat. Mohave 5, F-1
Pro.: /bòri'ǽnə/
The Borianna Mine is notable because Arizona's first tungsten was discovered here c. 1904. The mine, active for fifty years, is still producing.

Ref.: 4, p. 325; Harris. Map: GH-8 (Boriena).

## BOUNDARY CONE

El.: c. 1800'     Loc.: Mohave 5, C-1.5
Lt. Joseph Christmas Ives in 1857 named this huge white rhyolitic cone because the 35th Parallel goes through its center.

**v.n. Elephant's Tooth**
Ref.: Harris; Housholder; 121, p. 70. Maps: C-10; E-4; GH-9.
**a.n. Boundary Cone Wash**   Loc.: At Boundary Cone     Mohave
Ref.: 62, p. 180.

## BREON

Loc.: Not known
Paul Breon was postmaster at Mohave City in 1877 and had a store there.

P.O. est. April 6, 1883. Allan H. Grant, p.m. Discont. February 19, 1885.
Ref.: Barnes; P.O. Records. Map: None.

## BRIDGE CANYON

El.: c. 4000'     Loc.: Mohave 4, DE-3.2-3.7
The dam site in this canyon is the proposed location of a hydroelectric dam to help prevent the silting up of Lake Mead.

Ref.: Colorado River APHS Files. Maps: GH-6; GH-8.
**a.n. Bridge Canyon Rapids**     Map: GH-1     Mohave

## BULLHEAD CITY

El.: c. 600'     Loc.: Mohave 3, A-11
Bullhead City, a private development, was begun in 1945 with the erection of a service station. Most Davis Dam employees live at this place. The name is derived from its proximity to Bullhead Rock, now largely concealed by the waters of Davis Dam.

P.O. est. August 2, 1946. William T. Hopkins, p.m.
Ref.: Hornbuckle; P.O. Records. Map: GH-4.
**a.n. Bulls Head Peak**   Loc.: T. 21 N., R. 20 W.     Mohave
    **Bulls Head**     Loc.: At Davis Dam     Mohave

## BULLRUSH WASH (sic)

El.: c. 4000'     Loc.: Mohave 2, CF-3.2-4.6
A large swamp formerly at this location was filled with bulrushes.

Ref.: Barnes. Map: C-12.

## BURCH PEAK

El.: c. 6000'     Loc.: Mohave 6, B-3
Tom Burch in the 1870's had a mine called the Esmeralda about sixty miles south of Kingman. He also worked other claims in the area and was still there as late as 1882.

Ref.: Harris. Maps: C-12; GH-6; GH-8.

## BURRO CREEK

El.: c. 1500'   Loc.: Mohave 6, DG-5; Yavapai 2, BA-1-5
A scouting party from Camp Tollgate discovered this stream in July 1869, and it was named by the army officers. The precise reason for so doing is not given. However, when prospectors and miners decided to call it quits, as they were frequently forced to do by lack of luck or by trouble with Indians, they often turned their burros loose. Their wild burro descendants are considered something of a nuisance today in parts of Mohave County. The presence of wild burros may well have led to the naming of Burro Creek and other places carrying the designation "Burro."

Ref.: *Weekly Arizona Miner*, July 24, 1869; 3:1. Maps: C-5; C-6; C-11 (Sycamore or Burro Creek).

## CACTUS PASS

El.: c. 4000'     Loc.: Mohave 4, CD-9.7
Lt. Amiel W. Whipple on January 30, 1854, named the pass "at the urgent request of Dr. Bigelow, because he had found there numerous specimens of this, his favorite plant."

Ref.: 114, II, 214; 177, p. 208. Maps: C-4; E-12; E-20.

## CANE BEDS

El.: c. 1000'     Loc.: Mohave 2, D-1.4
Seeking new places in which to settle, Mormons sent John D. Lee in 1852 to explore southern Utah and land to the south of it. Lee made his way to the bottom lands of the Virgin River, the Virgin Bottoms, and thence to the junction of the Virgin River with Ash Creek.

By 1868 a small settlement had been begun at the former Virgin Bottoms. Because of wild cane, the community was designated Cane Beds. By 1910 the population had dwindled to five, but it has since increased again so that there is now a small community here.

P.O. est. June 15, 1917. Cora H. Cox, p.m. Discont. April 18, 1945.
Ref.: 70, pp. 25, 42; P.O. Records. Maps: C-12; GH-8.
**a.n. Cane Springs**     Map: C-12     Mohave
    **Cane Springs Wash**   Loc.: T. 18 N., R. 13 W.     Mohave
    **Cane Canyon**     Map: B-4     Coconino

## CASTLE PEAK

El.: c. 6000'     Loc.: Mohave 1, E-10
Descriptive.
Ref.: Barnes. Map: C-12.
**a.n. Castle Peak**     Loc.: T. 7 N., R. 15 E.     Gila

## CASTLE ROCK BAY

El.: 1100'     Loc.: Mohave 5, BC-5.5
The bay takes its name from the fact that before the Colorado was dammed, Castle Rock stuck up at low stages of

the river. The rock looked like a castle. Locally, the rock was also known as Mohave Rock or Pulpit Rock.

About three miles from Kingman just off Rt. 93 there is a place known descriptively as Castle Rocks. However, the owner of the place referred to it always as the Garden of the Gods.

Ref.:   Housholder; 4, p. 336. Map: GH-12.

## CAVE CANYON

El.: c. 6000′                    Loc.: Mohave 2, BC-9.2

Numerous caves exist in the four-mile length of this canyon. In the canyon is Columbine Falls, so named because the cliffs on each side of the falls are covered with columbine.

v.n. **Columbine Canyon**

Ref.:   Barnes. Maps: GH-6; GH-8.

## CEDAR

El.: c. 4000′                    Loc.: Mohave 6, C-3

Mining operations near the summit of the Hualapai Mountains caused the establishment of a post office at a ranch. Much cedar grew in the area.

v.n. **Cedarville**          Map: C-7

P.O. est. September 24, 1895. Ira M. George, p.m. Discont. July 31, 1911.

Ref.:   Babcock; P.O. Records; 100, p. 25; 62, p. 16. Maps: C-7; C-8.

The word "cedar" occurs descriptively in many place names. A few are listed below:

a.n. **Cedar Basin**          Map: GH-3              Mohave
     **Cedar Mountain**                              Coconino
     El.: 7057′. Loc.: T. 31 N., R. 6 E.
     **Cedar Creek**          Map: GD-10              Gila

P.O. est. November 1, 1946. Mrs. Virginia A. Kirkpatrick, p.m. Discont. December 15, 1949.

Ref.:   P.O. Records.

**Cedar Flat**          Map: GD-11              Gila
**Cedar Mountain**      Loc.: T. 13 N., R. 6 E.     Yavapai
**Cedar Canyon**        Map: GH-3              Mohave
**Cedar Springs**       Loc.: T. 24 N., R. 19 E.    Navajo

This was the first trading post in the Hopi Buttes area, established by Jake Tobin in the 1880's.

P.O. est. April 1, 1910. Charles Hubbell, p.m. Name changed to Tees To (q.v.), June 18, 1930.

Ref.:   167, p. 29; P.O. Records.

## CERBAT

El.: c. 4000′                    Loc.: Mohave 3, E-9.2
Pro.:   /serbæt/ or             Coco-Maricopa and Mohave:
        /serbət/                "big horn mountain sheep"

Now completely gone, Cerbat was at one time an important mining community, named because of its location in the Cerbat Mountains (see *a.n.* below). The mining town arose in the late 1860's following the discovery of such mines as the Golden Gem, the Cerbat, the Esmeralda, and the Vanderbilt. A small smelter was erected at Cerbat one-half mile below the Cerbat Mine, which was opened in 1869.

In 1871 Cerbat was made the county seat for Mohave County in place of Hardyville (q.v.). The county seat was again moved in 1873, this time to Mineral Park (q.v.).

P.O. est. as Cerbat, December 23, 1872. William Cory, p.m. Name changed to Campbell, June 25, 1890. John H. Campbell, p.m. Name changed to Cerbat, October 24, 1902. Discont. June 15, 1912.

Ref.:   100, p. 13; 177, p. 212; 62, pp. 19, 91; 169, p. 6; P.O. Records; Charles Metcalf, Letter, March 10, 1906 (APHS Files). Maps: C-2; C-7 (Campbell); C-9; GH-8.

a.n. **Cerbat Mountains**   Loc.: Same as for Cerbat      Mohave

The Cerbat Mountains extend for about thirty miles. Lt. Amiel W. Whipple in 1854 applied the name Cerbat Range to these mountains and also to the present Hualapai Mountains on the south plus the White Hills to the north. This is the range described by Fr. Francisco Garcés on June 9, 1775, as Sierra Morena (Spanish: "blackish" or "swarthy mountains").

a.n. **Cerbat Canyon**       Map: GH-3              Mohave
     **Cerbat Peak**         Map: GH-3              Mohave
     **Cerbat Wash**         Map: GH-3              Mohave

## CHARCOAL CANYON

El.: c. 3000′                    Loc.: Mohave 3, E-9.5

Wherever there were miners, there was a need for sharpening tools. The word "charcoal" used in place names sometimes has the significance it does in the case of Charcoal Canyon, for it was in this place that charcoal was prepared for use in blacksmithing.

Ref.:   Harris. Map: GH-3.

## CHEMEHUEVI VALLEY

El.: c. 600′                     Loc.: Mohave 5, A-3.5-7
Pro.:   /čimowéyvi/

Lt. Amiel W. Whipple on February 23, 1854, told about the beauty of the valley occupied by the Chemehuevis Indians, many of whom swam the Colorado River, bringing grain and vegetables to the explorer's party. Probably an offshoot of the Piute Indians, the Chemehuevis were a Shoshonean tribe who formerly lived on the east bank of the Colorado River. This former quiet little valley is now under the water of the lake formed by Parker Dam.

Ref.:   177, p. 232; 88, p. 242; Harris. Maps: GH-9; GH-11; GH-12.

## CHEROKEE

El.: c. 6000′                    Loc.: Mohave 4, DE-6.2

If there was a specific reason for the use of this name, it is not known in the area today. It was necessary for the railroad to name the various section houses and watering stations along its roadbed, and many names were used merely for the sake of attaching some designation to points on the line. This may be the case with Cherokee.

Ref.:   Barnes. Maps: C-11; GH-6.

## CHERUM PEAK

El.: 6978′                       Loc.: Mohave 3, D-8.3
Pro.:   /šrʌm/

The highest point in the Cerbat Mountains, Cherum Peak is named for a principal chief of the Hualapai Indians, who in 1875 with other chieftains of the tribe visited Col. August V. Kautz (Brevet Maj. Gen.) to give assurance of the peaceful intent of the Indians in leaving the Colorado River

Agency and to ask permission for the tribe to return to and remain in their own mountainous country. Kautz advised Cherum to talk to J. A. Tonner, Indian Agent on the Colorado River Reservation, since Kautz had no authority in the matter. Cherum told the army officer that the Indians had left the Colorado River Agency because his people were dying, there was no grass, their horses had nearly all perished, and the tribe, instead of getting twenty-four beeves a week, had been cut down to seven. (cf. Camp Beale Springs).

In January 1874 six hundred twenty Hualapais had been ordered to the hot river bottom reservation. The Indians promptly took to the hills, but at the insistence of their friend, Capt. Thomas Byrne, they went peaceably to the Colorado River Reservation, having a promise that Byrne would go also. Capt. Byrne was transferred to a camp at La Paz to keep an eye on his Indian friends and to be in charge of issuing rations. Within a few months the Hualapai tribe was greatly decimated and half its horses were dead. In March 1875 during the absence of Capt. Byrne, Tonner told the Indians that rations would no longer be distributed by Byrne at La Paz and that thereafter rations would be issued only at the Indian agency headquarters, forty-five miles north of La Paz. Tonner then issued short rations. The Indians apparently made ready to follow his orders, but instead of going to Tonner's headquarters, they headed for their own native mountains. At this juncture, Cherum called on Col. Kautz. The Indians never returned to the Colorado River Agency.

Ref.:    169, pp. 97, 98, 113. Maps: C-13; GH-3.

## CHLORIDE

El.: 4009′                          Loc.: Mohave 3, D-8.1
Chloride was named because of the type of silver ore found in the area.

Of the several mining communities which sprang up in this area in the 1860's and 1870's, Chloride was not only the first, but it is the only one which survives.

Chloride was a mining camp in 1864. With the opening of additional mines, the camp developed into a town, and by 1900 it had a population of two thousand. The earliest prospectors in the district were time and again driven away by Indians, but the richness of the ores always brought the miners back. The first locations were made in 1863 at Silver Hill, where the Hualapai Indians laid their hands on their first guns, using them to kill four miners at Silver Hill Camp. One was shot, and two others were killed by the Indians' throwing stones down the mining shaft.

P.O. est. March 27, 1873. Robert H. Choate, p.m. Wells Fargo Station, 1903.
Ref.:    62, pp. 51-52; 89, pp. 81, 82; Schroeder; P.O. Records. Map: GH-3.

## CLACK

El.: c. 6000′                        Loc.: Mohave 3, E-8.7
                                     3 miles s. of Mineral Park.
The Clack brothers, who had a lease on the land, named the post office at the Oro Plata mine for their family. This place has since disappeared.

P.O. est. July 20, 1898. John W. Babson, p.m. Discont. August 26, 1899.
Ref.:    Barnes; P.O. Records; Babcock. Map: None.

## COOPER POCKETS

El.: c. 6000′                        Loc.: Mohave 2, A-5
                                     N.w. of Mount Trumbull c. 30 miles.
A sheepman named Cooper once used these water holes, c. 1862-1874.

Ref.:    Barnes. Map: None.

## COTTONWOOD BASIN

El.: c. 1000′                        Loc.: Mohave 3, A-8
Cottonwood Basin was formed when Cottonwood Island, named descriptively, disappeared under waters impounded by Davis Dam. Lt. Joseph Christmas Ives named the island on his trip up the Colorado River in 1857.

Cottonwood Station was a way-stop on the route from Searchlight, Nevada, to Mineral Park.

Ref.:    Harris; Burns; 87, p. xliv. Map: E-20.
         There are too many place names using "cottonwood" for a full list to be included. However, those below are examples:

**a.n. Cottonwood Valley**                              Mohave
         Loc.: Where Colorado River emerges from Black Canyon. Named by Ives in 1857.

Ref.:    100, pp. 37-38; 121, p. 78.

| **Cottonwood Creek** | Loc.: T. 3 S., R. 11 E. | Pinal |
| **Cottonwood Canyon** | Map: GE-5 | Graham |
| **Cottonwood Mountain** | Loc.: Sec. 2, T. 7 S., R. 21 E. | Graham |
| **Cottonwood Canyon** | Map: GF-2 | Greenlee |
| **Cottonwood Spring** | Map: GB-1 | Cochise |
| **Cottonwood** | | Pinal |

P.O. est. November 9, 1881. Charles D. Henry, p.m. Discont. February 4, 1884.
Ref.:    P.O. Records.

## CROZIER

El.: c. 4000′                        Loc.: Mohave 4, C-7.1
Samuel Crozier had one of the first cattle ranches in Mohave County in the early 1870's in the area where the Crozier section house on the A.T. & S.F. R.R. is now located. Crozier was said to have sold Peach Springs, located on the Hualapai Indian Reservation and a principal source of water for the Hualapai Indians, to the A. & P. R.R. in 1882. Years later c. 1927 this led to a law suit by the Hualapais against the railroad. The Indians claimed that Crozier never lived anywhere near the springs in question and so had no right to a homestead claim in the area.

A Hualapai Indian who was a cowhand for Crozier adopted his employer's surname, replacing his Indian name of Haka with the name Kate Crozier. Kate Crozier served as a scout under Generals Crook, Miles and Willcox. In 1927 Kate Crozier testified that Sam Crozier did not, in fact, sell Peach Springs, but did sell Truxton Springs to the railroad, the latter water being on Crozier's ranch. Kate Crozier also said that the spring which was sold was that which ran at the former Crozier Station, called (in 1927) Truxton Canyon Station.

Sam Crozier was a close friend of Charlie Spencer and in early 1888 was trustee of Spencer's estate (*see* Spencer Canyon).

Wells Fargo Station, 1907.

Ref.: Harris; 169, pp. 156, 256, 270. Map: C-10.

## CYCLOPIC WASH

El.: 4500'  Loc.: Mohave 3, G-4.6

Cyclopic Wash takes its name from the former presence of the Cyclopic Mine, which was discovered in the early 1880's by men named Patterson, Rowe, and Glen, who c. 1896 leased it to a Seattle company. The name was applied to a post office which was established to give mail service to miners.

P.O. est. July 7, 1905. Robert Nickel, p.m. Discont. February 15, 1917.

Ref.: P.O. Records; 62, p. 124. Map: C-12 (P.O.).

**a.n. Cyclopic**

P.O. est. September 19, 1914. Stanley C. Bagg, p.m.

## CYGNUS MOUNTAIN

El.: c. 4000'  Loc.: Mohave 6, FG-7

On January 25, 1854, Lt. Amiel W. Whipple wrote that he had named a range of snow-topped mountains "Cygnus Mountain." Although Whipple does not state his reason for so doing, it may be that the white-backed range in some way reminded him of a swan.

This is the same mountain which Marcou in 1857 called Whipple Mountain. It is a curious fact that several men tried to honor Whipple by naming peaks and mountains after him, but the name never became attached permanently to any mountain in Arizona. For instance, Ives in 1857 appears to have called The Needles (*q.v.*) "Mount Whipple," and in 1858 Beale so named a peak south of the junction of the Puerco and Little Colorado Rivers.

Ref.: 177, pp. 200, 234 (Note 4). Maps: C-4; E-20.

## DAVIS DAM

El.: c. 700'  Loc.: Mohave 3, A-10

Located in Pyramid Canyon (*q.v.*), Davis Dam was originally called Bullhead Dam because of a rock formation at the dam site. The project to construct the dam was authorized in April 1941, and construction began a year later on the earth-and-rock filled embankment with its concrete spillway, intake system, and power plant. The dam was renamed in 1941 for Arthur Powell Davis, Director of Reclamation 1914-1923, who was among the group responsible for the beginning of the Colorado River development.

Work on Davis Dam was interrupted by World War II, but was resumed in 1946. In January 1950 the first water began to be stored. The dam rises two hundred feet from its foundation and about one hundred forty feet from the river bed.

P.O. est. in Clark Co., Nevada, but shifted to Mohave County December 1, 1950. Discont. August 31, 1954.

Ref.: "Davis Dam Power Plant," U. S. Dept. of Interior, Bureau of Reclamation, Region 3, Boulder City, Nevada, February 1953; Hornbuckle; P.O. Records. Map: GH-4.

## DAVIS, MOUNT

El.: c. 2000'  Loc.: Mohave 3, A-8

Lt. Joseph C. Ives, who passed through this area in 1858, may have named the mountain for Jefferson Davis, who was Secretary of War for the United States from 1853 to 1857.

Ref.: Barnes. Maps: C-4; E-20.

## DEAN PEAK

El.: c. 8000'  Loc.: Mohave 4, A-11

In 1877 William (Bill) Dean located a mine near this peak, later selling it and leaving the country to investigate mining prospects elsewhere.

Ref.: 151, p. 257; Harris. Map: C-12.

## DELAWARE SPRING

Loc.: Doubtful

Lt. Edward Fitzgerald Beale named a spring in Engles Pass (between Truxton and White Rock springs) for Dick, a Delaware Indian, who was a member of Beale's exploring party in 1857-58.

Ref.: Barnes. Map: None.

## DELLENBAUGH, MOUNT

El.: 6650'  Loc.: Mohave 4, DE 7-1

Maj. John Wesley Powell named this mountain for Frederick S. Dellenbaugh, the artist of the second Grand Canyon expedition in 1871-72.

Ref.: 41, p. 259; 42, p. 310. Map: C-6; C-12.

## DELUGE WASH

El.: c. 2500'  Loc.: Mohave 6, CD-3.5

The story is that a prospector named Tom Burch had a camp in this wash. It was destroyed by a cloudburst in 1873. Others think the name of the prospector was Diamond Joe Reynolds, whose name in reality may have been Joe Diamond.

Ref.: Barnes; Harris; 100, p. 22. Maps: C-7; C-11.

## DIAMOND BUTTE

El.: 6250'  Loc.: Mohave 2, A-6.6

Frederick Dellenbaugh, artist and topographer with Maj. John Wesley Powell's second Grand Canyon expedition, applied the name "Diamond Butte" because near it Powell's party found an ant-hill covered with quartz crystals which sparkled like diamonds.

Ref.: 41, p. 192. Maps: C-3; E-20.

## DIAMOND CANYON

El.: c. 1500'  Loc.: Mohave 4, F-3. Coconino 3, CA-7-8

While it is known that Lt. Joseph Christmas Ives, who explored the possibilities of navigation on the Colorado River, used the name for this canyon, its origin is not known. On April 5, 1858, Lt. Ives and Dr. John S. Newberry came to the western end of the Grand Canyon at Diamond Peak. Before the construction of a railroad from Williams to the Grand Canyon in 1907, tourists viewed the Grand Canyon at its western end where the canyon walls are two thousand feet high. Following a ten-hour trip by horse-drawn stage they stayed at the Wooden Diamond Creek Hotel. When the hotel was abandoned, it disappeared piece by piece as Indians and ranchers carried away the frame building.

Ref.:   Barnes; 4, p. 323. Maps: C-3; C-12; E-20.

## DIAMOND JOE

El.: c. 1500'                    Loc.: Mohave 6, D-9
Diamond Joe Reynolds, whose name in reality may have been Joe Diamond, was a prospector who located a mine at this place. It is said that he once owned the Diamond Joe Mississippi River steamboat line and that he was also the owner of the Congress Mine (Yavapai Co.). Diamond Joe, as a place, is now abandoned. (cf. Deluge Wash).

Ref.:   Babcock; Barnes. Map: C-12.

## DIXIE

El.: c. 2500'                    Loc.: Mohave 1, AC-21
                    Arizona Strip along the Virgin River.
Mormons from Utah called this area Dixie because the climate was warmer than that in Utah. Here they raised grapes, apples, and other fruit. The region was also noted for its wine.

Ref.:   41, pp. 163-164. Map: None.

**a.n. Dixie National Forest**                    Mohave
    (Now part of Coconino National Forest).

## DOUDSVILLE

El.: c. 500'                    Loc.: Mohave 5, A-2.4
Pro.:  /dáwdi^vil/
Milo Doude was a prospector and miner.

Ref.:   Harris. Maps: C-9; C-10.

## DUNCAN

El.: c. 3000'                    Loc.: Mohave 4, A-1.5
Tap Duncan was an old time cowman who bought his ranch from Wellington Starkey c. 1904 and called his place the Diamond Bar Ranch. Prior to that time, the place had been called Grass Springs and was the location of the O. K. and Excelsior mines, located in the 1880's. The OK Wash takes its name from one of the mines.

Ref.:   Harris; 62, p. 121. Map: GH-6 (Ranch).

## DUTCH FLAT

El.: c. 2000'                    Loc.: Mohave 5, EF-5.6
Dutch Flat, from which the Dutch Flat Road takes its name, was so called because several Dutch and German families lived here. One of the men had a mine in this area.

Ref.:   Housholder; Harris. Map: GH-2.

## EL DORADO, CAMP

El.: c. 1000'                    Loc.: Mohave 3, A-4
A short-lived army post, El Dorado Camp was established on January 15, 1867, and abandoned on August 24, 1867. It probably was named because of its proximity to El Dorado Canyon, site of some of the earliest placer gold finds along the Colorado River, but on the California side of the river.

It was at this point that a ferry was established on the Arizona side, with the name El Dorado Cañon being applied to the post office located here to serve travelers and miners. P.O. est. January 17, 1865. Frank S. Alling, p.m. Discont. September 27, 1867.

Ref.:   85, p. 497; 75, p. 132; 100, p. 37; 62, p. 218; P.O. Records. Map: C-1.

**a.n. El Dorado Pass**            El.: c. 2700'            Mohave
    A pass through the Black Mountains on road to White Hills.

## ELEPHANT HILL

El.: 150'                    Loc.: Mohave 3, A-5.7
                    N. of Mt. Davis at a bend in the Colorado River
                    Near T. 26 S, R. 22 W.
Dr. John S. Newberry of the Ives Expedition in 1857, reported finding a perfect tooth of *Elephas primigenius* at the base of this eminence.

Ref.:   Barnes. Map: None.

## ELEPHANTS TOOTH

El.: c. 2500'        Loc.: Mohave 5, BC-1 T. 19 N, R. 20 W.
The name is descriptive of a prominent rhyolite plug southeast of Oatman. Because it is silhouetted against the Black Mountains, its whiteness is very marked. (cf. Boundary Cone).

Ref.:   170, p. 77. Map: None.

## ENGLE'S PASS

El.: c. 4000'                    Loc.: Mohave 4, BC-7.5
On October 8, 1857, Lt. Edward Fitzgerald Beale wrote of making a gentle descent through a canyon about two hundred yards wide, with the sides at some places eight hundred feet high. Beale named the canyon Engle's Pass after Capt. Engle, U.S.N.

Ref.:   12, p. 69. Map: E-12 (Unnamed pass through which Beale's route goes).

## FERN SPRING

El.: c. 6000'                    Loc.: Kanab Canyon
The name Fern Spring derives from the fact that the water from the spring drops from a place about eight feet high in the canyon wall, and the area surrounding it on the wall is covered with Maiden's Hair fern.

Capt. George M. Wheeler in 1872 said that Fern Spring was a pool in Kanab Canyon in a place so narrow that the sun reached the canyon bed for only two hours during the day.

**v.n. Dripping Spring**
Ref.:   175, I, 52. Map: None.

## FISHBACK

El.: c. 5000'                    Loc.: Mohave 3, BC-9.5
                    S. of road above Union Pass.

This is a sharp ridge.

Ref.:   Ferra. Map: None.

## FLATROCK SPRING

El.: c. 6000'                    Loc.: Mohave 4, B-6
There is a large flat rock standing on its edge near the spring.
Ref.: Barnes. Map: GH-8.

## FLORES WASH

El.: c. 4000'                    Loc.: Mohave 3, CD-8.5
                      N.W. of Cerbat above Sacramento Valley.
Pro.: /flóres/
First located in 1871 by prospectors from Nevada, the mine which gives Flores Wash its name was abandoned because of Indian troubles and did not begin operation again until c. 1876. Once known as Five Forks Mine, the property was sold in 1888 to the Flores Mine Company of Philadelphia, which worked it until 1893. The mine has not been worked since that time.
Ref.: 62, p. 96. Maps: None.
**a.n. Flores Gulch**                    Mohave

## FORTIFICATION ROCK

El.: c. 3000'                    Loc.: Mohave 3, A-1
In 1857 Lt. Joseph C. Ives, on his expedition to determine the navigable headwaters of the Colorado River, mentioned climbing to the top of Fortification Rock for a view of the great bend of the Colorado River. Capt. George M. Wheeler in 1871 referred to this isolated peak as Fortification Mountain. The name most commonly in use today is Fortification Hill.
Ref.: 169, p. 18; 173, I, 159; Housholder. Maps: E-4; GH-6; GH-8.

## FRANCONIA

El.: c. 1200'                    Loc.: Mohave 5, CD-3.5
Formerly a section house on the A.T. & S.F. R.R., this place was named after Frank Smith, son of F. W. Smith, a general superintendent of the railroad. In 1956 nothing remained but a sign at this place.
Ref.: Barnes; Babcock. Map: GH-9.

## FRANKLIN HEATON RESERVOIR

Loc.: Mohave 2, A-5.3. Southern end Hurricane Ledge.
The Heaton family was among the first to settle in the Arizona Strip country. About 1865 Franklin Heaton of Pipe Springs used this place for watering stock.
Ref.: Barnes. Map: None.

## FRANK MURRAY'S PEAK

El.: c. 2000'    Loc.: Mohave 5, B-1 35°05'56", 114°28'25"
Lt. Edward Fitzgerald Beale on October 14, 1857, described a single peak rising above the nearby mountains and named it Frank Murray's Peak. Beale's party followed a rough pass at the base of this peak, finding Indian trails, a few rude dwellings, a field of pumpkins and a fine spring. At the foot of this pass, Beale's party discovered Mohave Indians. He described them as "a fine-looking, comfortable, fat and merry set; naked except for a small piece of cotton cloth around the waist, and though barefooted [they] ran over

the sharp rock as easily as if shod with iron. We were soon surrounded on all sides by them. Some had learned a few words from trafficking with the military posts, 250 miles off, and one of them saluted me with: 'God damn my soul eyes.' 'How de do! How de do!' "
Ref.: 12, pp. 73-75. Map: None.
**a.n. Murray's Spring**                    Mohave
      This is the source of Meadow Creek (q.v.) and was named by Beale on January 24, 1858.
Ref.: 169, p. 5, (Note 5).

## FREE'S WASH

El.: c. 5000'                    Loc.: Mohave 4, A-9-10
When Gov. A. P. K. Safford made his trip through the territory of Arizona in 1875, he noted stopping at Free's Wash between Mineral Park and Greenwood City where he met and talked with Cherum, chief of the Hualapai Indians. (cf. Cherum Peak). Some travelers mistook the sound of the name Free's and referred to the place as Freeze Wash. Actually, the name seems to have come from the name of John Free, a prospector in that area.

In 1890 Free's Wash was the scene of a Hualapai "ghost dance" held by Levy-Levy's band. The ghost dances began in 1889 as a part of a belief by some Indians that their Messiah was due to arrive. The dancers dressed in white and danced for several days until they fell exhausted, at which stage they were supposed to see visions concerning their Messiah.
Ref.: Babcock; *Arizona Miner,* June 6, 1875, 1:4; 169, p. 172; Harris; 158, p. 68. Maps: GH-8; GH-15 (Fries Wash).

## FRISCO

El.: 3000'                    Loc.: Mohave 3, B-10.6
The mining town connected with the Frisco mine at one time housed several hundred people.
P.O. est. May 5, 1913. Cornelius J. Falvey, p.m. Discont. July 15, 1915.
Ref.: P.O. Records; Barnes; Housholder. Maps: F-2; GH-8.
**a.n. Frisco Peak**                    Mohave

## GABRIEL'S SPRING

El.: c. 4000'        Loc.: Probably in Truxton Canyon.
Lt. Edward Fitzgerald Beale is said to have named this location, but for what reason has not yet been ascertained.
Ref.: Barnes. Map: None.

## GADDIS SPRING

El.: c. 5000'                    Loc.: Mohave 3, EF-9.3
Pro.: /gédəs/
The spring takes its name from the owner of the ranch, O. D. M. Gaddis. His full name was Oregon Dakota Montana Gaddis. He was at one time postmaster in Kingman.
Ref.: Harris. Map: GH-3.

## GENTILE SPRING

El.: c. 6000'                    Loc.: Mohave 3, F-11
Sometimes referred to as Railroad Spring, Gentile Spring may have taken its name from the fact that the Mormons

often referred to others than themselves as Gentiles. In 1872 Capt. George M. Wheeler noted that the Gentiles "generally made small settlements convenient to mine districts and established ranches along routes of communication."

**v.n. Gentle Spring**

Ref.:   174, p. 32. Map: C-7 (Gentle Spring).

## GERMA

El.: c. 2500′                         Loc.: Mohave 5, A-1.
                                      S.w. of Oatman 2½ miles.
About 1896 a mine was discovered nearly three-fourths of a mile east of Vivian and slightly above it. It was owned by the German-American Mining Company of Los Angeles c. 1900. The Germa Mine was closed in 1906 because of a lack of water to run the mill on a double shift, the only economically feasible way the mine could operate. It is a ghost mining camp today.

P.O. est. January 20, 1903. Isaac D. Hilty, p.m. Discont. February 27, 1906.

Ref.:   P.O. Records; 62, p. 186; Harris. Map: None.

**a.n. German-American Wash**                            Mohave

## GLENWOOD

El.: c. 2500′             Loc.: Mohave 6, DE-6.2
             12 miles east of McCrackin mine on Sandy Creek.
Long since vanished, Glenwood had one hundred residents in 1876. It was a mining community.

Ref.:   55, p. 579. Map: None.

## GOLCONDA

El.: c. 3500′                       Loc.: Mohave 3, DE-9
Johnny Boyle owned and named the Golconda mine, all operations at which were wiped out by fire. The camp was idle for many years, but there was some activity here in 1956.

P.O. est. December 8, 1909. William Pound, p.m. Discont. February 28, 1918.

Ref.:   P.O. Records; Barnes; Babcock; Harris. Maps: C-11; C-12.

## GOLD BASIN

El.: c. 3000′                     Loc.: Mohave 3, DE-2.8
Valuable minerals were discovered in the Gold Basin district during the early 1870's. The basin-like terrain and the fact that it contained gold are clues to the name. The non-availability of supplies and the scarcity of fuel and water to work the mines kept the area from developing. Nevertheless, there were enough miners to warrant a post office. The region enjoyed renewed activity c. 1903 under the name Basin.

P.O. est. as Gold Basin, September 20, 1890. Michael Scanlon, p.m. Discont. January 4, 1894. Re-est. as Basin, March 17, 1904. Eugene D. Chandler, p.m. Discont. June 15, 1907.

Ref.:   P.O. Records; 62, pp. 16, 118-119. Map: C-9.

## GOLDFLAT

El.: c. 2500′                    Loc.: Mohave 3, E-11.5
Descriptive.

P.O. est. December 22, 1908. Jacob A. Hamme, p.m. Discont. July 15, 1910.

Ref.:   P.O. Records. Map: C-10.

## GOLDROAD

El.: 2900′                       Loc.: Mohave 5, B-1
The famous Gold Road mining district extends from the meadows (cf. Meadow Creek) across the top of the mountain range and down to the valley on the west slope. The principal mining camp for the district, Goldroad was on the western slope of the range about a mile below the crest. The district was long known for the presence of minerals, which were first found in 1860 by John Moss and his party. Ore from the Moss Mine was treated at the Moss mill seven miles to the west. In the 1880's with the discovery of rich ores in the Cerbat Mountains, mining activity ceased in the Goldroad area. However, as the value of gold increased, activity re-opened c. 1902. It was in this year that the big strike was made.

The story is that Joe Jerez, a Mexican prospector, drifted into Kingman looking for a grubstake. Henry Lovin, a prominent citizen, gave him $12.50 in food. Jerez took off for the hills and spent his first night in the Gold Road district. The next morning Jerez found that his burros had strayed from camp. While searching for them, the Mexican picked up a piece of quartz which showed pure gold. He immediately set up a monument and staked out a claim. When Jerez had the piece assayed, it ran forty ounces in gold to the ton. The result was a stampede to the Goldroad district. Lovin and Jerez sold out their claim for $50,000. A later owner sold the same location for $275,000. By 1906 a French syndicate was in control, having paid a half million for one-fourth of the stock. A year later, however, the high cost of power and the low grade of the ore caused the mine to be closed.

In 1949 the remains of the mining operations and community were razed to save taxes. Today the casual visitor sees merely the ghostly ruins of the once successful camp. Down below on the flat are the remains of what was once called Mexican Town.

P.O. est. March 24, 1906. Edward A. Shaw, p.m. Discont. October 15, 1942.

Ref.:   P.O. Records; Babcock; 62, pp. 16, 152, 154-155; 170, p. 74. Maps: C-10; GH-6; GH-8.

**a.n. Gold Road Gulch**                                 Mohave
      Loc.: S.e. of Goldroad Mine ½ mile.
Ref.:   62, p. 164.

   **Gold Road Pass**     El.: 5000′. Map C-12      Mohave
   Same as Sitgreaves Pass (q.v.).
Ref.:   62, p. 152.

## GRAND WASH CLIFFS

El.: c. 6000′                    Loc.: Mohave 1, AC-7.8-5.5
The cliffs take their name from the Grand Wash. The Grand Wash trough was formed by the "faulting and tilting of a large crust block." The valley it forms (Grand Wash Valley)

is marked by detritus-broken rocks and bare sand which has collected over millions of years. The edge of this great valley is bordered by the Grand Wash Cliffs. Although the cliffs appear at a distance to be vertical, this is not the case. The cliffs rise like steps from the lowland area to the high plateaus.

**v.n. Grand Cliffs Range**

Ref.   "Lake Mead," U. S. Government Printing Service, 1955, No. 0-351918; 100, pp. 13, 30; 132, p. 188. Map: C-6.

## GRANITE PEAK

El.: c. 4000'                    Loc.: Mohave 6, BC-2.5
Descriptive.

Ref.:   Harris. Maps: C-10; GH-8.
The word *granite* is used descriptively in many place names, some of which are given below:

**a.n. Granite**          Map: C-12                    Yavapai
P.O. est. April 10, 1903. Earl G. Norton, p.m. Discont. October 11, 1904.

| | | |
|---|---|---|
| **Granite Mountains** | Map: C-12 | Pima |
| **Granite Park** | Loc.: T. 30 N., R. 9 W. | Coconino |
| **Granite Peak** | El.: 7387'. Loc.: T. 19 S., R. 19 E. | Cochise |
| **Granite Peak** | Map: E-20 | Yavapai |

This peak was once called Gurley Mountain for John A. Gurley, appointed first territorial governor of Arizona by Abraham Lincoln in March 1863. Gurley died before getting west of the Mississippi. Probably the only place in Arizona currently carrying his name is Gurley Street in Prescott.

Another name for Granite Mountain was Sierra Prieta, so noted by J. Ross Browne in his trip to Arizona in 1864.

Ref.:   87, p. 301.

| | | |
|---|---|---|
| **Granite Knob** | El.: 6625'. Map: GM-23 | Yavapai |
| **Granite Point** | Map: E-3 | Yuma |
| **Granite Spur** | Map: GN-6 | Yuma |
| **Granite Wash Mountains** | Map: GN-6 | Yuma |

## GRAPEVINE CREEK

El.: c. 2500'                    Loc.: Mohave 3, F-1-4
Along part of the creek bed there is a marshy area where there are grapevines.

Ref.:   Harris. Maps: GH-6 (wash); GH-8 (wash).
The word *grapevine* occurs descriptively in place names. Two examples are given here:

**a.n. Grapevine Spring**          Map: E-20                    Gila
This is the spring on the Salt River described by King S. Woolsey in 1864.

| | | |
|---|---|---|
| **Grapevine Spring** | Loc.: T. 6 N., R. 4 E. | Maricopa |

## GRASS MOUNTAIN

El.: c. 6000'                    Loc.: Mohave 1, E-8.2
This mountain was usually covered with good grass.

**v.n. Grassy Mountain**

Ref.:   Barnes. Map: C-12.

## GREENWOOD

El.: c. 2500'                    Loc.: Mohave 6, DE-5.6
Greenwood took its name from the many palo verde trees in the area. When Gov. A. P. K. Safford visited the mining community in 1875, he mentioned a ten-stamp mill to assist in the work of the Greenwood gold mine. At that time the

community had about thirty houses and a population of approximately three hundred. Many residents probably were living in tents. Greenwood soon vanished because of the poor quality of the ores at the mine.

Ref.:   *Arizona Miner*, March 26, 1875, 4:1; June 4, 1875, 1:4-5; 89, pp. 146-147; 87, p. 252. Maps: E-20; GH-8 (Greenwood School).

**a.n. Greenwood Peak**          Map: C-12                    Mohave

## GREGGS FERRY

El.: c. 1500'                    Loc.: Mohave 3, E-1
Tom Gregg located this ferry about eighty miles due north of Kingman. According to Asa Harris, when Scanlon left his own ferry Gregg took over its operation, at which time Scanlon Ferry (q.v.) was called Gregg Ferry. However, at an earlier date the two ferries were separate.

Ref.:   Harris; 100, p. 17. Maps: C-10; C-12 (Gregg Ferry: 2 miles n. of Scalon Ferry); C-13; GH-6 (Scanlon Ferry).

## GRIFFITH

El.: c. 2500'                    Loc.: Mohave 5, E-1
The first name for this location on the railroad was Sacramento Siding, which was changed c. 1883 to Drake, the name of a chief engineer. On November 14, 1930, the name was changed to Griffith, the name of a bridge gang foreman. All that remains at this point is a section house.

Ref.:   Barnes; Harris. Maps: C-6 (Drake); C-13.

## GROOM PEAK

El.: c. 4000'                    Loc.: Mohave 6, C-4.9
Bob Groom (cf. Groom Creek, Yavapai) had mining claims near the peak which today bears his name.

Ref.:   Barnes. Maps: C-12; GH-8.

## GROSSMAN PEAK

El.: c. 5000'                    Loc.: Mohave 5, C-5
A. G. Grossman at one time did placer mining near this peak. A printer, he also ran the *Needle's Eye* at Needles, California.

**v.n. Crossman Peak**

Ref.:   Barnes. Maps: C-10 and C-11 (Crossman Peak); GH-8.

## HACKBERRY

El.: c. 4000'                    Loc.: Mohave 4, C-7.5
When Lt. Edward Fitzgerald Beale came through this area he named a spring Gardiner Spring, which may be the same as the Hackberry Spring. Not until the 1870's was the name Hackberry Spring supplied. In that year William Ridenour, Sam Crozier, Isaac Putnam, and John Kits found a rich vein of ore one and a half miles west of the spring. The men named the mine the Hackberry Mine for the beautiful tree beside the spring under which they found shelter and shade during their search for a mine. The four men built a stone house beside the spring. With the discovery of the mine it was not long before Hackberry developed into a prosperous mining town with a population of over one hundred people. In the summertime hackberry trees attract millions of birds

which eat its abundant fruit. Indians, too, gather its sweet berries. Hackberry wood, however, is valueless, since it does not burn and rots rapidly.

P.O. est. July 9, 1878. Alonzo E. Davis, p.m. Wells Fargo Station, 1885.

Ref.: P.O. Records; *Weekly Arizona Miner*, March 5, 1875, 2:2; 89, pp. 87, 146; 87, p. 252; 122, p. 216; 100, pp. 20, 78. Map: C-6.

**a.n. Hackberry Mountain**      Map: C-12      Yavapai
Named c. 1878. Descriptive.

## HACKS CANYON

El.: c. 6000'      Loc.: Mohave 2, EF-5.5-5.7
Chris Heaton owned a spring in this canyon. He sold it to a man named Haskell Jolly, who raised horses here for a number of years. The settlers called Jolly "Hack" and applied the name to the canyon where Jolly had his horses.

Ref.: Barnes. Maps: GH-6; GH-8.

## HARDY MOUNTAINS

El.: c. 2000'      Loc.: Mohave 3, C-11.9
A group of low-lying hills about three miles in diameter and rising six hundred feet above the terrain is named for the Hardy Mine, which was discovered in the early 1860's by William H. Hardy of Kingman (cf. Hardyville). The mine was a steady producer on a small scale.

Ref.: 62, pp. 153, 176-177, 179. Map: GH-6.

**a.n. Hardy Camp**      Mohave
     **Hardy Wash**      Mohave

## HARDYVILLE

El.: c. 500'      Loc.: Mohave 3, A-11.2
In 1864 Capt. William H. Hardy established a little community on the Colorado River nine miles above Fort Mohave. His move was a smart one, for his place was at the practical head of navigation on the river, and this meant that it immediately became a shipping point for goods brought by boat up the river to be shipped overland to the mines in the Cerbat Mountains and elsewhere. By 1870 there were twenty people living at Hardyville.

The county seat for Mohave county was at Mohave City in 1864. Hardyville was nearby, and the county seat was at Hardyville in early 1872. In November 1872 Hardyville was destroyed by fire. However, it was rebuilt and in 1906 was still considered an important mining camp. Few traces remain of Hardyville today.

**v.n. Hardy's Landing**

P.O. est. January 17, 1865. William H. Hardy, p.m. Discont. February 19, 1883.

Ref.: Charles Metcalf, Letter, March 10, 1906 (APHS Files); 7, p. 614, (Note 5); *Weekly Arizona Miner*, November 30, 1872, 2:4; *Arizona Miner*, September 21, 1864, 3:2; 89, p. 147; 87, pp. 43, 252; 62, p. 16; Babcock; Harris; APHS Files; P.O. Records. Maps: C-1; C-4; E-20; GH-4.

## HARPER

El.: c. 1000'      Loc.: Mohave 5, A-1.
Jesse Harper was the first settler in this area. He ran a ferry across the river.

Ref.: Harris; Housholder. Map: GH-9.

**a.n. Harper's Slough**      Map: C-10      Mohave

## HARRIS

El.: c. 3500'      Loc.: Mohave 3, EF-11
George W. Harris was an engineer on the A.T. & S.F. R.R.

Ref.: Harris (no relation). Maps: GH-6; GH-8.

## HARRY EDWARD'S MOUNTAIN

Loc.: Mohave 5, B-11.6. 35°03'39", 114°25'42", Camp 28.
Lt. Edward Fitzgerald Beale on October 12, 1857, wrote of seeing a rugged mountain to the south, which he named Harry Edward's Mountain after a member of his party.

Ref.: 12, p. 72. Map: None.

## HAVILAND

El.: c. 1500'      Loc.: Mohave 5, D-3
While the origin of this name has not yet been determined, it is known that the presence of clay had nothing to do with it. There is currently a section house only at this place.

**v.n. Havilin**

Ref.: Housholder; Babcock. Map: GH-14.

## HEADGATE ROCK DAM

El.: c. 1500'      Loc.: Mohave 3, A-1
The presence of Headgate Rock near the northern end of the Great Colorado Valley at the site of the dam resulted in the name.

Ref.: 100, p. 47; "Hoover Dam," U. S. Department of the Interior, Bureau of Reclamation, n.d. Map: None.

## HENNING

El.: c. 1500'      Loc.: Mohave 5, E-5
A. E. Henning was in charge of the general water service for the railroad between Needles and Albuquerque. Today Henning is a section house only.

P.O. est. February 28, 1884. John H. Mollering, p.m. Discont. February 5, 1886.

Ref.: Barnes; P.O. Records. Maps: C-6; C-7.

## HIDDEN CANYON

El.: c. 4000'      Loc.: Mohave 1, C-5.5
The inaccessibility of this canyon resulted in its name.

Ref.: Barnes. Map: GH-8.

## HOOVER DAM

El.: 640' at river bed      Loc.: Mohave 3, A-1
Prior to the construction of Hoover Dam, the Colorado River was subject to wild rampaging floods second to none. The first step in Colorado River control was a meeting in 1922 of representatives of the seven states within the boundaries of which the Colorado River Basin lies, and at that time the Colorado River Compact was drafted. Six years later in 1928, the United States Congress passed the Boulder Canyon Project authorizing the construction of the spectacular dam. Originally the dam was supposed to have been placed in Boulder Canyon, hence the name Boulder Canyon Dam or Boulder Dam. However, the dam was actually erected in Black Canyon, with work beginning in 1931. The dam was dedicated in 1935. It is the highest dam in the

western hemisphere, being 726.4 feet high. The name was officially changed to Hoover Dam to honor ex-president Herbert Hoover, by an act of the Eightieth Congress on April 30, 1947.

The creation of the dam wiped out all traces of the old Hardin Ferry known to have been in operation in 1877 at the mouth of the Virgin River.

Ref.: 4, pp. 147, 337, 338; 100, pp. 15, 26, 36; 127, p. 168; "Hoover Dam," U. S. Dept. of Interior, Bureau of Reclamation, n.d. Maps: C-13 (Boulder Dam); GH-6; GH-8.

**a.n. Boulder Basin** Mohave
Loc.: Between Hoover Dam and Boulder Canyon.
The western-most of the three basins occupied by Lake Mead.

## HORSESHOE RAPIDS

El.: c. 500′ Loc.: Mohave 3, AC-1
At the foot of the Grand Canyon and head of Black Canyon. On September 24, 1871, Capt. George M. Wheeler named the bend in the river at this place Horseshoe Rapids because of its shape. He noted that the walls of the canyon rose fully seventeen hundred feet.

Ref.: 175, I, 159. Map: None.

## HOUSHOLDER PASS

El.: c. 2000′ Loc.: Mohave 3, A-3
In the early 1930's when engineers were trying to build a road to Hoover Dam for use during the construction period, Ross Housholder of Kingman, an engineer, located and put through the pioneer roads. For this reason Percy Jones (the locating engineer on the dam) and his associates called the pass by Housholder's name.

Ref.: Housholder. Map: GH-6.

## HUALAPAI

El.: c. 4000′ Loc.: Mohave 4, A-8
Pro.: /wálpay/
Hualapai Indians lived in this area (cf. Hualapai Indian Reservation).

Ref.: Barnes. Map: C-12.

## HUALAPAI INDIAN RESERVATION

Loc.: Mohave 4, AF-3-6
Pro.: /wálpay/
Originally, the Hualapai were a tribe of Yumas living on the middle portion of the Colorado River above the Mohave Indians' locale, and from the river well into the interior of Arizona in the Hualapai, Sacramento and Yavapai Valleys and in the Cerbat and Aquarius Mountains. Later they moved entirely into the interior mountains. Their name has also been rendered as Walapai and as Hualapai.

The Hualapai stubbornly resisted incursions by white men, but after prolonged and severe struggles, the Indians agreed to move to the reservation on the Colorado River (cf. Cherum Peak), but their troubles did not end there. They finally were permitted to return to their native mountains where on January 4, 1883, a reservation was established

for them. Acreage was added on June 2, 1911, and on May 12, 1912, but the latter addition was revoked on July 18, 1913. Total acreage is currently 997,045. In 1889 there were seven hundred twenty-eight Hualapai Indians on the reservation, but by 1910 the number had dropped to four hundred ninety-eight. In 1957 there were an estimated six hundred forty Indians using the reservation, with headquarters at Peach Springs (q.v.)

Ref.: Graser; 88, II, 899; "Annual Report of the Arizona Commission of Indian Affairs, 1954, 1955, 1956," p. 15. Maps: D-10; GH-1.

**a.n. Hualapai Mountains** Mohave
El.: c. 7000′. Loc.: Ts. 16-20 n., Rs. 15, 16 W.
**Hualapai Peak** Mohave
El.: 8268′. Loc.: T. 20, N., R. 15 W.
**Hualapai Rapids** Mohave
Loc.: Below mouth of Grand Canyon.
The rapids are formed by boulders in Hualapai Wash. (see below).
**Hualapai Valley** Map: GH-3 Mohave
**Hualapai Wash** Loc.: T. 28 N., R. 17 W. Mohave
**Hualapai, Old Fort** Map: E-20 Yavapai
This was a stage station on the road to Prescott. Mrs. Summerhayes referred to it as "old Camp Hualapai" and mentioned its being a very pleasant resting place for travelers.
P.O. est. November 22, 1882. Charles A. Behm, p.m. Discont. April 2, 1883, when name was changed to Juniper (cf. Juniper, Yavapai).

Ref.: 158, p. 72, 72 (Note 20).

## ICEBERG CANYON

El.: c. 2000′ Loc.: Mohave 3, E-1
In 1871 Capt. George M. Wheeler is reported to have applied the term "iceberg" to this canyon because of the shape of its northern wall. Another observer reports that Iceberg Canyon is cut through the base of a tilted block. This may have resulted in the resemblance to an iceberg.

Ref.: 42, p. 298; 100, p. 19. Maps: E-20; GM-7.

## IVANPATCH SPRING

El.: c. 2500′ Loc.: Mohave 1, D-5
At head of Andrus Canyon.
Piute: "small spring coming out of white saline soil with grass growing all around the place"
Descriptive.

**v.n. Ivanpah**
Ref.: 151, p. 394; Barnes. Map: None.

## JAP SLOUGH

El.: c. 500′ Loc.: Mohave 5, B-1.5
An oriental gardener raised truck produce at this point. The damming of the river caused the disappearance of the location.

Ref.: Housholder. Map: GM-9.

## JOHNSON SPRING

El.: c. 4000′ Loc.: Mohave 3, E-10.2
Johnson Spring was named for Jack Johnson, who discovered the C.O.D. Mine. Johnson was in this locality in 1882.

Ref.: Harris. Maps: C-6; C-7.

**a.n. Johnson Canyon** Mohave

## KAIBAB PIUTE RESERVATION

El.: c. 5500'                    Loc.: Mohave 2, DG-1-3;
                                 Coconino 1, BC-1-2.5
Pro.: /káybæb páy uwt/
This reservation of 121,000 acres was set aside on October 16, 1907, in part, and in full on July 17, 1917. Tribal offices are at Moccasin. There are an estimated ninety-six members of the Kaibab band of Piute Indians in the seventeen families on this reservation.
Ref.: "Annual Report of the Arizona Commission of Indian Affairs, 1954, 1955, 1956," p. 17. Maps: C-10; GH-6.

## KASTER

El.: c. 1500'                    Loc.: Mohave 5, E-1
Dr. Kaster was a surgeon for the S.F. R.R. in the 1880's. Kaster apparently never had any other name (cf. Griffith). It is today a section house on the railroad.
Ref.: Harris; Barnes. Map: C-10.

## KATHERINE

El.: c. 1100'                    Loc.: Mohave 3, A-10
J. S. Bagg of Kingman discovered the Katherine Mine c. 1920 and named it for his sister. The mine was extremely active, and as a result a community developed nearby. Activity continued from 1921 through 1942, although after 1929 the mine was not going at its full capacity.
P.O. est. December 21, 1921. Alva C. Lambert, p.m. Discont. June 5, 1929.
Ref.: P.O. Records; Housholder; Burns; Hornbuckle. Map: GH-6.

**a.n. Katherine Beach**    Loc.: On the Colorado River    Mohave
Katherine Beach is the older name for the present Lake Mohave Resort. It was named for the Katherine Mine which lies one wash further north over the ridge.
Ref.: "Davis Dam and Power Plant," U. S. Department of the Interior, Bureau of Reclamation, Region 3, Boulder City, Nevada, January 1, 1954.

**Katherine Wash**         Map: GH-4           Mohave
**Katherine Boat Landing**                     Mohave
Loc.: 2 miles from Lake Mohave Resort.

## KEYSTONE

El.: c. 4500'                    Loc.: Mohave 3, D-8.7
The Keystone No. 1 and No. 2 locations were the second to be made in 1870 in the Mineral Park district. The mill went into operation in 1876, continuing until about 1882, when production fell off. The station named Keystone for shipping ore on the A.T. & S.F. R.R. branch line is now abandoned.
Ref.: Babcock; 62, p. 80; 102, p. 50. Map: GH-3.

## KINGMAN

El.: 3336'                       Loc.: Mohave 3, E-10.1
When the railroad was constructed through this area in the 1880's, Lewis Kingman was the locating engineer. He named this location after himself. The coming of the railroad placed the town of Kingman in a position of great importance which resulted in its being selected in 1887 as the fourth and permanent county seat for Mohave County. It is today the most important city in the county.

P.O. est. March 22, 1883. Edward F. Thompson, p.m. Wells Fargo Station, 1885. Incorporated January 21, 1952.
Ref.: Patey; P.O. Records. Map: C-6.

**a.n. Kingman Mesa**                          Mohave
**Kingman Wash**                               Mohave
Loc.: Enters Lake Mead about 2 miles above Hoover Dam. Sometimes referred to as Dead Man Wash.

## KLONDYKE MILL

El.: c. 500'                     Loc.: Mohave 3, A-7.5
In October 1898 Dick Blythe and William and George Cooke (brothers) located the Klondyke Mine. They soon sold it and in November of the same year built a mill, with two batteries of five stamps being installed in 1899. Fuel was supplied by the Indians, who sold the miners driftwood at $5 per cord.

In 1905 the ore was assayed at $8 per ton, a considerable drop from its original assay of from $20 to $38 per ton. The mine is now covered by water from Davis Dam.
Ref.: Housholder; Babcock; Harris. Maps: C-9; GH-6.

**a.n. Klondyke**          El.: c. 1500'. Map: GH-6          Mohave

## KOHINOOR SPRING

El.: c. 4000'                    Loc.: Mohave 4, B-4.6
The spring was named for a nearby mine.
Ref.: Barnes. Map: C-13.

## LINCOLNIA

El.: c. 500'                     Loc.: Mohave 5, A-1.6
The Cottonia Land and Cotton Company owned the construction camp at which Edmund Lincoln established a store which was not, however, a trading post in the usual sense of the word. The original name of Cottonia for the post office in the store honored the company owning the land. However, the first postmaster soon changed the name to one reflecting his own surname. The place has been out of existence for nearly four decades.
P.O. est. as Cottonia, May 12, 1910. Edmund Lincoln, p.m. Changed to Lincolnia, April 13, 1911. Discont. October 31, 1912.
Ref.: Harris; P.O. Records; Housholder. Map: C-12.

## LITTLEFIELD

El.: c. 1500'                    Loc.: Mohave 1, A-1.1
Three miles east of the Nevada and five south of the Utah state lines, Littlefield is in the extreme northwestern corner of Arizona. Here, led by Henry W. Miller in the mid 1860's, came Mormons seeking a place to make an agricultural settlement. Although some referred to the place as Millersburg, the abundance of beaver and troubles with their dams led to naming the place Beaver Dams. In 1867 the river flooded, destroying the colonists' efforts, and the place was abandoned. Ten years later, more settlers began to arrive and a permanent settlement was effected. When the post office department turned down the name "Beaver Dams," the applicants came up with the name Littlefield, because of the numerous small farms in the vicinity.
P.O. est. October 25, 1894. Matilda Frehner, p.m.

Ref.:   102, p. 54; P.O. Records; 112, pp. 117-118. Maps: C-8; GH-8.

**a.n. Beaver Dam Creek**       Maps: C-12; E-20        Mohave
**Beaver Dam Mountains**                               Mohave
Loc.: From junction Beaver Dam Creek and Virgin River n.e. into Utah.

## LIVERPOOL LANDING

El.: c. 500'                    Loc.: Mohave 3, A-9
There were many landings along the Colorado River where ores were shipped from mines in the area. It is worth noting that many of these landings were the names of cities to which ores were shipped for smelting. However, no definite proof of such an origin for this name has been found.

Ref.:   Housholder. Maps: C-7; E-20; GH-11.

## LOPEANT

El.: c. 4000'                   Loc.: Mohave 2, C-1.
                                Near Utah line w. of Cane Springs.
The origin of this name has not yet been ascertained.
P.O. est. January 26, 1921. Mrs. Mattie W. Ruesvo, p.m. Discont. June 14, 1922.

**v.n. Topeat**
**Topeant**

Ref.:   P.O. Records; Barnes. Map: None.

## LOST BASIN

El.: c. 1000'                   Loc.: Mohave 3, E-2.5
Descriptive. This small basin is nearly surrounded by little hills. In 1906 the community in the basin was listed as an important mining camp.
P.O. est. July 11, 1882. Michael Scanlon, p.m. Discont. January 13, 1891.
Ref.:   P.O. Records; Babcock; Harris. Maps: C-6; C-12.
The remoteness of places often leads to using the word "lost" in naming them.

**a.n. Lost Creek**        Loc.: T. 28 N., R. 14 W.    Mohave
**Lost Spring**            Map: C-12                  Mohave
**Lost Spring Mountain**   Loc.: T. 41 N., R. 8 W.    Mohave

## LOUISE

El.: 3500'                      Loc.: Mohave 3, F-10
The now-vanished section house at this place was named for the daughter of the general manager and vice president of the railroad, A. G. Wells.

Ref.:   Barnes; Babcock. Map: C-13.

## LYONSVILLE

El.: c. 2500'                   Loc.: Mohave 5, BC-1.
                                Below Virginia City ½ mile (near Oatman).
Apparently Lyonsville was one of those projected communities which never developed. Residents of Virginia City said that Lyonsville consisted "of one house to be built and the skeleton of a corral."

Ref.:   87, p. 252. Map: None.

## MAYSWELL CANYON

El.: c. 4000'                   Loc.: Mohave 3, E-9.8
In the early days (c. mid-1860's) when mines were first being prospected in this area, George May dug a well in the canyon now called Mayswell Canyon. He later sold his mine and went into the cattle business.

Ref.:   Harris. Map: GH-3.
**a.n. Maywell Wash**                                  Mohave
Ref.:   62, p. 115.
**Mayswell Peak**          Map: GH-3                  Mohave

## McCONNICO

El.: c. 3000'                   Loc.: Mohave 3, E-11
The railroad line was built in the Detrital Wash for the benefit of the mines in the Cerbat area. S. B. McConnico was vice president and general manager of the Arizona & Utah R.R. in 1901.

Ref.:   David Myrick, letter, September 23, 1959; Babcock; Barnes. Map: C-9.

## McCRACKIN MINE

El.: c. 3000'                   Loc.: Mohave 6, C-7
One of the most famous mines of its time, the McCrackin was discovered on August 17, 1874, by Jackson McCrackin (b. South Carolina, 1821; d. December 14, 1904), who came to Arizona in 1861. In its single immense vein, the McCrackin mine had silver ore which assayed at from sixty to six hundred dollars per ton. By 1877 the mine was the best equipped in Arizona with ores being handled at nearby Greenwood (q.v.). By 1880 over six million dollars had been derived from the ores.

Somewhere along the line, the *i* in McCrackin's name gave place to an *e*, so that the *Arizona Sentinel* noted that everything about the mine was well known except the correct spelling of its name.

P.O. est. May 16, 1908. John L. Witley, p.m. Discont.?
Ref.:   92, p. 199; 105, p. 199; *Arizona Sentinel*, July 6, 1878, 1:2; 87, p. 162; P.O. Records. Maps: C-12; E-20; GH-8.

**a.n. McCracken Peak**    El.: 3410'. Map: C-12       Mohave

## MEAD, LAKE

El.: c. 1200'                   Loc.: Mohave 3, AF-1
Construction of Hoover Dam (q.v.) for the first time permitted control of the lower Colorado River which before the dam was built was subject to awesome and violent floods. The reservoir for Hoover Dam was named Lake Mead for Dr. Elwood Mead, Commissioner of Reclamation from 1924 to 1936.

Lake Mead is the world's largest man-made reservoir by volume. It has five hundred fifty miles of shoreline, one hundred twenty-five of which border Mohave County, and the lake extends fifteen miles upstream. Beneath its waters are all the old ferry landings along this part of the Colorado River.

The Lake Mead Recreational Area includes Lake Mead and Lake Mohave.

Ref.:   "Hoover Dam," U. S. Dept. of the Interior, Bureau of Reclamation, n.d. Maps: GH-6; GH-8; GH-15.

## MEADOW CREEK

El.: c. 2500'                   Loc.: Mohave 5, CD-1-2
In 1857 Lt. Joseph Christmas Ives reported that he named Meadow Creek because after an arduous climb over the Black Mountains, his party suddenly came upon the heading to this creek below which the ravine formed "a snug mead-

ow carpeted with grass and fringed on one side with a growth of willows that bordered the stream." To refresh his half-starved animals and to rest his men, Ives stayed here nearly two days.

Many years later (1906) the mining mill for the Gold Road district used water from the company's well at the Meadows at the same place where Ives rested his mules and Beale his camel train.

v.n. **Aguage de San Pacifico** (Garcés)
Ref.: Ives; 169, pp. 5 (Note 5), 5; 62, pp. 156-7. Map: GH-15.

## MERIWITICA CANYON
El.: c. 2500'                    Loc.: Mohave 4, CB-2.2-3.2
Pro.: /mærowítikə/ or /mætowítikə/
The canyon is a gash in the surrounding plateau. A thousand feet down in the canyon there is some garden land which the Hualapais cultivate. The name refers to the formation made by a deposit of travertine in the canyon floor which has resulted in a five hundred-foot cliff.

In 1872 and 1873 during the troubles with the Hualapai Indians about sixty of the Hualapais enlisted as Indian scouts to fight against the Apaches. However, when the order came to remove the Hualapais from Mohave County to the Colorado River bottoms, half of the scouts deserted and went with the rest of the tribe to what was called Mut-a-witt-a-ka Canyon where they hid. The tribe was starved out and compelled to go to the Colorado River Indian Reservation about February 2, 1874.
Ref.: Dobyns; 4, p. 323; 169, p. 211. Map: GH-1.

## MILKWEED SPRING
El.: c. 1600'                    Loc.: Mohave 4, D-4
Charles Spencer (cf. Spencer Canyon) claimed ownership of Milkweed Spring in early 1881 and hence may have named it, since he was the first white man to live in this area. The name is well applied, for milkweed grows abundantly along Milkweed Creek.
Ref.: 169, p. 135. Map: C-13.

a.n. **Milkweed Tank**    Loc.: T. 26 N., R. 11 W.              Mohave

## MILLTOWN
El.: c. 800'                    Loc.: Mohave 5, A-2
In 1903 the Mohave Gold Mining Company bought the Leland mine and began development on a large scale. One phase was the installation of a forty-stamp mill eleven miles southeast of the mine, to which the name Milltown became attached. A pumping plant on the Colorado River two miles below Needles pumped water about six miles to the mill. A narrow gauge railroad was constructed from the Colorado at Needles to Milltown, with freight and ore crossing the river to Needles (in California) by ferry, to make connection with the S.F. R.R. Cattle roaming the open range posed a real problem which necessitated putting a gate across the track. This meant that on every trip the engineer had to stop the train, open the gate, move the train through, close the gate and then proceed on his way. During a severe flood the Colorado washed out all but two miles of the track.
Ref.: 62, p. 183; Housholder. Maps: C-10; GH-9.

## MINERAL PARK
El.: 4200'                    Loc.: Mohave 3, E-8.5
The first mine located in the Mineral Park district was discovered in 1870. Other locations soon were made, including the Keystone (q.v.), which gave rise to a thriving community which took its name from its being situated in a beautiful park-like basin between mountains rich in minerals. In 1873 Mineral Park was for a brief time the seat of Mohave County. Production in the mines dwindled in the years following 1882, although in 1906 Mineral Park was still listed as an important mining camp. It is now abandoned.
P.O. est. December 13, 1872. Alder Randall, p.m. Discont. June 15, 1912.
Ref.: 62, pp. 16, 80; Babcock; P.O. Records. Maps: C-2; E-20; GH-6; GH-8.

a.n. **Mineral**    Loc.: Below Mineral Park on r.r.        Mohave
This was a station for unloading mining materials and for shipping ores.
P.O. est. September 28, 1908. John R. Sears, p.m. (deceased). Rescinded December 17, 1908.

## MOCCASIN SPRING
El.: 4500'                    Loc.: Mohave 2, E-2
William B. Maxwell was at this spring before 1864, but left in 1866 because of continuing troubles with the Indians. Thereafter the spring was used infrequently by Mormon pioneers. According to legend, moccasin tracks found in the sand near the spring gave rise to the name Moccasin Spring.
Ref.: 112, p. 97. Maps: C-10; E-20.

a.n. **Moccasin**    Loc.: Sec. 31, T. 41 N., R. 4 W.        Mohave
A day school, a dozen houses, and headquarters for the Kaibab Piute Indian Reservation (q.v.) comprises the community of Moccasin.
P.O. est. June 11, 1909. Charles C. Heaton, p.m.
Ref.: P.O. Records; 4, p. 282..

## MOCKINGBIRD
                                    Loc.: Not known
Origin not yet determined.
P.O. est. February 8, 1907, William F. Ward, p.m. Rescinded March 25, 1907.
Ref.: P.O. Records. Map: None.

## MOHAVE, FORT
El.: 541'                    Loc.: Mohave 5, A-1
Pro.: /mówhaviˆ/            Mohave: *hamol*, "three";
                                    *avi*, "mountains"
In January 1859, Col. William Hoffman was instructed to locate a place for a fort to be used in a campaign to subdue the Mohave Indians, a handsome, well-built, and at one time extremely war-like branch of the Yuma Indian tribe. Hoffman was told to establish the fort in California on the Mohave River or at the ford where the main trail crossed the Colorado River at Beale's Crossing. Finding the Mohave River dry, Hoffman established Camp Colorado at the crossing. Maj. Lewis Addison Armistead was placed in charge on April 26, and by May 1 had renamed the location Fort Mohave. The post was abandoned in 1861 at the outbreak of the Civil War, but was re-established in May 1863 as Camp Mohave. In 1890 the old fort was turned over for use as an Indian school.

The history of the Fort Mohave Indian Reservation is closely allied with that of the fort itself. An area of 5,572 acres was set aside on March 30, 1870, by General Orders 19 issued by the headquarters of the Military Division of the Pacific. This was followed on September 19, 1880, by an Executive Order establishing the reservation in Arizona, with additional land being added from time to time. Total acreage is now 38,382, occupied by approximately three hundred seventy-five Indians. Agency headquarters are at Parker and the Mohave tribal offices are at Needles, Calif.

Ref.: *Weekly Alta California*, May 28, 1859, n.p. (APHS File); 87, pp. 313-314; 8, pp. 249, 277 (Note); 105, p. 90; 75, p. 145; 111, p. 152; "Annual Report of the Arizona Commission of Indian Affairs, 1954, 1955, 1956," p. 14. Maps: C-1; E-11; GH-9; GH-12.

**a.n. Mohave City**          Map: C-1          Mohave

After the limits of the military reservation had been defined in 1864, a settlement began on the outskirts of the reservation. It came to be known as Mohave City. In 1866 it was made the county seat of Mohave County and a post office was established. However, in the fall of 1869, the reservation was extended so that the town of Mohave was engulfed. A thirty-day notice was given to residents to leave the town. Many claims were made against the government because of this. Apparently the residents of Mohave City won, for the census of 1870 lists one hundred fifty-nine residents in the community. There is nothing left at this location today.

P.O. est. October 8, 1866. James P. Bull, p.m. Discont. October 31, 1938.

Ref.: 52, IV, 12; *Arizona Miner*, April 13, 1872, 1:4; P.O. Records.

| Mohave Canyon | Map: GN-9 | Mohave |
|---|---|---|
| Mohave Creek | Map: C-12 | Mohave |
| Mohave, Lake | Map: GH-4 | Mohave |

Created by waters of Davis Dam (*q.v.*).

| Mohave Mountains | Map: GN-12 | Mohave |
|---|---|---|
| Mohave Peak | Map: C-12 | Mohave |
| Mohave Rock | Map: GH-9 | Mohave |
| Mohave Spring | Map: GH-11 | Mohave |
| Mohave Valley | Maps: GH-9; GH-10 | Mohave |
| Mohave Wash | Map: GH-11 | Mohave |

## MONUMENT CANYON

El.: c. 3000'          Loc.: Mohave 1, A-10

This is a canyon of wild and picturesque scenery with vivid colors, according to Dr. John S. Newberry, who was with Lt. Joseph C. Ives' party during the exploration of the Colorado River in 1857-58.

Ref.: Barnes. Map: GH-6.

## MOSS HILL

El.: c. 2500'          Loc.: Mohave 3, B-11.9

The Moss Hills are named for Capt. John Moss (b. 1823; d. April 1880), a prospector and an agent to the Mohave Indians. In 1863 or 1864, he located the famous Moss Mine, about one and a half miles away from the Moss Hills. He was shown the location of gold diggings by the Mohave chief Iretaba, who was grateful to Moss for his friendly services. He found visible gold out-croppings about where he sank the shaft. From a hole only ten feet in diameter and

depth, he is reported to have taken out a quarter of a million dollars in gold, which he spent in developing the mine. He died in poverty.

Ref.: *Arizona Weekly Enterprise*, April 18, 1891, 1:3; 25, p. 70; 62, pp. 153, 170. Map: GH-6 (Mine).

## MUSIC MOUNTAIN

El.: 3971'          Loc.: Mohave 3, C-5.3

When Lt. Joseph Christmas Ives (d. November 12, 1868) in 1854 sought the head of navigation of the Colorado River, he named this peak Music Mountain because the exposed strata appeared similar to a huge sheet of music or a musical staff. The name was placed on his map, but as the mountain was not conspicuous, it was overlooked by pioneers. Later the name was misapplied to another and more conspicuous peak ten miles west. It is the latter Music Mountain to which Capt. George M. Wheeler refers in his report of his expedition in the early 1870's. The Music Mountain area was a stronghold of the Hualapais and it was good prospecting ground for miners.

Ref.: 87, p. 50; 175, III, 47, (Note 199); 62, p. 16. Maps: E-20 (C-4).

## NEEDLES, THE

El.: c. 650'          Loc.: Mohave 5, B-4.1

Lt. Amiel W. Whipple named The Needles, a group of three sharp peaks in a massive surrounding group of lower hills. The Needles are the "three mountains" referred to in the translation of the word *Mohave* (cf. Fort Mohave).

Because of its adjacency to these peaks, the settlement on the A.T. & S.F. R.R. across the river in California was called Needles. Prior to the construction of a railroad bridge across the river, the shipping point on the Arizona side was known both as Red Rock and as Mellen. The later name was that of Capt. Jack Mellen, a Colorado River steamboat pilot. The station at Mellen was established in 1891.

The maps reveal either a shifting or a confusion of names in connection with this location. GLO 1883 shows Powell on the Arizona side of the river at this location. GLO 1903 shows Powell shifted inland on the railroad a few miles, and Mellen at the former location of Powell. A further change in name is revealed on GLO 1912, when Mellen has been replaced by the name Topock /towpak/, which is still in use. The origin of Topock has not yet been learned. In 1956 Powell consisted of a section house.

P.O. est. as Needles, February 15, 1883. Augustus A. Spear, p.m. Since Needles was in California, a change had to be made, so the name was changed to Powell, October 11, 1883. Discont. July 9, 1886. Re-est. as Mellen, March 26, 1903. Emilie O. Holstein, p.m. Discont. April 30, 1909. Wells Fargo Station, 1903. Re-est. as Topock, March 6, 1916. Enos H. Norton, p.m.

**v.n. Red Crossing**

Ref.: *Arizona Sentinel*, May 9, 1891, 3:4; 177, p. 234, (Note 4); 87, p. 275; 100, p. 27; 62, p. 15; P.O. Records. Maps: See entry above, E-4; GH-9; GH-12.

**a.n. Topock Bay**          Map: GH-12          Mohave
**Powell Lake**          Maps: GH-9; GH-10          Mohave

Several places in Arizona are named for Maj. John Wesley Powell, who led exploring parties through the Grand Canyon in 1869 and again in 1871-72.

**Powell Peak**          El.: 2353'. Map: GH-9          Mohave

## NEW LONDON

El.: 3800'                        Loc.: Mohave 3, DE-9.5
Deserted mine shafts are all that remain today to indicate
the location of what was in the mid-1880's a prosperous
mining community. The mine was closed about 1893 and
the equipment removed.
Ref.: Harris; 62, p. 105. Map: C-6.

## NEW VIRGINIA

El.: c. 2500'                        Loc.: Mohave 6, DE-6
Following the Civil War many veterans made their way
to the West to find a new life. They brought with them many
of the place names from their native states. This may well
be the origin of the name for this locality.
In 1877 six to seven hundred people were living in what
was sometimes called Virginia City. The inhabitants de-
pended on the McCrackin Mine (q.v.) for their existence,
since the mill for the McCrackin Mine was in New Virginia.
Ref.: *Arizona Sentinel,* July 6, 1878, 1:2; 87, pp. 251-52; 55,
      p. 579. Map: E-20.

## NIGGER HEAD

El.: c. 4000'                        Loc.: Mohave 3, D-8.8
This is a big mountain which is as black as coal. It lies
below Mineral Park.
Ref.: Harris. Map: GH-3.

## NODMAN CANYON

El.: c. 3500'                        Loc.: Mohave 3, E-7.4
One of the signers of the petition sent on January 13, 1877,
to Gen. August V. Kautz from Mineral Park was Fred Nodman. The petition sought to have the Hualapais stop killing
the white men's cattle. This would indicate that Nodman
was a stockman.
Ref.: 169, p. 115. Map: GH-3.

## NUTT, MOUNT

El.: c. 5000'                        Loc.: Mohave 3, C-11.9
The origin of this name has not yet been ascertained. It
first appears on GLO 1887. On GLO 1921, the name is corrupted to Mount McNutt, and on GLO 1933 to Mount Nut.
Ref.: 62, p. 23. Maps: See entry.

## OATMAN

El.: c. 2400'                        Loc.: Mohave 5, B-1
Oatman was initially called Vivian, which in turn took its
name from the finding of the Vivian Mine about one-fourth
mile below the present town. The mine was discovered c.
1902 by a half-breed Mohave Indian, Ben Taddock, who
while riding along the trail saw glittering free gold on the
ground and immediately located a claim. In 1903 he sold
his location to Judge E. M. Ross and Col. Thomas Eqing,
who in 1905 sold it to the Vivian Mining Company, which
had headquarters in Los Angeles. In the three year period
from 1904 to 1907, over three million dollars in gold was
taken from this area. The resultant town of Vivian had two
banks, ten stores, and a Chamber of Commerce.

In 1910 Ely Hilty, Joe Anderson, and Daniel Tooker discovered an extremely rich mine, calling it the Oatman Claim.
The town, already large, proceeded to boom to even greater
proportions, growing still larger when another rich claim
was discovered in February 1915.

It is interesting to note that a wealthy Mohave Indian named
John Oatman was heavily interested in mining in this area.
He claimed to be the son of Olive Oatman, who with her
brother Lorenzo, was a survivor of the Oatman Massacre
(cf. Oatman Flat, Maricopa). While there is a possibility
that the name of Vivian was changed to Oatman because of
the presence of John Oatman, local legend prefers the story
that Oatman was named for John's mother, Olive Oatman.
One source states that Olive Oatman and her sister were
hidden at the Ollie Oatman Spring, which is one-half mile
north of the townsite.

Today Oatman, which once had a population of eight thousand, is a town of relatively few people. It is set in a valley
of jagged red rock spires and hogbacks surrounded by pink
mining tailings which are eroding with age.
P.O. est. as Vivian, March 1, 1904. James H. Knight, p.m.
Name changed to Oatman, June 24, 1909.
Ref.: 170, pp. 77, 78; 4, p. 236; *Yuma Daily Sun,* November
      20, 1953, II:2, 3-4; *Arizona Republican,* April 30, 1922,
      5:1; *Mohave County Miner* (Kingman), "Mining Edi-
      tion," July 20, 1919, I:10:1; 62, pp. 180, 195; P.O.
      Records. Map: C-10.
a.n. Vivian Wash                                    Mohave

## OLD MAN MOUNTAIN

El.: c. 2500'            Loc.: Mohave 3, C-10. On n. side
                         of the road at Ferra Ranch in Union Pass.
Jonathan Draper Richardson named this mountain descrip-
tively c. 1885. It is a rock column with a single "eye" in it.
Ref.: Ferra. Maps: None.

## OLD TRAILS

El.: c. 2500'                        Loc.: Mohave 5, BC-1.1
To commemorate the famous old trails which tied together
early communities or various districts of the expanding
United States, the National Old Trails Association cooperated with the Daughters of the American Revolution in
marking old trails. Old Trails settlement was on one of
these routes. Both Lt. Edward Fitzgerald Beale and Lt. Lorenzo Sitgreaves passed near here. It is possible that there
is a connection between the name Old Trails and the National Old Trails Association's widely-publicized plan at
about the time the settlement was started.
P.O. est. as Oldtrails, February 29, 1916. Erne S. Statton, p.m.
Discont. July 21, 1925.
Ref.: P.O. Records; Becker. Map: C-12.

## OWEN

El.: c. 2500'                        Loc.: Mohave 6, DE-4
Now an abandoned mining camp, Owen was named for
John ("Chloride Jack") Wren Owen (b. Illinois, 1824),
who came to Arizona with the California Column in 1864.
In 1870 he was stationed at Camp Crittenden, and later he

served as Deputy Collector of Customs at Maricopa Wells. At the time of his death on November 4, 1877, he was treasurer of Maricopa County.

There is some question whether the Owen discussed above is actually the same person as Chloride Jack Owen, inasmuch as no evidence has been found as yet to link John Wren Owen with the mining district purportedly named for Chloride Jack.

P.O. est. as Owens, April 4, 1899. Nellie C. Cornwall, p.m. Discont. August 31, 1914.

Ref.: P.O. Records; John W. Owen File, APHS; Barnes; Babcock. Maps: C-9; C-12.

**a.n. Owens Peak**            Mohave

Ref.: 100, p. 24.

**Owens Mining District**     Map: C-4      Mohave

## PA-A-COON SPRINGS

El.: c. 2500'            Loc.: Mohave 1, BC-6.25
                      Piute: "water that boils up"

Descriptive.

**v.n. Pah-guhn Springs**
     **Pah Coon Springs**
     **Pakoon Springs**

Ref.: Barnes; MNA; 87, p. xlvii. Map: C-9.

## PAINTED CANYON

El.: c. 500'            Loc.: Mohave 3, A-8
Lt. Joseph Christmas Ives in February 1857 was so struck by the colors in this canyon that he named it Painted Canyon. Here, according to Ives, "Various and vivid tints of blue, brown, white, purple, and crimson were blended with exquisite shading upon the gateways and inner walls, producing effects so novel and surprising as to make the cañon, in some respects, the most picturesque and striking of any of these wonderful mountain passes."

Ref.: 121, p. 79. Maps: E-4; E-20.

## PAINT POTS

El.: c. 2500'           Loc.: Mohave 3, A-1
This area on the shore of Lake Mead is very much eroded and is brilliantly colored.

Ref.: None. Map: GH-6.

## PEACH SPRINGS

El.: 4800'            Loc.: Mohave 4, F-6
The name is probably descriptive. It has been noted that although early explorers such as Fr. Francisco Garcés visited these springs, no mention was made of peach trees, but that when Mormon missionaries were in this vicinity in the 1850's, a child planted some peach pits and trees developed. Peach Tree Springs was called Pozos de San Basilio ("St. Basil's Wells") by Fr. Garcés on June 15, 1775. Lt. Edward Fitzgerald Beale passed over the same route and on September 17, 1858, called the place Indian Spring. The Udell party camped here on April 23, 1859, dubbing the place Hemphill Camping Ground Springs. When the railroad tracks were laid in the early 1880's, a watering station was established three miles southwest of Peach Tree Springs and the station was called Peach Springs.

There are apparently three springs or groups of springs in Peach Spring Canyon, the upper group being used for years by Hualapais for watering stock, but by 1930 the springs were so filled in as to be nearly useless. The fact that the railroad took over the springs led to an extended lawsuit by the Hualapais against the railroad in the late 1920's (cf. Crozier).

P.O. est. July 12, 1887. Jacob Cohenour, p.m. Wells Fargo Station, 1885.

**v.n. Pah-Wash**
     **Pabroach Spring**
     **New Creek**
     Same as Peach Springs Draw. Called New Creek by Ives.

Ref.: 87, pp. xlvii, xlvi; 169, pp. 235, 8-9, 8 (Note 12); 4, pp. 322-23; 165, pp. 53, 72; P.O. Records. Maps: C-4; C-5.

## PEACOCK SPRING

El.: c. 1300'          Loc.: Mohave 4, B-8
On March 31, 1857, Lt. Joseph C. Ives and his party took their course east. The day was extremely hot and the mules, which had not had enough to drink for four days, were in great distress. The trainmaster for the party, G. H. Peacock, rode in advance and discovered a spring of sweet water near the road. The Mohave chief Iretaba, who was acting as a guide, gave no sign that he knew such a place existed, although the Indians had been in the habit of stopping at another spring a few miles farther on. The location of Peacock Spring on GLO 1869 is identical with that given for Truxton Spring on GLO 1883.

Ref.: 169, p. 18; 121, p. 6. Map: C-1.

**a.n. Peacock Mountains**      Map: C-4      Mohave
     **Peacock Peak**    El.: 6268'. Loc.: T. 22 N., R. 14 W.    Mohave

## PERKINS, MOUNT

El.: 5500'            Loc.: Mohave 3, B-6
The origin of this name has not yet been learned. Mount Perkins is actually a group of ridges extending miles north of Union Pass to El Dorado Pass, where the mass culminates in the peak known as Mount Perkins.

Ref.: 62, p. 22. Maps: A-7; C-12.

## PIERCE FERRY

El.: c. 1200'          Loc.: Mohave 3, F-0.1
Although called "Pierce," this ferry was established by Harrison Pearce in December 1876, for use by Mormons and others wishing access from Utah to the rich mines of Mohave County. Dellenbaugh wrote of seeing a stone building called Fort Pierce, used by settlers in defense against Shivwits and Uinkarets Indians. (cf. Pearce Mountain, Navajo.)

In 1956 Pierce Ferry had long since disappeared under the waters of Lake Mead, and a fishing camp had replaced the old buildings.

**v.n. Colorado Crossing**

Ref.: Babcock; 112, p. 96; 41, p. 191. Maps: C-8; GH-6; GH-8.

**a.n. Pierce Mill Canyon**            Mohave
     Loc.: S. of ferry 12 miles, in Lost Basin.

Ref.: 62, p. 150.

     **Pierce Wash**                  Mohave
     Loc.: Rises close to Utah line at Cave Springs near Vermillion Cliffs and flows w. to Virgin River.

## PIGEON CANYON

El.: c. 4000'                    Loc.: Mohave 1, BC-8
The first Mormons in this region found large flocks of wild
pigeons.

Ref.:   Barnes. Map: C-12.

**a.n. Pigeon Spring**        Map: C-11                    Mohave

## PILOT ROCK

El.: 1500'                    Loc.: Mohave 3, A-5-6
This point was used by travelers and steamboat captains as
a guide in navigation.

Ref.:   Barnes. Maps: A-7 (Pilot Knob); GN-25.

## PIPE SPRING

El.: c. 6000'                    Loc.: Mohave 2, E-2-3
In 1858 a party of Mormon missionaries led by Jacob Hamblin stopped at this place, which offered the only available
water for a radius of sixty miles in any direction. William
("Gunlock Bill") Hamblin was a real sharpshooter. His
companions wagered that he could not shoot a hole through
a handkerchief at fifty paces. His attempt to do so resulted
in the cloth merely giving away without any hole. Irritated
by this, the sharpshooter bet that he could shoot the bottom
out of Dudley Leavitt's pipe. Leavitt, a sensible man, put
the pipe on a rock and Hamblin shot the bottom neatly out
of it. From this came the name Pipe Spring. The next day
the party left this place to continue explorations.

In 1863 Dr. James M. Whitmore visited the country, and
entranced by its luxurious grass decided to raise cattle there.
He and his brother-in-law, Robert McIntyre, made themselves a dugout on the east side of a small hill near Pipe
Spring. Both he and his companion were killed by Indians
in the winter of 1865-1866.

In April 1870 B. P. Windsor, acting for the Mormons, bought
the property from Mrs. Whitmore and in 1873 the Mormons
formed a cooperative livestock association called the Windsor Castle Livestock Growers Association. Brigham Young
instructed that a fort be constructed at Pipe Spring (cf.
Fredonia, Coconino). It was called Windsor Castle.

Over-grazing and periods of drought devastated the land
which at one time was a true sea of grass. Today the land
is nearly barren.

In 1932 Pipe Spring National Monument, a forty-acre tract,
was set aside in order to preserve an outstanding example
of how the pioneers protected themselves. It is interesting
to note that the first telegraph line in northern Arizona was
that running from Kanab to Pipe Spring.

**v.n. Yellow Rock Spring**
    This was the Indian name for this location.

Ref.:   5, Johnreed Lauritzen, "Pipe Spring: A Monument to
        Pioneers," pp. 1, 3, 4; 112, p. 98; 70, pp. 44-45; 41, pp.
        169, 185-186; 4, p. 283. Maps: C-5; C-7; GH-15.

**a.n. Pipe Valley Wash**        Loc.: T. 40 N., R. 5 W.        Mohave
    **Pipe Springs Wash**                                        Mohave

Ref.:   41, p. 185.

## PITTSBURGH LANDING

El.: c. 1000'                    Loc.: Mohave 5, C-6.5
The old landings along the Colorado River, where steamers
used to unload their freight and take on ores for trans-ship-
ment to smelting centers, have long since disappeared. Pittsburgh Landing was one of these. The origin of the name
is not known. (See Liverpool Landing.)

Ref.:   Housholder. Maps: C-7 (Shows Liverpool Landing,
        which was not the same as this); E-20; GH-15; GH-6.

**a.n. Pittsburg Flat**        El.: 440'. Map: GH-11        Mohave

## POTTS MOUNTAIN

El.: 3377'                    Loc.: Mohave 6, CD-7.5
John C. Potts was a pioneer in the Prescott area in the very
early days before it became the territorial capital. He moved
to Mohave county where he became sheriff c. 1893.

Ref.:   Barnes; Harris; 102, p. 71. Maps: C-11; GH-15.

## POVERTY KNOLL

El.: c. 6000'                    Loc.: Mohave 1, E-6.2
On GLO 1879, this location is named descriptively Solitaire
Butte. Not until GLO 1933 is the name changed, and it
then shows as Poverty Mountain with a Poverty Knoll just
northeast of it. Why the change of name was made has not
yet been ascertained.

Frederick S. Dellenbaugh named Solitaire Butte because of
its lonely, dark, and forbidding appearance.

Ref.:   42, p. 310. Maps: See entry above. GH-8.

## PYRAMID CANYON

El.: c. 600'                    Loc.: Mohave 3, A-10
Lt. Joseph Christmas Ives in 1858 named this canyon because near the rapids was a natural pyramid nearly thirty
feet tall. The canyon is about three hundred feet deep and
eight miles long.

In order to provide mail services for miners at the Sheeptrail Mine, a post office was established which was later
known as Pyramid because of its location.

P.O. est. as Sheeptrail, October 29, 1898. John C. Dexter, p.m.
Name changed to Pyramid, June 30, 1899. Discont. October 2,
1901.

Ref.:   100, p. 39; 62, p. 16; P.O. Records. Map: C-10.
        The word *pyramid* is used descriptively in a few Arizona
        place names.

**a.n. Pyramid Mountains**        Loc.: T. 23 N., R. 13 E.        Navajo
    **Pyramid Peak**            Loc.: T. 5 N., R. 2 E.        Maricopa
    **Pyramid Peak**            Loc.: T. 4 N., R. 13 W.        Yuma

## QUARTERMASTER CANYON

El.: c. 3000'                    Loc.: Mohave 4, BC-1.5
This canyon takes its name from a Hualapai Indian called
"Quartermaster," who lived in this canyon in the early
1900's to c. 1930.

Ref.:   Euler (MNA). Maps: D-12; GH-6; GH-8.

## RABBIT PATCH

El.: c. 3350'                    Loc.: Mohave 3, F-11
In this area are located the houses of prostitution of Kingman.

Ref.:   Anonymous.

## RAILROAD PASS

El.: c. 3300′  Loc.: Main pass through Cerbat Mts. on n. and Hualapai Mts. on s.
Fr. Francisco Garcés camped in this pass in the mid-1770's. The next white man known to have been at this location was Lt. Amiel W. Whipple in 1854, followed by Lt. Joseph Christmas Ives in 1857. Ives called it Railroad Pass and recommended its use when tracks should be laid. This is the pass through which the railroad now goes.
Railroad Pass appears to be identical with what Lt. Edward Fitzgerald Beale called Engle's Pass on October 8, 1857, but there remains some question about this.

Ref.: Babcock; 169, pp. 5 (Note 5), 17. Map: None.

## ROARING RAPIDS

El.: c. 500′  Loc.: Mohave 3, A-2.7
The name is descriptive of the nature of these rapids in Black Canyon. They were so severe that steamboat captains did not attempt to navigate through them in order to go farther up the Colorado River. However, in 1866 Captain Rodgers took the steamship *Esmeralda,* which was 97 feet long and drew three and a half feet of water, up as far as Callville near the mouth of the Virgin River. This was higher than Lt. Joseph Christmas Ives had gone in 1857. Rodgers went through Roaring Rapids in seven minutes.

Ref.: 42, pp. 173-174. Map: E-4.

## ROCKY BUTTE

El.: c. 6000′  Loc.: Mohave 4, C-5
Descriptive.

Ref.: Barnes. Map: C-12.

## SACRAMENTO VALLEY

El.: c. 3000′  Loc.: Mohave 3, C-7-10
As early as 1857, some prospectors from Sacramento, California, were at the site of the present town of Chloride where, as a result of the rainy season, the high grass and field flowers reminded them so strongly of their home that they named the area the Sacramento Valley. Some mining locations were found, but abandoned quickly because of trouble with the Hualapai Indians.

The area is sometimes called the Detrital-Sacramento Valley or simply the Detrital /ditraytəl/ Valley. The most frequent usage today is merely Sacramento Valley. The name Detrital derives from the fact that the valley is filled with geologic debris. The valley is approximately one hundred thirty miles long by five to fifteen miles wide.

Ref.: Babcock; Housholder; 55, p. 346; 76, p. 66. Maps: C-2; C-12; E-20; GH-3.
a.n. Detrital Wash  Map: GH-6  Mohave
This used to be called Death Valley Wash from Chloride north to the Colorado River.
Ref.: Housholder.
Death Valley Lake  Map: B-5  Mohave
Sacramento Wash  Map: GH-12  Mohave

## SAEVEDRA SPRINGS

El.: c. 4000′  Loc.: Mohave 3, E-11. 35° 09′12″, 114° 11′25″.
Saevedra was a Mexican guide for Lt. Edward Fitzgerald Beale's party. On October 7, 1857, Beale was so disgusted with Saevedra that he referred to him as an "old wretch and a constant source of trouble to everyone, and his entire and incredible ignorance of the country renders him totally unfit for any service. I keep him moving, however, on all occasions, by way of punishment for putting himself upon us as a guide." Beale was in a not very much better humor on October 12 when he wrote that Saevedra had found a spring. Beale said that he was pleased because it was the first thing old Saevedra had found that "he had started to look for since our departure from Albuquerque." Beale also noted that that spring was a good one, since it afforded water for any number of animals. An emigrant party camped at this spot on August 23, 1858, noting that it lay thirty-eight miles west from White Rock Spring.
v.n. Savadras Spring
Saavedra Springs
Savedra Spring
Ref.: 165, p. 41; 12, p. 67, 27. Map: None.

## SALT SPRINGS WASH

El.: c. 600′  Loc.: Mohave 3, D-1-3
Descriptive. Salt or brackish springs are at the head of this wash.
Ref.: Barnes. Map: GH-15.

## SANDY

Loc.: Probably on Big Sandy River
The origin of this name is probably associated with its location, but this has not been definitely determined as yet.
P.O. est. June 8, 1892. Mrs. Nellie C. Hunt, p.m. Discont. January 8, 1900.
Ref.: P.O. Records. Map: None.

## SANTA CLAUS

El.: 3384′  Loc.: Mohave 3, D-9
Santa Claus is a subdivision which has never fully developed. Nevertheless, it is nationally known. The subdivision was begun by Mrs. Ninon Talbot, who weighed nearly three hundred pounds. As a real estate dealer in Los Angeles, she advertised herself as the biggest in the business. She moved to Kingman and soon thereafter started the Santa Claus subdivision on the road to Hoover Dam north of Kingman. The imaginative architecture of the buildings at Santa Claus are a joy to both children and adults. The buildings were designed by Ed Talbot, who had been associated with the motion picture business.

Mrs. Talbot made Santa Claus a famous place by her policy of sending Christmas cards to every caller. She took the trouble to note license numbers and to trace the addresses of the car owners who stopped at Santa Claus.

Ref.: Housholder. Map: GH-3.

## SANTA MARIA RIVER

El.: c. 3000'                    Loc.: Mohave 6, FG-8
Pro.:   /sántə maríyə/ or
/sǽntəmaríyə/
Lt. Amiel W. Whipple called this river the Rio Santa Maria
since, as he noted, this was the name that Spanish map
makers applied to the entire Bill Williams River. Juan de
Oñate in 1604 apparently was the first white man to see
and to name this river. He followed it to its junction with
the Colorado, calling the latter the Rio Grande de Buena
Esperanza. Oñate called the Santa Maria the Rio de San
Andres. Possibly he did so because he may have visited the
area on November 30, which is St. Andrew's Day. The Spaniards customarily named locations according to the saint's
day on which a Spaniard first visited the locality.
Ref.:   177, pp. 216, 216 (Note 27); 7, p. 348. Maps: C-11;
        GH-6; GH-8.

**a.n. Santa Maria Mountains**                                    Mohave
       **Santa Maria Canyon**                                     Mohave

## SANUP PLATEAU

El.: 6200'                      Loc.: Mohave 4, DF-1.2
                *Sannup* "married Indian man," or the "male
                            equivalent for squaw"
The reason for using this name has not been learned. The
word is apparently not one used by southwestern Indians.
Ref.:   Barnes; Lenon. Maps: C-5; E-20.

**a.n. Sanup Peak**                                               Mohave

## SCANLON FERRY

El.: c. 500'                    Loc.: Mohave 3, E-1
The ferry was established about 1881 (cf. Greggs Ferry).
Mike Scanlon was a prospector in the White Hills. At one
time he served as Mohave County Supervisor and was prominent in county affairs just prior to 1900. In 1912 when
Emery Kolb and his brother made the trip down the length
of the Colorado River to its mouth, they reported that the
ferry was "in charge of a Cornish man, who also had as
pretty a little ranch as one could expect to find in such an
unlikely place."
Ref.:   Babcock; 98, pp. 273-74; 112, p. 97. Maps: C-10; GH-6.

## SCATTERVILLE

                                Loc.: Not determined.
In late 1877 new buildings were going up all along the Sandy
for a distance of three miles and the name Scatterville had
been given to the location. This is probably the area which
developed into the town of Signal (*q.v.*).
Ref.:   *Arizona Miner*, November 2, 1877, 1:6. Map: None.

## SCREWBEAN SPRING

El.: c. 2500'                   Loc.: Mohave 5, G-6.5
A lone screwbean tree at this location gave the spring its
name.
Ref.:   Harris. Maps: C-13; GH-11.

## SECRET PASS

El.: c. 3400'                   Loc.: Mohave 3, CD-11
On GLO 1887, Secret Spring is shown tucked back in the
hills to the south of Union Pass about seven miles. Secret

Pass appears only on GLO 1921 where it is shown directly
north of Secret Spring. Barnes notes that there was a Secret
Mine at this location. The fact that a post office briefly
existed here lends credence to his report.
P.O. est. October 20, 1916. Ada Webster, p.m. Discont. May
15, 1917.
Ref.:   P.O. Records; Harris; 62, p. 23; Barnes. Map: C-12.

## SEPARATION RAPID

El.: c. 1500'                   Loc.: Mohave 4, DE-2.5
Separation Rapid when it was encountered by Maj. John
Wesley Powell's Grand Canyon 1869 expedition was so
turbulent and obviously fraught with extreme danger that
Seneca and W. H. Howland, and William Dunn elected
to leave the main body of the expedition. The rapid was
first called Catastrophe Rapid by Dr. A. H. Thompson
of Powell's party (cf. Ambush Water Pocket).
Ref.:   Shellbach File; 41, p. 242. Map: GH-6.

## SHARPS BAR

El.: c. 1000'                   Loc.: Mohave 3, A-2.5
C. M. Sharp, a Swiss miner, had a mine at this place in the
early 1880's. More recently a man named Sandy Harris
had placers at the same location. During the 1930's when
the depression was forcing many people to fend for themselves and to live as best they could, several people were
in this area placering gold, which led to the name of Placer-
ville for their small settlement.
Ref.:   Barnes; Harris (no relation); Housholder. Map: GN-6
        (Sandy Harris Placers).

## SHIPLEY

El.: c. 4000'                   Loc.: Mohave 4, F-5.5
Shipley was a blind siding which was used by the Shipley
brothers, who were drilling wells in the vicinity for the
railroad.
Ref.:   Barnes; Harris. Maps: GH-6; GH-8.

## SHIVWITS PLATEAU

El.: 6300'                      Loc.: Mohave 1, DE-4-8
The Shivwits Indians were a Piute tribe living formerly in
the area which today bears their name. In 1873 there were
one hundred eighty-two of these Indians, but by 1909 only
one hundred eighteen were still living in southwestern Utah.

**v.n. Shiwitz Plateau**
     **Sheavwitz Plateau**

Ref.:   88, II, 552; 151, p. 689; 100, p. 30. Maps: C-4; C-10;
        E-26.

## SHORT CREEK

El.: c. 5000'                   Loc.: Mohave 2, C-1
The town takes its name from a very short creek in T. 41
N., R. 7 W.
The Mormon settlement of Short Creek was in existence
in 1872.
P.O. est. June 26, 1914. Lydia M. Covington, p.m.
Ref.:   47, p. 53; A. H. Thompson, "Diary," July 8, 1872, *Utah
        Historical Quarterly*, p. 89 (Shellbach File); Barnes;
        P.O. Records. Map: C-12.

## SIGNAL

El.: c. 1500′                    Loc.: Mohave 6, DE-6.2
The town of Signal came into being in 1877 with the completion of the mill for the Signal Mine, one of the most famous of its day. Signal was about nine miles from both the McCrackin and Signal Mines.

Signal as a mining community may be considered typical of many in early Arizona, except that it was larger than the majority. In its heydey it had stores, workshops, hotels, and saloons. The townsite was surveyed by Richard Gird. When the town was only eight months old, it had two hundred buildings and a population of nearly eight hundred. A brewery supplied beer for the thirsty miners. A visitor to the location in February 1878 commented that the isolation of the camp was almost inconceivable, adding that Los Angeles at that time was scarcely "considered a city and if it contained any wholesale houses they were unimportant. Freight from San Francisco was originally brought by steamer around the California peninsula up into the mouth of the Rio Colorado, but at this time it came by rail to the west side of the river at Yuma, and thence by barge up the river to Aubrey Landing, where it was loaded on wagons and hauled by long mule teams thirty-five miles upgrade to Signal. The merchants considered it necessary to send orders six months before the expected time of delivery . . . and up to this time the nearest post office was Ehrenberg on the Colorado River, fifty miles away."

Ed Schieffelin brought his first ores from Tombstone to Signal to run an assay. As a result of this, Richard Gird became interested in the Tombstone mining ventures and many miners flocked from Signal to Tombstone (q.v., Cochise).

Signal remained prosperous for many years. Today, however, it is practically deserted.

P.O. est. October 15, 1877. Thomas E. Walter, p.m. Discont. May 14, 1932.
Ref.: Housholder; *Arizona Sentinel*, October 13, 1877, 2:3; July 6, 1878, 1:2, 3; 87, pp. 251-252; 140, pp. 8-9. P.O. Records. Maps: C-4 (Signal City); C-12; E-20.
**a.n. Signal Canyon**                                    Mohave
Loc.: Where the Big Sandy leaves the town of Signal.
Ref.: 100, p. 52.
**Signal Peak**           Map: C-12                       Mohave
As was the case with many such peaks throughout the country, this peak was used by Indians for making signals.
Ref.: Barnes.
The following is a list of place names using the word Signal in a fashion similar to that for Signal Peak listed above. Whether the places were actually used by Indians is frequently not documented.
**Signal Butte**                                         Maricopa
El.: 1715′. Loc.: Sec. 13, T. 1 N., R. 7 E.
**Signal Butte**        El.: 590′. Map: GN-15            Yuma
**Signal Mountain**     Loc.: T. 1 S., R. 14 E.          Pinal
**Signal Peak**    Loc.: S.W. corner T. 1 S., R. 15 E.  Gila
This is the Signal Peak mentioned in King S. Woolsey's June 1864 report, according to Barnes.
**Signal Peak** (No. 2)                                   Gila
Loc:. Sec. 13, T. 1 S., R. 12 E.

**Signal Peak**                                          Pinal
El.: 2277′. Loc.: Sec. 29, T. 5 S., R. 7 E.
**Signal Peak**      El.: 4640′. Loc.: T. 1 S., R. 18 W.  Yuma
There are many signs of Indian use here.
**Signal Peak**             Map: B-7                      Gila
**Signal Mountain**   El.: 2180′. Map: GG-18            Maricopa
**Signal Mountain**                                      Yuma

## SITE SIX

El.: c. 400′                      Loc.: Mohave 5, CD-6.6
During World War II (c. 1943) an airfield was constructed at this location as an auxiliary to the base at Kingman. The name came from its place in the construction series of airstrips. Site Six is now used by Colorado River fishermen.
Ref.: Housholder. Map: GN-25.

## SITGREAVES PASS

El.: 3600′                        Loc.: Mohave 5, CD-0.5
Lt. Edward Fitzgerald Beale was the first white man to lead a group through this pass on October 15 and 16, 1857. Beale came through again with his party on January 24, 1858. Beale called the pass John Howell's Pass, after a member of his party. The next group to go through was led by Lt. Joseph Christmas Ives on March 25, 1858. Ives named the pass Sitgreaves after Lt. Lorenzo Sitgreaves, the first American military man to explore a route across northern Arizona. However, Sitgreaves himself never went through the pass. He used Union Pass (q.v.), on November 5, 1851. As Sitgreaves Pass is above the formerly important mining town of Oatman, it is sometimes referred to as Oatman Pass.
Ref.: 4, p. 325; 12, pp. 77-78; 169, p. 5 (Note 5). Maps: C-12; E-4.
**a.n. Sitgreaves Mountain**     Loc.: T. 23 N., R. 4 E.   Coconino
Capt. Sitgreaves visited this mountain in 1852.
**Sitgreaves National Forest**      Navajo, Apache and Coconino
This forest area was created in 1898 as the Black Mesa Forest Reserve and was re-designated under its present name in 1906.

## SPEARS LAKE

El.: 452′                          Loc.: Mohave 5, A-2.5
Augustus A. Spear was a brother of Benjamin S. Spear, the first and only postmaster at Beale Springs from 1873 to 1876. Gus Spear served as an Indian scout and established a ranch about four miles east of the Colorado River, from which the lake took its name. Ben Spear had the sutler's store at Fort Mohave and later at Mineral Park. Ben was also active as a prospector during the 1860's and later.
Ref.: Harris; 62, p. 190. Map: GH-10.

## SPENCER CANYON

El.: c. 2800′                      Loc.: Mohave 3, D-1
Charley Spencer (d. 1866) was one of the best known guides for exploring parties in the early territorial days of Arizona. He served as a guide for Capt. George M. Wheeler's expedition in the 1870's. Prior to that time he had raised cattle in the Sacramento Valley in the late 1860's. When other cattlemen began to crowd the range

and trouble with sheepmen developed there, he moved into the country behind Music Mountain (*q.v.*).

Spencer was a very close friend of the Hualapai Indians and married a Hualapai woman. Frequently Spencer served as an interpreter between the government people and the Hualapais. He also served as an Indian scout and was a mining partner with another famous scout, Dan O'Leary. Because of the trouble which he had with stockmen, Spencer was very active in helping to establish the Hualapai Indian Reservation to protect his Indian relatives and himself and their cattle from white cattlemen. Spencer built a house in Meriwitica Canyon. He made a mistake in being partners with a man named Cohan, with whom he had a serious quarrel over livestock. Spencer told Cohan that if he ever came onto the Hualapai Reservation, Spencer would kill him. The two men met in Truxton Canyon where they had another quarrel about an acre of ground and Cohan killed Spencer. Sam Crozier acted as executor for Spencer's estate (cf. Crozier).

Ref.:   Daniel O'Leary File, APHS; 169, pp. 127, 156, 347-348. Maps: C-4; GH-1.

**a.n. Spencer Creek**          Map: C-7          Yavapai
Among his other activities, Spencer carried the U. S. mail from Camp Willow Grove to Hardyville. He was attacked on this creek on March 23, 1868, by Hualapai Indians and was badly wounded. Spencer was wounded at least six times while acting as a guide and Indian scout.
Ref.:   Barnes.

## STOCKTON HILL
El.: 4800'          Loc.: Mohave 3, E-9.5
The mines in the vicinity of Stockton were among the first to be discovered in the 1860's; this would seem to indicate that Stockton Hill derived its name in the same manner that Sacramento Valley did — by the fact that Californians comprised the majority of miners in the area. However, Stockton Camp—which gave the name to the hill—did not become active until c. 1880. Both the camp and the hill were named by a Scotsman, Johnny McKinsey. Furthermore, miners in the area (1880) were either Arizonans or Cornishmen.

There were more Cornishmen (called "Cousin Jacks" because of their habit of thus greeting each other) in this section of Mohave County than elsewhere in Arizona. Exceedingly clannish, the Cousin Jacks refused to permit other miners to work with them. To enforce their wishes, the Cornishmen were a bit careless about letting something lethal fall on any miner who had the temerity to attempt to work in the mines with the Cousin Jacks.

P.O. est. as Stockton Hill March 7, 1888. William H. Lake, p.m. Discont. July 11, 1892.
Ref.:   Harris; P.O. Records; 62, p. 107; 76, p. 68; 87, pp. 160, 252. Maps: C-4; GH-3 (Stockton Mine).

## STONE FERRY
El.: c. 1400'          Loc.: Mohave 3, A-1
A man named Stone established this ferry.
Stone or Stone's Ferry was one of the principal crossings for traffic from Utah into northwestern Arizona. It should

not be confused with Bonelli's crossing (*q.v.*), which was at the mouth of Detrital Wash within two or three miles of Stone Ferry. There is, however, a possibility that Bonelli ran this ferry for a short period. Both Bonelli and Stone Ferry are now under the waters of Lake Mead.
Ref.:   Housholder; 55, p. 552; 112, p. 97; 127, p. 158. Maps: C-4; E-20.

## SURPRISE CANYON
El.: c. 5000'          Loc.: Mohave 4, D-1-2
Frederick Dellenbaugh said that Surprise Valley was named by Beaman and Riley in January 1872. The canyon takes its name from the valley.
Ref.:   Barnes. Maps: GH-6; GH-8.

## SWEENEY
Loc.: Not known.
The origin of this name has not yet been ascertained.
P.O. est. February 14, 1906. James E. Bond, p.m. (Refused commission. Office never in operation). Discont. May 23, 1906.
Ref.:   P.O. Records. Map: None.

## SWICKERT SPRING
El.: c. 4000'          Loc.: Mohave 3, DE-7
Although this name is listed as "Swicker," it should be Swickert after a prospector by that name who camped at the spring whenever en route for supplies to Chloride from his mine in Nevada.
Ref.:   Housholder. Map: GH-3.

## TEMPLE BAR
El.: 2500'          Loc.: Mohave 3, C-1
Temple Bar is one of a number of sand and gravel cliffs. It was named The Mormon Temple in the early 1870's by Daniel Bonelli (cf. Bonelli's Crossing Mohave).
Ref.:   100, p. 35; George S. Perkins, *Pioneers of the Western Desert*, p. 36. Map: C-12.

**a.n. Temple Wash**          Mohave
Loc.: Drains into Lake Mead from nearly opposite the Temple (above).
**v.n. Temple Bar Wash (corruption)**

## THIMBLE MOUNTAIN
El.: c. 4000'          Loc.: Mohave 5, C-1
Descriptive.
Ref.:   Barnes. Map: C-12.

## TIPTON, MOUNT
El.: 7364'          Loc.: Mohave 3, D-6.8
A Lt. Tipton was a member of Lt. Joseph Christmas Ives' expedition of 1858.
Ref.:   Barnes. Maps: C-4; E-4; E-20.

## TODD BASIN
El.: c. 1500'          Loc.: Mohave 3, E-9
About 12 miles from Chloride.
John Todd was a miner. In 1906 Todd Basin was one of the most important mining locations in the county.
Ref.:   Harris; 62, pp. 16, 20. Map: None.

## TOROWEAP VALLEY

El.: c. 2500'　　　　　Loc.: Mohave 2, B-9.7-6.6
　　　　　　　　　　　　Piute: "gully; dry wash"
Frederick Dellenbaugh noted that the Uinkarets called this valley "Toroweap." He also mentioned that on its eastern side was the Toroweap Fault, which created the Toroweap Cliffs, a wall approximately eight hundred feet high. There was an old trail through the Toroweap (Tuweap) Valley to the Colorado River, and Maj. John Wesley Powell went down it to investigate the peaks of the volcanic field in the valley. Dr. A. H. Thompson of Powell's party named the valley from the Indian designation.

Ref.: A. H. Thompson, "Diary," *Utah Historical Quarterly* (Shellbach File); 41, p. 192; 132, pp. 186, 188; 70, p. 21. Maps: C-6; C-7; C-8; C-12 (Tornado Valley); C-9; C-10 (Torroweap Valley); C-11; C-13; C-14; GC-6 (Toroweap Valley).

a.n. Tuweep　　　　Map: GC-6　　　　Mohave
This post office served ranchers in this part of the Arizona Strip.
P.O. est. June 27, 1929. Mabel K. Hoffpauir, p.m. Discont. December 31, 1950.
v.n. Torowip Cliffs
Mu-koon'-tu-weap　　　　Piute: "straight canyon"
Ref.: P.O. Records; 133a, pp. 13, 111.

## TORTILLA FLAT

El.: c. 1500'　　　　　Loc.: Mohave 6, E-8
Pro.: /tortíyə/　　　　Spanish: "omelet; pancake"
In the early 1880's a Mexican settlement existed on the mesa north of New Virginia (*q.v.*) where "the leading industries are said to be raising watermelons, making adobes, and keeping bit saloons."
Ref.: 87, p. 252; Barnes. Map: None.

## TROUT CREEK

El.: c. 3500'　　　　　Loc.: Mohave 6, D-1.5
Lt. Amiel W. Whipple called the present Trout Creek "Bill Williams Fork" in error. Trout Creek is one of the three largest streams which empty into the Big Sandy.
Ref.: 177, p. 212; 100, p. 50. Maps: C-4; E-20.

## TRUMBULL, MOUNT

El.: 8028'　　　　　Loc.: Mohave 2, AB-7.7
When Lt. Joseph Christmas Ives visited this area in 1858 he called a group of mountains, which today bear individual names, the North Side Mountains. Maj. John Wesley Powell visited this same area during his exploration of the Grand Canyon in 1871-1872 and named the three major volcanic peaks of the North Side Mountains after individuals. One was named for Senator Lyman Trumbull, U.S. Senator, Illinois, 1854-1871 (See *a.n.* below).
P.O. est. April 6, 1920. Lillian D. Iverson, p.m. Discont. July 31, 1954.
Ref.: P.O. Records; 41, pp. 186, 187; 133, p. 131. Maps: C-1; E-20 (North Side Mountain); C-4.
a.n. Emma, Mount　　El.: 7698'. Map: GC-6　　Mohave
This is the largest of the volcanic peaks; it was named by Powell for his wife.

Ref.: 47, pp. 103, 104.
Logan, Mount　　El.: c. 7500'　　　　Mohave
This is the third peak, named by Powell for U. S. Senator John Logan.
v.n. Logan Peak
Ref.: Barnes; 41, p. 192.

## TUCKET CANYON

El.: c. 4000'　　　　　Loc.: Mohave 2, D-7-9
Tucket Canyon was named because of its being in the Tucket Mining District. Through corruption, the name has been changed to Tuckup Canyon.
Ref.: Maps. Map: C-10.
a.n. Tuck Up Point　　　Map: GC-6　　　Mohave
Rocky Point　　El.: 5987'. Map: GC-6　　Mohave
Tuckup Trail　　　　　　　　　　Mohave

## TURQUOISE MOUNTAIN

El.: c. 4400'　　　　　Loc.: Mohave 3, E-9
Turquoise was mined here and at other places near Mineral Park. The turquoise was shipped to New York where it was sold in rough form for use in making jewelry.
Ref.: Harris; 62, p. 218. Map: GH-3.

## TRUXTON CANYON

El.: 3880'　　　　　Loc.: Mohave 4, AF-5.5-6
On October 28, 1851, Lt. Lorenzo Sitgreaves dispatched a reconnoitering party to find running water. The party returned to report finding a band of Yampais (Yavapais) encamped upon the creek which today is called Truxton Wash. The guide, Antoine Leroux, learned from these Indians that the Sitgreaves party was approaching the Colorado River. On October 30, Sitgreaves named the creek the Yampai, an attempt to spell "Yavapai."

The presence of cliffs along the eastern edge of the stream led to applying the name Yampai Cliffs to them. Today these are called the Grand Wash Cliffs.

On January 27, 1858, Lt. Edward Fitzgerald Beale spent the day at what he called Truxton Spring. He described the spring as being "a beautiful one; the water pouring over the rock is received in a basin of some 20 feet diameter and 8 or 10 deep." His party stayed at this place all day, shoeing their mules and resting their exhausted animals. His party had a brush with Indians here, a not uncommon occurrence for visitors, since the Indians made use of the springs. It is probable that Beale named the spring for his wife, whose maiden name was Truxton. Beale speaks of leaving Truxton Spring on January 28, traveling to White Rock Spring and entering a wide valley which led to Hemphill's Spring.

Maps for the area are confusing, for the names shift freely. GLO 1869 shows a Peacocke Spring and emerging from it to empty into Red Lake is a stream called Yampa Creek. The route followed by Lt. Joseph Christmas Ives crosses the creek about a mile northwest of the spring. Smith 1879 (Map E-20) shows a Truxton Spring with Peacock Spring approximately a mile and a half to the west. Peacock Spring still apparently empties into Red

Lake. There is also a Truxton Valley shown. On GLO 1883, Peacock Spring has disappeared, Truxton shows as a station on the railroad, and Yampai Creek is shown taking a southwesterly direction between Peach Springs and Truxton. This is true until GLO 1892 when Truxton disappears altogether. It reappears again on GLO 1903, but the name Yampai has disappeared. On GLO 1912 what was formerly Yampai Creek shows as Truxton Wash. Truxton Wash is the same wash which was followed by Fr. Garcés on June 10, 1775. He called it the Arroyo de San Bernabe.

In 1883 the A.&P.R.R. put in a large pump and tank at Truxton Springs, thus eliminating the necessity of hauling water two hundred miles for use in steam engines. Truxton for many years served as an important watering place on the railroad. This led to a suit with the Hualapai Indians (cf. Crozier). Today there is only a section house at Truxton, diesel engines having eliminated the watering stops.

Today there is a new community called Truxton developing a mile west of Peach Springs. It was established in October 1951 when D. J. Dilts built a restaurant and service station at this point. There are now five families living in Truxton, and two additional property owners who have not yet moved in. Dilts named his little settlement for the Truxton railroad siding and Truxton Canyon two miles to the west because he felt that the name Truxton was well known. Dilts came to Arizona in July 1942, as a supervisor with the S.F.R.R.

Ref.: Dilts; 169, pp. 7, 216; 150, p. 15; 62, p. 19; 12, pp. 78, 79; 131, Entry for 1889; 112, p. 13. Maps: C-1 (Peacocke Spring); C-5 (Truxton); C-9 (Truxton); C-11 (Truxton Wash); E-20 (Truxton Spring, Truxton Valley, and Peacock Spring).

**a.n. Truxton Plateau**                                          Mohave
   The edge of the Truxton Plateau is formed by Cottonwood Cliffs and Aquarius Cliffs.

   **Yampai**                                                    Yavapai
   This railroad location is on the Yampa Divide, hence its name.

P.O. est. May 15, 1901. Robert L. Barry, p.m.

Ref.: P.O. Records.


## UINKARETS MOUNTAINS

El.: c. 6000'                          Loc.: Mohave 2, AC-6-8
                                       Piute: "region of pines"
These mountains are the same as those called by Lt. Amiel W. Whipple on January 1, 1854, the High Mountains. They also correspond to the North Side Mountains including Logan, Emma, and Trumbull (q.v.) Maj. John Wesley Powell reported that Uinkarets was the name of a Piute band living in the area.

There are one hundred eighteen volcanic cones surrounding the three larger mountains.

Ref.: 133a, p. 13. Maps: C-12; E-20 (North Side Mountains).
**a.n. Uinkaret Plateau**       Map: C-15                  Mohave


## UNION

El.: c. 4000'                          Loc.: Mohave 3, DE-9.2
The name Union was given to this station on the Arizona and Utah Railroad because at this point the old road from Union Pass crossed the valley to reach mines in the Cerbat Mountains.

Ref.: Barnes. Maps: C-9; C-10; C-11; C-12 (Union Station); C-13; C-14.
**a.n. Union Basin**       Maps: C-4; E-20                 Mohave
   Union Basin is one of three depressions which collect waters from Grand Wash in the Cerbat District.
Ref.: 62, pp. 91, 98.


## UNION PASS

El.: 3680'                          Loc.: Mohave 3, C-D-10
Capt. Lorenzo Sitgreaves, the first American military man to lead an exploring expedition across northern Arizona to the Colorado River, crossed the Black Mountain Range through this pass on November 5, 1851. Why it is called Union Pass has not yet been ascertained.

When rich mines opened up in the Cerbat Mountains, Union Pass became an extremely important route for those who wished to reach the mining communities on the east side of the Sacramento Valley. In 1871 the Union Pass Station was managed by U. E. Dolittle. A ferry on the Colorado River provided access to mines near Searchlight, Nevada. There was as much traffic with miners getting supplies at Chloride and taking them west over the pass to Nevada as there was in the opposite direction.

Ref.: *Weekly Miner*, June 30, 1871, 2:2; 169, p. 5 (Note 5); 100, p. 25; Barnes. Maps: C-5; C-12; E-20; GH-6.


## UTE MOUNTAINS

El.: c. 4000'                          Loc.: Mohave 5, CD-1
Pro.: /uwt/
The Ute Indians made their home in the vicinity of this range.

Ref.: Barnes. Map: C-10.


## VALENTINE

El. c. 3800'                          Loc.: Mohave 4, CD-7.5
The agency for the Hualapai Indians is located at Valentine. At one time this place was called Truxton Canyon Sub-agency, established on December 22, 1898, in Truxton Canyon. It is not the same place as Truxton although a post office at the Truxton Canyon Sub-agency was set up under the name Truxton. On May 14, 1900, six hundred sixty acres of land were set aside and an Indian school built on the land. These buildings are now used as agency headquarters. When the school was still in operation the post office was on agency land, which accounts for the fact that the first Indian agent, Henry Ewing, was made postmaster when the Truxton Canyon post office was established. When the Indian school was discontinued, the post office was moved a mile away and because of the change of location it was necessary to change the name of the post office,

which was no longer on agency ground. It was then called Valentine in honor of Robert G. Valentine, Commissioner of Indian Affairs from 1908 to 1910.

P.O. est. as Truxton, January 10, 1901. Henry P. Ewing, p.m. Name changed to Valentine, February 24, 1910.

Ref.: Harris; Glaser; 169, p. 202; 4, p. 323; P.O. Records. Map: C-11.

## VIRGIN RIVER

El.: c. 3000'                              Loc.: Mohave 2, AD-21
            Piute: *Pah'reah* "water that tastes salty"
The name Rio Virgen is an old one, but the reasons for its name are lost. It was apparently named by Escalante in 1776.

There is a Virgen Salt Well near where the Virgin River joins the Colorado. Although the well is in Nevada, it is mentioned because it is the only place known in which the Spanish word *virgen* survives in connection with the river. Also it may account for the brackish taste of the river water. A later map of Escalante's route shows the name Rio Sulfureo de las Piramides. It is a coincidence that Thomas Virgin explored this river with Jedediah Smith in the 1820's.

Ref.: 175, III, 109-110; Barnes; George S. Perkins, *Pioneers of the Western Desert*, p. 60. Maps: C-1 (Santa Clara River) Above the Colorado River, marked Rio Virgen; C-4 (Rio Virgen); E-20 (Virgin River).

**a.n. Virgin Canyon**                                        Mohave
The river runs through this canyon, which was visited by Capt. George M. Wheeler on October 1, 1871. Wheeler says he named the canyon because it was the first "entirely new ground" his party had explored. Wheeler apparently did not know Maj. John Wesley Powell had gone down it as far as the Virgin River. Wheeler was going up in the opposite direction.

Ref.: 175, I, 161; 42, pp. 297-298; 100, p. 34.

**Virgin Basin**                                             Mohave
This is the middle basin of the three occupied by Lake Mead. It is sometimes erroneously called Middle Basin or Middle Lake.

## VOCK CANYON

El.: c. 4000'                              Loc.: Mohave 3, E-8.1
Pro.: /vowk/
Chris Vock was a cook for rodeo cowboys. He developed the spring at this location and began raising cattle in the canyon.

Ref.: Harris. Map: GH-3.

| **a.n. Vock Spring** | Map: GH-3 | Mohave |
| Vock Wash | Map: GH-3 | Mohave |
| Vock Wash, Left Fork | Map: GH-3 | Mohave |

## VULCAN'S THRONE

El.: 5108'                                 Loc.: Mohave 2, BC-9.5
Vulcan's Throne is in the Toroweap Valley. It is a volcanic cone which towers about six hundred feet high on the brink of the Inner Gorge. It is, however, just one of one hundred sixty-nine small volcanos in the immediate vicinity. The point was named by Clarence Dutton in 1880.

Ref.: 47, pp. 4, 92; Shellbach. Map: GC-6.

## WAUBA YUMA DISTRICT

El.: c. 3000'                              Loc.: Mohave 6, AD-5
Pro.: /wábəyúwmə/
The first important discovery of mineral in this area was made c. 1865 by prospectors under the leadership of John Moss. The group located mines in what they called the Wauba Yuma District, after the chief of the Hualapai Indians (cf. Camp Willow Grove). Indians soon drove the miners from the area and the name Wauba Yuma for the area was lost. Capt. George M. Wheeler camped on a wash in this area in 1871 on the east side of the mountains. Soon a group of prospectors from San Francisco moved in. To honor the explorer, the prospectors named their first location the Wheeler Lode. The name for the wash, Wheeler Wash, soon came into being.

Ref.: 62, p. 139; Harris. Maps: C-1; C-13 (Wheeler Wash).

## WEEPING CLIFFS

El.: c. 1500'                             Loc.: Mohave 1, AB-10.4
Water drips constantly from these cliffs.

Ref.: U. S. Geographic Board Decision (not dated) (State Library Files). Map: GH-6.

## WHITE CLIFFS CREEK

El.: c. 4000'                             Loc.: Mohave 4, FC-9-10
Lt. Amiel W. Whipple was responsible for naming this stream White Cliffs Creek. He wrote of passing with his party down the bed of the creek and noting that the hills on either side were of coarse granite with a noticeable amount of feldspar, which doubtless accounts for the white appearance. Whipple's account mentions a Big Horn Spring, which according to his description must have been about twelve miles above where Trout Creek joins the Little Sandy to form the Big Sandy. However, Big Horn Spring does not show on any maps examined.

Whipple named Big Horn Spring because of mountain sheep which were "frightened away" when Whipple's party approached.

Ref.: 177, p. 212; Barnes. Maps: C-7, C-8 (entirely Mohave County); C-12 (Cottonwood Creek); C-13 (Knight Creek with Cottonwood Creek moved one stream farther north); C-14 (Knight Creek); C-4 (White Cliffs Creek. Cottonwood Springs is shown at the head of this Creek. Doubtless the creek took its name from the spring); C-5 (Cottonwood Spring. The creek is unnamed.); C-1 (Cottonwood Creek in Yavapai County at the Willows, north of Fort Rock. The creek bears the name Canon Creek. Mohave and Yavapai.); E-20 (White Cliffs Creek).

## WHITE HILLS

El.: c. 2500'                              Loc.: Mohave 3, B-4
The White Hills is a group of low, gentle hills rich in minerals. In May 1892 Henry Shaffer made the first mining location. Shaffer was shown a piece of rich silver ore by Hualapai Jeff, an Indian, who revealed the source of the ore.

By July 23, 1892, a town named White Hills was in the boom stages, at that time already having about two hundred residents, a store, four saloons, three restaurants and fifty tents. By 1894 the town was owned by the White Hills Mining Company and had a population of fifteen hundred. The company was sold in 1895 to an English firm which went heavily in debt to set up production for the mines. The company could not make its final payment and the property was put up at sheriff's sale. The original owner, Root, bought it back with the help of D. H. Moffat. In 1898 peak production was obtained, but thereafter veins began to produce less.

It is a curious fact that water cost one dollar per barrel in the town of White Hills, but a flash flood on August 5, 1899 completely flooded the mine shafts. From that time on, White Hills was on its way to becoming the ghost town which it very nearly is today.

P.O. est. October 20, 1892. William H. Taggart, p.m. Discont. August 15, 1914.

Ref.: *Arizona Sentinel*, July 23, 1892, 1:3; 62, pp. 20, 127; P.O. Records; 170, pp. 79, 80, 81. Map: C-7.

## WHITMORE WASH

El.: c. 5000′          Loc.: Mohave 2, A-9.8
Whitmore Wash is named for a man who had a ranch which Frederick Dellenbaugh visited in 1872. This is the same ranch mentioned by Dr. A. H. Thompson as being on the Uinkaret Plateau near Mount Trumbull.

Ref.: 41, p. 188; A. H. Thompson, "Diary," entry for March 23, 1872, *Utah Historical Quarterly* (Shellbach File). Map: B-5.

a.n. Whitmore Point     Loc.: T. 40, N. R. 5 W.          Mohave

## WHITNEY

El.: c. 2500′          Loc.: Mohave 6, D-2.9
In 1874 Colonel Buell surveyed a townsite which he called Whitney for a former state geologist of California.

Ref.: *Arizona Citizen*, September 26, 1874, 1:4. Map: GH-6 (Whitney School).

## WICKYTYWIZ

Loc.: Not known
At one time the famous Indian scout and guide, Charles Spencer, lived in this canyon with the kinsmen of his Hualapai wife. Why the canyon is named Wickytywiz has not yet been ascertained.

Ref.: 22, p. 451. Map: None.

## WIKIEUP

El.: c. 2500′          Loc.: Mohave 6, D-3.5
Pro.: /wíki˄p/
The term "wikieup" is frequently applied to brush shelters built by Indians in the Southwest, particularly those constructed by Apaches.

Originally it was proposed that the post office of Wikieup be called Sandy, but there was already a post office by that name, and it could not be used. The second name proposed was Owens. Owens shows on GLO 1933 as being two miles south of Wikieup. The name probably derived from the fact that there was an Owens Ranch which in turn may

have originated before 1879 in the mining district in that area called the Owens District. When neither the name Sandy nor Owens could be used for the post office, the name was changed to Wikieup because there was an Indian tepee at a spring close by. At that time it was spelled Wickiup.

The canyon in the area is called Wickiup Canyon; by a curious corruption on GLO 1909, this shows as Wake-up Wash.

P.O. est. April 22, 1922. William F. Buchanan, p.m.

Ref.: Rosenberger, Letter, February 1, 1956; "U. S. Geographic Board Decision, May 6, 1941," p. 4; P.O. Records. 88, II, 950. Maps: C-13, See entry; E-20 (Owens District).

## WILD BAND POCKET

El.: c. 4000′          Loc.: Mohave 2, F-4
Frederick Dellenbaugh tells of visiting this place but finding no water. However, while on the way to water nearby, his group saw a band of at least twenty wild horses "spinning across the plain one behind another like a train of railway cars, a huge stallion playing locomotive." Clarence E. Dutton said the shallow valley was known as the "Wild Band Pockets" because of horses which gathered at the rain pools.

This is apparently the same place which Bolton refers to in connection with Escalante's visit of 1776, saying that the name was given because wild horses watered here. Bolton calls it Wild Band Pools.

Ref.: 41, p. 251; 47, p. 80; Barnes. Maps C-6; C-7 (Wild Band Pools).

## WILLCOX

Loc.: Not known
The origin of this name has not been learned.

P.O. est. October 1, 1923. Harry O. Parks, p.m. Discont.?

Ref.: P.O. Records. Map: None.

## WILLOW BEACH

El.: c. 1500′          Loc.: Mohave 3, A-2.7
Descriptive name for a small settlement.
Maps: GH-6; GH-8.

## WILLOW GROVE, CAMP

El.: c. 4000′          Loc.: Mohave 4, EF-9.5
Camp Willow Grove was established on August 23, 1864, and discontinued on June 30, 1869. Troops withdrew in September. In a report dated 1869, Camp Willow Grove was noted as being an extremely unhealthy place. To say the least, forage for livestock was scant since about thirty-five cattle starved to death there during one winter, although "they had free access to the haystack at all times."

v.n. Warm Creek
    Willows

Ref.: 85, pp. 429, 557; 75, p. 161; 175, III, 206; *Citizen*, August 15, 1874, 1:4; 169, p. 89. Map: E-20.

**a.n. Willow Grove Springs**     Map: E-20     Mohave

Martha Summerhayes noted that there was a small group of willow trees at this place, hence the name. In 1864 this location was referred to as Willow Spring, where J. Hundredmark and Company had established a place for travelers on October 24. In 1866 George Leihy, Superintendent of Indian Affairs, reported that Hualapai Indians, under their chief Wauba Yuma, killed Edward Clower who had been left in camp by his companions. This upset the treaty which William Hardy (cf. Hardyville, Mohave County) had made with Wauba Yuma. Sam Miller of Prescott, a freighter, heard of Clower's death at the Willows. Miller then murdered Wauba Yuma. He thereby precipitated the arduous and long campaign against the Hualapais.

P.O. est. Willow Ranch, February 12, 1880. Edwin Imey, p.m. Discont. June 10, 1880.

Ref.: 158, p. 70; *Arizona Miner*, November 23, 1864, 4:1; 169, p. 35; 111, p. 193; P.O. Records.

## WILSON, MOUNT

El.: 5500'     Loc.: Mohave 3, A-1

The origin of the name has not been ascertained. The Mount Wilson group extends for about twenty-five miles from Boulder Canyon to El Dorado Pass.

Ref.: 62, p. 22; 100, p. 25. Maps: C-6; GH-8.

## WITCH WATER POCKET

El.: c. 6000'     Loc. : Mohave 2, AB-7

Piute: *Innupin* or *Oonupin Picabu*, "witch water pocket"

Frederick Dellenbaugh writes of camping at a rocky pool and of being told by an Indian named Chuar that Indians believed that the water-pocket was a "favourite haunt of witches. These were often troublesome and had to be driven away or they might hurt one." Maj. Clarence Dutton described it as a weird spot with "jagged masses of black lava still protruding through rusty, decaying cinders . . . The pool itself might well be deemed the abode of witches . . ."

Ref.: 41, p. 251; 47, p. 84. Maps: C-5; E-20.

## WOLFHOLE

El.: 4600'     Loc.: Mohave 1, E-2.3

Shivwits: *Shina-bitz-spits*, "coyote spring"

Maj. John Wesley Powell translated the Indian word for *coyote* as *wolf* when he named this spring.

P.O. est. July 3, 1918. Dexter M. Parker, p.m. Discont. April 20, 1927.

Ref.: Barnes; 122, p. 202, Plate XI; P.O. Records. Maps: C-12; GH-6; GH-8.

**a.n. Wolfhole Dry Lake**     Mohave

## WONSITS PLATEAU

El.: c. 4000'     Loc.: Mohave 2, AB-2-3

Uinkarets: *Wonsits Tiravu*, "Antelope Plain"

Frederick Dellenbaugh noted that Maj. John Wesley Powell used a translation of the Uinkarets name for this area in giving it a name. Antelope were the chief source of large game food for the Piutes. Antelope existed in great herds at the time that Powell's party went through, but the animals have since vanished.

Ref.: 41, pp. 254-255; 70, p. 37. Maps: C-3; C-4 (Wonsits Tiravu).

## YUCCA

El.: 2000'     Loc.: Mohave 5, E-1.6

Pro.: /yʌkə/

There is a particularly fine stand of Joshua tree type of yucca in this area. The settlement of Yucca is a small town just off the main highway.

The yucca (*yucca arvorescens*) which is sometimes called the "Joshua tree," grows prolifically near Yucca and increasingly so in the White Hills to the southeast. During the days when mines were active in the White Hills and Gold Basin areas, yucca wood was used for fuel to operate the hoists.

P.O. est. August 28, 1905. Louis Janc, p.m. Wells Fargo Station, 1885.

Ref.: Harris; 62, p. 15; P.O. Records. Map: GH-14.

# ARIZONA PLACE NAMES

# NAVAJO COUNTY

*Hopi mesa and farmers — Navajo weaver — Mormon farmers with their first dam.*

## NAVAJO COUNTY:

Pro.: /nǽvəho/

Navajo County has an area of 6,343,040 acres which is laid off in a fifty-mile-wide stretch two hundred twenty-five miles long. Holbrook *(q.v.)* is the county seat. Navajo, a part of the original Apache County, became an entity on March 21, 1895. The enactment of the bill followed a two months' fight, with the bill being held up by a filibuster. It finally passed within a few moments of adjournment on the last day of the session. Will C. Barnes, author of the bill, is responsible for the name being Navajo instead of Colorado County.

The name Navajo has been interpreted in several ways. Currently it is thought that the word derives from *nava,* "field," and *ajo,* a Spanish suffix indicating that the article in question is small. Thus Navajo may mean a somewhat worthless field. Early Spaniards along the Rio Grande were familiar with the term *Apachu* ("strangers") and *de Nabahu* ("of the cultivated fields"). In writing they changed the "h" to "j" for Navajo and the "u" into the current "e" of *Apache.* A pueblo ruin of pre-Spanish period known to the Tewa Indians as Navahu was found in the northwest corner of New Mexico. The man who found these ruins and investigated them (Hewett) conjectured that the term *Apachu de Navahu* referred to a band which invaded the Tewa area at this spot, hence the name.

The principal industries of Navajo County include lumbering, farming, livestock raising, trading with the Indians, and the producing of Indian crafts.

# ADAIR

El.: c. 5000'          Loc.: Navajo 3, G-5.5
George Bagnall, a shoemaker, lived here in what was called Bagnall Hollow (sec. 21, T. 10 N, R. 21 E) from about 1881 to 1885. When Bagnall left, Aaron Adair moved into the locality where he planned to farm. The nature of the country was such that local people began calling the place Fools Hollow, since only a fool would attempt to farm there. However, it was not long before a settlement became established, taking the name Adair. It has since vanished.
P.O. est. December 4, 1899. Jesse D. Brady, p.m. Discont. July 14, 1906.
Ref.: Barnes. Maps: B-9; C-10.

**a.n. Adair Spring**      Loc.: Feeds into lake at Lakeside    Navajo
This springs flows at the rate of one million gallons daily.
Ref.: 4, p. 450.

**Adair Wash**      Loc.: Sec. 12, T. 9 N., R. 21 E.      Navajo

# AGATHLA NEEDLE

El.: 6825'          Loc.: Navajo 1, F-3
Pro.: /ʔaghassáˇ/      Navajo: "much wool"
Heading toward Utah, a traveler entering Monument Valley finds the landscape dominated by a great black igneous needle. Kit Carson called it El Capitan because it commands the entrance to the valley. The needle towers fifteen hundred feet above the surrounding landscape. At the base of a volcanic shaft, according to the Navajo Bead Chant, Indians once killed a herd of antelope and set about cleaning the hides to make clothing. According to the story, so many hides were scraped against the rock that it became known as "The Place of Wool and Hair." It is possible that this rock was Agathla.

**v.n. Lana Negra** (Macomb, 1860 map) (Spanish: "black wool")
Ref.: Burcard; 65, p. 18; 73, p. 205; 96, p. 6; 166, p. 51; 167, p. 53. Maps: C-10; D-4; GI-4.

**a.n. El Capitan Flat**      Map: GI-5      Navajo
**El Capitan Wash**      Maps: GI-4; GI-5      Navajo

# APACHE BUTTE

El.: c. 4000'          Loc.: Navajo 2, D-11.5
Pro.: /əpǽčí/
Will C. Barnes named this butte. It was here in 1883 that Barnes and J. W. Benham had trouble with Mexican sheep herders. Help arrived at the critical moment.
Ref.: Barnes. Maps: C-9; GI-11.

# APACHE, FORT

El.: 5600'          Loc.: Navajo 3, H-11
Pro.: /əpǽčí/
In 1870 Maj. John Green, the commanding officer of Camp Goodwin (q.v., Graham) selected a new camp site which he believed would avoid the malaria prevalent at the older camp. The new post was established under the name of Camp Ord on May 16, 1870, with Green in charge. Originally named Ord in honor of Gen. Edward Otho Cresap Ord (d. July 22, 1883), it was changed on August 1, 1870, to Camp Mogollon, possibly because of its location on a mesa surrounded by hills running to the plateau which forms the first line of Mogollon range. The second name had the distinction of lasting six weeks, giving way on September 12 to Camp Thomas, probably after Maj. Gen. George Henry Thomas (d. March 28, 1870). This name too was destined to be shortlived, for as the camp gradually developed from a raw state to the status of a permanent military post, another name was applied on February 2, 1871, when the place was designated Camp Apache. Its location, only a mile away from the headquarters of the soon-to-be established Indian reservation, bespeaks the fact that the post lay in the heart of the Apache country and justly earned its new name. During the Indian fighting era, the camp was in a commanding position between the areas occupied by Apaches and Navajos. The final change in name came on April 5, 1879, with the shift from Camp to Fort Apache. The fort entered civilian life in 1924 when it was turned over to the Indian Service for use as a school.
P.O. est. as Camp Apache February 8, 1873. John A. Meredith, p.m. Changed to Fort Apache, August 13, 1879. Frank Staples, p.m.
Ref.: 22, p. 142; 75, pp. 123, 147; 38, p. 165, (Note 7); 111, p. 156; 105, p. 97; 175, III, 218; *Weekly Arizona Miner,* February 25, 1871, 2:3; *Tucson Citizen,* February 8, 1873, 3:2; *Tucson Citizen,* December 10, 1870, 3:5. Maps: A-7; C-2; GD-6.

# APACHE, FORT, INDIAN RESERVATION

El.: c. 6000'          Loc.: Navajo 3, GH-10
Pro.: /əpǽčí/
Maj. John Green of Fort Apache reported in 1870 on the feasibility of setting up a reservation for the various Apache tribes. As a result, the Fort Apache Indian Reservation was established by Executive Order November 9, 1871, for the Arivaipa, Chiricahua, Coyotero, Mimbreno, Mogollon, Pinaleno, and Tsiltaden Apaches, with 1,681,920 acres being set aside for their use. There was no political unity among these tribes, and even within them there were subdivisions of local groups, each led by its own chief. As many as thirty households, usually related by marriage or by membership in a clan, made up a local group. The failure of the government to recognize that such groups might well be hostile and better kept apart led to trouble when attempts were made to herd them onto the reservation without regard for ancient enmities and customs. Today the old group distinctions have nearly vanished.

Headquarters for the reservation was located at Camp Apache, on the opposite side of the White River from Fort Apache. Today the headquarters and the adjacent community are known as Whiteriver. Part of the reservation was separated to form the San Carlos Indian Reservation by Executive Order of a later date.
Ref.: 88, II, 374; 28, p. 155. Maps: C-2 (White River Indian Reservation); C-10 (Fort Apache Indian Reservation).

# ARIPINE

El.: 6500'          Loc.: Navajo 3, B-8
A Mormon settlement, begun in 1883, this locality was first called Joppa at the suggestion of Mrs. Lucy O. Flake. For some years there was no activity here. New settlers

brought a new name into use through the combination of the first three letters of Arizona, plus the fact that the settlement was located at the edge of pine timberland.
P.O. est. as Joppa, May 28, 1912. Mrs. Lucy O. Flake, p.m. Discont. May 15, 1913. Re-est. as Aripine August 25, 1922. Grace M. Turley, p.m.
Ref.: 102, p. 12; 167, p. 148. Maps: B-9; C-12 (Joppa); C-13.

## AWATOBI

El.: c. 6000'                       Loc.: Navajo 1, E-15
Pro.: /àwat?owbíˆ/        Hopi: "high place of the bow people"
The Hopi name Awatobi indicates that the Bow Clan lived here. The name was first applied by Fewkes. Today drifting sands cover this site, but when Pedro de Tobar and Lopez de Cardenas of Coronado's expedition in 1540 first visited this Hopi village, Awatobi was an active community. That it was an important place is attested by the fact that on August 20, 1629, Fr. Francisco de Porras—accompanied by Andres Gutierrez, Cristobal de la Concepcion, and Francisco de San Buenaventura—started a Franciscan mission here. In honor of the saint's day on which the mission was begun, it was named San Bernardino. The Hopis resisted the attempt at Christianization and also the oppression practiced by the Spaniards, this resulting in 1629 in the poisoning of Fr. Porras.
Efforts to Christianize the Indians continued until the great Hopi uprising of 1680, at which time the population of Awatobi was about eight hundred. Fr. Figueroa was murdered and no further attempts at missionary work occurred until about 1700 when Fr. Garaycoechea baptized seventy-three people at Awatobi. The community was friendly to the missionaries, although no mission was re-established. Hopis from Walpi and Mishongnovi, alarmed by this friendliness toward the Spaniards, in November 1700 attacked Awatobi at night, killing most of its inhabitants. Awatobi as a town ceased to exist as of that night.
v.n. St. Bernardo          (San Bernards)
Ref.:    MNA; Director of Peabody Museum, *Franciscan Atatovi.*
    **Aguato, Ahuato, Zaguato** (Espejo, 1583);
    **Zuguato** (Hinton, 1878) **Talla-Hogan** (Mindeleff, 1886)
    Talahogan ("house at the water"): The name comes from the fact that a hogan was located at Talahogan Spring close to Awatobi Spring. The flow of water is such that the area has supported cliff dwellers, Hopis and Navajos at different times.
Ref.:    Bartlett; 54, p. 617; 11, p. 51; 71, pp. 134, 154, 190, 195; 88, I, 119, 120, 561. Maps: D-1; D-4; E-11.
a.n. Awatobi Mesa                                       Navajo

## AZANSOSI MESA

El.: c. 7000'                       Loc.: Navajo 1, BD-1-2
Pro.: /asdᶎã:ts?ósí/        Navajo: "slim woman"
Herbert Gregory gave the name Azansosi to the mesa in honor of Mrs. John (Louisa) Wetherill, who with her husband established the first trading post in this locality. The Navajos called Mrs. Wetherill "Asthonsosie", ("slender woman") of which Gregory's name may be considered a phonetic corruption.
v.n. Asthonsosie Mesa
Ref.: 71, p. 47. Maps: D-1; D-4.

## BAKABI

El.: 6583'                          Loc.: Navajo 1, B-12
Pro.: /bá:kavwiˆ/        Hopi: "place of the jointed reed"
Hotevilla (q.v.), a Hopi town, was established in 1906, a year noted for the severity of its winter. One group of dissidents who had left Oraibi (q.v.) to found Hotevilla wished to return at the end of the first difficult year to the mother village of Oraibi, but on being refused admittance, they settled near Hotevilla and founded their own settlement, calling it Bakabi.
v.n. Bacabi
    Bacovi
    Bacobi
Ref.:    Hopi Constitution; 4, p. 412; 29, p. 47; 81, p. 7; 167, p. 7. Maps: D-4; D-1; C-12.
a.n. Bakavi Springs          Loc.: At Bakabi          Navajo

## BARDGEMAN WASH

El.: c. 6000'                       Loc.: Navajo 2, C-5.5
Joe Bardgeman dug a well here c. 1888. He ran cattle, a fact which roused the ire of Navajos who considered the range theirs. Herbert Gregory noted that the wells consisted of two holes, "each about 6 feet deep." The wash takes its name from the wells.
Ref.: 71, pp. 39, 161. Map: D-1 (Bargeman Wells).

## BEAR SPRINGS

El.: c. 5500'     Loc.: Navajo 2, H-11. T. 11 N., R. 17 E.
This name is derived from the fact that a bear was roped and killed here during a roundup in the middle 1880's.
Ref.: Barnes. Map: None.

## BEGASHIBITO

El.: c. 6000'                       Loc.: Navajo 1, AB-4-5
Pro.: /bégašibəto?/        Navajo: *begashi,* "cow"
                                                *bito,* "water"
Cows water here.
v.n. Bako-shi-gito
    Beki-shibito
Ref.: 71, p. 190. Maps: D-1; D-4.
a.n. Begashibito Brook                                   Navajo
Ref.: 71, p. 92.
    Begashibito Valley                                  Navajo
Ref.: 71, p. 42.

## BETATAKIN

El.: c. 7500'                       Loc.: Navajo 1, CD-5
Pro.: /ᶀitát?ahkin/        Navajo: "house on the edge;
                                            side hill house"
In the three hundred sixty acre tract of the Navajo National Monument (cf. Navajo Mountain, Coconino) are three spectacular cave pueblos. Of these, the most accessible to the casual visitor is Betatakin. The initial view of the ruin from the Sandal Trail along the canyon rim, at Betatakin Point, is breath-taking. Far below and set well back in a wind-carved cave large enough to house our nation's capitol rests a magnificent two hundred room cliff dwelling. It is estimated to be seven centuries old and is the second largest ruin in Navajo National Monument. It

is so remote that it was not seen by a white man until 1909 when John Wetherill and Dr. Byron Cummings visited it. The canyon in which it is located is referred to both as Betatakin Canyon and as the Tsegi branch of Laguna Canyon.

**v.n. kin Lani** ("many houses") old Navajo name.

P.O. est. January 6, 1932. Mrs. Elizabeth C. Rorick, p.m. Discont. February 28, 1934 (presumably at the monument headquarters).

Ref.: 71, p. 190; 167, p. 140; 5, Jim and Sally Brewer, "Navajo National Monument," pp. 3, 4; 4, pp. 422, 38. Map: GI-11.

**a.n. Sandal Trail**
This is a path marked by sandal tracks painted on the bare rocks.

## BIDAHOCHI BUTTE

El.: c. 6700'     Loc.: Navajo 2, GH-5
Pro.: /bidÁho·čiy˘:ʔ/     Navajo: "many red streaks up its slope"

From 1888 to 1892, Julius Wetzler had a trading post here. Behind the store on the mountain is the red scar of a rock slide, hence the name. Gradually the name has come to include the valley and nearby pueblo ruins.

**v.n. Biddehoche**
   **Bita Hache**
   **Bitahochee**
   **Biddahoochee**
   **Bitahotsi**

Ref.: 71, pp. 153, 190; 88, p. 149. Maps: D-1; D-6.

**a.n. Bidahochi Spring** (cf. Indian Wells). Map: D-4     Navajo

## BIG DRY WASH

El.: c. 6000'     Loc.: Navajo 3, A-2-1;
Navajo 2, AC-14-10; Coconino 5, HF-13-14

On July 17, 1882, Indian scouts and troops finally caught up with Apaches who had escaped from the San Carlos Reservation and gone on a series of raids against settlers. Five troops of cavalry—massed from Fort Whipple, Camp Verde, and Fort Apache—encountered the half hundred Indians on what the official report called "Big Dry Wash or Chevelon's Fork." Capt. George M. Wheeler had used the name Big Dry Fork in 1871.

The battle lasted four hours and proved to be the last major Indian battle in Arizona, excepting lesser guerilla trouble with Geronimo a few years later. The place of the battle is sometimes called Battleground Ridge.

Ref.: 175, III, 587; 85, p. 447; 127, p. 6. Maps: B-2 (Chevelon's Fork Canyon); C-7; C-12.

**a.n. Clear Creek** Map: GD-11     Coconino
In 1851 this stream was called Big Dry Fork by Capt. Lorenzo Sitgreaves. A camp for travelers existed at Big Dry Fork Crossing. To differentiate this part of the stream from the Clear Creek on the Verde slope, the former is referred to as East Clear Creek, whereas lower in its course it is called Clear Creek. The names are descriptive.

Ref.: Barnes.

   **Clear Canyon** Map: B-9     Coconino

## BIG MOUNTAIN

El.: 7000'     Loc.: Navajo 3, H-8
Descriptive.

Ref.: None. Maps: C-12; D-3.

**a.n. Big Canyon** Loc.: Sec. 19, T. 7 N., R. 22 E.     Navajo

## BILLIE CREEK

El.: c. 5000'     Loc.: Navajo 3, IH-7-6
Billie Scorse, after whom this creek was named, was an eccentric Englishman who lived on its banks for several years.

Ref.: Barnes. Map: B-9.

## BIRD SPRINGS

El.: c. 5000'     Loc.: Navajo 2, A-7
Pro.: /tsídiy˘:toʔí/     Navajo: tsidiito i "bird spring"

Navajos traveling between the Moqui Butte country and Leupp used this spring as an outstanding landmark and watering place until the development of watering facilities by the Indian Service reduced its importance.

Ref.: 167, p. 9. Map: None.

## BLACK CANYON

El.: c. 7500'     Loc.: Navajo 3, A-5
Descriptive. The view of this canyon from the valley below gives an impression of a black line.

Ref.: Barnes. Maps: B-7; B-9.

## BLACK MESA

El.: 7000'     Loc.: Navajo 1, G-10-11
Descriptive. The "fingers" of this roughly hand-shaped mesa form the Hopi Mesas on which the Hopi Villages lie. Actually, Black Mesa is like a huge "island"—two hundred fifty miles in circumference—which rises about two thousand feet above the surrounding plain. Capt. John G. Walker in 1858 referred to it as Mesa de las Vacas (Spanish: "cows' mesa") in his report to the War Department.

**v.n. Black Mountain**

Ref.: 16, p. 58; 166, p. 106; 167, p. 10. Maps: C-4; D-1; E-20 (Mesa la Vaca).

## BLUE CANYON

El.: c. 6000'     Loc.: Navajo 1, AB-10
Pro.: bikʰoh: hodowətʔež/     Navajo: Bikoo hodo tl izh, "blue canyon"

The name Blue Canyon scarcely does justice to the huge pale blue pillars and striped sides of this canyon, where magnificently sculptured blue formations rise abruptly from the broad canyon floor.

The first school for the western Navajo country was started in this vicinity in 1895 under the jurisdiction of Maj. Constant Williams, Acting Navajo Agent.

**v.n. Dot-Klish Canyon**
   **Boo-koo-dot-klish**

Ref.: MNA; 71, pp. 88, 190, 191; 167, p. 13. Maps: C-12; D-4.

## BOUCHE'S FORK

El.: c. 6000'                          Loc.: Navajo 3, FG-4-1
                                       Navajo 2, H-14-13
Origin not discovered to date.
**v.n. Silver Creek**          Map: C-5
Ref.:   None. Maps: C-1; E-10; E-11; E-12.
**a.n. Bouche's Mesa**          Map: E-10                Navajo

## BRIGHAM CITY

El.: c. 3000'                          Loc.: Navajo 2, AB-9
Five Mormon communities were destined to develop from
the arrival of a party of emigrants on March 24, 1876, in
the vicinity of the present Joseph City (q.v.). One member
of that party was Jesse O. Ballinger. With a small group he
established Ballinger's Camp, or Ballinger. In September,
1878, the name was changed to Brigham City after the
Mormon leader, Brigham Young. Soon there was a flourishing colony of nearly three hundred people, some of
whom operated a grist mill which had been donated by
Mormons in Utah for the use of the new colonies on the
Little Colorado River. However, things did not go well and
by 1881 the settlement had been broken up with the permission of the Mormon church. By 1890 only one family
remained at the site.
P.O. est. April 10, 1878. James T. Woods, p.m. Discont. May
5, 1882.
Ref.:   Richards; 112, p. 146; 171, pp. 1, 2. Maps: C-4; E-20.

## BROOKBANK CANYON

El.: c. 6000'                          Loc.: Navajo 3, A-5
J. W. Brookbank settled here in 1884, later moving to Holbrook.
Ref.:   Richards. Map: B-9.
**a.n. Brookbank Point**          Map: B-7                Navajo

## BRUSH MOUNTAIN

El.: c. 6000'                          Loc.: Navajo 3, A-8.2
Descriptive. In some places in Arizona the brush is so
thick that a rabbit couldn't get through on its hands and
knees. "Brushy" or "brush" are often used in place names.
A few are listed below.
Ref.:   None. Map: B-7.

| a.n. Brushy Canyon | Map: GD-2 | Gila |
| Brushy Hollow | Maps: GD-2; GD-7 | Gila |
| Brushy Top Mountain | Map: B-7 | Gila |
| Brushy Mountain | Map: B-9 | Apache |
| Brushy Mountain Spring | Map: B-9 | Apache |
| Brushy Can | Map: GB-9 | Cochise |
| Brushy Canyon | Map: GB-22 | Cochise |
| Brushy Creek | Map: GB-5 | Cochise |
| Brushy Basin | Map: B-7 | Maricopa |
| Brushy Basin Canyon | Map: GD-2 | Gila |
| Brushy Basin Spring | Map: B-7 | Maricopa |
| Brushy Mountain | Map: B-7 | Maricopa |
| Brushy Spring | Map: GK-12 | Maricopa |
| Brush Mountain | Map: B-7 | Navajo |

## BUCKSKIN WASH

El.: c. 6000'                          Loc.: Navajo 3, BC-4
In 1879 Lehi Heward (b. August 7, 1851; d. December 2,
1926) moved to Arizona, settling in St. Joseph. He hauled
freight to the settlement from Albuquerque, N.M. In 1883
he moved to this wash near Heber, which takes its name
from the fact that Heward dressed in buckskins. Here he
lived until 1887 when he moved to Pine and later to Tuba
City, still later establishing a homestead on Dry Lake
(c. 1906), where he lived until 1925.
Ref.:   Glenn Heward, Letter, 1956. Maps: B-9; C-13.

## BURRO SPRINGS

El.: c. 6000'                          Loc.: Navajo 2, B-2
The origin of this name has not been learned.
Availability of water has always been the key to travel in
Arizona. This fact formerly made Burro Springs impor-
tant, for the spring was known to travelers on the Winslow-
Oraibi road. Sinking tanks in the rock and covering the
water supply with poles insured its permanence and pota-
bility.
Ref.:   71, p. 142. Maps: C-12; D-4.

## CANYON BUTTE

El.: c. 5000'                          Loc.: Navajo 2, C-11
Capt. George M. Wheeler in 1873 spoke of this butte as
being a "conspicuous basaltic cone" having a number of
small canyons near its base, from whence came the name
of the butte itself.
Ref.:   175, III, 638, 647. Maps: C-3; E-18, E-11.

## CARR LAKE

El.: c. 5500'                          Loc.: Navajo 2, HI-11-12
E. W. Carr had a dam here in 1899. There is no longer a
lake, since the area which was dammed up has filled in.
Ref.:   Branch; Grigsby. Map: GI-8.
**a.n. Carr Lake Draw**          Map: GI-8                Navajo

## CHAISTLA BUTTE

El.: c. 6800'                          Loc.: Navajo 1, F-3
                                       Navajo: "beaver pocket"
Descriptive.
**v.n. Cha-ez-kia**
Ref.:   71, pp. 152, 191. Map: GI-4.

## CHAKPAHU

El.: c. 6000'          Loc.: Navajo 2, FG-1. In Jadito Valley.
                                       Hopi: "little water"
Descriptive.
In 1901 archaeologists undertook work on this large ruin
which is on the mesa rim, northwest side of the valley.
Ref.:   80, pp. 18, 19, 20; 88, I, 564. Map: None.

## CHEDISKI MOUNTAIN

El.: c. 6000'                          Loc.: Navajo 3, B-7
Pro.: /tsédezˢʔ ay/          Apache: "solid object that juts out"
                          or "white mountain that sits back alone"
Descriptive. This is one of the few Apache place names
used by non-Indians.
Ref.:   Davis; Uplegger. Maps: B-7; D-3.

## CHEVELON CREEK

El.: c. 5000′      Loc.: Navajo 2, CA-10.1-14
Pro.: /čévələn/
Early maps show Chevalon Fork to the east of Big Dry Wash (q.v.), but the name gradually shifted until Chevelon Creek (or Fork) is now synonymous with the old Big Dry Wash. Capt. Lorenzo Sitgreaves, on October 2, 1851, wrote that the stream got its name from that of a trapper called Chevalon who died after eating some poisonous root along its banks. The name is spelled in various ways, some used herein.

This same stream was also known as East Clear Creek. Here in July 1882 Apaches planned to roll boulders down on pursuing soldiers, but Al Sieber's scouts discovered the ambush and avoided it. Capt. Adna Romanza Chaffee had his men cross the canyon and surround the Indians.

v.n. Shevlon
     Chevlon Creek
Ref.: 111, p. 117; 150, p. 7; 4, p. 457; 22, p. 145. Maps: B-9; C-4; C-9; C-13.
a.n. Chevlon's Butte    El.: 5230′. Maps: C-6; C-7    Coconino
     Chevelon Butte        (same)

## CHILCHINBITO (SPRING)

El.: c. 6500′      Loc.: Navajo 1, F-8
Pro.: /tsiy˘ščinbi:ʔtó/    Navajo: "water in the sumacs"
The sumac growing around this spring is the kind used by Navajo women in basketry.

When John and Louisa Wetherill were considering building a trading post, they were urged by an old Navajo to build at Chilchinbito, but they did not do so. It was here that Piutes pursuing a Navajo were themselves ambushed. Their bones are now used in the Enemy Chant, or the War or Squaw Dance.

v.n. Bitterweed Springs
Ref.: 65, p. 77; 167, p. 38. Map: C-10.
a.n. Chilchinbito Canyon               Navajo
     Chilchinbito Creek             Navajo

## CHUCK BOX LAKE

El.: c. 6000′      Loc.: Navajo 3, B-7
Cowboys on a roundup far from headquarters take a chuck wagon along. At this lake in about 1887 or 1888 the Waters Cattle Company's range foreman found the going so tough that the chuck box had to be unpacked and abandoned. Another story is that Capt. George Nice, first Indian Service Ranger on the Fort Apache Indian Reservation, kept a supply box here.

Ref.: Barnes; Davis. Maps: B-7; D-3.

## CHURCH ROCK

El.: c. 7000′      Loc.: Navajo 1, G-4
The igneous lava plug which is Church Rock rises abruptly from the valley floor. The name is descriptive.
Ref.: 71, p. 37; 167, p. 121. Map: D-1.

## CIBECUE CREEK

El.: 5200′      Loc.: Navajo 3, C-8-7
Pro.: /cíʾbisuw/    Apache: "reddish bottom land"
It was at an old Indian village on Cibicu (sic) Creek in the late summer of 1881 that serious trouble arose among the

Coyotero Apaches. A medicine man, Nokay Delklinne (also spelled Nock-e-da-klin-ny), conducted ghost dances of increasing frenzy. He was promising the Apaches to raise their leader Diablo from the dead. Diablo would then lead them in victory against the white man. Rumors of an impending uprising led Col. Eugene Asa Carr with six officers, seventy-nine soldiers, and twenty-three Indian scouts to attempt the arrest of Nokay Delklinne at Cibicu on August 30, 1881. Opposed were more than three hundred hysterically excited Indians who stood by while their medicine man submitted to arrest. While Carr was making camp, his own Indian scouts turned against him and opened fire. Capt. Edmund C. Hentig was killed immediately. The troops retreated down the creek, but before the battle ended, ten privates had been killed. Forty-seven Apaches were taken prisoner. Three of the mutinying Indian scouts were hanged at Fort Grant on March 3, 1882; two others were sent to Alcatraz.

Carr apparently was responsible for applying the name "Cibicu" to the place of battle, having gotten the name from an Apache.

Currently Cibecue has a store, a school and Apache dwellings. This community is about two and a half miles north of the site of the battle.

P.O. est. March 18, 1910. Agnes M. Chambers, p.m.
Ref.: Uplegger; Davis; 4, p. 465; 39, p. 111; 111, pp. 232, 233; 157, p. 125. Maps: B-7; C-2; E-18; GD-1.

## CLAY SPRINGS

El.: c. 6000′      Loc.: Navajo 3, E-5
This spring emerges from a clay bank.
P.O. est. March 12, 1917. Dora Petersen, p.m.
Ref.: Barnes. Maps: B-9; C-12.

## CLY BUTTE

El.: 5789′      Loc.: Navajo 1, H-1
An old Navajo chief, Cly, died in 1934 and was buried at the foot of the butte which bears his name. Navajo custom calls for all of a man's possessions to be destroyed at his death, so Cly's horse, sheep, goats and cattle were killed and his saddle destroyed at this place.
Ref.: 96, pp. 117-118. Map: GI-1.

## COMA-A SPRING

El.: c. 6000′      Loc.: Navajo 2, B-3.5
It was at this spring in the 1880's that the Hopis, on the insistence of their Indian agent, said they would settle to prevent the Navajos from taking over the Hopi reservation. The Navajos burned the Hopi houses, the ruins of which may still be seen.

Although the water from the spring is not good, at one time it probably served a large population as evidenced by the extensive prehistoric ruins in the area.

v.n. Comar Spring (Springs)
     Kaibito
Ref.: Colton; 71, pp. 191, 137, 153. Maps: C-9; D-4.

## COOLEY MOUNTAIN

El.: c. 7000'                    Loc.: Navajo 3, H-5.5
Corydon E. Cooley (d. March 18, 1917) was a scout at
Camp Apache in 1872. He had a ranch well-known to
travelers (cf. McNary, Apache) where the road forked,
one branch going to Horsehead Crossing near the present-
day Holbrook, and the other toward what is now Springerville.
Ref.:   22, p. 178; Barnes. Map: B-9.

## CORDUROY CREEK

El.: c. 5000'                    Loc.: Navajo 3, G-7
In 1880 troops from Fort Apache put logs along the edge
of the creek, making a corduroy road.
Ref.:   Barnes. Map: D-3.

## DEBEBEKID LAKE

El.: c. 5000'                    Loc.: Navajo 1, E-8
Pro.: /dibebibe?ek?id/          Navajo: "sheep lake"
Descriptive. A Navajo sheep watering place.
v.n. Te-ye-ba-a-kit
Ref.:   7, p. 191. Maps: D-4; C-6 (Te-ye-ba-a-kit); C-12.

## DECKER WASH

El.: c. 6000'                    Loc.: Navajo 3, D-4
Z. B. Decker, a Mormon, ran sheep here in the 1880's.
Ref.:   Barnes. Map: A-7.

## DEER SPRING MOUNTAIN

El.: c. 3000'                    Loc.: Navajo 3, H-8.5
A spring at the foot of this mountain was used by deer.
Ref.:   Cone Webb. Map: D-3.
a.n. Deer Creek          Map: GD-6                    Gila

## DIGGER CREEK

El.: c. 6000'                    Loc.: Navajo 2, I-7
Bands of wild horses used to dig for water, found here
about eighteen inches beneath the surface. Twenty or thirty
men in this region owned about ten mares each. The mares
roamed the wide open range and within a few years there
were huge herds of wild ponies. Smarter in their own way
than emigrants, who not infrequently died of thirst along
this route, the wild horses could be seen teaching their
offspring to dig for water.
v.n. Digger Wash
Ref.:   Branch; Grigsby. Map: GI-11.

## DILKON

El.: c. 7000'                    Loc.: Navajo 2, E-5-6
Pro.: /čéžindĩlko:hi/           Navajo: "smooth black rock"
Dropping the first part of the Navajo name resulted in
Dilkon. This is a location which seems to have changed
its name as often as it changed hands. Because of a nearby solitary desert landmark, it was first known as Castle
Butte, described as having a resemblance to a "ruined
medieval stronghold, having a causeway flanked by towers,
above which [loom] embattlements and casements."

The name was changed to Stiles when a cattleman, J. Barnett (Barney) Stiles, operated a trading post intermittently
here. In 1914 McPherson C. Maddox opened the first post
office, naming it for himself. The next owner was Justus
W. Bush, who in 1919 applied the name Dilcon (sic), taking it from a translation of the Navajo name for the butte
back of the store.
P.O. est. January 15, 1914. McPherson C. Maddox, p.m.
Changed to Castle Butte, September 25, 1916. Changed to
Dilkon, December 17, 1920. Discont. January 13, 1943.
Ref.:   Richards; MNA; 71, pp. 137, 140; 167, p. 50; 36, p. 58.
        Maps: C-6 (Castle Butte); C-13 (Dilkon).
a.n. Chimney Butte                                   Navajo
    Descriptive; highest landmark in the vicinity.

## DINNEBITO

El.: c. 6000'                    Loc.: Navajo 1, AB-12-13
Pro.: /ḍinéḅitó?/               Navajo: dine, "people";
                                bito, "water; spring"
Descriptive.
v.n. Denabito
    Denebito
    Tinebito
Ref.:   71, pp. 154, 191; 167, p. 50. Maps: D-4; C-12.
a.n. Dinnebito Wash      Map: GI-11                   Navajo
Ref.:   71, p. 38.

## DODSON WASH

El.: c. 6000'                    Loc.: Navajo 3, EG-4-2.3
Rube Dodson, a Mormon, was a cattleman and farmer
who used this canyon in the 1880's.
Ref.:   Barnes. Map: B-9.

## ECHO CAVE RUIN

El.: c. 5600'                    Loc.: Navajo 1, G-2
In this cave, in Monument Valley, the echo consists of
from "eight to sixteen separate echoes, the number depending upon the weather." Extensive Indian ruins are in this
cave.
Ref.:   96, pp. 118-119. Map: GI-1.

## EGLOFFSTEIN BUTTE

El.: c. 5500'                    Loc.: Navajo 2, DE-3
Frederick F. W. von Egloffstein was a topographer with
Lt. Joseph C. Ives' expedition in 1858.
Ref.:   71, p. 191; 121, p. 21. Map: C-12.

## FIRST HOLLOW

El.: c. 6000'                    Loc.: Navajo 3, H-7
This is one of four parallel, short canyons which enter Big
Canyon. They were named by cattlemen who trailed cattle
from the R-14 Ranch (q.v., Gila) to McNary.
Ref.:   Barnes; Davis. Map: B-9.
a.n. Second Hollow       Map: D-3                     Navajo
    Third Hollow         Map: D-3                     Navajo
    Fourth Hollow        Map: D-3                     Navajo

## FIRST KNOLL

El.: c. 6000'          Loc.: Navajo 3, H-6
James Flake gave this name to the solitary knoll first encountered en route from Snowflake to Holbrook. Those he called "Second" and "Third" apparently were never mapped.

Ref.: Barnes. Map: B-9.

## FIRST MESA

El.: c. 6000'          Loc.: Navajo 1, E-14
This is the first of the Hopi Mesas encountered when one is traveling from New Mexico toward the west. In 1858 Lt. Joseph Christmas Ives recorded what was probably the first visit for an American citizen to this mesa which, however, had been known to the Spaniards since 1540.

Ref.: 78, p. 6. Map: D-1.

**a.n. First Mesa Spring**          Navajo
Loc.: At base of First Mesa, sec. 14, T. 28 N., R. 18 W.
Ref.: 71, p. 155.

**Second Mesa**     Maps: D-1; C-12     Navajo
P.O. est. March 15, 1939. Noble O. Guthrie, p.m.

**Second Mesa Wash**          Navajo
Loc.: Tributary to First Mesa Wash
Ref.: 71, p. 39.

## FIVE BUTTES

El.: c. 6000'          Loc.: Navajo 2, H-7
Descriptive.

Ref.: Barnes. Maps: GI-11; C-12.

## FORESTDALE

El.: c. 6000'          Loc.: Navajo 3, FG-6.5
When Mormons first came into what is now southern Navajo County in late 1877, they settled at Forest Dale, inadvertently locating on Indian reservation land. Oscar Cluff was the first settler. He was joined by his brother Alfred who named the place in February 1878. By Christmas 1879 only three families were still living at the location, because others had left in fear of trouble with the Apaches over the ownership of the land. Gen. E. A. Carr of Fort Apache invited the Mormons to colonize, assuring them that Forest Dale was not on reservation land. When the Indians in May 1882 came to plant corn, their wrath brought on troubles which were solved by a treaty giving the Indians thirty acres. This was upset by the arrival of Lt. Charles Bare Gatewood (later to win fame in the campaign against Geronimo). Gatewood ordered the settlers to leave the area by the following spring, and before the summer of 1883, white men had deserted Forest Dale.
There are today a store and tourist accommodations at Forestdale

Ref.: 112, pp. 170, 172-173. Map: A-13.

**a.n. Forestdale Canyon**     Map: B-7     Navajo

## FRENCH BUTTE

Loc.: Navajo 2, D-7. S. of Castle Butte and s.e. of French Spring.
Franklin French, stockman and miner, married one of the widows of John D. Lee. The Frenches lived at Hardy Station (*See* Havre) twenty-four miles west of Holbrook, where they ran the section house. French spent much time prospecting in the Grand Canyon. He later moved to Winslow where he died.

Ref.: Barnes; 36, Map; 71, p. 153. Map: A-7.

**a.n. French Spring**     Loc.: 2 miles e. of French Butte     Navajo

## GIANT CHAIR

El.: c. 6500'          Loc.: Navajo 2, B-2
Descriptive. Hopis call this *Hoyapi*, "Big Hopi House." Hopis favor this location for catching eagles which they keep captive for their feathers.

Ref.: 29, p. 44; 71, p. 154; 167, pp. 65, 66. Maps: A-7; C-10; D-4.

## GOODWATER

El.: c. 5850'          Loc.: Navajo 2, H-8
Most well water in this region is salty. However, when Dick Grigsby's brother dug a well here in 1912, he found very good water. There is a trading post here.

Ref.: Branch; Grigsby. Map: GI-8.

## GRASSHOPPER

El.: c. 6000'          Loc.: Navajo 3, BC-7.8
(Head of Salt River Draw, Ft. Apache Res.)
Ruins as extensive as those at Point of Pines (*q.v.*, Gila) exist in the vicinity of Grasshopper. This place was named by stockmen because of the hordes of grasshoppers. It is a stockmen's station with an adobe house which was built in 1918 by a sheepman named Jaques.

Ref.: Davis. Map: D-3.

## GYPSUM CREEK

El.: c. 6000'          Loc.: Navajo 1, H-2
Barnes says there is a "huge bed of gypsum on this stream." Gregory notes that the water is totally unpalatable, but says nothing about the gypsum bed.

Ref.: 71, p. 49. Map: GI-1.

## HAVRE

El.: c. 5200'          Loc.: Navajo 2, C-11
Originally this section house was called Hardy after the man who was the first superintendent of telegraphing on the A. & P. R.R. The location of another place on the railroad by the same name caused a change from Hardy to Havre.

The ruins of pueblos built by the Patki, Kukuch, and Piba-Tabo (of the Hopi Kokop clan) are in this area.

Ref.: Barnes; 88, II, 902. Maps: C-12 (Hardy); C-13.

## HAYSTACK BUTTE

El.: c. 7000'          Loc.: Navajo 2, DE-6
Descriptive.

Ref.: Barnes. Maps: D-1; GI-11.

**a.n. Haystack Peak**     Map: C-12     Yuma

## HEBER

El.: c. 6000'                    Loc.: Navajo 3, BC-5
Pro.: /híyber/
The Mormon migration to Arizona in 1876 and 1877 drew two companies of emigrants from Arkansas. Destitute, some of these families were assigned to Little Colorado River settlements. John W. N. Scarlett was sent to Allen's Camp, but in 1883 he withdrew and founded Heber, which takes its name from that of Heber C. Kimball, Chief Justice of the State of Deseret in 1883. Today Heber is a thriving lumber community.

P.O. est. September 11, 1890. James E. Shelley, p.m.
Ref.:  Richards; 112, p. 155; 171, p. 4. Maps: B-7; C-7.

## HIGGINS TANK

El.: c. 5500'                    Loc.: Navajo 2, E-12
                                 S.w. of Holbrook 10 miles.
A horse rancher, J. M. Higgins, caught flood waters here by constructing a dirt tank c. 1888.

Ref.:  Barnes. Map: None.

## HOLBROOK

El.: 5080'                       Loc.: Navajo 2, FG-11
John W. Young in 1882 named a new railroad station Holbrook in honor of H. R. Holbrook.

Prior to the establishment of the new station, Young—a railroad contractor—had maintained headquarters in 1881 at a place two miles east of the future Holbrook. There was a little community at this earlier location prior to Young's arrival. Juan Padilla had built the first house immediately east of Horsehead Crossing (above the junction of the Puerco and Little Colorado Rivers) in 1871, but after a short time had put Berado Frayde in charge of his saloon. Since Frayde used only his first name, the place soon came to be known as Berado's. All comers—penniless or wealthy—found food at Berado's. A haphazard store keeper, Frayde priced every item at fifty cents, regardless of its true value. Berado's Station was the main crossing point for travelers to the south. This may account for the fact that Mormons built two additional stores at the location.

In 1881 the crews laying railroad tracks put down the first rails at Berado's, soon extending the track toward the west. A year later Holbrook came into being and Berado's began to disappear. Berado himself moved to Albuquerque. Gradually Horsehead Crossing disappeared and Holbrook grew in importance. Holbrook became the county seat in 1895. Today it is the supply point for numerous ranches and trading posts and is also the distribution point for mail to seventy-six post offices served via five Star Routes and one special routing, each community representing a post office off the main line railroad.

P.O. est. September 18, 1882. James H. Wilson, p.m. Wells Fargo Station, 1885.
Ref.:   112, p. 163; 167, p. 72; 87, p. 296; 4, p. 313; 29, p. 45; Richards; Grigsby; W. S. Hulet, Postmaster of Holbrook, Letter, 1956. Map: GI-11.

## HOMOLOBI

El.: c. 4000'      Loc.: Navajo 2, A-10. On n. side of Little
                              Colorado River at Winslow.
Pro.:   /howmówləowvi^/        Hopi:  "place of the breast-
                                       like elevations"
According to Hopi tribal history, "Homolobi" refers to the ruins of five towns which were abandoned when irrigation brought alkali to the surface and destroyed any hope of successful agriculture. The Mormons encountered the same difficulty with alkali when they irrigated lands in their settlements along the Little Colorado River.

Ref.:   88, p. 558; 111, pp. 6, 46. Map: None.

## HOP MOUNTAIN

El.: c. 7000'                    Loc.: Navajo 3, F-7
Wild hops grow abundantly in this region.
Ref.:   Barnes. Map: C-12.
**a.n. Hop Canyon**          Map: B-9                    Navajo

## HOPI BUTTES

El.: c. 6000'      Loc.: Navajo 2, H-5-6. Navajo 2, E-7-7.9
Pro.:   /hówpi^/
On September 7, 1857, Lt. Edward Fitzgerald Beale wrote of the conical points of these buttes, which he called Rabbit Hills. Another writer referred to them as Rabbit-Ear Butte, a descriptive name. Herbert Gregory made a plea for the return to their earlier Spanish name of Moqui Buttes, but transcribed it into the more acceptable use of Hopi for the name of the Indians. The Mexicans called these peaks Cerritos Azules, from which may have come the term "Blue Peaks" used on Macomb's map of 1860.

The Hopi Buttes are the scene each June of eagle hunting by men from some of the Hopi clans. The feathers are used in making prayer sticks.

Ref.:   *Masterkey,* 19:89-94, May 1945 (APHS); 4, p. 314; 12,
        p. 45; 36, p. 101; 71, p. 37, (Note 1); 167, p. 101. Maps:
        E-20; E-12 (Rabbit Hills).

## HOPI INDIAN RESERVATION

Loc.: Wholly surrounded by Navajo Indian Reservation.
                                 Includes Hopi Mesas.
Pro.:   /hówpi^/
An Indian agency was maintained for this area at Fort Defiance from 1869 to 1875. On December 16, 1882, land was specifically set aside for use by Hopi Indians, the assigned acreage being enlarged to the present 631,194 acres on January 8, 1900. About six hundred seventy-five families, consisting of approximately three thousand Hopis, are estimated to be more or less permanent residents on the reservation.

Ref.:   *Hopi Constitution;* 7, p. 547; 88, II, 374; "Annual Report
        of the Arizona Commission of Indian Affairs, 1954, 1955,
        1956," p. 9. Maps: C-5 (Moqui Indian Reservation);
        D-1.

## HOPI VILLAGES

El.: c. 6000'
Pro.: /hówpiˆ/          Hopi: *hopitu,* "the peaceful ones"

| Names | Location | Pronunciation |
|---|---|---|
| Awatobi (*q.v.*) | Navajo 1, E-15 | /awátʔowbíˆ/ |
| Bakabi (*q.v.*) | Navajo 1, B-12 | /báːkavwiˆ/ |
| Kawaioku (*q.v.*) | Navajo 2, F-1.5 | |
| Hotevilla (*q.v.*) | Navajo 1, AB-13 | /hówˆtvʷelə/ |
| Kuchaptuvela | Not known | |
| Polacca (*q.v.*) | Navajo 1, DE-14.5 | /pówlaˆkaka/ |
| Moenkopi | Coconino 2, D-11 | /mównəkapki/ or /mównkapi/ |
| Walpi (*q.v.*) | Navajo 1, DE-14.3 | /wálːəpiˆ/ |
| Mishongnovi (*q.v.*) | Navajo 1, C-14.5 | |
| | | r |
| Oraibi (*q.v.*) | Navajo 1, BC-12.9 | /owžᴀyviˆ/ |
| Sikyatki (*q.v.*) | Navajo 1, DE-14.3 | /siˆkⁱᴧpkiˆ/ |
| Sipaulovi (*q.v.*) | Navajo 1, E-14.5 | /šipówləviˆ/ or /sówlowəpaviˆ/ |
| Tewa (*q.v.*) | Navajo 1, DE-13.3 | /téowˆa/ |
| Shungopavi (*q.v.*) | Navajo 1, C-14 | /səmówwəpaviˆ/ |
| Sichomovi (*q.v.*) | Navajo 3, EF-1 | /sitówməoviˆ/ |

A barefooted friar, Marcos de Niza, was the first white man known to have seen the Hopi Villages. He first heard of their existence when word was sent back to him by the Negro Estevan that there were to the northwest wondrous cities with large houses several stories high. Estevan was, of course, referring to what the Spaniards called the Seven Cities of Cibola (the Zuñi villages of New Mexico), to the west of which lay the Hopi Villages.

Marcos de Niza hastened to catch up with his advance scout. On May 9, 1539, the friar entered the wilderness near the present-day Fort Apache Indian Reservation, and while in this region he was brought word of Estevan's death at the hands of the Indians. Fr. Marcos, attended only by a limited number of Indians, feared entering the Seven Cities alone. He viewed them from a distance, going from there to investigate reports of settlements to the west —the Hopi Villages—where it was rumored the inhabitants used implements of gold. Marcos de Niza was determined to see, if only from a distance, what the fabled province looked like, and this he did from the entrance of what is known today as the Jadito (or Jeddito) Valley.

Fr. Marcos soon returned to Mexico City. At once rumors sprang up about fabulous wealth to be had for the asking at the Seven Cities of Cibola. Within a matter of weeks, Viceroy Mendoza of Mexico was organizing an expedition. On February 23, 1540, a gala army, with Francisco Vasquez de Coronado at its head, took off for the wilds to the north. The adventurers had all the trappings of court—shining armor, vizored head-pieces, footmen carrying harquebuses; servants, tents, tons of supplies carried by a thousand horses and mules, and herds of sheep, swine and cattle to feed to the army en route. The going was rough and supplies dwindled rapidly. The shining armor was abandoned to rust by the wayside. Months later, on July 7, 1540, a dedraggled and discouraged band entered a Zuñi village. Here was the first of the dreamed about Seven Cities of Cibola, and as the culmination of a dream, the miserable town of stone and mud was a dismal failure. How the name Cibola came to be attached to the towns has not

definitely been established, but it is conjectured that it came from a word meaning "buffalo," and that buffalo may have roamed as far west as the Zuñi towns in the sixteenth century. Mexican natives may have used the name for the region because it was the only place in which they had seen buffalo, since the animals were not known in either Mexico or California.

Before the disappointed Spaniards left the area, they sent Don Pedro de Tobar to investigate the rumors concerning villages to the west. His party met hostile Indians in a region of broken mesas and lovely valleys. Fr. Juan de Padilla, who was with the Spaniards, reported that he had heard the name Totonteac used for the region, but the exploring party called it Tucano or Tusayan. Concerning the name Tusayan, Frank Hamilton Cushing states that the Zuñis formerly called two of the largest Hopi towns "Usaya-kye or people of Usaya. Hence T-usayan." Their first view of the Jadito Valley must have caused the Spaniards to lift up their hearts, for it was a golden view where even today the ground is strewn with tons of yellow potsherds and mounds of Mesa Verde golden sandstone. It has been conjectured that Indians with no knowledge of metals, but only of color, may have had the golden sands in mind when they told the Spaniards that "gold" existed everywhere in the region. The investigating Spanish party found several villages, but failed to record their names in full. None of the villages, however, was at that time atop the mesas where they perch today. One source lists the names of some of the villages seen by the Spaniards as Kawaiku, Awatobi, Sityatki, Kuchaptuvela (Old Walpi), old Shungopovy, old Mishongnovi, and Oraibi.

The hostile Hopi soon accepted the exploring party and discussed with it the nature of the surrounding land. From them Tobar learned that a great river lay several days' journey to the west. It was, of course, the Colorado River (*q.v.,* Grand Canyon). The visiting Spaniards soon departed, and it was many years before white men again entered the Hopi Villages.

The Province of Tusayan was visited in 1583 by Fr. Espejo, who called the region Mohoce and mentioned only five pueblos. He was followed late in 1598 by Juan de Oñate, who made the Indians into complete vassals. The missionizing period began shortly thereafter, and in 1629 a mission was established in Tusayan (cf. Awatobi).

The term *Mohoce* was also rendered by the Spaniards as Moki and as Moqui, terms detestable to the Hopi since in their tongue it means "dead." Nevertheless, the name continued to exist and it was picked up by Americans. It was used until 1895 when the Smithsonian Institution adopted the correct name of Hopi, the name used by the tribe for its own people.

The movement of entire villages from lowland to mesa top apparently began at the time of the Pueblo Uprising in 1680 when the Hopi and other pueblo Indians ousted the Spaniards in a bath of blood. It has been said that the Hopi feared Spanish retribution and hence the Indians moved to impregnable positions on the mesa tops, abandoning their former villages. Probably they feared the Navajo for when attack came, it was by Navajos, not Spaniards. The mesa top villages proved effective defense against attack.

Ref.:   Shellbach; 1, p. 75; 7, pp. 47, 547; 10, p. 38, (Note 1); 21, p. 185; 71, p. 16; 80, p. 20; 88, I, 560, 561; 177, p. 156, (Note 12); 182, pp. 356, 357, 359, 361, 362, 377. Maps: D-1; D-4; E-11; E-18; E-23.

## HOSKININNI MESA

El.: c. 6000'                          Loc.: Navajo 1, CD-1
Pro.: /háskəniyniy/
After the end of the Navajo campaign (cf. Fort Defiance, Apache) Chief Hoskinnini, one of the last of the Navajos, led his people and flocks to this area, where he lived until his death in 1909. He was reputed to have a rich silver mine. (cf. Mitchell Butte, Apache).

Ref.:   4, p. 423; 71, p. 47; 65, p. 15. Map: D-4.

## HOTEVILLA

El.: c. 6600'                          Loc.: Navajo 1, AB-13
Pro.: /hów˟tv ͮwelə/                    Hopi: "scraped back"
The Hopi name comes from the former Hotevilla Spring which, being in a low cave, often took the skin off the back of anyone entering. Here in 1906 the conservative party settled after it lost the tug of war at Oraibi (q.v.). In the following year, part of the group formed Bakabi (q.v.).

P.O. est. July 24, 1916. Emory A. Marks, p.m.

v.n. Hotevila

Ref.:   Hopi Constitution; 29, p. 47; 167, p. 75. Maps: D-1; D-4.

## HOUSE OF HANDS

El.: c. 6000'                          Loc.: Navajo 1, H-2
When the area termed the Valley of Mystery was explored for the first time in 1949, one of the first of the ruins to be investigated was found to have hundreds of hand prints painted in white on the cliff wall.

v.n. House of Many Hands

Ref.:   96, pp. 15-16. Map: GI-2.

## HOWELL MESA

El.: c. 6448'                          Loc.: Navajo 1, A-12
Edward E. Howell made the "first geologic traverse" of this area for the Wheeler expedition in 1873.

v.n. Cedar Mesa

Ref.:   Gregory, p. 39, (Note 2), 191. Maps: D-1; D-4.

## INDIAN WELLS

El.: c. 5500'                          Loc.: Navajo 2, G-11
Navajos dug a well here at their regular camping place on the road to Keams Canyon and Holbrook. Rev. William R. Johnson started a mission here in 1912, there already being a store and post office at the locality. (cf. Bidahochi Butte).

P.O. est. April 1, 1910. Hubert Richardson, p.m.

Ref.:   Burcard; Barnes; 73, p. 166; 167, p. 77. Maps: C-11; D-1; D-6.

## IRON SPRING

El.: c. 6000'                          Loc.: Navajo 3, A-4
Named in 1887 by Will C. Barnes because the water is strongly impregnated with iron.

Ref.:   Barnes. Maps: C-12; D-1.

## IVES MESA

El.: c. 6000'                          Loc.: Navajo 2, D-7
Lt. Joseph Christmas Ives in 1858 traversed this mesa with his surveying crew.

Ref.:   71, p. 191; 151, p. 394. Maps: A-7; C-12; D-1; GI-11.

## JADITO WASH

El.: c. 6700'                          Loc.: Navajo 2, DG-3-1
Pro.: /jédito/           Navajo: jado, "antelope"; to, "water"
This is one of four long washes carrying water from Black Mesa (Apache County) through the Hopi butte country to the Little Colorado River.

The first white man to visit the Jadito Valley was Don Pedro de Tobar of the Coronado Expedition in 1540. T. V. Keams (cf. Keams Canyon) was apparently the first to show interest in the extensive archaeological sources of the valley, probably in the late 1870's.

P.O. est. as Jeddito, February 16, 1921. Alma G. Roberts, p.m. Discont. February 28, 1934.

Ref.:   71, pp. 38, 155; 80, pp. 17, 18. Maps: A-7; C-6 (Jettyto Spring); C-12.

a.n. Antelope Spring     Loc.: Sec. 14, T. 29 N., R. 18 E.     Navajo
    Jadito Canyon         Loc.: T. 27 N., R. 20 E.              Navajo
Ref.:   151, p. 395.
    Jadito Spring                                                Navajo
Ref.:   71, p. 154.

v.n. Jetto-to Spring
    Jeddito Spring
Ref.:   MNA.

## JAQUES MOUNTAIN

El.: c. 7000'                          Loc.: Navajo 3, I-7
An isolated butte named for Sanford Jaques, a sheepman and early settler.

Ref.:   Barnes. Maps: GI-11; B-9.

## JOSEPH CITY

El.: 5083'                             Loc.: Navajo 2, E-10
On March 24, 1876, Mormon emigrants arrived at their approximate destination on the Little Colorado River. From this group three settlements were formed (See Brigham City; Sunset), one of which was begun by William Coleman Allen (b. February 14, 1843; d. March 17, 1926). At the point where the march ended, Allen City arose. The first name for the city, or rather Allen's Camp, was Cumorah, for the name of the hill where were found the gold plates from which the Book of Mormon was translated. A drawing was held to name the colony. One name suggested was Ramah City, but both this and Cumorah gave way on May 26, 1876, to Allen Camp or Allen's City. The community was located on the eastern outskirts of the present Joseph City. Here the Mormon colonists built a fort of cottonwood logs, the start of the oldest Mormon colony in Arizona.

On January 21, 1878, the name was changed to St. Joseph, after the Mormon prophet Joseph Smith. Railroad officials soon requested that the name be changed to Joseph City to avoid confusion with the St. Joseph already on the railroad in Missouri.

In 1878 the residents of Joseph City, Brigham City, and Sunset cooperated in establishing the Mormon Dairy (cf. Mormon Lake, Coconino). They also operated the first sawmill in the region. Determination and sheer grit account for the fact that the settlers of Joseph City refused to abandon their colony despite severe hardships, not the least of which was maintaining dams they used for irrigation. Four other Mormon settlements vanished, but Joseph City kept doggedly on against what must have seemed overwhelming handicaps. By 1894 seven dams had been constructed and had been washed out by the flooding Little Colorado River. This caused a Mormon official to call Joseph City the "leading community in pain, determination and unflinching courage in dealing with the elements around them." More dams were destined to be washed out, but at last a dam was built in 1939 which has withstood the devastating torrents of the rampaging river.

P.O. est. as Saint Joseph, February 21, 1878. John McLaws, p.m. Changed to Joseph, October 31, 1898. Changed to Joseph City, December 19, 1923.

Ref.: *Holbrook Argus*, September 17, 1898, 5:3; Richards; Wiltbank; 29, p. 46; 112, pp. 139, 140; 167, p. 82; 171, pp. 4, 11, 18, 41, 7; 4, p. 314. Maps: C-5 (St. Joseph); C-11 (Joseph City); E-20 (San Joseph).

## KAWAIOKU

El.: c. 6000'      Loc.: Navajo 2, F-1.5

On rim of Antelope Mesa 3 miles e. and s. of Awatobi. In 1540 when Don Pedro de Tobar was advancing through the Hopi region with a party of one horseman and a few foot soldiers, he attacked this village and destroyed it. The village was reoccupied some time before Luxan's visit in 1582, but was finally abandoned before 1598. Today it is an important Hopi ruin.

**v.n. Kawaika**

Ref.: 10, p. 38, (Note 5); 80, p. 21; 88, I, 564. Maps: None.

## KAYENTA

El.: 5700'      Loc.: Navajo 1, E-F-4.1
Pro.: /káyəntə/ or /káəntə/
In 1910 John and Louisa Wade Wetherill established a trading post at Kayenta, the name of which is the American way of rendering the Navajo *tyende*. The Navajo word refers to a deep spring, about three miles away from the post, which forms a boghole in which wild animals and stock mired when they came for water. The Wetherills and their partner Colville first called their post Oljeto, but soon changed the name to Kayenta. There is a sizeable community at Kayenta today, since it is the last point in Arizona nearest to the uranium prospects in Monument Valley and on the Navajo Reservation.

P.O. est. as Oljeto, January 31, 1911. John Wetherill, p.m. Name changed to Kayenta, March 21, 1911.

Ref.: Barnes' Notes; Burcard; P.O. Records; 96, p. 48. Maps: D-1; C-12.

## KEAMS CANYON

El.: 6800'      Loc.: Navajo 1, F-15
Hopi: *pongsikvi*, "government town"
In the 1860's a trading store was opened in the present Keams Canyon by Billy Dodd, brother of the agent for the Navajos at that time. The location, then known as Peach Orchard Spring, did not take on its present name until the coming of Thomas Varker Keams (b. England, 1843; d. England, November 30, 1904), who was agent in charge of the Navajos beginning June 4, 1872. Keams had served with Kit Carson in the Navajo campaign, later acting as an interpreter to the Navajos and moving on into Hopi country where he started the first permanent white settlement.

In 1886 twenty Hopi chieftains requested the federal government to establish a school for Hopi children, and a year later a school was started in Keams Canyon where Keams had a trading post. Here in 1899 a separate Hopi Agency was established, moving to its present site in 1902 from the trading post area two miles down the canyon.

P.O. est. March 12, 1883. Alex M. Stephen, p.m.

Ref.: 16, p. 126; 36, pp. 210-11; 71, p. 192; 167, p. 83. Maps: C-6 (Keam's Cañon); C-9 (Keam Canyon).

## KEET SEEL

El.: c. 7500'      Loc.: Navajo 1, CD-3.7
Pro.: /kíts?iy˘:lí/      Navajo: "empty houses"
Keet Seel is an Indian cliff dwelling ruin which is believed to have been built between 1274 and 1286 A.D. Its three hundred fifty rooms are the best preserved ruin in the Navajo National Monument.

**v.n. Kiet Seel**
(preferred by the Museum of Northern Arizona)
**Kietzeel**
**Kit siel**
**Kit sil**

Ref.: 151, p. 420; 167, p. 140; 71, pp. 44, 157. Map: GI-11.

**a.n. Keet Seel Spring**      Navajo
**Keet Seel Canyon**      Navajo

## KINNEY MOUNTAIN

El.: c. 8500'      Loc.: Navajo 3, H-8
This was named for J. P. Kinney, forest officer, U. S. Indian Service. Kinney was first chairman of the Branch of Forestry for the Indian Service and is considered the father of forestry law in the United States. He is currently with the Justice Department in Washington, D.C.

Ref.: Barnes; Davis. Map: B-9.

## LAKESIDE

El.: 7000'      Loc.: Navajo 3, H-6-7
Three lakes nearby give this place the name of Lakeside. When the Mormon settlement was begun in the early 1880's, it was known as Fairview. The damming of Showlow Creek created a true lake which caused the change in name to Lakeside. The settlement had also been referred to as Woodland, although the maps show Woodland as being in the next range (23 E). Adair Spring (cf. Adair) is a source for the lake.

The first sawmill in the region began its migrations in 1876 when it was built on Mount Trumbull and then shipped to the vicinity of Mormon Lake. From there it was moved to Pinedale and later it was moved from there to Lakeside.

P.O. est. October 5, 1906. John L. Fish, p.m.

Ref.:  29, p. 55; 4, p. 450. Maps: B-9; C-10.

## LAVA SPRING

El.: c. 6600'                    Loc.: Navajo 2, G-4-5

This spring emerges from under a lava flow.

Ref.:  71, p. 153. Map: C-12.

## LINDEN

El.: c. 5000'                    Loc.: Navajo 3, F-5.5

At first the small Mormon settlement (begun c. 1878) at this location was called Juniper, the name being changed to Linden, in all probability on account of the long-leaf cottonwoods lining nearby Linden Wash.

P.O. est. August 18, 1891. David E. Adams, p.m. Discont. May 31, 1958.

Ref.:  167, p. 148. Maps: B-9; C-8 (7 miles northwest of Show-low); C-9 (8 miles west of Showlow).

## LITTLE COLORADO RIVER

Loc.: Crosses Apache, Navajo, and part of Coconino County.

The Coronado Expedition in 1540 assigned Lt. Garcia Lopez de Cardenas to explore to the west from the Zuñi Villages. Cardenas left records which are somewhat confusing in connection with what rivers he designated by name. For instance, his Rio Vermejo ("Red River") might have been either the Zuñi River or the Little Colorado. However, there is a strong possibility that he was referring to the Zuñi River by that name, since he used the term Rio del Lino ("Flax River") for another stream, and it is a fact that others later used the same appellation when speaking of the Little Colorado River, because of wild flax growing on its banks. In 1604 Juan Mateo de Oñate used the word *colorado* ("red") for the Little Colorado. When Fr. Francisco Garcés saw the same stream on June 28, 1776, he called it Rio Jaquesila and also referred to it as Rio San Pedro. The valley Garcés refers to in his diary on July 18 as the Valle del Lino ("Wild Flax Valley") may well have been that of the Little Colorado River, although this has not been established as a fact.

When Lt. Amiel W. Whipple saw the stream in 1854 he found it was generally called the Flax River, but even the name was in transition to Chiquito Colorado ("Little Colorado") and its anglicized form, the name which it carries today.

Ref.:  35, pp. 354, 355 (Note 36), 410; 175, I, 149, 178, Part II, 26 (Note); 7, pp. 88 (Note 21), 154-155; 18, p. 113; 42, p. 93; 21, p. 269. Map: All of region traversed by river.

## LOKASKAL SPRING

El.: #1: c. 7000'          Loc.: #1: Navajo 1, F-11
  #2: c. 6000'             Loc.: #2: Navajo 2, G-5
Pro.: /lók?a:ʰsika:d/        Navajo: "clump of reeds"

Descriptive. Several springs on the Navajo Reservation have this name.

v.n. Lokasakal
     Lukasakad
     Lokasakad

Ref.:  71, pp. 112, 153, 155, 193. Maps: A-7 (No. 1); C-6; C-12 (No. 1); D-4 (No. 1 & No. 2).

## LOLOMAI POINT

El.: c. 7000'                    Loc.: Navajo 1, E-5
                                 Hopi: "good"

Lolomai was a prominent Oraibi chief.

Ref.:  71, p. 193. Maps: C-12; D-1.

## LONE PINE DAM

El.: 6000'          Loc.: Navajo 3, F-3. Near Taylor.

Descriptive. In 1940 this was the largest earth dam in Arizona, storing water to irrigate seventeen hundred acres of land. It is a noted refuge for wild ducks.

Ref.:  4, p. 449. Map: None.

## LONG LAKE

El.: c. 5000'                    Loc.: Navajo 3, H-5.5

Descriptive. The Navajo name has an identical translation (*Be'ek'id hónééz*: "long pond").

Ref.:  73, p. 186. Maps: B-9; C-12.

## LULULONGTURQUI

El.: c. 6000'                    Loc.: Navajo 2, F-2
                                 East side of Jadito Valley.
          Hopi: "Bull Snake Point"; "plumed serpent mound"

A medium-sized ruined pueblo, Lululongturqui was excavated in 1901. It is called "Peacock Ruin" at the Jadito store and at one time was better known by that name.

v.n. Lululongturkwi

Ref.:  MNA; 80, p. 20; 88, p. 778. Map: None.

## MAL PAIS SPRING

El.: c. 2000'                    Loc.: Navajo 2, FG-6.1
Pro.: /mǽl pays/                 Spanish: "bad land"

So called because of volcanic nature of area.

Ref.:  71, p. 153. Maps: A-7; C-12.

## MANILA

El.: c. 5000'                    Loc.: Navajo 2, D-10.4

Lt. Amiel W. Whipple had his Camp 79 near here. The location later became a station on the S.F. R.R. It was named during the Spanish-American War after the chief city and capital of the Philippines.

P.O. est. June 6, 1912. Clarence G. Wallace, p.m. Discont. June 15, 1918.

Ref.:  177, p. 157 (Note 13); Barnes. Map: C-11.

## MARCOU MESA

El.: c. 6000'　　　　　　Loc.: Navajo 2, DG-8.5-10
Pro.: /markuw/
Named for Jules Marcou, who was geologist for Lt. Amiel W. Whipple's expedition in 1858.
Ref.: 71, p. 193; 151, p. 501. Map: C-13.

## MARSH PASS

El.: 6750'　　　　　　Loc.: Navajo 1, D-5.3
While it has been suggested that this pass was named for a Professor Marsh of Yale University, it seems more likely that the name had a descriptive origin because as late as 1907 the pass had a chain of swamps and lakes, since drained by a deep arroyo. The arroyo was caused by erosion as a result of over-grazing and the cutting of ever-deeper wagon ruts through the pass.

**v.n. La Puerta Limita**
("limited opening") (Macomb Map, 1860)
Ref.: MNA; 71, p. 36; 167, p. 93. Maps: D-1; C-12.

## MASIPA SPRING

El.: c. 2000'　　　　　　Loc.: Navajo 1, BC-5.7
Pro.: /masíupa/　　　　Hopi: "gray spring"
Shungopa Spring, which used to supply the Hopi village of Shungopovi with water, failed following a minor earthquake in 1870. Since then Masipa Spring has been the water source. It is also known as Shanto Spring, but Masipa is preferred because the Navajo name Shanto ("sandy spring") occurs in several additional locations.
Ref.: Colton; 167, p. 146. Maps: D-4 (Shato); D-1 (Shonto).

## MERRICK BUTTE

El.: c. 5000'　　　　　　Loc.: Navajo 1, GH-1.3
Accompanying the Navajos on their trek into exile following their conquest by Col. Kit Carson were two soldiers named Merrick and Mitchell. These men noted the magnificent silver worn by the Indians and decided to return to Monument Valley, the area where they thought the source of the ore must be. They found the source, but it was not until 1879 that they located someone to finance extracting the ore. The men returned to the mine despite previous warnings by the Piutes to stay out. The Indians shot at Mitchell as he emerged with ore samples from the mine. Merrick sprang to his horse and galloped off. He was caught and killed at the foot of the great butte which today bears his name.

One version relates that Mitchell was the one who escaped and was later shot (cf. Mitchell Butte).
Ref.: 65, p. 96; 96, pp. 27-30. Map: GI-1.

## MILPA CREEK

El.: c. 6000'　　　　　　Loc.: Navajo 3, HG-11.5-12.4
Pro.: /míˆlpa/　　Spanish: "small corn or grain field"
This former stream has apparently disappeared.
Ref.: Lenon. Maps: C-4; E-20.

## MISHONGNOVI

El.: c. 6000'　　　　　　Loc.: Navajo 1, CD-14.2
Hopi: "the other of two sandstone columns remains standing"
The odd name refers to the fact that one of two irregular sandstone columns here has fallen. The original pueblo stood west of the present village and was one of the colonies of the old Tusayan (cf. Hopi Villages). It was abandoned prior to 1680 when the present town was built.
The Franciscans had a *visita* called San Buenaventura at the old site from 1629 to 1680.

**v.n.**　　Several, chief of which are given here:

　Mashongniovi
　Beunaventura　　　（Vargas, 1692)
　Manzana　　　　　(Schoolcraft)
　Masagnebe　　　　(Garcés, 1776)

Ref.: *Hopi Constitution*; 4, p. 412; 29, p. 44; 71, p. 193; 88, pp. 564, 871; 151, p. 523. Map: D-4.

## MITCHELL BUTTE

El.: 6382'　　　　　　Loc.: Navajo 1, FG-1.1
With his partner Merrick, Mitchell was a twenty-one year old prospector who was killed by Piutes, according to a story told by a Navajo chieftain, Hoskininibegay. One version relates that Merrick was killed immediately at the entrance to a rich silver mine in Monument Valley and that Mitchell escaped to another butte where he was discovered and killed by the Indians. Navajos who helped find the bodies of the two men reported that the prospectors had used water belonging to the Piutes. The Indians deliberately picked a quarrel at the mining location with the two men. (cf. Merrick Butte).
Ref.: 4, p. 423; 65, p. 95; 96, pp. 31, 33. Map: GI-2.

**a.n. Mitchell Butte Wash**　　　　　　　　　Navajo
**Mitchell Mesa**　　El.: 6570'. Map: GI-1　　Navajo

## MITTEN BUTTE

El.: 6210'　　　　　　Loc.: Navajo 1, G-1.1
From a distance, a formation like a pair of mittens towers eight hundred feet above the valley. The Navajos refer to these formations as the Big Hands, once powerful but now stilled. They say that power may some day return to the hands to rule beyond the limits of Monument Valley.
Ref.: 4, pp. 423-24; 71, p. 193; 96, p. 117. Maps: GI-11; C-12.

## MITTEN PEAK

El.: 6600'　　　　　　Loc.: Navajo 2, GH-8.5
Frank A. Zuck of Holbrook named this peak in 1897 because of its appearance. While acknowledging this name, Gregory called the volcanic shaft Pilot Peak. Locally it is sometimes called Rabbit Mountain because its north slope —unlike its steep south side—is a rabbit haven.

**v.n. Pilot Rock**
Ref.: Branch; 71, p. 34. Maps: C-12; GI-8.

## MONUMENT PASS

El.: c. 6500'　　　　　　Loc.: Navajo 1, F-3.3
The pass into Monument Valley is lined with a variety of monuments bearing descriptive names. Going north, one sees immediately to the west Castle Rock and Setting Hen.

To the east are the Emperor with his pronged "crown," the Stage Coach and the Bear and the Rabbit facing each other.

Ref.:   4, p. 424; 71, p. 193. Maps: C-9; D-4.

## MONUMENT VALLEY

El.: 4800' to 5200'          Loc.: Navajo 1, FH-1-2
Mesas, spires, and buttes rise abruptly from the floor of this spectacular valley. Conspicuous monuments often rise nearly one thousand feet above the mile-high valley.

Ref.:   71, p. 48. Map: C-10.

## MORGAN MOUNTAIN

El.: c. 6000'          Loc.: Navajo 3, HG-6.4
William Morgan was a sheepman here in the 1880's.

Ref.:   Barnes. Maps: A-7; B-9.

## MYSTERY, VALLEY OF

El.: c. 6000'          Loc.: Navajo 1, F-1.5
The so-called Valley of Mystery was entered by white men for the first time in 1949. It is the site of well preserved prehistoric ruins.

Ref.:   96, pp. 15-16. Map: GI-2.

## NAAHTEE CANYON

El.: 6500'.          Loc.: Navajo 2, G-4.2
Pro.: /náʔadiˆːh/          Navajo:  "without eyes"; "toadstool causes blindness"
John Wetherill said this should be spelled Na-ettee.
P.O. est. November 22, 1916. Harry W. Wetsel, p.m. Discont. August 31, 1932.

Ref.:   102, p. 62; Maps: C-12; F-3.

## NAKAI CANYON

El.: c. 5300'          Loc.: Navajo 1, CD-3.2-1
Navajos refer to Mexicans as "No-kai." Nakai Creek is one of the principal tributaries to the San Juan River.

v.n. Nokai Canyon
Ref.: 6, p. 11. Maps: GI-1; GI-11.
a.n. Nokai Creek                                          Navajo
     Nakai Mesa                                           Navajo
     Nakai Mesa          Map: GI-1                        Navajo

## NASH CREEK

El.: c. 2500'          Loc.: Navajo 3, GH-12.3-11.7
Lafayette P. Nash (b. Berlin, Ohio, November 19, 1846; d. March 13, 1914) was twice wounded during the Civil War, the second wound resulting in a permanent limp. Following the war, Nash went to Ohio Wesleyan University until his funds gave out, going from there to New Orleans and working on river steamers. He arrived in Arizona in 1867, following employment on the Union Pacific R.R. in Nevada. Nash worked first for Michael Goldwater at Ehrenberg, freighting later for Goldwater between La Paz, Ehrenberg, and Prescott. In 1876 he went to Signal (q.v., Mohave), and when the McCrackin mine shut down, moved with his bride to the Tonto Basin country, living there for three years before establishing a ranch in Strawberry Valley in 1881. Nash had the government contract

to supply beef to Fort Apache in 1892, and while in that capacity he was attacked by an Apache with a large butcher knife. Nash quelled him with one blow of a meat cleaver, as a result of which Nash was tried and the case dismissed. The family moved to Phoenix and opened a store. In 1910 Nash was appointed the first justice of the peace in Miami, serving until his death.

Ref.:   W. B. Nash, Jr., Letter, November, 1956. Map: C-12.
a.n. Nash Point          El.: 6527'. Maps: B-7; GM-19          Gila

## OBED

El.: c. 4000'          Loc.: Navajo 2, DE-10.2
The party of Mormon emigrants which arrived on the Little Colorado River on March 24, 1876, rapidly split into groups which formed the nuclei of four colonies. One of these was Obed, with George Lake as its leader. Obed is a character in the *Book of Mormon*. The site selected was swampy and malarial and, being in the path of the Little Colorado, particularly subject to rampaging flood stages. Before March 1877, the residents of Obed had joined other nearby Mormon communities and Obed was no more. The strongly built fort, however, remained standing for years, being used as a cattle corral by the Aztec Cattle Company until the building was torn down in 1895.

v.n. Lake's Camp
Ref.:   Richards; Barnes; 112, p. 147; 171, p. 2. Map: C-6.
a.n. Obed Spring                                          Navajo

## OLJETO WASH

El.: c. 5100'          Loc.: Navajo 1, E-1-2
Pro.: /oːljéːtó/          Navajo:  *olja,* "moon"; *to,* "water"
The anglicized name, Moonlight Water, comes from the translation of the Navajo. Oljeto Wash is one of the four principal tributaries to the San Juan River.

Ref.:   6, p. 11. Maps: GI-5; GI-11 (Moonlight Creek).

## ORAIBI

El.: 6497'          Loc.: Navajo 1, BC-12.9
Pro.: /owžáyviˆ/          Derived from Hopi name for a particular rock, *Orai,* plus *bi,* "the place of"
Oraibi vies with Acoma, New Mexico, for the honor of being the oldest continuously inhabited town in the United States. Pottery sherds indicate occupancy of Oraibi since c. 1150 A.D. Old Oraibi is atop the mesa, while the newer town is at its foot. Apparently Luxan (of the Espejo Expedition) was the first to document the name of the older town, reporting that on April 24, 1583, his party arrived at "Olalla," which he said was the largest of the Hopi towns. Since there are at least forty-nine variant spellings of the name, Luxan's attempt cannot be considered too far-fetched.

Oraibi's population once numbered in the thousands, but was decimated by smallpox, drought, and the creation of the newer towns of Hotevilla and Bakavi (q.v.). The new towns developed because of dissension between the conservatives and liberals of Oraibi about education for their children. The argument was settled by a tug of war, with the losers having to move out. Near Oraibi on the Hotevilla trail is a line cut in the rock commemorating this event. Lower (New) Oraibi had been settled before the dissension. It is called Kia-Kocho-movi (or Kiquchmovi) because of the spring by that name from which the people draw their water.

Old Oraibi is now nearly in ruins.

P.O. est. as Oraibi August 11, 1900. Changed to Oraibi, April 11, 1901.

**v.n. Oraybe**

Ref.:    Colton; 29, p. 43; 81, pp. 1, 4, 8; 167, p. 110. Maps: C-9; D-4.

**a.n. Oraibi Butte**                                                               Navajo

Ref.:    71, p. 194.

**Oraibi Wash**                                                                    Navajo

## OVERGAARD

El.: c. 6000'                           Loc.: Navajo 3, BC-4.5

Overgaard is a Mormon community near Snowflake. The origin of the name has not yet been ascertained.

P.O. est. October 14, 1938. William T. Shockley, p.m.

Ref.:    P.O. Records. Map: F-6.

## PAT MULLEN PEAK

El.: c. 7000'                                    Loc.: Navajo 3, I-6.
                                        Sec. 11, T. 9 N., R. 23 E.

Pat Mullen was a pioneer stockman.

Ref.:    Barnes. Map: None.

## PENZANCE

El.: c. 6000'                           Loc.: Navajo 2, EF-11

There is a rock quarry here still used by the railroad for riprap. Local belief is that the place was named for Penzance on the coast of England, where there is also a quarry. The name was given to the place in 1888 by the S.F. R.R.

Ref.:    John L. Westover, Joseph City, Letter, December 3, 1955; Barnes. Map: B-9.

## PHOENIX PARK CANYON

El.: c. 7000'                           Loc.: Navajo 3, BC-6-7

The canyon and the nearby Phoenix Park Wash were named by James Stinson, who had cattle in the area as early as 1873. Stinson, who lived in Phoenix, called his ranch at the head of the wash Phoenix Park, a name which gave way to Holcomb (or Hokum) when Stinson sold out to Daniel Boone Holcomb.

Ref.:    Barnes. Map: B-9.

## PINEDALE

El.: 6500'                              Loc.: Navajo 3, D-5

In 1879 Niels Mortenson began a Mormon settlement at this location. At first known as Mortenson, it was also referred to as Percheron because of the stallion of that breed which Mortenson and the Petersons brought in with them. By 1888, however, the settlement was called Pinedale, its name today.

P.O. est. April 18, 1888. Lydia C. Bryan, p.m.

Ref.:    112, pp. 168, 169. Maps: B-9; C-7.

**a.n. Mortenson Wash**           Map: B-9                     Navajo

## PINETOP

El.: c. 7000'                           Loc.: Navajo 3, H-7

William L. Penrod (b. 1831; d. August 21, 1916) and his family moved to the region of Show Low in 1878. They arrived from Utah and settled in a house which had already been constructed in 1886 by a bachelor, Johnny Phipps (d. 1890). Phipps ran a saloon for the colored soldiers from Fort Apache. When Phipps died, Walt Rigney took over the bar and the colored boys began calling the place Pinetop, a name which they used for Rigney himself. When the post office was established, the name Pinetop was given to it, thus banishing the name Penrod. Until 1906 the residents were mainly the thirteen Penrod children.

P.O. est. December 19, 1891. Edward E. Bradshaw, p.m.

Ref.:    Rollin Fish, as told to him by Penrod himself in 1905, Letter, 1955; 4, p. 450. Maps: B-9; C-8.

## PINON

El.: 6497'                              Loc.: Navajo 1, F-11.2

Pro.:  /pinyówn/     Spanish: "a pine bearing edible nuts"

In 1858 the first Americans crossed through this area. They were Capt. John G. Walker and his Mounted Rifles. Walker described the place as a broken, inaccessible region, largely uninhabited, a statement which holds true to this day. In 1912 Lorenzo Hubbell built a trading post at a time when the crop of piñon nuts was extra large, hence he called the place Piñon.

P.O. est. November 1, 1952. Fletcher Corrigan, p.m.

Ref.:    Thomas F. Corrigan (son), Letter, November 1955; 167, p. 113. Maps: A-13; F-13.

## PIUTE CREEK

El.: c. 6000'                           Loc.: Navajo 1, BA-3-1

Pro.:  /páyuwt/

One of the four principal tributaries which flow north to the San Juan River, Piute Creek reflects in its name the fact that the area was once home ground for Piute Indians.

**v.n. Paiute**

Ref.:    6, p. 11; 71, p. 194. Map: D-4.

**a.n. Piute Mesa**       El.: c. 7200'. Map: GI-10       Navajo
**Paiute Canyon**         Map: D-4                        Navajo

## POLACCA

El.: c. 5500'                           Loc.: Navajo 1, DE-14.5

Pro.:  /powla^kaka/                    Hopi: "butterfly"

Tom Polacca, a Tewa Indian from Hano, moved down from the mesa top to its base in 1890 and established the village which is named for him.

P.O. est. February 16, 1901. Richard J. Barnes, p.m.

Ref.:    167, p. 116; P.O. Records. Maps: C-9; D-1.

**a.n. Polacca Wash**                                              Navajo

Loc.: Junction of Wepo and First Mesa Washes, 10 miles n.w. Polacca.

Ref.:    71, p. 38.

## PORRAS DIKES

El.: 5685'                          Loc.: Navajo 1, FG-3.5
Fr. Francisco de Porras was a Franciscan missionary to the
Hopis from 1629 until killed by Indians in 1633. Gregory
named these geological dikes after him.
Ref.: 71, p. 194. Maps: GI-4; D-4.

## PORTER CREEK

El.: c. 6000'        Loc.: Navajo 3-IG-8-7. T. 9 N, R. 25 E.
James Porter was a pioneer sheepman here.
Ref.: Barnes. Map: None.

**a.n. Porter Mountain**          Map: B-9                  Navajo

## PORTER TANK

El.: c. 6000'                      Loc.: Navajo 2, EF-11-10
A dry wash named for Jack Porter, who c. 1887 located
rock tanks for a sheep camp here.
Ref.: Barnes. Map: C-13.

## POST OFFICE HILL

El.: c. 6000'                      Loc.: Navajo 3, GH-8-9
                                   Sec. 2, T. 7 N, R 23 E.
This ridge was known by its name of Post Office Hill at least
as early as 1878. Hinton's *Handbook* states that it was the
location of a white man's grave. Killed by Apaches, the
man was remembered by them whenever they passed, for
they took time to place a rock on the grave mound which
was "about twenty feet square at the base and four feet
high." Barnes says Apaches told him that the stone-placing
was "talk" with the next Indian passing.
Ref.: 112, p. 244; Barnes. Map: None.

**a.n. Post Office Canyon**        Map: GI-11                Navajo
    When the roads were in bad shape during inclement weather,
    the mules pulled from Fort Apache to a shack in Post Office
    Canyon, half-way to Show Low. The mail was left in the
    hut to be picked up by a team from the opposite direction.
    The origin of the name for the hill as well as the canyon
    may derive from this fact.
    Ref.: Davis.

## POTATO WASH

El.: c. 6000'                      Loc.: Navajo 3, C-2.5-1
                                   Navajo 2, C-14-11
Will C. Barnes raised potatoes in this wash 1888-1895.
Barnes named it.
Ref.: Barnes. Maps: B-9; GI-11; C-12.

**a.n. Potato Field Draw**         Map: B-9                  Navajo

## PYRAMID BUTTE

El.: c. 6000'                      Loc.: Navajo 2, D-6.5
Descriptive.

**v.n. Pyramid Mountain**
Ref.: 71, p. 136. Maps: D-4; C-13.

## RAINBOW FOREST

El.: c. 5500'                      Loc.: Navajo 2, I-12
The brilliant colors back of the Petrified National Monument headquarters give this area its name. It has been
so called since first seen by early white visitors.
Ref.: Branch. Map: GI-8.

## RED TOP MOUNTAIN

El.: c. 6000'                      Loc.: Navajo 3, DE-6.5
This mountain has a bright red sandstone top.
Ref.: Barnes. Map: B-9.

## REIDHEAD

El.: c. 6300'                      Loc.: Navajo 3, FG-4.5
In 1878 John Reidhead, a Mormon, settled here, remaining
until 1883. He bought the location from Herman Woolf
(cf. Woolf's Crossing, Coconino), who had obtained it from
an unknown Mexican. Because of beavers found here, the
place was initially called Beaver Ranch. It was also known
as Lone Pine Crossing because of a single yellow pine growing at the Reidhead Crossing.
Ref.: 55, p. 573; 112, p. 169. Map: GI-11 (Lone Pine Reservoir).

## RICHARDS LAKE

El.: 6000'                         Loc.: Navajo 2, C-13
J. W. Richards ("Billie St. Joe") c. 1902 diverted flood
waters from Black Canyon into this crater, forming a
sizeable tank for his cattle.
Ref.: Barnes; Richards. Map: D-1.

## SANENCHECK ROCK

El.: 6680'                         Loc.: Navajo 1, BC-1.5
                                   Navajo: "thief rock"
An isolated rock peak.

**v.n. Sanenecheck Rock**
Ref.: Barnes; 71, p. 194; 151, p. 666. Maps: C-12; D-4; GI-11.

## SAULS

El.: c. 6000'                      Loc.: Navajo 2, I-8-9
                              On county line at Carrizo Creek.
Lt. John Gatewood, when enlisting Indian scouts, often
replaced their difficult Apache names with others. At least
as early as 1882 the name Saul was that of the Indian who
lived at this point.
Ref.: Barnes. Map. None.

## SEGEKE BUTTE

El.: c. 6000'                      Loc.: Navajo 1, AE-1-3
                                   Navajo: "square rock"
Descriptive.
Ref.: 71, p. 194; 151, p. 680. Map: D-4.

## SEGI MESAS

El.: 8065'                         Loc.: Navajo 1, AE-1-3
Pro.: /tséyi?/                     Navajo: "canyons" or
                                   "mesas trenched by canyons"
A series of mesas cut by canyons forms the Segi Mesas.
Included in the group are Skeleton Mesa (highest elevation, 8065'), a triple mesa cut by canyons. Azansosi Mesa
and Hoskininni Mesa lie one thousand feet lower and give
the entire series the appearance of steps. The area was at
one time the center of the cliff dwellers' population and
today contains extensive ruins in good preservation.

**v.n. Tsegi Mesas**
Ref.: 71, pp. 36, 47, 48; 151, p. 680. Maps: C-12; D-4.

## SEVEN MILE HILL

El.: c. 7000'    Loc.: Navajo 3, HI-12. T. 5 N, R. 23 E.
This hill lay seven miles along the road to Fort Thomas
from Fort Apache. Here on August 30, 1881, a band of
Apaches massacred and burned four Mormons caught at
the top of the hill. The same Indians that afternoon caught
and killed an army telegraph-line repair crew near Black
River. Two days later, on September 2, Col. Carr left Fort
Apache with Troop E and Cibicu Charley as a guide, drawing closer to the Indian campfires near the hill. It was on
this night ride that the bodies of the four Mormons were
discovered. The scouting party was relieved to escape
without trouble (cf. Cibecue Creek).

Ref.: 39, pp. 127, 133. Map: None.

a.n. Seven Mile Canyon    Loc.: Heads at Seven Mile Hill    Navajo

## SHATO SPRING

El.: c. 7400'    Loc.: Navajo 1, B-6
Pro.: /sã:?toho/    Navajo: "sunshine water spring";
that is, "water on south side of rock wall"
Navajos say that Kit Carson's soldiers visited this place in
1864. There are several springs by this name on the Navajo
Reservation. The best known location, however, is that
of the Shanto Trading Post, started in 1915 by John Wetherill and Joe Lee, who sold to Harry Rorick.

The former lush meadow with its small lakes disappeared
following the washing out of natural earth dams in 1912.
Shato Spring is near the center of the Shato Plateau.

v.n. Shonto Plateau
Shonto Spring
Ref.: 71, pp. 43, 195; 151, p. 685; 167, p. 145. Maps: D-1;
D-4; C-11.

a.n. Shato Canyon    Navajo
Shonto Hill    Navajo
Loc.: On road to Navajo National Monument
Ref.: 5, p. 6.

## SHONES CROSSING

El.: c. 6000'    Loc.: Navajo 3, G-4
A one-legged, discharged Fort Apache cavalryman, John
Shone, located his cattle ranch at this point about 1879. It
was the crossing for the stage line to Fort Apache.

v.n. Shoens Crossing
Ref.: Barnes. Map: B-9.

## SHOW LOW

El.: 6500'    Loc.: Navajo 3, GH-5.5
Corydon E. Cooley (d. March 18, 1917), a government
scout with Gen. George Crook in 1872 and 1873, married the daughter of Chief Pedro of the White Mountain
Apaches, and in 1875 established his home on Show Low
Creek. His place soon gained a name for having comfort,
plenty, and cleanliness not often found by pioneer travelers.
Marion Clark was Cooley's partner in the venture, but
later Clark decided the arrangement would not work. The
two men agreed to play a game of Seven-up to decide who
should move. As the last hand was dealt Cooley needed a
single point to win. Clark, running his hands over the
cards, is said to have stated, "If you can show low, you

win." Cooley threw down his hand and replied, "Show low
it is." The words immediately became the identifying name
for the location. Clark, the loser, moved up the creek to
establish a ranch near Pinetop.

In 1881 Cooley sold half interest to Henry Huning of Las
Lunas, New Mexico. The two men extended their interests
to cattle and lumber, and to a store for travelers. In 1890
they agreed to disagree, selling out to W. J. Flake, who
wished to establish a Mormon settlement. Cooley moved
back onto the Apache reservation where he later died.

P.O. est. August 19, 1880. Corydon E. Cooley, p.m.
Ref.: 4, p. 442; 112, p. 168. Maps: B-9; C-6; GI-11.

a.n. Show Low Creek    Map: B-9    Navajo

## SHUMWAY

El.: c. 6000'    Loc.: Navajo 3, G-4
On February 4, 1864, Charles Shumway was the first Mormon to cross the Mississippi during the Mormon exodus,
and he was one of one hundred forty-three pioneers who
arrived in Salt Lake the following summer with Brigham
Young. According to Barnes, Shumway settled in Arizona
at an early date.

P.O. est. January 9, 1893. James Pearce, p.m. Discont. October
11, 1956.
Ref.: Barnes; 112, p. 167. Maps: B-9; C-8.

a.n. Shumway Ruin    Loc.: 40 miles s. of Holbrook    Navajo
A prehistoric pueblo of the long house type.
Ref.: 88, II, 560.

## SHUNGOPOVI

El.: c. 6000'    Loc.: Navajo 1, C-14
Pro.: /səmówəpavi^/    Hopi: "a place of chumoa —
a kind of grass or reed"
In their missionizing efforts, the Spaniards founded San
Bartolome in this Hopi settlement in 1629. Nearby at an
ancient spring was an Indian settlement, Old Shongopovi.
The pueblo which sprang up in 1680 was the scene in that
same year of the martyrdom of Fr. Joseph de Truxillo and
the complete destruction of the mission. It is at this village
that the annual Snake Dance occurs in August.

P.O. est. Chimopovy June 24, 1926. Mrs. Marietta Eubank, p.m.
Name changed to Shungopowy (sic), May 1, 1934. Discont. June
30, 1942.

F. W. Hodge lists fifty-six variant spellings for this Second
Mesa village, only the most widely differentiated of which
are given below:

v.n. Xongopavi    (36, p. 103, Note 1)
Shongopovi    (Spring) (71, pp. 155, 195)
Comupavi    (Oñate) (1598)
Jongopabi    (Vargas – 1692)
Shimopavi    (Bandelier, 1890)
Showmowth-pa    (Domenech, 1860)
Shu-muth-pa    (Whipple, 1877)
San Bartolome de Xongopavi
(Vetancourt, 1694)
San Bernardo de Jongopabi
(Vargas, 1692)
Ci-mo-pavi    (Fewkes, 1892)

Ref.: 4, p. 412; 29, pp. 43, 44; 88, I, 553; 36, p. 103 (Note 1);
88, p. 564. Maps: C-1; D-4; E-11.

## SICHOMOVI

El.: c. 6000'                    Loc.: Navajo 3, EF-1
Pro.: /sitów˘məoviˆ/        Hopi: "place of the mound of
                                      the wild currant bush"
When Walpi (q.v.) became too crowded, apparently some
of the residents formed a suburb which took its name from
wild currant bushes growing on a knoll. Although the date
of its founding is not known, Sichimovi (sic) was in existence by 1782 when Morfi spoke of it as having been
founded recently.
Ref.:   29, p. 44; 71, p. 195; 78, p. 6. Map: C-3.

## SIKYATKI

El.: c. 6000'                    Loc.: Navajo 1, DE-14.3
Pro.: /siˆkⁱʌpkiˆ/          Hopi: "yellow house"
Sikyatki is a ten- to fifteen-acre ruined pueblo of the Fire-
wood (Kokop) Hopi clan, and spreads over two knolls.
Tradition says it was destroyed by warriors from Walpi
and perhaps from other Hopi villages. The reason for the
name "yellow house" is not known to present-day Hopis.
Sikyatki apparently predates the coming of the Spaniards.
Ref.:   83, p. 63; 88, II, 572. Maps: E-18; E-20 (Seecho-wah-
        wee).

## SILVER CREEK

El.: c. 6000'                    Loc.: Navajo 3, FH-4-12.5
                                Navajo 2, GH-14-12.5
                                Town: Navajo 3, HI-6.3
Early settlers named the location Silver Creek because the
stream was clear and silvery. It was referred to as Silver
Creek by Martha Summerhayes in 1875.
P.O. est. October 27, 1905. Rafael Carrillo, p.m. Discont. July
6, 1932.
Ref.:   Barnes; 158, p. 125. Maps: B-9; C-6; C-11 (town).

## SINKS, THE

El.: c. 6000'                    Loc.: Navajo 3, E-2
A series of earth depressions varying from twenty-five feet
deep and a few feet across to others over nine hundred feet
in diameter, these holes collect rainwater which sinks rapidly into the ground.
Ref.:   4, pp. 448-449. Maps: A-7; C-9.

## SIPAULOVI

El.: c. 6000'                    Loc.: Navajo 1, E-14.2
Pro.: /sowlówəpaviˆ/ or    Hopi: "The place of mosquitoes"
      /sowpáulaviˆ/
The Hopi meaning of the name Sipaulovi is misleading.
Actually, the name derives from the fact that the largest
clan is composed of some of the people who formerly lived
at Homolobi, which was abandoned because of mosquitoes.
Other residents came from Shongopovi. The village was
founded c. 1750.
v.n. Shipaulovi
     Ah-le-la
        (Whipple Pacific RR Reports, 1856, Suni name)
     Shipolovi
     Sha-pah-lah-wee
Ref.:   Hopi Constitution; 88, II, 551, 562. Maps: C-3; D-1;
        E-18; GI-11.

## SMITH BUTTE

El.: c. 6000'                    Loc.: Navajo 2, E-8.4
Bill A. Smith was a cattleman who had a cow camp at
Smith Spring, six miles east, c. 1890.
v.n. Black Rock Spring        (descriptive)
Ref.:   Barnes; 71, p. 153. Maps: C-12; GI-11.

## SNOWFLAKE

El.: 5600'                       Loc.: Navajo 3, FG-2.6
When Martha Summerhayes traveled through here in 1875,
the location was a ranch owned by James Stinson. Mrs.
Summerhayes said that many so-called ranches were mere
adobe ruins, but since it was necessary to have names on
maps, the names of former owners remained on deserted
ranches. Such ranches were usually located near a spring
or creek and so became travelers' camp sites.
In July 1878, William J. Flake bought the land from Stinson. That autumn twelve destitute families arrived and
Flake gave them temporary shelter. With a group, Erastus
Snow (b. North Carolina, July 3, 1839) arrived at the
Kartchner ranch nearby in September. Flake's place was
selected as the townsite and it was given the name Snow
Flake after its two founders.
When Apache County was created in 1879, Snow Flake
was its first county seat. Snow Flake retained that honor
only until the fall election when the county government
was moved to St. Johns.
P.O. est. June 27, 1881. William D. Kartchner, p.m. Changed to
Snowflake, September 17, 1906.
Ref.:   4, p. 448; 112, pp. 164, 165; 158, p. 125; APHS Files.
        Maps: B-9; C-5; E-20.

## SPOTTED MOUNTAIN

El.: c. 6000'                    Loc.: Navajo 3, A-8.8
Bunches of timber form "spots" on this mountain.
Ref.:   Barnes. Map: B-7.

## SQUASH MOUNTAINS

El.: c. 7000'                    Loc.: Navajo 1, GH-11
This group of mountains was named at least by 1879 when
it appears on the Smith map. A later writer said the mountains dominated the foreground (referring to what he called
Squash Blossom Butte) like "an inverted bloom that the
storm of aeons had carved and a million rare sunsets tinted.
Indians reverence the squash blossom as a symbol of frui-
tion . . . It is found in Navajo silver-work . . . and
when one goes into Hopiland, he finds it imitated in the
dressing of their maids' hair. So they named this altar."
Ref.:   36, p. 63. Map: E-20.

## STANDARD

El.: c. 6000'                    Loc.: Navajo 3, EF-5.5
In 1922 the Standard Lumber Company built a sawmill
here. A post office was established for the convenience of
the logging crews.
P.O. est. October 17, 1924. Mrs. Agnes J. Cheshire, p.m. Discont. October 15, 1938.
Ref.:   Barnes; P.O. Records. Map: C-13.

## STEPHEN BUTTE

El.: c. 6000'  Loc.: Navajo 2, E-3.2
A. M. Stephen, an ethnologist who lived for many years at Keams Canyon, is buried here.
Ref.: Barnes; 71, p. 195. Maps: D-4; GI-11.

## STINSON WASH

El.: c. 6000'  Loc.: Navajo 3, D-4.5
James Stinson had a ranch here from 1873 to 1878. (cf. Snowflake.)
Ref.: Barnes. Map: B-9.
**a.n. Stinson Valley**  Navajo
Name used by pioneers for site of Snowflake.

## SUNFLOWER BUTTE

El.: c. 6000'  Loc.: Navajo 2, G-7
Sunflowers of skin and wood, made by prehistoric Indians, were found in abundance here.
Ref.: Barnes quoting "Report 65," U. S. Bureau Ethnology. Map: D-4.

## SUNSET

El.: c. 4000'  Loc.: Navajo 2, A-9
Sunset was one of five Mormon settlements which developed from the Mormon immigration of 1876 (cf. Joseph City). The name is said to have come from Sunset Gap to the west (cf. Sunset Crossing).

Lot Smith and Lorenzo Roundy led the colonists to a place where there were ancient Indian ruins. For a brief time, the settlers were upstream two miles from their final location at Sunset. At Sunset the Mormons built a fort of drift cottonwood logs. Poor soil and undependable irrigation forced the colonists to abandon Sunset by 1878. The last to leave were Lot Smith and his family, who departed in 1888. Today only a graveyard remains on a hill to the northeast of the vanished settlement.
P.O. est. July 5, 1876. Alfred M. Derrick, p.m. Discont. November 23, 1887.
Ref.: MNA; 112, p. 142; 167, p. 153; 171, p. 1. Maps: C-4; E-20.

## SUNSET CROSSING

El.: c. 4000'  Loc.: Navajo 2, A-9
The route followed by Lt. Edward Fitzgerald Beale (April 7, 1858) and later by Capt. George M. Wheeler in the 1870's, crossed the Little Colorado River on a rocky ledge which formed a ford. It lay on the route from the east to Camp Verde, Fort Whipple, and other places in Arizona and farther west, via Sunset Gap, a pass through the mountains to the southwest twenty miles from Winslow. The crossing was the only one having a rock bed, and it was used by stages going east and west.

At Sunset Crossing William Blanchard and J. H. Breed operated a store during the period when the railroad was being built (1878-1883). From their names, Sunset Crossing was also known as Blanchard Crossing and as Breed's Crossing. Here William Blanchard and Joe Barrett were found murdered in December 1881. The murderers—"Thick-lipped Joe" Waters and William Campbell—were caught, jailed at St. Johns, and lynched.
Ref.: Barnes; Richards. Map: C-5.

## SUPPLY, CAMP

El.: 6000'  Loc.: Navajo 2, FG-11
One mile e. of Holbrook.
When Col. Kit Carson was on an expedition against the Navajos in 1863, he is said to have established a temporary camp at this place.
Ref.: Barnes; 105, pp. 97-98. Map: None.
**a.n. Camp Sunset**  Navajo
Loc.: Supposedly in same locality as Camp Supply.
Ref.: 111, p. 157.

## TAYLOR

El.: 5700' (No. 2)  No.1: Navajo 2, D-10.2
No. 2: Navajo 3, FG-3.1
Two settlements called Taylor have resulted in some confusion concerning their histories as well as the origins of their names.

The first Taylor was established on the Little Colorado River, about three miles west of the present Joseph City, on January 22, 1878, when John Kartchner and eight Mormon families from Utah attempted to put up dams in order to irrigate. When their fifth dam washed out in July, the pioneers gave up trying to establish a colony, moving to Silver Creek to a locality known at that time as Bagley, after Daniel Bagley, who had already settled there. The new residents wanted to call their settlement Walker, but the post office department required another name, since there was already a Walker post office in Arizona. The settlers then selected the name Taylor to honor John Taylor, English-born president of the Church of Jesus Christ of Latter-day Saints, who had been wounded in 1844 by the mob which killed Joseph Smith.
P.O. est. March 28, 1881. Jesse N. Perkins, p.m.
Ref.: 4, p. 449; 112, pp. 148, 166, 167. Maps: B-9 (No. 2); C-5 (No. 2).

## TEAS TOH

El.: c. 5500'  Loc.: Navajo 2, E-3.8
Pro.: /tʔiyˇstó/  Navajo: *tees* "cottonwood trees"; *to,* "water"
Descriptive. When the Cedar Springs (*q.v.*) store and post office was abandoned in 1930, operations were moved to Juan Lorenzo Hubbell's trading post at nearby Teas Toh.
P.O. est. as Tees To, June 18, 1930. Discont. February 29, 1934.
**v.n. Tees Too**
Ref.: Barnes. Maps: D-1; C-13.

## TEWA

El.: c. 6000'  Loc.: Navajo 1, DE-13.3
Pro.: /téowˇa/
When the Spaniards returned to the Rio Grande area in the 1690's (following their rout from the region in the Pueblo uprising of 1680), a group of Indians from a New Mexican

pueblo called Tsawarnum-a-bive (now La Puebla) sought refuge. These refugees settled on First Mesa c. 1700. The name Hano was applied to them as a contraction of the word *anopi*, meaning "eastern people." Although they have intermarried with the Hopi, these people still speak their native tongue, Tewa.

P.O. est. August 10, 1900. Sarah E. Abbott, p.m. Rescind. January 15, 1901.

**v.n. Tegua**

Ref.: Colton; 29, p. 44; 71, pp. 191, 195; 88, pp. 531, 591. Maps: C-4; E-11.

**a.n. Tewa Spring**   Loc.: Sec. 11, T. 28 N., R. 18 E.        Navajo

## TOHADISTOA SPRING

El.: c. 5500′                Loc.: Navajo 1, GH-10
                   Navajo: "bubbling water is heard"
Descriptive.

**v.n. To-hah-le-tis-ta**

Ref.: 71, pp. 155, 196; 151, p. 760. Map: D-4.

## TOREVA

El.: c. 6000′                Loc.: Navajo 1, C-14.2
                   Hopi: *toriva* "crooked" or "twisted"
The village takes its name from a spring which emerges in a twisted way from the earth.

P.O. est. October 1, 1900. Frank D. Voorhees, p.m. Discont. July 24, 1937.

Ref.: 71, pp. 39, 159. Maps: C-9; D-4; D-6.

## TOVAR MESA

El.: c. 6000′                Loc.: Navajo 2, CD-2 AB-4
In 1540 Coronado sent Pedro de Tobar (or Tovar) with a party to explore the Hopi pueblos. Apparently Herbert Gregory was the first to apply the name to the mesa.

Ref.: 71, pp. 38, 196; 151, p. 764. Maps: C-12; D-4.

## TSAY-YAH-KIN

El.: c. 6000′                Loc.: Navajo 1, F-1.5
Pro.: /tséya·kin/      Navajo: "house under the rock"
First discovered by white men in late 1949, Tsay-yah-kin lies in a vast cliff hanging over the head of a box canyon. It has been visited by few white people, but obviously housed many early Indians.

Ref.: 96, p. 16. Map: A-7.

## TSEGI CANYON

El.: c. 6000′                Loc.: Navajo 1, DC-5-4
Pro.: /tséyiʔ/    Navajo: "in between the rocks"; "canyon"
Navajos use *tsegi* as generally descriptive of deep canyons with sheer walls. In the 1880's John Wetherill (cf. Kayenta) and his brothers explored this canyon. Near the turn of the twentieth century this canyon was called Laguna Canyon because its broad floor held several lakes, now gone. A flood in 1912 washed out dams along the canyon floor and began erosion now down to depths of over fifty feet.

Ref.: 5, p. 6; 71, pp. 192, 47 (Plate XIV); 167, p. 140. Map: D-1.

**a.n. Laguna Creek**                               Navajo
Loc.: Rises at Boiling Springs and flows to Chinle Wash Springs in Tsegi Canyon.
Ref.: 4, p. 423.

**Upper Laguna Creek**    Map: GI-3               Navajo
Ref.: Colton.

## TURKEY SPRINGS

El.: c. 6000′                Loc.: Navajo 3, AB-5.2
In May 1886, Will C. Barnes camped overnight with an old trapper named Woolf (cf. Woolf's Crossing, Coconino), who had just found a clutch of wild turkey eggs. As the springs had no names, the men agreed to call them Turkey Springs.

Ref.: Barnes. Map: B-6.

## TWIN BUTTES

El.: 5685′                Loc.: Navajo 2, I-6
Descriptive. These buttes are typical of the Hopi Buttes, which are remnants of a volcanic region much older than the San Francisco Mountains.

**v.n. Twin Mesas
    Zañi Mountain**

Ref.: 29, p. 45; 71, pp. 153, 196; 151, p. 776. Map: D-4.

## TWIN LAKES

El.: c. 6000′                Loc.: Navajo 3, A-5.5
Descriptive. These are small crater lakes.

Ref.: Barnes. Maps: B-7; B-9; C-12.

## TWIN WASH

El.: c. 5300′                Loc.: Navajo 2, F-10.8-11.1
After crossing the Painted Desert, the twin arms of this double wash merge just before arriving at U. S. Highway 66.

Ref.: Branch. Map: GI-8.

## TYENDE CREEK

El.: c. 6000′                Loc.: Navajo 1, CH-3.5
Pro.: /tʰyeʔnde·h/    Navajo: "where they fell into a pit";
                         i.e., where animals bog down
This is the bog hole near Kayenta (*q.v.*).
Tyende Creek is the longest perennially flowing stream in the area, emerging from Laguna Canyon at Marsh Pass and flowing thence north to the rim of Monument Valley on to Chinle Valley, eventually reaching the San Juan River.

**v.n. Ta enta Creek
    Laguna Creek
    Kayenta Creek**

Ref.: 71, pp. 36, 87, 196; 167, p. 166. Maps: C-11 (Laguna Creek); C-12; D-4; GI-3.

**a.n. Tyende Mesa**                               Navajo

## WALPI

El.: 6225′                Loc.: Navajo 1, DE-14.3
Pro.: /wálːəpiˆ/      Hopi: *wala* "gap"; *opi* "place of"
Walpi takes its name from a gap on the mesa on which it is located. Below the present site on the northwest side of the mesa is Old Walpi, now a ruin. It was first called Walpi

but later called Kuchaptuvela, "gray slope" (Hopi: "ash hill terrace"). It was still occupied when visited by Fr. Espejo on April 21, 1583, but was abandoned c. 1629 when the inhabitants moved to Kisakobi ("ladder place town") farther up the mesa. Kisakobi in turn was abandoned in 1680 when the present Walpi was built. The Spanish mission at Kisakobi was destroyed during the Hopi uprising in 1680, thus ending efforts to Christianize Hopis. The efforts were not resumed until after Arizona became part of the United States.

The move to the mesa top was probably made in fear of reprisals by the Spaniards, who never came, but the new and safer location proved its worth when nomadic Indians attacked the Hopis and devastated their fields, while the Hopi perched safely on their mesa tops.

v.n. **Gaspe**    (name applied by Espejo to Old Walpi)
**Ash Hill Terrace**
Ref.:   78, p. 5; 88, I, 703, 731; 88, II, 901; 151, p. 800. Maps: C-3 (Wolpi); E-11 (Gualpi).
a.n. **Walpi Spring**   Loc.: Sec. 15, T. 28 N., R. 18 E.    Navajo
Ref.:   71, p. 155.

## WASHBOARD CREEK

El.: c. 5000′          Loc.: Navajo 2, FH-13.4-1.2
Where this dry wash crossed the old stage road to Fort Apache it was cut up "like a washboard" with small arroyos.
Ref.:   Barnes. Map: GI-11.

## WEPO SPRINGS

El.: c. 6000′          Loc.: Navajo 1, FG-11
Pro.: /wíphowya/          Hopi: "onion"
Certain ceremonial races begin at Wepo Springs, especially the opening of the snake ceremony. Terraced gardens here are worth noting; their presence indicates that at one time there must have been much more water than there is today.
v.n. **Wipho**
Ref.:   88, II, 963 Colton; 71, p. 155; 151, p. 807. Map: D-4.
a.n. **Wepo Valley**          Navajo
**Wepo Wash**   Loc.: Tributary to First Mesa Wash    Navajo
Ref.:   71, p. 39.

## WETHERILL MESA

El.: 6160′          Loc.: Navajo 1, GH-1-2
Named for John Wetherill (cf. Kayenta).
Ref.:   MNA. Map: GI-1.

## WHITE CAVE SPRING

El.: c. 6000′          Loc.: Navajo 2, GH-3.3
A cave of light colored rock is the source of this spring.
Ref.:   Barnes. Maps: A-1; C-10.

## WHITE CONE

El.: c. 6000′          Loc.: Navajo 2, FG-2.5
White Cone is a peak of light sandstone which the Navajos call *Hakaltizh* ("penis head").
Ref.:   73, p. 319; 167, p. 171. Maps: C-9; D-4.
a.n. **White Cone Spring**          Navajo
Ref.:   71, p. 153.

## WHITE RIVER

El.: c. 6000′-4000′          Loc.: Apache 3, B-10-A-11;
                                    Navajo 3, H-10
The East Fork of the White River (rises T. 6 N., R. 26 E.) joins the North Fork of the White River (rises T. 7 N., R. 26 E.) at Fort Apache to form the White River. An early name for this stream was the Sierra Blanca River. Currently, the North Fork is often called Snake Creek, and its long-pronged tributary is called Smith Cienega.
v.n. **White Mountain Creek**
Ref.:   175, I, 62; Wentz; Wiltbank; 22, p. 142. Maps: B-9; C-2 (White Mountain River); C-10.
a.n. **Whiteriver** *(q.v.)*          Navajo
Headquarters for the Fort Apache Indian Reservation. *(q.v.).*

## WHITERIVER

El.: c. 4000′          Loc.: Navajo 3, H-10
Whiteriver is the present headquarters for the Apache Indian Reservation, on the north fork of the White River.
P.O. est. as White River November 19, 1896. Effie W. Russell, p.m.
Ref.:   P.O. Records; Davis. Map: C-9.

## WILD HORSE LAKE

El.: c. 6000′          Loc.: Navajo 3, AB-5.5
Daniel Boone Holcomb (cf. Phoenix Park Canyon) built a corral here to capture wild horses.
Ref.:   Barnes. Maps: C-14; B-9.

## WILD HORSE WASH

El.: 5500′          Loc.: Navajo 2, I-9-9.4
Wild horses at one time abounded in this area. (Cf. Digger Creek).
Ref.:   Grigsby. Map: GI-8.

## WILFORD

El.: c. 6000′          Loc.: Navajo 3, AB-4.5
Named in honor of President Wilford Woodruff of the Mormon church, Wilford was a small and prosperous settlement established in 1883 by John Bushman and others from St. Joseph. Two years later the wash went dry and Wilford's residents moved to Heber, where they found more abundant water.
Ref.:   Barnes; 112, p. 155. Map: B-3.
a.n. **Wilford Spring**   Map: B-9          Navajo

## WINSLOW

El.: 4856′          Loc.: Navajo 2, AB-9.8
In November 1881, the coming of the A. & P. R.R. (now the S.F.R.R.) marked the end of the importance of Sunset Crossing *(q.v.)* as a trading center when the railroad established a terminal at the site of the present Winslow.
Already on the site was F. G. Demerest, a hotel man, who had a tent here in late 1880. He was soon followed by J. H. Breed, formerly of Sunset Crossing. Opinions vary as to whether the town took its name from that of a prospector named Tom Winslow who, while living at Meyer in 1920,

said that Winslow was named for him, or whether the city was named for Gen. Edward Winslow, president of the old St. Louis and San Francisco R.R., which was associated with the new transcontinental line.

P.O. est. January 10, 1882. U. L. Taylor, p.m. Wells Fargo Station, 1885.

Ref.:   APHS; Richards, Diary; 167, p. 174. Maps: C-5; GI-11.

## WOODRUFF

El.: c. 5000'                    Loc.: Navajo 2, H-12.8
First settlers in this area were Luther Martin and Felix Scott, c. 1870, who settled two miles south of the present village. In 1876 Mormons from Allen's Camp (cf. Joseph City) looked over the land, but took no steps to obtain it. Then in 1877 came Ammon M. Tenney who decided to settle. He arrived shortly after Lewis P. Cardon with a few other families, and for about a year the place was known as Tenney's Camp. In February 1878, the name Woodruff was adopted to honor President Wilford Woodruff of the Mormon church. Time and again river dams broke under the impact of the turbulent Little Colorado River. Dams washed out a total of seven times between 1880 and 1890.

P.O. est. May 14, 1880. James Deans, p.m.

**v.n. Black Peak**

Ref.:   Richards; 112, pp. 161, 162; 167, pp. 176, 177. Maps: C-5; B-9; E-20.

**a.n. Woodruff Butte**          El.: 5616'                    Navajo
A volcanic cone, Woodruff Butte is sacred to the Navajos, whose medicine men climb the butte to collect jimson weed for ceremonial use.

## WOOLHOUSE MOUNTAIN

El.: c. 6000'                    Loc.: Navajo 2, H-2.6
Manuel Candelaria of Concho built a warehouse for storing wool here c. 1884.

Ref.:   Barnes. Map: B-2.

**a.n. Woolhouse Tank**          Map: B-9          Navajo

## YEI BICHEI MESA

El.: 5200'                    Loc.: Navajo 1, GH-2
A formation at the northern tip of this mesa gives it the name. The formation bears a similarity to the appearance of a group of Navajo dancers lined up in the nine-day healing ceremony, the Yei Bichei.

Ref.:   96, pp. 88, 119. Map: GI-1.

## ZENIFF

El.: c. 5000'                    Loc.: Navajo 3, CD-2
Originally, this location was known as Dry Lake because of its adjacency to a basin which when filled with flood drainage waters was used by thousands of range stock in the 1880's. Later the area was converted to a farming region which took the name of Zeniff, after a character in the *Book of Mormon*. In 1956 there were fewer than five people living at Zeniff.

P.O. est. September 20, 1922. John A. Bowler, p.m. Discont. July 15, 1933.

**v.n. Big Dry Lake**          (Richards)

Ref.:   Richards. Maps: C-13; D-1.

## ZILLESA MESA

El.: c. 6000'                    Loc.: Navajo 1, EF-11
            Navajo:  "mountain surrounded by bare soil"
This is a round butte, more like a mesa than a peak.

**v.n. Zillesa Peak**
     **Amusovi Mesa**          (Hopi name)

Ref.:   MNA; 71, p. 40; 151, p. 833. Maps: C-12; D-4.

## ZILNEZ MESA

El.: c. 7000'                    Loc.: Navajo 1, BC-3.4
                              1
Pro.:   /dzišnne:z/     Navajo:  *dzil*, "mountain"; *nez*, "long"
Descriptive.

**v.n. Zillnez**
     **Zihl Nez**
     **Zilth Nez Mesa**

Ref.:   71, pp. 48, 197; 151, p. 833; 5, p. 2. Maps: C-11; D-1; D-4.

## ZILTAHJINI MESA

El.: c. 7000'                    Loc.: Navajo 1, CD-10.5
                              1
Pro.:   /dzišdahžin/     Navajo:  "standing cranes"
Origin not yet ascertained.

**v.n. Zilh-tah-jini Peak**          (C-6)

Ref.:   Barnes; 71, p. 40. Maps: C-6; C-12; D-4.

# PIMA COUNTY

*Padre Kino and Indians — San Xavier — Butterfield Mail Stage in Tucson.*

## PIMA COUNTY:
Pro.:  /píymə/

In the days of Spanish missions in Arizona, Pima County was part of an area known as Pimeria Alta (Spanish: "upper Pima land"). Fr. Eusebio Kino in May 1704, suggested that another name to be given to the region, and that it be called thereafter New Philippines. Later, when the United States annexed the huge region then known as New Mexico, southern Arizona was included in Doña Ana County, which stretched all the way from the Colorado River eastward to the present New Mexican border. Then came the War Between the States, and Sylvester Mowry (cf. Mowry Mine, Santa Cruz) proposed on his map of Arizona in 1860 that the name Ewell County be given to what is now Pima and Santa Cruz counties. The name was that of Capt. Richard S. Ewell (*See* Fort Buchanan, Santa Cruz). None of the early names, however, was destined to take hold.

On November 8, 1864, the first territorial legislature for Arizona created four counties, of which Pima was one. The name was given because the county was the home of the Pima Indians. The Pima Indians are a peaceful agricultural tribe. Their name came from a nickname given them by the Spaniards because these Indians used the word *pim* to indicate negation. The descendants of the Pima Indians of Pimeria Alta now have the Pima and San Xavier Indian Reservations, and their cousins have the Papago Reservation.

As originally constituted, Pima County included all land south of the Gila River and east of Yuma (roughly all that part of the United States acquired from Mexico in the Gadsden Purchase). Gradually the huge county diminished as other counties were carved from it. Parts were cut off in forming Maricopa, Pinal, and Cochise counties, and more was lost when Graham County was formed. Currently Pima County has 5,914,240 acres. Its county seat has always been Tucson.

Whatever industries are found in other Arizona counties will be found in Pima County, with the possible exception of extensive lumbering, although at one time (in the 1870's) lumber was hauled from the Santa Rita Mountains.

## ACHI

El.: c. 1500'                           Loc.: Pima 2, EF-3.1
Pro.: /áčə/                              Papago: "ridge"
This is a small permanent Papago village.

v.n. Archi; Achie    (corruption)
Ref.:   128, p. 5. Map: D-8.

## AGUA DULCE MOUNTAINS

El.: c. 1500'                           Loc.: Pima 1, BC-6
Pro.: /ágwa dúwlsey/                    Spanish: "sweet water"
These mountains take their name from the Agua Dulce
Spring on the Sonoyta River across the border in Mexico.
The water in the spring is soft and sweet, hence the name.
This spring was referred to by Lt. N. Michler in 1854.

v.n. Sonoyta Mountains
     Sierra de Agua Dulce   (Lumholtz)
Ref.:   Ketchum; Hensen; 51, p. 115. Map: A-7.

a.n. Agua Dulce Pass   Loc.: In Ajo Mountains          Pima
     Kino passed through at least seven times, but gave the pass
     no name.

v.n. Sweet Water Pass
Ref.:   Hensen.

## AGUIRRE PEAK

El.: 4947'                              Loc.: Pima 3, BC-11
Pro.: /agíyriy/
Inasmuch as the name Aguirre Peak does not appear on
maps until GLO 1909, nor the name Aguirre prior to GLO
1892, the name of Aguirre Peak probably derives from its
adjacency to the Buenos Ayres Ranch, owned by Pedro
Aguirre. His brother Epifanio was killed many years earlier
across the border in Mexico.
Pedro Aguirre (b. Mexico, June 21, 1835) came to Arizona
in 1859. With his brothers he ran various stage lines. In
1870 he established the ranch where he built a large dam
c. 1886. This created Aguirre Lake.
There has for many years been Indian ranching at Aguirre
Lake.
P.O. est. as Buenos Ayres, February 6, 1892. Beatrice Aguirre,
p.m. (cf. La Osa).
Ref.:   APHS Files; 141, p. 53; 128, pp. 4, 32; 151, p. 170;
        P.O. Records. Map: GJ-9.

a.n. Aguirre Pass      Map: GJ-4                        Pima
     Aguirre's Station                                 Pima
     Loc.: On the stage road from Tucson to Quijotoa.
     This was a dry camp in 1884.
Ref.:   155, p. 78.

     Aguirre Valley                                    Pima
     Loc.:Waterman Mountains and Roskruge Mountains on
     east; Vaca Hills and Santa Rosa Mountains on west.
Ref.:   128, p. 18.

## AGUIRRE VAYA

El.: c. 4000'                           Loc.: Pima 3, B-3.5
Pro.: /agirəwáha/
This is a temporary Papago village named after a Mexican
ranger.
Ref.:   128, p. 12. Map: D-8.

a.n. Aguirre Wash                                      Pima
     Loc.: This wash flows n.w. by Aguirre Vaya.
Ref.:   128, p. 27.

## AHE VONAM

El.: c. 2500'                           Loc.: Pima 2, DE-4
Pro.: /a?ey ownəm/                      Papago: "hat on both ends"
Descriptive. The mountain looks like a hat from either of
its two sides.

When the Brownell Mine was active, the post office here
was Brownell, after Frank Brownell, a Civil War veteran
and miner in the Quijotoa Range. He also had a store.
When the post office was discontinued, the name soon
reverted to the Indian designation.

P.O. est. as Brownell April 3, 1903. Frank Brownell, p.m.
Discont. December 15, 1911.

v.n. Aaivonam
Ref.:   Barnes; Kirk Bryan Notes; P.O. Records; 128, p. 5.
        Maps: C-10 (Brownell); D-8.

a.n. Brownell Mountains                                Pima
     Brownell Peak                                     Pima
     Brownell Valley                                   Pima

## AJO

El.: 1751'                              Loc.: Pima 1, E-2.6
Pro.: /áho/                             Papago: au'auho, "paint"
A similarity between the sound of the Papago word for
this locality and the Spanish word ajo for many years led
to misapprehension concerning the origin of the name of
present-day Ajo. The Papago Indians used au'auho in connection with the mines at Ajo because the ores were a
source of red paint which the Papagos used to decorate
themselves. This was so noted by one of the earliest American travelers in the region. Nevertheless, the fact that the
Mexican miners pronounced the word without the double
pronunciation of the au of the Papago resulted in a word that
sounded much like ajo. This, added to the fact that the Ajo
lily (the root of which looks and tastes much like a spring
onion) grows abundantly in this area, led to the belief that
the locality was named Ajo because of the wild lilies.

The first American citizen to notice the mining possibilities
in the region was Capt. Peter R. Brady, who was with the
surveying party for the Thirty-Second Parallel railroad in
1853. When the party broke up in San Francisco, Brady
was influential in organizing a group of men to explore
mining possibilities at Ajo. This group soon had shipped
out all the rich, easily-smelted ores from Ajo's mines. Despite the fact that the remaining ores were unquestionably
rich, there was no satisfactory way to reduce them economically, and for many years the treasure in copper at
the Ajo mines remained relatively untouched. The hills
with their rich exposed ores were a speculators' paradise.

In 1910 the population—including Mexicans, Indians and
American citizens—was fifty people. The main business
among these people was grazing cattle. Lack of water was
a serious problem and poverty rampant. In February 1911,
there were only four Americans at what later came to be
known as Old Ajo. However, Ajo was on the verge of becoming a boom town. With the discovery of a leaching
process which made it possible to work the ores efficiently
and inexpensively, Ajo entered into a prosperous period.

The New Cornelia Copper Company was organized, a
smelter built, and wells dug. From three to five thousand
people were employed by the mines.

The battle between the few old timers in Old Ajo and the
powerful mining company was soon joined. The old town
of Ajo was far too close to huge deposits of low grade ore
which the copper company wanted to develop. The company located its own town a mile to the north, which it
proposed to call Cornelia. However, nearly all of Old Ajo
burned down, and the name Ajo became attached to the
new town (cf. Clarkstown).

P.O. est. August 29, 1900. John H. Hovey, p.m.

Ref.:   Kirk Bryan Notes; *Ajo Copper News,* XXXIX (October
21, 1954), Insert A:1:2,5; 101, p. 69; 46, pp. 157, 159;
104, p. 80; 34, p. 367; P.O. Records. Map: GJ-1.

**a.n. Ajo Range**                                                      Pima
   **Mount Ajo**   El.: 4843'. Loc.: In Ajo Range.          Pima
   **Ajo Peak**     El.: 2617'. Map: GJ-1               Pima
   There are four sharp-pointed peaks in this group. The one
   furthest to the north is known as Peñasco Peak, descrip-
   tive of the fact that it rises by a series of cliffs, to a pillar
   of rock.
   Ref.:  34, p. 208.

   **Little Ajo Mountains**     Map: GJ-1                      Pima

## AK CHUT VAYA

El.: c. 2500'                          Loc.: Pima 2, G-10.8
Pro.: /ák tit vʷàhya/          Papago: "well in wash"
Descriptive. This is a small Papago village.
Ref.:  128, p. 3. Map: GJ-15.

## ALDONA

El.: 2800'
                                       Loc.: Pima 4, BC-4.8
                                       E. of Tucson 5 miles.
This location on the railroad was named for Alfred S.
Donau, who came to Arizona in 1883. Al Donau was a
cattleman, real estate agent, and merchant.
Ref.:  Barnes. Map: None.

## ALI AK CHIN

El.: c. 1500'                          Loc.: Pima 2, A-10
Pro.: /awaᵏčín/          Papago: "little mouth of wash"
This Papago village (or temporal) and charco (pond) is
named descriptively, since the location is at the small mouth
of a wash.

**v.n. La Quintuna**

(probably Spanish corruption of Papago pronunciation).
Ref.:  Kirk Bryan Notes; 128, p. 7. Map: D-8.

**a.n. La Quintuna Valley**                                     Pima
   Loc.: Ali Ak Chin is in this valley.
   So named by Kirk Bryan.
Ref.:  Kirk Bryan Notes; 128, p. 17.

## ALI CHUK SON

El.: 2589'                             Loc.: Pima 2, GH-7.6
Pro.: /ari čuksówn/          Papago: "foot of the little
                                              black hills"
The name of this large Papago village is descriptive. It has
cultivated fields at the base of a small lava hill.

**v.n. Tucsoncito**   "Little Tucson" (Spanish corruption)
Ref.:  34, p. 407; Kirk Bryan Notes; 128, p. 1. Maps: GJ-12;
D-8 (Ali Chukson).

## ALTAR VALLEY

El.: c. 4000'                          Loc.: Pima 3, FC-4.3-12.8
Pro.: /altar/
In 1693 Fr. Kino passed through this area on a missionizing
journey during which he made brief stops. With his lieutenant, Juan Mateo Manje, he stopped at a place they
called El Altar, where the river disappeared in the sand.
The Altar River has its source near the Mexican boundary
and flows south, whereas the Altar Valley heads near the
same place, but extends north.

**v.n. Baboquivera Plain**          (Pumpelly)

Ref.:   U. S. G. B. "Decision, July 1, 1936–June 30, 1937," p.
4; 120, p. 278. Maps: A-6; C-10.

**a.n. Altar Wash**     Maps: GJ-2; GJ-8                      Pima

## ALVAREZ MOUNTAINS

El.: 3248'; 2830'                      Loc.: Pima 2, EF-8.7-9.5
Pro.: /ǽlvərez/
These mountains were named for a Mexican rancher here
in the early days.
Ref.:  Ketchum. Maps: GJ-12; GJ-15.

## AMOLE PEAK

El.: 4683'                             Loc.: Pima 2, G-3.5
Pro.: /əmówliy/          Spanish: "soap root"
This peak first appeared on the Roskruge map (1893) as
Wasson Peak, named for John A. Wasson (b. 1833, d. January 16, 1909) a newspaper man, who arrived in California
in 1852, coming to Arizona at a later date which is not
known. During the establishment of Arizona's public school
system, Wasson was right hand man to Gov. A. P. K. Safford. Wasson started the *Arizona Citizen* and was its editor
and publisher for many years.

Despite the fact that there are no more yucca plants (from
which soap is occasionally made) at this peak than elsewhere, the name was changed from Wasson Peak by Eldred
D. Wilson and his partner Jenkins when a prospector told
them the name was Amole Peak.

Ref.:   3a, p. 33; 115, p. 253; G.E.P. Smith, Letter to U. S.
Board on Geographic Names, November 3, 1939. Maps:
B-3 (Amole and Wasson); C-7; C-12; C-9; C-15 (Was-
son Peak); GJ-6 (Amole).

**a.n. Amole**                                                      Pima
   El.: 3917'. Loc.: On railroad e. of Tucson 33 miles.
   Named because of innumerable yucca (amole) in area.
Ref.:   Barnes; APHS Names File. Maps: B-3; C-13 (Amoli).

## ANDRADE'S RANCH

El.: c. 4000'                          Loc.: Pima 4, E-7.4
Pro.: /andrádiˆ/
In the early 1870's Jose Andrade (d. September 27, 1902)
homesteaded a ranch in Davidson Canyon. It was a favorite
spot for Apaches lurking in wait to attack travelers on the
road from Tucson to Fort Crittenden or to Tombstone.
Ref.:   *Arizona Star,* September 30, 1902, 1:6. Maps: GJ-16;
GL-3.

## ANEGAM

El.: c. 1500'                    Loc.: Pima 2, E-2.3
                        Papago: *an*, "slender tree"; plus locative
                            "place of many desert willows"
Descriptive. Anegam is a small permanent Papago village.
It was visited by Fr. Kino in 1698 and again in 1699. In
1858 ninety-six Indians were living in Anegam.
Ref.:   Kirk Bryan Notes; 128, p. 16; 34, p. 191; 70, pp. 398-
        399; 19, I, 205. Maps: A-13; D-8; D-11 (Anekam);
        GJ-16.
**a.n. Anegam Wash**   Loc.: Same as for Anegam         Pima

## ARCH CANYON

                    Loc.: Pima 1, F-6.4 (approximate).
                            In Ajo Mountains.
The presence of a double arch gives this canyon its name.
The larger arch measures one hundred and twenty-five feet
by thirty feet high with another directly on top of it measur-
ing ten feet by six feet. The canyon is in the Organ Pipe
Cactus National Monument.
Ref.:   Hensen. Map: None.

## ARIVACA

El.: c. 3500'                    Loc.: Pima 3, E-11.6
Pro.: /ǽrivákə/ or             Pima: *alivapk*, "little reeds" or
      /ǽrivǽkə/                         "little fence water"
It seems likely that the hypothesis advanced by Kirk Bryan
concerning the origin of the name Arivaca is the correct
one. According to Bryan the current name is a Mexican
corruption of the Indian name. He points out that *vapk* or
*vakera* means "reeds" or "fence water." The first part of
the name may be from the Indian word *ali*, thus resulting
in *alivapk*, which corrupts into Arivaca. Hodge notes Arivaca as being a former "Piman village . . . dating from
prior to 1733" and that the Pimas abandoned it in 1751
during the Pima Revolt. In the intervening years it had been
*visita* of Guevavi (*q.v.*, Santa Cruz).
In 1777 an application was made by a man named Ortiz
for a grant covering the whole of the valley. A grant for
La Aribac was given to Tomas and Ignacio Ortiz. Final
title was awarded on July 2, 1833. Despite the awarding of
the grant, Arivaca was a deserted ranch in 1835. During
the surveying by the Boundary Commission in 1854, Lt.
N. Michler also described it as a deserted ranch, in hills
rich with minerals.
In December 1856, Charles Debrille Poston noted in his
*Journal* that he had bought the estate of Arivaca from
Tomas and Ignacio Ortiz for $10,000 in gold (cf. Cerro
Colorado).
P.O. est. April 10, 1878. Noah W. Bernard, p.m.
Ref.:   P.O. Records; Kirk Bryan Notes; 88, I, 87; 72, 118; 51,
        p. 119; 138, p. 6; 131. Map: GJ-2.
**a.n. Arivaca Creek**     Map: GJ-2                     Pima
     **Arivaca Wash**      Map: GJ-2                     Pima

## ARTESA MOUNTAINS

El.: c. 2800'                    Loc.: Pima 2, FG-8
Pro.: /artíyžə/
The origin of the name is not known.
This is a group of mountains which Lt. N. Michler in 1854
referred to as the Sierra Arteza.

Ref.:   51, pp. 71, 72. Map: GJ-12.
**a.n. Artesa**          El.: 2490'. Map: GJ-12          Pima
     The Papago village by this name was established c. 1907.
     Its Indian name is Komoktetuvávosit (Papago: "where the
     turtle was caught").
Ref.:   Kirk Bryan Notes; 34, p. 352.

## AVRA VALLEY

El.: c. 2500'                    Loc.: Pima 3, E-2
Pro.: /ǽvrə/                    Spanish: "open"
The Avra Valley is the northern portion of the Altar Valley
(*q.v.*). The southern portion of this valley is sometimes re-
ferred to as the Arivaca Valley. Mexicans referred to it as
"La Abra."
A post office existed in this valley for a short time.
P.O. est. January 6, 1932. Mrs. LaVera Lacey, p.m. Discont.
January 20, 1933.
Ref.:   G. E. P. Smith, Letter from George C. Martin, Board
        on Geographic Names, December 31, 1936; U. S. G. B.
        "Decision, July 1, 1936, 1937," p. 4; Mrs. Mary B.
        Aguirre File, APHS. Map: A-7.

## BABOQUIVARI PEAK

El.: 7730'                       Loc.: Pima 3, C-9.4
Pro.: /babokíyvəriˆ/           Papago: *vav*, "mountain";
                               *kívolik*, "narrow in the middle"
The anglicized name for this peak is a corruption of the
Papago word, generally taken to mean "a neck between two
heads," as it clearly is when seen from the south. This was
the same peak which Fr. Kino's lieutenant, Juan Mateo
Manje, described as looking like a "tall castle, situated on
the top of a high peak, for which reason we called it
Noah's Ark." Others who saw the outstanding peak also
gave it names different from its Indian appellation. In 1863
Maj. D. E. Ferguson called it Papago Peak and referred to
it in his report as Picacho de Baboquivari. Lt. N. Michler of
the Boundary Survey party in 1854 said that the name
meant "water on the mountains," which indicates that he
may have confused the Papago explanation for the tanks
on top of the mountain with their name for the peak itself.
Ref.:   Kirk Bryan Notes; 34, p. 380; 51, p. 119. Maps: C-2;
        E-2; E-20; GJ-9.
**a.n. Baboquivari Mountains**   Map: GJ-9              Pima
     **Baboquivari**                                    Pima
     The Figueroa Ranch on the west side of the Baboquivari
     Mountains at one time maintained a post office.
P.O. est. as Baboquivari, September 11, 1890. Charles Bent,
p.m. Discont. July 3, 1893.
**Baboquivari Canyon**    Map: GJ-9                      Pima
**Baboquivari Valley**    Map: GJ-15                     Pima
**Baboquiveri Plain**
Same as Altar Valley (*q.v.*) (Pumpelly).
**Baboquivari Wash**      Map: GJ-12                     Pima
**Baggiburi Buta**   Loc.: s.e. of Baboquivari Mountain  Pima
This place was visited by Kino in 1698.
Ref.:   20, p. 399.

## BATAMOTE MOUNTAINS

El.: c. 2000'                    Loc.: Pima 1, FG-1
Pro.: /bátamówtey/
These mountains were named for the Batamote Well, which
in turn took its name from the presence of a plant called
*batamote*. The plant is a dense green bush which grows

where there is moisture. Batamote Well was a stopping place on the long dry journey from the Gila River to the mines at Ajo. At Batamote Well, Thomas Childs and his father maintained a well, known locally as Ten Mile Well.

Ref.:   Ketchum; Kirk Bryan Notes; 34, p. 359. Map: GJ-1.

## BATES WELL

El.: c. 1500′                              Loc.: Pima 3, DE-4.8
At one time there was a small community at this location consisting of a mine, a store and a few residences. The east well of two was dug by a man named Bates in the 1890's. The west well was dug by C. A. Puffer in 1913. The fact that a man named Ruby Daniels laid claim to the east well and its vicinity has led some people to apply the term Daniels Ranch to the area. Others refer to the wells as Growler Wells because the Growler Mine is one and a half miles distant. Mexicans, who are unable to pronounce Bates with facility, have corrupted the name to El Veit (Pro.: /veyt/). The Daniels brothers removed most of their cattle from this area in 1920 following the drought.

Ref.:   Kirk Bryan Notes; 34, p. 418. Map: A-6.

## BIGELOW PEAK

El.: c. 8000′                              Loc.: Pima 4, D-2.1
Lt. John Bigelow, Jr., served as a cavalry scout in the Santa Rita Mountains in the early 1870's. Bigelow led a command in pursuit of Apaches in 1885 to Stockton Gap (q.v., Graham County).

Another possible source of the name is from that of Dr. J. M. Bigelow of Ohio, who served as physician and botanist for the railroad survey made by Lt. Amiel W. Whipple. Bigelow also served with the Boundary Survey Commission at an earlier date.

Ref.:   Barnes; 177, p. 10. Map: B-3.

## BLANCA, SIERRA

El.: c. 4000′                              Loc.: Pima 2, CE-4.5
Pro.:  /siéra blánkə/       Spanish: "white mountain"
The name of these mountains is descriptive of the grey and white granite formations of which they consist. In 1858 there was a Papago village by this name which had fifty inhabitants, but it is not known whether it was close to these mountains.

Ref.:   34, p. 231; 88, II, 565. Maps: C-9; GJ-16.

## BOWLEY

El.: c. 3600′                              Loc.: Pima 3, D-6.1
Bowley was a stage station on the road to the mines in the Quijotoa region in 1883. By 1920 the place existed merely as an abandoned ranch.

v.n. Bawley
Ref.:   Barnes; 34, p. 376; 155, p. 78. Map: C-7.

a.n. Bawley Wash                                          Pima
    Loc.: Adjacent to Bawley Ranch. Maps: GJ-4; GJ-8.
    The old Bawley Ranch shows on the 1893 Roskruge map.
    The name was corrupted to Brawley Wash despite the fact
    that the wash is not named on the Roskruge map.
Ref.:   G. E. P. Smith, Letter to U. S. Geological Survey, December 9, 1936.

## BROOKLYN

El.: c. 3000′                              Loc.: Pima 2, DE-5.9
A townsite was laid out in conjunction with the Brooklyn Mine, the owner of which was a native of Brooklyn, New York.

Ref.:   Barnes. Map: C-7.

## BROWN CANYON

El.: c. 3000′                              Loc.: Pima 3, EC-8.7-9
Rollin C. Brown (b. Indiana, October 24, 1844; d. May 5, 1937) arrived at Tucson on March 6, 1873. Sometime after 1879, he moved to a ranch at the foot of the east side of the Baboquivari Mountains, in what came to be known as Brown's Canyon.

Ref.:   Rollin C. Brown File, APHS. Map: GJ-8.

a.n. Brown Wash            Map: GJ-8                      Pima

## BUELL

El.: c. 4200′                              Loc.: Pima 4, F-7
                                           E. of Tucson 29 miles.
John H. Buell may have been the person for whom this point on the railroad was named, inasmuch as he laid out what was known as Buell's Addition. He was in Tucson in 1878.

Ref.:   Robert Alpheus Lewis File, APHS; Barnes. Map: None.

## BUTTERFLY PEAK

El.: c. 5500′      Loc.: Pima 4, DE-1.4. E side of Santa
                   Catalina Mountains 3 miles from Soldier Camp.
A Natural Area was established here to preserve one of the largest varieties of trees and shrubs to be found anywhere in the Southwest.

Ref.:   33, p. 14. Map: None.

## CABABI

El.: c. 2100′                              Loc.: Pima 2, FG-5.6
                   Papago: "hidden springs"
Hinton noted that the mine on the mountain by this name, which he called the Cabibi (sic) Mine, was as famous as the Ajo Mine.

P.O. est. March 12, 1883. Robert H. Choat, p.m. Discont. June 4, 1884.

v.n. Cahuabi
    This is the place where Pumpelly noted the location of a
    rich silver mine, the other being located at what he called
    "T Ajo."
Ref.:   Barnes; 87, p. 227; 134, p. 38; P.O. Records. Maps: A-7; C-7.

## CAMELBACK MOUNTAIN

El.: 2572′                                 Loc.: Pima 1, E-2.7
Descriptive.
Ref.:   None. Map: GJ-1.

## CANOA

El.: c. 3200'  Loc.: Pima 4, A-9.6
Pro.: /kanówə/  Spanish-American: "a trough for carrying irrigation water"

This was the place where people crossed the Santa Cruz River. The Canoa Ranch is one of the oldest in the Santa Cruz Valley. In 1775, Fr. Francisco Garcés noted the existence here of a Papago rancheria, now vanished.

In addition to their ownership of the Arivaca Land Grant (cf. Arivaca) Tomas and Ignacio Ortiz obtained a grant in 1821 from the Mexican government to the Canoa Land Grant under the name San Ignacio de la Canoa. In Spanish the word designates "canoe," and it has been suggested that there may at one time have been an irrigation or watering trough hewn from a large tree, hence the name, since such a trough resembles a canoe.

In 1860 Pumpelly noted the presence of a corral and inn at the crossing of the Santa Cruz River. This place had been built by a company of Maine lumbermen, under a leader named Tarbox, which was operating a lumber camp in the Santa Rita Mountains. It may well be that the terrible Apache troubles began as a result of an incident at this location when a group of Mexicans came in 1861 to enlist aid to overtake Apaches who had stolen the Mexicans' stock. The lumbermen joined the Mexicans and ambushed the Apaches at Canoa. The Apaches fled, leaving the stolen stock. Within a month Apaches attacked Canoa and killed all the settlers there. The miners and lumbermen, however, were at work and did not discover the devastation until they returned to their residences. Tarbox was killed in the raid.

In January 1869, the Canoa Land Grant passed into the hands of men named Maish and Driscoll, who at that time took over its seventeen thousand acres. Canoa is still a productive ranch.

Ref.: Kirk Bryan Notes; *Arizona Star,* February 19, 1880; APHS Files; 134, p. 7; 52, II, 54, 55-56; 35, p. 74, (Note 5); 26, p. 419. Maps: E-18 (Canoe Crossing); E-20 (Canoe); GJ-14; GL-3.

a.n. **Canoa Ranch**  Santa Cruz
This is a smaller ranch located in Santa Cruz County.
**Canoa Canyon**  Map: B-3  Pima
**Canoa Wash**  Map: GJ-7  Pima

## CARSON PLAINS

The fact that Kit Carson crossed the Arizona desert along the course of the Gila River led to the former use of the name Carson Plains for the desert in southern Arizona.

Ref.: Barnes. Map: None.

## CATHEDRAL ROCK

El.: 8400'  Loc.: Pima 4, CD-2.5
Descriptive. The Spanish name for this high point in the fore range of the Catalinas is "La Iglesia," which means "the church."

Ref.: 3a, p. 44; Barnes. Map: GJ-13.

## CAT MOUNTAIN

El.: 3854'  Loc.: Pima 3, E-5.7
The variant name for this mountain is Cat Back, which is descriptive.

Ref.: Lenon. Map: GJ-11.

## CEBADILLA MOUNTAIN

El.: c. 4000'  Loc.: Pima 4, DE-3
Between Rincon Mountains and Santa Catalina Mts.
Pro.: /sébədíyə/  Spanish: "wild lily"

This name first appears on the Roskruge map of 1893 and was applied to the small mountain because of the abundance of wild lilies called *cebadilla* which grow around springs at the mountain base. The bulbs are not unlike small green onions in taste and smell, hence the name.

Ref.: G. E. P. Smith. Map: None.
(Roskruge, 1893: Barnes — "Ceballeta")

## CERRO COLORADO

El.: 4240'  Loc.: Pima 3, FG-10.9
Pro.: /sérow kolorádo/  Spanish: "red hill"

In 1854 Charles Debrille Poston and Herman Ehrenberg visited Arizona to investigate mining possibilities. During their visit they spent some time near Tubac where they found old abandoned mines worth reworking. Poston thereupon went to the East Coast in 1855 and by March 1856 had organized the Sonora Exploring and Mining Company. The company bought the old Arivaca Ranch (cf. Arivaca) and secured title to mines in the Santa Rita Mountains east of Tubac. Included in their purchases was Cerro Colorado where there were twenty-nine silver mines. The name Cerro Colorado was used by Mexicans to describe the conical red hill, a landmark in the area.

The most famous of the mines in the Cerro Colorado group was the Heintzelman Mine, named for Samuel P. Heintzelman, president of the mining company. The superintendent was John Poston, brother of Charles Poston. Despite the richness of the mines, many difficulties were encountered and the mines failed to pay off. Chief among the difficulties was trouble with Apache Indians, whose depredations forced the mine owners to abandon their holdings following the withdrawal of federal troops in the summer of 1861. In addition there was trouble with the native Mexican workers, some of whom murdered John Poston.

Soon after the end of the Civil War, miners began returning to Arizona and by 1870 there were fifty-eight people living at Cerro Colorado. In 1880 reduction works were constructed at Arivaca. The mines remained active for many years, but today are deserted and in ruins.

P.O. est. April 17, 1879. William S. Read, p.m. Discont. April 15, 1911.

Ref.: 87, pp. 221-222; 25, pp. 264-265, 269-270; 87, p. 43; 134, p. 17; 105, p. 194; P.O. Records. Map: GJ-2.

a.n. **Cerro Colorado Mountains**  Map: GJ-2  Pima
**Cerro Colorado Wash**  Map: GJ-2  Pima

## CHIAWULITAK

El.: c. 3000'                    Loc.: Pima 2, H-7.4
Pro.: /čiuwli ták/          Papago: "barrel cactus sits"
This is a Papago village with a descriptive name.
**v.n. Jeowic**           (corruption)
Ref.: 128, p. 12. Map: GJ-12.

## CHICO SHUNIE WELL

El.: c. 2000'                    Loc.: Pima 1, DE-3
Pro.: /číyko súwniˆ/
This place was a Papago village which was named for
Francisco Shunie, "Chico" being a nickname for Francisco.
He was a Papago Indian who dug a well and established a
family group at this point many years ago. For several
years his descendants lived at the point, but one by one
they too drifted away or died, except for one or two re-
maining relatives.
Ref.: Ketchum. Map: GJ-1.

## CHILDS

El.: 1428'                    Loc.: Pima 1, EF-1.4
Tom Childs, Sr. (b. Mississippi, 1822) joined the rush to
California in 1856 and lived an adventurous life in the
West and Southwest. By 1890 he was a rancher in the Ajo
area. His son, Tom Childs, Jr., (b. Yuma, June 10, 1870;
d. February 5, 1951) accompanied his father to Ajo in
1884, and spent the remainder of his life in this area. The
station on the railroad is among several places named for
Childs.
Ref.: *Ajo Copper News*, XXXIX (October 21, 1954), 7:7.
      Map: GJ-1.
**a.n. Child's Mountain**   El.: 2910'. Map: GJ-1          Pima
      **Child's Valley**        Map: GJ-1                 Pima

## CHOULIC

El.: c. 2300'                    Loc.: Pima 2, GH-10.1
Pro.: /čúˆlə/          Papago: "corner"
This is a Papago Indian village.
**v.n. Chulik**
Ref.: 128, p. 1; Kirk Bryan Notes; 34, p. 408. Map: GJ-15.

## CHUILI SHAIK

El.: c. 3800'                    Loc.: Pima 3, B-8.7
Pro.: /čiúl ə šay/          Papago: "willow thicket"
This is a descriptive name for a Papago village, the upper
one of three in Fresnal Canyon. It was probably among
villages visited by Fr. Kino in 1699.
Ref.: 34, p. 407; 128, p. 1. Map: GJ-15.
**a.n. Ventana**          Loc.: Sec. 14, T. 11 S., R. 1 E.      Pima
                                        Spanish: "window"
      A Papago village said to have been named for a rock nearby
      about four hundred feet high.
**v.n. White's Well**
      A well dug by Wesley White which produced only salt
      water.
Ref.: Barnes; 2, p. 8.
**a.n. Ventana Canyon**   Loc.: Sec. 18, T. 12 S., R. 14 E.      Pima
      This canyon is named because of a hollow through the
      mountain near the skyline north of Tucson.
Ref.: G. E. P. Smith.
**v.n. Window, The**

## CHUI VAYA

El.: 3163'                    Loc.: Pima 3, B-10.9
Pro.: /čiú wà?a/          Papago: "cave well"
This is a summer village of the Papagos.
Ref.: Jones. Map: GJ-9.

## CHUKUT KUK

El.: c. 1500'                    Loc.: Pima 2, DE-9.2
Pro.: /čúkut ku/          Papago: "owl hoots"
This is a Papago village which is reported to have had one
hundred forty families in 1865. Apparently Mexicans translated the Papago name into the word familiar to them, the
Nahuatl word *tecolotl*, meaning "ground owl." This word
was rendered as Tecolote when applied to the village.
Ref.: 128, p. 3; 88, II, 713; 34, p. 392. Map: D-8.
**a.n. Chukut Kuk Wash**   Loc.: Drains n.w. past Chukut Kuk   Pima
**v.n. Big Wash**
      **Tecolote Valley**                                    Pima
      Loc.: Upper course of Chukut Kuk Wash.
Ref.: 128, p. 17.

## CHUTUM VAYA

El.: c. 3800'                    Loc.: Pima 3, BC-10.1
Pro.: /čútum wà?ə/          Papago: "bear well"
This is a summer rancheria used by the Papagos.
Ref.: 128, p. 2. Map: GJ-9.
**a.n. Chutum Vaya Pass**     Map: GJ-9          Pima
      **Chutum Vaya Wash**     Map: GJ-9          Pima
Ref.: 128, p. 24.

## CIENAGA, LA

El.: c. 3800'                    Loc.: Pima 4, EF-6.5
Pro.: /la siyénegə/     Spanish: "swampy or marshy place"
On a map made by Captain Overman, the entire valley from
Tucson to the pass between the end of the Rincons (Sierra
de Santa Catalina) bears the name Cienegos de los Pinos.
This same designation is carried on another map as Cienegas de los Pinos. The only change on GLO 1869 is to the
name Cienegas de las Pimas. The name Cienaga first appears on the GLO 1876. In 1883 when the railroad came
through and established a station, the name Pantano appears close to the old and vanished location of Cienaga.

The name of the stage station established in 1858 by the
Butterfield Overland Stage line at this point was descriptive; it was sometimes called Cienaga Springs. Several visitors to this place have noted the fact that it had sweet and
cool water. The adobe buildings of the stage station were
abandoned when Butterfield dropped its stage line through
southern Arizona. It did not take long for the buildings
to fall into ruins, caused in part by a devastating fire. The
First California Volunteers camped here on June 21, 1862,
noting that there had been a fire some time between the
closing of the route and that date.

Following the Civil War, the Cienega again became a stage
station, frequently subjected to Apache attack. Here in
1867 W. A. ("Shotgun") Smith and three companions were
attacked by Indians. All but Smith were killed. He used his
shotgun to such advantage that he killed or wounded about

eight Apaches. In 1870 when the point was called Miller's Station, the mail carrier and a man named Scott Young were butchered Apache style and the station again destroyed.

With the coming of the railroad, Cienaga ceased to exist for the simple reason that the railroad tracks passed over the foundation of the old stage station buildings (cf. Pantano).

Ref.: 32, II, 152, 153; 111, p. 164; 52, V, 289-290; *Weekly Arizona Miner*, September 3, 1870, 2:2; *Arizona Citizen*, April 24, 1875, 1:4. Maps: C-1 (Cunejo del los Pimas); E-20; E-6 (Cienega de las Pimas); E-11; E-17; E-18 (Cienega de los Pinos).

**a.n. Cienaga Creek**                                              Pima
   Loc.: Joins Rincon Creek to form Pantano Wash.

## CIMARRON MOUNTAINS

El.: c. 2500'                    Loc.: Pima 2, DC-2.5-1.4
Pro.: /símeràn/                  Spanish: "sheep"
Mexicans refer to mountain sheep as *cimarron*. Early documents allude repeatedly to wild mountain sheep throughout western Arizona.

Ref.: Barnes. Map: GJ-16.

## CLARKSTOWN

El.: c. 1800'                    Loc.: Pima 1, EF-2.7
When the New Cornelia Copper Company built a company-owned town (cf. Ajo), opposition developed to living in the new location. Sam Clark (b. England, January 15, 1871; d. October 3, 1933) proceeded to lay out a townsite on some mining claims near the reduction works of the mining company. This place was referred to as Clarkston or Clarkstown. The copper company refused to sell water to the residents of Clarkstown, who retaliated by deepening a test shaft for a new mining location to get water. Their community was more popular in 1916 and 1917 than the mining company town. Clarkstown then had about one thousand residents, but the place went into a decline towards the end of 1917.

Meanwhile the residents of Clarkstown applied for a post office. Because of the great popularity of President Woodrow Wilson, they desired to call their post office either Wilson or Woodrow, but both names were ruled out by the Post Office Department. The residents got around this by reversing the name Woodrow and came up with the name Rowood. One month after the townspeople got their name for the post office, it was changed to Samclark, but this name did not stick.

In 1931 Clarkstown was almost completely destroyed by fire. Following this, what was left of the community was moved to Ajo. The post office survived for many years, the Rowood post office being moved to Gibson nearby but retaining the name Rowood.

P.O. est. as Rowood January 21, 1918. Kallulah H. Holcumb, p.m. Changed to Samclark, February 26, 1918 (Rescinded). Discont. November 30, 1955.

Ref.: Ketchum; *Ajo Copper News*, XXXIX (October 21, 1954), 2:4; 34, pp. 358, 559. P.O. Records. Map: GJ-1.

## COCHIBO

El.: c. 1000'                    Loc.: Pima 1, H-7
Pro.: /kówčiybo/    Papago: *kochi*, "a pig"; *vo*, "a well"
A Papago called Slim Joe Manuel owned this stock watering place. It consisted of two wells between which were a small corral and some huts.

Ref.: 34, p. 412. Map: A-7.

## COCORAQUE BUTTE

El.: c. 2500'                    Loc.: Pima 3, E-4.1
Pro.: /kokorakey/
The origin of this name is not known. However, there is a Cocoraque Ranch at the base of this butte.

Ref.: None. Map: GJ-4.

## COLOSSAL CAVE

El.: c. 4000'                    Loc.: Pima 4, E-6.1
This cave was discovered in 1879 by an American named Ross. It contains evidences of occupancy by Indians.
In 1884 a S.P.R.R. train was robbed and the robbers trailed to this cave. They escaped.

Ref.: None. Maps: A-13; B-3.

## COMOBAVI

El.: c. 3800'                    Loc.: Pima 2, GH-0.1
Pro.: /còwmwáhi/    Papago: *kom*, "hackberry tree"; *vaxia*, "well"
This name is a Spanish corruption of the Papago name for a rancheria. The well here is a hole dug in the sandy bed of an arroyo. Hackberry trees occur frequently in Papago legends and in place names on the Papago Indian Reservation.

Comobavi is one of the oldest winter rancherias, reported to have had eighty families in 1871.

**v.n. Comohuabi**
Ref.: Kirk Bryan Notes; 34, pp. 45, 365; 128, p. 12. Maps: C-15; D-8.
**a.n. Comobavi Mountains**    Maps: C-7; C-12    Pima
   **Comobavi Pass**                                Pima
   Loc.: N.w. to s.e. along Combobavi Wash and n. and s. Comobavi Mountains.    Pima
Ref.: 128, p. 21.
   **Comobavi Wash**                                Pima
   Loc.: Heads in Comobavi Mountains, a tributary to Seels Wash.
Ref.: 128, p. 25.

## CONTINENTAL

El.: 2625'                       Loc.: Pima 4, AB-9.8
The Continental Rubber Company in 1914 purchased part of the old Canoa Land Grant. The company planned to grow guayule, which yields guayule rubber. A railroad siding, post office, and headquarters for the operation were established at Continental.

P.O. est. January 11, 1917. Stanley Morse, p.m. Discont. February 5, 1929.

Ref.: P.O. Records; Barnes; APHS Names File. Maps: B-3; GJ-16.

## CONTZEN PASS

El.: c. 3200'                    Loc.: Pima 3, G-3.4
This pass was probably named for Fritz Contzen (b. Germany, February 27, 1831; d. May 2, 1909), who came to Arizona with the Boundary Survey party in 1856.
Ref.:   105, p. 143; 112, III. Map: GJ-6.

## CORNELIA, ARROYA

El.: c. 1500'                    Loc.: Pima 1, FE-3.5-1.5
The Arroya Cornelia or Cornel apparently did not exist prior to 1916. It was probably named for the New Cornelia Copper Company. The name Rio Cornez which appears on current maps is not known in the Ajo vicinity. The mine company was named by Col. Greenway (cf. Ajo).
Ref.;   Ketchum. Map: GJ-16 (Rio Cornez).

## CORONADO NATIONAL FOREST

Loc.: Pima 4, BG-1-5 & BD-8-10
Cochise 1, AB-12-12.9
The forest was named for Francisco Vasquez de Coronado, who journeyed in 1540 to the Zuñi and Hopi villages through parts of what is today the Coronado National Forest.

At least fourteen different shifts in government land were made before the Coronado National Forest, part of which lies in New Mexico, attained the form which it has today. The first move was the creation on April 11, 1902, of the Santa Rita Forest Reserve, followed in July of that year by the Santa Catalina Forest Reserve. On July 30 of the same year was added the Chiricahua Forest Reserve. On November 3, 1906, was formed the Baboquivari Forest Reserve, followed the next day by the Huachuca Forest Reserve and on November 7 by the formation of the Tumacacori Forest Reserve. The Peloncillo Forest Reserve came into being on November 5, 1906. On May 25, 1907, the Dragoon National Forest was created.

The seven original forest reserves went through their first consolidation in 1908, on the same day. On July 2, the Baboquivari, Huachuca and Tumacacori Forest Reserves were consolidated into Garcés National Forest. At the same time, the Santa Rita, Santa Catalina, and Dragoon Reserves became the first to bear the name of Coronado National Forest. The same day, a third consolidation was made when the Chiricahua and Peloncillo Reserves became the Chiricahua National Forest.

The first increment to the Coronado National Forest occurred on April 17, 1911, when Garcés was added to it. Chiricahua National Forest joined the Coronado family on July 6, 1917.

The final move took place on July 1, 1953, when 425,674 acres of Crook National Forest were transferred to Coronado National Forest from the Santa Teresa, Galiuro, Mount Graham, and Winchester divisions of Crook National Forest. Total acreage is 1,317,659.
Ref.:   47, p. 34. Maps: B-2; B-3.

## CORTARO

El.: 2156'                    Loc.: Pima 3, H-2.9
Pro.:   /kortǽro/or /kortáro/
The area occupied today by the Cortaro Farms was at one time covered by a heavy growth of mesquite and ironwood. The trees were cut off for local use, hence the name from the Spanish cortar, "to cut."
P.O. est. July 16, 1920. Richard C. Hunter, p.m.
Ref.:   P.O. Records; Barnes. Map: GJ-6.

## CORWIN

El.: c. 3000'                    Loc.: Pima 4, B-7.5
The origin of this name has not been ascertained.
P.O. est. October 1, 1912. Archibald W. Roberts, p.m. Discont. February 15, 1915.
Ref.:   P.O. Records. Map: C-12.

## COWLIC

El.: 2098'                    Loc.: Pima 2, EF-8.5
Pro.:   /kawlik/                    Papago: "hill"
Cowlic is a medium-sized Papago village, named because of its adjacency to a small hill.
v.n Kavolik
Ref.:   128, p. 14; Kirk Bryan Notes. Map: GJ-12.

## CRATER, THE

El.: c. 2000'                    Loc.: Pima 1, E-1
A basin formed by erosion in horizontal lava flow has created a formation which looks like a volcanic crater, hence the name.
Ref.:   Kirk Bryan Notes. Map: C-12.
a.n. Crater Mountains        Map: C-10                    Maricopa
      Crater Tank            Loc.: In the crater          Pima
Ref.:   Kirk Bryan Notes.

## CRUZ

El.: c. 2800'                    Loc.: Pima 4, CD-6
When this point on the railroad was first established it was called Esmond, but the reason for so doing is not known. In 1912 the name was changed to Cruz by dropping Santa from the name of the Santa Cruz River. The name was changed to save time in telegraphy.
Ref.:   Barnes. Maps: C-12 (Cruz); GJ-13 (Esmond).

## CUMERO MOUNTAIN

El.: 4697'                    Loc.: Pima 3, D-1.3
Pro.:   /kuwméro/                    Spanish: "hackberry tree"
The north slopes of this mountain have many hackberry trees.
Ref.:   Barnes. Map: GJ-7.
a.n. Cumero Canyon        Map: GB-12                    Pima

## DAVIDSON CANYON

El.: c. 3800'                    Loc.: Pima 4, DE-8.4-6.8
In 1871 a watering place in this canyon was known as Davidson Spring. Here on August 22, 1872, Lt. Reid T. Stewart and Corporal Black were killed by Apaches. The name Davidson, according to Hinton, was that of a pioneer who was also killed by Apaches.
Ref.:   22, p. 107; 87, p. 232. Map: GL-3.

## DeLONG PEAK

El.: c. 6000'                    Loc.: Pima 4, E-4
Sidney DeLong was post trader at Fort Bowie in 1878. He
was a well-known merchant and trader in Tucson where
he had served as mayor in 1871.
Ref.: Barnes. Map: C-8.

## DESERT WELL

El.: 1969'                    Loc.: Pima 3, F-6.6
Desert Well (or Wells) in 1879 was reportedly a money
maker for its owners since it offered the only opportunity
to get water for many miles in either direction. For this
reason it was a camping place for freighters and others and
served as a team changing station for stage coaches. Travelers paid twenty-five cents per head to water stock.
P.O. est. as Desert, May 10, 1880. Charles H. Labaree, p.m.
Discont. September 2, 1885.
Ref.: 140, pp. 28-29; P.O. Records. Maps: C-5 (Desert Station); E-20 (Desert Station); E-18.

## DEVINE, MOUNT

El.: 4788'                    Loc.: Pima 2, GH-5
When George Roskruge surveyed Pima County in 1893
he named this peak for John J. Devine, who in 1890 had
silver mines in this area.
Ref.: Barnes. Map: GJ-5.

## DIAZ PEAK

Loc.: In Organ Pipe Cactus National Monument
The peak was named c. 1942 for Melchior Diaz, a member
of Coronado's expedition in 1540. Diaz made a trip overland to the mouth of the Colorado River, thus being the
first white man to travel through what is now the Organ
Pipe Cactus National Monument area. On the return journey, a greyhound began harassing the sheep herded by
Diaz' men for food along the way. When the animal refused to desist, Diaz rode at it with his lance. The lance
caught in the ground and ran through Diaz' kidney. He died
before his men could transport him to the main body of
the expedition.
Ref.: Hensen; 182, p. 407. Map: None.

## DOBBS STATION

Loc.: Not definitely ascertained.
In 1880 E. W. Dobbs was a stage driver who also maintained a station on the road to Quijotoa. His place was
also called Half-way House. Here passengers stopped to
have dinner.
Ref.: Rollin C. Brown File, APHS; 155, p. 79. Map: None.
a.n. Dobbs Butte        Map: C-12              Pima
    Dobbs Wells        Map: C-13              Pima

## DOWLING

El.: c. 1500'                    Loc.: Pima 1, EF-8.1
Dowling was a mining camp which also had an adobe
custom house. It was named for Pat Dowling, a miner
who had a smelter here. By 1915 the place was abandoned.
Ref.: Kirk Bryan Notes; 26, p. 421. Map: C-10.

## EMERY PARK

El.: c. 2500'                    Loc.: Pima 4, B-5.3
The Emery family lived at this location, hence the name.
P.O. est. September 21, 1928. Camilla M. Emery, p.m. Name
changed to Butland, January 2, 1931. Rescinded, December 24,
1931. Discont. September 30, 1952.
Ref.: Barnes; P.O. Records. Maps: C-13; GJ-16.

## EMPIRE MOUNTAINS

El.: c. 5000'                    Loc.: Pima 4, EF-8-8.7
Walter Vail established the Empire Ranch in 1876 about
fifteen miles south of the present-day Pantano. Vail pur-
chased his land from E. N. Fish, and applied the name
Empire because he said the ranch would be an empire.
The ranch was located in a small canyon which soon came
to be known as Empire Gulch.
In 1879 Jerry Dillon, who had claims on the nearby moun-
tains, named the Empire Mountains after the ranch.
P.O. est. as Empire Ranch, May 7, 1879. John N. Harvey, p.m.
Discont. May 3, 1880. Re-est. as Empire, June 21, 1880. George
C. Alger, p.m. Discont. April 19, 1881.
Ref.: Barnes; APHS Files; P.O. Records. Map: GL-3.

## ESCUELA

El.: c. 4000'                    Loc.: Pima 4, A-5
Pro.: /eskwéylə/            Spanish: "school"
A government school for Indians is located at this place,
hence the name.
P.O. est. July 10, 1907. Haddington G. Brown, p.m. Discont.
October 31, 1942.
Ref.: Barnes; P.O. Records. Maps: B-3; C-10; GJ-16.

## ESPERANZA

El.: c. 4000'                    Loc.: Pima 3, G-8.6
Pro.: /ésperànzə/            Spanish: "hope"
The Esperanza Ranch probably was the location for the
post office which was established in this area.
P.O. est. February 26, 1884. Hiram W. Blaisdell, p.m. Discont.
October 9, 1884.
Ref.: P.O. Records. Map: GJ-14.
a.n. Esperanza Wash    Map: GJ-14                Pima

## FAGAN, MOUNT

El.: 6175'                    Loc.: Pima 1, D-8.1
Michael Fagan, a cattleman and prospector, in 1880 owned
a ranch near this mountain. At one time Fagan was a
partner of David Harshaw (cf. Harshaw, Santa Cruz).
Ref.: APHS Files; Barnes. Map: GL-3.

## FLOWING WELLS

El.: 3100'                    Loc.: Pima 4, AB-4
Emerson Oliver Stratton bought land c. 1885 about where
the current day Flowing Wells district is located. Stratton
planned to use the land for farming. The name was descriptive of the quantity of water available.
Ref.: Emerson O. Stratton ms., APHS. Map: None.

## FRESNAL

El.: 4200'                                    Loc.: Pima 3, AB-9-10
Pro.: /freznǽl/                          Spanish: "ash grove"
Fresnal was a Papago village visited by Pumpelly in 1860.
In 1863 Charles Debrille Poston's *Indian Affairs Report*
stated that there were three hundred eighty-five Indians living in the ravine. A year later, J. Ross Browne called it a
"small Mexican town containing some ramshackle adobe
huts built in the past twenty-four months." He conjectured
that this was done because Fresnal was a convenient place
where water existed for use in reducing ores stolen from
nearby mines.

There are currently reported to be at least eighteen dug
wells scattered along four miles in the canyon. There are
also three Papago villages. They are Chiuli Shaik (*q.v.*),
Tshiuli (Papago: "willow forest" *seik*: forest), and Pitoikam ("sycamore place"). It is from a translation of the
last named place that Fresnal Canyon probably takes its
name. This was interpreted by Lumholtz as meaning "where
there are ash trees." Pitoikam is the largest of the three
communities.

Ref.: 88, I, 476; 134, p. 40; 25, p. 281; 26, p. 422; Kirk Bryan
        Notes; 128, p. 1. Map: GJ-3.

| a.n. Fresnal Creek | | Pima |
|---|---|---|
| Fresnal, Cerro del | Map: GJ-7 | Pima |
| Fresnal Wash | Map: GJ-12 | Pima |

There is a second Fresnal Wash near Baboquivari. Fresnal
Creek is a variant name for this wash.

| Fresnal Wash | Map: GJ-8 | Pima |
|---|---|---|
| Fresno Canyon | Map: GJ-14 | Pima |
| Fresno Spring | Map: B-3 | Pima |
| Fresno Wash | Map: GJ-7 | Pima |

## GADSDEN PEAK

El.: c. 2500'                                    Loc.: Pima 1, F-6.5
                                N.w. of Organ Pipe Cactus National
                                Monument headquarters ½ mile.
This peak, formerly known as West Twin Peak, was renamed in 1953. This was done because that year was the
centennial of the Gadsden Purchase (cf. Gadsden, Yuma).
Formerly West Twin Peak was one of two which were
misnamed since the peaks are distinctly unlike each other.
Ref.: Hensen. Map: None.

## GATES PASS

El.: c. 3500'                                    Loc.: Pima 3, E-5.1
Tom Gates came to southern Arizona in 1865. This is the
pass through the Tucson Mountains on the road to Old
Tucson (*q.v.*).
Ref.: Barnes. Map: GJ-11.

## GIBSON

El.: c. 1500'                                    Loc.: Pima 1, E-2.6
Matthew Ellsworth Gibson, Sr., laid out a townsite on a
group of mining claims north of those held by the New
Cornelia Copper Company. Gibson and his family arrived

in the vicinity in 1912. When Clarkstown was nearly
burned out in 1931, the Rowood post office was moved to
Gibson. The current name of the place is North Ajo.
Ref.: Ketchum; 34, p. 358; *Ajo Copper News*, XXXIX (Octo-
        ber 21, 1954), 5:3. Map: GJ-1.

| a.n. Gibson Arroyo | Map: GJ-1 | Pima |
|---|---|---|

## GREATERVILLE

El.: 5280'                                    Loc.: Pima 4, D-9.5
Following the discovery of placer gold in this area in 1874,
miners rushed to the location and the town of Greaterville
developed. The mining district was organized on March
17, 1875, but apparently was never recorded. Scarcity of
water made it necessary to work placers by rocker and
long tom. Water was brought in canvas or goatskin bags
from Gardner Canyon, four miles away.

By 1881 the gold had nearly played out and miners began
to desert the camp. Others left because of Indian attacks.
From 1886 to 1900 Greaterville was dead on its feet. It
enjoyed a revival when a hydraulic plant was installed in
nearby Kentucky Gulch, but the renewed activity lasted
only a few months. Today Greaterville consists of a half
dozen Mexican houses.

During its heyday Greaterville had more than an occasional
visitor show up along what was known as the Renegade's
Route, so named because it was used by men who sought
to avoid the law while on their way from the border to
Tucson or vice versa. Such men camped near Greaterville.
P.O. est. January 3, 1879. Thomas Steele, p.m. Discont. June
30, 1946.

Ref.: P.O. Records; 119, pp. 158-159; Seibold. Map: GL-3.

| a.n. Greaterville Gulch | Map: B-3 | Pima |
|---|---|---|

## GROWLER MOUNTAINS

El.: c. 2500'                                    Loc.: Pima 1, CE-1-5-6.6
The Growler Mountains took their name from the nearby
Growler Mine, which was discovered and named by Fred-
eric Wall. He named the mine for a prospector called John
Growler.

Ref.: Barnes; Kirk Bryan Notes. Maps: C-8; GJ-16.

| a.n. Growler Pass | Loc.: T. 14 S., R. 6 W | Pima |
|---|---|---|
| Growler Peak | Map: C-12 | Pima |
| Growler Well | cf. Bates Well | Pima |

## GU ACHI

El.: 2180'                                    Loc.: Pima 2, E-3.3
Pro.: /gu áči/          Papago: *gu*, "big"; *achi*, "narrow ridge"
Gu Achi was visited by Fr. Kino in 1698 and referred to
by him as "the great rancheria of Adid." He also called it
San Francisco del Adid. It was then and remains today
a great Papago community, the largest of the summer
rancherias. A farming community, it spreads over several
miles.

v.n. Santa Rosa del Achi
     Kuarchi (corruption)
     Kuat-shi (corruption)

Ref.: 128, p. 5; 34, pp. 391-392; 20, p. 398. Maps: D-8; D-11
        (Kuatshi).

| a.n. Gu Achi Peak Loc.: Near s. end Santa Rosa Mountains Pima |
|---|

Ref.: 128, p. 36.

## GUIJAS MOUNTAINS

El.: c. 4000'  Loc.: Pima 3, CD-10.8-11
Spanish: "rubble" or "conglomerate"
This small group of mountains was called the Sierra del Pais by Lt. N. Michler in 1854. Possibly this was a misprint, since on the Boundary Survey map they show as the Sierra del Mal Pais ("mountains of bad country"). These mountains were later renamed for the Las Guijas Mine which was active in the 1860's and 1870's. The name describes the conglomerate in which placer gold may be found.
Ref.: 34, p. 379; 51, p. 119. Map: GJ-2.
**a.n. Las Guijas Wash**    Map: GJ-2    Pima

## GUNSIGHT

El.: c. 2500'  Loc.: Pima 1, G-4.5
The Gunsight Mine was located on November 25, 1878, by a man named Myers and three others. The mine was named because of its location near a mountain with a striking resemblance to a gun sight with the "barrel" of the gun being formed by a ridge. The gunsight portion of this formation looks like a flat whisky bottle seen sideways. The first name for the mining community in this area was Allen or Allen City, named for John Brackett Allen (b. Maine, 1818; d. June 13, 1899) the merchant for the camp. He first came to Arizona in 1857 and returned in 1862 with the California Column. Thereafter he settled near Yuma, had a store at Maricopa Wells, and finally moved to Tucson. Allen seems to have followed the mining camps in establishing his stores. His name crops up time and again in the history of mining communities of Pima County. In his later years he lived in Florence.

Gunsight is a ghost town today.

P.O. est. as Allen, July 5, 1882. John B. Allen, p.m. Discont. November 11, 1886. Re-est. as Gunsight, June 27, 1892. Samuel Sutherland, p.m. Discont. January 6, 1896.
**v.n. Montezuma Head**
The gunsight part of the formation also resembles the head and shoulders of a man, hence the name Montezuma Head.
Ref.: P.O. Records; John Brackett Allen File, APHS; Emerson O. Stratton ms., p. 21 (APHS); Lenon; *Arizona Weekly Citizen*, November 5, 1882, 4:5; Jordan. Map: GJ-8.
**a.n. Gunsight Hills**    Pima
Loc.: T. 14 S., R. 3, 4 W., T. 15 S., R. 3, 4 W.
**Gunsight Mountain**    Map: GJ-8    Pima
**Gunsight Pass**    Loc.: In Gunsight Hills    Pima
**Gunsight Valley**    Loc.: N.e. of Gunsight Hills    Pima
**Gunsight Ranch**    Loc.: W. of Gunsight Mine 2 miles    Pima
Originally this was at a well dug by a man named Haynes and so was known as Haynes Well. Because goats were raised here for many years, it is also sometimes referred to as Goat Ranch. A man named Blair owned it c. 1925, during which period it was called the Blair Ranch. The Papago name for this place is Schuchuli ("many chickens").
Ref.: Kirk Bryan Notes; 26, p. 337; 128, p. 8.
**Gunsight Wash**    Loc.: E. of Bates Well 3 miles    Pima
**Gunsight Well**    Loc.: T. 14 S., R. 3 W.    Pima

## GU OIDAK

El.: c. 1500'  Loc.: Pima 2, E-7.7
Pro.: /guw óyda/  Papago: *gu,* "big"; *oidak,* "field"
Descriptive. This is a large Papago village.
Ref.: 128, p. 14. Maps: D-8; D-11.
**a.n. Gu Oidak Valley**    Pima
Loc.: Quijotoa Valley on w. to Kupk Hills
**Gu Oidak Wash**    Loc.: Drains Gu Oidak Valley    Pima

## GURLI PUT VO

El.: c. 2500'  Loc.: Pima 2, EF-4.9
Pro.: /gúli putwó/  Papago: *guli,* "old man"; *put,* "dead"
*vo,* "water hole"
The Papago name is sometimes rendered as Kolipatvawka. The name dates back at least to 1912, but even then no one could remember who the "dead old man" was. Ordinarily ponds are owned by members of a Papago village, but in this case the water hole was owned by a single person, hence the name.
**v.n. Kolipatvooka** (corruption)
Ref.: 128, p. 5; Barnes. Map: D-8.

## GUTHRIE MOUNTAIN

El.: c. 5500'  Loc.: Pima 4, E-2.6
John D. Guthrie served as supervisor for the Coronado National Forest prior to 1921.
Ref.: Barnes. Map: GJ-13.

## GU VO

El.: c. 2200'  Loc.: Pima 1, H-6
Pro.: /gu'wow/  Papago: *gu,* "big"; *vo,* "charco"
Descriptive. This village has a large pond thirteen hundred feet long in a wide sweeping curve. The charco is from fifteen to thirty feet wide and fills only with flood waters. Fr. Kino visited here in 1701.
**v.n. Cuvo**
**Kuvo**
**Kerwo**
Ref.: Kirk Bryan Notes; 19, I, 7, 292. Map: D-8.
**a.n. Gu Vo Hills**    Pima
Loc.: E. of Ajo Range and s.w. of Mesquite Mts.
**Gu Vo Pass**    Pima
Loc.: Runs e. and w. through Gu Vo Hills.

## HALI MURK

El.: c. 1500'  Loc.: Pima 2, C-6.8
Pro.: /haˡmək/  Papago: "squash burned"
Hali Murk is a Papago village consisting of about fifteen houses. The place is used as a summer rancheria with extensive fields under cultivation.
**v.n. Hardimui** (corruption)
Ref.: 128, p. 10. Map: D-8.

## HART

El.: c. 3200'  Loc.: Pima 4, A-9.2
S. of Tucson about 30 miles.
In January 1878 William Hart (d. 1899) came to Arizona from Rochester, New York, with John A. Rockfellow (cf. Rockfellow Dome, Cochise). He established a ranch on the railroad.
Ref.: 140, p. 199. Map: None.

## HELVETIA

El.: c. 4400′                    Loc.: Pima 4, C-7.5

It is thought that before the Civil War minerals were probably already being located in what later became the Helvetia area. In the late 1870's L. M. Grover located the Old Dick, Heavy Weight, and Tallyho claims which, however, were not opened for development until 1881. In 1880 the first mine to be worked in the district was the Old Frijole, owned by John Weigle and William Hart. The group of claims in this region was obtained by the Helvetia Copper Company of New Jersey in the early 1890's, under whose operation the community of Helvetia took shape, continuing its existence until December 2, 1901. Two years later, in November 1903, the Helvetia Copper Company of Arizona took over and operated the mines, continuing until 1911, when the low price of copper closed down the mines. For some years the place remained relatively inactive, but in 1956 work again resumed.

The Columbia Copper Camp was among those in the Helvetia district.

P.O. est. December 12, 1899. Charles M. Coon, p.m. Discont. December 31, 1921.

Ref.:   133a, pp. 25, 96, 97; 76, p. 47; P.O. Records. Map: GL-3.

a.n. **Helvetia Wash**        Loc.: At Helvetia                Pima
    **Old Dick Hill**     Loc.: Near the Helvetia Basin         Pima
    **Frijole Mine**      Loc.: Near Helvetia                   Pima
    Located by John A. Rockfellow while camped on west slope of the Santa Rita Mountains. He named it because frijoles (beans) were then considered the one thing necessary in camp, and he suggested the mine might supply the beans for a while.

Ref.:   140, p. 59.

## HICKIWAN

El.: c. 2400′                    Loc.: Pima 1, H-2.3
Pro.: /ʔigᵏiwan/                Papago: "zig zag"

Since the Papago word *hic* may mean "rough" or may refer to hair which has been cut short, the supposition is that there is a local story about a jagged haircut which gave the name to this village. What the story is has not been ascertained. This may be the place which Fr. Kino visited in 1699 and to which he gave the name San Geronimo. In October 1781 it was visited by Fages who said the place was called Tachitoa or Cerro de la Pirigua.

v.n. **Hikivo Perigua**          (Lumholtz)
    **Hikibon**
    **Hikuwan**

Ref.:   128, p. 8; 20, p. 435. Map: D-8.

a.n. **Hickiwan Valley**                                       Pima
    Loc.: S. and s.w. of Sauceda Mountains.
    **Hickiwan Wash**   Loc.: Drains Hickiwan Valley           Pima

## HORSE MOUNTAIN

                Loc.: Said to be north by east of Ajo,
                          but not definitely known.

Semi-wild range horses graze on this mountain, which is very rocky and rugged. Horses go higher than cattle for forage because horses have better feet and are also able to range more miles for water. The grass high on this mountain attracts them, hence the name.

Ref.:   Ketchum. Map: None.

## HORSESHOE

El.: c. 2500′                    Loc.: Pima 2, D-5.5

Kirk Bryan noted the presence of a placer gold mine, a store and a post office at this place. The mine, long since deserted by those who located it, was worked desultorily by Papagos. This may be the same place referred to as Horseshoe Bend, which is mentioned as being in the Quijotoa Mountains. The Papago name for this place according to Bryan was Komaktjivurt, meaning "gray soil," a reference to the presence of caliche.

Ref.:   Kirk Bryan Notes; 155, p. 59. Maps: C-12; D-11.

a.n. **Horseshoe Basin**        Map: C-10                      Pima

## HOTASON VO

El.: c. 2000′                    Loc.: Pima 1, H-4
Pro.: /hòdeyšownwów/            Papago: "foot of rocky"
                                         hill charco"

The Spanish translation for the name of this Papago village is approximately the same as the Papago translation into English: Charco de la Piedra, meaning "charco of the stone." The pond lies in rocks at the base of the hills.

Ref.:   128, p. 8; 34, pp. 423-424. Map: D-8.

## HUERFANO BUTTE

El.: c. 4000′                    Loc.: Pima 4, C-8.5
Pro.: /wærfáno/                 Spanish: "orphan"

This little butte stands off all by itself in a lonely fashion, hence the name. It was at this place that Mrs. Larcena Pennington Page was wounded and pushed over the cliff by Apache Indians. Mrs. Page was left for dead and lay for several days in a coma. The Indians had lanced her and taken her shoes, which they then wore, in this way duplicating her tracks and leading her would-be rescuers to pass by the place where she lay half conscious. Despite the fact that the Indians had also stoned her, she recovered sufficiently to make her way back to her own home in the bitter cold without shoes, food, or water.

Ref.:   104, p. 150. Map: GL-3.

## IRENE

El.: 3327′                      Loc.: Pima 4, E-6.8

The origin of the name Irene for this point on the railroad has not been ascertained. Locally the point is known as Three Bridges, since one railroad goes under another and also under the highway.

Ref.:   Lenon. Map: GJ-13.

## JAYNES

El.: c. 2300′                    Loc.: Pima 4, A-3.2

Inasmuch as this point on the railroad was named c. 1890, there is some doubt that it was so named for Allen B. Jaynes who in 1916 was editor of the *Tucson Citizen*. However, the place may have been named for him.

P.O. est. July 21, 1922. Hubert E. Hunts, p.m. Discont. May 17, 1924.

Ref.:   Barnes; P.O. Records. Map: GJ-6.

## KAKA

El.: c. 1500'                    Loc.: Pima 2, B-1.2
Pro.: /kagkə/                    Papago: "clearing"
This is a medium sized permanent Papago village. It is said to have been visited by Fr. Kino in 1698 and again in 1700. He referred to it as El Gaga.

**v.n.** Cazoln      (Wheeler survey) (corruption)
         Cacate                  (corruption)
Ref.: 128, p. 8; 20, pp. 398-399; 34, p. 11. Map: D-8.

**a.n.** Kaka Valley                            Pima
    Loc.: Bounded on n. by Sand Tank Mountains; w. by Sauceda Mountains; e. by Castle Mountains.
    Kaka Wash      Loc:. Drains Kaka Valley      Pima

## KELLOGG PEAK

El.: 8385'                    Loc.: Pima 4, D-2
This mountain, which shows as Mount Lee on the Roskruge Map of 1893, was probably named for William Kellogg, who owned a ranch on its northeast slope c. 1900. His brother, Alexander Kellogg, worked on the north slope of the Santa Catalina Mountains.
Ref.: G. E. P. Smith; APHS Names File. Map: GJ-13.

## KIMBALL PEAK

El.: c. 6000'                    Loc.: Pima 4, BC-2.6
Fred E. A. Kimball (b. New Hampshire, October 22, 1863; d. February 4, 1930) arrived in Tucson in the spring of 1899 and went to work as a reporter on the *Arizona Star*. In 1900 he had a general store at Helvetia. Kimball spent much of his spare time in endless explorations of the Santa Catalina Mountains.
Ref.: F. E. A. Kimball File, APHS; 151, p. 427. Map: GJ-13.

## KINO PEAK

El.: 4800'                    Loc.: Pima 1, D-5.2
Pro.: /kíyno/
The name Kino Peak was applied to the highest peak in the Growler Range c. 1942 by William Supernaugh, then superintendent of the Organ Pipe Cactus National Monument. This was done to honor Fr. Eusebio Francisco Kino, often referred to as the "Padre on horseback." Kino was a tireless missionary among the Papagos from 1694 until his death in 1711.
Ref.: Hensen. Map: None.

**a.n.** Kino          Map: GJ-6                    Pima

## KITT PEAK

El.: 6875'                    Loc.: Pima 3, AB-7.5
In 1893 when George Roskruge was surveying Pima County, he had an Indian named Kit with his party as cook and general roustabout. Kit was known as a "character." It seems possible that Roskruge may have named the peak for Kit, particularly since on Roskruge's own map the name appears as Kits Peak. However, there is also the possibility that the peak may have been named either for Roskruge's sister, Mrs. William F. Kitt, or for his nephews. On maps the name appears on GLO 1896 as Kitts Peak, disappears from GLO 1903, and reappears as Kits Peak on GLO 1909 through 1921, thereafter not appearing on GLO maps.

In 1958 Kitt Peak was designated as the site for the new National Observatory.
Ref.: Barnes; Mrs. George F. Kitt. Maps: C-8; C-10; C-11; C-12; GJ-3.

## KOHI KUG

El.: c. 4000'                    Loc.: Pima 3, AB-8.8
Pro.: /ków˘hiˆ kù/                Papago: "mulberry stands"
Kohi Kug is a temporary Papago village. This is the place which Lumholtz referred to as Ventana. However, Ventana is actually another Papago village (cf. Chiuli Shaik). The Indian Service Map for 1915 shows a Ventana Ranch at this location.

**v.n.** Koxikux                (corruption)
Ref.: 128, p. 1. Map: GJ-3.

## KOMELIK

El.: c. 2500'                    Loc.: Pima 2, GH-9.8
Pro.: /kówmˡək/                  Papago: "flats"
Bolton commented that he believed the place visited by Fr. Kino in 1698 and called by him Cubit Tubig was perhaps Komelik, which was at that time at a somewhat different location. Komelik is a Papago village.

Ref.: 128, p. 1; 20, pp. 398-399 (Note 1). Map: GJ-15.

**a.n.** Komelik Pass                            Pima
    Loc.: Between Slate Mountains on n. and Santa Rosa Mountains on s.
Ref.: 128, p. 21.

## KO VAYA

El.: c. 2500'                    Loc.: Pima 2, G-6
Pro.: /kə? wahə/                 Papago: "badger well"
This is a winter Papago rancheria. The Spanish rendered the name incorrectly as Cobabi. Lt. Juan Mateo Manje referred to this place as Cups.
In 1863 about three hundred fifty Indians were living here when Pumpelly noted the presence of an abandoned mine which he called Cahuabi.

**v.n.** Kavavaik
Ref.: 128, p. 5; 34, p. 365; Kirk Bryan Notes. Map: GJ-5.

**a.n.** Ko Vaya Hills      Map: GJ-5            Pima
**v.n.** Cobabi Mountains
Ref.: Kirk Bryan Notes.

**a.n.** Ko Vaya Wash                            Pima
    Loc.: Flows w. and n.w. toward Ko Vaya

## KUAKATCH

El.: c. 2500'                    Loc.: Pima 1, G-5.2
Pro.: /kúəkəᶜ/                   Papago: "end of mountain"
Descriptive. At one time this village was called Wall's Well or Pozo de Frederico because here Frederick Wall dug a well in connection with the Growler Mine which he discovered and named.
Kuakatch has been described as "the most beautiful and comfortable spot between Tucson and Sonoyta." The well is protected to keep out wandering stock. It is fringed with

green mesquite, palo verde, and desert willows. All of this lies at the peak which is called both Gunsight (q.v.) and Montezuma's Head.

When mining activities ceased in this region the Papago Indians moved in and made use of the abandoned well. It is a favorite camping spot of the Indians when they are harvesting saguaro cactus fruit.

Ref.:   Netherlan; Hensen; Kirk Bryan Notes; 128, p. 7; 91, p. 74. Map: D-8.

**a.n. Kuakatch Pass**                                          Pima
Loc.: S.e. to n.w. between Ajo Range and Gunsight Hills.

**Kuakatch Wash**                                              Pima
Loc.: A tributary of Growler Wash; flows by Kuakatch.

## KUM VO

El.: c. 1500'                    Loc.: Pima 2, BC-7.3
Pro.:  /kówmwow/        Papago: "hackberry charco"
There is a water hole at this location and hackberry trees in the vicinity. This is a small Papago village which has a white adobe church and several houses.

**v.n. Comovo**
**Pato**                              (Spanish: "duck")
According to Kirk Bryan this small village was sometimes referred to as Pato because that was the name of the principal Indian living at the place.

**Santa Cruz**
This name was sometimes used because it is the name of the church.

Ref.:   Kirk Bryan Notes; 34, p. 369; 128, p. 10. Map: D-8.

**a.n. Kom Vo Valley**                                         Pima
Loc.: S. of Quijotoa Valley between Mesquite Mountains and Kupk Hills.

**v.n. Comovo Valley**
**Bajio Comovo**                    (corruption)
Ref.:   Kirk Bryan Notes; 128, p. 17.

## LAGUNA

El.: c. 2500'                       Loc.: Pima 3, G-9.3
The Laguna Stage Station on the road to Sacaton in 1869 had a population of about eighty-five pioneers. Distinguished guests were met here by the elite of Tucson who escorted them to the Old Pueblo.

The fact that the stage station lay nine miles from Tucson led to its being called Nine Mile Waterhole.

Ref.:   *Weekly Arizonan*, May 22, 1869, 3:1; APHS Files. Map: A-2 (Nine Mile Station).

## LAGUNA, SIERRA DE

El.: c. 4800'                       Loc.: Pima 1, G-7.3
                      Spanish: "mountains of the lake"
This was the name which was given to this portion of the Ajo Mountains by Lt. N. Michler in 1854.

Ref.:   50, I, 72. Map: None.

## LEMMON, MOUNT

El.: 9150'                         Loc.: Pima 4, CD-2.2
In June 1882 Dr. J. G. Lemmon (d. 1917) of the Lemmon Herbarium of Oakland, California, arrived in Arizona with his bride on a trip to study flora on this mountain. Finding

himself unable to ascend it from the south, Lemmon went to Oracle where with Emerson Oliver Stratton, he ascended Oracle Road up the mountain. In honor of the Lemmons, Stratton named the peak Mount Lemmon.

P.O. est. June 29, 1945. Hurst B. Amyx, p.m.

Ref.:   Emerson O. Stratton ms., p. 63, (APHS); P.O. Records. Map: GJ-13.

**a.n. Lemmon Canyon**                                        Pima

## LESNA PEAK

El.: 4717'                      Loc.: Pima 3, DE-12.5
Pro.:  /léysnə/                    Spanish: "awl"
Lesna Peak is the highest in the group known as the La Lesna Mountains. The reason for the name has not been ascertained.

**v.n. Cerritos de los Linderos**
Ref.:   50, I, 122 (1857); Kirk Bryan Notes; 128, p. 33. Map: GJ-7.

## LOCOMOTIVE ROCK

El.: 2166'                         Loc.: Pima 1, E-3.2
When viewed from the north this peak bears a striking resemblance to the front end of a steam locomotive. Locally it is sometimes referred to as Locomotive Peaks.

Ref.:   Kirk Bryan Notes; 34, p. 210. Map: GJ-1.

## LOGAN

El.: c. 2500'                       Loc.: Pima 2, DE-5.5
In 1885 Logan City was a mining center for the Quijotoa Mining District, and it supplied water for nearby mines. Following the mining discovery on Ben Nevis Mountain in 1883, J. T. and W. R. Logan, brothers, dug the well. The brothers hit water on April 8, 1884. Within a very short time there were nearly two hundred adobe houses in Logan City and in other communities nearby.

Logan is today an abandoned mining camp.

Ref.:   155, pp. 63, 65, 66, 67; 128, p. 5. Map: C-7.

## LORD, MOUNT

El.: 3825'                          Loc.: Pima 3, E-2.6
George J. Roskruge named this peak on his 1893 map of Pima County for Charles Lord, his neighbor. Lord (b. Watertown, Wisconsin, March 12, 1858) was a member of Lord & Williams, well-known Tucson merchants and freighters.

Ref.:   APHS Names File. Map: C-8.

## LOWELL, FORT

El.: 2530'                          Loc.: Pima 4, BC-3.8
The first Camp Lowell was established by Col. West and the California Volunteers on May 20, 1862, and was located at what is now the corner of Scott and 14th Streets in Tucson. It was named in honor of Brig. Gen. Charles R. Lowell, Sixth U. S. Cavalry, who was killed in a Civil War battle in 1862. The original Camp Lowell was established when the California Volunteers were chasing the Confederate Column. Once established, the camp existed for two years. It was abandoned on September 15, 1864,

and re-occupied in May 1865. On August 29, 1866, it was declared a permanent post and given the name Camp Lowell.

There was a great need for a good water supply for the post and also for hay to feed the horses. For this reason in 1873 Camp Lowell was moved to the site occupied by its ruins today about seven miles from the center of Tucson. It is interesting to note that it was established because there was running water in the Rillito and there was an abundant growth of hay nearby. The move to the new post was made on March 18, 1873. Within a short time Camp Lowell became an important community having two weekly papers, a public school, a church and the usual increment of places of entertainment for the soldiers. The fact that the new post had permanent quarters was a relief to the military, which up to that time had been housed in brush shelters and cloth tents. Fort Lowell, as it was then known, continued to have great importance until the Apaches were subdued in the early 1880's. The post was abandoned in 1886. The adobe buildings fell into ruins, the shade trees died from lack of attention, and only a small community continued to exist at the old location. It has long since merged with Tucson.

Currently Fort Lowell has been somewhat restored. Further disintegration is being prevented.

P.O. est. as Fort Lowell, July 6, 1911. Muli Ignacio, p.m. Discont. March 5, 1912.

Ref.: *Arizona Citizen*, March 2, 1872, 3:2; 75, p. 142; 87, pp. 270, 312; 32, II, 60. Maps: C-2; E-12 (Troops); E-18; E-20; GJ-13.

## LUKEVILLE

El.: c. 1500′       Loc.: Pima 1, EF-8.2. In Organ Pipe Cactus Natl. Monument on international border.
This small village lies on sixty-seven acres owned by Charles Luke of Phoenix.

P.O. est. July 16, 1949. Mrs. Leona Daisy Hocker, p.m.

Ref.: *Phoenix Gazette*, July 5, 1949, n.p. (State Library Files); P.O. Records. Map: None.

## McCLEARY PEAK

El.: 7000′       Loc.: Pima 4, D-9.2
William B. McCleary located a ranch in this area c. 1879 (cf. Rosemont).

Ref.: 151, p. 483. Map: B-3.

**a.n. McCleary Camp**       Pima
Loc.: Lower part of Stone Cabin Canyon
In 1909 this was the principal mining settlement in the Madera Canyon region. It lay twelve miles south of Helvetia and here mail for Helvetia miners was received three times a week.
Ref.: 133a, p. 167.

**McCleary Canyon**       Map: GL-3       Pima

## MADERA CANYON

El.: c. 6000′   Loc.: Pima 4, AC-9-10; Santa Cruz 7, E-1
Pro.: /mədérə/       Spanish: "lumber"
The name Madera Canyon goes back at least to 1820, when it was mentioned in the record of the Canoa Land Grant as the point from which measurements were taken.

This canyon was later sometimes referred to as White House Canyon. The location of the white house which gave this canyon its variant name was near the middle of Madera Canyon at an elevation of 5260 feet where the canyon emerges into the plain. Theodore Welish built it in the 1880's. Welish also owned a store in Tucson by the same name.

From the very first incursions of white men, Madera Canyon was noted for its fine timber. In 1858 Larcena Pennington married John Hempstead Page, who with his partner Capt. Reynolds, whipsawed lumber in Madera Canyon, hauling from there to Tucson. In 1860 Mrs. Page persuaded her husband to take her to the lumber camp for her health. It was here that she was captured and dragged off by Apaches (cf. Huerfano Butte).

P.O. est. April 29, 1929. Katherine M. Dusenberry, p.m. Discont. August 31, 1942.

Ref.: *Book of Records of Pima County, 1820-1873*, APHS; APHS Names File; 56, p. 12; 133a, p. 175; P.O. Records. Maps: B-3; C-13 (town); GL-3.

## MAISH

El.: c. 3000′       Loc.: Pima 3, FG-5.4
The Maish and Driscoll Cattle Company of Tucson had a ranch here.

**v.n. Marsh**       (corruption)
Ref.: Barnes. Maps: C-7; C-10 (Marsh).

## MAISH VAYA

El.: c. 2400′       Loc.: Pima 2, DE-7.7
Pro.: /máyš wahə/       Papago: "covered well"
Maish Vaya is a small Papago village with houses in two main groups strung out along an arroyo. The group of houses at the west wells is sometimes referred to as Covered Wells, a translation of the Papago name. In 1884 it was a mining center, the three wells of which furnished water for nearby mines. A townsite was laid out in that year by M. J. Walsh, J. M. Kinley, R. D. Ferguson, M. M. Rice, and M. Redding. As mining declined, the area returned to being an Indian village.

**v.n. Maish-vaxia**
**Maisk**
**Babaho**       (Wheeler)
Ref.: 128, p. 5; Kirk Bryan Notes; 34, p. 366; 155, p. 77. Maps: C-13 (Covered Wells); D-8; D-11 (Maispvaxia).

## MARANA

El.: 1990′       Loc.: Pima 3, F-1.6
Pro.: /məránə/ or       Spanish: "tangle"; "impassable
/mərǽnə/       because of briars and brambles"
As has been noted elsewhere (cf. Cortaro) the valley in which Marana is located was once noted for its extremely thick mesquite and other desert growth. The name Marana first appears on the railroad on GLO 1909. Meanwhile, the land was being cleared under the auspices of a man named Post, whose native state was Michigan. In 1910 there was a small farming community known as Postvale, northwest of Tucson on the Santa Cruz River, where a post office was established. As the railroad name for this

point was Marana, the name Postvale was changed after a few years to correspond with the stop at which the mail was dropped, and the post office at Postvale was consolidated with that at Marana, which involved a slight shift in position.

P.O. est. as Postvale, October 15, 1920. Frank Clark, p.m. Marana p.o. est. May 17, 1924. Jesse M. Dills, p.m. Postvale consolidated with Marana February 1, 1925.
Ref.:    Barnes; APHS Names File; P.O. Records. Map: C-10.

## MARTINEZ HILL

El.: 2850′                              Loc.: Pima 4, AB-5.6
Pro.:  /martíynez/
This small hill opposite San Xavier Mission on the east side of the Santa Cruz River was owned by the Martinez family when the San Xavier Indian Reservation was established in the early 1880's. Although other families were made to leave the reservation, Martinez was able to substantiate his squatter's rights and retain about fifteen acres which reached across the valley to the hill. The Santa Cruz River at that time passed on the west side of the hill, but it has since changed its course.

Martinez' daughter, Maria, married a jeweler named Berger. After Martinez died, the property passed to his daughter and the name Berger Hill came into use. Berger later served as Indian agent on the reservation, obtaining his post with the promise that he would sell his tract to the Indian Service. Documentary evidence has not yet been located to substantiate this.

v.n. Sahuarito Butte
Ref.:   G. E. P. Smith, "Report on Place Names," APHS, November 15, 1941, November 15, 1947; 128, p. 40. Map: GJ-13.

## MELENDRETH PASS

El.: 5500′                              Loc.: Pima 4, D-9.5
A Mexican named Melendrez built a stone and adobe house at this spot. The name "Melendreth" is probably an American approximation of the sound of his name.
Ref.:   Barnes. Map: C-10.

## MENEGERS LAKE

El.: c. 1500′                          Loc.: Pima 1, H-9
Joe Meneger homesteaded at this location during World War I, taking out rights to six square miles. He built a dam to create a water hole. The dam was completed shortly after 1920. In the 1930's he sold his township to the Papago Indian Reservation.
Ref.:   Ketchum; Kirk Bryan Notes. Map: C-13 (Meneger's Dam).

## MICA MOUNTAIN

El.: 8590′                              Loc.: Pima 4, F-4.2
This mountain has large mica outcroppings.
Ref.:   Barnes. Map: GJ-13.

## MINERAL HILL

El.: 3650′                              Loc.: Pima 4, AB-6.5
In 1920 Mineral Hill was a mining camp with a store and a post office on the route then commonly used from Tucson

to Nogales. When the new road was built, Mineral Hill lost its minor importance.
Ref.:    26, p. 351; 34, p. 374. Map: GJ-14.

## MONTAZONA PASS

El.: c. 2500′           Loc.: Pima 2, E-2. Between Cimarron
                        Mts. on n. and Sheridan Mts. on s.
This name is derived from the Montana-Arizona Mining Company which c. 1933 was involved in an unsavory swindle.
Ref.:    128, p. 21. Map: None.

## MONTE CRISTO

El.: c. 2500′                          Loc.: Pima 2, E-1
This was the post office used by the Monte Cristo Mine.
P.O. est. August 14, 1922. Mattie L. Megson, p.m. Discont. October 8, 1923.
Ref.:    P.O. Records; Barnes. Map: F-3.

## MORAS, LAS

El.: c. 4000′                          Loc.: Pima 3, C-10.7
Pro.:  /las mórəs/          Spanish: "mulberries"
The Las Moras Ranch was so named because of the presence of mulberry trees. One of the oldest ranches in the valley, it has changed hands several times.
Ref.:    34, p. 377. Map: GJ-9.
a.n. Moras Wash, Las    Maps: GJ-9; GJ-2              Pima
     Moras Well, Las    Loc.: T. 20 S., R. 7 E.       Pima
v.n. Moros Well, Los

## MORENA, SIERRA DE

El.: 4345′                             Loc.: Pima 2, G-11.4
Pro.:  /siyérədey moréynə/    Spanish: morena "black"
It is possible that these hills took their name from the location of the Morena Mine here in 1873.
Ref.:    Barnes. Maps: C-15; D-8 (Morena Mountain); GJ-18.

## NARIZ MOUNTAINS

El.: c. 4000′                          Loc.: Pima 1, G-9.1
Pro.:  /naríys/               Spanish: "nose"
Descriptive. These mountains are the ones referred to by Lt. N. Michler in 1854 as the Sierra de la Nariz.
A Papago village by the name Nariz existed in 1863, with a population of about two hundred fifty. The precise location of this village is not known, but it may be associated with the Nariz Mountains.
Ref.:    51, p. 122; Kirk Bryan Notes; 155, p. 79; 88, II, 28. Maps: C-10; E-20 (Sierra de la Naril).
a.n. Nariz Flats    Loc.: At base of Nariz Mountains    Pima
     Here in 1699 Fr. Kino camped near Rainwater Lakes. It was on this trip that he established a cattle ranch at Sonoyta.
Ref.:    20, pp. 410-411.

## NEW VIRGINIA

El.: 2450′                             Loc.: Pima 2, DE-4.8
In December 1884, the New Virginia Townsite Company platted New Virginia, which rapidly became an active mining center. It is probable that it was named for the

highly successful Virginia City in Nevada. The community ceased to exist when the mines closed down a few years later.

Ref.: 155, pp. 68, 69; APHS Names File. Map: C-7.

## NINE MILE PEAK

El.: c. 4000'                    Loc.: Pima 1, H-4.3
This prominent lava butte lies nine miles east of the old Gunsight Mine, hence its name.

Ref.: Kirk Bryan Notes; Barnes. Map: C-10.

## NOLIA

El.: 2374'                       Loc.: Pima 2, F-6.8
Pro.: /nówəliy/             Spanish: *noria,* "well"
Nolia is a corruption of the Spanish name for this place. Nolia, a Papago village, is located in one of the oldest mining areas in southern Arizona.

v.n. Nolic
    Noli

Ref.: Kirk Bryan Notes; 128, p. 14; 34, p. 352. Maps: C-13; D-8; D-11 (Noolik); GJ-5.

## NOT VAYA

El.: c. 4000'                    Loc.: Pima 3, C-6.8
Pro.: /náwt wahə/          Papago: "pampas grass well"
Descriptive. This is a small Papago village.

Ref.: 128, p. 12. Map: D-8 (Nawt Vaya).

a.n. Not Vaya Pass                                        Pima
    Loc.: Runs e. and w. between Coyote Mountains on s. and Dobb's Buttes on n.
Ref.: 128, p. 21.

## OLD TUCSON

El.: c. 3000'                    Loc.: Pima 3, G-4.4
"Old Tucson" was originally built as a location set for the motion picture "Arizona" in the early 1940's. It is a replica of Tucson in the 1860's and is being maintained as a tourist attraction.

Ref.: None. Map: None.

## OLIVE

El.: c. 4000'                    Loc.: Pima 4, H-8
Olive was the post office for Olive Camp, a mining community occupied by mine employes and the James Kilroy Brown family, and owned by S. B. Conway of Boston in the 1880's. The camp was named for Olive Stephenson (b. July 24, 1858), who married Brown. The Browns arrived in Arizona on December 24, 1879, at Casa Grande. They moved to Tucson in July 1880, and later to Olive Camp. The mine was sold in the late 1880's.

P.O. est. March 4, 1887. Owen J. Doyle, p.m. Discont. May 23, 1892.

Ref.: P.O. Records; Olive Brown File, APHS. Map: C-6.

## ORGAN PIPE CACTUS NATIONAL MONUMENT

Loc.: Pima 1, CG-4-9
The arms of the organ pipe cactus branch from a central point close to the ground and grow straight and tall to form a cluster resembling organ pipes. The organ pipe cactus is found in abundance within the 330,687 acres of desert mountains and plains of the monument. This accounts for the land having been set aside as a national monument in 1937. It is notable not only for the organ pipe cactus, but also for the fact that it contains a magnificent reserve of virgin desert growth.

Ref.: 183, pp. 1, 2, 3; 5, Natt, N. Dodge, "Godfather of the Organ Pipes." Maps: GJ-16; GJ-18.

## ORO, CANADA DEL

El.: c. 2300'-2500'              Loc.: Pima 4, BA-2-3
Pro.: /kanyádə del oro/          Spanish: "dale" or
                                  "sheepwalk"; *oro,* "gold"
The name Cañada del Oro is an old one. The first specific mention of this canyon is recorded in connection with the activities of Capt. C. R. Wellman, who conducted military operations in this vicinity from June to November 1862. In 1877 Hiram C. Hodges reported that the Cañada del Oro contained rich placer gold deposits where there was evidence of work done many years prior to American occupation. The canyon was the scene of many Apache encounters. Typical was the attack made by three hundred Indians on a Tully and Ochoa wagon train on May 10, 1872, in which five men were killed, several wounded and all the mules taken. The wagons were burned.

The road from Tucson to old Camp Grant ran through the canyon.

v.n. Canyon del Oro

Ref.: 71, p. 166; William Whelan Log, APHS; 89, p. 66; 22, p. 53; 111, p. 166. Maps: E-18; E-20 (Gold Cañon); GJ-6.

a.n. Cañada del Oro Wash  Map: GJ-13               Pima
    Cañada del Oro      Loc.: Not known            Pinal
P.O. est. March 28, 1881. Jose D. Camacho, p.m. Discont. October 12, 1882.
Ref.: P.O. Records.

## OSA, LA

El.: c. 3500'                    Loc.: Pima 3, C-12.7
Pro.: /la osə/                   Spanish: "bear"
La Osa is one of the oldest ranches in Arizona. At Rancho de la Osa, a Mexican cowboy roped and killed a silver-tipped bear and her cub, hence the name La Osa. This name was maintained when Col. W. S. Sturges bought the ranch and made it the headquarters of the La Osa Cattle Company in 1885. The ranch has changed hands many times. It continues to be a working cattle ranch, and in addition is now also a guest ranch.

Although there may be no immediate connection, it is worth noting that the De La Osa family has for generations been prominent in Santa Cruz County and in Sonora.

When the mail was discontinued the papers were sent to Buenos Ayres (*q.v.*) a nearby ranch with a post office. The latter post office changed its name to La Osa in 1903.

P.O. est. as La Osa, May 26, 1890. Paul N. Roth, p.m. Discont. December 12, 1899.

Ref.: P.O. Records; Barnes; Lenon; Escalante. Map: GJ-9.

a.n. Osa Wash, La        Map: GJ-9                 Pima
    Maps: C-7; C-12; GJ-9.

## OURY, MOUNT

El.: c. 6000'                    Loc.: Pima 4, F-6
Pro.: /yúwriy/
The Oury brothers were prominent citizens in Tucson. All
three brothers were born at Abingdon, Virginia. The oldest
was William S. (b. Aug. 13, 1816). William took part in
the Mexican War and then went to California during the
Gold Rush. He came to Arizona in 1857 as the first agent
for the Butterfield Overland Stage. It was William who
was a leader in the Camp Grant Massacre (cf. Old Camp
Grant, Pinal).

The second brother was named Marcus (b. February 3,
1821; d. 1865). His name may have been Marius. He was
killed by Apaches near Tucson, which accounts in part for
the hatred his brother William bore toward Apaches.

The third brother was named Granville (b. March 12,
1825). He, like William, went to California in 1849. Grant,
as he was called, came to Arizona in 1859. By 1860 he
was Chief Justice of the Supreme Court for the Provisional
Government of Arizona. He resigned the same year. During
his lifetime he attained eminence as a lawyer and a politician. It was he who in 1857 led the party that went to
the relief of the Crabb expedition (cf. Filibuster, Yuma).
Ref.:   Oury File, APHS. Map: C-8.

## PALO ALTO

El.: c. 2500'                    Loc.: Pima 3, EF-8.1
Pro.: /pǽlo ǽlto/                Spanish: "high tree"
Palo Alto was the post office for the Palo Alto Ranch. In
1907 there was a very tall mesquite in front of the house.
P.O. est. August 3, 1925. Walter A. Jost, p.m. Discont. March
1, 1928.
Ref.:   Willson; P.O. Records. Map: C-12 (Palo Alto Ranch);
GJ-16.

## PAN TAK

El.: c. 4000'                    Loc.: Pima 3, C-6.5
Pro.: /bᴾan ták/                 Papago: "coyote sits"
This Papago village is sometimes referred to as Coyote.
It was so known as a watering place in 1864.
Ref.:   128, p. 12; 25, pp. 284, 285. Map: GJ-10.

a.n. Coyote Field          Map: GJ-10                Pima
     Coyote Mountains      Map: GJ-10                Pima
v.n. Pan Tak Mountains
                     Maps: GJ-3; GJ-4; GJ-8
a.n. Coyote Pass           Map: GJ-9                 Pima
     Coyote Wash           Map: GJ-9                 Pima
     Pan Tak Pass          Map: GJ-3                 Pima
     Pan Tak Wash          Map: GJ-3                 Pima

## PANTANO

El.: 3547'                       Loc.: Pima 4, EF-7.1
Pro.: /pæntǽnow/                 Spanish: "swamp" or "body of
                                 water at head of a valley"
When the railroad came through in the early 1880's, the
tracks were laid across the old stage station at Cienega
(q.v.) and a new point for the convenience of the residents
in the area was established at Pantano a mile and a half

to the east of the vanished Cienega. The name, in all probability, was derived from the fact that it was closely related
descriptively to Cienega.
P.O. est. July 2, 1880. Lyman W. Wakefield, p.m. Discont. April
30, 1952. Wells Fargo Station, 1885.
Ref.:   P.O. Records; 32, II, 152. Maps: B-3; C-5; GL-3.
a.n. Pantano Wash          Map: GJ-13                Pima
     Pantano Wash is formed by the junction of Rincon Creek
     with Cienega Creek.
Ref.:   133a, p. 43.

## PAPAGO INDIAN RESERVATION

Loc.: Stretches for 60 miles along international boundary
and north-south about 90 miles in southwestern part of state.
Pro.: /pǽpəgo/        Pima:  papah, "beans"; ootam, "people"
Although contact by Americans with Papago Indians has
existed since the 1850's, the Papago Reservation was the
last permanent reservation to be formed in the United
States. This occurred in 1916 with the establishment of the
agency headquarters at Sells. However, land had been set
aside for Papagos at San Xavier on July 1, 1874. Thereafter from time to time additional acreage was added to
form the Gila Bend (q.v., Pinal) portion as well as to round
out the present 2,774,536 acres of the reservation. It is the
second largest in the nation, the last allotment having been
made on June 13, 1939.

The name Papago is thought to have come from the Pima
name papah and ootam, borne out by the fact that the
Papagos are a Piman tribe and eat beans of various trees
such as those of the screwbean and mesquite. Currently
about eight thousand Papagos are on this reservation.
Ref.:   88, II, 200, 374; "Annual Report of the Arizona Com-
        mission of Indian Affairs, 1954, 1955, 1956," pp. 11-12.
        Map: D-8.
a.n. Papagueria
     This name was used by travelers in the region occupied by
     the Papago Indians, including northern Mexico.

## PASQUA VILLAGE

El.: 2500'              Loc.: Pima 4, B-4.1. In Tucson.
Pro.: /pǽskwə/
Pasqua is the largest Yaqui village in Arizona. The Yaqui
Indians came to Arizona to escape exile by the Mexican
government, which wished to move them from their home
on the Yaqui River in Sonora to the tropical regions of
central Mexico. Their villages in the United States and
elsewhere are noted for their religious festivals, particularly
those at Easter time.
Ref.:   Gillmor. Map: None.

## PIA OIK

El.: c. 2000'                    Loc.: Pima 1, H-7.5
Pro.: /piyóy?/          Papago:  "no fields" or "no one farms"
Despite the translation of its name, Pia Oik is a medium-
sized permanent village of the agricultural Papago Indians.
Ref.:   128, p. 7. Map: D-8.
a.n. Pia Oik Pass                                    Pima
     Loc.: Extends w. to e. between n. and s. masses of Gu Vo
     Hills.

Ref.:   128, p. 21.

**Pia Oik Valley**                                      Pima
Loc.: Bounded on w. by Gu Vo Hills; on e. by Mesquite Mountains.
Ref.:   128, p. 18.

**Pia Oik Wash**                                        Pima
Loc.: Heads at Ajo Range and flows e. and s. past Pia Oik.

## PINKLEY PEAK
El.: c. 4843'          Loc.: Pima 1, E-6.7
The most prominent peak in the Puerto Blanco Mountains was named for Frank Pinkley, first superintendent at the Casa Grande National Monument and later head of the Southwestern Monuments Association.
Ref.:   Hensen; U. S. G. B. "Decision No. 4501, 02, 03," p. 6. Map: None.

## PISINIMO
El.: c. 1500'          Loc.: Pima 2, C-6.5
Pro.:   /pəsiynmow/        Papago: "brown bear head"
Pisinimo is a summer rancheria of the Papago Indians. Most of its houses are substantially built of adobe.
P.O. est. August 7, 1939. Rescinded, October 19, 1939.
Ref.:   34, p. 354; P.O. Records; 128, p. 10. Maps: C-12; D-8; D-11 (Picinemoi).

## PITAHAYA CANYON
El.: c. 3000'      Loc.: Pima 1, F-5.4. N. end of Ajo Mts. in Organ Pipe Cactus National Monument.
Pro.:   /pi'təhayə/
Saguaro cactus in notable numbers is in this small valley. Pitahaya is an old name for saguaro cactus. A. A. Nichol apparently named this canyon c. 1930 while collecting botanical specimens.
The canyon is sometimes erroneously called Grass Canyon because of luxuriant grass which springs up during the rainy season.
Ref.:   Hensen; William Supernaugh, Letter, March 5, 1956. Map: None.

**a.n. Pitahaya Region**
Early travelers in territorial days and before used this name for southern Arizona.

## PITOIKAM
El.: c. 3800'          Loc.: Pima 3, A-9.2
Pro.:   /pitwiᵏəm/        Papago: "sycamore place"
This is one of three villages in Fresnal Canyon (cf. Fresnal).
Ref.:   128, p. 1. Map: GJ-3.

## POINT OF MOUNTAIN
El.: c. 1900'          Loc.: Pima 3, FG-1.7
Because of its abundant water, this place was a noted stage and freighting station, with large groves of mesquite. As late as 1908, the buildings were in a fair state of preservation, but the ruins are now completely demolished.

**v.n. Pointer Mountain**
Ref.:   32, II, 161-162; 25, p. 131. Maps: A-2; C-1; E-18; E-20; E-2; E-11; E-12 (Charcos de los Pimas).

## POLVO
El.: c. 2500'          Loc.: Pima 4, BC-4.7
Pro.:   /pálvo/            Spanish: "dust"
Descriptive.
Ref.:   Barnes. Map: GJ-16.

## POSO BUENO
El.: c. 3000'          Loc.: Pima 3, D-8
Pro.:   /pozo bwéyno/
The origin of this name has not been ascertained.
P.O. est. November 11, 1890. Hubbard W. Larabee, p.m. Discont. November 11, 1895.
Ref.:   P.O. Records. Map: C-7.

## POSO, EL
                                      Loc.: Not known
The origin of this name has not yet been ascertained.
P.O. est. June 19, 1879. Damacio Garcia, p.m. Discont. October 18, 1880.
Ref.:   P.O. Records. Map: None.

## POSTA QUEMADA CANYON
El.: c. 4000'          Loc.: Pima 4, EF-5.2
Pro.:   /posta keymádə/      Spanish: "burned post"
The old stage road to Tucson ran down this canyon. At one time the stage station burned, hence the name. The name dates back at least to 1875.
Ref.:   APHS Names File; Barnes. Map: B-3.

## POZO VERDE
El.: c. 4800'          Loc.: Pima 3, C-11.9
Pro.:   /pózo vérdiˆ/      Spanish: pozo, "well"; verde, "green"
In 1699 Fr. Kino called this water tank Guvo Verde because of its greenish color (Papago: guvo, "well"). Lt. N. Michler of the Boundary Survey party in 1854 wrote of following the old trail around the southern base of the Sierra del Pozo Verde to the Agua del Pozo Verde (showing a shift to the Spanish name).

For many years the location of this water tank was indeterminate. On GLO maps from 1903 to 1912, it is shown in Sonora, Mexico, but on GLO 1921, the well is on the border but in the United States, east of the Papago Reservation, its correct location.

According to Papago legend, Pozo Verde is the region where there is a cave formerly occupied by an ogress called Haw-auk-aux (Cruel Old Woman). To appease her voracious appetite, the ogress ate all the wild animals and then took to cannibalism. This was too much for the Papagos. They consulted their Spirit of Goodness and on his advice invited the old woman to a big dance. She danced until she fell into exhausted sleep, whereupon Spirit of Goodness threw her over his shoulder and deposited her in a cave. While she continued to sleep, the Indians piled the cave high with wood which they set on fire. The ogress perished. It is said that one can still see the footprints of Spirit of Goodness near the cave in which the old woman was burned.

**v.n. Chutukivahia**    (J. W. Fewkes: Papago, "green spring")
Ref.: Kirk Bryan Notes; 20, pp. 281, 408, 409-410; 51, p. 121; 34, p. 10. Maps: C-12; E-18; E-20.

**a.n. Pozo Verde Mountains**                                    Pima
Loc.: From border to Sec. 35, T. 21 S., R. 7 E.

## PUERTO BLANCO MOUNTAINS

El.: c. 2000'                    Loc.: Pima 1, ED-7.5-6.5
Pro.: /pwérto blánko/            Spanish: *puerto,* "door"
                                          *blanco,* "white"
The Puerto Blanco Mountains are so named because an old Spanish trail crosses the international boundary and heads northward through a pass known as the Puerto Blanco, a descriptive name. The pass is located at a spring called Dripping Spring, also descriptive. Because of this spring, the range of mountains has since the early 1890's been called the Dripping Springs Range by American prospectors.

There is some question concerning whether the pass known as the Puerto Blanco is actually that in the mountain range or is one which lies to the west of the Organ Pipe Cactus National Monument Headquarters where two white rocks form a pass over low mountains.

Ref.: Hensen; Ketchum; 5, Dodge, pp. 2, 5; 26, p. 410; U. S. G. B. "Decision No. 4501, 02, 03," p. 6; Kirk Bryan Notes. Maps: C-12; GJ-16.

## PUNTA DEL AGUA

El.: 2450'                    Loc.: Pima 4, AB-6
Pro.: /pántə del ágwa/        Spanish: "point of water"
It was at this place that the waters of the Santa Cruz River formerly rose to the surface after having traversed its course underground for some miles. The name, therefore, was descriptive. The water and place have long since disappeared, but at the time the Punta del Agua existed, the waters of the Santa Cruz from here ran through the community of Tucson before disappearing into the sand. Punta del Agua was apparently a stopping place for travelers. It was owned by a German (Fritz Contzen, cf. Contzen Pass) and his wife, and their place was noted for the solid old-fashioned meals obtainable there. In 1859 Punta del Agua was referred to as a "hacienda of the San Xavier Mining Company."

Ref.: 23, p. 326; *Weekly Arizonan,* April 21, 1859, 3:1. Maps: C-2; E-18; E-20.

## PUSCH RIDGE

El.: c. 4500'                    Loc.: Pima 4, B-2-3
George Pusch (b. Germany, June 24, 1847), a well-known cattleman, was naturalized in Tucson on May 24, 1876. Pusch established the Steampump Ranch near the ridge which bears his name. A steam pump was used to raise water from the well.

Ref.: *Pima County Great Register, 1894;* Pusch (son); Barnes. Maps: C-13; GJ-18; GJ-13 (Steampump Ranch).

## QUIJOTOA

El.: c. 3000'                    Loc.: Pima 2, E-5
Pro.: /kiyhowtów?/    Papago: *Kia Hoa Toak,* "carrying
                                      basket mountain"
The name Quijotoa is a Spanish corruption of the Papago name. The Papago women carry ollas on their backs in a specially shaped baskets. The top of nearby Ben Nevis Mountain (See *a.n.*) resembles such a basket, and because of this the name Quijotoa was used by Indians and adopted by prospectors.

In 1863 there were about three hundred eighty-five Indians living at this location. Apparently mining went on in this region as early as 1774 when it is reported that ores were shipped to Baja California, for reduction. Mining work of great importance here in 1879 with the discovery of copper, and in 1883, when even better deposits were uncovered, Quijotoa surged forward as a mining center. A townsite known as Quijotoa City was laid out under the ownership of Charles H. Beckwith and George L. Rognon. Other townsites also sprang into existence (cf. New Virginia and Logan). By 1885 the ores were exhausted and Quijotoa went into a decline. It has now almost completely vanished.

P.O. est. December 11, 1883. Ransom Gibson, p.m. Discont. August 31, 1942.

**v.n. Tnijotobar**    (Bailey, 1858)
    **Kihatoak**    (Russell, 1908)
Ref.: P.O. Records; 128, p. 5; 88, II, 340; 155, p. 71; *Arizona Mining Index,* January 26, 1884, 3:6. Maps: C-5; D-8.

**a.n. Ben Nevis Mountain**    Map: C-7    Pima
The Papago appellation for this mountain consisted of Kia Hoa Toak for one part of it, Gah-kotkh, ("crooked") for the remainder. With the coming of English-speaking miners to the area, other names were soon applied, such as Peer Mountain. The name Peer was that of a mining claim held by McKay on the mountain. S. A. Manlove called it Ben Nevis in honor of Alexander McKay, a Scotchman, who was the first man to climb the mountain. Manlove borrowed the name from Keats' poem with its reference to rugged and precipitous heights.
Ref.: 155, pp. 17, 18, 24; 34, p. 392.

**Quijotoa Mountains**                                    Pima
**Quijotoa Pass**                                         Pima
Loc.: Extends w. to e. between Quijotoa Mtns. and Brownell Mts. on n.
**Quijotoa Valley**                                       Pima
Loc.: W. of Quijotoa Mtns. and e. of Gu Vo Hills.
**Quijotoa Wash**                                         Pima
Loc.: Heads on n.e. side of Quijotoa Mtns. and extends n.e. past Quijotoa.

## QUINLIN MOUNTAINS

El.: c. 5000'                    Loc.: Pima 3, CD-9
James Quinlin (b. Maine; d. 1892) arrived in Tucson in 1865. Quinlin had a stage station on the line from Tucson to Quijotoa in 1884, where teams were changed and watered. At various times he had mines in this region and was also a freighter. His name was applied to these mountains by Roskruge when the latter surveyed Pima County in 1893, Quinlin's stage station having been at their northern base.

Ref.: Barnes; APHS Names File; 155, p. 79. Maps: GJ-3; C-11.

## QUITOBAQUITO

El.: c. 2000'                                Loc.: Pima 1, D-7.5
Pro.: /kíyto baki'yto/        Papago: *ki-to-bac,* "house ring
                                            spring" (see entry below)
Formerly, there was a settlement called Quito Baquito in
Sonora, Mexico, but the famous Quito Baquito Springs are
just within the United States. Their name indicates in
*ki-to-bac* a "watering place" to which is joined the designation indicating "first ring of thatch in a circular Papago
house," so that the name means "house ring spring." Part
of this seems to have been lost or changed somewhat, so
that the addition of the Spanish diminutive *quito* resulted
in the final form of the name. There was a larger town
called Quito Bac south of Sonoyta in Mexico, and this may
have led to the addition of *quito* for the smaller settlement
just south of the Arizona boundary.

Another theory concerning the origin of the name is that
the *bac* (or *baq*) portion is derived from the Papago word
for "spring," to which has been added the Spanish diminutive ("little spring," Quitobaq). To this in turn may have
been added a further diminutive to produce the final name,
Quito Baquito.

To further confuse the picture is the comment made by
Lumholtz that Papagos called this place Alivaipai ("little
springs"), but called the town farther in Mexico, Baketa
("reeds").

Whatever the origin of the name, Quitobaquito had its
first Spanish visitor when Melchior Diaz stopped to rest
here in 1541 on his trip to the Colorado River. Later the
spot was an important stop on the Camino del Diablo. Fr.
Kino called the Sonoran village San Luis de Bacapa or San
Luis Beltram de Bacapa. In 1774 Fr. Francisco Garcés
maintained the saint's name but changed the rest to San
Luis de Quitobac.

The pond formed by waters emerging from the old spring
contains rare Percy minnows, a desert fish found at only
one other place in Arizona.

Ref.: Hensen; W. J. McGee, "Old Yuma Trail," *National
      Geographic Magazine,* XII (1901), 105, Note; 34, pp.
      2, 426-27; 35, p. 487, (Note 33); 51, p. 115; 5, Dodge,
      pp. 5, 7. Maps: E-18; E-20 (Quitovaquito); E-2; E-17.

**a.n. Quito Baquito Mountains**      Maps: C-12; E-2          Pima

## REALES, LOS

El.: c. 2800'                                Loc.: Pima 4, AB-5.6
Pro.: /los reyáləs/       Spanish: a kind of coin (see below)
Los Reales was a reduction point for mines owned by a
man whose first name was Domingo, but whose last name
has not been ascertained. At this point Domingo had his
home as did also several Mexicans who worked for him,
forming a community called Los Reales. It is believed that
the name came from the fact that Domingo paid his workers with Mexican money, using coins called *reales,* two of
which were worth twenty-five cents. It is conjectured that
the workman would say it was time to pick up "our los
reales," hence the name for the community.

Los Reales is said to have been in existence c. 1865 and
that at one time nine families lived at this place. In 1881
it had two stores, several houses and a blacksmith's house.
When the Santa Cruz River changed its course and left Los
Reales high and dry, the town died of dessication. Piece by
piece the buildings were pulled down to provide materials
for those who wished to build elsewhere. In 1937 all that
remained was a rapidly weathering cemetery.

Ref.: "Ghost Town Is Recalled Here," *Arizona Daily Star,*
      June 30, 1937, in Bernice Cosulich Clipping Book,
      APHS; also *Arizona Star,* June 27, 1937. Map: None.

## REDINGTON

El.: c. 2600'                                Loc.: Pima 4, FG-1.8
The Redfield brothers settled approximately six miles south
on the San Pedro River from where the present community
of Redington is now located. The earlier community was
located by Henry and Lem Redfield in 1875 and they
established a post office at their ranch. Since the Post Office
Department would not accept the name Redfield for the
office, the brothers coined the name Redington.

In the next several years, outlaws used the vicinity of Redington when hiding out from the law. In 1883 some of
these bandits robbed a stage and committed a murder a
mile and a half north of the old Riverside stage station.
Tracked to the Redfield ranch, Joe Tuttle was found with
much of the loot; he was with Lem Redfield. Both men
and Frank Carpenter, who had also been caught, were
imprisoned at Florence where Tuttle confessed that he and
Charlie Hensley committed the crime and that Redfield
was to be cut in on the loot for hiding the money. Redfield
denied the accusation. His brother Henry, deciding that
Lem's life was in danger, went to Florence with seven men
and a Deputy United States Marshal to take Lem to
Phoenix for safety's sake. Aroused, the citizens of Florence
immediately lynched Lem Redfield and Joe Tuttle. There
has been much doubt that Redfield had any part in the
crime for which he was lynched.

P.O. est. October 7, 1879. Henry F. Redfield, p.m. Discont. December 31, 1940.

Ref.: William Whelan File, APHS; 131, pp. 27-28; P.O. Rec-
      ords. Maps: C-5; GB-18.

## RICE PEAK

El.: 7577'                                   Loc.: Pima 4, D-1
Gen. Elliott Warren Rice was one of the owners of the
Southern Belle and other Pima County mines in the early
1880's.

Ref.: APHS Files; *Arizona Star,* April 28, 1881, (APHS).
      Maps: C-8; C-13; GJ-16; GJ-18; GK-18.

## RILLITO CREEK

El.: 2500'                                   Loc.: Pima 4, DB-3
Pro.: /riyíy˘to/                   Spanish: "little river"
Descriptive. The fact that there was living water in Rillito
Creek led to the establishment of Fort Lowell on its banks
(cf. Lowell, Fort). There is water in this stream bed today
only following heavy rainfall. The name Rillito is an old
one, being found first on the Military Map of 1875.

Ref.: 151, p. 642; 22, pp. 53, 55. Maps: C-2; E-18; GJ-6;
      GJ-13.

**a.n. Rillito**          El.: 2069'. Map: B-3          Pima

Rillito appears on the railroad on GLO 1903. There was a community called Rieletto which had thirty-two people according to the census of 1870, but it is not known whether this has any connection with the location on the railroad. The name of Rillito was changed to Langhorne after the family by that name which resided there. It retained this name four years.

P.O. est. as Rillito, July 13, 1905. Catherine E. Langhorne, p.m. Changed to Langhorne, September 21, 1908. Changed to Rillito, December 7, 1912.

Ref.: Barnes; P.O. Records; 87, p. 43.

## RINCON MOUNTAINS

El.: c. 7500'          Loc.: Pima 1, F-4-5
Pro.: /rinkan/          Spanish: "corner"
Two possible reasons have been suggested for the naming of the Rincon Mountains. One source states that the mountains took their name from a family which had a cattle ranch in the area in the 1880's. On the other hand, the name may possibly be descriptive, since the mountains form a definite inside corner.

Ref.: APHS Names File. Maps: B-3; C-6; GJ-13; GB-12.

**a.n. Rincon Creek**          Map: GK-13          Pima
  **Rincon Peak**          El.: 8465'. Map: GK-13          Pima
  **Rincon Valley**          Map: GK-13          Pima

## ROBLES JUNCTION

El.: c. 2900'          Loc.: Pima 3, E-5.8
Pro.: /robleys/          Spanish: "oak"
In 1884 Bernarbe Robles ran a stage line from Tucson to Quijotoa, as well as one to Gunsight. A stage station on that line existed at his ranch, which was known as Spanish Ranch and as Robles Ranch. Where the road divides to go to Sasabe or to Sells from Tucson is Robles Junction. Currently it is frequently referred to as Three Points inasmuch as the Robles holdings were sold c. 1920 and the road is three-pronged here.

Ref.: 155, pp. 69, 78. Maps: C-7; GJ-4.

**a.n. Robles Pass**          Map: GJ-11          Pima

## ROSEMONT

El.: c. 4200'          Loc.: Pima 4, D-8.8
An early name for Rosemont was McCleary Camp, after the locator of the claims.

Rosemont was located in the southeastern part of the Helvetia (q.v.) district and may possibly have had some claims in the late 1870's and early 1880's. They were owned by William McCleary (cf. McCleary Peak), who in 1894 sold them to L. J. Rose. The Rosemont Mining and Smelting Company in turn was sold in 1896 to the Lewisohn brothers of New York City. The smelters were closed down at Rosemont in 1907 during an industrial depression.

P.O. est. as Rosemont, September 27, 1894. William B. McCleary, p.m. Discont. May 31, 1910.

Ref.: 133a, pp. 24-25, 128; Barnes; APHS Names File; P.O. Records. Maps: B-3; C-8; GL-3.

## ROSKRUGE MOUNTAINS

El.: 3738'          Loc.: Pima 3, CD-2-4
Pro.: /raskruwj̃/
George J. Roskruge (b. England, April 10, 1845; d. July 27, 1928) came to the United States in 1870, living for the next two years in Denver. From there he arrived in Prescott in 1872, where he served as cook and chainman to Omar H. Case, Deputy U.S. Surveyor for Arizona and New Mexico. Later Roskruge became a surveyor. He moved to Tucson where he lived for forty-five years. In 1893 he surveyed Pima County, applying many place names to the map, including his own for the Roskruge Mountains.

Ref.: Kirk Bryan Notes; Lenon; 55, p. 457, (Note 5); 112, III. Maps: C-8; GJ-4.

## SABINO CANYON

El.: c. 2700'-3700'          Loc.: Pima 4, CD-2.8-4
Pro.: /sabíyno/
According to a man who was born and raised in this canyon, the name came from the fact that a type of desert shrub known as *sabino* or *savino* grows abundantly in it. Sabino Canyon is currently a recreation area.

Ref.: Juan Figueroa. Map: GJ-3.

**a.n. Sabino Canyon**          Map: GJ-3          Pima
  **Sabino Wash**          Maps: GJ-3; GJ-8          Pima
  **Sabino Otero Land Grant Claim**          Map: C-6          Pima
  This claim lay in T. 20 S., R. 13, 14 E. Therefore it does not seem to have any connection with Sabino Canyon (*a.n.* above) in T. 18 S., R. 8 E. The Otero claim was one of those disallowed by the U. S. Land Court.

## SAGUARO NATIONAL MONUMENT

El.: 2800'-3500'          Loc.: Pima 4, DG-4-5
Pro.: /sawáro/
In 1933 the Saguaro National Monument was created to preserve approximately ninety-nine square miles which include a thick stand of saguaro cactus.

Ref.: 5, Dodge, "The Wilderness of Unreality," p. 3. Maps: C-14; GJ-13.

## SAHUARITA

El.: 2540'          Loc.: Pima 4, B-7.2
Pro.: /sawaríytə/          Spanish: "little saguaro"
James Kilroy Brown arrived in Arizona on December 24, 1879, en route to the Sahuarita Ranch south of Tucson. The ranch was the hub of a settlement which sprang up around the school house. It soon became a stage station on Pedro Aguirre's line between Tucson, Arivaca, and the mines in the Quijotoa region, and the ranch house was turned into a hotel. Why Hinton should have referred to this place as Columbus has not yet been learned.

Brown, the owner of the Sahuarita Ranch, was associated with the Olive Mining Company (cf. Olive Camp). He sold the ranch holdings c. 1886. After the sale of the ranch the post office was discontinued and Sahuarita fell into decline. However, in 1911 the railroad established a station here and somewhat later the post office was re-established. Today Sahuarita has an active cotton gin and numerous accommodations for cotton workers.

**v.n. Saurita**

P.O. est. as Sahuarito September 4, 1882. James K. Brown, p.m. Discont. July 11, 1886. Re-est. as Sahuarita October 15, 1911, Tomasa G. Dumont, p.m.

Ref.: Mrs. J. K. Brown, ms., APHS; 87, pp. xxxiii, xxiv; P.O. Records. Maps: B-3; C-2; C-12; E-20.

**a.n. Sahuarita Wash**                                                                    Pima

Loc.: Heads in Santa Rita Mountains, extending n. past Sahuarita.

## SAMANIEGO PEAK

El.: 5591'                        Loc.: Pima 3, F-8
Pro.: /səmaniyéygo/

This peak was probably named by George Roskruge, since it first appears on his 1893 map of Pima County.

Mariano G. Samaniego (b. Mexico, July 26, 1844; d. after 1885) was naturalized an American citizen under the terms of the Gadsden Purchase. He lived in New Mexico until coming to Tucson in 1869 where he then lived until his death. A freighter, cattleman, and stage line operator, Samaniego had a stage line between Tucson and Oro Blanco.

Ref.: APHS Names File; 112, III; Barnes. Maps: C-8; C-12; GJ-14.

**a.n. Samaniego Hills**            Map: C-12                      Pima
  **Samaniego Ridge**            Map: GJ-13                     Pima

## SAN COSME

El.: c. 2500'        Loc.: Pima 4, H-7 (approximate only)
Pro.: /san kazmey/

Fr. Kino named a now-vanished rancheria north of San Xavier del Bac on the Santa Cruz River, San Cosme. It shows on the map of 1702 as Cosmas.

On March 3, 1757, Fr. Bernard Middendorf established a mission at this point, called San Cosme de Tucson. Apparently it did not long remain a mission, but soon became a *visita,* or rancheria visited by missionaries from time to time. Some time during the 1760's Fr. Alfonso Espinosa resided at this place, making it once again a mission in all but name. At this time it apparently had a large population.

Ref.: 88, II, 428; 145, pp. 112, (Note 3). Map: None.

## SAN JUAN SPRING

El.: c. 3635'                      Loc.: Pima 3, AB-7.2
Pro.: /sãn hwãn/            Spanish: "Saint John"

San Juan Springs is a winter rancheria. The spring at this location supplies water for the Papagos.

Ref.: 128, p. 2; 26, p. 426. Maps: C-12 (San Juan); D-8; GJ-3.

**a.n. San Juan Canyon**            Map: GJ-3                      Pima
  **San Juan Pass**              Map: GJ-3                      Pima
  **San Juan Wash**            Maps: GJ-3; GJ-8              Pima

## SAN LUIS

El.: c. 2500'                      Loc.: Pima 2, FG-5.6
Pro.: /san luwis/            Spanish: "Saint Louis"

San Luis is a small Papago village.

Ref.: 128, p. 14. Map: GJ-5.

**a.n. San Luis Canyon**            Map: B-3                       Pima
  **San Luis Mountains**      Maps: GJ-2; GJ-7              Pima

These mountains are named for the San Luis Mine.

Ref.: Barnes.

**San Luis Wash**                   Map: GJ-2                      Pima

## SAN MIGUEL

El.: 2477'                        Loc.: Pima 3, A-11.3
Pro.: /san migeyəl/        Spanish: "Saint Michael"

San Miguel is a Papago village established by the Indians c. 1914. In 1915 it had both a Catholic and a Presbyterian mission.

P.O. est. June 15, 1917. Elizabeth T. Wolfe, p.m. Discont. June 15, 1918.

Ref.: 128, p. 3; Kirk Bryan Notes; P.O. Records. Map: GJ-15.

**a.n. San Miguel Wash**            Map: GJ-8                      Pima

## SAN SERAFIN

                                  Loc.: Not precisely known.
Pro.: /san særfin/          Spanish: "Holy Seraph"; also
                                          St. Francis of Assisi

In 1698 Fr. Kino came across a Pima rancheria which he referred to as San Rafael del Actum el Grande, which was the Spanish way of rendering a saint's name plus the Papago name for the location. The Papagos apparently called it Akchin, meaning "arroyo's mouth." This "Great Akchin" was so named to set it apart from a Small Akchin in the Santa Rosa Valley.

The name San Serafin is an old one. It appears as San Serafin de Actum in Juan Mateo Manje's report in 1700 and it shows as S. Serafin on Fr. Kino's map of 1701.

For some reason that is not known, this village was gradually deserted by the Indians until finally it was used only as a summer rancheria by one or two families. Even these c. 1901 abandoned the place. However, by 1917 it had been re-occupied, this having occurred apparently in 1914. One source says that this place was also referred to as La Quituni (q.v.).

**v.n. Guactum**                    (Manje, 1701)
  **San Serafino del Napcul** (Anza and Fonte, 1780)

Ref.: 128, p. 5; 88, II, 453; 34, pp. 412-413. Map: None.

## SANTA CATALINA MOUNTAINS

El.: c. 8000'-9100'              Loc.: Pima 4, DE-2-3
Pro.: /santə catəliýnə/ or /sæntə cætəliýnə/

In 1697 Fr. Kino visited a now-vanished Papago rancheria near what is today Tucson, and called the place Santa Catalina Cuitchibaque. It was here in 1756 that Fr. Bernard Middendorf attempted unsuccessfully to establish a mission, being dissuaded from this because of the cruelty of the Indians. The name Santa Catalina, or Catarina, was applied by Fr. Kino to the mountains bordering the valley to the north and east. Since it was customary for missionaries to name localities for the saint's day on which such places were first visited, it may well be that Fr. Kino gave these mountains their name on the same day (St. Catherine's day) on which he christened the Indian village nearby. Lt. John G. Parke in 1854 referred to the range as the Santa Catarina Mountains, whereas Lt. N. Michler in the same year called them the Sierra de Santa Catarina. The

name continued in use, sometimes being given as Santa
Catrina at least until 1880. Gradually, however, the name
Santa Catalina came into use.

Ref.:  88, I, 371; 20, 503; 124, p. 24; 51, p. 118. Maps: C-1;
       C-4; C-5; E-2; E-11; E-12 (Sierra de la Santa Catarinas);
       E-6 (Santa Catarinas Mountains); E-20 (Santa Catalina
       Mountains); GJ-13; GK-18.

a.n. **Santa Catalina Forest Reserve**                          Pima
      This forest preserve was set aside by presidential proclama-
      tion on July 2, 1902.

Ref.:  55, p. 730.

        **Catalina**                  Loc.: Not yet located      Pima
P.O. est. February 9, 1917. Edwin P. Bernard, p.m.

        **Santa Catalina Natural Area**                          Pima
        The 4,454 acres of this area were set aside in 1927 to main-
        tain original conditions which could be studied by foresters,
        livestock men, and scientists, as well as by the general
        public.

Ref.:  33, p. 13.

        **San Catalina**          Loc.: Near American Flag      Pinal
P.O. est. April 21, 1882. Louis S. Goodman, p.m. Discont.
September 11, 1882.

Ref.:  P.O. Records.

## SANTA RITA EXPERIMENTAL RANGE

El.: c. 3000'                          Loc.: Pima 4, C-8.5
In 1903 the Santa Rita Experimental Range was set aside
along the western slope of the Santa Rita Mountains. Controlled grazing is permitted in this area. The experiments
are designed to improve rangeland management and also
to increase profits in the handling of range livestock. Experiments in the area also include those with deer.

Ref.:  33, p. 9; APHS Files. Map: GI-3.

## SANTA ROSA MOUNTAINS

El.: c. 2500'                          Loc.: Pima 1, G-7.8-8.4
The origin of this name has not yet been ascertained. On
the Lumholtz map and GLO 1912 they show as the Sierra
Santa Rosa at the southern end of the Ajo Mountains.

Ref.:  Kirk Bryan Notes; 128, p. 36. Map: GJ-16.

a.n. **Santa Rosa Valley**      Map: GJ-15             Pima
v.n. **Bajia Santa Rosa**

Ref.:  Kirk Bryan Notes; 128, p. 17.

a.n. **Santa Rosa Wash**                        Pima and Pinal
      Loc.: T. 15 S., R. 7 E., to T. 6 S., R. 4 E.

## SAN XAVIER DEL BAC

El.: 2525'                          Loc.: Pima 4, A-6
Pro.:  /sanəfir del bak/        Spanish: St. Francis Xavier
                                Pima: *baq*, "well"
The name San Xavier del Bac is the usual missionary com-
bining of a saint's name with a local Indian word. In this
case the saint's name was applied by Fr. Kino. While Kino
was a student at Hala in 1663, he was so ill that it was
thought that he would not live. Kino vowed that if God
permitted him to live he would devote his life to his patron
saint, San Francisco Xavier, "the Apostle of the Indies," by
joining the Society of Jesus and serving as a missionary in
foreign lands. Kino began to carry out his vow when he
entered the novitiate in 1665. Ultimately he found himself

bound for Pimeria Alta, a term covering the northern section of lands occupied by the Pima Indians (in this case
northern Sonora and what is now Pima, Pinal, Maricopa,
Graham, and parts of Cochise counties in Arizona). In
1692 Kino visited the Pima village to which he gave the
saint's name San Xavier plus the Pima locative *del Bac*.
In 1697 there were eight hundred thirty Indians living in
one hundred seventy-six houses.

Here on April 28, 1700, Kino wrote in his diary that he had
brought in cattle and founded a cattle ranch in January
1697, and that on April 28, 1700 ". . . we began the
foundations of a very large and spacious church and house.
All the many people working with much pleasure and zeal,
some in excavating for the foundations, others in hauling
many and very good stone of tezontle from a little hill
which was about a quarter of a league away." This church
of the mission, however, is not the present church. The old
mission was destroyed during the Pima Indian revolt of
1751. In 1767 the Franciscan Order replaced the Jesuits. A
year later, a famous Spanish missionary arrived. He was
Fr. Francisco Garcés, who served here for eight to ten
years. The old mission building had been destroyed by
Apaches who in later raids stole all the mission livestock.
Although Garcés was often absent on exploratory trips, the
mission at San Xavier was slowly rebuilt. The present
church was built between the years 1783-1797. It has often
been described as the best preserved and most beautiful of
all missions in the Spanish Southwest.

Today the San Xavier Mission is a part of the San Xavier
Indian Reservation. Adjacent to the mission is the Indian
village of San Xavier. In 1870 one hundred eighty people
were living at this place. A post office was established for
their convenience.

P.O. est. August 7, 1915. Forman M. Grant, p.m. Discont. May
31, 1917.

Ref.:  Kirk Bryan Notes; 88, II, 463; 20, pp. 33, 34, 265, 268,
       498, 507; 19, I, 122, 235, 263; 7, pp. 379-380; 5F, p.
       177; 128, p. 43; 87, p. 43; P.O. Records. Maps: C-1;
       E-2; E-11; GJ-11; GJ-13.

a.n. **San Xavier Mountains**      Map: GJ-14             Pima

## SASABE

El.: 3566'                          Loc.: Pima 3, C-12.8
Pro.:  /sásəbey/ or        Indian:: "head or parent valley"
       /sǽsəbiy/                          (see below)
Concerning the origin of the name Sasabe, Mrs. Mary B.
Aguirre, who came to Arizona in the 1860's, said that it was
an Indian name. At that time it applied to Sasabi Flat which
was at the head of an immense plain. A possible variant name
which is probably closer to Indian phonetics is that of a rancheria called Sasabac on the Gila River in 1774. The present
border town of Sasabe is not that which was in existence
in the 1860's. In fact, it is necessary to analyze maps fairly
closely in order to trace the shifting of this place name from
one locality to others. The earliest printed reference to Sasabi
Flat was in an 1862 newspaper article discussing a proposed
post office at Sasabi Flat where, the newspaper stated,
existed nothing but a few Mexicans in a small hovel not in
the United States, but really in Mexico. The Mexicans took

care of stage mules. Apparently this post office was not established. This was probably the same place as that shown on the 1879 Smith map as Zasabe, eight miles south of the border on the road to Libertad. However, there is a Sasabi Flat shown on GLO 1876 two miles north of the international boundary and an equal distance northwest of Boundary Monument 13. This latter place disappears from maps until GLO 1887, when it is given as Sasabe Flat, and indications are that a small community was at this place. There was a post office here from 1869 until 1878 (see below).

Two other place names are so closely interwoven with that of Sasabe that they must be discussed simultaneously. They are La Osa (q.v.) and Buenos Ayres (cf. Aguirre Peak) and it is the shifting of their post offices and names which requires that they be discussed together. All three places occur for the first time on GLO 1896, on which Buenos Ayres is four miles northwest of Sasabi Flat and La Osa is southwest of the flat on the Mexican border. Sasabi Flat then disappears from maps until GLO 1909, when Sasabe replaces the name of La Osa on the boundary line. This same map shows a Sasabe in Mexico, two miles to the southeast. This is what is considered the "old border town." On GLO 1921 for the first time appears San Fernando at the site of the old La Osa. This is the Sasabe of today, the "new border town."

The present Sasabe took shape as a private development under hard-working Carlos Escalante, nephew of Don Fernando Serrano, Sr. Don Fernando escaped from Mexico during the 1910 Madero Revolution and surveyed six hundred acres where he settled in 1913 as a cattleman. Here, on what was known as the old Reveil Ranch, settled Carlos Escalante in 1916. In the same year a new port of entry was established with the erection of three tents. This was necessary because of the lack of water at the old Sasabe. Young Escalante labored to erect quarters for residents from old Sasabe, who were moving into his little private village, which he named San Fernando in honor of his uncle. The name was changed later because of confusion in mails with the post office at San Fernando, California. Mr. and Mrs. Escalante have created by their efforts a town which in 1957 had a population of sixty-five, a school, a Catholic church, and on its outskirts the U. S. Customs House which was built in 1935-36.

P.O. est. as Sasabe Flat, August 16, 1869. Juan Elias, p.m. Name changed to Providence Wells, July 30, 1878. Discont. October 21, 1878. Re-est. as Sasabe, February 6, 1892. Mrs. Beatrice Aguirre, p.m. Name changed to La Osa, February 24, 1903. Name changed to Sasabe, August 23, 1905. Teofilo Aros, p.m. Discont. June 30, 1914. P.O. est. as San Fernando, April 21, 1919. Reyes M. Pacho, p.m. Name changed to Sasabe, February 10, 1926.
Ref.:   Mrs. Carlos M. Escalante; Mrs. Mary B. Aguirre ms., APHS; *Weekly Arizonan*, November 20, 1862, 2:2; 52, VIII, 139; 34, p. 378; 88, II, 468; P.O. Records. Maps: GK-16; GK-18.

**a.n. Sasabe, Arroyo del**          Map: GJ-9                      Pima

## SAWMILL CANYON
El.: 3969'                               Loc.: Pima 4, CB-9
It was in this canyon that Henry Lazard (b. France, October 30, 1831; d. March 11, 1895) with his partner, Sam

Hughes, maintained a sawmill. Lazard arrived in Arizona in 1858 and by 1860 was a partner with Hughes. In 1869 the men erected a sawmill in the Santa Rita Mountains, employing twenty-four teams to haul lumber. The mill burned in 1870, but Lazard bought another.

Lazard was something of a character. A small, excitable man, he was totally deaf and apparently believing everyone else was too, he customarily talked in a voice which could be heard two blocks away. Lazard lived extremely well, importing French wine by the barrel for the sake of his health.

**v.n. Dowdle Canyon**
      This was so called after David Dowdle, who had a ranch nearby. This name appeared on the Roskruge map of 1893.
Ref.:   Barnes; Henry Lazard File, APHS. Map: GL-3.

## SECUNDINO WELL
El.: c. 3200'                            Loc.: Pima 3, D-10
Pro.: /sèkuwndíyno/
This well was dug somewhat earlier than 1912 by a Mexican named Secundino. There is also a spring at this location.
Ref.:   Barnes; Kirk Bryan Notes. Map: GJ-2.

## SELLS
El.: 2674'                               Loc.: Pima 2, FG-7.8
On GLO 1909 this location shows as Artesa at the north end of the Artesa Mountains. Thereafter that name disappears. However, c. 1920 Kirk Bryan noted that a new town of Artesa was located a mile from Indian Oasis. It may be, however, that when Joseph Meneger dug the first well the older settlement shifted somewhat to Indian Oasis, so called because it was the only place where there was permanent water.

In 1918 the name of the post office was changed to Sells, so named for Cato Sells, who was then commissioner of Indian Affairs. Inasmuch as the post office was located on federal land, it took an act of Congress to change the name. The location was becoming important following the construction of government buildings as headquarters for the Papago Indian Reservation.

P.O. est. as Indian Oasis, August 11, 1909. Joseph Menager, p.m. (sic). Discont. May 16, 1919. P.O. est. as Sells, December 14, 1918. Joseph Menager declined appointment; William G. Power appointed April 26, 1919.
Ref.:   Kirk Bryan Notes; 26, p. 393; 128, p. 14; P.O. Records. Map: GJ-12.

**a.n. Sells Valley**                                            Pima
      Loc.: Bounded on e. by Artesa Mountains; n. and part of s. by Comobabi Mountains; extends into Gu Oidak Valley on s.w.
   **Sells Wash**           Maps: GJ-12; GJ-3                   Pima

## SENITA PASS
El. c. 3500'                             Loc.: Pima 1, E-7.2
                             S. end of Puerto Blanco Mountains.
Pro.: /səníytə/
There are several senita cacti found in this pass, hence the name. Senita is popularly known as the "old man cactus" because of its bearded appearance.
Ref.:   Hensen. Map: None.

## SENTINEL PEAK

El.: c. 3100'          Loc.: Pima 4, B-4.2
This is the mountain which is called "A" Mountain, because students at the University of Arizona have made a huge A on its side and annually take a day off to white-wash the stones forming the letter. The name Sentinel is descriptive of the fact that pioneers used to watch for hostile Indians from this point. The Spanish name for it was Picacho del Sentinela (cf. Tucson.)
Ref.:  Barnes. Map: None.

## SHAOTKAM

El.: c. 1500'          Loc.: Pima 2, AB-9.2
Pro.:  /šowətkəmš/        Papago: "sweet potato"
The name is descriptive of an edible root which grows in the vicinity of Shaotkam, a small Papago village. The Spanish name for it is Los Camotes (Spanish: "sweet potato").
Ref.:  Kirk Bryan Notes; 128, p. 7. Map: D-8.

## SHEEP TANK

El.: c. 2500'          Loc.: Pima 1, C-2.3
This rock tank on the north side of Sheep Peak is probably so named because of the presence of wild mountain sheep.
Ref.:  26, p. 427. Map: C-13.

## SHERIDAN MOUNTAINS

El.: c. 2500'          Loc.: Pima 2, DE-2-3
This irregular group of small mountains was named for Gen. Philip Sheridan.
Ref.:  Barnes. Maps: C-12; D-8; GJ-16.

## SIERRITA MOUNTAINS

El.: c. 4500'          Loc.: Pima 3, F-7.3
              Spanish:  sierrita, "little mountains"
Despite the fact that these low lying hills are a limited area which is roughly circular and about seven miles in diameter, their topography is the sierra type, hence the redundant name.
Ref.:  34, p. 252. Map: B-3.

## SIKORT CHUAPO

El.: c. 2500'          Loc.: Pima 1, G-3
Pro.:  /síkərt čiəpʌ/       Papago: "round spring"
The Spanish name for this location is Pozo Redondo ("round well"). A man named Redondo dug a round well here c. 1910 at the east end of Redondo Canyon. He overstocked the range, thus making it necessary to remove his cattle from the Papago reservation. Papagos then established a year-around rancheria at the well.
Ref.:  Kirk Bryan Notes; Netherlan; 128, p. 8; 34, p. 423. Map: D-8.
a.n. Pozo Redondo Mountains                    Pima
   Loc.: W. and n. Gunsight Hills; w. of Sikort Chuapo Mts.
Ref.:  128, p. 30.
   Pozo Redondo Valley                         Pima
    Loc.: W. of Sikort Chuapo Mts.; e. of Pozo Redondo Mts.
Ref.:  128, p. 17.
    Sikort Chuapo Mountains                    Pima
    Loc.: N. of Gunsight Valley; w. of Hickiwan Valley.
Ref.:  128, p. 30.

   Sikort Chuapo Pass                          Pima
   Loc.: On Sikort Chuapo Wash between Gunsight Hills on w. and Sikort Chuapo Mts. on e.
Ref.:  128, p. 22.
   Sikort Chuapo Wash                          Pima
   Loc.: Heads in Gunsight Hills, goes n.w. to Sikort Chuapo, to Childs Wash, 6 miles ne. of old Rowood.
Ref.:  128, p. 23.

## SIL NAKYA

El.: c. 2000'          Loc.: Pima 2, G-4.1
Pro.:  /si'l nakhy/       Papago: "saddle hangs"
Bryan thinks that Sil is a corruption of the Spanish word silla meaning saddle.

Bolton thinks that this place is the location of the point called Cups by Manje in 1693 during the visit of Fr. Kino.
v.n. San Lorenzo
Ref.:  128, p. 12; Kirk Bryan Notes; 20, p. 281. Map: GJ-5.
a.n. Sil Nakya Hills          Map:GJ-5          Pima
   Sil Nakya Pass                              Pima
   Loc.: N. to s. along Sil Nakya Wash between Sil Nakya Hills.
Ref.:  128, p. 22.
   Sil Nakya Valley     Loc.: S. of Sil Nakya Hills    Pima
   Sil Nakia Wash                              Pima
   Loc.: Heads in n. Comobabi Mountains, n.w. by Sil Nakya as tributary to Santa Rosa Wash.
Ref.:  128, p. 28.

## SILVERBELL

El.: c. 4000'          Loc.: Pima 3, CD-2
The origin of the name for the Silverbell Mine has not yet been ascertained. It has had intermittent postal service. Currently the mine is active.
P.O. est. August 18, 1904. Roger W. Warren, p.m. Wells Fargo Station, 1906.
Ref.:  Barnes; P.O. Records. Maps: C-8 (mine); C-10; GJ-16.
a.n. Silverbell Mountains                      Pima
   Silverbell Valley                           Pima
   Loc.: N. of Waterman Mts., s. of Silverbell Mts.

## SIOVI SHUATAK

El.: c. 1500'          Loc.: Pima 1, H-7.1
Pro.:  /siowl šuətə/       Papago: "sweet water"
This is a small Papago village.
v.n. Cochibo
   Con Quien        (see Coon Canyon, a.n.)
   Sweetwater
Ref.:  128, p. 7. Map: D-8.
a.n. Siovi Shuatak Pass                        Pima
   Loc.: N. and s. along Siovi Shuatak Wash.
   Siovi Shuatak Wash                          Pima
   Loc.: Heads in Ajo Range, extending e. by Siovi Shuatak and s. into Mexico.
   Coon Canyon                                 Pima
       Loc.: In Ajo Mountains s. of Gunsight
Jose Maria Ochoa was a Papago leader from 1870 to 1885. His nickname was Con Quien (Spanish: "with whom"). Probably the Indian spent much of his time playing the card game by that name, which was popular with Indians

in Arizona. The name Con Quien applied to the village and canyon in some manner was corrupted to Coon Canyon, the name by which it is known today.

Ref.: Barnes.

## SOLDIER CAMP

El.: c. 7000'                              Loc.: Pima 4, D-2

In 1882 this place was called Turkey Roost because of birds roosting thickly in the low branching pines. When soldiers were tracking Geronimo in 1885, they camped at this spot, hence the later name.

Ref.: Emerson O. Stratton ms., p. 70, APHS; 2, p. 49. Map: B-3.

**a.n. Soldier Canyon**          Map: GJ-13                   Pima

This was the beginning of the mountainous part of the Old Soldier Trail used by details of soldiers.

**Soldier Trail**          Loc.: In Soldier Canyon          Pima

## SONOITA MOUNTAINS

El.: c. 1500'                              Loc.: Pima 4, EF-8
Pro.: /sənóytə/

This small range of mountains takes its name from the nearby Sonoyta River in Mexico. Fr. Kino passed near here in 1699.

Ref.: 34, p. 211; Hensen. Maps: C-10; GJ-18.

## SOUTH MOUNTAIN

El.: c. 4000'                              Loc.: Pima 2, DE-7

South Mountain lies near the southern end of the Quijotoa Range. It rises sheer, composed of purplish-red sheets of lava combined in columns.

Ref.: 34, p. 231. Map: A-7.

## SPUD ROCK

El.: 8590'                              Loc.: Pima 4, F-4.2

William H. Barnett and Jim Miller, engineers for the S.P. R.R. raised potatoes and cabbage on a little place close to this rock. The men called it Spud Rock for their major crop, potatoes.

By a coincidence, the rock itself looks like an enormous potato. It is clearly visible in the mountains north of the main highway between Tucson and Benson.

Ref.: Barnes. Map: GJ-13.

## STEVENS MOUNTAIN

El.: 4411'                              Loc.: Pima 3, EF-8

This mountain is so named because of its adjacency to the Stevens Ranch. Stevens, as it was sometimes called, was noted for its excellent water which emerged from an artificial tunnel fifty feet long in a hillside from which the water was pumped to the ranch house.

Ref.: 34, p. 373; 26, p. 353. Map: GJ-8.

## STOA PITK

El.: c. 2500'                              Loc.: Pima 2, A-1.5
Pro.: /tówa pit/                          Papago: "white clay"

There are white clay deposits in the neighborhood of this Papago village, hence the name.

Ref.: 128, p. 8. Maps: C-12 (Toapit); D-11 (Toapit); GJ-16.

## STOCKHAM

El.: 2700'                              Loc.: Pima 4, A-2.8 N.w. of Tucson 2 miles.

This point on the railroad has now been engulfed by the city's suburbs. The siding was named for John Stockham, Jr., who worked with a railroad bridge gang and owned land at this point c. 1904.

Ref.: Barnes; Jordan. Maps: C-13; GJ-16.

## STONE CABIN

The precise location of Stone Cabin post office has not been determined, but it is likely that it existed in Stone Cabin Canyon.

P.O. est. December 28, 1880. John P. Zimmerman, p.m. Discont. February 16, 1881.

Ref.: P.O. Records. Map: None.

**a.n. Stone Cabin Canyon**          Map: GL-3                   Pima

## STRATTON CAMP

El.: c. 7000'                              Loc.: Pima 4, D-1.8

This summer camp was named for Emerson Oliver Stratton, a cattleman and miner in Arizona in the 1880's and thereafter. He sold a claim to the people who formed the Stratton Copper Company.

Ref.: Barnes; APHS; *Tucson Citizen*, May 28, 1917, n.p. (APHS). Map: B-3.

**a.n. Stratton Canyon**          Maps: GK-4; GK-18; GJ-13          Pima

This canyon was sometimes referred to as Stratton Gulch. It was named c. 1880. Stratton owned the Pandora Ranch which was incorporated with the Inner-Ocean Cattle Company in 1885.

Stratton spent much time building roads for access to the mines.

Ref.: Emerson O. Stratton ms., pp. 57, 70, APHS.

**Stratton Wash**          Map: GK-4                   Pima

## SUMMERHAVEN

El.: 6500'                              Loc.: Pima 4, D-1.8

In 1882 William Reed and a man named Carter homesteaded here, but failed to prove up the land. They called the place Carter's Camp. Somewhat later Frederick E. A. Kimball (cf. Kimball Peak) was instrumental in establishing a summer colony with a descriptive name.

P.O. est. May 26, 1924. Frederick E. A. Kimball, p.m. Discont. October 14, 1929.

Ref.: Emerson O. Stratton ms., p. 63, APHS; F. E. A. Kimball File, APHS; P.O. Records. Maps: B-3; GJ-13.

## TANQUE VERDE

El. c. 3000'                              Loc.: Pima 4, D-3.8
Pro.: /tánkə veˈrdi/ or                   Spanish: "green tank"
      /tǽnki veˈrdi/

The name Tanque Verde dates back to the 1860's. In 1858 William Oury (cf. Mount Oury) bought cattle from a drover headed for California. Later Oury brought in four hundred blooded Kentucky cattle and transferred his herd to Tanque Verde where he had a ranch. Two or more fairly large water holes containing green algae are the source of the name. The holes are at the base of Tanque Verde Ridge, a northwestern extension of the Rincon Mountains.

The present-day small community of Tanque Verde is not the same as that which appears on GLO 1892 adjacent to Fort Lowell. The post office was at the earlier location.
P.O. est. December 1, 1888. Manuel L. Martinez, p.m. Discont. March 26, 1892.
Ref.: G. E. P. Smith; Juan Figueroa; 105, pp. 227-28; P.O. Records. Map: GJ-13.

**a.n. Tanque Verde Canyon**   Map: GJ-13                          Pima
Forms course of Tanque Verde Creek or Wash.

> **Tanque Verde Hot Springs**                                  Pima
> In 1872 Gov. A. P. K. Safford and his party visited these springs. They may have been at the place designated on GLO 1909 as Hot Springs or Fuller's Hot Springs. The Agua Caliente Ranch owned by Ed Bullock in 1889 was at Fuller's Hot Springs, and Agua Caliente Creek emerges from the springs. Today the location is known as Agua Caliente Hill.

> **Fuller Pass**        Map: C-7                               Pima
> **Agua Caliente Creek**                                        Pima
> (See *a.n.* Tanque Verde Hot Springs).

> **Fuller Canyon**                                              Pima
> Loc.: Between Agua Caliente and Soldier Canyon.
> **Agua Caliente Hill**   El.: 5350'. Map: GJ-13                Pima
> (See *a.n.* Tanque Verde Hot Springs).

Ref.: G. E. P. Smith; *Tucson Citizen*, April 13, 1872, 3:2; *Arizona Star*, July 2, 1899, 4:2.

## TINAJA PEAK

El.: 4515'                              Loc.: Pima 3, G-8.9
Pro.: /tináha/
Descriptive.                           Spanish: *tinaja*, "tank"
Ref.: Barnes. Map: GJ-14.

## TONOKA

El.: c. 3000'                          Loc.: Pima 1, G-6
Pro.: /tənuykə/
Tonoka is a Papago village. Although its name has a Spanish origin, its meaning is not known. It has been said by some that the word means *knee*.
**v.n. Barajita**  (corruption)
Ref.: 128, p. 7; Kirk Bryan Notes; 34, p. 412. Maps: C-12 (Tonoco); D-11.
**a.n. Barajita Valley**                                         Pima
Loc.: E. of Ajo Range and w. of Gu Vo Hills.
Ref.: 128, pp. 17, 19.
**v.n. Gunoka Valley**

## TOPAWA

El.: 2043'                             Loc.: Pima 2, FG-9
Pro.: /tòwpáow/       Papago: "it is a bean"
This large Papago village was close to the route followed by Fr. Kino in 1699. It is today an important headquarters for Catholic missionary work on the reservation. The name derives from the fact that the Indian boys played a game using a red bean which they called "mawi."
**v.n. Topahua**
P.O. est. June 14, 1917. Thomas S. Throssell, p.m. Discont. November 24, 1917. Re-est. February 7, 1925. Bonaventure Oblasser, p.m.
Ref.: Barnes; 128, p. 1; 20, p. 410; P.O. Records. Maps: C-12; D-8; D-11.
**a.n. Topawa Hills**      Map: GJ-12                            Pima
**Topawa**          Maps: GJ-3; GJ-12                            Pima

## TORTOLITA MOUNTAINS

El.: c. 4127'          Loc.: Pima 3, GH-1.2; Pima 4, AB-1.2
Pro.: /tortəlíytə/
The reason for the naming of these hills has not yet been ascertained. This is the same locality which in 1775 was called by Font, Llano del Azotado because near here a muleteer who attempted to desert was flogged (Spanish: *azotado*, "one who has been flogged").

In these hills Cochise and his band of Apaches attacked the Gatchell-Curtis wagon train. Here too a military detachment was ambushed with only one soldier escaping. He later became separated from the other civilian survivors. According to Lt. John Bourke, the men sent to look for the lost soldier never found him, but they did find his tracks and those of a huge mountain lion. Following the tracks they found a place where there were signs of a struggle and then of something having been dragged off.
Ref.: 35, p. 82 (Note 13); 22, pp. 39-40. Maps: C-15; GJ-6.

## TOTAL WRECK

El.: c. 4600'                          Loc.: Pima 4, EF-8
John T. (Jerry) Dillon came to Arizona from New Mexico in 1876. In 1877 he discovered the first silver mines in the Empire Mountains and located the Total Wreck mining claims. When he found this location, he had no mining notices of ownership with him and went to obtain some. He was asked to give a name for the place, whereupon he described it as being a "big ledge, but a total wreck, the whole hillside being covered with big boulders of quartz which have broken off the ledge and rolled down." From that came the name Total Wreck. Dillon, a cowboy, sold the property to the Empire Mining and Development Company and it was in turn sold for taxes to Vail and Gates c. 1883. A fairly large mining community developed at this location. The mine has been worked from time to time since 1907.
P.O. est. August 12, 1881. Nathan R. Vail, p.m. Discont. November 1, 1890.
Ref.: Jerry Dillon and Green File, APHS; 133a, p. 142. Maps: C-5; GL-3.

## TUCSON

El.: 2390'                             Loc.: Pima 4, AB-4.2
Pro.: /tuwsán/ or /túwsan/
The Papago name for Sentinel Mountain (*q.v.*) is Chuk Shon, referring to the fact that the base of the mountain has a darker color than the summit. The Papagos customarily name their villages after distinctive landmarks, and an old Indian village was once located at the base of this mountain. Spanish pronunciation was an approximation of the Papago name, Tuqui Son or, in its current form, Tucson. Hodge states that Tu-uk-so-on means "black base." The rancheria at this point has long since disappeared.

That there was prehistoric civilization where present-day Tucson exists is beyond question. When the Pima County Court House was constructed in Tucson in 1928, workmen excavating for the footings not only uncovered a part of the old presidio wall, but also found evidence of prehistoric civilization. Again in December 1954, workmen excavating for a proposed building found the northern wall for the same presidio and below it a Hohokam pit house dating at least to 900 A.D. The ruins were covered and plans for a new building abandoned.

Records have much to say about Tucson. Its first mention by a Spanish missionary was that made by Fr. Kino in 1697. However, the place to which Kino referred was about three miles north of the present courthouse and hence outside the orginal town limits by a considerable distance. This was San Augustín de Oiaur. Kino noted that it was on the banks of the Santa Cruz River, which was then running with some force, and that between that point and San Xavier del Bac was the most thickly populated and fertile spot in the whole Santa Cruz Valley. It is to be noted that Kino did not apply the word Tucson to this place. Co-existent with this place was Chuk Son near Sentinel Peak (see above).

Many years passed and with them vanished the supremacy of the Jesuits, who fell out of favor with the Spanish court. The Franciscan order took the place of the Jesuit in Arizona, and in 1751 the Indian settlement of Chuk Son became a *visita* of San Xavier del Bac. During the Pima revolt (1751), both the *visita* and the mission were abandoned. A few years later, Fr. Francisco Garcés was sent into southern Arizona. It was he who, to protect the peaceful Indians against the raiding Apaches, caused a small pueblo with a church and a wall to be constructed for defense in 1769. The fact that there was a wall completely around this small community is the origin of the currently used nickname for Tucson, the Old Pueblo. The name San Augustín del Tuquison was transferred to this place to distinguish it from the nearby Chuk Son (or Kuck Son) which was called San Augustín de Pueblito de Tucson. The latter place was reported to have two hundred families in 1772, but by 1774 only eighty families remained. To protect the missions and the peaceful Indians the Spaniards had previously established a detachment of the military at Tubac (*q.v.*, Santa Cruz County). In 1776 these soldiers were moved to San Augustín de Tucson.

In 1822 Tucson was in the newly created Mexico. Tucson was the military outpost of Mexico until the area in which the settlement was located became part of the United States with the Gadsden Purchase in 1853. Apache troubles in the Santa Cruz Valley caused Tucson's population to fluctuate and after 1848 to increase because of refugees from Tubac and Tumacacori seeking safety within its environs. In 1846 the Mormon Battalion passed through under Gen. Philip St. George Cooke. It was at this time that the Mexican presidio moved permanently from the Old Pueblo.

In 1856 the U. S. Government sent four companies of the First Dragoons, who stayed a very brief time at Tucson before being moved to the vicinity of Calabasas in October. It is this fact which has led to some confusion about the date of the establishment of the post office at Tucson (cf. Fort Buchanan, Santa Cruz).

In the summer of 1861, Tucson had a total of sixty-eight American voters. This handful of men assembled in a convention and elected a "territorial delegate" (Granville Oury,

cf. Mount Oury) to the Confederate Congress. In February 1862, Confederates from Texas under Capt. Sherod Hunter marched unopposed into the Old Pueblo. Their stay was a brief one, for they retreated on May 20 before the oncoming California Volunteers, who entered the town and raised the flag of the United States. In June, James H. Carleton, Commander of the California Column, reached Tucson, and Arizona, which had since August 1861 been part of the Confederacy, returned to the Union.

Two years later in May 1864, Gov. John N. Goodwin (who had recently taken up his duties as the first actual governor of Arizona Territory) declared Tucson a municipality, which was tantamount to its incorporation. There was much haggling to establish the permanent capital for the territory at various places and Tucson exerted pressure for her own selection. In 1867 by a majority of a single vote, Tucson became the territorial capital, but in 1877 the capital was moved back to Prescott.

In 1879 thousands of people flocking to the Tombstone District had their effect on the economy of Tucson, which began to emerge from being a tiny sleepy village into its life as a city. The fact that it was sleepy applied mostly to the daylight hours, for Tucson had a reputation of being wide open, rough, and ready. A favorite story was that concerning the tenderfoot from the East who stepped down from a dusty stage trip at four o'clock in the morning. He made tracks for the nearest bar, which wasn't difficult to locate. The tenderfoot made some comment about it being late for the bar to be open, to which the bartender replied that it was late for the night before last, but "just the shank of the evening for tonight."

P.O. est. July 13, 1865. Mark Aldrich, p.m. Wells Fargo Station, 1879. Incorporated February 7, 1877.

Ref.:   Fr. Bonaventure Oblasser, Letter to Frank C. Lockwood, May 5, 1935; 88, II, 111; 7, pp. 369, 381-382, 496, 513-514; 35, p. 78, (Note 11); 20, pp. 376-377; 50, p. 67; 105, pp. 323, 147; 52, III, pp. 71-72; 140, p. 32; 22, p. 83; *Arizona Star*, February 24, 1955, 4:1; P. O. Records. Map: All of Southern Arizona after 1850.

There are at least forty different ways to spell the name Tucson. A few are listed below.

v.n. **Tueson**

　　 **Toison**

　　 **Stjoekson**

　　 **Stycson**

a.n. **Barrio Libre, El**　　Loc.: Center of downtown Tucson　　Pima
Many of Tucson's Spanish-Americans live in this area.

　　 **Tucson Mountains**　　Maps: GJ-6; GJ-11　　　　　　　Pima
v.n. **Sierra Frente Negra** (Spanish: "black faced mountains")
Ref.:   35, p. 81 (Note 13).


## TUMAMOC HILL

El.: c. 3200'　　　　　　　　　　　　Loc.: Pima 4, AB-4.3
　　　　　　　　　　　　　　　　　　Papago: "horned toad hill"
On this hill in 1902 was constructed a laboratory for research in desert botany. The buildings are now used as the Geochronology Laboratories of the University of Arizona.

Ref.:   92, p. 321; Kirk Bryan Notes. Map: GJ-11.

## VAIL

El.: 3220'                          Loc.: Pima 4, DE-6.5
Walter Vail, a cattleman with large holdings, gave the
railroad the right of way through his property in 1880,
and the railroad point from which supplies were freighted
to mines was named for him.
P.O. est. February 26, 1901. Harry A. Mann, p.m. Wells Fargo
Station, 1903.
Ref.:   APHS Names File; P.O. Records. Map: GJ-13.

## VAMORI

El.: 2248'                          Loc.: Pima 2, D-9
Pro.: /váməri/                     Papago: "swamp"
This name is descriptive of the low basin in which this
Papago village is located.
Ref.:   128, p. 3; Kirk Bryan Notes. Map: GJ-15.
**a.n. Vamori Valley**      Map: GJ-15                  Pima
Ref.:   128, p. 19.
        **Vamori Wash**       Maps: GJ-12; GJ-15         Pima
**v.n. Valshni Wash**            (corruption)
Ref.:   128, p. 24.

## VIOPULI

El.: 2686'                          Loc.: Pima 3, DE-6.2
Pro.: /wiyowpʌl/                   Papago: "wild tobacco"
This Papago village was sometimes called San Pedro, c
1914, but the correct name is Viopuli. This refers to a kind
of tobacco grown by the Indians in the vicinity.
Ref.:   128, p. 12; Kirk Bryan Notes. Map: GJ-4.
**a.n. Viopuli Wash**       Map: GJ-4                   Pima

## VIRGINIA CITY

El.: c. 3000'                       Loc.: Pima 2, DE-5.8
Virginia City was one of several townsites laid out in connection with the Quijotoa mining communities (cf. Quijotoa). It was owned by W. J. Dougherty, W. R. Gleason,
and L. D. Chilson. It lay to the south of Logan City. Another
development was called Brooklyn, which was on the north
of Logan.
Ref.:   155, pp. 70-71. Map: C-7.

## WATERMAN MOUNTAINS

El.: 3825'                          Loc.: Pima 3, DE-3
In 1893 when surveying Pima County, George Roskruge
named the peak in these mountains Abbie Waterman Peak
for the mine of the same name which in 1880 was the lead-

ing producer in the Silver Bell District. J. C. Waterman
named the mine for one of his two daughters.
Ref.:   76, p. 46; Emerson O. Stratton ms., APHS. Maps: A-7;
        C-10; GJ-16.
**a.n. Waterman Pass**                                 Pima
        Loc.: Between Waterman Mountains and Roskruge Mts.

## WELDON

El.: c. 2500'                       Loc.: Pima 2, EF-6.5
The Weldon Mine was highly successful and at one time
there were several thousand people living at Weldon. Wel-
don vanished and in its place is San Antone, a location
used by a few Papago families as a winter rancheria.
P.O. est. September 17, 1904. J. Wight Giddings, p.m. Discont.
May 15, 1912.
Ref.:   26, p. 324; P.O. Records. Map: C-10.

## WOLFLEY HILL

El.: c. 3500'                       Loc.: Pima 2, EF-10.7
Lewis Wolfley, a resident of Tucson, was sworn in as Arizona's ninth territorial governor (including John Gurley,
who never assumed office) on March 28, 1889.
Ref.:   APHS Files; 128, p. 33; Parkman. Maps: A-7; C-13;
        GJ-15.

## WOOD'S RANCH

El.: c. 3300'                       Loc.: Pima 4, CD-6.5
This ranch was owned by John M. Wood. A post office was
established here for the convenience of residents in the
vicinity.
P.O. est. July 2, 1884. John M. Wood, p.m. Discont. October
7, 1884.
Ref.:   Barnes; P.O. Records. Maps: C-5; E-20.

## WRIGHTSTOWN

El.: c. 2700'                       Loc.: Pima 4, CD-4
This place was on the ranch owned by Frederick C. Wright.
P.O. est. as Wrightstown, February 11, 1914. Frederick C.
Wright, p.m. Discont. September 21, 1921.
Ref.:   P.O. Records; G. E. P. Smith. Map: B-3.

## WRONG MOUNTAIN

El.: 7767'                          Loc.: Pima 1, F-4.3
Government surveyors c. 1910 first took this mountain to
be Rincon Peak. When they discovered their mistake, they
named it Wrong Mountain.
Ref.:   Barnes. Map: GJ-13.

# PINAL COUNTY

*Mines — the ore train of wagons — glimpse of modern smelter — cotton raising.*

## PINAL COUNTY:
Pro.: /pinǽl/

Pinal County was formed on February 1, 1875, from parts of Maricopa and Pima Counties. The name may have been derived from that of the Pinal Apaches or possibly from the pine groves in the lofty mountains. Pinal County underwent slight modification in 1877 to correct a boundary error, and it also lost the Globe District of southern Gila in 1881. Its present area is 3,441,920 acres. Included in it are the Gila River (forming part of its boundary) and part of the San Carlos Indian Reservation. Pinal County varies in its characteristics from the agricultural land around its county seat at Florence to the mountains where many rich mining discoveries have been made.

## ADAMSVILLE

El.: 1441'  Loc.: Pinal 1, H-6.1

Charles S. Adams (b. Ohio 1834) established the town of Adamsville in 1866. An energetic man, Adams laid out a ditch to irrigate a quarter section of land. He also surveyed for a town site and gave land to all who wished to build. In addition to this he operated a highly successful saloon and store. The result was that a village soon came into being. Here in 1869 Nick and William Bichard established a flour mill and a store. Their mill was the only one between Tucson and California, and William Bichard and Company supplied many of the Arizona forts with flour. This was in the period when Maricopa Wells (*q.v.*) was declining and the town of Florence was yet to get started.

By 1870 there were four hundred people at Adamsville. When the local residents petitioned for a post office, they requested the name Adamsville, but instead were given the name Sanford for Capt. George B. Sanford of the First U.S. Cavalry, who by 1871 had been transferred elsewhere. This was done according to one report at the instance of Richard McCormick, a politician who disliked Adams. Meanwhile, Adams himself had left the area and was living in Prescott. Nevertheless, although the post office records bore the name Sanford, local people continued to call the town Adamsville, which led to some confusion when the overland mail stages made Sanford a stop in 1871 and 1872.

Adamsville did not last very long. By 1920 it had become merely a dilapidated double row of roofless houses with a single Mexican family living in one partially preserved room. Even this is now gone and the land is privately owned.

P.O. est. as Sanford, January 24, 1871. Larkin W. Carr, p.m. Discont. January 26, 1876.

Ref.: Emerson O. Stratton ms., APHS; 1870 Census; *Arizona Miner*, April 29, 1871; June 17, 1871; *Arizona Citizen*, March 2, 1872; 105, p. 343; 87, p. 43; 111, p. 275; 34, p. 386. Maps: C-2; E-20 (Sanford); GK-10.

## AGENCY PEAK

El.: c. 2000'  Loc.: Pinal 1, E-5.8

This peak is close to the headquarters of the Gila River Indian Reservation.

Ref.: None. Map: GK-25.

## ALMA

El.: c. 2500'  Loc.: Pinal 2, G-8.5

The reason for this name has not yet been learned.

P.O. est. May 12, 1891. Frank M. Doll, p.m. Discont. August 22, 1898.

Ref.: Barnes; P.O. Records. Map: C-7.

## AMERICAN FLAG

El.: c. 4400'  Loc.: Pinal 2, F-11.5

Isaac Lorraine, a native of Martinique, located the American Flag Mine in the late 1870's. Lorraine not only developed the mine but c. 1882 established a cattle ranch known as the American Flag Ranch. Here he lived for about eight years as a miner and cattleman before moving to Phoenix to enter the real-estate business.

The American Flag Mine was the first in the area to be developed. By 1880 enough people were in the area to warrant a post office. The Richardson Mining Company bought the American Flag Mine in 1881.

P.O. est. December 20, 1880. Peter F. Loss, p.m. Discont. July 16, 1890.

Ref.: Emerson O. Stratton ms., APHS; 131, pp. 24-25. Maps: B-3; C-5.

a.n. American Hill  El.: 4842'. Maps: GK-4; GK-18  Pinal
American Flag Springs  Maps: GK-4; GK-18; GK-30  Pinal

## APACHE JUNCTION

El.: c. 1500'  Loc.: Pinal 1, G-1.8
Pro.: /əpǽči/

Apache Junction is a small but growing settlement at the west end of the Apache Trail (*q.v.*, Gila) from which it takes its name.

P.O. est. August 15, 1950. Mrs. Marie L. Porter, p.m.

Ref.: None. Map: F-12.

## APACHE LEAP

El.: 4833'  Loc.: Pinal 2, G-4.1
Pro.: /əpǽči/

The legend associated with this location is that in the 1870's a cavalry detachment from Camp Pinal caught seventy-five Indians on the edge of the cliff which bears the name Apache Leap. Rather than surrender, the Indians plunged to their deaths. No official reports of this incident have been located to date.

Ref.: 4, p. 349. Maps: GK-10; GK-29.

## ARIVAIPA CANYON

El.: c. 3000'  Loc.: Pinal 2, IF-8
Pro.: /ǽrəváypə/  Nevome Pima: *aarivapa*, "girls"

The origin of this name is not known, but it is conjectured that the Arivaipa Apaches may have earned the name because of some now unknown unmanly act. These Indians made Arivaipa Canyon more or less permanent headquarters. However, they wandered afield, raiding into Mexico. They are said to have destroyed every town in northern Mexico as far north as the Gila River prior to 1853. A fierce though small group, the Arivaipas exterminated the large tribe of Sobaipuri Pimas (cf. Sopori Ranch, Pima) toward the end of the eighteenth century. The Apaches were in turn badly decimated by the old Camp Grant massacre (cf. Old Camp Grant). In 1872 the remaining Arivaipas were transferred to the San Carlos Reservation.

Gen. Thomas Kearney in 1847 traveled down the Arivaipa Canyon Indian trail into the San Pedro Valley. The canyon is a deep, wild gorge cut by Arivaipa Creek. Indian ruins are said to dot its eighteen mile length.

Ref.: 88, I, p. 87; 111, p. 92; 87, p. 234. Maps: C-12; E-20; GE-5; GK-3.

a.n. Arivaipa Creek  Pinal and Graham
Maps: E-20; GE-5; GK-3; GK-15; GK-17.

In 1697 Fr. Kino wrote of the visit of Indian chiefs from Busac and Tubo, noting that they came from villages on an arroyo called Babiteoida (Arivaipa Creek). The stream apparently ran with water, as at least one reference calls it the Arivaypa River.

Ref.:   20, p. 367; 76, p. 13.

**Fort Arivaypa**                                    Pinal
(cf. Old Camp Grant).

**Arivaypa Mountains**              Pinal and Graham
Records of military skirmishes in Arizona reveal that a
fight with Indians took place in the Arivaipa Mountains
on February 4, 1869. Another such engagement took place
on April 28, 1874. Arivaypa Mountains do not show on
maps examined. However, it may be assumed that the
name refers to the mountains at the north end of the present-day Galiuro Mountains through which Arivaipa Canyon winds.
Ref.:  85, pp. 440-443.

**Arivaipa Springs**                                Pinal
In March 1872 a military camp was established at this
point. (See Old Camp Grant).

**Arivaipa Valley**                                Graham
This is called Grass Valley on the Smith Map of 1879.

## ARIZOLA

El.: 1451'                          Loc.: Pinal 1, F-8.1
The town of Arizola was established by a man named
Thomas from Carthage, Missouri. He coined the name
from the first four letters of Arizona plus his daughter's
name Ola.

In January 1891, Arizola was developing as a new town.
Here the "Baron of Arizona," Peralta-Reavis, established
headquarters for his vast "holdings." There is much folklore
in connection with this man, including the statement that he
dressed his children in royal purple velvet, monogrammed
with coronets. Reavis claimed ownership of all water and
mineral rights over a huge area by right of an ancient Spanish land grant. His bold scheme brought him millions, as
railroads and mines paid him for quit claim deeds. The
fraud was ultimately exposed.

P.O. est. April 29, 1892. Julia S. Fishback, p.m. Discont.
September 26, 1904.
Ref.:   Barnes; *Arizona Enterprise,* January 3, 1891, 3:3; 112,
        p. 30; Donald M. Powell, Reference Librarian, U. of A.
        Maps: C-8; GK-29.

## ARNETT CREEK

El.: c. 2600'                       Loc.: Pinal 2, BC-3.2-4.3
The Arnett Ranch was the headquarters for the Arnett family c. 1885, hence the name for the creek.
Ref.:   Barnes; Craig. Maps: C-10; GK-21; GK-29.
**a.n. Arnett Canyon**        Map: GK-10                Pinal

## BAPCHULE

El.: c. 1500'                       Loc.: Pinal 1, D-4.5
Pro.:  /bæpčúwliy/
The Indian name for this place is said to mean "squaw with
a long pointed nose."
P.O. est. June 26, 1931. Mrs. Myra Martin, p.m.
Ref.:   State Library Files; P.O. Records. Map: C-13.

## BARKERVILLE

El.: c. 4000'                       Loc.: Pinal 2, D-8.5
The post office for the Barker cattle ranch and its neighborhood was on the old stage road from Tucson to Florence.

P.O. est. as Barkerville, February 1, 1924. Mrs. Ruth E.
Barker, p.m. Discont. December 15, 1933.
Ref.:   Barnes; P.O. Records. Maps: C-13; GK-2; GK-31.

## BARRETT, FORT

El.: c. 1200'                       Loc.: Pinal 1, E-4.7
In 1862 at the Pima Villages, the Federal troops of the
California Column were informed that a Confederate detachment under Lt. Jack Swilling was somewhere ahead of
it, on the route to Tucson. Lt. James Barrett with twelve
men was sent in pursuit of Swilling. He caught up with the
Confederates at Picacho on April 15. Barrett and two Federal privates were killed; the Confederates also lost two men,
with two others being captured (See Picacho). Meanwhile,
the main body of Federal troops was following Barrett.
Word was brought back to the Union men when they were
apparently east of the Pima Villages that Barrett had been
killed. The troops proceeded to throw up a breastwork, apparently anticipating a Confederate attack. They named
their defense post Fort Barrett in honor of the dead officer.
Fort Barrett was a recognized military post, established May
31, 1862, and abandoned on July 23 of the same year.
There has been much speculation upon the location of Fort
Barrett. It has been found on a single map, which further
indicates the temporary nature of the location.
Ref.:   75, p. 124; 105, p. 87; 166, p. 153; 32, II, 167; 52, II,
        88, 102. Map: E-17.

## BATESVILLE

El.: c. 1500'                       Loc.: Pinal 2, EF-6.2
In 1893 Bates, Newman and Company, of which J. T. Bates
was a member, was a mining concern. The company attempted to start a town at this location, advertising town
lots for sale in the *Tucson Arizona Enterprise* on July 27,
1893. Whether or not a town actually developed is not
known.
Ref.:   Barnes. Map: None.
**a.n. Bates Canyon**      Maps: GE-5; GK-3              Pinal

## BELGRAVIA

El.: c. 1500'                       Loc.: Pinal 2, D-4.8
The first name for the mill site of the Ray-Hercules Mining
Company was Hercules. This was soon changed by Mr.
Adams of the company to Belgravia, the name of a suburb
of Johannesburg, South Africa, his native home. The little
Arizona settlement has completely disappeared.

P.O. est. April 15, 1918. Frederick O. Locke, p.m. Discont.
June 19, 1930.
Ref.:   Barnes; APHS Names File; P.O. Records. Map: C-12.

## BELL BUTTE

El.: c. 2000'                       Loc.: Pinal 2, B-4.7
Its adjacency to the Silver Bell Mine gave this butte its name.
Ref.:   Barnes. Map: C-12.

## BIG WASH

El.: c. 3500'-2200'                 Loc.: Pinal 2, ED-11-12
It is.
Ref.:   None. Maps: GK-4; GK-7; GK-18; GK-20; GK-30.

## BITTER WELL (SIF VAYA)

El.: c. 1500'                    Loc.: Pinal 1, B-10.5
Pro.: /siy vaha/          Papago: *sif,* "bitter"; *vaya* "well"
Descriptive. Sif Vaya is the correct name for the small Pag-ago village sometimes referred to as Bitter Well.
Ref.:   Kirk Bryan Notes; 34, p. 395; 128, p. 16. Maps: C-12; D-11 (Siovaxia).
**a.n. Bitter Well Mountains**   Map: C-12                    Pinal
Ref.:   *Weekly Arizona Enterprise,* February 25, 1892, 3:5.

## BLACKWATER

El.: c. 1500'                    Loc.: Pinal 1, F-5.3
Barnes relates that the Pima Indians kept "calendar sticks," a method of preserving their history. The calendar sticks relate that in the early 1870's there was a Pima Indian known as Old Man Blackwater, hence the name.
Blackwater was a stage station at least as early as 1875.
P.O. est. April 18, 1907. Samuel Pinkley *(sic)* p.m. Discont. February 28, 1931.
Ref.:   *Weekly Arizona Miner,* June 18, 1875, 3:1; Barnes. Maps: C-10; GK-33.
**a.n. Blackwater Chapel**   Map: GK-15                    Pinal

## BLUE WATER

El.: c. 1500'                    Loc.; Pinal 1, G-7.5
Blue Water was established as a stage station in the latter part of 1859 when the stage company sank a well at this point. The army made good use of the grass and water at the station in 1862. Blue Water was still a stage station in 1867, the land then being owned by Samuel B. Wise. In 1870 he apparently sold this station to a stage driver named Baker, who handled the stages between Blue Water and Tucson. Baker's possession was very short. With his family, he was murdered at the station in 1871 by a Mexican employee who escaped to Sonora.
Blue Water was still in use as a stage station at least as late as 1879. Nothing remains of it today.
Ref.:   32, II, 164-165; 23, p. 25; 55, p. 448; 111, p. 276; *Weekly Arizonan,* June 11, 1870, 3:4. Maps: C-2; C-5 (Two locations. Also a Blue Water Station in Gila Co.); E-20.

## BON

El.: 1298'                    Loc.: Pinal 1, D-6.7
Pro.: /bown/
The first three letters of the last name of H. G. Bonorden, chief dispatcher for the S.P.R.R., were used to name this point on the railroad.
Ref.:   Barnes. Map: GK-5.

## BRADY WASH

El.: c. 3000'-2000'                    Loc.: Pinal 2, CB-8-9
Richard Garnett Brady owned the Brady Ranch c. 1880. He was the son of Peter Rainesford Brady (cf. Ajo, Pima). Young Brady moved to Tucson in 1890.
Ref.:   Emerson O. Stratton File, APHS; 112, III. Map: GK-33.

## BRANDENBURG MOUNTAIN

El.: 4367'                    Loc.: Pinal 2, H-7.1
J. C. Brandenburg settled on Arivaipa Creek in the early 1880's. He was a farmer who sold his produce in Mammoth.
Ref.:   Barnes; Woody. Maps: GK-30; GK-3.

## BRANNAMAN

El.: c. 1500'                    Loc.: Pinal 2, DE-6
Patrick Brannaman, a cattleman, established Brannaman's Ranch c. 1900. The ranch was also known as the Branna-man-Scott Ranch. The railroad passed through it.
John Brannaman located the Pioneer Mine on the south side of the Pinal Mountains in 1887. Shortly thereafter he was involved in a severe fight and was so badly beaten that he died. His widow and four sons remained in Globe, where his wife kept a boarding house.
Ref.:   Barnes (Notes); APHS Files. Map: GK-23.

## BULLDOG MINE

El.: c. 1500'                    Loc.: Pinal 1, GH-1
The name for this mine was derived from its location near a rock formation which resembled an enormous bulldog. The blowing up of the rock in 1895 led to confusion in mining claims, since many mines were located with refer-ence to their distance and direction from the "bulldog."
Ref.:   Barnes (Notes); *Phoenix Gazette,* November 20, 1895 (State Library Files). Map: GG-6.
**a.n. Bulldog Wash**   Map: GG-6    Maricopa and Pinal

## BURNS

El.: c. 2000'                    Loc.: Pinal 2, F-7.1
A cattleman named Burns was in this location in 1898.
Ref.:   Barnes. Map: GK-23.

## BUTTE, THE

El.: 4293'                    Loc.: Pinal 2, HG-5.8
Descriptive. The name for The Butte is elemental in its simplicity. This must have appealed to the miners who estab-lished a camp nearby, for they called their post office and little settlement Butte. The community was started in late December 1881 or in January 1882 eighteen miles east of Florence. The Pinal Consolidated Mining Company erected reduction works at this location.
P.O. est. April 16, 1883. Maurice B. Fleishman, p.m. Discont. June 23, 1886.
Ref.:   *Arizona Weekly Enterprise,* January 7, 1882, 2:5. Map: GK-6.
**a.n. Butte Spur**   Loc.: On r.r. 25 miles e. of Florence    Pinal

## CAMERON

El.: c. 1500'                    Loc.: Pinal 1, G-7.8
14 miles e. of town of Casa Grande on r.r.
In 1924 Amos Hess laid out a townsite which he named for United States Senator Ralph H. Cameron (cf. Bright Angel Creek, Grand Canyon).
Ref.:   Barnes. Map: None.

## CAMPAIGN CREEK

El.: c. 5000'                                         Loc.: Pinal 2, B-1
                        Maricopa 2, K-6-7; Gila 1, GF-9-10
Locally it is believed that in 1873 United States troops used
points along this creek as campaign headquarters during
Gen. George Crook's regime.

Ref.:    Barnes. Maps: A-7; GK-16.

## CASA BLANCA

El.: c. 1200'                                     Loc.: Pinal 1, CD-4.6
                                           Spanish: "white house"
Casa Blanca is a prehistoric ruin near the old Pima Villages.
It is not to be confused with Casa Grande *(q.v.)*. Another
name for Casa Blanca was Montezuma's Castle or Casa
Montezuma. In addition to the ruin there was a Pima village called Baaki (Pima: "ancient house") with about fifty
houses and five hundred thirty-eight residents in 1858. Their
number dropped to three hundred fifty by 1869.

A trader, Ammi White, had a stage station here in 1858.
He was a native of Maine, and he is said to have had the
first steam operated flour mill in the area.

P.O. est. as Bah Ki, June 13, 1916. Singleton I. Martin, p.m.
Discont. December 31, 1926.

**v.n. A-vuc-hoo-mar-lish**

    According to the Pacific Railroad Report (1856) this was
    the Maricopa Indian name for Casa Blanca.

Ref.:    88, I, 11, 104, 209, 211, 167-168. Maps: C-12; F-3
         (Vah Ki); E-17; E-20; GK-11.

## CASA GRANDE NATIONAL MONUMENT

El.: 1405'                                        Loc.: Pinal 1, E-7.8
                            Spanish: "big house"; "great house"
In the early days the Casa Grande ruins were frequently
referred to as the Casa Montezuma. The ruin was thought
to have been one of the places occupied by the Nahuatl or
Aztecs in their migration from the north into the valley of
Mexico. However, the Pima Indians, in whose territory the
ruins lie, have a legend that the structures were erected by
Civano, who was either a chief or a deity of the Pima, from
whence their name Civano or House of Civano for the place.
Casa Grande National Monument is one of at least eight
separate village sites in the area. Apparently the first white
man to visit it was Fr. Kino, who performed the mass inside
the ruin in November 1694. Juan Mateo Manje in his
diary left an interesting and detailed description of the ruins.
The years after 1700 wrought havoc on the buildings, the
central one of which is four stories high. In order to preserve
the ruins from further depredations by man and the elements, Casa Grande was made a national park on March
2, 1889, and was established as a national reservation on
June 22, 1892. Finally on August 3, 1918, it was made into
a national monument, containing four hundred and seventy-
two acres.

Ref.:    88, p. 209, 210-211; 183, Frances Elmore, "Casa Gran-
         de," p. 1; 4, p. 40. Maps: E-11; E-18; E-20; GK-5;
         GK-25; GK-27.

**a.n. Casa Grande**        El.: 1398'. Maps: C-7; GK-27        Pinal
    The thriving and prosperous town of Casa Grande was
    so named by the railroad because at the time of its naming
    it was the closest community on the railroad to the Casa
    Grande ruins.

P.O. est. September 10, 1880. Jery Fryer, p.m. Wells Fargo
Station, 1885.
Ref.:    Prather.
    **Casa Grande Mountains**     El.: 1450'. Map: GK-27     Pinal
    This small range is sometimes referred to as the Arizola
    Mountains because of its proximity to the small com-
    munity by that name.
Ref.:    34, p. 240.

## CATALINA

                                                  Loc.: Not known.
The origin of this name has not been ascertained.
P.O. est. January 4, 1881. John T. Young, p.m. Discont. June
19, 1896.
Ref.:    Barnes; P.O. Records. Map: None.

## CHIAPUK

El.: c. 2500'                                    Loc.: Pinal 1, C-11.5
Pro.: /číəpʌk/                              Papago: "spring"
The Papago village of Chiapuk was at one time referred to
as Copperosity because of its being near the Copperosity
Mine. The name Copperosity is supposed to have been de-
rived from the custom of prospectors asking each other,
"How's your copperosity?" — to which a second miner would
reply, "Just staked her out and here she is."

Ref.:    U. S. G. B. "Decision 1940-41" (State Library Files);
         128, p. 16; 102, p. 29; 26, p. 371. Maps: C-13 (Copper-
         osity); D-8; GG-17.
**a.n. Copperosity Hills**                Map: GG-17                Pinal
Ref.:    128, p. 34.

## CHUICHU

El.: 1455'                                        Loc.: Pinal 1, E-9.1
Pro.: /čúw čuw/                              Pima: "caves"
Chuichu is a small Pima village. The name comes from its
proximity to natural caves. The current spelling of the name
is a corruption of the Kohatk Pima name *Tschuhutsho*, or
*Tjuitjo*.

**v.n. Chiu Chuschu**   (corruption)       Maps: C-12; GK-5
Ref.:    Kirk Bryan Notes; 26, pp. 371; 34, p. 391; U. S. G. B.
         "Decision 1940-41." Maps: C-12; D-8; GK-5.

## COCHRAN

El.: c. 2000'                                     Loc.: Pinal 2, B-5.1
Named for its first postmaster.

P.O. est. January 3, 1905. John S. Cochran, p.m. Discont.
January 15, 1915.
Ref.:    Barnes; P.O. Records. Map: C-10.

## COMET PEAK

El.: 2694'                                          Loc.: Pinal 2, B-4
A mine in the area gave its name to this peak.
Ref.:    Barnes. Maps: C-13; GK-10.

## COOLIDGE

El.: 1400'                    Loc.: Pinal 1, G-6.5
Coolidge, a prosperous agricultural center, came into existence when the Coolidge Dam was constructed and water was made available for irrigation in the vicinity of the town. (cf. Coolidge Dam, Gila).
P.O. est. June 14, 1926. Mrs. Dora H. Nutt, p.m.
Ref.:  P.O. Records. Maps: C-13; C-14.

## COPPER CREEK

El.: 4010'                    Loc.: Pinal 2, HG-9.5
The location of the Yellow Bird claim in 1863 was the start of mining in the Copper Creek Area. The first ore found was silver, but underlying veins changed sharply in formation to copper ores. In 1917 operation ceased and the mines remained dormant until 1933 when they were bought by the Arizona Molybdenum Corporation.
P.O. est. March 6, 1906. Bell E. Sibley, p.m. Discont. August 31, 1942.
Ref.:  Mammoth File, APHS. Maps: C-13; GK-7; GK-18; GK-19; GK-30.

## COPPEROPOLIS

El.: c. 2000'      Loc.: Pinal 1, AB-11-12 (approximate)
This short-lived copper settlement and mine had an ambitious name. This may be the same place as Copperosity (cf. Chiapuk).
P.O. est. October 17, 1884. Edward G. Hellings, p.m. Discont. September 4, 1885.
Ref.:  Barnes. Map: None.

## CROZIER PEAK

El.: 4273'                    Loc.: Pinal 2, D-6.9
Crozier was a prospector and mine owner who had claims on this peak.
Ref.:  Barnes. Maps: C-12; GK-8; GK-31.

## CRYSTAL CAVE

El.: c. 2500'                    Loc.: Pinal 2, FG-8
                             S.e. of Winkelman 10 miles.
The name Crystal Cave is descriptive of this cavern, discovered in early 1929 by Mr. Logan and Mr. Rhodes. The cavern has two rooms, the first over three hundred feet long and the second over four hundred feet long. The walls and roof of the cave are of gypsum interspersed with shale and many beautiful crystals.
Ref.:  Mammoth File, APHS. Map: None.

## DEER CREEK

El.: c. 2700'                    Loc.: Pinal 2, FH-6
In the 1880's the discovery of coal in Deer Creek Basin (Loc.: T. 4 S., R. 18 E.) led to attempts by speculators to have this land separated from the San Carlos Indian Reservation to which it belonged. Their attempts were unsuccessful.
Ref.:  22, p. 441. Maps: C-12; GK-6.

## DeNOON

El.: c. 4000'      Loc.: Pinal 2, A-2.5 (Approximate)
In 1888 Judge J. DeNoon Reymert owned a mine for which a mill was erected at DeNoon.
P.O. est. March 19, 1890. John Knight, p.m. Discont. April 1, 1891.
Ref.:  Barnes. Map: None.

## DESERT PEAK

El.: 1969'                    Loc.: Pinal 2, C-10
Descriptive.
Ref.:  Barnes; 87, p. 269. Maps: C-3; C-12; E-20.
**a.n. Desert Range Peak**        Map: C-12              Pinal

## DOCK

El.: c. 1500'                    Loc.: Pinal 1, E-4.9
                             Pima: *dahk,* "nose"
Apparently Pima Indians referred to this railroad point as *American dahk* ("American nose").
Ref.:  Barnes. Map: GK-33.

## DONNELLY WASH

El.: c. 2400'-2200'            Loc.: Pinal 2, AB-5.4-6.4
This wash takes its name from the location of the Donnelly cattle ranch on its course. In 1879 Donnelly was living in what was referred to as Donnelly Canyon. The Donnelly Ranch is the site of a spring which Fr. Kino visited in 1697, naming it San Gregorio. Kino's party did not find enough water at this spring for all their horses and so traveled two leagues downstream where they camped opposite the present-day town of Price.
**v.n. Donley Canyon**   (corruption)
Ref.:  20, p. 368. Maps: C-13; GK-10.

## DOS NARICES MOUNTAIN

El.: c. 4000'                    Loc.: Pinal 2, DE-8
                        W. of Old Camp Grant 12 miles.
Pro.: /dos naríysəs/          Spanish: "two noses"
In the early 1870's, two adjacent peaks which resembled noses were known by the name Dos Narices. The name seems to have vanished.
Ref.:  22, p. 31. Map: None.

## DOUBLE PEAKS

El.: 2283'                    Loc.: Pinal 1, C-9
Descriptive.
Ref.:  U. S. G. B. "Decision, 1940-41," p. 17. Map: GK-5.
**a.n. North Butte**        Maps: C-12; GK-10        Pinal
    This is one of two buttes on either side of the Gila River. They are sometimes referred to locally, according to their position, as North or South Butte.
**South Butte**        El.: 2815'. Maps: C-12; GK-10        Pinal

## DROMEDARY PEAK

El.: 2500'                    Loc.: Pinal 2, A-3.5
Descriptive.
Ref.:  Barnes. Map: GK-10.

## DURHAM WASH

El.: c. 2000'                                           Loc.: Pinal 1, I-9.5
The Durham cattle ranch was near the head of this wash.
Ref.: 26, p. 421. Map: GK-24.

## ELOY

El.: 1572'                                              Loc.: Pinal 1, G-9.1
Pro.: /íyloy/
Eloy does not appear on GLO maps until 1921. As late
as 1918 there was no town or settlement of any kind in
the vicinity of the present Eloy, but merely a section of
land belonging to the railroad and bearing the name Eloy.
Agriculture was restricted to the raising of some cattle.
In the same year W. L. Bernard, J. E. Myer, and John Alsdorf bought land from a man named Trekell to establish
a townsite. The three men purchased the east half of the
section named Eloy and drilled a well. They subdivided the
area and called the proposed development Cotton City,
which soon had an administration building and store. The
same men bought land west of Eloy and divided it into
tracts for raising cotton. An application was made for a post
office at Cotton City, but the name was rejected in favor
of Eloy to maintain simplicity of routing, since the railroad
would carry the mail and already had the name Eloy on
its records.
Why the railroad named a section Eloy has not yet been
ascertained. Locally a tall tale has come into existence. According to the legend, the railroad came through and someone connected with it took one look at the surrounding
barren waste and named the location "Eloi," supposedly the
Spanish pronunciation of the Biblical quotation, "Eli, Eli,
lama sabachthani?" The meaning of this is, of course, "My
God, My God, why hast thou forsaken me?" There is apparently no basis for this story.
P.O. est. May 1, 1919. George L. Stronach, p.m. Incorporated
August 1950.
Ref.: Alsdorf. Maps: C-12; GK-9; GK-27.

## ENID

El.: 1283'                                              Loc.: Pinal 1, A-8.3
The origin of this name has not yet been ascertained.
Ref.: Barnes. Maps: C-10; GG-10.

**a.n. Enid Mountains**                            Maricopa and Pinal
These mountains lie parallel to the Estrella Mountains
(q.v.).
Ref.: 34, p. 398.

## ESTHWAITE

El.: c. 2400'                                           Loc.: Pinal 2, A-3.4
The origin of this name has not been ascertained.
P.O. est. June 23, 1919. Richard H. Mattison, p.m. Discont.
December 15, 1919.
Ref.: P.O. Records. Map: C-12.

## ESTRELLA MOUNTAINS

El.: 4503'                                              Loc.: Pinal 1, A-4
Pro.: /estréyə/                                        Spanish: "star"
The earliest recorded name for the Sierra Estrella was that
given by Fr. Francisco Garcés in 1775 when he referred
to them as the Sierra de San Joseph de Cumars. Cumars

means "broad" or "thick" in Pima language. Why the
mountains should have the name Estrella is not known. The
Pima Indians called this small range the Kamatuk, or in
its anglicized form, Komatke.
The small Pima village of Komatke is located at the foot
of the mountains and the Pima name for it is Kamatuk
Wutca ("below or at the foot of Kamatuk"). The English
name for the village is St. Johns because of St. John's Chapel,
a half mile to the west.

**v.n. Komertkewotche**
P.O. est. as Komatke December 22, 1915. Herman Alis, p.m.
Discont. May 31, 1944.
Ref.: Kirk Bryan Notes; 34, p. 398; 88, I, 724. Maps: C-2;
E-17; E-18 (Sierra de la Estrella); E-20 (Santa Es-
trella).

**a.n. Maricopa Mountains**                          Maricopa and Pinal
El.: 2767'. Maps: GG-7; GG-13
The name Maricopa Mountains was apparently not applied
to this range until after the battle between the Yuma In-
dians and the Maricopas in this vicinity in 1851. In that
year the mountains were known in the Maricopa language
as We-al-hus, the meaning of which is not known. The
Maricopa Mountains at one time included the Estrella
Mountains or Sierra Estrella.
Ref.: Arizona Gazette, August 1, 1883, 3:3.

**Maricopa Peak**      El.: 4084'. Map: GG-7.        Maricopa
**Estrella Valley**                                Pinal and Maricopa
The valley between the Sierra Estrella and the Maricopa
Mountains has many hills. The old road to the west lay
along the base of the Estrella Mountains.
The plain at the foot of the Estrella Mountains was used
by many explorers and gradually the crossing came to be
known as the Jornado de las Estrellas (Spanish: "The day's
journey of the stars"). Later the military telegraph and the
Butterfield Overland Stage route crossed from Maricopa
Wells to Gila Bend, using the same road.
Ref.: 34, p. 399; 34, p. 236.

**Estrella**              Maps: C-12; GG-13           Maricopa
This siding on the railroad has existed since 1881.
P.O. est. as Estrella Hill, January 2, 1919. Roy L. Crowley,
p.m. Name changed to Estrella, January 2, 1933. Discont. July
15, 1944.

## FIVE POINTS MOUNTAIN

El.: 5491'                                              Loc.: Pinal 2, C-2
The five points which give this mountain its name are
easily seen when one is driving on the road from Miami
to Globe. It was the origin of the name for the Five Points
Mining Company.
Ref.: Craig. Maps: GD-10; GK-33.

## FLAT TOP MOUNTAIN

El.: 3666'                                              Loc.: Pinal 2, E-7.3
Descriptive.
Ref.: None. Map: GK-15.

## FLORENCE

El.: 1493'                                              Loc.: Pinal 1, HG-5.9
The first settler in the future Florence was its founder, Levi
Ruggles, who came to Arizona as an Indian agent in 1866.
The first house in Florence was built in the same year.
Agricultural activity in the valley increased rapidly, and by

1868 the settlers of the upper Gila River decided that a name was needed for the community. Gov. Richard Mc-Cormick was requested to name the town and selected the name Florence after his sister. By 1870 the census showed two hundred eighteen people living at Florence. Levi Ruggles took out a patent for the plat of the town and filed it on October 30, 1875.

The completion in 1921 of the Ashurst-Hayden Diversion Dam on the Gila River made sufficient water available for irrigation in the Florence area so that the community rapidly surged to importance as an agricultural center. The construction of Coolidge Dam consolidated the importance of Florence. It has been the county seat since the formation of Pinal County on February 1, 1875.

P.O. est. August 19, 1869. Thomas R. Ewing, p.m. Wells Fargo Station, 1879.

Ref.: 7, p. 625, (Note 10); 87, p. 43; 4, p. 293. *Weekly Arizona Miner*, October 31. 1868, 2:5; APHS Files. Maps: C-2; E-20; GK-20.

a.n. Florence Junction        Map: GK-20                          Pinal
    Passengers from Florence journeyed to this point in order
    to board the train to the east or west.
P.O. est. July 9, 1934. Mrs. Velma Caldwell, p.m.

Ref.: Barnes; P.O. Records.

## FORDVILLE

El.: c. 3000'                          Loc.: Pinal 2, FG-9
There is a possibility that Fordville was the post office for the Ford Mine.

P.O. est. March 15, 1880. William A. Cunningham, p.m. Discont. June 7, 1880.

Ref.: None. Maps: GK-18; GK-30 (Ford Mine).

## FOREMAN WASH

El.: c. 4000'         Loc.: Pinal 2, DE-9 (Approximate)
The Foreman Wash was so named because of the Foreman cattle ranch at the head of Suffering Gulch.

Ref.: 34, p. 383; 26, p. 422. Map: None.

## GOLDEN PALISADES

El.: c. 1500'                          Loc.: Pinal 1, C-11.5
The origin of this name has not yet been learned.

P.O. est. April 7, 1915. Arthur H. Elliott, p.m. Discont. February 28, 1918.

Ref.: P.O. Records. Map: F-2.

## GOLDFIELD

El.: c. 2500'                          Loc.: Pinal 1, H-1
Goldfield is today a ghost town. It was established by George U. Young in 1893, and for that reason was also referred to as Youngsberg. Why it was called Goldfield is not known.
P.O. est. October 7, 1893. James L. Patterson (deceased). Office activated March 12, 1894. J. G. Peterson, p.m. Discont. November 2, 1898.

Ref.: Phoenix Chamber of Commerce, "List of Ghost Towns," November 26, 1948; Barnes; P.O. Records. Maps: C-9; GK-33.

## GOLDMINE MOUNTAIN

El.: c. 1600'                          Loc.: Pinal 1, FG-4.1
According to local stories, a gold mine long ago was operating on the peak, hence its name.

Ref.: Barnes. Map: GK-25.

## GONZALES PASS

El.: 2651'                          Loc.: Pinal 2, A-3.2
The road passes over a summit at this point. It was apparently used by a freighter named Gonzales.

Ref.: Craig. Maps: GK-21; GK-29.

a.n. Gonzales Pass Canyon        Maps: GK-21; GK-29        Pinal

## GOVERNMENT HILL

El.: 5445'                          Loc.: Pinal 1, BC-1.6
A government surveying party placed a bench mark on this hill. Thereafter cowboys and settlers began speaking of the location as Government Hill.

Ref.: Barnes. Maps: GK-14; GK-29.

## GRANT, CAMP (OLD)

El.: 2500'                          Loc.: Pinal 2, F-8
Because of its location on Arivaipa Creek, this post was called Fort Arivaypa in late 1859 when it had a small garrison. It became a military fort on May 8, 1860, with its first name giving way on August 6 to Fort Breckenridge, after the vice president of the United States. In 1861 Fort Breckenridge was burned when troops were withdrawn for service elsewhere during the Civil War.

When the post was re-established on May 29, 1862, it was called Fort Stanford for Leland Stanford, then governor of California. It became Fort Grant on November 1, 1865, but by 1872 it was being called Camp Grant. There is, however, some evidence that between October 1863 and July 1865 the name reverted to Fort Breckenridge, or at least that name was used in some references examined. When the new Camp Grant (q.v., Graham) was established, the one in Pinal County came to be known as Old Camp Grant. The Camp Grant Massacre, in which men from Tucson and its vicinity raided and massacred Arivaipa Apaches who were being held at the post, occurred at Old Camp Grant in 1871. One hundred eighteen Indians were slain.

P.O. est. August 19, 1869. George Cox, p.m. Moved to new Camp Grant (q.v., Graham).

Ref.: Barnes; 7, p. 497; 85, pp. 477, 482; 75, pp. 126, 154; 157, pp. 1-2, 15-16. Richard Lord File, APHS. Maps: C-1; E-11 (Camp Breckenridge); E-17; E-18.

a.n. Camp Grant Wash                                              Pinal
    Maps: C-12; GK-22; GK-30; GK-31
    So named because the wash lay across the river from Old
    Camp Grant.
Ref.: APHS Files.

## GREENES RESERVOIR

El.: c. 1500'                          Loc.: Pinal 1, F-11
William Cornell Greene endeavored to dam the Santa Cruz River near where it joined the Gila River c. 1909. He spent a large sum of money erecting an earth work dam. When this dam was inspected by Frank Jordan, he told Mr. Greene

that the dirt had been placed on the wrong side of the dam, making it possible for animals to burrow and that thereby the dam structure would be weakened and there would be leaks. Nevertheless, plans to irrigate the surrounding area with Santa Cruz River water were continued. These included the construction of a store at the dam site.

The dam did wash out and was never successfully rebuilt. The reservoir is no longer in existence, but the dikes remain. This has the unfortunate effect of causing flood waters to back up, creating in the Eloy area a very shallow and widespread pond referred to locally as Lake Eloy.

Ref.:    APHS Files; Jordan; Stanfield. Maps: C-12; GK-9.

**a.n. Greenes Wash**                                            Pinal
    Loc.: Sec. 25, T. 9 S., R. 6 E. Joins Santa Rosa Wash to form Santa Cruz Wash.
    This is the outlet for the old Greene Reservoir.
Ref.:    128, p. 26.

## GU KOMELIK

El.: c. 1600'                          Loc.: Pinal 2, C-12
Pro.:  /guw kówməli?/              Papago: gu, "big"; komelik, "flats"
The village of Gu Komelik was established by the Papagos at the site of a well abandoned by an American stockman. The Papagos cultivate crops in the big fields.

**v.n. Kukomalik**
      **Komalik**
Ref.:    128, p. 16; 34, p. 391. Maps: D-8; D-11; GK-28.

## HARRINGTON

El.: c. 2000'      Loc.: Pinal 2, F-6.6 (Approximate)
The Harrington family located at this ranch in 1879. They maintained a stage station between Dudleyville and Winkelman.
Ref.:    Barnes. Map: None.

## HAYDEN PEAK

El.: c. 1500'                          Loc.: Pinal 1, EF-5.7
This peak was named for Charles Trumbull Hayden (cf. Tempe, Maricopa).
Ref.:    APHS Files; Barnes. Maps: C-10; GK-25.

## HERMOSILLO

El.: c. 1400' Loc.: Pinal 1, EF-7.8. e. Casa Grande 3 miles.
Pro.:  /ermosíyo/
This was a developing community in 1891. Nothing else is known concerning it.
Ref.:    Barnes. Map: None.

## HEWITT CANYON

El.: c. 2500'                          Loc.: Pinal 2, A-1.6-2.8
The Hewitt family ranch gave this canyon its name.
Ref.:    Barnes; Craig. Maps: GK-10; GK-16; GK-21.

**a.n. Hewitt Ridge**    Maps: GK-21; GK-29              Pinal
      **Hewitt Station**   Maps: GK-21; GK-29              Pinal

## HOLY JOE PEAK

El.: 5415'                          Loc.: Pinal 2, H-8.5
Holy Joe was an old prospector prone to preaching sermons. His last name has not been ascertained.
Ref.:    Barnes. Maps: C-12; GK-15; GK-30.

**a.n. Holy Joe Canyon**       Map: GK-15              Pinal
      **Holy Joe Pasture**     El.: 4802'. Map: GK-15     Pinal
      **Holy Joe Springs**     Map: GK-30              Pinal
      **Holy Joe Wash**        Map: GK-15              Pinal

## HORMIGUERO

Loc.: Between Casa Blanca and Huchiltchik on Gila River Reservation, 1863
Pro.:  /ormigéro/              Spanish: "ant hill"
The Spanish name is in all probability a translation of the Pima *Statannyik* ("many ants"). Hodge suggests that the place may have been identical with or closely related to Ormejea, since the two villages were adjacent.

Through corruption in the name, it apparently came to be known as Hermho, although there is some doubt concerning whether the two places are the same.

P.O. est. as Hermo, May 17, 1901. Lewis D. Nelson, p.m. Discont. September 12, 1901. (Never in operation).
Ref.:    88, I, 569; 88, II, 149, 635; 129; P.O. Records. Map: None.

## HUGGINS PEAK

El.: 4356'                          Loc.: Pinal 2, H-5.8
Bud Ming of Ray told Barnes that this peak was near the former's ranch. It was called Quartzite Peak until about 1910 when Albert Crockett began calling it by its present name, borrowed from that of a mountain in New Mexico. In 1915 Ming gave government surveyors the name Huggins Peak. However nearby is a Quartzite Mountain (El.: 4869'; Map GK-6).
Ref.:    Barnes. Map: GK-6.

## HUTTON PEAK

El.: 5615'                          Loc.: Pinal 2, C-2.5
Oscar Hutton (d. November 1, 1873) in 1870 was acting as a packer and a guide for troops at Old Camp Grant (cf. Hutton Butte, Grand Canyon).
Ref.:    Barnes. Maps: C-3; E-20; GD-4; GD-10.

## IRON MOUNTAIN

El.: 6056'                          Loc.: Pinal 2, B-1.6
This mountain was named for Robert A. Irion, who brought cattle to Arizona from Colorado in 1877. He pronounced his name "Iron." Mr. Irion settled in the vicinity of the mountain bearing the misspelling of his name. He took up his location on what is now Pinal Ranch (cf. Camp Pinal).
Ref.:    Craig (stepdaughter). Maps: C-9; GK-16; GK-29.

**a.n. Iron Canyon**         Maps: GD-10; GK-29          Pinal
      **Iron Canyon Spring**  Map: GD-10              Pinal

## J. K. MOUNTAIN

El.: c. 4000'                    Loc.: Pinal 2, C-1.4
John Kennedy arrived in Arizona from Kansas in 1876. He
ran the J-K Brand on the mountain which carries his initials.
Ref.:   Woody; Craig. Map: GK-33.

## JACK RABBIT

El.: c. 1500'                    Loc.: Pinal 1, D-10.8
            Pima:  *tat,* "foot"; *mumeri,* "run"; *kut,* "where"
Jackrabbit is the name generally used today for an old summer rancheria of the Kohatk Pimas. The original name
seems to have been Tat Momoli. The Indian name derived
from the fact that the residents are said to have been the
first Pimas to hold foot races.

In 1875 the Jack Rabbit Mine was discovered by Emerson
O. Stratton and Al Robard. A silver mine, it produced well
for several years. When a well was dug four miles north of
the mine, it was called Jack Rabbit Well, and locally the
tendency increased to use the name Jack Rabbit in referring to government activities at Tat Momoli.

**v.n. Taht Mahmelia**      (corruption)
**Tatamúmerikut**      (corruption)
Ref.:   34, p. 391; 128, p. 16; 26, p. 371; Emerson O. Stratton
        ms., APHS; Kirk Bryan Notes. Maps: C-12; D-8; D-11;
        GK-28.
**a.n. Tat Momoli Mountains**     Map: GK-28             Pinal
**Tat Momoli Pass**   Loc.: Tat Momoli is in this pass   Pinal
**Tat Momoli Wash**   Loc.: Part of Tat Momoli Pass      Pinal
**v.n. Jack Rabbit Wash**

## JERUSALEM MOUNTAIN

El.: 5290'                    Loc.: Pinal 2, H-5.3
Cattlemen in the area of this peak used to round up strays
which had wandered onto the Apache Reservation. Extra
saddle horses were held at this peak while some of the men
scouted the area. The cowboys began calling the trip "going
to Jerusalem," hence the name.
Ref.:   Barnes. Map: GK-6.
**a.n. Jerusalem Canyon**     Map: GK-6               Pinal

## KANE SPRINGS

El.: c. 4000'                    Loc.: Pinal 2, D-4
The origin of this name has not been learned.
It was at this point that Pearl Hart (b. Ontario, Canada
1881) and her companion, Joe Boot, robbed a stage at the
turn of the road as it rises toward the mountain above the
Gila River. Pearl, who had led a rough life as a mining
camp cook and who had actually done mining herself, had
enlisted Joe Boot's aid in obtaining money for her sick
mother. After robbing the stage, they escaped but were soon
overtaken about twenty miles from Benson. Boot was given
thirty years in prison. Pearl made friends with a jail trusty
who cut a hole one night through the light plaster jail wall
and pulled Pearl through. They fled to Lordsburg where she
was arrested, thus putting an effectual stop to her organizing
a cutthroat gang. She was sent to the prison at Yuma for
five years, but was soon paroled because that institution was
not equipped to take care of women. She was released when

she promised to leave Arizona. Her next conflict with the
law occurred in Kansas, where she was charged with abetting
pickpockets. She then disappeared from the scene.
Ref.:   *Cosmopolitan Magazine,* XXVII (October 1899) (Woody
        Files); *Coconino Sun,* November 25, 1899 (Woody
        Files). Map: B-7.
**a.n. Kane Springs Canyon**     Map: B-7             Pinal

## KEARNY

El.: c. 2500'                    Loc.: Pinal 2, C-5.5
Upon construction of its Leach-Precipitation-Flotation installation at this location, the Ray Mines Division of the
Kennecott Copper Company in 1958 began constructing
a community to house plant workers and their families,
totalling about 3500 people. The town is named for General
Philip Kearny, who explored along the Gila River in 1849-
50.
Ref.:   *Arizona Republic,* "Arizona Days and Ways," Novem-
        ber 9, 1958. Map: None.

## KELVIN

El.: c. 2000'                    Loc.: Pinal 2, CD-5
On the site of the present-day Kelvin the Riverside stage
station was established in 1877 on the Globe-Florence road.
The old stage station is still in existence.
Kelvin was so named by Lord Gordon after Kelvin Grove,
Scotland. The town was constructed as the Ray Mining
Company reduction works and office headquarters. Since
it is the junction point which connects the main line with
the branch to Ray, the place is also known as Ray Junction.
P.O. est. as Riverside October 17, 1877. Charles D. Putnam,
p.m. Changed to Kelvin, April 25, 1900. Wells Fargo Station,
1904. Discont. January 31, 1956.
Ref.:   *Florence Tribune,* October 21, 1899, 3:1; State Library
        Files; P.O. Records. Maps: C-4; C-9; C-12; E-20
        (Riverside); GK-23 (Kelvin).

## KENILWORTH

El.: c. 1400'                    Loc.: Pinal 1, G-6.2
                    W. of Florence 7 miles, on Gila River.
Judge Richard E. Sloan filed for a section next to that
owned by Thomas Davis with whom he combined holdings
when a nearby canal was ready to deliver water for irrigation purposes. The men planned to have a single ranch under
Davis' management. Because Davis had been born within
a few miles of the old castle made famous by Sir Walter
Scott, the men named the ranch Kenilworth.
Their plans were hounded by continued drought, and they
were forced to give up the project c. 1894.
P.O. est. September 21, 1891. Thomas C. Graham, p.m. Discont. January 11, 1895.
Ref.:   153, pp. 65, 69, 70. Map: None.

## KING'S CROWN PEAK

El.: 5541'                    Loc.: Pinal 2, BC-2.6
The peak lies above the location of the Silver King Mine
(*q.v.*) and is rounded at the top. However, this did not inter-
fere with the miners' notion that the Silver King deserved
a crown. Therefore they named the peak King's Crown Peak.
Ref.:   Craig. Maps: GK-10; GK-29.

## KOHATK

El.: 1639′                              Loc.: Pinal 1, B-11.1
Pro.: /gᵏowhat/    Pima: "where a hollow has been made"
                                (by water or other means)
Although the origin of the name Kohatk is not accurately
known, the history of Kohatk deserves mention. In September 1698, Fr. Kino with Capt. Diego Carrasco passed
through the village of Kohatk, which Kino called San Boni-
facio del Coati y del Sibuoidag. Kino was on his way down
the Gila River, searching for a quicksilver mine reported to
him by Sobaipuri Indians.

By 1865 the village was being referred to as Cojate and
had one hundred three families. The location of the town
may have shifted slightly at times, but it has always remained
roughly in the same general area.

**v.n. Quajote**     (corruption)
Ref.: Kirk Bryan Notes; 34, pp. 9, 391; 88, I, 322; 128, p.
   16. Maps: C-12 (Quajote); D-8; GG-17; GK-28.

| a.n. Quajota Wash | Map: GK-9 | Pinal |
| v.n. Kohatk Wash | Maps: GG-17; GK-28 | Pinal |
| a.n. Kohatk Valley | | Pinal |

   Loc.: S. and s.e. of Vekol Mts. Drained by Kohatk Wash.

## LEROY

El.: c. 2000′    Loc.: Pinal 1, AB-11. In Bitter Well Mts.
The townsite for the mining community associated with the
Great Eastern Mining Company was laid out by Leroy O.
Chilson. The surveyor's first name was given to the camp.
Ref.: Barnes. Map: None.

## LITTLE GILA RIVER

El.: c. 1500′                              Loc.: Pinal 1, GE-6-5
Pro.: /híylə/
Descriptive. This thirty-five mile long branch used to fill
when the Gila River flooded.
Ref.: Barnes. Maps: C-11; GK-12; GK-25.

## MAGMA

El.: c. 1500′                              Loc.: Pinal 1, GH-5
Magma was the junction point on the Arizona Eastern Railroad leading to the Magma Mine, owned by the Magma
Copper Company. The name for the company may have
been derived from the fact that the word *magma* signifies
a type of molten rock material turned into igneous rock.
According to the mine superintendent in the 1930's, there
was much igneous rock in the mine.

The first name for this mine was the Silver Queen, which
was recorded on December 4, 1871. While it antedates the
finding of the famous Silver King Mine, the legend is that
prospectors realized it was not big enough to be the king.
The original locators let the claim lapse.

P.O. est. as Magma, August 13, 1915. George H. Parker, p.m.
Discont. April 30, 1928.
Ref.: Barnes; Woody; Craig; 170, p. 84; APHS Names File.
   Map: C-12.

## MAMMOTH

El.: 2353′                              Loc.: Pinal 2, G-9.6
The first mine in the Mammoth district was located by
Frank Shultz, who was in Arizona at least as early as 1883.

The location at the Mammoth Mine was being worked as
early as December 27, 1873, by E. M. Pearce, C. O. Brown,
and Tully, Ochoa and Co. The Mammoth Mine, sometimes
referred to as the Old Mammoth Mine, was located at what
was sometimes called Mammoth Camp, or Shultz after its
locator.

It was not possible to work the ores at the mine site. A stamp
mill for this purpose was built on the San Pedro River and
this place was called Mammoth. The gold ores from the
Shultz or Mammoth Mine were transported to the mill town
by buckets suspended from a wire cable; the returning buckets were filled with water for the mining camp.

In 1895 the Shultz or Mammoth Mine changed hands, and
work stopped while a new system of milling was introduced. This was the beginning of the last gold mining revival in Arizona except for that during the Depression when
individuals placered for gold. Mammoth enjoyed renewed
importance in 1936 when molybdenum production was
begun.

P.O. est. as Schultz, July 12, 1894. Mrs. Lizzie Schneider, p.m.
Discont. April 21, 1902.
P.O. est. as Mammoth, June 23, 1887. Lewis Ezekiels, p.m.
Ref.: Mammoth File, APHS; 119, p. 47; 4, p. 89; *Arizona
   Citizen,* December 27, 1873, 3:2. Maps: C-7; GK-18;
   GK-30.

| a.n. Shultz Spring | Map: GK-18 | Pinal |
| Mammoth Mine | Maps: GK-18; GK-30 | Pinal |
| Mammoth Wash | Maps: GK-18; GK-30 | Pinal |

## MANLYVILLE

El.: c. 4000′                              Loc.: Pinal 2, F-9
In 1880 Joseph Chamberlin and his sons established the
Willow Spring Ranch in the valley through which Camp
Grant Wash runs. Here one of the sons, Manly R. Chamberlin, established a post office, calling it Manlyville after
himself. The mail was carried on a pony which made trips
between Tucson and the Riverside Stage Station until a
four-horse coach was later substituted and the place made
a stage stop.

P.O. est. March 18, 1881. Manly R. Chamberlain *(sic),* p.m.
Discont. July 5, 1888.
Ref.: 119, pp. 40-41. Maps: C-5 (Incorrect location); C-6.

## MARICOPA

El.: 1175′                              Loc.: Pinal 1, B-5.8
Pro.: /mǽrikópə/
When the railroad built the branch line joining Phoenix
to the main transcontinental route, a community known as
Maricopa Junction sprang up at the point where the two
lines joined. While at first it had been proposed to run the
line north from Maricopa Station (*q.v.*), such a route would
have left Tempe without railroad facilities. In order to keep
its subsidy, the railroad company agreed to so establish the
line that it would give Tempe a railroad outlet, and consequently the branch line was started at Maricopa Junction,
not at Maricopa Station (now Heaton), but this in turn
was the death knell for the old Maricopa Station. The name
Maricopa Junction was dropped in 1887, since the old
Maricopa Station had been wiped out of existence as a

stage-railroad junction. The change left only one Maricopa on the line. The post office at the older Maricopa Station (q.v.) was moved here when Maricopa Station became Heaton. Wells Fargo Station, 1885.

Ref.: Barnes; *Phoenix Herald*, July 7, 1887, 2:1. Maps: C-7; C-12; GG-10.

## MARICOPA (AK CHIN) INDIAN RESERVATION

El.: 1225'                    Loc.: Pinal 1, BC-5-7
Pro.: /mǽrikópə akčin/

This reservation for Papago and Pima Indians was established on May 28, 1912, for the Maricopa band of Papago Indians. Currently about one hundred thirty-nine Indians live on its 21,840 acres. Tribal headquarters are at Ak Chin.

Ref.: "Annual Report of the Arizona Commission of Indian Affairs, 1954, 1955, 1956," p. 7. Maps: C-11; C-12 (Ak Chin); GK-1.

## MARICOPA STATION

El.: 1133'                    Loc.: Pinal 1, AB-5.4
Pro.: /mǽrikópə/

Not to be confused with the present Maricopa nor with Maricopa Wells, Maricopa Station was the junction point where the S.P.R.R. passengers disembarked to take the stage line south to Tucson and Tombstone or north to Phoenix, Prescott, and other points. This was prior to the existence of railroad connections to the points named. For a time, until the establishment of a railroad line, Maricopa Station enjoyed importance, as it was thought that the railroad would probably go north from that point. For this reason a military telegraph line (which had been located at the older Maricopa Wells) was moved to Maricopa Station, as was also the post office of Maricopa Wells, the post office name then being changed to Maricopa.

When it was thought that the railroad would run north to Phoenix from Maricopa Station, a boom in land values took place. The name Maricopaville was given to the proposed community where a successful sale of lots occurred on May 12, 1879, attended by two hundred and sixteen special train passengers. The plans did not develop (*See* Maricopa) and the boom died. Maricopa Station lost its name and became Heaton. It is today a railroad siding.

P.O. est. May 7, 1879. Charles Wellhoff, p.m.

Ref.: Barnes; Kirkland ms., APHS; 26, p. 376; 102, p. 45. Maps: C-3; E-20; GG-10.

## MARICOPA WELLS

El.: c. 1500'                    Loc.: Pinal 1, B-4.3
Pro.: /mǽrikópə/

Maricopa Wells was of great importance to travelers, not only during the time of the Spanish padres but also in the days following the Gadsden Purchase. Coues was of the opinion that the spot called by Fr. Kino in 1694 San Andres Coata was near Maricopa Wells, if not at the precise spot. It is also probable that in November 1775, Fr. Francisco Garcés was at Maricopa Wells, which he called Las Lagunas del Hospital. The name arose from the fact that members of his crew drank bad water in pools, hence the name Hospital Lagoon. The fact that Garcés referred to a number of pools instead of a single well is considered significant, since the only place in the entire area known to have a number of such pools or wells was in the vicinity of Maricopa Wells itself.

It is reported that when the Mormon Battalion passed through this country under Col. Philip St. George Cooke in December 1846, the battalion camped at Maricopa Wells and proceeded to dig out several pools. There were then signs of Indian habitation of long standing. Later when emigrants began to cross the country, Maricopa Wells came into immediate importance because it was the last water before the pioneers set out across the rugged and waterless stretch of country between that point and what was then called Tezotal (cf. Gila Ranch, Maricopa) forty miles further west.

In 1857 Maricopa Wells was made an intermediate station on the San Antonio and San Diego mail route. Here the eastbound coaches met the westbound and mails were exchanged, with each turning back to its point of origin. The station itself consisted of a shelter and a brush corral. A year later the Butterfield Overland Stage erected adobe buildings and a larger corral. At that time water in the six to eight wells was reported good. The Pima Indians who originally inhabited the place brought in their relatives and a trading post was established. The Indians made a good living supplying overland emigrant trains with the forage which many had to carry in order to cross the dreaded Forty Mile Desert (Pinal and Maricopa Counties).

Maricopa Wells was a center of activity. In addition to a detachment of soldiers, there were often from twenty to four wagons, each with a team of from eight to twenty mules. Added to this were emigrant trains, their members bartering with Indians for supplies. In turn the Indians bartered with the keeper of the trading post. By 1870 there were sixty-eight permanent residents at Maricopa Wells. The station at that time was run by James A. Moore, who had sold out half of Maricopa Wells to Larkin W. Carr on November 24, 1869. In 1873 the military telegraph line arrived. With the coming of the railroad, however, Maricopa Wells began to slide into obscurity.

The water table in the Santa Cruz Cienega lowered as agriculture expanded in the valley. Today little remains of what was once a principal station on the Butterfield Stage route. Seven well holes are still visible.

P.O. est. as Maricopa, April 13, 1858. Francis J. Mullen, p.m. Discont. March 16, 1859. Re-established as Maricopa Wells, November 21, 1865. P.O. transferred to Maricopa Station (q.v.).

Ref.: 35 pp. 110 (Note 13), 109; 32, II, 169-170; 25, pp. 102-103; 51, p. 117; Kirkland ms., APHS; Emerson O. Stratton ms., APHS; APHS Names File; 111, p. 275; 87, p. 43; 88, II, 423. Maps: C-2; C-8; E-9; E-17; E-18; E-22; GG-10.

## MASON'S VALLEY

El.: c. 3500'                    Loc.: Pinal 2, CD-2.5

The fact that the name Mason's Valley is found on an 1869 map appears to eliminate the possibility that it was named for Charles G. Mason, co-discoverer of the Silver King

Mine, who was in Colorado at least until 1873. There is a much stronger possibility that the valley was named for an army officer—perhaps Julius Wilmot Mason, although documentary evidence has not yet been found to substantiate this theory.

Ref.:   Barnes; Woody. Maps: C-1; E-18; E-20.

## MASTENS PEAK

                                                        Loc.: Not known.
N. K. Masten was president of the Maricopa and Phoenix Railroad. This peak is reported to be on the divide between Superior and the Pinal Mountains.

Ref.:   Barnes. Map: None.

## MAULDIN

                                                        Loc.: Unknown
P.O. est. April 11, 1941. Mrs. Katherine M. Gordon, p.m. Discont. September 30, 1943.

Ref.:   P.O. Records.

## McCLELLAN WASH

El.: 1305'                                      Loc.: Pinal 1, F-5-6
The McClellan family settled on this wash.

Ref.:   Barnes. Maps: GK-24; GK-25; GK-27.

**a.n. McClellan Flats**          El.: 1450'                        Pinal
Ref.:   122, p. 215, Plate XXI.

## MESAVILLE

El.: c. 2500'                                   Loc.: Pinal 2, F-8
After Old Camp Grant had been removed from its first location, a small settlement existed at or near its site. The original proposal was to name the place Dodsons after its first postmaster, but the post office would not approve that name. Therefore the petitioners for the post office requested the name Mesaville, which was descriptive.

P.O. est. June 6, 1878. Joseph N. Dodson, p.m. Discont. March 13, 1888.

Ref.:   Barnes. Maps: C-5; C-8.

## MINERAL CREEK

El.: c. 3500'                                   Loc.: Pinal 2, CD-3-5;
                                                      Gila 1, HG-13-14
In November 1846, Maj. William H. Emory and his Boundary Survey party camped at the mouth of what was a dry creek except for a spring flowing from under the sand at the junction of two washes. Emory noted "many indications of gold and copper ores." He then named the stream Mineral Creek.

Ref.:   50, p. 78. Maps: C-1; E-1; E-11; GD-4; GD-10; GK-23.
        Although there is no documentary evidence to support the assumption, it may well be that the following place names were applied because of the presence or supposed presence of minerals:

**a.n. Mineral Butte**        El.: 1910'. Map: GK-25                Pinal
**Mineral Mountain**    El.: 3350'. Map: GK-10                Pinal
**Mining Mountain**     El.: 3949'. Map: GK-15                Pinal

## MONTEZUMA'S HEAD

El.: 2406'                                      Loc.: Pinal 1, A-4.9
Descriptive, particularly when viewed from the east.

Ref.:   Barnes. Maps: C-12; E-18; GG-10.
        Probably because it was once thought that Aztecs passed through Arizona on their way to Mexico, the name of the Aztec chief Montezuma was given to many place names. The following may be instances of this:

**a.n. Montezuma Peak**          El.: 4337'. Map: GG-10            Pinal
**Montezuma Store**                                              Pinal
        Loc.: 12 miles s. Florence on old Tucson Road.
        Owned by Austin and Dempsey.
Ref.:   Barnes.
**Montezuma's Tank**    Loc.: W. of Casa Grande                Pinal
        Named by Fr. Kino in 1698, but earlier called by him Aljibe.
Ref.:   20, p. 394 (Note 1).
**Montezuma**                      Map: E-20                    Pinal
        Barnes says p.o. est. 1880, Joseph Collingwood, p.m.
**Montezuma Head**                 Map: C-12                 Maricopa
**Montezuma Head**                 Map: C-12                    Pima
**Montezuma Cave**                                              Pima
        Loc.: 6 miles from Fresnal settlement.
**Montezuma's Chair**              Map: C-12                  Navajo
**Montezuma Sleeping**             Map: C-12                 Maricopa

## MORGAN'S FERRY

El.: c. 1500'                                   Loc.: Gila 1, B-4
Henry Morgan (b. Wisconsin c. 1841; d. October 15, 1908) arrived in Arizona on March 18, 1864. For a short time he was an engineer at Maricopa Wells, but soon located a trading post and ferry on the river to the north of the wells. Morgan's Ferry became the best known crossing of the Gila River on the road from Prescott to Tucson. His ferry and property were washed away on August 26, 1881. Morgan had learned Indian dialects and thereafter served as an interpreter.

Ref.:   Henry Morgan File, APHS; Emerson O. Stratton ms.,
        p. 9, APHS; State Library Files; *Weekly Arizona Miner*,
        February 2, 1875, 4:1. Map: E-20 (Ferry).

## MUNN

El.: 1575'                                      Loc.: Pinal 2, A-5.1
This location on the Pacific and Eastern railroad was named for the man who was in charge of construction for this branch in 1903.

Ref.:   Barnes. Map: GK-33.

## NAVISKA

El.: 1948'                                      Loc.: Pinal 2, H-11.8
The origin of the name for this siding on the railroad is not known.

Ref.:   Barnes. Map: GK-24.

## NEEDLE'S EYE

El.: c. 2500'                                   Loc.: Pinal 2, H-4.2
Coolidge Dam was built at the Needle's Eye, which is a narrow place in the canyon of the Gila River.

Ref.:   Barnes. Map: B-7.

## NEWMAN PEAK

El.: 4508'                              Loc.: Pinal 1, H-9.6
Newman Peak is the highest in the Picacho Mountains (cf. Picacho). A plaque at its base relates that it was named for a soldier killed in the only battle of the Civil War to take place in Arizona. However, another plaque in the area commemorating the battle does not list Newman's name (cf. Barrett, Fort).

Ref.:   Plaques mentioned above. Maps: C-12; GK-24.

## NINETY-MILE DESERT

El.: c. 1500'-2300'              Loc.: Pinal 1, AI-6-12
The Ninety-Mile Desert was the stretch of barren land which dusty travelers followed between Maricopa Wells and Point of Mountain, north and west of Tucson. There was a notable change in desert growth after the travelers passed Point of Mountain (q.v., Pima).

Ref.:   25, p. 131. Map: None.

## NUGGET CANYON

El.: c. 5200'                          Loc.: Pinal 2, FG-11
In 1879 the Nugget Mine was located in the southerly branch of the Peppersauce Gulch.

Ref.:   Emerson O. Stratton ms., APHS, p. 51. Maps: C-13; GK-4; GK-19.

## NUNEZ

El.: 1335'                              Loc.: Pinal 1, D-7.1
Pro.: /núwnyez/
This small location on the S.P.R.R. was established c. 1900. It is reportedly named after Ventura Nuñez, who murdered G. R. Whistler at Burkes Station (q.v., Maricopa) on July 7, 1874.

Ref.:   Barnes. Maps: C-10; GK-5.

## OCATILLA (sic)

El.: 1692'                              Loc.: Pinal 1, H-9.9
Pro.: /ókətíyə/              Spanish: "coach whip"
The name of this location on the S.P.R.R. is probably derived from the presence of the ocotillo shrub. The ocotillo is not a cactus, but it is one of the most distinctive of southwestern plants. During most of the year it bears no leaves on its cluster of what looks to be long, slender, thorny, and nearly dead sticks. However, when there is sufficient moisture every long branch begins to bear bright green leaves and in the spring a veritable flame tip of red flowers breaks out at the end of each branch.

Ocotillo is used for fence enclosures. It takes root easily. It is also used to support thatched roofs of ramadas ("sun shelters").

Ref.:   46, pp. 254-257. Map: GK-24.

## OLBERG

El.: c. 1500'                          Loc.: Pinal 1, F-5.2
Col. C. R. Olberg was chief engineer of the Indian Bureau at the time that he was in charge of the construction of Coolidge Dam. Olberg supervised the building of diversion dams for the Indian lands. The small town of Olberg came into existence in 1903 and was at one time a very busy place with machine shops, a trading post, and a post office.

P.O. est. June 2, 1927. Joseph O. Willett, p.m. Discont. August 31, 1938.

Ref.:   Hayden; Prather; Tempe News, November 27, 1903, 4:1. Map: GK-33.

## ONEIDA

El.: c. 1500'                          Loc.: Pinal 1, F-6.8
                       N.w. of Signal Peak, 1½ miles
Oneida was a station established in late 1858 or early 1859 by the Butterfield Overland Stage Company. Many men connected with the establishment of the stage line came from upper New York State. It is highly probable that Oneida was named for the home town of one such person.

Ref.:   32, II, 165. Map: None.

## ORACLE

El.: 4514'                              Loc.: Pinal 2, F-10.8
Albert Weldon made the trip to the western part of the United States via the Horn in his uncle's ship, The Oracle. Weldon was doing assessment work for the Oracle Mine c. 1880, building a brush camp where Oracle exists today. In 1881 Weldon and Alexander McKay built a one-room adobe house in the hollow below the mine.

The town of Oracle did not begin developing until the Apache Mine began working. Oracle then served as the halfway point between Apache Camp (Pinal) and Tucson. However, the settlement still did not have a name. By January 1882, there were about eight dwellings at what was called Summit Spring or Oracle Camp. Among the early settlers were Mr. and Mrs. Edwin S. Dodge, who started a lodging house at the Arcadia Ranch, so named because their partner, Jack Aldwinkle, was a Nova Scotian. When Dodge applied for a post office he desired to use the name Arcadia, but this was rejected and the name Oracle was selected in its place, so named for the ship in which young Weldon had come around the Horn.

P.O. est. December 28, 1880. James Branson, p.m.

Ref.:   Emerson O. Stratton ms., APHS, p. 54; Weekly Arizona Enterprise, January 14, 1882, 3:3. Maps: C-5; GK-30.

a.n. Oracle Hill          El.: 5290'. Map: GK-30        Pinal
       Oracle Junction                                          Pinal
       Loc.: Turn-off from Tucson-Florence Highway to Oracle.
       Oracle Ridge                                  Pinal and Pima
       El.: 7505'. Maps: GK-19; GK-30.

## ORIZABA

El.: 1628'                              Loc.: Pinal 1, CD-10.7
Reportedly the camp for the Orizaba Mine was so named for a Papago Indian who was still working in the area in 1903.

P.O. est. September 25, 1888. John Reiss, p.m. Discont. August 11, 1893.

Ref.:   Barnes. Maps: C-7; GK-28.

## OTIS
Loc.: Not known.
The origin of this name has not yet been learned.
P.O. est. January 13, 1893. Thomas C. Carey, p.m. Discont.
August 19, 1893.
Ref.:   P.O. Records. Map: None.

## OWL HEAD
El.: c. 3600′                          Loc.: Pinal 2, C-10
In 1879 William H. Merrit and E. Walker established a
mining camp at this location. The name is descriptive of
two nearby buttes which look like large owl heads.
P.O. est. July 10, 1930. Mrs. Josie M. Guss, p.m. Discont.
August 15, 1933.
Ref.:   Emerson O. Stratton ms., APHS, p. 44; Barnes. Maps:
C-12 (Owl Head Butte); C-13.

## PALMA, LA
El.: c. 1500′                          Loc.: Pinal 2, GH-7.3
Pro.: /la palmə/                     Spanish: "the palm"
In 1927 a new townsite was laid out at this location.
Ref.:   *Arizona Daily Star*, May 1, 1927, p. 6 (APHS). Map:
GK-33.

## PALO VERDE MOUNTAINS
El.: 2029′                            Loc.: Pinal 1, AB-6.4
Pro.: /pǽlo vérdiˆ/                   Spanish: *palo*, "stick";
                                      *verde*, "green"
Descriptive. The palo verde is a cousin of the mesquite
and screwbean trees. There is a notable absence of rough
bark on the palo verde, except on those which are very
old or on the main trunk and the largest branches. The
bark is smooth and remains green the year round, including the smallest twigs, hence the name.
Ref.:   15, p. 174. Maps: GG-10; GK-1.
**a.n. Palo Verde**        Loc.: T. 1 S., R. 4 W.          Maricopa
     This small settlement takes its name from its location in
     the Palo Verde Hills where the first settlers noted the
     presence of many palo verde trees.
P.O. est. June 4, 1910. William Walton, p.m.
Ref.:   141, pp. 27, 216; Barnes.

## PARKER'S PEAK
El.: c. 3000′                         Loc.: Pinal 2, C-4
This peak was probably named for Tom Parker, a pros-
pector who had claims in the vicinity. The name first ap-
pears on GLO 1876.
Ref.:   Barnes. Maps: C-3; C-4; E-20 (Packers Peak).

## PEACH ORCHARD
El.: c. 2000′    Loc.: Pinal 1, I-3.5. N.w. across canyon
                       from Silver King Camp in 1877.
Peach Orchard was the name for a mining camp consisting
of a few rock houses. A miner planted several peach trees
which gave the place its name. Apparently the place was
just getting started in the early fall of 1875 under the
name of Peachville. Two additional small communities
were also beginning at that time. They were Brownsville
(Nuggetville), and Happy Hollow.
Ref.:   Barnes; 87, p. xlvii; *Weekly Arizona Miner*, September
3, 1875, 2:3. Map: None.
**a.n. Peachville Mountain**      El.: 4843′. Map: GK-29          Pinal
     **Peachville Wash**          Map: GK-29                      Pinal

## PEPCHILTK
Loc.: N.e. of Casa Blanca.
Pima: "concave"
A family of Pima Indians having concave noses lived at
this location. The first recorded name for the place was
Pepchalk in 1872. The place was still in existence in 1902.
Ref.:   88, II, 22. Map: None.

## PEPPERSAUCE WASH
El.: c. 4400′-2600′                   Loc.: Pinal 2, GH-11
In the mid 1880's there was a well-traveled trail between
Oracle and the Apache Mine Camp. On his way to Apache
Camp Louie Depew stopped to eat lunch. He was very
fond of pepper sauce, a bottle of which he had with him.
He left the sauce and his comrades at Apache Camp joshed
him about his loss. They named the wash.
**v.n. Peppersauce Canyon**      Map: GK-19          Pinal
     **Peppersauce Gulch**                           Pinal
Ref.:   Emerson O. Stratton ms., APHS, p. 62. Maps: GK-4;
GK-30; GK-20.

## PICACHO
El.: 3382′                            Loc.: Pinal 1, H-9.8
Pro.: /pikáčow/                      Spanish: "peak; point"
On October 29, 1775, Fr. Francisco Garcés wrote of passing the Cerro de Tacca, a conspicuous landmark. He apparently got the name from the Pima Indians living in the
vicinity, as they referred to this outstanding peak as *Tcacca*
or *Taceo* (probably from *Ta-kgu*, "iron"). There are many
"picachos" in Arizona, since the name is used indiscrim-
inately for any outstanding peak. The location of *tinajas*
(shallow pools) at the Picacho, and the fact that it lay half-
way between Tucson and the Gila River, no doubt helped
contribute to its importance to early travelers. By some it
was called the Picacho del Tucson.

The first American military unit to camp in Picacho Pass
was the Mormon Battalion on December 17, 1846. Later,
Picacho Pass was the scene of the only Civil War battle
to be fought in Arizona. On April 15, 1862, sixteen Confederate cavalrymen of Capt. Sherod Hunter's command
were with Lt. Jack Swilling when they were overtaken by
Lt. James Barrett and a dozen soldiers. During the skirmish
Barrett was killed, as were Pvt. George Johnson and Pvt.
William S. Leonard of the Union forces. Two Confederates, whose names are not known, were killed and two
others taken prisoner. (Not all accounts agree concerning
the Confederates.)

Picacho Pass was also important because Picacho Station
was in it. It served both as a Butterfield Overland Stage
station and as a place where emigrant trains camped. The
Picacho Station lay approximately one mile southeast of
the present Wymola siding on the S.P.R.R.
Ref.:   35, p. 84, (Note 21); 87, p. 180; 25, p. 130; 51, pp.
117-118; 7, p. 514; 111, p. 163; 32, II, 163. Maps: E-17;
E-18 (Picacho del Tucson); GK-24.
**a.n. Picacho**        Maps: GK-9; GK-24          Pinal
     This is the present-day community on the main highway
     between Phoenix and Tucson.

P.O. est. January 26, 1881. Manuel S. Ramirez, p.m. Discont. June 5, 1907.

> This station may have been at the old Picacho Station location. The post office was re-established at its current location on February 21, 1929.

**Picacho Mountains**          Map: GK-24          Pinal

> The Pima name for these mountains is *Tcacca* (see main entry).

Ref.:   Kirk Bryan Notes.

**Picacho Lake**          Pinal

> Reservoir for the Casa Grande canal system.

Ref.:   Barnes.

## PIMA VILLAGES

El.: c. 1200'          Loc.: Pinal 1, A-3.6
Pro.:   /píymə/

The Pima or, as they were sometimes called, Pimo Villages consisted of a string of Indian settlements extending from Casa Blanca westward on either side of the Gila River in the same area which is today occupied by the Gila River Indian Reservation. The principal towns included some still in existence today, such as Sacaton, Snaketown, and Santan, which, however, did not have these same names in the early days.

Apparently the Azul (Spanish: "blue") family held precedence over other Indians in the area. In 1851 their chief was Cielo Azul, who was succeeded by his son, Antonio Azul. The fact that the Pimas were always friendly toward Americans and put themselves out to supply emigrants and military groups with forage made their villages an important stopping place on the early southern transcontinental route. This probably accounts for the fact that Ammi White established a flour mill at Casa Blanca, then a Pima village.

Ammi White was an Indian trader in the Pima Villages. Capt. Sherod Hunter and his Texas Confederates confiscated fifteen hundred sacks of wheat and arrested Mr. White on March 3, 1862. While engaged in this action. Hunter's men heard of the approach of Capt. McCleave and nine men of the First California Cavalry. The Union men were captured without the firing of a gun and both Capt. McCleave and Trader White were sent to the Rio Grande as Confederate captives.

P.O. est. as Pimo Village, June 21, 1859. Silas St. John, p.m. Discont. December 6, 1871.

Ref.:   48, p. 207, (Note 14); 137, p. 228; 159, pp. 222-223, (Note 22); 111, pp. 275, 162. Maps: C-2; E-1; E-11; GG-10.

## PINAL

El.: 2529'          Loc.: Pinal 2, B-3.1
Pro.:   /pinǽl/

When the Silver King Mine became important in the mid-1870's, it was necessary to construct a smelter to work the ores. The mill town was located where William G. Arnett had located earlier because of the presence of water, below the high butte known as Picket Post. When the settlement first came into being, it was known as Picket Post because of its adjacency to the butte. (For further information about military operations and the origin of the name Picket Post, cf. Pinal, Camp).

The town began to grow in 1877 and by March 1878 had permanent stone and adobe buildings. It bustled with hundreds of prospectors and miners and became an important stage station on the road to Globe. In 1879 the name was changed from Picket Post to Pinal, also referred to as Pinal City. The community disappeared quickly when work closed down at the Silver King Mine in 1888 (cf. Silver King). Today the old mining town, which once had two thousand residents, is the site of the Thompson Southwest Arboretum, founded by William Boice Thompson as an experimental station for plant research.

P.O. est. as Picket Post, April 10, 1878. William W. Benson, p.m. Name changed to Pinal, June 27, 1879. Discont. November 28, 1891. Wells Fargo Station, 1875.

Ref.:   *Arizona Sentinel,* October 6, 1877, 2:2; March 2, 1878; 2:3; July 5, 1879, 2:2; 25, p. 263; Emerson O. Stratton ms., APHS; 77, p. 343. Maps: C-4; E-20 (Picket Post P.O.); GK-10.

## PINAL, CAMP

El.: c. 4500'          Loc.: Pinal 2, C-2.3
Pro.:   /pinǽl/

On November 28, 1870, a military post was established in the Pinal Mountains under the name of Infantry Camp, with Gen. George Stoneman as commanding officer. The camp was established in what was referred to as Mason's Valley at the headwaters of Mineral and Pinto creeks. The name was changed on April 4, 1871, to Camp Pinal.

The nearby butte was called Picket Post, probably because soldiers were placed on picket to watch for Indians.

The Stoneman Grade was built at this time by U. S. troops. It began on what was called Picket Post Creek, currently referred to as Queen Creek, at the site of Infantry Camp. This trail became of immense importance to the residents of the Globe area, although it was never more than five miles long and travelers made their way beyond it as best they could.

Stoneman had planned to make Pinal Camp a permanent post, but when he was relieved of his command and Gen. George Crook took his place, the project was abandoned in August 1871. That there may have been some attempt to locate a community at the site of the old camp is attested to by a dispatch in the *Arizona Miner* for April 6, 1872 (1:4), which speaks of an Indian raid at Pinal City. However, apparently a permanent location by a settler was not made at this place until 1877. In that year Robert A. Irion located his ranch headquarters at the site of the old Camp Pinal. Since that time the location has been known as Pinal Ranch. Pinal Ranch was an important stopping place for travelers.

Ref.:   Craig (Irion's stepdaughter); 75, p. 148; 85, pp. 511, 533. Maps: E-20; E-18; GD-4; GD-10.

## POSTON BUTTE

El.: c. 1500'                    Loc.: Pinal 1, HI-5.7
Pro.: /pówstən/
Charles Debrille Poston (b. Kentucky, April 20, 1825; d. June 24, 1902) came to Arizona in 1857 with the Sonora Mining Company of Gen. S. P. Heintzelman.

Poston is known as the "Father of Arizona" because it was due largely to his personal efforts that the Territory of Arizona was created by act of President Abraham Lincoln. According to Poston's own words as expressed in his private *Journal,* he was able to get the bill passed by offering political plums to the men needed to pass it in Congress. He pointed out that this probably would not have been possible had not the Union been in a state of civil war at the time, since Arizona had many southern sympathizers living within her confines. When all the plums had been distributed, Poston suddenly realized he had been so assiduous that he had forgotten to take care of his own needs. He was thereupon appointed the first Superintendent of Indian Affairs (cf. Colorado River Indian Reservation, Yuma and Mohave). In 1877 Poston was appointed to the U. S. Land Office, which was then in Florence. Meanwhile, he had traveled around the entire world and had been much struck by the sun worship which he had encountered while in Egypt. It is perhaps best to take his own words for what he intended to do with the work he began on what he called Primrose Hill. Poston states that late in 1877 he noted that Primrose Hill was much like the pyramids of Egypt and that he then began preparing his own tomb on the hill. He sank a shaft for the tomb about thirty feet to solid rock and constructed a road to the top of the hill where he also had a well dug on the south side. Many authors speak of this project as Poston's plan to erect a temple to the sun.

Poston's wish to be buried at Poston Butte was not fulfilled at the time of his death. He died in a state very close to poverty in Phoenix in 1902. A few years later the State Legislature voted $100 for a tombstone to be placed on Poston's grave. However, attempts to locate his grave in the pauper's flat where he had been buried were not successful.

In 1925 Poston's supposed remains were re-buried under a monument at the top of Poston's Butte, a long overdue honor for Arizona Territory's first delegate to Congress.

An early name for Poston's Butte, Stiles Hill, was taken from the name of William Stiles who settled near its base. He was the father of Billy Stiles, who was involved in a train robbery near Tombstone. The younger Stiles was captured.

Ref.:    Preston Mercer, *"Desert Scrapbook," Yuma Daily Sun,* LIV (August 8, 1954), III, 2:4; Emerson O. Stratton ms., APHS, p. 28; Charles D. Poston, *Journal;* 104, pp. 77-78. Maps: C-10; GK-10.

## PRICE

El.: 1574'                       Loc.: Pinal 2, A-5.3
There are two possible origins for the name of Price. William Price was a merchant in Florence who supplied many of the needs of the contractors during the building of the railroad in 1903. On the other hand, B. S. Price worked with George Tisdale, the general contractor for the construction of the line in the same year.

P.O. est. March 18, 1909. Henry Zeuner, p.m. Discont. March 15, 1923.
Ref.:    Barnes; P.O. Records. Maps: C-10; GK-10.

## QUEEN CREEK

El.: c. 4500'-2000'        Loc.: Pinal 1, G-4-2; Pinal 2, AC-4
Queen Creek rises in the Pinal Mountains and drains toward the Gila River, but its waters disappear in the sand before it reaches the river. Until the Silver Queen Mine was located, the creek was known as Picket Post Creek. It runs through what is called either Queen Canyon or Queen Creek Canyon. The community of Queen was in Queen Canyon, probably near the Silver Queen Mine.

P.O. est. April 21, 1881. Charles H. Miller, p.m. Discont. September 5, 1881.
Ref.:    Craig; Woody; 3A, p. 21. Maps: C-11; E-18; E-20; GK-10; GK-21; GK-25; GK-29.
a.n. Queen Station       Maps: GK-21; GK-29        Pinal
      Queen Creek        Maps: C-12; GK-25         Maricopa
P.O. est. March 21, 1913. Frank E. Ross, p.m. Discont. July 31, 1916.

## RABBIT

El.: 3600'                       Loc.: Pinal 2, E-9.7
This was the post office for the Rabbit Ranch.
P.O. est. January 13, 1893. Andrew J. Doran, p.m. Discont. June 21, 1905.
Ref.:    P.O. Records. Maps: GK-2; GK-31.

## RANDOLPH

El.: 1560'                       Loc.: Pinal 1, GH-7.4
This railroad location was named for Col. Epes Randolph, long-time vice-president and general manager of the S.P.R.R.

P.O. est. July 18, 1925. Channing E. Babbitt, p.m.
Ref.:    Barnes. Maps: C-13; F-13.
a.n. Randolph Canyon          Map: GK-10               Pinal

## RAWHIDE MOUNTAIN

El.: c. 4000'                    Loc.: Pinal 2, I-6
A Mexican goat herder on this mountain wore rawhide sandals and lived like a miser. He is reported to have slept on rawhide.
Ref.:    Barnes. Map: B-7.

## RAY

El.: 2024'                       Loc.: Pinal 2, CD-4.3
The Ray Copper Company was organized in 1882 and reportedly a small settlement was so called by a man named Bullinger after a mine named for his sister somewhat earlier. Although the first copper mining took place at Ray in the 1880's and some silver mining was done earlier than that, large scale operations did not begin until 1911. To prepare for large scale operations, in 1909 the town of Ray was

constructed by the Arizona Hercules Copper Company, on the property belonging to the Hercules Townsite Company. Open pit operations were begun at Ray in 1947.

P.O. est. September 8, 1889. Charles R. Clauberg, p.m.

Ref.:   123, p. 91; Barnes; *Arizona Gazette,* August 10, 1909, 8:2; P.O. Records. Maps: GD-13; GK-23.

| **a.n.** **Ray Junction** | Map: C-10 | Pinal |
|---|---|---|
| **Ray Hill** | Map: GK-23 | Pinal |
| **Ray Spring Hill** | El.: 4536′. Map: GK-18 | Pinal |

## RED ROCK

El.: 1867′                              Loc.: Pinal 1, I-11

A red butte is near this station on the S.P.R.R.

At one time the branch line to the smelter for the Silver Bell Mine had its junction with the S.P.R.R. at Red Rock. P.O. est. as Red Rock, June 14, 1887. Joseph W. Haskin, p.m. Changed to Redrock, November 30, 1895. Changed to Red Rock, June 1, 1950. Wells Fargo Station, 1890.

Ref.:   Jordan; P.O. Records. Maps: C-5; GK-24.

## REYMERT

El.: 3160′                              Loc.: Pinal 2, A-3.6
Pro.:   /ráymert/

J. D. Reymert had a mine at this location. A post office was established for the convenience of the miners.

P.O. est. June 6, 1890. Mrs. Elisa Reymert, p.m. Discont. May 27, 1898.

Ref.:   P.O. Records; Barnes; APHS Files; Craig. Maps: C-7; GK-10.

## RIPSEY HILL

El.: 3937′                              Loc.: Pinal 2, CD-6.5

Ripsey Hill is named for the owners of the Ripsey Ranch who ran cattle at least as early as 1910 in this area.

Ref.:   Barnes. Maps: C-10; GK-31 (Ripsey Ranch).

| **a.n.** **Ripsey Spring** | Map: GK-23 | Pinal |
|---|---|---|
| **Ripsey Wash** | | Pinal |

Maps: GK-8; GK-10; GK-31; GK-23.

## ROBLAS BUTTE

El.: 3110′                              Loc.: Pinal 2, A-2.7
Pro.:   /róbləs/

A Mexican by the name of Roblas or Robles is said to have had a ranch on the eastern slope of this butte many years ago.

Ref.:   Barnes. Maps: GK-21; GK-29.

| **a.n.** **Roblas Canyon** | Maps: GK-21; GK-29 | Pinal |
|---|---|---|

Ref.:   Barnes.

## ROCK BUTTE

El.: c. 2000′                              Loc.: Pinal 1, F-4.6
Descriptive.

Ref.:   Barnes. Maps: C-10 (Rock Peak); C-12.

## ROCK HOUSE MOUNTAIN

El.: 3672′                              Loc.: Pinal 2, H-4.9

A rock house used to exist at the foot of this mountain.

Ref.:   Barnes. Maps: C-12; GK-6.

| **a.n.** **Rock House Canyon** | Map: GK-6 | Pinal |
|---|---|---|

## SACATE

El.: 1128′                              Loc.: Pinal 1, BC-4.4
Pro.:   /zakátey/

The word *sacate* is derived from the Nahuatl word designating the type of grass preferred by horses and cattle as distinguished from *sacaton,* which consists of weeds, brush, and other herbage not fit for forage. In 1775 Fr. Francisco Garcés wrote of the growth of *sacate* in the area where the Indian village of Sacate is located today. However, the name does not occur on maps examined until GLO 1892 whereon it shows as Sacaton Station north of Maricopa on the branch line to Phoenix. This name was changed to Sacate, probably to obviate confusion with the town of Sacaton which was a stage station on the early Butterfield Overland Stage route and which continues as a village on the Pima Indian Reservation (cf. Sacaton).

Ref.:   35, p. 87, (Note 24). Maps: C-12; GG-10.

## SACATON

El.: 1274′                              Loc.: Pinal 1, E-5.3
Pro.:   /sakətówn/ or /sǽkətown/

Although the Nahuatl word from which *sacaton* is derived refers to coarse and generally inedible forage, in this part of Arizona sacaton (*Sporobolus wrightii*) is a type of forage which grows to the height of a mule's back. Such grass was noted as existing in abundance when emigrants were first crossing this part of what is now Arizona.

The Pima designation for the very old and still extant settlement at Sacaton was Uturituc ("the corner") because of its situation where the new and old stream branches of the Gila River coincided. In 1775 Fr. Francisco Garcés called it both Vturituc and San Juan Capistrano. A still earlier name was that bestowed by Fr. Kino in 1696; Kino interpreted the Indian name of Tudacson as Soacson, which has gradually changed into Sacaton. Kino also refers to La Encarnacion, which Hodge notes was in the neighborhood of the present-day Sacaton.

In 1857 Sacaton was the extreme end of the stage line between it and Fort Yuma. It was also a station on the Butterfield Overland Stage route, being the next along the way from Oneida. The road followed a pass between Thin Mountain (El.: 1750′) and the Sacaton Mountains. The stage station lay one and a quarter miles to the east of present-day Sacaton. The community has long been the headquarters for the Pima Indian Reservation. This village is not to be confused with the former Sacaton Station, now known as Sacate (*q.v.*)

P.O. est. as Sacaton, January 6, 1871. Peter Forebac, p.m. Discont. March 11, 1873. Re-est. as Pima Agency, February 1, 1875. Howard C. Christ, p.m. Changed to Sacaton, January 3, 1876.

Ref.:   122, p. 199; 88, II, 877-878, 647; 141, p. 97; 20, p. 284; 35, p. 88, (Note 28); 32, II, 165-166. Maps: E-18 (Pima Agency); E-17; E-20; E-6 (Zacatone Camp); GK-25.

| **a.n.** **Sacaton Ranch** | Maps: GK-15; GK-20; GK-30 | Pinal |
|---|---|---|

P.O. est. as Sacaton, September 23, 1895. Nannine B. Young, p.m. (No P.O. Record for this.)

Ref.:   Barnes.

| **Sacaton Butte** | Map: GK-13 | Pinal |
|---|---|---|
| **Sacaton Mountain** | Maps: GK-13; GK-25; GK-27 | Pinal |
| **Sacaton Peak** | Map: GK-25 | Pinal |

## SADDLE BACK MOUNTAIN

El.: 4233'                    Loc.: Pinal 2, G-6.5
In 1854 Antisell applied this descriptive name to a mountain in the Galiuro Mountains.
Ref.:   128, p. 146; 175, III, 509. Maps: A-7; C-12; E-11.

a.n. **Saddle Mountain**    Loc.: T. 11 S., R. 21 E.    Graham
**Tilted Peak**    Loc.: N. end of Pinalenos Mts.    Pinal
Antisell called this peak "Saddleback Mountain," but it is not the same as "Saddle Back Mountain" mentioned above. The current name of Tilted Peak is descriptive.

## SAN MANUEL

El.: c. 3500'                    Loc.: Pinal 2, GH-10.5
Pro.: /san manuwell/ or /sæn mænuwel/
San Manuel is a company-owned copper mining town established c. 1953.
P.O. est. April 1, 1954. Joe H. Cittadini, p.m.
Ref.:   P.O. Records. Map: GK-19.

## SANTAN

El.: c. 1300'                    Loc.: Pinal 1, EF-4.8
Pro.: /sántan/
Santan is a corruption for the Spanish name Santa Ana. It is a Pima settlement near Sacaton.
When the Pimas located at this place, the Papagos called their location Santa Ana, the normal pronunciation of which is "Santana." According to the Pima "calendar sticks" the settlement was in existence as early as 1857.
P. est. ? Discont. February 29, 1932.
Ref.:   Barnes. Maps: C-13; GK-25.

a.n. **Santan Mountains**    El.: 3093'. Map: C-12    Pinal

## SASCO

El.: 1806'                    Loc.: Pinal 1, H-11.6
A branch line from Red Rock on the railroad led to the smelter for the Silver Bell Mine. The smelter was located on a small but prominent hill. Its name was derived from the initials of the Southern Arizona Smelting Company. The place is now in ruins and the branch line of the railroad has been torn up.
P.O. est. July 10, 1907. Charles O. Matthews, p.m. Discont. September 15, 1919.
Ref.:   Jordan; Barnes; 26, p. 367. Maps: C-10; GK-24.

## SAWTOOTH MOUNTAINS

El.: c. 2500'                    Loc.: Pinal 1, EF-10.7
Descriptive.
Maps:   C-12; GK-9; GK-28.

a.n. **Sawtooth Ridge**    Maps: GK-14; GK-16; GK-29    Pinal
**Sawtooth Mountain**    Loc.: T. 6 N., R. 23 E.    Apache

## SCOTT MOUNTAIN

El.: 5115'                    Loc.: Pinal 2, D-4
George Scott was one of the signers of the papers for the Globe Mining District in November 1875. He had a ranch eight miles up the Gila River from the old Riverside Station, which is Kelvin today. It is probable that the mountain was named for him.
Ref.:   Woody. Maps: C-10; GK-33.

## SHOPISHK

El.: c. 1450'                    Loc.: Pinal 1, C-9
Pro.:   /sápič/                    Papago: "pass"
This is the correct name for the location sometimes called Ko-opke (Papago: "place of the dam") where the Indians built a dam prior to 1915.
Ref.:   2, p. 16; Kirk Bryan Notes. Maps: C-12 (Koopke); D-8.

a.n. **Shopishk Valley**    Pinal
Loc.: Between Silver Reef Mts. on w. and reservation boundary on e.
Ref.:   128, p. 19.

## SILVER KING

El.: c. 4000'                    Loc.: Pinal 2, B-2.6
The Silver King Mine was discovered on March 24, 1875, by Isaac Copeland, William Long, Charles Mason, and Ben Reagen. All four men were farmers who during that time of the year when farmers had time on their hands, engaged in prospecting. Long and Copeland were among those who had located the Globe Ledge two years prior to the discovery of Silver King. They discovered the second mine on their return from a trip to the Globe Mine.

According to the story, a soldier named Sullivan was among the many who worked on the construction of Stoneman's Grade (cf. Camp Pinal). He found a piece of black rock which was curiously heavy and soft, and while on a visit in Florence he showed his find to Charles G. Mason, reporting that he found the object near the foot of the grade. Sullivan, whose enlistment had expired, then left the area without giving further information. Mason kept the story in mind, and while he and his three companions were on their way back from Globe to their farm land, William Sampson, who was with the party, was killed by Apaches, and Copeland slightly injured. The men managed to save Sampson's body. (This may be the body which was concealed in large old earthen ovens at Camp Supply.) Meanwhile, one of the animals belonging to the party strayed. It was found standing on an outcropping of chloride of silver, the "black rock" of Sullivan.

The discovery was so rich that the owners decided they had found the king of mines, hence its name. There was an immediate stampede of those wishing to cash in on the bonanza, and the community of Silver King was the result. Stamp mills were put up at Picket Post (cf. Pinal). By 1888, however, the boom was nearing its end. All that remains today are a few small stone buildings and a mine half filled with water.
P.O. est. December 21, 1877. S. B. Chapin, p.m. Discont. May 15, 1912.
Ref.:   89, pp. 118-119; 170, pp. 85, 93, 86; Woody. Maps: C-4; C-12; E-20; GD-9; GK-10; GK-29.

a.n. **Silver King Wash**    Maps: GK-29; GK-21    Pinal

## SILVER REEF MOUNTAINS

El.: 2471'                    Loc.: Pinal 1, E-9.8
The now abandoned Silver Reef Mine was located on a reeflike ledge. This resulted in the name for these mountains.
Ref.:   Stanfield. Maps: C-12; GK-28.

**a.n. Silver Reef Pass**                                 Pinal
    Loc.: Between Silver Reef Mts. and Tat Momoli Mts.
**Silver Reef Wash**    Map: GK-28                Pinal
    The Silver Reef Pass winds along this wash.
**Silver Reef Valley**                                    Pinal
    Loc.: S. of Silver Reef Mts. and e. of Tat Momoli Mts.

## SLATE MOUNTAINS

El.: 3300'    Loc.: Pinal 1, D-11-12
Both the name Slate Mountains and its Spanish name of
Sierrita Prieta (Spanish: "black; little mountains") are
descriptive.
Ref.: Barnes; 34, p. 243. Maps: C-10 (Sierra Prieta); GK-28.

## SLINKARD SPRINGS

    Loc.: Not known
Pro.: /slǽnkerd/
In 1889 Frank Slinkard, Tom Deloche and Fin Clanton
robbed a Chinese merchant named Sam Gee, who had
gardens at the Pringle Ranch where he was robbed. Clanton
had a deformed hand for which he used special gloves. The
robbers were identified by the fact that Clanton carelessly
dropped a glove for his deformed hand near the robbed safe.
Ref.: Byrnes; State Library File clipping (Unidentified). Map:
None.

## SNAKETOWN

El.: 1175'    Loc.: Pinal 1, CD-4.1
Snaketown is a Papago Indian village. The Pima word
"Ska-kaik" means "many rattle snakes."
Ref.: Barnes. Map: GK-13.

## SOLDIERS GRAVE

    Loc.: Somewhere n. of Blue Water Station and below
            Sacaton Butterfield Overland Stage station.
This is the place where Charles C. Genung stopped in 1864
in connection with his pursuit of a renegade Mexican murderer. According to Barnes, Genung caught the man and
disposed of him "according to local customs." Why it is
called "soldier's grave" has not been learned.
Ref.: 52, IV, 51; Barnes. Map: None.

## SOMBRERO BUTTE

El.: 5670'    Loc.: Pinal 2, HI-10.2
Pro.: /sombréyro/    Spanish: "hat"
Descriptive. This was also the name of the settlement at
the base of the butte.
P.O. est. June 18, 1919. Clara Johnson, p.m. Discont. May 31,
1945.
Ref.: Barnes; P.O. Records; 119, pp. 51, 56. Maps: C-12;
GE-1.

## SONORA

El.: 2250'    Loc.: Pinal 2, C-4.5
Pro.: /sanorə/
Mexican employees of the Ray Consolidated Copper Com-
pany established and named this settlement after the Mexi-
can state of Sonora adjacent to the Arizona boundary.
P.O. est. January 29, 1912. Frank Abril, p.m.
Ref.: APHS Names File. Maps: C-12; GD-13; GK-23.
**a.n. Sonora Hill**    El.: 2637'. Maps: GD-13; GK-23    Pinal

## SPINE, THE

El.: c. 2000'    Loc.: Pinal 2, G-4.9
This sharp ridge resembles a spine, hence the name.
Ref.: Barnes. Map: GK-10.

## STANFIELD

El.: c. 1300'    Loc.: Pinal 1, C-7.8
The first name for Stanfield was Summerland.
The thriving agricultural community of Stanfield exists on
land which was homesteaded by Nixon W. Stanfield prior
to 1915. He donated eighty acres to form a school district
which was given his name. The first store was built in 1943
at the east of the present town.
Two years later another store was built and came to be
known as Table Top, the name being taken from the nearby
mountain. When the residents in the area petitioned for a
post office, they conferred with Mrs. Bess Prather, then
post mistress at Casa Grande, and the name Stanfield was
selected. Some residents still refer to one end of the town
as Table Top.
P.O. est. as Summerland, May 6, 1914. Nixon W. Stanfield,
p.m. Discont. June 15, 1918.
P.O. est. as Stanfield, August 1, 1948. Earle Ellsworth, p.m.
Ref.: John D. Lannin (Ellsworth's son-in-law); Prather.
    Maps: C-12; F-2 (Summerland); GK-33.

## STEAMBOAT MOUNTAIN

El.: c. 3500'    Loc.: Pinal 2, DE-5.1
Descriptive, as are other names given below.
Ref.: Barnes. Maps: C-10; GD-13; GK-33.
**a.n. Steamboat Peak**    Map: C-12    Mohave
**Steamboat Rock**    Map: GH-11    Mohave
**Steamboat Wash**    Map: B-7    Pinal
    Takes its name from nearby Steamboat Mountain.

## SUPERIOR

El.: 2888'    Loc.: Pinal 2, B-3
According to Barnes, the first name of Superior was Hastings, a name found by Barnes on an 1882 map of the Pioneer
Mining District. A community developed at the location of
the Silver Queen Mine. The Queen proved more enduring
than the Silver King, since when the silver ores played out
at the Queen, large underlying deposits of copper were discovered.
In 1910 the Magma Copper Company took over the Silver
Queen properties. Prior to that date the townsite of Superior
had been laid out by George Lobb c. 1900. The community
was named Superior because its livelihood was dependent
upon the operation of the Arizona and Lake Superior Mining Company. In 1904 the town was described as having
many tents and primitive board houses, as well as a store,
boarding house, blacksmith shop, and post office. There
were few permanent dwellings. In 1914 the Magma Copper
Company constructed a huge smelter and from that time
on Superior's place in the roster of Arizona communities
was well secured as long as copper continues to be found
in the area.
P.O. est. December 9, 1902. George Lobb, p.m.
Ref.: Barnes; *Arizona Blade,* April 2, 1904, 1:2; 4, p. 349.
    Maps: C-9; GK-29.

## SUPERSTITION MOUNTAINS

El.: 5057'                                Loc.: Pinal 1, H-1

The Pima Indians have a legend concerning a great flood, the foam of which caused the broad white streak in the limestone extending for several miles along the face of the rough Superstition Mountains. Because of this legend, the Spanish referred to these mountains as the Sierra de la Espuma ("mountains of foam"). Their current name may be attributed to the stories told by the valley-dwelling Indians that the mountains were bad medicine, since no one who entered them ever returned. This was probably true, because Apaches watched for strangers from the peaks and ambushed any who dared enter the mountains. The United States cavalry disproved the legends concerning the disappearance of men. At least two skirmishes with Apaches occurred in the Superstition Mountains from which the military men emerged with few casualties.

Like other mining states, Arizona has its own store of lost mine tales, and that of the Lost Dutchman Mine is one of the best known (cf. Weaver's Needle).

Ref.:   4, p. 350; 111, p. 22; Barnes: 85, pp. 438, 440. Maps: C-10; E-18; E-20; GK-10.

**a.n. Superstition Peak**          El.: 5057'                Pinal
Highest peak in the Superstition Mountains.

## SUPPLY, CAMP

El.: c. 3300'                            Loc.: Pinal 2, B-3.3
                                         S. of present Superior 2 miles.

This was the location of the supply point for the military men who in 1870 were engaged in building Stoneman's Grade (cf. Pinal Camp). Earthen ovens were built here. It was in one of these that a body was buried (cf. Silver King.)

Ref.:   178, p. 85; Woody. Map: None.

## SWEETWATER

El.: c. 1200'                            Loc.: Pinal 1, DE-4.6

In 1868 George F. Hooper and Company had a store located at this place. Hinton listed it as a stage station.

Ref.:   *Weekly Arizona Miner*, October 24, 1868, 4:4; 87, p. xx. Maps: C-5; GK-11.

**a.n. Sweetwater Store Indian Trading Post**    Map: GK-11    Pinal

## TEAPOT MOUNTAIN

El.: 3400'                               Loc.: Pinal 2, CD-4
Descriptive.

**v.n. Tea Kettle Mountain**
Ref.:   3a, p. 379; Barnes. Map: GK-23.

## TELEGRAPH CANYON

El.: c. 2600'                            Loc.: Pinal 2, B-3-2
The first telegraph line to Superior traversed this canyon.
Ref.:   Craig. Map: GK-21.

## TIGER

El.: 3150'                               Loc.: Pinal 2, FG-9.9
The community at Tiger took its name from the mine.
P.O. est. March 15, 1939. Thomas Leo Chapman, Jr., p.m. Discont. November 26, 1954.
Ref.:   P.O. Records. Map: GK-18.

## TOLTEC

El.: 1504'                               Loc.: Pinal 1, FG-8.7
Pro.:  /tówltek/

This small community on the S.P.R.R. was named for pre-Aztec Indians. Frank Hamilton Cushing c. 1888 was among the first to make a scientific study of the Indians in the area of Casa Grande and, of course, Toltec. It was Cushing who classed the prehistoric Indians of that region with the Toltecs. Later investigations have demonstrated that the supposed relationship in fact did not exist.

P.O. est. June 24, 1892. Julia S. Fishback, p.m. Order rescinded August 24, 1892. P.O. re-established May 19, 1910. Discont. July 31, 1922.

Ref.:   153, 1-52. Maps: C-7; GK-27.

**a.n. Toltec Buttes**                                        Pinal
Loc.: N. of road, three low-lying hills, ½ mile w. of Toltec.

## TOM MIX WASH

El.: c. 2000'                            Loc.: Pinal 2, AB-8.4
The popular western star of cowboy pictures, Tom Mix (b. January 6, 1880; d. October 12, 1940) was killed when his car went out of control and turned over in this wash.
Ref.:   None. Map: GK-33.

## TORTILLA MOUNTAINS

El.: 4170'                               Loc.: Pinal 2, D-7.2
Pro.: /tortíyə/          Spanish: "omelet; pancake"

These mountains were so designated by Maj. William H. Emory in 1853. In 1872 Arch R. Marvine of the Wheeler expedition described the low scattered hills as having "occasional high table-topped buttes." He called the highest Tortilla Butte.

Ref.:   175, III, 224. Maps: C-2; E-18 (Sierra Tortillata); E-6 (Tortillata Mountains); E-2 (Sierra Tortilato); GK-2; GK-23; GK-30.

**a.n. Tortilla Creek**          Map: GK-29                Pinal

## TROY

El.: 3644'                               Loc.: Pinal 2, D-4.5

When this mining community first began to develop, it was known as Skinnerville, after a local resident. When it was taken over by the Troy-Manhattan Copper Mine, the name was changed. The owners of the company came from the places named in the company title.

P.O. est. August 5, 1901. Frank W. Hutchings, p.m. Discont. September 15, 1910.

Ref.:   Barnes. Maps: C-9; GD-13.

**a.n. Troy Mountain**          El.: 4910'. Maps: C-10; GD-13    Pinal

## TURNER

                                         Loc.: Pinal 1, I-1
The origin of this name has not yet been learned.
P.O. est. October 21, 1880. George Danforth, p.m. Discont. December 7, 1880.
Ref.:   P.O. Records. Map: A-2 (Directory for map only).

## TUSONIMO

El.: c. 1550'    Loc.: Pinal 1, D-7.8 (approximate).
Four leagues w. of Casa Grande ruins.
When Fr. Kino visited this Indian village in 1697, he found
it was called El Tusonimo, which he renamed La Encarnacion since he arrived there "to say mass on the first Sunday
in Advent." Lt. Juan Mateo Manje wrote that the town of
"Tucsonimon . . . is so named from a great heap of horns,
from the wild or sylvan sheep, which appears like a hill;
and from the number that there are of the animals, they
make the common subsistence of the inhabitants."
This is the place which later came to be known as Sacaton
(q.v.).
Ref.:  9. pp. 265-266; 19, I, 128; 88, II, 854; 86, p. 16; 20, p.
372. Map:None.

## VAIVA VO

El.: c. 1400'    Loc.: Pinal 1, BC-8.5
Pro.: /wàyva wów?/    Papago: "cocklebur charco"
Because of its meaning when translated, Vaiva Vo is some-
times referred to as Cocklebur. This place may correspond
to the San Angelo del Botum of Fr. Kino.
Ref.:  128, p. 16; Kirk Bryan Notes. Maps: C-12; D-8; D-11;
GK-33.

a.n. Vaiva Hills    Pinal

## VALLEY FARMS

El.: c. 1500'    Loc.: Pinal 1, H-6.3
Descriptive.
P.O. est. June 27, 1942. Ruth E. Wright, p.m.
Ref.:  P.O. Records. Map: GK-33.

## VEKOL MINE

El.: 3625'    Loc.: Pinal 1, B-11
Pima: "grandmother"
John D. Walker in 1864 organized a company composed
entirely of Pima Indians to help fight the Apaches. Walker
remained among the Pimas as a trader and established his
residence near them, learning their language and becoming
their close friend. The Pimas told him about the existence
of an old Indian silver mine which they themselves probably called Vekol (references examined not clear on this
point). Walker told his friend Peter R. Brady in Florence
about the existence of the mine, which Walker had not
seen. This displeased the Indians, who refused to show the
latter the location—if he were accompanied by anyone other
than his own brother. Walker promised to keep the secret,
and his brother, he and the Indians went at night secretly
to find the mine. However, Brady followed them and put
in his appearance almost at the moment of the Indians'
revealing the location of the rich mine. Walker thereupon
admitted Brady to part ownership. This was in 1880. In
1883 the three men—Peter R. Brady, Lucien E. Walker and
John D. Walker—were offered $150,000 for the mine, but
they did not sell.
By 1886 a mining community of about thirty families
had developed. It was unique in that it contained no saloons. By 1912 the settlement and mine were abandoned.

P.O. est. September 25, 1888. William T. Day, p.m. Discont.
October 30, 1909.
Ref.:  104, pp. 82-83; 153, pp. 36-37; APHS Files; *Arizona
Journal Miner*, October 1, 1908, 3:3; Kirk Bryan Notes.
Maps: C-7; GG-17.

a.n. Walker Butte    El.: 1988'. Maps: E-20; GK-25    Pinal
Up until at least 1879 the name for this butte was Cheene
(Pro.: /čiýniy/ Pima: "bird beak"), a descriptive name for
a sharp peak located on this butte.
Ref.:  Barnes.

Vekol Mountains    Map: GG-17    Pinal
v.n. Bitter Well Mountains
a.n. Vekol Valley    Map: GK-1    Maricopa
Vekol Wash    Map: GK-1    Pinal and Maricopa

## WEAVER'S NEEDLE

El.: 4535'    Loc.: Pinal 1, H-1.4
It is thought, but has not been definitely proved, that
Weaver's Needle is named for the scout Pauline Weaver.
On the other hand, the rock looks like a needle formerly
used by weavers.
Weaver's Needle figures in several legends about the Lost
Dutchman Mine in the Superstition Mountains. The needle
is said to be a landmark pointing the way to the mine,
which has never been found.
The folklore connected with the Lost Dutchman Mine is
nearly endless. Typical is the legend concerning a Mexican
lover who, while fleeing from his sweetheart's angry father,
took refuge in the Superstition Mountains where he found
an immense gold deposit. He returned to his home in Mexico and in order to take advantage of the mine before the
land became a part of the United States through the Gadsden Purchase, the young man led his entire community
north to the Superstitions. Every member of the party is
said to have loaded himself with gold and then set out
for Mexico. Apaches ambushed and killed the entire party,
said to have numbered four hundred men, with the exception of two small boys. These children grew to manhood retaining the secret of the mine. With a third partner
they returned to the mine, but had barely begun to dig
when a Dutchman with a long white beard appeared. They
made the mistake of telling him about the mine, whereupon he murdered the young men. This was in 1870.
In the ensuing years many people attempted to trail the
Dutchman to his mine. None succeeded, and at least eight
are reputed to have died at the prospector's hands. He
himself died c. 1884 without revealing the secret of his
mine except to one neighbor. The neighbor was unable to
follow the directions and the Lost Dutchman Mine earned
its name.
Ref.:  4, pp. 163-164; Barnes; Willson. Maps: E-18; E-20; GK-
10.

## WHITE HORSE PASS

El.: c. 2000'    Loc.: Pinal 1, D-10. T: 8 S., R. 5 E.
in Silver Reef Mts.
Near the pass is a white rock formation like a horse's
head.
Ref.:  Barnes. Map: None.

## WHITLOW CANYON

El.: c. 3000'                    Loc.: Pima 2, A-2-3
Charles Whitlow had a ranch at the head of this canyon where he raised cattle and had a stage station.
Ref.:   Barnes. Map: GK-10.

## WYMOLA

El.: 1775'                    Loc.: Pinal 1, HI-10.3
The railroad siding at Wymola was one of the first places to be named on the S.P.R.R. in 1881. The origin of the name has not been ascertained.
Ref.:   Barnes. Maps: C-12 (Wynola); C-13; GK-24.

## YOUNGBERG

El.: c. 1500'                    Loc.: Pinal 1, G-1.4
Youngberg was named for George U. Young, secretary of Arizona Territory, 1909-1910. The place served as a post office for the Goldfield Mine, which until 1898 had its own post office.
P.O. est. June 8, 1921. Rolla W. Walling, p.m. Discont. October 30, 1926.
Ref.:   Barnes; P.O. Records. Map: F-3.

## ZELWEGER

El.: c. 2400'                    Loc.: Pinal 2, BC-5.1
John Zelweger, Sr., was a cattleman in this area.
Ref.:   Barnes. Map: C-10.

# SANTA CRUZ COUNTY

*Old-time mining — Spanish arrastra — bringing up ore with windlass — the Mowry Mine.*

## SANTA CRUZ COUNTY:

Pro.: /sántə cruwz/ or /sǽntə cruwz/

On March 15, 1899, the smallest of Arizona's counties was created out of parts of Pima and Cochise Counties. It was Santa Cruz County, with Nogales as its seat of government. Names which had been proposed for the new county included Papago County and Grant County, but both were set aside in favor of the name taken from that of the Santa Cruz River, which traverses the county. The area of the county is 797,240 acres.

Historically, Santa Cruz County is interesting, for it encompasses early explorations and missionizing by the Spaniards as well as later explorations by Americans in the mid-nineteenth century. Emigrants hustling to the West Coast during the California gold rush left their imprint on the future Santa Cruz County. Its story is replete with tales of mining and of Apache warfare.

Santa Cruz County counts agriculture and mining among its industries. Its county seat, Nogales, is the major Arizona port of entry from Mexico.

## ALISO SPRING

El.: c. 4000'  Loc.: Santa Cruz CE-2.3
Pro.: /alí'so/  Spanish: "alder tree"
Descriptive. This spring is capable of handling from three hundred to four hundred and fifty head of stock.

Ref.: 26, p. 417. Map: B-3.

## ALTO

El.: 4650'  Loc.: Santa Cruz F-2
Spanish: "high"
The post office for the Alto Mine was located where mining discoveries had been made c. 1687. Mines here were worked by Spaniards and Mexicans until about 1857 when Apaches drove out everyone in this area. Alto came back to life again in 1875 as the Gold Tree Mine owned by Mark Lully, who sold it c. 1880. It was then known as the El Plomo Mine. The hill on which the mine was located was called El Plomo by the early Spaniards because the deposits contained lead (plomo: "heavy"). It is not known when the name was changed to Alto. There was a ranch here in 1955.

P.O. est. March 6, 1907. A. W. Larson, p.m. Rescinded June 10, 1907. Re-est. June 6, 1912. Minnie A. Bond, p.m. Discont. December 30, 1933.

Ref.: 138a, pp. 196, 197, 198; P.O. Records. Maps: C-12; C-14; GL-1.

**a.n. Alto Gulch**  Santa Cruz

## ALUM CANYON

El.: c. 4000'  Loc.: Santa Cruz F-3
Alum Canyon is so named because water in the creek which flows through the canyon contains alum that imparts a bitter taste to the water. At La Jarilla Mine in the canyon is a crude adobe smelter similar to those used by early Mexican and American miners to extract metals from ores. At one time there was an Alum Mine (in the 1850's) which had apparently brilliant prospects as a producer, but these were dissipated by the Civil War and by Apache depredations.

**v.n. Alum Gulch**

Ref.: 138a, pp. 22-23. Maps: GL-2; GL-3.

## AMADO

El.: 2885'  Loc.: Santa Cruz D-1
Pro.: /əmádo/
In 1910 Manuel H. Amado established a store and post office at a station on the Tucson-Nogales branch of the S.P.R.R. The Amado family had long been active in southern Arizona.

P.O. est. as Amadoville, June 17, 1910. Manuel H. Amado, p.m. Name changed to Amado, February 27, 1920. Discont. March 7, 1958.

Ref.: Barnes; APHS Files. Maps: C-11; C-12; GL-5.

## AMERICAN PEAK

El.: 5241'  Loc.: Santa Cruz G-3.5
American Peak was named for the American Mine, a mile and a half to the southwest of Harshaw (q.v.). The mine was discovered c. 1880. It produced more than $80,-000 in ore.

Ref.: 138a, pp. 256-277. Maps: B-3; GL-2.

## ASHBURN MOUNTAIN

El.: c. 5000'  Loc.: Santa Cruz GH-3
Oscar F. Ashburn (d. 1924), Walter Vail and Gates owned the Monkey Springs Ranch bought from Rollen R. Richardson. During Vail and Ashburn's ownership, the ranch was referred to as the Ashburn Ranch (cf., Hughes Mountain, Santa Cruz). Patagonia (q.v.) is on the old Ashburn homestead.

Ref.: Lenon; APHS Files. Map: B-3.

## ATASCOSA MOUNTAINS

El.: c. 5000'  Loc.: Santa Cruz C-4
Pro.: /atəskósə/  Spanish: atasco, "an obstruction to passage"
In 1854 Lt. N. Michler of the Boundary Survey Commission wrote that the Sierra Atascosa was said to be rich in minerals. He also noted that the name meant "miry," but that to his eyes it looked like an "upheaved, boiling, volcanic pool." From their eastern face the Atascosa Mountains form such an abrupt barrier that the descriptive nature of the name seems self-evident.

Ref.: 51, pp. 119, 68. Map: GL-4.

**a.n. Atascosa Canyon**  Map: GL-4  Santa Cruz
**Atascosa Peak**  El.: 5440'. Maps: E-20; GL-4  Santa Cruz
**Atascosa Spring**  Loc.: Sec. 24, T. 23 S., R. 11 E.  Santa Cruz

## AZTEC

El.: 4850'  Loc.: Santa Cruz F-3
Aztec was the post office for the Aztec mining prospect where there was also a mill.

P.O. est. December 6, 1878. Christian Foster, p.m. Discont. June 6, 1883.

Ref.: Barnes; Lenon; 138a, p. 263. Maps: A-2; E-20 (Aztec Mill).

**a.n. Aztec Gulch**  Santa Cruz

## BACA FLOAT NO. 3

El.: c. 4000'  Loc.: Santa Cruz DF-3-5
Pro.: /bákə/
The correct name for this twelve-mile-square area is the Luis Maria Baca Land Grant No. 3. Luis Maria Cabeza de Baca was a lineal descendant of Alvarado Cabeza de Vaca, to whom the King of Spain granted a large tract of land in what is now New Mexico. The fact that others later settled on this land led to disputes which the United States Court of Private Land Claims undertook to settle. The land was, as a matter of fact, occupied by the city of Las Vegas, New Mexico. A compromise was reached whereby Luis Maria de Baca was permitted to select out of the public domain five separate areas consisting of 100,-000 acres each.

The original Baca Float Grants were made by Act of Congress on June 21, 1860. The third area selected by de Baca, Baca Float No. 3, was located incorrectly by surveyors in 1866 to the northeast of where it should have been. When the error was later discovered and the Float relocated, it overlapped several other grants which court action had already confirmed in Santa Cruz County. Lengthy litigation ended in the Supreme Court where the cases were settled in favor of Baca's heirs. It was many, many years before matters were finally settled satisfactorily. Meanwhile, the rich land went largely unsettled because of the insecurity of land titles. When the case was resolved, rapid development of this part of the Santa Cruz Valley was assured. Baca Float No. 5 is in Yavapai County, as is also No. 2 (identical with Red Butte, Yavapai County).

Ref.: Lenon; Glannon; 124, pp. 371-72. Maps: B-3; C-9.

## BELLOTA CANYON

El.: c. 4500'                                   Loc.: Santa Cruz CD-4
Pro.: /beyótə/                          Spanish: bellota, "acorn"
Acorns are found in this canyon.

Ref.: Seibold. Map: GL-4.

**a.n. Bellota Spring**          Map: B-3              Santa Cruz
**Tres Bellotas**                                           Santa Cruz
    Spanish: "three acorns," referring to the tree rather than to the nuts themselves.

    **Tres Bellotas Canyon**       Map: GJ-7            Santa Cruz
    This is a stock watering place on the Mexican boundary ten miles east of Sasabe, where there are two wells about a mile apart. Mexicans collect the nuts, which are entirely edible.

Ref.: Glannon; Lenon; 26, p. 428.

## BENEDICT, MOUNT

El.: c. 4000'                                     Loc.: Santa Cruz E-4
In 1872 on John Benedict's ranch two men were discovered murdered by Indians.

An early name for this mountain was Helmet Mountain (descriptive).

Ref.: Lenon; *Arizona Citizen,* August 24, 1872, 2:4. Maps: C-10; GL-2.

## BISCUIT MOUNTAIN

El.: c. 4000'                                     Loc.: Santa Cruz I-1
The top of this mountain looks very much like a folded-over (Parker House) roll.

Ref.: Lenon. Map: GL-1.

## BLOXTON

El.: c. 4000'                                     Loc.: Santa Cruz F-3
This station on the Benson-Nogales branch of the S.P.R.R. was named by Denton G. Sanford (across whose ranch the railroad ran) for Robert V. Bloxton, his brother-in-law. Bloxton ran sheep in this vicinity in 1881. The siding was used as late as 1915 for loading ore from the 3-R Mine. Sanford's ranch is now the Circle Z Ranch.

Ref.: APHS Files. Map: GL-6.

**a.n. Circle Z Mountain**   Loc.: At the Circle Z Ranch   Santa Cruz
**v.n. Bloxton, Mount**
Ref.: Seibold.

## BOND CANYON

El.: c. 5200'                                   Loc.: Santa Cruz EF-2.5
Bond Canyon was named for Josiah Bond, a mining engineer who c. 1910 relocated the mines at Alto Canyon, where his wife served as postmistress.

Ref.: Lenon; 138a, p. 207. Map: GL-1.

## BRUCE, MOUNT

El.: c. 6000'                                     Loc.: Santa Cruz HI-1
Charles M. Bruce, manager for the Babocomari Cattle Company, had headquarters near the base of this mountain. He served in 1893 as Secretary for Arizona Territory. This mountain was named for him prior to 1899 by the Pima County Board of Supervisors. A bronze tablet was erected on the north face of Mount Bruce c. 1913.

Ref.: Barnes; APHS Names File. Map: C-12.

**a.n. Bruce Canyon**          Map: C-12               Santa Cruz
    The old Indian trail into Mexico ran along this canyon, at the mouth of which Bruce had his headquarters.

Ref.: APHS Files.

## BUCHANAN, FORT

El.: c. 5000'                                    Loc.: Santa Cruz G-1.6
Troops which had been sent to Tucson in the late fall of 1856 remained only long enough to receive orders to establish a camp near what is today Patagonia. In November 1856, Maj. Enoch Steen completed the formal establishment of what was known as Camp Moore. It is possible that this was named for Lt. I. N. Moore, who was in charge of a company of infantry.

The name was changed on November 17 to Fort Buchanan to honor James Buchanan, then President of the United States. It is significant that the postmaster for this location was Elias Brevoort. At that time Tucson was a small and unimportant location, and it would seem that the post office established as "Tucson" on December 4, 1856, moved with the troops in November to the new location, particularly since Brevoort came from New Mexico specifically to be a sutler for the troops. The name "Tucson" for the post office was changed to Fort Buchanan on June 5, 1857, with Elias Brevoort remaining as postmaster. The delay is not surprising, considering slowness of communication, the dragging tendency of red tape and the vast distance between Washington and Arizona.

Southern Arizona was noted for its sympathy with the developing Confederate cause. In the late 1850's, the Secretary of War for the United States pursued a policy throughout the nation of placing as many stores as possible where they might conceivably fall into Southern hands at a later date. Fort Buchanan became the depository of more than a million dollars in military supplies, the plan being to have them seized by the Confederate Column which was to march from Texas to lay hands on the rich silver mines of Arizona and the gold of California. The Confederate plans were not destined to be fulfilled. The first step toward closing Fort Buchanan occurred with the abandonment of its post office on October 21, 1860. Early in July 1861, Moore—now a captain—received orders from the headquarters of the Department of New Mexico to burn Fort Breckenridge and then Fort Buchanan. On July 21, 1861, under the command of Lt. Richard Lord, Fort Buchanan was completely destroyed.

P.O. est. as Tucson, December 4, 1856. Elias Brevoort, p.m. Name changed to Fort Buchanan, July 5, 1857. Discont. October 21, 1860.

Ref.: 85, pp. 483, 525; 111, p. 150; Richard S. C. Lord, Lt., APHS File; 75, p. 126; P.O. Records. Maps: C-1; E-11; E-17; GL-3.

## BUENA VISTA LAND GRANT

El.: c. 4000'                      Loc.: Santa Cruz EF-5
Pro.: /bwéynə víystə/        Spanish: "good view"
This Mexican land grant was made on October 24, 1831, to Doña Josefa Morales. It consisted of 18,640 acres and was known as the Maria Santissima del Carmen Land Grant. Following the Gadsden Purchase, the United States Land Grant Court confirmed 7,128 acres of the grant to men named Maish and Driscoll.

Ref.: Barnes; 55, p. 428. Maps: C-12; C-5; GL-2.

## CALABASAS

El.: c. 3400'                      Loc.: Santa Cruz DE-3.6
Pro.: /kǽləbǽsəs/ or /káləbasəs/    Spanish: "calabashes"
When Fr. Kino was in southern Arizona in the late 1600's, there was a Sobaipuri rancheria at this location. It shows as San Gaetan on the 1701 Kino map; another name for it was San Cayetano de Calabazas. Until 1784 it was a *visita* of Guevavi (q.v.). Here in 1797 were erected a church and house for the priest. From 1784 to 1797, Calabasas was probably a *visita* of Tubac.

Sometime between 1797 and 1828, Calabasas became a ranch. By 1851 the hacienda was in ruins, according to Commissioner Bartlett of the United States Boundary Survey party. Bartlett conjectured that the place was named Calabasas because of the number of wild gourds in the valley. Apparently the old Rancho de la Calabasas was at one time prior to 1853 the property of Gov. Gandara of Sonora, Mexico, and later it was used as a Mexican military post, convenient for troops because the ranch was on the main road from Hermosillo, Mexico, to the interior of Arizona.

Another possible origin of the name is that given by Reid, who on February 8, 1857, attributed the name to an old yellow adobe house on the right bank of the Santa Cruz River at its juncture with Sonoita Creek.

In 1856 United States First Dragoons were quartered at the old Calabasas ranch. The troops stayed until 1858, with Maj. Enoch Steen commanding. For a while thereafter Calabasas was deserted, but it came back to life following the Civil War when in 1864 Fort Mason (cf. Fort McKee) was established. Troops were again withdrawn in 1866 and Calabasas dozed into somnolence. The sleeping ended when it was rumored the railroad planned to put a branch to Mexico and that it would pass through Calabasas. There were those who firmly believed that Calabasas would boom as the port of entry, and the rush was on. The finest brick hotel in the territory was built. A tent city sprang up overnight. Before long, the tents were folded and silently stolen away when the railroad chose to make Nogales its point of entry.

The name survives in the Calabasas School District.

P.O. est. as Calabazas, October 18, 1866. Edward N. Fish, p.m. Discont. August 31, 1868. Re-est. April 26, 1880. Discont. August 15, 1913. Wells Fargo Station, 1885.

Ref.: 88, I, 187; Lenon; 105, pp. 341-342; 23, pp. 327, 328. Maps: C-1; E-20; GL-2.

a.n. **Calabasas Canyon**          Map: GL-4          Santa Cruz
**San Cayetano Mountains**                          Santa Cruz
El.: c. 6000'. Map: GL-3.

v.n. **San Coyotano Range** (Hinton)
**Arroyo de San Geyetano**
Loc.: 5 miles s. of Tubac; so called in 1866.
Ref.: 52, IV, 132.

**Calabazas P.O.** (Kitchen Ranch)                   Santa Cruz
GLO 1869 shows two places by the name Calabasas. One of these is the location of the Calabasas discussed above. The other is the Peter Kitchen Ranch (q.v.). It was unquestionably this post office which was established as Calabazas on June 11, 1873, Peter Kitchen, p.m. In 1878, John A. Rockfellow was seeking payment for ore sent to San Francisco. There was a pack of mail waiting for him at the post office called Monument on the Benedict Ranch. In it was the long awaited draft in payment for the ore.

Ref.: 140, p. 26. Map: C-4 (Monument).

## CALERA CANYON

El.: c. 3500'                      Loc.: Santa Cruz C-1
Pro.: /kalérə/                 Spanish: "lime"
There is a lime kiln in this canyon.

v.n. **Calera Draw**
**Lime Kiln Canyon**
Ref.: Lenon. Map: GL-5.

## CAMERON, CAMP

El.: c. 4000'                      Loc.: Santa Cruz D-1.5
When Calabasas (q.v.) was found to be an unhealthy site for the further housing of troops, Camp Cameron was established on October 1, 1866, sixteen miles east and northeast of Calabasas. The post was abandoned on March 7, 1867. Camp Cameron was named for Simon Cameron, Secretary of War under President Lincoln and an uncle of the Cameron brothers who became prominent cattle raisers in the San Rafael Valley, 1882-1890.

Ref.: Barnes; 75, p. 127; 85, p. 45; John S. Billings, *A Report of Barracks and Hospitals with Description of Military Posts,* Washington, D. C.: Government Printing Office, 1870, p. 473. Maps: C-5; E-18.

## CAMERON PASS

El.: c. 6000'                      Loc.: Santa Cruz I-3
This place was named for Colin and Brewster Cameron, noted cattle raisers in the San Rafael Valley from 1882 to 1890.

Ref.: Barnes. Map: C-11.

## CANELO HILLS

El.: c. 6000'                      Loc.: Santa Cruz GH-2-3
Pro.: /kəníʼlo/ or /kənélo/    Spanish: "cinnamon"
No documentary evidence has as yet been uncovered to trace the name of the Canelo Hills to a date earlier than GLO 1896, when they first appear as the Canille Mountains. Maps for the period of the Gadsden Purchase apply

the name Sierra de la Santa Cruz to what was probably later divided into the Patagonia Mountains and the Canelo Hills. The earlier name in all likelihood came from the community of Santa Cruz just below the border in Sonora. From 1896 the Canelo Hills disappear from maps until GLO 1909. The name is descriptive of the fact that the hills have a light brown color not unlike that of cinnamon.

Ref.:   G. E. P. Smith, Letter to Board on Geographic Names, July 16, 1941; APHS Names File. Maps: C-8; GB-13; GL-3.

**a.n. Canelo**              Map: C-12              Santa Cruz
    This is a small community store today.
P.O. est. as Canille, August 22, 1904. Robert A. Rodgers, p.m. Discont. April 10, 1924.

**Canelo Pass**          Map: GL-2              Santa Cruz

## CARMEN

El.: c. 3800'                    Loc.: Santa Cruz CD-2-3
In November 1918 Mrs. Carmen Zepeda set up a trading store and homesteaded about three hundred acres here. She was the sole resident at what has since developed into a small community named for her.

Ref.:   Mrs. Carmen Zepeda. Maps: B-3; C-11.

## CHIMINEA MOUNTAIN

El.: c. 4000'                    Loc.: Santa Cruz B-3.5
Pro.: /čímǝnèyǝ/                Spanish: "chimney"
Descriptive of type of out-crop. "Chimney" is a mining term.

Ref.:   Barnes; Lenon. Map: B-3.

**a.n. Chimney Canyon**      Maps: GJ-2; GL-4; GL-5      Santa Cruz

## COMMISSION

El.: 4000'                      Loc.: Santa Cruz H-4
In 1864, a French mining engineer named F. Biertu reported that there were fifteen houses at the village called Commission. The community was the center for workers in the old Mowry mine about a mile distant. It is worth noting that the Mowry settlement had two locations, the other being on Mowry Wash.

Ref.:   Hayes; 118, pp. 74, 75. Map: None.

## CRITTENDEN, FORT

El.: c. 5000'                    Loc.: Santa Cruz G-1.6
The fact that Camp Crittenden was constructed on a hill overlooking the site of abandoned Fort Buchanan (q.v.) has led many to confuse the two posts. In his annual report, Gen. Irvin McDowell on September 14, 1867, reported that "General Crittenden has recommended the building of a permanent camp near the site of old Fort Buchanan, where there are many adobes, made before the war and which can be used in new buildings. When built, the post at Tubac will be discontinued." McDowell was referring to Gen. Thomas Leonidas Crittenden, 32nd Infantry, who had served as a general of volunteers during the Civil War. He was breveted a brigadier general of the regular forces on March 2, 1867, and served as military commander for southern Arizona 1867-1868. The new camp, named for Crittenden, was established on March 4, 1867. On June 8, 1872, it was announced that Camp Crittenden was to be

abandoned because of unhealthy conditions. Three weeks later a newspaper article stated that the camp was in the process of breaking up.

Ref.:   52, V, 251; 85, p. 339; *Weekly Arizona Miner,* June 8, 1872, 2:1, June 29, 1879, 2:1; 75, p. 130. Maps: C-3; E-20; GL-3.

**a.n. Crittenden**          Maps: C-6; GL-3          Santa Cruz
Casa Blanca, Spanish: "white house," the earliest known name for this location, is recorded in the field notes of T. F. White, a surveyor, in late 1876, under a notation, "Casa Blanca, an adobe." This would indicate that the name is descriptive, although White said nothing further. Casa Blanca was in existence as early as 1860 when it had a post office. In January 1866, some Mexicans set up a mescal factory here, but were stolen out of business. Two members having been killed, the others abandoned the project.
The proximity of this place to Fort Crittenden underwrote its existence as a community. The census of 1870 reported fifty-two residents in Casa Blanca. Meanwhile the abandoned post office was reopened in 1873 and, as was customary, under the new name of Crittenden. The year coincides fairly closely with the abandonment of Fort Crittenden (see above). In the late 1890's Rollen R. Richardson (who owned the land) moved the trading post, the town, and the railroad station to what is now Patagonia (q.v.). The station had in former years been important to the Harshaw and Mowry Mines. There had also been a mill at Crittenden in the late 1870's.
P.O. est. as Casa Blanca, January 12, 1860. Thomas Hughes, p.m. Discont. October 9, 1861. Re-est. as Crittenden, June 11 1873. Thomas Hughes, p.m. Name changed to Casa Blanco (sic) April 27, 1882. Name changed to Crittenden, July 26, 1882. Discont. January 23, 1901. Wells Fargo Station, 1885.

Ref.:   Lenon; Seibold; P.O. Records; *Arizona Mining Index,* May 31, 1843, 3:2; 52, IV, 130-131; 87, p. 43; 138a, p. 239.

**a.n. Casa Blanca Canyon**      Map: GL-3          Santa Cruz
**Casa Blanca Creek**    Loc.: T. 21 S., R. 16 E.    Santa Cruz
**v.n. Josephine Creek**

## DEVIL'S CASH BOX

El.: 3500'                      Loc.: Santa Cruz D-2
The mineral deposits found in this mile-long ridge are said to have given it the name of Devil's Cash Box. This may be a corruption of Devil's Cache.

Ref.:   Lenon; 138a, p. 185. Map: GL-1.

**a.n. Devil's Throne**    Loc.: Near Devil's Cache    Santa Cruz
This formation looks like an over-stuffed chair with a horseshoe-shaped "back" of rolling land lying around a flat piece of ground which forms the "seat."

Ref.:   Lenon.

## ELGIN

El.: 4710'                      Loc.: Santa Cruz HI-1.6
It has been suggested that the home town of the local storekeeper was Elgin, Illinois.

P.O. est. February 12, 1910. Reuben C. Collie, p.m.

Ref.:   Seibold; Lenon. Map: C-10.

## ENREQUITA

El.: c. 4000'                    Loc.: Santa Cruz AB-4.3
                                Spanish: "Harriet"
The origin of this name has not yet been learned.

P.O. est. May 7, 1866. Charles H. Lord, p.m. Discont. June 24, 1867.

Ref.:   Barnes; P.O. Records. Map: E-20.

## FRAGUITA, MOUNT

El.: c. 5000'                    Loc.: Santa Cruz A-3
Pro.: /frəgíytə/                    Spanish: "forge"
The first name for this mountain was Roddick Mountain, named for Thomas G. Roddick (b. Ohio 1836; d. June 1879). Roddick went to California during the gold rush days and came to Arizona in 1865. In 1874 he was living in the Oro Blanco Mining District where he was co-owner of the Yellow Jacket Mine. At the time of his death, he had a half interest in the Sahuarita Ranch.

At a later date a forge was found on this mountain. This resulted in its current name.

Ref.:   Thomas G. Roddick File, APHS; APHS Names File; Barnes. Maps: B-3; C-13.
**a.n. Fraguita Wash**          Map: GJ-2                    Pima

## GARDNER CANYON

El.: 5500'                       Loc.: Santa Cruz EF-1
One of the early pioneers in what is now Santa Cruz County was Thomas Gardner (b. Buffalo, New York, April 13, 1820; d. March 26, 1909). Gardner came to Arizona in 1859. For a time he had cattle near what is now Lochiel, but after 1867 moved his herd close to the present day Patagonia where he remained until 1872. In that year he established his Apache Spring Ranch about forty miles south of Tucson in the foothills of the Santa Ritas, where he remained until 1896.

Ref.:   Thomas Gardner File, APHS; Reminiscences of Mrs. Mary Gardner Kane, APHS. Map: GL-3.

## GLENCOE

El.: 4000'                       Loc.: Santa Cruz H-5
The origin of this name has not been learned.

P.O. est. January 12, 1889. Lauretta A. Reppy, p.m. Discont. September 13, 1890.
Ref.:   P.O. Records. Map: None.

## GROSVENOR PEAK

El.: 5000'                       Loc.: Santa Cruz EF-2.6
In 1861 H. C. Grosvenor (b. Ohio, 1820), manager of the Santa Rita Mine, was killed by Apaches. Grosvenor Peak does not appear on maps examined, but on GLO 1921 the name Josephine Peak seems to be in the position which was probably occupied by the older Grosvenor Peak. However, the name has survived in Grosvenor Hills (Map: GL-3).

Ref.:   87, p. 190. Map: None.

## GUAJOLOTE FLAT

El.: 5800'                       Loc.: Santa Cruz FG-4.5
Pro.: /wahalówtey/                    Spanish: "turkey"
This flat was named for the old Guajolote Mine, located here in 1880. It was then called the "old lode."

Ref.:   Seibold; 138a, p. 294; T. R. Sorin, *Handbook of Tucson and Surroundings* (1880), p. 20, Map: GL-2.
**a.n. Guajolote Wash**     Loc.: Drains Guajolote Flat     Santa Cruz

## GUEVAVI

El.: c. 4000'                    Loc.: Santa Cruz E-4.4
Pro.: /wevávi^/ or /gwevávе/
The first Spanish mission to be established in what became Arizona was that at Guevavi. In January 1691, Fr. Kino wrote of visiting this rancheria and remaining five days to baptize infants and adults, thereafter returning to Cocospera, Sonora. At Guevavi Kino founded the mission Los Angeles de Guevavi, typical of the establishments which the Spanish Jesuits created to help Christianize the Indians in a practical way. Kino noted in his diary on April 24, 1700, that there were eighty-four sheep and goats, a field of wheat, maize and beans, and an adobe house for the priest, whom the natives were looking forward to welcoming. In 1701 the priest came in the person of Fr. Juan de San Martin to found a mission which had Tumacacori (q.v.) and Bacoancos as *visitas*. (Bacoancos is Buena Vista, q.v.) A church was soon constructed—a small one at first, later replaced by a larger structure. Guevavi endured as a mission for many years. In 1763 Fr. Ignatius Pfeffercorn was its priest, having under his care the *visitas* of Sonoitac, Calabazas, Tumacacori, and Arivaca. The mission at Guevavi, with other church establishments, had been plundered by Indians in 1750, but was reoccupied in 1752. While Pfeffercorn was its priest, Guevavi had a hundred and eleven Indians on its premises. It was abandoned prior to 1784 when Tumacacori became the head mission for the area.

Its days as a mission had ended, but Guevavi later became the site of a ranch and is still one. Here in 1856 during an Apache attack the owner, Rafael Saavedra, lost his life in the valiant rescue of a woman whom the Indians had seized.

Very little remains of Guevavi Mission today. Fortunately, its present owners have recognized the value of the slight traces and have fenced them for protection against depredations by vandals.

**v.n. Guebavi**
   **Gusubac** (Rudo Ensayo, 1763)
   This is a Pima name meaning "great water."

   **San Felipe de Jesus Guevavi**
   **San Miguel de Jesus Guevavi** (Jesuit name after 1782)
   **San Rafael** (Jesuit name)
   **Santos Angeles** (Franciscan name)
   **San Luis Guebavi** (Venegas, 1759)
   **Huavabi Ranch**

Ref.:   Jones; Lenon; Glannon; 20, pp. 265, 512; 105, p. 35; 145, pp. 18, 45; 35, p. 257, (Note 1); 72, p. 110; 88, I, 511; 7, pp. 384, 385; 52, IV, 131. Map: E-17 (Guebavi).
**a.n. Guebabi Canyon**          Map: GL-2                    Santa Cruz

## HARDSHELL

El.: 5150'                       Loc.: Santa Cruz G-3.8
The post office for the Hardshell Mine was about a mile south-southwest of Harshaw (q.v.) in Hardshell Gulch where ore was discovered in 1879 by Jose Andrade and David Harshaw. It was bought in 1880 by Rollen R. Richardson.

P.O. est. January 21, 1901. John C. Smith, p.m. Discont.?
Ref.:   138a, p. 269. Map: GL-2.

## HARSHAW

El.: c. 5000'                                    Loc.: Santa Cruz G-3.75
In December 1873, David Tecumseh Harshaw was a cattle-
man in the San Pedro Valley where his cattle were roaming
over the Chiricahua Indians' range. Indian Agent Thomas
J. Jeffords asked Harshaw to remove his stock. Harshaw
moved over into what is now Santa Cruz County at a location which the Mexicans then called and still call Dur-
asno because of peach trees in the area. Here Harshaw
located and developed mines. By 1880 there was a lively
mining camp with several stores at Harshaw, but mining
activity gradually died out and by 1909 there were only a
few families still living in the once prosperous village.
P.O. est. April 29, 1880. Dan B. Gillette, Jr., p.m. Discont.
February 28, 1903.
Ref.: Lenon; 76, p. 32; 138a, p. 246; *Arizona Citizen*, December 30, 1873, 3:3. Maps: B-3; C-5; GL-2.

a.n. Harshaw Creek          Maps: GL-2; GL-3          Santa Cruz
    The importance of Harshaw was due largely to the exist-
    ence of the Hermosa Mine three-fourths of a mile south
    and southeast of the Harshaw Mine. This mine was first
    located in 1877 and was sold c. 1879 to the Hermosa Min-
    ing Company of New York, which built a twenty-stamp
    mill at Harshaw. The mill was in operation until 1881. In
    1887 the company sold the mine to James Finley of Tucson
    for $600. Finley died c. 1903 and work ceased at the mine.
Ref.: 133a, p. 272.

a.n. Hermosa Hill                                    Santa Cruz
    Hermoso Hill            Map: GL-2                Santa Cruz
    Hermoso Canyon         Map: GL-2                Santa Cruz

## HOPKINS, MOUNT

El.: 8572'                                    Loc.: Santa Cruz EF-1.25
Gilbert W. Hopkins (b. New York, 1830; d. March 1,
1865) was a young mining engineer for the Santa Rita
Mining Company. Hopkins first came to Arizona in 1859.
He served as a member of the territorial legislature and
as superintendent of the Maricopa Copper Mines prior to
coming to the Santa Ritas, where in 1865 he was killed
by Apaches.
Ref.: 87, p. 190; Gilbert W. Hopkins File, APHS. Maps: C-8;
    GL-3.

## HUGHES MOUNTAIN

El.: c. 5000'                                    Loc.: Santa Cruz G-1.8
In 1867 Thomas Hughes started a ranch near Fort Crittenden at the base of a high ridge known today as Hughes
Mountain. Between 1867 and 1876, the Apaches killed
twenty-two men on the Hughes ranch. During one attack
in March 1874, the Indians went so far as to seize the
ranch itself. Hughes, away at the time, crept back after
nightfall and successfully liberated about one hundred
hogs to prevent their slaughter by the Indians.
Hughes Ranch has had several names. The first name for
it was Cuevacita (Spanish: "little cave") because of a
number of caves near a spring on the property. This name
was given to it by a Spanish-American named Apodaca,
who owned the ranch in partnership with "Frenchie" Laz-
zard. Hughes was said to have had a half-wit working for
him, and the cowboys joshingly said that Hughes had

bought a monkey and was training him to be a cowboy.
This may be the origin of the name Monkey Springs Ranch
which Asburn and Vail used when they bought the ranch
from its second owner. However, there is a Monkey Springs
shown on the 1875 map of *Arizona As It Is*.
No documentary evidence has been uncovered to indicate
that the name Monkey Springs is a corruption of the name
of Fr. Kino's lieutenant, Juan Mateo Manje. When Rollen
R. Richardson bought the ranch in 1883, he named it the
Pennsylvania Ranch for his native state.
Ref.: Mary Gardner Kane File, APHS; Barnes; Thomas
    Gardner File, APHS; Rollen R. Richardson File, APHS;
    111, p. 201; 55, p. 467. Maps: A-2 (Monkey Springs);
    GL-1; GL-3; GL-6.

a.n. Monkey Canyon          Map: GL-3          Santa Cruz

## JOSEPHINE PEAK

El.: 8435'                                    Loc.: Santa Cruz EF-1.5
George Roskruge, who did much surveying in southern
Arizona in the early 1890's, named this peak for Josephine
Pennington, one of the four daughters of Jim Pennington.
Elias Green Pennington and his family of twelve mother-
less children arrived at old Fort Buchanan in June 1857.
The family was in dire straits, completely tired out by their
long journey, and it was at this point that they dropped
out of the emigrant train which was headed for California.
Larcena Pennington was seriously ill, and while waiting
for her to recover, the father and his two sons (Jim and
Jack) contracted to deliver wild hay to the fort. Larcena
recovered and in December 1858 married John Hempstead
Page of Tucson (cf. Madera Canyon). She was the only
member of the family to remain in Arizona.
The Pennington family moved often during their stay in
southern Arizona. In 1860 they had a stone house near
the Mexican border. In 1869 they were living at Tubac.
Apaches killed Jim Pennington and his son, Green Pen-
nington. The remaining members of the family moved to
Tucson, but soon the elder Pennington decided to go to
California. Again bad luck plagued him, for another daugh-
ter came down with pneumonia at the Point of Mountain
Station and shortly thereafter she died in Tucson.
Ref.: R. H. Forbes, Letter to James McClintock, April 5,
    1920 (State Library Files); 56, pp. 3, 10, 12, 31. Map:
    GL-3.

a.n. Josephine Canyon          Maps: GL-3; GL-5          Santa Cruz

## KITCHEN RANCH, PETE

El.: 4250'                                    Loc.: Santa Cruz DE-5
One of the most colorful characters in southern Arizona
was Pete Kitchen (b. Covington, Kentucky, 1819; d. August 5, 1895). His life was one long adventure. Kitchen
served as a wagoner during the war with Mexico. After
having been mustered out in Oregon, he joined the rush to
the California gold fields. In 1854 Pete showed up in
southern Arizona where he began ranching at the Canoa
Ranch on the Santa Cruz River. When troops were withdrawn during the Civil War and Apache depredations went
unchecked, Kitchen's holdings were wiped out by Indians.
He spent the next four years in Sonora. The war ended,

Kitchen returned to the Santa Cruz Valley to find it in a state of desolation. It was shortly after this that he settled on Potrero Creek at his El Potrero Ranch, where he remained from 1869 to 1876 and perhaps later.

Having been driven out of business once by Indians, Pete Kitchen was determined that there should be no repetition of earlier events. Accordingly he built a ranch house which was attacked by Apaches many times, never successfully. This was due in part to the fact that a parapet was built around the edge of its roof where a sentinel was constantly posted. The men plowing in the fields carried rifles, cocked and loaded, swung from their plow handles. In addition, every man and boy had one or two revolvers on his person. The war-like aspect of the ranch did not extend inside the home where travelers were made welcome while women carded, spun and sewed. On the outside were peaceful sounds—the blacksmith at his anvil, the wagon maker checking equipment, the saddler discussing his trade with a vaquero. Often the peace was broken by Indian raids. Apaches killed and wounded Kitchen's employees, stole his stock, and studded the skins of his pigs with arrows. On June 8, 1871, they killed his son, but the determined Kitchen refused to join others who fled from the valley in fear of Indians.

A prospector as well as a rancher, Pete Kitchen in 1878 owned the Kitchen Mine fifteen miles south of Arivaca, selling his interest in October 1879. At another time he prospected in Sonora where he found no wealth but plenty of trouble, barely emerging with his life. It was this which led to the saying once popular in Tucson when something turned out a fruitless quest, that one "got what Pete Kitchen brought back from Sonora."

In his later years, Kitchen lived in relative poverty in Tucson where he died.

Ref.: 22, p. 78; 153, p. 84; Pete Kitchen File, APHS; *Arizona Daily Star*, February 24, 1955, 9:1; "Letter from Sec'y of Interior transmitting certain papers regarding the Sopori Land Grant," pp. 47-48, APHS. Map: E-20.

**a.n. Nogales Wash**      Loc.: GL-2      Santa Cruz
A variant name for Potrero Creek.

## LITTLE, CAMP STEPHEN D.

El.: 4000'      Loc.: Santa Cruz E-5
In 1910 during the Madero Revolution in Mexico, a garrison of infantry was established on the northern outskirts of Nogales, Arizona. So far as is known, this camp had no name. The 12th Infantry arrived in Nogales on April 27, 1914, under Col. William H. Sage. On November 26, 1915, a Negro soldier named Stephen D. Little was killed in a battle against Pancho Villa. The name of the military establishment was then changed to Stephen D. Little. The camp was finally abandoned in 1931.

At one time more than thirteen thousand troops were stationed in and around Nogales. Four or five battles took place within the town itself.

Ref.: Jones; *Outguard*, I, 8, 1:1; 25, p. 212. Map: None.

## LOCHIEL (LA NORIA)

El.: c. 5000'      Loc.: Santa Cruz H-5.25
Pro.: /lokíyəl/      Spanish: *noria*, "well"
The Richard Harrison family came to Arizona in 1879, staying briefly in Tucson before moving to La Noria where several wells had been dug without obtaining water. Apparently this place was so close to what later became Lochiel that the two were practically identical. On the exact site of the present-day Lochiel was one well, the Lenora water hole. A post office existed at La Noria for the better part of a year. It was probably about a mile and a half north-northeast of Lochiel where, in 1884, the post office was re-established as Lochiel, being so named by Colin Cameron, one of the owners of the San Rafael Land Grant. Although Colin and Brewster Cameron came to Arizona from Pennsylvania, they named the place for the family's original home in Scotland. Natives in the area continued to refer to the place as La Noria and Mexican-Americans today continue to use that name. This may account for the fact that on GLO 1887 the name is Lochiel, whereas on GLO 1886 it is La Noria. When the International Boundary was re-surveyed in the 1890's, the line cut the village of La Noria exactly in two. GLO 1912 shows La Noria on the Mexican side of the boundary. In 1909 the post office name was changed to La Noria.

P.O. est. as La Noria July 24, 1882. Richard Harrison, p.m. Discont. 1883. P.O. est. as Lochiel, October 6, 1884. Abner B. Elder, p.m. Name changed to San Rafael March 1, 1888. Discont. October 4, 1888. Re-est. as La Noria, December 17, 1909. Discont. September 30, 1911.

Ref.: Mary Harrison Chalmers ms., APHS; Glannon; Lenon; P.O. Records; Barnes. Maps: C-5; C-11 (La Noria); C-6 (Lochiel).

## LUTTRELL

El.: 5000'      Loc.: Santa Cruz H-5
In 1880 Henry Holland located a claim in Duquesne Gulch, which he sold to Dr. J. M. Luttrell shortly thereafter. Dr. Luttrell was a member of a party of men from California who developed a mining camp which was named for Luttrell, superintendent of the mine.
P.O. est. August 23, 1880. Harrison Fuller, p.m. Discont. February 19, 1883.
Ref.: 138a, p. 388. Map: C-5.

## MANZANA

El.: 4817'      Loc.: Santa Cruz BC-4.6
Pro.: /manzənə/ or /mænzænə/      Spanish: "little apple"
Probably this name is a corruption of *manzanita*. This is based on the fact that there is a Manzanita Spring (Map: GL-4) on the south side of the mountain and also because dense manzanita grows on the mountain.
Ref.: Barnes. Map: GL-4.

## McKEE, CAMP

El.: 3500'      Loc.: Santa Cruz DE-3.9
In 1854 when America took possession of the territory included in the Gadsden Purchase of December 1853, a Mexican fort existed about two miles from Calabasas. Here

in 1856 dragoons under Maj. Enoch Steen were quartered temporarily (cf. Calabasas and Fort Buchanan). The fort was formally occupied in 1865 as a military post by members of the First Battalion of Native Cavalry (organized among Californians). The troop, recruited near Santa Barbara, was led by Capt. Thomas Young, when it moved into southern Arizona and took up headquarters. The men established Fort Mason on August 21, 1865, naming it for Gen. John S. Mason of the California Volunteers, who was military commander of Arizona 1865-1866. In early 1866 troops of the regular forces were stationed at Fort Mason. The name Fort Mason was changed to Camp McKee on September 6, 1866. Because of sickness among the men the camp was abandoned on October 1, 1866, when the troops were shifted to old Fort Buchanan.

Ref.: 85, p. 421; 75, p. 143; 105, p. 98; 111, pp. 168-169; 52, IV, 99; 52, II, 195. Maps: E-18; E-20 (Old Fort Mason).

## MOWRY MINE

El.: 5500'                              Loc.: Santa Cruz G-4
Sylvester Mowry (d. October 25, 1871), a native of Rhode Island, was graduated from West Point Military Academy in 1852. He resigned from the service as a first lieutenant on July 31, 1858. When he resigned his commission he was stationed at Fort Crittenden. He purchased the Patagonia Mine (cf. Patagonia) for which he had been negotiating with fellow-officers. The Patagonia Mine was an old one, but was rediscovered in the fall of 1858 by a Mexican herder who sold it for a pony and several articles of little value to army officers at Fort Crittenden. The list of their names is an interesting one. It includes Capt. Richard S. Ewell (cf. Ewell Springs, Cochise); Lt. I. N. Moore (cf. Fort Buchanan); Lt. Richard M. Lord, Col. James W. Douglass, and others. Lt. Lord and one other sold their interests to Elias Brevoort, postmaster at Fort Buchanan, who resigned as postmaster to serve as superintendent of the mine. When the French engineer F. Biertu made his report on the mine, he stated that Brevoort was a poor manager and that as a result the potentially rich mine was costing the owners more than they were getting from it. There were lengthy arguments among them. Finally they agreed to disagree and called the whole thing off by selling the mine to Sylvester Mowry.

It is not known why these men called the mine Patagonia. There is not the slightest resemblance in landscape to the famed Patagonia at the tip of South America. Mowry lost no time in changing the name to the Mowry Mine. He employed over one hundred men and shipped out $1,500,000 in ore.

In June 1862, Mowry was seized as a Southern sympathizer and imprisoned for almost six months. At the end of that time he was discharged, the opinion of the court being "there was no evidence against him," to prove he actively supported the Confederacy. Nevertheless, Mowry had drawn up a map showing how Arizona was to be partitioned by the Confederacy. Meanwhile, the government receiver for the mines had made the property unworkable by

extensive and deliberate damage to the equipment. In 1864 Mowry was still trying to get the Federal Government to relinquish his property.

Mowry was an indefatigable worker for the advancement of Arizona. He was twice elected delegate to Congress. Congress, however, refused to seat him because Arizona was not a territory. A highly cultured man, Mowry traveled widely.

The mine gradually fell into disuse. It was acquired by relocation in the early 1880's, being sold by the new owners (Fish and Silverburg of Tucson) to Steinfeld and Swain, Tucson merchants. These men in the late 1890's reopened the old workings. They in turn sold the mine in 1904. There was a short period of renewed activity, but that too diminished to the vanishing point.

P.O. est. as Patagonia, May 7, 1866. Charles E. Mowry, p.m. Discont. June 24, 1867. Re-est. May 24, 1880. J. W. Davis, p.m. Discont. November 22, 1880. P.O. est. as Mowry, June 23, 1905. Violet Van Norman, p.m. (deceased); Dorette D. Davis, p.m. Discont. July 31, 1913.

v.n. **Corral Viego Mine:** same as old Mowry Mine (1879)
Ref.: 105, p. 196. Maps: C-1; E-20; GL-1; GL-2.

| a.n. | | | |
|---|---|---|---|
| **Mowry Flat** | El.: 5500.' | Loc.: At Mowry Mine | Santa Cruz |
| **Mowry Wash** | | Map: GL-2 | Santa Cruz |
| **Patagonia Mountains** | | Map: GL-2 | Santa Cruz |

## NOGALES

El.: 3689'                              Loc.: Santa Cruz E-5
Pro.: /nogǽləs/ or /nogáləs/        Spanish: "walnuts"
The name Nogales is an old one, being found on maps examined from 1859 consecutively to the present, with the exception of GLO 1883, on which it appears as Isaacson. When the Boundary Survey Commission was doing its work in the early 1850's, the surveying crew established an observatory at Los Nogales. Many years later Brig. Gen. Frank Wheaton said that as a youth of eighteen he served with the Corps of Engineers on the boundary and that it was he who in his report recommended that the monument at this spot be named Los Dos Nogales because of two walnut trees, one on either side of the boundary line. (Wheaton was commissioned a first lieutenant of the 1st Cavalry on March 3, 1855). Whether there was a stock ranch existing at Los Nogales at this time is not clear, but it is entirely possible. That such a ranch did exist four years later is attested to by the fact that the Nogales Rancho was listed as a stop on the route to Sonora.

On early maps Los Nogales shows just a little north of the boundary on the main road into Sonora. A stock farm was still in existence here in 1869; it shows on GLO 1869 as Nugales. Late in 1879 or early in 1880 the S.P.R.R. from Benson to the border and from Guaymas, Sonora, to Nogales neared completion. Attracted by the possibility of business during the railroad construction period, Jacob Isaacson (b. Goulding, Russia, December 9, 1853; d. December 29, 1928) appeared on the scene at the International Boundary. He was an itinerant peddler who had been in Arizona since 1875. Isaacson built a small store and storehouse straddling the International Boundary Line. As the railroad men moved in, they made his place a headquarters and the name Isaacson was attached to the post office in his store. Here Isaacson remained for three years, making a name for himself as a highly educated linguist, musician, and successful business-man. When the last golden railroad spike was placed in September 1882 to connect the two ends of the railroad line, Isaacson helped drive it home. With the work completed, a temporary lull fell on the border community. Isaacson, a businessman to his marrow, moved on to greener fields in Mexico City and vanished from the local scene. He died in Detroit in 1928.

Meanwhile, the little community on the border struggled for existence. American residents were referring to the place as Line City, but the name was not destined to take hold. Late in 1882 the railroad called the station Nogales and the *Arizona Star* said that would probably settle the matter. The citizens petitioned to have the post office name changed from Isaacson to Nogales and this was done.

Nogales has become the largest international city on the Arizona-Sonora border. Today the name Los Dos Nogales is again applicable because there is a Nogales, Arizona, and also a Nogales, Sonora, the two being separated by the International Boundary Fence. From its beginnings of a box-car railroad station and a community of several tents and a few mud huts, Nogales has grown into a large, pros-perous and attractive city. It is the county seat.

P.O. est. as Isaacson, May 31, 1882. Jacob Isaacson, p.m. Name changed to Nogales, June 4, 1883. James Breeden, p.m. Wells Fargo Station, 1885. Incorporated July 22, 1893.

Ref.: Jones; Glannon; Jacob Isaacson File, APHS; 51, pp. 31, 176, 177; 111, p. 114; 32, p. 328; *Weekly Arizonan,* May 21, 1859, 3:1; *Tombstone Prospector,* November 17, 1896, 4:4; *Phoenix Herald,* October 4, 1882, 3:2; *Ari-zona Republican,* November 21, 1896, 2:1. Maps: C-1; C-5 (Isaacson); E-11; E-12; GL-2.

**a.n. Nogales Pass**                           Santa Cruz

   **Nogales Wash**        Map: GL-2          Santa Cruz
   Variant for Potrero Creek.

# NOONVILLE

El.: 4159'                       Loc.: Santa Cruz B-4.25
                                  18 miles west of Nogales.
Capt. John N. Noon, a native of Ireland, discovered the Noon Mine in 1879 and moved to the location in 1887. Noonville is sometimes referred to as Noon Camp.

P.O. est. as Noonville, October 31, 1888. Alonzo E. Noon, p.m. Discont. July 21, 1890.

Ref.: Barnes; P.O. Records; 7, p. 628 (Note 13). Map: None.

# OLD GLORY MINE

El.: 4370'                       Loc.: Santa Cruz B-4
When the owners of the American Flag Mine applied for a post office at their mining community, they asked for the name American Flag. However, the name had already been used at the American Flag Mine in Pinal County and therefore was rejected by the Post Office Department. The owners of the mine thereupon petitioned for and obtained the name Oldglory. It is reported that resentment arose over the name, but if so, it must have had slow growth be-

cause the name continued as a single word for the ensuing sixteen years, following which the name was changed to Old Glory. This place is abandoned today.

P.O. est. as Oldglory, January 15, 1893. William E. Ward, p.m. Name changed to Old Glory, November 23, 1909. Discont. August 14, 1915.

Ref.: Lenon; Barnes; P.O. Records. Maps: C-9; C-12; GJ-7.

# ORO BLANCO

El.: 4002'                       Loc.: Santa Cruz B-3.5
Pro.: /oro blánko/             Spanish: "white gold"
In 1873 the *Arizona Citizen* reported that the mineral vein at Oro Blanco had been worked so early that in some places large oak trees had grown on the scene of obvious mining activity. In 1873 mining was resumed. The mine lay so close to the International Boundary that it was necessary to run a survey line to be sure it lay in Arizona.

P.O. est. October 2, 1879. William J. Ross, p.m. Discont. April 30, 1915.

Ref.: *Arizona Citizen,* December 27, 1873, 3:3; P.O. Records. Maps: B-3; C-4; E-20; GJ-7.

**a.n. Oro Blanco Wash**      Maps: GJ-2; GJ-7         Santa Cruz

# PAJARITO MOUNTAINS

El.: 5100'                       Loc.: Santa Cruz CD-5
Pro.: /paharí⁀to/             Spanish: "small bird"
These mountains were so called when the Boundary Survey Commission mapped this part of the Gadsden Purchase in 1853. Maj. William H. Emory noted that the Sierra del Pajarito was a part of the Arizona Mountains, a system which lay in Mexico and extended north of the proposed boundary. These mountains were also frequently referred to as the Arizone Mountains.

The name for the Pajarito Mountains probably came from the fact that there is a butte between fifty and seventy-five feet high (Loc.: northeast ¼, northwest ¼, section 11, T. 24 S, R. 12 E.) which is today called Pajarito Peak (El.: 4490'). The formation looks like a little bird sitting on the side of the mountain, and in fact is still referred to by cowmen as Pajarito.

Emory also noted that the eastern slope of the Sierra del Pajarito was called Los Nogales.

**v.n. Oro Blanco Mountain**               Santa Cruz
   When mines in this area began to be re-worked at the Oro Blanco Mine (cf. Oro Blanco) the mountains quite natural-ly were referred to as the Oro Blanco Mountains.

Ref.: 87, p. 225.

   **Oro Blanco Peak**                    Santa Cruz
   This is the same as Pajarito Peak. See Oro Blanco Moun-tains.

Ref.: Lenon; 51, pp. 120, 69; 151, p. 582. Maps: B-3; E-3; GL-4.

**a.n. Pajarito**                           Santa Cruz
   Loc.: In Pajarito Mountains, but not as yet definitely located by the editor.
   This was apparently a mining community which developed at about the same time as Oro Blanco.

P.O. est. January 3, 1881. John M. McArthur, p.m. Discont. April 9, 1883.

Ref.: P.O. Records.

## PARKER CANYON

El.: c. 5000'                    Loc.: Santa Cruz HI-5.2-4.4
William Parker (b. Tennessee, August 9, 1824; d. 1923)
was of Scotch-Irish descent. Parker took part in the California gold rush and en route his party lost the main road;
as a result Parker first saw the place where he later returned
to settle—Parker Canyon. Parker made good in California
and returned to Missouri for his wife and children, taking
them c. 1870 to Phoenix, without ever living in Texas
as has sometimes been said. In 1881 the family moved to
Parker Canyon to avoid the "congestion" in population developing at Phoenix. He is buried in Parker Canyon.

P.O. est. as Parker Canon, April 14, 1912. Louis K. McIntyre,
p.m. Name changed to Parker Canyon, January 1, 1928. Discont. January 18, 1929.

Ref.: Mrs. Emily Parker Gray (great-granddaughter), Letter,
March 18, 1956; P.O. Records. Maps: C-12; GL-2.

## PATAGONIA

El.: 4050'                        Loc.: Santa Cruz FG-2.8
Pro.: /pǽtəgowníyə/
The history of the contemporary town of Patagonia is
closely connected with that of Crittenden (q.v.). The town
of Crittenden was owned by Rollen R. Richardson, who
owned all the land in the area.

Rollen Rice Richardson (b. Shippenville, Pa., July 10,
1846) served in the Civil War, following which he entered
the oil business in Pennsylvania. He sold out in 1880 and
in 1883 bought the Monkey Springs Ranch. He also bought
out squatters at old Camp Crittenden. He thereupon called
the entire holdings the Pennsylvania Ranch. Here in 1890
he was running twelve thousand head of cattle in partnership with L. V. Gormley and Alex Harrison. The drought
forcing him out of business, he sold to Vail, Gates, and
Ashburn, reserving about five hundred acres of land where
Patagonia is today. While the date of his death has not
been ascertained, it is known that he was dead by 1940.
In 1896 Richardson decided to move the entire town of
Crittenden into the then marshy area where Patagonia exists today. He proposed to call the new town Rollen, but
its residents—who had no choice about being moved to the
new location—balked at that name. They chose Patagonia
because the nearby mountains had that name. Since the
petition for a post office had to be signed by them, Patagonia it was, whether Richardson liked it or not.

Locally some people ascribe the origin of the name Patagonia to Indians' having big feet. However, there is no
archaeological evidence to support this legend. As a matter
of fact, the Patagonia Mine from which the mountains and
the town take their name was itself named in 1858 by a
group of American army officers who bought it from a
Mexican. Mexicans as late as 1879 called the mine Corral
Viego (cf. Mowry Mine).

P.O. est. March 3, 1900. Mamie M. Cretin, p.m. Wells Fargo
Station, 1903. Incorporated, 1948.

v.n. Rollintown

Ref.: Lenon; P.O. Records; Rollen R. Richardson File, APHS;
Tucson Citizen, November 11, 1896, 1: (APHS Names
File). Maps: C-9; GL-3.

## PECK CANYON

El.: 3760'                        Loc.: Santa Cruz BD-3-4
This canyon was named for A. L. Peck, who lived near its
upper end. On April 27, 1886, Peck's wife, while holding
her baby in her arms, was killed by Apaches and a second
child carried off. It was later recovered. Peck thereupon left
the canyon.

The next resident was a Polish miner named Joseph Piskorski. Gradually the name Polaco, erroneously spelled Palaco
(a corruption based on Piskorski's being a "Pollack") came
into use, as did also the name Piskorski for the canyon.
By decision of the Geographic Board on Names June 24,
1930, the name Peck Canyon was officially designated.

Ref.: Lenon; Barnes; 151, p. 594. Maps: B-3; GL-4.

a.n. Peck Pass                    Map: C-12                Santa Cruz

## PENA BLANCA DAM

El.: 3800'                        Loc.: Santa Cruz CD-4-5
Pro.: /péynyə blánkə/            Spanish: "white rock"
Descriptive. Plans for the original dam had to be altered
because it was found that a fault in one of the rocks made
it impossible to construct the dam at that point. The plans
were replaced by those for an earth dam at an elevation
just above four thousand feet. The dam was completed in
late 1957, and a fishing and recreation area was developed
upon completion of the dam.

Ref.: Lenon; Arizona Star, February 24, 1955, 3:1. Map:
GL-4.

a.n. Peña Blanca Spring           Map: GL-4                Santa Cruz

## PESQUIERA CANYON

El.: 4500'                        Loc.: Santa Cruz CD-5-4.5
Pro.: /peskiyærə/ or /peskiyérə/
Capt. M. H. Calderwood of the California Volunteers was
in command at Calabasas in 1865. One evening while he
was on the parade grounds, a Mexican rode up to him and
requested permission to camp. Calderwood was astonished
the next morning to see not a single camper, but the entire
army of Gov. Ignacio Pesquiera of Sonora, including servants and personal property. Pesquiera had fled from Mexico with Maximilian's French troops scorching his heels.
Before long the French troops were withdrawn from Sonora
and Pesquiera returned to assume control of Mexico. While
he was in Arizona he was the guest of Col. Charles W.
Lewis, commandant at Tubac. The harboring of foreign
forces on American soil came close to costing Lewis his
commission.

The Pesquiera family has many descendants living in Santa
Cruz County.

Ref.: Lenon; Charles W. Lewis File; APHS; 52, IV, 190-191.
Map: GL-4.

## PETE MOUNTAIN

El.: 5000'                        Loc.: Santa Cruz DE-1.6
This mountain, sometimes referred to as Old Pete Mountain, was named for Peter Gabriel (b. Prussia, 1838; d.
July 29, 1898). By July 1870, Gabriel was a prospector
in Prescott. He moved into southern Arizona where he

worked for a time near the mountain which bears his name. He moved to Pinal County where he served as sheriff for three terms. In June 1888, in a Florence saloon he had a gun fight with Joseph Phy during which eleven shots were fired. Phy was hit four times and Pete twice. The gun battle was the culmination of a long-standing feud. Gabriel died at his Monitor Mine in Pinal County.

**v.n. Elephant Head**

One part of Pete Mountain is a towering bare rock which resembles the head of an elephant. Indians used to take captives to this point and throw them down.

**Diablo Mountain**

This mountain is a part of the entire group known as Pete Mountain. It is located in Sec. 6, T. 20 S., R. 12 E. The folklore of Santa Cruz County has many references to devils, but it is not known which tale led to naming this mountain "Diablo."

Diablo Mountain appears as Mount Waldeck Peak on the GLO Field notes for 1905. It is conjectured that Waldeck (or Walldeck) may have been a member of the surveying crew.

Ref.: Barnes; Seibold; Lenon; Peter Gabriel File, APHS. Maps: C-11; GL-3.

**a.n. Elephant Head Mine**     Santa Cruz

This mine was named for the nearby Elephant Head formation.

P.O. est. July 10, 1914. Henry W. Williams, p.m. Discont.?

Ref.: Jones; P.O. Records.

# RAMONOTE PEAK

El.: 6047'     Loc.: Santa Cruz CD-3.8
Pro.: /ramanówtey/
It is reported that a Mexican named Ramon was herder here during the early territorial days and that his eyes were blind to ownership of stock near his camp. The suffix *ote* means "large" or "grand."

**v.n. Ramanote Peak** (corruption)
Ref.: Barnes. Map: GL-4.

**a.n. Ramonote Canyon**     Map: GL-4     Santa Cruz

# REVENTON RANCH

El.: c. 5000'     Loc.: Santa Cruz DE-1
GLO 1869 shows Reventon as seven miles east of north of Tubac. The ranch was occupied in 1859 by Elias Brevoort, who had come to Arizona to be the sutler at the new Fort Buchanan. This substantiates the fact that he was attached to the military unit which the post office "Tucson" was to serve, later to be changed to Fort Buchanan (q.v.). Browne reports that Brevoort was later sent by the Quartermaster's Department into Mexico to recover some wagons and teams belonging to the Federal Government. He adds succinctly, "The wagons and teams remained and so did Brevoort." *The Weekly Alta Californian* on May 28, 1859, reported that the ranch was owned by men named Mercer and Dodson. In 1860 Raphael Pumpelly noted that "Reventori" was a fortified ranch. It became a true fort in the middle of 1864 when three companies of the First California Cavalry were stationed at it temporarily. It was in this same year that Browne noted that Jimmy Caruthers took squat-

ter's rights at the palatial ranch dwelling after the disappearance of Brevoort southwards, but that the Apaches drove Caruthers out of the Santa Cruz Valley as they had the majority of other settlers. Browne noted that the house was deserted and the ranch a ruin when he visited it in 1864. That Reventon Ranch was an old one is shown by the fact that in 1864 the oldest Mexicans and Indians in the area were unable to remember its beginnings.

**v.n. Revanton** (corruption)
**Revantano** (corruption)     Map: E-20
Ref.: *Arizona Miner*, July 6, 1864; 2:3; 134, p. 45; 25, pp. 256, 259; 105, pp. 222-223. Map: C-1.

# RHODES RANCH

El.: c. 4000'     Loc.: Santa Cruz CD-2
William Rhodes (cf. Rhodes Ranch, Yuma) in 1861 was residing in the Santa Cruz Valley where the withdrawal of troops had left local ranchers and miners prey to the Apaches. Leaving Tubac one morning, Rhodes and a Mexican planned to hunt horses. They arrived at the Canoa Ranch, which was then serving as an inn. All was safe there at the time. When Rhodes and his companion returned to the Canoa at noon they found three Americans and a Papago slaughtered. The attack was so recent that more than one hundred mounted Apaches were still near. The Indians attacked Rhodes and the Mexican, and the latter escaped to Tubac on his fast horse, but Rhodes' horse failed and Rhodes felt the sting of an arrow in his arm. He threw himself to the ground, ran to a thicket, and hid in a dry water hole. Here he spread out his revolver cartridges and caps. He then broke off the arrow, pulled out the shaft and buried his bleeding arm deep in the earth to stop the flow. Cooly, calmly, precisely, Rhodes picked off the Indians one by one, re-loading after each shot. The Indians waited until Rhodes had fired six times. Then, believing his weapon empty, they charged. Rhodes killed two more Indians. The Apaches tried the same ruse a second time with similar results. The Apaches admired strength and courage, and in respect for Rhodes they retreated after their second attack. Apaches never bothered him thereafter. True, he did not give them much chance, for he soon left the Santa Cruz Valley.

**v.n. Roods Ranch**

Charles D. Poston called this the William B. Roods Ranch in a letter to State Historian Joseph Farrish.

Ref.: 34, p. 371. Map: E-20.

# RUBY

El.: 4219'     Loc.: Santa Cruz BC-3.6
Ruby was the post office which was established at the Montana Mine at what was known as Montana Camp. Here in January 1895, came Julius F. Andrews (b. Ohio, April 10, 1853) to take charge of the camp store which he ran for the next eighteen years. When mining activity took an upsurge c. 1909, an application was made for a post office, the one at Oro Blanco then being inactive. Andrews named the post office in honor of his wife, whose maiden name

was Lille B. Ruby. Andrews sold out his interest in the store in 1913, moving to Tucson where he lived to be more than eighty-eight years of age.

The proximity of Ruby to the international border was an open invitation to trouble with renegades. In 1914 the store was being operated by the Frazier brothers, Canadians. Both were murdered at the store. In 1921 a couple named Pearson was murdered by Mexican bandits who also attempted to murder their child, but an aunt grabbed the three-year-old and hid with it in a canyon. The murderers were caught and convicted. En route to prison at Florence, they killed the sheriff and escaped, but were again caught by a posse from Nogales.

The Montana Mine, which was one of the original ones on the mining properties in the area, was in existence at least as early as 1880. At one time it was owned by the Eagle Picher Company, and there were more than two thousand people in Ruby. Adobe buildings were reroofed and temporary buildings erected. These were taken down when the company moved. In 1946 Hugo Miller of Nogales obtained the property, selling out in 1956. The mines are once again entering a phase of activity.

P.O. est. April 11, 1912. Julius S. Andrews, p.m. Discont. May 31, 1941.

Ref.: G. E. P. Smith; Mrs. Hugo Miller; APHS Files. Maps: C-12; GL-4.

**a.n. Montana Peak**    El.: 5380'. Map: GL-4    Santa Cruz
**Ruby Peak**    El.: 5061'. Map: GL-4    Santa Cruz

## SALERO HILL

El.: 5500'    Loc.: Santa Cruz F-2
Pro.: /saléro/    Spanish: "salt cellar"

Salero Hill was so named because the Salero Mine is located a third of the way up its face. The mine is reputed to be one of the oldest in southern Arizona. It is said to have been worked by Jesuits in the 17th century, although no documentary evidence has been found to substantiate this. However, it is known that it was worked from about 1828 to 1830 and later, by Mexicans.

Regarding the origin of the name Salero, Hinton related a legend that the "Padres at St. Joseph's" (i.e. San José de Tumacacori) were expecting a bishop to visit them and that he was something of a *bon vivant* who had complained of the lack of salt for his dinner. The priests thereupon are said to have fashioned a salt cellar from a piece of ore taken from the Salero Mine, hence its name. What they may have done about the salt is another story, since there are no salt deposits in this region.

Historically, Salero Mine may be taken as an example of the extreme hardships imposed by Apaches in the late 1850's and early 1860's. In 1857 John W. Wrightson of the *Cincinnati Enquirer* and his brother William became owners of the old mine, forming the Salero Mining Company in 1858 with John Wrightson as manager; H. C. Grosvenor, engineer (cf. Grosvenor Peak); Raphael Pumpelly, geologist; and Gilbert W. Hopkins, mineralogist (cf. Mount Hopkins). The company had headquarters at Tubac. Of the four leading figures in the mine's ownership, only Pumpelly escaped death at the hands of Indians.

In 1865 the company went out of business. Following the Civil War, difficulties were encountered with Baca Float No. 3 *(q.v.)* land titles. The mine was relocated by John E. McGee c. 1876 but he was unable to hold it because of title difficulties. However, while McGee was in the area, the old Hacienda de Santa Rita (which had been abandoned on June 15, 1861, following a fierce Apache battle) again became the center of a small community near which was Camp Toltec, headquarters for the syndicate which McGee had organized. In one year alone more than one thousand mining locations were made in this vicinity.

Land ownership difficulties continuing, the area again fell into disuse. From that time the Salero Mine showed sporadic activity, being re-organized as the Salero Mines Company c. 1900.

Ref.: Lenon; *Arizona Sentinel*, June 29, 1878, n.d. (APHS File); 25, p. 230; 138a, pp. 194-195; 87, p. 203; 87, p. 202. Maps: B-3; C-6.

**a.n. Salero**    Santa Cruz
P.O. est. August 13, 1884. Lizzie E. Durand, p.m. Discont. April 17, 1890.

## SANFORD

El.: 3650'    Loc.: Santa Cruz EF-3.4

Denton G. Sanford (b. New York, March 7, 1833; d. January 23, 1885) came to Arizona in 1862 where he homesteaded a ranch near present-day Patagonia. On November 14, 1878, he bought at public sale at the Florence Land Office what is now the Circle Z Ranch, obtaining a patent to the land on April 30, 1879. He died of malaria. After his death the ranch came to be known as the Circle Z.

Ref.: Lenon; Denton G. Sanford File, APHS. Map: GL-2.

## SAN RAFAEL DE LA ZANJA LAND GRANT

El.: c. 4000'    Loc.: Santa Cruz EF-5
Pro.: /san rafáyal dey la zánha/    Spanish: "Saint Raphael of the Ditch"

In May 1825, the Mexican government granted land to Manuel Bustello. Many years later this land was owned by cattlemen Colin and Brewster Cameron (c. 1889). According to a newspaper account there was a ruin called by Roskruge in 1887 the "Old San Rafael Ruins" about three miles to the north of the Cameron ranch.

Ref.: Barnes; *Weekly Arizona Enterprise*, January 31, 1891, 1:3-9. Map: C-6.

**a.n. San Rafael**    Maps: C-7; E-20; GL-2    Santa Cruz
P.O. est. March 1, 1888. Mrs. Katherine F. Cameron, p.m. Discont. October 4, 1888. Re-established, March 25, 1913. Robert N. Keaton, p.m. Discont. May 31, 1917.
Ref.: P.O. Records.

## SANTA CRUZ RIVER

Loc.: Traverses Santa Cruz County, Pima, and Pinal to Santa Cruz Cienega.
Pro.: /sánta cruwz/ or /sǽnta cruwz/

One of the oldest place names in Arizona is that of the Santa Cruz River. It was referred to by that name by Fr. Kino in the late 1690's, and the name has been in use ever since. The river rises in Arizona and flows for a short distance south into Sonora, Mexico, after which it swings back toward the north. Its course, now largely dry, becomes lost in the Santa Cruz Cienega. Formerly the stream had living water as far north as the outskirts of Tucson.

Ref.: 19, II, 249; 87, pp. 183, 184. Maps: All of area which river traverses.

## SANTA RITA MOUNTAINS

El.: 9000'                          Loc.: Santa Cruz EF-4.2
The origin of the name has not yet been ascertained.
When the United States Boundary Commission in 1851 passed through this part of the future Gadsden Purchase, Commissioner Bartlett noted that this magnificent range of lofty mountains was called the Santa Rita Mountains. Their name first appears on maps examined as the Sierra de las Santa Rita.

In writing about these mountains, Hinton noted that east and north of Tubac there was a bold spur which formed a "skirmish line for the three great mounts of peaks in which the range finds its combination." He referred to this point as Sentinel Peak. This is probably the same as Picacho del Diablo.

Ref.: 5a; 87, p. 189. Maps: C-2; GL-3.

## SARDINA PEAK

El.: 5506'                          Loc.: Santa Cruz C-2
A Mexican named Sarvinia lived for years near this peak. With reference to the peak his name gradually was anglicized to Sardina.

Ref.: Barnes. Map: GL-5.

## SHIBELL, MOUNT

El.: c. 5000'                       Loc.: Santa Cruz DE-3
Pro.: /šaybél/
Charles A. Shibell (b. St. Louis, Mo., August 14, 1841; d. October 21, 1908) first saw Arizona when he was a teamster for Gen. J. H. Carleton in 1862. Upon his discharge nearly a year later, Shibell returned to Tucson. He served as sheriff in 1876. His vocation shifted from miner and rancher to merchant and hotel man toward the latter part of his life.

Ref.: APHS File; 112, III. Maps: B-3; C-12.

## SONOITA

El.: 4865'                          Loc.: Santa Cruz GH-1.4
Pro.: /sonóytə/    Papago: "place where corn will grow"
In 1859 a traveler noted that the entire Sonoita Valley was golden with grain and that one field alone contained one hundred and fifty acres of corn. Hinton noted that corn grew as high and as lushly in the Sonoita Valley as it did in Missouri bottomlands and that the Sonoita River rose to the ground and disappeared several times within twelve miles of Camp Crittenden. In 1856 Col. Gray referred to the stream as the "Sonoita or Clover Creek."

The first recorded notation by Fr. Kino of the name Sonoita in documents examined is dated February 1700. The Sobaipuri Chief, Coro, met Kino here at the settlement which Coro established in 1698 when he moved his people

from Quiburi (q.v., Cochise County) to a settlement called by Jesuits, Los Reyes. Coro moved his people to this point following their decided victory against Apaches, whose swift vengeance Coro feared. This place was on Sonoita Creek about two or three miles southwest of Patagonia. Hodge says that this place was a visita of Guevavi. There were ninety-one people living here at what was called Sonoita, during the time of the Pima revolt in 1751. It became a visita of Tubatama, Sonora, in 1768, but within twenty years was deserted.

A small Mexican Land Grant known as San Jose de Sonoita extended along both sides of Sonoita Creek. It was sold to Leon Henores on May 15, 1825. When this land became part of the United States through the Gadsden Purchase, the United States Land Court confirmed 7,592 acres of the grant.

Like other areas in southern Arizona, the Sonoita Valley because of trouble with Apaches in the period 1861-1876 was nearly uninhabited by white men.

The present day community of Sonoita is of relatively recent origin, having come into existence in 1882 when it was established on the newly constructed railroad line. When the newer community of Sonoita was established on the railroad to the east of the old Sobaipuri rancheria, a post office was established.

**v.n. Los Reyes de Sonoydag**
P.O. est. May 8, 1912. Clara L. Hummel, p.m.

Ref.: *Arizona Citizen*, June 1, 1872, 2:3; 20, pp. 385-386; 88, II, 391, 616; 4, p. 26; 55, p. 428; 19, I, 233; 91, p. 86; 87, p. 214; 101, p. 51. Maps: C-10; GL-3.

## SOPORI RANCH

El.: 3250'                          Loc.: Santa Cruz CD-1
The name Sopori is probably a corruption of the name for the Sobaipuri Indians, a now vanished tribe (See Arivaipa Canyon, Pinal).

The Pima Indians for many years had a rancheria in the vicinity of Sopori Ranch on the Altar Road. The name of this rancheria according to the *Rudo Ensayo* (1763) was Sepori. This place contained eighty families in 1871. In 1851 there was a silver mine and a ranch here twelve miles northwest of Tubac, being worked by Col. James Douglass. There was a spring at this place known as the Ojo del Agua de Sopori in 1854; at one time it was used to irrigate what was known as the Sopori Valley in which the spring and ranch lay. The ranch was on the route to Arivaca, according to Michler in 1854.

The Sopori Ranch consisted of 21,000 acres including the Sopori Mining Company holdings. According to F. Biertu's report in 1861, the mining company was incorporated with a capital of one million dollars with Lt. Sylvester Mowry as one of the principal share holders. This would place it among the Arivaca mines.

In 1861 Raphael Pumpelly reported that as a result of Apache raids Sopori Ranch was deserted. The climaxing attack was made by the same band of Apaches which unsuccessfully tried to kill William B. Roods (see Rhodes Ranch). Roods heard them shout, "Sopori! Sopori!" when they left him after a fierce battle. Sopori Ranch must have come back into use again following Apache troubles, for Hinton refers to the ranch as having much timber.

Ref.:  Barnes; Kirk Bryan Notes; 88, II, 510; 134, p. 47; 137, pp. 192, 193; 87, p. 221; 51, p. 119; 118, p. 81; 25, p. 260. Maps: C-1; E-17; E-18.

a.n. Sopori Wash          Map: GL-5          Santa Cruz
     Sopori Peak          Map: B-3           Santa Cruz
     Sopori Land Grant    Map: C-6           Santa Cruz
     Among the Mexican land grants rejected by the United States Land Courts following the Gadsden Purchase was this claim for 142,721 acres.

Ref.:  Barnes.

## TUBAC

El.: 3250'                         Loc.: Santa Cruz D-2.1
Pro.: /tuwbǽk/ or      Pima or Papago: *tu,* meaning not known;
      /tuwbák/                    *bac,* "house" or "ruins";
The community known today as Tubac is at a different location from that of the earlier Tubac mentioned in many records. The first townsite lay in the extreme northwest corner of Baca Float No. 3, whereas the present town lies entirely outside the Float.

It is possible that the older Tubac is that referred to in 1763 as Tucubavi, a *visita* of Guevavi. Fr. Bonaventure Oblasser believes that the Spanish attempt to pronounce the Papago "Chuevak" came out as *Tubac.* The name Tubac does not appear until after the Pima Indian revolt in 1750. In 1752 the Spaniards established a presidio and a mission called St. Gertrude de Tabac or San Ignacio de Tubac. There were fifty military men stationed here. By 1754 there were four hundred and eleven residents. Capt. Juan B. de Anza was commandant. Incidentally, it was from Tubac that de Anza led an expedition to California, founding San Francisco.

In 1776 the presidio was transferred to Tucson, thus leaving the residents in the Santa Cruz Valley without military protection. The fact that repeated petitions returned no troops to Tubac led the inhabitants to establish their own garrison of Pima Indians. It is reported that in 1828 a silver mine was worked in this vicinity and that a military garrison was again sent to Tubac. This, of course, was following the creation of Mexico from the old Spanish domain. When the United States Boundary Survey party passed through Tubac in 1851, Bartlett reported that in 1850 it had served temporarily as a stopping place for a party of Mormons on their way to California. The Mormons had liked the place so well that they planned to stay, but the following year (1851) was very dry, forcing them to abandon Tubac. Bartlett states that he met this party at Santa Isabel in California. He also said that Tubac itself was half deserted and half in ruins. Three years later, Lt. N. Michler wrote that Tubac was completely deserted, stating that "the wild Apache lords it over this region, and the timid husbandman dares not return to his home."

Tubac was rejuvenated when Charles DeBrille Poston arrived in 1856 with about three hundred and fifty men, mostly miners from Texas. In his *Journal,* Poston said that headquarters for the Sonora Mining and Exploring Com-

pany were established in the abandoned Spanish presidio at Tubac in September of that year. Tubac enjoyed a period of relative prosperity with Poston leading an almost baronial existence. It was during this era that Arizona's first newspaper, *The Arizonan,* was begun on a press brought by William Wrightson of the *Cincinnati Enquirer* around the Horn and then from the west coast of Mexico to Tubac. The withdrawal of federal troops for service in the Civil War was a signal to the Apaches for renewed violent activity and the prosperity of Tubac fell into the same ruin that visited other places in the Santa Cruz Valley.

By 1908 almost all of the old Tubac presidio had disappeared.

P.O. est. February 21, 1859. Frederick Hulseman, p.m. Discont. November 30, 1942.

Ref.:  Lenon; Fr. Bonaventure Oblasser, Letter to Frank C. Lockwood, May 5, 1935; 72, p. 141; 35, p. 69, (Note 2); 34, p. 14; 87, p. 184; 149, p. 203; 89, p. 18; 7, pp. 383, 382; 112, p. 56; 51, p. 118; 88, II, 830; 131; 86, pp. 38, 39. Maps: B-3; C-1; E-6; E-11.

a.n. Tubac Creek          Map: GL-5          Santa Cruz
     Tubac Range                             Santa Cruz
     Variant name for Atascosa Mountains (*q.v.*).

Ref.:  87, p. 180.

## TUMACACORI NATIONAL MONUMENT

El.: c. 3500'                      Loc.: Santa Cruz CD-2-3
Pro.: /tuwmǝkǽkoriˆ/           Pima: *tsu-ma-ka-kork,* "curved peak"
The Indian name Tumacacori derives from the fact that a mountain to the west appears to slant somewhat.

In 1691 Fr. Kino with Fr. Salvatierra visited Tumacacori, which was then a large Pima town where the Indians prepared three brush shelters for the priests, in one of which mass was said. Here Kino was visited by the head men from the Sobaipuri settlement at Bac, asking the Jesuits to visit their people. This later led to the building of the church at San Xavier del Bac (*q.v.,* Pima). However, in 1691, the time was not ripe for the establishment of missions, so in 1697 Tumacacori was set up as a *visita* of Guevavi, known as San Cayetano Tumapacori.

Following the Pima Rebellion in 1751 and the establishment of a presidio at Tubac (*q.v.*), Tumacacori began to emerge from obscurity. Jesuits were expelled from all Spanish dominions in 1767 and Franciscans took over the mission chain in northern Sonora. The ever-active Apaches caused the abandonment of Guevavi as a mission in 1773. It was in this year that San Jose de Tumacacori became the headquarters mission. It reached its period of fullest activity in the last decade of the 18th century and the first two of the 19th. The church which can be seen in ruins today was just taking shape in 1800. By 1822 it was in use, but fierce Apache raids between 1830 and 1840 led to its abandonment. It has never been re-occupied. The first Americans to visit the place noted early in the 1850's that fear prevented the use of the structure except by two or three Germans, who did not remain long. It began to decay. In 1907 Will C. Barnes, then an assistant U. S. forester, suggested that Tumacacori Mission be made into a national monument. This was done by presidential proclamation in 1908. The national monument comprises ten acres of ground.

P.O. est. July 14, 1905. Fred A. Edward, p.m. Rescinded September 12, 1905. Re-established April 16, 1947. Paul Pyron Valenzuela, p.m.

Ref.: "Tumacacori Nat'l. Monument," Washington, D. C. Department of Interior, n.d., pp. 1-4; 20, p. 264; 88, II, 836-837; 51, p. 118; 5, Lewis R. Kaywood "Tumacacori," p. 2.

v.n. St. Joseph's Mission

Ref.: 87, p. 191. Maps: B-3; C-1; E-11 (Tumacacori).

a.n. Tumacacori de las Calabasas y Guebavi Land Grant        Santa Cruz
       Map C-4.
       In 1806 the Spanish Government made this grant to Juan Laguna, governor of the Indian pueblo of Tumacacori. Laguna never took up his land and in 1844 the Government of Mexico sold the land at auction. Following the Gadsden Purchase, this land grant was rejected in its entirety.

Ref.: Barnes.

### Tumacacori Mountains        Santa Cruz

El.: 6500'. Maps: GL-4; GL 5.
This range of mountains is in reality an extension of the Pajarito Mountains (q.v.). and of the Atascosa Mountains (q.v.). The United States Geographic Board established that the term Tumacacori applies to that portion of the range extending from (and including) Diablito Mountain to Peak Canyon.

Ref.: 34, p. 251; *Geographic Board Report, July 1, 1941*, p. 9

## VALEVIEW

Loc.: Not known.

The origin of this name has not been learned.

P.O. est. July 21, 1922. Clifford F. Peterson, p.m. Discont.?

Ref.: P.O. Records. Map: None.

## WALKER CANYON

El.: 5700'        Loc.: Santa Cruz CD-5-6

William Henry Walker (b. Watsonville, California, January 16, 1859; d. August 25, 1944) came to Arizona in 1886 and settled in the canyon which bears his name. He later moved to a ranch near Calabasas which was involved in title difficulties in connection with the Baca Float Land Grant (q.v.). Mr. Walker's wife was the sister of the Owens brothers, one of whom was killed by Geronimo. Mrs. Walker once spent a night hidden in a tree to avoid marauding Indians.

Ref.: Virgil Walker, Letter, March 1956. Map: GL-4.

## WASHINGTON CAMP

El.: 5500'        Loc.: Santa Cruz GH-4.5

The mining camps at Washington and Duquesne are so closely allied both in physical location and in history that they scarcely can be treated separately.

Mining in the early part of the 19th century left ruins of old Mexican adobe smelters in this area. In 1862 an important mine, the San Antonio, was discovered. Apache troubles kept the region from becoming very populous. However, a few white pioneers were living there in the late 1860's or early 1870's. Among them was Thomas Gardner (cf. Gardner Canyon). However, it was another twenty years before the camp became a mining center. The surge to importance began with the location of the Bonanza Mine by Thomas Shane and N. H. Capen in the early 1880's. They sold their claim to a Mr. Hensley who in turn sold it to the Duquesne Company c. 1889.

Meanwhile, in the early 1880's Washington Camp also developed. It appears that one of the early mines was called the Washington Mine, hence the name. Mount Washington first appears on GLO 1883, but the name Washington or Washington Camp does not appear until GLO 1887. The mountain is then shown about one mile northwest of the camp. At no time on GLO maps from 1883 to 1896 does the name Duquesne appear. As Duquesne, the second mining camp, began to develop, the two camps were situated about three-quarters of a mile apart. Near them were at least eighty claims covering sixteen hundred acres of mining ground. A half-dozen mines were actually in operation with their ores being reduced at Duquesne Camp. Several dwellings lay between the two camps. The headquarters for the Duquesne Mining and Reduction Company (home office: Pittsburgh, Pa.) was at Duquesne and the reducing plant at Washington. Gradually the two camps fell into inactivity. In 1940 a new mill was constructed and activity was resumed.

P.O. est. as Washington, May 13, 1880. William B. Hopkins, p.m. Name changed to Duquesne, June 6, 1890; rescinded October 28, 1890. Name changed to Duquesne August 17, 1904. Discont. February 14, 1920.

Ref.: 138a, pp. 321, 322, 327; 76, p. 43; *Arizona Star*, February 24, 1955, 9:5. Maps: C-1; C-6 (Washington); C-10 (Duquesne); E-20 (San Antonio).

a.n. Duquesne Gulch        Santa Cruz
       Washington Gulch        Santa Cruz

## WRIGHTSON, MOUNT

El.: 9432'        Loc.: Santa Cruz EF-1.1

In 1864 when J. Ross Browne traveled through southern Arizona, he mentioned the two main peaks of the Santa Rita Mountains, calling them descriptively "The Teats." These are the two mountains which are today known as Mount Hopkins (q.v.) and Mount Wrightson. Browne was in southern Arizona in the same year in which William Wrightson, manager of the Salero Mining Company, was killed by Apaches. Hopkins was also killed, but at another time.

Mount Wrightson shows on the Smith map (1879), but GLO 1887, 1892, and 1896 give two names to it, "Old Baldy or Santa Rita Peak." The name Old Baldy, which can be taken as descriptive considering the nature of the peak, came from the nickname of Capt. Richard S. Ewell, who was at Fort Buchanan (from 1857 to 1860). He was a great favorite and because of his youthful but bald head, his men are said to have named the peak Old Baldy in his honor. By 1881 the mountain was generally being called Mount Wrightson, although this name fails to appear with one exception for many years thereafter on maps. Hinton referred to it as "Mount Wrightson or Old Baldy." It is thought by some that the mountain was named Wrightson to honor the two brothers who lost their lives while mining in southern Arizona, John being killed by Mexicans, and

William by Apaches. On the Lenon map of Santa Cruz County, Mount Wrightson is shown southeast of a small, high peak marked "Old Baldy."
GLO 1903 shows Old Baldy and Mount Hopkins, but the map of 1909 reverses their position. Mount Wrightson does not appear until GLO 1933.
Ref.:   APHS Names File; Unidentified Clipping, November 1881 (Sharlot Hall Museum); 25, p. 25; 104, pp. 179, 180; 87, p. 183. Maps: B-3; C-5 (Santa Rita Peak); C-9 (Old Baldy); C-13 (Mt. Wrightson); GL-1; GL-3.

## YANK'S CANYON

El.: c. 4000'                    Loc.: Santa Cruz B-4
When military supplies were being hauled in southern Arizona, much of the freighting was done by two teamsters known as Hank and Yank. Their names were Hank Hewitt and Yank Bartlett.
Ref.:   Lenon; Theobald. Map: GL-4.

**a.n.** **Yank's Spring**         Map: GL-4             Santa Cruz

## YELLOW JACKET MOUNTAIN

El.: 4750'                    Loc.: Santa Cruz AB-3.5
This mountain was named after the Yellow Jacket Mine which was located by Thomas G. Roddick (d. June 1879) who came to Arizona in 1865 and lived in the Oro Blanco Mining District in 1874. He had two physicians when he died and they had a row over what caused his death. Upon the demise of the patient the case went into court where one doctor broke his cane over the head of the other. An autopsy on Roddick was ordered. The verdict as to the cause of death was that it was due to a "complication of diseases."

Ref.:   Thomas G. Roddick File, APHS. Map: GL-1.

**a.n.** **Yellowjacket Mine**       Map: GJ-7             Santa Cruz
      **Yellowjacket Mountain**    Map: B-3              Santa Cruz
      **Yellow Jacket Spring**     Map: GJ-2             Santa Cruz

# YAVAPAI COUNTY

*Fort Whipple — Pauline Weaver — Jerome.*

## YAVAPAI COUNTY:

Pro.: /yǽvəpay/

Yavapai is the name of an Indian tribe. The Yavapais take their name from *enyaeva* ("sun") and *pai* ("people"). The tribe, formerly referred to as Apache-Mohave Indians, is a branch of the Yuman family. The remnants of the Yavapai tribe were shifted from one reservation to another until they finally drifted back to their original home on the Verde River. On November 27, 1901, Camp McDowell Military Reservation was assigned for their use.

Yavapai County was among the four created by the first Arizona Territorial Legislature on November 8, 1864. The county area was so tremendous that subsequently it was divided to form six complete counties and parts of others. As originally established, Yavapai County reached from the New Mexico line on the east to the middle of the Gila River on the south and north to the Utah boundary. Its western boundary has not changed since its creation. From Yavapai as originally constituted have been formed Gila, Maricopa, Coconino, and Apache Counties, the last named having since been cut into Apache and Navajo counties. Despite its reduction in area, Yavapai remains larger than the state of New Jersey. Current county acreage is 5,179,240.

The county seat is Prescott, which from 1864 to 1867 and again from 1877 to 1889 also served as the territorial capital.

The history of Yavapai County is studded with stories about fabulous placers and mines, about Indian fights, and about pioneer settlements. Yavapai has always been a noted mining and stock raising county. In 1930 the county enclosed nearly forty per cent of the patented mineral area of Arizona. This is still largely true, despite uranium developments elsewhere in the state.

## ABRA

El.: 4439'                        Loc.: Yavapai 2, H-1
Pro.: /ábrə/                      Spanish: "gorge"
Descriptive.
Twenty-nine miles south of Ash Fork is Abra, a small station on the railroad, near a deep canyon.

Ref.: Barnes. Map: GM-13.

## AGUA FRIA RIVER

El.: c. 3800'          Loc.: Yavapai 3, BE-10.2-3.2
Pro.: /agwa fríyə/        Spanish: "cold water"
It is likely that the name for this river is descriptive, although currently much of its bed is dry.

Ref.: None. Maps: C-1; C-2; GM-11; GM-12; GM-15.

**a.n. Agua Fria Peak**          Map: B-6      Yavapai and Maricopa
   **Agua Fria Valley**   El.: c. 4000'. Maps: C-4; E-20    Yavapai
   In 1875 a stage station and post office existed at this location on the Black Canyon road. The station was in operation as early as 1872 and earlier – in 1869 – the Bowers brothers had a flour mill here (cf. Dewey).

P.O. est. May 15, 1875. Dennis J. Marr, p.m. Name changed to Aguafria, July 22, 1893. Discont. January 11, 1895.

**v.n. Agua Frio**

Ref.: Barnes; P.O. Records.

## ALEXANDRA

El.: c. 5500'               Loc.: Yavapai 3, B-8.3
T. N. Alexander, Ed Peck, and Col. H. A. Bigelow were prominent miners in the early days of Yavapai County. Mrs. T. N. Alexander (b. 1828; d. 1898) was the first white woman to visit the mine in the Bradshaw Mountains where the mining community of Alexandra, named in her honor, developed. Alexander and Bigelow laid out the townsite.

P.O. est. as Alexandria, August 6, 1878. Joseph S. Drew, p.m. Discont. March 25, 1896.

Ref.: Thomas Matthew Alexander File, Sharlot Hall Museum, Prescott; P.O. Records. Maps: C-4; GM-3.

## AMERICAN RANCH

El.: c. 5000'               Loc.: Yavapai 2, G-3.8
James Harrison Lee (d. 1915) owned a ranch, known both as the Lee Ranch and as the American Ranch, on the road from Ehrenberg to Prescott. His place was a stage stop. Lee lived here for many years, finally selling out his cattle and brand in early 1898.

Barnes relates a story about a sack of poisoned flour being left in the store, which was then permitted to remain open to the depredations of the Indians. Later a scouting party found twenty-four dead and fourteen very sick Indians in a nearby camp.

Ref.: 14, p. XXV; Barnes; APHS Files; *Southwest Stockman,* January 28, 1898, 5:1. Map: GM-8.

**a.n. American Valley**                             Yavapai
   Loc.: Valley of American Ranch.
   The body of Jacob Smith, who had been murdered by Indians, was found in this valley by a party of soldiers.

Ref.: *Arizona Miner,* March 5, 1870, 3:2.

## ANTELOPE PEAK

El.: 5766'                      Loc.: Yavapai 2, EF-8.3
In 1865 Richard McCormick wrote of the settlement of Weaver as being at the foot of Antelope Hill. It was on the top of this hill in 1863 that members of Pauline Weaver's expedition found an incredibly rich deposit of gold. Abraham Harlow Peeples related that the party camped on the slope of this mountain, about eighty-five miles northwest of the present city of Phoenix, and here Peeples killed three antelope, from which came the name Antelope Mountain. Peeples jerked the meat and while it was drying a few members of the party indulged in sporadic prospecting. They struck it rich in the creek bed the very first day and named the arroyo Weaver Gulch.

While the miners were working in the creek bed, a Mexican climbed to the two thousand foot summit of the mountain to the east of the gulch, and there in a small saddleback of the mountain, in less than one acre of ground, lay nugget gold barely beneath the surface of the earth. In under three months men took out over one hundred thousand dollars in nugget gold. This led to the name Rich Hill, which contemporaries said lay between the forks of Antelope Creek on the west and Weaver Creek on the east. The only tool used by the prospectors was a knife to force the gold out of crevices and pockets. The knife wielders worked busily and well so that within two years the placers were exhausted. Through some cartographical error, maps dated from 1904 show Antelope Peak six miles north by west of Weaver and four miles from Rich Hill.

**v.n. Antelope Hill**

Ref.: Richard McCormick, *Arizona, Its Resources and Prospects,* p. 17; New York, 1865; APHS Files; 111, p. 111; 89, pp. 64-65; 87, p. 98. Maps: C-5; C-11 (Antelope Peak and Rich Hill); E-20; GM-6.

**a.n. Antelope Creek**   Maps: C-1; GM-3; GM-6; GM-11   Yavapai
   **Antelope Range**                                Yavapai
   This is what Lt. George M. Wheeler called the Weaver Mountains.

Ref.: 87, p. 301.

   **Antelope Valley**      Map: GM-6                Yavapai
   The first name for Antelope Valley was Stanton. The history of Stanton is an outstanding example of a ruthless and bloody climb to power. When the vicinity of Antelope Hill became important as a mining location, it was inevitable that a community would develop which would be important as a stage station. Such a station did develop under the name of Antelope Station, run by William Partridge. There was also a store owner named G. H. Wilson. There was no love lost between the two men because Wilson's pigs had broken into Partridge's place. Stanton, who sought to run things in the vicinity, played up the feud in order to get rid of both men. He bribed Mexicans to tell Partridge that "the owner of the pigs is out to get you," whereas actually their owner (Wilson) had said in public that he would pay any damages. In an era and place where self-preservation was the rule, Partridge hesitated not a moment in shooting Wilson on sight. He was, of course, imprisoned. With two down and one store owner – Timmerman – to go, Stanton connived to get rid of Timmerman. Having done so, Stanton then arranged for the stage road to run by his own place, thereby cornering the trade that his victims had built up. One of his first acts was to rename the town after himself. Stanton's nefarious deeds continued until the end of

his life, which came abruptly in 1886 when he was murdered by a Mexican who was avenging his insulted sister.

Despite Stanton's desire to maintain his name as that of the town, other citizens in the community managed to have the name changed to Antelope Valley after the name Stanton had been official only six months.

P.O. est. as Stanton, March 5, 1875. Charles P. Stanton, p.m. Changed to Antelope Valley, September 1, 1875. Charles C. Genung, p.m. Discont. December 13, 1890.

Apparently the office was re-established as Stanton sometime between 1891 and the final discontinuance of the office under the name Stanton on May 23, 1905. This changing back to Stanton probably occurred about 1896 when mining activity in the region showed a sharp and renewed upswing. Stanton is today a ghost town. In 1959 the location was purchased by The Saturday Evening Post. The town, renamed Ulcer Gulch, was to become a prize in an advertising contest.

Ref.:   170, p. 72; 58, p. 71; *Daily Arizona Miner*, December 20, 1897, 4:4; *Arizona Daily Star*, May 25, 1959. Maps: C-4; GM-6.

**Antelope Wash**        Map: GM-17                    Yavapai

## ANVIL ROCK

El.: 5700'                    Loc.: Yavapai 1, B-6.6
This huge volcanic rock resembles a blacksmith's anvil.

Ref.: *Arizona Miner*, September 30, 1871, 2:2. Maps: C-4; C-12; E-20.

**a.n. Anvil Rock Station**                                Yavapai
In 1881 this was a stage station near the rock.
Ref.:   87, p. xxiv.

## APACHE

Pro.: /əpǽči/                    Loc.: Not known.
The origin of this name has not yet been learned.

P.O. est. January 7, 1873. John A. Meredith, p.m. Discont. August 11, 1875.

Ref.: P.O. Records. Map: None.

## ARIZONA CITY

El.: c. 4000'                    Loc.: Yavapai 3, BC-6.2
This is reported to have been a small mining camp on Big Bug Creek.

Ref.: Barnes. Map: None.

## ARRASTRA CREEK

El.: 2540'                    Loc.: Yavapai 3, C-9
Pro.: /ərǽstrə/        Spanish: a drag mill for grinding ores
In the early days of mining in Yavapai County and elsewhere, many miners used arrastras to work their ores. The remains of primitive ore grinding stones have led to the naming of several places in Arizona. A few are listed below. There are various ways of spelling the name.

Ref.: Allan.

**a.n. Arrastre Creek**                                Yavapai
     Maps: GM-3; GM-4; GM-6; GM-10.
**Arrastre Wash**        Map: GM-9                    Yavapai
**Arrastra Mountain**    Map: GH-6                    Mohave

## ASH FORK

El.: 5144'                    Loc.: Yavapai 1, H-4.2
Freighters who carried materials to Jerome traveled part of the way along Ash Creek, so named because of a group

of small ash trees. The creek divided into three forks at its mouth and all rejoined at the place where the original town of Ash Fork was constructed, where a stage depot existed under the ash trees. The freighters and operators of the stage line to Phoenix agitated for a more convenient freight and passenger terminal than that at Williams. In October 1882, the railroad company announced that a second siding west of Williams would be established; by November both passengers and freight were disembarking at Ash Fork. According to one source, the original name proposed for the new depot was Ash Canyon, but the name Ash Fork was more suitable. The original town burned c. 1893 and the present town was then begun on the other side of the tracks at its present location.

Whether the name should be spelled as one word or two has been a matter of controversy for many years. It occurs today in both forms.

P.O. est. as Ash Fork, April 2, 1883. Henry W. Kline, p.m. Name changed to Ashfork, September 17, 1894. Wells Fargo Station, 1885. Name changed to Ash Fork, June 1, 1950.

Ref.:   Kelly; 61, p. 39; P.O. Records. Maps: C-5; GM-1.

**a.n. Ashfork Draw**        Maps: B-4; GM-8                    Yavapai
**Ashfork Field**        Map: B-4                    Yavapai

## AULTMAN

El.: c. 4000'                    Loc.: Yavapai 3, EF-5
At least as early as 1885 there was a post office under the name Aultman in connection with the Conger mill in the Middle Verde section of Yavapai County. Aultman was a man who lived there. Today nothing remains of the Aultman settlement.

P.O. est. July 9, 1885. Charles A. Bush, p.m. Discont. February 21, 1923.

Ref.:   Barnes; R. W. Wingfield; Goddard; P.O. Records. Maps: C-6; C-12.

## AZATLAN

                    Loc.: None
The first Arizona territorial legislature in 1864 found the delegates from the first district trying to establish the territorial capital anywhere but in Prescott. So strong were these gentlemen in their insistence that a capital be established elsewhere that they suggested building a town to be called Azatlan at the junction of the Verde and Salt Rivers. The place never existed in more than name. Barnes, however, says there was a mining camp by this name six miles south of Prescott in 1866.

Ref.: Barnes.

## AZTEC PASS

El.: c. 6000'                    Loc.: Yavapai 2, D-1
Lt. Amiel W. Whipple and his men struggled up the east side of the mountains toward this pass through a snowstorm. When they reached the top they encountered such a gale that they had to cling together in order to avoid being blown away. To the right of the men lay mountains at the base of which were found ruins. The presence of these ruins caused the party to call the mountains the Aztec Range, after Indians thought at one time to have lived in Arizona.

One member of the party, Mr. Campbell, climbed a hill several hundred feet above the ridge of the pass and found at its top a ruin at least twenty-five feet wide at one end and twenty at the other, with the walls still five feet high. Its entrance was almost inaccessible and it commanded a full view of the pass. Their imaginations stirred by the ancient ruins, Whipple's party gave the name Aztec Pass to the place.

v.n. Juniper Mountains

Ref.: 178, pp. 91, 94; 177, pp. 192, 198-199, 194 (Note 11); Dobyns. Maps: C-5; C-12; E-11.

## BAGDAD

El.: 4100'          Loc.: Yavapai 2, AB-7.5

Bagdad was named for the mining claim located January 1, 1882, by W. J. Pace and J. M. Murphy. In 1883 John Lawler bought the Bagdad claim.

In 1955 there was an active open pit copper mine here.

P.O. est. February 26, 1910. Henry A. Geisendorfer, p.m. Discont. July 15, 1913. Re-est. July 12, 1944.

Ref.: Willson; P.O. Records; C. A. Anderson, E. A. Scholz, J. D. Strobell, Jr., *Geology and Ore Deposits of the Bagdad Area*, U. S. Govt. Printing Office, 1955. Maps: C-11; GM-2.

## BALD HILL

El.: 4684'          Loc.: Yavapai 2, A-1.2

Descriptive.

Ref.: None. Map: GM-13.

| a.n. Bald Hill | El.: 3801'. Map: GM-3 | Yavapai |
|---|---|---|
| Bald Hill | El.: 6193'. Map: GM-21 | Yavapai |
| Bald Hill | El.: 6161'. Map: GM-9 | Yavapai |
| Bald Hill | El.: 6177' | Yavapai |
| Bald Mountain | El.: 6092'. Map: GM-19 | Yavapai |
| Bald Knob | El.: 5041'. Map: GB-15 | Cochise |
| Bald Ridge | El.: 5939'. Map: GB-24 | Cochise |
| Bald Hill | Map: B-9 | Coconino |

## BANGHARTS

El.: c. 6000'          Loc.: Yavapai 2, H-1.5

In 1866 George W. Banghart (d. July 1895) established a stage station here. His numerous daughters proved a great attraction.

Ref.: Barnes. Maps: C-7; C-8.

## BATTLE FLAT

El.: 5740'          Loc.: Yavapai 3, AB-8

In May 1864, five white men held an estimated one hundred and fifty Indians at bay. The men included Fred Henry, Stuart M. Wall, DeMarion Scott, Samuel Herron, and Frank Binkley, who had camped on this small open area. The fight lasted for three hours. Fred Henry was wounded in the arm, but was able to go for help. Before he returned with assistance the Apaches had abandoned the fight. Frank Binkley was blinded in one eye and Sam Herron was so severely wounded that he died nine days later.

Ref.: 55, p. 385; *Arizona Star*, February 4, 1899, 1:6. Maps: GM-3; GM-20.

## BAYARD

El.: c. 5000'          Loc.: Yavapai 3, A-9.5

Bayard was a mining camp named for James A. Bayard, secretary of Arizona Territory in 1887.

P.O. est. May 25, 1888. William B. Long, p.m. Discont. April 24, 1897.

Ref.: P.O. Records; Barnes. Map: C-8.

## BEAR

El.: 4311'          Loc.: Yavapai 3, A-1

While the railroad was being built, a bear was shot here. This is the shipping point for flagstone which is freighted in huge pieces to points throughout the United States.

Ref.: Barnes; Schnebly. Map: GM-5.

The presence of bear or the fancied resemblance to a bear has led to the use of the word in several place names, probable instances of which are listed below:

| a.n. Bear Mountain | El.: 6288'. Map: GM-21 | Yavapai |
|---|---|---|
| Bear Spring (Ojo del Oso) | Map: GB-11 | Apache |
| Bear Canyon | Map: GB-24 | Cochise |
| Bear Creek | Map: GB-6 | Cochise |
| Bear Gulch | Map: GB-6 | Cochise |
| Bear Springs | Map: E-20 | Cochise |
| Bear Canyon | Loc.: Baboquivari Mts. | Pima |
| Bear Mountain | Loc.: T. 2 N., R. 30 E. | Greenlee |
| Bear Valley | | Greenlee |
| Bear Wallow Creek | | Greenlee |

Loc.: T. 3 N., R. 28 and 29, E.

Pete Slaughter (cf. Slaughter Mountain, Graham) in 1884 drove cattle into this valley and saw numerous bears with wallows along the creek where the bears came to ward off pesky flies.

Ref.: Barnes.

**Bear Springs**          Navajo

Loc.: 3 miles n. Steamboat Canyon on e. side Steamboat Canyon Wash.

**Bear Wallow**          Map: GJ-3          Pima

This name was in existence by 1880.

Ref.: Emerson O. Stratton ms, APHS.

**Bear Well(s)**          Loc.: 7 miles s. of Fresnal          Pima

There are two dug wells here, one twenty and the other twenty-nine feet deep. Their Papago name is Tjotonvaxiaka ("bear's well").

**Bear Valley**          Santa Cruz

Loc.: T. 23 S., R. 11 E. and T. 22 S., R. 11 E.

This area of relatively low ridges is west of the Atascosa Mountains.

**Bear Hills**          Map: C-12          Yuma

**Bear Springs**          Map: GB-6          Cochise

In 1854 Lt. John G. Parke noted six springs which make up this location. Here on May 5, 1871, Lt. Howard B. Cushing, three soldiers, and several civilians were killed by Chiricahua Apaches.

Ref.: 34, pp. 26-27; 22, p. 105.

**Bear and the Rabbit**          Navajo

Loc.: In Monument Pass; rock formation.

**Bear's Ears**          Navajo

Loc.: In Monument Pass; rock formation.

## BEAVER CREEK

El.: c. 4500'          Loc.: Yavapai 3, GF-3.5-4.5

Early settlers found many beaver along Beaver Creek. The presence of beaver frequently led to incorporating the word in place names.

**v.n. Wet Beaver Creek**
Ref.:  Barnes; 11, p. 25. Map: GM-21.

**a.n. Beaverhead**                                           Yavapai
   Early pioneers had a camp at Beaverhead on the old road
   from Camp Verde to Flagstaff. The cabin was still in existence in 1894 when Fewkes reported its presence.

Ref.:  APHS Files.

   **Beaverhead Flat**      Map: B-6               Yavapai
   **Beaver Dam Wash**                            Apache
   Loc.: North of Little Colorado River in western Apache
   County.

   **Beaver Canyon**        Map: B-9               Coconino
   **Beaver Creek Crossing**
   The descent to the crossing on this creek was very steep
   and abrupt. Beaver Creek was described by Hinton as being
   a large stream of permanent water with a rocky bed and a
   good crossing.

Ref.:  87, p. xxxvi.

## BELL ROCK

El.: 5228'                    Loc.: Yavapai 3, FG-2.1
This rock has a liberty bell shape.

Ref.:  Schnebly; 29, p. 53. Map: GM-21.

**a.n. Bell Rock Spring**     Map: B-8               Yavapai

## BELL'S CANYON

El.: c. 4000'                 Loc.: Yavapai 3, EF-6.5
Bell's Canyon has been described as "one of the roughest
granite mountains on earth." It was also one of the roughest
to try to go through during the days of Indian troubles, for
it was a natural ambush pocket. Here on May 3, 1865,
Richard Bell, Cornelius Sage, and Charles Cunningham were
killed by Indians. A year later George W. Leihy, who had
succeeded Charles D. Poston as superintendent of Indian
Affairs, was murdered by Indians, as was also his clerk,
W. H. Evarts. The first man known to have been killed in
the canyon was Bell, hence the name.

Ref.:  52, VII, 2, 128; *Weekly Arizona Miner*, April 16, 1875,
       2:2; *Arizona Miner*, November 30, 1866, 2:3; 111, pp.
       188-189. Map: GM-6.

## BIG BUG

El.: c. 4300'                 Loc.: Yavapai 3, B-7
The first miners who came into this area from Walker's
Diggings in 1863 found enormous bugs after which they
named the creek. The bugs still abound. They are large,
dark brown, and shiny flying beetles about the size of a
walnut. The creek was named before the establishment of
the famous Big Bug District or its Big Bug lode. The mining
community of Big Bug took its name from the creek on
which it was located.

P.O. est. as Bigbug, March 31, 1879. William A. Muncy, p.m.
Changed to Red Rock November 28, 1879. Amos C. Stedman,
p.m. Changed to Big Bug, March 29, 1881. Changed to Bigbug,
August 22, 1895. Discont. March 31, 1910.

Ref.:  Thompson; Merritt; P.O. Records; *Weekly Arizona
       Miner*, June 5, 1869, 3:2. Maps: C-4; E-20.

**a.n. Bigbug Creek**   Maps: GM-3; GM-11; GM-20    Yavapai
   **Big Bug Mesa** El.: 7000'. Maps: GM-3; GM-20   Yavapai

## BLACK CANYON

El.: c. 5000'                 Loc.: Yavapai 3, CD-7-10
Black Canyon takes its name from the malpais (Spanish:
"bad land," i.e., volcanic) formation of its walls which have
a black appearance. The canyon was used by stage drivers
and freighters, since the road along its bottom connected
military forts in the early days. The Black Canyon highway
follows the old road, but is cut through the high sides of
the canyon. At points one can look down to the canyon
floor and see signs of the old trail.
Black Canyon Hill was a formidable part of the journey
along the canyon. Not only did it afford a convenient place
for hold-ups, but it was also a dangerous one-way grade
with few turnouts to permit passing. To avoid the possibility
of meeting on the hill, stage drivers announced their coming with blasts on long tin horns; two blasts acknowledged
that someone was coming from the opposite direction.
Occasionally thunder or other noises made hearing the horns
impossible. When as a result two stages met at an impassable
place, "the 'up' team was unhitched, two men grasped the
tongue of the vehicle and rolled it downhill until reaching
a place where it could be passed."
The current community of Black Canyon (El.: 2000') is
on the Black Canyon highway. Here a post office was established in 1894 under the name of Cañon, but was closed in
1906. Locally it was also referred to as Goddard's after its
first postmaster. For a time the area was served by a post
office at Rock Springs (q.v.) but when that office closed,
a new post office was opened under the name of Black Canyon. The residents selected the name because the locality
had been known as Cañon, the Black Canyon is located
just west of the community, and the community is on the
new Black Canyon highway.

P.O. est. as Cañon, May 19, 1894. Charles A. Goddard, p.m.
Discont. October 17, 1906. P.O. est. as Black Canyon June 1,
1955, Mrs. Alma K. Amann, p.m.

**v.n. Bumblebee Canyon**
Ref.:  Amann; Schnebly; Slipher; 16, p. 306; P.O. Records.
       Maps: E-20; GM-3; GM-4; GM-15.

**a.n. Black Canyon Station**   Maps: GM-9; GM-12    Yavapai
   In 1875 this was a stage station where the Agua Fria River
   crossed the Black Canyon road.

Ref.:  Theobald.

## BLACK FOREST

El.: c. 6000'                 Loc.: Yavapai 1, H-5-6
In 1854 Lt. Amiel W. Whipple named the mesa west of Bill
Williams Mountain Black Forest because of the vast extent
of cedar in the area.

**v.n. Black Mesa**
Ref.:  44, p. 180; 165, p. 53; 177, p. 89. Maps: C-6; E-12;
       E-20.

## BLACK MOUNTAIN

El.: 6000'                    Loc.: Yavapai 3, EF-1
George Black, a successful saloon keeper and cattleman,
was an early settler in the Flagstaff area.

Ref.:  Slipher. Map: C-13.

**a.n. Black Pass**           Map: B-8               Coconino
   **Black Springs**         Map: GC-3              Coconino

## BLIND INDIAN CREEK

El.: 3500'　　　　　　Loc.: Yavapai 2, H-9
When the first prospectors entered this area in the 1860's, an old blind Indian was camped on this creek, hence its name.

Ref.:　Barnes. Maps: GM-6; GM-20; GM-22.

## BLOODY BASIN

El.: 3077'　　　　　　Loc.: Yavapai 3, F-9
According to local legend Bloody Basin earned its name because of numerous Indian fights which occurred in it. There are many Indian ruins in the Basin. The area is topographically extremely rough and even today it is not uncommon for people to become lost in it. During the spring of 1949 a family was lost here and nearly froze before being found.

Ref.:　Schnebly. Maps: C-9; GM-19.

## BLUEBELL

El.: 4620'　　　　　　Loc.: Yavapai 3, BC-7
The Bluebell Mine was at one time an extremely important copper mine about a mile west of the small railroad station of Bluebell. The station was named for the mine. An aerial tram was used to carry the ore from the mine to the siding, from which the ore was transhipped for smelting to the Humboldt Smelter. Bluebell is today a ghost town.

Ref.:　Glannon; 4, p. 305. Maps: GM-11; GM-25.

## BLUE MOUNTAIN

El.: 5550'　　　　　　Loc.: Yavapai 2, BC-4.5
Descriptive.

Ref.:　Barnes. Map: GM-2.

## BOGGS RANCH

El.: c. 6000'　　　　　　Loc.: Yavapai 3, BC-6.3
Theodore W. Boggs (b. c. 1836, Independence, Missouri; d. June 7, 1905) had this ranch in the middle 1860's. He came to Arizona in 1863 and later with others on a prospecting party he discovered the Mexican Gulch Mine. The Boggs Ranch served as a stage station.

Ref.:　APHS Files. Maps: C-10; C-11.

## BOLADA

El.: c. 6000'　　　　　　Loc.: Yavapai 2, H-8
Pro.:　/bówleydə/ or /bowládə/
A post office was established at Bolada in order to serve miners in the area. There were three families living in Bolada, their names being Bones, Lane and Dandrea. By using the first two letters of each name, the name for the post office was coined. There is nothing remaining of Bolada today, although the Dandrea family still lives nearby.

P.O. est. February 24, 1921. Alice Bones, p.m. Discont. August 20, 1932.

Ref.:　P.O. Records; Barnes; Theobald. Map: F-3.

## BOTKIN

El.: 6000'　　　　　　Loc.: Yavapai 3, C-2.2
Robert Botkin was a section foreman on the United Verde and Pacific Railroad. The switch station, now vanished, was named for him.

Ref.:　Barnes. Map: C-10.

## BOULDER CREEK

El.: c. 4000'　　　　　　Loc.: Yavapai 3, BC-9.8-10.2
Descriptive. At one time there was a mining town called Boulder Creek (T. 15 N., R. 10 W.), which is now gone.

Ref.:　Barnes. Maps: GM-2; GM-3; GM-7.

## BOWERS RANCH

El.: c. 4000'　　　　　　Loc.: Yavapai 3, C-6
King S. Woolsey was the original owner of what came to be known as the Bowers Ranch. When Woolsey sold the property to Nathan Bowers, a stockman of Prescott, Bowers built stone-walled corrals and part of his house from stone taken from what was once a prehistoric dwelling at this spot. Bowers' home lay on the road between Prescott and the Verde Valley, a route which was noted for its history of encounters with Indians. Since Bowers' place was half way between the two terminal points, it was sometimes referred to as Half-Way House. The place was often attacked by Indians, but never successfully. It once served as a gathering point for an expedition led by King S. Woolsey against Apaches.

Ref.:　*Arizona Sentinel*, May 24, 1874, 1:2; 111, p. 189; 52, II, 263; 22, pp. 165-66. Map: E-20.

## BRADSHAW MOUNTAINS

El.: 9000'　　　　　　Loc.: Yavapai 3, BC-9.8
The Bradshaw Mountains take their name from William D. Bradshaw, who came to Arizona from California c. 1863 (*See* Bradshaw Ferry or Olive City, Yuma). While Bradshaw's brother Isaac was running the ferry, Bill Bradshaw was out prospecting and exploring. On one of his trips he led a small party into the mountains to which he gave his name. In the fall of 1863 the Bradshaw brothers first discovered some of the rich minerals in the Bradshaw Mountains; the new mining district was named the Bradshaw District in their honor. William Bradshaw, a heavy drinker, cut his throat with a razor during a fit of delirium tremens at La Paz, where he is buried in an unmarked grave.

Because of the rich silver finds, these mountains were sometimes referred to as the Silver Range in the early days. By 1871 there was a sufficient number of miners and prospectors in the Bradshaw Mountains to warrant the laying out of a townsite on top of Bradshaw Mountain above Poland's cabin (cf. Poland). The community of Bradshaw lay on the trail from Prescott to the Tiger and Eclipse Mines. The townsite was surveyed by O. H. Case and was called Bradshaw City; it lay just under Mount Wasson. At one time it had five thousand residents, but now it is nearly deserted.

P.O. est. July 1, 1874. Noah C. Sheckells, p.m. Discont. December 15, 1874.

Ref.: *Arizona Miner,* September 21, 1864, 2:2; April 29, 1871, 2:2; 87, p. 254; 52, III, 88-89; 4, p. 307; P.O. Records. Maps: C-3 (city); C-12; GM-3; GM-4; GM-7.

## BRADY BUTTE

El.: 4400'   Loc.: Yavapai 3, C-7. Sec. 19, T. 12 N., R. 1 W.
Francis Brady worked a mine at this place c. 1881.

Ref.: Barnes. Map: None.

## BRIGGS

El.: 2759'                              Loc.: Yavapai 3, A-10
Briggs was a mining camp. The reason for the name has not yet been ascertained.

P.O. est. December 30, 1890. Emory W. Fisher, p.m. Discont. March 20, 1907.

Ref.: Barnes; Gardner; P.O. Records. Maps: C-7; GM-3.

## BROOKLYN PEAK

El.: 5379'                              Loc.: Yavapai 3, EF-9.2
The Brooklyn Mine was the origin for the name of this peak.

Ref.: Barnes. Map: GM-19.

## BUENO

El.: 5258'                              Loc.: Yavapai 3, AB-7.4
Pro.: /bwéyno/
The Bully Bueno Mine was located at this place in 1872.

P.O. est. June 27, 1881. Marion A. Vickroy, p.m. Discont. June 1, 1893.

Ref.: P.O. Records; Barnes. Maps: C-5; E-20; GM-3.

## BULLARD PEAK

El.: c. 3600'                           Loc.: Yavapai 2, A-10
A prospector named Bullard had a mine about five miles south of Bullard Peak for many years.

Ref.: Barnes. Map: C-11.

**a.n. Bullard Wash**   Loc.: T. 11 N., R. 13 W.                Yavapai

## BUMBLE BEE

El.: 2509'                              Loc.: Yavapai 3, CD-9
The first prospectors who entered this area in 1863 found a bumblebee nest full of honey in the cliffs along the creek. The bees objected in the usual way to being disturbed, and the prospectors named the place Bumble Bee Creek.

In the early days a stage station was run by a man named Mr. Bobs where Bumble Bee community is now located. Mr. Snyder bought the place from Bobs c. 1887. When the post office was established the name Bumble Bee was selected. In 1948 it was a town of about sixty persons. The fourteen buildings were owned privately. The town was put up for sale in April 1949. Bumble Bee is today an abandoned place.

P.O. est. as Bumblebee, February 3, 1879. William D. Powell, p.m.

Ref.: G. E. P. Smith; Barnes; Sharlot Hall Museum Files; P.O. Records. Maps: C-4; GM-3; GM-4.

**a.n. Bumble Bee Creek**   Maps: GM-3; GM-4; GM-11   Yavapai
   **Bumblebee Creek**      Map: B-7                   Gila
   Many bumblebees are found at the Bumblebee Tank and along the creek.

## BURNT RANCH

El.: 5125'   Loc.: Yavapai 2, I-4. N.e. of Prescott 7 miles.
Jake Miller and a single companion in 1865 built a small log cabin northeast of Prescott where Miller spent his time making pine timber shakes for use in Prescott.

The fact that the cabin was in a grassy area led Judge E. W. Wells to arrange with Miller to take care of Wells' cattle, herding them by day and corraling them at night. Once when Miller went to bring in the cattle, he noticed a raven fly up from the brush. It was followed by a second and then a third raven. Looking intently at the brush, Miller observed the head of an Indian. He hurriedly rounded up the cattle and headed toward the corral, whereupon several Indians broke out in open pursuit. Miller stopped them temporarily by shooting the first one. Miller's bulldog at once jumped on the dead Indian and began worrying the body, thus delaying the other Indians who stopped to fight off and kill the dog. This gave Miller time to get the cattle into the corral and himself into the cabin where he and his friend prepared themselves for an attack. It came swiftly.

Finally Miller had but a single bullet left. The practice in those days was for a man to use his last shot on himself, but in this instance Miller decided to risk it in an effort to kill the Indian chief, thus ending the fight, since Indians characteristically ceased fighting when they lost their leader. Cautiously Miller poked his rifle through a bit of chinking, only to have the gun caught by an Indian outside. In jumping back, Miller recovered his rifle and also laid his hand on an old forgotten horse pistol loaded with buckshot. The next time he looked through a higher hole he found the chief was lying directly below, watching the hole in the chinking through which the rifle had previously been pushed. Miller fired the pistol. The Indian sprang up and backward about twenty feet and fell dead. The marauding Indians immediately took to their heels, with Miller defiantly firing his final bullet at their retreating backs.

When the mail carrier passed by that evening and stopped to water his mules, Miller sent word by him to Wells to come and get his cattle. The cattle were then taken into Prescott. Miller went with them. That same night the Indians burned the cabin and the corral to the ground. From this incident came the name Burnt Ranch.

When Gen. George Crook was assigned to a new command from that which he had so successfully held in Arizona, a farewell gathering was held for him at Burnt Ranch. Hundreds walked to listen to the words of the new commander Gen. August V. Kautz, who bade Crook farewell.

Ref.: 52, V, 211-315; 22, p. 239. Map: None.

## CACTUS BASIN

El.: c. 4000'                          Loc.: Yavapai 3, E-8
Descriptive. The basin is thickly overgrown with prickly pear cactus.

Ref.: West. Map: GM-11.

Many place names in Arizona use the word "cactus" descriptively. A few are given below:

**a.n. Cactus Mountain**      Map: GM-21              Yavapai
   **Cactus Ridge**      El.: 6799'. Map: GD-9         Gila

**Cactus Flat**          Loc.: S. of Safford          Graham
Cactus Flat is a small community, the correct name of which is Lebanon (q.v., Graham). However, Cactus Flat is now in general local use.

**Cactus**          Loc.: E. of Phoenix 8 miles          Maricopa

**Cactus**          Loc.: N. of Phoenix 12 miles, T. 3 N., R. 3 E.
P.O. est. May 4, 1918. William Hyatt, p.m.
Ref.:  P.O. Records.

**Cactus Plains**                                                  Yuma
El.: 2000'. Loc.: Near Bill Williams River

## CAMEL ROCK

El.: c. 4000'          Loc.: Yavapai 3, FG-1-2
          S. end of Oak Creek.

Descriptive. This is a humpbacked rock. A trail leads to the top of this rock, from which a magnificent view can be had.

**v.n. The Camel**
Ref.:  Schnebly; 29, p. 52. Map: None.

## CAPITOL BUTTE

El.: 6347'          Loc.: Yavapai 3, F-1
The origin of this name has not been ascertained. At one time it reportedly was called "George Otey's Tombstone" because that gentleman frequently said he wished to be buried there.

Ref.:  Barnes. Map: GM-21.

## CASTLE CREEK

El.: 2500'          Loc.: Yavapai 3, BA-12-11
          Yavapai 2, HG-11-10

The creek bed lies in a canyon which has castellated rock walls. The Wickenburg stage road used to follow the creek bed for miles.

Ref.:  Barnes. Maps: C-8; GM-3; GM-4; GM-7.

**a.n. Castle Hot Springs**                                        Yavapai
El.: 1800'. Maps: C-10; C-6 (Hot Springs).
Although one story says that Charles Craig and his men moved southward following a battle with the Apaches and discovered Castle Hot Springs on November 4, 1867, no documentation of this discovery has been uncovered. However, the discovery of the springs by George Monroe (d. December 23, 1897) and Ed Farley in 1874, following which the two men made a trail to the springs, is authenticated by a story in the *Weekly Arizona Miner*, June 15, 1877, Supplement, 1:1. On May 27, 1877, according to the same article, the springs were re-located by Jesse Jackson, who had expressed his intention of settling at the place. The same article notes that the main spring issues from granite rock at the head of a small canyon and that it has a temperature of about 150° F., which drops about 20° within two hundred yards. The waters were reported able to clean all dirt from a "miner's shirt after a three month's prospecting tour in about five minutes," no mean feat. The first name for the springs was Monroe Springs. The place has since developed into a resort.
P.O. est. as Hot Springs, May 22, 1891. Minnie Grove, p.m. Name changed to Castle Hot Springs, May 1, 1936.
Ref.:  "Apaches and the Magic Waters," *Arizona Magazine*, February, 1914, p. 6; P.O. Records; *Weekly Arizona Miner*, June 15, 1877, Supplement, 1:1; *Arizona Journal Miner*, December 27, 1897, 4:2.

**Monroe Canyon**          Map: GM-19          Yavapai

## CATOCTIN

El.: c. 5000'          Loc.: Yavapai 2, G-5.7
The Catoctin Mine gave the name to the post office established to provide mail service to miners.
P.O. est. December 29, 1902. Henry N. Tharsing, p.m. Discont. July 15, 1920.
Ref.:  Barnes; P.O. Records. Maps: C-12; GM-6.

## CHAPARRAL

El.: c. 6000'          Loc.: Yavapai 3, A-5.8
Pro.: /sǽpərǽl/          Spanish: "bramble bushes; evergreen oaks"

A mine in this vicinity was located in dense chaparral. Chaparral was a shipping point on the railroad.
P.O. est. as Chaparral, May 24, 1894. Harman B. Hanna, p.m. Discont. December 31, 1917.

**v.n. Chapara Gulch**
Ref.:  P.O. Records; Barnes; 151, p. 209. Maps: GM-11; GM-12; GM-15; GM-20.

**a.n. Chaparral Gulch**          Map: GM-3          Yavapai

## CHASM CREEK

El.: c. 4000'          Loc.: Yavapai 3, EF-6
Pro.: /čæsəm/ or /kǽsəm/
Descriptive.
Ref.:  Dugas. Map: GM-19.

## CHERRY CREEK

El.: c. 2500'          Loc.: Yavapai 3, DF-3.9
The former abundance of wild cherry trees lining this canyon is gone today.

That Cherry Creek was known by this name at least as early as October 1868 is attested to by the fact that a scouting excursion was held along this creek by members of the First and Eighth Cavalry and the Fourteenth and Thirty-Second Infantry accompanied by Indian scouts. Hinton referred to it as Wild Cherry Creek.

Ref.:  85, p. 432; 87, p. xxxvii. Maps: C-6; GM-3; GM-6; GM-9; GM-12; GM-7; GM-21; GM-22.

**a.n. Cherry**          El.: 5996'. Map: GM-12          Yavapai
The name of this small community also came from the former abundance of wild cherry trees. By curious coincidence, several years after the naming of this location the Norville Cherry family arrived from Texas. This has led to some confusion concerning the origin of the name.
P.O. est. March 3, 1884. Cecilia DeKuhn, p.m. Discont. March 15, 1943.
Ref.:  Allen; Frier; Schnebly; P.O. Records.

**Cherry Creek Station**          Map: GM-9          Yavapai
Cherry Creek is the name of the railroad station at the town of Dewey (q.v.). Wells Fargo Station, 1903.
Ref.:  162, p. 3.

## CHILDS

El.: c. 2500'          Loc.: Yavapai 3, H-7
Childs is a transformer plant of the Arizona Power Co. It was named for a rancher in the vicinity.
P.O. est. October 17, 1912. Landon H. Woodmansee, p.m. Discont. April 15, 1915.
Ref.:  Barnes; P.O. Records. Maps: C-12; F-2.

## CHINO VALLEY

El.: c. 4000'                    Loc.: Yavapai 2, H-3
Pro.: /číyno/                    Spanish: *chino*, "curly hair"
When Lt. Amiel W. Whipple came through this valley in January 1854, he noted that it had an abundant growth of grama grass which was called by local Mexicans "de china." For this reason Whipple called the valley Val de China or Chino. The grass had a somewhat curly appearance, which may account for its name. Until at least September 1871, the valley was known as the Chino Valley and was so recorded in accounts of official scouts or encounters with Indians. Gradually, however, it came to be called Big Chino Valley and is so referred to in newspaper dispatches of 1897.

Settlement in the rich valley was steady and by 1879 there was a need for a post office.

P.O. est. as Chino, October 6, 1879. Benjamin A. Wade, p.m. Discont. July 25, 1891.

Ref.:   178, pp. 15, 90; 85, p. 347, 433; 177, p. 188, (Note 5); *Arizona Journal Miner*, November 16, 1897, 4:2; P.O. Records. Maps: C-5; C-7; C-12; GM-13; GM-14; GM-15; GM-17.

a.n.   **Big Chino Wash**       Maps: GM-14; GM-15        Yavapai
   **Chino Creek**                                Yavapai and Coconino
   Loc.: T. 26 N., R. 6 W. to T. 17 N., R. 1 W.
   **Chino Wash**           Map: GM-15              Yavapai
   **Chino**               Loc.: W. of Seligman 4 miles     Yavapai
   **Chino Valley**          Map: C-12              Yavapai
   Where the narrow gauge branch of the United Verde and Pacific Railroad to Jerome joins the Prescott and Arizona Central (later the Santa Fe) a small community developed with the descriptive name of Junction.

P.O. est. as Junction, June 7, 1895. George C. West, p.m. Wells Fargo Station, 1903. Name changed to Jerome Junction, December 23, 1914. Name changed to Chino Valley, April 11, 1923.
Ref.:   Gardner; Theobald; 162, p. 9; P.O. Records.

## CIENEGA

El.: 5550'                    Loc.: Yavapai 1, D-6.9
Pro.: /sénəkiy/
The Cienega Ranch was a stopping place on the road from Camp Verde to Prescott at the head of Cienega Creek. The old stone house is still in use.

P.O. est. April 25, 1877. George W. Hance, p.m. Discont. November 15, 1892.

Ref.:   Barnes; Schnebly, Goddard; P.O. Records. Maps: C-4; GM-23.

a.n.   **Cienega Creek**    Maps: GM-9; GM-11; GM-19    Yavapai
In 1868 T. J. Buckman had founded a permanent camp at Fort Rock (*q.v.*). When Indians stole his stock, Buckman tracked and caught up with them, but continued trailing until the Indians stopped for the night. Buckman and his son waited until dawn to shoot the Apaches, who were then feasting on one of Buckman's horses. After the fight, Buckman discovered there was a spring where the Apaches had feasted. Thus Buckman may be said to be the white man who found Cienega Spring. Near here in 1870 the cavalry established a post. In the same year Henry Mehrens filed a claim at Cienega Spring.

Ref.:   Cienega Spring File, APHS.

## CLARK, CAMP

El.: c. 4000'                    Loc.: Yavapai 2, H-3
Established in December 1863, Camp Clark was the original Fort Whipple. When Fort Whipple was moved in 1864 to its permanent location, Major Willis issued general orders stating that the old Fort Whipple would henceforth be known as Camp Clark after John H. Clark, the Surveyor General who first visited the place in August 1863.

Camp Clark may be considered the first temporary capital of Arizona. For a time after the establishment of Fort Whipple, Fort Clark, as it came to be known, was maintained as a sub-post.

Ref.:   *Arizona Miner*, May 25, 1864, 2:4; 111, pp. 166, 155. Map: E-22.

## CLARKDALE

El.: 2568'                    Loc.: Yavapai 3, D-2
William A. Clark was a senator from Montana, 1901-1907. While he was visiting the New Orleans Exposition, he saw samples of ore from the United Verde Mines. Finding that an interest could be purchased, he then visited the mines at Jerome. The result was an investigation for a possible site for the proposed Clarkdale Smelter. Suitable land was found on what was known as the Jordan Ranch, where ground was broken in 1910 and the first furnace put into operation on May 26, 1915. The town of Clarkdale was laid out in 1914. As a mining community, Clarkdale went out of existence at the same time as Jerome and for the same reasons (cf. Jerome). Several years later the town was bought by Earle P. Halliburton. It is currently enjoying a renascence as a community for retired people.

P.O. est. February 8, 1913. LaMont Coleman, p.m.

Ref.:   4, p. 332; 127, pp. 12, 14; Schnebly; P.O. Records. Maps: C-12; GM-5.

## CLEARWATERS

El.: c. 4000'                    Loc.: Yavapai 2, H-1
This small station on the Arizona and Prescott Railroad was named for the Clearwaters family, which resided here.
P.O. est. June 9, 1887. David W. Clearwaters, p.m. Discont. November 14, 1887.
Ref.:   Barnes; P.O. Records. Map: C-6.

## CLEATOR

El.: c. 4000'                    Loc.: Yavapai 3, B-8
Pro.: /klíyter/
The name Cleator is relatively recent. It arose in one of the first places to be occupied in Yavapai County. The first name was Turkey Creek, because of numerous wild turkeys. The Turkey Creek Mining District was organized in 1864. By 1869 the miners petitioned for a post office. A settlement developed within the next two years midway between Prescott and the Bradshaw mines where two men had established a stage station. At the turn of the century the community of Turkey Creek found itself on the branch railroad from Prescott to the Crown King mine.

Apparently Turkey was near the present Cleator. James P. Cleator was the second postmaster at Turkey, being appointed to that position on February 14, 1913. When the post office was moved to a new location forty-four miles southeast of Prescott, Cleator and his partner resided there. Cleator acquired the town from his partner in 1925. Today it is practically a ghost town which was offered for sale in April 1949. It then consisted of twenty houses, a grocery, service station, saloon, and water works and had about sixty residents.

P.O. est. as Turkey Creek, July 15, 1869. James A. Flanagan, p.m. Discont. September 20, 1869. Re-est. as Turkey, March 21, 1903. Levrett P. Nellis, p.m. Name changed to Cleator, May 1, 1925. James P. Cleator, p.m. Discont. July 15, 1954.

Ref.: *Weekly Arizona Miner,* July 22, 1871, 3:3; *Weekly Arizona Democrat,* March 20, 1880, 2:2; Sharlot Hall Museum Files; State Library Files; P.O. Records. Maps: C-1 (Turkey Creek District); C-10 (Turkey Creek); C-12 (Turkey); C-13 (Cleator); GM-11.

a.n. Turkey Canyon          Map: GM-18          Yavapai

## CLEMENCEAU

El.: 3300'                    Loc.: Yavapai 3, E-2.9
Pro.: /klémensòw/

When the United Verde Extension Mining Company located and built smelting works in 1917, the name Verde was given to the place. Following World War I, it was deemed wise to eliminate Verde as the name of a post office and railroad station, since there were many other "Verdes" in the area. At the suggestion of George E. Tener, vice-president of the company, the name of Georges Clemenceau, the French Minister of War, was given to the former Verde. This was done to commemorate the part which Clemenceau played in helping the Allies to win the war. In his will Clemenceau left to the town "a vase designed by Chaplet in a light lilac color." The vase and a letter from Clemenceau are now in the Clemenceau High School in Cottonwood.

The smelter at Clemenceau was closed permanently in January 1937.

P.O. est. as Verde, October 10, 1917. Jesse M. Foster, Jr. p.m. Name changed to Clemenceau, July 3, 1920. Discont. July 31, 1954.

Ref.: Schnebly; 151, p. 224; 4, pp. 331-332; "The Naming of Clemenceau, Arizona," James S. Douglas, *Prescott Courier,* a reprint, but without identification (State Library Files); APHS Names File; P.O. Records. Maps: C-12; GM-12.

## COLUMBIA

El.: c. 3500'                    Loc.: Yavapai 3, F-9.4
Columbia was a mining camp which took its name from a nearby mine.

P.O. est. September 25, 1894. M. Joseph Nolan, p.m. Discont. July 31, 1915.

Ref.: Gardner; Barnes; P.O. Records. Maps: C-8; GM-3.

## CONGRESS

El.: c. 3000'                    Loc.: Yavapai 2, E-8.9
Dennis May (d. October 13, 1907) discovered and named the Congress Mine in 1883. By 1897 there were four hundred twenty-five men employed at the mine. The mining community consisted of an upper and lower town. The

mine is said to have been owned by Diamond Jim Reynolds who died here in March 1891. Today Congress is a ghost town.

As a result of mining activity at Congress, Congress Junction developed on the railroad. When Congress was discontinued as a post office, the name was then moved to Congress Junction, which is today a cattle shipping point. (cf. Martinez).

P.O. est. as Congress, January 19, 1889. Charles A. Randall, p.m. Discont. August 31, 1938. P.O. est. at Congress Junction, March 23, 1906. Oliver L. Geer, p.m. Name changed to Congress, November 1, 1938. Wells Fargo Station (Congress Junction), 1904.

Ref.: APHS Files; Barnes; *Arizona Journal Miner,* October 12, 1897, 1:3, 4; *Arizona Sentinel,* October 16, 1907, 2:3; Hayden; P.O. Records. Maps: C-7; C-10 (Congress and Congress Junction).

## CONNEL GULCH

El.: c. 6000'                    Loc.: Yavapai 2, DC-2.2-3.1
Pro.: /kanél/

George Connel came to this area in 1873 and established a cattle ranch on upper Walnut Creek. He used the pitchfork brand.

v.n. Cottonwood Creek
   Barnes points out that Cottonwood is actually another creek which heads toward Connel Gulch and joins it farther down.

Ref.: Barnes; Rosenberger. Maps: C-10; GM-16; GM-23.

a.n. Connel Mountains
   El.: 5750'. Maps: GM-16; GM-23.          Yavapai

## CONSTELLATION

El.: c. 4000'                    Loc.: Yavapai 2, G-10
Constellation was the post office for the mining camp of the Constellation Mine.

P.O. est. April 29, 1901. William F. Roberts, p.m. Discont. January 31, 1939.

Ref.: Barnes; Gardner; P.O. Records. Maps: C-9; GM-6.

## COPPER BASIN

El.: c. 5000'                    Loc.: Yavapai 2, G-5.2
The area of Copper Basin was so named because of the presence of copper claims within it. In 1864 Charles C. Genung mentioned having passed the grave of a man named Millen, who was partner with a man named Leigh in copper claims within this basin.

It was on the Copper Basin Trail that the old scout, Pauline Weaver, (*See* Weaver Pass, Yuma; Weaver, Yavapai) was shot by Indians in 1865. Although Weaver did not die of the wound, he did not have much longer to live. He died c. 1866 near Camp Verde where he had been a scout. Weaver refused to go to the hospital or into a house, so the soldiers erected a tent over the outdoorsman and under this he died.

A small mining community by the name of Copper Basin was established in this area (Sec. 21, T. 13 N, R. 3 W.) to serve the copper and gold miners.

P.O. est. August 4, 1888. Duncan M. Martin, p.m. (not confirmed). Discont. January 18, 1890. P.O. est. July 28, 1891, Charles O'Malley, p.m. Discont. May 3, 1893.

Ref.: 52, IV, 49; 111, p. 111; P.O. Records. Maps: GM-3; GM-6; GM-7; GM-10; GM-22.

**a.n. Copper Basin Wash**   Maps: GM-6; GM-8; GM-10   Yavapai

**Copper Basin Road Spring**   Map: GM-10       Yavapai

**Copper Canyon**       Map: GM-21       Yavapai
This is the deepest cut (200 feet) in the Black Canyon Highway. The old stage road along the canyon floor can be seen from this point. Copper Canyon had its name at least as early as 1864 when King S. Woolsey mentioned it in his report.
Ref.: 52, III, 258-259.

**Copper**           Map: GM-13       Yavapai
This is a small station nineteen miles north of Prescott on the Ash Fork-Phoenix branch of the A.T. & S.F. R.R.
P.O. est. August 2, 1902. Rose Roberts, p.m. Order rescinded March 2, 1905 (Never in operation).
Ref.: P.O. Records.

**Copper Mountain**   El.: 5018'. Maps: GM-3; GM-11  Yavapai

**Copperopolis**       Map: GM-3       Yavapai
According to one source, Copperopolis was a "copper-metropolis which didn't metrop."
P.O. est. October 17, 1884. Edward E. Hellings, p.m.
Ref.: 102, p. 29; Barnes; P.O. Records.

**Copperopolis Creek**   Map: GM-3       Yavapai

## CORDES
El.: 3762'               Loc.: Yavapai 3, C-7.8
Pro.: /kórdes/
Before the railroad arrived at this spot, the place was called locally Antelope Station. When the railroad came through the residents asked for a continuance of the name, but this was refused because there was already an Antelope on the line. John H. Cordes then named the location after his family.
P.O. est. June 9, 1886. John H. Cordes, p.m. Discont. November 15, 1944.
Ref.: Barnes; P.O. Records. Maps: C-6; GM-3; GM-11.

**a.n. Cordes Cabin**       Map: GM-4       Yavapai

**Cortes Peak**       El.: 4233'. Map: GM-11   Yavapai
This name is a corruption of the correct name.

## CORNVILLE
El.: c. 3500'               Loc.: Yavapai 3, E-3
The original name for this location was the Pitchner Place. As a settlement formed around this location, the Verde Valley residents suggested that it be named Coaneville for a pioneer family named Coane. The name was submitted to the post office department in Washington, but was returned as Cornville.
P.O. est. July 9, 1885. George A. Kingston, p.m.
Ref.: Barnes; Schnebly; P.O. Records. Maps: C-6; GM-21.

## COTTONWOOD
El.: 3310'               Loc.: Yavapai 3, EF-2.6
In 1874 soldiers from Camp Verde were stationed at an adobe house where Cottonwood stands today, but they had no name for the place. Gradually as settlers moved in, a community developed and took its name from a circle of sixteen large cottonwoods growing about a quarter of a mile away from the river.

The location of the community in the center of the 1500 mile-square Verde Valley contributed greatly to its growing importance; however, malaria and dysentery were severe problems in the early days. Mosquitoes rose in thick clouds from the stagnant pools left by the flooding river after it had receded. The only medicine available was quinine at four dollars an ounce, to be had only when it was in surplus at Camp Verde.

By 1879 several families were living in the community, including the Nichols, Van Deerens, Hawkins, Strahans, and others. It is a curious fact that each of the families named had nine children, making a total of fifty-four altogether. The adobe building once used by soldiers was turned into a schoolhouse.

Today Cottonwood is a thriving community, but both the adobe building and the cottonwoods have long since disappeared.
P.O. est. March 6, 1879. William H. Michael, p.m.
Ref.: Stemmer; Willard; 127, pp. 41, 153; P.O. Records. Maps: C-6; GM-9; GM-12.

## COURT HOUSE BUTTE
El.: c. 6000'          Loc.: Yavapai 3, G-2.1
Descriptive. This is a large square rock, sometimes referred to erroneously as Cathedral Rock.
Court House Butte was named by a settler, Bill James, c. 1876.
Ref.: Barnes; Schnebly; Colton. Map: GM-21.

## COX
El.: c. 6000'      Loc.: Yavapai 2, H-5. Near Prescott.
The origin of this name has not yet been learned.
P.O. est. July 18, 1883. William Durbin, p.m. Discont. December 17, 1883.
Ref.: P.O. Records. Map: None.

## C.P. BUTTE
El.: c. 4000'         Loc.: Yavapai 3, EF-9-10
                       T. 9 N., R. 5 E.
Col. C. P. Roundtree had a mine at this butte, which has his initials for its name.
Ref.: Barnes. Map: None.

## CRAIG
El.: 3764'               Loc.: Yavapai 2, G-8.1
The name for this post office was a shortening of the last name of its first postmaster.
P.O. est. August 13, 1894. George W. Craighead, p.m. Discont. May 15, 1903.
Ref.: P.O. Records. Map: GM-6.

## CROOK CITY
Loc.: "On east branch of Hassayampa near Maple Gulch"
In 1875 Crook City consisted of about fourteen miners' cabins strung out along the Hassayampa River. The little settlement was named for the General Crook Mine in this vicinity, which in turn was named for Gen. George Crook, the famous Indian fighter.

Ref.: *Weekly Arizona Miner,* April 30, 1875, 3:4. Map: None.

a.n. Crook Canyon      Maps: GM-3; GM-20      Yavapai
v.n. Crooks Canyon

## CROOKTON

El.: c. 6000'      Loc.: Yavapai 1, E-3.3
This point on the railroad was named for Gen. George Crook (*See* Crook National Forest, Gila).

Ref.: Barnes. Maps: B-4; GM-24.

## CROSS MOUNTAIN

El.: 6625'      Loc.: Yavapai 1, A-4.7
In 1854 Lt. Amiel W. Whipple named this mountain because it forms a perfect cross.

Ref.: 178, p. 95; Rothwell; 57, p. 200. Maps: C-6; GM-24.

## CROWN KING

El.: c. 6000'      Loc.: Yavapai 2, A-9.2
Although Crown King is today a ghost town, in the 1880's it was a very active mining camp. It took its name from the first mine in the vicinity.

P.O. est. June 29, 1888. George P. Harrington, p.m. Discont. May 15, 1954. Wells Fargo Station, 1904.

Ref.: Barnes; Schnebly; P.O. Records. Maps: C-7; GM-3; GM-7.

## CROWN POINT

El.: 4635'      Loc.: Yavapai 2, H-9.7
Active in the early 1900's, Crownpoint (*sic*) was a mine lying between Crown King on top of the mountain and Goodwin near its base. It was named by its discoverers after the Crownpoint Mine at Gold Hill, Nevada.

P.O. est. January 12, 1900. R. J. Bignell, p.m. Discont. December 22, 1903.

Ref.: Gardner; Barnes; P.O. Records. Maps: C-9; GM-6.

## CRUICE

El.: 5126'      Loc.: Yavapai 1, GH-4.9
Pro.: /kruws/
This station on the Ashfork-Prescott branch of the A.T. & S.F. R.R. was named for S. P. Cruice, Assistant General Freight Agent for the railroad.

Ref.: Barnes. Map: GM-1.

## CURTISS

El.: c. 4300'      Loc.: Yavapai 3, BC-6.7
The origin of this name has not yet been ascertained.
P.O. est. November 27, 1891. Marvin A. Baldwin, p.m. Discont. March 23, 1895.

Ref.: P.O. Records. Map: C-7 (Curtis).

## DATE

El.: 3367'      Loc.: Yavapai 2, D-7.8
At one time this railroad point was named Date Creek after the stream which rises nearby. The railroad company shortened the name.

Ref.: Barnes. Map: C-9.

## DATE CREEK, CAMP

El.: 3726'      Loc.: Yavapai 2, D-7
In 1863 Charles C. Genung and others came upon what was later to be called Date Creek. The men were struck at once by the beauty of the place, a green meadow with grass four feet or more in height and scattered cottonwood groves. Through the meadow ran a stream of clear water which the Indians called Ah-ha Carsona, meaning "pretty water." According to another source, the Apache name for the sink about twenty miles below the old fort was A-ha-Ca-son, meaning "sinking waters." White men applied the name to Date Creek because of the abundance of wild dates or yucca in the area, the name for yucca being "da-tal."

The richness of the Date Creek vicinity attracted both white man and Indian, and conflict was inevitable. The first recorded skirmish occurred on September 5, 1869, and from that time forward there were frequent Indian attacks on wagon trains, detachments of troops, and individuals. Even earlier, Camp McPherson had been established in nearby Skull Valley. It was named for Brig Gen. James Birdseye McPherson, who was killed on July 22, 1864, at Atlanta, Georgia. The post was established in late 1864 by the California Volunteers; regular troops arrived in 1866 to protect the settlers of Skull Valley.

In 1867 McPherson was abandoned; the command was moved and the name of the new location changed to Camp Date Creek on July 15. Camp Date Creek was at the junction of the north and south forks of the creek. According to one source the camp was established by California Volunteers at Date Creek in 1864, but troops moved in 1866 twenty-five miles to the north to Camp McPherson and returned to the original camp in 1867. The final location was arrived at in 1868 on the south bank of Date Creek, twenty-six miles from Wickenburg. The name was officially changed to Camp Date Creek on November 23, 1868, by order of Gen. H. W. Halleck.

A temporary reservation was established at Date Creek by Vincent Colyer in 1871 and in June rations were issued to two hundred twenty-five Indians. The number increased to almost one thousand from various tribes. The entire group was moved to Camp Verde in May 1873, for a brief stay, being removed from there in March 1875. The reservation at Date Creek was abolished in July 1872, by order of Gen. O. O. Howard. In 1874 the Secretary of War restored the lands to the public domain, agreeing that the Camp Date Creek Reservation was of no use whatever for military purposes.

The withdrawal of the reservation and of troops did not mean the end of Date Creek, despite the fact that in April 1875, there were only two men here caring for sheep. Nevertheless, a post office for the convenience of settlers continued to exist for several years.

P.O. est. March 1, 1872. George H. Kimball, p.m. Discont. October 18, 1880. Wells Fargo Station, 1879.

Ref.:    Farrish, VIII, 10; Willson; 52, IV, 36; 85 pp. 434, 521; 105, p. 94; APHS Names File; *Prescott Courier,* July 21, 1917 (State Library Files); *Weekly Arizona Miner,* December 12, 1868, 2:2; *Tucson Citizen,* January 23, 1875, 1:4; *Weekly Arizona Miner,* April 16, 1875, 2:2; P.O. Records. Maps: C-2; C-14; E-22.

**a.n. Date Creek Mountains**    El.: 4500'.  Map: GM-6    Yavapai

## DAVIS

El.: c. 6000'                                    Loc.: Yavapai 3, B-2.8

An abandoned station on the United Verde and Pacific Railroad, this place was named for a teamster who hauled lumber to it for shipment from the sawmill at the base of Mingus Mountain.

Ref.:    Barnes. Map: C-10.

## DAVIS, MOUNT

El.: 8000'                                    Loc.: Yavapai 2, H-6.3

The Civil War had its repercussion among miners in Arizona. Northern sympathizers applied the name Union Peak, today known as Mount Union, to an eminence of 7971'. Southern sympathizers, not to be outdone, proceded to name a nearby peak for Confederate President Jefferson Davis.

Ref.:    Barnes. Map: GM-20.

## DEADMAN CREEK

El.: c. 3500'                                    Loc.: Yavapai 3, IG-9.5

Boyd Dougherty and Judge Reiley found an unidentified dead man in this area.

Ref.:    Barnes. Map: GM-19.

**a.n. Deadman Creek, South Fork**    Map: GM-19    Yavapai

## DEFIANCE

                                                  Loc.: Unknown.

P.O. est. January 6, 1875. William F. M. Arny, p.m. Discont. November 9, 1875.

Ref.:    P.O. Records. Map: None.

## DEL RIO SPRINGS

El.: 4384'                                    Loc.: Yavapai 2, H-1.8

Pro.:  /del ríyə/

Although no documentary evidence has been uncovered to prove that the temporary army encampment at Del Rio was ever called Ft. Whipple, it is apparently true that troops stationed at this spot were removed from here in 1864 to the newly established Ft. Whipple. One officer, however, did not accompany the troops to the new fort. He was Robert Postle (*Pro.: /Pówstal/*), (b. England 1840; d. April 1871), who was dismissed from service on December 31, 1863. Postle settled down at the springs. He filed claim to his land on January 13, 1865. He lived a lonely life until 1866 when the David Wesley Schivers family from Missouri stopped at Del Rio in their covered wagon. One of their five children was Hannah, a girl of fourteen. She soon married Postle. When Hannah was barely nineteen, her husband died and there began for her a difficult life as a pioneer woman who was determined to rear her children, prove up her homestead, and live out her life at Del Rio. She was eminently successful.

Early travelers mentioned stopping at Postles Ranch, the main house of which was a large adobe built on the site of the old military establishment.

The abundant water supply at Del Rio Springs caused the city of Prescott to buy the ranch after the disastrous city fire of 1900. The water was piped to Prescott. In 1910 the Santa Fe Railroad purchased the 3,520 acres of Del Rio Ranch to serve as a dairy ranch for the Fred Harvey hotels and to provide winter pasture for the mules from the Grand Canyon. At one time the Santa Fe hauled water from the deep wells at Del Rio to the Grand Canyon, one hundred thirty miles away. In 1956 the Santa Fe Railroad offered the ranch for sale.

Ref.:    *Prescott Evening Courier,* January 18, 1956, 1:8; *Arizona Miner,* March 13, 1869, 2:1; 115, pp. 1-4; 153, p. 131; 87, p. xxxvii (Postal's Ranch). Maps: C-9; GM-9.

## DEVILS WINDPIPE

El.: c. 3200'                                    Loc.: Yavapai 3, HG-5.5

The narrow and deep nature of this canyon resulted in its name.

Ref.:    Barnes; Goddard. Map: GM-21.

## DEWEY

El.: 4556'                                    Loc.: Yavapai 3, BC-5.1

In the early days when a stage station was run at this place by Darrel Duppa, the location was known as Agua Fria (*q.v.*). The post office for Agua Fria was discontinued in 1895. According to post office rule, an office could not reopen under its old name. Therefore, when the post office was re-established in 1898, the name Dewey was selected. There is some question as to whether it was named for Rear Admiral Dewey or for a pioneer settler in the vicinity. It is to be noted also that the name of the railroad station was and still is Cherry Creek, but this name was in use elsewhere as a post office, and so could not be used.

P.O. est. July 18, 1898. Fred Hiltenbrandt, p.m.

Ref.:    *Arizona Journal Miner,* September 24, 1898. 4:1; Barnes; 4, p. 304; P.O. Records. Maps: C-9; GM-9.

## DRAKE

El.: 4607'                                    Loc.: Yavapai 2, H-2.5

The railroad shipping point was named for W. A. Drake, an engineer who constructed the line. Today it is a major shipping point for some of the finest flagstone quarried in the United States.

P.O. est. November 9, 1936. Frank Schiel, p.m. Discont. April 15, 1939.

Ref.:    Barnes; Schnebly; P.O. Records. Map: C-13.

## DUGAS

El.: 3957'                                    Loc.: Yavapai 3, FG-6

Fred Dugas has been at the Dugas Ranch since 1879. He considers his place the geographical center of Arizona. As more settlers moved in, a need for a post office developed and the Dugas family, which had come from California and lived in Prescott several years before moving to the ranch, conducted the post office in their home.

P.O. est. November 11, 1925. Mrs. Gertrude H. Dugas, p.m. Discont. June 15, 1938.

Ref.:    Dugas; P.O. Records. Map: GM-19.

## ELLIOT, MOUNT

El.: 7000′      Loc.: Yavapai 3, A-6.1
A. G. Elliot located a mine in this area in September 1874.
Ref.: Barnes. Maps: GM-3; GM-20.

## ENTRO

El.: 5132′      Loc.: Yavapai 3, A-4.3
This railroad point lies at the entrance to a small canyon through which the road passes, hence the name.
Ref.: Barnes. Map: GM-9.

## EQUATOR

El.: 4000′      Loc.: Yavapai 3, CD-4.1
The reason for the name of this mining camp has not yet been ascertained.
P.O. est. December 12, 1899. Arthur Woods, p.m. Discont. September 22, 1903.
Ref.: Barnes; P.O. Records. Map: C-9.

## ESTLER

El.: 4500′      Loc.: Yavapai 3, E-7.1
Estler Monroe (d. c. 1895) had a cattle ranch and lived in this area.
Ref.: West; Dugas. Map: GM-11.

## EUGENE GULCH

El.: c. 5000′      Loc.: Yavapai 3, AB-6
A man whose name was either Eugene or Eugenia operated a placer mine in this gulch. There was also a Eugene Station on the branch railroad to the Poland Mine.
Ref.: Barnes. Maps: GM-3; GM-20.

## FAIR OAKS

El.: 5100′      Loc.: Yavapai 2, EF-3.3
A grove of live oak trees at the site of this stage station resulted in its name. Also, W. W. Ross, a druggist of Prescott, and a Henry Clay planted an orchard here.
Ref.: Barnes. Map: GM-16.

## FIELDS

El.: c. 6000′      Loc.: Yavapai 1, A-1
Billy Fields was a Santa Fe brakeman who lost both arms in an accident near this point.
Ref.: Barnes. Map: None.

## FLORES

El.: c. 2500′      Loc.: Yavapai 2, E-10
Pro.: /flóres/      Spanish: "flowers"
When the railroad was being laid, the desert in this vicinity was covered with many flowers.
Ref.: Barnes. Map: None.

## FOOLS GULCH

El.: c. 4000′      Loc.: Yavapai 2, EF-8.8
Fools Gulch was so named because the first prospectors in the area were deemed fools for expecting to find gold in the formation displayed in this gulch. Later a post office by this name was established to serve the Planet-Saturn mine.

P.O. est. January 15, 1897. William A. Clark, p.m. Discont. October 30, 1897.
Ref.: Barnes; P.O. Records. Map: GM-6.
a.n. Fools Canyon      Map: GM-6      Yavapai

## FORREST

El.: c. 5000′      Loc.: Yavapai 3, BC-6.7. Near Bigbug.
In 1882 Henry F. Forrest had a small cattle ranch at this location. (See Forrest, Cochise)
P.O. est. as Forest, April 21, 1882. Henry A. Marsh, p.m. Discont. September 5, 1882.
Ref.: Barnes; P.O. Records. Map: None.

## FORT ROCK

El.: 4900′      Loc.: Yavapai 1, A-4.8
During the year 1866 the mail carrier between Prescott and Hardyville had an escort of soldiers for protection against Indians. One day in the fall of that year the three soldiers and Poindexter (the mail carrier) arrived at the place which came to be called Fort Rock. The station was kept by a man named J. J. Buckman, whose son Thad (about fifteen years old) had that day made a stone playhouse a little over a foot high in front of his father's cabin. Early the next morning as the mail carrier was getting ready to leave, Indians attacked. Their shots came so rapidly that Buckman and McAteer, one of the soldiers, were unable to return to the cabin, and they sought protection inside the stone playhouse. The boy, the mail carrier, and Ed May (another soldier) got into the cabin. Having defective guns, the mail carrier and the soldier spent the day loading guns for the young boy who did the shooting. The two men would lift the boy to a loophole from which he would shoot. Meanwhile, out in front on the other side of the cabin the men in the stone playhouse were holding the Indians at bay. It was no mean job, for there were more than a hundred Hualapais attacking the little group of white men. The fight continued all day. It is not known what part the third soldier played in the battle.

The name Fort Rock was inevitable. Nevertheless, apparently the first post office at this area was called Mount Hope (q.v.). Fort Rock was a well-known stage station for many years.
P.O. est. as Mount Hope, June 22, 1876. E. S. Smith, p.m. Name changed to Fort Rock, May 12, 1879. S. L. Bacon, p.m. Discont. November 12, 1879.
Ref.: 52, IV, 133-134; 158, p. 71; 87, p. xxxviii; P.O. Records. Maps: C-3; E-20; E-13.

## FOSTER

     Loc.: Not known.
The origin of this name has not yet been learned.
P.O. est. April 26, 1887. Philander J. Schofield, p.m. Discont. November 12, 1888.
Ref.: P.O. Records. Map: None.

## FRANCIS CREEK

El.: 3020′      Loc.: Yavapai 2, A-2.9-3.1
John W. Francis was a sheepman who lived in Flagstaff.
Ref.: Barnes; Thompson. Map: C-12.

## FRITSCHE RANCH

El.: 4500'                        Loc.: Yavapai 1, FG-6.7
H. W. Fritsche was a stockman.

P.O. est. October 26, 1912. Sidney Fritsche, p.m. Discont. April 15, 1918.

v.n. Fritchie

Ref.: Barnes. Maps: C-12; GM-14.

## FULLER

Loc.: On East Verde River, but not definitely located. The post office at Fuller, which actually never was in operation, was named for the Fuller family, local cattlemen.

P.O. est. March 5, 1898. Oscar Townsend, p.m. Discont. January 30, 1899.

Ref.: Barnes; P.O. Records. Map: None.

a.n. Fuller Seep          Map: GD-9          Yavapai

## GALLES

Loc.: Unknown.
Galles was the name of a post office which was never actually in operation.

P.O. est. June 19, 1899. Rose Roberts, p.m.

Ref.: P.O. Records. Map: None.

## GEMINI PEAK

Loc.: Yavapai 2, A-1
Lt. Amiel W. Whipple in 1854 described this as a "remarkable mountain rising 2,000 feet about its sides . . . and, in the centre, cut as it were into two equal peaks; hence called the Gemini."

Ref.: 177, p. 199; 178, p. 94. Maps: C-5; E-20.

## GENUNG MOUNTAIN

El.: c. 4600'                    Loc.: Yavapai 3, F-8.8
                                 N. of Yarnell 1 mile.
At one time referred to as Boulder Mountain, Genung Mountain is near the ranch owned by Charles C. Genung, which he established in the 1860's. It is still in his family. The mountain was renamed in his honor in June 1939.

Ref.: "List of Place Names Submitted for Decision June 21, 1939," Place Names Committee of Arizona Pioneers' Historical Society. Map: None.

a.n. Genung Springs       Map: GM-6          Yavapai

## GILBERT

El.: 4370'                        Loc.: Yavapai 2, GH-10
The post office which served the King Solomon Mine was named for its first postmaster.

P.O. est. November 17, 1899. William J. Gilbert, p.m. Discont. October 31, 1903.

Ref.: Barnes; P.O. Records. Map: GM-6.

## GLASSFORD HILL

El.: 6177'                        Loc.: Yavapai 3, B-5
In the early 1880's Lt. William A. Glassford used this hill as a heliograph station to send messages east via Baker Butte to Fort Union in New Mexico. Glassford was responsible for establishing the system of heliograph stations in southern Arizona and southwest New Mexico under Gen. Nelson A. Miles.

v.n. Bald Hill

Ref.: Barnes; 151, p. 326. Map: GM-15.

## GLEED

El.: 5452'                        Loc.: Yavapai 1, FG-3.6
C. S. Gleed was a director for the Santa Fe Railroad from 1900 to 1920.

Ref.: Barnes. Map: B-4.

## GOLDWATER LAKE

El.: c. 6000'                     Loc.: Yavapai 2, H-5.5
Goldwater Lake, which supplies Prescott with water, is actually two lakes. The upper lake was built in 1933 and covers approximately thirty-five acres. The lower was constructed at a later date. Both lakes are named for Morris Goldwater, a prominent citizen and one-time mayor of Prescott.

Ref: Jackson. Map: GM-20.

## GOODWIN

El.: c. 6000'                     Loc.: Yavapai 2, HG-6.7
The post office for residents in the vicinity of Goodwin played a game of hop-scotch over the years, moving from one location to the other, but never any great distance. It was first established at Goodwin (GLO 1896). Meanwhile a post office was established prior to the closing of the Goodwin office, at Maxton, five miles northwest. Both offices landed eventually at Venezia, three miles north of Goodwin. The game came full circle when the post office went back to Goodwin in 1935. Goodwin's post office came to an end in 1943. Goodwin is a ghost town today. The reason for the name Maxton has not yet been learned. "Venezia" is said to have been named at the instance of an Italian settler, F. Scopal, for his native city.

P.O. est. at Goodwin, April 13, 1894. Sarah E. Randolph, p.m. Discont. February 28, 1915. Mail to Maxton. P.O. est. at Maxton, July 6, 1901. Marilla T. Alwens, p.m. Changed to Venezia, April 16, 1916. Don J. Tomlinson, p.m. Changed to Goodwin, June 1, 1935. Discont. September 30, 1943.

Ref.: P.O. Records; Barnes. Maps: C-8 (Goodwin); (C-10 Maxton); GM-20 (Venezia).

## GOODWIN CITY

El.: 5355'                        Loc.: Yavapai 2, H-5
Prior to the time that Prescott was established as the Arizona territorial capital, several miners on Granite Creek located on a mesa known as Goose Flat. This was in 1863 when Gov. John N. Goodwin's party had just arrived in the newly created territory. The miners named their area Goodwin in the governor's honor. John N. Goodwin was Arizona's second governor, but the first actually to arrive in the territory He was born in the state of Maine, from which he was elected in 1860 to the United States Congress. When the Territory of Arizona was created, Goodwin was named Chief Justice, but following the death of Arizona's first governor, John Gurley, Goodwin stepped up into the position of territorial governor on August 20, 1863. Goodwin served as governor until 1865, at which time he was elected delegate to represent Arizona in Congress. He disappeared from the Arizona scene, never to return.

Goodwin City had scarcely been laid out when Prescott was selected as the site for the territorial capital. Thereafter Goodwin was sneeringly referred to as Gimletville, and it soon vanished.

Some years later a mining camp by the name of Goodwin was established.

When the Goodwin post office was discontinued, the mail was then forwarded to Maxton (See Goodwin). This indicates the two localities were not identical. They also show separately on the GLO map of 1909. At a much later date the community of Venezia (See Goodwin) had its name changed to Goodwin, but this also was not the same location as the original Goodwin mining camp.

P.O. est. April 13, 1894. Sarah E. Randolph, p.m. Discont. February 28, 1915.

Ref.: *Arizona Miner,* April 6, 1864, 2:3; *Arizona Republic,* December 11, 1889, 4:4; 52, III, 187-188; P.O. Records. Map: None.

a.n. **Goodwin Spring** (cf. Goodwin Canyon, Cochise) Cochise Gov. John N. Goodwin is said to have used this spring at one time.

## GOVERNMENT CANYON

El.: 5750'     Loc.: Yavapai 2, H-5

When federal troops were in the Territory of Arizona, it was customary to apply the term "government" to places utilized by soldiers. Government Canyon was a pathway used by troops returning to Fort Whipple from scouting excursions.

Ref.: Merritt. Map: GM-15.

a.n. **Government Sawmill**     Yavapai
Loc.: On route from Fort Whipple to Camp Verde.
**Government Springs** Maps: GM-6; GM-10; GM-4 Yavapai
This name was in use in the early 1860's.

Ref.: Schroeder.

**Government Spring Gulch**     Map: GM-11     Yavapai

**Government Spring Wash** Maps: GM-4; GM-11     Yavapai
General Kirk and troops under his command camped at these springs while on a journey after recapturing horses stolen from Camp Hualapai.

Ref.: Barnes.

## GRAND VIEW

El.: 4084'     Loc.: Yavapai 2, E-6.3

Where the highway tops Yarnell Hill the view warrants its descriptive name.

Ref.: None. Maps: C-9; GM-6.

## GRANITE DELLS

El.: 5125'     Loc.: Yavapai 2, HG-4.2

An early name for this place was Point of Rocks, a descriptive name for the place where Granite Creek becomes a freak of nature with miniature hills, mountains, and valleys. In the early days it was a dangerous spot because it formed a perfect place for Indian attacks. The mail rider was frequently attacked here. In 1867 the place was owned by Louis A. Stevens (d. 1878). While he was attending legislative meetings in Prescott, Apaches attacked his ranch on September 20, 1867. Mrs. Stevens sent word to him to stay in town but to send her ammunition.

Today Granite Dells is a recreation area which includes lakes, a clear stream, shade trees, and picnic areas.

Ref.: Barnes; *Arizona Miner,* April 6, 1872, 1:1; September 21, 1867, n.p., n.d.; 22, p. 160; APHS Files. Map: GM-15.

## GRASSHOPPER FLAT

El.: 4500'     Loc.: Yavapai 3, FG-1-1.2

Grasshoppers used to exist here by the millions.

Ref.: Schnebly. Map: GM-21.

## GRAYBACK MOUNTAIN

El.: 6300'     Loc.: Yavapai 3, F-1.2

The top of the mountain back is gray. This seems to be a recent name for what was formerly called Capital Butte, a large red butte with gray on top. Old-timers call it Gray Mountain.

Ref.: Schnebly; Colton; 127, p. 116. Map: B-6.

a.n. **Grayback Mountains**     Map: C-12     Yavapai

## GRIEF HILL

El.: c. 4000'     Loc.: Yavapai 3, EF-4.8

Army records reveal that several engagements with Indians took place at Grief Hill, the first on December 11, 1866, and the second on May 6, 1869. However, the name apparently does not come from a military engagement. The fact is that there are still today ten graves on Grief Hill, and had the victims been soldiers their bodies would have been returned to the nearest army camp. In 1954 a group of Verde pioneers climbing this hill found and carried back to Camp Verde the rusted parts of wagons, apparently made in the 1860's. This later fact coupled with the presence of graves indicates that at least one battle was with civilians, although the possibility of there having been a small military escort is not precluded.

An account of a battle in January 1866, says that the march from Fort Whipple to Camp Lincoln (later Camp Verde) was a bad one, partially because of a three-day delay at Grief Hill occasioned by bad weather. One section of the party consisted of ten pack animals carrying provisions. This group was attacked while descending Grief Hill. The Indians destroyed several provision packs, but the military escort escaped. The best estimate at this late date is that Grief Hill earned its name for two reasons: because of the difficulty of hauling freight over it in inclement weather, and because of the danger of Indian attack. Ordinarily the Grief Hill road was not used by civilian wagons, which used instead the Fossil Creek road where the highway runs today.

Ref.: Goddard; 127, "Introduction," p. 7; 85, p. 427, 433; 52, IV, 102. Maps: GM-21; GM-24.

a.n. **Grief Hill Wash**     Map: GM-21     Yavapai

## GROOM CREEK

El.: 7000'     Loc.: Yavapai 3, A-5

Col. Bob Groom (b. Kentucky, August 24, 1824; d. January 21, 1899) came to Arizona in 1862. Although he lived principally by prospecting and mining, Groom was also a surveyor who surveyed the townsite of Prescott. He was a member of the first Arizona Territorial Legislature.

An increasing number of residents settled in the Groom Creek area, but few chose to remain the year round because of the severity of the winters. However, by 1901 there were enough families at the location of the present Groom Creek settlement to warrant establishing a post office. The name selected was Oakdale, because of the situation of the community in a grove of oaks. Officially the name lasted about six weeks, at which time it was changed to Groom Creek. Currently, about thirty-five people live at Groom Creek the year around. During the summer months, the colony numbers into the hundreds. The townsite for Groom Creek City was recorded in Prescott in 1903.

P.O. est. as Oakdale, July 1, 1901. Clara B. Riley, p.m. Name changed to Groom Creek, August 19, 1901. Discont. January 31, 1942.

Ref.: P.O. Records; Jackson; *Prescott Courier*, July 21, 1917, (State Library Files); Robert Groom File, APHS. Maps: C-9; GM-3; GM-20.

**a.n. Grooms Hill**            Map: GM-6                Yavapai

## HARRINGTON

El.: c. 5000'            Loc.: Yavapai 3, BC-9.5
George P. Harrington operated the Oro Bell Mine near this post office. He also served as second postmaster at this location.

P.O. est. April 4, 1904. Robert G. Scherer, p.m. Discont. August 31, 1918.

Ref.: Willson [April 4]; P.O. Records. Map: C-10.

## HASKELL SPRING

El.: c. 3200'            Loc.: Yavapai 3, DE-2.3
In Verde Valley near Clarkdale.
Lt. Harry Haskell, Twelfth U.S. Infantry, was in charge of a group of Indians who, c. 1873, had to be moved from this spring, where they had lived for many years, to the San Carlos Indian Reservation.

Ref.: Barnes; Schnebly. Map: None.

## HAYNES

El.: c. 4000'            Loc.: Yavapai 2, C-7
The shipping point on the railroad was named for Lloyd C. Haynes, superintendent of the Big Stick Mine.

P.O. est. April 4, 1908. John R. Roberts, p.m. Name changed to Date Creek, December 13, 1921. This is not the same Date Creek as that of importance in earlier days (cf. Date Creek Camp).

Ref.: Barnes; APHS Names File; P.O. Records. Map: C-9.

## HECLA

El.: c. 4000'
Loc.: Yavapai 3, CD-6
Sec. 3, T. 13 N., R. 2 E.
The Hecla Mine gave this mining camp its name. The presence of a big stone corral also led to its being called Stone Corral.

P.O. est. March 3, 1893. John H. Hutchins, p.m. Discont. October 3, 1894.

Ref.: Barnes; P.O. Records. Map: None.

## HELL CANYON

El.: 4900'            Loc.: Yavapai, H-5.4-7
The name Hell Canyon dates back at least to a military skirmish on July 3, 1869. In a military report of November 25, 1872, the same location is referred to as "Red Rocks or Hell Canyon." The name is a just one, for the sides and floor of this not very deep canyon are extremely rough. Nevertheless, this canyon was part of the route from the old Beale Trail into Chino Valley in the early days.

Ref.: Benham; 85, pp. 434, 438; APHS Names File. Maps: C-9; GM-1; GM-9; GM-13; GM-19.

## HICKEY MOUNTAIN

El.: 7619'            Loc.: Yavapai 3, C-3
Dennis Hickey had a potato ranch on Mingus Mountain in the early 1880's. He also ran a ditch into the valley for irrigation.

**v.n. Hickory Mountain** (corruption)  Map: GM-12        Yavapai
Ref.: Barnes; Stemmer. Map: GM-12.

## HIGH BALL WATER

El.: c. 4000'            Loc.: Yavapai 3, E-7
E. of Dugas 5 miles.
High Ball Water is a spring at the end of the flat country where the truckers begin to "highball" their trucks in order to get up and over the divide.

Ref.: Dugas. Map: None.

## HILLSIDE

El.: 3853'            Loc.: Yavapai 2, D-6.2
Descriptive. The post office was at the mine first, but later was moved down to the community of Hillside. The latter was a railroad station on Date Creek. The community was named for the Hillside Mine located by John Lawler and B. T. Riggs in 1887.

P.O. est. July 31, 1888. John W. Archibald, p.m. Wells Fargo Station, 1904.

Ref.: Willson; C. A. Anderson, E. A. Scholz, J. D. Strobell, Jr., *Geology and Ore Deposits of the Bagdad Area*, U. S. Gov't Prtg. Office, 1955; P.O. Records. Maps: C-9; C-12; GM-2; GM-6.

**a.n. Hillside Rocks**        Map: GM-2                Yavapai

## HITT WASH

El.: c. 5000'            Loc.: Yavapai 2, EF-1.3-1.9
James Hitt lived near this stream c. 1880.
Ref.: 151, p. 367. Maps: GM-17; GM-23.

## HOLMES CANYON

El.: c. 5000'            Loc.: Yavapai 3, DE-9.5
R. J. Holmes, Jr. (d. April 26, 1931) ran cattle in the Bloody Basin (*q.v.*) region for many years.

Ref.: Barnes. Map: GM-25.

**a.n. Holmes Creek**        Loc.: T. 9 N., R. 4 E.        Yavapai

## HUALAPAI, CAMP

El.: 6000'            Loc.: Yavapai 2, DE-1
Pro.: [wálpay/
On March 26, 1869, Col. William Redmond Price wrote

to Col. John P. Sherburne of the Department of California that he had conferred in Prescott with Gen. Thomas C. Devin and that since the Hualapai Indians were quiet, a temporary camp should be established in the vicinity of the Toll Gate with two companies under Price's command, plus additional cavalry from Prescott. Col. Price also recommended having a permanent camp at this location. On May 9, 1869, the camp was established. The post was situated in a pass of the Aztec Mountains on a level mesa overlooking Walnut Creek. The name Toll Gate derived from the fact that the location was on the toll road between Prescott and Hardyville, which belonged to Capt. William H. Hardy (*See* Hardyville, Mohave). A gate on the road enabled the owner to collect tolls. On October 4, 1870, the name was changed to Camp Hualapai. The post was abandoned on July 31, 1873.

P.O. est. as Camp Hualapai, January 13, 1873. D. T. Foster, p.m. Name changed to Charmingdale, January 30, 1879. Samuel C. Rodgers, p.m. Discont. November 18, 1880.

Ref.: 169, pp. 86-87, 90; 85, p. 551; *Tucson Citizen*, July 19, 1873, 2:1; *Arizona Miner*, November 25, 1871, 2:2; March 14, 1879, 3:1; 38, p. 174 (Note 3); 105, p. 96; P.O. Records. Maps: C-2; C-12 (Old Fort Hualapai); E-20 (Old Camp Hualapai).

## ILGES, CAMP

Loc.: On Rio Verde.

In 1873 Maj. Guido Ilges was a member of the Seventh Infantry. He was transferred to the Fifth Infantry in 1879.

Ref.: 85, p. 562. Map: None.

## IRON KING

El.: 5000'          Loc.: Yavapai 3, B-5.5

The post office at Iron King was first established under the name Blanchard, probably after W. H. Blanchard. When the Iron King Mine became important, the name of the post office was changed. For some years the mine was not in operation. Currently it is owned by the Shattuck-Denn Mining Company and the smelter is in operation.

P.O. est. as Blanchard, August 17, 1903. Annie M. Williams, p.m. Changed to Iron King, June 11, 1907. Alfred H. Glenn, p.m. Discont. July 15, 1912.

Ref.: Schnebly; P.O. Records. Maps: C-10; GM-12; GM-15.

## IRON SPRINGS

El.: 6400'          Loc.: Yavapai 2, G-9.7

At one time Iron Springs served as a stage station on the road between Phoenix and Wickenburg. The name is descriptive of the taste of the water in the springs. On analysis, the water proved to have no iron, although the sands about the springs were filled with it. Phoenix residents c. 1890 began building summer cottages at this location.

P.O. est. as Ironsprings, June 22, 1900. Elmer Hawley, p.m. Name changed to Iron Springs, June 1, 1950. Wells Fargo Station, 1903.

Ref.: Barnes; 4, p. 288; P.O. Records. Maps: C-9; GM-6, GM-8.

**a.n. Iron Spring Wash**     Maps: GM-2; GM-8          Yavapai

## ISLAND MESA

El.: c. 4000'          Loc.: Yavapai 3, D-1

Sycamore Creek flows on both sides of this mesa, turning it into an "island."

Ref.: Barnes. Map: GM-9.

## IVES PEAK

El.: 3856'          Loc.: Yavapai 2, A-8

There is a possibility that this peak is named for Lt. Joseph Christmas Ives, who was with Lt. Amiel W. Whipple in 1853 when the latter's party passed through this area. The name Ives Peak first appears on Smith 1879 map. This seems to throw into doubt the chance that the peak was named for Eugene S. Ives, at the turn of the century a mine owner and prominent Arizona politician.

Ref.: Barnes; Willson. Maps: C-5; E-20.

## JACK'S CANYON

El.: c. 5000'          Loc.: Yavapai 2, GH-3-2

C. M. (Jack) Montgomery, Al Doyle, and John Marshall constructed a trail from Montgomery's ranch to the area below between 1882 and 1884. At first the trail in the canyon was called Jack's Trail, but the name gradually shifted to Jack's Canyon.

Clay Park is on the site of the old Jack's Ranch.

Ref.: Barnes; Schnebly. Map: B-8.

**a.n. Jack's Gulch**          Map: B-6          Yavapai

## JEROME

El.: 5435'          Loc.: Yavapai 3, CD-2.7

The copper mines which existed in the Jerome area were known to white men at least as early as 1582 when Fr. Espejo and Farfán were exploring in this area. Their description of the mines was identical to the description of the Indian workings found when the United Verde Company was incorporated in 1883. It is certain that the Indians had worked the ores in the Jerome area, probably using them for pigment.

In 1873 some prospectors came to the Verde Valley and began working at the site of Jerome. John Ruffner held claim to the property, which he later leased to Gov. Frederick A. Tritle of Arizona. To develop the property, Tritle interested Eugene Jerome of New York, who agreed to finance the project provided that the camp be named for him. Jerome was treasurer of the company in 1883. True development of the area had to await the arrival of the railroad tracks at Ash Fork, when the mining interests established a road from Ash Fork to the mine so that a smelter could be brought in. In 1886 W. A. Clark of Montana purchased the properties, installed a new smelter, and made a narrow gauge rail connection with the main railroad.

It is difficult to give an elevation for this community perched on the side of a mountain, for the highest building stands fifteen hundred feet above the lowest. Five times flames have raced through the community. The fire of September 1898 consumed the entire business section. For mutual protection against fires, the citizens incorporated the community in 1899.

The year 1925 marked the beginning of the end for Jerome as a mining community. When two hundred fifty pounds of dynamite were used to blast the Black Pit, the entire town began to shift at the rate of about three-eighths of an inch per month. The concrete jail skidded slowly three hundred feet across the highway and tumbled onto its side below street level. Jerome's citizens shored up the buildings in various distinctive ways and Jerome continued to prosper. In 1929 there were fifteen thousand people living in the city. As the price of copper declined, so did the population, and in 1938 the United Verde Extension Company (Inc. March 8, 1899) was dissolved.

Today Jerome is nearly deserted, but Jerome's remaining citizens are preserving the community and have established a museum.

P.O. est. September 10, 1883. Fred F. Thomas, p.m. Incorporated as a city, 1908.

Ref.:  Schnebly; 11, pp. 22-23; 127, pp. 12, 14; 4, pp. 333-335; 170, p. 104; *Jerome Mining News*, April 30, 1899, 1:3 (State Library Files); P.O. Records. Maps: C-6; GM-5; GM-9; GM-12.

a.n. Jerome Canyon          Map: GM-8          Yavapai

## JERSEY

El.: 5772'                    Loc.: Yavapai 2, H-6.7
Jersey was the post office for the Jersey Lily Mine, the owner of which was a great admirer of Lily Langtry, the English actress.

P.O. est. March 6, 1895. William H. Ferguson, p.m. Discont. July 31, 1909.

Ref.: Barnes; P.O. Records. Maps: C-8; GM-20.

## JOE'S HILL

El.: 4030'                    Loc.: Yavapai 3, D-9.3
This location was named for Joe Mayer (cf. Mayer).

Ref.:  102, p. 49. Map: GM-24.

## JOSH MOUNTAIN

El.: 5956'                    Loc.: Yavapai 2, F-4
Edward and Clint Draper settled to the southwest of this mountain on the D-1 Ranch c. 1875 and named the mountain for their father, Joshua Draper.

Ref.: Barnes. Map: B-6.

a.n. Josh Spring          Map: GM-8          Yavapai

## JUNIPER

El.: c. 5000'                    Loc.: Yavapai 3, DE-1
At one time known as old Camp Hualapai (*q.v.*) this place was a stopping point for travelers. The name was changed to Juniper in 1883.

P.O. est. February 8, 1883. Charles A. Behm, p.m. Discont. July 15, 1910.

Ref.:  Gardner; 129; P.O. Records. Map: C-6.
    "Juniper" is a descriptive word used in many place names. A few examples are given below.

| a.n. Juniper Flat | El.: 6112'. Maps: GD-6; GD-5 | Gila |
| Juniper Gulch | Maps: GM-3; GM-7; B-6 | Yavapai |
| Juniper Mesa | Map: GM-23 | Yavapai |
| Juniper Mountains | | Yavapai |
| El.: 6750'. Maps: GM-23; GM-18 | | |
| Juniper Spring | Map: GE-1 | Graham |
| Juniper Spring | Map: GM-20 | Yavapai |

## KELLY

Loc.: Not known.
Charles I. Kelly owned a small mine and ranch on which he attempted to have a post office established. The name entered the official records on November 12, 1888, but Kelly was not commissioned and the post office was abandoned on January 30, 1889.

Ref.: P.O. Records; Barnes. Map: None.

## KING CANYON

El.: 4100'                    Loc.: Yavapai 3, B-1
The King brothers raised horses in this area from 1898 to 1910.

Ref.: Barnes. Map: GM-13.

| a.n. King Peak | Map: GM-2 | Yavapai |
| King Canyon Tank | Map: B-6 | Yavapai |
| King's Ranch | Map: GM-9 | Yavapai |

According to Barnes, Thomas R. King (d. Feb. 2, 1932) of California established this ranch c. 1883. Later his nephews joined him and managed the ranch for several years, raising horses.

Ref.: Barnes.

| King Springs | Map: GM-13 | Yavapai |

## KIRBY

Loc.: Near Tip Top Mine
The origin of this name has not yet been learned.

P.O. est. May 23, 1883. William C. Dawes, p.m. Discont. April 28, 1884.

Ref.: Barnes; P.O. Records. Map: None.

## KIRKLAND

El.: 3927'                    Loc.: Yavapai 2, F-6.3
William H. Kirkland (b. Virginia, July 12, 1832; d. January 1, 1899) came to live in Arizona in 1856 and is said to have been the man who raised the first American flag in Tucson when the Mormon Battalion went through in 1846. He settled in Tucson where in 1860 he and his fiancée were the first American couple to be married in Arizona. Three years later Kirkland, his wife and two children moved to the valley which today bears his name. By 1864 the Kirklands had a stage station which soon became noted for its excellent meals. Kirkland made a good living at farming and mining until 1868, at which time he and his family moved to Phoenix.

By 1869 at least twenty-five hundred acres of land had been claimed by settlers in the valley and a post office was soon established. In 1894 the railroad extended its line through the valley and named its small station Kirkland after the original settler.

P.O. est. as Kirkland Valley, April 5, 1871. John W. Kelsey, p.m. Discont. April 26, 1880. Re-est. as Kirkland, October 24, 1895. Thomas M. Earnhart, p.m. Wells Fargo Station, 1903.

Ref.:  P.O. Records; 25, p. 292; 105, p. 143; 4, p. 289; 115, pp. 73-74, 77; *Arizona Journal Miner*, January 10, 1899, 4:1; *Weekly Arizona Miner*, February 13, 1869, 2:1. Maps: C-3; GM-6.

a.n. Kirkland Creek          Maps: GM-6; GM-16          Yavapai

# LANE MOUNTAIN

El.: 7150'                    Loc.: Yavapai 3, A-9
James Madison Lane was a miner in this vicinity in 1876.
Ref.:  Barnes. Map: GM-7.

**a.n. Lane Spring**          Map: GM-7          Yavapai

# LOGAN MINE

El.: 5019'                    Loc.: Yavapai 3, E-5
Originally the Logan Mine was called the Isabella Mine,
having been so named for the youngest daughter of Charles
E. Hitchcock in 1875. Later it was apparently operated by
a man named Logan.
Ref.:  *Weekly Arizona Miner,* May 28, 1875, 3:2; Barnes.
      Map: GM-8.

**a.n. Logan Wash**          Map: GM-8          Yavapai

# LONESOME VALLEY

El.: 5017'                    Loc.: Yavapai 3, B-4.1-4.7
About ten miles south of Prescott is the valley which in
1879 was called Lonesome Valley because "not a living
creature was seen upon its many thousand acres."
Ref.:  *Arizona Sentinel,* May 24, 1879, 1:2. Maps: C-10; GM-
      9; GM-15.

# LONGFELLOW RIDGE

El.: 6791'                    Loc.: Yavapai 2, H-7.2-8
The ridge was named for the nearby Longfellow Mine list-
ed by Hinton in 1877.
Ref.:  Barnes. Map: GM-20.

**a.n. Longfellow Ridge Spring**    Map: GM-20    Yavapai

# LYNX CREEK

El.: 6225'                    Loc.: Yavapai 3, AB-7.3-8
In 1863 Capt. Joseph Walker led an expedition to prospect
in the interior of Arizona. Early in May 1863, five members of his party went up what came to be known as Lynx
Creek. While other members of the group hunted, Sam
Miller washed a pan of dirt, thus accidentally finding gold.
The main body of men was waiting on the Hassayampa for
word from the advance group, and that camp was broken
up immediately and moved to the new location. At the
new location on May 10, 1863, the Pioneer Mining District
was formed. At that time the river was called by the Indians the Ookilsipava River. Some time between that date
and September of the same year, the name became Lynx
Creek. The story is that Sam Miller found a lynx in the
creek and when he leaned down to pick it up, it suddenly
sprang at him, wounding his arm. Sam threw the animal
to the ground and kicked it to death. Lynx were not uncommon in this vicinity in the early days.
Ref.:  19, p. 3; *Weekly Alta Californian,* September 26, 1863
      (APHS); 19, pp. 4, 7, 8; Unidentified clipping, Sharlot
      Hall Museum, Prescott. Maps: C-2; GM-3.

# MacDONALD          Loc.: Apparently near Jerome.

The origin of this name has not yet been ascertained.
P.O. est. April 4, 1904. Fred H. Gorham, p.m. Discont. July
20, 1905.
Ref.:  P.O. Records. Map: None.

# MAHONE PEAK

El.: 7499'                    Loc.: Yavapai 2, A-1
Jim Mahone was a Hualapai Indian who served as a scout
and guide under Gen. George Crook. According to Mahone, Geronimo did "a lot of killing of United States Army
white men, and so forth, like that," and Mahone was called
on by the General to help clean up the trouble. The Indian
was drawing a government pension in 1931, at which time
he was known to be between ninety and one hundred years
of age.
Ref.:  169, pp. 247-248. Maps: C-9; C-12 (Mohon Mountain);
      C-13; C-8.

# MARION

El.: c. 4000'                 Loc.: Yavapai 2, H-8-9
In June 1871, a new mining community in the Bradshaw
Mountains was named for John H. Marion of Prescott.
The first structure, a store, was completed by July 1. The
town never seems to have amounted to much.
John H. Marion (b. Louisiana, 1835; d. 1891) arrived in
California in the late 1850's and worked as a printer on a
weekly newspaper. He moved to Arizona in 1865 in search
of gold, but after a year or so of prospecting and brushes
with the Indians, he located permanently in Prescott. In
1866 he became part owner of the *Prescott Miner* and continued to edit it for several years.
Ref.:  *Weekly Arizona Miner,* June 17, 1871, 3:2; July 18,
      1871, 2:3; 52, V, 347, 350. Map: None.

# MARTIN MOUNTAIN

El.: 6433'                    Loc.: Yavapai 2, EF-5
This was named for John C. Martin of Prescott, who became
a resident in 1892. He owned and published the *Arizona
Journal Miner* for many years.
Ref.:  Barnes. Map: GM-16.

**a.n. Martin Spring**       Maps: GM-6; GM-22        Yavapai
      **Martin Peak**       El.: 2300'. Map: C-12     Yavapai

# MARTINEZ

El.: c. 5000'                 Loc.: Yavapai 3, DE-9.2
Pro.:  /martíynes/
Martinez was a stage station in Martinez Valley on the
road from Ehrenberg to Camp McDowell via Date Creek.
It was named because of a Mexican who worked a placer
and kept stock here in 1862. By 1885 Martinez was gone
and the only two residents were men named Dennis May
and Frink. As the region became better settled, a post office
was established. By 1906 the place was being referred to
locally as Congress Junction (*q.v.*) and the post office name
was changed accordingly.
P.O. est. as Martinez, October 3, 1895. Edward Zeigler, p.m.
Changed to Congress Junction, March 23, 1906.
Ref.:  P.O. Records; 87, p. xxvii; *Prescott Journal Miner,*
      April 3, 1906, 8:4; *Weekly Prescott Courier,* November
      6, 1885 (Sharlot Hall Museum). Maps: C-9; C-10.

**a.n. Martinez Creek**       Map: GM-6          Yavapai

## MASSICKS

El.: c. 4000'                    Loc.: Yavapai 3, B-4
This post office took its name from that of its second post-
master, Thomas G. B. Massicks.
P.O. est. March 6, 1895. Peter Meade, p.m. Discont. March 6,
1899.
Ref.:   P.O. Records. Map: C-8.

## MAYER

El.: 4371'                       Loc.: Yavapai 3, B-3.6
Joe Mayer located c. 1882 at the point which bears his name.
He established a store and saloon in addition to a stage
station. The place rapidly became a trading center for the
surrounding agricultural and mining area.
P.O. est. January 11, 1884. Sarah B. Mayer, p.m. Wells Fargo
Station, 1903.
Ref.:   *Arizona Journal Miner*, January 4, 1888, 4:3; APHS
        Files; 4, p. 305. Maps: C-6; GM-3; GM-11.

## McCABE

El.: 5237'                       Loc.: Yavapai 3, B-8
John H. Marion (*See* Marion) discovered the mine at this
point, but was driven out by Indians. The mine was idle
until 1883 when it was re-located by Frank McCabe, who
sold half interest to Judge E. W. Wells and J. H. Packer.
By 1898 there was a flourishing mining town at McCabe.
It is a ghost town today.
P.O. est. December 31, 1897. Mrs. Marion C. Behn, p.m. Dis-
cont. October 31, 1917.
Ref.:   *Arizona Prospector*, "McCabe Mine, Its Early History,"
        May 4, 1901, 1:4; *Arizona Journal Miner*, January 10,
        1898, 4:2; 115, p. 63; Platten; P.O. Records. Maps: C-9;
        GM-3.

## McCLOUD MOUNTAIN

El.: 4500'                       Loc.: Yavapai 2, C-6.2
These mountains are named for a settler whose name may
have been spelled McLeod.
Ref.:   Barnes. Maps: C-10; GM-6.

## McGUIREVILLE

El.: c. 4000'                    Loc.: Yavapai 3, F-4
McGuireville was named for Gene McGuire.
Ref.:   Goddard. Map: GM-24.

## MEATH

El.: c. 5000'                    Loc.: Yavapai 1, H-5.2
Meath is an old English name which was suggested to rail-
road officials by the Rev. Meany of Prescott.
Ref.:   Barnes. Maps: B-6; C-13; GM-1.

| a.n. Meath Dam | Map: GM-1 | Yavapai |
| Meath Wash | Map: GM-1 | Yavapai |

## MEESVILLE

El.: c. 6000'                    Loc.: Yavapai 3, A-8
James Mees located at this point in 1880. He had a small
mine and ran the post office.
P.O. est. November 28, 1881. James Mees, p.m. Discont. Sep-
tember 2, 1885.
Ref.:   Barnes; P.O. Records. Map: C-6.

## MESCAL GULCH

El.: 6011'                       Loc.: Yavapai 3, CD-3
Pro.:   /méskæl/            Spanish: "century plant"
There is still a forest of century plants in this gulch. Apaches
used to have mescal pits here for baking the cactus.
Charley Yavapai, a chieftain who lived near Sedona, told
of an Indian fight between the Hualapais and the Yavapais
in Mescal Canyon. The battle lasted two days, with the
Yavapais killing all the Hualapais except six or seven who
escaped temporarily but were overtaken in the Chino Valley.
As a result of this battle, no Indians would go back to the
canyon or near Mingus Mountain (in which the canyon
lies) for fear of the ghosts of the dead.
Ref.:   127, p. 124; Barnes; Schnebly. Maps: GM-5; GM-9;
        GM-12.

## MIDDELTON

El.: c. 4000'                    Loc.: Yavapai 3, BC-7-8
Named for the Middelton family, Middelton was at the
end of the branch railroad running to the Bradshaw Mountain mines. The first postmaster had an annual salary of
$5.71.
P.O. est. May 8, 1903. George Middelton, p.m. Discont. January 8, 1908. Wells Fargo Station, 1904 (Middleton).
Ref.:   129; P.O. Records. Map: C-10.

## MIDNIGHT MESA

El.: 5000'                       Loc.: Yavapai 3, HI-9.5
Black volcanic rock gives this place its name.
Ref.:   Barnes. Map: GM-25.

## MILLER VALLEY

El.: 5438'                       Loc.: Yavapai 2, H-4.9
Samuel C. Miller established a ranch in this valley. The
ranch was known as Miller's Ranch and also as Burnt Ranch
(*q.v.*). Miller (b. Peoria, Illinois, November 4, 1840; d. October 12, 1909) came to Arizona in 1861. Following experiences as a prospector (*See* Lynx Creek), Miller engaged in
the freighting business. In April 1869, Brig. Gen. Thomas
C. Devin in his report on the Hualapais said that in 1866
Miller "treacherously and causelessly killed" Wauba Yuma,
chief of the Hualapais, and thus precipitated hostilities between the Hualapais and the whites. It was an uprising which
had not been quelled by late 1869.
Miller continued freighting until the coming of the railroads,
just prior to which time he sold out and located his ranch
in what is now known as Miller Valley.
Ref.:   52, II, 261-262; APHS Files; 169, p. 91. Map: GM-15.

| a.n. Miller Creek | Maps: GM-8; GM-15 | Yavapai |
| Miller Mountain | El.: 4352'. Map: GM-2 | Yavapai |

## MINGUS MOUNTAIN

El.: 7720'                       Loc.: Yavapai 3, CD-3.4
William Mingus (b. c. 1851; d. November 1911) was a
well-known mine owner and miner on the mountain which
bears his name. His body was found near Prescott in his
camp.

Mingus Mountain was known as Bee Mountain to the Yavapai Indians, none of whom would go near it for fear of the ghost of the dead in Mescal Gulch (q.v.) where an Indian fight between the Hualapais and Yavapais occurred many years ago.

Ref.: *Prescott Courier*, November 25, 1911, 8:3; 127, p. 124; Willard. Maps: C-10; GM-9; GM-12.

## MINNEHAHA

El.: 5449'          Loc.: Yavapai 3, A-9
Charles Taylor (b. New York, c. 1824; d. June 6, 1891) was a member of the Joseph C. Walker prospecting party, arriving in Arizona in 1863. He recorded several claims and by May 21, 1875, was living at his own ranch on Minnehaha Creek, Minnehaha Flat. The name Minnehaha was taken from a mine by that name.

P.O. est. June 21, 1880. Charles Taylor, p.m. Discont. December 31, 1910.

Ref.: Charles Taylor File, APHS; P.O. Records. Maps: C-9; GM-3.

a.n. Minnehaha Creek  Maps: C-5; GM-6; GM-7; GM-22  Yavapai
Minnehaha Flat     Maps: GM-3; GM-7       Yavapai
Minnehaha Spring    Map: GM-7          Yavapai
Hiawatha                        Yavapai
Loc.: Not known, but near Minnehaha. Mentioned as being a hill named "after the mythical Indian maiden (sic) . . . the subject of a poem by Longfellow."

Ref.: *Weekly Arizona Miner*, September 19, 1879, 2:2.

## MINT VALLEY

El.: c. 5000'          Loc.: Yavapai 2, GH-4-3
A man named McKee settled in this area in the late 1860's, but a three year drought coupled with Indian trouble forced him to leave. He liked the mint which grew along the stream in the valley, hence his name for the area.

v.n. Mint Creek

Ref.: *Arizona Miner*, January 20, 1872, 2:1. Maps: C-12 (Mint Creek); E-20; GM-24.

a.n. Mint Wash     Maps: GM-8; GM-17     Yavapai

## MISERY, FORT

El.: 5355'          Loc.: Yavapai 2, HG-5
When Gov. John N. Goodwin and his party arrived at the capital of the newly created Arizona Territory, it was necessary to provide quarters for them. The first house to be erected in Prescott was a two-room log cabin built by Manuel Yersera, who accompanied the military escort. He stopped his loaded teams at the spot where Granite Street turns to cross Granite Creek in Prescott and he did not budge an inch when selecting the spot on which to erect a log house. The following May, surveyors for the town lived in the house when they were surveying Prescott.

The house was next used by Judge Howard, and one legend says that the building received its name because of the manner in which the judge meted justice. A second story is that when the building was converted in 1864 into a boarding house, the quality of the food resulted in the name Fort Misery. The boarding house for fifty men was run by an American woman called the Virgin Mary. There is some doubt about her real name, though it may have been Mary Brown, listed in the Arizona census of 1864 as having been born in Texas and as having lived in Arizona for the preceding eight years. She died on Lynx Creek in 1880. It is said that her nickname was due to her many charities.

Fort Misery No. 2 was built in the early 1870's. The vicinity of the buildings was known as Happy Valley, possibly because the buildings were the scene of many gay times. Happy Valley was probably where the Sharlot Hall Museum exists today.

Ref.: Garrett; 52, III, 205-206; Virgin Mary File, APHS; *Weekly Arizona Miner*, December 19, 1868, 3:3; November 26, 1875, 3:2. Map: GM-7.

## MONTEZUMA CASTLE

El.: 3200'          Loc.: Yavapai 3, F-4.2
Montezuma Castle is a prehistoric cliff dwelling on the right bank of Wet Beaver Creek. Although legend used to claim that this place was once occupied by Aztecs, there is no ground for this belief and no reason to connect it with the Indian chief Montezuma, who was murdered in 1519 on the site of Mexico City.

In the early part of the Eleventh Century, Indians began to locate in the high limestone cliff on Wet Beaver Creek, in its numerous caves and erosion pockets. In one of these they created the five-story structure known as Montezuma Castle. By 1400 A.D. the Indians had abandoned most of the pueblos in the Verde Valley. Antonio de Espejo entered the Verde Valley almost two hundred years later (c. 1583), but apparently did not see Montezuma Castle. The first white visitor is unknown, although by 1860 the structure was a familiar one to the white men who were drifting into the valley to take up agriculture.

By 1895 it was apparent that unless something was done, Montezuma Castle would probably collapse. It was repaired by the Arizona Antiquarian Association. On December 8, 1906, President Theodore Roosevelt proclaimed Montezuma Castle a National Monument, today an area of five hundred twenty acres.

Ref.: 88, pp. 935-936; 24, Earl Jackson, pp. 3-6; Cook (Supt. of Nat'l. Monument). Maps: C-10; C-12; GM-21.

a.n. Montezuma Well  Maps: C-12; GM-21     Yavapai
Montezuma Well is a detached portion of Montezuma Castle National Monument. The visitor will find it a complete surprise, for from the base of the hill one would never suspect that a body of water lay within miles of the place. The hill in which the well is located has been eroded by Beaver Creek so that on one side it forms a cliff. It is necessary to climb the crater-like mound. From the brink of this "crater," one looks across four hundred and seventy feet to the other side as well as down to a vast circular well about eighty feet below. Although it appears to be a volcanic crater, the well has in fact been created in the limestone by underground water having loosened the top of the cavern, which then fell in. Divers have explored the depth of the well and found it to be on an average of fifty five feet deep. Around the sides of the well are the remains of a dozen Indian cliff dwellings.

On the flat adjacent to the well, settlers erected an old adobe fort which had a well inside, thus making it possible for the pioneers to withstand the attacks of Indians without suffering from thirst. A settlement known as Montezuma City grew up in this area in 1864. This was the site of the Wales Arnold Ranch, which was constructed from stones taken from the nearby pueblo ruins. The ranch fort was torn down by its new owner in 1952.

P.O. est. October 20, 1892. Amanda Mehrens, p.m. Discont. July 19, 1893.

Ref.:   Dugas; 161, p. 134; *Arizona Miner*, October 26, 1864; 1:1; 22, p. 166; 107, pp. 127-128; 88, p. 936; P.O. Records.

## MUCHOS CANONES

El.: c. 5000'                         Loc.: Yavapai 3, C-4-5
                            Near head of Santa Maria River.
Pro.: /muwčos kanyównes/    Spanish: "many canyons"
The name derives from the fact that five canyons unite at this point. Here on September 25, 1872, Companies B, C, and K of the Fifth Cavalry with Indian scouts under Col. Julius Wilmot Mason overtook a band of Hualapai Indians who had attempted to murder Gen. George Crook during a conference at Date Creek. The Indians lost more than forty men in the ensuing fight.

Ref.:   85, p. 438; 132, p. 170; 111, p. 220. Map: None.

## MUDDY CANYON

El.: c. 6000'                         Loc.: Yavapai 1, BA-7-5
The name Muddy Canyon is probably descriptive of its condition during the rains.

Hinton noted this as a stage station where the road was good, wood abundant and where water was to be found in a canyon three hundred yards to the right of the road. He also noted that an old government camping ground existed three miles beyond the Camp near Muddy Canyon. There was an army skirmish in Muddy Canyon on March 22, 1866.

Ref.:   87, p. xxiv. Maps: C-4; C-7; E-20.

## MULDOON CANYON

El.: c. 4000'                         Loc.: Yavapai 3, FG-3
Farrell Teirnen wes a soldier at Camp Verde who was known as "Muldoon." When he was discharged, he ran cattle in the canyon which bears his name.

Ref.:   Barnes. Map: GM-13.

**a.n. Muldoon Tank**        Map: GM-13              Yavapai

## MULE SHOE BEND

El.: 2500'                            Loc.: Yavapai 3, G-7.9
Descriptive.

Ref.:   Barnes. Map: C-12.

## NELSON

El.: c. 6000'                         Loc.: Yavapai 1, A-1
Fred Nelson was a conductor on the construction train of the Santa Fe Railroad when the track was laid in 1883. At that time he was living with his family in what was called a "boarding car" on the train. Nelson noticed the presence of fine lime and other construction materials near the location which today bears his name. He started several quarries and also a lime kiln which is still operating.

P.O. est. March 23, 1904. William Carey, p.m. Discont. July 15, 1954. Wells Fargo Station, 1906.

Ref.:   Kelley; 169, pp. 214, 216; P.O. Records. Maps: C-10; GM-24.

**a.n. Nelson Mesa**          Map: GM-2               Yavapai

## OAKS AND WILLOWS

El.: c. 6000'                         Loc.: Yavapai 1, C-7
Descriptive.
Oaks and Willows was a stage station which later became headquarters camp for the Perrin Livestock Company of Williams.

Ref.:   Barnes. Maps: E-13; E-20.

## OCOTILLO

El.: c. 4000'                         Loc.: Yavapai 3, B-8
Pro.: /okotíylə/             Spanish: "coach whip"
The presence of ocotillo in this area resulted in the selection of the name for the post office.

P.O. est. January 13, 1916. Pearl Orr, p.m. Discont. May 30, 1925.

Ref.:   Barnes; P.O. Records. Map: C-12.

## OCTAVE

El.: c. 3500'                         Loc.: Yavapai 2, F-9.4
Pro.: /ákteyv/
In 1863 Octave was laid out as a placer camp, at which time it was claimed by eight men, hence the name. The Octave Mine was closed at the end of World War II and the camp was demolished in order to reduce taxes.

At one time approximately three thousand people lived at Octave. According to post office records, Octave and Weaver were the same place. As a matter of fact, the two locations were adjacent to each other (*See* Weaver). Weaver in 1899 was inhabited largely by Mexicans and the town was in such a dissolute state that the people at large asked that the town be stamped out.

P.O. est. as Weaver, May 26, 1899. Roger W. Aaren, p.m. Name changed to Octave, April 19, 1900. David J. Jones, p.m. Discont. December 31, 1942.

Ref.:   Barnes; 170, p. 69; P.O. Records. Maps: C-9; GM-6.

## ORO

El.: c. 4000'                         Loc.: Yavapai 3, AB-9
Pro.: /óro/                  Spanish: "gold"
Oro was the post office for the Oro Belle Mine.

P.O. est. June 20, 1904. Benjamin Heller, p.m. Discont. March 6, 1907.

Ref.:   Willson; G. E. P. Smith; P.O. Records. Map: None.

## PALACE STATION

El.: 5856'                            Loc.: Yavapai 2, H-7
Palace Station, one of the oldest structures made by white men in Arizona, served as a stage station at Spencer Spring on the Senator Trail from Prescott to Phoenix. Spencer Spring was owned by the Spencer family. The stage station was abandoned about 1910.

Ref.:   Theobald; Willson. Map: GM-20.

## PAMELA

El.: c. 6000'                         Loc.: Yavapai 2, GH-4-5
The origin of this name has not yet been learned.

P.O. est. November 28, 1881. Fernando Nellis, p.m. Discont. April 27, 1883.

Ref.: P.O. Records. Map: None.

## PAN

El.: c. 5200′  Loc.: Yavapai 1, E-3.1

A short name for a short railroad switch.

Ref.: Barnes. Map: C-11.

## PARTRIDGE CITY

El.: c. 4000′  Loc.: Yavapai 2, D-9

Partridge City was actually a store and stage station owned by William Partridge.

William Partridge (b. England, 1825; d. September 12, 1899) arrived in Arizona in 1864. In 1877 he built the stage station which according to Hinton was called Partridge City. As a result of a feud, Partridge in the late fall of that year shot G. H. Wilson (See Antelope Peak, a.n. Antelope Valley). Partridge, sent to Yuma Prison, was pardoned in 1880. He then returned to Stanton.

Ref.: William Partridge File, APHS; 87, p. xxi. Map: None.

## PAULDEN

El.: 4407′  Loc.: Yavapai 2, H-1

The son of the first postmaster at this point was killed accidentally. His name was Paul and the post office was named for him. In 1956 Paulden consisted of a residence, a truck service stop and a few tourist cabins.

**v.n. Midway Grocery**

P.O. est. February 13, 1926. Orville T. Pownall, p.m.

Ref.: Barnes; P.O. Records. Map: C-13.

## PECK MINE

El.: c. 3000′  Loc.: Yavapai 3, C-7.3

Edmond George Peck (b. Canada, Dec. 28, 1834; d. December 13, 1910) came to Arizona in 1863. When Peck retired from service as a scout and guide for troops at Fort Whipple, he lived in Prescott. He was shown some rich silver ore which prompted him to reveal that he knew where tons of equally good ore existed. As a result of this conversation T. M. Alexander, C. C. Bean, William Cole, and Peck located the Peck Mine.

According to Fish the first three men were prospecting while Peck was hunting for a deer. He found a very heavy rock which, when tested, proved rich silver ore. In 1875 the Peck Mine was a leading one in Arizona Territory. In the three-year period to 1878 it produced $1,200,000 in silver, but in the latter year a lawsuit was begun over the mine. It dragged on and on, and Peck died a poor man. From 1879 to 1910, he prospected unsuccessfully at various places in the vicinity of the mine.

Ref.: 55, p. 539; 52, II, 263, 264; 76, p. 48. Map: E-20.

**a.n. Peck Canyon**  Maps: GM-3; GM-20  Yavapai

**Peck Lake**  El.: 3332′. Map: GM-9  Yavapai
The Indian name for this small lake is *Hatalacva* (Yavapai: "crooked water"). The water of this lake is of subterranean origin. According to one story the lake was formed by workmen who turned the Verde River from its natural channel by cutting through a ridge and putting in levees to keep the lake from overflowing.

**v.n. Bass Lake**

Ref.: Peck (Ranger at Tuzigoot National Monument. No relation to E. G. Peck); Stemmer; Clipping, unidentified, at Sharlot Hall Museum.

**a.n. Peck Spring**  Map: GM-20  Yavapai

## PEEPLES VALLEY

El.: 4500′  Loc.: Yavapai 2, F-8

Abraham Harlow Peeples (b. North Carolina, June 11, 1822; d. January 29, 1892) came to Arizona from California by way of Yuma in 1863. At Yuma he organized a prospecting expedition with Pauline Weaver as guide. The party made its way across Arizona to Rich Hill (q.v.) where gold placers were found.

In 1865 Peeples had a ranch in the valley which bears his name, but he left prior to 1870, in which year he was a saloon keeper in Wickenburg. His ranch was probably purchased by Charles C. Genung.

**v.n. People's Ranch**

P.O. est. October 18, 1875. Charles Genung, p.m. (cf. Yarnell).

Ref.: APHS Names File; *Arizona Miner*, June 10, 1871, 3:2; 85, p. 426; 4, p. 290; 25, p. 292; 87, p. 44; P.O. Records. Maps: C-6; E-20; GM-6.

## PERKINSVILLE

El.: 3847′  Loc.: Yavapai 3, BC-1

James Baker, a Montana prospector, settled on the Verde River about 1876. His herd of cattle increased to about ten thousand, of which he shipped out more than seven thousand following a drought. He later entered partnership with John G. Campbell, using the 76 brand. Baker retained the land after the cattle had all been sold.

On July 5, 1899, Marion Alexander Perkins (d. June 30, 1927) a Texas stockman, sold his Texas ranch holdings and set out for a new location farther west. He finally arrived at the Baker and Campbell 76 Ranch, which he soon bought. He returned to New Mexico for cattle which had been driven in from Texas and arrived on his new ranch on November 1, 1900.

When the Santa Fe Railroad built a branch from Drake to Clarkdale, the line ran across part of the Perkins' property where the station was named Perkinsville. After Perkins died, his outfit was continued as a unit by his four children until 1936. Today Nick Perkins, his four sons and daughter own the land.

P.O. est. August 24, 1925. Mrs. Annie N. Perkins, p.m. Discont. August 1, 1939.

Ref.: Robert E. Perkins, Letter, December 16, 1955. 115, pp. 42, 45, 47, 49, 50; P.O. Records. Maps: C-11; GM-5; GM-9.

## PICA

El.: 5247′  Loc.: Yavapai 1, B-1.6

Pro.: /píykə/

The original name of this small station on the A.T. & S.F. R.R. was Picacho. However, another station by the same name on the S.P.R.R. made it necessary to change one of the names to avoid confusion in freight shipments. Officers

from the two railroad lines matched coins to see which name would be changed and the Santa Fe lost. The name was changed to Pica.
Ref.:   Barnes. Map: C-10.

## PICACHO

El.: 7260'                                    Loc.: Yavapai 1, EF-4
Pro.: /pikáčo/                              Spanish: "peak"
Lt. Amiel W. Whipple in 1854 mentioned crossing Lt. Lorenzo Sitgreaves' trail, from which the Picacho lay about twenty-five miles west. From that point Whipple's party traveled to Picacho Spring where his men rejoined the main body of his expedition at the south end of the Picacho.
**v.n. Picacho Butte**
Ref.:   177, pp. 178, 189, 190. Maps: C-2 to C-13 (inclusive).

## PIEDMONT

El.: 3345'                                    Loc.: Yavapai 2, DE-8.4
This railroad station was named because of the variety of colors on the nearby mountains.
Ref.:   Barnes. Map: C-9.

## PINEVETA

El.: 5300'                                    Loc.: Yavapai 1, FG-3.8
Pro.: /páyn víytə/
This station was named because of its presence at the edge of cedar country. Nearby is Pineveta Peak.
Ref.:   Barnes. Maps: C-5; E-11; E-22; E-23.
**a.n. Pineveta Peak**        Maps: C-5; E-22              Yavapai
   **Pineveta Canyon**       Maps: B-4; B-6               Yavapai

## PINTO MESA

El.: 5408'                                    Loc.: Yavapai 3, EF-4.7
Pro.: /pínto/            Spanish: "painted" with reference to a
                                                       horse only
A pinto horse or cow ran on Pinto Mesa.
Ref.:   Barnes. Maps: GM-21; GM-25.

## PLACERITA

El.: 5300'                                    Loc.: Yavapai 2, GH-8
Pro.: /plæceríytə/              Spanish: "little placer"
The post office serving the area of Placerita Gulch was referred to in 1898 as Placeritas in a newspaper story concerning a robbery of the post office.
The name of both the gulch and the post office probably came from the location of placer mines in the area. Gold was found here by Mexicans in 1868-69.
P.O. est. February 1, 1896. Louis H. Herron, p.m. Discont. August 15, 1910.
Ref.:   P.O. Records; *Arizona Journal Miner*, March 10, 1898, 4:1; Barnes; Platten; 87, p. 101. Maps: C-9; GM-6.
**a.n. Placerita Gulch**      Maps: GM-6; GM-10             Yavapai

## POLAND

El.: 5500'                                    Loc.: Yavapai 3, A-8.7
Davis Robert Poland (b. Tennessee, 1834; d. February 23, 1882) came to Arizona in 1864. By 1871 he had a cabin in the Bradshaw Mountains just below the then new town of Bradshaw, and the following year he located the Poland

Mine for which a post office was later opened. Poland also raised cattle. A community named Poland Junction developed on the railroad about five miles from the mine.
P.O. est. November 16, 1901. James R. Sias (deceased). Frank Lecklider apptd. January 6, 1902. Discont. February 15, 1913. Wells Fargo Station, 1903.
Ref.:   Barnes; Davis Robert Poland File, APHS; P.O. Records. Maps: C-9; C-12; GM-3; GM-20 (Poland Junction).
**a.n. Poland Creek**        Maps: GM-3; GM-4; GM-7          Yavapai

## POWELL SPRINGS

El.: c. 4000'      Loc.: Yavapai 3, EF-4-5. Cherry Creek area.
Powell Springs was named for William Dempsey Powell (b. January 1, 1846; d. 1936) who lived here from 1875 on. He was a miner but later became a prominent stockman in the Flagstaff area.
Ref.:   Mrs. Frier (daughter). Map: None.

## PRAIRIE

El.: 5136'                                    Loc.: Yavapai 1, H-5.6
Descriptive. This is a railroad siding in flat country.
Ref.:   Barnes. Map: GM-24.

## PRESCOTT

El.: 5347'                                    Loc.: Yavapai 2, H-5
A variety of circumstances contributed to the formation of the northern Arizona city of Prescott. Possibly the first contributing factor was the discovery of gold in the Walker District by the Pauline Weaver party organized by Abraham Harlow Peeples at Yuma in 1863. On December 29, 1863, the territorial governor's party arrived in the newly created Arizona Territory. (*See* Navajo Springs, Apache). In his proclamation, Gov. John N. Goodwin stated that the seat of government would be at or near Fort Whipple, to which the Gubernatorial Party immediately proceeded. The fort had been established only a month earlier. On January 22, 1864, Gov. Goodwin and his party arrived at Fort Whipple. In May the seat of government was moved from the fort to a spot approximately eighteen miles to the southwest and by July a town was taking shape on Granite Creek.

Among the first settlers was Joseph Ehle (b. New York, March 1813; d. November 1912) with his wife, one son, and five daughters. They arrived on July 28, 1864. Ehle and his wife before coming to Arizona had lived in Iowa from which they moved to Colorado in 1860. In 1865 Ehle established a ranch in Skull Valley, where he had the government road station. The next year, however, he returned to Prescott.

Prescott developed rapidly. In 1865 it was described as built exclusively of wood and inhabited almost entirely by Americans. Both these facts made it unique among early communities in Arizona. Meanwhile, on May 30, 1864, the citizens held a meeting on Granite Creek and established the town. They selected the name Prescott to honor William Hickling Prescott (b. Massachusetts, 1796; d. Boston 1859), a historian noted for his books about the Aztecs and for his translations of Spanish works. When the town was laid out, the residents named many of the streets after others closely identified with the history of the Southwest, such as Coronado, Whipple, Aubrey, Leroux, and Walker.

In July 1864 was held the first of the Fourth of July celebrations which still continue as the annual Prescott Frontier Days and Rodeo. The first rodeo in the world is said to have been held at Prescott on July 4, 1888.

Whether or not Prescott would remain the permanent territorial capital caused many a ruckus in the legislatures of 1864-5-6. Some representatives favored Tucson, considering it a more important community. They were able to carry the legislative vote, but the governor from year to year proclaimed that the legislature would be convened at Prescott as the temporary seat of government. However, by a majority of one vote in 1867 Tucson was made the capital and the ensuing five legislative sessions were held in that city. Ten years after the change (1877) Prescott was again made the capital, an honor which it lost permanently in 1889 to Phoenix.

As was frequently the case in Arizona in the early days, fire devastated Prescott. In 1900 a drunken miner overturned a kerosene lamp in a lodging house. The next year Prescott provided for an adequate water system by purchasing Del Rio Springs (q.v.).

In its early days Prescott had various names associated with it. One of these was Fleuryville, a name applied to the west side of Granite Creek. The name Fleuryville came from that of Judge Henry W. Fleury (d. 1896), who had his headquarters there. It was also referred to as Gránite by its first citizens.

P.O. est. August 25, 1863. Hiram W. Reed, p.m. Wells Fargo Station, 1879. Prescott incorporated January 3, 1881.

Ref.:    55, p. 568; 7, pp. 522, 526; 52, IV, 19; 115, pp. 136-137; 4, pp. 237-238; *Arizona Miner*, September 7, 1864, 1:1; P.O. Records. Maps: C-1; E-12; E-22; GM-9; GM-15.

**a.n. Prescott National Forest**                                          Yavapai
Maps: C-7; GM-2; GM-5; GM-6; GM-8; GM-9; GM-10; GM-11; GM-12; GM-13; GM-20; GM-22; GM-23.
Created as the Prescott Forest Reserve, May 10, 1898. Verde Forest Reserve created December 30, 1907. Prescott and Verde Forest Reserve consolidated under the name of Prescott National Forest, July 2, 1908. Additional acreage added, October 22, 1934, transferred from Tusayan National Forest to Prescott National Forest to make total acreage of 1,456,313.
Ref.:    120, p. 35.

## PROVIDENCE

El.: 5500′                          Loc.: Yavapai 3, AB-8.5
The origin of this name has not yet been learned.
P.O. est. April 4, 1899. Bradford M. Crawford, p.m. Discont. October 25, 1904. Wells Fargo Station, 1903.
Ref.:    P.O. Records. Maps: C-9; GM-3.

## PUNTENNEY

El.: 3840′                          Loc.: Yavapai 3, CD-1
George Puntenney came to Arizona from Colorado in 1879. It was he who built the first lime kiln at this location. The Puntenney Lime Company was sold in 1929 to John T. Sheffield and Alfred Paul (*See* Paul Spur, Cochise).

P.O. est. as Puntney, May 20, 1892. George Puntenney, p.m. Name changed to Puntenney, date unknown. Discont. September 30, 1932.
Ref.:    Barnes; Garrett; Eli Puntenney File, APHS; *Builder and Contractor*, October 30, 1929 (APHS File); P.O. Records. Maps: C-8; C-12.

## RAMSGATE

El.: 5092′                          Loc.: Yavapai 2, G-4.7
The railroad runs more than one crooked mile between this spot and Iron Springs, hence the name Ramsgate because of twisting, as in a ram's horn. Ramsgate is a siding on the railroad.
Ref.:    Barnes; Garrett. Map: GM-8.
**a.n. Ramsgate Spring**          Map: GM-8          Yavapai

## RAWLINS, CAMP

El.: c. 5000′                          Loc.: Yavapai 2, E-2
In 1870 Camp Rawlins was a subpost to Whipple Barracks in Williamson's Valley. It was probably named for John Aaron Rawlins, Secretary of War from March 11, 1869, until his death on September 6, 1869. The post was established in February 1870 and abandoned in September of the same year.
Ref.:    85, p. 537; 75, p. 50. Maps: C-5; E-20.

## REIMER PEAK

El.: 5038′                          Loc.: Yavapai 3, E-6.1
Pro.: /ríymer/
Gus Reimer was a sheepman who grazed his flocks in this area.
**v.n. Reamer Peak**
Ref.:    Barnes. Map: C-13.
**a.n. Reimer Draw**          El.: 5038′. Map: GM-19          Yavapai

## RELIABLE

El.: 4300′                          Loc.: Yavapai 3, B-8
The post office for the mining camp took its name from the Old Reliable Mine.
P.O. est. May 13, 1890. Mrs. Margaret C. Liston, p.m. Discont. April 20, 1895.
Ref.:    Barnes; P.O. Records. Maps: C-7.

## RICE PEAK

El.: 5333′                          Loc.: Yavapai 3, EF-8
Pro.: /ráysiˆ/ or /rays/
This peak is probably named for Willard Rice (d. January 2, 1899) who arrived in 1864 as a miner. On January 1, 1865, he was employed as a guide by Lt. Charles A. Curtis. He also served as a scout for Lt. Abeyta in 1867. On this peak the New Mexico Volunteers fought with Apaches and were licked thoroughly by the Indians. Willard Rice was not killed in this battle. Rice later served as a guide for Capt. George M. Wheeler in his expedition.
Ref.:    Dugas; 52, III, 329; File, Sharlot Hall Museum, Prescott. Map: GM-19.
**a.n. Rice Spring**                                                      Yavapai
Loc.: This spring is in the canyon near Rice Peak.

## RICH-IN-BAR

El.: 3000'                    Loc.: Yavapai 3, D-9.1
This was the name of a gold mine in Agua Fria Canyon.
Its locator, a man named Zika, was optimistic, hence the
name.

P.O. est. as Richinbar, July 30, 1896. John H. Webb, p.m.
Discont. March 15, 1912.

Ref.: Barnes; *Prescott Courier,* July 21, 1917 (Sharlot Hall
    Museum Files); P.O. Records. Maps: C-9; GM-3.

## RIMROCK

El.: 3639'                    Loc.: Yavapai 3, G-3.7
Rimrock is a ranch and post office. A formation of rimrock
makes the bank of Beaver Creek on which the ranch is
located.

P.O. est. February 18, 1929. Ella Laudermilk, p.m.
Ref.: Barnes; Schnebly; P.O. Records. Maps: C-13; GM-21.

## ROCK BUTTE

El.: 5435'                    Loc.: Yavapai 1, H-6.6
Descriptive. The name is also applied to the railroad siding nearby.

Ref.: Barnes. Maps: C-10; C-12 (Rock Butte Station); GM-
    13.

## ROCK SPRINGS

El.: c. 4000'                    Loc.: Yavapai 3, CD-10.2
Rock Springs was named in 1921 by Ben Warner because
here the spring emerged from the rocks.

P.O. est. February 1, 1938. Ben Warner, p.m. Discont. May
31, 1955.

Ref.: Ben Warner, Letter, March 1, 1956; P.O. Records.
    Maps: F-6-F-13 (inclusive); GM-25.

## ROK

El.: c. 4800'                    Loc.: Yavapai 1, H-6.5
Because this railroad point is near Rock Butte the station
should probably have been called by that name. However,
the name was abbreviated to Rok for clarity and celerity
in telegraphy.

Ref.: Barnes. Maps: C-13; GM-1.

## ROVER PEAK

El.: 5285'                    Loc.: Yavapai 3, F-10.9
The peak was named for the Red Rover Mine at its base.
The mine opened in 1880.

Ref.: Barnes. Map: GM-19.

## RUSSELL

El.: 5491'                    Loc.: Yavapai 3, BC-2.5
Russell (first name not known) was a superintendent for
the railroad sidetrack on the Jerome narrow gauge railroad
to the Jerome mines.

Ref.: Barnes. Maps: C-10; GM-5; GM-9.

a.n. **Russell Hill**          Map: B-6          Yavapai
    **Russell Spring**        Map: GM-21        Yavapai

## RUTHERFORD

El.: 2400'                    Loc.: Yavapai 3, F-5.3
This place was named for O. H. Rutherford, who was a
close friend of the Hopper family who gave it the name.
Rutherford lived in Jerome.

P.O. est. September 14, 1907. Elizabeth Hopper, p.m. Discont.
May 25, 1911.

Ref.: Barnes Notes; P.O. Records. Map: C-10.

## ST. MATTHEWS (SIC) MOUNTAIN

El.: 6310'                    Loc.: Yavapai 3, B-2.6
Marion Alexander Perkins (*See* Perkinsville) said a young
woman once climbed this peak. She left a card on top asking
that the name St. Matthew be applied and Perkins began
using that name.

Ref.: Barnes. Maps: B-6; C-13; GM-13.

## SAYER'S

El.: c. 2500'                    Loc.: Yavapai 2, F-10
This place was named for its first postmaster.

P.O. est. November 17, 1908. George Sayer, p.m. Discont. July
13, 1913.

Ref.: P.O. Records. Maps: C-10; F-2.

## SEAL MOUNTAIN

El.: 5116'                    Loc.: Yavapai 2, GH-9.4
This is the mountain which is said to have been used for
the background on the first Arizona Territorial Seal, which
showed a miner standing by his wheelbarrow with a pick
and shovel beside him and auriferous hills in the background.
Whereas the nation as a whole trusted in God, early Arizonans used the motto *"Ditat Deus"* ("God Enriches"). In
1864 a new seal was authorized, using the San Francisco
Mountains in the background. This second seal was put
in use apparently about 1883 and was used until 1890.
A new seal was adopted when Arizona became a state in
1912. The only thing remaining on it from the early seals
is the *Ditat Deus.*

Ref.: Barnes. Maps: GM-22; GM-6.

## SECRET MOUNTAIN

El.: c. 5000'                    Loc.: Yavapai 3, EF-1
This mountain was named by W. W. Van Deren. It is a
narrow, low hogback between Secret Canyon and Low
Canyon.

Ref.: Barnes. Map: GM-24.

## SEEPAGE MOUNTAIN

El.: 6230'                    Loc.: Yavapai 2, E-2.7
The name is descriptive of the seepage on the south and
east sides of the mountain.

Ref.: Barnes. Map: GM-23.

a.n. **Seepage Canyon**      Maps: GM-16; GM-23      Yavapai

## SELIGMAN

El.: 5242'                    Loc.: Yavapai 1, D-3
Pro.: /sǝlíygmǝn/
In 1886 when the line from Prescott to the main railroad

was completed, the junction of this line with the main one at its northern end was known as Prescott Junction, where a new town quickly sprang up. When the Ash Fork branch of the railroad was built, the older Prescott branch was abandoned and the rails removed. However, Prescott Junction continued to exist and gradually came to be known as Seligman because the Seligman brothers (New York bankers who were connected with the A. & P. R.R.) owned the Hash Knife Cattle Company.

The A. & P. R.R. reorganized in May 1897, with the result that Williams was abandoned as its western terminus and Seligman selected in its stead. In July the S.F. R.R. emerged from the reorganization. The round house at Williams was dismantled and moved to Seligman.

P.O. est. November 9, 1886. James Daly, p.m. Wells Fargo Station (Prescott Junction), 1887.

Ref.: P.O. Records; Barnes; *Prescott Weekly Courier*, August 6, 1886, 3:1, 2; 61, p. 66. Maps: C-6; C-12; GM-25.

**a.n. Seligman Canyon**      Map: GM-2      Yavapai

## SENATOR

El.: c. 6000'      Loc.: Yavapai 2, H-6.4

The Senator Mine apparently gave this location its name. The mine was in existence as early as 1878 when it had a ten-stamp mill to run ores which assayed $85 per ton in gold. The mining-community was important enough to rate a school.

P.O. est. November 1, 1915. Mary Wills, p.m. Discont. October 22, 1918.

Ref.: Barnes; *Arizona Journal Miner*, November 16, 1897, 4:2; P.O. Records. Map: C-12.

## SHERIDAN MOUNTAIN

El.: 6199'      Loc.: Yavapai 2, E-3

Tom Sheridan is said to have lived in the Williamson Valley from which he moved to Sheridan Mountain in 1877. He raised horses.

Ref.: Barnes. Maps: C-13; GM-16; GM-24.

## SHIPP MOUNTAIN

El.: c. 5000'      Loc.: Yavapai 2, C-4.9

Jeff Shipp had a cattle ranch in this area c. 1880, with headquarters known as the Cienega Ranch on the Santa Maria River.

Ref.: Barnes. Maps: B-6; C-12; C-13.

**a.n. Big Shipp Mountain**      El.: 5184'. Map: GM-24      Yavapai
   **Little Shipp Mountain**      Map: GM-24      Yavapai

## SIERRA PRIETA

El.: c. 5000'      Loc.: Yavapai 2, G-3-5

Pro.: /siyérə priyétə/      Spanish: "black mountains"

In referring to the mountains near Prescott, Gilbert (a member of Wheeler's survey party) called the range the San Prieto and remarked that it showed very little lava near Prescott but became "eruptive in character" in the vicinity of "Postal's Ranch" (Postle's). Hinton referred to the range as the Sierra Prieta, the name in use today.

**v.n. Granite Range**      Maps: C-6, E-20

Ref.: 175, III, 125; 87, pp. 51, 301. Maps: A-7; C-3; C-11 (Sierra Prieta); C-2 (San Prieto); CM-8.

**a.n. Prieta**      El.: 5920'      Yavapai
   Probably so named because near the Sierra Prieta.

Ref.: 25, p. 255.

**Prieta Range**      Loc.: T. 9 N., R. 8 E.      Yavapai
   A black volcanic formation, covered with cedar brush.

## SILVER MOUNTAINS

El.: 6120'      Loc.: Yavapai 2, H-9.4

Silver Mountains so appears for the first time on the Hamilton map of 1866 (*See* Bradshaw Mountains). The name derived from rich silver deposits in the mountains.

Ref.: Barnes. Maps: C-10; GM-3; GM-7.

## SIMMONS

El.: c. 4500'      Loc.: Yavapai 2, FG-2

A man named Simmons homesteaded at this point c. 1864, establishing a stage station. This was probably the same man as the first postmaster, William J. Simmons. However, when the post office was established at Simmons Station, the office was called Wilson. The name underwent several changes as listed below. According to one newspaper account (*Citizen*, November 1, 1873, 2:3) the place once bore the name Vitty, but post office records do not substantiate this.

P.O. est. as Wilson, January 20, 1871. William J. Simmons, p.m. Name changed to Williamson Valley, October 9, 1873. Mrs. Betsy Zimmerman, p.m. (*See* Williamson Valley). Name changed to Simmons, July 5, 1881. Stephen Breon, p.m. Discont. April 21, 1931.

Ref.: *Citizen*, November 1, 1873, 2:3; *Prescott Weekly Courier*, August 6, 1886, 3:1, 2; *Weekly Arizona Miner*, August 13, 1875, 3:1; April 29, 1871, 1:3; P.O. Records; Platten. Maps: C-5; C-3 (Williamson's); GM-17 (Simmons).

**a.n. Simmons Peak**      El.: 5758'. Map: GM-17      Yavapai

## SKELETON RIDGE

El.: 5953'      Loc.: Yavapai 3, G-8

This is a narrow, sharp ridge with rib-like branches.

Ref.: Barnes. Map: GM-19.

## SKULL VALLEY

El.: 4112'      Loc.: Yavapai 2, F-5.4

Many stories are told concerning the origin of the name Skull Valley. There is documentation to demonstrate that the name dates back at least to 1864 when the first gubernatorial party arrived in the future Prescott (*q.v.*). While it is a fact that there were several severe battles with Indians after the arrival of white men in Skull Valley, the name actually derives from the fact that the first white man who entered it found piles of bleached Indian skulls. The skulls were found by soldiers in Captain Hargraves' company of the First California Volunteers, while escorting Coles Bashford to Tucson in March 1864. The skulls were the remnants of a bitter battle between Apaches and Maricopas in which the latter were the victors. It is reported that the Apaches had stolen stock from the Pima villages and were pursued by the Maricopas. The dead were left where they fell.

At least thirty-five more skulls were added to the bleaching bones as a result of a fight on August 12, 1866, in which six freighters (the chief of whom was a Mr. Freeman) five citizens, and four soldiers battled more than one hundred Indians. The fight took place not more than three miles from the Skull Valley Station. Apparently the Indians were those who had stopped the same party from proceeding on its way on the first day of the month, forcing them to return to Camp McPherson, as the Skull Valley Station was called. A private citizen rode back to the post for help when the Indians appeared. He returned accompanied by Lt. Oscar Hutton, who demanded to know why the Indians had stopped the train. The Indians replied as they had once before, that the water, the grass, and the country belonged to them and that all whites must leave the valley within the week. After sharp words on both sides, the battle was joined. When the bloody conflict ended, twenty-three Indians lay dead in the immediate vicinity and several more were found at some distance from the battleground. These too were left where they fell.

P.O. est. April 26, 1869. John C. Dunn, p.m. Wells Fargo Station, 1903.

Ref.: P.O. Records; *Arizona Miner*, January 20, 1872, 2:2; Unidentified clippings dated October 4, 1895 (Sharlot Hall Museum); 169, pp. 37-39; 26, p. 381, (Note 1). Maps: C-4 (Scull Valley); GM-6; GM-8.

a.n. Skull Valley Wash     Maps: GM-6; GM-8         Yavapai

## SMITH CANYON

El.: 3195'                           Loc.: Yavapai 2, FD-3-4
John and William Smith were cattlemen who used the Dumbbell brand in this area in the 1880's.

Ref.: Barnes. Map: GM-16.

a.n. Smith Mesa          Map: GM-16               Yavapai

## SMITHVILLE

El.: c. 4000'                         Loc.: Yavapai 3, EF-4-5
                                    E. of Prescott 33 miles.
Smithville was a mining community named for A. M. Smith, superintendent of the Golden Era Mining Company. It was established in mid-1879 on mining company property.

Ref.: *Weekly Arizona Miner*, September 19, 1879, 2:2. Map: None.

## SORENSON

Loc.: Not known, except near Hillside on Santa Maria River.
Postal records show that a Sorenson post office was established in Mohave County on July 13, 1903, with Benjamin F. Ferris, p.m. This order was rescinded on December 16, and less than two weeks later (on December 27) a Sorenson post office was established in Yavapai County with Peter V. Sorenson as postmaster. This may indicate that an error had occurred in the original postal orders. Undoubtedly the place was named for its postmaster. Sorenson as a post office went out of business on June 6, 1904.

Ref.: P.O. Records. Map: None.

## SPRUCE MOUNTAIN

El.: 7693'                            Loc.: Yavapai 2, H-6
Descriptive. Locally the trees on this mountain are referred to as spruce, but they are actually Douglas fir. "Spruce" occurs descriptively in several place names, instances of which are given below.

Ref.: Gardner. Map: GM-20.

a.n. Spruce Canyon          Map: GM-8                Yavapai
    Spruce Mountain      El.: 7690'. Map: GM-3       Yavapai
    Spruce Wash             Map: B-6                 Yavapai

## STEHR LAKE

El.: c. 2700'                         Loc.: Yavapai 3, H-7
Frederick W. Stehr was treasurer for the Arizona Power Company, which constructed the power plant on Fossil Creek.

Ref.: Barnes. Map: GM-19.

## STINSON MOUNTAIN

El.: 6411'                            Loc.: Yavapai 3, DE-2
The mountain took its name from a settler called Stinson who settled near here in 1872.

Ref.: Barnes; Rosenberger. Maps: GM-23; GM-24.

a.n. Stinson Wash           Map: GM-23               Yavapai

## STODDARD

El.: 3906'                            Loc.: Yavapai 3, GH-6.4
The Stoddard-Binghamton Mine was owned by Isaac T. Stoddard, who named the mine for his native town in New York. Stoddard was secretary of Arizona Territory, 1901-1907. Although the mine is still in operation, the community which served it is now gone.

P.O. est. December 15, 1882. George N. Birdsall, p.m. Discont. September 15, 1927.

Ref.: Barnes; Schnebly; APHS Names File; P.O. Records. Maps: C-5; C-12; GM-3.

a.n. Stoddard Spring        Map: GM-11               Yavapai

## STORM RANCH

El.: 5163'                            Loc.: Yavapai 3, A-4.3
As was frequently the case for remote areas, the rancher at this location, James P. Storm, had a post office for the convenience of his neighbors. Storm later served as Yavapai County Treasurer.

P.O. est. June 20, 1894. James P. Storm, p.m. Discont. January 23, 1901.

Ref.: Barnes; APHS Names File; P.O. Records. Map: GM-15.

## STRICKLAND WASH

El.: 4800'                            Loc.: Yavapai 2, F-3-4
George Arnold Strickland settled in this area and operated the Simmons Stage Station in the late 1870's. Later he began a sheep ranch and built troughs at the spring in this wash.

Ref.: Barnes. Maps: GM-8; GM-17.

a.n. Strickland Spring     Loc.: In Strickland Wash     Yavapai

## SULLIVAN

El.: c. 6000'  Loc.: Yavapai 1, D-5
J. W. (Jerry) Sullivan (b. Canada 1844) arrived at Prescott in December 1868. Headquarters for his cattle ranch were at this location. Sullivan was also the name of a station on the now abandoned Prescott and Arizona Railroad.
Ref.: Barnes; APHS Names File. Map: C-7.

| a.n. Sullivan Buttes | Map: GM-17 | Yavapai |
| Sullivan Lake | El.: 4348'. Map: GM-13 | Yavapai |

## SULLIVAN SPRING

El.: 5758'  Loc.: Yavapai 2, H-8.9
Matthew Sullivan was a miner who had a claim in this area.
Ref.: Barnes. Map: GM-7.

## SULTAN

Loc.: Not known, but near Hillside.
This was the name of a mine owned by a champagne salesman named La Montagne.
P.O. est. May 6, 1903. Harry La Montagne, p.m. Discont. June 27, 1904.
Ref.: Gardner; P.O. Records. Map: None.

## SWILLING GULCH

El.: c. 6500'  Loc.: Yavapai 3, AC-7.8
What comes close to being the ugliest place name in Arizona was no doubt named for Jack W. Swilling, who came to Arizona in 1859 (See Gillette, Maricopa). The Swilling Ranch was on this gulch.
Ref.: None. Maps: C-4 (Swilling Ranch); E-20; GM-3.

## SYCAMORE CANYON

El.: c. 5000'-3000'  Loc.: Yavapai 3, DE-7.3
Many localities in Arizona bear the word "sycamore" in their designations because of the presence—either now or in the past—of the largest of desert trees, particularly beautiful because of the irregular manner in which their white trunks lean and their white limbs branch and spread. Sycamore Canyon is but one such place name. At its mouth a community developed which for a brief time had a post office. The creek in Sycamore Canyon is a very long and beautiful one.
P.O. est. as Sycamore, October 16, 1911. Ethell Rosenberger, p.m. Discont. September 30, 1912.
Ref.: Schnebly; Barnes; P.O. Records; 92, pp. 381, 388, 389. Map: C-11.

| a.n. Sycamore Canyon | Map: GD-14 | Gila |
| Sycamore Canyon Wilderness Area | Map: GM-16 | Yavapai |
| Sycamore Creek | Map: B-9 | Coconino |
| Sycamore Creek | Map: GG-3 | Maricopa |
| Sycamore Creek | Maps: GD-11; GD-15 | Gila |

The Sycamore Creek named by King S. Woolsey is now generally known as Cook Creek (q.v.).

| Sycamore Creek | Map: GE-1 | Graham |
| Sycamore Mesa | Map: GM-16 | Yavapai |
| Sycamore Creek | Loc.: T. 15 N., R. 13 W. | Mohave |
| Sycamore Pass | Map: B-6 | Yavapai |
| Sycamore Rim | Map: GM-16 | Yavapai |
| Sycamore Spring | Maps: GD-5; GD-14 | Gila |

## TANGLE CREEK

El.: 3077'  Loc.: Yavapai 3, FH-9.3-10
The crooked course of this creek and the tangle of underbrush lining its banks probably resulted in the name.
Ref.: Barnes. Map: GM-19.

| a.n. Tangle Peak | El.: 3582'. Map: GM-19 | Yavapai |

## TAPCO

El.: 3500'  Loc.: Yavapai 3, DE-2.1
The first letters of the words "The Arizona Power Company" were combined to give the name to this station on the railroad.
Ref.: Barnes. Map: GM-5.

## THIRTEEN MILE ROCK

El.: 5514'  Loc.: Yavapai 3, H-5.1
This prominent rock is on the old military road thirteen miles east of Camp Verde; hence the name.
Ref.: Barnes; Goddard. Map: GM-21.

| a.n. Thirteen Mile Spring | Map: B-8 | Yavapai |

## THOMPSON VALLEY

El.: c. 4000'  Loc.: Yavapai 2, DE-5-5.7
Under the name Tompkins Valley (probably a corruption) this place is listed as the site of an army skirmish on November 10, 1869. By March 1870, settlers were coming to Thompson Valley. The valley was named for Maj. John Thompson of the First New Mexico Volunteers. Thompson had several skirmishes with Indians in this area.
Ref.: Arizona Miner, June 10, 1871, 3:2; Weekly Arizona Miner, March 12, 1870, 3:1; 85, p. 434. Maps: C-10; GM-6.

## TIGER

El.: 6500'  Loc.: Yavapai 2, H-9
In 1880 the Tiger Mine (from which the entire district took its name) was one of the richest silver mines in Arizona Territory. It was said to have been the first silver mine of importance discovered in northern Arizona. Today Tiger is a ghost town.
Ref.: Theobald; 76, p. 50. Maps: E-20 (Tiger District); GM-7.

| a.n. Tiger Canyon | Map: GM-4 | Yavapai |
| Tiger Creek | Map: GM-7 | Yavapai |

## TIP TOP

El.: 2500'  Loc.: Yavapai 3, BC-10.3
The Tip Top mine was discovered in 1875. The name is said to have come from the fact that it was a "tip top" prospect as a mine. From the point of view of small-time miners, who were referred to as "chloriders," it was a very good place from which to haul rock for reduction at nearby mills.

In 1897 Tip Top had a sufficient number of residents so that it had a school. It is a ghost town today, but in 1956 the remains of the community still extended at least three-fourths of a mile along the canyon.
P.O. est. as Tip Top Mine, March 4, 1879. Winthrop A. Rowe, p.m. Discont. November 18, 1879.

P.O. est. as Tip Top, August 12, 1880. Edwin G. Wager, p.m. Discont. February 14, 1895.

Ref.: P.O. Records; Schnebly; Theobald; 76, p. 51; *Daily Arizona Journal Miner*, November 16, 1897, 4:2. Maps: C-5; C-6 (Maricopa County); C-8; C-12; GM-3 (Yavapai County).

## TOWER MOUNTAIN

El.: 6100'                    Loc.: Yavapai 3, AB-8.5
George W. Tower mined in this locality in 1873. He later owned what was called the Potato Ranch.

Ref.: Barnes. Maps: C-10; GM-3.

| **a.n. Tower Creek** | Maps: B-6; GM-3; GM-20 | Yavapai |
| Tower Ranch | Map: GM-3 | Yavapai |

## TRITLE, MOUNT

El.: 7793'                    Loc.: Yavapai 2, H-6.4
Pro.: /tráytʌl/ or /tráytļ/
Frederick A. Tritle (b. Pennsylvania, August 7, 1833; d. May 1906) came to Arizona for his health in 1880. He was sworn in as Arizona's seventh territorial governor (including Gov. Gurley, who died before taking office) on February 6, 1882, serving until May 5, 1886. Tritle had extensive mining interests in Arizona.

Ref.: Garrett; 55, p. 635. Maps: GM-3; GM-20.

## TURRET PEAK

El.: 5848'                    Loc.: Yavapai 3, EF-8.5
In his autobiography, Gen. George Crook notes that Turret Mountain (now Turret Peak) was so called because of its shape. Crook also tells the story of a battle which took place in 1872 between federal troops under Maj. George Randall and a band of Apaches. The troops were pursuing the Indians who had taken refuge on top of Turret Mountain. The soldiers reconnoitered and discovered the peak was a circular mountain which rose into a column and that there was but one feasible means of climbing it. Nevertheless, the soldiers made their way up by crawling on their stomachs, reaching the summit just before the sun rose. Undetected, they crawled close to the Indians and as day broke, charged into the Indian camp. The Indians were so completely taken by surprise in what they had considered their entirely safe retreat that they panicked, some of them even jumping off the precipice. These, to use Crook's words, "were mashed into a shapeless mass."

None of the Indian men survived, but some of the Indian women told Maj. Randall that theirs was the band of Indians which had recently killed three white men on the Hassayampa. Taylor, one of the white men, had been tortured with typical Apache ingenuity. His body had been stuck full of splinters which were then set on fire.

Ref.: 38, p. 178. Maps: C-5; E-20; GM-19.

## TUSCUMBIA MOUNTAINS

El.: 6672'                    Loc.: Yavapai 3, AB-3.3
The mountains took their name from the Tuscumbia Mine located by James Burd Wilson and James McLane, one of

whom had lived in Tennessee on the Tuscumbia River and the other of whom had come from Alabama where there was a town by this name.

Ref.: Barnes. Maps: GM-3; GM-20.

| **a.n. Tuscumbia Creek** | Maps: GM-3; GM-20 | Yavapai |

## TUZIGOOT NATIONAL MONUMENT

El.: 3478'                    Loc.: Yavapai 3, DE-2
Pro.: /túwziˆguwt/
The forty-two acres of the Tuzigoot National Monument contain at least three pueblos which in turn have a total of more than one hundred and ten rectangular rooms. Only part of the complete dwelling area has been restored.

Archaeologists estimate that people lived at Tuzigoot from the tenth through fourteenth centuries, attaining a high degree of culture. Evidences of this culture can be seen in the museum at the monument, which has an excellent pottery display, bead work, shell and turquoise mosaics, and a display of stone and bone implements used by the pueblo's former residents.

The first white man thought to have visited the area was Don Antonio de Espejo in 1583. Hundreds of years later white residents in the area began restoring the ancient dwellings. The name Tuzigoot was selected by Apaches themselves, who translated it as "crooked water," taking the name from Peck's Lake (*q.v.*) below the pueblo. Tuzigoot Hill with its museum and collections was given to the federal government by citizens in the area. On July 25, 1939, Tuzigoot was made into a national monument.

Ref.: 5, Jack Cotter, "Tuzigoot National Monument," pp. 4-6; Peck (Ranger at Tuzigoot); 4, pp. 38-39, 332. Map: GM-24.

## VALLEY

El.: 4573'                    Loc.: Yavapai 2, H-2
This point on the railroad took its name from the fact that it was located at the head of Chino Valley.

Ref.: Barnes. Map: GM-9.

## VENTURA

Loc.: Near Wagoner.
The origin of this name has not yet been ascertained.

P.O. est. June 1, 1908. Forrest McKinley, p.m. Discont. November 13, 1908.

Ref.: P.O. Records. Map: None.

## VERDE, CAMP

El.: 3147'                    Loc.: Yavapai 3, F-4.8
Pro.: /vérdi/
In June 1865, nine men left Prescott to explore the Verde Valley in order to found an agricultural settlement. As a result of their explorations a small colony soon began on the Verde River at the junction of the Verde and Clear Fork about three and one-half miles below the present town of Camp Verde. This took place in February and a private fort was built which was called Camp Lincoln. Apparently when a garrison was established for soldiers in this area, the Army Fort also took the name Fort Lincoln. This occurred late in 1865, although officially the post

was not established until January 1866, having prior to that time merely contained a garrison detached from Fort Whipple.

Within a short time it became apparent that Fort Lincoln was on the wrong side of the river and that it was situated in a particularly unhealthy spot which, incidentally, was on a mesa too small to accommodate the number of buildings required. By the middle of 1866 at least half of the soldiers went on strike because they had been in service almost a year without receiving a cent of pay. By the twenty-ninth of the same month, Capt. H. S. Washburn reported that he had a command consisting solely of five enlisted men, all more or less sick. He had to call upon the settlers to help him protect government property. Two weeks later only two enlisted men remained, both ill. Despite its troubles, Fort Lincoln struggled along.

On November 23, 1868, Gen. Henry Wager Halleck changed the army post name to Camp Verde because there were two Lincolns in the list of army camps. Two years later, Gen. George Crook, who was noted for his interest in seeing that the army establishments were located in healthful spots, selected a site one mile south and in 1871 the camp was moved. Little work was done on the new post until 1873. The name was changed for the last time in 1879 to Fort Verde. In 1884 the military land holdings were turned over to the Department of the Interior.

P.O. est. as Camp Verde, March 14, 1873. George W. Hance, p.m.

Ref.: Goddard; 127, pp. 5, 6, 8, 106; 52, IV, 109; 75, p. 158; 87, p. 316; 38, p. 166, (Note 8); 105, p. 94; *Weekly Arizona Miner*, December 12, 1868, 2:2; P.O. Records. Maps: C-2; E-13; GM-21.

**a.n. Rio Verde Reservation**　Map: GM-21　Yavapai
Vincent Colyer in 1871 used this location as a temporary reservation.
Ref.: 52, VIII, 12; 85, p. 538.

**Verde Hot Springs**　Map: GM-19　Yavapai
A resort has developed at these hot springs.
Ref.: Goddard.

**Verde National Forest**　Yavapai and Coconino
Loc.: Both sides of Verde River.
Established 1907; combined with Prescott National Forest, 1909.

**Verde River**　Maps: E-11 and others Yavapai and Coconino
The Verde River has been known by various names, the earliest recorded being that of Don Antonio de Espejo who, according to Luxan, on May 8, 1583, called it the El Rio do los Reyes (Kings' River). The next name which occurs is on the Disturnell Map for 1847, which gives it the name San Francisco River. In 1853 Lt. Amiel W. Whipple called the headwaters of the Verde the Bill Williams Fork. Meanwhile, the Indians called their river by a descriptive name which meant "Green." The name derived from the color of malachite on its banks. The first Mexicans and Spaniards who used the river soon translated the Indian name into the Spanish equivalent, *verde*. The Verde River area was the scene of numerous fights of settlers and troops against Indians.
Ref.: Schroeder; 11, p. 30; 177, p. 178, (Note 20); 5, p. 6.

**Verde Valley**　Map: GM-15　Yavapai
Lt. Amiel W. Whipple in 1853 made specific mention of the rich agricultural possibilities of the valley of the Rio

Verde. However, Yavapais and Apaches had long since discovered such possibilities and were fairly thickly settled in the valley and this made it difficult for white men to take over.
Ref.: 117, p. 195; 127, p. 5.

**Verde**　Map: C-4　Yavapai
P.O. est. June 24, 1878. George W. Hull, p.m. Discont. September 21, 1880. (*See* Clemenceau).

## WAGONER

El.: c. 3500'　Loc.: Yavapai 2, G-8.6
Ed Wagoner founded the town which bore his name.
P.O. est. June 6, 1893. Minerva Wagoner, p.m.
Ref.: *Arizona Journal Miner*, March 27, 1899, 4:1; P.O. Records. Maps: C-8; GM-6; GM-22.

## WAGON TIRE FLAT

El.: c. 5000'　Loc.: Yavapai 1, H-6.9
An old wagon tire was for years leaning against a tree on this flat.
Ref.: Barnes. Map: GM-1.

**a.n. Wagon Tire Dam**　Map: GM-13　Yavapai
**Wagon Tire Wash**　Maps: GM-1; GM-13　Yavapai

## WA KOTA

Loc.: Not known.
The reason for this name has not yet been learned.
P.O. est. September 25, 1913. Louis G. Ochsenreiter, p.m. Discont.?
Ref.: P.O. Records. Map: None.

## WALKER

El.: 6300'　Loc.: Yavapai 3, A-6.5
Capt. Joseph Reddeford Walker (b. 1798; d. 1876) in 1863 led a gold prospecting expedition into Yavapai County, as a result of the success of which the town of Walker came into being.

Capt. Walker was a noted guide, having in 1853 led an expedition from Great Salt Lake to California. Later he served with Col. Kit Carson in New Mexico during the campaigns against the Navajo Indians. Walker found gold in Yavapai County in 1861, but at the time preferred to go to California rather than to remain to investigate his find further. Two years later Walker returned with thirty-four men and began prospecting on Lynx Creek (*q.v.*) His mining location was sometimes referred to as Walker Diggings. Always restless, Walker did not remain long in Arizona, but went again to California in 1867. Today the community carrying his name is a ghost town.

There is some confusion in various documents concerning a second Joseph R. Walker on the 1863 expedition. The latter, however, was Joseph Rutherford Walker, a nephew of Capt. Walker.

P.O. est. December 15, 1879. William L. Lewis, p.m. Discont. September 30, 1940.

Ref.: *Weekly Arizona Miner*, June 5, 1869, 3:2; *Arizona Miner*, November 27, 1869, 2:2; State Library Files; 4, p. 304; 111, pp. 109-110; P.O. Records. Maps: C-6; GM-3; GM-20.

**a.n. Walker Gulch**　Map: GM-3　Yavapai
**Walker's Pass**　Loc.: Not known　Yavapai

## WALKER MOUNTAIN

El.: 5885'                        Loc.: Yavapai 3, H-6
This mountain, as well as Walker Basin and Walker Creek, was named for a bachelor who was in the area in the late 1870's. Whether he was a nephew of Capt. Joseph Reddeford Walker has not been ascertained.
Ref.: R. W. Wingfield, Letter, February 11, 1956. Map: GM-21.

## WALNUT GROVE

El.: 3469'                        Loc.: Yavapai 2, GH-8
In 1864 a town was laid out and several buildings erected at what came to be known as Walnut Grove. The name may have come from the fact that the community was two miles south of Walnut Canyon where there are still many wild walnut trees. The name Walnut Grove may be descriptive. By 1870 it had forty residents.

Barnes relates that Walnut Dam near Walnut Grove was built by Alexander O. Brodie (later governor of Arizona). The dam burst and seventy lives were lost.
P.O. est. June 24, 1874. Jane Oswald, p.m. Discont. April 30, 1915.
Ref.: P.O. Records; Kelly; 87, pp. 187, 44; *Arizona Miner,* May 11, 1864, 3:1. Maps: C-2 (Walnut Grove District); C-4; E-20; GM-6; GM-10.
**a.n. Walnut Creek**         Maps: GM-17; GM-23          Yavapai
There was a stage station on the Prescott-Mohave Road known as Walnut Creek.
Ref.: Barnes.
   **Walnut Creek, North Fork**      Map: GM-23          Yavapai
   **Walnut Creek, South Fork**      Map: GM-23          Yavapai

## WATSON LAKE

El.: c. 5000'                     Loc.: Yavapai 2, H-4.4
This is an artificial lake which was named for Senator James W. Watson, a Republican senator from Indiana, who was president of the Arizona Land and Irrigation Company in 1916.
Ref.: Merritt. Map: GM-15.

## WATSON PEAK

El.: c. 6000'                     Loc.: Yavapai 3, AB-9.5
Henry Watson mined in this vicinity in 1882.
Ref.: Barnes. Maps: B-6; C-13.
   **a.n. Watson Spring**      Maps: GM-3; GM-20          Yavapai

## WEAVER

El.: c. 5000'                     Loc.: Yavapai 2, FG-9.2
While Capt. Joseph Walker's party was exploring for mines in Yavapai County in 1863, the Abraham Harlow Peeples' party with Pauline Weaver as guide was traveling across the territory from Yuma. One night some horses strayed from the Peeples' party and one or more Mexicans went out to find them. When the Mexicans returned, they brought nuggets found on a nearby mountain. Before breakfast Peeples picked up $7,000 in loose gold.

This rich find was on what was then known as Indian Creek, which shortly came to be called Weaver Creek. In 1864 Weaver (the community) was described as a "pic-turesque little hamlet stretching along Indian Creek in a gorge of the mountain. [The buildings are] adobe, reed, mud and stone, two-thirds of them covered with wagon sheets . . ." The place was also called Weaverville.

The rich placers soon played out and by the 1890's the population at Weaver Camp was entirely Mexican. It was a hangout for thieves and murderers. In 1898 a newspaper article called for the town to be wiped out because it was the headquarters for a cutthroat gang whose leader was known as the "King of Weaver," then an old and blind man, the degenerate remains of thirty years of lawlessness. What residents were left in Weaver stampeded nearby to Congress and by January 1899 only two or three people still remained in Weaver (*See* Octave). Weaver is a ghost town today.
P.O. est. May 26, 1899. Roger W. Warren, p.m. Changed to Octave (q.v.) almost immediately.
Ref.: 4, p. 290; 76, p. 56; 170, p. 70; 25, p. 292; *Hartford Evening Press,* Hartford, Connecticut, June 20, 1864; *Arizona Journal Miner,* November 28, 1898, 4:1; November 29, 1898, 1:5; January 30, 1899, 4:1; P.O. Records. Maps: C-10; C-11.
**a.n. Weaver Gulch**         Loc.: At Weaver          Yavapai
The first encounter with Indians in this area occurred in December 1863.
Ref.: 111, p. 25.
   **Weaver Mountains**                                   Yavapai
   Maps: C-6; C-8; C-10; C-9 (Weaver's Mountains); E-20; GM-6.
   Hinton says these mountains were so called by Capt. George M. Wheeler, but were known locally as the Antelope Range.
Ref.: 87, p. 301.
   **Weaver Peak**            Map: C-12          Yavapai
   **Weaver Pass**                                Yuma
   El.: 1306'. Maps: C-6; C-7; C-8; C-9; E-20; GN-21; GN-5. Although the Weaver Mining District shows as early as GLO 1869, Weaver Pass does not appear on maps examined until the military map of 1875 (E-18: Sheet No. 3). It disappears from maps after 1903 until the issuance of USGS maps listed above.

## WEBB

                              Loc.: Not known, but near Prescott.
The origin of this name has not yet been learned.
P.O. est. January 8, 1892. John A. Webb, p.m. Discont. May 13, 1892.
Ref.: P.O. Records. Map: None.

## WEST CEDAR MOUNTAIN

El.: 5512'                        Loc.: Yavapai 3, F-9.5
Descriptive. It lies two miles west of East Cedar Mountain.
Ref.: Barnes. Map: GM-19.

## WHIPPLE, FORT

El.: c. 5000'                     Loc.: Yavapai 2, H-4.8
The first step towards protecting miners in the Yavapai area was taken under General Orders No. 27 dated at Santa Fe on October 23, 1863, which established a new Military Department called the District of Northern Arizona. This was followed by the establishment of a small garrison at Postle's ranch under Maj. Edward B. Willis with Captains Hargrave and Benson and two companies of California Volunteers on December 23, 1863.

When Gov. John N. Goodwin and his party arrived in Arizona Territory in late December 1863, a proclamation was read at Navajo Springs (*q.v., Apache*), which established the seat of the territorial government in the vicinity of what was called Fort Whipple, apparently established as Whipple Barracks. The location may not have been known by the name Fort Whipple at that time. By gubernatorial proclamation the seat of government was soon moved to a new community called Prescott *(q.v.)* and Whipple Barracks was established. When the new post was established in the vicinity of Prescott, it was known as Prescott Barracks and also as Fort Whipple. Fort Whipple was occupied first on May 18, 1864.

Both the earlier Whipple Barracks and Camp (or Fort) Whipple were named for Brig. Gen. Amiel Weeks Whipple, who died on May 7, 1868, of wounds received in the battle of Chancellorsville, Virginia. As second lieutenant in the topographical engineers, Whipple (b. Massachusetts 1818) had been a member of the group which surveyed the boundary between the United States and Mexico in 1849. His observatory for work at the Colorado and Gila River junction was atop the hill where Fort Yuma was later established. From October through December 1851, he was surveying down the Gila River to the Colorado River. From 1853 to 1856, Whipple explored a possible route for a railroad to the Pacific.

When Gen. George Crook was inspecting posts in Arizona, he found that Fort Whipple was fairly typical of the miserable state of such establishments. Lt. John G. Bourke described Fort Whipple as being a "ramshackle, tumble-down palisade of unbarked pine logs . . . supposed to 'command' something, exactly what, I do not remember, as it was so dilapidated that every time the wind rose we were afraid that the palisade was doomed. The quarters for both officers and men were also log houses, with the exception of one single-roofed shanty . . . constructed of unseasoned, unpainted pine planks, and there it served as General Crook's headquarters . . ."

Despite these poor beginnings, Whipple became the center of social life for Prescott and headquarters for the Department of Arizona. The Department was established April 15, 1870; it included Arizona and all of California south of a "line drawn eastward from Point Concepcion." Under General Orders No. 19 dated October 10, 1871, the Quartermaster's depot was changed to a depot to be used for repairs and to be known as Whipple Depot. In 1879 there were two parts to the post, one known as Fort Whipple and the other as Prescott Barracks, both of which, according to one authority, were combined into Whipple Barracks. For a short time the Department of Arizona included the military district of New Mexico, but in 1887 all headquarters were moved to Los Angeles, despite the vigorous protests of the citizens of Arizona. The post was discontinued in 1898 and then re-garrisoned in 1902. Whipple Barracks was rejuvenated in 1904, but even this did not serve to retain the small garrison of troops. The inevitable was put off for a few years, but in 1912 the post

was abandoned when troops were sent from there to the Mexican border. The year 1922 saw the military reservation transferred to the Secretary of the Treasury for use in the Public Health Service. Today old Fort Whipple is used as a Veterans' Hospital.

P.O. est. as Whipple, February 12, 1887. Charles H. Allaback, p.m. Discont. May 24, 1898.

Ref.:  85, p. 535; 177, pp. 7, 9; 7, p. 522; 75, p. 160; 127, p. 3; 22, p. 160; 87, pp. 255, 256; 4, p. 288; 38, p. 173, (Note 1); 111, pp. 155, 156; *Arizona Miner*, November 4, 1871; 3:3; March 9, 1864, 3:2; P.O. Records. Maps: C-1; E-22; GM-9; GM-15.

a.n. **Whipple Valley**                                    Yavapai
According to a story in the *Arizona Miner* of December 26, 1868 (2:2) Indians had driven settlers out of all the valley in the Prescott area with the exception of Rufus E. Farrington, who was then living in Whipple Valley.

## WHIPSAU

El.: c. 3200'                          Loc.: Yavapai 2, H-10.2
According to its postmaster, Whipsau was a community serving as headquarters for several mining companies, chief of which was the Whipsau Mine. The postmaster also served as storekeeper, banker, mine auditor, and peacemaker.

The mine was named because timbers were whipsawed for use in it.

P.O. est. June 15, 1900. John G. Spangler, p.m. Discont.?

Ref.:  Barnes. Map: None.

a.n. **Whipsau Creek**        Maps: B-6; GM-24        Yavapai
**Whipsau Gulch**   Loc.: Same as for Whipsau Creek   Yavapai

## WHITE SPRUCE MOUNTAIN

El.: c. 7690'                          Loc.: Yavapai 3, A-6
A dense grove of trees formerly here resulted in the name.

v.n. **Spruce Mountain**   Maps: GM-24; GM-25

Ref.:  Barnes. Maps: GM-24; GM-25.

a.n. **West Spruce Mountain**   Maps: GM-24; GM-25   Yavapai

## WILLIAMSON VALLEY

El.: c. 4000'                          Loc.: Yavapai 2, FH-2-1.2
Lt. Robert Stockton Williamson, who served with the topographical engineers with Lt. Joseph C. Ives' party in Arizona in 1854, surveyed the valley which was named for him.

When the military establishment was created at Camp Tollgate (*See* Camp Hualapai) settlers began to flock to Williamson Valley and by December 1869 many new buildings were going up. By March 1870 at least twenty-seven ranches existed in the area. Five years later a newspaper noted that the place was thickly settled. Williamson Valley was approximately seventeen miles west of Camp Tollgate.

P.O. est. at a place called Wilson, January 20, 1871. Name and location changed to Williamson Valley, October 9, 1873. For full information about post office for Williamson Valley, See Simmons.

Ref.:  APHS Names File; *Weekly Arizona Miner*, December 25, 1869, 3:2; January 15, 1870, 3:2; March 12, 1870, 3:1; April 9, 1875, 2:3; P.O. Records. Maps: C-6; GM-17.

a.n. **Williamson Valley Wash**   Maps: GM-13; GM-17   Yavapai

## WILLOW CREEK

El.: c. 6000'                    Loc.: Yavapai 2, HG-5-4
Descriptive. This name was given to the stream in 1864 by
J. D. Monihon.

Ref.:   Barnes. Maps: C-11; GM-8; GM-9; GM-15.

**a.n. Willow Creek**          El.: 5000'. Map: GM-3-4          Yavapai
**Willow Creek Reservoir**     Map: GM-15                      Yavapai
**Willow Lake**                                                Yavapai
Loc.: North and left of Willow Creek.
**Willow Springs**   Maps: GM-8; GM-16; GM-20   Yavapai
It was at this point that J. D. Monihon located his place.
This is also said to be the same as Oakley Springs (Ref.
Garrick, Mallery, *B.A.E.,* "4th Annual Report," 1886).
**Willow Springs Basin**      Map: GM-19                       Yavapai
**Willow Spring Gulch**       Map: GM-19                       Yavapai
**Willow Valley**   Loc.: Near Thumb Butte          Yavapai
General Osborn had a house in Willow Valley. The place
was noted for its conviviality.
Ref.:   *Weekly Arizona Miner,* February 13, 1869, 2:1.

## WOOD, CAMP

El.: c. 6000'                    Loc.: Yavapai 2, D-2
The first name for the present Camp Wood was Kymo.
This name came from the fact that Paul Wright, a native
of Kentucky, married a woman from Missouri, and in
honor of their two states he gave the name Kymo to the
small settlement.

Locally it is thought the name Kymo applied to the place
from about 1880. In early 1890's a cavalry captain named
Wood camped here while on a scouting expedition and the
area gradually came to be known as Camp Wood. When
the post office was re-established in 1926, this was the name
selected, since postal regulations would not permit the second use of the name Kymo.

P.O. est. as Kymo, April 29, 1893. Robert H. Ferguson, p.m.
Discont. July 26, 1907. P.O. re-est. as Camp Wood, July 21,
1926. Harry S. Knight, p.m.

Ref.:   Gardner; Rosenberger; APHS Names File; P.O. Rec-
        ords. Maps: C-13; C-8 (Kymo); GM-23.

**a.n. Camp Wood Mountain**    Map: GM-23                       Yavapai
**Wood Canyon**                                                 Yavapai
This was named for Miles L. Wood (d. November 30, 1938)
an army contractor who had a wood and hay camp. Wood
came to Arizona in 1865.

Ref.:   Barnes; APHS Files.

**Wood's Canyon**   Loc.: Sec. 6, T. 12 N., R. 9 E.     Yavapai
This was named for John Wood, who had a ranch here in
1875. He ran the 101 brand.

Ref.:   Barnes.

## WOODCHUTE MOUNTAIN

El.: 7500'                    Loc.: Yavapai 3, C-2.7
Mining in Arizona was no problem, but local smelting of
the ores called for vast amounts of fuel. Fuel in the Jerome
smelters was supplied by timber from Woodchute Mountain. The logs were cut and sent sliding down the mountain via a log chute. The lumber was used for open roasting to remove sulphur from the ores. Between the resultant

killing fumes and the unceasing demand for timber, the
mountain is now denuded of wood.
Later, mines in the mountain caved in. This forced the
mine owners to find a new location for the smelter. It was
built at Clarkdale *(q.v.).*

Ref.:   Stemmer; 170, p. 103. Maps: GM-5; GM-12.

## YAEGER CANYON

El.: c. 6000'                    Loc.: Yavapai 3, BC-3.4
Louis Yaeger (b. 1877; d. May 9, 1911), a sheepman and
miner, had a mine in this canyon. The road which ran
through it was used by twenty-mule-team freight wagons.

Ref.:   West. Maps: GM-9; GM-12; GM-15.

**a.n. Yaeger**          Loc.: T. 14 N., R. 1 E.          Yavapai
This is a station on the branch line of the A.T. & S.F. R.R.

## YARBO WASH

El.: c. 5000'                    Loc.: Yavapai 3, C-4-6.5
Apparently this was named for the Yarbo Mine. There
used to be a stamp mill for gold on this wash. The wash
was named prior to 1900, but the exact date is not known.
**v.n. Yarber Wash** (corruption)

Ref.:   West. Maps: GM-3; GM-9; GM-11; GM-12.

## YARNELL

El.: c. 5000'                    Loc.: Yavapai 2, D-8.7
The community of Yarnell and Yarnell Hill (El.: 4877')
both take their names from the Yarnell family, which was
among the earliest to settle in this area. Harrison Yarnell
(d. Aug. 11, 1916) located and worked the Yarnell Mine,
which he sold c. 1892.

P.O. est. as Yarnell, October 18, 1892. Frank McKean, p.m.
Discont. April 30, 1911. Re-established as Peeples Valley,
August 14, 1928. Name changed to Yarnell December 1, 1933.

Ref.:   P.O. Records; Barnes; State Library Files; APHS Files;
        4, p. 289. Maps: C-8; C-13 (Peeples Valley); GM-6.

**a.n. Yarnell Spring**          Map: GM-6          Yavapai

## YAVA

El.: c. 4000'                    Loc.: Yavapai 2, D-5.8
Pro.: /yǽvə/
Yava is in a stock raising and agricultural district. The
post office was opened by petition, the signatures having
been obtained by the first postmaster, William W. Davis.
Several names were submitted for the post office, with
Yava being the first on the list. This name was coined by
Mr. Davis from the first four letters of Yavapai.

P.O. est. May 8, 1916. William W. Davis, p.m. Discont. February 28, 1954.

Ref.:   Davis, Diary; interview; P.O. Records. Maps: C-12;
        GM-24.

## ZONIA          Loc.: Not known, but near Kirkland.

The origin of this name has not yet been ascertained.

P.O. est. February 9, 1900. John M. McCaffrey, p.m. Discont.
December 13, 1900.

Ref.:   P.O. Records. Map: None.

# YUMA COUNTY

*Gold-panning along the Colorado — steamboating on the river.*

## YUMA COUNTY:

Pro.: /yúwmə/

While Arizona was still a part of the Territory of New Mexico, that portion which is now Yuma County was part of the vast extent of Doña Ana County. A name proposed for this section when Sylvester Mowry (See Mowry Mine, Santa Cruz) was making a map of Arizona in 1860 was Castle Dome County, doubtless for the famous Castle Dome mining district (See Castle Dome). However, when Yuma County was created by act of the first Arizona territorial legislature on November 8, 1864, it was decided to name the new county for its chief Indian inhabitants, the Yuma tribe.

There has been some confusion regarding the origin of the name Yuma. It seems probable that it does not, as has been suggested, reflect the title of a hereditary chief Yahmayo ("son of the captain"), but that the word *Yuma* derives from the habit this tribe had of making huge fires to induce rain, creating a tremendous amount of smoke in the process,' and that their name in consequence comes from the Old Spanish word *umo,* meaning "smoke."

Yuma is the only one of the four original counties in Arizona which still retains its original boundaries. The county encompasses 6,390,400 acres. The first county seat was at La Paz *(q.v.),* but since 1870 it has been at Yuma *(q.v.),* the principal city in the county. Mining from the first was among the chief industries of Yuma county. Today agriculture is also of prime importance.

# ADAM'S WELL

El.: c. 2500'                              Loc.: Yuma 4, A-3
Samuel Adams (b. Pennsylvania, 1828; d. 1915) came to
Arizona in 1863. He established himself at the south end
of the Castle Dome Mountains on the trail that went across
the desert. Here he dug a well about ninety feet deep, which
provided the only water in that district.

Adams won the nickname "Steamboat" because of his en-
thusiasm for developing the Colorado River for use by
ocean-going ships. He ran for the state legislature on a
river-development platform, but received only thirty-one
votes.

Adams claimed to have made a trip through the Grand
Canyon by himself prior to the time that. Maj. John Wesley Powell and his expedition came through (1869).

Ref.: APHS Files; Preston Mercer, *Yuma Daily Sun*, "Desert
    Scrapbook," (October 30, 1954), II:2:4. Map: C-11.

# ADONDE

El.: c. 500'                               Loc.: Yuma 3, F-6.2
Pro.: /ədóndey/                           Spanish: "where"
A siding still exists at this location where the S.P.R.R. first
came through on January 9, 1879. During the days of
the steam railroad, the company used wells at this location to water its engines. The location was an old one, having been used as a stage station for many years.

Ref.: 105, p. 311; Lenon. Maps: GN-26; GN-24; E-20.

# AGUILA

El.: 2180'                                Loc.: Yuma 4, F-6
Pro.: /əgílə/                             Spanish: "eagle"
The small former settlement of Aguila took its name from
the nearby Aguila Mountains. The mountains are named
because an eagle's beak and eye can be discerned in the
rock formation. There is still a siding on the railroad at
Aguila.

Ref.: Monson; Lenon; 4, p. 359. Map: GN-1 (Aguila Moun-
    tains).

# ALAMO

El.: c. 1500'                             Loc.: Yuma 2, D-1
Pro.: /ǽləmow/ or /áləmo/                 Spanish: "cottonwood"
At one time Alamo Crossing on the Bill Williams River
from Mohave to Yuma County was an important place,
but by 1953 only two individuals were living there. The
name derived from the former presence of large cottonwoods.

P.O. est. as Alimo, November 23, 1899. Joseph B. Tappan,
p.m. Rescinded December 15, 1900. Re-est. as Alamo, March
30, 1911. Vincent M. Devine, p.m. Discont. December 31,
1918.

Ref.: Dobyns; Willson; P.O. Records. Maps: C-11; GN-11.
    The word "Alamo" is used descriptively in several place
    names. A few are listed below:
**a.n. Alamo Springs**     Loc.: T. 7 N., R. 11 W.      Apache
**Alamo Spring**           Loc.: T. 1 N., R. 16 W.      Yuma
This is a noted spring used by prospectors for many years.

Ref.: Monson; Willson; 181, p. 116; 141, p. 199.

**Alamo Ranger Station**     Map: GD-14                Gila
In 1954 this place was sold to private owners who have
converted it into offices and apartments.

Ref.: Woody.
    **Alamo**                Loc.: S. of Phoenix 15 miles    Maricopa
Alamo was the first station on the stage line from Phoenix
to Maricopa Wells. Viall Ransom was the owner and keeper
in 1881.

Ref.: Barnes.
    **Alamo Canyon**                                        Pima
Loc.: In Organ Pipe Cactus National Monument.
There used to be cottonwoods one-third of the way from
the north end of the Ajo Mountains.

Ref.: Hensen.
    **Alamo Mountains**                                     Pima
Named for Alamo Canyon and Alamo Spring. There is a
scenic road in the canyon.

**v.n. Big Ajo Mountains**

Ref.: Hensen.
**a.n. Alamo Canyon**          Map: GL-4              Santa Cruz
    **Alamo Mine**             Map: GJ-7              Santa Cruz
    **Alamos**          Loc.: On Santa Cruz River    Santa Cruz
A former rancheria, probably of the Sobaipuri. This place
was visited and named by Fr. Kino c. 1697.

Ref.: 88, I, 35.

# ANKRIM'S LANDING                        Loc.: Not known.
Capt. William Ankrim (d. March 1859) was one of the
early steamboat men on the Colorado River. He had been
active in driving sheep to the California market, at one
time herding 22,000 of the animals to the West Coast.
During one trip he had a battle with Apache Indians in
which he reported killing nearly forty and losing five of
his own party. He also stated that the Indians used both
clubs and firearms and that they had gold bullets.

When Ankrim decided to become a steamboat pilot he was
a partner with William Jaeger, who ran a ferry across the
Colorado. Subsequently, Ankrim bought out Capt. George
A. Johnson's interest in the ferry company, in which Ankrim was active until his death.

The Colorado steamer *Uncle Sam* sank at Ankrim's Landing on June 22, 1853.

Ref.: 159, pp. 213, 258, 262, 269. Map: None.

# ANTELOPE HILL

El.: 816'                                 Loc.: Yuma 3, H-6
In 1854 Lt. N. Michler reported that Antelope Peak lay
on his route. The peak is about a mile by a half-mile wide
and rises steeply, forming a striking sandstone eminence.
Although Antelope Hill was not one of the original Butterfield Overland Stations of 1857, a station was built here by
John Kilbride and shows on the 1859 itinerary for the
overland stage. Subsequently, the Antelope Hills Stage
Station became Tacna (*q.v.*).

For the past twenty-five years an Easter Sunrise Service
has been held at the base of this hill. The service is supposed to have originated with Indians. An Indian cemetery
on the knoll back of Antelope Hill is still being used.

Ref.: 141, p. 23; 181, p. 171; 51, p. 105; Mrs. Kelland; Fr.
    Figueroa ms., APHS. Maps: C-1; E-2; GN-24.

## ANVIL MOUNTAIN

El.: c. 3304'                    Loc.: Yuma 2, FG-10.4
Descriptive.

Ref.: Barnes. Maps: A-7; C-13.

**a.n. Anvil Rock** (*q.v.*)     Loc.: T. 19 N., R. 8 W.        Yavapai

**Anvil Rock — Station**     Loc.: Same as above        Yavapai
The Anvil Rock Station is just north of Luis Maria Baca
Land Grant. The *Arizona Gazetteer*, 1881, states, "There is
a stage station near this rock by the same name. About 68
miles northwest of Prescott. C. P. Wilder, owner and station keeper."

Ref.: Barnes.

## ARABY

El.: 141'                       Loc.: Yuma 3, M-14
The name may have been derived from the fact that the
surrounding country resembles an Arabian desert.
A railroad section house and an alfalfa dehydrating plant
exist at this small place today.

Ref.: Mercer; 102, p. 12. Map: GN-11.

## ARCH TANK

El.: c. 1500'                   Loc.: Yuma 1, E-14
                                Sec. 2, T. 3 S., R. 19 W.
This tank, which has in front of it a natural arch about
seven feet high, has been described as one of the most
beautiful natural tanks in the world, but it is extremely inaccessible as it lies in a steep-walled narrow canyon.

Ref.: Monson. Map: None.

## AVALON

El.: 216'                       Loc.: Yuma 3, C-6
The origin of this name has not yet been learned.

When the railroad yards were getting too large to be ac-
commodated in Yuma itself, they were moved to this location. The yards were still extant in 1956. Lettuce sheds rose
around this location.

Ref.: Mercer. Maps: C-11; GN-11 (Ivalon).

## AZTEC

El.: c. 500'                    Loc.: Yuma 4, F-4
The name of this small railroad work stop and settlement
comes from the nearby Aztec Hills. The S.P.R.R. station
was established in 1881 to provide a watering stop for
engines.

P.O. est. September 12, 1889. Charles A. Dallman, p.m. Wells
Fargo Station, 1890. Discont. July 30, 1900.

Ref.: Johnson; 141, p. 78; P.O. Records. Maps: C-7; GN-11.

**a.n. Aztec Hills**     Maps: GN-1; GN-2        Yuma

## BAKER PEAKS

El.: 1416' and 1409'            Loc.: Yuma 4, A-7
There is little doubt that the name for Baker Peaks came
from the presence of Baker's ranch in 1875 at Baker's
Tanks, a natural waterhole on the old trail from Mexico
through the pass formed by the two peaks. The tanks were
originally a series of stream potholes just north of the old
road.

A band of renegade Mexicans was active in this vicinity
in 1875. One of these men, Chavez, was employed by
Baker. Chavez broke horses for Baker without pay for two
months. He was seen and recognized by a herder for King
S. Woolsey. Woolsey in turn reported it to a man named
Colvig, who planned to capture the bandit. Colvig shot
Chavez in the back when the latter ran for his arms. As a
result of this action, Mexicans of Chavez' band attacked
King Woolsey's ranch, looking for Colvig.

**v.n. Baker Butte**

Ref.: 136, p. 169; *Weekly Arizona Miner*, December 3, 1875,
     4:3; December 17, 1875, 1:6; Mrs. Kelland. Maps: GN-
     13; GN-24; GN-11.

## BARAGAN MOUNTAINS

El.: 1289'                      Loc.: Yuma 4, E-1.5
Pro.: /barag)n/
Frank Baragan was a Mexican rancher who dug Baragan's
well (Sec. 18, T. 5 S., R. 11 W.), which he used to water
his stock.

Ref.: Lenon; 141, p. 201. Maps: GN-11; GN-7.

## BATTLESHIP MOUNTAIN

El.: c. 1500'                   Loc.: Yuma 2, BC-3
Descriptive.

Ref.: Willson. Map: GN-11.

**a.n. Battleship, The**                Grand Canyon (Coconino)
    El.: 5867'. Maps: GC-1; GC-7.

## BEAR HILLS

El.: c. 1500'                   Loc.: Yuma 2, AB-7-8
William Bear was the first postmaster at Harrisburg. These
mountains are named for him. When he died, Bill Bear's
body was carried to his grave as he had requested—on a
burro.

Ref.: Willson. Map: GN-11.

## BLACK MESA

El.: c. 900'                    Loc.: Yuma 1, H-10
Descriptive. The mesa is of metamorphic gneiss or schist.

Ref.: Mercer. Map: GN-11.

## BLACK PEAK

El.: 1656'                      Loc.: Yuma 1, F-3.4
Descriptive. The word "black" is frequently used descriptively (see *a.n.* below).

Map: GN-11.

**a.n. Black Butte**     Loc.: T. 6 N., R. 7 W.        Maricopa
**Black Butte**     El.: 1782'. Map: GK-27        Pinal
**Black Canyon Spring**     Map: GM-12        Yavapai
**Black Draw**     Map: GB-17        Cochise
**Black Gap**     Map: GG-16        Maricopa
Pass formed by two volcanic hills. Black Gap Station on
the Cornelia and Gila Bend R.R. is in this pass.
**Black Hill**     El.: 2948'. Map: GM-3        Yavapai
**Black Hills**     Map: GE-6        Graham
**Black Hills**        Graham and Greenlee
(Variant name for Peloncillo Mountains).
**Black Hills**     Loc.: T. 7, 8 S., R. 16 E.        Pinal
**Black Hills Tank**     Map: GM-5        Yavapai
**Black Hill Wash**     Map: GM-11        Yavapai

| Black Knob | El.: 5824'. Map: GB-2 | Cochise |
| Black Mesa | El.: 4355'. Maps: GD-11; GD-14 | Gila |
| Black Mesa | Loc.: T. 8, 9 N., R. 4 E. | Maricopa and Yavapai |

Sometimes called Cook Mesa for William (Billy) Cook, a cattleman.
Ref.: Barnes.

| Black Mesa | El.: 3125'. Map: GG-11 | Maricopa |
| Black Mesa | El.: 4172'. Map: GG-3 | Maricopa |
| Black Mesa | Loc.: W. of Bill Williams Mtn. | Yavapai |

Named by Lt. Amiel W. Whipple.

| Black Mountain | Loc.: Top of Ash Flat | Graham |

Five sheep herders were killed here by cowpunchers in the 1880's.
Ref.: Jennings.

| Black Mountain | El.: 3016'. Map: GJ-1 | Pima |
| Black Mountain | El.: 5298'. Maps: GK-2; GK-30 | Pinal |
| Black Mountain | Loc.: T. 11 N., R. 3 W. | Yavapai |
| Black Mountains | El.: 4972'. Map: GM-10 | Yavapai |
| Black Mountain Wash | Map: GD-9 | Gila |
| Black Peak | El.: 4780'. Map: GD-4 | Gila |
| Black Peak | Loc.: T. 22 S., R. 10 E. | Pima |
| Black Point | Map: GK-10 | Pinal |
| Black River | | Graham and Gila |

Loc.: Part of boundary between White River Apache and San Carlos Apache reservations.

| Black Rock Point | El.: 7520'. Map: GA-5 | Apache |
| Blackrock Wash | Maps: GA-13; GA-14 | Apache |
| Black Tank | Map: GN-16 | Yuma |

Charles C. Genung reported that this tank was used by an 1863 prospecting party.
Ref.: 52, IV, 35.

## BLAISDELL

El.: 186'　　　　Loc.: Yuma 3, D-5.7
There were two Blaisdells concerned with the pioneer history of Yuma during Arizona territorial days. One was Ira Blaisdell, who was in Yuma in 1879. He was successful in getting the S.P.R.R. to permit him to manage the water pump and supply the city of Yuma with water.
The second pioneer was Hiram W. Blaisdell, who was the engineer of two canals in the area, and it was probably for the latter that the small railroad station was named.

P.O. est. March 23, 1896. John E. McIver, p.m. Discont. December 18, 1905. Wells Fargo Station, 1903.

Ref.: Kline; Fr. Figueroa ms., (APHS), pp. 68, 69; P.O. Records. Maps: GN-6; GN-26.

## BLALACK

El.: c. 500'　　　　Loc.: Yuma 3, CD-5.8
　　　　About 6 to 8 miles east of Yuma.
Pro.: /bléylæk/
Blalack is reported to have been the name of a local land owner. The former small store and community known as Blalack has vanished and the area is now a farming section. The country store for the area is known as Gila Center Store.

P.O. est. April 22, 1928. Mrs. Alice M. Noyes, p.m. Discont. October 31, 1933.

Ref.: Barnes; P.O. Records. Maps: C-13; GN-11 (Gila Center).

## BOOT PEAK

El.: c. 1500'　　　　Loc.: Yuma 3, D-4.4
Lt. Joseph Christmas Ives named this Boot Mountain in 1857.
Ref.: 121, p. 21. Maps: C-5; E-20; E-4.

## BOUSE

El.: c. 500'　　　　Loc.: Yuma 2, A-5
The original name of this location was Brayton, so named for John Brayton Martin, who kept the Brayton Commercial Company which was the store for the Harqua Hala (sic) Mine. Local residents changed the name of Brayton to Bouse.

There is some question whether the place was named for Thomas Bouse, a trader and storekeeper, or for George Bouse, a miner and truck gardener. Possibly it was named for both men. According to a news story in 1909, George Bouse of the Bouse Townsite, Land and Improvement Company purchased 1,600 acres of land for cultivation.

P.O. est. as Brayton, May 14, 1906. William E. Enos, p.m. Name changed to Bouse, November 27, 1907. Wells Fargo Station, 1907.

Ref.: Barnes; Arizona Star, January 15, 1909, 3:4; P.O. Records; 4, p. 369; 141, p. 202. Maps: C-10; GN-28.

| a.n. Bouse Hills | Map: C-12 | Yuma |
| Bouse Wash | Map: GN-12 | Yuma |

## BOWYER PEAK

El.: 2125'　　　　Loc.: Yuma 1, E-8
Joe Bowyer owned the nearby mine from which the peak takes its name.
Ref.: Barnes. Map: GN-11.

## BRADFORD WELL

El.: c. 1500'　　　　Loc.: Yuma 2, D-8.3
Thomas W. Bales owned several cattle wells in this vicinity, of which Bradford Well is one.
Ref.: 141, p. 203. Map: GN-11.

## BRYAN MOUNTAINS

El.: 2000'　　　　Loc.: Yuma 4, F-9.3-10.6
These mountains were named by Eldred D. Wilson of the University of Arizona in 1930 for Kirk Bryan, author of articles and books on the geology of southwestern Arizona.
Ref.: 181, p. 155. Map: GN-11.

## BUCK MOUNTAIN

El.: c. 700'　　　　Loc.: Yuma 4, A-3-9.6
Descriptive. Bighorn mountain sheep are frequently seen on this mountain.

v.n. Buck Peak
Ref.: 181, p. 162; Monson. Yuma: U.S.G.S. 1923.
a.n. Buck Mountain Tank　　　　Yuma
　Loc.: Sec. 16, T. 12 S., R. 16 W.
　The Fish and Wildlife Service developed this tank and named it for the nearby mountain in 1949.
Ref.: Monson.

## BUCKSKIN MOUNTAINS

El.: 3137'                    Loc.: Yuma 2, AE-1-2.5
The origin of this name has not been learned. These mountains are in reality a continuation of the Aubrey Hills of Mohave County.
Ref.: 100, p. 28. Maps: C-10; GN-11.

## BUTLER MOUNTAINS

El.: 1300'                    Loc.: Yuma 3, F-9
Eldred D. Wilson named this short range in 1930 for Dr. G. M. Butler, then Dean of the College of Mines of the University of Arizona.
Ref.: 181, p. 179. Map: GN-11.

## BUTLER VALLEY

El.: c. 1500'                 Loc.: Yuma 2, CD-3.9
Sam Butler and his brother c. 1888 were miners living in Butler Valley, named for them.
Ref.: 141, p. 205; Barnes. Maps: C-12; GN-11.

a.n. **Butler Pass**        Loc.: T. 8 N., R. 15 W.            Yuma
**Butler Well**        Loc.: T. 8 N., R. 14 W.            Yuma
The Butler brothers dug and maintained a well which supplied water for the Clara Mine.

v.n. **Clara Well**

## CABEZA PRIETA MOUNTAINS

El.: 2500'                    Loc.: Yuma 4, AC-9-10
Pro.: /kəbéysə priéytə/      Spanish: "black head"
The Cabeza Prieta Mountains are descriptively named because of a black lava-capped peak near the center of this twenty-two mile range.
Ref.: Mercer; Lenon; 181, p. 162. Maps: E-12; E-17.

a.n. **Cabeza Prieta Pass**      Loc.: N. end of range        Yuma
The old trail from Mexico went through here.

**Cabeza Prieta Tank**    Loc.: Sec. 9, R. 15 W., T. 13, S.   Yuma
One of these tanks was developed by the Fish and Wildlife Service in 1948.
Ref.: Monson; 181, p. 162.

## CAMINO del DIABLO

El.: 1000'-100'   Loc.: Desert Road across southern Arizona, part of northern Mexico and through Yuma County to the Gila River near Yuma.
Pro.: /kami·no del diyáblo/      Spanish: "Devil's Road"
The first white man to establish a trail across southern Arizona and northern Mexico toward the West Coast was Fr. Kino on his missionary trip to the Colorado River in the late 1690's.

Thousands of others attempted to follow roughly the same route and hundreds met with disaster. As a matter of fact, the so-called "Road of the Devil" was scarcely worthy of the name *road* since it wandered at traveler's will from waterhole to waterhole, and shifting sands at times made portions of it impassable so that roundabout means to reach the waterholes had to be found. The trail, such as it was, dipped into Mexico and returned to Arizona at Quitobaquito, south of the present Ajo. From here it went northwest through the Tinajas Altas to Yuma. The toll of

dead along this *camino* may never be known, but it is known that hundreds died from hunger, thirst, and fatigue. In the Tinajas Altas Mountains and elsewhere in certain portions of southern Arizona deep wagon ruts and other signs of the old road may still be found.
Ref.: 4, pp. 389-90; 181, pp. 177-78. Maps: C-17; E-2; E-20 (Not named); GN-11.

## CASTLE DOME

El.: 3793'                    Loc.: Yuma 3, G-1
The highest point in the Castle Dome Mountains was called Capital Dome by soldiers at Fort Yuma in the 1850's. The name, however, soon corrupted to Castle Dome Peak. The group of hills was sometimes called Castle Dome Range. The area in which the peak is located was of little interest prior to 1863, but in that year two miners named Conner and Jacob Snively organized the Castle Dome Mining District. They found much evidence of earlier mining, the antiquity of which was attested to by slow-growing ironwood and palo verde trees of large size growing in the mouths of old pits and on piles of mining refuse. The veins did not prove as rich as had been anticipated, and most prospectors soon moved on. Several years later (c. 1875) Colorado steamboat captains became interested in the mines. They shipped the ores via steamer to Yuma from Castle Dome Landing. After 1883 the district became relatively inactive.

Castle Dome City was laid out directly west of the mountains at what was called the Pitoti, so named because of a weed found growing only in that vicinity. This is the place which later was known as Castle Dome Landing.

P.O. est. as Castle Dome, December 17, 1875. William P. Miller, p.m. Discont. December 4, 1876. Re-est. as Castle Dome Landing, August 6, 1878. Andrew H. Cargill, p.m. Discont. June 16, 1884.
Ref.: Lenon; 87, p. 251; 181, pp. 77, 85-87; *Arizona Miner*, April 6, 1864; 2:3; P.O. Records. Maps: E-4; E-17; GN-11; GN-15.

a.n. **Castle Dome Plain**      Map: GN-26                  Yuma
**Castle Dome Mountains**                                  Yuma
El.: c. 3000'. Loc.: T. 1 N. to T. 7 S., R. 18 W.

**Castle Rock Dam**  Loc.: Sec. 30, T. 4 S., R. 17 W.      Yuma
This dam was built by the Fish and Wildlife Service in 1952, and it was named for the nearby Castle Dome Mountains.
Ref.: Monson.

## CEMENTOSA TANKS

El.: c. 2500'                 Loc.: Yuma 2, B-10
The conglomerate forming this natural waterhole has cement-like qualities.

v.n. **Cemetosa Tanks**

Ref.: Barnes; 141, p. 205; 181, p. 116. Maps: A-7 (Cemetosa); GN-11.

## CEMETERY RIDGE

El.: c. 1500'                 Loc.: Yuma 2, F-11
This sixteen-mile-long and two-mile-wide, low range was the scene of the killing of several prospectors in the 1870's, according to local stories. Their bodies are said to be buried on the ridge, which is also known as Cemetery Hills.

The highest point in the range is Nottbusch Butte in the southeastern portion. It is several hundred feet higher than the average of the surrounding hills (cf. Nottbusch Butte).

Ref.: Barnes; 181, p. 142. Maps: C-12 (Cemetery Hills); GN-11.

## CENTENNIAL

El.: c. 1500'                          Loc.: Yuma 2, E-7

Centennial took its name from its location on Centennial Wash (Yuma and Maricopa Counties) which is supposed to be one hundred miles long, including that portion which is also called Cullen Wash.

Apparently Centennial was an outgrowth of a place called Orville, which was on the Gila River near Palomas. The fact that this name gave way to Plomosa would seem to indicate that ores were handled at this place, since the Spanish meaning of Plomosa is "heavy metal."

P.O. est. as Orville, February 2, 1880. William B. Ready, p.m. Changed to Plomosa, April 8, 1880. J. Coleman, p.m. Changed to Centennial, July 13, 1881. George A. Ellsworth, p.m. Discont. March 26, 1886.

v.n. Orrville (Barnes)

   Harqua Hala (q.v.)

Ref.: *Weekly Arizona Miner,* September 26, 1879, 3:1; Barnes; Lenon; P.O. Records; 13, p. 39. Maps: C-5 (Centinel); E-18 (Oroville).

a.n. Plomosa Mining District                               Yuma
   Loc.: E. of Ehrenburg 35 miles on the Colorado River.
   This district first came to attention in 1862 and was still well known in the 1880's as a place for placer gold mining.
   Ref.: 76, p. 75.

## CHAIN TANK

El.: c. 2000'                          Loc.: Yuma 3, GH-1
                                       Sec. 35, T. 4 S., R. 17 W.

Chain Tank is known to be at least twenty feet deep. Prospectors many years ago decided to make use of the water. This they did, fastening a rope over a rock projection on the lip of the tank and then pulling a chain up over the projection. The men climbed hand over hand by the chain and put in a pipe to siphon the water. The chains are in two lengths, the lower being thirty feet long and the upper forty feet, hence the name.

The sides of the tank are so steep that it used to form a death trap for game. A tunnel has been put in the tank to enable game which falls in to escape as well as to enter safely at the lower level in order to get water.

Ref.: Monson. Map: None.

## CHOCOLATE MOUNTAINS

El.: 2500'        Loc.: Yuma 1, BC-14; Yuma 3, CD-1

This low, twenty-five mile long range is chocolate colored. It was named by Dr. John C. Newberry of Lt. Joseph Christmas Ives' expedition in 1857.

Ref.: 181, p. 74; 121, p. 24. Maps: E-4; GN-11; GN-18; GN-20; GN-23.

a.n. Chocolate Canyon                                      Yuma
Ref.: 100, p. 49.

## CIBOLA

El.: c. 250'                          Loc.: Yuma 3, A-12
Pro.: /sibówlə/

The reason for using this name has not been learned. (For its origin, (*See* Hopi Villages, Navajo.)

The small community of Cibola probably developed because Colorado River steamers used to unload freight and take on wood for boilers at a landing here. The residents at Cibola sold beef, eggs, and produce to the steamer crews, and a farming area began developing. There was also a ferry which crossed the river to Blythe, California. At one time the Rhodes Ranch (*q.v.*) was at this location. In 1957 enterprising farmers took matters in their own hands and constructed a bridge for farm trucks to cross the river. The matter did not come to public attention until owners of small boats complained the bridge was too low to permit their passage under it.

P.O. est. February 28, 1903. Louis W. Bishop. p.m. Discont. September 15, 1933.

Ref.: Barnes; Mercer; 32, II, 183; *Phoenix Herald,* October 18, 1888, I:3 (APHS); Theobald; Blythe Chamber of Commerce, "Cruise Bulletin," October 10, 1954, 162, p. 17; 37, pp. 131-132, 135; P.O. Records. Maps: C-8; GN-4.

a.n. Cibola Lake   Loc.: Lower end of Cibola Valley        Yuma
   The lake was created by the building up of the river bed after the Imperial Dam was closed in 1938.
   Cibola Valley       Maps: GN-4; GN-18                    Yuma

## CINNABAR

El.: c. 600'                          Loc.: Yuma 1, E-10

This mining location was thought to contain cinnabar, from which it took its name.

Ref.: Barnes; Lenon. Map: GN-11.

## CLANTON'S WELL

El.: c. 400'                          Loc.: Yuma 2, F-11.2

Thomas Newton Clanton, a native of Missouri, came to Arizona in 1877 as a rancher at Bigbug, moving from there to Phoenix in 1880. He later (1885) contracted to build ten miles of canals at Buckeye (*q.v.,* Maricopa), and in 1888 moved to that community. He also dug the well which bears his name, and the name gradually extended to the Clanton Hills twenty-five miles north of Palomas. The importance of the well was due to its being the only one in the region.

Ref.: 112, III; 141, p. 23; 181, pp. 142, 144. Map: GN-11.

## CLARA PEAK

El.: 2400'                            Loc.: Yuma 3, E-1

Sterling Winters located and named the Clara Mine, from which the peak takes its name. A later name was Carrigan Peak, after T. J. Carrigan, a prospector.

v.n. Klara Peak (corruption)
   Karrigan Peak (corruption)
   Kerrigan Peak (corruption)
Ref.: Barnes. Maps: C-12 (Carrigan); C-11.

a.n. Carrigan Well      El.: 1100'. Map: GN-16             Yuma
v.n. Osborne Well
   E. S. Osborne, who dug this well, sold it to T. J. Carrigan.
a.n. Clara Well    Cf. Butler Valley, a.n. Butler Well     Yuma
   Osborne Wash        Map: GN-16                          Yuma

## CLIP

El.: c. 450'                                    Loc.: Yuma 3, C-1
Clip was the shipping point for the Silver Clip Claim five
miles north of the town of Silent. The Clip Mill Site at
Clip had a ten-stamp mill about eight miles northwest of
the mine. The mill began production in 1883.

The Clip Mine, as it came to be called, was discovered in
the early 1880's and was operated by men named Anthony
G. Hubbard and Bowers until April 1887, producing by
that time more than a million dollars in silver. From 1887
until 1925 the mine was relatively inactive, but in the
latter year some of the ore from the mine was milled at
Norton's Landing and a one-hundred-ton cyanide mill was
built at the mine. However, none of the later operations
really succeeded.

P.O. est. February 6, 1884. Anthony G. Hubbard, p.m. Discont.
October 13, 1888.
Ref.:   181, pp. 52, 56; P.O. Records. Maps: C-7; GN-18.
**a.n. Clip Wash**          Map: GN-18                    Yuma

## COLFRED

El.: 328'                                       Loc.: Yuma, 4-B-6
Pro.: /kalfréd/
The treasurer of the S.P.R.R. in 1881 was Col. Fred
Crocker. The name was taken from his military title and
first name.
Ref.:   Barnes. Map: GN-13.

## COLORADO, CAMP

El.: c. 500'                                    Loc.: Yuma 1, F-2.8
Camp Colorado was established on November 24, 1868,
and abandoned in 1871. It is not the same as the Camp
Colorado established by Col. William Hoffman (cf. Fort
Mohave, Mohave). On the Department of Arizona Map,
Sheet No. 3 (1875) this place shows as Old Camp Colo-
rado, indicating that it had been abandoned by then as
a sub-post for Fort Yuma.
Ref.:   145, p. 490; 27, p. 152; 28, p. 128. Maps: C-2; E-18.

## COLORADO RIVER (MOHAVE-CHEMEHUEVI) RESERVATION

El.: c. 300'                                    Loc.: Yuma 1, CE-3-9
                                                (partly in California)
Charles Debrille Poston (*See* Poston Butte, Pinal) was the
first Indian superintendent for Arizona. In 1864 he selected a location on the Colorado River bottom to be set
aside as the second Indian reservation in Arizona. On
March 3, 1865, the reservation was established to serve
the needs of the Hualapais, Yavapais, and tribes along the
Colorado River, under the phrase "Indians of said river
and its tributaries."

Poston suggested what may have been the first attempt by
Americans to irrigate in Arizona with waters of the Colorado River. Between 1867 and 1874, Indians assisted in
digging a nine-mile canal. However, the results were so
unsatisfactory that the Indians began to lose their belief
in the white man's ability to get things done. As a result,
some Indians living away from the river refused flatly to
move down to the river bottom reservation.

By an interesting extension of the intent of the phrase
"and its tributaries" as applying to Indians who could use
the reservation, it has been possible to resettle Navajo and
Hopi Indians on the reservation, since waters from both
the Navajo and the Hopi reservations drain into the Colorado River. On February 3, 1945, the Colorado River
Tribal Council authorized settlement by Indians from other
tribes, and on September 1, 1945, sixteen Hopi families
arrived. The resettlement area is believed capable of sup-
porting about two thousand families under the long range
plan. By the close of 1954, one hundred eleven Navajo
and Hopi colonists had settled on the reservation.

The reservation contains 265,858 acres, of which 126,860
is potential farming land. Currently a total of about eleven
hundred Indians reside on the reservation, with agency
and tribal headquarters at Parker.

Ref.:   88, II, 374; 141, pp. 39, 41; "Annual Report of the Ari-
        zona Commission of Indian Affairs, 1954, 1955, 1956,"
        p. 13. Maps: GN-3; GN-11.

## COPPER MOUNTAINS

El.: 2808'                                      Loc.: Yuma 3, H-8
Descriptive. There is much copper staining on the volcanic
rocks of this range.
Ref.:   181, p. 164; Lenon. Maps: GN-11; GN-13; GN-24;
        GN-26.

## CORONA MOUNTAIN

El.: 1675'                                      Loc.: Yuma 2, C-3
There was a mine near this mountain called the Corona
Mine.
Ref.:   Barnes. Map: GN-11.

## CORONATION PEAK

El.: 1422'                                      Loc.: Yuma 3, I-5.4
Travelers across Arizona in the 1850's and later never
failed to notice the striking Coronation Peak, so named
because the "peaks bear a strong resemblance to those of
a mitered crown, and seen in the glow of the setting sun,
would readily suggest the idea of that gilded emblem of
royalty."

John Russell Bartlett of the U.S. Boundary Survey Commission in 1852 made a sketch of the peak, calling it Pagoda Mountain, and noting that its three points closely
resembled "the tops of Hindu pagodas."

The early descriptive name "Coronation Peak" was not
destined to endure. The name "Klotho's Temple" was applied by DeLancey Gill, artist on the Old Yuma Trail exploration party in November, 1900. Klotho is one of the
three Fates.

**v.n. Klothos Temple**
    **Clothos Temple**
    **Clothopas Temple**
Ref.:   25, p. 78; 181, p. 318; 9, p. 188; 31, p. 175; 87, p. 173;
        W. J. McGee, "Old Yuma Trail," *National Geographic
        Magazine*, XII (April 1, 1901), 140. Maps: C-9; C-10;
        C-12; C-13; E-20; GN-6; GN-11.

## COWBELL LAKE

El.: c. 220'                      Loc.: Yuma 3, AB-1
                                  Sec. 2, T. 4 S., R. 24 W.

This lake is home ground for a cow which wears a bell around her neck. She has been in the vicinity for some time and at the end of 1956 was still hanging around.

Ref.: Monson. Map: None.

## CULLING'S WELL

El.: c. 500'                      Loc.: Yuma 2, F-5

This place shows as Cullen's Well on all maps examined except GLO 1921, which calls it Cullin's. The correct name, however, is Culling, since it was a stage station kept by Charles C. Culling where the road from Ehrenburg forked to go toward Wickenburg. Martha Summerhayes wrote of stopping at Cullen's (sic) ranch in 1875 and enjoying a "delicious supper of stewed chicken, and fried eggs, and good bread, and then Mrs. Cullen put our boy to bed in Daniel's crib . . ."

When Joe Drew was station keeper here, he "grieved that several deaths from thirst had occurred only a few miles from the station." Drew therefore began raising a lantern each night above the well frame, and one evening "an almost spent lad . . . on the point of lying down to die, had seen in the distance a glimmer of light from the windows of the station house," and creeping onward, found water and safety at the well.

A similar story is told about Baker Peak, Yuma County.

P.O. est. as Culling's, October 17, 1896. Joseph S. Drew, p.m. Discont. March 6, 1902.

Ref.: 87, p. xxvii; 158, p. 154; 111, p. 278; P.O. Records. Maps: C-2 through C-8; C-10; C-12.

**a.n. Cullen Wash**                                         Yuma
Loc.: Upper part of Centennial Wash (cf. Centennial)
Ref.: 141, p. 39.

## CUNNINGHAM PASS

El.: c. 750'                      Loc.: Yuma 2, E-4-4.5

After having been a sailor, Charles Cunningham arrived in this area in the mid-1860's. He was a miner and a friend of the Indians. Despite the latter fact, on May 3, 1871 he was a victim of an ambuscade in Bell's Canyon (q.v. Yavapai). When the Indians discovered that they had killed their friend, they did not mutilate his body as they did those of his three companions.

Ref.: APHS Names File; Arizona Miner, May 3, 1871. Map: GN-11.

**a.n. Cunningham Mountain**     El.: 3314'. Map: GN-5     Yuma

## DATELAND

El.: 434'                         Loc.: Yuma 4, E-4.6

A large grove of date trees was the source of the name for Dateland, which was built about 1930 by Mrs. William Harrison. The grove of date trees still exists, but the work buildings and large residence do not. A few buildings are still standing.

Ref.: Johnson; 4, p. 39. Map: GN-11.

## DESERT STATION

El.: c. 400'                      Loc.: Yuma 2, FG-10

In 1875 Desert Station was owned by Englishmen named Hunt and Dudley, according to Martha Summerhayes. She also noted that the place was clean and attractive, an unusual fact for a stage station in Arizona. The name remained on maps as Desert Station for many years, finally changing to Desert Well, which was referred to as a stage station southwest of Vicksburg where a well had originally been dug one hundred twenty feet deep.

Ref.: 158, p. 156; 141, p. 207; 87, p. xxvii. Maps: C-5; C-6; C-7; C-8; E-18; E-20; GN-11.

## DOME

El.: 288'                         Loc.: Yuma 3, E-5

Dome first appears in 1875 as Gila City on maps examined. It is not the same as Castle Dome City (cf. Castle Dome).

Gila City was a bonanza development which began in 1858 when Jacob Snively found rich deposits of placer gold. Before long, one thousand prospectors swarmed through the surrounding canyons and gulches. Only four or five permanent adobe buildings were erected, with the remainder of the town's population finding refuge in temporary quarters, either tents or roughly built structures. J. Ross Browne said, "Enterprising men hurried to the spot with barrels of whiskey and billiard tables; Jews came with ready-made clothing and fancy wares; traders crowded in with wagons of pork and beans; and gamblers came with cards and monte-tables. There was everything in Gila City within a few months but a church and a jail . . ."

Gila City was nearly obliterated by a flood in 1862. Nevertheless, miners still thronged in the area, recovering the magic metal by dry washing, but by 1865 the great wealth had been taken out of the ground. By 1872 Gila City consisted of a single house, a stable, and a corral.

When the railroad line came through the southern part of Arizona, a siding was constructed approximately one and a half miles east of the old Gila location. The siding was given the name of Dome, apparently because when river boats ceased operation in 1883, this siding became the most important mining-shipping point for the Castle Dome and other mines. The establishment of the railroad siding at Dome was the death blow to Castle Dome Landing (cf. Castle Dome).

By 1890 Dome had enough residents to establish a post office.

A second post office called Monitor had been established two years earlier on the outskirts of old Gila City. Monitor was so named because it was at the mouth of Monitor Gulch, noted for rich placers. In October 1893, the Monitor post office was the scene of the murder of the postmaster and another man. A postal inspector was instructed to conduct the post office affairs until another postmaster could be found. He reported for duty, but remained only a few days, then left, recommending that the post office be discontinued because letters were received there only occasionally. Why the post office should have been continued is a mystery, but it survived for more than a decade.

P.O. est. at Gila City, December 24, 1858. H. Busch, p.m. Discont. July 14, 1863. P.O. est. at Dome, December 16, 1892. William S. Hodges, p.m. Name changed to Gila, March 3, 1904. Name changed to Dome, May 16, 1905. Wells Fargo Station, 1904. P.O. est. at Monitor, December 3, 1890. Albert S. Potter, p.m. Discont. March 3, 1904.

> Variant name for Gila City: Snivelly's Stage Station (on Butterfield route).

Ref.: 141, p. 10; 181, pp. 86, 208; Preston Mercer, "Desert Scrapbook." *Yuma Daily Sun,* XLVIII (August 26, 1953), II:2:3; 52, I, 296; 4, pp. 76-77; Lenon; Theobald; P.O. Records. Maps: GN-10; GN-26; GN-11.

## DOME ROCK MOUNTAINS

El.: 3314'                          Loc.: Yuma 1, D-8-10
This range is not to be confused with the Castle Dome Mountains to the southeast.

In 1854 Lt. N. Michler, a member of the Boundary Survey Commission, reported that about forty-five miles northeast of Fort Yuma was Avie Tok-a-va or Dome Mountain, which he also referred to as Sierra de San Pedro, describing it as "a solid rock many feet in height, and resembling the dome of a cathedral. Some god is supposed to inhabit this range. Near it is a second peak, called the 'Broken Dome.'" The topography of the military map for the Department of New Mexico (1859) shows a range as the "Sierra Mo-Quin-To-Ora or Dome Mountains . . ." Whether this is actually the Castle Dome Mountains or the Dome Rock Mountains it is not possible to say because of the rough approximations of the topographical work.

**v.n. La Paz Mountains**
   **Dome Rock Range**
Ref.: 51, pp. 104, 105. Maps: C-4; C-5; E-20; GN-5; GN-23.

## DRIPPING SPRINGS

El.: c. 650'                          Loc.: Yuma 1, G-9.2
Descriptive. (Not same location as Dripping Springs in Tinajas Altas.)

Ref.: Barnes. Map: GN-11.

**a.n. Dripping Springs Mountain        Map: E-20        Pinal**
   This range s.e. of Globe on n. side of Gila River takes its name from a spring. The range is called the Mescal Mountains on the U.S.G.S. 1910 Ray map.
Ref.: Barnes.

**Dripping Spring        Maps: GM-3; GM-11        Yavapai**
**Dripping Spring Amphitheater        Grand Canyon, Coconino**
On Boucher Trail (Cf. Boucher Creek, Grand Canyon).

**Dripping Spring Trail        Grand Canyon, Coconino**
Maps: GC-1; GC-7.
Cf. Boucher Creek, Grand Canyon.

## EAGLE LANDING

El.: c. 500'                          Loc.: Yuma 1, FG-2.2
This was the shipping point used by the Planet Mine.
Ref.: Barnes. Maps: C-12; GH-11.

## EAGLETAIL MOUNTAINS

El.: c. 1700'                          Loc.: Yuma 2, F-9-10
The Eagletail Mountains are named because Eagletail Peak is in them. Eagletail Peak consists of three shafts which bear a striking resemblance from one viewpoint to the tail feathers of an eagle.

Ref.: Parkman; Monson; 141, p. 22. Maps: C-6; C-7; C-8; C-13; E-18; E-20.

**a.n. Eagletail Valley                          Yuma**
Ref.: 141, p. 40.

## E.C.P. PEAK

El.: c. 4000'                          Loc.: Yuma 2, F-4
This mountain takes its name from the fact that it is on the *E*ast side of *C*unningham *P*ass, hence the letters E.C.P.

Ref.: Lenon. Map: GN-11.
**a.n. W. C. P. Peak                          Yuma**
   Loc.: On west side of Cunningham Pass

## EHRENBERG

El.: 274'                          Loc.: Yuma 1, C-9.3
Herman Ehrenberg, a graduate of Freyburg University, was a German engineer who came to Arizona with Charles Debrille Poston in 1854. In 1863 Ehrenberg surveyed a town on the Colorado River called Mineral City. Mineral City and Ehrenberg were apparently not identical, but adjacent to each other. Ehrenberg lay between Mineral City and Olive.

In October 1866, Herman Ehrenberg was shot at Dos Palmas, California, on the road to La Paz from San Bernardino. The town bearing his name was established soon thereafter, one reason for its coming into existence undoubtedly being that the Colorado River shifted its course and left La Paz high, dry, and useless as a steamboat shipping point.

In 1870 Ehrenberg had two hundred thirty-three residents and was considered the principal landing for freight to be shipped overland to Prescott. According to Hinton, the town consisted of "one straggling street of adobe houses facing the river . . ." All that remains of Ehrenberg today is the old cemetery and the scarcely visible foundations of a few buildings.

P.O. est. September 20, 1869. Joseph Goldwater, p.m. Discont. December 31, 1913. Re-est. 1958. Wells Fargo Station, 1879.

Ref.: 87, p. 251; *Arizona Miner,* October 23, 1866, 2:1; 7, pp. 616, and 616, (Note 6); 52, IV, 59; 105, p. 142; P.O. Records. Maps: C-2; C-3; C-5; C-6; C-7; C-8; E-18; E-20; GN-11.

**a.n. Ehrenberg Wash        Map: GN-5        Yuma**

## ELKHART

El.: c. 600'                          Loc.: Yuma 2, F-5.9
A temporary siding used while the tunnel was being constructed in this place, Elkhart was named for the tunnel foreman.

Ref.: Barnes. Map: GN-11

## ENGESSER PASS

El.: c. 1000'                              Loc.: Yuma 2, BC-11.3
The pass was named for a man named Engesser, who owned
the Engesser Mine in Section 18 nearby.

Ref.: Monson. Map: GN-11.

## EXPLORER'S PASS

El.: c. 500'                               Loc.: Yuma 3, CD-4.6
Where the Chocolate Mountains close in on the waters of
the Colorado River, in 1857 Lt. Joseph Christmas Ives and
his party came to a narrow canyon which they called Explorer's Pass, after the *USS Explorer,* the steamboat which
the Ives party used to explore the head of navigation on
the Colorado River.

Seven miles farther up the river the *USS Explorer* ran into
another narrow and deep canyon, which the party called
the Purple Hills Pass, after a hill of that color on the
California side of the river.

Ref.: 42, p. 164; 121, p. 47. Maps: E-4; E-18.

## FARRAR PEAK

El.: 2900'                                 Loc.: Yuma 1, DE-9.1
This may be the same peak which shows on Lenon's map
for Yuma County as Sawtooth Mountain, a descriptive
name.

Barnes suggests that the name Farrar Peak should be
spelled Ferra Peak, after Juan Ferra. When Pauline Weaver
brought to Fort Yuma gold which he had found in the
vicinity of the future La Paz, a party went to Weaver's
camp with Don Jose M. Redondo. Each man searched
various gulches for placer gold. When the men went south
again to Laguna and reported the richness of their individual discoveries, forty miners prepared to go to the new
locations. Among them was Juan Ferra, whose gold find-
ings in Ferra Gulch in February 1862, proved to be the
most valuable made. The news spread quickly and a veritable stampede of miners began. It lasted until early 1864,
when the placers were exhausted. Today Ferra Gulch is
called Farrer Gulch.

Ref.: 52, II, 293-294. Maps: GN-5; GN-11.

## FILIBUSTER'S CAMP

El.: c. 500'                               Loc.: Yuma 3, GH-6
Henry A. Crabb was married to a member of a prominent
Sonoran family, and while visiting his wife's relatives in
1856, he met and talked to Pesqueira, who at that time
hoped to unseat Gandera, the legally elected governor of
Sonora. Pesqueira suggested that Crabb bring a thousand
Americans to help with the proposed revolution and in return Crabb was to be given a strip of territory along the
border between Mexico and Arizona. Apparently Crabb
had no difficulty raising his little army and it proceeded
to the spot on the Gila River called Filibuster's Camp.

Pesqueira, however, not waiting for Crabb's help, was already governor of Sonora. He denied any connection with
Crabb, going beyond that to actually rousing the Mexican

government against Crabb and attacking him at Caborca.
More than half of Crabb's advance contingent of one hundred men was killed or wounded. Crabb surrendered on
promise of immunity. The promise was kept just long
enough to get Crabb and his remaining men under control. They were then butchered and Crabb's head was sent
to Mexico City as evidence of Pesqueira's own loyalty.
The nine hundred men who awaited news of the advance
party disbanded at once and only twenty-seven Americans
started from Tucson to get relief to Crabb. They arrived
too late.

In 1858 the Butterfield Overland Stage line established a
station at Filibuster's Camp, but abandoned it in late 1859.
Ref.: 87, pp. 36, 37; Lenon. Maps: E-7; E-20; E-21.

## FORTUNA

El.: 775'                                  Loc.: Yuma 3, E-7.8
                 Spanish: "fortune, chance, fate"
The rich vein of the La Fortuna Mine was discovered
c. 1893 by Charles Thomas, William Holbert, and two
additional prospectors. However, gold had been known to
exist in this locality for many years. The La Fortuna Gold
Mining and Milling Company was organized in 1896 and
built a twenty-stamp mill, which was the hub of the little
community of Fortuna. Between 1896 and the end of 1904,
over two and one-half million dollars in gold was taken
from the mine. After 1904 the mine was worked intermittently until 1924. The place has since been ransacked of
surface property and the shafts are caved in.

P.O. est. September 30, 1896. John Doan, p.m. Discont. November 4, 1904.

Ref.: P.O. Records; 181, pp. 189-190. Maps: GN-6; GN-26;
GN-11.

| a.n. Fortuna Wash | Map: GN-26 | Yuma |
| Fortuna Station | Loc.: Sec. 31, T. 8 S., R. 21 W. | Yuma |

## GADSDEN

El.: 150'                                  Loc.: Yuma 3, A-7.9
Early in 1915 a cotton-growing community was established
at Gadsden. It was named either for the Gadsden Purchase
or for James Gadsden, the Secretary of State under whom
the purchase was made.

P.O. est. July 15, 1915. William M. Davison, p.m.

Ref.: P.O. Records; Barnes. Map: GN-11.

## GAEL

El.: 349'                                  Loc.: Yuma 4, A-6
Named for Robert Gael, who was in charge of pumping
water for trains at this place.

Ref.: Barnes. Maps: GN-11; GN-13.

## GILA MOUNTAINS

El.: 3150'                                 Loc.: Yuma 3, DG-6-9
Pro.: /híylə/
In 1854 Lt. N. Michler said the Sierra de la Gila extended
above the junction of the Colorado and Gila Rivers. At a
later date the name became Gila Mountains, and the range

was not considered to extend beyond the Gila River on the north. For a time the range was referred to as the Gila City Mountains, during the boom days of that community, but the word "City" did not persevere.

Ref.: 181, pp. 181-183; 51, p. 104. Maps: C-5; E-3 (Sierra de la Gila); E-20; E-18; GN-6; GN-24; GN-26.

**a.n. Gila Valley**          Map: GN-26                          Yuma

## GLYNNS FALLS

El.: c. 350′          Loc.: Yuma 4, D-7.1
The origin of this name has not yet been learned.

The falls are formed by a series of rock tanks which are of no particular importance and seldom hold enough water to form falls.

Ref.: Mercer. Map: GN-11.

## GREAT COLORADO VALLEY

El.: c. 500′          Loc.: Yuma 1, GC-1-9
The Great Colorado Valley is the largest of the many basins through which the Colorado River extends, stretching from Aubrey Canyon to the Chocolate Mountains (Yuma County).

Ref.: 100, p. 45. Map: E-20.

## HALFWAY BEND

El.: c. 300′          Loc.: Yuma 1, CD-3.5-9
Lt. Joseph Christmas Ives in 1857 named the Half-way Mountains in California, from which the bend takes its name. This was the point at which Charles Debrille Poston in 1864 suggested an Indian reservation be established (cf. Colorado River Reservation). When the reservation was established in 1865, the first agents in charge were John C. Dunn and Herman Ehrenberg (cf. Ehrenberg).

In making a report on this location, the chief engineer said the Indians called a slough here Mad-Ku-Dap, the mean-of which has not yet been learned.

Ref.: 55, p. 525; 52, III, 169; APHS Files. Map: None.

## HARCUVAR MOUNTAINS

El.: c. 4700′          Loc.: Yuma 2, CF-4.5-5
Pro.: /hárkuwvar/          Mohave: "sweet water" or *aha*, "water"; *coo-bar*, "there is very little"
The Harcuvar Mountains first show as the Huacavah. On GLO 1869 there is a spot in these mountains marked Har-couver Water. By 1875 the name had settled to Harcuvar Mountains, but on the Public Surveys Map of 1874 it had been shown as the Harquar Mountains. Harcuvar Peak is on GLO 1921.

Ref.: 100, p. 14; APHS Names File; Willson. Maps: See entry above.

**a.n. Harcuvar**          Loc.: S. of Salome 2 miles          Yuma
A station on the Parker branch of the A.T. & S.F. R.R.

**Harcuvar**          Map: C-7          Maricopa

P.O. est. May 5, 1890. Frank Nicholson, p.m. Discont. August 19, 1893.

## HARQUAHALA MOUNTAINS

El.: 5672′          Loc.: Yuma 2, D-7.2
Pro.: /hárkwəheylə/ or          Mohave: "running water" or
/hárkuwheylə/          *Ah-ha-qua-hale:* "water there is, high up"
An earlier name for the mountains was Penhatchapet (1865), probably because on their south slope was a spring called Pen-Hatchai-pet Water. By 1869 this same spring was being called Hocquahala Springs, and the name was gradually used to include the mountains themselves. The attempts of white men to wrap their tongues around this word has resulted in various spellings, among them Hua-cahella Mountains and Har-qua-halle Mountains. They are, name and all, the most massive in central-western Arizona.

In 1869 it was reported that a Pima Indian had found gold in the Hacquehila Mountains. Later the Harquahala Mine was located in these mountains nine miles south of Salome. The mine, which once sold for $1,335,000, is now deserted.

Ref.: 52, IV, 11; *Weekly Arizona Miner*, January 23, 1869, 2:1; July 31, 1869, 1:2; 100, p. 14; 141, p. 209; Willson. Maps: C-2; E-17; E-18.

**a.n. Harquahala Mountain**          El.: 5669′. Maps: C-7; E-20          Yuma
In 1932 a scientific observatory was on this highest peak in the Harquahala Mountains.

**Little Harquahala Mountains**          Yuma
Loc.: S. and s.w. of Harquahala Mts.

**Harqua Hala**          Map: GG-18          Yuma
This mining community was on the site of the old Centennial (*q.v.*). (See also: Harrisburg).

P.O. est. March 5, 1891. Horace E. Harris, p.m. Discont. August 31, 1918. Re-est. as Harqua, June 6, 1927. Mrs. Margaret E. Ward, p.m. Discont. December 31, 1932.

Ref.: P.O. Records.

## HARRISBURG

El.: c. 1500′          Loc.: Yuma 2, F-7
In 1886 Capt. Charles Harris, a Canadian who had served with northern forces in the Civil War, started the town of Harrisburg in company with Gov. Frederick A. Tritle. The men hauled a five-stamp mill from Prescott to be used in connection with ores from the Socorro Mine (cf. Socorro Peak) and from other nearby mines. Harrisburg was established on the site of the old Centennial stage station, which on GLO 1892 shows as Harqua Hala.

At the Harrisburg cemetery (three miles west from Salome) there is a memorial to mark where Indians in 1849 massacred a party of California emigrants, whose bones were found months later by another party of gold-seekers. The finders carried the bones to the top of the Harrisburg cemetery knoll and buried them.

P.O. est. February 9, 1887. William Bear, p.m. Discont. September 4, 1906.

Ref.: Barnes; 100, p. 11; 4, p. 361; *Prospect*, June 15, 1901, 8:1; 2:3 (APHS); P.O. Records. Maps: C-7; C-5.

**a.n. Harrisburg Valley**          Yuma
Ref.: 141, p. 14.

## HARWOOD

El.: c. 500'                    Loc.: Yuma 3, C-1
                               Above Yuma 28 miles.
Colonel Harwood was a member of the Gila Canal Company, and the landing on the Colorado River at the head of the Colorado and Gila Canal was named after this man by Capt. Jack Mellen, a Colorado River steamboat captain.

Ref.:    Barnes. Map: None.

## HATCHTON

                               Loc.: Not known.
Origin not yet ascertained.
P.O. est. November 30, 1921. Frank E. Black, p.m. No further data; not now in operation.

Ref.:    P.O. Records. Map: None.

## HAVASU LAKE

El.: 450'                       Loc.: Yuma 1, FC-1;
                               Mohave 5, AE-3-8.2
Pro.: /hǽvəsuw/
Named for the Havasupai Indians, Havasu Lake is the reservoir for Parker Dam (q.v.). Havasu Lake is one mile wide and forty-five miles long. The Havasu Lake National Wildlife Refuge borders the lake.

Ref.:    None. Maps: GH-10; GH-12; GN-16.

## HOPE

El.: c. 1100'                   Loc.: Yuma 2, C-7
In 1909 the *Arizona Gazette* noted that under the name of Johannesberg a new town had sprung into existence at this location. It was short-lived. When in 1920 the main highway changed its route from Vicksburg to bypass the location of old Johannesberg, merchants moved from Vicksburg to the new location and named it "Hope" to reflect their own wishes for renewed business. No other explanation for the name has been uncovered.

Ref.:    Lenon; *Arizona Gazette,* November 4, 1909, 11:7. Map: GN-11.

## HYDER

El.: 536'                       Loc.: Yuma 4, FG-2.2
The origin of the name Hyder has not yet been ascertained. It is known, however, that it has no significance in Egyptian.

Ref.:    Mahomet Radwan, Graduate student, University of Arizona. Map: GN-7.

## IBEX PEAK

El.: 2125'                      Loc.: Yuma 1, G-7
Locally there used to be stories about ibex being in this vicinity, but actually the animals were the ewes of mountain sheep. The ewes had long, straight horns. There also used to be on this peak a group of domestic goats which had gone wild. Their horns also resembled those of ibex.

Ref.:    Mercer. Map: GN-11.

## IMPERIAL DAM

El.: c. 300'                    Loc.: Yuma 3, D-3.5
Imperial Dam was named for Imperial Valley, California, the largest area served by water routed from the Colorado River through the All-American Canal. Originally the dam site was known as Cocopah Damsite No. 3.

Ref.:    William J. Williams, Bureau of Reclamation, Boulder City, Nevada, Letter, June 4, 1956. Maps: GN-11; GN-26.

a.n. Imperial National Wildlife Refuge    Map: GN-18    Yuma
     Imperial Reservoir              Map: GN-26    Yuma

## IMPERIAL WELL

El.: c. 1000'                   Loc.: Yuma 3, DE-5-6
                               Sec. 17, T. 8 S., R. 21 W.
This well has no connection with the Imperial Valley in California. The well was owned by Alberto Imperial.

Ref.:    141, p. 210. Map: None.

## INDEPENDENCE, CAMP

El.: c. 220'     Loc.: Yuma 3, C-5.5. E. bank of Colorado
                 River near junction with Gila River.
Camp Independence was established under the command of Lt. Thomas W. Sweeney, who had as his contingent one non-commissioned officer and nine men. He established the camp on June 6, 1851. In connection with the name, Sweeney states, "As touching myself it is an appropriate name for though I am not

            Monarch of all I survey
     My orders there are none to dispute."

Replacing this camp, Fort Yuma was established in December 1851 on the California side of the Colorado.

Ref.:    151, pp. 52, 54-55. Map: None.

## INGALLS LAGOON

El.: c. 250'                    Loc.: Yuma 3, B-7
Capt. Frank S. Ingalls (b. Maine, 1851; d. 1927) came to Arizona in 1882. Ingalls, who had been in Prescott serving as Surveyor General of the Territory, was sent to Yuma to take charge of the territorial prison in 1883. He began a company farm on what came to be known as Ingalls Lagoon. Ingalls sought to discover what produce would grow best in the Yuma area.

Ref.:    Mrs. Addie Ingalls Kline (daughter). Maps: GN-11; GN-26.

## KIM

El.: c. 400'                    Loc.: Yuma 4, D-5
The president of the S.P.R.R., Epes Randolph, had on his private railroad car a Chinese cook named Kim. The siding was named for the cook. Kim had never seen his "town," and on one trip Randolph offered to let Kim be dropped off to see it. The train stopped; Kim dropped off. The Randolph private train pulled away. There was nothing at "Kim" except the cook and the railroad spur. However, Randolph had arranged for the next train through to pick Kim up. When the Chinese was asked how he liked his town he replied, "Fine! Fine! Lots of room to grow."

Ref.:    Lenon. Maps: GN-8; GN-11.

## KOFA

El.: 1700'                              Loc.: Yuma 4, C-3.8
Pro.: /kówfə/
The King of Arizona Mine Company had a "branding iron"
which was used to mark company property. The iron read
"K of A." When a post office name for the community was
being discussed, someone spotted the branding iron and
the name Kofa resulted.

In 1896 Charles E. Eichelberger discovered the King of
Arizona Mine, which he developed in partnership with
H. B. Gleason and Epes Randolph. The availability of
water in order to work ores was a problem. For a while
the ores were shipped to a five-stamp mill near Mohawk
on the Gila River. Late in 1897 water was located at a
depth of one thousand feet five miles south of the mine.
The mine was closed temporarily in order to build a cyanide plant. The mine was then very active until July, 1910,
its total production amounting to over three and one half
million dollars. In 1909 Charles Eichelberger sold out to
Col. Eugene S. Ives.

P.O. est. June 5, 1900. Lewis N. Alexander, p.m. Discont.
August 27, 1928.

Ref.: Lenon; 181, pp. 109-110; P.O. Records. Map: GN-11.

**a.n.** King Valley                                          Yuma
   Loc.: Between Kofa Mountains and Castle Dome Mountains.

   **Kofa Butte**     Loc.: T. 2 S., R. 16 W. in north part     Yuma
   Kofa Butte has the appearance of an old tailings dump. This
   leads to its also being called Mud Mountain, since tailings
   are sometimes referred to as "mud."
   Ref.: Monson.

   **Kofa Mountains**          El.: 1800'                        Yuma
   This is a variant name for the S. H. Mountains (q.v.).

   **Kofa Queen Mine**     Loc.: Sec. 6, T. 1 S., R. 17 W.       Yuma
   Every king must have his queen, and the Kofa Queen Mine
   is the partner to the King of Arizona.

   **Kofa Queen Canyon**   Loc.: Same as Kofa Queen Mine  Yuma

   **Kofa Well**       Loc.: Sec. 22, T. 2 S., R. 17 W.         Yuma
   The well location where the mine had its cyanide mill is of
   particular interest because it is a physical demonstration of
   how the land was stripped in order to supply fuel to run the
   various mining operations in the state of Arizona. The
   physical evidence is a tremendous pile of ironwood ashes
   which still exists at Kofa Well site.
   Ref.: Monson.

## LAGUNA

El.: c. 200'                            Loc.: Yuma 3, CD-4.4
Pro.: /lagúwnə/              Spanish: "pond"
The original small community of Laguna is now the site
of Laguna Dam.

In May 1864 several new towns (including Laguna) were
started along the Colorado River as a result of gold placering. There were, as a matter of fact, two Lagunas below
the present Laguna Dam; they were called First and Second
Lagunas. Despite the fact that many miners left the area
when rich discoveries were made near Ehrenberg, Laguna
survived for many years. It was owned by R. J. Duncan
c. 1894.

In 1902 the Reclamation Act provided for the construction of Laguna Dam to introduce irrigation on a large
scale near Yuma. By 1907 water was being impounded. The
crest of the dam measures 4,780 feet and its height is forty
feet. During the construction period, workers reported finding placer nuggets and coarse gold in potholes a hundred
feet above the river.

P.O. est. as Lagune, August 3, 1909. Robert G. Weatherstone,
p.m. Discont. December 20, 1928.

Ref.: Mercer; 52, II, 294; 4, p. 273; 181, p. 217; APHS
   Names File; *Arizona Miner,* May 11, 1864, 3:1; P.O.
   Records. Maps: C-9; C-1; E-20; GN-26.

**a.n.** Laguna Reservoir            Map: GN-26               Yuma

   Laguna Mountains       Maps: GN-9; GN-26           Yuma
   These mountains are also known as the San Pablo Moun-
   tains.
   Ref.: 181, p. 211.

## LA PAZ

El.: c. 500'                            Loc.: Yuma 1, CD-8.5
Pro.: /la páz/                    Spanish: "peace"
According to one source, the first name for La Paz was
Pot Holes. In January 1862 a party of prospectors led by
Pauline Weaver found gold in the Arroyo de la Tenaja.
The discovery was made on January 12, which is the Feast
of our Lady of Peace, hence the name La Paz. A boom
mining town quickly developed, having at one time over
five thousand residents.

La Paz was made the county seat for Yuma County in
1862, but lost that honor in 1870 when the records were
taken down the Colorado on the steamer *Nina Tilden* to
Arizona City (cf. Yuma). A change in the course of the
Colorado River in 1869 brought commercial disaster to
La Paz, which was left high and dry. By 1872 it was fast
on its way to becoming a ghost town.

P.O. est. January 17, 1865, Charles A. Phillips, p.m. Discont.
March 25, 1875. Wells Fargo Station, 1870.

Ref.: 111, p. 106; Preston Mercer, "Desert Scrapbook," *Yuma
   Daily Sun,* LXXXV (April 12, 1954), 11:2; Figueroa
   ms., APHS; 52, I, 297; 105, p. 333; *Weekly Arizona
   Miner,* April 6, 1872, 2:3; 87, pp. 250-251; P.O. Records.
   Maps: C-1; E-17; GN-11.

**a.n.** La Paz Arroyo              Maps: C-12; GN-5           Yuma
   La Paz Mountain    El.: 1325'. Maps: C-12; GN-5       Yuma

## LA PAZ, CAMP

El.: c. 500'                            Loc.: Yuma 1, CD-8.4
In January 1869 one company of soldiers was detached
for duty at La Paz on the Indian reservation. This may be
the same place which was referred to as Camp Lincoln in
1864. Apparently Camp La Paz was used intermittently,
for the *Weekly Arizona Miner* in 1874 noted that on May
30, Camp Beale Springs (q.v., Mohave) had been abandoned and that La Paz had been recognized as a new military post. It was not the same as Camp Colorado (q.v.).

Ref.: *Weekly Arizona Miner,* January 9, 1869, 1:3; 111, p.
   152; 85, p. 516. Map: E-18.

## LECHUGUILLA DESERT

El.: c. 600'                    Loc.: Yuma 3, H-7.9-11
Pro.: /lečuwgiˆyə/              Spanish: "frill; ruff"
The Spanish name for the century plant or agave is lechuguilla. This name is probably derived from the fact that the spinate slender leaves of a century plant form a ruff at its base. Many century plants exist on this desert. There are many varieties of the plant in Arizona.

Ref.:   Monson; Mercer; Barnes. Maps: C-9; C-10; C-11; GN-24; GN-26.

## LeSAGE

El.: c. 500'                    Loc.: Yuma 4, E-4.7
LeSage was a private development built by a man named Hayter. It consisted of no more than a building and some agricultural development. LeSage went out of existence when it burned c. 1931. The nearby railroad siding was first known as Musina, but residents in the area asked to have its name changed to LeSage.

P.O. est. September 22, 1928. Sylvester H. Jansen, p.m. Discont. October 31, 1931.

Ref.:   Johnson; Barnes; P.O. Records. Map: F-3.

## LIGHTHOUSE ROCK

El.: 250'                       Loc.: Yuma 3, AB-0.8
Dr. John S. Newberry of Ives' expedition in 1857 called this Light-House Rock. It has apparently always served as a navigation aid to white men on the Colorado River. A circular rock pinnacle, the rock blocked the center of the river so that steamers were forced to go one side or the other according to the amount of water in either channel. However, the building of dams has caused the Arizona channel to silt up so that now the Colorado River lies entirely on the California side of Lighthouse Rock.

Ref.:   Blythe Chamber of Commerce "Cruise Bulletin," October 10, 1954; 121, p. 24; 100, p. 49; Mercer. Maps: C-10; GN-18.

## LIGURTA

El.: 230'                       Loc.: Yuma 3, EF-6.1
Pro.: /ligértə/
The origin of this place name is not known. However, it is worth noting that it bears a close resemblance phonetically to lagarto (Spanish: "lizard") and that lizards abound in the area. The more recent name Fossil Point came from the finding here on October 31, 1917, of fossil bones buried on the land bordering the Gila River.

Ref.:   Willson; 141, p. 75. Maps: C-10; C-11; C-12; GN-6; GN-26.

## LINSKEY

El.: 781'                       Loc.: Yuma 1, FG-4.9
This small station on the branch line of the main railroad was named for a track foreman, Pat Linskey, of the Arizona and Chloride Railroad.

Ref.:   APHS Names File; Barnes. Map: GN-12.

## LITTLE HORN MOUNTAINS

El.: c. 3200'                   Loc.: Yuma 2, DE-10-11
The Little Horns are so named because they are smaller than the nearby Big Horn Mountains. Both ranges harbor bighorn mountain sheep.

Ref.:   Barnes; 181, p. 131. Map: GN-11.

## LONE MOUNTAIN

El.: c. 1500'                   Loc.: Yuma 2, EF-8.3
Descriptive.

Ref.:   Barnes. Map: C-12.

a.n. Lone Mountain Well   Loc.: Sec. 17, T. 3 N., R. 11 W.   Yuma
Isolated landmarks often use "lone" for their names. Some instances are given below:

Lone Butte Loc.: Palomas Plain, w. edge of Yuma Co.   Yuma
Lone Cedar Mesa      El.: 4698'. Map: GE-5      Graham
Lone Hill            Map: GJ-13                 Pima
Lone Mountain        Map: GB-13                 Cochise
Lone Mountain        El.: 2500'. Map: GG-11     Maricopa
Lonesome Peak        Loc.: T. 1 N., R. 18 W.    Yuma
Lone Tree                                       Cochise

## LOVE

El.: c. 2000'                   Loc.: Yuma 2, F-5.6
Ernest Love was killed in World War I. His father was a Santa Fe engineer, and after the war the station name, formerly Lockhart, was changed to Love. The reason for the name Lockhart has not been ascertained.

Ref.:   Lenon; Willson; Barnes. Maps: C-12 (Lockhart); C-13 (Love); GN-11.

## LOW MOUNTAINS

El.: c. 2500'                   Loc.: Yuma 2, F-4.2
Descriptive.

Ref.:   None. Map: GN-11.

## MARTINEZ LAKE

El.: c. 200'                    Loc.: Yuma 3, D-2-2.6
Pro.: /martíˆnez/
Gabriel Martinez is a Spanish gentleman seventy-eight years old in 1956, who is still living in Yuma. Martinez ran cattle at this location. His ranch headquarters are now under the waters of the lake, hence its name.

Ref.:   Monson. Map: GN-11.

## McMULLEN VALLEY

El.: c. 2000'                   Loc.: Yuma 2, DEF-5.7-5
James McMullen was a stage driver on the route from Yuma to Ehrenberg. He later turned prospector, spending much of his time in McMullen Valley. Occasionally the name "Grace Valley" is applied to this area, for Grace Salome Pratt, whose husband (H. B. Pratt) tried to start an agricultural colony in the Salome portion of the valley (cf. Salome).

Ref.:   Barnes; Lenon; APHS Names File. Maps: E-20; GN-11.

a.n. McMullen                                    Yuma
Loc.: On the Ehrenberg-Prescott stage route.
This was a stage station run by James McMullen.

## McVAY

El.: c. 1500'          Loc.: Yuma 2, B-6.1

All that remains at McVay today is a loading area, which may be used for loading ores or possibly granite. A man named McVay is reported to have been the first to drill a well for the railroad at this location.

Ref.: Barnes. Maps: C-13; GN-11.

## MESQUITE WELL

El.: 2500'          Loc.: Yuma 2, DE-6.4

Pro.: /meskíyt/

Mesquite Well served as a stage station as early as 1875, being kept by a solitary Mexican with one lone burro for company.

Mesquite is found in dense groves along water courses in Arizona. Its maximum height is from thirty to forty feet and in diameter it usually does not exceed two feet and more often is much less than that.

Mesquite wood has figured largely in pioneer life in Arizona. The tough tree was used for building corrals, bridges, and shelters, and miles of mesquite posts for fences crisscrossed parts of the state. Thousands of trees were consumed as fuel for mine smelters.

Ref.: 158, p. 155; 141, p. 213; 122, pp. 214, 215. Map: None.

Considering its importance as the "pioneer's wood," mesquite naturally occurs often in place names, a few examples of which are given below:

| a.n. Mesquite | Map: B-3 | Pima |

**Mesquite**          Maricopa
Loc.: In 1876 near Hayden's Ferry (Barnes).

**Mesquite Charcos**          Pima
Loc.: North of La Nariz, Sonora, nine miles, near border in Arizona.

The Papago name is Vatjeki ("small waterhole"), because the charco was made by digging it out with a basket.

Ref.: Kirk Bryan Notes.

| **Mesquite Creek** | Loc.: T. 2 N., R. 9 E. | Maricopa |
| **Mesquite Flat** | Map: GD-15 | Maricopa |
| **Mesquite Mountains** | Loc.: T. 16, 17 S., R. 1, 2 E. | Pima |
| **Mesquite** | Loc.: North of Nogales | Santa Cruz |
| **Mesquite Jim Well** | El.: 564'. Map: GN-15 | Yuma |
| **Mesquite Springs** | | Mohave |

Loc.: c. 10 miles n. of Union Pass.
While in pursuit of Mohaves, Col. William Redwood Price and his men stopped here to rest on September 29, 1868.

Ref.: 169, p. 57.

**Mesquite Tank**          Pima
Loc.: S.w. face of highest part of Mesquite Mtns.
The water in this tank is there the year around because the well-concealed tank is in a cave. It is possible for a horse to enter and drink, but the opening is so narrow that the animal must back out.

Ref.: Kirk Bryan Notes.

| **Mesquite Wash** | Map: B-7 | Maricopa |

## MIDDLE WELL

El.: c. 500'          Loc.: Yuma 4, B-1.9

Middle Well lies half way between the railroad and the Kofa Mine.

Middle Well, now dry and abandoned, was originally developed to supply water for the King of Arizona Mine,

but was never used except by Abel Figueroa, who bought the well for his stock when the mine closed.

Ref.: Lenon; Monson; 141, p. 214. Maps: C-13; GN-11.

## MIDWAY

El.: c. 1500'          Loc.: Yuma 2, E-4.5

Midway was on the Arizona and Swansea Railroad. Half way between Bouse and Swansea, the spot was frequently used by prospectors as a camping site.

Ref.: 141, p. 215. Maps: C-11; GN-11.

## MILTON          Loc.: Unknown.

P.O. est. December 20, 1887. Charles J. Taylor, p.m. Discont. May 22, 1891.

Ref.: P.O. Records.

## MING

El.: c. 500'          Loc.: Yuma 3, H-6

Frank Ming was mayor of Yuma for many years (c. 1920). Since Ming Spur does not appear on maps until GLO 1933, it is probable that it was named for him rather than for Dan Ming, a cattleman who lived in Graham County in the 1880's, but never in Yuma County.

Ref.: Kline; Lenon. Maps: C-13; GN-11; GN-24.

## MISSION CAMP

El.: c. 500'          Loc.: Yuma 3, GH-6

John Killbride built the stage station at Mission Camp. In 1860, when forty-six years old, he was a blacksmith at the Ajo Copper Mine. He died in 1871.

One source states that the name for Mission Camp came from the fact that the station was built at the site of an ancient mission ruin. Barnes says that according to Charles Debrille Poston, the U.S. Boundary Commission camped at this place and their "mission" gave the place its name. However, Mission Camp does not appear on maps prior to 1869.

Killbride sold his interest in the station to Peter Reed in December 1870. On December 24, 1870, three renegade Mexicans murdered James Lytle (a stage driver), Thomas Oliver (the cook), and "Charles" Reed, the station manager. Another paper reported that Mrs. Reed was also murdered. The murderers took everything of value when they left.

Ref.: Fr. Figueroa, Letter of March 11, 1936, in APHS Files; *Weekly Arizona Miner*, January 7, 1871, 2:1; Barnes; John Killbride File, APHS. Maps: A-8; C-1; C-2; E-18; E-20.

## MOHAWK

El.: 545'          Loc.: Yuma 4, C-5.5

In 1869 Mohawk was not the same place as Mission Camp. The latter is thirty miles west northwest of Mohawk Station. The original stage station was also not the same as the Mohawk on GLO 1903 (twenty-two miles to the west-southwest of Chrystoval).

The original Mohawk Station was so named by men who created the Butterfield Overland stage route. Many came from New York State and brought place names from there to Arizona. As a stage station, Mohawk vanished. The name came to be applied to the valley in which the stage station was first located. Long before this time, the name had first been applied to Mohawk Gap lying between Texas Hill on the east and Antelope Hill on the west, now known as Mohawk Pass. This same place shows as Mohawk on Smith Map 1879, the first map to use the name Mohawk Range for the mountains bordering the western side of the valley. These mountains were known in the early days as the Big Horn Mountains. The highest point in this range was called Mohawk Mountain or Mohawk Peak.

In the 1880's the present Mohawk was established and the population was sufficient to require a post office. In 1956 Mohawk consisted of a section station on the railroad, a service station, a motel and a single residence. According to post office records, Chrystoval was changed to Mohawk as of September 30, 1905 (cf. Stoval).

P.O. est. June 25, 1890. George W. Norton, p.m. Wells Fargo Station (sometimes called Summit) 1903.

Ref.: 32, II, 184; 181, p. 148; APHS Names File; John Kill-bride File, APHS; P.O. Records. Maps: C-1; C-4; C-10; GN-13; GN-8; GN-15.

## MUGGINS MOUNTAINS

El.: 1500′  Loc.: Yuma 3, F-4-5

The Muggins Mountains are said to have been named for a burro owned by an early-day prospector.

Ref.: Lenon; 136, p. 218. Maps: GN-6; GN-24; GN-26.

a.n. Coronation Peak (q.v.)  Yuma
Loc.: Highest point in Muggins Mts.

Muggins Tank  Loc.: In Muggins Mountains  Yuma
Ref.: 141, p. 215.

## NEW WATER

El.: c. 1500′  Loc.: Yuma 1, E-9.5

New Water Pass is now called Livingston Pass by the Fish and Wildlife Service. The name Livingston comes from the fact that a man by that name is currently living in New Water Pass.

The New Water Pass took its name from the New Water Well (R. 15 W., T. 2 N., approximately Sec. 19). The well is a very old one and probably got its name from the fact that it was developed at the time when new mines were being found in that section of Yuma County.

Ref.: Monson. Maps: A-7; C-3.

a.n. New Water Mountains  Yuma
New Water Pass  Yuma
Maps: C-6 through C-9; C-11; C-12

## NINE MILE STATION

El.: c. 500′  Loc.: Yuma 3, D-6

This station was nine miles east of Yuma on the road which dipped south and thence to Tucson.

Ref.: 87, p. xxx (Nine-mile Water). Maps: E-18; E-20.

## NORTON

El.: 312′  Loc.: Yuma 4, B-4.6

The late appearance of Norton on maps suggests that it was named for its second postmaster, Charles G. Norton. Nor-

ton was an engineer who was responsible for the first irrigation canal at Wellton.

Norton Tank first appears on maps in 1912, and the community of Norton in 1921 when it is shown a mile and a half south of the tank location, on the railroad tracks. Immediately opposite it across the tracks is the name Growler, which may indicate that Growler and Norton were in reality the same place. The community has now disappeared except for a few crumbling adobe walls.

P.O. est. May 1, 1914. Robert L. Wallace, p.m. Discont. May 20, 1925.

Ref.: Mercer; P.O. Records. Maps: C-11 through C-14; GN-15.

## NORTON'S LANDING

El.: c. 400′  Loc.: Yuma 3, B-1

Norton's Landing was a steamer landing on the Colorado River where supplies for the Red Cloud Mine were unloaded and where freight teams from Yuma stopped on their travels. George W. Norton (b. Indiana, August 9, 1843) came to Arizona in 1877 with the railroad construction crews, in charge of the building of the first bridge across the Colorado. Having finished that assignment, he turned mining man, owning the Pacific and the Silent mines. He still later entered politics and took up farming, following those activities with real estate interests in Yuma in 1912.

Norton's Landing has been gone for years, but the Red Cloud Mine is still being worked.

P.O. est. June 4, 1883. Jacob D. Dettlebach, p.m. Discont. March 13, 1894.

Ref.: 112, III; Mercer; Willson; APHS Names File; Blythe Chamber of Commerce "Cruise Bulletin," October 10, 1954; 181, p. 52; P.O. Records. Maps: GN-18; GN-11.

## NOTTBUSCH BUTTE

El.: c. 1000′  Loc.: Yuma 2, F-12

J. Fred Nottbusch owned the small community of Palomas, which was located at this butte. He had a hotel building and a store and kept bees. The town was sold about 1940, and little by little, pilferers carted the entire place away.

Nottbusch owned about three hundred acres of land in this area. He also owned the Nottbusch or Silver Prince Mine, from which considerable ore was taken in 1912.

Ref.: Lenon; Mercer; 181, p. 128. Map: GN-11.

a.n. Nottbusch Valley  Yuma
Loc.: Between Cemetery Ridge and Clanton Hills.

Nottbusch Peak  Loc.: Same as Palomas Peak  Yuma

## OCOTILLO

El.: c. 1000′  Loc.: Yuma 2, B-11
West side of Kofa Mountains.

Pro.: /okətíyo/  Spanish: "coach whip"

The mining camp is now gone, although some of the old buildings still remained in 1956. The place took its name from the presence of ocotillo which, however, is not found more abundantly here than elsewhere in the area.

Ref.: Mercer. Map: None.

## OLIVE CITY

El.: c. 500'                                   Loc.: Yuma 1, C-9
Originally this location near the La Paz Ferry was called
Olivia and was so named, according to one reference, by
Myron Angel, who was the founder of the town and who
wished to honor Olive Oatman (*See* Oatman Flat, Maricopa). Olive City was perhaps better known by the name
Bradshaw's Ferry, which was operated by William D. Bradshaw and his brother Isaac. Travelers who crossed the Colorado at this place found that Olive City was merely one
house about twelve by ten feet, which was covered with brush
and sided with willow poles. Considering its flimsy construction, it is no wonder that all signs of this single building
have long since disappeared. The ferry crossing was typical
of many along the lower Colorado River.

Ref.: *Quarterly of California Historical Society,* XII, (March,
1933), 16; Preston Mercer, "Desert Scrapbook," *Yuma
Daily Sun,* LXII (October 30, 1954), II:2:3; 52, IV, 34.
Map: E-20.

## O'NEILL PASS

El.: c. 500'                                   Loc.: Yuma 4, F-12.8
Dave O'Neill was an old prospector who c. 1916 died of
exposure and over-exertion in the pass in which he is buried
and which bears his name. His burros walked to Papago
Well after his death, which led the people living there to
investigate and find his body.

Ref.:   Monson; Kirk Bryan Notes; 34, p. 419. Map: GN-11.

**a.n. O'Neill Hills**   Loc.: W. of Papago Well 4 miles   Yuma

## PACIFIC CITY

El.: c. 500'                                   Loc.: Yuma 3, BC-1. Near Silent.
Pacific City was a stage stop on the Yuma-Ehrenberg run
in the 1880's. It was probably named for the Pacific Mine
nearby.

P.O. est. November 30, 1880. Paul Billeck, p.m. Discont. December 20, 1880.

Ref.:   Preston Mercer, "Desert Scrapbook," *Yuma Daily Sun,*
LXXII (October 30, 1954), I:3:2; P.O. Records. Map:
None.

## PALM CANYON

El.: 2500'                                   Loc.: Yuma 1, G-12
Descriptive. This is one of the few places in Arizona where
native palm trees are found. The palms are of the species
*Washingtonia arizonica.* Their appearance in thirty-foot wide
Palm Canyon against the red-rock walls is exceedingly lovely.
The old name was Fish Tail Canyon, because of a fishtail
fork at the head of the canyon. Old Palm Canyon is south
and east of the present Palm Canyon and has palms at its
bottom. Palms are also found in Four Palms Canyon on the
north side of Signal Peak.

Ref.:   Monson; 4, p. 469; 15, p. 60. Map: GN-11.

## PALOMAS

El.: c. 600'                                   Loc.: Yuma 4, E-3.6
Pro.: /palómas/                               Spanish: "doves"
Flocks of white-wing doves are always found here during
the summer months. Palomas was first known as Doanville,
for John Doan, a pioneer in the district. The community

is now gone and the entire area is under cultivation.

P.O. est. as Doanville, November 22, 1889. Frank S. Schultz,
p.m. Name changed to Palomas, April 18, 1891. Discont.
August 31, 1938.

Ref.:   P.O. Records; Barnes; 141, p. 216; Johnson. Map: GN-2.

**a.n. Palomas Mountains**   El.: 1900'. Map: GN-30   Yuma
**Palomas Plain**   Maps: GG-5; GN-7   Yuma

## PARKER

El.: 413'                                   Loc.: Yuma 1, E-3
When the Colorado River Agency was established (cf.
Colorado River Reservation) it was necessary to have a
post office for the area. The name "Parker" was selected
to honor Gen. Eli Parker, then Commissioner of Indian
Affairs. Parker is on GLO 1879.

When the railroad came through in 1905, the location of
Parker was moved four miles up river to the new railroad
crossing. It is a curious fact that the locating engineer
was Earl H. Parker, so that the new location had a double
origin for its name.

P.O. est. January 6, 1871. John H. Salt, p.m. This P.O. probably operated in connection with the Indian Agency. Wells
Fargo Station, 1908.

Ref.:   169, p. 312; P.O. Records; *Weekly Arizona Miner,* April
29, 1871, 1:3; *Arizona Sentinel,* November 8, 1873, 3:4;
98, p. 294. Maps: C-4; GN-16.

**a.n. Parker Dam**   Maps: GN-16; GH-11   Yuma
Parker Dam is a desilting basin for the Colorado River
aqueduct and also helps with flood control. Construction
was begun on July 29, 1937, and finished on September 1,
1938. Only some eighty-five feet of the dam show above
the surface, but workmen dug down two hundred thirty-five
feet in order to place the concrete foundation. Waters
diverted from the dam supply many communities in southern California.

Ref.:   "Parker Dam and Power Plant," U. S. Dept. of Interior,
Bureau of Reclamation, Boulder City, Nevada. January
1, 1954.

## PATIO

El.: c. 290'                                   Loc.: Yuma 3, B-5.5
Pro.: /pátio/
The railroad yard at 4th Street and Madison Avenue in
Yuma was given the Spanish name "Patio," the latter being
considered more euphonious than "yard." Engineers on
the railroad from Gila to Yuma always signed their train
books, "Arrived Patio such-and-such an hour," thus never
actually officially arriving in Yuma itself.

Ref.:   Lenon. Map: None.

## PEDRICKS

El.: c. 140'                                   Loc.: Yuma 3, A-8
The origin of this name has not yet been learned.
On the outline map prepared by Captain Overman of "A
Route for Cattle Drovers, etc." this place shows on the
Sonora border and is called Patricks. It appears as Pedricks
later, but disappears from all maps after 1879. "Old Man"
Pedricks supplied wood for Colorado River steamers. He
grossed about $5,000 a year.

**v.n. Pedricks**
      **Pedrichs**
      **Padricks**
Maps:   C-1; E-17; E-18; E-20.

## PEMBROKE

El.: c. 500'                     Loc.: Yuma 4, B-5.6
The origin of this name has not been learned. A railroad well existed at this place.

Ref.: 141, p. 78. Maps: GN-11; GN-13.

## PINACATE VALLEY

El.: c. 200'                     Loc.: Yuma 4, EF-12
Pro.: /pinəkáte/     Spanish: corruption of Aztec *pinacatl,*
                                  "small ground beetle"
This valley, most of which lies in Mexico, is filled with lava flow. Beetles in large numbers are found in the valley, hence its name. Known to scientists as *Eleodes ornatus,* the beetle responds by standing on its head when it is disturbed.

Ref.: 34, p. 420; Barnes. Map: GN-11.

## PINTO TANK

El.: 1250'                     Loc.: Yuma 4, E-10.6
Pro.: /pínto/
Jim Chappo, who ran cattle in the Pinto Mountains prior to 1920, always referred to this tank as Pinto Tank. However, others have called it Heart Tank because it is a pothole (seven feet deep by ten long) which has a heart-like appearance when filled with water to a certain level.

As is often the case with natural water holes, this tank was a death trap for animals which fell in while attempting to drink when the water level was low. In 1940 the Fish and Wildlife Service put in a dam to deepen the tank and also blasted out a ramp which animals could use as an exit in case they tumbled in.

Ref.: 181, p. 158; Mercer; Monson. Map: C-12 (Heart Tank).

## PLANET

El.: c. 2500'                     Loc.: Yuma 2, A-1
The Planet Mine, one of the first copper mines to be worked to any extent by Americans in Arizona, was discovered in April 1864 by Richard Ryland. The small community which sprang up about the mine took the name of Planet. A way station for travelers soon developed which lasted for many years.

P.O. est. March 28, 1902. Edward H. Webb, p.m. Discont. March 31, 1921.

Ref.: 87, p. 157; APHS Files; P.O. Records; *Arizona Sentinel,* June 15, 1878, 2:2. Map: GN-11.

**a.n. Planet Peak**     Loc.: T. 10 N., R. 17 W.     Yuma

## PLAYAS, LAS

El.: c. 1000'                     Loc.: Yuma 4, EF-12.7
Pro.: /las pláyəs/          Spanish: "flat area"
Reporting on the boundary survey work in 1854, Lt. N. Michler noted a low mesquite flat which he called Las Playas, saying that it contained water holes, filled during the rainy season. The bed of a temporary lake forms a good example of a *playa* or flat area which is occasionally flooded.

Ref.: 50, I, 115; 34, p. 106. Maps: C-12; E-2; E-11; E-12.

## PLOMOSA

El.: c. 1500'                     Loc.: Yuma 1, F-9.2
Pro.: /plomówsə/          Spanish: "lead-colored"
Mining in the Plomosa District began as early as 1862 with a great deal of placer gold being found during the early days. The name is descriptive (see *a.n.* below).

Ref.: 76, p. 75. Map: GN-11.

**a.n. Plomosa Mountains**     Map: GN-12     Yuma
This range has many lead-bearing mines.

## POLARIS

El.: c. 1500'                     Loc.: Yuma 2, A-12
The post office at Polaris was so named because it was located at the North Star Mine, said to have been discovered by reference to the North Star in 1909.

P.O. est. June 17, 1909. William R. Wardner, p.m. Discont. July 31, 1914.

Ref.: Monson; Lenon; Barnes; P.O. Records. Maps: A-7; C-11.

**a.n. Polaris Mountain**     Yuma
Loc.: The North Star Mine is at the foot of this mountain.

## POLHAMUS     Loc.: Not known. Possibly Mohave County.

Capt. Tom M. Polhamus (b. April 7, 1828; d. January 16, 1922) was a Colorado River steamboat captain. According to his letterhead, he stored goods awaiting shipment at the landing known as "Polhamus," probably his own home, and accepted shipments for overland freighting at Ehrenberg and also at Hardyville in Mohave County.

Ref.: *Arizona Sentinel,* May 9, 1891, 1:2; Barnes. Map: None.

## POSA PLAIN, LA

El.: c. 500'                     Loc.: Yuma 1, F-5.5-7.2
Pro.: /la pózə/          Spanish: *pozo:* "well"
The name for this plain probably may be attributed to the presence of two wells called Los Posos which appear in this valley on GLO 1867, due east of La Paz. There are no other wells of importance in this valley. The name shifted back and forth through the years, applying to the wells and then again to the valley and vice versa. Not until GLO 1892 do both names show, and then as Posas Valley and Los Poses.

**v.n. Deep Well**
Los Poses is twelve hundred feet deep.

Ref.: Monson; Willson. Maps: See entry. Also: E-20 (Posas Valley); GN-14; GN-11; GN-23.

## POSTON

El.: c. 500'                     Loc.: Yuma 1, D-4.4
Pro.: /pówstən/
Poston was named for Charles Debrille Poston (cf. Poston Butte, Pinal) first Superintendent for Indian Affairs in Arizona and directly responsible for the establishment in 1865 of the Colorado River Reservation *(q.v.)* on which this place is located.

During World War II, Poston was created as a relocation camp for twenty thousand Japanese. Today it is one small building which is used as a post office for residents of the area.

P.O. est. June 14, 1949. Mrs. Agnes Savilla, p.m.

Ref.: Savilla; P.O. Records. Map: F-12.

## POZOS, LOS

El.: c. 500'                                Loc.: Yuma 1, F-8.5
Pro.: /los pózos/        Spanish: "water pockets; wells"
A Yuma rancheria existed at this place in 1776. The word
*pozos* or *posos* is found frequently on early maps where
waterholes existed. These were of extreme importance to
travelers across the desert.

Ref.:   88, II, 288. Maps: C-1; E-20.

**a.n. Posas Valley**                                        Yuma
**v.n. Posas Plain**

## QUARTZ KING

El.: 500'                                     Loc.: Yuma 1, F-3
Quartz King was a mining camp.

P.O. est. October 24, 1907. Willard W. McCune, p.m. Discont.
June 15, 1910.

Ref.:   Barnes; P.O. Records. Maps: C-10 (Quartzking); GN-
        11.

## QUARTZSITE

El.: 879'                                   Loc.: Yuma 1, F-8.8
The town of Quartzsite is located on the site of old Fort
Tyson, a privately owned fort built in 1856 by Charles
Tyson for protection against Indians. Because of the water
which existed at this place, Tyson's Wells soon became
a stage station on the road from Ehrenberg to Prescott.
In 1875 Martha Summerhayes described this place as being
the most melancholy and uninviting that she had seen, saying that it "reeks of everything unclean, morally and phy-
sically . . ."

Although Hinton lists Tyson's as being the same place as
Los Posos (*q.v.*), maps show that the two were separate,
Los Posos lying about four miles to the east of Tyson's.
Gradually as the stage lines disappeared, Tyson's Wells
was abandoned.

In 1897 the development of mining in the area resulted in
a small boom. It was reported that Tyson's Wells had
three stores, two saloons, and a short-lived post office.

Apparently when it became necessary to re-open the post
office because of renewed mining activity, a new name had
to be found since the post office did not permit offices to
re-open under formerly used names. Therefore, George
Ingersoll suggested the name Quartzite, since quartzite is
actually found in the vicinity, but quartz is not. However,
the post office in error apparently added an *s* to the name.
The resulting "Quartzsite" erroneously implies that quartz
is found locally. Actually Quartzsite is approximately nine
miles east of the old Tyson's Wells which lay nineteen
miles from Ehrenberg. Therefore a different name was
doubly suitable.

Travelers through Quartzsite today may visit the grave of
Hadji Ali, who was a camel driver for Lt. Edward Fitzgerald Beale on his trip across Arizona. Hadji Ali (b.
Syria c. 1829; d. December 16, 1902) who was known as
Philip Tedro in later years, came to Arizona as a camel
driver in 1856. When camels were abandoned for use of
transportation of supplies, Tedro kept several animals and
used them to haul freight in southern Arizona. He was
then living in Arizona City. In 1868 he turned the animals
loose near Gila Bend. For many years it was reported that
camels were seen in the mountains and other parts of southwestern Arizona. The simple headboard for his grave was
replaced by the present stone monument and plaque in
1934. His name has been anglicized to "Hi Jolly."

P.O. est. as Tyson's, June 6, 1893. Michael Welz, p.m. Discont.
September 21, 1895. P.O. est. September 19, 1896. George U.
Ingersoll, p.m.

Ref.:   4, p. 361; 158, p. 157; *Arizona Sentinel,* June 19, 1897,
        2:1; 87, p. xxxvii; 151, p. 628; Preston Mercer "Desert
        Scrapbook," *Yuma Daily Sun,* LVI, LV (October 7,
        1953), II:2:4; (October 5, 1953), 10:2; Arizona Bu-
        reau of Mines; P.O. Records. Maps: C-8 (Tyson); C-9
        (Quartzite); GN-15.

**a.n. Tyson Wash**        Maps: GN-5; GN-23                     Yuma

## RADIUM HOT SPRINGS

El.: c. 240'                                Loc.: Yuma 3, H-5.1
Descriptive.
Dr. C. A. Eaton of Yuma began developing the thermal
springs at this place in 1930 as a health resort. It is not
now commercially active.

Ref.:   181, p. 220. Maps: GN-24; GN-26.

## RANEGRAS PLAIN

El.: c. 1500'                              Loc.: Yuma 2, BE-7-10
The reason for the name has not yet been discovered. The
name for this area first appears on the military map for
1875 as Hanegras Plain. It then disappears from maps
until Smith 1879, after which it is off again until GLO
1887 on which it appears as Ranegras. The change may
well have been a draftsman's error in transcribing the *H*
and making it into an *R*. Nevertheless, "Ranegras" has
appeared on all GLO maps since 1892.

Ref.:   Maps examined. Map: A-7. See entry above.

## RAVEN BUTTE

El.: c. 1000'                                 Loc.: Yuma 3, G-9
Hornaday said that very tame and trusting ravens existed
here in abundance.

Ref.:   Barnes; 181, p. 178. Map: GN-11.

## RHODES RANCH

El.: c. 450'                                 Loc.: Yuma 3, CD-9
It is probable that the correct spelling of William Rhodes'
name is Rodes or Roods. Rhodes had a ranch just above
the Barriers, a rapid in the Colorado River and the name
is "Rhodes" on maps showing the location. In a newspaper
article the name is spelled William B. Roods.

When Rhodes first came to Arizona from Kentucky in
1855, he had a cattle ranch in southern Arizona (cf.
Rhodes Ranch, Santa Cruz). He left the valley because
of trouble with Indians and established a ranch on the
Colorado River. During a rising flood on April 29, 1870,
Rhodes drowned while attempting to cross the Colorado
with a companion named Poindexter, who also drowned.
Their boat struck a snag and capsized.

Rhodes' Ranch was still in fairly good condition in 1899, but it has since been destroyed by treasure seekers as a result of rumors of treasure hidden somewhere either in or near the old adobe house. This is today the location of Cibola (*q.v.*).

Ref.: Barnes; *Arizona Miner*, May 7, 1870, 2:4; Blythe Chamber of Commerce "Cruise Bulletin," October 10, 1954; Lenon. Maps: C-1 (Rodes); C-3; C-4; E-18; E-20.

## ROLL

El.: c. 600′          Loc.: Yuma 4, A-4.8
John H. Roll homesteaded in this farming section. Currently, Roll is a growing community with an insecticide and fertilizer plant, a school, store, and other facilities.

P.O. est. November 3, 1926. John H. Roll, p.m.

Ref.: Barnes; Mercer; P.O. Records. Maps: GN-11; GN-15.

a.n. Roll Valley                          Yuma
This is the local name for the Mohawk Valley.

Ref.: Mercer.

## ROUND KNOB

El.: c. 2500′          Loc.: Yuma 4, B-1
Descriptive.

Ref.: Barnes. Map: C-12.
The descriptive use of the word "round" occurs in many place names. Examples are given below:

a.n. Round Mountain          Map: B-6          Coconino
Round Mountain Spring          Map: B-6          Coconino
Round Mountain          Loc.: T. 10 S., R. 32 E.          Greenlee
Roundtop          El.: 6000′. Maps: GI-11; C-12          Navajo

## SALOME

El.: c. 1500′          Loc.: Yuma 2, D-6.2
Pro.: /səlówmiˆ/
The town of Salome was established in late 1904 by Charles H. Pratt. Pratt was speculating on where the railroad would lay its tracks, and missed it by a mile so that the community had to be moved to its present location. In the venture with Pratt were Earnest and Dick Wick Hall, the latter a widely known wit. Dick Wick Hall was responsible for the story that the town was named because Mrs. Grace Salome Pratt, on taking off her shoes, found the sand burned her feet, hence the slogan, "Salome where she danced."

P.O. est. April 14, 1905. Etta Von Stauffer, p.m. Wells Fargo Station, 1906.

Ref.: *Prescott Journal Miner*, August 21, 1906, 5:4; *Arizona Sentinel*, August 29, 1906, 3:3; *Phoenix Enterprise*, January 12, 1905, 3:3; P.O. Records. Maps: C-10; C-11; GN-11.

a.n. Salome Peak          Loc.: T. 6 N., R. 14 W.          Yuma

## SAN LUIS

El.: 136′          Loc.: Yuma 3, GH-6
Pro.: /san luwíys/          Spanish: "Saint Louis"
The reason for this name has not yet been ascertained. San Luis is a thriving small community lying on both sides of the border.

Ref.: None. Maps: C-13; GN-11.

## S. H. MOUNTAINS

El.: 4000′          Loc.: Yuma 1, G-11-14; Yuma 2, 11-13
The name S. H. Mountains is preferred by local residents, although recent maps have tended to use the name Kofa for this short range. There are at least three stories concerning the possible origin of the name S. H. Mountains. The first, which dates back further than the other two, is that told by an Arizona pioneer, Charles B. Genung. The story is that when the California Column came into Arizona via Ehrenberg, it passed to the north of these mountains and the soldiers noticed a string of large peaks, each with a small one located behind and between it and the next peak. The soldiers were quick to notice the resemblance to outhouses and promptly referred to the mountains as the S. H. Mountains. As more women moved into the territory and asked about what the letters S. H. meant, it became necessary for the oldtimers, who were delicate about such things, to invent an answer. Therefore they told the women that the name was Short Horn. At the turn of the century the S. H. Mountains were called the Short Horn Mountains. The second story merely changes the California Column to prospectors in the vicinity, the explanation of the name remaining the same.

The third story is that given by Darton, who said that the name came from Stone House. Although no documentary evidence has been uncovered to substantiate this, it is worth noting that on GLO 1912 there is a Stone Cabin Gap Wash lying north of Palomas and terminating apparently in the S. H. Mountains. The only Stone Cabin found, however, is on GLO 1921, and this place is sixteen miles west of the S. H. Mountains (*See* Stone Cabin.)

Ref.: State Library Files; 181, p. 106; 4, p. 470. Maps: C-12; GN-11.

## SHEEP MOUNTAIN

El.: c. 2000′          Loc.: Yuma 3, F-7.3
Bighorn mountain sheep were formerly here.

Ref.: Barnes. Map: GN-11.

## SIERRA PINTA

El.: 2700′          Loc.: Yuma 4, DF-10-11
Pro.: /siyéra píˆntə/          Spanish: "painted mountains"
The gneisses at the southern end of this range are blackish, while the northern end is grayish-white granite. The contrast gives the mountains a painted look.

Ref.: Mercer; 181, pp. 157-158. Maps: C-10; C-11.

## SILENT

El.: c. 500′          Loc.: Yuma 3, BC-1
Charles Silent was an Associate Justice of the Territorial Supreme Court in 1880.

The town of Silent was named for the Silent Mining Claim in the Silver Mining District. A small smelter erected at Silent in 1880 operated intermittently for about three years. The Silver Mining District was not active until 1879 at which time George Sills, Neils Johnson, George W. Norton, and Gus Crawford relocated many of the claims which had been abandoned, and organized this district.

P.O. est. November 8, 1880. Charles T. Norton, p.m. Discont. March 13, 1884.

Ref.:  Willson; 181, p. 52; P.O. Records. Maps: C-5 through C-8.

### SMITH PEAK

El.: 4957'                              Loc.: Yuma 2, F-3
Pete Smith had a claim on the peak which bears his name.

**v.n. Pete Smith Peak**

Ref.:  Barnes. Maps: C-12; GN-11.

### SOCORRO PEAK

El.: 5681'                              Loc.: Yuma 2, F-6.8
Pro.: /səkóro/            Spanish: "succor; help"
In the 1880's, the Socorro Mine was located on this mountain by people from Socorro, New Mexico. The peak is the highest in the Harquahala Mountains.

Ref.:  Barnes. Maps: C-12; C-13; GN-11.

### SOMERTON

El.: 101'                               Loc.: Yuma 3, B-7
In 1898 residents in the agricultural area south of Yuma met to discuss founding a town to provide facilities for the increasing number of residents. A site on the Algodones Land Grant was selected and the place was named Somerton at the suggestion of Capt. A. D. Yocum, who reportedly named it for his native town.

P.O. est. December 23, 1898. Minnie E. Case, p.m.

Ref.:  *Yuma Sun*, September 30, 1898, 5:1; *Arizona Sentinel*, January 24, 1900, 3:3; P.O. Records. Maps: C-9; GN-11; GN-26.

### STONE CABIN

El.: c. 600'                            Loc.: Yuma 1, F-13
Now in ruins, Stone Cabin was apparently built to provide a way station for travelers on the old Dome-Quartzsite Road.

Ref.:  Lenon; 181, p. 97. Maps: C-12; GN-11.

### STOVAL

El.: 776'                               Loc.: Yuma 4, D-5
Pro.: /stowvál/
In order to trace the many changes in name which this location has undergone, a fairly close analysis of maps must be given.

The first name appears as Grinnel Station, south of the Gila River, on GLO 1869. The station was so named for Henry Grinnel, its first keeper, who worked for the Butterfield Overland Stage. On this same map is Texas Hill Camp. Grinnel is so close to Maricopa County that subsequent maps reveal it may actually have been in Maricopa rather than in Yuma. However, by 1875 Grinnel Station had ceased to exist, and in its place is Stanwix (*q.v.*, Maricopa), while Texas Hill Camp is shown southwest of Teamsters Camp. Texas Hill proved to be a durable name, for on all subsequent maps studied (until GLO 1892) Stanwix is replaced by Texas Hill. In 1892 Texas Hill has

disappeared and in its place is the name Chrystoval, which in turn yields to Stoval on GLO 1909.

As to why the place names shifted, the following may be the explanation. Texas Hill was a stage station, so named because a party of Texas emigrants was said to have been killed at the hill. Texans are also known to have had cattle here in the early days. By 1888 the place rated a post office, called Chrystoval.

The change to Chrystoval may have occurred as follows: The first postmaster of Chrystoval was Oscar F. Thornton, who started a farmers' colony here c. 1882. The land was so fertile that Thornton called the farming section Christvale, a name which the railroad was slow to accept as a substitute for Texas Hill Station. When the railroad finally agreed to a change in name, it accepted Chrystoval, which c. 1911 was shortened to Stoval to facilitate telegraphing. A newspaper article relates that Crystoval in 1899 was a new settlement which was begun in November 1888 by twenty-five families from St. Louis on four thousand acres of land. The article mentions that there were three preachers and not one saloon in the community.

P.O. est. as Chrystoval, September 25, 1888. Oscar F. Thornton, p.m. Name changed to Stoval, May 26, 1913. Discont. March 31, 1916. Wells Fargo Station, called Texas Hill, 1888.

Ref.:  Barnes; Mercer; P.O. Records; 32, II, 183; 162, p. 17; 37, pp. 131-32, 135; *Phoenix Herald*, October 18, 1888, I:3 (APHS); Theobald; *Arizona Daily Star*, April 20, 1889, 4:2. Maps: A-4; C-1; C-7; C-10; E-18; GN-30.

**a.n. San Cristobal Valley**                                    Yuma
    Maps: GN-1; GN-2; GN-8; GN-30.
    Prior to its appearance on GLO 1933, this valley was considered a n.w. extension of Mohawk Valley.

Ref.:  141, p. 206.

### SWANSEA

El.: 2000'                              Loc.: Yuma 2, B-1.5
Prior to the establishing of the smelting town of Swansea, ores were shipped from northern Yuma County and southern Mohave County as far as Swansea, Wales, for smelting. Possibly miners wanted to continue shipping their ores to "Swansea," and so named this community. When it was first begun, the place was called Signal, but soon changed to Swansea.

P.O. est. March 25, 1909. Stella Siprell, p.m. Discont. June 28, 1924.

Ref.:  Lenon; 141, p. 223; *Arizona Daily Star*, January 15, 1909, 4:4. Maps: C-10 through C-14; GN-11.

### TACNA

El.: 340'                               Loc.: Yuma 4, A-6
Pro.: /tǽknə/
Tacna is what may be termed a "floating" place name which has been in and out of existence and which has shifted position somewhat on the maps. The first name for this location in 1859 was Antelope Hill (*q.v.*), a stage station. With the coming of the railroad, the name Tacna was applied to a post office here, but it soon went out of existence, and the place was apparently not inhabited by white men.

In the early 1920's Max B. Noah arrived from Texas and set up business under a tree, with a barrel of gasoline and a hand pump. Noah was noted for his tall stories, and apparently it was he who began circulating a story that in the seventeenth century a Greek priest named Tachnapolis came from California to Arizona and spent his last days with the Indians who shortened his name to Tachna or Tacna. Efforts to substantiate this legend have all so far led to a single source—Max B. Noah. Noah picked up the name Tacna from the old railroad siding, and used the name when he applied for a post office at the community which he was busily establishing. He did so well with community building that he was able to sell a complete town, at public auction in 1941. His restaurant, Noah's Ark, was known to thousands of travelers.

Another restaurant was started four miles east of Tacna by Joe E. Ralph (d. c. 1934), who called his place Ralph's Mill. After Tacna town had been sold, the post office was moved to Ralph's Mill. Today a road sign at this point reads "Ralph's Mill-Tacna P.O." The name on the old railroad siding was also relocated at Ralph's Mill, and replaced by Noah at the older location.

P.O. est. as Tacna, January 9, 1888. Edwin Mayes, p.m. Discont. July 22, 1898. Re-est. June 4, 1927. Max B. Noah, p.m.
Ref.: Kelland; P.O. Records. Maps: GN-11; GN-24.

## TANK MOUNTAINS

El.: 3200'                     Loc.: Yuma 4, DE-1-2
Several natural water tanks exist in these mountains, hence the name.

| v.n. Frenchman Mountains | (N.w. half of range) |
| Puzzles Mountains | (e. half of range) |

Ref.: 181, p. 123. Map: C-12.
a.n. White Tanks     Maps: C-10; C-11                     Yuma

## TEAMSTER'S CAMP

El.: c. 500'                     Loc.: Yuma 4, E-3.7
Apparently Teamster's Camp was established fairly late as a stage station. Although the derivation of its name is not known, it is worth speculating on the fact that the turn-off to the old road to the Ajo district lay about four miles west, and perhaps teamsters of freight wagon trains used this as a stopping place.
Ref.: 87, p. xx. Maps: C-2; C-4; E-18; E-20.

## TINAJAS ALTAS

El.: c. 1500'                     Loc.: Yuma 2, H-10
Pro.: /tənéyhasáltəs/     Spanish: tinajas, "water pools"; altas, "high"
These tanks were visited by Fr. Kino in 1698 and called Agua Escondida ("Hidden Water") because of their location among the rocks. In 1702 Kino again visited them, and also tanks in the Gila Mountains where he was stopped by a cloudburst. He said that the latter tanks looked as though they had been made by skilled hands. He named these tanks Aguaje de los Alquives (aguaje, "rapid current of spring water"; alquives, meaning not known).

Jacobo Sedelmayr may have visited Tinajas Altas on No-

vember 23, 1750, for his description applies: a "spot in which there were three tanks of high elevation." The next documented reference is that made by Lt. N. Michler in 1854, who wrote that Mexicans called the tanks "Tinejas Altas . . . natural wells formed in the gulleys, arroyos on the sides of the mountains, by dams composed of fragments of rocks and sand washed down by heavy rains . . . there are eight of these tinejas, one above the other, the highest two extremely difficult to reach . . ." The tanks were much used by emigrants on the Camino del Diablo. The name used by Americans today is Dripping Springs.

| v.n. Tinechas | Map: C-5 |
| La Tinaoca | Kino Map, 1701 |
| Tinajualto | Maps: C-6; C-7; C-8 |
| Tinejas Altos | Map: C-9 |
| Tinejas de Candelaria | Anza & Font, 1776 |

Ref.: 145, p. 68; 51, p. 114; 4, p. 389; 20, pp. 412, 413; 181, pp. 177-178; 88, II, 754; 34, p. 414; 19, pp. 253, 254 (Note). Map: E-2. Also see variant names above.
a.n. Tinajas Altas Mountains                     Yuma
El.: 2400'. Maps: C-12; GN-26.
The route from Wellton south to Tinajas Altas Mountains is known as Smugglers' Trail because it was used by liquor smugglers during prohibition days. The pass which separates the Tinajas Altas Mountains from the Gila Mountains is called Cipriano Pass, named for Cipriano Ortega, who had a well in the area. Until 1921 these mountains show as part of the Lechuguilla Mts.
Ref.: 34, p. 426; Kirk Bryan Notes.

## TRIGO MOUNTAINS

El.: 3000'                     Loc.: Yuma 1, AE-12-14; Yuma 3, AF-1-2
Pro.: /tríygo/                     Spanish: "wheat"
Indian wheat known as "trigo" (Plantheo ignota) grows abundantly in these mountains. It is a grass much favored by cattle. Locally these mountains are called the Chocolate Mountains because of their color, with the southern portion being referred to as the Dome Rock Range. Only the portion northwest of the Chocolate Mountains is locally called Trigo Mountains.

Ref.: 181, pp. 18, 50. Maps: C-11; E-20 (Chocolate and Dome Rock Mountains); GN-18; GN-23; GN-4.

| a.n. North Trigo Peaks | Map: GN-23 | Yuma |
| South Trigo Peaks | Map: GN-23 | Yuma |
| Trigo Pass | Map: GN-23 | Yuma |
| Trigo Wash | Map: GN-23 | Yuma |

## TULE MOUNTAINS

El.: c. 1500'                     Loc.: Yuma 4, AD-9.5-12
Pro.: /túwli/                     Spanish: "reed"
Only about four miles of the Tule Mountains lie in Arizona, the remainder being in Mexico. The older name for these mountains was Mesa de Malpais (Spanish: "badlands") and it in turn was even earlier the Sierra Del Tule. On GLO 1903, however, the name changes to Tule Mountains. On GLO 1921 (C-12), there is a further shift to Cabeza Prieta Mountains (Spanish: "black head mountains"), which—like the name Malpais—may be attributed to the volcanic terrain. A further separation took place so that currently the Tule Mountains are considered as be-

ing separated from today's Cabeza Prieta Mountains by a broad low pass through which wound the old Camino del Diablo (*q.v.*). It is this separation which leaves the Tule Tank (see below) in the Cabeza Prieta Mountains, although it was the tank which originally gave the range its name.

Ref.:   181, p. 160.   Maps: C-6; E-3.

**a.n. Tule Tank**      Loc.: Sec. 10, T. 14 S., R. 15 W.      Yuma
Two miles north of the Mexican line is the tank which was used by emigrants on the Camino del Diablo in the 1850's and later. Lt. N. Michler in 1853 reported that the tanks were so called because of the few "scattered blades of coarse grass growing in their vicinity." Travelers early learned to recognize signs of water in desert country. One was that where tules grew, water lay either on or close to the surface. There is no longer such growth at this particular point.

Ref.:   51, p. 114; Mercer.

> **Tule Lagoon**          Map: GN-26          Yuma
> **Tule Desert**                              Yuma
> Loc.: East of and adjacent to Tule Mountains.

## TURTLE BACK MOUNTAIN

El.: c. 1500′                          Loc.: Yuma 4, FG-1
Descriptive.

**v.n. Pass Mountain**    Descriptive.   Map: A-7
Ref.:   Barnes.   Map: GN-11.

## UTTING

El.: c. 500′                           Loc.: Yuma 2, B-6
Charles Utting was a Rough Rider in the Spanish-American War. There is nothing visible at Utting today from the highway except a few cropworkers' cabins.

Ref.:   Barnes.   Map: GN-11.

## VICKSBURG

El.: 1382′                             Loc.: Yuma 2, C-6.8
Victor E. Satterdahl started a store at this location. In the late 1890's when he applied for a post office, he used his first name to produce "Vicksburg" for the location.

P.O. est. November 15, 1906. Victor E. Satterdahl, p.m. Wells Fargo Station, 1907.

Ref.:   4, p. 369; Barnes; 141, p. 225; P.O. Records. Maps A-7; C-10.

## VINEGARON WELL

El.: c. 500′                           Loc.: Yuma 2, D-9.5
Pro.:   /vínəgarown/
Vinegaron is an old name for this well, the reason for which is not known. A vinegaron is a harmless insect which somewhat resembles a scorpion. There are not known to be more vinegarons at this location than elsewhere.

Ref.:   Mercer; 141, p. 225.   Map: GN-11.

**a.n. Vinegaron Wash**      Map: GN-10      Yuma

## VIRGIN BASIN

El.: c. 800′                           Loc.: Yuma 3, G-1
This is an old name for a place which is noted for its virginal beauty.

Ref.:   Monson.   Map: GN-11.

## VIRGIN PEAK

El.: c. 2500′                          Loc.: Yuma 2, D-11
The origin of the name Virgin Peak has not yet been ascertained.

Ref.:   None.   Map: GN-11.

## WELLTON

El.: 354′                              Loc.: Yuma 3, G-6.1
When the railroad came through this region, wells were needed to supply trains with water. Several deep wells were sunk, hence the name Wellton.

Just west of Wellton on the Gila River is the location which Fr. Kino referred to in 1699 as San Pedro.

P.O. est. August 4, 1904. Benjamin M. Lee, p.m. Wells Fargo Station, 1909.

Ref.:   Barnes; 4, p. 389; 20, pp. 413-414; P.O. Records. Maps: GN-24; GN-26.

**a.n. Wellton Hills**      El.: 1195′. Map: GN-24      Yuma
     **Wellton Mesa**          Map: GN-24          Yuma

## WENDEN

El.: c. 1500′                          Loc.: Yuma 2, E-6
Wenden was established as Wendendale in 1905 by Otis E. Young, after his home town in Pennsylvania, where he owned a farm called Wendendale.

P.O. est. as Wendendale, August 3, 1905. Harry B. Hanna, p.m. Changed to Wenden, August 7, 1909. Wells Fargo Station, 1907.

Ref.:   APHS File; 102, p. 89; P.O. Records.   Map: GN-11.

## WHITE WELL

El.: c. 500′                           Loc.: Yuma 4, E-7
Wesley White struck salt water at one hundred ten feet when he dug this well.

Ref.:   Barnes.   Maps: GN-11; GN-8.

## WINCHESTER PEAK

El.: c. 2500′                          Loc.: Yuma 2, CD-6.4
Josiah Winchester owned the Desert Mine in this locality c. 1910.

Ref.:   Barnes.   Maps: C-11; C-12; GN-11.

## YAQUI TANKS

El.: c. 2300′                          Loc.: Yuma 2, B-11.8
Pro.:   /yǽk i/ or /yáki/
In the early 1900's, a Yaqui Indian used to lie in wait for mountain sheep and deer which watered at these tanks. He sold their meat to the cook at the Kofa Mine.

Ref.:   Monson.   Map: GN-11.

## YUMA

El.: 213′                              Loc.: Yuma 3, BC-5.5
Pro.:   /yúwmə/
The reason for the name Yuma remains obscure. One group feels that the name is a corruption of the Yuma title "Yahmayo," which means "son of the captain" and that this name may have been applied to the entire tribe by early Spanish missionaries who misunderstood the word. Still others think that the name Yuma may be a corruption of

the Spanish word *fumar* ("to smoke.") According to Dr. Bertha Bascom, an expert in Spanish linguistics, the name Yuma could not be derived from "fumar" but might have come from the Old Spanish word *umo,* meaning "smoke." Smoke has long been associated with the Yuma Indians. The name Yuma may relate to the habit of the tribe of building huge fires along the river banks.

One of the chief divisions of Yumas, the Cocopa Indians, used to live on both sides of the Colorado River. Old Fort Yuma was near the center of the territory in which the Indians lived.

Probably the first white man to pass the site of the future Yuma was Fernando de Alarçon, who in 1540 sailed part way up the Colorado River. Over one hundred years later, Fr. Eusebio Francisco Kino explored the area (1691), while searching for a route to California. In the fall of 1700 Kino, who was curious to know whether Lower California was an island or a peninsula, made a trip down the Colorado River to what is now southwest Arizona. When he reached the Yuma rancheria opposite what was to become Fort Yuma, he named it San Dionisio because it was on that saint's day that he arrived. This name is given as "Doonysio" on Kino's map of 1701. Kino did not establish a mission at this point.

On December 4, 1775, Fr. Francisco Garcés came to what he called the "Pueblo de la Concepcion," a strait between two low hills through which the united Gila and Colorado rivers flowed. Garcés established a mission for the Indians and it was here, after Garcés had spent more than a year attempting to get the Spaniards in Mexico City to follow through on promises to the Yuman Chief Palma, that the Indians murdered the priest on July 17, 1781.

With the discovery of gold in California and the migratory move being made by Americans to the West Coast, it was inevitable that an emigrant route should be found through southern Arizona. The United States was negotiating with the government of Mexico to facilitate the location of such a route. In this preliminary boundary survey in 1849, Lt. Amiel W. Whipple pitched camp on the future site of Fort Yuma, California. Although some sources mention that this was the site of the old Mission of Puerta de la Concepcion which had been founded in 1780 by Garcés, it seems clear that the mission itself was on the Arizona side of the river. Nevertheless, the first American officer, (Maj. Samuel P. Heintzelman) on this spot noted that in 1851 the "rough stone foundation of the houses, with their earthen ruins, could be traced."

Before the coming of the United States troops to this location, a ferry had been established and was in operation on June 28, 1849, one mile below the site of the future fort. The community attached to this enterprise was Jaegerville (so named for Louis Jaeger, its owner). Jaegerville was located on the California side of the river.

The first projected community on the Arizona side was Colorado City. Charles Debrille Poston and some friends were en route to California in 1854 seeking to raise capital for mining, but when the party reached the Colorado River and the ferry belonging to Jaeger, they were told that the fare would be about $25. Poston's group had no money. The men took counsel with themselves in order to meet the situation. At Poston's suggestion, an engineer set to work with instruments and other members of the group ran around with signal staffs, laying out a city in squares and streets and making up a map which, incidentally, had provisions for a steam ferry landing. Jaeger's curiosity got the best of him and over he came to find out what was going on. Poston, a born promoter, convinced Jaeger that the place had a good future, with the result that the German bought several lots and the surveying party got free transportation across the river as part payment for a single lot. Poston on arriving in San Diego registered Colorado City as a community, and in San Francisco sold its plans and acreage for $10,000.

As emigrants to California began arriving on the banks of the Colorado River, the community began to develop at Colorado City on the Arizona side. It had brisk trade with Fort Yuma on the California side, where the first tents had been pitched in 1850 (*See* Camp Independence). Fort Yuma was named for the local Indians, and as the fort grew, so did Colorado City. However, by 1861 the little community still had only a few permanent buildings and a post office, the name of which in 1858 had been changed to Arizona (in the territory of New Mexico). In 1862 a devastating flood swept the community away and when it again took shape, it was established on higher ground. One of its new residents was Jaeger, since Jaegerville too had gone to oblivion in the Colorado River rampage. Jaeger had suffered another serious blow to his fortunes when the federal troops burned his ferry boats. The federals feared that the Confederates invading Arizona might well reach the Colorado River and seek to use the boats for passage. Jaeger resumed his ferry business with headquarters at Arizona, T. N.M., remaining in business until the railroad put an end to commercial boating on the Colorado.

The post office at the community on the Arizona side of the river was discontinued as a result of Civil War events. When it was re-established, post office rules required that a new name be used. The next name for the location was the one still in use—Yuma, taken from that of Fort Yuma. However, at the first opportunity, citizens had the name shifted to Arizona City. Opponents of the name change began agitating to have the name become permanently Yuma, and this was accomplished in 1873.

By 1870 more than eleven hundred people were living at Yuma. It was the most important community in the southwestern part of Arizona and logically was selected to be the county seat to replace La Paz (*q.v.*). The county records were shipped on the steamer *Nina Tilden* from La Paz to Yuma, which continues to be the county seat.

Yuma's importance grew with the establishment of the first territorial prison at Yuma in 1876. In 1909 the prison was transferred to Florence in Pinal County. Today Yuma is one of Arizona's most important cities and the heart of a rich agricultural area.

No book about Arizona would be complete without the ancient story beloved by military men in early Yuma: a soldier died and, of course, went to hell. He had to return to Yuma for his blankets.

P.O. est. as Colorado City, December 2, 1857. John B. Dow, p.m. Name changed to Arizona (in the territory of new Mexico), March 17, 1858. Discont. June 8, 1863. Re-est. as Yuma, October 1, 1866. Francis Hinton, p.m. Name changed to Arizona City, October 28, 1869. Name changed to Yuma, April 14, 1873. Wells Fargo Station (oldest in Arizona), 1865. Arizona City incorporated, March 11, 1871. Changed by legislative action to Yuma, February 3, 1873.

Ref.: 104, pp. 47-48; 134, p. 60; *Citizen,* January 25, 1873, 1:2; January 23, 1875, 1:4; 7, pp. 489, 616; 4, p. 272; 87, p. 249; 105, p. 333; 88, II, 431; 35, p. 548; 20, pp. 438-439; 159, pp. 50-51, 221; *Weekly Alta Californian,* July 30, 1859 (APHS); P.O. Records. Maps: GN-11; GN-26.

**a.n. Yuma Desert**                    Map: GN-6                    Yuma

**Yuma Indian Reservation**            Map: GN-19                  Yuma

This reservation, which is partly in California, was established on September 27, 1917, as the Cocopa Reservation. It consists of 527 acres on which at present about fifty-five Indians live, with another estimated two hundred residing in the Yuma Valley. The Cocopas are a division of the Yuman family which in 1604-1605 lived near the mouth of the Colorado River. They later moved gradually slightly north, but still remained in Mexico where Maj. Samuel P. Heintzelman in 1856 reported seeing them near the United States boundary line.

Ref.: "Annual Report of the Arizona Commission of Indian Affairs, 1954, 1955, 1956," pp. 14-15; 88, I, 319.

**Yuma Heights**              Map: GN-26                         Yuma

This suburb of Yuma has been in existence since c. 1920.

**Yuma Hills**                                                  Yuma

In 1854 Lt. N. Michler said his camp was "opposite the military post, on the left bank of the Colorado, between the Plutonic Ridge on the east, and a low range of sand and gravel hills, called the Yuma hills, on the west; these latter end abruptly at the water's edge."

Ref.: 51, p. 103.

**Yuma Mountains**              Map: C-12                        Yuma

**Yuma Wash**          Maps: GN-19; GN-20; GN-23                 Yuma

A Colorado steamer landing used to be at the mouth of this wash. Here freighters often remained overnight, as did also cattlemen driving their herds from Cibola *(q.v.)* to Yuma.

Ref.: Blythe Chamber of Commerce "Cruise Bulletin," October 10, 1954.

# BIOGRAPHICAL INFORMATION

The following section is devoted to thumbnail biographical sketches of people whose knowledge of and interest in Arizona names and history have qualified them to contribute materially to information in this volume. Occasionally the list includes not only those personally interviewed by the editor, but also some of the many who have taken time to send information by mail.

ADAMS, W. G. (BILLY): In the early 1920's Billy Adams and his wife built a tourist camp, among the earliest in the United States, at Winona, where Mr. Adams is now a well-known cattleman.

ALLAN, HUGH: Hugh Allan belongs to a family that was among the first to settle in the Cherry Creek (Yavapai County) area. For many years he has carried mail between Dewey and outlying areas.

ALSDORF, JOHN: John Alsdorf and two partners arrived c. 1919 at what is now Eloy. It was then merely a name applied by the railroad to an unoccupied section of land. Mr. Alsdorf died in 1959.

AMANN, ALMA K. (MRS.): Mrs. Amann is acting postmaster at Black Canyon.

ANDERSON, MARGARET (MRS.): One of the oldest pioneers in Flagstaff, Mrs. Anderson has contributed much information about her area.

ASHURST, HENRY FOUNTAIN: For many years United States Senator for Arizona, Sen. Ashurst is the son of William Ashurst, among the first to settle in the Flagstaff area.

BABCOCK, HENRY: A resident of Kingman, Mr. Babcock has lived in the area for the past sixty years. He has numberless fascinating stories on place names and pioneer events.

BARTLETT, KATHERINE: As archeologist and historian who has written many articles on Spanish exploration in Arizona, Dr. Bartlett is in charge of the library of the Museum of Northern Arizona.

BECKER, JULIUS: The son of Gustav Becker, Julius Becker has spent his life in the Springerville region where his father and uncle established the Becker Mercantile Company about two decades before the turn of the century.

BENHAM, H. L.: A forest ranger for many years, Mr. Benham has been in the Williams vicinity since 1909.

BENNETT, FRED: Fred Bennett came to Arizona in 1896. His work as a deputy sheriff and as a cowboy has given him knowledge of place names in southern Arizona.

BENNETT, FRED (MRS.): Mrs. Bennett's father came to Watervale in 1879, living there until Tombstone was founded.

BRANCH, WILLIAM B.: Mr. Branch is Superintendent of the Petrified Forest National Monument. He has an intimate knowledge of the history of that area and its place names.

BROPHY, FRANK CULLEN: One of Arizona's leading bankers, Frank Brophy is the son of a man who came to Arizona c. 1881 and settled in Cochise County.

BRYANT, HAROLD C.: Mr. Bryant is a former Superintendent of Grand Canyon National Park. He is responsible for some place names in that area.

BUNCH, ALMA (MRS.): Mrs. Bunch is the daughter of a pioneer who settled in southeastern Coconino County in the 1880's.

BURCARD (FR. BURCARD FISHER, O.S.M.): Fr. Burcard of St. Michael's has worked among the Navajo Indians for many years and speaks the language fluently.

BURGESS, OPIE RUNDLE (MRS.): Mrs. Burgess, a long-time resident of the Bisbee vicinity, is an authority on the history of Cochise County. She has published many articles in this connection.

BURNS, ROBERT: A national park ranger, Mr. Burns was spending the last day of his assignment at Katherine Boat Landing in Mohave County when the editor was fortunate enough to meet him. Ranger Burns took the editor in a jeep on long-vanished roads to the site of the Katherine Mine and was very helpful in giving the history of place names in the area.

BURRALL, HARRY: An old-time ranger, Mr. Burrall has ridden the range in the Chiricahua Mountains and adjacent valleys for over half a century. He has named places in the region.

BUTLER, MOLLY: The daughter of Noah Butler, who with his family settled in the Greer area in 1888. Molly Butler has a close knowledge of place names near Greer.

BYRNES, GENEVIEVE (MRS.): A native Arizonan, Mrs. Byrnes was born c. 1880 near Globe. Her family came to Arizona in 1878.

CHUBB, MERRILL D.: Dr. Chubb, a member of the faculty of the University of Kansas, has climbed more buttes and temples in the Grand Canyon than any other living person. He has an intimate knowledge of the Grand Canyon.

COLCORD, WILLIAM: Mr. Colcord lived on the Upper Gila for many years. He was interviewed by Mrs. Clara Woody.

COLTON, HAROLD S.: Dr. Colton is the now retired Director of the Museum of Northern Arizona at Flagstaff. He has an intimate knowledge of the Hopis and their culture.

CONRAD, JOHN F.: A pioneer in Flagstaff, Mr. Conrad knows the history of the area.

COOPER, CHESTER: Chester Cooper has spent almost his entire lifetime where his father settled in the vicinity of Roosevelt Lake. Mr. Cooper has been in the region over sixty years, having arrived in Arizona when he was twelve years old. He was interviewed by Mrs. Woody and the editor.

COREY, MARGARET LOUISE (MRS. WILLIAM): Mrs. Corey served for several years as secretary and treasurer of the Northern Branch of the Arizona Pioneers' Historical Society. She has a keen interest in and knowledge of the history of northern Arizona.

COREY, WILLIAM: Bill Corey is a ranger in the national forests of Coconino County.

CORRIGAN, THOMAS: Mr. Corrigan is the son of the first postmaster at Piñon.

COSPER, BILL: Born in January 1874, Bill Cosper came to Arizona when he was twelve years old and has lived in the Duncan region for the past sixty-nine years. He is a well-known and beloved cattleman.

CRAIG, MRS. DUDLEY I.: Mrs. Craig (née Gerald) first saw Arizona while riding in front of her father on a horse in 1878 when she was barely two years old. She has spent the remainder of her life in the area of Pinal Ranch.

CROXEN, FRED W.: Mr. Croxen has an enviable knowledge of Arizona based on many years' residence and service as a forest ranger. He contributed materially to the Will C. Barnes' *Arizona Place Names*, as well as to the present volume.

DARLING, CHARLES: Although Mr. Darling had been connected with the Havasu Lake Wildlife Refuge at Parker for only three years when seen by the editor, the nature of his work had given him valuable knowledge concerning place names and their origins.

DAVIS, SILAS O.: Mr. Davis worked with and lived among the Apache Indians of the Fort Apache Indian Reservation for many years. He was serving as recreation manager of the White Mountain Recreation Enterprise (owned and operated by the Apaches) at the time of his death in 1958. His thorough knowledge of the reservation area and its history was an invaluable source for place names.

DAVIS, WILLIAM W.: A pioneer in Thompson's Valley, Yavapai County, Mr. Davis was the first postmaster of Yava.

DEVORE, ALF: Mr. Devore is the son of a pioneer who settled in the Wheatfields district, later moving to Cherry Creek and then to Globe. Interviewed by Mrs. Woody.

DOBYNS, HENRY F.: An archaeologist, Mr. Dobyns knows the Papago language. He worked on Hualapai place names in connection with the Indian claims case for the Hualapai Indian Reservation.

DUGAS, FRED: An oldtime cowman who came to Arizona when he was "just a kid," Fred Dugas was eighty-seven when seen by the editor in late 1955. Dugas has spent all his years in Arizona at his own ranch in Yavapai County and knows the surrounding area as only a person who rides the range can.

EMPIE, HAL: Hal Empie, born in Safford, has lived in Duncan since 1934.

ESCALANTE, CARLOS: (MRS.): Mr. and Mrs. Escalante own the village of Sasabe on the Arizona border. They have created the town from nothing during approximately the past thirty-five years.

FARMER, MALCOLM F.: Formerly Assistant Director of the Museum of Northern Arizona, Mr. Farmer furnished information concerning forts and camps in Arizona.

FARNSWORTH, SOPHIE (MRS.): Mrs. Farnsworth arrived in Clifton toward the end of December 1898. She was born in Virginia City, Nevada.

FERRA, EDITH (MRS.): Mrs. Ferra was born in 1892 and came to Union Pass, Mohave County, in 1897, where she has lived ever since except for a period of some thirteen years spent in Ajo.

FITZGERALD, ED C.: County Treasurer for Greenlee County, Ed Fitzgerald came to Clifton in 1903. He was born in Solomonville.

FORD, FRANK: Mr. Ford has the distinction of having been born on Alcatraz Island. He has spent most of his life in the area of Jerome and Williams. He was sixty-eight years old in 1956.

FOSTER, GEORGE E.: Mr. Foster is the Director of affairs at Meteor Crater in Arizona. He has written many articles concerning the scientific aspects and the history of the crater.

FRAZIER, MRS. T. T.: Mrs. Frazier has had the store at Roosevelt, Arizona, for half a century. She was born in the area; her father was George Pemberton.

FRIER, DELLA POWELL (MRS.): Mrs. Frier is the daughter of one pioneer (William Powell, who homesteaded on Cherry Creek) and the widow of another (Thomas Conway Frier, who located in northern Arizona in 1884). In 1886 her husband established a ranch near Marshall Lake using the Bar D T (Della and Tom) brand.

FRITZ, FRED: Fred Fritz is a cattleman who is prominent both locally and nationally. He has served as President of the Senate of the State Legislature, being one of two men who have had that honor. He was interviewed by Miss Elizabeth Shannon.

FUCHS, JAMES R.: Mr. Fuchs prepared his Master's Thesis on the history of Williams, Arizona. He has furnished by correspondence much information needed on pioneers, events, and place names in that area. He is currently associated with the Truman Library in Independence, Missouri.

GARDNER, GAIL I.: Mr. Gardner was born in Prescott in 1892. During his boyhood he used to watch his father exchange goods for gold, using a scale in the store. The fact that his father could tell at a glance from which area the gold came has given Mr. Gardner an unusual background in the origin of many place names. For twenty-five years Gail Gardner was a Yavapai County cattle rancher.

GARRETT, NORMAN (MRS.): Mrs. Garrett has for several years worked for Senator Carl Hayden in connection with the history of pioneers in early territorial Arizona.

GILLETTE, VERNE: Mr. Gillette came to the Payson vicinity a half century ago after spending a year in Prescott. He has lived for many years near Globe. He was interviewed by Mrs. Woody and the editor.

GLANNON, THOMAS I.: A resident of Nogales for nearly two decades, Mr. Glannon is keenly interested in the history of southern Arizona and has amassed a fund of reliable information.

GLASER, RAPHAEL M.: Mr. Glaser is stationed at the Truxton sub-agency for the Hualapai Indians at Valentine, Arizona.

GODDARD, JESS: Mr. Goddard has been a rancher in Yavapai County for many years. He was president of the Verde Historical Society in 1956.

GRAY, B. W. (MRS.): Mrs. Gray is a resident of Odessa, Texas. She has provided authentic information concerning her grandfather, William Parker, of Parker Canyon, Santa Cruz.

GRIGSBY, DICK: An old-time cowman, Uncle Dick Grigsby knows the range north and south of Highway 66 in eastern Arizona.

HARRIS, ASA: "Ace" Harris was born in Oregon, being taken in 1870 from there when only a year old to San Francisco. When his mother remarried after his father's death, young Harris did not get along well with his stepfather. As a result, when he was ten years old, he joined a cattle outfit owned by a man named Lambert, who drove his stock to the Colorado River. There Lambert married an Indian woman and Harris remained with the couple until he was eighteen years old. Ace has led a venturesome life as a ranger, a deputy sheriff, and a United States Marshal. His work led him into every corner of Arizona Territory, which he describes as having been "a dumping ground for thieves, murderers, and cutthroats from Texas, California, and New Mexico."

HARRIS, W. M.: When just a young boy, Mr. Harris discovered Harris Cave in Apache County. He is now nearly ninety.

HART, LESS: As an early-day cattleman, Less Hart established his own ranch in the country southwest of Flagstaff. His knowledge of the ranges in that territory as well as elsewhere in the state is exhaustive. Mr. Hart was eighty-three in 1956.

HAYS, CARL D. W.: A resident of Columbus, New Mexico, Mr. Hays has contributed much valuable information concerning that part of Arizona which lies along the international boundary east and west of Nogales. Not only has he personally traveled along most of the boundary several times, but he has made a study of maps in connection with the Boundary Survey and early territorial period.

HENSEN, AL: Currently stationed at the Canyon de Chelly National Monument, Al Hensen was at the Organ Pipe Cactus National Monument when the editor dropped in. Mr. Hensen was extremely helpful in searching the files and in contributing information concerning the place names within the monument area.

HEWARD, GLEN B.: Mr. Heward (of Holbrook) furnished information concerning the life of his grandfather, Lehi Heward.

HICKS, MARK: Mrs. Clara Woody interviewed Mr. Hicks, who came to the Globe area c. 1886 and has spent his life there.

HINCHLIFFE, LOUISE M.: Miss Hinchliffe was extremely helpful in connection with the place names of the Grand Canyon. She is a member of the staff at the Naturalist's Headquarters.

HOCKDERFFER, GEORGE E.: Mr. Hockderffer is the grandson of a man who settled north of Flagstaff in 1885.

HOMER, PETER: Mr. Homer is the tribal council chairman for the Colorado River Indian Agency at Parker. The members of the tribal council were very helpful in supplying information.

HORNBUCKLE, DICK: Mr. Hornbuckle has been at Davis Dam since 1945. He knows the history of Davis Dam and its vicinity with accuracy and in detail.

HOUSHOLDER, E. ROSS: A resident of the Kingman area since 1916, Mr. Housholder is an engineer who has spent many years preparing an accurate map of Mohave County, in the process of which he has amassed knowledge concerning place names.

JACKSON, W. L.: Mr. Jackson has lived at Groom Creek as a year-around resident since about 1930.

JENNINGS, C. A.: Mr. Jennings is an oldtimer who has lived at Safford for several decades. As a child, Mr. Jennings spent some years at Fort Apache and at Fort Grant.

JOHNSON, BERT: Mr. Johnson has been a resident of northern Arizona for eighty-two years.

JOHNSON, HOWARD (MRS.): Mr. and Mrs. Johnson homesteaded at Aztec in 1926 when, she reports, there were no other residents in the area.

JONES, ADA E. (MRS.): Mrs. Jones has lived in Nogales for many years. She is a keen student of the history of Santa Cruz County, on which she has written several articles. Her clipping file furnished much valuable information.

JONES, ALDEN W.: Mr. Jones is the Assistant Superintendent of the Papago Indian Agency. His book on Papago place names is one of the basic references used in the current volume.

JORDAN, FRANK: When he was a boy ten years old, Frank Jordan accompanied his father in 1886 to take up a homestead at Oatman Flat. He has spent most of his life there.

KEENEY, K. A.: Mr. Keeney is Supervisor of the Coconino National Forest.

KELLAND, ROY: Mr. Kelland and his mother moved to Tacna from Missouri in May 1936.

KELLY, LEO: Mr. Kelly is an old-time railroad engineer who has the run out of Ash Fork, where he has lived for many years.

KENNEDY, JIM: A resident of Williams for the past sixty-five years, Jim Kennedy has led an active life during which he was influential in highway development in Arizona. He was eighty-five when he was visited by the editor in 1956.

KETCHUM, ED: A retired ranger, Ed Ketchum rode the border country for many years and in consequence has an intimate knowledge of names along the border.

KITT, EDITH O. (MRS.): Mrs. Kitt for many years was Executive Secretary of The Arizona Pioneer's Historical Society. Literally hundreds of entries in this volume reflect her knowledge of Arizona history and place names, for Mrs. Kitt made available to the editor her notes concerning where information could be found to expand the present volume. At her specific request, her name is not appended to entries, but wherever "APHS" is mentioned, her assistance may be assumed.

KLINE, ADDIE INGALLS (MRS.): The librarian at the Carnegie Library in Yuma, Mrs. Kline is the daughter of Frank Ingalls, a well-known pioneer.

KOLB, EMERY C.: Emery Kolb came to the Grand Canyon in 1902 from Pittsburgh, Pennsylvania, when he was twenty-one years old. He has explored and photographed the Grand Canyon for years, running the Colorado River at least twice.

LAURRIAU, JOHN (JUDGE): Born in Santa Fe, Judge Larriau was brought by his parents to Contention near Tombstone in 1880 when he was barely six months old. His family shortly thereafter moved to Fairbank. As a boy and young man, he used to deliver meat to Charleston.

LENON, ROBERT: An engineer, Bob Lenon has prepared maps of both Yuma and Santa Cruz Counties. Lenon's father was a railroad man based in Yuma. Robert Lenon has a fine collection of valuable volumes on early Arizona history.

MACIA, ETHEL (MRS. J. H.): Mrs. Macia was born in Tombstone c. 1881. She spent a brief time with her motherless brothers and sister at Pearce. Mrs. Macia has lived the rest of her life at Tombstone except for attendance at the University of Arizona. Her keen interest in the history of the Tombstone area is reflected in this volume. Mrs. Macia is known to thousands as the former proprietor of the Rose Tree Inn at Tombstone.

MANUEL, MARK: As Chairman of the Papago Council, Mr. Manuel made it possible for the editor to transcribe the Papago pronunciation for place names on the reservation.

McINTURFF, JEFF: Mr. McInturff, who was interviewed by Mrs. Clara Woody, was in the Pleasant Valley area in the early 1890's. He now lives near Globe.

McKINNEY, NORA (MRS.): Mrs. McKinney knows the Pleasant Valley area intimately inasmuch as she and her husband lived at the old Tewksbury ranch for twenty-three years. They lived in Clifton before moving to Pleasant Valley. Mrs. McKinney was interviewed by Mrs. Woody and the editor.

McMICKEN, K. V.: Mr. McMicken is vice-president of Goodyear Farms at Litchfield Park, Arizona.

MERCER, PRESTON M.: A sportsman, entomologist, and writer on the history of Yuma County, Preston Mercer supplied much valuable information. He has been writing historical articles for the past twenty-five years.

MERRITT, EVELYN B. (MRS.): Mrs. Merritt is interested in early Arizona territorial history. She is the author of a history of Prescott.

MILLER, DICK: Interviewed by Miss Elizabeth Shannon of Clifton, Dick Miller has been a trapper in that area for many years.

MONSON, GALE: Mr. Monson is in charge of the Fish and Wildlife Service for the Kofa and Cabeza Prieta Game Ranges. He has been in Arizona since 1934. Since the Fish and Wildlife Service is concerned with the maintenance and development of wildlife refuges and wildlife management areas, Mr. Monson's work has provided him with dependable and interesting knowledge of the game ranges.

MORRIS, EARL H.: An archaeologist, Mr. Morris investigated the Canyon de Chelly c. 1929.

MORSE, HELEN (MRS.): A lifetime resident of the Seligman area, Mrs. Morse is interested in its history and provided help on the origins of place names.

NASH, W. B., JR.: Mr. Nash's father was Lafayette P. Nash, who came to Arizona in 1881 and became one of Arizona's best known pioneers.

NETHERLAN, ALTON: A resident of Ajo, Mr. Netherlan was serving as Deputy County Attorney when seen by the editor in 1956.

NOBLE, LESLEY: Mr. Noble is a lifetime resident of Alpine. Noble Mountain was named for his father, who settled at its foot.

NUTTAL, JEAN McCLELLAN (MRS.): Mrs. Nuttal was born and raised near Dragoon. She is now living in Tombstone.

OLLSEN, LOUIS (MRS.): Mrs. Ollsen is the former Agnes Vineyard, who was born in Greenback Valley. She was interviewed by Mrs. Clara Woody.

PARKER, REV. CHARLES FRANKLIN: A frequent contributor to Arizona Highways, Rev. Parker is interested in place names throughout the state.

PARKMAN, I. H.: Mr. Parkman has been in Buckeye for the past sixty years. He originated the Old Settlers Club and started the museum at Buckeye.

PATEY, RALPH: At the time the editor was in Kingman, Mr. Patey was in charge of the Chamber of Commerce. Although a relatively new resident, Mr. Patey's keen interest in Mohave County had already resulted in a sound knowledge of the county's history.

PATTON, JAMES MONROE: In 1945, Mr. Patton wrote his Master's thesis at the University of Arizona on the history of Clifton, during the course of which he interviewed many oldtimers who have since died. He continues to maintain a lively interest in the history of Clifton and has contributed materially to the present volume.

PENROD, MR. AND MRS. JOHN RALPH: The Penrod family arrived in the Pinetop area in 1887.

PERKINS, R. E.: The Perkins family located at Perkinsville in 1900.

PERRY, EBEN P.: The Perry family moved to Perryville in 1929, the elder Perry having arrived in Arizona in 1875.

PHILLIPS, W. S.: Dr. Phillips is head of the Botany Department at the University of Arizona. He made available information concerning places of particular interest to botanists.

PIEPER, ERNEST: Mr. Pieper was born at Globe in 1891 and spent his childhood at Payson where he continued to live until he was about fifty years of age. He was interviewed by Mrs. Clara Woody and the editor.

PLATTEN, MARY FORD (MRS.): "Aunt Mary" Platten was born in 1869, the first American white child to be born on Kodiak Island, Alaska. As a child in Arizona she used to climb on Gen. George Crook's knee and question him about why he wore whiskers. For the record, he replied that he needed to protect his face against the weather during Indian campaigns. Mrs. Platten is the widow of Fred Platten, A Congressional Medal of Honor holder, who spent much of his life riding the ranges of northern Arizona, his wife many times accompanying him.

POLLOCK, TOM E.: A well-known pioneer and rancher, Tom Pollock owns the Grapevine Canyon Ranch.

PRATHER, BESS (MRS.): Mrs. Prather was for many years postmaster at Casa Grande. She is a prominent leader in women's activities in the state.

REILLY, PETER: Mr. Reilly has been a resident of the Clifton area for half a century.

RICHARDS, J. MORRIS: Mr. Richards is a well-known newspaper man. He is the grandson of Bishop J. W. Richards who came to Arizona c. 1877. (See St. Joseph) Mr. Richards is keenly interested in the history of Mormons in Arizona.

RIELL, ROBERT: Mr. Riell came to Globe in the 1890's. He was interviewed by Mrs. Clara Woody.

RIGGS, LILLIAN (MRS.): The daughter of one pioneer—Neil Erickson—and the widow of another—Ed Riggs—Mrs. Riggs has contributed invaluable information concerning the history and the place names of eastern and southeastern Cochise County. With her husband, she was the first to explore the Wonderland of Rocks, and through their joint efforts the Chiricahua National Monument was established.

ROSENBERGER, DOROTHY (MRS.): A long-time resident of Prescott and vicinity, Mrs. Rosenberger by correspondence has supplied needed information for Camp Wood and other areas in Yavapai County.

ROTHWELL, LYNN (MRS.): Mrs. Rothwell lives on a ranch near Seligman. She has supplied information concerning place names for that area.

SAVILLA, AGNES (MRS.): Mrs. Savilla is Secretary for the Mohave Tribal Council. Through her able assistance, information was obtained concerning Poston, Arizona, and the editor had the privilege of conferring with members of the tribal council. Unfortunately, time did not permit garnering the information which is still needed concerning Mohave place names. However, the tribal council has pledged its help in the future towards this objective.

SCHNEBLY, ELLSWORTH: Mr. Schnebly has a keen interest in and knowledge of place names in Oak Creek and in the Cottonwood area. His father came to Arizona in 1912.

SCHROEDER, ALBERT H.: An archaeologist, Mr. Schroeder is deeply interested in early Spanish names and in Arizona's territorial history. He has prepared many articles concerning the Spanish explorations. He was associated with the Southwestern National Monuments at Globe when visited on several occasions by the editor.

SCOTT, JAMES BOYCE: As County Attorney for Greenlee County, Mr. Scott has spent much time making abstracts for the Clifton area.

SECAKUKU, HALE: Hale Secakuku is the former Chairman for the Hopi Tribal Council. He was very helpful to the editor during a trip through the Hopi villages.

SEIBOLD, DORIS: A well-known folklorist of Santa Cruz County, Miss Seibold provided much information and many suggestions for the current volume.

SHANNON, ELIZABETH: The niece of Charles M. Shannon who was among the first to arrive in Clifton, Miss Shannon has a deep interest in the history of Greenlee County. She spent many hours interviewing pioneers and forwarding information to the editor.

SHELLBACH, LOUIS: A distinguished naturalist, Dr. Shellbach over the years has amassed a file of information on place names in the Grand Canyon. These were made available for use by the editor. Dr. Shellbach was the Naturalist at the Grand Canyon until late 1957.

SHREEVE, JIM: A former Supervisor of Apache County, Jim Shreeve has a vital interest in the history of the St. Johns area.

SIMMONS, MR. AND MRS. JESSE: Many years' residence in Greenlee County has given Mr. and Mrs. Simmons an accurate knowledge of the names of pioneers, their ranches or mines, and of brands used on the ranges—often reflected in place names. Mr. Simmons came to Clifton in 1904. Mrs. Simmons is a native Arizonan.

SISK, HANSON R.: Mr. Sisk is editor and publisher of the *Nogales Herald*. He has a deep interest in the history of Santa Cruz County.

SLAMON, JOHN (JUDGE): A long-time resident of Ash Fork, Judge Slamon contributed information concerning the history of the area and its place names.

SLIPHER, EARL O.: Dr. Slipher of the Lowell Observatory at Flagstaff has been in the area for many years. His interest in the history of northern Arizona has led him to make a collection of old photographs which proved helpful. Dr. Slipher's many interests include the origins of place names.

SMITH, G. E. P.: Dr. Smith has for many years been a member of the University of Arizona faculty. He is an authority on irrigation problems. His interest in place names dates back many years. Dr. Smith made available his notes on correspondence with the U. S. Geographic Board on names and reports amassed while chairman of the Place Names Committee of the Arizona Pioneers' Historical Society.

SMITH, MARK: Mr. Smith was born in Williams sixty-seven years ago and has spent his entire life there.

SPAIN, MADELINE (MRS.): Mrs. Spain supplied needed information in connection with Baker Butte and other place names in Yuma County.

SPARKS, GRACE (MRS.): A long-time resident of Yavapai County, Mrs. Sparks is now living in Santa Cruz County where she has been a prime agent in the establishment of the Coronado International Monument.

SPROAT, JOHN (MRS.): Mrs. Sproat and her husband moved to Winona in 1912, when there was no one else living there, although there was a railroad section house used occasionally. As a young woman, Mrs. Sproat with her first husband worked for Mr. and Mrs. Ed Riggs (see biography of Lillian Riggs) in Cochise County.

STANFIELD, W. A.: A lawyer, Mr. Stanfield is deeply interested in land matters in the vicinity of Eloy. His research has given him a solid knowledge of locations and their histories.

STEMMER, CHARLES C.: Charlie Stemmer is a well-known Arizona pioneer whose life as a cattleman and businessman has given him a background useful in determining the origin of place names.

STOUT, AL.: Mr. Stout has lived in the vicinity of Casa Grande for over half a century.

SUPERNAUGH, WILLIAM: Mr. Supernaugh was Superintendent at the Organ Pipe Cactus National Monument at the time when names were applied to places within that area in the early 1940's. Now stationed at Platte National Monument in Oklahoma, Mr. Supernaugh took time to send needed information to the editor.

SWEETING, HARRIET: Miss Sweeting was born on the Frisco River in Greenlee County, the daughter of Luther F. Sweeting, who bought Mason Greenlee's homestead and thereby acquired Evans Point. Miss Sweeting has a deep interest in the history of her native county.

SWITZER, W. H.: A well-known pioneer in Flagstaff, Mr. Switzer has been a leading spirit in the organization and functioning of the Northern Branch of the Arizona Pioneers' Historical Society.

SYKES, STANLEY: An Englishman who paused in northern Arizona en route to Australia when a very young man, Stanley Sykes spent the rest of his life in the vicinity of Flagstaff. He had a knowledge of northern Arizona which came from a long and active life. His contributions to the present volume are notable. Mr. Sykes died late in 1956.

TERRY, SID: Mr. Terry, a railroad man, arrived in Williams in 1907.

THEOBALD, JOHN: Few people in Arizona have the knowledge of their state's history comparable to that possessed by Mr. Theobald. He and his wife Lillian probably know more about territorial post offices, Wells Fargo stations, and the history of communication and transportation in the territorial period than anyone else.

THOMPSON, WILLIAM M.: Mr. Thompson has been a rancher near Dewey, Yavapai County. His wife, Mary Margaret, is the daughter of the late Frank C. Lockwood. Both Mr. and Mrs. Thompson contributed materially to the present volume.

UPLEGGER, REV. FRANZ: Pastor Uplegger has been a missionary to the San Carlos Apaches since 1919. For more than thirty years he has been working on an Apache grammar. (There is none now in existence.) His knowledge of the Apache language and of the reservation was extremely helpful. Rev. Uplegger is in his late eighties.

WALKER, VIRGIL: A resident of Nogales, Mr. Walker is the son of William Walker who came to Arizona in 1886.

WARNER, BEN: Mr. Warner has lived at Rock Springs, Yavapai County, since 1921.

WEBB, A. C.: As a small boy, Mr. Webb came to Arizona from Kansas c. 1890. He has ranched along and above Tonto Creek for many years. Mr. Webb was interviewed by Mrs. Clara Woody.

WENTZ, C. B.: Mr. Wentz, now retired, spent many years as a guide in the White Mountain country. His knowledge of the area is reflected in many place names covered in this volume.

WESTOVER, JOHN L.: Mr. Westover has been in Joseph City since at least 1897.

WILLARD, C. A.: Mr. Willard was ninety-seven years old when seen by the editor in 1955. His clear and keen memory of early Arizona dated back to the 1870's when he arrived at what is now Cottonwood.

WILLSON, ROSCOE G.: Mr. Willson is the well-known writer of a weekly column on Arizona history and places which appears in "Arizona Days and Ways" in the *Arizona Republic*. His knowledge of the state and of its pioneers has been extremely helpful in the preparation of the present volume.

WILSON, SID: Currently mayor of Tombstone, Sid Wilson is an oldtime cowboy who includes among his many adventures a trip to Europe in the early 1900's with Buffalo Bill's show. Mayor Wilson has been a cattleman on ranges all the way from the Grand Canyon to the border and knows a great deal about Arizona place names.

WILTBANK, MILO: A lifetime resident of Eager, Milo Wiltbank is an amateur historian and a collector of rare books and manuscripts about Arizona. He supplied much valuable information concerning Mormon settlements in northern Arizona.

WINGFIELD, R. W.: Mr. Wingfield manages the Wingfield Commercial Company at Camp Verde. His father came to that area in the late 1870's. Mr. Wingfield made notable contributions to the Will C. Barnes' *Arizona Place Names*, as well as to the current volume.

WOODY, CLARA (MRS.): Mrs. Woody is responsible for a great deal of the material included under Gila County. For the past thirty-five years she has made a study of the history of Gila County and has written several articles in that connection. During the preparation of the present volume, Mrs. Woody traveled from one end of Gila County to the other, looking up and interviewing pioneers for information on place names.

YOUNG, ROBERT W.: Mr. Young is Assistant to the General Superintendent of the Navajo Indian Reservation. He speaks Navajo fluently. It is largely due to his co-operation that it has been possible to expand the present volume to include many Navajo place names. Mr. Young spent several hours recording Navajo place names on a tape recorder for later phonetic transcription. He is the author of annual reports concerning Navajos and their reservation.

# MAP BIBLIOGRAPHY

Note: All maps on the following pages are United States Geological Survey maps unless otherwise noted.

### A: General Maps of Arizona

A-1: "Arizona," *Business Atlas*. Chicago: Rand McNally & Co., c. 1879.

A-2: "Arizona," *Business Atlas*. Chicago: Rand McNally & Co., 1881.

A-3: "Arizona," *Business Atlas*. Chicago: Rand McNally & Co., 1888.

A-4: "Arizona," *Business Atlas*. Chicago: Rand McNally & Co., 1893.

A-5: "Arizona: General Use Map." (Advance Sheet), SE/4. U.S.G.S., 1956.

A-6: "Arizona: General Use Map." (Advance Sheet), SW/4. U.S.G.S., 1956.

A-7: Darton, N. H., Arizona Bureau of Mines, and U.S.G.S. "Topographic Map of the State of Arizona." 1923.

A-8: Hodges, Hiram C., "Map of Territory of Arizona." *Arizona as It Is*. 1875.

A-9: "Southwestern United States." *The National Geographic Magazine*, XCIV (December 1948).

A-10: "State of Arizona." U.S.G.S. 1919; revised 1939.

A-11: "State of Arizona: General Highway Map." Division of Economics and Statistics, State Highway Department, Phoenix; 1955.

A-12: "State of Arizona: Land Management Map, Bureau of." U. S. Dept. of the Interior. 1953.

A-13: "Arizona Points of Interest and Touring." Chevron Gasoline Map, 1953.

A-14: "Map of Arizona." Rand McNally & Co., not dated: approx. 1882.

A-15: "Arizona." *Business Atlas*. Rand McNally & Co., 1898.

### B: National Forest Maps

B-1: "Coconino National Forest." U. S. Dept. of Agriculture, Forest Service. 1946.

B-2: "Coronado National Forest: East Half." Forest Service, Albuquerque, N. M. c. 1955.

B-3: "Coronado National Forest: West Half." Forest Service. Compiled, Washington, D.C., 1917. Revised and corrected 1955 (?).

B-4: "Kaibab National Forest." U. S. Dept. of Agriculture, Forest Service. 1949.

B-5: "Kaibab National Forest." Forest Service. Albuquerque, N. M. 1955.

B-6: "Map Covering Ranges 6 E. to 8 W. and Ts. 8 N. to 21 N., Coconino and Yavapai Counties; Traced by J. A. Schoedinger and F. G. Rawlins for Forest Service Regional Office, Albuquerque." Forest Service, Albuquerque, N. M., 1940.

B-7: "Map: Description: Range 2 E.–18 E. T 1 S.–13 N." Compiled by F. E. Landon and B. Elliott, 1943. Corrected July 1953." Forest Service, Alburquerque, N. M.

B-8: "Map: Description: Ts. 10 N.–26 N., R. 3 E.–13 E. Compiled by B. Elliott, January 1935. Retraced by F. G. Rawlins, May 1941. Corrected 1955." Forest Service, Albuquerque, N. M.

B-9: "Sitgreaves National Forest." Forest Service, Albuquerque, N. M. 1955.

### C: General Land Office Maps

C-1: "Map of the Territory of Arizona." Dept. of the Interior, General Land Office." November 1, 1869.

C-2: "Map of Arizona Showing Progress of Public Surveys to Accompany Surveyor General's Report, 1874."

C-3: "Territory of Arizona." Dept. of the Interior, General Land Office. 1876.

C-4: "Territory of Arizona." Dept. of the Interior, General Land Office. 1879.

C-5: "Territory of Arizona." Dept. of the Interior, General Land Office. 1883.

C-6: "Territory of Arizona." Dept. of the Interior, General Land Office. 1887.

C-7: "Territory of Arizona." Dept. of the Interior, General Land Office. 1892.

C-8: "Territory of Arizona." Dept. of the Interior, General Land Office. 1896.

C-9: "Territory of Arizona." Dept. of the Interior, General Land Office. 1903.

C-10: "Territory of Arizona." Dept. of the Interior, General Land Office. 1909.

C-11: "State of Arizona." Dept. of the Interior, General Land Office. 1912.

C-12: "State of Arizona." Dept. of the Interior, General Land Office. 1921.

C-13: "State of Arizona." Dept. of the Interior, General Land Office. 1933.

C-14: "State of Arizona." Dept. of the Interior, General Land Office. 1941.

C-15: "State of Arizona." Dept. of the Interior, General Land Office. 1897.

### D: Indian Country Maps

D-1: "Automobile Road Map of the Indian Country." Automobile Club of Southern California. Los Angeles, California: No date.

D-2: "Colorado Indian Reservation." Colorado River Agency, U. S. Indian Service, U. S. Dept. of the Interior, Parker, Arizona. No date.

D-3: "Fort Apache Indian Reservation." Dept. of the Interior, Office of Indian Affairs. 1938.

D-4: Gregory, Herbert. "Map." *The Navajo Country: A Geographic and Hydrographic Reconnaissance*. Washington: U. S. Gov't. Printing Office, 1916.

D-5: "Jurisdiction of Pima Agency, Arizona." n.p.; n.d.

D-6: "Navajo and Hopi Reservations: Arizona, Utah, New Mexico." Compiled and drawn by H. K. Boyd. Road Department Map. n.d.

D-7: "Navajo Country: Utah, Colorado, Arizona, and New Mexico." Dept. of the Interior, Office of Indian Affairs. 1937.

D-8: "Papago Indian Reservation." Dept. of the Interior, Office of Indian Affairs. 1944.

D-9: "San Carlos Indian Reservation." Dept. of the Interior, Office of Indian Affairs. 1945.

D-10: "Walapai Indian Reservation." Dept. of the Interior, Office of Indian Affairs. 1941.

D-11: Lumholtz, Carl. "Map showing Papago Rancherias Present and Past." Drawn by A. Briesemeister. c. 1912.

D-12: Dobyns, Henry. "Map of Hualapai Place Names in Mohave County."

### E: Military Maps
(These maps are given in chronological order.)

E-1: Parke, John G. "Map of the Territory of New Mexico." Assisted by Richard H. Kern. Santa Fe, N. M. 1851.

E-2: Emory, W. H. "Map No. 3: Boundary Between the United States and Mexico. Agreed upon by the Joint Commission, under the Treaty of December 30, 1853." Surveyed in 1855.

E-3: Weller, John B., and William H. Emory. "Map No. 4: Boundary Between the United States and Mexico. Agreed upon by the Joint Commission under the Treaties of Guadalupe Hidalgo; and December 30, 1853." Surveyed in 1849 and 1854-55.

E-4: Ives, Joseph Christmas. "Exploration of the Colorado River, 1858."

E-5: White, J. L. "Map of a Reconnaissance of the Colorado River from the Mouth of the Gila to Lat. 35° 18′ North." January 20, 1858.

E-6: Leach, J. B. "Map No. 1 of the El Paso & Fort Yuma Wagon Road, 1857-58." Department of the Interior: Pacific Wagon Roads.

E-7: Leach, J. B. "Map No. 2 of the El Paso & Fort Yuma Wagon Road, 1857-8" Department of the Interior: Pacific Wagon Roads.

E-8: Hutton, N. H. "Map No. 1 of the El Paso & Fort Yuma Wagon Road." Department of the Interior: Pacific Wagon Roads. 1857-8.

E-9: Hutton, N. H. "Map No. 2 of the El Paso & Fort Yuma Wagon Roads." Department of the Interior: Pacific Wagon Roads. 1857-8.

E-10: "A sketch map of the Colorado River showing communities located on the river and roads and trails crossing the river. Not identified as to author." No date. National Archives Map No. US 324-62.

E-11: "Territory and Military Department of New Mexico. Compiled in the Bureau of Topographical Engineers of the War Dept. . . . under the authority of Hon. J. B. Floyd, Sec. of War, 1859."

E-12: "Map of New Mexico: expressly prepared for Maj. Gen. M. C. Meigs, Q. Mast. Genl. U.S.A. in the Engineers Office at Hd. Qus. 5th Military Dist. Bvt. Captain Wm. Hoelcke, U.S.A. in charge." No date.

E-13: "Map of the area northwest of Prescott (Fort Whipple) showing route taken by scouting party, under Lieutenant Rich. C. Lord." National Archives Map No. US 324-78. No date.

E-14: "Map showing route from the headquarters at Fort Whipple near Prescott to Fort Whipple, January 28 to April 15, 1866." National Archives Map No. US 324-2.

E-15: "Sketch Map of Trail of Indian Scout from Ft. McDowell, A. T. Sept. 27 to Oct. 6, 1866."

E-16: Overman, T. C., "Outline Map showing a New Route from Texas to Fort Yuma, California for Cattle Droves and Trains En Route to California." c. 1867.

E-17: "A manuscript map of the southern portions of Arizona and New Mexico Territories, not dated." National Archives Map No. US 324 Port. 79.

E-18: "Department of Arizona. Revised 1875." Office of the Chief of Engineers, U. S. Army, Washington, D.C., 1876. First Lieut. J. C. Mallery, Corps of Engineers, Chief Engineer. Under the authority of Major General J. M. Schofield.

E-19: "Rough Sketch of Country passed over by Expedition, Comd. Maj. W. H. Brown, 5th Cav. . . . Original furnished by John G. Bourke, 2nd Lieut., 3rd Cav. Traced in Engineer Office, Mil. Div. Pacific, Aug. 13, 1873. Section of Salt River Canyon, Arizona, Scene of action, Dec. 28, 1872."

E-20: "Map of Arizona Territory." Prepared by authority of Bvt. Major General O. B. Willcox, Commanding Department, under the Direction of 1st Lieut. Fred A. Smith, Adjutant 12th Inftry., Engineer Officer D. A. 1879.

E-21: "Map of Portion of Arizona Territory. Showing Position of surveyed line of Southern Pacific Railroad." Carl F. Palmer, 1st Lieut. Corps of Engineers U.S.A., 1879. Engineer Office, Headquarters, Military Division of the Pacific. Department of California at Presidio of San Francisco, California, Jan. 21, 1879.

E-22: "Map of the Military Department of New Mexico." Drawn under the direction of the Brig. Gen. James H. Carleton by Capt. Allen Anderson, 5th U. S. Infantry. 1864.

E-23: W.603 Pt. 6, No. 2 (National Archives)

E-24: Record Group 77, W133, H 1 (National Archives)

### F: Postal Route Maps

F-1: "Map of that Portion of the United States of America West of the 102nd Meridian Exhibiting the Post Offices and Mail Routes." 1868.

F-2: "Post Route Map of the State of Arizona." January, 1917.

F-3: "Post Route Map of the State of Arizona." January, 1929.

F-4: "Post Route Map of the State of Arizona." December 1, 1931.

F-5: "Post Route Map of the State of Arizona." August 1, 1934.

F-6: "Post Route Map of the State of Arizona." July 15, 1938.

F-7: "Post Route Map of the State of Arizona." January 1, 1940.

F-8: "Post Route Map of the State of Arizona." April 1, 1941.

F-9: "Post Route Map of the State of Arizona." July 15, 1942.

F-10: "Post Route Map of the State of Arizona, September 15, 1946.

F-11: "Post Route Map: Arizona." September 15, 1948.

F-12: "Post Route Map: Arizona." November 1, 1951.

F-13: "Post Route Map: Arizona." October 15, 1953.

### G: County Maps
#### GA: APACHE COUNTY

GA-1: "Apache County." Board of Supervisors, Apache County, St. Johns 1918; corrected 1937.

GA-2: "Canyon de Chelly National Monument." 1937 and 1938.

GA-3: "Dinne Mesa NE: Arizona-Utah." (Advance sheet) 1953.

GA-4: "Dinne Mesa NW: Arizona-Utah." (Advance sheet) 1953.

GA-5: "Dinne Mesa SE." (Advance sheet) 1956.

GA-6: "Dinne Mesa SW." (Advance sheet) 1956.

GA-7: "Gigantes NE, Los." (Advance sheet) 1956.

GA-8: "Gigantes NW, Los." (Advance sheet) 1956.

GA-9: "Gigantes SE, Los." (Advance sheet) 1956.

GA-10: "Gigantes SW, Los." (Advance sheet) 1956.

GA-11: "Pastora Peak NE. Arizona-New Mexico-Utah." (Advance sheet) 1953.

GA-12: "Pastora Peak NW: Arizona-Utah." (Advance sheet) 1953.

GA-13: "Pastora Peak SE: Arizona-New Mexico." (Advance sheet) 1953.

GA-14: "Pastora Peak SW." (Advance sheet) 1956.

GA-15: "Petrified Forest National Monument." Edition of 1939.

GA-16: "Petrified Forest Quadrangle." Edition of 1912; reprinted 1947 with corrections.

GA-17: "Redrock Valley NE: Arizona-New Mexico." (Advance sheet) 1953.

GA-18: "Redrock Valley NW." (Advance sheet) 1956.

GA-19: "Redrock Valley SE: Arizona-New Mexico." (Advance sheet) 1956.

GA-20: "Redrock Valley SW," (Advance sheet) 1956.

GA-21: "Setsiltso Springs 2 NE: Arizona-Utah." (Advance sheet) 1952.

GA-22: "Setsiltso Springs 2 NW: Arizona-Utah." (Advance Sheet) 1952.

GA-23: "Setsiltso Springs 2 SE." (Advance Sheet) 1956.

GA-24: "Setsiltso Springs 2 SW." (Advance Sheet) 1956.

GA-25: "Apache County: General Highway Maps: 1956."

### GB: COCHISE COUNTY

GB-1: "Benson Quadrangle." Edition of January, 1915; reprinted 1948.

GB-2: "Bisbee Quadrangle." Edition of April, 1910; reprinted 1936.

GB-3: "Bisbee and Vicinity." Edition of 1906; reprinted 1948.

GB-4: "Bowie Quadrangle." Edition of 1950. Graham County also (GE) partly on this map.

GB-5: "Chiricahua Quadrangle: Arizona-New Mexico." 1917.

GB-6: "Cochise Head Quadrangle." 1950.

GB-7: "Cochise Quadrangle." Edition of 1943.

GB-8: "Dos Cabezas Quadrangle." Edition of 1943; reprinted 1948.

GB-9: "Douglas Quadrangle." Edition of October, 1914; reprinted 1946.

GB-10: "Dragoon Quadrangle." Edition of 1943; reprinted 1948.

GB-11: "Fisher Hills Quadrangle." Edition of 1944.

GB-12: "Happy Valley Quadrangle." Edition of 1945. Pima County also partly on this map.

GB-13: "Hereford Quadrangle." Edition of September, 1914; reprinted 1946.

GB-14: "Huachuca Quadrangle, Fort: 7.5 Minute Series." United States Department of Army, Corps of Engineers, 1948.

GB-15: "Official Map of Cochise County." Board of Supervisors, Cochise County, June 2, 1941.

GB-16: "Pearce Quadrangle." Edition of 1916; reprinted 1948.

GB-17: "Perilla Quadrangle: Arizona-New Mexico." Edition of 1919; reprinted 1948.

GB-18: "Redington Quadrangle." Edition of 1945. Graham and Pima Counties also partly on this map.

GB-19: "San Simon Quadrangle: Arizona-New Mexico." Edition of 1951. Greenlee County also partly on this map.

GB-20: "Tombstone District." Edition of March, 1906; reprinted 1942.

GB-21: "Tombstone and Vicinity." Edition of January 1908; reprinted 1948.

GB-22: "Vanar Quadrangle: Arizona-New Mexico." Edition of 1951.

GB-23: "Willcox Quadrangle." Edition of 1943. Graham.

GB-24: "Winchester Mountains Quadrangle." Edition of 1945. Graham County also partly on this map.

GB-25: "Cochise County: General Highway Maps: 1951."

GB-26: "Cochise County, Official Map of:" 1940.

### GC: COCONINO COUNTY

GC-1: "Bright Angel: 1903."

GC-2: "Coconino County." Barney, R. G., County Engineer, Flagstaff, Arizona: 1954.

GC-3: "Flagstaff." Edition of June, 1912; reprinted 1951.

GC-4: "Jacob Lake: 1940."

GC-5: "Lees Ferry: 1954." Paria Plateau No. 1 (Advance sheet; subject to correction).

GC-6: "Topographic Map of the Grand Canyon National Monument." Edition of 1944, Mohave County also partly on this map.

GC-7: "Topographic Map of the Grand Canyon National Monument: East Half." Edition of 1927; reprinted 1948.

GC-8: "Topographic Map of the Grand Canyon National Monument: West Half." Edition of 1927; reprinted 1948.

GC-9: "Coconino County: General Highway Maps: 1948."

### GD: GILA COUNTY

GD-1: "Blue House Mountain Quadrangle." United States Department of the Army, Corps of Engineers. Edition of 1951.

GD-2: "Diamond Butte Quadrangle." Edition of 1943.

GD-3: "Gila County, Map of." Milton, Julius, County Engineer. April 1921.

GD-4: "Globe Quadrangle." Edition of April, 1902; reprinted 1940.

GD-5: "Inspiration Quadrangle: 7.5 Minute Series." Edition of 1947.

GD-6: "McFadden Peak Quadrangle." United States Department of the Army, Corps of Engineers. Edition of 1950.

GD-7: "Miami Copper Belt." Edition of March, 1912.

GD-8: "Old Dominion Quadrangle." Edition of February, 1902; reprinted 1948.

GD-9: "Payson Quadrangle." Edition of 1942.

GD-10: "Pinal Ranch Quadrangle: 7.5 Minute Series." Edition of 1949.

GD-11: "Pine Quadrangle." Edition of 1934.

GD-12: "Promontory Butte Quadrangle." Edition of 1939; reprinted 1951.

GD-13: "Ray Quadrangle." Edition of February, 1910; reprinted 1948.

GD-14: "Rockinstraw Mountain Quadrangle." Edition of 1950.

GD-15: "Roosevelt Quadrangle." Edition of August, 1912; reprinted 1948.

GD-16: "Gila County: General Highway Maps: 1949."

### GE: GRAHAM COUNTY

GE-1: "Galiuro Mountains Quadrangle." Edition of 1943.

GE-2: "Graham County Map." Western Publishing Company, Portland, Oregon. 1955.

GE-3: "Graham Quadrangle, Mt." Edition of 1945.

GE-4: "Jackson Mountain Quadrangle." Edition of 1946.

GE-5: "Klondyke Quadrangle." Edition of 1943.

GE-6: "Sierra Bonita Ranch Quadrangle." Edition of 1943.

GE-7: "Graham County: General Highway Maps: 1949."

### GF: GREENLEE COUNTY

GF-1: "Clifton Quadrangle." Edition of September 1902; reprinted June 1914 with corrections.

GF-2: "Morenci Quadrangle: Arizona-New Mexico." Edition of March, 1915; reprinted 1946.

GF-3: "Greenlee County: General Highway Maps: 1949."

### GG: MARICOPA COUNTY

GG-1: "Camelback Quadrangle." Edition of December 1906; reprinted 1948.

GG-2: "Cashion Quadrangle." War Department, Corps of Engineers, U. S. Army. Edition of 1948.

GG-3: "Cave Creek Quadrangle." Edition of 1939; reprinted 1950.

GG-4: "Cotton Center Quadrangle." Edition of 1951.

GG-5: "Dendora Valley Quadrangle." Edition of 1951.

GG-6: "Desert Well Quadrangle." Edition of July 1906; reprinted 1946. Pinal.

GG-7: "Estrella Quadrangle." Edition of 1951.

GG-8: "Gila Bend Quadrangle." Edition of 1951.

GG-9: "Gila Butte Quadrangle." Edition of 1917; reprinted 1945. Pinal.

GG-10: "Maricopa Quadrangle." Edition of September 1915; reprinted 1946. Pinal County also partly on this map.

GG-11: "McDowell Quadrangle, Fort." Edition of December 1906; reprinted 1948.

GG-12: "Mesa Quadrangle." Edition of April 1915; reprinted 1942.

GG-13: "Mobile Quadrangle." Edition of 1951.

GG-14: "Phoenix Quadrangle." Edition of June 1914; reprinted 1946. Pinal County also partly on this map.

GG-15: "Sentinel Quadrangle." Edition of 1950.

GG-16: "Theba Quadrangle." Edition of 1951.

GG-17: "Vekol Mountains Quadrangle." Surveyed in 1938-1939. Pima and Pinal Counties also partly on this map.

GG-18: "Woolsey Peak Quadrangle." Edition of 1951.

GG-19: "Maricopa County: General Highway Maps: 1947."

GG-20: "Chandler." (Advance Sheet) 1956.

GG-21: "Fowler." (Advance Sheet) 1956.
GG-22: "Gila Butte." (Advance Sheet) 1956.
GG-23: "Guadalupe." (Advance Sheet) 1956.
GG-24: "Laveen." (Advance Sheet) 1956.
GG-25: "Lone Butte." (Advance Sheet) 1956.
GG-26: "Mesa." (Advance Sheet) 1956.
GG-27: "Phoenix." (Advance Sheet) 1956.
GG-28: "Tempe." (Advance Sheet) 1956.

### GH: MOHAVE COUNTY

GH-1: "Bridge Canyon: 1930."
GH-2: "Buck Mountains." Edition of 1929; reprinted 1947.
GH-3: "Chloride: 1954."
GH-4: "Davis Dam: Nevada-Arizona-California: 1952."
GH-5: "Hoover Dam: Nevada-Arizona: 1953."
GH-6: "Housholder's Base Map of Mohave County." Housholder, E. Ross, Kingman, Arizona; March 16, 1955.
GH-7: "Iceberg Canyon: Nevada-Arizona: 1953."
GH-8: "Mohave County, Map of." Mulligan, John S. (Registered architect), Kingman, Arizona; August, 1942.
GH-9: "Needles: Arizona-California." Edition of November, 1904; reprinted 1943.
GH-10: "Needles: Arizona-California: 1952."
GH-11: "Parker: Arizona-California." Edition of March, 1911; reprinted 1947.
GH-12: "Topock: Arizona-California: 1951."
GH-13: "Virgin Basin: Nevada-Arizona: 1953."
GH-14: "Yucca." Edition of 1929; reprinted 1947.
GH-15: "Mohave County: General Highway Maps: 1952."

### GI: NAVAJO COUNTY

GI-1: "Agathla Peak 1 NE: Arizona-Utah: 1956." (Advance sheet).
GI-2: "Agathla Peak 1 NW: Arizona-Utah: 1956." (Advance sheet).
GI-3: "Agathla Peak 1 SE: 1956." (Advance sheet)
GI-4: "Agathla Peak 1 SW: 1956." (Advance sheet)
GI-5: "Agathla Peak 2 NE: Arizona-Utah: 1956." (Advance sheet)
GI-6: "Agathla Peak 2 NW: Arizona-Utah: 1956." (Advance sheet)
GI-7: Agathla Peak 2 SE: 1956." (Advance sheet)
GI-8: "Petrified Forest." Edition of 1912; reprinted 1947 with corrections.
GI-9: "Petrified Forest National Monument: 1939."
GI-10: "Shato Spring 1 NE: 1956." (Advance sheet)
GI-11: "Navajo County: General Highway Maps: 1951."

### GJ: PIMA COUNTY

GJ-1: "Ajo." Edition of 1934; reprinted 1947.
GJ-2: "Arivaca: 1943." Santa Cruz.
GJ-3: "Baboquivari Peak: 1944."
GJ-4: "Cocoraque Butte." Edition of 1943; reprinted 1948.
GJ-5: "Comobabi: 1942."
GJ-6: "Cortaro: 1947."
GJ-7: "Oro Blanco: 1944." War Department. Santa Cruz.
GJ-8: "Palo Alto Ranch: 1943."
GJ-9: "Presumido Peak: 1943."
GJ-10: "San Vicente: 1948."
GJ-11: "San Xavier Mission." Edition of 1943; reprinted 1947.
GJ-12: "Sells." Edition of 1943; reprinted 1948.
GJ-13: "Tucson." Edition of 1905; reprinted 1947.
GJ-14: "Twin Buttes: 1948."
GJ-15: "Vamori: 1943."
GJ-16: "Pima County: General Highway Maps: 1947."
GJ-17: "Reddington Quadrangle."
GJ-18: "Official Map of Pima County Including Santa Cruz County, Arizona." Pima County Highway Department, January 1953.

### GK: PINAL COUNTY

GK-1: "Antelope Peak Quadrangle: 1948."
GK-2: "Black Mountain Quadrangle: 7.5 Minute Series: 1950." Department of Army.
GK-3: "Brandenburg Mountain Quadrangle: 7.5 Minute Series: 1950." Department of Army.
GK-4: "Campo Bonito Quadrangle: 7.5 Minute Series: 1949." Pima.
GK-5: "Casa Grande Quadrangle: 1924." Maricopa County also partly on this map.
GK-6: "Christmas Quadrangle." Edition of 1917; reprinted 1939. Gila County also partly on this map.
GK-7: "Clark Ranch Quadrangle: 7.5 Minute Series: 1949."
GK-8: "Crozier Peak Quadrangle: 7.5 Minute Series: 1950."
GK-9: "Eloy Quadrangle: 1948." Pima County also partly on this map.
GK-10: "Florence Quadrangle." Edition of 1907; reprinted 1950. Maricopa County also partly on this map.
GK-11: "Gila Butte: 1956." (Advance sheet)
GK-12: "Gila Butte NW: 1956." (Advance sheet) Maricopa County also partly on this map.
GK-13: "Gila Butte SE: 1956." (Advance sheet)
GK-14: "Haunted Canyon Quadrangle: 7.5 Minute Series: 1949."
GK-15: "Holy Joe Peak Quadrangle: 7.5 Minute Series: 1950."
GK-16: "Iron Mountain Quadrangle: 7.5 Minute Series: 1949." Maricopa County also partly on this map.
GK-17: "Lookout Mountain Quadrangle: 7.5 Minute Series: 1950."
GK-18: "Mammoth Quadrangle: 1951."
GK-19: "Mammoth Quadrangle: 7.5 Minute Series: 1949."
GK-20: "Peppersauce Wash Quadrangle: 7.5 Minute Series: 1949." Pima County also partly on this map.
GK-21: "Picketpost Mountain Quadrangle: 7.5 Minute Series: 1949."
GK-22: "Putnam Wash Quadrangle: 7.5 Minute Series: 1950."
GK-23: "Ray and Vicinity." Revised 1917; edition of 1919.
GK-24: "Red Rock Quadrangle: 1947."
GK-25: "Sacaton Quadrangle." Edition of 1907; reprinted 1948. Maricopa County also partly on this map.
GK-26: "Saddle Mountain Quadrangle: 7.5 Minute Series: 1950."
GK-27: "Signal Peak Quadrangle: 1924."
GK-28: "Silver Reef Mountains Quadrangle." Surveyed in 1939 and 1940. Pima County also partly on this map.
GK-29: "Superior Quadrangle: 1948." Gila County also partly on this map.
GK-30: "Winkelman Quadrangle." Edition of October 1913; reprinted 1946. Gila, Pima Counties also partly on this map.
GK-31: "Winkelman Quadrangle: 1951."
GK-32: "Winkelman Quadrangle: 7.5 Minute Series: 1950." Gila County also partly on this map.
GK-33: "Pinal County: General Highway Maps: 1949."
GK-34: "Maricopa." (Advance Sheet)
GK-35: "Montezuma Peak." (Advance Sheet)
GK-36: "Enid." (Advance Sheet)

### GL: SANTA CRUZ COUNTY

GL-1: "Lenon's Map of Santa Cruz County." Lenon, Robert; Patagonia, Arizona; 1950.
GL-2: "Nogales Quadrangle." Edition of 1905; reprinted 1947.
GL-3: "Patagonia Quadrangle: 1904."
GL-4: "Ruby Quadrangle: 1942."
GL-5: "Tubac Quadrangle: 1943." Pima County also partly on this map.
GL-6: "Santa Cruz County: General Highway Maps: 1947."

### GM: YAVAPAI COUNTY

GM-1: "Ash Fork: 1949." Department of Agriculture, Forest Service. Coconino.

GM-2: "Bagdad: 1948."

GM-3: "Bradshaw Mountains." Edition of February 1903; reprinted 1946. Maricopa County also partly on this map.

GM-4: "Bumblebee: 1950." Department of Agriculture, Forest Service.

GM-5: "Clarkdale: 1948." Coconino County also partly on this map.

GM-6: "Congress." Edition of 1904; reprinted 1948.

GM-7: "Crown King: 1950." Department of Agriculture, Forest Service.

GM-8: "Iron Springs: 1949." Department of Agriculture, Forest Service.

GM-9: "Jerome." Edition of 1905; reprinted 1922.

GM-10: "Kirkland: 1950." Department of Agriculture, Forest Service.

GM-11: "Mayer: 1949." Department of Agriculture, Forest Service.

GM-12: "Mingus Mountain: 1947."

GM-13: "Paulden: 1950." Department of Agriculture, Forest Service. Coconino County also partly on this map.

GM-14: "Picacho Butte." 1950. Department of Agriculture, Forest Service.

GM-15: "Prescott: 1948." Department of Agriculture, Forest Service.

GM-16: "Sheridan Mountain: 1950." Department of Agriculture, Forest Service.

GM-17: "Simmons: 1950." Department of Agriculture, Forest Service.

GM-18: "Turkey Canyon: 1950." Department of Agriculture, Forest Service.

GM-19: "Turret Peak." Edition of 1933; reprinted 1947. Gila, Maricopa, Coconino Counties also partly on this map.

GM-20: "Union, Mt.: 1949." Department of Agriculture, Forest Service.

GM-21: "Verde, Camp." Edition of 1936; reprinted 1949. Coconino County also partly on this map.

GM-22: "Wagoner: 1950." Department of Agriculture, Forest Service.

GM-23: "Wood, Camp: 1949." Department of Agriculture, Forest Service.

GM-24: "Yavapai County Map." Merritt, R. L., County Engineer. Prescott, Arizona, 1952.

GM-25: "Yavapai County: General Highway Maps: 1948."

## GN: YUMA COUNTY

GN-1: "Aguila Mountains." Edition of 1930; reprinted 1947.

GN-2: "Aztec." Edition of 1929, reprinted 1950 with corrections. Maricopa County also partly on this map.

GN-3: "Big Maria Mountains: California-Arizona: 1.5 Minute Series: 1951."

GN-4: "Cibola: Arizona-California: 1951."

GN-5: "Dome Rock Mountains: Arizona-California: 1933."

GN-6: "Fortuna." Edition of 1929, reprinted 1943."

GN-7: "Hyder." Edition of 1930, reprinted 1947. Maricopa.

GN-8: "Kim: 1931."

GN-9: "Laguna." Edition of 1929; corrected 1940; reprinted 1949.

GN-10: "Laguna: 1956." (Advance sheet)

GN-11: "Lenon's Map of Yuma County." Lenon, Robert. Patagonia, Arizona: 1952.

GN-12: "Linskey." Edition of 1930; reprinted 1947.

GN-13: "Mohawk." Edition of 1928; reprinted 1947.

GN-14: "Moon Mountain: Arizona-California." Edition of 1932; reprinted 1943.

GN-15: "Norton Quadrangle." Edition of 1928; reprinted 1947.

GN-16: "Parker Dam Area: California, San Bernardino Co.: 1950."

GN-17: "Paz Mountain, La: 1956." (Advance sheet)

GN-18: "Picacho: Arizona-California: 1951."

GN-19: "Picacho Peak: Grid Zone "F": California-Arizona: 1.5 Minute Series: 1945."

GN-20: "Red Hill." Edition of 1939; reprinted 1948.

GN-21: "Roll: 1956." (Advance Sheet)

GN-22: "Sawtooth Range: California-Arizona: 1.5 Minute Series: 1951."

GN-23: "Trigo Peaks." Edition of 1939; reprinted 1947.

GN-24: "Wellton." Edition of 1928; reprinted 1947.

GN-25: "Whipple Mountains: California-Arizona: 1.5 Minute Series: 1952."

GN-26: "Yuma." Edition of 1905; reprinted 1944.

GN-27: "Yuma: Grid Zone "F": California-Arizona-Mexico: 1942."

GN-28 "Yuma County: General Highway Maps: 1948."

GN-29: "Laguna." U.S.G.S. (Advance Sheet)

# BIBLIOGRAPHY

1. Abert, J. W. (Lt.) *Examination of New Mexico in the Years 1846-'47.* Executive Document No. 23, 30th Congress, 1st Session.
2. Antisell, Thomas. *Explorations and Surveys for a Railroad Route from the Mississippi River to the Pacific Ocean, 1853-56, VII, Part 2.* Washington: 1857.
3. *Arizona: 1887-1950.* Phoenix: Bank of Douglas, 1949.
3a. Arizona Geological Society. *Guide Book for Field Trip Excursions in Southern Arizona.* Tucson, Arizona: Geological Society of America (April), 1952.
4. *Arizona: A State Guide.* "American Guide Series." New York: Hastings House, 1940.
5. *Arizona's National Monuments.* Santa Fe, N.M.: Southwestern Monuments Association, 1945.
6. Baker, Arthur A. *Geology of the Monument Valley-Navajo Mountain Region, San Juan County, Utah.* Washington, D. C.: U. S. Government Printing Office, 1936.
7. Bancroft, Hubert Howe. *History of Arizona and New Mexico, II.* New York: The Bancroft Company, n.d.
8. Bandel, Eugene. *Frontier Life in the Army 1854-1861.* Bandel, Olga, and Richard Jente, trans. Bieber, Ralph, ed. Glendale, California: The Arthur H. Clark Company, 1932.
9. Bartlett, John Russell. *Personal Narrative: or Explorations and Incidents in Texas, New Mexico, California, Sonora and Chihuahua, I, II.* New York: D. Appleton & Company, 1854.
10. Bartlett, Katharine. "How Don Pedro de Tovar Discovered the Hopi and Don Garcia Lopez de Cardenas Saw the Grand Canyon, With Notes Upon Their Probable Route." *Plateau,* XII (January, 1940), 37-45.
11. Bartlett, Katharine. "Notes Upon the Route of Espejo and Farfán to the Mines in the Sixteenth Century." *New Mexico Historical Review* (January, 1942), pp. 21-36.
12. Beale, Edward Fitzgerald. *Wagon Road from Fort Defiance to the Colorado River.* House Executive Document No. 124, 35th Congress, 1st Session. Washington, D.C.: 1858.
13. Becker, Julius. "Statement by Julius W. Becker Relative to Highways Leading to and from Springerville, Arizona." Unpublished ms.
14. "Becker's 75th Anniversary Number." *Apache County Independence News,* XXXIX (August 31, 1951).
15. Benson, Lyman, and Robert A. Darrow. *A Manual of Southwestern Desert Trees and Shrubs.* Tucson, Arizona: University of Arizona, 1944.
16. Bentley, Harold Woodmansee. *A Dictionary of Spanish Terms, with Special Reference to the American Southwest.* New York: Columbia University Press, 1932.
17. Blake, William P. "Geological Report." *Pacific Railroad Report, V.* Washington: 1856.
18. Bolton, Herbert Eugene. *Coronado on the Turquoise Trail.* Albuquerque, N. M.: University of New Mexico Press, 1949.
19. Bolton, Herbert Eugene. *Kino's Historical Memoir of Pimeria Alta, I, II.* Berkeley, California: University of California Press, 1948.
19a. Bolton, Herbert Eugene. *Padre on Horseback.* San Francisco: The Sonora Press, 1932.
20. Bolton, Herbert Eugene. *Rim of Christendom: A Biography of Eusebio Francisco Kino, Pacific Coast Pioneer.* New York: The Macmillan Company, 1936.
21. Bolton, Herbert Eugene, ed. *Spanish Explorations in the Southwest (Original Narratives of Early American History) 1542-1706.* New York: Charles Scribner's Sons, 1916.
22. Bourke, John G. *On the Border with Crook.* New York: Charles Scribner's Sons, 1891.
23. Box, Michael J. *Adventures and Explorations in New and Old Mexico.* New York: 1869.
24. Breed, Jack. "Land of the Havasupai." *National Geographic Magazine, The,* XCIII (May 1948).
25. Browne, J. Ross. *A Tour Through Arizona, 1864.* New York: Harper & Brothers, 1869.
26. Bryan, Kirk. *Routes to Desert Watering Places in the Papago County: Arizona.* Water Supply Paper 490-D. Washington, D. C.: U. S. Government Printing Office, 1922.
26a. Bryan, Kirk. Personal notes taken while studying watering places in the Papago County. Unpublished.
27. Burns, Walter Noble. *Tombstone, An Iliad of the Southwest.* New York: Grosset & Dunlap, 1929.
28. Clum, Woodworth. *Apache Agent: The Story of John P. Clum.* Boston: Houghton Mifflin Company, 1936.
28a. Colquhoun, James. *Early History of Clifton-Morenic District.* London: William Clowes & Son, Ltd., 1935.
29. Colton, Harold S. and Frank C. Baxter. *Days in the Painted Desert and the San Francisco Mountains.* Flagstaff, Arizona: Coyote Range, 1927.
30. Colton, Harold S. "Grand Falls." *Museum Notes,* II (June 1930), 1-3.
31. Conklin, E. *Picturesque Arizona: Being the Result of Travels and Observations in Arizona During the Fall and Winter of 1877.* New York: Continental Stereoscope Company of New York, 1878.
32. Conkling, Roscoe P. and Margaret B. *The Butterfield Overland Mail, 1857-1869,* I, II. Glendale, California. The Arthur H. Clark Company, 1947.
33. *Coronado National Forest.* U. S. Department of Agriculture, Forest Service: Southwestern Region. Washington, D. C.: U. S. Government Printing Office, 1942.
34. Bryan, Kirk. *Papago Country, Arizona.* Water Supply Paper No. 499. Washington, D. C.: U. S. Government Printing Office, 1925.
35. Coues, Elliott, trans. *On the Trail of a Spanish Pioneer: The Diary and Itinerary of Francisco Garcés, 1775-1776.* New York: E. P. Harper, 1900.
36. Crane, Leo. *Indians of the Enchanted Desert.* Boston: Little, Brown and Company, 1929.
37. Cremony, John C. *Life Among the Apaches.* San Francisco: A. Roman & Company, 1868.
38. Crook, George. *General George Crook, His Autobiography.* Martin F. Schmitt, ed. Norman, Oklahoma: University of Oklahoma Press, 1946.
39. Cruse, Thomas. *Apache Days and After.* Caldwell, Idaho: The Caxton Printers, Ltd., 1941.
40. Cummings, Byron. "Turkey Hill Ruin." *Museum Notes,* II (May 1930), 6.
41. Dellenbaugh, Frederick S. *A Canyon Voyage: The Narrative of the Second Powell Expedition down the Green-Colorado River from Wyoming, and the Explorations on Land, in the Years 1871 and 1872.* New Haven: Yale University Press, 1926.
42. Dellenbaugh, Frederick S. *Romance of the Colorado River.* New York: G. P. Putnam's Sons, 1906.
43. Derby, George H. *Report to the Secretary of War, Communicating, in Compliance with a Resolution of the Senate, a Reconnaissance of the Gulf of California and the Colorado River, 1851.* Senate Executive Document No. 81, 32nd Congress, 1st Session. Washington, D.C.: 1852.
44. Ellsworth, Huntington. "Desert Laboratory, The." *Harper's Magazine,* CXXII (April 1911), 651-662.

45. Dobie, J. Frank, Mody C. Boatwright, and Harry H. Ransom, eds. *Coyote Wisdom.* Austin, Texas: Texas Folklore Society, 1938.

46. Dobyns, Henry F. "The Case of Paint vs. Garlic." *Arizona Quarterly, XI* (Summer 1955), 156-160.

47. Dutton, Clarence E. *Tertiary History of the Grand Canyon District: With Atlas.* Washington, D.C.: U. S. Government Printing Office, 1882.

48. Eccleston, Robert. *Overland to California on the Southwestern Trail: Diary of Robert Eccleston (1849).* Hammond, George P. and Edward H. Howes, eds. Berkeley, California: University of California Press, 1950.

49. Elliott, Wallace W. *History of Arizona Territory.* San Francisco: Wallace W. Elliott Company, 1884.

50. Emory, Wiliam H. *Notes of a Military Reconnaissance from Fort Leavenworth, in Missouri, to San Diego, in California, Including Part of the Arkansas, Del Norte, and Gila Rivers.* Executive Document No. 41. Washington, D.C.: Wendell and Van Benthuysen, Printers, 1848.

51. Emory, William H. *Report on the United States and Mexican Boundary Survey, I.* Washington, D.C.: Cornelius Wendell, Printers, 1857.

52. Farish, Thomas Edwin. *History of Arizona, I-VIII.* Phoenix: c. by Thomas Edwin Farish, 1915.

53. Favour, Alpheus H. *Old Bill Williams, Mountain Man.* Chapel Hill: University of North Carolina Press, 1936.

54. Fewkes, J. W. "Archeological Expedition to Arizona in 1895." *17th Annual Report, Bureau of American Ethnology, Part II.* Washington, D.C.: 1900.

55. Fish, Joseph. *History of Arizona.* Unpublished manuscript, Parts I and II.

56. Forbes, Robert H. *The Penningtons: Pioneers of Early Arizona.* N.p.: Arizona Archaeological and Historical Society, 1919.

57. Forrest, Earle R. *Arizona's Dark and Bloody Ground.* Caldwell, Idaho: Caxton, 1936.

58. Forrest, Earle R. and Edwin B. Hill. *Lone War Trail of Apache Kid.* Pasadena, California: Trail's End Publishing Company, Inc., 1947.

59. Foster, George E. *Arizona's Meteorite Crater.* N.p.: n.p., c. 1951.

60. Freeman, Lewis R. "Surveying the Grand Canyon of the Colorado." *National Geographic Magazine, The,* XLV (May 1924), 471-548.

61. Fuchs, James R. *A History of Williams, Arizona, 1876-1951.* Tucson, Arizona: University of Arizona, 1955.

62. Garrison, Lon. "A Camera and a Dream." *Arizona Highways,* XXIX (January 1953), 30-35.

63. "General Scheme of Arizona." *U. S. Post Office Department Railway Mail Service Guide (August 1938).* Washington, D.C.: U. S. Government Printing Office, 1938.

64. Gilbert, G. K. *Report of the Geology of Portions of New Mexico and Arizona Examined in 1873: U.S.G.S. Surveys West of 100th Meridian: Geology, III.* Washington, D.C.: 1875.

65. Gillmor, Frances, and Louisa Wade Wetherill. *Trader to the Navajos.* Albuquerque, N. M.: University of New Mexico Press, 1934.

66. "Government Cave." *Museum Notes, II* (December 1, 1929), 1-3.

67. Graham, J. D. *3rd Report of Lt. Col. J. D. Graham.* Senate Congressional Document No. 121, 32nd Congress, 1st session.

68. Gray, A. B. *Survey of a Route for the Southern Pacific Railroad on the 32nd Parallel.* Cincinnati: 1856.

69. Greenslet, Ferris. *The Lowells and Their Seven Worlds.* Boston: Houghton Mifflin Company, 1946.

70. Gregory, Herbert E. *Geology and Geography of the Zion Park Region: Utah and Arizona.* U. S. Geological Survey Professional Paper No. 220. Washington, D.C.: U. S. Government Printing Office, 1949.

71. Gregory, Herbert E. *The Navajo Country: A Geographic and Hydrographic Reconnaissance of Parts of Arizona, New Mexico, and Utah.* Water Supply Paper No. 380. Washington, D.C.: U. S. Government Printing Office, 1916.

72. Guitéras, Eusebio, trans. *Rudo Ensayo: 1763. Records of the American Catholic Historical Society of Philadelphia, V,* No. 2, 1894.

73. Haile, Fr. Berard. *A Stem Vocabulary of the Navaho Language.* St. Michaels, Arizona: St. Michaels Press, 1951.

74. Hall, Sharlot M. *First Citizen of Prescott: Pauline Weaver.* Introduction by Alpheus H. Favour. Prescott, Arizona: n.p., 1929.

75. Hamersly, Thomas H. S., ed. *Complete Regular Army Register of the United States: For One Hundred Years (1779 to 1879).* Washington, D.C.: T. H. S. Hamersly, 1880.

76. Hamilton, Patrick. *Resources of Arizona, The: A Manual of Reliable Information Concerning the Territory.* Prescott, Arizona: State of Arizona, 1881.

77. Hargrave, Lyndon L. "Elden Pueblo." *Museum Notes,* II (November 1, 1929), 1-3.

78. Hargrave, Lyndon L. "First Mesa." *Museum Notes,* III (February 1931), 1-6.

79. Hargrave, Lyndon L. "Influence of Economic Geography upon the Rise and Fall of the Pueblo Culture in Arizona, The." *Museum Notes,* IV (December 1931), 1-3.

80. Hargrave, Lyndon L. "Jeddito Valley and the First Pueblo Towns in Arizona to be Visited by Europeans, The." *Museum Notes,* VIII (October 1935), 17-23.

81. Hargrave, Lyndon L. "Oraibi: A Brief History of the Oldest Inhabited Town in the United States." *Museum Notes,* IV (January 1932), 1-8.

82. Hargrave, Lyndon L. "Shungopovi." *Museum Notes,* II (April 1930), 1-4.

83. Hargrave, Lyndon L. "Sikyatki." *Museum Notes,* IX (June 1937), 63-66.

84. Haws, Atella; Milo C. Wiltbank and Twylah Hamblin. *Church of Jesus Christ of Latter Day Saints: Dedicatory Services, May 6, 1951.* Eager, Arizona: Eager Ward, St. Johns Stake, 1951.

85. Heitman, Francis B. *Historical Register and Dictionary of the United States Army, from Its Organization, September 29, 1789, to March 2, 1903.* Washington, D.C.: U. S. Government Printing Office, 1903.

86. Hellenbeck, Cleve, and Juanita H. Williams. *Legends of the Spanish Southwest.* Glendale, California: The Arthur H. Clark Company, 1938.

87. Hinton, Richard J. *Hand-book to Arizona, The.* San Francisco: Payot, Upham & Company, n.d. Republished by Arizona Silhouettes, Tucson, Arizona, 1954.

88. Hodge, Frederick W. ed. *Handbook of American Indians North of Mexico, I, II.* Washington, D.C.: 1907.

89. Hodge, Hiram C. *Arizona as It Is, or The Coming Country.* New York: Hurd and Houghton, 1877.

90. Hoffmeister, Donald F. and Woodrow Goodpaster. *Mammals of the Huachuca Mountains.* Chicago: University of Illinois Press, 1954.

91. Hornaday, William T. *Campfires on Desert and Lava.* New York: Charles Scribner's Sons, 1908.

92. James, George Wharton, *Arizona, the Wonderland.* Boston: The Page Company, 1917.

93. James, George Wharton. *Grand Canyon of Arizona, The: How to See It.* Boston: Little, Brown, & Company, 1910.

94. James, George Wharton. *Indians of the Painted Desert Region.* Boston: Little, Brown, & Company, 1905.

95. Kitt, Edith O. and T. M. Pearce. "Arizona Place Name Records." *Western Folklore,* XI (October 1952), 284-287.

96. Klinck, Richard E. *Land of Room Enough and Time Enough.* Albuquerque, N. M.: University of New Mexico Press, 1953.

97. Kolb, Ellsworth and Emery Kolb. "Experiences in the Grand Canyon." *National Geographic Magazine, The,* XXVI (August 1914), 99-184.

98. Kolb, Emery L. *Through the Grand Canyon from Wyoming to Mexico.* New York: Macmillan Company, 1920.

98a. "Land of Cochise, The." *Pipeliner, The,* XV (Summer 1952), 56-67.

99. Lang, Walter B., ed. *First Overland Mail, The: Butterfield Trail, San Francisco to Memphis, 1858-1861.* Washington, D.C.: n.p., 1945.

100. Lee, Willis T. *Geologic Reconnaissance of a Part of Western Arizona.* Washington, D.C.: U. S. Government Printing Office, 1908.

101. Lee, Willis T. *Underground Waters of Salt River Valley, Arizona.* Water Supply and Irrigation Paper No. 136. Washington, D.C.: U. S. Government Printing Office, 1905.

102. Lloyd, Elwood. *Arizonology: Knowledge of Arizona.* Flagstaff, Arizona: The Coconino Sun, 1933.

103. Lockett, H. C. with photographs by Milton Snow. *Along the Beale Trail: A Photographic Account of Wasted Range Land.* Willard W. Beatty, ed. Lawrence, Kansas: Education Division, U. S. Office of Indian Affairs, 1938.

104. Lockwood, Frank C. *Life in Old Tucson, 1854-1864.* Tucson, Arizona: Tucson Civic Committee, 1943.

105. Lockwood, Frank C. *Pioneer Days in Arizona.* New York: The Macmillan Company, 1932.

106. Lumholz, Carl. *New Trails in Mexico.* New York: Charles Scribner's Sons, 1902.

107. Lummis, Charles F. *Some Strange Corners of Our Country.* New York: The Century Company, 1898.

108. "Madonna of the Trail, The." *Daughters of the American Revolution Magazine,* LXIII (July 1929), 399-404.

108a. Martin, Douglas. *Tombstone's Epitaph.* Albuquerque, N. M.: University of New Mexico Press, 1951.

109. Matthes, Francois E. Unpublished ms. of letter to Edward F. McKee, Park Naturalist, Grand Canyon, relative to place names; February 17, 1936. In Grand Canyon Naturalists Files.

109a. Matthes, Francois E.: Unpublished personal papers. Naturalists Headquarters, Grand Canyon.

110. Matthews, Washington. *Navaho Legends.* Boston: Houghton, Mifflin and Company, 1897.

111. McClintock James H. *Arizona: Prehistoric; Aboriginal; Pioneer, Modern.* I-III. Chicago: S. J. Clarke Publishing Company, 1916.

112. McClintock, James H. *Mormon Settlement in Arizona.* Phoenix: n.p., 1921.

113. McGee, W. D. "Old Yuma Trail." *National Geographic Magazine, The, XII* (March and April 1901), 103-107; 129-143.

114. Mollhausen, Baldwin. *Diary of a Journey from the Mississippi to the Coasts of the Pacific with a United States Government Expedition,* I-II. London: 1858.

115. Morgan, Learah Cooper, ed. *Echoes of the Past: Tales of Old Yavapai.* Prescott, Arizona: Yavapai Cow Belles, 1955.

116. Morris, Earl H. "Exploring in the Canyon of Death." *National Geographic Magazine, The,* XLVIII (September 1925), 263-300.

117. Mowry, Sylvester. *The Geography and Resources of Arizona and Sonora.* San Francisco: A. Roman & Company, 1863.

118. Mowry, Sylvester. *Geography and Resources of Arizona with Appendix.* Third edition. New York: 1864.

119. Muffley, Bernard W. *The History of the Lower San Pedro Valley in Arizona.* Unpublished M.A. Thesis. Tucson, Arizona: University of Arizona, 1938.

119a. Myers, John Myers. *Last Chance, The: Tombstone's Early Years.* New York: E. P. Dutton & Company, Inc., 1950.

120. *National Forest Facts: Southwestern Region.* Albuquerque, N. M.: U. S. Department of Agriculture, Forest Service, 1955.

121. Newberry, John S. *Report upon the Colorado River of the West, Explored in 1857-58 by Lt. J. C. Ives.* Washington, D.C.: 1861.

122. Nichol, A. A. *The Natural Vegetation of Arizona.* Technical Bulletin No. 68. Tucson, Arizona: University of Arizona, 1937.

123. Opler, Morris Edward. With an appendix of comparative references by David French. *Myths and Tales of the Chiricahua Apache Indians. Memoirs of the American Folk-Lore Society,* XXXVII (1942).

124. Parke, John G. "General Report of Exploration from the Pima Villages to the Rio Grande, 1854-5." *Pacific Railroad Reports, VII, Part 1.* Washington, D.C.: 1857.

125. Pattie, James Ohio. *Personal Narrative of James O. Pattie of Kentucky.* Reuben Gold Thwaites, ed. *Early Western Travels, XVIII.* Cleveland: Arthur H. Clark Company, 1905.

126. Patton, James Monroe. *The History of Clifton.* Unpublished M.A. Thesis. Tucson, Arizona: University of Arizona, 1945.

127. *Pioneer Stories of Arizona's Verde Valley.* N.p.: Verde Valley Pioneers Association, Inc., 1954.

128. *Place Names on the Papago, Gila Bend, and San Xavier Indian Reservations.* Sells, Arizona: Sells Indian Agency, U. S. Department of the Interior, Office of Indian Affairs, 1941 (?).

129. Post Office Department. *1903 U. S. Official Register, VII.* Washington, D.C.: Post Office Department.

130. *Records of Appointments of Postmasters, State of Arizona, 1896-1930. Record Group 28 (Microfilm).* General Services Administration, National Archives and Records Section, Washington, D.C., 1953.

131. Poston, Charles Debrille. *Personal Journal.* Unpublished manuscript in Sharlot Hall Museum of Historical Arizona, Prescott, Arizona.

132. Powell, John Wesley. *Explorations of the Colorado River of the West and Its Tributaries: Explored in 1869, 1870, 1871, and 1872.* Washington, D.C.: U. S. Government Printing Office, 1875.

133. Powell, John Wesley. *Report of Explorations in 1873 of the Colorado of the West and Its Tributaries.* Washington, D.C.: 1874.

134. Pumpelly, Raphael. *Across America and Asia: Notes of a Five Years' Journey Around the World and of Residence in Arizona, Japan and China.* New York: Leypoldt and Holt, 1870.

135. Ransome, Frederick Leslie. *Geology of the Globe Copper District, Arizona.* Washington, D.C.: U. S. Government Printing Office, 1903.

136. "Record of Heber Ward, Luna, New Mexico." Unpublished Manuscript.

137. Reid, John C. *Reid's Tramp: or a Journal of the Incidents of Ten Months' Travel Through Texas, New Mexico, Arizona, Sonora, and California.* Selma, Alabama: John Hardy & Company, 1858. Reprinted by The Steck Company, Austin, Texas, 1935.

138. Riggs, Harvey D. "Arivaca Is Old Arizona." *Arizona Publisher, The,* I (September 1955), 6.

138a. Schrader, Frank C. *Mineral Deposits of the Santa Rita and Patagonia Mountains, Arizona.* Washington, D.C.: U. S. Government Printing Office, 1915.

139. Robinson, Henry Hollister. *San Francisco Volcanic Field, The.* U. S. Geological Survey Professional Paper No. 76. Washington, D.C.: 1913.

140. Rockfellow, John A. *Log of an Arizona Trail Blazer.* Tucson, Arizona: Acme Printing Company, 1933.

141. Ross, Clyde P. *Lower Gila Region, Arizona, The.* Water Supply Paper No. 498. Washington, D.C.: U. S. Government Printing Office, 1923.

142. Russell, Henry Norris. "Meteor Crater." *Museum Notes,* IV (September 1931), 1-3.

143. "San Francisco Peaks." *Museum Notes,* III (September 1930), 1-4.

144. Sealock, Richard B. and Pauline A. Seely. *Bibliography of Place Name Literature.* Chicago: American Library Association, 1948.

145. Sedelmayr, Jacobo. *Jacobo Sedelmayr: Four Original Manuscript Narratives, 1744-1751.* Peter Masten Dunne, trans. Tucson, Arizona: Arizona Pioneers Historical Society, 1955.

146. Seibold, Doris Katherine. *Folk Tales from the Patagonia Area.* Tucson, Arizona: University of Arizona Bulletin No. 13 (October 1948).

147. Simpich, Frederick. "Along Our Side of the Mexican Border." *National Geographic Magazine, The,* XXXVIII (July 1920), 61-80.

148. Simpson, James H. *Journal of a Military Reconnaissance from Santa Fe, New Mexico, to the Navajo Country.* Philadelphia: Lippincott, Grambo and Company, 1852.

149. Sisk, Hanson Ray. "Historical Santa Cruz County." Nogales, Arizona: n.p., 1954.

150. Sitgreaves, Lorenzo. *Report of an Expedition Down the Zuni and Colorado Rivers.* Senate Executive Document No. 59, 33rd Congress, 1st Session. Washington, D.C.: Beverley Tucker, Senate Printer, 1851.

151. *Sixth Report of the United States Geographic Board: 1890 to 1932.* Washington, D.C.: U. S. Government Printing Office, 1933.

152. Slipher, V. M. "The Lowell Observatory." *Publications of the Astronomical Society of the Pacific,* XXXIX (June 1927), 143-154.

153. Sloan, Richard E. *Memories of an Arizona Judge.* Palo Alto, California: Stanford University Press, 1932.

154. Smith, T. B., ed. *Grammar of the Pima or Nevome.* New York: Library of American Linguistics, 1860-1864.

155. Stephens, Bascom A. "Quijotoa Mining District." N.p.: n.p., 1884.

156. Stevens, Robert Conway. *A History of Chandler, Arizona.* Unpublished M.A. Thesis. Tucson, Arizona: University of Arizona, 1954.

157. Stone, Jerome. *History of Fort Grant, The.* Unpublished M.A. Thesis Tucson, Arizona: University of Arizona, 1941.

158. Summerhayes, Martha. *Vanished Arizona: Recollections of My Army Life.* Milo Milton Quaife, ed. Chicago: The Lakeside Press, 1939 (reprint).

159. Sweeny, Thomas W. *Journal of Lt. Thomas W. Sweeny, 1849-1853.* Arthur Woodward, ed. Los Angeles: Westernlore Press, 1956.

160. Sykes, Godfrey. "Camino del Diablo, The." *Geographical Review,* XVII (1927), 62-74.

161. Tevis, James H. *Arizona in the '50's.* Albuquerque, N. M.: University of New Mexico Press, 1954.

162. Theobald, John Orr. *Wells Fargo & Company Stations and Agents in Territorial Arizona.* Unpublished manuscript. Phoenix: 1956.

163. Thompson, Alisson Harris. "Diary." *Utah Historical Quarterly,* VII (January, April, and July 1939).

164. "Tuba City and the Charlie Day Spring." *Museum Notes,* II (May 1931), 1-4.

165. Udell, John. *Journal of John Udell.* Jefferson, Ohio: Ashtabula Sentinel Steam Press, 1868.

166. Underhill, Ruth M. *Here Come the Navaho!* Lawrence, Kansas: United States Indian Service, 1953.

166a. United States Geographic Board

   a. "Decisions Rendered Between July 1, 1938, and June 30, 1939"

   b. Decisions Rendered Between July 1, 1939, and June 30, 1940."

   c. "Decisions Rendered Between July 1, 1940, and June 30, 1941."

   d. "Decisions Rendered Between July 1, 1941, and June 30, 1943."

   e. "Decisions: #4301: Rendered Between July 1, 1943, and October 31, 1943."

   f. "Decisions #4303: Rendered Between October 31, 1943, and December 1943."

   g. "Decisions #4501,2,3: Rendered January, February, March 1945."

   h. "Decisions #4510,11,12: Rendered October, November, December 1945."

   i. "Decisions #4607,8,9: Rendered July, August, September 1946."

   j. "Decisions #4701,2,3.: Rendered January, February, March, 1947."

   k. "Decisions #4708,9: Rendered August, September 1947."

   l. "Decisions #4801-06: Rendered Between January and June 1948."

   m. "Decision List #5003: January, February, March 1950; May 1950."

   n. "Decisions on Names in the United States and Alaska Rendered During April, May, and June 1950; August 1950."

   o. "Decisions #4910,4911,4912: October, November, December 1949; January 1950."

   p. "Decision #19: May 4, 1932."

   q. "Decisions Rendered Between July 1, 1936, and June 30, 1937."

167. Van Valkenburgh, Richard; Lucy Wilcox Adams, and John C. McPhee, eds. *diné bike'yah.* Window Rock, Arizona: Navajo Service, Office of Indian Affairs, 1941.

168. Verkamp, Margaret M. *History of Grand Canyon National Park.* Unpublished M.A. Thesis. Tucson, Arizona: University of Arizona, 1940.

169. *Walapai Papers: Historical Reports, Documents, and Extracts from Publications Relating to the Walapai Indians of Arizona.* Senate Document No. 273. 74th Congress, 2nd Session. Washington, D.C.: U. S. Government Printing Office, 1936.

170. Wells, Muriel Sibell. *Bonanza Trail, The: Ghost Towns and Mining Camps of the West.* Bloomington, Indiana: Indiana University Press, 1953.

171. Westover, Adele B. and J. Morris Richards. *Brief History of Joseph City, A.* Winslow, Arizona: The Winslow Mail, 1951.

172. Wheeler, George M. *Annual Report upon the Geographical Explorations and Surveys West of the 100th Meridian, etc., Appendix of Annual Report of the Chief of Engineers for 1875.* Washington, D.C.: U. S. Government Printing Office, 1875.

173. Wheeler, George M. *Preliminary Report of Explorations and Surveys South of the Central Pacific R.R., Principally in Nevada and Arizona.* Washington, D.C.: 1872.

174. Wheeler, George M. *Progress-Report Upon Geographical and Geological Explorations and Surveys West of the One Hundredth Meridian in 1872.* Washington, D.C.: U. S. Government Printing Office, 1874.

175. Wheeler, George M. *Report Upon the Geographical and Geological Explorations and Surveys West of the One Hundredth Meridian, in Charge of First Lieutenant George M. Wheeler.* Washington, D.C.: U. S. Government Printing Office, 1875.

176. Whipple, Amiel W. *Itinerary: Explorations and Surveys for a Railroad Route from the Mississippi River to the Pacific Ocean: Route Near the 35th Parallel in 1853 and 1854.* Washington, D.C.: 1854.

177. Whipple, Amiel W. *Itinerary of Lieutenant A. W. Whipple During His Explorations for a Railway Route from Fort Smith to Los Angeles in the Years 1853 & 1854,* published under following title: *Pathfinder in the Southwest, A,* Grant Foreman, ed. and annotater. Norman, Oklahoma: University of Oklahoma Press, 1941.

178. Whipple, Amiel W. *Report of Explorations and Surveys to Ascertain the Most Practical and Economical Route for a Railroad from the Mississippi River to the Ocean, 1853-54,* I-VII. Washington, D.C.: 1854.

179. Whitfield, J. S., and J. S. Diller. "Mineralogical Notes on Dumortierite from Harlem, N. Y., and Clip, Arizona." *American Journal of Science,* XXXVII (1889), 216-219.

180. Williams, Oran A. *Settlement and Growth of the Gila Valley as a Mormon Colony, 1879-1900.* Unpublished M.A. Thesis. Tucson, Arizona: University of Arizona, 1937.

181. Wilson, Eldred D. *Geology and Mineral Deposits of Southern Yuma County, Arizona.* University of Arizona Bulletin (February 15, 1933), IV, No. 2. Arizona Bureau of Mines, Series No. 7, Bulletin No. 134. University of Arizona, Tucson, Arizona.

182. Winship, George Parker. *Coronado Expedition, 1540-1542, The 14th Annual Report,* Bureau of American Ethnology, Washington, D.C.

183. Young, Robert W. *Navajo Yearbook of Planning in Action, The.* Window Rock, Arizona: Navajo Agency, 1955.

# MAPS

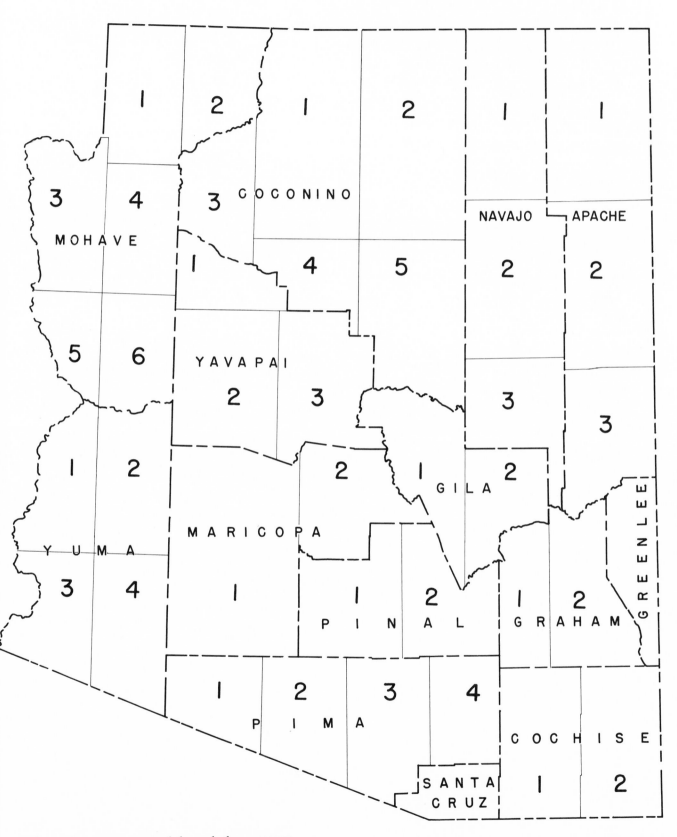

These maps were prepared through the generous
cooperation of Mr. Robert T. O'Haire, Assistant
Minerologist, Arizona Bureau of Mines

410

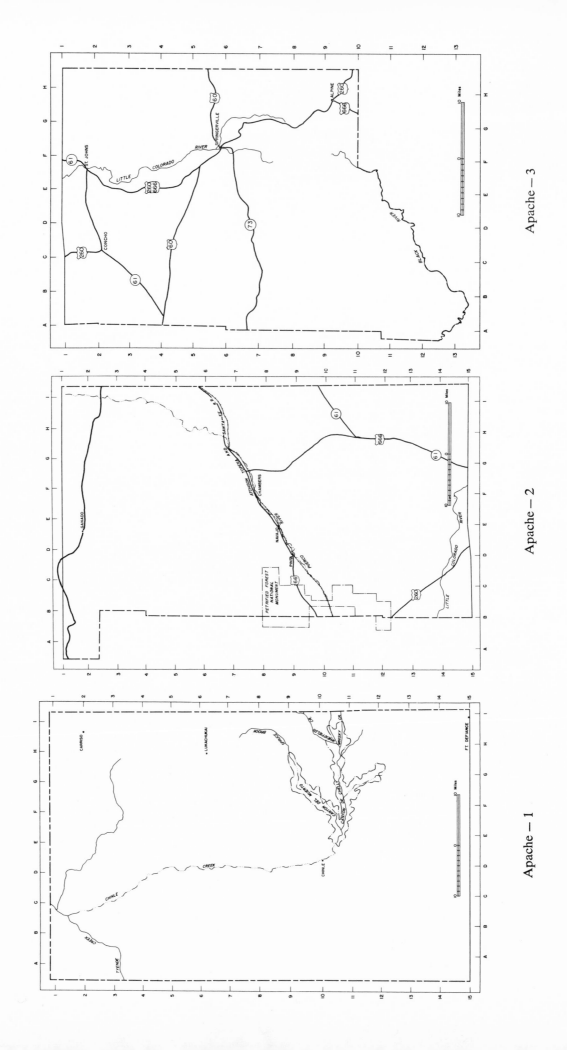

Apache — 1

Apache — 2

Apache — 3

411

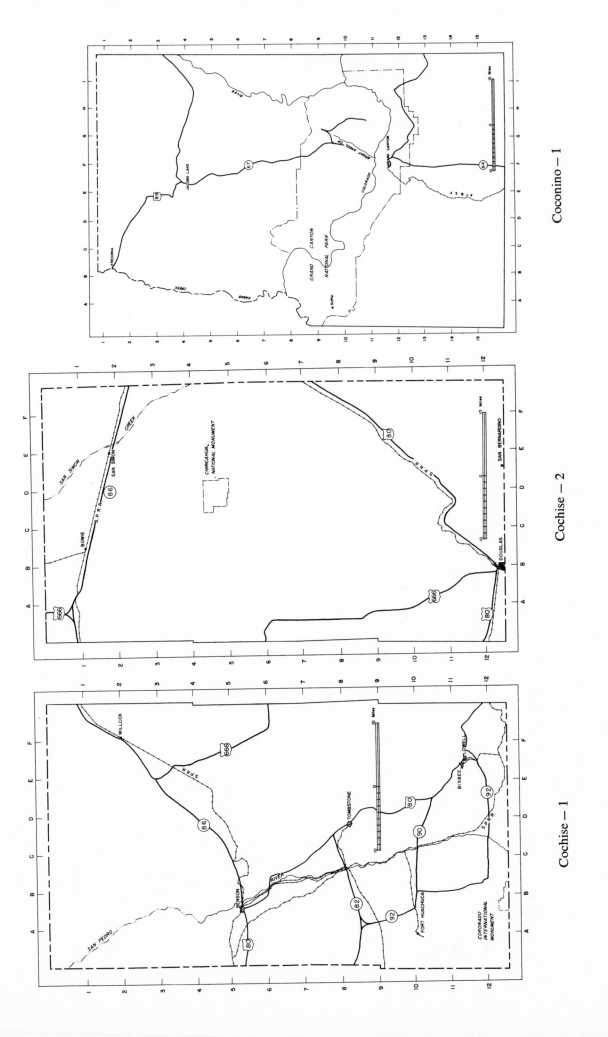

Cochise – 1

Cochise – 2

Coconino – 1

412

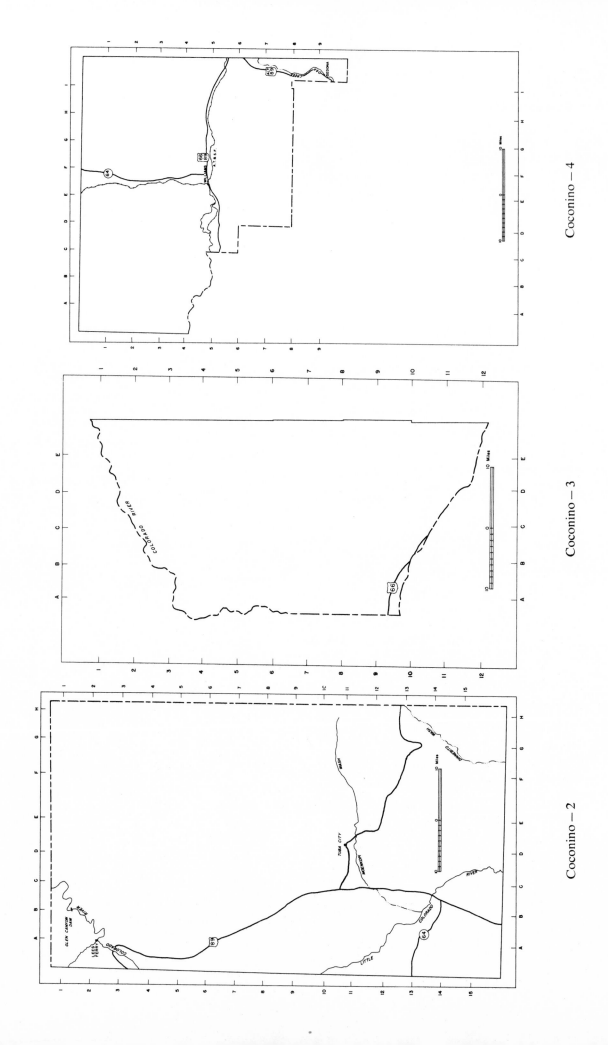

Coconino – 4

Coconino – 3

Coconino – 2

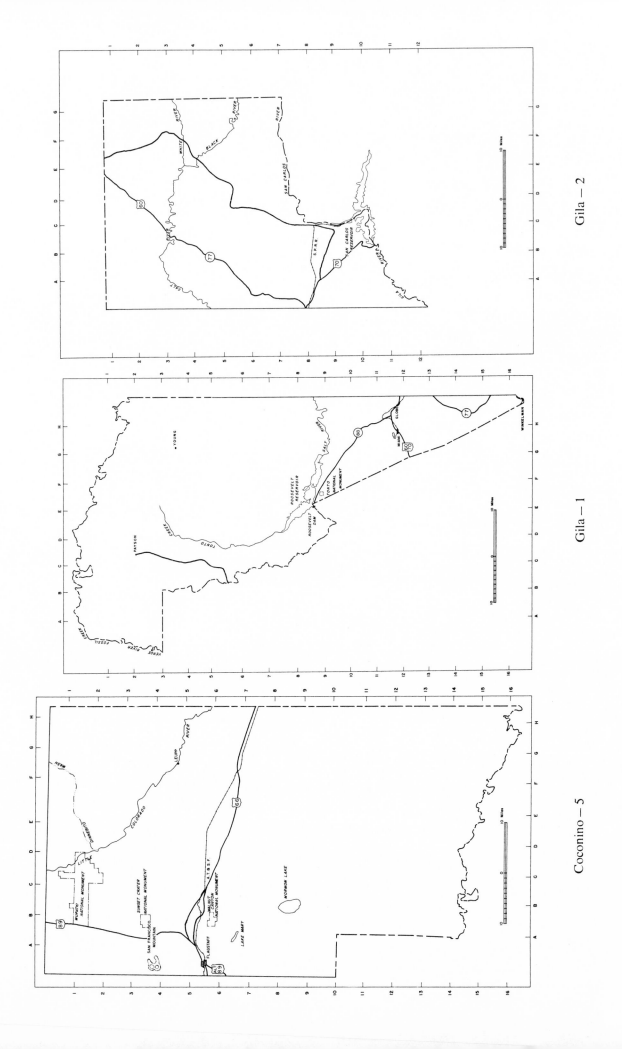

Gila – 2

Gila – 1

Coconino – 5

414

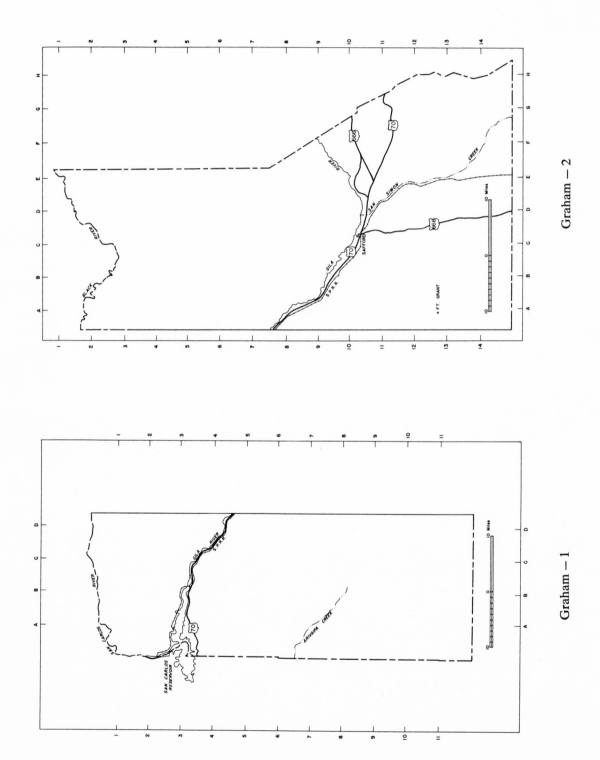

Graham – 2

Graham – 1

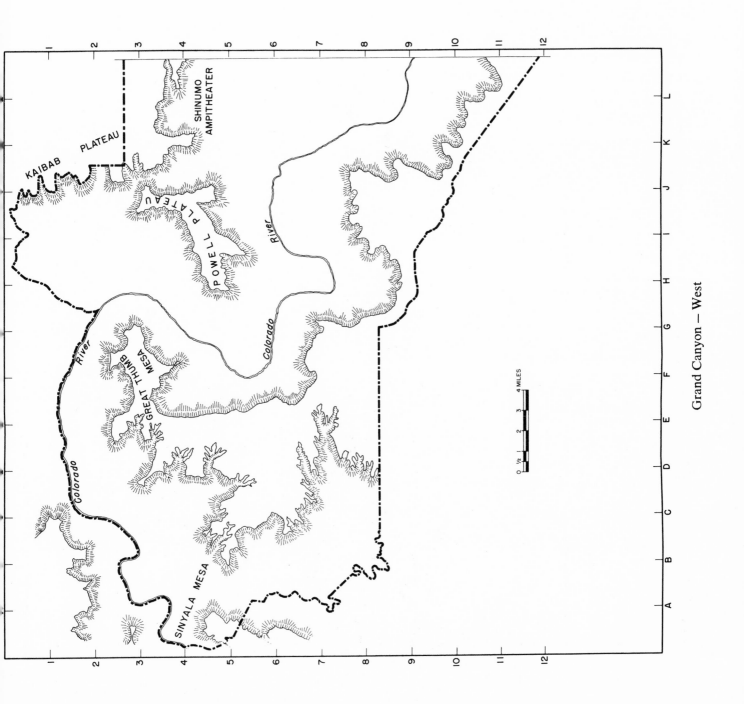

Grand Canyon — West

416

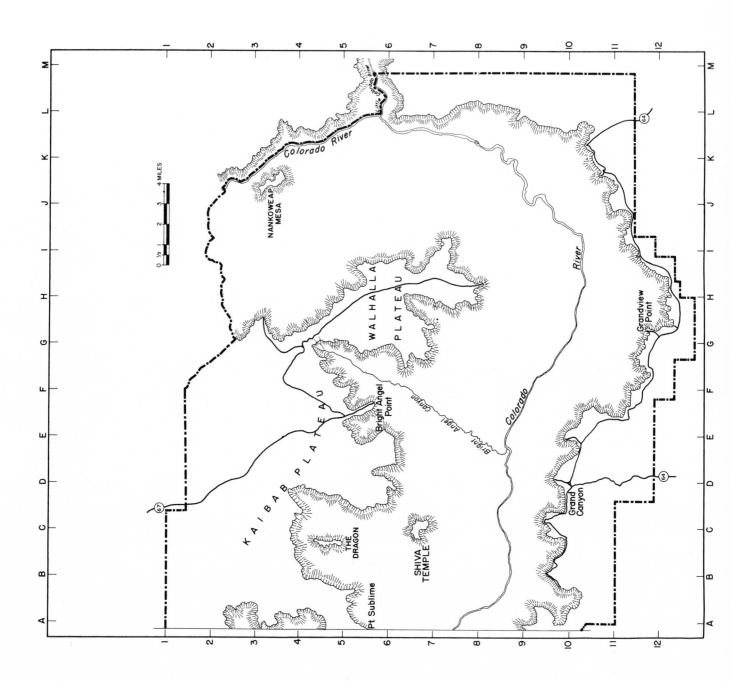

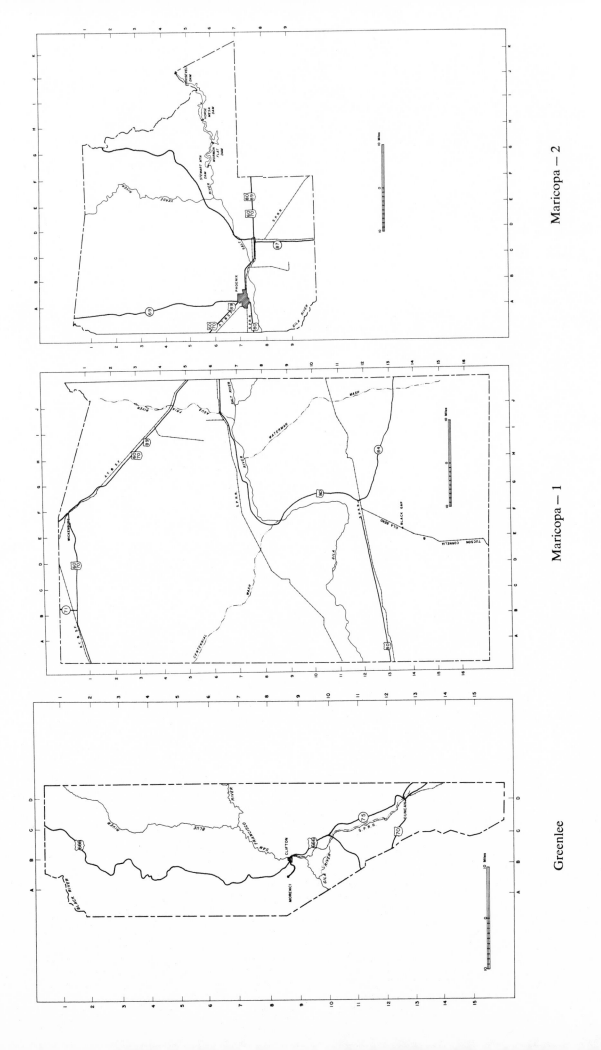

417

Maricopa – 2

Maricopa – 1

Greenlee

418

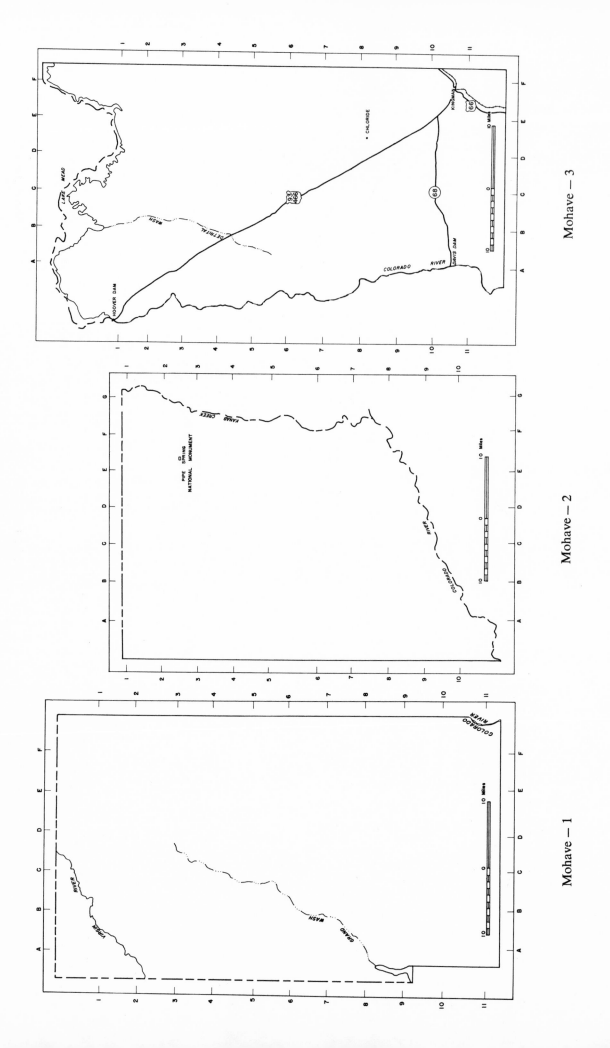

Mohave – 3

Mohave – 2

Mohave – 1

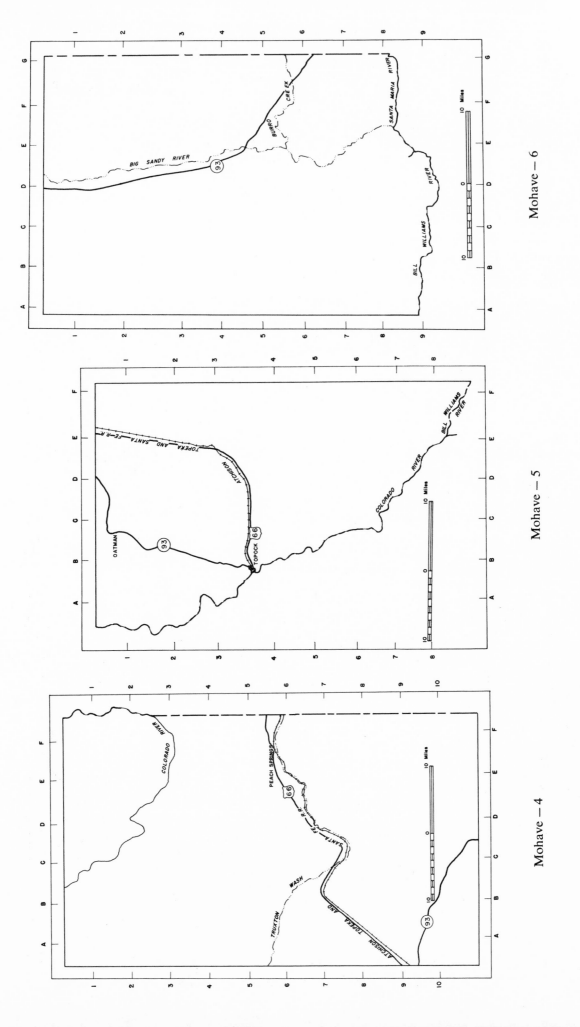

419

Mohave — 6

Mohave — 5

Mohave — 4

420

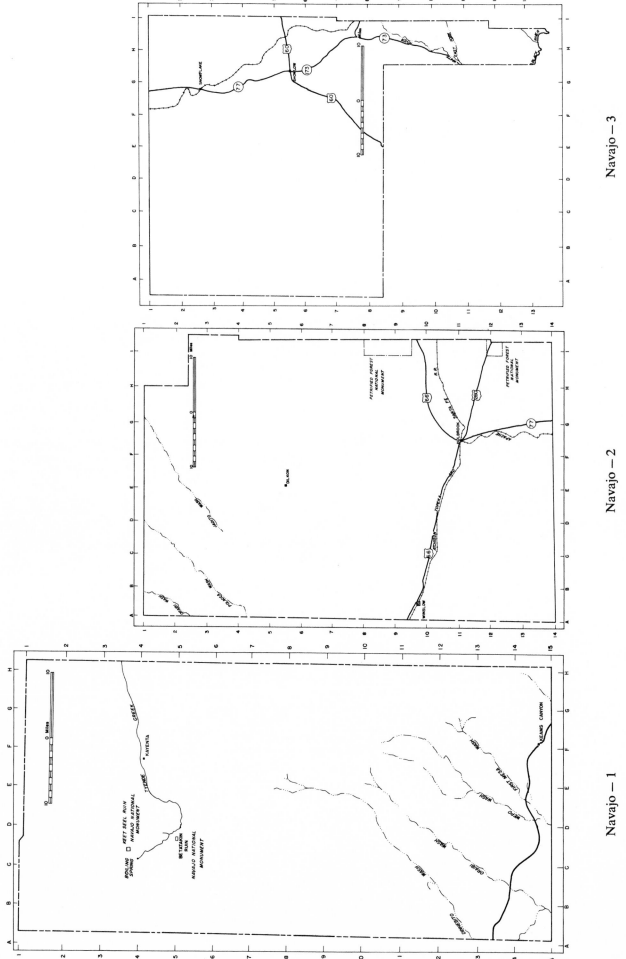

Navajo – 1

Navajo – 2

Navajo – 3

421

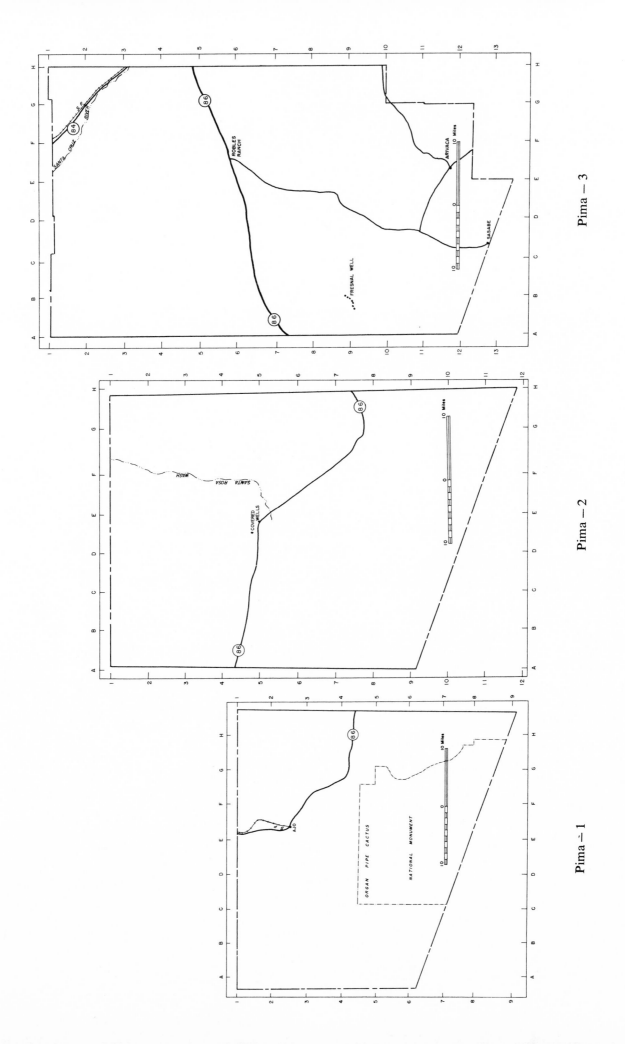

Pima — 3

Pima — 2

Pima — 1

422

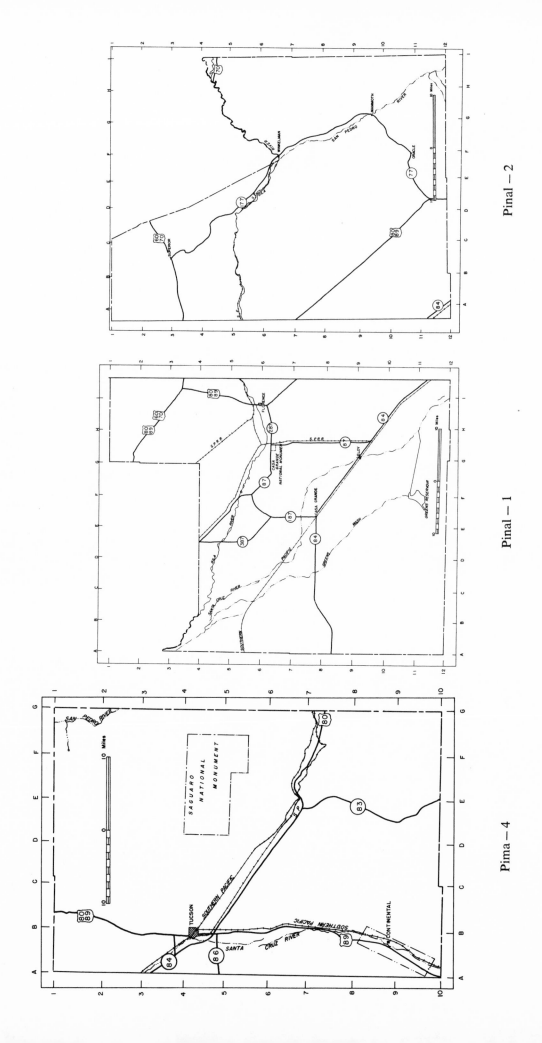

Pinal – 2

Pinal – 1

Pima – 4

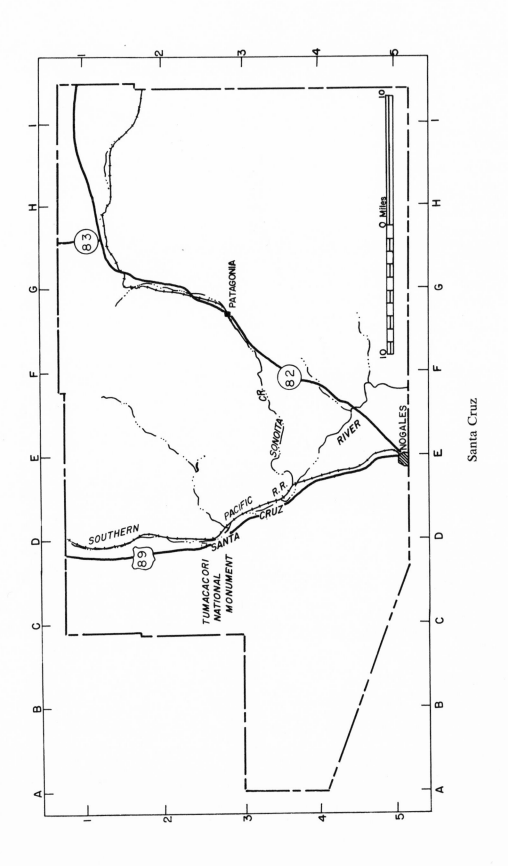

Santa Cruz

424

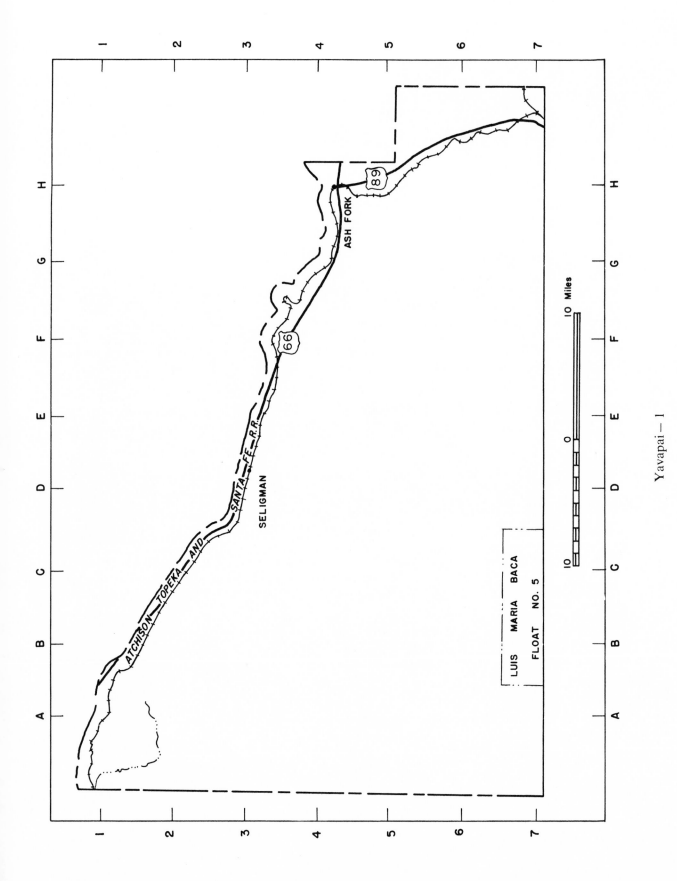

Yavapai — 1

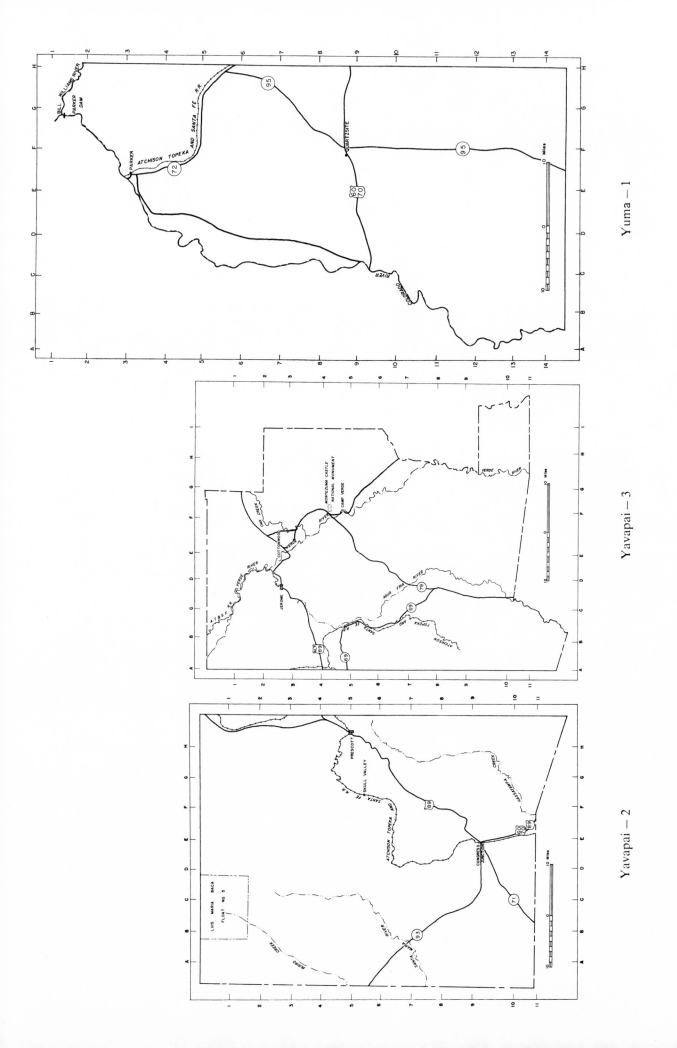

425

Yuma – 1

Yavapai – 3

Yavapai – 2

426

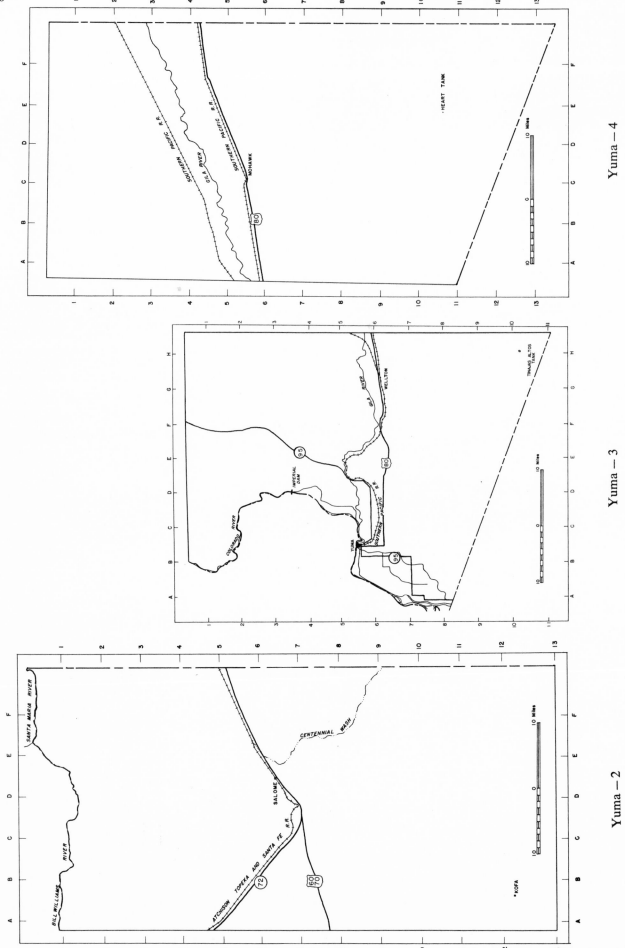

Yuma – 4

Yuma – 3

Yuma – 2

# INDEX

AJAX HILL ..............................COCHISE
AJO .......................................PIMA
Ajo, Mount ..................................Pima
    See: AJO, PIMA
Ajo Peak ....................................Pima
    See: AJO, PIMA
Ajo Range ...................................Pima
    See: AJO, PIMA
AKABA, MOUNT ..........GRAND CANYON, COCO
Akchin ......................................Pima
    See: SAN SERAFIN, PIMA
AK CHUT VAYA ...........................PIMA
Alameda, Rio de la .........................Apache
    See: LITTLE COLORADO RIVER,
Alamo .....................................Maricopa
    See: ALAMO, YUMA
ALAMO ...................................YUMA
Alamo Canyon ................................Pima
    See: ALAMO, YUMA
Alamo Canyon ..........................Santa Cruz
    See: ALAMO, YUMA
Alamo Crossing ..............................Yuma
    See: ALAMO, YUMA
Alamo Mine ............................Santa Cruz
    See: ALAMO, YUMA
Alamo Mountains .............................Pima
    See: ALAMO, YUMA
Alamo Ranger Station .........................Gila
    See: ALAMO, YUMA
Alamos ................................Santa Cruz
    See: ALAMO, YUMA
Alamo Spring ...............................Apache
    See: ALAMO, YUMA
Alamo Spring ...............................Yuma
    See: ALAMO, YUMA
ALARCON TERRACE .......GRAND CANYON, COCO
ALCOVE CANYON ........................APACHE
ALDER CANYON .......................COCONINO
ALDER CREEK ........................GREENLEE
ALDER CREEK .........................MARICOPA
Alder Lake ..............................Coconino
    See: ALDER CANYON, COCONINO
Alder Peak ..............................Greenlee
    See: ALDER CREEK, GREENLEE
ALDONA ....................................PIMA
Aleh-zon ......................................XV
ALEXANDER, CAMP ....................MOHAVE
ALEXANDRA .........................YAVAPAI
Alexandria .................................Yavapai
    See: ALEXANDRA, YAVAPAI
ALGODON ................................GRAHAM
Algodones Land Grant ........................Yuma
    See: SOMERTON, YUMA
ALHAMBRA ...........................MARICOPA
ALI AK CHIN ...............................PIMA
ALI CHUK SON .............................PIMA
ALICIA ..................................MARICOPA
Alimo .......................................Yuma
    See: ALAMO, YUMA
ALISO CREEK ................................GILA
ALISO SPRING .......................SANTA CRUZ

Alivaipai ....................................Pima
    See: QUITO BAQUITO, PIMA
Aljibe .......................................Pinal
    See: MONTEZUMA'S HEAD, PINAL
Alkali Flats ................................Cochise
    See: WILLCOX, COCHISE
ALLAH ..................................MARICOPA
ALLAN LAKE .........................COCONINO
Allen .......................................Pima
    See: GUNSIGHT, PIMA
Allen City ...................................Pima
    See: GUNSIGHT, PIMA
Allen's Camp ...............................Navajo
    See: JOSEPH CITY, NAVAJO
Allen's City ...............................Navajo
    See: JOSEPH CITY, NAVAJO
ALLENTOWN ............................APACHE
ALLIGATOR, THE ........GRAND CANYON, COCO
ALMA ......................................PIMA
ALMA .....................................PINAL
ALMA MESA ..........................GREENLEE
Alma Ward ..................................Apache
    See: ROUND VALLEY, APACHE
ALPHA ...................................MARICOPA
    See also: BURKES STATION, MARICOPA
ALPINE ..................................APACHE
ALSAP BUTTE .............GRAND CANYON, COCO
Altamount ................................Maricopa
    See: LIBERTY, MARICOPA
Alta Pimeria ................................Pima
    See: SAN XAVIER DEL BAC, PIMA
Altar, El ....................................Pima
    See: ALTAR VALLEY, PIMA
ALTAR VALLEY ...........................PIMA
Altar Wash ..................................Pima
    See: ALTAR VALLEY, PIMA
ALTO .................................SANTA CRUZ
Alto Gulch .............................Santa Cruz
    See: ALTO, SANTA CRUZ
Alum .................................Santa Cruz
    See: ALUM CANYON, SANTA CRUZ
ALUM CANYON .....................SANTA CRUZ
Alum Gulch ............................Santa Cruz
    See: ALUM CANYON, SANTA CRUZ
ALVAREZ MOUNTAINS .....................PIMA
AMADO ...............................SANTA CRUZ
Amadoville ............................Santa Cruz
    See: AMADO, SANTA CRUZ
Amarilla, Cienega ..........................Apache
    See: CIENEGA AMARILLA, APACHE
AMBERON FLAT ........................APACHE
Amberon Point .............................Apache
    See: AMBERON FLAT, APACHE
AMBOY ..................................MOHAVE
AMBUSH WATER POCKET ...............MOHAVE
AMERICAN FLAG .......................MOHAVE
AMERICAN FLAG .........................PINAL
American Flag Ranch .........................Pinal
    See: AMERICAN FLAG, PINAL
American Flag Springs ........................Pinal
    See: AMERICAN FLAG, PINAL

American Hill ............................Pinal
　　See: AMERICAN FLAG, PINAL
American Mine .......................Santa Cruz
　　See: AMERICAN PEAK, SANTA CRUZ
AMERICAN PEAK ...................SANTA CRUZ
AMERICAN RANCH ....................YAVAPAI
American Valley .......................Yavapai
　　See: AMERICAN RANCH, YAVAPAI
Amity, Fort ..........................Apache
　　See: ROUND VALLEY, APACHE
Amity Ward ..........................Apache
　　See: ROUND VALLEY, APACHE
Amole ...............................Pima
　　See: AMOLE PEAK, PIMA
AMOLE PEAK .........................PIMA
"A" Mountain .........................Pima
　　See: SENTINEL PEAK, PIMA
AMSTER .............................GILA
Amusovi Mesa ........................Navajo
　　See: ZILLESA, NAVAJO
Ana, Doña, County ......................XV
ANCHA, SIERRA .......................GILA
Ancha Experimental Forest, Sierra ..........Gila
　　See: ANCHA, SIERRA, GILA
Ancha Forest Reserve, Sierra ..............Gila
　　See: ANCHA, SIERRA, GILA
Ancha Mines, Sierra ....................Gila
　　See: ANCHA, SIERRA, GILA
ANDERSON CANYON ...............COCONINO
Anderson Mesa .......................Coconino
　　See: ANDERSON CANYON, COCONINO
Anderson Point .......................Coconino
　　See: ANDERSON CANYON, COCONINO
Anderson Spring ......................Coconino
　　See: ANDERSON CANYON, COCONINO
ANDRADE'S RANCH ....................PIMA
Andrews Spring .......................Coconino
　　See: TWIN SPRINGS, COCONINO
Andrus Canyon .......................Mohave
　　See: ANDRUS SPRING, MOHAVE
Andrus Draw .........................Mohave
　　See: ANDRUS SPRING, MOHAVE
ANDRUS SPRING .....................MOHAVE
Andrus Spring, Lower ...................Mohave
　　See: ANDRUS SPRING, MOHAVE
Andrus Spring, Upper ...................Mohave
　　See: ANDRUS SPRING, MOHAVE
ANEGAM ............................PIMA
Anegam Wash ........................Pima
　　See: ANEGAM, PIMA
Anekam .............................Pima
　　See: ANEGAM, PIMA
Angeles de Guevavi, Los .................Santa Cruz
　　See: GUEVAVI, SANTA CRUZ
ANGELL ...........................COCONINO
Angel Plateau ..............Grand Canyon, Coco
　　See: INDIAN GARDEN, GRAND CANYON
ANGORA ............................GILA
ANITA ............................COCONINO
Anita Mines .........................Coconino
　　See: ANITA, COCONINO
ANKRIM'S LANDING ...................YUMA

ANNADALE ..........................MOHAVE
ANTARES ...........................MOHAVE
Antelope Hill ........................Yavapai
　　See: ANTELOPE PEAK, YAVAPAI
ANTELOPE HILL .......................YUMA
Antelope Hills Stage Station ..............Yuma
　　See: ANTELOPE HILL, YUMA
ANTELOPE HOUSE ....................APACHE
ANTELOPE LAKE ...................COCONINO
Antelope Mesa .......................Navajo
　　See: KAWAIOKU, NAVAJO
Antelope Mountain ....................Yavapai
　　See: ANTELOPE PEAK, YAVAPAI
ANTELOPE PEAK ....................YAVAPAI
　　See also p. XVII
Antelope Peak ........................Yuma
　　See: ANTELOPE HILL, YUMA
Antelope Plain .......................Mohave
　　See: WONSITS PLATEAU, MOHAVE
Antelope Point .......................Apache
　　See: ANTELOPE HOUSE, APACHE
Antelope Range ......................Yavapai
　　See: WEAVER, YAVAPAI
　　See also: ANTELOPE PEAK, YAVAPAI
ANTELOPE SPRING ...................COCHISE
Antelope Spring ......................Coconino
　　See: FLAGSTAFF, COCONINO
Antelope Spring ......................Navajo
　　See: JADITO WASH, NAVAJO
Antelope Station ......................Yavapai
　　See: CORDES, YAVAPAI
　　See: ANTELOPE PEAK, YAVAPAI
Antelope Valley ......................Yavapai
　　See: ANTELOPE PEAK, YAVAPAI
Antelope Wash .......................Yavapai
　　See: ANTELOPE PEAK, YAVAPAI
ANVIL MOUNTAIN ....................YUMA
ANVIL ROCK ........................YAVAPAI
　　See also: ANVIL MOUNTAIN, YUMA
Anvil Rock Station ....................Yavapai
　　See: ANVIL MOUNTAIN, YUMA
　　ANVIL ROCK, YAVAPAI
A One Crater ........................Coconino
　　See: A ONE (A 1) MOUNTAIN,
　　COCONINO
A ONE (A 1) MOUNTAIN ..............COCONINO
A 1 Ranch Spring .....................Coconino
　　See: A ONE (A 1) MOUNTAIN, COCONINO
APACHE ...........................COCHISE
APACHE ...........................YAVAPAI
APACHE BUTTE .....................NAVAJO
Apache, Camp ........................Navajo
　　See: APACHE, FORT, NAVAJO
Apache Camp ........................Pinal
　　See: ORACLE, PINAL
Apache Canyon .......................Graham
　　See: APACHE PEAKS, GILA
APACHE CAVE .....................MARICOPA
APACHE COUNTY .......................2
Apache Creek ........................Greenlee
　　See: APACHE GULCH, GREENLEE
Apache Creek ........................Maricopa
　　See: APACHE CAVE, MARICOPA

APACHE, FORT .........................NAVAJO

APACHE, FORT, INDIAN RESERVATION ......NAVAJO

Apache Gap .........................Maricopa
    See: APACHE CAVE, MARICOPA

Apache Grove ......................Greenlee
    See: APACHE GULCH, GREENLEE

APACHE GULCH .....................GREENLEE

APACHE INDIAN RESERVATION,
    FORT ........................NAVAJO, Gila

APACHE JUNCTION ....................PINAL

APACHE, LAKE ........................APACHE

Apache Lake ........................Maricopa
    See: HORSE MESA, MARICOPA
        APACHE CAVE, MARICOPA

APACHE LEAP ..........................PINAL

APACHE MAID MOUNTAIN .....COCONINO, Yavapai

Apache Mine .........................Pinal
    See: ORACLE, PINAL

Apache Mountains ......................Gila
    See: APACHE PEAKS, GILA
        ROCKINSTRAW MOUNTAIN, GILA

APACHE NATIONAL FOREST ......APACHE, Greenlee

APACHE PASS .........................COCHISE

Apache Peak ........................Cochise
    See: APACHE PASS, COCHISE

Apache Peak .......................Maricopa
    See: APACHE CAVE, MARICOPA

Apache Peak .........................Pinal
    See: APACHE PEAKS, GILA

APACHE PEAKS ..........................GILA

APACHE POINT ..........GRAND CANYON, COCO

Apache, Sierra ........................Gila
    See: ROCKINSTRAW MOUNTAIN, GILA

Apache Spring ......................Cochise
    See: APACHE PASS, COCHISE

Apache Spring ......................Graham
    See: APACHE PEAKS, GILA

Apache Spring ......................Maricopa
    See: APACHE CAVE, MARICOPA

Apache Spring Ranch ...............Santa Cruz
    See: GARDNER CANYON, SANTA CRUZ

APACHE TRAIL ..............  .....GILA, Maricopa
    See also: APACHE CAVE, MARICOPA

APEX ..............................COCONINO

APIARY WELL .......................MARICOPA

Apostoles, Rio de los ....................Gila
    See: GILA RIVER, GILA

Apple Ranch .........................Gila
    See: ELLISON, GILA

Aquarius Cliffs ......................Mohave
    See: AQUARIUS MOUNTAINS, MOHAVE

Aquarius, Mount .....................Mohave
    See: AQUARIUS MOUNTAINS, MOHAVE

Aquarius Mountain ...................Mohave
    See: AQUARIUS MOUNTAINS, MOHAVE

AQUARIUS MOUNTAINS ..................MOHAVE

Aquarius Plateau ....................Mohave
    See: AQUARIUS MOUNTAINS, MOHAVE

Aquarius Range .....................Mohave
    See: AQUARIUS MOUNTAINS, MOHAVE

ARABY ...............................YUMA

ARAVAIPA ...........................GRAHAM

Arcadia Ranch .........................Pinal
    See: ORACLE, PINAL

ARCH CANYON .........................PIMA

Archi ................................Pima
    See: ACHI, PIMA

ARCH TANK ...........................YUMA

AREY ..............................COCONINO

Aribac, La ...........................Pima
    See: ARIVACA, PIMA

ARIPINE .............................NAVAJO

Aritutoc ...........................Maricopa
    See: OATMAN FLAT, MARICOPA

ARIVACA ..............................PIMA

Arivaca Creek .........................Pima
    See: ARIVACA, PIMA

Arivaca Valley ........................Pima
    See: ALTAR VALLEY, PIMA
        AVRA VALLEY, PIMA

Arivaca Wash .........................Pima
    See: ARIVACA, PIMA

ARIVAIPA CANYON .................PINAL, Graham

Arivaipa Creek ..................Pinal, Graham
    See: ARIVAIPA CANYON, PINAL

Arivaipa Springs ....................Graham
    See: ARIVAIPA CANYON, PINAL

Arivaipa Valley .....................Graham
    See: ARIVAIPA CANYON, PINAL

Arivaypa, Fort ........................Pinal
    See: GRANT, CAMP (OLD), PINAL

Arivaypa Mountains ..............Pinal, Graham
    See: ARIVAIPA CANYON, PINAL

Arivaypa River ..................Pinal, Graham
    See: ARIVAIPA CANYON, PINAL

ARIZMO .............................COCHISE

ARIZOLA .............................PINAL

Arizola Mountain ......................Pinal
    See: CASA GRANDE, PINAL

Arizona ...............................XV

Arizonac ..............................XV

Arizonac, Real de ......................XV

Arizona City .......................Maricopa
    See: GILLESPIE DAM, MARICOPA

ARIZONA CITY ........................YAVAPAI

Arizona City .........................Yuma
    See: YUMA, YUMA

Arizona Mountains .................Santa Cruz
    See: PAJARITO MOUNTAINS, SANTA CRUZ

ARIZONA, PLATEAU OF .................COCONINO

Arizona Plateau .......................XIII

ARIZONA STRIP .............COCONINO, Mohave
    See also: COCONINO COUNTY, p. 60

ARK BASIN ...........................MOHAVE

ARKILL .............................GRAHAM

ARLINGTON .........................MARICOPA

Arlington Mesa .....................Maricopa
    See: ARLINGTON, MARICOPA

Arlington Valley ...................Maricopa
    See: ARLINGTON, MARICOPA

ARMER ................................GILA

Armer and Tanner Winter Camp ..........Gila
    See: ARMER, GILA

AUBREY LANDING ........................MOHAVE

Aubrey Peak .................................Mohave
    See: AUBREY LANDING, MOHAVE

AUBREY SPRING ........................COCONINO

Aubrey Spring ...............................Mohave
    See: AUBREY LANDING, MOHAVE

Aubrey Valley ...............................Mohave
    See: AUBREY LANDING, MOHAVE

Aubry City .................................Mohave
    See: AUBREY LANDING, MOHAVE

Audley ....................................Mohave
    See: AUBREY LANDING, MOHAVE

Audrey ....................................Mohave
    See: AUBREY LANDING, MOHAVE

AULTMAN ...............................YAVAPAI

AVALON ...................................YUMA

Avansada, Mesa de la ........................Cochise
    See: SAN BERNARDINO LAND GRANT,
    COCHISE

Avie Tok-a-va ...............................Yuma
    See: DOME ROCK MOUNTAINS, YUMA

AVONDALE .............................MARICOPA

AVRA VALLEY. .............................PIMA

A-vuc-hoo-mar-lish ...........................Pinal
    See: CASA BLANCA, PINAL

AWATOBI .................................NAVAJO
    See also: KAWAIOKU, NAVAJO

Awatobi Mesa ...............................Navajo
    See: AWATOBI, NAVAJO

Awatobi Spring ..............................Navajo
    See: AWATOBI, NAVAJO

AWATOVI CREEK ..........GRAND CANYON, COCO

Awatubi Crest ...................Grand Canyon, Coco
    See: AWATOVI CREEK, GRAND CANYON

Awatuvi Creek ..................Grand Canyon, Coco
    See: AWATOVI CREEK, GRAND CANYON

AYER POINT ..............GRAND CANYON, COCO

AZANSOSI MESA ........................NAVAJO

AZATLAN ...............................YAVAPAI

Aztec .....................................Cochise
    See: WILGUS, COCHISE

AZTEC ................................SANTA CRUZ

AZTEC ...................................YUMA

Aztec Gulch ..............................Santa Cruz
    See: AZTEC, SANTA CRUZ

Aztec Hills .................................Yuma
    See: AZTEC, YUMA

AZTEC PASS .............................YAVAPAI

AZTEC PEAK ................................GILA

Azul, Rio ..................................Coconino
    See: BILL WILLIAMS MOUNTAIN, COCONINO

Azul, Rio ..................................Greenlee
    See: BLUE RIVER, GREENLEE

Azul, Sierra ................................Apache
    See: BLUE RANGE, APACHE

Azul, Sierra ...............................Greenlee
    See: BLUE RIVER, GREENLEE

Azul, Sierra ...............................Yavapai
    See: VERDE, CAMP, YAVAPAI

Baaki .....................................Pinal
    See: CASA BLANCA, PINAL

Babacanora .................................Cochise
    See: BABOCOMARI, COCHISE

Babacomari Land Grant .......................Cochise
    See: BOABOCOMARI, COCHISE

Babaho ....................................Pima
    See: MAISH VAYA, PIMA

BABBIT BILL TANK .....................COCONINO

Babbitts ..................................Coconino
    See: BABBIT BILL TANK, COCONINO

Babbit Spring ..............................Coconino
    See: BABBIT BILL TANK, COCONINO

Babiteoida ............................Pinal, Graham
    See: ARIVAIPA CANYON, PINAL

BABOCOMARI ...........................COCHISE

Babocomari Creek ............................Cochise
    See: BABOCOMARI, COCHISE

Babocomari River ...........................Cochise
    See: BABOCOMARI, COCHISE

Baboquivari .................................Pima
    See: BABOQUIVARI PEAK, PIMA

Baboquivari Canyon ...........................Pima
    See: BABOQUIVARI PEAK, PIMA

Baboquivari Forest Reserve .....................Pima
    See: CORONADO NATIONAL FOREST, PIMA

Baboquivari Mountains .........................Pima
    See: BABOQUIVARI PEAK, PIMA

BABOQUIVARI PEAK .......................PIMA

Baboquivari Valley ...........................Pima
    See: BABOQUIVARI PEAK, PIMA

Baboquivari Wash ............................Pima
    See: BABOQUIVARI PEAK, PIMA

Baboquivera Plain ............................Pima
    See: BABOQUIVARI PEAK, PIMA
    ALTAR VALLEY, PIMA

Bacabi ....................................Navajo
    See: BAKABI, NAVAJO

BACA FLOAT #3 ......................SANTA CRUZ

Bacobi ....................................Navajo
    See: BAKABI, NAVAJO

Bacovi ....................................Navajo
    See: BAKABI, NAVAJO

Badger Canyon ..............................Coconino
    See: BADGER CREEK, COCONINO

BADGER CREEK .........................COCONINO

Baecker Butte ..............................Coconino
    See: BAKER'S BUTTE, COCONINO

BAGDAD .................................YAVAPAI

Baggiburi Buta ..............................Pima
    See: BABOQUIVARI PEAK, PIMA

Bagley ....................................Navajo
    See: TAYLOR, NAVAJO

Bagnall ...................................Navajo
    See: ADAIR, NAVAJO

Bagnall Hollow ..............................Navajo
    See: ADAIR, NAVAJO

Bah Ki ....................................Pinal
    See: CASA BLANCA, PINAL

Bajia Santa Rosa ............................Pima
    See: SANTA ROSA MOUNTAINS, PIMA

Bajio Comovo ...............................Pima
    See: KUM VO, PIMA

BAT CANYON ...........................APACHE
BAT CANYON ..........................GREENLEE
Bat Cave ................................Greenlee
   See: BAT CANYON, GREENLEE
Bates Canyon ..............................Pinal
   See: BATESVILLE, PINAL
BATESVILLE ...............................PINAL
BATES WELL ...............................PIMA
Bat Rock ................................Apache
   See: BAT CANYON, APACHE
BATTLE FLAT ..........................YAVAPAI
BATTLEGROUND .........................APACHE
Battleground, The ..........................Graham
   See: CEDAR SPRINGS, GRAHAM
Battle Mountain ...........................Mohave
   See: BATTLESHIP MOUNTAIN, MOHAVE
Battle Ridge ..............................Coconino
   See: SYCAMORE CANYON, COCONINO
BATTLESHIP, THE .......................APACHE
Battleship, The .................Coconino, Grand Canyon
   See: BATTLESHIP MOUNTAIN, YUMA
BATTLESHIP MOUNTAIN .................MOHAVE
BATTLESHIP MOUNTAIN ....................YUMA
Bat Trail ................................Apache
   See: BAT CANYON, APACHE
Bawley ....................................Pima
   See: BOWLEY, PIMA
Bawley Wash ..............................Pima
   See: BOWLEY, PIMA
BAYARD .................................YAVAPAI
Beachville ................................Coconino
   See: FLAGSTAFF, COCONINO
BEALE POINT .............GRAND CANYON, COCO
BEALE SPRINGS, CAMP ...................MOHAVE
Beal's Crossing ............................Mohave
   See: MOHAVE, FORT, MOHAVE
Bean .....................................Cochise
   See: BOWIE, COCHISE
Bean Canyon ..............................Cochise
   See: BOWIE, COCHISE
Bean City ................................Cochise
   See: BOWIE, COCHISE
BEAR ..................................YAVAPAI
Bear Canyon ..............................Cochise
   See: BEAR, YAVAPAI
Bear Canyon ..............................Greenlee
   See: BEAR CREEK, GREENLEE
Bear Canyon ...............................Pima
   See: BEAR, YAVAPAI
Bear Creek ................................Cochise
   See: BEAR, YAVAPAI
BEAR CREEK ...........................GREENLEE
BEARDSLEY ...........................MARICOPA
Bear Gulch ...............................Cochise
   See: BEAR, YAVAPAI
BEAR HILLS ...............................YUMA
   See also: BEAR, YAVAPAI
Bear Mountain ............................Greenlee
   See: BEAR CREEK, GREENLEE
Bear Mountain .............................Yavapai
   See: BEAR, YAVAPAI

Bear and the Rabbit .......................Navajo
   See: BEAR, YAVAPAI
Bear's Ears ...............................Navajo
   See: BEAR, YAVAPAI
Bear Spring ...............................Apache
   See: BEAR, YAVAPAI
Bear Springs ..............................Coconino
   See: ELDEN MOUNTAIN, COCONINO
Bear Springs ..............................Cochise
   See: BEAR, YAVAPAI
BEAR SPRINGS ..........................NAVAJO
   See also: BEAR, YAVAPAI
Bear Springs ...............................Pima
   See: BEAR, YAVAPAI
Bears Well (s) .............................Pima
   See: BEAR, YAVAPAI
Bear Valley ...............................Greenlee
   See: BEAR, YAVAPAI
Bear Valley ..............................Santa Cruz
   See: BEAR, YAVAPAI
Bear Wallow ...............................Pima
   See: BEAR, YAVAPAI
BEAUCHAMP PEAK ......................APACHE
BEAUFORD MOUNTAIN .................MARICOPA
BEAUTY, CAMP ..........................APACHE
Beauty Springs ...........................Graham
   See: INDIAN HOT SPRINGS, GRAHAM
Beaver Canyon ............................Coconino
   See: BEAVER CREEK, YAVAPAI
   See: HAVASU CANYON, GRAND CANYON
BEAVER CREEK ........................YAVAPAI
Beaver Creek Crossing ......................Yavapai
   See: BEAVER CREEK, YAVAPAI
Beaver Dam Creek ..........................Mohave
   See: LITTLEFIELD, MOHAVE
Beaver Dam Mountains ......................Mohave
   See: LITTLEFIELD, MOHAVE
Beaver Dams ..............................Mohave
   See: LITTLEFIELD, MOHAVE
Beaver Dam Wash ..........................Apache
   See: BEAVER CREEK, YAVAPAI
Beaver Falls ...................Grand Canyon, Coco
   See: HAVASU CANYON, GRAND CANYON
Beaverhead ...............................Yavapai
   See: BEAVER CREEK, YAVAPAI
Beaverhead Flat ...........................Yavapai
   See: BEAVER CREEK, YAVAPAI
Beaver Ranch .............................Navajo
   See: REIDHEAD, NAVAJO
Becker Creek ..............................Apache
   See: SNOWSTAKE, CREEK, APACHE
BECKER LAKE ...........................APACHE
BEDIVERE POINT ..........GRAND CANYON, COCO
Bed Rock Camp ...............Grand Canyon, Coco
   See: BASS CAMP, GRAND CANYON
BED ROCK CANYON .......GRAND CANYON, COCO
Bed Rock Rapids ...............Grand Canyon, Coco
   See: BED ROCK CANYON, GRAND CANYON
Bee Mountain .............................Yavapai
   See: MINGUS MOUNTAIN, YAVAPAI
Begashibito Brook .........................Navajo
   See: BEGASHIBITO CANYON, NAVAJO
BEGASHIBITO CANYON ........NAVAJO and Coconino

Big Shipp Mountain .........................Yavapai
    See: SHIPP MOUNTAIN, YAVAPAI
BIG SPRINGS ...........................COCONINO
Big Wash .......................................Pima
    See: CHUKUT KUK, PIMA
BIG WASH .................................PINAL
Bilas .........................................Graham
    See: BYLAS, GRAHAM
BILLIE CREEK ...........................NAVAJO
BILLINGS .................................APACHE
Bill Williams Fork .........................Mohave
    See: TROUT CREEK, MOHAVE
        BILL WILLIAMS MOUNTAIN, COCONINO
Bill Williams Fork .........................Yavapai
    See: VERDE, CAMP, YAVAPAI
BILL WILLIAMS MOUNTAIN .............COCONINO
Bill Williams River .........................Mohave
    See: BILL WILLIAMS MOUNTAIN, COCONINO
Billy Moore's Station ......................Maricopa
    See: AVONDALE, MARICOPA
BINGHAM PEAK .......................GREENLEE
Birch Mesa ......................................Gila
    See: BURCH MESA, GILA
BIRD SPRINGS ...........................NAVAJO
BISBEE .....................................COCHISE
Bisbee Junction ..............................Cochise
    See: BISBEE, COCHISE
BISCUIT MOUNTAIN .......SANTA CRUZ, COCHISE
BISCUIT PEAK ...........................GRAHAM
Bishop, The ...................................Cochise
    See: CHIRICAHUA MOUNTAINS, COCHISE
BISHOP KNOLL ..............................GILA
BISHOP SPRINGS .......................COCONINO
Bissel Point .....................Grand Canyon, Coco
    See: COMANCHE POINT, GRAND CANYON
Bitahotsi .......................................Navajo
    See: BIDAHOCHI BUTTE, NAVAJO
BITSIHUITOS BUTTE ....................APACHE
BITTER SPRINGS ......................COCONINO
Bitterweed Springs ...........................Navajo
    See: CHILCHINBITO, NAVAJO
BITTER WELL (SIF VIA) ....................PINAL
Bitter Well Mountains .........................Pinal
    See: BITTER WELL, PINAL
        VEKOL MINE, PINAL
Black Bill Flat ..............................Coconino
    See: BLACK BILL PARK, COCONINO
BLACK BILL PARK .....................COCONINO
Black Butte ..................................Maricopa
    See: BLACK PEAK, YUMA
Black Butte .....................................Pinal
    See: BLACK PEAK, YUMA
Black Canyon .................................Mohave
    See: BLACK MOUNTAINS, MOHAVE
BLACK CANYON ........................NAVAJO
    See also: IRON SPRING, NAVAJO
BLACK CANYON .........................YAVAPAI
Black Canyon Hill ............................Yavapai
    See: BLACK CANYON, YAVAPAI
Black Canyon Range .........................Mohave
    See: BLACK MOUNTAINS, MOHAVE

Black Canyon Spring .........................Yavapai
    See: BLACK PEAK, YUMA
Black Canyon Station .........................Yavapai
    See: BLACK CANYON, YAVAPAI
BLACK CREEK ...........................APACHE
Black Creek Canyon ..........................Apache
    See: BLACK CREEK, APACHE
Black Creek Valley ...........................Apache
    See: BLACK CREEK, APACHE
BLACK DIAMOND .......................COCHISE
Black Diamond Peak ..........................Cochise
    See: BLACK DIAMOND, COCHISE
Black Diamond Peak and Station ..............Cochise
    See: BLACK PEAK, YUMA
Black Draw ...................................Cochise
    See: BLACK PEAK, YUMA
BLACK FALLS ..........................COCONINO
BLACK FOREST ..........................APACHE
BLACK FOREST .........................YAVAPAI
Black Gap ...................................Maricopa
    See: BLACK PEAK, YUMA
Black Gap Station ...........................Maricopa
    See: BLACK PEAK, YUMA
Black Hill ....................................Yavapai
    See: BLACK PEAK, YUMA
Black Hills ..................................Coconino
    See: BLACK FALLS, COCONINO
Black Hills ........................Graham, Greenlee
    See: BLACK PEAK, YUMA
Black Hills .....................................Pinal
    See: BLACK PEAK, YUMA
Black Hills Tank .............................Yavapai
    See: BLACK PEAK, YUMA
Black Hill Wash .............................Yavapai
    See: BLACK PEAK, YUMA
BLACK JACK CANYON ..................GREENLEE
Blackjack Mountain ..............................Gila
    See: BLACK PEAK, YUMA
Black Jack Spring ...........................Greenlee
    See: BLACK JACK CANYON, GREENLEE
Black Knob ...................................Cochise
    See: BLACK PEAK, YUMA
Black Knob ..................................Coconino
    See: BLACK FALLS, COCONINO
Black Lake ....................................Apache
    See: BLACK CREEK, APACHE
BLACK MESA .............................APACHE
    See also: JADITO WASH, NAVAJO
Black Mesa ..................................Coconino
    See: MOGOLLON RIM, COCONINO
Black Mesa .......................................Gila
    See: BLACK PEAK, YUMA
Black Mesa ..................................Maricopa
    See: BLACK PEAK, YUMA
Black Mesa ...................................Mohave
    See: BLACK MOUNTAINS, MOHAVE
BLACK MESA ............................NAVAJO
    See also: BLACK MESA, APACHE
Black Mesa ....................................Yavapai
    See: BLACK PEAK, YUMA
    See also: BLACK FOREST, YAVAPAI
BLACK MESA ...............................YUMA

BLUE RIVER .........................GREENLEE
BLUE SPRING .......................COCONINO
BLUE WATER ..........................PINAL
BLY .................................COCONINO
BOARD TREE SADDLE ....................GILA
Bodaway Mesa .......................Coconino
    See: BODOWAY MESA, COCONINO
BODOWAY MESA .....................COCONINO
BOG CREEK ...........................APACHE
BOGGS RANCH .......................YAVAPAI
BOLADA ..............................YAVAPAI
BON ...................................PINAL
BOND CANYON ....................SANTA CRUZ
Bonelli Ferry .........................Mohave
    See: STONE FERRY, MOHAVE
Bonelli Landing ......................Mohave
    See: BONELLI'S CROSSING, MOHAVE
BONELLI'S CROSSING ..................MOHAVE
BONEYARD, THE ......................APACHE
BONITA .............................GRAHAM
BONITA CREEK .......................GRAHAM
BONITA LAVA FLOW .................COCONINO
BONITA RANCH, SIERRA ..............GRAHAM
BONITO CANYON ......................APACHE
BONITA CREEK ........................APACHE
BONITO CREEK ........................APACHE
Bonito, Rio .........................Graham
    See: BONITA CREEK, GRAHAM
Boo-koo-dot-klish ....................Navajo
    See: BLUE CANYON, NAVAJO
BOOT HILL ..........................COCHISE
BOOT LAKE ..........................COCONINO
BOOT PEAK ...........................YUMA
BOQUILLAS ..........................COCHISE
BORIANNA MINE .....................MOHAVE
Boriena .............................Mohave
    See: BORIANNA MINE, MOHAVE
Born, Lake .........................Coconino
    See: BOOT LAKE, COCONINO
Borne, Lake ........................Coconino
    See: BOOT LAKE, COCONINO
BOSQUE ............................MARICOPA
BOSTON MILL ........................COCHISE
BOTKIN .............................YAVAPAI
Bottom City ........................Maricopa
    See: LEHI, MARICOPA
BOTTOMLESS PITS ...................COCONINO
BOUCHER CREEK .........GRAND CANYON, COCO
Boucher Rapids ............Grand Canyon, Coco
    See: BOUCHER CREEK, GRAND CANYON
Boucher Trail .............Grand Canyon, Coco
    See: BOUCHER CREEK, GRAND CANYON
BOUCHE'S FORK .......................NAVAJO
Bouche's Mesa .......................Navajo
    See: BOUCHE'S FORK, APACHE
Boulder Basin .......................Mohave
    See: HOOVER DAM, MOHAVE
Boulder Canyon ......................Mohave
    See: HOOVER DAM, MOHAVE
Boulder Canyon Dam ..................Mohave
    See: HOOVER DAM, MOHAVE

BOULDER CREEK .........GRAND CANYON, COCO
BOULDER CREEK .......................YAVAPAI
Boulder Dam .........................Mohave
    See: HOOVER DAM, MOHAVE
Boulder Mountain ....................Yavapai
    See: GENUNG MOUNTAIN, YAVAPAI
BOUNDARY CONE ......................MOHAVE
Boundary Cone Wash ..................Mohave
    See: BOUNDARY CONE, MOHAVE
BOUNDARY RIDGE ........GRAND CANYON, COCO
BOURKE POINT ..........GRAND CANYON, COCO
BOUSE ...............................YUMA
Bouse Hills .........................Yuma
    See: BOUSE, YUMA
Bouse Wash .........................Yuma
    See: BOUSE, YUMA
BOWERS RANCH .......................YAVAPAI
BOWIE .............................COCHISE
BOWIE, FORT ........................COCHISE
Bowie Mountain, ....................Cochise
    See: BOWIE, FORT, COCHISE
Bowie Reservation, Fort .............Cochise
    See: BOWIE, FORT, COCHISE
BOWLEY ..............................PIMA
BOWYER PEAK ........................YUMA
Box Canyon .........................Maricopa
    See: FISH CREEK, PINAL
Boxing Glove, The ..................Cochise
    See: CHIRICAHUA MOUNTAINS, COCHISE
BOYLES ............................GREENLEE
BOYSAG POINT ..........GRAND CANYON, COCO
BRADFORD WELL ......................YUMA
BRADLEY POINT .........GRAND CANYON, COCO
Bradshaw ...........................Yavapai
    See: BRADSHAW MOUNTAINS, YAVAPAI
Bradshaw City ......................Yavapai
    See: BRADSHAW MOUNTAINS, YAVAPAI
BRADSHAW MOUNTAINS .................YAVAPAI
Bradshaw's Ferry ...................Yuma
    See: OLIVE CITY, YUMA
BRADY BUTTE .......................YAVAPAI
Brady House .......................Cochise
    See: PICK-EM-UP, COCHISE
BRADY PEAK ...........GRAND CANYON, COCO
BRADY WASH ..........................PINAL
BRAHMA TEMPLE .........GRAND CANYON, COCO
BRANDENBURG MOUNTAINS ..............PINAL
BRANNAMAN ..........................PINAL
BRANNOCK ..........................COCHISE
Brawley Wash .......................Pima
    See: BOWLEY, PIMA
Brayton .............................Yuma
    See: BOUSE, YUMA
Breckenridge, Fort .................Pinal
    See: GRANT, CAMP (OLD), PINAL
BRECKENRIDGE SPRING ................COCONINO
Breed's Crossing ...................Navajo
    See: SUNSET CROSSING, NAVAJO
BREEZY POINT ..........GRAND CANYON, COCO
BREON ..............................MOHAVE
BREWERY GULCH ......................COCHISE

Buenos Ayres ........................Pima
   See: SASABE, PIMA

Buffalo Creek ........................Apache
   See: BLACK RIVER, APACHE

Buffalo Crossing ........................Apache
   See: BLACK RIVER, APACHE

Buford Canyon ........................Graham
   See: BUFORD HILL, GRAHAM

BUFORD HILL ........................GRAHAM

Buford, Mount ........................Maricopa
   See: BEAUFORD MOUNTAIN, MARICOPA

Bugui Aquimuri ........................
   See: COLORADO RIVER,
     GRAND CANYON, COCO

Bule Park ........................Apache
   See: BUELL PARK, APACHE

Bullard Canyon ........................Greenlee
   See: BULLARD PEAK, GREENLEE

BULLARD PEAK ........................GREENLEE

BULLARD PEAK ........................YAVAPAI

Bullard Wash ........................Yavapai
   See: BULLARD PEAK, YAVAPAI

BULLDOG MINE ........................PINAL

Bulldog Wash ........................Pinal, Maricopa
   See: BULLDOG MINE, PINAL

BULLHEAD CITY ........................MOHAVE

Bull Head Rock ........................Mohave
   See: BULLHEAD CITY, MOHAVE

BULL RUN ........................COCHISE

BULLRUSH WASH ........................MOHAVE

Bulls Head ........................Mohave
   See: BULLHEAD CITY, MOHAVE

Bulls Head Peak ........................Mohave
   See: BULLHEAD CITY, MOHAVE

Bully Bueno Mine ........................Yavapai
   See: BUENO, YAVAPAI

BUMBLE BEE ........................YAVAPAI

Bumblebee Canyon ........................Yavapai
   See: BLACK CANYON, YAVAPAI

Bumblebee Creek ........................Gila
   See: BUMBLE BEE, YAVAPAI

BURCH MESA ........................GILA

BURCH PEAK ........................MOHAVE

BURCH PUMPING STATION ........................GILA
   See also: MIAMI, GILA

Burger ........................Maricopa
   See: BURGER WELL, MARICOPA

BURGER WELL ........................MARICOPA

BURKES STATION ........................MARICOPA

BURNED PUEBLO ........................COCONINO

BURNS ........................PINAL

BURNT RANCH ........................YAVAPAI

BURNT STUMP MESA ........................GREENLEE

BURNT WELLS ........................MARICOPA

BURRO CANYON ..........GRAND CANYON, COCO

BURRO CREEK ........................MOHAVE

Burro, Mount ........................Grand Canyon, Coco
   See: BURRO CANYON, GRAND CANYON

Burros ........................Cochise
   See: TOMBSTONE, COCHISE

BURRO SPRINGS ........................NAVAJO

Busac ........................Pinal, Graham
   See: ARIVAIPA CANYON, PINAL

Bush, Fort ........................Apache
   See: ALPINE, APACHE

Bush Valley ........................Apache
   See: ALPINE, APACHE

Butland ........................Pima
   See: EMERY PARK, PIMA

BUTLER CANYON ........................APACHE

BUTLER MOUNTAINS ........................YUMA

Butler Pass ........................Yuma
   See: BUTLER VALLEY, YUMA

BUTLER VALLEY ........................YUMA

Butler Well ........................Yuma
   See: BUTLER VALLEY, YUMA

BUTTE, THE ........................PINAL

Butte ........................Pinal
   See: BUTTE, THE, PINAL

Butte City ........................Maricopa
   See: TEMPE, MARICOPA

BUTTERFLY MOUNTAIN ........................MARICOPA

BUTTERFLY PEAK ........................PIMA

Butte Spur ........................Pinal
   See: BUTTE, THE, PINAL

Buzzard Ranch ........................Maricopa
   See: BIG HORN, MARICOPA

BUZZARD ROOST CANYON ........................GILA

Buzzard Roost Mesa ........................Gila
   See: BUZZARD ROOST CANYON, GILA

Buzzard Roost Wash ........................Greenlee
   See: BUZZARDS ROOST CANYON, GREENLEE

BUZZARDS ROOST CANYON ........................GREENLEE

BYLAS ........................GRAHAM

CABABI ........................PIMA

CABEZA PRIETA MOUNTAINS ........................YUMA

Cabeza Prieta Pass ........................Yuma
   See: CABEZA PRIETA MOUNTAINS, YUMA

Cabeza Prieta Tank ........................Yuma
   See: CABEZA PRIETA MOUNTAINS, YUMA

Cabezua, Rio ........................Grand Canyon, Coco
   See: HAVASU CANYON, GRAND CANYON

Cabibi Mine ........................Pima
   See: CABABI, PIMA

Cacate ........................Pima
   See: KAKA, PIMA

Cactus ........................Maricopa
   See: CACTUS BASIN, YAVAPAI

CACTUS BASIN ........................YAVAPAI

Cactus Flat ........................Graham
   See: ALGODON, GRAHAM
   See also: CACTUS BASIN, YAVAPAI

Cactus Mountain ........................Yavapai
   See: CACTUS BASIN, YAVAPAI

CACTUS PASS ........................MOHAVE

Cactus Plains ........................Yuma
   See: CACTUS BASIN, YAVAPAI

Cactus Ridge ........................Gila
   See: CACTUS BASIN, YAVAPAI

Cahuabi ........................Pima
   See: CABABI, PIMA, KO VAYA, PIMA

CALABASAS ........................SANTA CRUZ

Carbon Creek .......................Grand Canyon, Coco
    See: CARBON BUTTE, GRAND CANYON
CARDENAS BUTTE ........GRAND CANYON, COCO
Cardenas Creek .....................Grand Canyon, Coco
    See: CARDENAS BUTTE, GRAND CANYON
Carino Canyon .............................Apache
    See: PINE SPRINGS, APACHE
Carleton Lake ..............................Coconino
    See: MORMON MOUNTAIN, COCONINO
Carlos Range, Sierra .............................Gila
    See: MESCAL MOUNTAINS, GILA
Carlos, Rio de .................................Gila
    See: SAN CARLOS RIVER, GILA
CARL PLEASANT DAM .................MARICOPA
CARMEN ...........................SANTA CRUZ
Carnero Creek ...............................Apache
    See: CARNERO LAKE, APACHE
CARNERO LAKE ...........................APACHE
Carpenter ...................................Greenlee
    See: BOYLES, GREENLEE
Carpenter Ranch ...............................Greenlee
    See: BOYLES, GREENLEE
CARR CANYON ...........................COCHISE
Carrigan Peak .................................Yuma
    See: CLARA PEAK, YUMA
Carrigan Well .................................Yuma
    See: CLARA PEAK, YUMA
CARRIZO ..................................APACHE
Carrizo ....................................Navajo
    See: CARRIZO, APACHE
    See: CHUSCA MOUNTAINS, APACHE
    See: FOUR CORNERS, APACHE
Carrizo Butte .................................Navajo
    See: CARRIZO, APACHE
Carrizo Creek ...............................Apache
    See also: LITHODENDRON CREEK, APACHE
Carrizo Mountains ...........................Apache
    See also: CHUSKA MOUNTAINS, APACHE
Carrizo Ridge .................................Navajo
    See: CARRIZO, APACHE
Carrizo Wash ...............................Apache
    See: CARRIZO, APACHE
Carrizo Wash ...............................Navajo
    See: CARRIZO, APACHE
CARR LAKE ..............................COCONINO
CARR LAKE ...............................NAVAJO
Carr Lake Draw .................................Navajo
    See: CARR LAKE, NAVAJO
Carr Mountain .................................Gila
    See: CARR PEAK, GILA
Carr Peak ..................................Cochise
    See: CARR CANYON, COCHISE
CARR PEAK ..................................GILA
CARSON MESA ...........................APACHE
CARSON PLAINS ........PIMA, Pinal, Yuma, Maricopa
Carter's Camp ...............................Pima
    See: SUMMERHAVEN, PIMA
Casa Blanca ..................................Apache
    See: WHITE HOUSE, APACHE
CASA BLANCA ...........................PINAL
Casa Blanca .................................Santa Cruz
    See: CRITTENDEN, FORT, SANTA CRUZ

Casa Blanca Canyon ........................Santa Cruz
    See: CRITTENDEN, FORT, SANTA CRUZ
Casa Blanca Creek .........................Santa Cruz
    See: CRITTENDEN, FORT, SANTA CRUZ
Casa Blanco ...............................Santa Cruz
    See: CRITTENDEN, FORT, SANTA CRUZ
Casa Grande ...................................Pinal
    See: CASA GRANDE NATIONAL
        MONUMENT, PINAL
Casa Grande Mountains ...........................Pinal
    See: CASA GRANDE NATIONAL
        MONUMENT, PINAL
CASA GRANDE NATIONAL MONUMENT .......PINAL
Casa Montezuma ...............................Pinal
    See: CASA BLANCA, PINAL
        CASA GRANDE NATIONAL
        MONUMENT, PINAL
Casaba ....................................Maricopa
    See: GOODYEAR, MARICOPA
Casacade Creek ...............................Coconino
    See: CATARACT CANYON, COCONINO
Cascades ....................................Coconino
    See: GRAND FALLS, COCONINO
Casas de San Pedro .............................Cochise
    See: SAN PEDRO RIVER, COCHISE
CASCABEL ................................COCHISE
Cascades ....................................Coconino
    See: GRAND FALLS, COCONINO
CASHION ...............................MARICOPA
Cashner Cabin ...............................Coconino
    See: CASNER MOUNTAIN, COCONINO
Casner Cabin ..................................Coconino
    See: CASNER MOUNTAIN, COCONINO
CASNER MOUNTAIN .....................COCONINO
Casner Park ...................................Coconino
    See: CASNER MOUNTAIN, COCONINO
Cassadore Creek ...............................Gila
    See: CASSADORE MESA, GILA
CASSADORE MESA ...........................GILA
Cassadore Mountain .............................Gila
    See: CASSADORE MESA, GILA
Cassadore Springs ...............................Gila
    See: CASSADORE MESA, GILA
CASTLE BUTTE .........................COCONINO
Castle Butte ..................................Navajo
    See: DILKON, NAVAJO
CASTLE CREEK ...........................YAVAPAI
CASTLE DOME ...........................COCHISE
CASTLE DOME ...........................MARICOPA
CASTLE DOME ..............................YUMA
Castle Dome City ...............................Yuma
    See: CASTLE DOME, YUMA
Castle Dome County ...............................366
    See: YUMA COUNTY
Castle Dome Landing .............................Yuma
    See: CASTLE DOME, YUMA
Castle Dome Mountains ...........................Yuma
    See: CASTLE DOME, YUMA
Castle Dome Peak ...............................Yuma
    See: CASTLE DOME, YUMA
Castle Dome Plain ...............................Yuma
    See: CASTLE DOME, YUMA

CHALENDER ...........................COCONINO
Challe, Canyon de el .....................Apache
   See: CHELLY, CANYON DE, APACHE
CHAMBERS ...............................APACHE
Chambers Wash ...........................Apache
   See: CHAMBERS, APACHE
CHAMISO ................................COCHISE
CHANDLER ..............................MARICOPA
Chandler Heights ........................Maricopa
   See: CHANDLER, MARICOPA
Chandler Junction .......................Maricopa
   See: CHANDLER, MARICOPA
Chandler Ranch ..........................Maricopa
   See: CHANDLER, MARICOPA
CHAOL CANYON ......................COCONINO
Chaol Creek ............................Coconino
   See: CHAOL CANYON, COCONINO
Chapara Gulch ..........................Yavapai
   See: CHAPARRAL, YAVAPAI
CHAPARRAL ...........................YAVAPAI
Chaparral Gulch .........................Yavapai
   See: CHAPARRAL, YAVAPAI
Charco de la Piedra .......................Pima
   See: HOTASON, VO, PIMA
CHARCOAL CANYON ....................MOHAVE
Charcos de los Pimas ......................Pima
   See: POINT OF MOUNTAIN, PIMA
CHARLESTON ..........................COCHISE
CHARLIE DAY SPRING ................COCONINO
Charmingdale .............................Yavapai
   See: HUALAPAI, CAMP: YAVAPAI
CHASE CREEK ........................GREENLEE
CHASM CREEK .........................YAVAPAI
Chave Spring ...........................Coconino
   See: CHAVES PASS, COCONINO
Chaves Crossing ........................Coconino
   See: CHAVES PASS, COCONINO
CHAVES PASS ..........................COCONINO
Chaves Pass Ruin ......................Coconino
   See: CHAVES PASS, COCONINO
      CHUBWICHALOBI, COCONINO
Chavez Pass ...........................Coconino
   See: CHAVES PASS, COCONINO
CHEDISKI MOUNTAIN ....................NAVAJO
Chegui, Sierra de ...........................Apache
   See: CARRIZO MOUNTAINS, APACHE
CHELLY, CANYON DE.. ....................APACHE
Chelly, Rio de .............................Apache
   See: CHELLY, CANYON DE, APACHE
CHEMEHUEBI POINT ......GRAND CANYON, COCO
CHEMEHUEVI VALLEY ...................MOHAVE
Chennele, Cañon ...........................Apache
   See: CANYON DE CHELLY, APACHE
CHEOPS PYRAMID ........GRAND CANYON, COCO
CHEROKEE ..............................MOHAVE
Cherry ...................................Yavapai
   See: CHERRY CREEK, YAVAPAI
CHERRY CREEK ...........................GILA
CHERRY CREEK ..........................YAVAPAI
   See also: DEWEY, YAVAPAI
Cherry Creek Station ......................Yavapai
   See: CHERRY CREEK, YAVAPAI

Cherry Flat Recreational Area ...................Gila
   See: CHERRY CREEK, GILA
Cherry Springs ................................Gila
   See: CHERRY CREEK, GILA
CHERUM PEAK .........................MOHAVE
Cheto ....................................Apache
   See: SANDERS, APACHE
Chevalon Butte .........................Coconino
   See: CHEVELON CREEK, NAVAJO
Chevalon Creek .........................Navajo
   See: CHEVELON CREEK, NAVAJO
Chevalon Fork ..........................Navajo
   See: CHEVELON CREEK, NAVAJO
Chevelon Butte .........................Coconino
   See: CHEVELON CREEK, NAVAJO
Chevelon Canyon .......................Navajo
   See: CHEVELON CREEK, NAVAJO
CHEVELON CREEK .....................NAVAJO
Chevez Pass ...........................Coconino
   See: CHAVES PASS, COCONINO
Chevlon's Butte ........................Coconino
   See: CHEVELON CREEK, NAVAJO
Chevlon Creek .........................Navajo
   See: CHEVELON CREEK, NAVAJO
CHEYAVA FALLS ..........GRAND CANYON, COCO
CHIAPUK ..............................PINAL
CHIAVRIA POINT ..........GRAND CANYON, COCO
CHIAWULITAK ............................PIMA
Chichilticalli ............................Graham
   See: PUEBLO VIEJO, GRAHAM
CHICO SHUNIE WELL ......................PIMA
CHIKAPANGI MESA .........GRAND CANYON, COCO
Chikapanagi Point .........Grand Canyon, Coco
   See: CHIKAPANGI MESA, GRAND CANYON
Chila ......................................Gila
   See: GILA RIVER, GILA
Chilchinbito Canyon ........................Navajo
   See: CHILCHINBITO, NAVAJO
Chilchinbito Creek ........................Navajo
   See: CHILCHINBITO, NAVAJO
CHILCHINBITO (Spring) ....................NAVAJO
CHILDS ...................................PIMA
CHILDS .................................YAVAPAI
Child's Mountain ............................Pima
   See: CHILDS, PIMA
Child's Valley ..............................Pima
   See: CHILDS, PIMA
CHILITO .................................GILA
CHIMINEA MOUNTAIN .................SANTA CRUZ
Chimney Butte ..........................Navajo
   See: DILKON, NAVAJO
Chimney Canyon ......................Santa Cruz
   See: CHIMINEA MOUNTAIN, SANTA CRUZ
CHIMNEY ROCK CANYON ...............GREENLEE
Chimopovy ...............................Navajo
   See: SHUNGOPOVI, NAVAJO
CHINA PEAK ............................COCHISE
China, Val de ............................Yavapai
   See: CHINO VALLEY, YAVAPAI
Chinaman's Head ...........................Cochise
   See: CHIRICAHUA MOUNTAINS, COCHISE
CHINDE MESA ...........................APACHE

Cienega, Sierra ..................................Coconino
    See: SAN FRANCISCO PEAKS, COCONINO
Cienegas de los Pinos ...........................Pima
    See: CIENAGA, LA, PIMA
Cienegos de los Pinos ...........................Pima
    See: CIENAGA, LA, PIMA
Cieneguilla Chiquita ...........................Apache
    See: BLACK CREEK, APACHE
Cieneguilla de Juanito ..........................Navajo
    See: WHEATFIELDS CREEK, NAVAJO
CIMARRON MOUNTAINS .....................PIMA
Ci-mo-pavi .......................................Navajo
    See: SHUNGOPOVI, NAVAJO
CINCH HOOK BUTTE ....................COCONINO
Cinder Hill ......................................Coconino
    See: HOGBACK MOUNTAIN, COCONINO
CINNABAR ....................................YUMA
Cipriano Pass and Well ...........................Yuma
    See: TINAJAS ALTAS, YUMA
Circle Prairie ..................................Graham
    See: POINT OF PINES, GRAHAM
Circle Z Mountain ...........................Santa Cruz
    See: BLOXTON, SANTA CRUZ
Circle Z Ranch ..............................Santa Cruz
    See: BLOXTON, SANTA CRUZ
        SANFORD, SANTA CRUZ
CITADEL, THE .........................COCONINO
CITY CREEK .................................GILA
Civano ...........................................Pinal
    See: CASA GRANDE, PINAL
CLACK .......................................MOHAVE
Clanton Hills ...................................Yuma
    See: CLANTON'S WELL, YUMA
CLANTON'S WELL ...........................YUMA
CLARA PEAK ................................YUMA
Clara Well .......................................Yuma
    See: CLARA PEAK, YUMA
        BUTLER VALLEY, YUMA
CLARK, CAMP ...........................YAVAPAI
CLARKDALE ..............................YAVAPAI
Clark, Fort ......................................Yavapai
    See: CLARK, CAMP, YAVAPAI
CLARK PEAK ............................GRAHAM
Clarkston ........................................Pima
    See: CLARKSTOWN, PIMA
CLARKSTOWN .............................PIMA
CLARK VALLEY .......................COCONINO
Clark's Valley ...................................Coconino
    See: CLARK VALLEY, COCONINO
CLARKVILLE ..........................COCONINO
CLAY PARK ............................COCONINO
    See also: JACK'S CANYON, YAVAPAI
CLAYPOOL ..................................GILA
CLAY SPRINGS ...........................NAVAJO
Clear Canyon ....................................Coconino
    See: BIG DRY WASH, NAVAJO
Clear Creek .....................................Coconino
    See: BADGER CREEK, COCONINO
        WEST CLEAR CREEK, COCONINO
        BIG DRY WASH, COCONINO
CLEARWATERS .........................YAVAPAI
CLEATOR ..................................YAVAPAI

CLEMENCEAU ...........................YAVAPAI
CLEMENT POWELL BUTTE ..GRAND CANYON, COCO
CLIFFS ...................................COCONINO
Cliff Town .......................................Greenlee
    See: CLIFTON, GREENLEE
CLIFTON ..................................GREENLEE
Clifton Hot Springs ..............................Greenlee
    See: CLIFTON, GREENLEE
CLINE .........................................GILA
Cline Creek .....................................Gila
    See: CLINE, GILA
Cline Mesa ......................................Gila
    See: CLINE, GILA
CLINTS WELL ..........................COCONINO
CLIP ..........................................YUMA
Clip Mill Site ...................................Yuma
    See: CLIP, YUMA
Clip Wash .......................................Yuma
    See: CLIP, YUMA
CLOSTERMEYER LAKE ..................COCONINO
Clothopas Temple ...............................Yuma
    See: CORONATION PEAK, YUMA
Clothos Temple ..................................Yuma
    See: CORONATION PEAK, YUMA
Clough Cienega ..................................Apache
    See: McNARY, APACHE
Clover Creek ..................................Santa Cruz
    See: SONOITA, SANTA CRUZ
Cluff Cienega ...................................Apache
    See: McNARY, APACHE
Cluff Peak ......................................Graham
    See: McNARY, APACHE
CLY BUTTE ...............................NAVAJO
Coal Canyon .....................................Navajo
    See: COAL MINE CANYON, COCONINO
COAL MINE CANYON ...................COCONINO
COALSON CANYON ......................GREENLEE
Coanini Creek .......................Grand Canyon, Coco
    See: HAVASU CANYON, GRAND CANYON
Cobabi ...........................................Pima
    See: KO VAYA, PIMA
Cobabi Mountains ................................Pima
    See: KO VAYA, PIMA
COBRE GRANDE MOUNTAINS .............GRAHAM
COCHIBO ......................................PIMA
    See also: SIOVI SHUATAK, PIMA
COCHISE ....................................COCHISE
COCHISE BUTTE ...........GRAND CANYON, COCO
Cochise Canyon ..................................Cochise
    See: GOODWIN CANYON, COCHISE
COCHISE COUNTY.. ...........................28
Cochise Head ....................................Cochise
    See: COCHISE, COCHISE
Cochise Memorial Park ...........................Cochise
    See: COCHISE, COCHISE
Cochise Peak .....................................Cochise
    See: CORONADO NATIONAL MEMORIAL,
        COCHISE. Also: COCHISE, COCHISE
Cochise Stronghold ..............................Cochise
    See: HORSESHOE CANYON, COCHISE
    Also: COCHISE, COCHISE
COCHRAN ....................................PINAL

Connor Canyon .................................Gila
    See: ROSE CREEK, GILA

Connor Creek ..................................Gila
    See: ROSE CREEK, GILA

Con Quien ....................................Pima
    See: SIOVI SHUATAK, PIMA

CONQUISTADOR AISLE ............GRAND CANYON

CONSTELLATION ........................YAVAPAI

CONTENTION ............................COCHISE

Contention City .............................Cochise
    See: CONTENTION, COCHISE

CONTINENTAL ..............................PIMA

CONTINENTAL MOUNTAIN .............MARICOPA

CONTZEN PASS .............................PIMA

Cook Mesa (Black Mesa) ...........Maricopa and Yavapai
    See: BLACK PEAK, YUMA

COOLEY MOUNTAIN ......................NAVAJO
    See also: McNARY, APACHE

Cooley, Ranch ...............................Navajo
    See: McNARY, APACHE

COOLIDGE.. ...............................PINAL
    See also: COOLIDGE DAM, GILA

COOLIDGE DAM ....................GILA and Pinal

Coon Canyon ................................Pima
    See: SIOVI SHUATAK, PIMA

COON CREEK ...............................GILA

Coon Creek Butte ............................Gila
    See: COON CREEK, GILA

Coon Mountain ............................Coconino
    See: METEOR CRATER, COCONINO

COOPER POCKETS .......................MOHAVE

Cooper Ranch ................................Gila
    See: RAMER RANCH, GILA

COPE BUTTE ..............GRAND CANYON, COCO

Copper .....................................Yavapai
    See: COPPER BASIN, YAVAPAI

COPPER BASIN ..........................YAVAPAI

Copper Basin Road Spring .....................Yavapai
    See: COPPER BASIN, YAVAPAI

Copper Basin Wash ..........................Yavapai
    See: COPPER BASIN, YAVAPAI

Copper Camp ................................Gila
    See: COPPER HILL, GILA

Copper Canyon ..............................Yavapai
    See: COPPER BASIN, YAVAPAI

COPPER CENTER .........................COCHISE

COPPER CREEK ............................PINAL

Copper City ..................................Gila
    See: COPPER HILL, GILA

Copper Glance ..............................Cochise
    See: SUNNYSIDE, COCHISE

Copper Gulch .................................Gila
    See: COPPER HILL, GILA

COPPER HILL ...............................GILA

COPPER KING MOUNTAIN ..............GREENLEE

COPPER MOUNTAIN ...................GREENLEE

Copper Mountain .............................Yavapai
    See: COPPER BASIN, YAVAPAI

COPPER MOUNTAINS ......................YUMA

Copper Queen Mine ...........................Cochise
    See: BISBEE, COCHISE

COPPEROPOLIS ...........................PINAL

Copperopolis .................................Yavapai
    See: COPPER BASIN, YAVAPAI

Copperopolis Creek ...........................Yavapai
    See: COPPER BASIN, YAVAPAI

Copperosity ..................................Pinal
    See: CHIAPUK, PINAL

Copperosity Hills .............................Pinal
    See: CHIAPUK, PINAL

COPPERPLATE GULCH ..................GREENLEE

CORDES ..................................YAVAPAI

Cordes Cabin ................................Yavapai
    See: CORDES, YAVAPAI

CORDUROY CREEK .......................NAVAJO

CORE RIDGE ............................COCONINO

Corgett Wash ...............................Maricopa
    See: CORGIAT WASH, MARICOPA

CORGIAT WASH ........................MARICOPA

Corino Canyon ..............................Apache
    See: PINE SPRINGS, APACHE

CORK ....................................GRAHAM

CORN CREEK ..........................COCONINO

Cornel Arroya ................................Pima
    See: CORNELIA, ARROYA, PIMA

Cornelia ....................................Pima
    See: AJO, PIMA

CORNELIA, ARROYA .......................PIMA

Cornez, Rio .................................Pima
    See: CORNELIA ARROYA, PIMA

CORNFIELDS .............................APACHE

CORNVILLE ..............................YAVAPAI

CORONA MOUNTAIN .......................YUMA

Coronado ..................................Greenlee
    See: CORONADO MOUNTAIN, GREENLEE

CORONADO BUTTE ...............GRAND CANYON

Coronado Creek ............................Greenlee
    See: CORONADO MOUNTAIN, GREENLEE

Coronado Gulch ............................Greenlee
    See: CORONADO MOUNTAIN, GREENLEE

CORONADO MOUNTAIN ................GREENLEE

CORONADO NATIONAL FOREST ..PIMA, Pinal, Cochise,
                        Santa Cruz

CORONADO NATIONAL MEMORIAL ........COCHISE

Coronado Ridge .............................Greenlee
    See: CORONADO MOUNTAIN, GREENLEE

CORONATION PEAK ........................YUMA
    See also: MUGGINS MOUNTAINS, YUMA

Corral Viego Mine ..........................Santa Cruz
    See: MOWRY MINE, SANTA CRUZ

CORTA ..................................COCHISE

CORTARO .................................PIMA

Cortes Peak .................................Yavapai
    See: CORDES, YAVAPAI

CORVA ..................................COCONINO

CORWIN ...................................PIMA

Cosmas ....................................Pima
    See: SAN COSME, PIMA

Cosmino Caves .............................Coconino
    See: COSNINO CAVES, COCONINO

Cosnina, Rio del ............................xxxxxx
    See: COLORADO RIVER, GRAND CANYON, COCO

Cosnino ....................................Coconino
    See: COSNINO CAVES, COCONINO

CRYSTAL CREEK ..........GRAND CANYON, COCO
CRYSTAL PEAK .........................GRAHAM
Crystall Rapid .....................Grand Canyon, Coco
   See: CRYSTAL CREEK, GRAND CANYON
Cubit Tubig ........................................Pima
   See: KOMELIK, PIMA
Cuevacita ...............................Santa Cruz
   See: HUGHES MOUNTAIN, SANTA CRUZ
Cullen's .................................Yuma
   See: CULLING'S WELLS, YUMA
Cullen's Well .............................Yuma
   See: CULLING'S WELLS, YUMA
Cullen's Wells ........................Coconino
   See: KERLINS WELL, COCONINO
Cullen Wash ..............................Yuma
   See: CENTENNIAL, YUMA
        CULLING'S WELLS, YUMA
CULLING'S WELLS .........................YUMA
Cullin's ...................................Yuma
   See: CULLING'S WELLS, YUMA
Cumero Canyon .............................Pima
   See: CUMERO MOUNTAIN, PIMA
CUMERO MOUNTAIN .......................PIMA
CUMMINGS MESA .....................COCONINO
Cumorah ...................................Navajo
   See: JOSEPH CITY, NAVAJO
Cunejo de los Pimas ........................Pima
   See: CIENEGA, LA, PIMA
Cunningham Mountain .......................Yuma
   See: CUNNINGHAM PASS, YUMA
CUNNINGHAM PASS .........................YUMA
Cups ......................................Pima
   See: KO VAYA, PIMA, SIL NAKYA, PIMA
Curnutt ....................................Gila
   See: LIVINGSTON, GILA
CURTISS ..................................YAVAPAI
CURVO ...................................COCHISE
CUTTER ....................................GILA
Cuvo ......................................Pima
   See: GU VO, PIMA
CYCLOPIC WASH .......................MOHAVE
CYGNUS MOUNTAIN .....................MOHAVE

Dagger Basin ...............................Gila
   See: DAGGER PEAK, GILA
Dagger Canyon .............................Gila
   See: DAGGER PEAK, GILA
DAGGER PEAK ...............................GILA
Dagger Spring ...............................Gila
   See: DAGGER PEAK, GILA
DAHL ....................................COCHISE
DANA BUTTE ..............GRAND CANYON, COCO
DANE CABIN .........................COCONINO
Dane Canyon ...........................Coconino
   See: DANE CABIN, COCONINO
Dane Ridge .............................Coconino
   See: DANE CABIN, COCONINO
Dane Spring ............................Coconino
   See: DANE CABIN, COCONINO
Daniels Ranch ..............................Pima
   See: BATES WELL, PIMA
DARK CANYON .......................GREENLEE

DARWIN PLATEAU .........GRAND CANYON, COCO
DATE ....................................YAVAPAI
Date Creek ...............................Yavapai
   See: DATE, YAVAPAI
   See also: DATE CREEK, CAMP, YAVAPAI
DATE CREEK, CAMP .....................YAVAPAI
Date Creek Mountains ......................Yavapai
   See: DATE CREEK, CAMP, YAVAPAI
DATELAND ................................YUMA
DAVENPORT HILL ....................COCONINO
Davenport Lake ........................Coconino
   See: DAVENPORT HILL, COCONINO
Davenport Peak .........................Yavapai
   See: DAVENPORT HILL, COCONINO
Davenport Ranch .......................Maricopa
   See: DAVENPORT HILL, COCONINO
Davenport Wash .................Maricopa, Yavapai
   See: DAVENPORT HILL, COCONINO
DAVIDSON CANYON .........................PIMA
Davidson Spring ............................Pima
   See: DAVIDSON CANYON, PIMA
DAVIS ..................................YAVAPAI
DAVIS DAM .............................MOHAVE
DAVIS, MOUNT ..........................MOHAVE
DAVIS, MOUNT ..........................YAVAPAI
Day's Camp ................................Pima
   See: QUIJOTOA, PIMA
DAZE ..................................COCONINO
Daze Lake ..............................Coconino
   See: DAZE, COCONINO
DEAD BOY POINT ..........................GILA
DEADMAN CREEK .......................YAVAPAI
Deadman Creek, South Fork ..................Yavapai
   See: DEADMAN CREEK, YAVAPAI
DEADMAN FLAT .......................COCONINO
   See also: DONEY PARK, COCONINO
DEADMAN GAP .......................MARICOPA
Deadman Ridge ...........................Graham
   See: DEADMAN'S CANYON, GRAHAM
DEADMAN'S CANYON ....................GRAHAM
Deadman's Peak ..........................Graham
   See: DEADMAN'S CANYON, GRAHAM
Deadman Tank ..........................Coconino
   See: DEADMAN FLAT, COCONINO
Deadman Wash ..........................Coconino
   See: DEADMAN FLAT, COCONINO
Deadman Wells .........................Coconino
   See: DEADMAN FLAT, COCONINO
DEAD RIVER ..............................APACHE
   See also: CARRIZO CREEK, APACHE
Dead Wash ...............................Apache
   See: DEAD RIVER, APACHE
DEAN PEAK .............................MOHAVE
Death Valley Lake ........................Mohave
   See: SACRAMENTO VALLEY, MOHAVE
Death Valley Wash ........................Mohave
   See: SACRAMENTO VALLEY, MOHAVE
DEBEBEKID LAKE .......................NAVAJO
DECKER WASH ..........................NAVAJO
Deep Well ................................Yuma
   See: POSA PLAIN, LA, YUMA

Dix Mesa ...................................Greenlee
    See: DIX CREEK, GREENLEE
DOAK ..........................................GILA
Doanville ...................................Yuma
    See: PALOMAS, YUMA
Dobbs Butte .................................Pima
    See: DOBBS STATION, PIMA
DOBBS STATION ............................PIMA
Dobbs Wells .................................Pima
    See: DOBBS STATION, PIMA
DOCK .........................................PINAL
Dodsons ......................................Pinal
    See: MESAVILLE, PINAL
DODSON WASH ...........................NAVAJO
DOME .........................................YUMA
Dome Mountain ..............................Yuma
    See: DOME ROCK MOUNTAINS, YUMA
DOME ROCK MOUNTAINS ...................YUMA
Dome Rock Range ............................Yuma
    See: DOME ROCK MOUNTAINS, YUMA
Doña Ana County ..............................XV
    See: PIMA COUNTY, YUMA COUNTY
Doney Crater ...............................Coconino
    See: DONEY PARK, COCONINO
Doney Mountain ............................Coconino
    See: DONEY PARK, COCONINO
DONEY PARK ...........................COCONINO
Doneys Cone ...............................Coconino
    See: DONEY PARK, COCONINO
Doniphan Pass ...............................Apache
    See: CHUSKA MOUNTAINS, APACHE
Donley Canyon ...............................Pinal
    See: DONNELLY WASH, PINAL
DON LUIS .................................COCHISE
Donnelly Canyon .............................Pinal
    See: DONNELLY WASH, PINAL
DONNELLY WASH .........................PINAL
Doonysio .....................................Yuma
    See: YUMA, YUMA
DORADO, EL, CAMP .....................MOHAVE
Dorado, El Cañon ............................Mohave
    See: DORADO, EL, CAMP, MOHAVE
Dorado, El, Pass ............................Mohave
    See: DORADO, EL, CAMP, MOHAVE
DORSEY GULCH ........................GREENLEE
Dos Cabezas ................................Cochise
    See: DOS CABEZAS PEAKS, COCHISE
Dos Cabezas Mountains ......................Cochise
    See: DOS CABEZAS PEAKS, COCHISE
DOS CABEZAS PEAKS .....................COCHISE
Dos Cabezos ................................Cochise
    See: DOS CABEZAS PEAKS, COCHISE
DOS NARICES MOUNTAIN ..................PINAL
DOS PALMAS WELL ....................MARICOPA
Dot-Klish Canyon ............................Navajo
    See: BLUE CANYON, NAVAJO
DOUBLE ADOBE .........................COCHISE
DOUBLE BUTTE ......................MARICOPA
DOUBLE CIRCLE RANCH ...............GREENLEE
DOUBLE PEAKS ...........................PINAL
DOUBTFUL CANYON .....................COCHISE

Doubtful Pass ...............................Cochise
    See: DOUBTFUL CANYON, COCHISE
Doubtful Pass Station ........................Cochise
    See: DOUBTFUL CANYON, COCHISE
DOUDSVILLE ............................MOHAVE
DOUGLAS ...............................COCHISE
DOVE SPRING .........................COCONINO
Dowdle Canyon ..............................Pima
    See: SAWMILL CANYON, PIMA
DOWLING ...................................PIMA
DOX CASTLE ...............GRAND CANYON, COCO
Doyle Peak .................................Coconino
    See: DOYLE SADDLE, COCONINO
DOYLE SADDLE ........................COCONINO
Dragoon .....................................Cochise
    See: DRAGOON MOUNTAINS, COCHISE
DRAGOON MOUNTAINS ...................COCHISE
Dragoon National Forest .....................Cochise
    See: CORONADO NATIONAL FOREST, PIMA
Dragoon Pass ...............................Cochise
    See: DRAGOON MOUNTAINS, COCHISE
Dragoon Peak ..............................Cochise
    See: DRAGOON MOUNTAINS, COCHISE
Dragoon Summit ............................Cochise
    See: DRAGOON MOUNTAINS, COCHISE
Dragoon Wash ..............................Cochise
    See: DRAGOON MOUNTAINS, COCHISE
Drake .......................................Mohave
    See: GRIFFITH, MOHAVE
DRAKE ...................................YAVAPAI
DREW'S STATION .........................COCHISE
Dripping Spring ...............Coconino, Grand Canyon
    See: DRIPPING SPRINGS, YUMA
DRIPPING SPRING ...........................GILA
Dripping Spring .............................Mohave
    See: FERN SPRING, MOHAVE
Dripping Spring .............................Pima
    See: PUERTO BLANCO MOUNTAINS, PIMA
Dripping Spring .............................Yavapai
    See: DRIPPING SPRINGS, YUMA
Dripping Spring Amphitheater ......Coconino, Grand Canyon
    See: DRIPPING SPRINGS, YUMA
Dripping Spring Mountain .....................Gila
    See: DRIPPING SPRING RANGE, GILA
Dripping Spring Mountain .....................Pinal
    See: DRIPPING SPRINGS, YUMA
Dripping Spring Mountains ....................Pima
    See: PUERTO BLANCO MOUNTAINS, PIMA
DRIPPING SPRING RANGE ...................GILA
Dripping Springs .................Grand Canyon, Coco
    See: BOUCHER CREEK, GRAND CANYON
DRIPPING SPRINGS ........................YUMA
Dripping Springs Range .......................Pima
    See: PUERTO BLANCO MOUNTAINS, PIMA
Dripping Spring Trail .........Coconino, Grand Canyon
    See: DRIPPING SPRINGS, YUMA
DRIPPING SPRING WASH ...................GILA
DROMEDARY PEAK ........................PINAL
DRY BEAVER CREEK ...................COCONINO
    See: WET BEAVER CREEK, COCONINO
Dry Canyon .................................Apache
    See: WATER CANYON, APACHE

Edwards Spring .................................Gila
    See: EDWARDS PEAK, GILA
EGLOFFSTEIN BUTTE .....................NAVAJO
Egypt ......................................Maricopa
    See: GOODYEAR, MARICOPA
EHRENBERG ...............................YUMA
EHRENBERG POINT .......GRAND CANYON, COCO
Ehrenberg Wash ...............................Yuma
    See: EHRENBERG, YUMA
Elaine Castle .....................Grand Canyon, Coco
    See: BEDIVERE POINT, GRAND CANYON
Elden, Mount ...............................Coconino
    See: ELDEN MOUNTAIN, COCONINO
ELDEN MOUNTAIN .....................COCONINO
Elden Pueblo ...............................Coconino
    See: ELDEN MOUNTAIN, COCONINO
Elden Spring ...............................Coconino
    See: ELDEN MOUNTAIN, COCONINO
        BABBIT BILL TANK, COCONINO
Elephant Head ...........................Santa Cruz
    See: PETE MOUNTAIN, SANTA CRUZ
Elephant Head Mine .....................Santa Cruz
    See: PETE MOUNTAIN, SANTA CRUZ
ELEPHANT HILL .........................MOHAVE
ELEPHANT LEGS .......................COCONINO
ELEPHANTS TOOTH .......................MOHAVE
    Also see: BOUNDARY CONE, MOHAVE
ELEVATOR MOUNTAIN .................GREENLEE
ELFRIDA ...................................COCHISE
ELGIN ..................................SANTA CRUZ
ELKHART ...................................YUMA
Ellen, Mount ................................Mohave
    See: TRUMBULL, MOUNT, MOHAVE
ELLIOTT, MOUNT ......................YAVAPAI
ELLISON ......................................GILA
Ellison Creek .................................Gila
    See: ELLISON, GILA
ELOY ........................................PINAL
Eloy, Lake ...................................Pinal
    See: GREENES RESERVOIR, PINAL
ELVES CHASM .............GRAND CANYON, COCO
EMERY .....................................GRAHAM
Emery City ..................................Cochise
    See: BOSTON MILL, COCHISE
EMERY PARK ...............................PIMA
EMIGRANT CANYON .....................COCHISE
Emigrant Hills ...............................Cochise
    See: EMIGRANT CANYON, COCHISE
Emigrant Pass ...............................Cochise
    See: EMIGRANT CANYON, COCHISE
EMIGRANT SPRINGS .....................APACHE
Emma, Mount ................................Mohave
    See: TRUMBULL, MOUNT, MOHAVE
Empire Gulch .................................Pima
    See: EMPIRE MOUNTAINS, PIMA
EMPIRE MOUNTAINS .......................PIMA
Empire Ranch .................................Pima
    See: EMPIRE MOUNTAINS, PIMA
Encarnacion, La ...............................Pinal
    See: SACATON, PINAL
    See also: TUSONIMO, PINAL
ENEBRO MOUNTAIN .....................GREENLEE

ENGESSER PASS ...........................YUMA
ENGLE'S PASS .............................MOHAVE
ENGLE WELL ...........................MARICOPA
ENID ........................................PINAL
Enid Mountains .....................Pinal and Maricopa
    See: ENID, PINAL
ENNIS ...................................MARICOPA
ENREQUITA ...........................SANTA CRUZ
ENTERPRISE .............................GRAHAM
ENTRO ...................................YAVAPAI
EPLEY'S RUINS ...........................GRAHAM
EQUATOR .................................YAVAPAI
ERICKSON .................................COCHISE
ESCALA ...................................GRAHAM
Escalante Basin .................Grand Canyon, Coco
    See: ESCALANTE CREEK, GRAND CANYON
ESCALANTE CREEK ........GRAND CANYON, COCO
Escalante River .................Grand Canyon, Coco
    See: ESCALANTE CREEK, GRAND CANYON
Escritas Piedras Pintadas, Sierra ...............Maricopa
    See: PAINTED ROCKS, MARICOPA
ESCUDILLA MOUNTAIN ...................APACHE
Escudillo, Sierra ...............................Apache
    See: ESCUDILLA MOUNTAIN, APACHE
ESCUELA ....................................PIMA
Esmond .......................................Pima
    See: CRUZ, PIMA
ESPEJO BUTTE ...........GRAND CANYON, COCO
Espejo Creek .....................Grand Canyon, Coco
    See: ESPEJO BUTTE, GRAND CANYON
ESPEJO SPRING .........................COCONINO
ESPERANZA ..................................PIMA
Esperanza Wash ...............................Pima
    See: ESPERANZA, PIMA
ESPERO ...................................GREENLEE
Espuma, Sierra de la ...........................Pinal
    See: SUPERSTITION MOUNTAINS, PINAL
ESTHWAITE .................................PINAL
ESTLER ....................................YAVAPAI
Estrella ....................................Maricopa
    See: ESTRELLA MOUNTAINS, PINAL
Estrella Hill .................................Maricopa
    See: ESTRELLA MOUNTAINS, PINAL
ESTRELLA MOUNTAINS .............PINAL, Maricopa
Estrella, Sierra ...............................Pinal
    See: ESTRELLA MOUNTAINS, PINAL
Estrella Valley ...............................Pinal
    See: ESTRELLA MOUNTAINS, PINAL
EUCLID ...................................MARICOPA
EUGENE GULCH .........................YAVAPAI
Eugene Station ...............................Yavapai
    See: EUGENE GULCH, YAVAPAI
Eureka Mountain ...............................Graham
    See: EUREKA SPRINGS, GRAHAM
EUREKA SPRINGS .........................GRAHAM
Evans .......................................Greenlee
    See: EVANS POINT, GREENLEE
EVANS POINT ...........................GREENLEE
Ewee-Tha-Quaw-Ai ...............................Gila
    See: ANCHA, SIERRA, GILA
Ewell County ...................................256

FLY'S PEAK ....................................COCHISE
Fools Canyon ...............................Yavapai
    See: FOOLS GULCH, YAVAPAI
FOOLS GULCH ...........................YAVAPAI
Fools Hollow .................................Navajo
    See: ADAIR, NAVAJO
FORDVILLE ...................................PINAL
FOREMAN WASH .........................PINAL
FOREPAUGH ..............................MARICOPA
Forepaugh Peak ...........................Maricopa
    See: FOREPAUGH, MARICOPA
FOREST DALE ...........................NAVAJO
Forestdale Canyon ..........................Navajo
    See: FOREST DALE, NAVAJO
Forestdale Creek ...........................Navajo
    See: FORESTDALE, NAVAJO
FOREST LAGOONS .....................COCONINO
FORREST ....................................COCHISE
FORREST ....................................YAVAPAI
FORT ROCK ................................YAVAPAI
FORT VALLEY ...........................COCONINO
Fortification Hill ...........................Mohave
    See: FORTIFICATION ROCK, MOHAVE
Fortification Mountain ....................Mohave
    See: FORTIFICATION ROCK, MOHAVE
FORTIFICATION ROCK ..................MOHAVE
FORTUNA ....................................YUMA
Fortuna Mine, La ...........................Yuma
    See: FORTUNA, YUMA
Fortuna Station .............................Yuma
    See: FORTUNA, YUMA
Fortuna Wash ...............................Yuma
    See: FORTUNA, YUMA
Forty-mile Desert .................Maricopa, Pinal
    See: MARICOPA WELLS, PINAL
    DESERT STATION, MARICOPA
FOSSIL CREEK ...............................GILA
Fossil Point .................................Yuma
    See: LIGURTA, YUMA
Fossil Springs ................................Gila
    See: FOSSIL CREEK, GILA
FOSTER ....................................YAVAPAI
FOUR BAR FOUR MESA ...............GREENLEE
FOUR CORNERS ...........................APACHE
Fourmile Creek .............................Graham
    See: FOUR MILE PEAK, GRAHAM
FOUR MILE PEAK .........................GRAHAM
FOURMILE SPRING .......GRAND CANYON, COCO
Four Palms Canyon .........................Yuma
    See: PALM CANYON, YUMA
FOUR PEAKS .....................MARICOPA, Gila
FOURR CANYON ...........................COCHISE
Fourth Forest ...............................Apache
    See: FIRST FOREST, APACHE
Fourth Hollow ...............................Navajo
    See: FIRST HOLLOW, NAVAJO
Fourth of July Butte ......................Maricopa
    See: FOURTH OF JULY WASH, MARICOPA
FOURTH OF JULY WASH ...............MARICOPA
FRAESFIELD MOUNTAIN ...............MARICOPA
FRAGUITA, MOUNT ..................SANTA CRUZ

Fraguita Wash ...............................Pima
    See: FRAGUITA, MOUNT, SANTA CRUZ
FRANCIS CREEK ...........................YAVAPAI
FRANCONIA ...............................MOHAVE
FRANKENBURG ...........................MARICOPA
FRANKLIN ...................................GREENLEE
FRANKLIN HEATON RESERVOIR .......MOHAVE
FRANK MURRAY'S PEAK .................MOHAVE
Fraser's Station .............................Maricopa
    See: FISH CREEK, PINAL
Frederico, Pozode ...........................Pima
    See: KUAKATCH, PIMA
FREDONIA ...................................COCONINO
FREE'S WASH ...............................MOHAVE
Freeze Wash ................................Mohave
    See: FREE'S WASH, MOHAVE
Freezeout Creek .............................Apache
    See: POKER MOUNTAIN, APACHE
FREEZEOUT CREEK .......................GRAHAM
Freezeout Mountain ........................Graham
    See: FREEZEOUT CREEK, GRAHAM
Fremont, Mount ...........................Coconino
    See: FREMONT PEAK, COCONINO
FREMONT PEAK ...........................COCONINO
    See also: DOYLE SADDLE, COCONINO
Fremont Saddle .............................Coconino
    See: CORE RIDGE, COCONINO
FRENCH BUTTE ...........................NAVAJO
FRENCH JOE CANYON ....................COCHISE
French Joe Peak .............................Cochise
    See: FRENCH JOE CANYON, COCHISE
Frenchman Mountains .......................Yuma
    See: TANK MOUNTAINS, YUMA
French Spring ...............................Navajo
    See: FRENCH BUTTE, NAVAJO
Frente Negra, Sierra .........................Pima
    See: TUCSON, PIMA
Fresco River ................................Apache
    See: SAN FRANCISCO RIVER, APACHE
FRESNAL ....................................PIMA
Fresnal Canyon .............................Pima
    See: FRESNAL, PIMA
Fresnal, Cerro del ...........................Pima
    See: FRESNAL, PIMA
Fresnal Creek ...............................Pima
    See: FRESNAL, PIMA
Fresnal Wash ...............................Pima
    See: FRESNAL, PIMA
Fresno Canyon .............................Pima
    See: FRESNAL, PIMA
Fresno Spring ...............................Pima
    See: FRESNAL, PIMA
Fresno Wash ................................Pima
    See: FRESNAL, PIMA
Fries Wash ..................................Mohave
    See: FREE'S WASH, MOHAVE
Frijole Mine ................................Pima
    See: HELVETIA, PIMA
FRISCO ....................................APACHE
    See also: ALPINE, APACHE
FRISCO ....................................MOHAVE
FRISCO CANYON ...........................GREENLEE

GERONIMO, MOUNT ......................COCONINO
GIANT CHAIR ...........................NAVAJO
GIBSON ...............................MARICOPA
GIBSON ..................................PIMA
Gibson Arroyo ...........................Pima
    See: GIBSON, PIMA
Gibson Creek ............................Gila
    See: GIBSON PEAK, GILA
GIBSON PEAK ..............................GILA
Gibson Wash .............................Gila
    See: GIBSON PEAK, GILA
GIGANTES, LOS .........................APACHE
Gigantes Buttes, Los ...................Apache
    See: GIGANTES, LOS, APACHE
GILA BEND ............................MARICOPA
Gila Bend Indian Reservation ..........Maricopa
    See: GILA BEND, MARICOPA
Gila Bend Mountains ............Maricopa, Yuma
    See: GILA BEND, MARICOPA
Gila Bend Station .....................Maricopa
    See: GILA RANCH, MARICOPA
Gila Bonita ............................Graham
    See: BONITA CREEK, GRAHAM
Gila Center Store ........................Yuma
    See: BLALACK, YUMA
Gila City ................................Yuma
    See: DOME, YUMA
Gila City Mountains ......................Yuma
    See: GILA MOUNTAINS, YUMA
GILA COUNTY ...............................94
GILA PUEBLO ..............................GILA
GILA MOUNTAINS ..........................YUMA
GILA RANCH ...........................MARICOPA
Gila Range ..............................Gila
    See: MESQUITE SPRING, GILA
GILA RIVER ...............................GILA
GILA RIVER INDIAN RESERVATION ..MARICOPA, Pinal
Gila Station ..........................Maricopa
    See: GILA RANCH, MARICOPA
Gila Valley ..............................Yuma
    See: GILA MOUNTAINS, YUMA
GILBERT ..............................MARICOPA
GILBERT ...............................YAVAPAI
GILLESPIE .............................GRAHAM
GILLESPIE DAM ........................MARICOPA
Gillespie Wash .........................Graham
    See: GILLESPIE, GRAHAM
GILLETTE .............................MARICOPA
GILLILAND GAP ............................GILA
Gilson Creek ............................Gila
    See: ALISO CREEK, GILA
GILSON'S WELL ............................GILA
Gimletville ...........................Yavapai
    See: GOODWIN CITY, YAVAPAI
Gird Camp .............................Cochise
    See: TOMBSTONE, COCHISE
GISELA ...................................GILA
Gisela Mountain .........................Gila
    See: GISELA, GILA
Glance .................................Cochise
    See: SUNNYSIDE, COCHISE

GLASSFORD HILL .......................YAVAPAI
GLEED ................................YAVAPAI
GLEESON ..............................COCHISE
GLENBAR ..............................GRAHAM
GLEN CANYON .........................COCONINO
Glen Canyon Dam .......................Coconino
    See: GLEN CANYON, COCONINO
GLENCOE ..........................SANTA CRUZ
GLENDALE ............................MARICOPA
Glendale Springs ..............Grand Canyon, Coco
    See: HANCE CREEK, GRAND CANYON
GLENN, MOUNT .........................COCHISE
GLENWOOD .............................MOHAVE
GLOBE ...................................GILA
Globe City ..............................Gila
    See: GLOBE, GILA
Globe Hills .............................Gila
    See: GLOBE, GILA
Globe Ledge .............................Gila
    See: GLOBE, GILA
Globe Mine ..............................Gila
    See: OLD DOMINION MINE, GILA
GLYNNS FALLS ...........................YUMA
Goat Mountain .....................Maricopa, Yuma
    See: BIG HORN MOUNTAINS, MARICOPA
GOAT RANCH ..........................GREENLEE
Goat Ranch ..............................Pima
    See: GUNSIGHT, PIMA
GOBBLER POINT .......................GREENLEE
GOBBLERS PEAK .........................APACHE
Goddard's .............................Yavapai
    See: BLACK CANYON, YAVAPAI
GOLCONDA .............................MOHAVE
GOLD BASIN ...........................MOHAVE
Gold Cañon ..............................Pima
    See: ORO, CAÑADA DEL, PIMA
GOLDEN ..............................MARICOPA
GOLDEN PALISADES ......................PINAL
GOLDFLAT .............................MOHAVE
Goldfield .............................Maricopa
    See: GOLDFIELD MOUNTAINS, MARICOPA
GOLDFIELD .............................PINAL
GOLDFIELD MOUNTAINS ...............MARICOPA
GOLD GULCH .........................GREENLEE
GOLDMINE MOUNTAIN ...................PINAL
GOLDROAD .............................MOHAVE
Gold Road Gulch ........................Mohave
    See: GOLDROAD, MOHAVE
Gold Road Pass .........................Mohave
    See: GOLDROAD, MOHAVE
Gold Tree Mine ......................Santa Cruz
    See: ALTO, SANTA CRUZ
GOLDWATER LAKE ......................YAVAPAI
GONZALES PASS .........................PINAL
Gonzales Pass Canyon ...................Pinal
    See: GONZALES PASS, PINAL
GOODWATER ............................NAVAJO
Goodwin ...............................Cochise
    See: GOODWIN CANYON, COCHISE
GOODWIN ..............................YAVAPAI
GOODWIN, CAMP ........................GRAHAM

Grant Hill ...................................Graham
    See: GRANT, FORT, GRAHAM
Grant Wash, Camp .........................Pinal
    See: GRANT, CAMP (OLD), PINAL
GRANVILLE ..............................GREENLEE
Grapevine Canyon ...........................Gila
    See: GRAPEVINE SPRING, GILA
GRAPEVINE CREEK ...................MOHAVE
GRAPEVINE SPRING ................COCONINO
GRAPEVINE SPRING ........................GILA
Grapevine Spring ........................Maricopa
    See: GRAPEVINE CREEK, MOHAVE
Grass Canyon ...............................Pima
    See: PITAHAYA CANYON, PIMA
GRASSHOPPER ...........................NAVAJO
GRASSHOPPER FLAT ...................YAVAPAI
GRASS MOUNTAIN ......................MOHAVE
Grass Springs ..............................Mohave
    See: DUNCAN, MOHAVE
Grass Valley ...............................Graham
    See: ARIVAIPA CANYON, PINAL
Grass Valley ..................................Gila
    See: GISELA, GILA
GRASSY MOUNTAIN ....................GREENLEE
Grassy Mountain .........................Mohave
    See: GRASS MOUNTAIN, MOHAVE
Graveyard Canyon .........................Graham
    See: DEADMAN'S CANYON, GRAHAM
GRAVEYARD CANYON ......................GILA
Gray Mountain ............................Yavapai
    See: GRAYBACK MOUNTAIN, YAVAPAI
GRAYBACK MOUNTAIN .................YAVAPAI
Grayback Mountains ......................Yavapai
    See: GRAYBACK MOUNTAIN, YAVAPAI
GREASEWOOD ...........................APACHE
Greasewood Flat ..........................Apache
    See: GREASEWOOD, APACHE
GREASEWOOD MOUNTAIN .............GRAHAM
Greasewood Spring .......................Apache
    See: GREASEWOOD, APACHE
Great Akchin ...............................Pima
    See: SAN SERAFIN, PIMA
Great Arizona Crater .....................Coconino
    See: METEOR CRATER, COCONINO
Great Basin ..................................Gila
    See: NATURAL BRIDGE, GILA
GREAT COLORADO VALLEY ................YUMA
GREATERVILLE ............................PIMA
Greaterville Gulch ...........................Pima
    See: GREATERVILLE, PIMA
Great Thumb Mesa ..............Grand Canyon, Coco
    See: GREAT THUMB POINT, GRAND CANYON
GREAT THUMB POINT ......GRAND CANYON, COCO
Greenback Creek .............................Gila
    See: GREENBACK VALLEY, GILA
Greenback Peak ..............................Gila
    See: GREENBACK VALLEY, GILA
GREENBACK VALLEY .......................GILA
GREENES RESERVOIR ......................PINAL
Greenes Wash ...............................Pinal
    See: GREENES RESERVOIR, PINAL

GREENHAW ...........................COCONINO
Greenland Lake ..........................Coconino
    See: GREENLAND SPRING, GRAND CANYON
Greenland Plateau .......................Coconino
    See: GREENLAND SPRING, GRAND CANYON
Greenland Point .........................Coconino
    See: GREENLAND SPRING, GRAND CANYON
GREENLAND SPRING ..GRAND CANYON, COCONINO
GREENLEE COUNTY .........................162
Green, Mount ..............................Apache
    See: GREEN'S PEAK, APACHE
GREEN'S PEAK ...........................APACHE
Green Spot Draw ...........................Apache
    See: CARNERO LAKE, APACHE
Green Valley ................................Gila
    See: PAYSON, GILA
Green Valley Creek ...........................Gila
    See: PAYSON, GILA
Green Valley Hills ............................Gila
    See: PAYSON, GILA
GREENWOOD ............................MOHAVE
Greenwood Peak ...........................Mohave
    See: GREENWOOD, MOHAVE
GREER ....................................APACHE
Gregg Buttes .............................Maricopa
    See: DOUBLE BUTTES, MARICOPA
GREGGS FERRY .........................MOHAVE
GREY'S PEAK ...........................GREENLEE
GRIEF HILL .............................YAVAPAI
Grief Hill Wash ...........................Yavapai
    See: GRIEF HILL, YAVAPAI
GRIFFIN FLAT .............................GILA
GRIFFITH ...............................MOHAVE
Grinnell Station .............................Yuma
    See: STOVAL, YUMA
GRIPE ...................................GRAHAM
Gritetho ...................................
    See: COLORADO RIVER, GRAND CANYON
GROOM CREEK .........................YAVAPAI
GROOM PEAK ...........................MOHAVE
Grooms Hill ...............................Yavapai
    See: GROOM CREEK, YAVAPAI
GROSSMAN PEAK .......................MOHAVE
Grosvenor Hills .........................Santa Cruz
    See: GROSVENOR PEAK, SANTA CRUZ
GROSVENOR PEAK ...................SANTA CRUZ
Grove of Robinson, The .......................Gila
    See: CATALPA, GILA
Growler ....................................Yuma
    See: NORTON, YUMA
Growler Mine ...............................Pima
    See: GROWLER MOUNTAINS, PIMA
GROWLER MOUNTAINS ......................PIMA
Growler Pass ................................Pima
    See: GROWLER MOUNTAINS, PIMA
Growler Peak ................................Pima
    See: GROWLER MOUNTAINS, PIMA
Growler Well ................................Pima
    See: GROWLER MOUNTAINS, PIMA
Growler Wells ...............................Pima
    See: BATES WELL, PIMA
GU ACHI ...................................PIMA

Happy Valley .................................Yavapai
   See: MISERY, FORT, YAVAPAI

Haraquahala Mountain ......................Yuma
   See: HARQUAHALA MOUNTAINS, YUMA

Harcouver Water ............................Yuma
   See: HARCUVAR MOUNTAINS, YUMA

Harcuvar ....................................Yuma
   See: HARCUVAR MOUNTAINS, YUMA

HARCUVAR MOUNTAINS ...................YUMA

Harcuvar Peak ..............................Yuma
   See: HARCUVAR MOUNTAINS, YUMA

HARDEN CIENEGA .......................GREENLEE

Hardimui ....................................Pima
   See: HALI MURK, PIMA

HARDIN .................................MARICOPA

Hardin Ferry ...............................Mohave
   See: HOOVER DAM, MOHAVE

Hardscrabble Canyon .........................Gila
   See: HARDSCRABBLE MESA, GILA

HARDSCRABBLE MESA ......................GILA

HARDSCRABBLE WASH ..................APACHE

HARDSHELL ...........................SANTA CRUZ

Hardshell Gulch .......................Santa Cruz
   See: HARDSHELL, SANTA CRUZ

HARDY ..................................GREENLEE

Hardy ......................................Navajo
   See: HAVRE, NAVAJO

Hardy Camp ................................Mohave
   See: HARDY MOUNTAINS, MOHAVE

Hardy's Landing ...........................Mohave
   See: HARDYVILLE, MOHAVE

HARDY MOUNTAINS ......................MOHAVE

Hardy Wash ................................Mohave
   See: HARDY MOUNTAINS, MOHAVE

HARDYVILLE ...........................MOHAVE

Harosoma Ridge .....................Maricopa, Pinal
   See: GOLDFIELD MOUNTAINS, MARICOPA

HARPER .................................MOHAVE

Harper's Slough ............................Mohave
   See: HARPER, MOHAVE

Harqua .....................................Yuma
   See: HARQUAHALA MOUNTAINS, YUMA

Harqua Hala ................................Yuma
   See: HARQUAHALA MOUNTAINS, YUMA

Harquahala Mine ............................Yuma
   See: HARQUAHALA MOUNTAINS, YUMA

HARQUAHALA MOUNTAINS ................YUMA

Harquar Mountains ..........................Yuma
   See: HARCUVAR MOUNTAINS, YUMA

HARRINGTON ............................PINAL

HARRINGTON ..........................YAVAPAI

HARRIS .................................MOHAVE

HARRISBURG ............................YUMA

Harrisburg Valley ..........................Yuma
   See: HARRISBURG, YUMA

HARRIS CAVE ...........................APACHE

Harris Lake ................................Apache
   See: HARRIS CAVE, APACHE

HARRIS MOUNTAIN .....................COCHISE

HARRY EDWARD'S MOUNTAIN ...........MOHAVE

HARSHAW .............................SANTA CRUZ

Harshaw Creek .......................Santa Cruz
   See: HARSHAW, SANTA CRUZ

HART CANYON .........................COCONINO

Hart Mountain .............................Coconino
   See: HART CANYON, COCONINO

HART ......................................PIMA

HART PRAIRIE .........................COCONINO

Harte Prairie .............................Coconino
   See: HART PRAIRIE, COCONINO

HARWOOD ...............................YUMA

HASBIDITO CREEK ......................APACHE

Hasbidito Spring ..........................Apache
   See: HASBIDITO CREEK, APACHE

HASKELL SPRING .......................YAVAPAI

Hassayampa ...............................Maricopa
   See: HASSAYAMPA RIVER, MARICOPA

Hassayampa Plain .........................Maricopa
   See: HASSAYAMPA RIVER, MARICOPA

HASSAYAMPA RIVER ..........MARICOPA, Yavapai

Hassayampa Sink ..........................Maricopa
   See: HASSAYAMPA RIVER, MARICOPA

Hastings ...................................Pinal
   See: SUPERIOR, PINAL

HAT MOUNTAIN .......................MARICOPA

Hatalacva ..................................Yavapai
   See: PECK MINE, YAVAPAI

HATCHTON ...............................YUMA

Hattan Butte .....................Grand Canyon, Coco
   See: HATTAN TEMPLE, GRAND CANYON

HATTAN TEMPLE .........GRAND CANYON, COCO

Havasu Canyon .............................Coconino
   See: CATARACT CANYON, COCONINO

HAVASU CANYON .........GRAND CANYON, COCO

Havasu Creek .....................Grand Canyon, Coco
   See: HAVASU CANYON, GRAND CANYON

Havasu Falls .....................Grand Canyon, Coco
   See: HAVASU CANYON, GRAND CANYON

Havasu Hilltop ...................Grand Canyon, Coco
   See: HAVASU CANYON, GRAND CANYON

HAVASU LAKE ......................YUMA, Mohave

Havasu Lake National Wildlife Refuge ............Mohave
   See: HAVASU LAKE, YUMA

Havasupai Gardens ................Grand Canyon, Coco
   See: HAVASU CANYON, GRAND CANYON

Havasupai Indian Reservation ........Grand Canyon, Coco
   See: HAVASU CANYON, GRAND CANYON

Havasupai Point ..................Grand Canyon, Coco
   See: HAVASU CANYON, GRAND CANYON

Havasu Rapids ...................Grand Canyon, Coco
   See: HAVASU CANYON, GRAND CANYON

HAVILAND ...............................MOHAVE

Havilin ....................................Mohave
   See: HAVILAND, MOHAVE

HAVRE .................................NAVAJO

HAWKINS BUTTE .........GRAND CANYON, COCO

HAYDEN ..................................GILA

Hayden ....................................Maricopa
   See: MESA, MARICOPA

Hayden Junction ............................Pinal
   See: HAYDEN, GILA

Hayden's Butte ............................Maricopa
   See: TEMPE, MARICOPA

Hickiwan Wash ...........................Pima
    See: HICKIWAN, PIMA
Hickory Mountain .......................Yavapai
    See: HICKEY MOUNTAIN, YAVAPAI
HIDDEN CANYON .......................MOHAVE
Hieroglyphic Canyon ...................Maricopa
    See: HIEROGLYPHIC HILL, MARICOPA
Hieroglyphic Canyon .............Yavapai, Gila
    See: HIEROGLYPHIC HILL, MARICOPA
HIEROGLYPHIC HILL ...............MARICOPA
Hieroglyphic Mountains .........Maricopa, Yavapai
    See: HIEROGLYPHIC HILL, MARICOPA
Hieroglyphic Tanks .............Yavapai, Gila
    See: HIEROGLYPHIC HILL, MARICOPA
HIGGINS TANK .......................NAVAJO
HIGH BALL WATER ....................YAVAPAI
High Mountains .........................Mohave
    See: TRUMBULL, MOUNT, MOHAVE
HIGLEY ...............................MARICOPA
Hikibon ................................Pima
    See: HICKIWAN, PIMA
Hikivo Perigua ..........................Pima
    See: HICKIWAN, PIMA
Hikuwan ...............................Pima
    See: HICKIWAN, PIMA
Hila.. .................................Gila
    See: GILA RIVER, GILA
HILLCAMP ...............................GILA
HILLERS BUTTE ...........GRAND CANYON, COCO
HILLSIDE ..............................YAVAPAI
Hillside Rocks ..........................Yavapai
    See: HILLSIDE, YAVAPAI
HILLTOP ...............................COCHISE
Hill Top ...............................Gila
    See: HILLCAMP, GILA
HINDU AMPHITHEATER ....GRAND CANYON, COCO
HITT WASH .............................YAVAPAI
HOBBLE MOUNTAIN ...................COCONINO
Hoc-qua-hala Springs ....................Yuma
    See: HARQUAHALA MOUNTAINS, YUMA
HOGBACK MOUNTAIN ..................COCONINO
Hogtown ...............................Graham
    See: GLENBAR, GRAHAM
Hokum .................................Navajo
    See: PHOENIX PARK CANYON, NAVAJO
HOLBROOK .............................NAVAJO
Holcomb ...............................Navajo
    See: PHOENIX PARK CANYON, NAVAJO
HOLDEN LAKE .......................COCONINO
HOLDER ...............................GILA
Hole in the Rock ......................Maricopa
    See: PAPAGO STATE PARK, MARICOPA
Holladay Hot Springs ...................Graham
    See: INDIAN HOT SPRINGS, GRAHAM
HOLMES CANYON ......................YAVAPAI
Holmes Creek ...........................Yavapai
    See: HOLMES CANYON, YAVAPAI
HOLT .................................COCHISE
Holy Joe Canyon ........................Pinal
    See: HOLY JOE PEAK, PINAL
Holy Joe Pasture .......................Pinal
    See: HOLY JOE PEAK, PINAL

HOLY JOE PEAK .........................PINAL
Holy Joe Springs .......................Pinal
    See: HOLY JOE PEAK, PINAL
Holy Joe Wash ..........................Pinal
    See: HOLY JOE PEAK, PINAL
HOMOLOBI .............................NAVAJO
HONEYMOON CABIN ...................GREENLEE
HOOKER'S HOT SPRINGS ...............COCHISE
HOOVER ...............................MARICOPA
HOOVER DAM .........................MOHAVE
HOPE .................................YUMA
Hope, Mount ...........................Yavapai
    See: FORT ROCK, YAVAPAI
HOPE WINDOW .........................APACHE
HOPI BUTTES ..........................NAVAJO
HOPI INDIAN RESERVATION .............NAVAJO
HOPI MESAS ...........................NAVAJO
    See also: BLACK MESA, NAVAJO
HOPI POINT ..............GRAND CANYON, COCO
HOPI VILLAGES ........................NAVAJO
Hopi Wall ...............Grand Canyon, Coco
    See: HOPI POINT, GRAND CANYON
Hop Canyon ............................Navajo
    See: HOP MOUNTAIN, NAVAJO
HOPKINS, MOUNT ...................SANTA CRUZ
HOP MOUNTAIN .........................NAVAJO
HORMIGUERO ...........................PINAL
Horse Camp .............................Gila
    See: HORSE MOUNTAIN, GILA
Horse Camp Canyon ......................Gila
    See: HORSE MOUNTAIN, GILA
Horse Camp Creek .......................Gila
    See: HORSE MOUNTAIN, GILA
Horse Camp Seep ........................Gila
    See: HORSE MOUNTAIN, GILA
Horse Canyon ...........................Gila
    See: HORSE MOUNTAIN, GILA
HORSE CANYON ........................GREENLEE
Horse Creek ............................Maricopa
    See: HORSE MESA, MARICOPA
HORSEFALL CANYON ...................COCHISE
Horsehead Crossing .....................Navajo
    See: HOLBROOK, NAVAJO
HORSE MESA ...........................MARICOPA
Horse Mesa Dam .........................Maricopa
    See: HORSE MESA, MARICOPA
HORSE MOUNTAIN .......................GILA
HORSE MOUNTAIN .......................PIMA
HORSESHOE ...........................PIMA
    See also: QUIJOTOA, PIMA
Horseshoe Basin ........................Pima
    See: HORSESHOE, PIMA
HORSESHOE BEND .......................GILA
Horseshoe Bend .........................Pima
    See: HORSESHOE, PIMA
HORSESHOE CANYON ....................COCHISE
HORSESHOE CIENEGA ...................APACHE
Horseshoe Hill .........................Coconino
    See: HORSESHOE LAKE, COCONINO
HORSESHOE LAKE ......................COCONINO

HUERFANO BUTTE ..........................PIMA

HUGGINS PEAK ...........................PINAL

HUGHES MOUNTAIN ...............SANTA CRUZ

HULL MOUNTAIN ......................COCONINO

Hull Spring ................................Coconino
    See: HULL MOUNTAIN, COCONINO

Hull Wash .................................Coconino
    See: HULL MOUNTAIN, COCONINO

Humboldt Mountain .........................Maricopa
    See: BEAUFORD MOUNTAIN, MARICOPA

HUMMING BIRD SPRING ...............MARICOPA

Humphrey Mountain .........................Coconino
    See: CORE RIDGE, COCONINO

HUMPHREYS PEAK .....................COCONINO

HUNT ....................................APACHE

HUNT CANYON (NO. 1) ...................COCHISE

HUNT CANYON (NO. 2) ...................COCHISE

HUNTER'S POINT .........................APACHE

HURRICANE CREEK ......................APACHE

HUTCH MOUNTAIN .....................COCONINO

HUTTMAN WELL .....................MARICOPA

HUTTON BUTTE ..........GRAND CANYON, COCO

HUTTON PEAK ...........................PINAL

HUXLEY TERRACE .........GRAND CANYON, COCO

HYDER ...................................YUMA

Hyla .....................................Gila
    See: GILA RIVER, GILA


IBEX PEAK ...............................YUMA

ICEBERG CANYON ......................MOHAVE

Ice Caves ..................................Coconino
    See: SUNSET CRATER, COCONINO

ICEHOUSE CANYON .........................GILA

ILGES, CAMP ...........................YAVAPAI

IMPERIAL DAM ............................YUMA

Imperial National Wildlife Refuge ..................Yuma
    See: IMPERIAL DAM, YUMA

IMPERIAL POINT ...........GRAND CANYON, COCO

Imperial Reservoir ...........................Yuma
    See: IMPERIAL DAM, YUMA

IMPERIAL WELL .........................YUMA

INDEPENDENCE, CAMP ....................YUMA

Indian Creek ...............................Yavapai
    See: WEAVER, YAVAPAI

Indian Delia's Place ...........................Gila
    See: CONLEY POINTS, GILA

INDIAN GARDEN ..........GRAND CANYON, COCO

INDIAN GARDENS ......................COCONINO

INDIAN GARDENS .........................GILA

INDIAN HOT SPRINGS ....................GRAHAM

Indian Oasis ................................Pima
    See: SELLS, PIMA

Indian Spring ...............................Mohave
    See: PEACH SPRINGS, MOHAVE

Indian Village ...............................Maricopa
    See: KYRENE, MARICOPA

INDIAN WELLS .............................Navajo
    See also: BIDAHOCHE BUTTE, NAVAJO

Infantry Camp ...............................Pinal
    See: PINAL, CAMP, PINAL

INGALLS LAGOON ..........................YUMA

INITIAL POINT ..........................MARICOPA

Inner Basin .................................Coconino
    See: HUMPHREYS PEAK, COCONINO

Innupin Picabu ...............................Mohave
    See: WITCH WATER POCKET, MOHAVE

INSCRIPTION HOUSE ....................COCONINO

INSPIRATION .............................GILA

INSPIRATION POINT .........................GILA

Interior Valley ...............................Coconino
    See: HUMPHREYS PEAK, COCONINO

IRENE ...................................PIMA

Iron Canyon ................................Pinal
    See: IRON MOUNTAIN, PINAL

Iron Canyon Spring ...........................Pinal
    See: IRON MOUNTAIN, PINAL

IRON KING .............................YAVAPAI

IRON MOUNTAIN .........................PINAL

IRON SPRING ...........................NAVAJO

Iron Springs ................................Graham
    See: INDIAN HOT SPRINGS, GRAHAM

IRON SPRINGS .........................YAVAPAI

Ironsprings ................................Yavapai
    See: IRON SPRINGS, YAVAPAI

Iron Spring Wash ...........................Yavapai
    See: IRON SPRINGS, YAVAPAI

Isaacson ...............................Santa Cruz
    See: NOGALES, SANTA CRUZ

Isabella Mine ...............................Yavapai
    See: LOGAN MINE, YAVAPAI

ISIS TEMPLE ...............GRAND CANYON, COCO

ISLAND MESA ...........................YAVAPAI

Ivalon ....................................Yuma
    See: AVALON, YUMA

Ivanpah ...................................Mohave
    See: IVANPATCH SPRING, MOHAVE

IVANPATCH SPRING .....................MOHAVE

IVES MESA ................................NAVAJO

Ives Mountain ...............................Coconino
    See: BILL WILLIAMS MOUNTAIN, COCONINO

IVES PEAK .............................YAVAPAI

IVES POINT ................GRAND CANYON, COCO


Jabesua de San Antonio, Rio ..........Grand Canyon, Coco
    See: HAVASU CANYON, GRAND CANYON

JACK IN THE PULPIT ...................MARICOPA

JACK RABBIT .............................PINAL

Jack Rabbit Mine ...........................Pinal
    See: JACK RABBIT, PINAL

Jack Rabbit Wash ...........................Pinal
    See: JACK RABBIT, PINAL

Jack Rabbit Well ...........................Pinal
    See: JACK RABBIT, PINAL

JACK'S CANYON .........................YAVAPAI

Jack's Gulch ................................Yavapai
    See: JACK'S CANYON, YAVAPAI

JACK'S MOUNTAIN .........................GILA

JACKSON BUTTE ...........................GILA

Jackson Butte ...............................Graham
    See: JACKSON MOUNTAINS, GRAHAM

JACKSON MOUNTAINS ...................GRAHAM

Joy's Camp ................................Greenlee
    See: MORENCI, GREENLEE
JOYA, CAMP, LA ........................APACHE
JUAN MILLER CREEK ...................GREENLEE
Jump-off, The ...............................Gila
    See: TONTO, GILA
JUMP-OFF CANYON ........................GILA
Junction ....................................Yavapai
    See: CHINO VALLEY, YAVAPAI
Juniper .....................................Navajo
    See: LINDEN, NAVAJO
JUNIPER .................................YAVAPAI
    See also: HUALAPAI, CAMP, YAVAPAI
Juniper Flat ..................................Gila
    See: JUNIPER, YAVAPAI
Juniper Gulch ..............................Yavapai
    See: JUNIPER, YAVAPAI
Juniper Mesa ...............................Yavapai
    See: JUNIPER, YAVAPAI
Juniper Mountains ..........................Yavapai
    See: AZTEC PASS, YAVAPAI
    Also: JUNIPER, YAVAPAI
Juniper Spring ..............................Graham
    See: JUNIPER, YAVAPAI
Juniper Spring .............................Yavapai
    See: JUNIPER, YAVAPAI


KABITO PLATEAU .....................COCONINO
Kaibab ........................Grand Canyon, Coco
    See: KAIBAB PLATEAU, GRAND CANYON
Kaibab Forest .............................Coconino
    See: KAIBAB PLATEAU, GRAND CANYON
Kaibabits .................................Coconino
    See: KAIBAB PLATEAU, GRAND CANYON
Kaibab Mountains ..........................Coconino
    See: KAIBAB PLATEAU, GRAND CANYON
Kaibab National Forest .....................Coconino
    See: KAIBAB PLATEAU, GRAND CANYON,
        COCONINO NATIONAL FOREST, COCONINO
KAIBAB PIUTE INDIAN
    RESERVATION ..............MOHAVE and Coconino
KAIBAB PLATEAU ..........GRAND CANYON, COCO
Kaibab Trail ..................Grand Canyon, Coco
    See: KAIBAB PLATEAU, GRAND CANYON,
        PHANTOM RANCH, GRAND CANYON
Kaibito ....................................Navajo
    See: COMA-a SPRING, NAVAJO
Kaibito Plateau ............................Coconino
    See: KABITO PLATEAU, COCONINO
Kaibito Spring ............................Coconino
    See: KABITO PLATEAU, COCONINO
Kaivavwits ................................Coconino
    See: KAIBAB PLATEAU, GRAND CANYON
KAKA .......................................PIMA
Kaka Valley ..................................Pima
    See: KAKA, PIMA
Kaka Wash ....................................Pima
    See: KAKA, PIMA
Kamatuk .....................................Pinal
    See: ESTRELLA MOUNTAINS, PINAL
KANA-A CREEK .........................COCONINO
KANAB CANYON ..........GRAND CANYON, COCO

Kanab Creek ..............................Coconino
    See: KANAB, GRAND CANYON, COCONINO
Kanab Desert ..................Grand Canyon, Coco
    See: KANAB, GRAND CANYON, COCONINO
Kanab Plateau ..............................Mohave
    See: KANAB, MOHAVE
Kanab Point ................................Mohave
    See: KANAB, MOHAVE
Kanab Rapids .................Grand Canyon, Coco
    See: KANAB, GRAND CANYON
Kanav Spring .................Grand Canyon, Coco
    See: KANAB, GRAND CANYON
KANE SPRINGS ...........................PINAL
Kane Springs Canyon ..........................Pinal
    See: KANE SPRINGS, PINAL
KANGAROO HEADLAND ....GRAND CANYON, COCO
KANSAS SETTLEMENT ....................COCHISE
Karrigan Peak ................................Yuma
    See: CLARA PEAK, YUMA
KARRO ...................................COCHISE
KASTER ...................................MOHAVE
KATHERINE ...............................MOHAVE
Katherine Beach .............................Mohave
    See: KATHERINE, MOHAVE
Katherine Boat Landing .......................Mohave
    See: KATHERINE, MOHAVE
Katherine Wash ..............................Mohave
    See: KATHERINE, MOHAVE
Kavavaik .....................................Pima
    See: KO VAYA, PIMA
Kavolik ......................................Pima
    See: COWLIC, PIMA
Kawaika ....................................Navajo
    See: KAWAIOKU, NAVAJO
KAWAIOKU ................................NAVAJO
KAYENTA .................................NAVAJO
Kayenta Creek ..............................Navajo
    See: TYENDE CREEK, NAVAJO
KEAMS CANYON ..........................NAVAJO
    See also: JADITO WASH, NAVAJO
KEARNY ...................................PINAL
KEET SEEL ................................NAVAJO
Keet Seel Canyon ...........................Navajo
    See: KEET SEEL, NAVAJO
Keet Seel Spring ...........................Navajo
    See: KEET SEEL, NAVAJO
KELLOGG PEAK .............................PIMA
KELLY ..................................YAVAPAI
KELLY BUTTE ...............................GILA
Kelly's Peak .................................Gila
    See: KELLY BUTTE, GILA
KELTON ..................................COCHISE
KELVIN ....................................PINAL
KENDALL ................................MARICOPA
Kendrick, Mount ...........................Coconino
    See: KENDRICK PEAK, COCONINO
Kendrick Park .............................Coconino
    See: KENDRICK PEAK, COCONINO
KENDRICK PEAK .......................COCONINO
Kendrick Spring ...........................Coconino
    See: KENDRICK PEAK, COCONINO
KENILWORTH ..............................PINAL

Klothos Temple ................................Yuma
   See: CORONATION PEAK, YUMA
Knight Creek ......................Mohave, Yavapai
   See: WHITE CLIFFS CREEK, MOHAVE
KNOB MOUNTAIN .........................APACHE
KO VAYA ......................................PIMA
Ko Vaya Hills ..................................Pima
   See: KO VAYA, PIMA
Ko Vaya Wash ..................................Pima
   See: KO VAYA, PIMA
KOFA ........................................YUMA
   See also: S H MOUNTAINS, YUMA
Kofa Butte ....................................Yuma
   See: KOFA, YUMA
Kofa Mountains ................................Yuma
   See: KOFA, YUMA
Kofa Queen Canyon ............................Yuma
   See: KOFA, YUMA
Kofa Queen Mine ..............................Yuma
   See: KOFA, YUMA
Kofa Well ....................................Yuma
   See: KOFA, YUMA
KOHATK .....................................PINAL
Kohatk Valley ..................................Pinal
   See: KOHATK, PINAL
Kohatk Wash ..................................Pinal
   See: KOHATK, PINAL
KOHI KUG ....................................PIMA
KOHINOOR SPRING ......................MOHAVE
KOHL'S RANCH ............................GILA
KOLB NATURAL BRIDGE ........GRAND CANYON
Kolb Point ....................Grand Canyon, Coco
   See: KOLB NATURAL BRIDGE, GRAND CANYON
Kolipatvawka ..................................Pima
   See: GURLI PUT VO, PIMA
Kolipatvooka ..................................Pima
   See: GURLI PUT VO, PIMA
Komaktjivurt ..................................Pima
   See: HORSESHOE, PIMA
Komalik ......................................Pinal
   See: GU KOMELIK, PINAL
Komatke ......................................Pinal
   See: ESTRELLA MOUNTAINS, PINAL
KOMELIK ....................................PIMA
Komelik Pass ..................................Pima
   See: KOMELIK, PIMA
Komertkewotche ................................Pinal
   See: ESTRELLA MOUNTAINS, PINAL
Komoktetuvavosit ..............................Pima
   See: ARTESA MOUNTAINS, PIMA
Kom Vo Valley ................................Pima
   See: KOM VO, PIMA
Ko-opke ......................................Pinal
   See: SHOPISHK, PINAL
Koxikux ......................................Pima
   See: KOHI KUG, PIMA
KUAKATCH ...................................PIMA
Kuakatch Pass ..................................Pima
   See: KUAKATCH, PIMA
Kuakatch Wash ................................Pima
   See: KUAKATCH, PIMA
Kuarchi ......................................Pima
   See: GU ACHI, PIMA

Kuat-shi ......................................Pima
   See: GU ACHI, PIMA
Kuchaptuvela ..................................Navajo
   See: HOPI VILLAGES, NAVAJO
   See: WALPI, NAVAJO
Kuck Son ......................................Pima
   See: TUCSON, PIMA
Kukomalik ....................................Pinal
   See: GU KOMELIK, PINAL
KUM VO ......................................PIMA
Kuoitak ......................................Pima
   See: GU OIDAK, PIMA
Kuvo ........................................Pima
   See: GO VO, PIMA
Kwagunt Butte ..............Grand Canyon, Coco
   See: KWAGUNT VALLEY, GRAND CANYON
Kwagunt Canyon ............Grand Canyon, Coco
   See: KWAGUNT VALLEY, GRAND CANYON
Kwagunt Creek ..............Grand Canyon, Coco
   See: KWAGUNT VALLEY, GRAND CANYON
Kwagunt Hollow ............Grand Canyon, Coco
   See: KWAGUNT VALLEY, GRAND CANYON
Kwagunt Rapids ............Grand Canyon, Coco
   See: KWAGUNT VALLEY, GRAND CANYON
KWAGUNT VALLEY ........GRAND CANYON, COCO
Kymo ........................................Yavapai
   See: WOOD, CAMP, YAVAPAI
KYRENE ...................................MARICOPA

LA BARGE CANYON .....................MARICOPA
La Barge Creek ................................Maricopa
   See: LA BARGE CANYON, MARICOPA
LADYBUG PEAK ..........................GRAHAM
Lady Bug Saddle ..............................Graham
   See: LADYBUG PEAK, GRAHAM
LAGUNA ....................................PIMA
LAGUNA ....................................YUMA
Laguna Canyon, Tsegi Branch ..................Navajo
   See: BETATKIN, NAVAJO
   See: TSEGI CANYON, NAVAJO
Laguna Creek ..................................Navajo
   See: TYENDE CREEK, NAVAJO, TSEGI CANYON,
      NAVAJO, KAYENTA, NAVAJO
Laguna Dam ..................................Yuma
   See: LAGUNA, YUMA
Laguna Mountains ..............................Yuma
   See: LAGUNA, YUMA
Laguna Negra ..................................Apache
   See: BONITO CREEK, APACHE
Laguna Reservoir ..............................Yuma
   See: LAGUNA, YUMA
LAGUNA, SIERRA DE .......................PIMA
Lagunas del Hospital, Las ......................Pinal
   See: MARICOPA WELLS, PINAL
Lake's Camp ..................................Navajo
   See: OBED, NAVAJO
Lake Cochise ..................................Cochise
   See: WILLCOX, COCHISE
Lake Mary ....................................Coconino
   See: MARY, LAKE, COCONINO
      CLARK VALLEY, COCONINO
Lake Mary Spring ..............................Coconino
   See: MARY, LAKE, COCONINO

LESLIE CANYON ........................COCHISE
Leslie Creek ..........................Cochise
    See: LESLIE CANYON, COCHISE
Lesna Mountains, La .......................Pima
    See: LESNA PEAK, PIMA
LESNA PEAK ................................PIMA
LEUPP .................................COCONINO
Leupp Corners .....................Coconino
    See: LEUPP, COCONINO
LEWIS AND PRANTY CREEK ............MARICOPA
LEWIS, CAMP ................................GILA
LEWIS SPRINGS ........................COCHISE
LEWISTON ..............................COCHISE
LIBERTY ..............................MARICOPA
Lida Creek ...........................Greenlee
    See: LYDA CREEK, GREENLEE
LIGHT .................................COCHISE
LIGHTHOUSE ROCK ......................YUMA
LIGHTNING MESA ......................GREENLEE
LIGURTA .................................YUMA
Lime Kiln Canyon .................Santa Cruz
    See: CALERA CANYON, SANTA CRUZ
Limerick .............................Graham
    See: CORK, GRAHAM
LIMESTONE CANYON ..................COCONINO
Limestone Mountain ...................Cochise
    See: DRAGOON MOUNTAINS, COCHISE
Limestone Pasture ....................Coconino
    See: LIMESTONE CANYON, COCONINO
Limestone Spring .....................Coconino
    See: LIMESTONE CANYON, COCONINO
Limestone Tanks ......................Coconino
    See: LIMESTONE CANYON, COCONINO
Lincoln, Camp ........................Yavapai
    See: VERDE, CAMP, YAVAPAI
Lincoln, Camp ..........................Yuma
    See: LA PAZ, CAMP, YUMA
Lincoln, Fort ........................Yavapai
    See: VERDE, CAMP, YAVAPAI
Lincoln Point ...............Grand Canyon, Coco
    See: LIPAN POINT, GRAND CANYON
LINCOLNIA ..............................MOHAVE
LINDEN .................................NAVAJO
Linderos, Cerritos de los ................Pima
    See: LESNA PEAK, PIMA
Linden Wash ...........................Navajo
    See: LINDEN, NAVAJO
Line City .............................Santa Cruz
    See: NOGALES, SANTA CRUZ
Lino, Rio de ...........................Apache
    See: LITTLE COLORADO RIVER, APACHE
LINSKEY ................................YUMA
LIPAN POINT .............GRAND CANYON, COCO
LISCUM ...............................MARICOPA
Litchfield ...........................Maricopa
    See: AVONDALE, MARICOPA
LITCHFIELD PARK ....................MARICOPA
Litchton ............................Maricopa
    See: LITCHFIELD PARK, MARICOPA
LITHODENDRON CREEK ..................APACHE

Lithodendron Wash .....................Apache
    See: LITHODENDRON CREEK, APACHE
Little Ajo Mountains ......................Pima
    See: AJO, PIMA
Little Bog Creek .......................Apache
    See: BOG CREEK, APACHE
Little Bonito Creek ....................Apache
    See: BONITO CREEK, APACHE
LITTLE, CAMP (STEPHEN D.) .........SANTA CRUZ
Little Carrizo Wash ....................Navajo
    See: CARRIZO, APACHE
LITTLE COLORADO RIVER .................NAVAJO
Little Dragoon Mountains ..............Cochise
    See: DRAGOON MOUNTAINS, COCHISE
Little Elden Spring ...................Coconino
    See: ELDEN MOUNTAIN, COCONINO
LITTLEFIELD ...........................MOHAVE
LITTLE GIANT ..............................GILA
LITTLE GILA RIVER .......................PINAL
LITTLE GREEN VALLEY ......................GILA
Little Harquahala Mountains .............Yuma
    See: HARQUAHALA MOUNTAINS, YUMA
LITTLE HORN MOUNTAINS ..................YUMA
Little Leroux Spring ..................Coconino
    See: LEROUX SPRING, COCONINO
Little L.O. Canyon ....................Coconino
    See: GARLAND PRAIRIE, COCONINO
Little L.O. Spring Canyon .............Coconino
    See: GARLAND PRAIRIE, COCONINO
Little Mount Elden ...................Coconino
    See: DRY LAKE, COCONINO
Little Nankoweap Creek .........Grand Canyon, Coco
    See: NANKOWEAP BUTTE, GRAND CANYON
Little Oraibi .........................Coconino
    See: MOENKOPI, COCONINO
Little Salt River Valley ..................Gila
    See: CATALPA, GILA
Little Shipp Mountain .................Yavapai
    See: SHIPP MOUNTAIN, YAVAPAI
Little Steve's Ranch ..................Greenlee
    See: DOUBLE CIRCLE RANCH, GREENLEE
Little Table Mountain ...................Pinal
    See: TABLE MOUNTAIN, COCONINO
Little Table Top Mountain ...............Pinal
    See: TABLE MOUNTAIN, COCONINO
LITTLE TROUGH CREEK ...................GILA
Little Valley ........................Coconino
    See: MARY, LAKE, COCONINO
LIVEOAK ..................................GILA
Liveoak Gulch ...........................Gila
    See: LIVEOAK, GILA
Liveoak Shaft ...........................Gila
    See: LIVEOAK, GILA
LIVERPOOL LANDING ....................MOHAVE
LIVINGSTON ...............................GILA
Livingston Pass ........................Yuma
    See: NEW WATER, YUMA
Llano del Azotado .........................Pima
    See: TORTOLITA MOUNTAINS, PIMA
LOCHIEL (La Noria) ..................SANTA CRUZ
LOCKETT LAKE .........................COCONINO

Lululongturkwi .......................... Navajo
    See: LULULONGTURQUI, NAVAJO
LULULONGTURQUI ......................NAVAJO
LUPTON ...............................APACHE
Lupton Wash .............................Apache
    See: LUPTON, APACHE
LUTTRELL ........................SANTA CRUZ
LYDA CREEK .........................GREENLEE
Lyda Springs ...........................Greenlee
    See: LYDA CREEK, GREENLEE
LYELL BUTTE ..............GRAND CANYON, COCO
Lyman .................................Apache
    See: LYMAN DAM, APACHE
LYMAN DAM ...........................APACHE
Lyman's Project .........................Apache
    See: LYMAN DAM, APACHE
Lyman Reservoir .........................Apache
    See: LYMAN DAM, APACHE
LYNX CREEK .........................YAVAPAI
LYONSVILLE ...........................MOHAVE

MAC DONALD ........................COCHISE
MAC DONALD ........................YAVAPAI
Mack Morris Mill ...........................Gila
    See: STANTON, GILA
Maddox .................................Navajo
    See: DILKON, NAVAJO
MADERA CANYON .............PIMA and Santa Cruz
Mad-Ku-Dap ..............................Yuma
    See: HALFWAY BEND, YUMA
MAGMA ................................PINAL
Magma Mine ...............................Pinal
    See: MAGMA, PINAL
Magnesium Springs ......................Graham
    See: INDIAN HOT SPRINGS, GRAHAM
MAHAN MOUNTAIN ...................COCONINO
MAHONE PEAK ........................YAVAPAI
MAIDEN'S BREAST, THE ....GRAND CANYON, COCO
Maine .................................Coconino
    See: PARKS, COCONINO
MAISH .................................PIMA
Maish-vaxia ...............................Pima
    See: MAISH VAYA, PIMA
MAISH VAYA ...........................PIMA
Maisk ...................................Pima
    See: MAISH VAYA, PIMA
Maispvaxia ...............................Pima
    See: MAISH VAYA, PIMA
Maley .................................Cochise
    See: WILLCOX, COCHISE
Maley Canyon ...........................Cochise
    See: WILLCOX, COCHISE
MALEY CORRAL .....................GREENLEE
Maley Gap ..............................Greenlee
    See: MALEY CORRAL, GREENLEE
MALLERY GROTTO ........GRAND CANYON, COCO
MAL PAI ...............................APACHE
Mal-pais Butte ...........................Apache
    See: BLACK PINNACLE BUTTE, APACHE
MALPAIS MOUNTAIN ...................GREENLEE
MAL PAIS SPRING ......................NAVAJO

MAMMOTH ...............................PINAL
Mammoth Camp ............................Pinal
    See: MAMMOTH, PINAL
Mammoth Mine ............................Pinal
    See: MAMMOTH, PINAL
Mammoth Wash ............................Pinal
    See: MAMMOTH, PINAL
MANILA ...............................NAVAJO
MANLYVILLE ...........................PINAL
MANSFIELD, CAMP .......................APACHE
MANU TEMPLE ...........GRAND CANYON, COCO
MANY FARMS .........................APACHE
Manzana .................................Navajo
    See: MISHONGNOVI, NAVAJO
MANZANA ........................SANTA CRUZ
Manzanita Creek ...................Grand Canyon, Coco
    See: MANZANITA POINT, GRAND CANYON
MANZANITA POINT .........GRAND CANYON, COCO
Manzanita Spring .......................Santa Cruz
    See: MANZANA, SANTA CRUZ
MANZORA .............................COCHISE
MAPLE CANYON .......................GREENLEE
Maple Peak ............................Greenlee
    See: MAPLE CANYON, GREENLEE
MARANA .................................PIMA
Marble Canyon ...................Grand Canyon, Coco
    See: MARBLE GORGE, GRAND CANYON
Marble Flats .....................Grand Canyon, Coco
    See: MARBLE GORGE, GRAND CANYON
MARBLE GORGE ..........GRAND CANYON, COCO
Marble Hills ............................Coconino
    See: WHITE HORSE HILLS, COCONINO
MARCOS TERRACE .........GRAND CANYON, COCO
MARCOU MESA ..........................NAVAJO
Maria Santissima del Carmen Land Grant ........Santa Cruz
    See: BUENA VISTA LAND GRANT, SANTA CRUZ
MARICOPA ...............................PINAL
    See also: MARICOPA WELLS, PINAL
MARICOPA COUNTY .........................174
MARICOPA (AK CHIN) INDIAN RESERVATION .PINAL
Maricopa Junction ..........................Pinal
    See: MARICOPA, PINAL
Maricopa Mountains ...................Pinal, Maricopa
    See: ESTRELLA MOUNTAINS, PINAL
Maricopa Peak ...........................Maricopa
    See: ESTRELLA MOUNTAINS, PINAL
MARICOPA POINT .........GRAND CANYON, COCO
MARICOPA STATION .....................PINAL
MARICOPA WELLS ......................PINAL
Maricopaville .............................Pinal
    See: MARICOPA STATION, PINAL
MARIJILDA CANYON .....................GRAHAM
Marijilda Creek ..........................Graham
    See: MARIJILDA CANYON, GRAHAM
MARINETTE ..........................MARICOPA
MARION ..............................YAVAPAI
MARION POINT ...........GRAND CANYON, COCO
MARKEEN MOUNTAIN ...................GREENLEE
Maroni, Fort ...........................Coconino
    See: FORT VALLEY, COCONINO

McCOLLUM RANCH ....................COCONINO
    See also: COLEMAN LAKE, COCONINO
McCONNICO ............................MOHAVE
McCracken .............................Mohave
    See: McCRACKIN MINE, MOHAVE
McCracken Peak .......................Mohave
    See: McCRACKIN MINE, MOHAVE
McCRACKIN MINE ......................MOHAVE
McCullum Ranch .......................Coconino
    See: COLEMAN LAKE, COCONINO
McDONALD FORT ...........................GILA
McDonald Mountain ........................Gila
    See: McDONALD FORT, GILA
McDonald Pocket ..........................Gila
    See: McDONALD FORT, GILA
McDowell .............................Maricopa
    See: McDOWELL, FORT, MARICOPA
McDowell Canyon .....................Maricopa
    See: McDOWELL, FORT, MARICOPA
McDOWELL, FORT .....................MARICOPA
McDowell, Fort, Indian Reservation .......Maricopa
    See: McDOWELL, FORT, MARICOPA
McDowell Mountain ...................Maricopa
    See: McDOWELL, FORT, MARICOPA
McDowell Pass .......................Maricopa
    See: McDOWELL, FORT, MARICOPA
McDowell Peak .......................Maricopa
    See: McDOWELL, FORT, MARICOPA
McFadden Creek ...........................Gila
    See: McFADDEN HORSE MOUNTAIN, GILA
McFADDEN HORSE MOUNTAIN ...............GILA
McFadden Peak ............................Gila
    See: McFADDEN HORSE MOUNTAIN, GILA
McFadden Spring ..........................Gila
    See: McFADDEN HORSE MOUNTAIN, GILA
McGUIREVILLE .........................YAVAPAI
McIntosh .................................Gila
    See: MESQUITE SPRING, GILA
McKAY'S PEAK .........................APACHE
McKEE, CAMP ......................SANTA CRUZ
McKinnon Point ..........Grand Canyon, Coco
    See: WIDFORSS POINT, GRAND CANYON
McLELLAN ...........................COCONINO
McLellan Dam ........................Coconino
    See: McLELLAN, COCONINO
McLellan Reservoir ...................Coconino
    See: McLELLAN, COCONINO
McMillan .................................Gila
    See: McMILLANVILLE, GILA
McMILLANVILLE .........................GILA
McMullen ................................Yuma
    See: McMULLEN VALLEY, YUMA
McMULLEN VALLEY ......................YUMA
McNARY ...............................APACHE
McNEAL ...............................COCHISE
McNutt, Mount ........................Mohave
    See: NUTT, MOUNT, MOHAVE
McPherson, Camp .....................Yavapai
    See: DATE CREEK, CAMP, YAVAPAI
McQUEEN ............................MARICOPA
McVAY .................................YUMA
MEAD ................................MARICOPA

MEAD, LAKE ...........................MOHAVE
MEADOWS, THE .........................APACHE
Meadows ..............................Mohave
    See: MEADOW CREEK, MOHAVE
MEADOW CREEK ........................MOHAVE
MEADOW VALLEY CREEK ...................GILA
MEATH ...............................YAVAPAI
Meath Dam ...........................Yavapai
    See: MEATH, YAVAPAI
Meath Wash ..........................Yavapai
    See: MEATH, YAVAPAI
Medicine Cave ........................Coconino
    See: MEDICINE VALLEY, COCONINO
MEDICINE VALLEY .....................COCONINO
MEESVILLE ............................YAVAPAI
MELENDRETH PASS .........................PIMA
Melendrez ...............................Pima
    See: MELENDRETH PASS, PIMA
Mellen ...............................Mohave
    See: NEEDLES, THE, MOHAVE
MENEGER'S LAKE .........................PIMA
Mericitica ...........................Mohave
    See: MERWITICA CANYON, MOHAVE
MERIDIAN ...........................MARICOPA
MERIDIAN BUTTE .......................APACHE
MERIWITICA CANYON ....................MOHAVE
Merlin Abyss ...............Grand Canyon, Coco
    See: BEDIVERE POINT, GRAND CANYON
MERRIAM CRATER .....................COCONINO
Merriam Mountain ....................Coconino
    See: MERRIAM CRATER, COCONINO
MERRILL CRATER .....................COCONINO
Merrill Creek .........................Graham
    See: MERRILL PEAK, GRAHAM
Merrill Mountain ....................Coconino
    See: MERRILL CRATER, COCONINO
MERRILL PEAK .........................GRAHAM
MERRICK BUTTE ........................NAVAJO
MESA ...............................MARICOPA
MESA BUTTE .........................COCONINO
Mesa Butte .................Grand Canyon, Coco
    See: SHINUMO ALTAR, GRAND CANYON
Mesa City ...........................Maricopa
    See: MESA, MARICOPA
MESAVILLE .............................PINAL
MESCAL ...............................COCHISE
Mescal Canyon .......................Cochise
    See: MESCAL, COCHISE
Mescal Canyon.. .....................Yavapai
    See: MESCAL GULCH, YAVAPAI
Mescal Creek ........................Cochise
    See: MESCAL, COCHISE
MESCAL GULCH .......................YAVAPAI
MESCAL MOUNTAINS ..................GILA, Pinal
Mescal Spring .......................Cochise
    See: MESCAL, COCHISE
Mescal Warm Spring .....................Gila
    See: MESCAL MOUNTAINS, GILA
MESCALERO POINT ........GRAND CANYON, COCO
Mesquite ...........................Maricopa
    See: MESQUITE WELL, YUMA

Mineral ............................................Mohave
    See: MINERAL PARK, MOHAVE
Mineral Butte ........................................Pinal
    See: MINERAL CREEK, PINAL
Mineral City .........................................Yuma
    See: EHRENBERG, YUMA
MINERAL CREEK ...........................APACHE
MINERAL CREEK ......................PINAL, Gila
MINERAL HILL .............................PIMA
Mineral Mountain ....................................Pinal
    See: MINERAL CREEK, PINAL
MINERAL PARK ..........................MOHAVE
MING ........................................YUMA
Mingkard Mountains ..............................Mohave
    See: VIRGIN RIVER, MOHAVE
MINGUS MOUNTAIN .....................YAVAPAI
MINGVILLE ..............................GRAHAM
Mining Mountain .....................................Pinal
    See: MINERAL CREEK, PINAL
MINNEHAHA ...........................YAVAPAI
Minnehaha Creek ..................................Yavapai
    See: MINNEHAHA, YAVAPAI
Minnehaha Flat ....................................Yavapai
    See: MINNEHAHA, YAVAPAI
Minnehaha Spring ..................................Yavapai
    See: MINNEHAHA, YAVAPAI
Mint Creek .........................................Yavapai
    See: MINT VALLEY, YAVAPAI
MINT VALLEY ..........................YAVAPAI
Mint Wash ..........................................Yavapai
    See: MINT VALLEY, YAVAPAI
MIRAGE, EL ............................MARICOPA
Miraflores (River) ...............................Gila, etc.
    See: GILA RIVER, GILA
MIRAMONTE ............................COCHISE
MISERY, FORT .........................Yavapai
Misery, Fort, Number 2 ...........................Yavapai
    See: MISERY, FORT, YAVAPAI
MISHONGNOVI .........................NAVAJO
MISSION CAMP ..........................YUMA
MISTAKE PEAK ........................GREENLEE
MITCHELL BUTTE ......................NAVAJO
Mitchell Butte Wash ...............................Navajo
    See: MITCHELL BUTTE, NAVAJO
Mitchell Mesa .......................................Navajo
    See: MITCHELL BUTTE, NAVAJO
MITCHELL PEAK .......................GREENLEE
MITTEN BUTTE ........................NAVAJO
MITTEN PEAK .........................NAVAJO
Mix Wash, Tom .......................................Pinal
    See: TOM MIX WASH, PINAL
Moa Ave .............................................Coconino
    See: MOE AVE, COCONINO
MOBILE ...............................MARICOPA
Moccasin ...........................................Mohave
    See: MOCCASIN SPRING, MOHAVE
MOCCASIN SPRING ......................MOHAVE
MOCKINGBIRD ..........................MOHAVE
MODOC MOUNTAIN .....................GREENLEE
Modred Abyss .....................Grand Canyon, Coco
    See: BEDIVERE POINT, GRAND CANYON

MOE AVE ...............................COCONINO
Moe Ave Springs ..................................Coconino
    See: MOE AVE, COCONINO
Moehavi .............................................Coconino
    See: MOE AVE, COCONINO
Moen Abi ............................................Coconino
    See: MOE AVE, COCONINO
Moenave .............................................Coconino
    See: MOE AVE, COCONINO
Moenavi .............................................Coconino
    See: MOE AVE, COCONINO
Moencopi Wash ....................................Coconino
    See: MOENKOPI, COCONINO
Moencopie ..........................................Coconino
    See: MOENKOPI, COCONINO
Moenkapi ...........................................Coconino
    See: MOENKOPI, COCONINO
MOENKOPI ..............................COCONINO
Moenkopi Plateau ..................................Coconino
    See: MOENKOPI, COCONINO
Mogollon Buttes ...........................Coconino, Navajo
    See: MOGOLLON RIM, COCONINO
Mogollon, Camp .....................................Apache
    See: APACHE, FORT, APACHE
Mogollon Mesa .....................................Coconino
    See: MOGOLLON RIM, COCONINO
Mogollon Plateau ..................................Coconino
    See: MOGOLLON RIM, COCONINO
MOGOLLON RIM ...COCONINO, Navajo, Apache, Yavapai
Mohatuk .............................................Maricopa
    See: SALT RIVER, GILA
Mohave, Camp ......................................Mohave
    See: MOHAVE, FORT, MOHAVE
Mohave Canyon .....................................Mohave
    See: MOHAVE, FORT, MOHAVE
Mohave City ........................................Mohave
    See: MOHAVE, FORT, MOHAVE
MOHAVE COUNTY ............................200
Mohave Creek .......................................Mohave
    See: MOHAVE, FORT, MOHAVE
MOHAVE, FORT .........................MOHAVE
Mohave, Indian Reservation, Fort ................Mohave
    See: MOHAVE, FORT, MOHAVE
Mohave Lake ........................................Mohave
    See: MOHAVE, FORT, MOHAVE
Mohave Mountains ..................................Mohave
    See: MOHAVE, FORT, MOHAVE
Mohave Peak ........................................Mohave
    See: MOHAVE, FORT, MOHAVE
MOHAVE POINT ...................GRAND CANYON
Mohave Point .......................................Mohave
    See: MOHAVE, FORT, MOHAVE
Mohave Rock ........................................Mohave
    See: MOHAVE, FORT, MOHAVE
        CASTLE ROCK BAY, MOHAVE
Mohave Spring ......................................Mohave
    See: MOHAVE, FORT, MOHAVE
Mohave Valley ......................................Mohave
    See: MOHAVE, FORT, MOHAVE
Mohave Wash ........................................Mohave
    See: MOHAVE, FORT, MOHAVE
MOHAWK ................................YUMA

Morenci Hot Springs ........................Greenlee
  See: MORENCI, GREENLEE
MORGAN MOUNTAIN ......................NAVAJO
MORGAN'S FERRY ..........................PINAL
Moritz Hill ......................................Coconino
  See: MORITZ LAKE, COCONINO
MORITZ LAKE .........................COCONINO
MORMON BEND ..........................APACHE
Mormon Canyon ...............................Coconino
  See: MORMON MOUNTAIN, COCONINO
MORMON CROSSING ...................COCONINO
  See also: GRAPEVINE SPRING, COCONINO
Mormon Dairy ..................................Coconino
  See: MORMON MOUNTAIN, COCONINO
Mormon Dairy Spring .........................Coconino
  See: MORMON MOUNTAIN, COCONINO
MORMON FLAT ..........................MARICOPA
Mormon Flat Dam .............................Maricopa
  See: MORMON FLAT, MARICOPA
Mormon Lake ...................................Coconino
  See: MORMON MOUNTAIN, COCONINO
MORMON MOUNTAIN ...................COCONINO
Mormon Ridge ..................................Coconino
  See: MORMON MOUNTAIN, COCONINO
Mormon Road ...................................Coconino
  See: MORMON MOUNTAIN, COCONINO
     HOUSE ROCK, COCONINO
Moroni, Fort ....................................Coconino
  See: FORT VALLEY, COCONINO
Moros Well, Los ...................................Pima
  See: MORAS, LAS, PIMA
MORRISTOWN ...........................GRAHAM
MORRISTOWN ..........................MARICOPA
Morse Canyon ...................................Cochise
  See: TURKEY CREEK, COCHISE
Mortenson ........................................Navajo
  See: PINEDALE, NAVAJO
Mortenson Wash .................................Navajo
  See: PINEDALE, NAVAJO
MOSS HILL ...............................MOHAVE
Mountain District ..................................XIII
Mount Whipple ..................................Mohave
  See: CYGNUS MOUNTAIN, MOHAVE
Mowry Flat ....................................Santa Cruz
  See: MOWRY MINE, SANTA CRUZ
MOWRY MINE ........................SANTA CRUZ
Mowry Wash ...................................Santa Cruz
  See: MOWRY MINE, SANTA CRUZ
Moyencopi .......................................Coconino
  See: MOENKOPI, COCONINO
MUAV CANYON ...........GRAND CANYON, COCO
Muav Saddle ......................Grand Canyon, Coco
  See: MUAV CANYON, GRAND CANYON
MUCHOS CANONES ........................YAVAPAI
Mud Mountain ....................................Yuma
  See: KOFA, YUMA
MUD SPRINGS ...........................COCHISE
Mud Springs .......................................Graham
  See: INDIAN HOT SPRINGS, GRAHAM
Mud Springs Canyon ............................Cochise
  See: MUD SPRINGS, COCHISE
MUD SPRINGS CANYON .................GREENLEE

Mud Springs Draw ..............................Cochise
  See: MUD SPRINGS, COCHISE
MUDDY CANYON .........................YAVAPAI
MUERTO, CANYON DEL ....................APACHE
  See also: CHELLY, CANYON DE, APACHE
MUERTOS, LOS .........................MARICOPA
Mueykava .........................................Maricopa
  See: MOIVAVI, MARICOPA
MUGGINS MOUNTAINS ......................YUMA
Muggins Tank ......................................Yuma
  See: MUGGINS MOUNTAINS, YUMA
Mu-koon-tu-weap ...............................Mohave
  See: TOROWEAP VALLEY, MOHAVE
MULDOON CANYON .......................YAVAPAI
Muldoon Tank ...................................Yavapai
  See: MULDOON CANYON, YAVAPAI
Mule Gulch .......................................Cochise
  See: MULE MOUNTAINS, COCHISE
MULE HOOF BEND .......................YAVAPAI
MULE MOUNTAINS ..........................COCHISE
Mule Pass ........................................Cochise
  See: MULE MOUNTAINS, COCHISE
Mule Pass Gulch .................................Cochise
  See: MULE MOUNTAINS, COCHISE
Mule Pass Mountain .............................Cochise
  See: MULE MOUNTAINS, COCHISE
MULE SHOE BEND ........................YAVAPAI
MULLEN WELLS .........................MARICOPA
MULLIGAN PEAK .........................GREENLEE
Mummy Cave ......................................Apache
  See: MUMMY HOUSE, APACHE
MUMMY HOUSE ...........................APACHE
Munds ............................................Mohave
  See: MUNDS PARK, COCONINO
Munds Canyon ...................................Coconino
  See: MUNDS PARK, COCONINO
Munds Draw ......................................Yavapai
  See: MUNDS PARK, COCONINO
Munds Mountain .................................Coconino
  See: MUNDS PARK, COCONINO
MUNDS PARK ..........................COCONINO
Munds Spring .....................................Coconino
  See: MUNDS PARK, COCONINO
Munds Trail .......................................Coconino
  See: MUNDS PARK, COCONINO
MUNN ......................................PINAL
Munson Cienega ..................................Graham
  See: SAN JOSE, GRAHAM
Munsonville ......................................Graham
  See: SAN JOSE, GRAHAM
Murderer's Grave ...............................Maricopa
  See: KENYON STATION, MARICOPA
Murray's Spring .................................Mohave
  See: FRANK MURRAY'S PEAK, MOHAVE
MUSIC MOUNTAIN .........................MOHAVE
Musina ...........................................Yuma
  See: LE SAGE, YUMA
Mustang Mountains ..............................Cochise
  See: WHETSTONE MOUNTAINS, COCHISE
Mut-a-witt-a-ka ................................Mohave
  See: MERIWITICA CANYON, MOHAVE
MYRTLE ........................................GILA

OLIVE CITY ...............................YUMA
Olivia ....................................Yuma
    See: OLIVE CITY, YUMA
Oljeto ...................................Navajo
    See: KAYENTA, NAVAJO
OLJETO WASH ..........................NAVAJO
Ollie Oatman Spring ....................Mohave
    See: OATMAN, MOHAVE
Omer ...................................Apache
    See: ROUND VALLEY, APACHE
          SPRINGERVILLE, APACHE
Omer Ward ..............................Apache
    See: ROUND VALLEY, APACHE
150 Mile Canyon ...............Grand Canyon, Mohv.
    See: 140 MILE CANYON, GRAND CANYON
140 MILE CANYON .........GRAND CANYON, COCO
135 Mile Rapids ...................Grand Canyon, Coco
    See: 140 MILE CANYON, GRAND CANYON
ONEIDA .................................PINAL
Onion Creek ............................Cochise
    See: ONION SADDLE, COCHISE
Onion Creek Saddle .....................Cochise
    See: ONION SADDLE, COCHISE
ONION SADDLE ........................COCHISE
O'NEAL SPRING .......................COCONINO
O'Neill Hills .............................Yuma
    See: O'NEILL PASS, YUMA
O'NEILL PASS ..........................YUMA
O'NEIL BUTTE ............GRAND CANYON, COCO
O'NEIL SPRING ...........GRAND CANYON, COCO
Ookilsipava ..............................Yavapai
    See: LYNX CREEK, YAVAPAI
Oonupin Pinabu .........................Mohave
    See: WITCH WATER POCKET, MOHAVE
Oparsoitac .............................Maricopa
    See: UPASOITAC, MARICOPA
Opdyke Tanks ..........................Coconino
    See: RATTLESNAKE TANKS, COCONINO
ORACLE .................................PINAL
Oracle Camp .............................Pinal
    See: ORACLE, PINAL
Oracle Hill ...............................Pinal
    See: ORACLE, PINAL
Oracle Junction ...........................Pinal
    See: ORACLE, PINAL
Oracle Ridge .........................Pinal, Pima
    See: ORACLE, PINAL
ORAIBI .................................NAVAJO
Oraibi Butte .............................Navajo
    See: ORAIBI, NAVAJO
Oraibi Wash .............................Navajo
    See: ORAIBI, NAVAJO
ORANGE BUTTE .......................COCHISE
Oraybe ..................................Navajo
    See: ORAIBI, NAVAJO
Ord, Camp ..............................Apache
    See: APACHE, FORT, APACHE
Ord Creek ...............................Apache
    See: SNOWSTAKE CREEK, APACHE
ORD, MOUNT ..........................APACHE
ORD, MOUNT ...................GILA, Maricopa
See also: ORD, MOUNT, APACHE

Ord Mine ................................Gila
    See: ORD, MOUNT, GILA
ORDERVILLE CANYON .................COCONINO
OREJANO CANYON ...................GREENLEE
ORGAN PIPE CACTUS NATIONAL MONUMENT  PIMA
Origin of Life Cave .......................Apache
    See: NEWSPAPER ROCK, APACHE
ORIZABA ................................PINAL
Ormejea .................................Pinal
    See: HORMIGUERO, PINAL
Oro ....................................Greenlee
    See: OROVILLE, GREENLEE
ORO ...................................YAVAPAI
Oro Belle Mine ..........................Yavapai
    See: ORO, YAVAPAI
ORO BLANCO .......................SANTA CRUZ
Oro Blanco Mountain ...................Santa Cruz
    See: PAJARITO MOUNTAINS, SANTA CRUZ
Oro Blanco Peak ......................Santa Cruz
    See: PAJARITO MOUNTAINS, SANTA CRUZ
Oro Blanco Wash ......................Santa Cruz
    See: ORO BLANCO, SANTA CRUZ
ORO, CAÑADA DEL .......................PIMA
Oro, Cañada del (P.O.) .....................Pinal
    See: ORO, CAÑADA DEL, PIMA
Oro, Canyon del ...........................Pima
    See: ORO, CAÑADA DEL, PIMA
Oro Wash, Cañada del .......................Pima
    See: ORO, CAÑADA DEL, PIMA
Oronai Mountain .......................Maricopa
    See: GOLDFIELD MOUNTAINS, MARICOPA
OROVILLE .............................GREENLEE
Orrville .................................Yuma
    See: CENTENNIAL, YUMA
Ortega Draw ............................Apache
    See: ORTEGA LAKE, APACHE
ORTEGA LAKE .........................APACHE
Ortega Wash ............................Apache
    See: ORTEGA LAKE, APACHE
Orville ..................................Yuma
    See: CENTENNIAL, YUMA
OSA, LA .................................PIMA
Osa Wash, La .............................Pima
    See: OSA, LA, PIMA
Osborne ................................Cochise
    See: BISBEE, COCHISE
Osborne Wash ............................Yuma
    See: CLARA PEAK, YUMA
Osborne Well .............................Yuma
    See: CLARA PEAK, YUMA
OSIRIS TEMPLE ..................GRAND CANYON
Otero Canyon ..........................Maricopa
    See: OTERO CREEK, MARICOPA
OTERO CREEK ........................MARICOPA
Otero Spring ...........................Maricopa
    See: OTERO CREEK, MARICOPA
OTIS ...................................PINAL
OURY, MOUNT ..........................PIMA
OUTLAW MOUNTAIN ..................COCHISE
Outlaw Spring ...........................Cochise
    See: OUTLAW MOUNTAIN, COCHISE
OVERGAARD ...........................NAVAJO

Papago Creek ......................Grand Canyon, Coco
    See: PAPAGO POINT, GRAND CANYON
PAPAGO INDIAN RESERVATION ........PIMA, Pinal
Papago Mountains ...........................Maricopa
    See: SAUCEDA MOUNTAINS, MARICOPA
Papago Park ...............................Maricopa
    See: PAPAGO STATE PARK, MARICOPA
Papago Peak ................................Pima
    See: BABOQUIVARI PEAK, PIMA
PAPAGO POINT .............GRAND CANYON, COCO
Papago Saguaro National Monument .............Maricopa
    See: PAPAGO STATE PARK, MARICOPA
PAPAGO STATE PARK ...................MARICOPA
Papagueria ............................Pima, Pinal
    See: PAPAGO INDIAN RESERVATION, PIMA
PARADISE ..............................COCHISE
PARADISE VALLEY ....................MARICOPA
Paria Plateau ...............................Coconino
    See: PARIA RIVER, COCONINO
PARIA RIVER ..........................COCONINO
Paria Valley ................................Coconino
    See: PARIA RIVER, COCONINO
Parishawampitts Canyon .....................Coconino
    See: PARRISSAWAMPITTS SPRING, COCONINO
PARK ..................................APACHE
PARKER ................................YUMA
Parker Butte ..................................Gila
    See: RENO, CAMP, GILA
PARKER CANYON ....................SANTA CRUZ
Parker Creek .................................Gila
    See: RENO, CAMP, GILA
Parker Dam .................................Yuma
    See: PARKER, YUMA
PARKER'S PEAK ...........................PINAL
PARKS ...............................COCONINO
Parks Lake .................................Graham
    See: WHITLOCK VALLEY, GRAHAM
Parrissawampitts Canyon .....................Coconino
    See: PARRISSAWAMPITTS SPRING, COCONINO
PARRISSAWAMPITTS SPRING .............COCONINO
Parson Canyon ...............................Graham
    See: PARSONS PEAK, GRAHAM
PARSONS PEAK .......................GREENLEE
PARTRIDGE CITY ......................YAVAPAI
PARTRIDGE CREEK ....................COCONINO
Partridge Ravine ..............................Coconino
    See: PARTRIDGE CREEK, COCONINO
Partridge Wash ..............................Coconino
    See: PARTRIDGE CREEK, COCONINO
PASQUA VILLAGE .......................PIMA
Pass Mountain ...............................Yuma
    See: TURTLE BACK MOUNTAIN, YUMA
PASTORA PEAK ..........................APACHE
Pastura Peak ................................Apache
    See: PASTORA PEAK, APACHE
Pat Burns Cienega ............................Cochise
    See: PAT HILLS, COCHISE
PAT CREEK ...........................GREENLEE
PAT HILLS .............................COCHISE
PAT KNOLLS ...........................APACHE

Pat Mesa ...................................Greenlee
    See: PAT CREEK, GREENLEE
Pat Mountain ................................Greenlee
    See: PAT CREEK, GREENLEE
PAT MULLEN PEAK .......................NAVAJO
PATAGONIA .........................SANTA CRUZ
Patagonia Mountains .......................Santa Cruz
    See: MOWRY MINE, SANTA CRUZ
Patagonia Post Office (1866) .................Santa Cruz
    See: MOWRY MINE, SANTA CRUZ
PATIO .................................YUMA
Pato ......................................Pima
    See: KUM VO, PIMA
Patos, Los, River ............................Greenlee
    See: SAN FRANCISCO RIVER, GREENLEE
Patricks ...................................Yuma
    See: PEDRICKS, YUMA
PATTIE BUTTE .............GRAND CANYON, COCO
PAUL SPUR ............................COCHISE
PAULDEN .............................YAVAPAI
PAYA POINT .............GRAND CANYON, COCO
PAYSON .................................GILA
Paz, La ....................................Yuma
    See: LA PAZ, YUMA
Paz Arroyo, la ...............................Yuma
    See: LA PAZ, YUMA
Paz Mountain, La .............................Yuma
    See: LA PAZ, YUMA
Paz Mountains, La ............................Yuma
    See: DOME ROCK MOUNTAINS, YUMA
PEACH ORCHARD ..........................PINAL
Peach Orchard Spring ..........................Navajo
    See: KEAMS CANYON, NAVAJO
Peach Spring Canyon ...........................Mohave
    See: PEACH SPRINGS, MOHAVE
PEACH SPRINGS ..........................MOHAVE
Peache Springs Draw ..........................Mohave
    See: PEACH SPRINGS, MOHAVE
Peach Tree Spring .............................Mohave
    See: PEACH SPRINGS, MOHAVE
Peachville .................................Pinal
    See: PEACH ORCHARD, PINAL
Peachville Mountain ...........................Pinal
    See: PEACH ORCHARD, PINAL
Peachville Wash ..............................Pinal
    See: PEACH ORCHARD, PINAL
Peacocke Spring ..............................Mohave
    See: TRUXTON CANYON, MOHAVE
Peacockes Spring .............................Mohave
    See: PEACOCK SPRING, MOHAVE
Peacock Mountains ............................Mohave
    See: PEACOCK SPRING, MOHAVE
Peacock Peak ................................Mohave
    See: PEACOCK SPRING, MOHAVE
Peacock Ruin ................................Navajo
    See: LULULONGTURQUI, NAVAJO
PEACOCK SPRING ........................MOHAVE
    See also: TRUXTON CANYON, MOHAVE
PEARCE ...............................COCHISE
Pearce Hill .................................Cochise
    See: PEARCE, COCHISE

Picacho Pass ..............................Pinal
  See: PICACHO, PINAL
Picacho del Sentinela ......................Pima
  See: SENTINEL PEAK, PIMA
Picacho Spring ..........................Yavapai
  See: PICACHO, YAVAPAI
Picacho Station ...........................Pinal
  See: PICACHO, PINAL
Picacho del Tucson ........................Pinal
  See: PICACHO, PINAL
Picinemoi ................................Pima
  See: PISINIMO, PIMA
PICK-EM-UP .........................COCHISE
PICKET CANYON .....................COCHISE
Picket Park ..............................Cochise
  See: PICKET CANYON, COCHISE
Picket Post ...............................Pinal
  See: PINAL, PINAL
Picket Post Creek .........................Pinal
  See: PINAL, CAMP, PINAL
         QUEEN CREEK, PINAL
Pico del Aguila .........................Maricopa
  See: AGUILA, MARICOPA
Picture Rocks ..........................Maricopa
  See: PAINTED ROCKS, MARICOPA
PIEDMONT ...........................YAVAPAI
PIEDRA ..............................MARICOPA
PIERCE FERRY .......................MOHAVE
Pierce, Fort ............................Mohave
  See: PIERCE FERRY, MOHAVE
Pierce Mill Canyon ......................Mohave
  See: PIERCE FERRY, MOHAVE
Pierce Wash ............................Mohave
  See: PIERCE FERRY, MOHAVE
Pierce Wash ............................Navajo
  See: PEARCE MOUNTAIN, NAVAJO
PIGEON CANYON .....................MOHAVE
PIGEON CREEK ......................GREENLEE
Pigeon Spring ..........................Mohave
  See: PIGEON CANYON, MOHAVE
Pilot Knob .............................Mohave
  See: PILOT ROCK, MOHAVE
PILOT ROCK .........................MOHAVE
Pilot Rock .............................Navajo
  See: MITTEN PEAK, NAVAJO
PIMA ................................GRAHAM
Pima Agency .............................Pinal
  See: SACATON, PINAL
PIMA COUNTY ...........................256
PIMA POINT ............GRAND CANYON, COCO
PIMA VILLAGES .......................PINAL
Pimeria Alta ..............................256
PINACATE VALLEY ....................YUMA
PINACLE RIDGE .....................GRAHAM
Pinal ..................................Gila
  See: PINAL MOUNTAINS, GILA
PINAL ................................PINAL
PINAL CAMP .........................PINAL
Pinal City ...............................Pinal
  See: PINAL, PINAL
PINAL COUNTY ..........................288

PINAL CREEK ...........................PINAL
Pinal Discovery ...........................Gila
  See: BIG JOHNEY GULCH, GILA
PINAL MOUNTAINS ......................GILA
Pinal Peak ...............................Gila
  See: PINAL MOUNTAINS, GILA
Pinal Peak .............................Greenlee
  See: PINAL MOUNTAINS, GILA
Pinal Ranch ..............................Pinal
  See: PINAL, CAMP, PINAL
PINALENO MOUNTAINS .................GRAHAM
PINE .................................GILA
Pine Butte ...............................Gila
  See: PINE SPRINGS, COCONINO
Pine Creek ............................Coconino
  See: TURKEY CREEK, COCONINO
Pine Creek ...............................Gila
  See: PINE SPRINGS, COCONINO
Pine Creek ............................Maricopa
  See: PINE SPRINGS, COCONINO
Pine Creek .............................Yavapai
  See: PINE SPRINGS, COCONINO
Pine Hollow ...........................Coconino
  See: PINE SPRINGS, COCONINO
Pine Mountain ..........................Yavapai
  See: PINE SPRINGS, COCONINO
Pine Plain Mountains .....................Graham
  See: PINALENO MOUNTAINS, GRAHAM
PINE SPRINGS .......................APACHE
PINE SPRINGS .....................COCONINO
  See also: MORMON MOUNTAIN, COCONINO
Pine Valley ..............................Gila
  See: PINE, GILA
Pineair ...............................Maricopa
  See: REAVIS, MARICOPA
PINEDALE ............................NAVAJO
PINERY CANYON .....................COCHISE
Pinery Creek ............................Cochise
  See: PINERY CANYON, COCHISE
Pinery Peak ............................Cochise
  See: PINERY CANYON, COCHISE
PINETOP .............................NAVAJO
PINEVETA ...........................YAVAPAI
Pineveta Canyon ........................Yavapai
  See: PINEVETA, YAVAPAI
Pineveta Peak ..........................Yavapai
  See: PINEVETA, YAVAPAI
PINEYON .............................APACHE
PINKLEY PEAK ..........................PIMA
PINNACLE MOUNTAIN .................MARICOPA
PINNACLE RIDGE .....................GRAHAM
PINON ...............................NAVAJO
Pinta ..................................Apache
  See: PINTO, APACHE
Pinta, Sierra ..........................Maricopa
  See: PAINTED ROCKS, MARICOPA
Pinta, Sierra ............................Yuma
  See: SIERRA PINTA, YUMA
PINTO ...............................APACHE
PINTO CREEK ...........................GILA
PINTO MESA .........................YAVAPAI

POLARIS ..................................YUMA

Polaris Mountain ............................Yuma
    See: POLARIS, YUMA

POLE KNOLL ...........................APACHE

POLHAMUS ..............................YUMA

POLLES MESA ..............................GILA

POLVO ......................................PIMA

POMERENE ............................COCHISE

Pomo, El ..............................Santa Cruz
    See: ALTO, SANTA CRUZ

POOL ....................................COCHISE
    See also: CASCABEL, COCHISE

POOL KNOLL ...........................APACHE

Pool Wash ................................Cochise
    See: POOL, COCHISE

POPPER WELL ....................MARICOPA

PORPHYRY MOUNTAIN ....................GILA

PORRAS DIKES .........................NAVAJO

PORTAL ................................COCHISE

Portal Peak ..............................Cochise
    See: PORTAL, COCHISE

PORTER CREEK .........................NAVAJO

Porter Mountain ..........................Navajo
    See: PORTER CREEK, NAVAJO

Porter Spring ...........................Coconino
    See: BRECKENRIDGE SPRING, COCONINO

PORTER TANK .........................NAVAJO

POSA PLAIN, LA ..........................YUMA

Posas Plain ................................Yuma
    See: POZOS, LOS, YUMA

Posas Valley ................................Yuma
    See: POZOS, LOS, YUMA
    POSA PLAIN, LA, YUMA

Poses, Los .................................Yuma
    See: POSA PLAIN, LA, YUMA

POSO, EL ...................................PIMA

POSO BUENO ..............................PIMA

Posos, Los .................................Yuma
    See: POSA PLAIN, LA, YUMA

POST CREEK ............................GRAHAM

Post Office Canyon .........................Navajo
    See: POST OFFICE HILL, NAVAJO

POST OFFICE HILL .....................NAVAJO

POSTA QUEMADA CANYON .................PIMA

Postles Ranch .............................Yavapai
    See: DEL RIO SPRINGS, YAVAPAI

POSTON ....................................YUMA

POSTON BUTTE ...........GRAND CANYON, COCO

POSTON BUTTE ...........................PINAL

Postvale ..................................Pima
    See: MARANA, PIMA

POTATO BUTTE ............................GILA

Potato Field Draw ........................Navajo
    See: POTATO WASH, NAVAJO

Potato Ranch .............................Yavapai
    See: TOWER MOUNTAIN, YAVAPAI

POTATO WASH ...........................NAVAJO

Pot Holes ..................................Yuma
    See: LA PAZ, YUMA

Potrero Creek ..........................Santa Cruz
    See: KITCHEN RANCH, PETE, SANTA CRUZ

Potrero Ranch, El ......................Santa Cruz
    See: KITCHEN RANCH, PETE, SANTA CRUZ

POTTER MESA ...........................APACHE

POTTER MOUNTAIN .....................COCHISE

Pottery Cave ..............................Apache
    See: HARRIS CAVE, APACHE

POTTS MOUNTAIN .......................MOHAVE

POVERTY KNOLL ........................MOHAVE

Poverty Mountain .........................Mohave
    See: POVERTY KNOLL, MOHAVE

Powell ...................................Mohave
    See: NEEDLES, THE, MOHAVE

Powell Lake ..............................Mohave
    See: NEEDLES, THE, MOHAVE

Powell Park .............................Coconino
    See: CLAY PARK, COCONINO

Powell Peak ..............................Mohave
    See: NEEDLES, THE, MOHAVE

POWELL PLATEAU .........GRAND CANYON, COCO

Powell Point ...............Grand Canyon, Coco
    See: POWELL PLATEAU, GRAND CANYON

Powell Spring ..............Grand Canyon, Coco
    See: POWELL PLATEAU, GRAND CANYON

POWELL SPRINGS .......................YAVAPAI

Powers ...................................Cochise
    See: RUCKER CANYON, COCHISE

POWERS BUTTE ........................MARICOPA

POZOS, LOS ................................YUMA

Pozo Blanco ...............................Pima
    See: DRIPPING SPRINGS, YUMA

Pozo Colorado .............................Pima
    See: SAUCEDA MOUNTAINS, MARICOPA

Pozo de Frederico .........................Pima
    See: KUAKATCH, PIMA

Pozo de la Rosa .........................Coconino
    See: PINE SPRINGS, COCONINO

Pozo Redondo .............................Pima
    See: SIKORT CHUAPO, PIMA

Pozo Redondo Mountains ...................Pima
    See: SIKORT CHUAPO, PIMA

Pozo Redondo Valley ......................Pima
    See: SIKORT CHUAPO, PIMA

Pozos de San Basilio ......................Mohave
    See: PEACH SPRING, MOHAVE

Pozo de Santa Isabel .....................Coconino
    See: RED HORSE WASH, COCONINO

POZO VERDE ...............................PIMA

Pozo Verde Mountains ......................Pima
    See: POZO VERDE, PIMA

Pozo Verde, Sierra del .....................Pima
    See: POZO VERDE, PIMA

PRAIRIE ................................YAVAPAI

PRATT ..................................MARICOPA

PRESCOTT ..............................YAVAPAI

Prescott Barracks .........................Yavapai
    See: WHIPPLE, FORT, YAVAPAI

Prescott Forest Reserve ....................Yavapai
    See: PRESCOTT, YAVAPAI

Prescott Junction .........................Yavapai
    See: SELIGMAN, YAVAPAI

Prescott National Forest ...................Yavapai
    See: PRESCOTT, YAVAPAI

Quartzite Peak .........................Pinal
    See: HUGGINS PEAK, PINAL
QUAYLE ..............................COCONINO
Queen ...................................Pinal
    See: QUEEN CREEK, PINAL
Queen Canyon ...........................Pinal
    See: QUEEN CREEK, PINAL
QUEEN CREEK ..................PINAL, Maricopa
Queen Creek Canyon .....................Pinal
    See: QUEEN CREEK, PINAL
Querino .................................Apache
    See: HELENA CANYON, APACHE
Querino Canyon .........................Apache
    See: HELENA CANYON, APACHE
QUIBURI ...............................COCHISE
QUIEN SABE CREEK ....................MARICOPA
Quien Sabe Peak .......................Maricopa
    See: QUIEN SABE CREEK, MARICOPA
Quien Sabe Springs ....................Maricopa
    See: QUINSABE CREEK, MARICOPA
QUIJOTOA ................................PIMA
Quijotoa City ............................Pima
    See: QUIJOTOA, PIMA
Quijotoa Mountains .......................Pima
    See: QUIJOTOA, PIMA
Quijotoa Pass ............................Pima
    See: QUIJOTOA, PIMA
Quijotoa Valley ..........................Pima
    See: QUIJOTOA, PIMA
Quijotoa Wash ............................Pima
    See: QUIJOTOA, PIMA
QUINLIN MOUNTAINS ......................PIMA
Quirino Canyon ..........................Apache
    See: HELENA CANYON, APACHE
QUITO BAQUITO ..........................PIMA
Quito Baquito Mountains ..................Pima
    See: QUITO BAQUITO, PIMA
Quito Baquito Springs ....................Pima
    See: QUITO BAQUITO, PIMA
Quitobac ................................Pima
    See: QUITO BAQUITO, PIMA
Quituna, La .............................Pima
    See: ALI AK CHIN, PIMA
Quituna Valley, La .......................Pima
    See: ALI AK CHIN, PIMA


RA, TOWER OF ...........................Yuma
RABBIT ................................PINAL
Rabbit Bill Tank .......................Coconino
    See: BABBIT BILL TANK, COCONINO
Rabbit-Ear Butte .......................Navajo
    See: HOPI BUTTES, NAVAJO
Rabbit Hills ...........................Navajo
    See: HOPI BUTTES, NAVAJO
RABBIT PATCH .........................MOHAVE
Rabbit Ranch ............................Pinal
    See: RABBIT, PINAL
Raccoon .................................Gila
    See: COON CREEK, GILA
RADIUM HOT SPRINGS ....................YUMA
RAGGED TOP ............................GILA

RAILROAD PASS ........................COCHISE
RAILROAD PASS .........................MOHAVE
Railroad Spring ........................Mohave
    See: GENTILE SPRING, MOHAVE
Rainbow Forest .........................Apache
    See: FIRST FOREST, APACHE
RAINBOW FOREST .......................NAVAJO
RAINBOW PLATEAU ....................COCONINO
RAINBOW VALLEY ......................MARICOPA
RAIN TANK ...........................COCONINO
Ralph's Mill .............................Yuma
    See: TACNA, YUMA
Ralph's Mill-Tacna P.O. ...................Yuma
    See: TACNA, YUMA
Ramah City .............................Navajo
    See: JOSEPH CITY, NAVAJO
Ramanote Peak .......................Santa Cruz
    See: RAMONOTE PEAK, SANTA CRUZ
Ramboz Camp .............................Gila
    See: RAMBOZ PEAK, GILA
RAMBOZ PEAK ...........................GILA
Ramboz Spring ...........................Gila
    See: RAMBOZ PEAK, GILA
RAMER RANCH ...........................GILA
RAMITA, LA ...........................COCHISE
Ramonote Canyon .....................Santa Cruz
    See: RAMONOTE PEAK, SANTA CRUZ
RAMONOTE PEAK ....................SANTA CRUZ
RAMSEY CANYON ......................COCHISE
Ramsey Peak ...........................Cochise
    See: RAMSEY CANYON, COCHISE
RAMSGATE .............................YAVAPAI
Ramsgate Spring ........................Yavapai
    See: RAMSGATE, YAVAPAI
RANCH CREEK ...........................GILA
Rancherias de San Diego ................Maricopa
    See: KENYON STATION, MARICOPA
Rancho de la Calabasas .................Santa Cruz
    See: CALABASAS, SANTA CRUZ
RANDOLPH ..............................PINAL
Randolph Canyon .........................Pinal
    See: RANDOLPH, PINAL
RANEGRAS PLAIN ........................YUMA
RATTLESNAKE BASIN ...................GREENLEE
Rattlesnake Camp .......................Greenlee
    See: RATTLESNAKE BASIN, GREENLEE
        STRAY HORSE CREEK, GREENLEE
Rattlesnake Canyon .....................Greenlee
    See: RATTLESNAKE BASIN, GREENLEE
Rattlesnake Creek ......................Greenlee
        STRAY HORSE CREEK, GREENLEE
Rattlesnake Gap ........................Greenlee
        STRAY HORSE CREEK, GREENLEE
RATTLESNAKE TANKS ..................COCONINO
RAVEN BUTTE ...........................YUMA
RAVENS PEAK ..........................COCHISE
RAWHIDE MOUNTAIN .....................PINAL
Rawhide Mountains ......................Mohave
    See: ARTILLERY MOUNTAINS, MOHAVE
RAWLINS, CAMP ........................YAVAPAI

R-14 RANCH ................................GILA
Rhoades ...........................Coconino
    See: PARKS, COCONINO
Rhoades Tank .......................Coconino
    See: PARKS, COCONINO
Rhodes ............................Coconino
    See: PARKS, COCONINO
RHODES RANCH ...................SANTA CRUZ
RHODES RANCH .....................YUMA
RHYOLITE CANYON ...................COCHISE
RIBBON FALLS ...........GRAND CANYON, COCO
RICE ...............................APACHE
Rice ................................Gila
    See: SAN CARLOS RIVER, GILA
RICE PEAK .......................PIMA, Pinal
RICE PEAK .........................YAVAPAI
Rice Spring .......................Yavapai
    See: RICE PEAK, YAVAPAI
Richards ...........................Navajo
    See: RICHARDS LAKE, NAVAJO
RICHARDS LAKE .....................NAVAJO
Richey .............................Apache
    See: NERO, APACHE
Rich Hill ..........................Yavapai
    See: ANTELOPE PEAK, YAVAPAI
RICH-IN-BAR ......................YAVAPAI
Richmond ...........................Cochise
    See: TOMBSTONE, COCHISE
RICHMOND BASIN ......................GILA
Richmond Mine .......................Gila
    See: RICHMOND BASIN, GILA
Richville ..........................Apache
    See: NERO, APACHE
Richville Valley ...................Apache
    See: NERO, APACHE
Rickerson, Fort .....................Coconino
    See: FORT VALLEY, COCONINO
Rieletto ............................PIMA
    See: RILLITO CREEK, PIMA
RIGG, CAMP .........................GILA
RIGGS CANYON .......................COCHISE
Riggs Seep .........................Cochise
    See: RIGGS CANYON, COCHISE
Rillito .............................Pima
    See: RILLITO CREEK, PIMA
RILLITO CREEK .......................PIMA
Rim, The ...........................Coconino
    See: MOGOLLON RIM, COCONINO
RIMMY JIMS ........................COCONINO
RIMROCK ...........................YAVAPAI
Rinconada ..........................Maricopa
    See: OATMAN FLAT, MARICOPA
Rincon Creek .......................Pima
    See: RINCON MOUNTAINS, PIMA
RINCON MOUNTAINS ...................PIMA
Rincon Peak ........................Pima
    See: RINCON MOUNTAINS, PIMA
Rincon Valley ......................Pima
    See: RINCON MOUNTAINS, PIMA
RIO DE FLAG .......................COCONINO
RIORDAN ...........................COCONINO
RIPSEY HILL .........................PINAL

Ripsey Spring .......................Pinal
    See: RIPSEY HILL, PINAL
Ripsey Wash .........................Pinal
    See: RIPSEY HILL, PINAL
RITTENHOUSE .......................MARICOPA
Riverside ...........................Pinal
    See: KELVIN, PINAL
ROARING SPRINGS .........GRAND CANYON, COCO
Roaring Springs Canyon ...........Grand Canyon, Coco
    See: ROARING SPRINGS, GRAND CANYON
ROARING RAPIDS .....................MOHAVE
ROBBER'S ROOST ....................COCONINO
Robbins Butte ......................Maricopa
    See: ROBERTS BUTTE, MARICOPA
ROBERTS BUTTE ....................MARICOPA
ROBERTS CIENEGA ...................COCHISE
Roberts Draw .......................Gila
    See: ROBERTS MESA, GILA
ROBERTS MESA .......................GILA
Robinson Crater ....................Coconino
    See: ROBINSON MOUNTAIN, COCONINO
ROBINSON MOUNTAIN ...............COCONINO
ROBLAS BUTTE ......................PINAL
Roblas Canyon ......................Pinal
    See: ROBLAS BUTTE, PINAL
ROBLES JUNCTION ....................PIMA
Robles Pass ........................Pima
    See: ROBLES JUNCTION, PIMA
Robles Ranch .......................Pima
    See: ROBLES JUNCTION, PIMA
ROCK BUTTE ........................PINAL
ROCK BUTTE .......................YAVAPAI
Rock Butte Station .................Yavapai
    See: ROCK BUTTE, YAVAPAI
ROCKFELLOW DOME ...................COCHISE
Rock, Fort .........................Yavapai
    See: FORT ROCK, YAVAPAI
Rock Horse Canyon ..................Gila
    See: ROCK HOUSE SPRING, GILA
Rock House .........................Gila
    See: ROCK HOUSE SPRING, GILA
Rock House Canyon ..................Gila
    See: ROCK HOUSE SPRING, GILA
Rock House Canyon ..................Pinal
    See: ROCK HOUSE MOUNTAIN, PINAL
Rock House Creek ...................Gila
    See: ROCK HOUSE SPRING, GILA
Rock House Hotel ...................Coconino
    See: HOUSE ROCK, COCONINO
ROCK HOUSE MOUNTAIN ...............PINAL
ROCK HOUSE SPRING ..................GILA
ROCKINSTRAW MOUNTAIN ..............GILA
Rock Peak ..........................Pinal
    See: ROCK BUTTE, PINAL
ROCK POINT ........................APACHE
ROCK SPRINGS .....................YAVAPAI
ROCK TOP MOUNTAIN ................COCONINO
Rock Top Spring ....................Coconino
    See: ROCK TOP MOUNTAIN, COCONINO
ROCKY BUTTE .......................MOHAVE
ROCKY GULCH ......................GREENLEE

SACRAMENTO PIT .........................COCHISE
Sacramento Range ........................Mohave
   See: BLACK MOUNTAINS, MOHAVE
Sacramento Siding ........................Mohave
   See: GRIFFITH, MOHAVE
SACRAMENTO VALLEY ..................MOHAVE
Sacramento Wash ........................Mohave
   See: SACRAMENTO VALLEY, MOHAVE
SADDLE BACK MOUNTAIN ...................PINAL
Saddle Canyon ...............Grand Canyon, Coco
   See: SADDLE MOUNTAIN, GRAND CANYON
Saddle Mountain ..........................Graham
   See: SADDLE BACK MOUNTAIN, PINAL
SADDLE MOUNTAIN .......GRAND CANYON, COCO
SAEVEDRA SPRINGS .....................MOHAVE
SAFFORD ...............................GRAHAM
SAGE PEAK ............................COCHISE
Saguaro Lake ...........................Maricopa
   See: STEWART MOUNTAIN, MARICOPA
SAGUARO NATIONAL MONUMENT ...........PIMA
SAHUARITA ...............................PIMA
Sahuarita Ranch ...........................Pima
   See: SAHUARITA, PIMA
Sahuarita Wash ............................Pima
   See: SAHUARITA, PIMA
Sahuarito Butte ...........................Pima
   See: MARTINEZ HILL, PIMA
St. Basil's Wells ........................Mohave
   See: PEACH SPRINGS, MOHAVE
St. Bernardo ...........................Navajo
   See: AWATOBI, NAVAJO
Saint Claire Mountain ...................Maricopa
   See: SAINT CLAIRE SPRING, MARICOPA
SAINT CLAIRE SPRING .................MARICOPA
Saint Claire Peak ......................Maricopa
   See: SAINT CLAIRE SPRING, MARICOPA
ST. DAVID ............................COCHISE
St. Gertrude de Tabac ...................Santa Cruz
   See: TUBAC, SANTA CRUZ
St. Joe Canyon ........................Coconino
   See: ST. JOE SPRING, COCONINO
ST. JOE SPRING ........................COCONINO
ST. JOHNS ...............................APACHE
St. Johns ..................................Pinal
   See: ESTRELLA MOUNTAINS, PINAL
St. John's Chapel ...........................Pinal
   See: ESTRELLA MOUNTAINS, PINAL
ST. JOHNS CREEK .........................GILA
St. Joseph's Mission ....................Santa Cruz
   See: TUMACACORI NATIONAL MONUMENT,
      SANTA CRUZ
ST. MATTHEWS MOUNTAIN ..............YAVAPAI
ST. MICHAELS ...........................APACHE
Sajini Butte ...............................Apache
   See: BLACK PINNACLE BUTTE, APACHE
Salado ..................................Gila
   See: SALT RIVER, GILA
Salado Reservoir ..........................Apache
   See: LYMAN DAM, APACHE
Salahkai Mesa .............................Apache
   See: BALUKAI MESA, APACHE

Salceda Mountains ....................Maricopa, Pima
   See: SAUCEDA MOUNTAINS, MARICOPA
Salee ....................................Apache
   See: TSEHILI, APACHE
Salem ...................................Apache
   See: ST. JOHNS, APACHE
Salero ...............................Santa Cruz
   See: SALERO HILL, SANTA CRUZ
SALERO HILL .......................SANTA CRUZ
Saletso Spring ...........................Apache
   See: SETSILTSO SPRING, APACHE
Salina ................................Maricopa
   See: PHOENIX, MARICOPA
Salinas ..................................Gila
   See: SALT RIVER, GILA
Salitre ..................................Graham
   See: GALIURO MOUNTAINS, GRAHAM
Salitre Negro, El ..........................Apache
   See: BLACK CREEK, APACHE
Salltso Spring ............................Apache
   See: SETSILTSO SPRING, APACHE
Sally May Canyon ..........................Gila
   See: SALOME CREEK, GILA
SALMON LAKE .........................COCONINO
SALOME ..................................YUMA
Salt Banks ...............................Gila
   See: SALT RIVER, GILA
SALT CREEK ...............................GILA
Salt Mountain ............................Gila
   See: SALT CREEK, GILA
SALT RIVER .......................GILA, Maricopa
SALT RIVER (P.O.) ......................MARICOPA
   See also: PHOENIX, MARICOPA
Salt River Canyon .........................Gila
   See: SALT RIVER, GILA
Salt River Draw ...........................Gila
   See: SALT RIVER, GILA
SALT RIVER INDIAN RESERVATION ......MARICOPA
Salt River Mountains .......................Gila
   See: SALT RIVER, GILA
Salt River Mountains ....................Maricopa
   See: SALT RIVER, GILA
Salt River Peak ...........................Gila
   See: SALT RIVER, GILA
Salt River Range ........................Maricopa
   See: SALT RIVER, GILA
SALT RIVER VALLEY ..................MARICOPA
SALT SPRING ..........................GREENLEE
SALT SPRINGS WASH .....................MOHAVE
Salumay ..................................Gila
   See: SALOME CREEK, GILA
Samaniego Hills ............................Pima
   See: SAMANIEGO PEAK, PIMA
SAMANIEGO PEAK ..........................PIMA
Samaniego Ridge ...........................Pima
   See: SAMANIEGO PEAK, PIMA
Samclark ..................................Pima
   See: CLARKSTOWN, PIMA
SAMPLE .................................COCHISE
San Agustin ...............................Pima
   See: TUCSON, PIMA
San Agustin de Oiaur .......................Pima
   See: TUCSON, PIMA

San Juan de Boquillas y Nogales ....................Cochise
    See: BOQUILLAS, COCHISE

San Juan de las Boquillas y Nogales Land Grant ...Santa Cruz
    See: NOGALES, SANTA CRUZ

San Juan Canyon ......................................Pima
    See: SAN JUAN SPRING, PIMA

San Juan Capistrano ..................................Pinal
    See: SACATON, PINAL

San Juan Pass ........................................Pima
    See: SAN JUAN SPRING, PIMA

SAN JUAN SPRING ..........................PIMA

San Juan Wash ........................................Pima
    See: SAN JUAN SPRING, PIMA

San Lorenzo ..........................................Pima
    See: SIL NAKYA, PIMA

SAN LUIS ..................................PIMA

SAN LUIS ..................................YUMA

San Luis de Bacapa ..................................Sonora
    See: QUITO BAQUITO, PIMA

San Luis Beltram de Bacapa ..........................Sonora
    See: QUITO BAQUITO, PIMA

San Luis Canyon ......................................Pima
    See: SAN LUIS, PIMA

San Luis de Quitobac..................................Pima
    See: QUITO BAQUITO, PIMA

San Luis Guebavi ................................Santa Cruz
    See: GUEVAVI, SANTA CRUZ

San Luis Mountains ...................................Pima
    See: SAN LUIS, PIMA

San Luis Wash ........................................Pima
    See: SAN LUIS, PIMA

SAN MANUEL ................................PINAL

SAN MIGUEL ................................PIMA

San Miguel de Jesus Guevavi .....................Santa Cruz
    See: GUEVAVI, SANTA CRUZ

San Miguel Wash ......................................Pima
    See: SAN MIGUEL, PIMA

SAN PABLO .............................MARICOPA

San Pablo Mountains ..................................Yuma
    See: LAGUNA, YUMA

San Pablo de Quiburi ...............................Cochise
    See: QUIBURI, COCHISE

SAN PEDRO .............................COCHISE

San Pedro ............................................Pima
    See: VIOPULI, PIMA

San Pedro ............................................Yuma
    See: WELLTON, YUMA

San Pedro Crossing .................................Cochise
    See: SAN PEDRO, COCHISE

San Pedro, Rio ................................Cochise, Pinal
    See: SAN PEDRO RIVER, COCHISE
    See: LITTLE COLORADO RIVER, NAVAJO

SAN PEDRO RIVER ..................COCHISE, Pinal

San Pedro River Station ............................Cochise
    See: OHNESORGEN STAGE STATION, COCHISE

San Pedro Settlement ...............................Cochise
    See: SAN PEDRO, COCHISE

San Pedro Springs ..................................Cochise
    See: SAN PEDRO, COCHISE

San Pedro Valley ...................................Cochise
    See: SAN PEDRO RIVER, COCHISE

San Prieto ..........................................Yavapai
    See: SIERRA PRIETA, YAVAPAI

San Rafael .......................................Santa Cruz
    See: GUEVAVI, SANTA CRUZ, SAN RAFAEL DE
    LA ZANJA GRANT, SANTA CRUZ
    See: LOCHIEL (LA NORIA), SANTA CRUZ

San Rafael del Actum el Grande .....................Pima
    See: SAN SERAFIN, PIMA

SAN RAFAEL DEL VALLE LAND GRANT ....COCHISE

SAN RAFAEL DE LA ZANJA
LAND GRANT .......................SANTA CRUZ

SAN SERAFIN ..............................PIMA

San Serafin de Actum .................................Pima
    See: SAN SERAFIN, PIMA

San Serafino del Napcul ..............................Pima
    See: SAN SERAFIN, PIMA

San Simon .........................................Cochise
    See: SAN SIMON VALLEY, COCHISE

San Simon Cienega ................................Cochise
    See: SAN SIMON VALLEY, COCHISE

San Simon Head ...................................Cochise
    See: SAN SIMON VALLEY, COCHISE
    Also: COCHISE, COCHISE

San Simon Peak ...................................Cochise
    See: SAN SIMON VALLEY, COCHISE

San Simon River ..................................Cochise
    See: SAN SIMON VALLEY, COCHISE

San Simon y San Judas ...........................Maricopa
    See: UPASOITAC, MARICOPA

SAN SIMON VALLEY ...............COCHISE, Graham

San Xavier ...........................................Pima
    See: SAN XAVIER DEL BAC, PIMA

SAN XAVIER DEL BAC ......................PIMA

San Xavier Mountains .................................Pima
    See: SAN XAVIER DEL BAC, PIMA

SANCHEZ ...............................GRAHAM

Sandal Trail ........................................Navajo
    See: BETATAKIN, NAVAJO

Sand Tanks ........................................Maricopa
    See: SAND TANK MOUNTAIN, MARICOPA

SAND TANK MOUNTAINS ...............MARICOPA

Sand Tank Wash ...................................Maricopa
    See: SAND TANK MOUNTAIN, MARICOPA

SANDERS ...............................APACHE

SANDY ...................................MOHAVE
    See also: WIKIEUP, MOHAVE

SANDY BOB CANYON .......................COCHISE

SANENCHECK ROCK ........................NAVAJO

Sanenecheck Rock .....................................Navajo
    See: SANENCHECK ROCK, NAVAJO

Sanford .............................................Pinal
    See: ADAMSVILLE, PINAL

SANFORD ............................SANTA CRUZ

Santa Catalina Cuitchibaque ..........................Pima
    See: SANTA CATALINA MOUNTAINS, PIMA

Santa Catalina Forest Reserve .........Pinal, Pima, Cochise
    See: CORONADO NATIONAL FOREST, PIMA
    SANTA CATALINA MOUNTAINS, PIMA

SANTA CATALINA MOUNTAINS ......PIMA and Pinal

Santa Catalina Natural Area ..........................Pima
    See: SANTA CATALINA MOUNTAINS, PIMA

Santa Catarina Mountains ............................Pima
    See: SANTA CATALINA MOUNTAINS, PIMA

Santa Catarina, Sierra de ............................Pima
    See: SANTA CATALINA MOUNTAINS, PIMA

SECRET MOUNTAIN ......................YAVAPAI
SECRET PASS ...........................MOHAVE
Secret Spring .......................................Mohave
    See: SECRET PASS, MOHAVE
SECUNDINO WELL .........................PIMA
SEDONA ..............................COCONINO
Sedro .............................................Apache
    See: ST. JOHNS, APACHE
Seecko-wah-wee ..................................Navajo
    See: SIKYATKI, NAVAJO
Seepage Canyon ...................................Yavapai
    See: SEEPAGE MOUNTAIN, YAVAPAI
SEEPAGE MOUNTAIN .....................YAVAPAI
Segatoa Spring ....................................Apache
    See: SEGETOA SPRING, APACHE
SEGEKE BUTTE .........................NAVAJO
SEGETOA SPRING .......................APACHE
SEGI MESAS ...........................NAVAJO
Sehili .............................................Apache
    See: TSEHILI, APACHE
SELIGMAN .............................YAVAPAI
Seligman Canyon ..................................Yavapai
    See: SELIGMAN, YAVAPAI
SELLS ..................................PIMA
Sells Valley .......................................Pima
    See: SELLS, PIMA
Sells Wash .........................................Pima
    See: SELLS, PIMA
SEMBRICH ............................COCHISE
SENATOR .............................YAVAPAI
SENITA PASS ...........................PIMA
SENTINEL .............................MARICOPA
Sentinel Butte .....................................Pima
    See: SENTINEL, MARICOPA
Sentinel Hill .....................................Maricopa
    See: SENTINEL, MARICOPA
SENTINEL PEAK ........................COCHISE
Sentinel Peak .....................................Maricopa
    See: SENTINEL, MARICOPA
SENTINEL PEAK ...........................PIMA
Sentinel Peak ...................................Santa Cruz
    See: SANTA RITA MOUNTAINS, SANTA CRUZ
Sentinel Wash ....................................Maricopa
    See: SENTINEL, MARICOPA
SEPARATION RAPID ......................MOHAVE
Sepori ...........................................Santa Cruz
    See: SOPORI RANCH, SANTA CRUZ
Sepulveda Creek ...................................Apache
    See: CONCHO, APACHE
SERVOSS .............................COCHISE
Set, Temple of .........................Grand Canyon, Coco
    See: SET, TOWER OF, GRAND CANYON,
SET, TOWER OF .............GRAND CANYON, COCO
SETSILTSO SPRING .......................APACHE
Seven Cities of Cibola .......................New Mexico
    See: HOPI VILLAGES, NAVAJO
Seven Mile Canyon .................................Navajo
    See: SEVEN MILE HILL, NAVAJO
SEVEN MILE CREEK .........................GILA
Seven Mile Crossing ................................Gila
    See: SEVEN MILE CREEK, GILA

SEVEN MILE HILL .........................NAVAJO
Seven Mile Mountain ................................Gila
    See: SEVENMILE CANYON, GILA
SEVENMILE CANYON ........................GILA
Seymour ..........................................Maricopa
    See: VULTURE, MARICOPA
Sezhini Butte .....................................Apache
    See: BLACK PINNACLE BUTTE, APACHE
Shaleys Fork ......................................Graham
    See: BONITA CREEK, GRAHAM
SHANNON MOUNTAIN ...................GREENLEE
SHANUB POINT ........GRAND CANYON, MOHAVE
SHAOTKAM ...............................PIMA
Shanto Spring .....................................Navajo
    See: MASIPA SPRING, NAVAJO
Sha-pah-lah-wee ...................................Navajo
    See: SIPAULOVI, NAVAJO
SHARPS BAR ...........................MOHAVE
Shashdits'inih ....................................Apache
    See: BLACK PINNACLE BUTTE, APACHE
Shato Canyon ......................................Navajo
    See: SHATO SPRING, NAVAJO
SHATO SPRING .........................NAVAJO
    See also: MASIPA SPRING, NAVAJO
Sheavwitz Plateau .................................Mohave
    See: SHIVWITS PLATEAU, MOHAVE
SHEEP CROSSING .......................APACHE
SHEEP DIP CREEK ......................APACHE
SHEEP HILL ..........................COCONINO
SHEEP MOUNTAIN .........................YUMA
Sheep Springs .....................................Apache
    See: SHEEP CROSSING, APACHE
Sheep Tank .......................................Coconino
    See: SHEEP HILL, COCONINO
SHEEP TANK ..............................PIMA
SHEEP WASH ...........................GREENLEE
Sheeptrail Mine ...................................Mohave
    See: PYRAMID CANYON, MOHAVE
SHELDON .............................GREENLEE
Sheldon Mountain .................................Maricopa
    See: SAWIK MOUNTAIN, MARICOPA
Sheno-mo ...........................Grand Canyon, Coco
    See: SHINUMO ALTAR, GRAND CANYON
SHERIDAN MOUNTAINS ......................PIMA
SHERIDAN MOUNTAIN .....................YAVAPAI
Shevlon Creek .....................................Navajo
    See: CHEVELON CREEK, NAVAJO
Shevlon's Fork ....................................Navajo
    See: CHEVELON CREEK, NAVAJO
S.H. MOUNTAINS ..........................YUMA
SHIBELL, MOUNT .....................SANTA CRUZ
Shimopavi .........................................Navajo
    See: SHUNGOPOVI, NAVAJO
Shina-bitz-spits ..................................Mohave
    See: WOLFHOLE, MOHAVE
SHINUMO ALTAR ..........GRAND CANYON, COCO
Shinumo Amphitheater .............Grand Canyon, Coco
    See: SHINUMO ALTAR, GRAND CANYON
Shinumo Canyon ...................Grand Canyon, Coco
    See: SHINUMO ALTAR, GRAND CANYON
Shinumo Creek ....................Grand Canyon, Coco
    See: SHINUMO ALTAR, GRAND CANYON

Silver Hill ...........................................Mohave
    See: CHLORIDE, MOHAVE
SILVER KING ...............................PINAL
Silver King Wash ............................Pinal
    See: SILVER KING, PINAL
SILVER MOUNTAINS .....................YAVAPAI
Silver Queen ..................................Pinal
    See: MAGMA, PINAL
Silver Range ...............................Yavapai
    See: BRADSHAW MOUNTAINS, YAVAPAI
SILVER REEF MOUNTAINS ..................PINAL
Silver Reef Pass .............................Pinal
    See: SILVER REEF MOUNTAINS, PINAL
Silver Reef Valley ...........................Pinal
    See: SILVER REEF MOUNTAINS, PINAL
Silver Reef Wash .............................Pinal
    See: SILVER REEF MOUNTAINS, PINAL
SILVERBELL .................................PIMA
Silverbell Mountains ..........................Pima
    See: SILVERBELL, PIMA
Silverbell Valley .............................Pima
    See: SILVERBELL, PIMA
SIMMONS ..................................YAVAPAI
Simmons Peak ..............................Yavapai
    See: SIMMONS, YAVAPAI
SIMPSON CREEK .........................APACHE
Sinagua, Sierra ...........................Coconino
    See: SAN FRANCISCO PEAKS, COCONINO
SINGLE STANDARD GULCH ...................GILA
SINKING SHIP ............GRAND CANYON, COCO
Sinks, The ..................................Apache
    See: CONCHO, APACHE
SINKS, THE ...............................NAVAJO
Sinyala Butte ...................Grand Canyon, Coco
    See: SINYALA CANYON, GRAND CANYON
SINYALA CANYON ........GRAND CANYON, COCO
Sinyala Mesa ...................Grand Canyon, Coco
    See: SINYALA CANYON, GRAND CANYON
Sinyala Mountain ...............Grand Canyon, Coco
    See: SINYALA CANYON, GRAND CANYON
Sinyala Rapids .................Grand Canyon, Coco
    See: SINYALA CANYON, GRAND CANYON
Siovaxia .....................................Pinal
    See: BITTER WELL, PINAL
SIOVI SHUATAK ............................PIMA
Siovi Shuatak Pass ...........................Pima
    See: SIOVI SHUATAK, PIMA
Siovi Shuatak Wash ..........................Pima
    See: SIOVI SHUATAK, PIMA
SIPAULOVI ...............................NAVAJO
SITE SIX .................................MOHAVE
SITGREAVES, MOUNT ...................COCONINO
Sitgreaves Mountain ........................Coconino
    See: SITGREAVES PASS, MOHAVE
SITGREAVES NATIONAL FOREST ..APACHE, Coconino,
                                    Navajo
    See also: SITGREAVES, MOUNT, COCONINO
             SITGREAVES PASS, MOHAVE
SITGREAVES PASS .......................MOHAVE
Sitgreaves Peak ...........................Coconino
    See: SITGREAVES, MOUNT, COCONINO

Six Mile Hill ...............................Cochise
    See: PEARCE, COCHISE
Sixteen Springs ...........................Coconino
    See: FAIN MOUNTAIN, COCONINO
Sixty Mile Canyon ......................Grand Canyon
    See: SIXTY-MILE CREEK, GRAND CANYON
SIXTY-MILE CREEK ........GRAND GANYON, COCO
Skeleton ...................................Maricopa
    See: APACHE CAVE, MARICOPA
SKELETON CANYON .....................COCHISE
Skeleton Cave .............................Maricopa
    See: APACHE CAVE, MARICOPA
SKELETON RIDGE .......................YAVAPAI
Skinnerville ..................................Pinal
    See: TROY, PINAL
Skull Cave ................................Maricopa
    See: APACHE CAVE, MARICOPA
Skull Mesa ................................Maricopa
    See: APACHE CAVE, MARICOPA
SKULL VALLEY ..........................YAVAPAI
Skull Valley Station .........................Yavapai
    See: SKULL VALLEY, YAVAPAI
Skull Valley Wash ..........................Yavapai
    See: SKULL VALLEY, YAVAPAI
SKUNK CREEK ...........................MARICOPA
SLATE CREEK ...............................GILA
Slate Lakes ................................Coconino
    See: SLATE MOUNTAIN, COCONINO
SLATE MOUNTAIN ......................COCONINO
SLATE MOUNTAIN .........................PINAL
SLAUGHTER MOUNTAIN ..................GRAHAM
SLEEPING BEAUTY PEAK ...................GILA
Sleeping Beauty Spring .........................Gila
    See: SLEEPING BEAUTY PEAK, GILA
Sleeping Mountain .........................Santa Cruz
    See: RED BUTTE, COCONINO
Sliker Hill ................................Coconino
    See: DUTTON HILL, COCONINO
SLINKARD SPRINGS .......................PINAL
Slough Reservoir ............................Apache
    See: LYMAN DAM, APACHE
Small Akchin .................................Pima
    See: SAN SERAFIN, PIMA
SMITH BUTTE ............................NAVAJO
SMITH CANYON ..........................YAVAPAI
Smith Cienega ...............................Apache
    See: WHITE RIVER, APACHE
Smith Mesa .................................Yavapai
    See: SMITH CANYON, YAVAPAI
SMITH'S MILL ...........................MARICOPA
SMITH PEAK ...............................YUMA
Smith Spring ................................Navajo
    See: SMITH BUTTE, NAVAJO
Smith Station ..............................Maricopa
    See: PHOENIX, MARICOPA
Smithville ..................................Graham
    See: PIMA, GRAHAM
SMITHVILLE .............................YAVAPAI
SMOOT LAKE ............................COCONINO
Smuggler's Trail ..............................Yuma
    See: TINEJAS ALTAS, YUMA

SPOTTED MOUNTAIN ......................NAVAJO

Spring Creek ..............................Coconino
    See: BADGER CREEK, COCONINO

Spring Gardens ............................Graham
    See: BUFORD HILL, GRAHAM

Springer's Store ...........................Apache
    See: SPRINGERVILLE, APACHE

SPRINGERVILLE .........................APACHE

Sprucedale ...............................Greenlee
    See: ESPERO, GREENLEE

Spruce Brook .............................Apache
    See: TSEHILI, APACHE

Spruce Canyon ...........................Yavapai
    See: SPRUCE MOUNTAIN, YAVAPAI

SPRUCE MOUNTAIN ....................YAVAPAI

Spruce Mountain .........................Yavapai
    See: WHITE SPRUCE MOUNTAIN, YAVAPAI

Spruce Wash .............................Yavapai
    See: SPRUCE MOUNTAIN, YAVAPAI

SPUD ROCK ...............................PIMA

SQUARE BUTTE .......................COCONINO

SQUARE BUTTE .........................GREENLEE

SQUARE MOUNTAIN ...................COCHISE

Square Mountain .........................Greenlee
    See: SQUARE BUTTE, GREENLEE

Square Peak ..............................Cochise
    See: SENTINEL PEAK, COCHISE

Square Top Hills ..........................Cochise
    See: SQUARE MOUNTAIN, COCHISE

Squash Blossom Butte .....................Navajo
    See: SQUASH MOUNTAINS, NAVAJO

SQUASH MOUNTAINS ...................NAVAJO

Squaw Butte ..............................Gila
    See: SQUAW CREEK, GREENLEE

Squaw Butte ..............................Yavapai
    See: SQUAW CREEK, GREENLEE

Squaw Canyon ............................Gila
    See: SQUAW CREEK, GREENLEE

Squaw Creek ..............................Graham
    See: SQUAW CREEK, GREENLEE

SQUAW CREEK .........................GREENLEE

Squaw Creek ..............................Yavapai
    See: SQUAW CREEK, GREENLEE

Squaw Creek Mesa ........................Yavapai
    See: SQUAW CREEK, GREENLEE

Squaw Creek Middle Fork ..................Yavapai
    See: SQUAW CREEK, GREENLEE

Squaw Creek North Fork ...................Yavapai
    See: SQUAW CREEK, GREENLEE

Squaw Creek South Fork ...................Yavapai
    See: SQUAW CREEK, GREENLEE

Squaw Flat ...............................Maricopa
    See: SQUAW CREEK, GREENLEE

Squaw Mesa ..............................Gila
    See: SQUAW CREEK, GREENLEE

Squaw Mountain ..........................Cochise
    See: SQUAW CREEK, GREENLEE

Squaw Mountain ..........................Yavapai
    See: SQUAW CREEK, GREENLEE

Squaw Peak ..............................Yavapai
    See: SQUAW CREEK, GREENLEE

Squaw Peak ..............................Gila
    See: SQUAW CREEK, GREENLEE

Squaw Peak ..............................Maricopa
    See: SQUAW CREEK, GREENLEE

Squaw Peak ..............................Mohave
    See: SQUAW CREEK, GREENLEE

Squaw Peak ..............................Yavapai
    See: SQUAW CREEK, GREENLEE

Squaw Peak ..............................Yuma
    See: SQUAW CREEK, GREENLEE

Squaw Tank ..............................Yuma
    See: SQUAW CREEK, GREENLEE

Squaw Tit ................................Yavapai
    See: SQUAW CREEK, GREENLEE

Squaw Tit Peak ...........................Maricopa
    See: SQUAW CREEK, GREENLEE

Squaw Tits ...............................Maricopa
    See: SQUAW CREEK, GREENLEE

STANDARD ...............................NAVAJO

STANFIELD ...............................PINAL

Stanford, Fort ............................Pinal
    See: GRANT, CAMP, (OLD), PINAL

Stanley ...................................Graham
    See: STANLEY BUTTE, GRAHAM

STANLEY BUTTE .........................GRAHAM

STANTON .................................GILA

STANTON POINT ...........GRAND CANYON, COCO

Stanton ..................................Yavapai
    See: ANTELOPE PEAK, YAVAPAI

Stanton Rapids ..............Grand Canyon, Coco
    See: STANTON POINT, GRAND CANYON

Stanvix Hall .............................Maricopa
    See: STANWIX, MARICOPA

STANWIX ...............................MARICOPA

STARK ....................................COCHISE

STAR VALLEY ..............................GILA

Statannyik ................................Pinal
    See: HORMIGUERO, PINAL

STEAMBOAT CANYON ..............APACHE, Navajo

STEAMBOAT MOUNTAIN ...................PINAL

Steamboat Peak ...........................Mohave
    See: STEAMBOAT MOUNTAIN, PINAL

Steamboat Rock ..........................Mohave
    See: STEAMBOAT MOUNTAIN, PINAL

Steamboat Wash ..........................Apache
    See: STEAMBOAT CANYON, APACHE

Steamboat Wash ..........................Pinal
    See: STEAMBOAT MOUNTAIN, PINAL

Steampump Ranch ........................Pima
    See: PUSCH RIDGE, PIMA

Steele Hills ...............................Cochise
    See: POINT-OF-MOUNTAIN, COCHISE

STEHR LAKE .............................YAVAPAI

STEPHEN BUTTE .........................NAVAJO

STEVENS MOUNTAIN ......................PIMA

Stevens Ranch ............................Pima
    See: STEVENS MOUNTAIN, PIMA

STEWARD POCKET .........................GILA

STEWART MOUNTAIN ...................MARICOPA

Stewart Mountain Dam ....................Maricopa
    See: STEWART MOUNTAIN, MARICOPA

Stewart Mountain Lake ....................Maricopa
    See: STEWART MOUNTAIN, MARICOPA

Stiles ....................................Navajo
    See: DILKON, NAVAJO

Summit Spring ........................Coconino
   See: SUMMIT MOUNTAIN, COCONINO
Summit Spring ...........................Pinal
   See: ORACLE, PINAL
Summit Valley .........................Coconino
   See: SUMMIT MOUNTAIN, COCONINO
Sumner ....................Grand Canyon, Coco
   See: SUMMER BUTTE, GRAND CANYON
SUNDAD ...............................MARICOPA
SUN FLOWER MESA ....................GREENLEE
SUNFLOWER BUTTE ......................NAVAJO
Sunflower Creek .......................Maricopa
   See: SUNFLOWER VALLEY, MARICOPA
Sunflower Ranch .......................Maricopa
   See: SUNFLOWER VALLEY, MARICOPA
SUNFLOWER VALLEY ...................MARICOPA
SUNGLOW ..............................COCHISE
SUNNYSIDE ............................COCHISE
Sunnyside Canyon .......................Cochise
   See: SUNNYSIDE, COCHISE
SUNRISE SPRINGS .......................APACHE
Sunset ................................Coconino
   See: SUNSHINE, COCONINO
SUNSET ...............................GRAHAM
SUNSET ...............................NAVAJO
Sunset, Camp ...........................Navajo
   See: SUPPLY, CAMP, NAVAJO
Sunset Canyon .........................Coconino
   See: JACKS CANYON, COCONINO
Sunset Canyon ..........................Graham
   See: SUNSET, GRAHAM
SUNSET CRATER .......................COCONINO
Sunset Crater National Monument .........Coconino
   See: SUNSET CRATER, COCONINO
Sunset Crossing .......................Coconino
   See: SUNSET PASS, COCONINO
SUNSET CROSSING .......................NAVAJO
SUNSET PASS ..........................COCONINO
   See also: JACKS CANYON, COCONINO
Sunset Peak ............................Graham
   See: SUNSET, GRAHAM
SUNSET PEAK .........................GREENLEE
SUNSHINE .............................COCONINO
SUPAI ................................COCONINO
Supai ......................Grand Canyon, Coco
   See: HAVASU CANYON, GRAND CANYON
SUPERIOR ..............................PINAL
SUPERSTITION MOUNTAINS ................PINAL
Superstition Peak ........................Pinal
   See: SUPERSTITION MOUNTAINS, PINAL
Supply, Camp ..........................Cochise
   See: PRICE, CAMP, COCHISE
      RUCKER CANYON, COCHISE
SUPPLY, CAMP .........................NAVAJO
SUPPLY, CAMP ..........................PINAL
SURPRISE CANYON .......................MOHAVE
Surprise Creek ..........................Apache
   See: SURPRISE VALLEY, APACHE
SURPRISE VALLEY .......................APACHE
SURPRISE WELL .......................MARICOPA
SWANSEA ...............................YUMA

SWEENEY ..............................MOHAVE
Sweet Water Pass .........................Pima
   See: AGUA DULCE MOUNTAINS, PIMA
SWEETWATER ...........................APACHE
Sweetwater ..............................Pima
   See: SIOVI SHUATAK, PIMA
SWEETWATER ...........................PINAL
Sweetwater Store Indian Trading Post .........Pinal
   See: SWEETWATER, PINAL
Sweetwater Wash ........................Apache
   See: SWEETWATER, APACHE
SWICKERT SPRING .....................MOHAVE
SWIFT TRAIL ..........................GRAHAM
SWILLING BUTTE ..........GRAND CANYON, COCO
SWILLING GULCH ......................YAVAPAI
Swisshelm .............................Cochise
   See: SWISSHELM MOUNTAINS, COCHISE
SWISSHELM MOUNTAINS .................COCHISE
Swisshelm Peak .........................Cochise
   See: SWISSHELM MOUNTAINS, COCHISE
SWITZER MESA ........................COCONINO
Sycamore .............................Yavapai
   See: SYCAMORE CANYON, YAVAPAI
SYCAMORE CANYON .....................YAVAPAI
Sycamore Canyon ..........................Gila
   See: SYCAMORE CANYON, YAVAPAI
Sycamore Canyon Wilderness Area ........Coconino
   See: SYCAMORE CANYON, YAVAPAI
Sycamore Creek ........................Coconino
   See: SYCAMORE CANYON, YAVAPAI
Sycamore Creek ...........................Gila
   See: COON CREEK, GILA
   Also: SYCAMORE CANYON, YAVAPAI
Sycamore Creek ..........................Graham
   See: SYCAMORE CANYON, YAVAPAI
Sycamore Creek ........................Maricopa
   See: SYCAMORE CANYON, YAVAPAI
Sycamore Creek .........................Mohave
   See: SYCAMORE CANYON, YAVAPAI
Sycamore Creek .........................Yavapai
   See: SYCAMORE CANYON, YAVAPAI
Sycamore Mesa .........................Yavapai
   See: SYCAMORE CANYON, YAVAPAI
Sycamore Pass .........................Yavapai
   See: SYCAMORE CANYON, YAVAPAI
Sycamore Rim ..........................Yavapai
   See: SYCAMORE CANYON, YAVAPAI
Sycamore Spring ..........................Gila
   See: SYCAMORE CANYON, YAVAPAI
Sydney ...............................Maricopa
   See: BUCKEYE, MARICOPA
Ta enta Creek ..........................Navajo
   See: TYENDE CREEK, NAVAJO
Table, The ..............................Gila
   See: TABLE MOUNTAIN, COCONINO
TABLE MOUNTAIN .....................COCONINO
Table Mountain ........................Greenlee
   See: TABLE MOUNTAIN, COCONINO
Table Mountain .........................Mohave
   See: TABLE MOUNTAIN, COCONINO
Table Mountain ..........................Pinal
   See: TABLE MOUNTAIN, COCONINO

Temple Wash .............................Mohave
    See: TEMPLE BAR, MOHAVE
Ten Mile Well .............................Pima
    See: BATAMOTE MOUNTAINS, PIMA
TENNEYS GULCH ....................COCONINO
Tenneys Spring ...................Coconino
    See: TENNEYS GULCH, COCONINO
Terminus ...............................XVIII
Terrenate, El ..........................Sonora
    See: SAN PEDRO RIVER, COCHISE
Terrenate, Rio ........................Sonora
    See: SAN PEDRO RIVER, COCHISE
Tesota ...............................Maricopa
    See: GILA RANCH, MARICOPA
Teuwalanki ...........................Coconino
    See: WUPATKI NATIONAL MONUMENT,
        COCONINO
Teviston ...............................Cochise
    See: BOWIE, COCHISE
TEWA ...................................NAVAJO
Tewa Spring ...........................Navajo
    See: TEWA, NAVAJO
Tex Canyon ...........................Cochise
    See: TEXAS CANYON, COCHISE
TEXAS CANYON .......................COCHISE
Texas Hill .............................Yuma
    See: STOVAL, YUMA
Texas Hill Camp .......................Yuma
    See: STOVAL, YUMA
Te-ye-ba-a-kit .........................Navajo
    See: DEBEKID LAKE, NAVAJO
Tezotal ...............................Maricopa
    See: GILA RANCH, MARICOPA
THATCHER .............................GRAHAM
THEBA .................................MARICOPA
THIMBLE MOUNTAIN ..................MOHAVE
Thin Mountain ..........................Pinal
    See: SACATON, PINAL
Third Forest ...........................Navajo
    See: FIRST FOREST, APACHE
Third Hollow ..........................Navajo
    See: FIRST HOLLOW, NAVAJO
Third Knoll ...........................Navajo
    See: FIRST KNOLL, NAVAJO
Third Mesa ............................Navajo
    See: FIRST MESA, NAVAJO
THIRTEEN MILE ROCK ..................YAVAPAI
Thirteen Mile Spring ...................Yavapai
    See: THIRTEEN MILE ROCK, YAVAPAI
THOMAS CREEK .......................GREENLEE
THOMAS, FORT .......................GRAHAM
Thomas, Mount .........................Apache
    See: BALDY, MOUNT, APACHE
Thomas, Peak ..........................Apache
    See: BALDY, MOUNT, APACHE
THOMPSON CANYON .......GRAND CANYON, COCO
THOMPSON PEAK .....................MARICOPA
THOMPSON POINT .........GRAND CANYON, COCO
Thompson Southwest Arboretum .............Pinal
    See: PINAL, PINAL
THOMPSON VALLEY ...................YAVAPAI
Thorburn Mountain .....................Coconino
    See: RED BUTTE, COCONINO

Thor's Hammer ..........................Cochise
    See: CHIRICAHUA MOUNTAINS, COCHISE
THOR'S HAMMER ..........GRAND CANYON, COCO
Thor Temple ...............Grand Canyon, Coco
    See: THOR'S HAMMER, GRAND CANYON
THOUSAND CAVE MOUNTAIN .............APACHE
THOUSAND WELLS ....................COCONINO
Three Bridges ...........................Pima
    See: IRENE, PIMA
THREE MILE LAKE ....................COCONINO
Three Peaks .............................Gila
    See: TRIPLETS, GILA
Three Points ............................Pima
    See: ROBLES JUNCTION, PIMA
THREE SISTERS BUTTES ..................COCHISE
THUMB BUTTE .........................GREENLEE
Thumb Butte ...........................Mohave
    See: THUMB BUTTE, GREENLEE
Thumb Butte ...........................Santa Cruz
    See: THUMB BUTTE, GREENLEE
Thumb Butte ...........................Yavapai
    See: THUMB BUTTE, GREENLEE
Thumb Butte ...........................Yuma
    See: THUMB BUTTE, GREENLEE
Thunder River ...............Grand Canyon, Coco
    See: TAPEATS CREEK, GRAND CANYON
Thunder Spring ..............Grand Canyon, Coco
    See: TAPEATS CREEK, GRAND CANYON
TIDWELL'S MILL .........................GILA
TIGER ...................................PINAL
TIGER ...................................YAVAPAI
Tiger Canyon ...........................Yavapai
    See: TIGER, YAVAPAI
Tiger Creek ............................Yavapai
    See: TIGER, YAVAPAI
Tiller Canyon ..........................Coconino
    See: MILLER CANYON, COCONINO
TILTED MESA ...............GRAND CANYON, COCO
Tilted Peak ............................Pinal
    See: SADDLE BACK MOUNTAIN, PINAL
TIMBER CAMP MOUNTAIN ...................GILA
TIMBUKTU .............................YUMA
TINAJA PEAK ............................PIMA
TINAJAS ALTAS ........................YUMA
Tinajualto ............................Yuma
    See: TINAJAS ALTAS, YUMA
Tinaoca, La ...........................Yuma
    See: TINAJAS ALTAS, YUMA
Tinebito ..............................Navajo
    See: DINNEBITO. NAVAJO
Tinechas ..............................Yuma
    See: TINAJAS ALTAS, YUMA
Tinechas Altas .........................Yuma
    See: TINAJAS ALTAS, YUMA
Tinejas ...............................Yuma
    See: TINAJAS ALTAS, YUMA
Tinejas Altos Mountains ..................Yuma
    See: TINAJAS ALTAS, YUMA
Tinejas de Candelaria ....................Yuma
    See: TINAJAS ALTAS, YUMA
TINTOWN ...............................COCHISE
TIP TOP ...............................YAVAPAI

Toroweap Cliffs .............................Mohave
   See: TOROWEAP VALLEY, MOHAVE
TOROWEAP VALLEY ......................MOHAVE
Torowip Cliffs ...............................Mohave
   See: TOROWEAP VALLEY, MOHAVE
TORRANCE WELL .....................MARICOPA
Tortilato Mountains ...........................Pinal
   See: TORTILLA MOUNTAINS, PINAL
Tortilla Butte ................................Pinal
   See: TORTILLA MOUNTAINS, PINAL
Tortilla Creek ......................Maricopa, Pinal
   See: TORTILLA FLAT, MARICOPA
       TORTILLA MOUNTAINS, PINAL
TORTILLA FLAT ......................MARICOPA
TORTILLA FLAT .........................MOHAVE
Tortilla Mountain ........................Maricopa
   See: TORTILLA FLAT, MARICOPA
TORTILLA MOUNTAINS .....................PINAL
Tortillata, Sierra (Mountains) ................Pinal
   See: TORTILLA MOUNTAINS, PINAL
TORTOLITA MOUNTAINS ...................PIMA
TOTAL WRECK ............................PIMA
Totem Pole ................................Cochise
   See: CHIRICAHUA MOUNTAINS, COCHISE
Totobit Tanks ............................Maricopa
   See: TOTOPITK, MARICOPA
Totonteac ................................Navajo
   See: HOPI VILLAGES, NAVAJO
TOTOPITK ...........................MARICOPA
Tourist .....................Grand Canyon, Coco
   See: HANCE CREEK, GRAND CANYON
Tousand Wells ...........................Coconino
   See: THOUSAND WELLS, COCONINO
Tovar Amphitheater, El .............Grand Canyon, Coco
   See: TOVAR TERRACE, GRAND CANYON
Tovar Hill, El ....................Grand Canyon, Coco
   See: TOVAR TERRACE, GRAND CANYON
TOVAR MESA ............................NAVAJO
Tovar Point, El ...................Grand Canyon, Coco
   See: TOVAR TERRACE, GRAND CANYON
TOVAR TERRACE ..........GRAND CANYON, COCO
TOWAGO POINT ...........GRAND CANYON, COCO
TOWER BUTTE ........................COCONINO
Tower Creek ...............................Yavapai
   See: TOWER MOUNTAIN, YAVAPAI
TOWER MOUNTAIN ......................YAVAPAI
Tower Ranch ...............................Yavapai
   See: TOWER MOUNTAIN, YAVAPAI
TRANSEPT, THE ...........GRAND CANYON, COCO
TRAVERTINE CANYON .....GRAND CANYON, COCO
Travertine Creek ..................Grand Canyon, Coco
   See: TRAVERTINE CANYON, GRAND CANYON
TRES ALAMOS ...........................COCHISE
Tres Alamos, Rio de .........................Cochise
   See: TRES ALAMOS, COCHISE
Tres Alamos Wash ..........................Cochise
   See: TRES ALAMOS, COCHISE
Tres Bellotas ...........................Santa Cruz
   See: BELLOTA CANYON, SANTA CRUZ
Tres Bellotas Canyon .....................Santa Cruz
   See: BELLOTA CANYON, SANTA CRUZ
Tres Cebollas ..............................Cochise
   See: BOWIE, COCHISE

Trigo, Canyon ..............................Apache
   See: MUERTO, CANYON DEL, APACHE
TRIGO MOUNTAINS ..........................YUMA
Trigo Pass ..................................Yuma
   See: TRIGO MOUNTAINS, YUMA
Trigo Wash .................................Yuma
   See: TRIGO MOUNTAINS, YUMA
TRIPLETS ..................................GILA
Triplet, Mount ..............................Gila
   See: TRIPLETS, GILA
Triplets Peaks ...............................Gila
   See: TRIPLETS, GILA
TRITLE, MOUNT .......................YAVAPAI
TRITLE PEAK ..............GRAND CANYON, COCO
TROUT CREEK ...........................MOHAVE
TROY ....................................PINAL
Troy Mountain ..............................Pinal
   See: TROY, PINAL
Truit Ranch ...............................Cochise
   See: McNEAL, COCHISE
Truman Point .............................Coconino
   See: ANDERSON CANYON, COCONINO
TRUMBULL, MOUNT ......................MOHAVE
Truxton ..................................Mohave
   See: VALENTINE, MOHAVE
       TRUXTON CANYON, MOHAVE
TRUXTON CANYON ......................MOHAVE
Truxton Canyon Station .....................Mohave
   See: CROZIER, MOHAVE
Truxton Canyon Sub-agency ..................Mohave
   See: VALENTINE, MOHAVE
Truxton Plateau ...........................Mohave
   See: TRUXTON CANYON, MOHAVE
Truxton Spring ............................Mohave
   See: TRUXTON CANYON, MOHAVE
       PEACOCK SPRING, MOHAVE
Truxton Springs ...........................Mohave
   See: CROZIER, MOHAVE
Truxton Valley ............................Mohave
   See: TRUXTON CANYON, MOHAVE
Truxton Wash ..............................Mohave
   See: TRUXTON CANYON, MOHAVE
Tsaile ....................................Apache
   See: TSEHILI, APACHE
Tsalee Creek ...............................Apache
   See: TSEHILI, APACHE
Tsalee Butte ...............................Apache
   See: TSEHILI, APACHE
Tsalee Pinnacle .............................Apache
   See: TSEHILI, APACHE
Tsali Creek ................................Apache
   See: TSEHILI, APACHE
Tsatsiltso Spring ............................Apache
   See: SETSILTSO SPRING, APACHE
TSAY-YAH-KIN ...........................NAVAJO
Tse-a-lee .................................Apache
   See: TSEHILI, APACHE
Tsegi Branch, Laguna Canyon ..................Navajo
   See: BETATAKIN, NAVAJO
TSEGI CANYON .........................NAVAJO
Tsegi Mesas ...............................Navajo
   See: SEGI MESAS, NAVAJO

Turkey Tanks ............................Coconino
    See: COSNINO CAVES, COCONINO
      SAN FRANCISCO PEAKS, COCONINO
TURNBULL, MOUNT ....................GRAHAM
TURNER ................................COCHISE
TURNER ................................PINAL
Turquoise ..............................Cochise
    See: GLEESON, COCHISE
TURQUOISE CANYON .......GRAND CANYON, COCO
Turquoise Mountain .....................Cochise
    See: GLEESON, COCHISE
TURQUOISE MOUNTAIN ..................MOHAVE
Turret Mountain ........................Yavapai
    See: TURRET PEAK, YAVAPAI
Turret Peak ........................Navajo, Gila
    See: NASH CREEK, NAVAJO
TURRET PEAK ..........................YAVAPAI
TURTLE BACK MOUNTAIN .................YUMA
TURTLE MOUNTAIN ......................COCHISE
TUSAYAN ..............................COCONINO
TUSAYAN ..............................NAVAJO
    See also: HOPI VILLAGES, NAVAJO
Tusayan Hill ....................Grand Canyon, Coco
    See: TUSAYAN RUIN, GRAND CANYON
Tusayan National Forest ....................Coconino
    See: COCONINO NATIONAL FOREST, COCONINO
TUSAYAN RUIN ............GRAND CANYON, COCO
Tuscumbia Creek .........................Yavapai
    See: TUSCUMBIA MOUNTAINS, YAVAPAI
TUSCUMBIA MOUNTAINS .................YAVAPAI
TUSONIMO ..............................PINAL
Tusonimon ..............................Pinal
    See: TUSONIMO, PINAL
Tuthill, Camp ..........................Coconino
    See: TUTHILL, FORT, COCONINO
TUTHILL, FORT ........................COCONINO
Tu-uk-so-on ............................Pima
    See: TUCSON, PIMA
Tuweap Valley ..........................Mohave
    See: TOROWEAP, VALLEY, MOHAVE
Tuweep ................................Mohave
    See: TOROWEAP VALLEY, MOHAVE
TUYE SPRING ..........................APACHE
Tuyey Spring ...........................Apache
    See: TUYE SPRING, APACHE
Tuzigoot Hill ..........................Yavapai
    See: TUZIGOOT NATIONAL MONUMENT,
      YAVAPAI
TUZIGOOT NATIONAL MONUMENT ........YAVAPAI
TWENTY-FOUR DRAW ....................APACHE
TWENTY-NINE MILE BUTTE .............COCONINO
Twenty-nine Mile Lake .....................Coconino
    See: TWENTY-NINE MILE BUTTE
Twenty-seven Mile Lake ....................Coconino
    See: TWENTY-NINE MILE BUTTE
TWIN BUTTES ..........................APACHE
Twin Buttes ............................Cochise
    See: TAYLOR BUTTE, COCHISE
TWIN BUTTES ..........................NAVAJO
TWIN LAKES ...........................NAVAJO
Twin Mesas ............................Navajo
    See: TWIN BUTTES, NAVAJO

TWIN SPRINGS .........................COCONINO
TWIN WASH ...........................NAVAJO
Two-Bar Canyon ........................Maricopa
    See: TWO-BAR RANCH, MARICOPA
Two-Bar Mountain .......................Gila
    See: TWO-BAR RANCH, MARICOPA
TWO-BAR RANCH ......................MARICOPA
Two Bar Ridge .........................Maricopa
    See: TWO-BAR RANCH, MARICOPA
T-ye-ba-a-kit ...........................Navajo
    See: DEBEKID LAKE, NAVAJO
TYENDE CREEK ........................NAVAJO
Tyende Mesa ...........................Navajo
    See: TYENDE CREEK, NAVAJO
Tyler .................................Cochise
    See: WEBB, COCHISE
Tyson's ...............................Yuma
    See: QUARTZSITE, YUMA
Tyson Wash ...........................Yuma
    See: QUARTZSITE, YUMA
Tyson's Wells ..........................Yuma
    See: QUARTZSITE, YUMA

Ugly Duckling ..........................Cochise
    See: CHIRICAHUA MOUNTAINS, COCHISE
UHUPAT OIDAK .......................MARICOPA
Uinkaret Plateau ........................Mohave
    See: TRUMBULL, MOUNT, MOHAVE
UINKARETS MOUNTAINS .................MOHAVE
    See: TRUMBULL, MOUNT, MOHAVE
UKWALLA POINT ..........GRAND CANYON, COCO
Ulcer Gulch ............................Yavapai
    See: ANTELOPE PEAK ..................YAVAPAI
UNCLE JIM POINT .........GRAND CANYON, COCO
Uncle Sam Gulch ........................Cochise
    See: UNCLE SAM HILL, COCHISE
UNCLE SAM HILL ......................COCHISE
Uncle Sam Mine ........................Cochise
    See: UNCLE SAM HILL, COCHISE
Union .................................Apache
    See: EAGAR, APACHE
UNION ................................MARICOPA
UNION ................................MOHAVE
Union Basin ............................Mohave
    See: UNION PASS, MOHAVE
Union, Mount ..........................Yavapai
    See: DAVIS, MOUNT, YAVAPAI
Union Park ............................Gila
    See: PAYSON, GILA
UNION PASS ...........................MOHAVE
Union Pass Station ......................Mohave
    See: UNION PASS, MOHAVE
Union Peak ............................Yavapai
    See: DAVIS, MOUNT, YAVAPAI
Union Ward ............................Apache
    See: ROUND VALLEY, APACHE
      EAGAR, APACHE
UPASOITAC ...........................MARICOPA
Updyke's Tanks ........................Coconino
    See: RATTLESNAKE TANKS, COCONINO
Upper Andrus Spring .....................Mohave
    See: ANDRUS SPRING, MOHAVE
Upper Crossing .........................Cochise
    See: SAN PEDRO, COCHISE

VINEYARD CANYON .....................COCONINO
Vineyard Mountain ...........................Gila
    See: VINEYARD CANYON, GILA
VIOPULI ..................................PIMA
Viopuli Wash ................................Pima
    See: VIOPULI, PIMA
Virgen, Rio ...............................Mohave
    See: VIRGIN RIVER, MOHAVE
Virgin Basin ..............................Mohave
    See: VIRGIN RIVER, MOHAVE
VIRGIN BASIN ...........................YUMA
Virgin Bottoms ............................Mohave
    See: CANE BEDS, MOHAVE
Virgin Canyon .............................Mohave
    See: VIRGIN RIVER, MOHAVE
VIRGIN PEAK ..............................YUMA
VIRGIN RIVER ..........................MOHAVE
Virginia City ..............................Mohave
    See: NEW VIRGINIA, MOHAVE
VIRGINIA CITY ............................PIMA
Vishnu Creek ....................Grand Canyon, Coco
    See: VISHNU TEMPLE, GRAND CANYON
VISHNU TEMPLE ..........GRAND CANYON, COCO
Vista Encantada .............Grand Canyon, Coco
    See: VISTA ENCANTADORA, GRAND CANYON
VISTA ENCANTADORA......GRAND CANYON, COCO
Vista, Sierra ...............................Cochise
    See: SIERRA VISTA, COCHISE
Vitty......................................Yavapai
    See: SIMMONS, YAVAPAI
Vivian ....................................Mohave
    See: OATMAN, MOHAVE
Vivian Wash ...............................Mohave
    See: OATMAN, MOHAVE
VOCK CANYON ...........................MOHAVE
Vock Spring ...............................Mohave
    See: VOCK CANYON, MOHAVE
Vock Wash .................................Mohave
    See: VOCK CANYON, MOHAVE
Vock Wash, Left Fork .........................Mohave
    See: VOCK CANYON, MOHAVE
Vokivaxia ..................................Pima
    See: SAUCEDA MOUNTAINS, MARICOPA
Voltz Crossing ..............................Navajo
    See: WOOLFS CROSSING, NAVAJO
Volunteer Canyon ..........................Coconino
    See: VOLUNTEER MOUNTAIN, COCONINO
VOLUNTEER MOUNTAIN .................COCONINO
Volunteer Spring ..........................Coconino
    See: VOLUNTEER MOUNTAIN, COCONINO
VOTA ....................................COCHISE
V T Park ....................Grand Canyon, Coco
    See: DE MOTTE PARK, GRAND CANYON
Vturituc ...................................Pinal
    See: SACATON, PINAL
VULCANS THRONE .......................MOHAVE
VULTURE ..............................MARICOPA
VULTURE MINE .........................MARICOPA
Vulture Range ............................Maricopa
    See: VULTURE MINE, MARICOPA
Vulture Siding .............................Maricopa
    See: MORRISTOWN, MARICOPA

Wachupe Mountains ..........................Cochise
    See: HUACHUCA, FORT, COCHISE
WADDELL .............................MARICOPA
WAGONER .............................YAVAPAI
Wagon Tire Dam ...........................Yavapai
    See: WAGON TIRE FLAT, YAVAPAI
WAGON TIRE FLAT .....................YAVAPAI
Wagon Tire Wash ..........................Yavapai
    See: WAGON TIRE FLAT, YAVAPAI
WAHL KNOLL ...........................APACHE
Wah-poo-ata ................................Gila
    See: STRAWBERRY VALLEY, GILA
Wainwright, Mount .........................Coconino
    See: WING MOUNTAIN, COCONINO
Wake-up Wash ..............................Mohave
    See: WIKIEUP, MOHAVE
WA KOTA .............................YAVAPAI
Waldeck Peak, Mount ....................Santa Cruz
    See: PETE MOUNTAIN, SANTA CRUZ
Wales Arnold Ranch .........................Yavapai
    See: MONTEZUMA CASTLE, YAVAPAI
Walhalla Plateau ..........................Coconino
    See: GREENLAND SPRING, GRAND CANYON
Walker.. ...................................Navajo
    See: TAYLOR, NAVAJO
WALKER ..............................YAVAPAI
Walker Basin ..............................Yavapai
    See: WALKER MOUNTAIN, YAVAPAI
Walker Butte ...............................Apache
    See: WALKER CREEK, APACHE
Walker Butte ...............................Pinal
    See: VEKOL MINE, PINAL
WALKER CANYON .....................SANTA CRUZ
WALKER CREEK .........................APACHE
    See also: MEXICAN WATER, APACHE
Walker Creek ..............................Yavapai
    See: WALKER MOUNTAIN, YAVAPAI
Walker Creek Valley ..........................Apache
    See: WALKER CREEK, APACHE
Walker Diggings ...........................Yavapai
    See: WALKER, YAVAPAI
Walker District ............................Yavapai
    See: PRESCOTT, YAVAPAI
Walker Gulch ..............................Yavapai
    See: WALKER, YAVAPAI
WALKER LAKE .........................COCONINO
WALKER MOUNTAIN .....................YAVAPAI
Walker's Pass .............................Yavapai
    See: WALKER, YAVAPAI
Wall's Well ................................Pima
    See: KUAKATCH, PIMA
Wallace ....................Grand Canyon, Coco
    See: HUXLEY TERRACE, GRAND CANYON
WALLEN, CAMP ..........................COCHISE
Wallen, Fort ...............................Cochise
    See: WALLEN, CAMP, COCHISE
Walnut ...................................Coconino
    See: WINONA, COCONINO
Walnut Canyon ............................Coconino
    See: WALNUT CANYON NAT. MONUMENT, COCO
    See also: SAN FRANCISCO PEAKS, COCONINO
Walnut Canyon ............................Yavapai
    See: WALNUT GROVE, YAVAPAI

West Fork, Little Colorado .......................Apache
    See: LITTLE COLORADO RIVER, NAVAJO
WEST PEAK ...............................GRAHAM
West Poker Mountain .........................Apache
    See: POKER MOUNTAIN, APACHE
West Spruce Mountain ......................Yavapai
    See: WHITE SPRUCE MOUNTAIN, YAVAPAI
West Twin Peak ................................Pima
    See: GADSDEN PEAK, PIMA
WET BEAVER CREEK ...................COCONINO
Wet Beaver Creek ...........................Yavapai
    See: DRY BEAVER CREEK, COCONINO
       BEAVER CREEK, YAVAPAI
WET-BOTTOM CREEK .................GILA, Yavapai
Wet-Bottom Mesa .............................Gila
    See: WET-BOTTOM CREEK, GILA
WETHERILL MESA ......................NAVAJO
Wheat Field ..................................Gila
    See: WHEATFIELDS, GILA
WHEATFIELDS ............................GILA
Wheatfields Canyon ..........................Apache
    See: WHEATFIELDS CREEK, APACHE
WHEATFIELDS CREEK ....................APACHE
Wheeler Load ...............................Mohave
    See: WAUBA YUMA DISTRICT, MOHAVE
WHEELER POINT ..........GRAND CANYON, COCO
Wheeler Wash ...............................Mohave
    See: WAUBA YUMA DISTRICT, MOHAVE
WHETSTONE MOUNTAINS ..................COCHISE
Whipple Barracks ............................Yavapai
    See: WHIPPLE, FORT, YAVAPAI
Whipple Depot ...............................Yavapai
    See: WHIPPLE, FORT, YAVAPAI
WHIPPLE, FORT .........................YAVAPAI
Whipple Mountain .............................Mohave
    See: CYGNUS MOUNTAIN, MOHAVE
Whipple Valley ..............................Yavapai
    See: WHIPPLE, FORT, YAVAPAI
WHIPSAU ...............................YAVAPAI
Whipsau Creek ...............................Yavapai
    See: WHIPSAU, YAVAPAI
Whipsau Gulch ...............................Yavapai
    See: WHIPSAU, YAVAPAI
WHISKEY CREEK ........................APACHE
WHITE CAVE SPRING .....................NAVAJO
White Cliff Creek .............................Mohave
    See: AQUARIUS MOUNTAINS, MOHAVE
White Cliff Valley ............................Mohave
    See: AQUARIUS MOUNTAINS, MOHAVE
White Cliffs .................................Mohave
    See: AQUARIUS MOUNTAINS, MOHAVE
WHITE CLIFFS CREEK ............MOHAVE, Yavapai
WHITE CONE ...........................NAVAJO
White Cone Spring ...........................Navajo
    See: WHITE CONE, NAVAJO
White Creek ...............Grand Canyon, Coco
    See: WHITE'S BUTTE, GRAND CANYON
WHITE HILL ...........................COCONINO
WHITE HILLS ...........................MOHAVE
White Hills ..................................Mohave
    See: WHITE HILLS, MOHAVE
WHITE HORSE HILLS ....................COCONINO

WHITE HORSE LAKE ...................COCONINO
WHITE HORSE PASS .......................PINAL
White Horse Spring ........................Coconino
    See: WHITE HORSE HILLS, COCONINO
White House Canyon ...........................Pima
    See: MADERA CANYON, PIMA
WHITE HOUSE RUINS ....................APACHE
WHITE MESA ...........................COCONINO
White Mountain Apache Indian Reservation ........Apache
    See: APACHE, FORT, INDIAN RESERVATION,
      APACHE
White Mountain Creek ........................Apache
    See: WHITE RIVER, APACHE
White Mountain Creek ...................Gila, Navajo
    See: WHITE RIVER, GILA
White Mountain Reservoir .....................Apache
    See: WHITE MOUNTAINS, APACHE
White Mountain River ...................Gila, Navajo
    See: WHITE RIVER, GILA
WHITE MOUNTAINS ...............APACHE, Greenlee
WHITE PICACHO .......................MARICOPA
WHITE RIVER ....................NAVAJO, Apache
WHITERIVER ............................APACHE
WHITERIVER ............................NAVAJO
    See also: WHITE RIVER, APACHE
White River ..................................Cochise
    See: WHITEWATER, COCHISE
White River ..................................Navajo
    See: FORT APACHE INDIAN RESERVATION,
      NAVAJO
WHITE RIVER .........................GILA, Navajo
Whiteriver ...................................Navajo
    See: FORT APACHE INDIAN RESERVATION,
      NAVAJO
WHITE SAGE WASH .....................COCONINO
WHITE SPRUCE MOUNTAIN ...............YAVAPAI
WHITE TANK ...........................MARICOPA
White Tanks ..................................Yuma
    See: TANK MOUNTAINS, YUMA
WHITE WELL .............................YUMA
WHITE'S BUTTE ............GRAND CANYON, COCO
White's Well ..................................Pima
    See: CHIULI SHIAK, PIMA
WHITEWATER ...........................COCHISE
Whitewater Draw ............................Cochise
    See: WHITEWATER, COCHISE
WHITING ..............................COCONINO
Whitlock Cienega ............................Graham
    See: WHITLOCK VALLEY, GRAHAM
Whitlock Hills ...............................Graham
    See: WHITLOCK VALLEY, GRAHAM
Whitlock Peak ...............................Graham
    See: WHITLOCK VALLEY, GRAHAM
Whitlock Sink ...............................Graham
    See: WHITLOCK VALLEY, GRAHAM
WHITLOCK VALLEY .....................GRAHAM
WHITLOW CANYON .........................PINAL
Whitmore Point ..............................Mohave
    See: WHITMORE WASH, MOHAVE
WHITMORE POOLS ......................COCONINO
WHITMORE WASH .......................MOHAVE
WHITNEY ...............................MOHAVE

WINSLOW ................................NAVAJO
Wintersburg ...............................Maricopa
    See: WINTERS WELL, MARICOPA
WINTERS WELL ........................MARICOPA
Wipho ....................................Navajo
    See: WEPO SPRINGS, NAVAJO
WISHBONE MOUNTAIN ..................APACHE
Witch Creek ...............................Cochise
    See: FIFE CANYON, COCHISE
WITCH WATER POCKET ..................MOHAVE
WITTMAN ..............................MARICOPA
Wittmore Springs ..........................Coconino
    See: WHITMORE POOLS, COCONINO
WODO, MOUNT ............GRAND CANYON, COCO
WOLFHOLE ..............................MOHAVE
Wolfhole Dry Lake ........................Mohave
    See: WOLFHOLE, MOHAVE
WOLFLEY HILL ...........................PIMA
WOLF MOUNTAIN .......................APACHE
Wonderland of Rocks .......................Cochise
    See: RIGGS CANYON, COCHISE
WONSITS PLATEAU ......................MOHAVE
Wonsits Tiravu ............................Mohave
    See: WONSITS PLATEAU, MOHAVE
WOOD, CAMP ...........................YAVAPAI
Wood, Camp, Mountain .....................Yavapai
    See: WOOD, CAMP, YAVAPAI
Wood Canyon ..............................Yavapai
    See: WOOD, CAMP, YAVAPAI
WOODCHUTE MOUNTAIN .................YAVAPAI
Woodland .................................Navajo
    See: LAKESIDE, NAVAJO
Wood's Canyon ............................Yavapai
    See: WOOD, CAMP, YAVAPAI
WOODRUFF ..............................NAVAJO
Woodruff Butte ............................Navajo
    See: WOODRUFF, NAVAJO
WOOD'S RANCH ...........................PIMA
WOODS CANYON ........................COCONINO
WOOLAROC ............................GREENLEE
Woolf Crossing ............................Coconino
    See: REIDHEAD, NAVAJO
WOOLFS CROSSING .....................COCONINO
WOOLHOUSE MOUNTAIN .................NAVAJO
Woolhouse Tank ...........................Navajo
    See: WOOLHOUSE MOUNTAIN, NAVAJO
WOOLSEY LAKE ..........................APACHE
WOOLSEY PEAK ........................MARICOPA
WOOLSEY POINT ..........GRAND CANYON, COCO
Woolsey Tank ..............................Maricopa
    See: WOOLSEY PEAK, MARICOPA
Woolsey Wash .............................Maricopa
    See: WOOLSEY PEAK, MARICOPA
WORKMAN CREEK ..........................GILA
Workman Creek Falls ........................Gila
    See: WORKMAN CREEK, GILA
Wotan's Throne ............................Coconino
    See: NEWBERRY MESA, COCONINO
WRIGHTSON, MOUNT ..................SANTA CRUZ
WRIGHTSTOWN ............................PIMA
WRONG MOUNTAIN ........................PIMA

WUPATKI NATIONAL MONUMENT .......COCONINO
Wupokabi ................................Apache
    See: GANADO, APACHE
WYMOLA ................................PINAL
Wynola ...................................Pinal
    See: WYMOLA, PINAL

Xara Springs, La ..........................Apache
    See: TANNER SPRINGS, APACHE
Xila
    See: GILA RIVER, GILA
Xongopavi ................................Navajo
    See: SHUNGOPOVI, NAVAJO

Yaeger ...................................Yavapai
    See: YAEGER CANYON, YAVAPAI
YAEGER CANYON ........................YAVAPAI
Yaeger Tank ...............................Maricopa
    See: JEAGER TANKS, MARICOPA
Yahdesut .................................Cochise
    See: CHIRICAHUA MOUNTAINS, COCHISE
YAKI POINT ........................GRAND CANYON
Yaki Trail ....................Grand Canyon, Coco
    See: PHANTOM RANCH, GRAND CANYON
YALE POINT ............................APACHE
Yampa Creek ..............................Mohave
    See: TRUXTON CANYON, MOHAVE
Yampai ...................................Yavapai
    See: TRUXTON CANYON, MOHAVE
Yampai Cliffs .............................Mohave
    See: TRUXTON CANYON, MOHAVE
Yampai Creek .............................Mohave
    See: TRUXTON CANYON, MOHAVE
Yampai Divide ............................Yavapai
    See: TRUXTON CANYON, MOHAVE
YANK'S CANYON ......................SANTA CRUZ
Yank's Spring ............................Santa Cruz
    See: YANK'S CANYON, SANTA CRUZ
Yaponcha Crater ..........................Coconino
    See: BONITA LAVA FLOW, COCONINO
YAQUI TANKS ............................YUMA
Yarber Wash ..............................Yavapai
    See: YARBO WASH, YAVAPAI
YARBO WASH ...........................YAVAPAI
YARNELL ...............................YAVAPAI
Yarnell Hill ...............................Yavapai
    See: YARNELL, YAVAPAI
Yarnell Spring ............................Yavapai
    See: YARNELL, YAVAPAI
YAVA ...................................YAVAPAI
YAVAPAI COUNTY .............................330
YAVAPAI POINT ..........GRAND CANYON, COCO
Yavapai Trail .........................Gila, Maricopa
    See: APACHE TRAIL, GILA
YEAGER CANYON .......................COCONINO
Yeager Lake ...............................Coconino
    See: YEAGER CANYON, COCONINO
YEI BICHEI MESA ........................NAVAJO
Yellow Jacket .............................Coconino
    See: HAPPY JACK, COCONINO
Yellow Jacket Mine ........................Santa Cruz
    See: YELLOW JACKET MOUNTAIN, SANTA CRUZ